EVIDENCE
CASES AND MATERIALS

Eighth Edition

■ ■ ■

by

Kenneth S. Broun
Henry Brandis Professor of Law Emeritus
University of North Carolina

Robert P. Mosteller
J. Dickson Phillips Distinguished Professor of Law
University of North Carolina

Paul C. Giannelli
Distinguished University Professor and
Albert J. Weatherhead, III & Richard W. Weatherhead Professor of Law
Case Western Reserve University

AMERICAN CASEBOOK SERIES®

Mat #41277992

American Casebook Series is a trademark registered in the U.S. Patent and Trademark Office.

COPYRIGHT © 1969, 1975, 1981, 1988, 1995 WEST PUBLISHING CO.
© West, a Thomson business, 2002, 2007
© 2014 by LEG, Inc. d/b/a West Academic Publishing
    444 Cedar St., Suite 700
    St. Paul, MN 55101
    1–877–888–1330

West, West Academic Publishing, and West Academic are trademarks of West Publishing Corporation, used under license.

Printed in the United States of America

ISBN: 978–0–314–28147–0

To

Margie

(K.S.B.)

Elizabeth

(R.P.M.)

Susan

(P.C.G.)

INTRODUCTION TO THE EIGHTH EDITION

The strengths of this book have always been in its insight into the origins of the evidence rules, which was a particular strength of its original authors Edward W. Cleary and John W. Strong. The new authors have built upon that strength at the same time we strive to give attention to contemporary issues in evidence law.

Since the last edition, the United States Supreme Court has decided half a dozen cases involving the Confrontation Clause under the testimonial statement approach of *Crawford v. Washington* (2004), which was a major focus of changes in the Seventh Edition. Substantial additions to the detailed notes regarding confrontation reflect those new developments.

New material concerning scientific evidence has also been added in this edition because of the dynamic nature of that particular area of evidence law—for example, the National Academy of Science's 2009 landmark report on forensic science. Indeed, throughout the text, an occasional new case and more frequently additions to notes have been made to bring a modern perspective to the discussion, but the pattern and flow of cases should feel familiar to those who have used the Seventh Edition.

In recognition of the importance of the Federal Rules of Evidence (now restyled) and state rules based upon them, principal cases and notes are largely directed to the application of those rules. Where possible, we have selected cases that illustrate how major issues are being dealt with under those rules. Where state law diverges significantly from Federal Rule treatment, notes generally examine the differences, although in a few situations a principal case illustrating the different treatment is included.

We also recognize the impact that modern technology has had both on the law of evidence and in the trial process. For the most part, the courts have not had much trouble adapting to new technologies, such as e-mail, computer simulations, social networking websites, and other internet issues. However, they have changed the way people live their lives and cases are tried. As a result, we acknowledge those changes and illustrate the application of doctrine with new technologies by our selection of cases and more generally by the discussion in the accompanying notes.

The current authors of the casebook owe a great debt to Professors Cleary and Strong, and we hope both in the continuity reflected in the book and its treatment of new areas we have lived up to the best tradition of their scholarly instincts and their keen interest in teaching.*

K.S.B.
R.P.M.
R.C.G.

---

* In an effort to make cases more readable, we have universally omitted all indication of the denial of certiorari and made similar minor alterations without notation.

SUMMARY OF CONTENTS

TABLE OF CONTENTS

———————

TABLE OF CASES

The principal cases are in bold type.

TABLE OF FEDERAL RULES OF EVIDENCE

CHAPTER 1[1]

CHARACTERISTICS OF THE ADVERSARY SYSTEM

■ ■ ■

■ ■ ■

A. THE ROLES OF THE JUDGE AND JURY

UNITED STATES V. BEATY
United States Court of Appeals, Third Circuit, 1983.
722 F.2d 1090.

JAMES HUNTER, III, CIRCUIT JUDGE:

Defendants John Ballouz and William Beaty appeal from their convictions on a number of drug-related offenses. The principal question presented in both cases is whether the trial judge, by his conduct, deprived the defendants of a fair trial. * * * After carefully reviewing the trial transcript, we conclude that the judge's conduct with regard to defendant Beaty, while sometimes unfortunate, did not rise to the level of prejudicial error. With respect to defendant Ballouz, however, we conclude that the trial judge's conduct was prejudicial. We will therefore reverse Ballouz's conviction and remand his case for a new trial.

* * *

I.   Facts

A brief recital of the evidence adduced at trial is helpful in considering defendants' claims. According to the Government, William Beaty asked a longtime friend, John Clark, if he would be interested in helping Beaty smuggle hashish into the United States. Clark was interested. Beaty explained that he needed a boat and a crew to ferry the hashish from the "mother ship" to shore. Clark arranged for Beaty to meet Robert Soleau, a commercial fisherman. Soleau agreed to provide the *Falcon* to carry the hashish, and a "safe boat," the *Tanqueray,* to carry

---

[1]   In the cases and materials throughout the chapter, some footnotes have been omitted and others have been renumbered. [Ed.]

people to count the bales of hashish and then return those people to shore separately from the drugs.

The operation was carried out on the night of October 9, 1981. Government witnesses testified that Ballouz was on the *Falcon* and Beaty was on the *Tanqueray*. Due to a combination of factors, the operation was unsuccessful. The weather was bad, the sea was rough, and the *Falcon* was overloaded. Eventually, after its crew was transferred to the *Tanqueray*, the *Falcon* sank. Government witnesses testified that Beaty was subsequently involved in two unsuccessful attempts to salvage the lost hashish.

Defendant Beaty presented no evidence. Defendant Ballouz presented an alibi defense. He testified that he lived in California, but had come to New Jersey the week of October 9th to surprise his parents for his birthday. He discovered only after his arrival that they had gone to California to surprise him. He testified that he could not have been on the *Falcon* because he spent the evening of October 9th having dinner with Mrs. Axelson, an old friend. He presented Mrs. Axelson, his father and brother, and Mr. Rumolo, an old friend, as witnesses.

II.   The Trial Judge's Conduct: Defendant Beaty

Beaty claims that the judge "chilled" his counsel, thereby denying Beaty effective assistance of counsel, by showing "favoritism" to the Government while constantly criticizing Beaty's counsel. He also claims that the judge's "favoritism" communicated the judge's belief in Beaty's guilt to the jury, thereby prejudicing Beaty and depriving him of a fair trial.

The law governing judicial participation in trials, while easy to state, is difficult to apply. On the one hand, it is clear that "[i]n a trial by jury in a federal court, the judge is not a mere moderator, but is the governor of the trial. * * * " *Quercia v. United States,* 289 U.S. 466, 469 * * * (1933). Indeed, this court has emphasized that:

> We have long abandoned the adversary system of litigation which regards opposing lawyers as players and the judge as a mere umpire whose only duty is to determine whether infractions of the rules of the game have been committed. A trial is not a contest but a search for the truth so that justice may properly be administered. For the purpose of eliciting the germane facts, a judge may on his own initiative and within his sound discretion interrogate witnesses.

Riley v. Goodman, 315 F.2d 232, 234 (3d Cir.1963) * * *. On the other hand, a judge must not "abandon his proper role and assume that of an advocate. * * * " *United States v. Green,* 544 F.2d 138, 147 (3d Cir.1976). We have cautioned that "[t]he judge's participation must never reach the point where 'it appears clear to the jury that the court believes the accused is guilty.' " *United States v. Nobel,* 696 F.2d 231, 237 (3d Cir.1982) (quoting *United States v. Robinson,* 635 F.2d 981, 984 (2d Cir.1980).

Unfortunately, "the manner in which interrogation should be conducted and the proper extent of its exercise are not susceptible of formulation in a rule." *United States v. Green,* 544 F.2d at 147 * * *.

The judge's conduct of this trial undeniably left much to be desired. Whether or not his conduct was ideal, however, is not the issue before us. We must determine whether his conduct was so prejudicial as to deprive defendant Beaty of a fair, as opposed to a perfect, trial. *See United States v. Parodi,* 703 F.2d 768, 776 (4th Cir.1983); *United States v. Robinson,* 635 F.2d at 984. A careful and detailed review of this trial record of more than 1600 pages satisfies us that, while the decision is not an easy one, Beaty has not made a sufficient showing of prejudice to require a new trial.

Initially, we note that the court's rebukes of Beaty's counsel, serious as some of them were,[2] occupy but a small portion of the extensive trial court record. Furthermore, the bulk of these rebukes occurred out of the presence of the jury. The record also reveals that these reprimands were far from unprovoked. Beaty's lawyer apparently believed that he should be allowed to elicit otherwise inadmissible hearsay on the grounds of relevance. He also believed that he could ask questions tending to impugn the veracity of the prosecution's witnesses without any good faith basis. The trial judge, quite correctly, flatly disagreed. The record reveals a judge who was increasingly frustrated by counsel's repeated attempts to do that which he had properly been forbidden to do.

When considered in this context, the only really serious altercation between the judge and Beaty's counsel is less troubling. The judge essentially cross-examined Beaty's counsel in the jury's presence concerning counsel's basis for a question that intimated that a prosecution witness was lying. We cannot condone the judge's conduct or say that the ensuing colloquy would not better have been conducted outside the jury's presence. But "misconduct by defense counsel may properly be taken into account by us in determining whether a defendant was prejudiced by the judge's response." *United States v. Robinson,* 635 F.2d at 985 * * *. In *United States v. Weiss,* 491 F.2d 460, 468 (2d

---

[2] For example, when Beaty's counsel, during cross-examination of a government witness, sought to question the witness as to whether he had lied under oath in an earlier, unrelated bankruptcy proceeding, the district court judge, after ruling that the question was improper, continued by asking Beaty's counsel: "Do you know he [the prosecutor] can put you on the stand and ask you the basis for the question?" Beaty's counsel charged that this suggestion by the court intimidated and chilled him. While we do not quarrel with the court's substantive ruling in the context in which it appears, we question the need for the district court judge to threaten defense counsel with taking the stand and responding to questioning by the prosecutor. Nor was this the only occasion on which the district court expressed itself in this same fashion.

Cir.1974), the Second Circuit recognized that, "Judges, while expected to possess more than the average amount of self-restraint, are still only human. They do not possess limitless ability, once passion is aroused, to resist provocation." We likewise reject any suggestion that defense counsel may inject reversible error into a trial by baiting the trial judge.

In considering Beaty's claim we also consider whether the judge exhibited partisanship by favoring Government trial counsel or holding them to lesser standards than those applied to counsel for the defendant. *See United States v. Robinson,* 635 F.2d at 985. He did not. The judge appeared to resolve all doubts concerning the admissibility of evidence in favor of the defense and repeatedly sustained defense objections to the prosecutor's questions. On occasion, he expressed disapproval of the prosecutor's conduct and, in general, he expected her to conform to a very high standard. Although we do not approve of the judge's rebukes of counsel, his relatively even-handed treatment of Government and defense counsel persuades us that his admonitions of Beaty's counsel did not convey a belief in Beaty's guilt to the jury.

Furthermore, we are persuaded that Beaty was not denied effective assistance of counsel because Beaty's counsel never acted as though he felt chilled. He zealously represented Beaty throughout. He extensively and vigorously cross-examined each prosecution witness. He pursued every possible avenue in testing their credibility and recollections. He frequently objected during the prosecutor's examinations. In sum, the record reveals no evidence that Beaty's counsel was chilled.

Beaty also claims that the judge frequently "rehabilitated" prosecution witnesses, and in so doing, conveyed to the jury his belief that they were credible. The questions complained of were designed to clarify testimony and pertained to no ultimate issue of fact for the jury. As such, they were proper unless they conveyed to the jury the judge's belief on the proper outcome of the trial. *Riley v. Goodman,* 315 F.2d at 235. Only one instance of questioning presents a sufficiently serious possibility of prejudice to merit further discussion. Defense counsel extensively elicited during cross-examination that Robert Soleau had previously lied under oath. At certain points in this lengthy cross-examination, Soleau's testimony became confused. The judge interrupted cross-examination to ask such questions as: "Did you tell any other lies to the Grand Jury other than trying to protect the names of the two men that you just gave?"; and "Did you at any time tell any lies to the authorities and falsely accuse anybody?" Given the extreme sensitivity of these questions, it might have been better for the judge to refrain altogether from asking them. Certainly he should have waited until after the prosecutor had had an opportunity on redirect examination to clear up any confusion. It may well have been error for the judge to interrupt cross-examination in this fashion. If it was, however, we do not believe that it rose to the level of prejudicial error.

We are unpersuaded that these questions implied to the jury that the judge believed Soleau. *See United States v. Parodi,* 703 F.2d at 776; *United States v. Robinson,* 635 F.2d at 986. Considered in isolation, they are nevertheless troublesome because a jury might think that a witness would be more likely to tell the truth to the judge than to counsel. The record reveals, however, that Beaty's counsel skillfully disproved any such inference. After Soleau told the judge that he had not lied other than to protect the names of "two men," Beaty's counsel impeached the witness by pointing out that he had actually lied to protect the names of three men. Thus neutralized, we do not believe that these questions prejudiced Beaty.

[handwritten margin note: PROBLEMATIC, BUT NOT IN THIS CASE BECAUSE]

The sheer length of this two week trial makes us cautious about investing any but the most inflammatory isolated statements with critical importance. We do not believe that a few summary questions or intemperate remarks assumed the same importance in the jury's mind as they naturally have in counsel's while preparing this appeal. *See United States v. Weiss,* 491 F.2d at 468. Although we acknowledge that this question is an uncomfortably close one, when the length of the trial and the overwhelming evidence of Beaty's guilt are considered, we are convinced that Beaty was not prejudiced by the judge's conduct.

[handwritten margin note: FINAL ON BEATTY]

III. The Trial Judge's Conduct: Defendant Ballouz

We cannot reach the same conclusion with respect to defendant Ballouz. The judge's conduct, always troublesome, became clearly prejudicial when he lengthily questioned three of Ballouz's four witnesses in a manner which Ballouz fairly labels as "cross-examination."[3] The court's vigorous participation in examining the defendant's witnesses, especially when contrasted with the complete freedom from hostile interruption of the prosecution's witnesses, must certainly have conveyed the judge's skepticism about Ballouz's alibi to the jury. * * *

We are particularly disturbed by the court's examination of Mrs. Axelson, the witness who testified that Ballouz spent the evening of October 9th with her. This exchange is reprinted in full in the Appendix to this opinion. Mrs. Axelson was the only witness (other than the defendant) whose testimony could not have been harmonized with the prosecution's version of the truth. She was therefore a "key" witness, and the jury's verdict ultimately rested on the jurors' evaluation of her credibility. We have long held that a judge must be extremely careful, especially when dealing with a key witness, to "minimize its own

---

[3]   For example, counsel for Ballouz called Ballouz's father as a witness. The entire direct examination dealing with the father's visit to San Francisco was transcribed in only four pages of testimony. The cross-examination took no more than one page. The court's examination, which occurred during redirect, consumed over eight pages of transcript.

questioning * * * to the end that any such judicial departure from the normal course of trial be merely helpful in clarifying the testimony rather than prejudicial in tending to impose upon the jury what the judge seems to think about the evidence." *Groce v. Seder,* 267 F.2d 352, 355 (3d Cir.1959). In this instance, the judge's questions cannot possibly be construed as "clarifying." They were completely unrelated to the offenses with which Ballouz was charged, the alibi which Ballouz offered, and the substance of Mrs. Axelson's testimony. Rather the judge asked Mrs. Axelson again and again how she had come to be a witness in the case. This lengthy cross-examination, which occupies four pages in the trial transcript, was a frontal attack on her credibility. The jury could not have helped but conclude that the judge simply did not believe Mrs. Axelson.

It is true that the judge instructed the jurors that, "I am not a partisan either way. I have no view. And you are to treat any questions put by me as though they had been put by anybody else." He also admonished them that they were the sole triers of fact and determiners of credibility. We do not believe, however, that the damaging impression created by the judge's questions was mitigated by these instructions. "[S]uch admonitions may offset [only] brief or minor departures from strict judicial impartiality." *United States v. Nazzaro,* 472 F.2d at 312–13 (quoting *United States v. Brandt,* 196 F.2d 653, 656 (2d Cir.1952)); *cf. United States v. Anton,* 597 F.2d 371, 375 (3d Cir.1979) ("Where a court has expressed its opinion on a pivotal issue in the case, and has expressed that opinion in a strong, unequivocal and one-sided fashion, abstract instructions regarding the jury's role as fact finder are not a sufficient remedy.").

The judge's overzealous examination was error. Because the evidence of Ballouz's guilt, in contrast to that of Beaty's guilt, was far from overwhelming we cannot conclude that this error did not prejudice Ballouz.[4] In such circumstances, the only remedy for the prejudice suffered by the defendant is to reverse the conviction and grant him a new trial. *See, e.g., United States v. Nazzaro,* 472 F.2d at 313; *United States v. Grunberger,* 431 F.2d 1062 (2d Cir.1970).

* * *

V. Conclusion

The conviction of defendant William Beaty will be affirmed. The conviction of defendant John Ballouz will be reversed, and his case remanded for a new trial.

---

[4] The testimony against John Ballouz consisted of the testimony of four co-conspirators and telephone toll records showing contact between Ballouz and Beaty, who were old friends. Three of the witnesses did not know Ballouz, and claim to have seen him only briefly on the evening of the rendezvous. The only witness who claimed to know Ballouz had not seen him for ten years before seeing him briefly on the night of the operation—when the witness was admittedly sick and drinking.

APPENDIX

Axelson—cross

THE COURT: How did you come to be a witness in this case, Ma'am?

THE WITNESS: How did I come to be an [sic] witness in this case?

THE COURT: That's what I asked you.

THE WITNESS: Because of the lawyer coming and asking me to be, which was telling the truth.

THE COURT: Oh, I see.

Was the first contact made from him to you or from you to him?

THE WITNESS: No. From the lawyer to me.

THE COURT: Did Mr. John Ballouz contact you before the lawyer did, or was it [sic] lawyer the first one?

THE WITNESS: Well, I had seen John before.

THE COURT: That isn't what I asked you, Ma'am.

THE WITNESS: I'm sorry.

THE COURT: Who first spoke to you about being a witness in this case?

THE WITNESS: Well, I think I approached them about that.

THE COURT: Oh, you approached somebody first?

THE WITNESS: Oh, yes, I managed to [sic] job. Gee, we were at the restaurant. I'd [sic] be willing to go as a witness.

THE COURT: You reached out for John Ballouz?

THE WITNESS: Yes.

THE COURT: Where was he when you reached out for him, Ma'am?

THE WITNESS: At my home.

THE COURT: He was in your home at that time?

THE WITNESS: Yes, he was.

THE COURT: Was he staying there?

THE WITNESS: No, no.

THE COURT: Was he just visiting you?

THE WITNESS: Visiting.

THE COURT: Who was he visiting there?

THE WITNESS: Me.

THE COURT: You?

THE WITNESS: Yes.

THE COURT: Not your daughter?

THE WITNESS: No. My daughter is married now.

THE COURT: When was it that he was visiting you that you mentioned to him about being a witness for him?

THE WITNESS: As I said, he always visited my home when he came to New Jersey.

THE COURT: Yes, but on what occasion was this? What month was this?

THE WITNESS: When he came home for the arraignment.

THE COURT: When was that?

THE WITNESS: The 1st of October—I don't know exactly when it was.

THE COURT: And where was he living when he came home for the arraignment?

THE WITNESS: Sausalito, California.

THE COURT: Did he stay overnight here in New Jersey, to your knowledge?

THE WITNESS: At his parents', probably. Not my home.

THE COURT: But he paid you a visit?

THE WITNESS: Yes.

THE COURT: The purpose of that was simply to come to see you?

THE WITNESS: Yes. Just to come to see us, which he always did.

THE COURT: Whenever he was in New Jersey?

THE WITNESS: Yes. Definitely.

THE COURT: When he happened to drop in you mentioned to him you could be a witness for him?

THE WITNESS: Yes.

THE COURT: Did you know the critical dates at that time?

THE WITNESS: I started from his birthday. It all sort of worked down. In the month of October it was a very specific month for me.

THE COURT: Yes, I know that you remember his birthday; is that correct?

THE WITNESS: I never forget helps [sic] birthday.

THE COURT: No. But do you also, at the time of his arraignment a year later, remember the day when the Falcon went down?

THE WITNESS: I don't know anything about the Falcon.

THE COURT: How did you know that you can be a witness for him, Ma'am, or that you would have anything useful to say?

THE WITNESS: Only that, you know—

THE COURT: I don't.

THE WITNESS:—if he was involved with this thing, how can he been there and at my home—be at the restaurant, too?

THE COURT: Be where, Ma'am?

THE WITNESS: Whatever this thing that is going with—

THE COURT: What did you know about this thing going with when you first spoke to him?

THE WITNESS: What I read in the newspaper.

THE COURT: You read it in the newspaper?

THE WITNESS: Yes.

THE COURT: Did you read the dates in the newspaper?

THE WITNESS: No.

THE COURT: Did you know what dates were important in this case?

THE WITNESS: No.

THE COURT: Did you know whether or not you could be of use to him as a witness?

THE WITNESS: Not then, really.

THE COURT: When you first spoke to him and told him that you would be a witness, did you have any idea whether you had any evidence to offer?

THE WITNESS: No. Not really.

THE COURT: All right. Thank you.

NOTES AND QUESTIONS

1. *Judicial Questioning.* Federal Rule 614(b) specifically approves interrogation of witnesses by the court. It does not, however, authorize questioning that demonstrates the court's partiality in the matter. See United States v. Tilghman, 134 F.3d 414, 416 (D.C.Cir.1998) ("Because juries, not judges, decide whether witnesses are telling the truth, and because judges wield enormous influence over juries, judges may not ask questions that signal their belief or disbelief of witnesses."); United States v. Filani, 74

F.3d 378, 385 (2d Cir.1996) ("these inquiries targeted the defendant's credibility and challenged his story more in the manner of a prosecutor than an impartial judge"); State v. O'Brien, 984 A.2d 879, 891–92 (N.J.2009) ("More damning was the judge's interruption of Dr. Verdon's testimony about defendant's lack of memory of the confession which Dr. Verdon attributed to defendant's being 'under the influence' of drugs. Expressing clear disbelief in the witness's conclusions, the judge even deconstructed the timeline of the day of the crime, including taking judicial notice of the time it takes to drive from Newark to Toms River, in an obvious effort to show that too much time had elapsed since defendant's last ingestion of drugs for him to have been under the influence when he initialed his statement. Those repetitive questions, which specifically suggested that the witness was testifying contrary to the documents in evidence, continued for six pages in the transcript and included the judge's question: 'And you call that under the influence?' "). Also, while permitting counsel to delay objection to the court's questioning until a time when the jury is not present, Rule 614(c) does not eliminate the requirement that an objection be made.

2. *Reversals rare.* As one may gather from *Beaty,* it is the extraordinary case where judicial action, even if apparently slanted strongly in favor of one party, produces a reversal. While the same standard—whether the trial is unfair—is generally applied in both criminal and civil contexts, reversals are rarer in civil cases. See, e.g., Handgards, Inc. v. Ethicon, Inc., 743 F.2d 1282, 1289 (9th Cir.1984) (very few cases outside criminal area find judicial misconduct); Ward v. Westland Plastics, Inc., 651 F.2d 1266, 1271 (9th Cir.1980) (new trial denied in discrimination case under Title VII, even though judge demeaned quality and relevance of plaintiff's evidence, suggested his own nondiscriminatory reasons for defendant's behavior, and disparaged congressional wisdom in creating cause of action). But cf. Maheu v. Hughes Tool Co., 569 F.2d 459, 471–72 (9th Cir.1977) ("glowing" comments by judge constituted personal character reference of plaintiff, whose credibility was crucial, denied defendant fair trial).

3. *View from above.* In ruling on the claim of improper judicial intervention, the appellate court's characterization of the purpose and effect of the judge's questioning is far from objectively certain. See, e.g., State v. Riley, 140 A.2d 543 (N.J.App.Div.), rev'd, 145 A.2d 601 (N.J.1958), where the intermediate appellate court ordered a new trial in the defendant's rape prosecution. The court concluded that the trial judge improperly assumed the role of an advocate in questioning the complaining witness and thereby communicated his opinion of the defendant's guilt. The state supreme court disagreed and affirmed the guilty verdict, characterizing the same questioning as necessary intervention by the judge who, because of his position, was particularly able to elicit sordid details from an anguished victim.

4. *Expressive conduct.* What should counsel do in a jury case if the judge shook her head during a witness' examination in a manner indicating disbelief? See Note, 61 Va.L.Rev. 1266 (1975); Annot., 49 A.L.R.3d 1186. In

United States v. Michienzi, 630 F.2d 455 (6th Cir.1980), a conviction was reversed because at the conclusion of an important government witness' testimony the judge shook his hand and told the jury he was an old friend. The problems of making an appropriate record of such conduct must not be overlooked. How should such a record be made? See Section B, infra.

5.   *Bench trials.* The absence of a jury would seem to eliminate, or at least reduce, the harm caused by undue participation by the judge. On what theory might undue participation by the judge call for reversal? See State v. Lawrence, 123 N.E.2d 271 (Ohio 1954); Note, 30 Notre Dame L.Rev. 689 (1955).

6.   *Jury questioning.* The Federal Rules neither explicitly authorize nor disallow the practice of juror questions. Rule 611(a) provides the only guidance by way of the statement that the court "should exercise reasonable control over the mode and order of examining witnesses." In United States v. Feinberg, 89 F.3d 333, 336 (7th Cir.1996), the court wrote: "The permissibility of witness questioning by jurors is a matter of first impression in this circuit. Every circuit to consider the practice has found it permissible in some circumstances. However, those same courts have expressed grave concerns about the practice. We agree that the practice is acceptable in some cases, but do not condone it. We share the reservations expressed by other courts." The court went on to note:

> Although questioning by jurors is "deeply entrenched" in American jurisprudence, concern over the practice is warranted. Witness questioning by jurors is fraught with risks. If permitted to go too far, examination by jurors may convert the jurors to advocates, compromising their neutrality. Jurors also may begin premature deliberation. Further, the practice "will often impale attorneys on the horns of a dilemma." Attorneys are faced with objecting to questions proffered by the arbiters that the attorneys are attempting to influence. The risk that an objection will alienate a jury is rather obvious. In cases such as this one, where jurors are permitted to blurt out their questions, the district court almost invites a mistrial. The district court leaves open the possibility that a juror will ask an impermissibly prejudicial question to which the witness responds before the judge is able to intervene. In the event of such a mishap, the entire trial may be rendered nothing more than a lesson in futility.

Id. at 336–37. See also United States v. Bush, 47 F.3d 511, 516 (2d Cir.1995) ("(1) jurors should be instructed to submit their questions in writing to the judge; (2) outside the presence of the jury, the judge should review the questions with counsel, who may then object; and (3) the court itself should put the approved questions to the witnesses."); Morrison v. State, 845 S.W.2d 882 (Tex.Crim.App.1992) (juror questioning disallowed in criminal cases); ABA Civil Trial Practice Standard 3 (2007) (setting forth procedure and jury instructions for juror questioning).

7. *Court witnesses.* Rule 614(a) authorizes the trial judge to call witnesses. See generally Saltzburg, The Unnecessarily Expanding Role of the American Trial Judge, 64 Va.L.Rev. 1 (1978). However, as with questioning witnesses, there are some, albeit largely undefinable, limits. In the extraordinary case when a judge crosses the boundary between the appropriate, though limited, role as a searcher for the truth and becomes a partisan, aiding one side by calling witnesses, such conduct becomes improper. See People v. Arnold, 772 N.E.2d 1140, 1145 (N.Y.2002) ("Although it does not appear from the record that the Trial Judge intended to give an advantage to either side, he abused his discretion in calling Sergeant Miller on a key issue when both parties chose not to. By calling Sergeant Miller, the court deprived defendant of the ability to request that the trier of fact draw a negative inference from the People's failure to produce an ESU [Emergency Services Unit] officer during its case. Loss of that inference, coupled with the generally damaging testimony of Sergeant Miller, create a significant probability that the verdict would have been affected had the error not occurred."). Rule 706 also permits the trial court to appoint an expert witness, who the judge can then call as a witness under Rule 614(a).

8. *Comparative law.* Professor Mirjan Damaska has written extensively comparing the "inquisitorial" and "adversary" systems: The Faces of Justice and State Authority: A Comparative Approach to the Legal Process (1986); Structures of Authority and Comparative Criminal Procedure, 84 Yale L.J. 480 (1975); Presentation of Evidence and Factfinding Precision, 123 U.Pa.L.Rev. 1083 (1975); Evidentiary Barriers to Conviction and Two Models of Criminal Procedure: A Comparative Study, 121 U.Pa.L.Rev. 506 (1973). Empirical efforts to evaluate the effectiveness and accuracy of the adversary system reach conflicting conclusions. Compare Thibaut, Walker & Lind, Adversary Presentation and Bias in Legal Decisionmaking, 86 Harv.L.Rev. 386 (1972); Lind, Thibaut & Walker, A Cross–Cultural Comparison of the Effect of Adversary and Inquisitorial Processes on Bias in Legal Decisionmaking, 62 Va.L.Rev. 271 (1976), with Vidmar & Laird, Adversary Social Roles: Their Effects on Witnesses' Communication of Evidence and the Assessments of Adjudicators, 44 J. Personality & Soc.Psychol. 888 (1983); Sheppard & Vidmar, Adversary Pretrial Procedures and Testimonial Evidence: Effects of Lawyer's Role and Machiavellianism, 39 J. Personality & Soc. Psychol. 320 (1980). As one might imagine, our adversary system has its critics, see, e.g., Van Kessel, Adversary Excesses in the American Criminal Trial, 67 Notre Dame L.Rev. 403 (1992), and defenders, see, e.g., Landsman, The Adversary System: A Description and Defense (1984).

STATE V. SHEEHAN
Court of Appeals of Utah, 2012.
273 P.3d 417.

CHRISTIANSEN, JUDGE:

Defendant Robert Michael Sheehan challenges his jury convictions for aggravated burglary * * * and aggravated assault * * *.

BACKGROUND

On December 11, 2006, the victim was attacked and seriously injured in her house. When the police arrived, the victim claimed that her attacker was a co-worker whom she had invited into her house earlier that night and who was in her house at the time of the attack. Based on the evidence at the scene, the police eventually eliminated that individual as a suspect despite the victim's initial identification of him as the attacker. During the initial investigation, an officer asked the victim if Sheehan could have assaulted her. The victim responded in the negative. However, during subsequent interviews in the days following the attack, the victim began to implicate Sheehan.

The only evidence that allegedly tied Sheehan to the scene of the attack was part of a bloody palm print found on a pillow case from the victim's bed. Before trial, Sheehan filed a motion requesting a hearing * * * to challenge the reliability and admissibility of the State's print evidence. Alternatively, he requested that the jury be instructed "that fingerprint identifications are opinions not facts and are not infallible." Also, in the alternative, Sheehan requested that "testimony of individualization" be excluded. * * *

On July 2, 2008, the trial court conducted a hearing at which the parties argued about the necessity of [an admissibility] hearing. Sheehan attempted to present the testimony of Dr. Simon A. Cole to dispute the reliability of the State's proposed print evidence. The court concluded that * * * Sheehan was not entitled to a * * * hearing to challenge the admissibility of the State's print evidence. * * *

Sheehan subsequently filed a motion requesting the court's permission for Dr. Cole to testify at trial. Sheehan asserted that the court should allow him "to present [expert] testimony challenging both the reliability of the methods employed by the State's expert in reaching her conclusions and the reliability of palm print evidence generally." Sheehan argued that, pursuant to Utah Rule of Evidence 702[5], "[d]ue process [allowed] Sheehan to attack the State's direct evidence against him, including the reliability of the specific methods used to determine a

---

[5]   [Utah R. Evid. 702 governs the admissibility of expert testimony, including its reliability. Ed.]

'match' of his palm print to a partial print found at the scene of the alleged crime."

On August 4, 2008, the court conducted a hearing on Sheehan's motion. During the hearing, Sheehan argued that it was "important that [he] have [his] own expert to come in and testify about the shortcomings of fingerprint identification," especially given the expected testimony from the State's expert that "there is a zero error rate" in making print identifications. Defense counsel stated, "[T]he [c]ourt determines admissibility, and ultimately the jury is going to decide the weight to give the evidence. We're not asking you to exclude the fingerprint evidence. We just want a fair chance to respond to the [State's] expert with our own expert." * * *

In denying Sheehan's motion, the court first addressed the weight of the evidence issue and stated that Sheehan could cross-examine the State's expert on whether mistakes can be made in fingerprint analysis. Sheehan responded to this ruling by arguing that, although he could cross-examine the State's expert on her response that the error rate is zero, he needed his own expert and that he was "entitled to under Rule 702 to come in and say, well, that's just simply not true; that's simply not accurate." In addressing the admissibility issue, the court once again relied on this court's decision in [State v. Quintana, 103 P.3d 168 (Utah 2005),] to exclude Dr. Cole's testimony.

Because the court excluded Dr. Cole's testimony, Sheehan's only option at trial was to attack the print evidence through cross-examination of the State's experts. The State called two experts to testify at trial, Trenton Gary Grandy and Elisa Macken–Farmer.

* * *

A.   The Trial Court Erred in Excluding Sheehan's Expert.

The trial court did not allow Sheehan's expert to testify at trial because the trial court found determinative *Quintana's* holding that the scientific principles underlying fingerprint comparison meet the threshold foundational requirements for admission in Utah courts. * * * However, * * * while the trial court acts as a gatekeeper to keep expert evidence that is not reliable from the fact finder, this threshold determination does not extend to exclude contradictory evidence. While it is true that a fingerprint expert's testimony about a fingerprint identification is considered sufficiently reliable to allow such evidence to be presented to a jury pursuant to *Quintana*, * * * and the trial court properly relied on this court's determination in *Quintana* to admit the State's expert testimony, * * * such a determination does not automatically exclude any contradictory expert testimony from trial, as long as the competing expert qualifies under rule 702. In fact, rule 702's advisory committee note states,

Contradictory evidence is not automatically excluded

When the trial court, applying this amendment, rules that an expert's testimony is reliable, this does not necessarily mean that contradictory expert testimony is unreliable. The amendment is broad enough to permit testimony that is the product of competing principles or methods in the same field of expertise. Contrary and inconsistent opinions may simultaneously meet the threshold; it is for the factfinder to reconcile—or choose between—the different opinions.

702 Rule Requirements

Utah R. Evid. 702 advisory committee note. Thus, rule 702 requires a trial court to independently evaluate whether the proposed expert's testimony meets the reliability threshold requirements under rule 702, rather than excluding one expert's testimony simply because it contradicts another expert's testimony that has already met the reliability threshold requirements. * * *

Because the trial court failed to independently evaluate whether Sheehan's expert's testimony was admissible under rule 702, the trial court misapplied rule 702 to exclude Sheehan's expert. Instead, the court essentially determined that because the State's print evidence was reliable for admissibility purposes, any evidence offered to challenge the State's print evidence at trial was necessarily unreliable. * * *

Trial court erred

Some of the trial court's confusion seemed to be based on its acceptance of the State's argument that the court alone determines whether expert testimony is reliable. Specifically, the State argued that Dr. Cole's testimony should be excluded because allowing contradictory evidence at trial impinged on the trial court's role to make a legal determination about the reliability of the evidence. Although a trial court makes a legal determination about the reliability of the expert's testimony under rule 702, such a determination is a threshold decision about admissibility. See Utah R. Evid. 702. Once the court determines that evidence is sufficiently reliable to be admitted at trial, the court may not then violate a defendant's constitutional rights to present an effective defense by excluding conflicting evidence or testimony that challenges that expert's opinion or credibility. See Crane v. Kentucky, 476 U.S. 683, 690–91 (1986) ("Whether rooted directly in the Due Process Clause of the Fourteenth Amendment, or in the * * * Confrontation clause[ ] of the Sixth Amendment, the Constitution guarantees criminal defendants a meaningful opportunity to present a complete defense.* * * That opportunity would be an empty one if the State were permitted to exclude competent, reliable evidence bearing on the credibility * * * when such evidence is central to the defendant's claim of innocence. In the absence of any valid state justification, exclusion of this kind of exculpatory evidence deprives a defendant of the basic right to have the prosecutor's case encounter and survive the crucible of meaningful adversarial testing." * * *) Thus, the trial court's legal determination that the State's expert

only deciding admissibility

testimony was admissible did not allow the court to then impinge on the jury's role as the fact finder by excluding the evidence that Sheehan may have used to challenge the credibility and weight of the State's expert testimony. * * *

Quite simply, there are two separate reliability determinations: admissibility, which is a legal determination the court makes, and the weight assigned to the evidence admitted at trial, which is a factual determination made by the fact finder. The court cannot impinge on the factual determinations correctly left to the finder of fact by excluding evidence or testimony because the court has made an incorrect legal determination that competing evidence is not reliable for admissibility purposes.

* * *

CONCLUSION

Although the trial court did not abuse its discretion in determining that the State's experts were allowed to testify at trial, the trial court erred in excluding Sheehan's expert witness, which may have been prejudicial. We reverse Sheehan's convictions and remand for a new trial * * *.

NOTES AND QUESTIONS

1. *"Admissibility v. weight."* Rule 104 allocates certain decisions to the trial judge. The judge decides issues of admissibility, which often include factual issues. For example, the admissibility of statements falling within the hearsay exception for declarations against interest, Rule 804(b)(3), depends upon the unavailability of the declarant—a question of fact if unavailability is based on the death of the declarant. Admissibility also depends upon whether the statement "possesses the required against-interest characteristics"—the application of a legal standard. Fed.R.Evid. 104 advisory committee's note. Once the court decides to admit the evidence, the jury decides what "weight" the evidence is to be accorded. Rule 104(e) preserves a party's right to challenge the evidence before the jury.

2. *Limited judicial role.* See Blake v. Pellegrino, 329 F.3d 43, 48 (1st Cir.2003) ("Rule 104(a) is inapposite here, for no foundational facts were in issue. Virtually by definition, foundational facts are those facts upon which the admissibility of evidence rests. * * * In this instance, those facts (e.g., the authenticity of the death certificate and the authority of the medical examiner to sign it) were never in dispute. The district court's problem did not go to any foundational fact, but, rather, to the very core of the evidence: its persuasiveness. Where, as here, a piece of evidence rests upon a proper foundation, Rule 104(a) does not permit a trial judge to usurp the jury's function and exclude the evidence based on the judge's determination that it lacks persuasive force.").

3. *Applicability of rules of evidence.* Should the judge, in taking evidence to aid in deciding questions of fact, be governed by the rules of evidence? Rule 104(a) states explicitly that in determining preliminary questions concerning the admissibility of evidence the judge is not bound by evidentiary rules with the exception of privilege. See Bourjaily v. United States, 483 U.S. 171 (1987) (court may consider alleged coconspirator statement itself in determining whether conspiracy exists preliminary to admissibility of the statement).

4. *Standard of proof.* Rule 104(a) does not specify the standard of proof to be observed in determining such preliminary questions. However, *Bourjaily*, note 3, supra, resolved that issue, holding that it must be established by a "preponderance of proof." 483 U.S. at 175–76.

- reasonable doubt
- preponderance
- clear/convincing

5. *Overlapping functions.* Sometimes the allocation of responsibility between judge and jury presents overlapping roles. For example, the hearsay exemption for coconspirator statements, Rule 801(d)(2)(E), requires the judge to determine the existence of a conspiracy as a prerequisite to admitting the statement; the "preponderance of evidence" standard applies. If the defendant is also charged with a substantive count of conspiracy, the jury will have to decide the existence of a conspiracy—using the "beyond a reasonable doubt" standard applicable in criminal trials. The judge does not inform the jury of the basis of the admissibility decision.

2,
how?
by observing if all elements might be satisfied?

6. *Out-of-court hearings.* Rule 104(c) requires that hearings on the admissibility of a confession shall be conducted outside the presence of the jury. The court has discretion to hold hearings to determine other preliminary questions under Rule 104 outside the presence of the jury. When would a judge exercise such discretion?

5th Amend. invoked?

HUDDLESTON v. UNITED STATES

Supreme Court of the United States, 1988.
485 U.S. 681.

CHIEF JUSTICE REHNQUIST delivered the opinion of the Court.

Federal Rule of Evidence 404(b) provides:

> "Other crimes, wrongs, or acts.—Evidence of other crimes, wrongs, or acts is not admissible to prove the character of a person in order to show action in conformity therewith. It may, however, be admissible for other purposes, such as proof of motive, opportunity, intent, preparation, plan, knowledge, identity, or absence of mistake or accident."

This case presents the question whether the district court must itself make a preliminary finding that the Government has proved the "other act" by a preponderance of the evidence before it submits the evidence to the jury. We hold that it need not do so. *Holding*

ISSUE

(handwritten margin note: Selling possession of stolen goods. 2 counts.)

Petitioner, Guy Rufus Huddleston, was charged with one count of selling stolen goods in interstate commerce, 18 U.S.C. § 2315, and one count of possessing stolen property in interstate commerce, 18 U.S.C. § 659. The two counts related to two portions of a shipment of stolen Memorex videocassette tapes that petitioner was alleged to have possessed and sold, knowing that they were stolen.

The evidence at trial showed that a trailer containing over 32,000 blank Memorex videocassette tapes with a manufacturing cost of $4.53 per tape was stolen from the Overnight Express yard in South Holland, Illinois, sometime between April 11 and 15, 1985. On April 17, 1985, petitioner contacted Karen Curry, the manager of the Magic Rent-to-Own in Ypsilanti, Michigan seeking her assistance in selling a large number of blank Memorex videocassette tapes. After assuring Curry that the tapes were not stolen, he told her he wished to sell them in lots of at least 500 at $2.75 to $3 per tape. Curry subsequently arranged for the sale of a total of 5,000 tapes, which petitioner delivered to the various purchasers—who apparently believed the sales were legitimate.

(handwritten margin note: "Rule 404(b)" "Similar acts")

There was no dispute that the tapes which petitioner sold were stolen; the only material issue at trial was whether petitioner knew they were stolen. The District Court allowed the Government to introduce evidence of "similar acts" under Rule 404(b), concluding that such evidence had "clear relevance as to [petitioner's knowledge]." App. 11. The first piece of similar act evidence offered by the Government was the testimony of Paul Toney, a record store owner. He testified that in February 1985, petitioner offered to sell new 12 black and white televisions for $28 apiece. According to Toney, petitioner indicated that he could obtain several thousand of these televisions. Petitioner and Toney eventually traveled to the Magic Rent-to-Own, where Toney purchased 20 of the televisions. Several days later, Toney purchased 18 more televisions.

The second piece of similar act evidence was the testimony of Robert Nelson, an undercover FBI agent posing as a buyer for an appliance store. Nelson testified that in May 1985, petitioner offered to sell him a large quantity of Amana appliances—28 refrigerators, 2 ranges, and 40 icemakers. Nelson agreed to pay $8,000 for the appliances. Petitioner was arrested shortly after he arrived at the parking lot where he and Nelson had agreed to transfer the appliances. A truck containing the appliances was stopped a short distance from the parking lot, and Leroy Wesby, who was driving the truck, was also arrested. It was determined that the appliances had a value of approximately $20,000 and were part of a shipment that had been stolen.

Petitioner testified that the Memorex tapes, the televisions, and the appliances had all been provided by Leroy Wesby, who had represented that all of the merchandise was obtained legitimately. Petitioner stated that he had sold 6,500 Memorex tapes for Wesby on a commission basis. Petitioner maintained that all of the sales for Wesby had been on a commission basis and that he had no knowledge that any of the goods were stolen.

[The Court explained that the circuit courts had divided on the issue. Some applied the "preponderance of evidence" standard, some the "clear and convincing evidence" standard, and still others applied a prima facie standard based on Rule 104(b).]

* * *

Federal Rule of Evidence 404(b)—which applies in both civil and criminal cases—generally prohibits the introduction of evidence of extrinsic acts that might adversely reflect on the actor's character, unless that evidence bears upon a relevant issue in the case such as motive, opportunity, or knowledge. Extrinsic acts evidence may be critical to the establishment of the truth as to a disputed issue, especially when that issue involves the actor's state of mind and the only means of ascertaining that mental state is by drawing inferences from conduct. The actor in the instant case was a criminal defendant, and the act in question was "similar" to the one with which he was charged. Our use of these terms is not meant to suggest that our analysis is limited to such circumstances.

Before this Court, petitioner argues that the District Court erred in admitting Toney's testimony as to petitioner's sale of the televisions. The threshold inquiry a court must make before admitting similar acts evidence under Rule 404(b) is whether that evidence is probative of a material issue other than character. The Government's theory of relevance was that the televisions were stolen, and proof that petitioner had engaged in a series of sales of stolen merchandise from the same suspicious source would be strong evidence that he was aware that each of these items, including the Memorex tapes, was stolen. As such, the sale of the televisions was a "similar act" only if the televisions were stolen. Petitioner acknowledges that this evidence was admitted for the proper purpose of showing his knowledge that the Memorex tapes were stolen. He asserts, however, that the evidence should not have been admitted because the Government failed to prove to the District Court that the televisions were in fact stolen.

Petitioner argues from the premise that evidence of similar acts has a grave potential for causing improper prejudice. For instance, the jury may choose to punish the defendant for the similar rather than the charged act, or the jury may infer that the defendant is an evil person inclined to violate the law. Because of this danger, petitioner maintains, the jury ought not to be exposed to similar act evidence until the trial court has heard the evidence and made a determination under Federal Rule of Evidence 104(a) that the defendant committed the similar act.

Rule 104(a) provides that "[p]reliminary questions concerning the qualification of a person to be a witness, the existence of a privilege, or the admissibility of evidence shall be determined by the court, subject to the provisions of subdivision (b)." According to petitioner, the trial court must make this preliminary finding by at least a preponderance of the evidence.

We reject petitioner's position, for it is inconsistent with the structure of the Rules of Evidence and with the plain language of Rule 404(b). Article IV of the Rules of Evidence deals with the relevancy of evidence. Rules 401 and 402 establish the broad principle that relevant evidence—evidence that makes the existence of any fact at issue more or less probable—is admissible unless the Rules provide otherwise. Rule 403 allows the trial judge to exclude relevant evidence if, among other things, "its probative value is substantially outweighed by the danger of unfair prejudice." Rules 404 through 412 address specific types of evidence that have generated problems. Generally, these latter Rules do not flatly prohibit the introduction of such evidence but instead limit the purpose for which it may be introduced. Rule 404(b), for example, protects against the introduction of extrinsic act evidence when that evidence is offered solely to prove character. The text contains no intimation, however, that any preliminary showing is necessary before such evidence may be introduced for a proper purpose. If offered for such a proper purpose, the evidence is subject only to general strictures limiting admissibility such as Rules 402 and 403.

Petitioner's reading of Rule 404(b) as mandating a preliminary finding by the trial court that the act in question occurred not only superimposes a level of judicial oversight that is nowhere apparent from the language of that provision, but it is simply inconsistent with the legislative history behind Rule 404(b). The Advisory Committee specifically declined to offer any "mechanical solution" to the admission of evidence under 404(b). Advisory Committee's Notes on Fed.Rule Evid. 404(b), 28 U.S.C.App., p. 691. Rather, the Committee indicated that the trial court should assess such evidence under the usual rules for admissibility: "The determination must be made whether the danger of undue prejudice outweighs the probative value of the evidence in view of the availability of other means of proof and other factors appropriate for making decisions of this kind under Rule 403." *Ibid.* see also S.Rep. No. 93–1277, p. 25 (1974) ("[I]t is anticipated that with respect to permissible uses for such evidence, the trial judge may exclude it only on the basis of those considerations set forth in Rule 403, *i.e.* prejudice, confusion or waste of time").

Petitioner's suggestion that a preliminary finding is necessary to protect the defendant from the potential for unfair prejudice is also belied by the Reports of the House of Representatives and the Senate. The

[handwritten margin note: 404b does not require preliminary finding by trial court that act in question occurred]

[handwritten margin note: Legislative intent is contrary to petitioner's assertion]

House made clear that the version of Rule 404(b) which became law was intended to "plac[e] greater emphasis on admissibility than did the final Court version." H.R.Rep. No. 93–650, p. 7 (1973). The Senate echoed this theme: "[T]he use of the discretionary word 'may' with respect to the admissibility of evidence of crimes, wrongs, or other acts is not intended to confer any arbitrary discretion on the trial judge." S.Rep. No. 93–1277, *supra,* at 24. Thus, Congress was not nearly so concerned with the potential prejudicial effect of Rule 404(b) evidence as it was with ensuring that restrictions would not be placed on the admission of such evidence.

Congress concerned with restrictions on admissions

We conclude that a preliminary finding by the court that the Government has proved the act by a preponderance of the evidence is not called for under Rule 104(a).[6] This is not to say, however, that the Government may parade past the jury a litany of potentially prejudicial similar acts that have been established or connected to the defendant only by unsubstantiated innuendo. Evidence is admissible under Rule 404(b) only if it is relevant. "Relevancy is not an inherent characteristic of any item of evidence but exists only as a relation between an item of evidence and a matter properly provable in the case." Advisory Committee's Notes on Fed.Rule Evid. 401, 28 U.S.C.App., p. 688. In the Rule 404(b) context, similar act evidence is relevant only if the jury can reasonably conclude that the act occurred and that the defendant was the actor. See *United States v. Beechum,* 582 F.2d 898, 912–913 (C.A.5 1978) (en banc). In the instant case, the evidence that petitioner was selling the televisions was relevant under the Government's theory only if the jury could reasonably find that the televisions were stolen.

relevant definition

404b Relevancy

Such questions of relevance conditioned on a fact are dealt with under Federal Rule of Evidence 104(b). *Beechum, supra,* at 912–913; see also E. Imwinkelried, Uncharged Misconduct Evidence § 2.06 (1984). Rule 104(b) provides:

> "When the relevancy of evidence depends upon the fulfillment of a condition of fact, the court shall admit it upon, or subject to, the introduction of evidence sufficient to support a finding of the fulfillment of the condition."

In determining whether the Government has introduced sufficient evidence to meet Rule 104(b), the trial court neither weighs credibility nor makes a finding that the Government has proved the conditional fact by a

---

[6] Petitioner also suggests that in performing the balancing prescribed by Federal Rule of Evidence 403, the trial court must find that the prejudicial potential of similar acts evidence substantially outweighs its probative value unless the court concludes by a preponderance of the evidence that the defendant committed the similar act. We reject this suggestion because Rule 403 admits of no such gloss and because such a holding would be erroneous for the same reasons that a preliminary finding under Rule 104(a) is inappropriate. We do, however, agree with the Government's concession at oral argument that the strength of the evidence establishing the similar act is one of the factors the court may consider when conducting the Rule 403 balancing. Tr. of Oral Arg. 26.

preponderance of the evidence. The court simply examines all the evidence in the case and decides whether the jury could reasonably find the conditional fact—here, that the televisions were stolen—by a preponderance of the evidence. See 21 C. Wright & K. Graham, Federal Practice and Procedure § 5054, p. 269 (1977). The trial court has traditionally exercised the broadest sort of discretion in controlling the order of proof at trial, and we see nothing in the Rules of Evidence that would change this practice. Often the trial court may decide to allow the proponent to introduce evidence concerning a similar act, and at a later point in the trial assess whether sufficient evidence has been offered to permit the jury to make the requisite finding. If the proponent has failed to meet this minimal standard of proof, the trial court must instruct the jury to disregard the evidence.

We emphasize that in assessing the sufficiency of the evidence under Rule 104(b), the trial court must consider all evidence presented to the jury. "[I]ndividual pieces of evidence, insufficient in themselves to prove a point, may in cumulation prove it. The sum of an evidentiary presentation may well be greater than its constituent parts." *Bourjaily v. United States,* 483 U.S. 171, 179–180 (1987). In assessing whether the evidence was sufficient to support a finding that the televisions were stolen, the court here was required to consider not only the direct evidence on that point—the low price of the televisions, the large quantity offered for sale, and petitioner's inability to produce a bill of sale—but also the evidence concerning petitioner's involvement in the sales of other stolen merchandise obtained from Wesby, such as the Memorex tapes and the Amana appliances. Given this evidence, the jury reasonably could have concluded that the televisions were stolen, and the trial court therefore properly allowed the evidence to go to the jury.

We share petitioner's concern that unduly prejudicial evidence might be introduced under Rule 404(b). See *Michelson v. United States,* 335 U.S. 469, 475–476 (1948). We think, however, that the protection against such unfair prejudice emanates not from a requirement of a preliminary finding by the trial court, but rather from four other sources: first, from the requirement of Rule 404(b) that the evidence be offered for a proper purpose; second, from the relevancy requirement of Rule 402—as enforced through Rule 104(b); third, from the assessment the trial court must make under Rule 403 to determine whether the probative value of the similar acts evidence is substantially outweighed by its potential for unfair prejudice, see Advisory Committee's Notes on Fed.Rule Evid. 404(b), 28 U.S.C.App., p. 691; S.Rep. No. 93–1277, at 25; and fourth, from Federal Rule of Evidence 105, which provides that the trial court shall, upon request, instruct the jury that the similar acts evidence is to be considered only for the proper purpose for which it was admitted. See *United States v. Ingraham,* 832 F.2d 229, 235 (C.A.1 1987).

Affirmed.

NOTES

1.   *Conditional relevance.* When dealing with a matter of "conditional relevancy," as in *Huddleston*, the judge still has a role, albeit a somewhat limited one, in determining whether the foundation evidence is sufficient for the jury to reasonably find the condition fulfilled. As *Huddleston* notes, however, the judge does not assess credibility of witnesses when making this decision. Moreover, the court may consider only evidence admissible under the rules of evidence since the jury will have only such evidence before it when it makes the final determination of the existence of the fact.

2.   *State positions.* Some jurisdictions have rejected the result in the *Huddleston* case with regard to the application of Rule 104(b). See, e.g., State v. Terrazas, 944 P.2d 1194, 1198 (Ariz.1997) ("[T]here are important reasons to apply a clear and convincing standard, rather than some lesser standard, to evidence of prior bad acts. Such evidence is quite capable of having an impact beyond its relevance to the crime charged and may influence the jury's decision on issues other than those on which it was received, despite cautionary instructions from the judge."); Minn.R.Evid. 404(b); Bigpond v. State, 270 P.3d 1244, 1250 (Nev.2012) ("the act is proven by clear and convincing evidence"); James v. State, 152 P.3d 255, 257 (Okla.Crim.App.2007) ("clear and convincing evidence"). The American Bar Association House of Delegates has endorsed a recommendation from its Criminal Justice Section that *Huddleston* be reversed and a clear and convincing standard adopted. 44 Crim.L.Rptr. (BNA) 2376 (Feb. 22, 1989). See also discussion in Ordover, Balancing the Presumptions of Guilt and Innocence: Rules 404(b), 608(b) and 609(a), 38 Emory L.J. 135 (1989).

NOTE ON PLAIN–MEANING JURISPRUDENCE

Beginning in the late 1980s, the Supreme Court employed a plain-meaning standard in interpreting the Federal Rules of Evidence. Such a method of "statutory interpretation" requires courts to follow a Rule's literal language unless ambiguous. Its primary interpretative tool is the statutory text itself, giving those words their ordinary meaning.

This mode of analysis is exemplified by *Huddleston*, where the Court held that Rule 104(b)'s very lenient standard of proof governed the determination of the defendant's involvement in other crimes that were offered by the government under Rule 404(b) to establish his guilty knowledge in the charged crime. Finding that imposing a higher standard of proof was inconsistent with the structure of the Rules and the "plain language" of Rule 404(b), the Court rejected substantial authority from the federal circuit courts that imposed special admission standards on other crimes evidence because of their special dangers of prejudice. Similarly, in Bourjaily v. United States, 483 U.S. 171 (1987), the Court used plain-meaning analysis in ruling that, contrary to longstanding pre-Rules practice, a putative coconspirator statement could be considered by the trial court in finding the existence of a conspiracy involving the person making the statement. The effect of the ruling was to permit the statement to be employed to help establish its own admissibility under Rule 801(d)(2)(E). See also United States v. Owens, 484 U.S. 554 (1988) (using plain meaning to interpret "subject to cross-examination" language of Rule 801(d)(1)).

However, despite the apparent dominance of this mode of analysis championed by Justice Scalia, the Court has also used quite traditional methodology, suggesting that it is not fully committed to plain-meaning analysis. See Old Chief v. United States, 519 U.S. 172 (1997) (citing advisory committee notes); Tome v. United States, 513 U.S. 150, 160 (1995) ("Our conclusion that Rule 801(d)(1)(B) embodies the common-law premotive requirement is confirmed by an examination of the Advisory Committee's Notes to the Federal Rules of Evidence. We have relied on those well-considered Notes as a useful guide in ascertaining the meaning of the Rules."); Green v. Bock Laundry Machine Co., 490 U.S. 504 (1989) (extensive examination of legislative history materials undertaken to determine whether Rule 403 applies in deciding if witness in civil case could be impeached with prior conviction under Rule 609(a)(1)).

The general effect of the plain-meaning method of interpreting the Federal Rules is to diminish the importance of extrinsic interpretative aids such as common law history, pre-Rules precedent, and general policy. See generally Becker & Orenstein, The Federal Rules of Evidence After Sixteen Years—The Effect of "Plain Meaning" Jurisprudence, the Need for an Advisory Committee on the Rules of Evidence, and Suggestions for Selective Revision of the Rules, 60 Geo.Wash.L.Rev. 857 (1992); Imwinkelried, A Brief Defense of the Supreme Court's Approach to the Interpretation of the Federal Rules of Evidence, 27 Ind.L.Rev. 267 (1993); Jonakait, The Supreme Court, Plain Meaning, and the Changed Rules of Evidence, 68 Tex.L.Rev. 745 (1990); Weissenberger, The Supreme Court and the Interpretation of the Federal Rules of Evidence, 53 Ohio St.L.J. 1307 (1992).

UNITED STATES V. ZOLIN

Supreme Court of the United States, 1989.
491 U.S. 554.

JUSTICE BLACKMUN delivered the opinion of the Court.

This case arises out of the efforts of the Criminal Investigation Division of the Internal Revenue Service (IRS) to investigate the tax returns of L. Ron Hubbard, founder of the Church of Scientology * * *.

[In the course of its investigation, the IRS sought access to documents that had been filed under seal in state court in connection with a suit by the Church of Scientology against one its former members. The suit charged that the former member had obtained documentary materials relating to Church activities, including two tapes, by unlawful means. The Church objected to production of the documents, *inter alia*, on the ground of attorney-client privilege. The IRS argued that the tapes fell within the crime-fraud exception to the privilege and urged the district court to listen to the tapes in making its privilege determination. Both the district court and the Ninth Circuit refused to apply the crime-fraud exception, finding no independent evidence to support it.]

* * * The specific question presented is whether the applicability of the crime-fraud exception must be established by "independent evidence" (i.e., without reference to the content of the contested communications themselves), or, alternatively, whether the applicability of that exception can be resolved by an *in camera* inspection of the allegedly privileged material. * * *

* * *

III

Questions of privilege that arise in the course of the adjudication of federal rights are "governed by the principles of the common law as they may be interpreted by the courts of the United States in the light of reason and experience." Fed.Rule Evid. 501. We have recognized the attorney-client privilege under federal law, as "the oldest of the privileges for confidential communications known to the common law." *Upjohn Co. v. United States*, 449 U.S. 383, 389 (1981). Although the underlying rationale for the privilege has changed over time, see 8 J. Wigmore, Evidence § 2290 (McNaughton rev. 1961),[7] courts long have viewed its central concern as one "to encourage full and frank communication between attorneys and their clients and thereby promote broader public interests in the observance of law and administration of justice." *Upjohn*, 449 U.S., at 389. That purpose, of course, requires that clients be free to "make full disclosure to their attorneys" of past wrongdoings, *Fisher v. United States*, 425 U.S. 391, 403 (1976), in order that the client may obtain "the aid of persons having knowledge of the law and skilled in its practice," *Hunt v. Blackburn*, 128 U.S. 464, 470 (1888).

The attorney-client privilege is not without its costs. Cf. *Trammel v. United States*, 445 U.S. 40, 50 (1980). "[S]ince the privilege has the effect of withholding relevant information from the factfinder, it applies only where necessary to achieve its purpose." *Fisher*, 425 U.S., at 403. The attorney-client privilege must necessarily protect the confidences of wrongdoers, but the reason for that protection—the centrality of open client and attorney communication to the proper functioning of our adversary system of justice—"ceas[es] to operate at a certain point, namely, where the desired advice refers *not to prior wrongdoing, but to*

---

[7] See also Hazard, An Historical Perspective on the Attorney–Client Privilege, 66 Calif.L.Rev. 1061 (1978); Developments in the Law–Privileged Communications, 98 Harv.L.Rev. 1450, 1455–1458 (1985).

future wrongdoing." 8 Wigmore, § 2298, p. 573 (emphasis in original); see also *Clark v. United States*, 289 U.S. 1, 15 (1933). It is the purpose of the crime-fraud exception to the attorney-client privilege to assure that the "seal of secrecy," ibid., between lawyer and client does not extend to communications "made for the purpose of getting advice for the commission of a fraud" or crime. *O'Rourke v. Darbishire*, [1920] A.C. 581, 604 (P.C.).

* * *

A

We consider first the question whether a district court may ever honor the request of the party opposing the privilege to conduct an *in camera* review of allegedly privileged communications to determine whether those communications fall within the crime-fraud exception. We conclude that no express provision of the Federal Rules of Evidence bars such use of *in camera* review, and that it would be unwise to prohibit it in all instances as a matter of federal common law.

(1)

At first blush, two provisions of the Federal Rules of Evidence would appear to be relevant. Rule 104(a) provides: "Preliminary questions concerning the qualification of a person to be a witness, *the existence of a privilege*, or the admissibility of evidence shall be determined by the court * * *. In making its determination it is not bound by the rules of evidence *except those with respect to privileges*." (Emphasis added.) Rule 1101(c) provides: "The rule with respect to privileges applies at all stages of all actions, cases, and proceedings." Taken together, these Rules might be read to establish that in a summons-enforcement proceeding, attorney-client communications cannot be considered by the district court in making its crime-fraud ruling: to do otherwise, under this view, would be to make the crime-fraud determination without due regard to the existence of the privilege.

Even those scholars who support this reading of Rule 104(a) acknowledge that it leads to an absurd result.

> "Because the judge must honor claims of privilege made during his preliminary fact determinations, many exceptions to the rules of privilege will become 'dead letters,' since the preliminary facts that give rise to these exceptions can never be proved. For example, an exception to the attorney-client privilege provides that there is no privilege if the communication was made to enable anyone to commit a crime or fraud. There is virtually no way in which the exception can ever be proved, save by compelling disclosure of the contents of the communication; Rule 104(a) provides that this cannot be done." 21 C. Wright & K.

Graham, Federal Practice & Procedure: Evidence § 5055, p. 276 (1977) (footnote omitted).

We find this Draconian interpretation of Rule 104(a) inconsistent with the Rule's plain language. The Rule does not provide by its terms that all materials as to which a "clai[m] of privilege" is made must be excluded from consideration. In that critical respect, the language of Rule 104(a) is markedly different from the comparable California evidence rule, which provides that "the presiding officer may not require disclosure of information *claimed to be privileged* under this division in order to rule on the claim of privilege." Cal.Evid.Code Ann. § 915(a) (West Supp.1989) (emphasis added). There is no reason to read Rule 104(a) as if its text were identical to that of the California rule.

* * *

We see no basis for holding that the tapes in this case must be deemed privileged under Rule 104(a) while the question of crime or fraud remains open. Indeed, respondents concede that "if the proponent of the privilege is able to sustain its burden only by submitting the communications to the court" for *in camera* review, Brief for Respondents 14–15 (emphasis in original), the court is not required to avert its eyes (or close its ears) once it concludes that the communication would be privileged, if the court found the crime-fraud exception inapplicable. Rather, respondents acknowledge that the court may "then consider the same communications to determine if the opponent of the privilege has established that the crime-fraud exception applies." *Id.*, at 15. Were the tapes truly deemed privileged under Rule 104(a) at the moment the trial court concludes they contain potentially privileged attorney-client communications, district courts would be required to draw precisely the counterintuitive distinction that respondents wisely reject. We thus shall not adopt a reading of Rule 104(a) that would treat the contested communications as "privileged" for purposes of the Rule, and we shall not interpret Rule 104(a) as categorically prohibiting the party opposing the privilege on crime-fraud grounds from relying on the results of an *in camera* review of the communications.

(2)

Having determined that Rule 104(a) does not prohibit the *in camera* review sought by the IRS, we must address the question as a matter of the federal common law of privileges. See Rule 501. We conclude that a complete prohibition against opponents' use of *in camera* review to establish the applicability of the crime-fraud exception is inconsistent with the policies underlying the privilege.

We begin our analysis by recognizing that disclosure of allegedly privileged materials to the district court for purposes of determining the merits of a claim of privilege does not have the legal effect of terminating the privilege. Indeed, this Court has approved the practice of requiring parties who seek to avoid disclosure of documents to make the documents available for *in camera* inspection, *see Kerr v. United States District Court for Northern District of Cal.*, 426 U.S. 394, 404–405 (1976), and the practice is well established in the federal courts. * * * Respondents do not dispute this point: they acknowledge that they would have been free to request *in camera* review to establish the fact that the tapes involved attorney-client communications, had they been unable to muster independent evidence to serve that purpose. Brief for Respondents 14–15.

Once it is clear that *in camera* review does not destroy the privileged nature of the contested communications, the question of the propriety of that review turns on whether the policies underlying the privilege and its exceptions are better fostered by permitting such review or by prohibiting it. In our view, the costs of imposing an absolute bar to consideration of the communications *in camera* for purpose of establishing the crime-fraud exception are intolerably high. * * *

B

We turn to the question whether *in camera* review at the behest of the party asserting the crime-fraud exception is always permissible, or, in contrast, whether the party seeking *in camera* review must make some threshold showing that such review is appropriate. In addressing this question, we attend to the detrimental effect, if any, of *in camera* review on the policies underlying the privilege and on the orderly administration of justice in our courts. We conclude that some such showing must be made.

Our endorsement of the practice of testing proponents' privilege claims through *in camera* review of the allegedly privileged documents has not been without reservation. This Court noted in *United States v. Reynolds*, 345 U.S. 1 (1953), a case which presented a delicate question concerning the disclosure of military secrets, that "examination of the evidence, even by the judge alone, in chambers" might in some cases "jeopardize the security which the privilege is meant to protect." *id.*, at 10. Analogizing to claims of Fifth Amendment privilege, it observed more generally: "Too much judicial inquiry into the claim of privilege would force disclosure of the thing the privilege was meant to protect, while a complete abandonment of judicial control would lead to intolerable abuses." *id.*, at 8. * * *

We think that the following standard strikes the correct balance. Before engaging in *in camera* review to determine the applicability of the crime-fraud exception, "the judge should require a showing of a factual basis adequate to support a good faith belief by a reasonable person," *Caldwell v. District Court*, 644 P.2d 26, 33 (Colo.1982), that *in camera* review of the materials may reveal evidence to establish the claim that the crime-fraud exception applies. * * *

C

The question remains as to what kind of evidence a district court may consider in determining whether it has the discretion to undertake an *in camera* review of an allegedly privileged communication at the behest of the party opposing the privilege. Here, the issue is whether the partial transcripts may be used by the IRS in support of its request for *in camera* review of the tapes.

The answer to that question, in the first instance, must be found in Rule 104(a), which establishes that materials that have been determined to be privileged may not be considered in making the preliminary determination of the existence of a privilege. * * *

* * * We conclude that the party opposing the privilege may use any nonprivileged evidence in support of its request for *in camera* review, even if its evidence is not "independent" of the contested communications as the Court of Appeals uses that term.[8]

D

In sum, we conclude that a rigid independent evidence requirement does not comport with "reason and experience," Fed.Rule Evid. 501, and we decline to adopt it as part of the developing federal common law of evidentiary privileges. We hold that *in camera* review may be used to determine whether allegedly privileged attorney-client communications fall within the crime-fraud exception. We further hold, however, that before a district court may engage in *in camera* review at the request of the party opposing the privilege, that party must present evidence sufficient to support a reasonable belief that *in camera* review may yield evidence that establishes the exception's applicability. Finally, we hold that the threshold showing to obtain *in camera* review may be met by using any relevant evidence, lawfully obtained, that has not been adjudicated to be privileged. * * *

It is so ordered.

JUSTICE BRENNAN took no part in the consideration or decision of this case.

---

[8] In addition, we conclude that evidence that is not "independent" of the contents of allegedly privileged communications—like the partial transcripts in this case—may be used not only in the pursuit of *in camera* review, but also may provide the evidentiary basis for the ultimate showing that the crime-fraud exception applies. We see little to distinguish these two uses: in both circumstances, if the evidence has not itself been determined to be privileged, its exclusion does not serve the policies which underlie the attorney-client privilege. * * *

NOTES AND QUESTIONS

1. *In camera review.* As *Zolin* demonstrates, when the preliminary question to be decided involves the existence of a privileged relationship, the determination becomes complicated because of the simultaneous demands to protect the arguably privileged information and to determine fairly whether any valid privilege exists. A delicate compromise between honoring and breaching the privilege often results. The Court's conclusion that an *in camera* review "does not destroy the privilege," 491 U.S. at 569, is critical in permitting this delicate compromise to proceed. In determining whether to conduct an *in camera* review, the court need not consider information offered by the party opposing review. In re Grand Jury Subpoena 92–1(SJ), 31 F.3d 826, 829–30 (9th Cir.1994).

2. *Sources.* For general treatments of the process of determining preliminary questions of fact, see Maguire & Epstein, Preliminary Questions of Fact in Determining the Admissibility of Evidence, 40 Harv.L.Rev. 392 (1927); Morgan, Functions of Judge and Jury in the Determination of Preliminary Questions of Fact, 43 Harv.L.Rev. 165 (1929); Morgan & Maguire, Looking Backward and Forward at Evidence, 50 Harv.L.Rev. 909, 913–18 (1937); Kaplan, Of Mabrus and Zorgs—An Essay in Honor of David Louisell, 66 Calif.L.Rev. 987 (1978). As to conditional relevancy, see Allen, The Myth of Conditional Relevance, 25 Loy.L.A.L.Rev. 871 (1992); Ball, The Myth of Conditional Relevancy, 14 Ga.L.Rev. 435 (1980); Nance, Conditional Relevance Reinterpreted, 70 B.U.L.Rev. 447 (1990); Seidelson, Conditional Relevancy and Federal Rule of Evidence 104(b), 47 Geo.Wash.L.Rev. 1048 (1979).

3. The attorney-client privilege and the crime-fraud exception to that privilege, which were at issue in *Zolin*, are examined in Chapter 15, Section B, infra.

B. PARTY RESPONSIBILITY

(1) OBJECTIONS: FEDERAL RULE 103(a)(1)

WILSON V. WILLIAMS

United States Court of Appeals, Seventh Circuit, En Banc, 1999.
182 F.3d 562.

EASTERBROOK, CIRCUIT JUDGE.

* * *

Jackie Wilson alleges in this suit under 42 U.S.C. § 1983 that James Williams, a guard at the Cook County Jail, attacked him without provocation and inflicted serious injuries. Williams contends that Wilson was the aggressor and that the force used in defense was reasonable under the circumstances. * * *

[Andrew Wilson, the plaintiff's brother, shot and killed two police officers. The plaintiff was an accomplice. Both Wilsons were serving terms of life imprisonment without possibility of parole, and both filed § 1983 suits contending that they were beaten (in separate incidents) while in custody before their convictions.] Andrew recovered a substantial judgment, Wilson v. Chicago, 120 F.3d 681 (7th Cir.1997), though he had trouble receiving a fair trial because the defendants harped on the nature of the crime he had committed. See Wilson v. Chicago, 6 F.3d 1233 (7th Cir.1993) (reversing an initial jury verdict in defendants' favor because the district judge failed to control inappropriate use of Andrew's criminal history).

Before the second trial of his civil suit began, Jackie Wilson asked the district judge to prevent Williams from informing the jury that he had been convicted of killing a police officer. * * * Nonetheless, the judge denied the motion *in limine*,[9] and when the trial began Wilson tried to make the best of his situation. His lawyer told the jury during his opening statement why Wilson was in custody and tried to use this to Wilson's advantage by arguing that Williams attacked Wilson because of the nature of Wilson's crime. Although Wilson's lawyer used the nature of the crime circumspectly, Williams's counsel had no reservations about the subject and invited the jury to rule against Wilson on emotional grounds. Practically the first words of counsel's opening statement were:

> I'd like to reintroduce the litigant, Jackie Wilson, cop killer, murdered a Chicago police officer who was on duty, Officer O'Brien. He also robbed Officer O'Brien. He was convicted of that. He also robbed Officer O'Brien's partner, Officer Fahey. He was also convicted of that. And, yes, that is the crime he was waiting trial on back in 1988 in the Cook County Jail.

Throughout the trial, Williams's lawyer did not miss an opportunity to remind the jury that Wilson had committed a despicable offense, and therefore must be a despicable person who should not collect a dime. Defense counsel was not satisfied with a suggestion that the jury should consider the conviction in connection with Wilson's credibility as a witness. The nature of the crime colored the trial. "Cop killer" was the refrain; defense counsel was inflammatory throughout; neutral language such as "criminally accountable because he participated in a robbery during which his brother Andrew shot two men" did not pass counsel's lips.

* * *

First in sequence is the question whether an objection at trial was necessary, given the district court's pretrial ruling that Williams would be

---

[9] [A motion *in limine* is a pretrial motion to exclude or admit evidence. "*In limine*" means "at the threshold." Ed.]

allowed to inform the jury that Wilson had been convicted, not simply of murder, but of killing a police officer. As the panel recognized, this court's precedents are in conflict. [An amendment to Fed.R.Evid. 103, adopted in 2000, states that a definitive pretrial ruling is sufficient to preserve the issue for appeal.]

One good example of a conditional [nondefinitive] ruling is a judge's statement that, if a litigant testifies, then the adverse party will be entitled to cross-examine in such-and-such a way. Until the condition has been satisfied by the testimony, the ruling has no effect. * * * Similarly, if the judge's pretrial ruling is tentative—if, for example, the judge says that certain evidence will be admitted unless it would be unduly prejudicial given the way the trial develops—then later events may lead to reconsideration, and the litigant adversely affected by the ruling must raise the subject later so that the judge may decide whether intervening events affect the ruling. An appeal in such a case without an objection at trial would bushwhack both the judge and the opponent. Objections alert the judge at critical junctures so that errors may be averted. When a judge has made a conditional, contingent, or tentative ruling, it remains possible to avert error by revisiting the subject.

[Definitive rulings, however, do not invite reconsideration.] When the judge makes a decision that does not depend on how the trial proceeds, then an objection will not serve the function of ensuring focused consideration at the time when decision is best made. A judge who rules definitively before trial sends the message that the right time has come and gone. [An objection is unnecessary to prevent error, and it may do little other than slow down the trial.] Sometimes an objection or offer of proof will alert the jury to the very thing that should be concealed. * * * Motions *in limine* are designed to avoid the delay and occasional prejudice caused by objections and offers of proof at trial; they are more useful if they can serve these purposes, which they do only if objections (and offers of proof) can be foregone safely.

[Treating a definitive ruling as sufficient to preserve the litigant's position for appeal also avoids laying a trap for unwary counselors] Many lawyers suppose that it is enough to raise an issue once and receive a definitive ruling. They may believe that raising the question again may annoy the judge. * * *

Conclusive pretrial rulings on evidence serve another useful end: they permit the parties to adjust their trial strategy in light of the court's decisions. Wilson wanted to keep the occupation of his victim out of the case, but if this could not be accomplished he wanted to introduce the evidence himself, if only to draw its sting. [Sensible adaptations could not be accomplished if Wilson had to wait until Williams offered the evidence, and then raise an objection, acting in the jury's eyes as if he had something to hide.] Waiting, objecting, and only then trying to make something of the subject not only would divest Wilson of the initiative but also would deprive him of an alternative theory of the case.

III.

* * *

A vital qualification is implicit in this way of putting the conclusion. Only arguments that were actually presented to the district court before trial are preserved for appeal—and then only if the district judge came to a definitive conclusion. A judge who expresses a tentative or conditional ruling can by that step require the parties to raise the issue again at trial. District judges thus are fully in charge of the process; they can require or excuse further exchanges on a subject by the way they express their rulings. A judge would do well to explain in the decision proper (or in the final pretrial conference) whether the conclusion is definitive, and whether consideration at trial is required, appropriate, or forbidden * * *; but if the judge does not elaborate, then we assume that an apparently unconditional ruling is conclusive.

Even if the ruling is unconditional, however, it resolves only the arguments actually presented. That much is clear from Fed.R.Evid. 103(a)(1), which requires a litigant to state a specific ground for an objection to evidence; grounds not presented cannot be raised later, else both judge and adversary are sandbagged (and preventable errors occur). There's a corollary to this point: a pretrial objection to and ruling on a particular use of evidence does not preserve an objection to a different and inappropriate use. Thus if the judge decides before trial that particular evidence can be used for impeachment, then there is no need to object at trial to this use; but a completely different use of the evidence is not covered by the ruling, and therefore fresh attention at trial (prompted by an objection) is essential if the error-prevention function of the contemporaneous-objection rule is to be achieved.

This is where Wilson's appeal founders. The district judge, asked before trial to forbid all reference to the occupation of the murder victims, said no. This meant at a minimum that Wilson could be cross-examined about the conviction when he testified on his own behalf. It also implied that Williams could present the testimony of another guard, Officer Cavallone, that Wilson stated during a trip to the infirmary after the altercation: "[Y]ou should have killed me when you had the chance. I already killed two Chicago police officers. My attorney is going to have a field day with this. I have no respect for the law. And the next thing we are going to do is take care of the blue shirts [guards] inside the jail." Williams offered this statement to corroborate his view that Wilson had a hostile and aggressive attitude, and either initiated the altercation or planned to invent a story for his attorney to have a "field day" with. Wilson denies saying any such thing to Cavallone, and he wanted the line "I already killed two Chicago police officers" redacted. The judge did not require this step. But beyond permitting Cavallone to testify to the full version of the statement, and permitting the use of the conviction to call Wilson's credibility as a witness into question, the ruling *in limine* did not sanction any particular use of evidence. In particular, the judge did not give Williams's counsel permission to introduce Wilson as a "cop killer," to describe the details of the crime, to seek sympathy for Wilson's victims, or to imply that people who commit heinous offenses are fair game in prison—all of which Williams's lawyer did, and without objection. The pretrial ruling did not say or imply that such uses (or misuses) of the evidence would be allowed. We reversed the verdict for defendants in the first trial of Andrew Wilson's § 1983 action precisely because defense counsel harped on the details of the murders and sought an emotional rather than reasoned evaluation of the facts. The defense strategy in Jackie Wilson's second trial was similar to that in Andrew Wilson's first— but the big difference is that Andrew Wilson's lawyers objected, and Jackie Wilson's did not. *Misuse* of evidence that has a proper use cannot be argued on appeal without a specific objection. See Fed.R.Evid. 103(a)(1).

A pretrial ruling is definitive only with respect to subjects it covers. Details of usage were not raised or resolved before trial. If the only problem were that Williams's counsel once said "cop killer" rather than a more neutral formulation, or repeated the statement when using the conviction for impeachment, we would be reluctant to say that objection has been forfeited. Misuse of evidence is a matter of degree, and litigants receive the benefit of the doubt in grey areas. But defense counsel strummed on "cop killer" as if it were a guitar rather than a bit of evidence; whatever line there was between proper and improper use was overstepped; objection never came, so forfeiture occurred and the plain-error standard governs. Fed.R.Evid. 103(d).

Plain error means an error that not only is clear in retrospect but also causes a miscarriage of justice. United States v. Olano, 507 U.S. 725, 736 * * * (1993). Wilson has not persuaded us that justice miscarried in his trial because of the way Williams used Wilson's crime. Blatant efforts to manipulate jurors' emotions and persuade them to ignore the facts and instructions often backfire. Wilson may have withheld objection in the hope that jurors would deem that Williams had overplayed his hand. Moreover, Wilson might have thought that Williams's efforts to hammer away on the cop-killer theme showed animus, and thus made Wilson's accusation against Williams more credible. Wilson had a weak case on damages, and success on liability depended on the resolution of a credibility contest. How the balance of advantage from the overuse of the cop-killer theme plays out in such a trial is difficult to say. The effects are not so inevitably baleful to the truth-finding function of trial that the problem must be deemed "plain error."

At last, in what must appear to be an afterthought, we tackle the issue that *has* been preserved: whether the district judge should have ruled before trial that the nature of Wilson's crime is inadmissible. As the Supreme Court observed in *Old Chief*,[10] the precise identity of a crime often creates a potential for prejudice that overwhelms its constructive value. Any legitimate use of the conviction by the defense would have been served by informing the jury that Wilson has been convicted of murder and sentenced to life imprisonment. The judge thus abused his discretion in denying the motion outright. But at oral argument before the court en banc, Wilson's lawyer disclaimed any contention that the district judge should have barred Cavallone from testifying that Wilson said "I already killed two Chicago police officers." With this statement in evidence, the district judge's error with the *Old Chief* issue is harmless. Williams's harping on the subject, and his implication that "cop killers" are not entitled to damages when guards behave as vigilantes, could not be thought harmless, but the lack of objection means that the misuse of the evidence has not been preserved for appellate review. As a result, the judgment is

AFFIRMED.

[Opinion of MANION, CIRCUIT JUDGE, concurring in part, dissenting in part, and concurring in judgment is omitted.]

WOOD, CIRCUIT JUDGE, with whom RIPPLE, CIRCUIT JUDGE, joins, dissenting in part.

While I agree with the *en banc* majority on the larger issues of law that this case presents, I am unable to concur with its finding that the errors that infected this trial do not require reversal. * * *

* * *

The place where I part company with the majority is in its application of these rules. To begin with, it is important to remember that there are two separate potential sources of reversible error in this case: the introduction of evidence concerning the victims of Wilson's crimes and the misuse of this evidence. With respect to the latter, because Wilson's failure to object to the improper use of the victim identity evidence led him to forfeit this point, * * * the question is how his appeal fares under the plain error standard of review of Fed.R.Evid. 103(d). A review of this transcript leaves no doubt that the error is clear in retrospect, and I do not understand the majority to assert otherwise. That leaves the question whether this was an error that "seriously affect[ed] the fairness, integrity, or public reputation of judicial proceedings," and thereby caused a miscarriage of justice. See United States v. Olano, 507 U.S. 725, 736 * * * (1993) (internal quotations deleted). In a brisk paragraph, the majority

---

[10] [Citing Old Chief v. United States, 519 U.S. 172 (1997), discussed in Chapter 7, Section C, infra. Ed.]

concludes that it did not, based solely on the fact that Wilson succeeded in finding a strategic use for the offensive information. * * * But this conclusion loses sight of the very point that lies behind the finding of forfeiture: far more was going on here than the simple act of making sure the jury knew what Wilson had done. Instead, defense counsel openly, repeatedly, and blatantly urged the jury to find against Wilson because of what lay in his past. The misuse of the evidence was so extreme and so pervasive that, even though Wilson forfeited his objection, I would find plain error and reverse on this ground.

Even if the misuse of the victim identity evidence did not rise to the level of plain error, there would remain the question whether the district court committed reversible error in permitting defense counsel to use the evidence at all. Here too, I agree with the majority at the beginning of its analysis, but not at the end. The district court abused its discretion in denying the motion *in limine* outright, because as the majority points out, any legitimate use of the conviction would have been served by informing the jury that Wilson had been convicted of murder and sentenced to life imprisonment. * * * Nevertheless, according to the majority, the fact that Wilson's lawyer at oral argument was not urging us to find that the judge should have barred Officer Cavallone from testifying that Wilson had proclaimed "I already killed two Chicago police officers," means that the district court's error was harmless. * * * In my view, however, this misunderstands the scope of counsel's comment at oral argument. The question we must ask is whether counsel would have objected to that part of Officer Cavallone's account if the judge had granted the motion *in limine* at the outset. To do otherwise would undermine the central holding of the majority opinion, that an objection at trial is unnecessary to preserve for appeal an issue addressed in a definitive *in limine* ruling. Given the wording of the *in limine* motion, I believe that the damaging statement would have been improper. Wilson's lawyers asked that "all evidence of Wilson's criminal conviction for Murder, together with all reference to those criminal proceedings and to any of the underlying conduct" be excluded from the trial. Accordingly, if the motion *in limine* had been granted (even if it had been limited to references to victim identity), as it should have been, Wilson's lawyer would have had a ground on which to object to Officer Cavallone's statement and likely would have done so. There is no question that Wilson's lawyer would have preferred to have tried this case without any mention at all, through Officer Cavallone or anyone else, about the identity of Wilson's victim. Under the proper perspective, I do not regard the error as harmless. Furthermore, again harking back to the theme of most of the majority's opinion, there is an important distinction between a single mention of the identity of the victim and an incessant mantra. From that perspective as well, the error that opened the door to the mantra cannot be regarded as harmless.

* * *

NOTES AND QUESTIONS

1. *Waiver or forfeiture?* See United States v. Olano, 507 U.S. 725, 733 (1993) ("Whereas forfeiture is the failure to make the timely assertion of a right, waiver is the 'intentional relinquishment or abandonment of a known right.'"). Nevertheless, courts and lawyers often do not make this distinction.

2. *Specific v. general objections.* Rule 103(a)(1) requires a party to state the "specific ground" for an objection. In Hafner Mfg. Co. v. City of St. Louis, 172 S.W. 28, 31 (Mo.1914), Justice Lamm paid his respects to the "three i's," incompetent, irrelevant and immaterial: "We think the time has come when, for the convenience of apt designation, this stereotyped objection may, without lowering the dignity of our case, be termed the '*3 i's.*' On a similar ground we may say these '*i's,*' like the mere germinating eyes of the potato, see not, and are of little or no sensible use in the administration of justice." Probably the all time record for generality of objection was set by the Kansas lawyer who objected "on all the grounds ever known or heard of." Johnston v. Clements, 25 Kan. 376, 379 (1881).

3. *Specificity requirement—wrong grounds.* Wigmore asserts, "a specific objection sustained (like a general objection) is sufficient, though naming an untenable ground, if some other tenable ground existed." 1 Wigmore, Evidence § 18, at 831 (Tillers rev. 1983). See also Hamling v. United States, 418 U.S. 87, 108 n.10 (1974) (suggesting that trial court's exclusion of expert testimony might be erroneous on grounds stated but sustainable on lack of expert qualifications); People v. Brown, 94 P.3d 574, 579 (Cal.2004) ("If a judgment rests on admissible evidence it will not be reversed because the trial court admitted that evidence upon a different theory, a mistaken theory, or one not raised below."). But compare 1 McCormick, Evidence § 52 (7th ed. 2013) (arguing that new trial appropriate where correct objection, if made, could have been obviated); Morgan, Basic Problems of Evidence 54 (1962) (same). The case authority is divided.

4. *Specificity requirement—parts.* With documents, the specificity requirement further demands that counsel indicate which particular portions are objectionable. See State v. Fox, 12 N.E.2d 413, 417 (Ohio 1938) ("Whenever evidence is offered which is only partially objectionable, the complaining party must point out the objectionable portion specifically."). Cf. Old Chief v. United States, 519 U.S. 172, 179 n.4 (1997) ("We see no impediment in general to a district court's determination, after objection, that some sections of a document are relevant within the meaning of Rule 401, and others irrelevant and inadmissible under Rule 402.").

5. *Continuing objections.* See State v. Henness, 679 N.E.2d 686, 693 (Ohio 1997) ("At times, a continuing objection is enough to preserve error. * * * However, it was not sufficient in this case. The existence of the marital privilege turns on the specific circumstances surrounding each allegedly privileged communication, e.g., whether a third party was present. Thus,

appellant had to object specifically so the circumstances could be determined.").

6. *"Apparent from the context" exception.* Rule 103(a)(1) recognizes an exception to the objection requirement where the ground for the objection is "apparent from the context." See United States v. Musacchia, 900 F.2d 493, 496–97 (2d Cir.1990) (exception invoked where review of transcript revealed counsel had specifically objected to similar questioning of another witness and asked that objection be deemed continuing). Can trial counsel ever assume that an appellate court will later find that the grounds for an objection were apparent from the context?

7. *Timeliness requirement (contemporaneous objection rule).* Ordinarily, objections must be made as soon as grounds to object become apparent, which is usually when the question is asked. Counsel cannot, as the courts are fond of saying, gamble on a favorable answer to an objectionable question and then move to strike if the result is disappointing.

8. *Motion to strike.* If circumstances prevent counsel from objecting before the witness answers, as where an objectionable answer is not responsive to the question or where the response is hastily given, a motion to strike is appropriate. Normally, in that situation counsel should also request and the court should give an instruction to the jury to disregard the inadmissible evidence. See also United States v. Achiekwelu, 112 F.3d 747, 754 (4th Cir.1997) ("Even when a district court admits evidence without objection, the district court has the discretion to grant a subsequent motion made after the close of the evidence to exclude the evidence.").

9. *Motions in limine.* Although not specifically mentioned in the Rules of Evidence, motions in limine are common. The decision to hold a pretrial hearing falls within the judge's discretion. As the principal case indicates, the court may also postpone a decision until trial. See United States v. LeMay, 260 F.3d 1018, 1028 (9th Cir.2001) ("The judge also reserved the Rule 403 decision until after the prosecution had introduced all its other evidence, in order to get a feel for the evidence as it developed at trial before ruling on whether LeMay's prior acts of child molestation could come in.").

10. *Judicial explanation.* If counsel is unable to understand the ground upon which his or her opponent objects to admission of evidence and asks for specification, the judge should indicate the ground specifically or require objecting counsel to do so. United States v. Dwyer, 539 F.2d 924 (2d Cir.1976).

11. *Common law "exceptions."* At common law, a party wishing to appeal an unfavorable ruling had a further obligation—i.e., to "except" to the ruling. Federal Civil Rule 46 and Criminal Rule 51, which are identical, provide, *inter alia*, that a party need not take a formal "exception" in order to review rulings or orders of the court.

12. *Making the record.* Even the best objections are obviously of no avail on appeal unless they appear in the record. United States v. Johnson, 542 F.2d 230, 234 n.8 (5th Cir.1976):

> Appellant's manner of preserving the point for appeal was irregular. No objection was ever made on the record. Instead, the objection was made and overruled in chambers with the court reporter absent. Later, the trial judge put into the record his recollection of the objection and his reason for overruling it.

> Because appellant failed in his obligation to make the record for appeal, he came dangerously close to losing his chance to argue to us his evidentiary point. Had appellant gone by the book, we would have had before us four items: (1) the original objection, (2) the government's response attempting to bring the elicited testimony within one or more of the exceptions to the bar against "other crimes" evidence, (3) the appellant's response to the government's position, and (4) the trial judge's ruling based on the arguments of both sides.

> Here we have only a general objection as restated by the trial judge and his decision to overrule based on the impeachment exception to the general rule of exclusion.

> If it is necessary to hear an objection outside the presence of the jury, this can be done without depriving this court of a record upon which to base its holding.

See also State v. Goodwin, 703 N.E.2d 1251, 1260 (Ohio 1999) ("[The defendant] did not make a pretrial motion to record all sidebars, nor does the record show that counsel for [the defendant] requested that all pretrial or bench conferences be recorded. In the absence of such a request, any possible error is waived."); State v. Keenan, 689 N.E.2d 929, 938 (Ohio 1998) (47 unrecorded sidebars).

13. *"Connecting up."* See Huddleston v. United States, 485 U.S. 681, 690 (1988) ("Often the trial court may decide to allow the proponent to introduce evidence concerning a similar act, and at a later point in the trial assess whether sufficient evidence has been offered to permit the jury to make the requisite finding. If the proponent has failed to meet this minimal standard of proof, the trial court must instruct the jury to disregard the evidence."). Is it the court's or opposing counsel's responsibility to raise the issue?

14. *Plain error.* Courts have been largely incapable of giving any concrete meaning to "plain error." In United States v. Marcus, 130 S.Ct. 2159, 2164 (2010), the Supreme Court wrote that "an appellate court may, in its discretion, correct an error not raised at trial only where the appellant demonstrates that (1) there is an error; (2) the error is clear or obvious, rather than subject to reasonable dispute; (3) the error affected the appellant's substantial rights, which in the ordinary case means it affected

the outcome of the district court proceedings; and (4) the error seriously affect[s] the fairness, integrity or public reputation of judicial proceedings." (internal quotation marks and citations omitted). See also Henderson v. United States, 133 S.Ct. 1121, 1130 (2013) ("The error must have affected the defendant's substantial rights and it must have seriously affected the fairness, integrity, or public reputation of judicial proceedings.") (citation omitted).

15. *Harmless error*. Although properly preserved, a technical infraction of the rules of evidence may prove unavailing because deemed harmless. See, e.g., Federal Civil Rule 61:

> Unless justice requires otherwise, no error in admitting or excluding evidence—or any other error by the court or a party—is ground for granting a new trial, for setting aside a verdict, or for vacating, modifying, or otherwise disturbing a judgment or order. At every stage of the proceeding, the court must disregard all errors and defects that do not affect any party's substantial rights.

See also Federal Criminal Rule 52(a) (Any error, defect, irregularity or variance which does not affect substantial rights shall be disregarded). Rule 103(a) is intended to leave these principles concerning harmless error unchanged. See Fed.R.Evid. 103(a) advisory committee's note.

WILLIAMS V. STATE
Texas Court of Criminal Appeals, 1977.
549 S.W.2d 183.

DALLY, COMMISSIONER.

This is an appeal from a conviction for the offense of robbery by firearm under the former penal code; the punishment is imprisonment for 25 years.

* * *

The appellant was represented by a court-appointed attorney at trial; however, he filed six pro se motions on his own behalf plus a pro se brief. In one pro se motion the appellant requested permission to "pick my own jury" and cross-examine the complaining witness. The trial court granted both requests. The appellant conducted the cross and direct examination of three witnesses and his attorney questioned the other witnesses. The appellant also made closing arguments to the jury at the guilt-innocence phase of the trial.

Appellant contends the court erred in failing to grant a mistrial after the complaining witness alluded to a prior extraneous offense allegedly committed by him. The appellant complains of the following testimony that occurred during the examination of the complaining witness:

"Q. (By Prosecutor): Except for the occasion when he came into your store once previously, before October the 24th of 1973, had you ever seen the man before?

"A. Yes, sir, I had.

"Q. Where?

"A. He had robbed me once before.

"Q. Well, that's not what I wanted.

"Okay. He has robbed you once before then? Is that true?

"A. Yes, sir.

"Q. And when did that happen?

"A. I don't remember the exact date.

"Q. And is that why you recognized him when he came back to rob you the second time?

"A. That is why.

"THE DEFENDANT: Objection, Judge, Your Honor.

"THE COURT: Sustained."

Testimony concerning this first robbery was brought out numerous other times before the jury without objection. The appellant himself questioned the complainant extensively concerning the first robbery. The court's charge instructed the jury not to consider testimony regarding other offenses that appellant may have committed unless it found beyond a reasonable doubt that the appellant committed the offenses and then only for the purpose of showing a common plan or systematic course of action, or in determining the identity, intent, motive, or malice of the defendant.

Appellant's only objection to this testimony was a general objection which does not preserve error for review. *Smith v. State*, 513 S.W.2d 823 (Tex.Crim.App.1974). Furthermore, appellant's objection was untimely and testimony concerning this first robbery was elicited by the appellant himself on cross-examination of the complainant. *Randolph v. State*, 502 S.W.2d 138 (Tex.Crim.App.1973). Appellant's objection was sustained and no further relief was requested; nothing is presented for review. * * *

Appellant's counsel on appeal argues in this ground of error that this Court should take into consideration the appellant's ignorance, as a layman, of the rules of evidence and procedure concerning preserving error and the rules excluding extraneous offenses. Appellate counsel recognizes that the appellant requested and was granted the right to conduct his own defense, but urges that permitting the appellant to conduct his own defense denied him a fair and impartial trial.

The United States Supreme Court has decided that an accused has the absolute right under the United States Constitution to defend himself without the benefit of counsel. *Faretta v. California*, 422 U.S. 806 (1975). In footnote 46 of *Faretta*, the Court said:

> "The right of self-representation is not a license to abuse the dignity of the courtroom. Neither is it a license not to comply with relevant rules of procedural and substantive law. Thus, whatever else may or may not be open to him on appeal, a defendant who elects to represent himself cannot thereafter complain that the quality of his own defense amounted to a denial of 'effective assistance of counsel.'"

The rules of evidence, procedure, and substantive law will be applied the same to all parties in a criminal trial whether that party is represented by counsel or acting pro se. * * * Grounds of error number one and three are overruled.

* * *

The judgment is affirmed.

Opinion approved by the Court.

NOTES AND QUESTIONS

1.   *Pro se defendants.* Why was the court in *Williams* not more inclined to protect the defendant, who was representing himself, from his own errors? What potential systemic problems might result from liberally forgiving procedural defaults in such circumstances? *[handwritten: EVERYONE WOULD ARGUE PRO SE TO HAVE RESULT THROWN OUT, MISTRIAL, ETC]*

2.   *Plain error.* A possible escape from the harshness of strict enforcement of procedural defaults exemplified in *Williams* may be found in the doctrine of "plain error." See the *Leech* case, Chapter 2, infra, and the notes following it. However, plain error with all its uncertainties is a woefully inadequate alternative to "protecting the record" by a properly made objection.

3.   *Standby counsel.* A standby counsel may be appointed to assist a pro se defendant. However, the accused will not be permitted to function as a co-counsel. See 3 LaFave et al., Criminal Procedure § 11.5(g) (3d ed. 2007) (noting that courts generally prohibit hybrid representation—i.e. accused acting as co-counsel). Why?

(2) OFFERS OF PROOF: FEDERAL RULE 103(a)(2)

UNITED STATES V. ADAMS

United States Court of Appeals, Tenth Circuit, 2001.
271 F.3d 1236.

KELLY, CIRCUIT JUDGE.

Defendant–Appellant Dale L. Adams was found guilty by a jury of possession of a firearm by a felon in violation of 18 U.S.C. § 922(g)(1), and sentenced to 51 months and three years supervised release. At trial, the government relied upon a series of incriminating statements made by Mr. Adams immediately following his arrest. On appeal, he contends that the district court's exclusion of expert testimony by a clinical psychologist denied his right to due process and a fair trial. * * * [The expert reported that Adams's low neurocognitive functioning and dependent personality structure strongly raised "the possibility, *given the conflicting explanations made by Mr. Adams and others,* that he was not telling the truth when he made incriminating statements to Wichita Police Officers and ATF agents. His statements that he was 'protecting a girlfriend' when he confessed to possession of the firearm is consistent with his personality and cognitive state, and indicative of his difficulty making appropriate and reasoned choices."]

* * *

Mr. Adams tried again at the onset of trial to admit the psychologist's report, claiming that it was relevant to Mr. Adams's mental condition and education, factors that could be considered in judging the credibility of his incriminating statements. Again, the government objected to the substance and timing of the evidence and again the court excluded it.

At trial, the government relied heavily on the incriminating statements that Mr. Adams made to the officers immediately following his arrest. Mr. Adams testified at trial, denying the veracity of his earlier confessions, and claiming that he lied to protect his girlfriend from incrimination. Nevertheless, the jury returned a guilty verdict.

Discussion

A. Adequacy of the Offer of Proof

At the outset we are faced with the question of whether Mr. Adams made an offer of proof to the trial court adequate to preserve the claimed error of excluding the psychologist's testimony. "Error may not be based on a ruling excluding evidence unless 'the substance of the evidence was made known to the court by offer [of proof] or was apparent from the context within which questions were asked.' " Inselman v. S & J Operating Co., 44 F.3d 894, 896 (10th Cir.1995) (quoting Fed.R.Evid. 103(a)(2)). On numerous occasions we have held that "merely telling the court the content of * * * proposed testimony' is not an offer of proof." Polys v. Trans–Colorado Airlines, Inc., 941 F.2d 1404, 1407 (10th Cir.1991) * * *. In order to qualify as an adequate offer of proof, the proponent must, first, describe the evidence and what it tends to show and, second, identify the grounds for admitting the evidence. Phillips v. Hillcrest Med. Ctr., 244 F.3d 790, 802 (10th Cir.2001); *Polys,* 941 F.2d at 1407. If the proponent's offer of proof fails this standard, then this court can reverse only in instances of plain error that affected appellant's substantial rights. *Phillips*, 244 F.3d at 802; Fed.R.Evid. 103(d).

A twofold purpose underlies these required showings. First, an effective offer of proof enables the trial judge to make informed decisions based on the substance of the evidence. *Polys*, 941 F.2d at 1406. Second, an effective offer of proof creates "a clear record that an appellate court can review to 'determine whether there was reversible error in excluding the [testimony].'" Id. at 1407 * * *.

Federal Rule of Evidence 103(a)(2) does not mandate a particular form for offers of proof. Instead, the rule invests the trial judge with discretion in determining the form of the offer. Fed.R.Evid. 103(b). There are at least four ways to make an offer of proof of testimony and achieve the purposes underlying the rule. 1 *McCormick on Evidence* § 51, at 216 n.9 (John W. Strong, 5th ed.1999). First, and most desirable from all standpoints except cost, the proponent may examine the witness before the court and have the answers reported on the record. *Id.*; 21 Charles Alan Wright & Kenneth W. Graham, *Federal Practice and Procedure* § 5040, at 214 (1977). The question and answer method necessitates excusing a jury, but this concern is not present when the offer of proof is made, as here, at a pretrial motion hearing. When the proponent proffers testimony in this manner, opposing counsel may be permitted "to cross-examine the witness to develop any factors which would put the proffered testimony in its true light." Wright & Graham § 5040, at 214.

The second, and least favorable, method for making an offer of proof of testimony is a statement of counsel as to what the testimony would be. *Id.* at 215. In this case, the colloquy between counsel and the district court was so lacking in detail that it is difficult to decipher why exclusion of the evidence might be error. During the hearing on the motion in limine, defense counsel stated that he had asked the examining psychologist to "look into whether or not [Mr. Adams's] personality, mental makeup, however you want to put it, would he be so inclined—given the testing that's done, would there be a possibility that he would give a false statement to the police." R.O.A. Supp. Vol. I, at 4. Counsel then proffered that the examining psychologist had "suggested in one of the paragraphs [of the report] * * * that his personality certainly is one that could have been—statements to the police could have been false." *Id.*

An offer of proof of testimony by counsel is the least favored method because of its potential to fall short of the standard required by the rules of evidence as well as the standard set out in *Phillips* and *Polys*. Defense counsel's offer of proof made during the colloquy with the judge illustrates the potential pitfalls of this method. Specificity and detail are the hallmarks of a good offer of proof of testimony, Wright & Graham § 5040, at 213, and conclusory terms, especially when presented in a confused manner, mark poor ones. * * *. Defense counsel hardly met the baseline requirement of " 'merely telling the court the content of * * * [the] proposed testimony.' " *Polys*, 941 F.2d at 1407. As for the additional requirements set out in *Phillips* and *Polys,* counsel did not explain the significance of the proposed evidence or what he expected the evidence to show. *Phillips*, 244 F.3d at 802; *Polys*, 941 F.2d at 1407. Nor did counsel clearly identify "the grounds for which [he] believes the evidence to be admissible." *Id.*

Documentary offers of proof comprise the third and fourth proper forms of proffering anticipated testimony. McCormick § 51, at 216 n.9. The first of these, and least common, is a statement written by examining counsel describing the answers the proposed witness would give if permitted to testify. *Id.* More common, and relevant to this case, the proponent of the evidence may introduce a "written statement of the witness's testimony signed by the witness and *offered as part of the record.*" *Id.* (emphasis added). In using either method of documentary proffer for anticipated testimony, "[i]t is suggested * * * that the writing be marked as an exhibit and introduced into the record for proper identification on appeal." *Id.* * * * Indeed the primary, formal reason for an offer of proof is "to preserve the issue for appeal by including the proposed answer and expected proof *in the official record of trial.*" McCormick § 51, at 216 n.9 (emphasis added).

On the morning of the pretrial hearing, counsel for Mr. Adams apparently sent a facsimile of the psychologist's report directly to the district court judge, who referred to the report during the hearing. * * * The report was not marked as an exhibit. "Documents and other exhibits are usually marked for identification and become part of the record on appeal, even if excluded." Wright & Graham § 5040, at 213. Nor was it filed as an exhibit to a pleading. The report is not part of the record below.

Merely sending a facsimile of the psychologist's report to the judge on the morning before the hearing unfortunately does not guarantee that the faxed item will actually be marked as an exhibit or filed and become part of the record. Our rules anticipate that when an appeal is based upon the challenge to the admission or exclusion of evidence, we be furnished not only with pertinent transcript excerpts, but also with pertinent trial exhibits that are part of the record. 10th Cir. R. 10.3(D)(1) & (2).

Mr. Adams has moved to supplement the record. The appellate rules allow supplementation of the record on appeal in instances where "anything material * * * is omitted from or misstated in the record by error or accident." Fed. R.App. P. 10(e)(2). Because the district court judge did make passing reference to a recently faxed psychologist's report, R.O.A. Supp. Vol. I, at 8, and because counsel as an officer of the court represents that this is the same report that was before the district court, and because the government does not oppose it, we will grant the motion.

We remind counsel, however, of the importance of a valid, properly presented, detailed, and recorded offer of proof when testimony is involved and of the importance of insuring that supporting documentary evidence be made part of the record.

* * *

[The court then upheld the exclusion of the evidence, in part because the prosecution was not notified until three days before trial, in violation of a discovery order.]

NOTES AND QUESTIONS

1. *Completeness of offer of proof.* See United States v. Crockett, 435 F.3d 1305, 1311–12 (10th Cir.2006) ("The proponent of excluded evidence does not satisfy his burden to make an offer of proof merely by telling the trial court the content of the proposed testimony. Rather, the proponent must explain what [he] expects [the evidence] to show and the grounds for which the party believes the evidence to be admissible."); Gruwell v. State, 254 P.3d 223, 232 (Wyo.2011) ("[W]e are unable to discern from the record the specific testimony that Appellant sought to elicit from Dr. Denison. Dr. Denison's report, if it existed, is not in the record.").

2. *"Apparent from the context" exception.* Rule 103(a)(2) recognizes an exception to the offer of proof requirement where the substance of the evidence is "apparent from the context." See Beech Aircraft Corp. v. Rainey, 488 U.S. 153, 174 (1988) (nature of proposed testimony of plaintiff on cross-examination by his own counsel "was abundantly apparent from the very questions" asked). Can trial counsel ever assume that an appellate court will later find that the substance of the offer is apparent from the context?

3. *Cross-examination.* See Ohio R.Evid. 103(A)(2) (providing that an "offer of proof is not necessary if evidence is excluded during cross-examination"); 1 McCormick, Evidence § 51 (7th ed. 2013) ("On cross-examination, the examining counsel is ordinarily assumed not to have had an advance opportunity to learn how the witness will answer, and the requirement of an offer will not usually be applied.").

4. *Pretrial hearings.* Sometimes extensive pretrial hearings are required. DNA evidence is illustrative. See United States v. Yee, 134 F.R.D. 161, 168 (N.D.Ohio 1991) ("hearings were held for approximately six weeks"); People v. Castro, 545 N.Y.S.2d 985, 986 (Sup.Ct.1989) ("This hearing took place over a twelve week period producing a transcript of approximately five thousand pages.").

5. *Talking objections.* Some judges prohibit "talking" objections and offers of proof in front of the jury. See United States v. Henderson, 409 F.3d 1293, 1298 (11th Cir.2005) (Defendant "argues that he could not have made an offer of proof at trial because the district judge did not permit bench conferences, requiring parties to reserve issues they did not wish to discuss before the jury to a time when the jurors were not required to be present in

court. Moreover, he indicates that the district judge also forbade 'speaking objections,' where the objecting party explains the basis for its objection, allowing the objecting party to voice only a very abbreviated basis for its complaint."). How should counsel deal with such a practice?

(3) APPEALS

LUCE v. UNITED STATES

Supreme Court of the United States, 1984.
469 U.S. 38.

Per curiam.

CHIEF JUSTICE BURGER delivered the opinion of the Court.

We granted certiorari to resolve a conflict among the Circuits as to whether the defendant, who did not testify at trial, is entitled to review of the District Court's ruling denying his motion to forbid the use of a prior conviction to impeach his credibility. *Issue*

I

Petitioner was indicted on charges of conspiracy, and possession of cocaine with intent to distribute, in violation of 21 U.S.C. §§ 846 and 841(a)(1). During his trial in the United States District Court for the Western District of Tennessee, petitioner moved for a ruling to preclude the Government from using a 1974 state conviction to impeach him if he testified. There was no commitment by petitioner that he would testify if the motion were granted, nor did he make a proffer to the court as to what his testimony would be. In opposing the motion, the Government represented that the conviction was for a serious crime—possession of a controlled substance. *FF / Motion Facts*

The District Court ruled that the prior conviction fell within the category of permissible impeachment evidence under Federal Rule of Evidence 609(a). The District Court noted, however, that the nature and scope of petitioner's trial testimony could affect the court's specific evidentiary rulings; for example, the court was prepared to hold that the prior conviction would be excluded if petitioner limited his testimony to explaining his attempt to flee from the arresting officers. However, if petitioner took the stand and denied any prior involvement with drugs, he could then be impeached by the 1974 conviction. Petitioner did not testify, and the jury returned guilty verdicts. *Dis of DC rule / DC rtg*

II

The United States Court of Appeals for the Sixth Circuit affirmed. *PH* 713 F.2d 1236 (1983). The Court of Appeals refused to consider petitioner's contention that the District Court abused its discretion in denying the motion *in limine* without making an explicit finding that the probative value of the prior conviction outweighed its prejudicial effect.

cod decision —

The Court of Appeals held that when the defendant does not testify, the court will not review the District Court's *in limine* ruling.

cir. split —

Some other Circuits have permitted review in similar situations;[11] we granted certiorari to resolve the conflict. 466 U.S. 903 (1984). We affirm.

III

It is clear, of course, that had petitioner testified and been impeached by evidence of a prior conviction, the District Court's decision to admit the impeachment evidence would have been reviewable on appeal along with any other claims of error. The Court of Appeals would then have had a complete record detailing the nature of petitioner's testimony, the scope of the cross-examination, and the possible impact of the impeachment on the jury's verdict.

A

A reviewing court is handicapped in any effort to rule on subtle evidentiary questions outside a factual context.[12] This is particularly true under Rule 609(a)(1), which directs the court to weigh the probative value of a prior conviction against the prejudicial effect to the defendant. To perform this balancing, the court must know the precise nature of the defendant's testimony, which is unknowable when, as here, the defendant does not testify.[13]

a

Any possible harm flowing from a district court's *in limine* ruling permitting impeachment by a prior conviction is wholly speculative. The ruling is subject to change when the case unfolds, particularly if the actual testimony differs from what was contained in the defendant's proffer. Indeed even if nothing unexpected happens at trial, the district judge is free, in the exercise of sound judicial discretion, to alter a

b

previous *in limine* ruling. On a record such as here, it would be a matter of conjecture whether the District Court would have allowed the Government to attack petitioner's credibility at trial by means of the prior conviction.

B

When the defendant does not testify, the reviewing court also has no way of knowing whether the Government would have sought to impeach with the prior conviction. If, for example, the Government's case is strong, and the defendant is subject to impeachment by other means, a prosecutor might elect not to use an arguably inadmissible prior conviction.

---

[11] *See, e.g., United States v. Lipscomb*, 226 U.S.App.D.C. 312, 332, 702 F.2d 1049, 1069 (1983) (en banc); * * * The Ninth Circuit allows review if the defendant makes a record unequivocally announcing his intention to testify if his motion to exclude prior convictions is granted, and if he proffers the substance of his contemplated testimony. See *United States v. Cook*, 608 F.2d 1175, 1186 (1979) (en banc).

[12] Although the Federal Rules of Evidence do not explicitly authorize *in limine* rulings, the practice has developed pursuant to the district court's inherent authority to manage the course of trials. See generally Fed.Rule Evid. 103(c); cf. Fed.Rule Crim.Proc. 12(e).

[13] Requiring a defendant to make a proffer of testimony is no answer; his trial testimony could, for any number of reasons, differ from the proffer.

Because an accused's decision whether to testify "seldom turns on the resolution of one factor," *New Jersey v. Portash,* 440 U.S. 450, 467 (1979) (BLACKMUN, J., dissenting), a reviewing court cannot assume that the adverse ruling motivated a defendant's decision not to testify. In support of his motion a defendant might make a commitment to testify if his motion is granted; but such a commitment is virtually risk free because of the difficulty of enforcing it.

Even if these difficulties could be surmounted, the reviewing court would still face the question of harmless error. See generally *United States v. Hasting,* 461 U.S. 499 (1983). Were *in limine* rulings under Rule 609(a) reviewable on appeal, almost any error would result in the windfall of automatic reversal; the appellate court could not logically term "harmless" an error that presumptively kept the defendant from testifying. Requiring that a defendant testify in order to preserve Rule 609(a) claims will enable the reviewing court to determine the impact any erroneous impeachment may have had in light of the record as a whole; it will also tend to discourage making such motions solely to "plant" reversible error in the event of conviction.

* * *

We hold that to raise and preserve for review the claim of improper impeachment with a prior conviction, a defendant must testify. Accordingly, the judgment of the Court of Appeals is

Affirmed.

JUSTICE STEVENS took no part in the consideration or decision of this case.

[JUSTICE BRENNAN, with whom JUSTICE MARSHALL joins, concurred.]

NOTES AND QUESTIONS

1. *Extending Luce.* The lower courts have been rather quick to extend *Luce* to situations outside of Rule 609 where the propriety of anticipated impeachment is challenged. See *United States v. Coumaris,* 399 F.3d 343, 348 (D.C. Cir.2005) ("Coumaris clearly waived his objection to the district court's *in limine* ruling by failing to call the character witnesses to testify. * * * We see no reason—and Coumaris has not suggested any—why [the *Luce*] considerations are not equally applicable when it is a character witness, rather than the defendant himself, who might have testified but for the *in limine* ruling."); *State v. Derby,* 800 N.W.2d 52, 58–59 (Iowa 2011) (collecting and analyzing state court cases that discuss or decide whether, or under what circumstances, an accused who does not testify is entitled to review of a trial court's ruling that evidence of prior convictions would be admissible to impeach the accused should he testify; noting further that a "strong majority of courts" have followed *Luce*).

2. *Constitutional issues.* Should *Luce* be inapplicable when impeachment would violate constitutional principles? Compare United States ex rel. Adkins v. Greer, 791 F.2d 590, 593–94 (7th Cir.1986) (*Luce* inapplicable to ruling on impeachment with unconstitutionally obtained confession), with Jordan v. State, 591 A.2d 875, 878 (Md.1991) (*Luce* applicable to claim that confession was involuntary). See also People v. Boyd, 682 N.W.2d 459, 466–67 (Mich. 2004) ("[D]efendant was required to testify to preserve for review his challenge to the trial court's ruling in limine allowing the prosecutor to admit evidence of defendant's exercise of his *Miranda* right to remain silent. Because the statement at issue in this case would have been properly admissible in one context, defendant's failure to testify precludes us from being able to determine whether the trial court's ruling was erroneous and, if so, whether the error requires reversal.").

3. *Rejecting Luce.* Some state courts have declined to follow *Luce*. See, e.g., Warren v. State, 124 P.3d 522, 527 (Nev.2005) ("But states declining to follow *Luce* maintain that the problem of meaningful review is unfounded when the record sufficiently demonstrates, through an offer of proof, the nature of the defendant's proposed testimony and that the defendant refrained from testifying when faced with impeachment by a prior conviction. Under such conditions, a reviewing court would have a sufficient record to conduct a harmless error analysis."); State v. Whitehead, 517 A.2d 373 (N.J.1986) (impeachment with prior conviction reviewable without defendant testifying); State v. Lamb, 365 S.E.2d 600, 607–08 (N.C.1988) (erroneous decision to permit impeachment of defendant with bad acts preserved for review in spite of defendant's decision not to testify).

4. Does *Luce* mean that, in order to preserve an issue of improper impeachment for appeal, the defendant or witness must in all cases have testified before the jury? The Supreme Court's concerns (1) that a trial court must know the precise nature of the defendant's testimony, which is unknowable when he or she does not testify, and (2) that the ruling remains tentative and subject to changes occasioned by later developments during trial prior to the moment of the defendant's testimony, may be met without the evidence being revealed to the jury. See United States v. Griffin, 818 F.2d 97, 105 (1st Cir.1987); United States v. Wexler, 657 F.Supp. 966, 970–71 (E.D.Pa.1987). What about the court's concern that the defendant in bad faith will "plant" error in the record, never intending to testify? Is this danger, which the Court suggests is not subject to remedy because of the difficulty of enforcing any commitment by the defendant to testify, limited to criminal litigation and specifically to impeachment of the defendant?

OHLER v. UNITED STATES

Supreme Court of the United States, 2000.
529 U.S. 753.

CHIEF JUSTICE REHNQUIST delivered the opinion of the Court.

* * *

Maria Ohler drove a van from Mexico to California in July 1997. As she passed through the San Ysidro Port of Entry, a customs inspector noticed that someone had tampered with one of the van's interior panels. Inspectors searched the van and discovered approximately 81 pounds of marijuana. Ohler was arrested and charged with importation of marijuana and possession of marijuana with the intent to distribute. Before trial, the Government filed motions *in limine* seeking to admit Ohler's prior felony conviction as character evidence under Federal Rule of Evidence 404(b) and as impeachment evidence under Rule 609(a)(1). The District Court denied the motion to admit the conviction as character evidence, but reserved ruling on whether the conviction could be used for impeachment purposes. On the first day of trial, the District Court ruled that if Ohler testified, evidence of her prior conviction would be admissible under Rule 609(a)(1). * * * She testified in her own defense, denying any knowledge of the marijuana. She also admitted on direct examination that she had been convicted of possession of methamphetamine in 1993. The jury found Ohler guilty of both counts * * *.

On appeal, Ohler challenged the District Court's *in limine* ruling allowing the Government to use her prior conviction for impeachment purposes. The Court of Appeals for the Ninth Circuit affirmed, holding that Ohler waived her objection by introducing evidence of the conviction during her direct examination. 169 F.3d 1200 (C.A.9 1999). We granted certiorari to resolve a conflict among the Circuits regarding whether appellate review of an *in limine* ruling is available in this situation. * * * We affirm.

Generally, a party introducing evidence cannot complain on appeal that the evidence was erroneously admitted. See 1 J. Weinstein & M. Berger, Weinstein's Federal Evidence § 103.14, 103–30 (2d ed.2000). Cf. 1 J. Strong, McCormick on Evidence § 55, p. 246 (5th ed. 1999) ("If a party who has objected to evidence of a certain fact himself produces evidence from his own witness of the same fact, he has waived his objection."). Ohler seeks to avoid the consequences of this well-established commonsense principle by invoking Rules 103 and 609 of the Federal Rules of Evidence. But neither of these Rules addresses the question at issue here. Rule 103 sets forth the unremarkable propositions that a party must make a timely objection to a ruling admitting evidence and that a party cannot challenge an evidentiary ruling unless it affects a substantial right. The Rule does not purport to determine when a party waives a prior objection, and it is silent with respect to the effect of introducing evidence on direct examination, and later assigning its admission as error on appeal.

Rule 609(a) is equally unavailing for Ohler; it merely identifies the situations in which a witness' prior conviction may be admitted for impeachment purposes. The Rule originally provided that admissible prior conviction evidence could be elicited from the defendant or established by public record during cross-examination, but it was amended in 1990 to clarify that the evidence could also be introduced on direct examination. [According to Ohler, it follows from this amendment that a party does not waive her objection to the *in limine* ruling by introducing the evidence herself.] However, like Rule 103, Rule 609(a) simply does not address this issue. There is no question that the Rule authorizes the eliciting of a prior conviction on direct examination, but it does no more than that.

Next, Ohler argues that it would be unfair to apply such a waiver rule in this situation because it compels a defendant to forgo the tactical advantage of preemptively introducing the conviction in order to appeal the *in limine* ruling. She argues that if a defendant is forced to wait for evidence of the conviction to be introduced on cross-examination, the jury will believe that the defendant is less credible because she was trying to conceal the conviction. The Government disputes that the defendant is unduly disadvantaged by waiting for the prosecution to introduce the conviction on cross-examination. First, the Government argues that it is debatable whether jurors actually perceive a defendant to be more credible if she introduces a conviction herself. Brief for United States 28. Second, even if jurors do consider the defendant more credible, the Government suggests that it is an unwarranted advantage because the jury does not realize that the defendant disclosed the conviction only after failing to persuade the court to exclude it. *Ibid.*

Whatever the merits of these contentions, they tend to obscure the fact that both the Government and the defendant in a criminal trial must make choices as the trial progresses. For example, the defendant must decide whether or not to take the stand in her own behalf. If she has an innocent or mitigating explanation for evidence that might otherwise incriminate, acquittal may be more likely if she takes the stand. Here, for example, petitioner testified that she had no knowledge of the marijuana discovered in the van, that the van had been taken to Mexico without her permission, and that she had gone there simply to retrieve the van. But once the defendant testifies, she is subject to cross-examination, including impeachment by prior convictions, and the decision to take the stand may prove damaging instead of helpful. A defendant has a further choice to make if she decides to testify, notwithstanding a prior conviction. [The defendant must choose whether to introduce the conviction on direct examination and remove the sting or to take her chances with the prosecutor's possible elicitation of the conviction on cross-examination.]

The Government, too, in a case such as this, must make a choice. If the defendant testifies, it must choose whether or not to impeach her by use of her prior conviction. Here the trial judge had indicated he would allow its use, but the Government still had to consider whether its use might be deemed reversible error on appeal. This choice is often based on the Government's appraisal of the apparent effect of the defendant's testimony. If she has offered a plausible, innocent explanation of the evidence against her, it will be inclined to use the prior conviction; if not, it may decide not to risk possible reversal on appeal from its use.

Due to the structure of trial, the Government has one inherent advantage in these competing trial strategies. Cross-examination comes after direct examination, and therefore the Government need not make its choice until the defendant has elected whether or not to take the stand in her own behalf and after the Government has heard the defendant testify.

Petitioner's submission would deny to the Government its usual right to decide, after she testifies, whether or not to use her prior conviction against her. She seeks to short-circuit that decisional process by offering the conviction herself (and thereby removing the sting) and still preserve its admission as a claim of error on appeal.

But here petitioner runs into the position taken by the Court in a similar, but not identical, situation in Luce v. United States, 469 U.S. 38 (1984), that "[a]ny possible harm flowing from a district court's *in limine* ruling permitting impeachment by a prior conviction is wholly speculative." Id., at 41. Only when the government exercises its option to elicit the testimony is an appellate court confronted with a case where, under the normal rules of trial, the defendant can claim the denial of a substantial right if in fact the district court's *in limine* ruling proved to be erroneous. In our view, there is nothing "unfair," as petitioner puts it, about putting petitioner to her choice in accordance with the normal rules of trial.

* * *

For these reasons, we conclude that a defendant who preemptively introduces evidence of a prior conviction on direct examination may not on appeal claim that the admission of such evidence was error.

The judgment of the Court of Appeals for the Ninth Circuit is therefore affirmed.

It is so ordered.

JUSTICE SOUTER, with whom JUSTICE STEVENS, JUSTICE GINSBURG, and JUSTICE BREYER join, dissenting.

The majority holds that a testifying defendant perforce waives the right to appeal an adverse *in limine* ruling admitting prior convictions for impeachment. The holding is without support in precedent, the rules of evidence, or the reasonable objectives of trial, and I respectfully dissent.

The only case of this Court that the majority claims as even tangential support for its waiver rule is *Luce v. United States* * * *.

This case is different, there being a factual record on which Ohler's claim can be reviewed. She testified, and there is no question that the *in limine* ruling controlled her counsel's decision to enquire about the earlier conviction; defense lawyers do not set out to impeach their own witnesses, much less their clients. Since analysis for harmless error is made no more difficult by the fact that the convictions came out on direct examination, not cross-examination, the case raises none of the practical difficulties on which *Luce* turned, and *Luce* does not dictate today's result.

A-

In fact, the majority's principal reliance is not on precedent but on the "commonsense" rule that "a party introducing evidence cannot complain on appeal that the evidence was erroneously admitted." * * * But this is no more support for today's holding than *Luce* is, for the common sense that approves the rule also limits its reach to a point well short of this case. The general rule makes sense, first, when a party who has freely chosen to introduce evidence of a particular fact later sees his opponent's evidence of the same fact erroneously admitted. He suffers no prejudice. * * * The rule makes sense, second, when the objecting party takes inconsistent positions, first requesting admission and then assigning error to the admission of precisely the same evidence at his opponent's behest. "The party should not be permitted 'to blow hot and cold' in this way." 1 J. Strong, McCormick on Evidence § 55, p. 246, n.14 (5th ed.1999).

Neither of these reasons applies when (as here) the defendant has opposed admission of the evidence and introduced it herself only to mitigate its effect in the hands of her adversary. Such a case falls beyond the scope of the general principle, and the scholarship almost uniformly treats it as exceptional. See, *e.g.,* 1 J. Wigmore, Evidence § 18, p. 836 (P. Tillers rev. 1983) ("[A] party who has made an unsuccessful motion in limine to exclude evidence that he expects the proponent to offer may be able to first to offer that same evidence without waiving his claim of error") * * *. The general thrust of the law of evidence, then, not only fails to support the majority's approach, but points rather clearly in the other direction.

With neither precedent nor principle to support its chosen rule, the majority is reduced to saying that "there is nothing 'unfair' * * * about putting petitioner to her choice in accordance with the normal rules of trial." * * * Things are not this simple, however.

Any claim of a new rule's fairness under normal trial conditions will have to stand or fall on how well the rule would serve the objects that trials in general, and the Rules of Evidence in particular, are designed to achieve. Thus the provisions of Federal Rule of Evidence 102, that "[t]hese rules shall be construed to secure fairness in administration, elimination of unjustifiable expense and delay, and promotion of growth and development of the law of evidence to the end that the truth may be ascertained and proceedings justly determined." A judge's job, accordingly, is to curb the tactics of the trial battle in favor of weighing evidence calmly and getting to the most sensible understanding of whatever gave rise to the controversy before the court. The question is not which side gains a tactical advantage, but which rule assists in uncovering the truth. Today's new rule can make no such claim.

purpose Rule 102

Previously convicted witnesses may testify honestly, but some convictions raise more than the ordinary question about the witness's readiness to speak truthfully. A factfinder who appreciates a heightened possibility of perjury will respond with heightened scrutiny, and when a defendant discloses prior convictions at the outset of her testimony, the jury will bear those convictions in mind as she testifies, and will scrutinize what she says more carefully. The purpose of Rule 609, in making some convictions admissible to impeach a witness's credibility, is thus fully served by a defendant's own testimony that the convictions occurred.

It is true that when convictions are revealed only on cross-examination, the revelation also warns the factfinder, but the timing of their disclosure may do more. The jury may feel that in testifying without saying anything about the convictions the defendant has meant to conceal them. The jury's assessment of the defendant's testimony may be affected not only by knowing that she has committed crimes in the past, but by blaming her for not being forthcoming when she seemingly could have been. Creating such an impression of current deceit by concealment is very much at odds with any purpose behind Rule 609, being obviously antithetical to dispassionate factfinding in support of a sound conclusion. The chance to create that impression is a tactical advantage for the Government, but only in the majority's dismissive sense of the term; it may affect the outcome of the trial, but only if it disserves the search for truth.

Allowing the defendant to introduce the convictions on direct examination thus tends to promote fairness of trial without depriving the Government of anything to which it is entitled. There is no reason to discourage the defendant from introducing the conviction herself, as the majority's waiver rule necessarily does.

H of Dissent

NOTES AND QUESTIONS

1.   *Rejecting Ohler.* Some state courts have declined to follow *Ohler*. E.g., State v. Swanson, 707 N.W.2d 645, 654 (Minn.2006) ("We recently rejected similar reasoning, stating that '[i]t is inconsistent with our precedent and with our notion of fairness to conclude that once a defendant chooses to

stipulate to evidence he was unsuccessful in getting excluded he has waived the opportunity to argue on appeal that the court erred in admitting the evidence.' "); Pineda v. State, 88 P.3d 827, 831 (Nev.2004) ("States that have rejected *Ohler* have done so because a trial court is fully aware of the proposed evidence and law when ruling on such evidence in limine, and it is a poor trial tactic for defense attorneys to wait for the prosecution to introduce such evidence on cross-examination. Given the nature of this tactical dilemma, these courts have held that a defendant may under such circumstances appeal a trial court's preliminary ruling conditionally admitting prior bad acts or convictions for impeachment purposes.").

2. *Invited error.* See People v. Wittrein, 221 P.3d 1076, 1082 (Colo.2009) ("Even though Dr. Stern's response was impermissible, we hold that the error was invited by defense counsel's questioning."); State v. Campbell, 738 N.E.2d 1178, 1188 (Ohio 2000) ("This court has found invited error when a party asked the court to take some action later claimed to be erroneous, or affirmatively consented to a procedure the trial judge proposed. But defense counsel did not suggest, request, or affirmatively consent to this procedure. * * * But invited error must be more than mere 'acquiesence in the trial judge's erroneous conclusion.' "); State v. Gary M.B., 676 N.W.2d 475, 480 (Wis.2004) ("Under the doctrine of strategic waiver, also known as invited error, '[a] defendant cannot create his own error by deliberate choice of strategy and then ask to receive benefit from that error on appeal.' ").

3. *"Fighting fire with fire."* Cross-examination on a matter, or introducing evidence to rebut it, has occasionally been held to waive objections to the matter previously made and overruled. See, e.g., State v. McKinney, 190 S.E.2d 30 (S.C.1972) (unless the objection is expressly reserved, cross-examination waives objection). However, the vast weight of authority is contra. 1 Wigmore, Evidence § 18, at 838 n.37 (Tillers rev. 1983). Parties objecting to admission may be held to waive the objection if they go beyond cross-examination and rebuttal of the evidence and affirmatively rely upon the inadmissible evidence and introduce similar evidence through their own witnesses. 1 Graham, Handbook of Federal Evidence § 103.4 (7th ed. 2012). Is this concept of waiver consistent with the Federal Rules of Evidence?

4. *"Opening the door."* The above concepts are related to, but are analytically distinct from, other situations that are sometimes included under the opening-the-door label. In this category, parties may, by their decision to open a specific issue such as character, permit response by an opponent that would have been barred absent their action under general concepts of relevancy or specific application of a rule, such as Rule 404(a) governing evidence of the character of the accused. See Chapter 8, Section C, infra. The distinction between this "door opening" concept and those discussed above is that there is nothing improper here about introduction of the new issue into the case. As a result, the analysis is a much more straightforward application of concepts of probativity weighed against prejudice, confusion, and

consumption of time, rather than the equitable concern of rough justice that infuses what passes for analysis under the other concepts.

When the first inquiry on an issue occurs during cross-examination, the door-opening principle does not operate because cross-examiners are not permitted to open the door for themselves. United States v. Mariani, 539 F.2d 915, 923–24 (2d Cir.1976). This limitation, however, is not generally applicable to matters "plainly within the scope of" direct examination or "reasonably suggested by" it. United States v. Havens, 446 U.S. 620, 627 (1980).

(4) LIMITED ADMISSIBILITY: FEDERAL RULE 105

CARBO v. UNITED STATES

United States Court of Appeals, Ninth Circuit, 1963.
314 F.2d 718.

[Carbo and others were convicted of extortion affecting commerce and of conspiracy. The case arose out of their efforts to secure managerial control of Don Jordan, a welterweight fighter, by bringing pressure to bear upon his manager, Donald Nesseth, and a local promoter, Jackie Leonard.]

MERRILL, CIRCUIT JUDGE.

* * *

Sica * * * objected to the introduction of testimony by Leonard and Nesseth to the effect that by reputation they knew of Sica as an "underworld" man and a "strong-arm" man. The objection was overruled. Sica assigns error in these respects.

In discussing the admissibility of evidence of bad moral character the Supreme Court in Michelson v. United States, 1948, 335 U.S. 469, 475, states:

> "Courts that follow the common-law tradition almost unanimously have come to disallow resort by the prosecution to any kind of evidence of a defendant's evil character to establish a probability of his guilt. * * * "

* * *

The nature of Sica's reputation was not introduced into the case for the purpose of characterizing him as a bad man likely to resort to the conduct with which he is charged. This was not the source of its relevance.

Instead the prosecution relied on the reputation of Sica as a probative fact enabling the jury to infer that Sica had intervened with Leonard and Nesseth knowing that his presence would instill fear in them and intending to manipulate this fear for the benefit of Carbo and Palermo; and further, to conclude that Carbo and Palermo had secured Sica's participation with full realization that his effectiveness was based upon the fear his reputation could inspire in the victims.

In cases of extortion based upon fear of violence the facts of fear, actual or anticipated, and of its reasonableness, are vital factors. To prove a substantive act of extortion it is essential to show the generation of fear in the victim. To prove a substantive act of attempted extortion it is necessary to prove an attempt to instill fear. To prove a conspiracy to extort it is necessary to show a plan to instill fear.

Here Sica stood in the position of a dangerous weapon to be used to strike fear into the hearts of Leonard and Nesseth. It was part of the prosecution's case to charge and to prove that the conspirators considered Sica to occupy this position. That Leonard and Nesseth considered him to be dangerous and that fear reasonably resulted from his appearance because of his reputation constituted relevant facts upon this part of the prosecution's case. * * *

It is true that (despite the precautionary steps taken by the judge as later discussed) the jury may have permitted this evidence to bear upon the probability of Sica's guilt. The question is whether this possibility renders such evidence unduly prejudicial and inadmissible. If so, the United States is precluded from establishing a material part of its case.

The question then is not whether the United States may use Sica's reputation as a sword against him, but whether he may himself make use of it as a shield to immunize himself from proof of the means by which the conspirators planned to frighten their victims into submission. If he may, then all who are known to live by violence are free to extort by the tacit threat of violence conveyed by their reputations; for the reasonableness of the resulting fear, as determined by its cause, may not be presented to the jury.

We cannot accept this result as a sound balance of the conflicting interests involved.

This, in our judgment (with such safeguards as were taken by the trial judge), is a proper case for application of what has been termed the "multiple admissibility doctrine." As stated in 1 Wigmore, Evidence (3d Ed., 1940), § 13, page 300:

> "When an evidentiary fact is offered for one purpose, and becomes admissible by satisfying all the rules applicable to it in that capacity, it is not inadmissible because it does not satisfy the rules applicable to it in some other capacity, and because the jury might improperly consider it in the latter capacity. This doctrine, although involving certain risks, is indispensible [sic] as a practical rule."

* * *

To avoid confusion of issues and to foreclose the jury from using the reputation evidence to convict defendants on the "bad man" theory, the court below, upon admitting the testimony in question, instructed the jury as to the limited consideration which might be given. The subject was again dealt with in the court's charge to the jury. We have no doubt but that to the maximum extent possible, prejudice flowing from any confusion of issues by the jury was eliminated.

* * *

We conclude that the district court did not err in * * * in admitting the evidence of Sica's reputation.

SHERMAN V. BURKE CONTRACTING, INC.
United States Court of Appeals, Eleventh Circuit, 1990.
891 F.2d 1527.

PER CURIAM:

Willie Lewis Sherman brought this suit against his former employer, Burke Contracting, Inc., and its president and principal owner, William Burke, (collectively Burke) seeking recovery for two acts of racial discrimination. * * * [After leaving Burke, Sherman] found work with another contractor, Palmer Construction Co. (Palmer). [He alleges] that Burke, in retaliation against him for complaining to the EEOC, persuaded Palmer to fire him.

* * *

To prove that Burke caused Palmer to fire him, Sherman introduced into evidence a tape recording of a conversation he had with Wade Palmer, the owner of Palmer Construction, a few weeks after he left Palmer's employ. In that conversation, which Sherman recorded without Wade Palmer's knowledge, Wade Palmer stated that William Burke had urged him to fire Sherman for complaining about Burke to the EEOC.[14]

Burke contends that the district court erred in permitting the recording to come before the jury because the recording was inaudible and its contents were hearsay. We find no error.

---

[14] The tape recording contains the following exchange: Sherman: "Alright sir, Mr. Wade you know when you were telling me about [how] Mr. Bill and Mr. John told you not to work me. [pause] You remember I was working that week with you and you were telling me * * *." Palmer: "Un, un, that ain't what I told you they didn't tell me not to work you. They said if they was me, they wouldn't work you, you turning it around. They can't tell me who to work and who not to work. They just said if I was you, he sued us and done us like he did, if I was you, I wouldn't. * * * Like he didn't tell me I couldn't work you, he just told me if it was him and you done sued him like you did, and all, you might turn around and sue me."

The controversy concerning the admissibility of the recording arose during Sherman's case-in-chief[15] when his attorney called Wade Palmer to the witness stand and asked him if William Burke had spoken to him about Sherman at any time during Sherman's employment with Palmer Construction. Counsel hoped that Palmer would say that a conversation had taken place and that William Burke had urged him to fire Sherman for complaining to the EEOC; this testimony would have been admissible as nonhearsay under Fed.R.Evid. 801(d)(2) (admission by party-opponent). When Palmer responded that there had been no such conversation, Sherman's attorney approached the bench and asked to discuss a matter out of the jury's presence. After the jury had been excused, counsel informed the court that Palmer had told Sherman that such a conversation had, in fact, taken place; that Sherman had surreptitiously recorded Palmer's statement to this effect; and that counsel wished to impeach Palmer by playing the recording before the jury.

The court concluded that the recording might be admissible as impeachment evidence and suggested that the proper course would be for counsel to call Sherman to the stand, in the jury's absence, and have him identify the recording. *See generally* Fed.R.Evid. 901. If Sherman identified it, he could then recall Palmer to the stand and confront him with the recording. Defense counsel made no objection to this procedure. Accordingly, with the jury still out, Sherman took the stand and identified the recording as the one he had made of his conversation with Wade Palmer a few weeks after the company had fired him.

At this point, Sherman's counsel argued that a sufficient predicate had been laid to introduce the recording into evidence for purposes of impeaching Palmer's statement that William Burke had not spoken to him about Sherman. Defense counsel objected, however, on the ground that portions of the recording were inaudible. The court found that the recording adequately revealed the relevant portion of the conversation between Sherman and Palmer and therefore overruled counsel's objection. The defense raised no objection on hearsay grounds; nor did counsel request a limiting instruction to inform the jury that the recording was admitted solely to impeach Palmer's testimony. The trial then resumed, with Sherman taking the stand and identifying the tape recording. The court admitted the recording into evidence and played it before the jury without any limiting instruction. * * *

---

[15] The controversy actually began prior to trial when Burke's counsel moved the court in limine to prevent Sherman from mentioning the tape recording in the jury's presence; counsel argued that the recording's contents were hearsay. The court reserved decision on the matter until trial, at which time Burke could renew his objection. As the text indicates, infra, after the court admitted the tape recording for purposes of impeachment, Burke objected on the ground that the recording was inaudible. Under the circumstances, we do not consider the motion in limine; rather, we review the objection made at trial and the court's ruling thereon.

Burke's second claim is that the recording was hearsay. We agree, as did the district court, which admitted the recording only for impeachment purposes. *See generally* Fed.R.Evid. 801(c). The court, however, gave no limiting instruction, and the defense failed to raise any objection on that point. In effect, then, the recording was received for the truth of its contents, and Sherman's counsel used it for that purpose—without any objection from the defense—in his closing argument to the jury. We believe that had defense counsel requested a limiting instruction, the court would have given one, having already recognized that the recording's sole value was as impeachment evidence. Burke now asks us to hold that its attorney had no duty to request a limiting instruction but that the court had a duty to give such an instruction on its own initiative. We refuse to so hold.

The relevant rule of evidence, Fed.R.Evid. 105, provides: "When evidence which is admissible as to one party or for one purpose but not admissible as to another party or for another purpose is admitted, the court, *upon request*, shall restrict the evidence to its proper scope and instruct the jury accordingly." (Emphasis added.) Under this rule, the court had a duty to instruct only "upon request." Since the court had no duty to give a limiting instruction in the absence of a request, we may reverse only if we conclude that the court's failure to give the instruction constituted plain error. *See United States v. Garcia*, 530 F.2d 650, 656 (5th Cir.1976).

We have found no civil case in which a federal appellate court has labelled as plain error a trial judge's failure to give a limiting instruction with respect to evidence that is admissible for some purpose.[16] Indeed, we have uncovered only a single case even addressing the issue. In that case, *Herndon v. Seven Bar Flying Serv., Inc.*, 716 F.2d 1322 (10th Cir.1983), the appellant argued that plain error occurred when a trial judge failed sua sponte to instruct a jury that evidence of subsequent remedial measures was not admissible to prove negligence. The Tenth Circuit recognized that such an instruction would have been appropriate if requested but held that, without such a request, reversal would be improper unless the trial court's failure to instruct constituted plain error. *Id.* at 1330. The court then concluded that the absence of an instruction in that case did not constitute plain error because it resulted in no manifest "miscarriage of justice." *Id.*; *cf. Wilson v. Attaway*, 757 F.2d 1227, 1242–43 (11th Cir.1985) (finding no plain error in trial judge's failure sua sponte to exclude relevant evidence on ground that danger of unfair prejudice outweighed probative value based on his holding that admission resulted in no manifest "miscarriage of justice"). Lawyers

---

[16] Appellants concede that the challenged evidence was admissible to impeach the credibility of relevant testimony: whether Palmer had talked with William Burke about Sherman while Sherman was an employee of Palmer Construction was pertinent to the merits of Sherman's case against Burke.

frequently choose for strategic reasons not to request limiting instructions. In order to find plain error in this context, therefore, a court must conclude that, as a matter of law, counsel's strategic choice resulted in a manifest miscarriage of justice. We cannot reach such a conclusion here. We therefore find no plain error in the trial court's decision to admit the tape-recorded statement for its nonhearsay purpose without a cautionary instruction.

* * *

AFFIRMED in part, REVERSED in part, and VACATED in part.

[CHIEF JUDGE TJOFLAT and SENIOR JUDGE ATKINS concurred specially on another issue.]

NOTES AND QUESTIONS

1. *Limiting instructions.* Concerning the problem of limiting and curative instructions, America's most famous trial lawyer once wrote:

> Few judges are psychologists, or they would realize that nothing can be stricken out of a human consciousness after being once let in. Judges seem to be quite unaware that it is a hard task to put anything into the average mind, and, once in, an impossible one to take it out. * * * If, after days or weeks or months of taking testimony, the judge decides that some item was not [admissible], he coolly tells the jury that they are to ignore this, that, and the other thing, probably without at all explaining his meaning of "ignore." The jury is so instructed, regardless of the fact that no one is able to know all the specific things that enter into his opinion, or take away, from an opinion already formed, any of the special facts, circumstances, guesses, or prejudices that go into its making.

Darrow, The Story of My Life 145 (Grosset's Universal ed.1960).

In O'Rear v. Fruehauf Corp., 554 F.2d 1304, 1309 (5th Cir.1977), after counsel had repeatedly brought out prejudicial matter contrary to court rulings, the judge put it more picturesquely: "You can throw a skunk into the jury box and instruct the jurors not to smell it, but it doesn't do any good."

2. *Multiple parties.* Problems of limited admissibility also arise when evidence is admissible against one party but not against a co-party. In Delli Paoli v. United States, 352 U.S. 232 (1957), the trial judge admitted a confession by one defendant which implicated his codefendant even though it was inadmissible against the codefendant. The Supreme Court held that no error was committed since the jury was instructed to consider the confession only against the confessing defendant. However, in Bruton v. United States, 391 U.S. 123 (1968), *Delli Paoli* was expressly overruled. The Court concluded that the risk that the jury would not follow the instruction was too great, and since the confessing defendant elected not to testify, the right of the nonconfessing defendant to confront the witnesses against him under the

Sixth Amendment was violated. The Court described the confession as "powerfully incriminating" and "devastating." See also Gray v. Maryland, 523 U.S. 185, 192 (1998) ("Redactions that simply replace a name with an obvious blank space or a word such as 'deleted' or a symbol or other similarly obvious indications of alteration * * * leave statements that * * * so closely resemble *Bruton's* unredacted statements that, in our view, the law must require the same result."); United States v. Schwartz, 541 F.3d 1331, 1352 n.64 (11th Cir.2008) ("This dilemma highlights the practical difficulties of redacting a codefendant statement without draining its meaning. A redaction is not a magic charm, an amulet against constitutional violation. Nor is it simple arithmetic. If done too liberally, redaction risks inaccuracy by eliminating words that played an integral role in establishing the statement's meaning. * * * If performed too sparingly, though, redaction jeopardizes the confrontation rights of the nonconfessing codefendant.").

What is the reach of *Bruton* when the impact of the codefendant's confession is less direct or where its independent impact is diminished by the admission of the defendant's own confession? For some answers to these questions, see Richardson v. Marsh, 481 U.S. 200 (1987) (Confrontation Clause not violated where direct references to nontestifying defendant omitted from codefendant's confession even though defendant is indirectly linked to the confession by other evidence); Cruz v. New York, 481 U.S. 186 (1987) (Confrontation Clause violated when codefendant's confession naming defendant is introduced even though defendant's own interlocking confession admitted, but since defendant's own confession properly admitted error may be rendered harmless). For further examination of confrontation issues, see Chapter 13, Section C, infra.

(5) NON–JURY TRIALS

CLARK V. UNITED STATES
United States Court of Appeals, Eighth Circuit, 1932.
61 F.2d 695, aff'd, 289 U.S. 1 (1933).

[Genevieve Clark was accepted and acted as a juror in a celebrated mail fraud case. After a seven week trial, the jury deliberated one week and was unable to reach a verdict. Throughout the deliberations the vote was eleven for conviction and one for acquittal, the lone vote being Mrs. Clark's. She was then adjudged guilty of contempt for withholding, on voir dire examination, information as to her previous associations with the accused and other aspects of bias and prejudice. On appeal, one of the grounds of error asserted was the admission in evidence of the deliberations in the jury room.]

KENYON, CIRCUIT JUDGE.

* * * There is no question here of impeaching the verdict of a jury. The question is the misconduct of one chosen as a juror. * * *

The testimony admitted of other jurors as to the statements and conduct of appellant in the jury room were admissible as bearing on the question of the falsity of answers given by her on the voir dire examination. No public policy requires the proceedings in the jury room to be kept secret under the circumstances here presented.

Assuming, however, that such testimony should have been excluded, there is exclusive thereof sufficient evidence in this record in our judgment to sustain the finding of the trial court as to criminal contempt. * * *

The fact that immaterial evidence may have been admitted does not necessarily require the reversal of a case where a court sits without a jury as a trier of fact, as there is a presumption that it acts only upon the basis of proper evidence. If there is not sufficient evidence to sustain the trial court if the improper evidence is disregarded, the presumption of course breaks down. In Swepston v. United States (C.C.A.) 251 F. 205, 209, referring to this question, the court said: "It is to be presumed that the court at last considered only the facts and circumstances that were in reality admissible and also calculated to support the judgments claimed; and this was in accord with settled rules of practice in cases tried without a jury." In Sinclair v. United States, 279 U.S. 749, 767 * * *, the court said: "Objections are offered to the admission of certain evidence. In answer, we need only refer to what was said in United States v. King, 7 How. 833, 854, 855 (12 L.Ed. 934): 'In some unimportant particulars, the evidence objected to was not admissible. But where the court decides the fact and the law without the intervention of a jury, the admission of illegal testimony, even if material, is not of itself a ground for reversing the judgment, nor is it properly the subject of a bill of exceptions. If evidence appears to have been improperly admitted, the appellate court will reject it, and proceed to decide the case as if it was not in the record.' " In Oates v. United States (C.C.A.) 233 F. 201, 205, it is said: "When a judge hears a case without a jury, he is supposed to act only on proper evidence, and if on review it is found that the evidence properly admitted justifies the decree it ought to be affirmed, and if not it ought to be reversed. * * * In all these and many other cases the rule laid down by Chief Justice Marshall in Field v. United States, 9 Pet. 202, 9 L.Ed. 94, has been followed: 'As the cause was * * * not tried by a jury, the exception to the admission of evidence was not properly the subject of a bill of exceptions. But if the District Court improperly admitted the evidence, the only effect would be that this court would reject that evidence, and proceed to decide the cause as if it were not on the record. It would not, however, of itself constitute any ground for a reversal of the judgment.' "

* * * The judgment of the court as to the contempt is affirmed, but the sentence is set aside and the case remanded to the trial court only for the purpose of resentencing.

Remanded.

GARDNER, CIRCUIT JUDGE (dissenting).

* * *

Finally, it is said in the majority opinion that the fact that immaterial evidence may have been admitted does not necessarily require a reversal of the case where the court sits without a jury, because there is a presumption that it acts only on the basis of proper evidence. There are two answers to this suggestion: First, if this evidence be excluded, there is no substantial evidence to sustain the judgment of the trial court, and the evidence is not only immaterial but is incompetent; and, second, that while it will ordinarily be presumed that the court sitting without a jury considers only the material and competent evidence, yet this is only a presumption, and it affirmatively appears in this case that the court did consider and did rely upon this very evidence. In the opinion of the trial court it is said: "During the deliberations of the jury, after the case was finally submitted, she announced that, since Mr. Horowitz had been unable to convince her of the guilt of the defendants, the other jurors could hardly expect to do so. She virtually closed her ears to the arguments of other jurors, and made a statement with respect to the government witness Cobel, the effect of which was to charge him with having given perjured testimony in a case in the South in an attempt to convict an innocent man. * * * Mrs. Clark, during the deliberations of the jury, expressed a wish that she might consult with her husband and secure his advice. She also made statements to the effect that she could not vote to send seven men to the penitentiary. The jury were out for approximately one week, and stood eleven for conviction, and one (Mrs. Clark) for acquittal." In another part of the opinion the court refers to the appellant's "unyielding attitude" in the jury room.

This conclusively shows that the trial court did not disregard nor exclude this incompetent evidence, and it is elementary that when facts appear presumptions vanish. A presumption cannot be weighed in the balance as against facts. * * *

NOTES AND QUESTIONS

1.   *Exclusion of evidence.* While, as *Clark* teaches, reversal will rarely result from admission of questionable evidence in a bench trial, the erroneous exclusion of evidence is treated the same in bench and jury trials. A professional finder of fact is no better able than a jury to consider evidence that was excluded. However, the greater danger of reversal when evidence is excluded from a bench trial does not mean that it is always foolish to object.

Parties do not need to worry about reversal on appeal unless they won below, and exclusion of persuasive, albeit inadmissible, evidence may be critical to a victory in the trial court. This is true even when the finder of fact is a judge, equipped with a sophisticated legal mind that we presume is capable of ignoring improperly admitted evidence.

2.   *Federal Rules.* The position set forth in *Clark* continues under the Federal Rules. See Harris v. Rivera, 454 U.S. 339, 346 (1981) (per curiam) ("In bench trials, judges routinely hear inadmissible evidence that they are presumed to ignore when making decisions."); Tampa Bay Shipbuilding & Repair Co. v. Cedar Shipping Co., 320 F.3d 1213, 1216 (11th Cir.2003) ("A district court's evidentiary rulings are not subject to reversal on appeal absent a clear abuse of discretion. This standard of deference is even greater when the objected-to evidentiary ruling is made during a bench trial because it is presumed that the district judge will rely only upon properly admitted and relevant evidence.").

3.   *Presumption rebutted.* See United States v. Poole, 640 F.3d 114, 118 (4th Cir.2011) ("At the outset, we observe that the district court's comments constitute error, because the court apparently gave some consideration to matters that were not in evidence in the case."); Petion v. State, 48 So.3d 726, 730 (Fla.2010) ("The initial presumption that a trial court has disregarded inadmissible evidence during a non-jury trial is well established in Florida. * * * However, this presumption can be rebutted through a trial court's express and specific finding of admissibility on the record or a statement on the record which discloses that the trial judge has actually relied upon the erroneous evidence to support the verdict or result.").

4.   *Sources.* Levin & Cohen, The Exclusionary Rules in Nonjury Criminal Cases, 119 U.Pa.L.Rev. 905 (1971); Davis, An Approach to Rules of Evidence for Nonjury Cases, 50 A.B.A.J. 723 (1964).

5.   The admissibility of evidence to impeach verdicts is considered in more detail in Chapter 16, Section B, infra.

CHAPTER 2[1]

LIMITATIONS OF THE ADVERSARY SYSTEM

■ ■ ■

■ ■ ■

NAPUE V. ILLINOIS
Supreme Court of the United States, 1959.
360 U.S. 264.

MR. CHIEF JUSTICE WARREN delivered the opinion of the Court.

At the murder trial of petitioner the principal state witness, then serving a 199–year sentence for the same murder, testified in response to a question by the Assistant State's Attorney that he had received no promise of consideration in return for his testimony. The Assistant State's Attorney had in fact promised him consideration, but did nothing to correct the witness' false testimony. The jury was apprised, however, that a public defender had promised "to do what he could" for the witness. The question presented is whether on these facts the failure of the prosecutor to correct the testimony of the witness which he knew to be false denied petitioner due process of law in violation of the Fourteenth Amendment to the Constitution of the United States.

The record in this Court contains testimony from which the following facts could have been found. The murder in question occurred early in the morning of August 21, 1938, in a Chicago, Illinois, cocktail lounge. Petitioner Henry Napue, the witness George Hamer, one Poe and one Townsend entered the dimly lighted lounge and announced their intention to rob those present. An off-duty policeman, present in the lounge, drew his service revolver and began firing at the four men. In the melee that followed Townsend was killed, the officer was fatally wounded, and the witness Hamer was seriously wounded. Napue and Poe carried Hamer to the car where a fifth man, one Webb, was waiting. In due course Hamer was apprehended, tried for the murder of the policeman, convicted on his plea of guilty and sentenced to 199 years. Subsequently, Poe was apprehended, tried, convicted, sentenced to death and executed. Hamer was not used as a witness.

---

[1] In the cases and materials throughout the chapter, some footnotes have been omitted and others have been renumbered. [Ed.]

Thereafter, petitioner Napue was apprehended. He was put on trial with Hamer being the principal witness for the State. Hamer's testimony was extremely important because the passage of time and the dim light in the cocktail lounge made eyewitness identification very difficult and uncertain, and because some pertinent witnesses had left the state. On the basis of the evidence presented, which consisted largely of Hamer's testimony, the jury returned a guilty verdict and petitioner was sentenced to 199 years.

Finally, the driver of the car, Webb, was apprehended. Hamer also testified against him. He was convicted of murder and sentenced to 199 years.

Following the conviction of Webb, the lawyer who, as former Assistant State's Attorney, had prosecuted the Hamer, Poe and Napue cases filed a petition in the nature of a writ of error *coram nobis* on behalf of Hamer. In the petition he alleged that as prosecuting attorney he had promised Hamer that if he would testify against Napue, "a recommendation for a reduction of his [Hamer's] sentence would be made and, if possible, effectuated."[2] The attorney prayed that the court would effect "consummation of the compact entered into between the duly authorized representatives of the State of Illinois and George Hamer."

* * *

This *coram nobis* proceeding came to the attention of Napue, who thereafter filed a post conviction petition, in which he alleged that Hamer had falsely testified that he had been promised no consideration for his testimony,[3] and that the Assistant State's Attorney handling the case had known this to be false. A hearing was ultimately held at which the former

---

[2]   In relevant part, his petition read as follows:

"After Hamer was sentenced your petitioner [the Assistant State's Attorney] well knowing that identification of Poe, Napue and Webb if and when apprehended would be of an unsatisfactory character and not the kind of evidence upon which a jury could be asked to inflict a proper, severe penalty, and being unable to determine in advance whether Poe, Napue and Webb would make confessions of their participation in the crime, represented to Hamer that if he would be willing to cooperate with law enforcing officials upon the trial of [*sic*] trials of Poe, Napue and Webb when they were apprehended, that a recommendation for a reduction of his sentence would be made and, if possible, effectuated.

"Before testifying on behalf of the State and against Napue, Hamer expressed to your petitioner a reluctance to cooperate any further unless he were given definite assurance that a recommendation for reduction of his sentence would be made. Your petitioner, feeling that the interests of justice required Hamer's testimony, again assured Hamer that every possible effort would be made to conform to the promise previously made to him."

[3]   The alleged false testimony of Hamer first occurred on his cross-examination:

"Q. Did anybody give you a reward or promise you a reward for testifying?

"A. There ain't nobody promised me anything."

On redirect examination the Assistant State's Attorney again elicited the same false answer.

"Q. [by the Assistant State's Attorney] Have I promised you that I would recommend any reduction of sentence to anybody?

"A. You did not."

Assistant State's Attorney testified that he had only promised to help Hamer if Hamer's story "about being a reluctant participant" in the robbery was borne out, and not merely if Hamer would testify at petitioner's trial. He testified that in his *coram nobis* petition on Hamer's behalf he "probably used some language that [he] should not have used" in his "zeal to do something for Hamer" to whom he "felt a moral obligation." The lower court denied petitioner relief on the basis of the attorney's testimony.

On appeal, the Illinois Supreme Court affirmed on different grounds over two dissents. 13 Ill.2d 566, 150 N.E.2d 613. It found, contrary to the trial court, that the attorney had promised Hamer consideration if he would testify at petitioner's trial, a finding which the State does not contest here. It further found that the Assistant State's Attorney knew that Hamer had lied in denying that he had been promised consideration. It held, however, that petitioner was entitled to no relief since the jury had already been apprised that someone whom Hamer had tentatively identified as being a public defender "was going to do what he could" in aid of Hamer, and "was trying to get something did" for him.[4] We granted certiorari to consider the question posed in the first paragraph of this opinion. * * *

First, it is established that a conviction obtained through use of false evidence, known to be such by representatives of the State, must fall

---

[4]   The following is Hamer's testimony on the subject:

"Q. [on cross-examination] And didn't you tell him [one of Napue's attorneys] that you wouldn't testify in this case unless you got some consideration for it?

"A. * * * Yes, I did; I told him that. * * *

"Q. What are you sentenced for?

"A. One Hundred and Ninety–Nine Years.

"Q. You hope to have that reduced, don't you?

"A. Well, if anybody would help me or do anything for me, why certainly I would.

"Q. Weren't you expecting that when you came here today?

"A. There haven't no one told me anything, no more than the lawyer. The lawyer come in and talked to me a while ago and said he was going to do what he could.

"Q. Which lawyer was that?

"A. I don't know; it was a Public Defender. I don't see him in here.

"Q. You mean he was from the Public Defender's office?

"A. I imagine that is where he was from, I don't know.

"Q. And he was the one who told you that?

"A. Yes, he told me he was trying to get something did for me.

"Q. * * * And he told you he was going to do something for you?

"A. He said he was going to try to. * * *

"Q. And you told them [police officers] you would [testify at the trial of Napue] but you expected some consideration for it?

"A. I asked them was there any chance of me getting any. The man told me he didn't know, that he couldn't promise me anything.

"Q. Then you spoke to a lawyer today who said he would try to get your time cut?

"A. That was this Public Defender. I don't even know his name. * * * "

under the Fourteenth Amendment, Mooney v. Holohan, 294 U.S. 103; Pyle v. Kansas, 317 U.S. 213 * * *. The same result obtains when the State, although not soliciting false evidence, allows it to go uncorrected when it appears. Alcorta v. Texas, 355 U.S. 28. * * *

The principle that a State may not knowingly use false evidence, including false testimony, to obtain a tainted conviction, implicit in any concept of ordered liberty, does not cease to apply merely because the false testimony goes only to the credibility of the witness. The jury's estimate of the truthfulness and reliability of a given witness may well be determinative of guilt or innocence, and it is upon such subtle factors as the possible interest of the witness in testifying falsely that a defendant's life or liberty may depend. As stated by the New York Court of Appeals in a case very similar to this one, People v. Savvides, 1 N.Y.2d 554, 557, 154 N.Y.S.2d 885, 887, 136 N.E.2d 853, 854–855:

> "It is of no consequence that the falsehood bore upon the witness' credibility rather than directly upon defendant's guilt. A lie is a lie, no matter what its subject, and, if it is in any way relevant to the case, the district attorney has the responsibility and duty to correct what he knows to be false and elicit the truth. * * * That the district attorney's silence was not the result of guile or a desire to prejudice matters little, for its impact was the same, preventing, as it did, a trial that could in any real sense be termed fair."

Second, we do not believe that the fact that the jury was apprised of other grounds for believing that the witness Hamer may have had an interest in testifying against petitioner turned what was otherwise a tainted trial into a fair one. As Mr. Justice Schaefer, joined by Chief Justice Davis, rightly put it in his dissenting opinion below, 13 Ill.2d 566, 571, 150 N.E.2d 613, 616:

> "What is overlooked here is that Hamer clearly testified that no one had offered to help him except an unidentified lawyer from the public defender's office. The jury could have concluded, and probably did conclude, that such an offer of help was unlikely to influence Hamer."

Had the jury been apprised of the true facts, however, it might well have concluded that Hamer had fabricated testimony in order to curry the favor of the very representative of the State who was prosecuting the case in which Hamer was testifying, for Hamer might have believed that such a representative was in a position to implement (as he ultimately attempted to do) any promise of consideration. That the Assistant State's Attorney himself thought it important to establish before the jury that no official source had promised Hamer consideration is made clear by his redirect examination, which was the last testimony of Hamer's heard by the jury:

"Q. Mr. Hamer, has Judge Prystalski [the trial judge] promised you any reduction of sentence?

"A. No, sir.

"Q. Have I promised you that I would recommend any reduction of sentence to anybody?

"A. You did not. [That answer was false and known to be so by the prosecutor.]

"Q. Has any Judge of the criminal court promised that they [sic] would reduce your sentence?

"A. No, sir.

"Q. Has any representative of the Parole Board been to see you and promised you a reduction of sentence?

"A. No, sir."

"Q. Has any representative of the Government of the State of Illinois promised you a reduction of sentence?

"A. No, sir."

We are therefore unable to agree with the Illinois Supreme Court that "there was no constitutional infirmity by virtue of the false statement." * * *

Reversed.

NOTES AND QUESTIONS

1.   *Other cases.* See Phillips v. Ornoski, 673 F.3d 1168, 1182–83 (9th Cir.2012) ("Over the course of his habeas proceedings Phillips has established that, contrary to her testimony and Minier's [prosecutor] statements, Colman was offered and received significant benefits from the state in exchange for testifying as she did. Phillips points to substantial, possibly life-saving benefits that Colman received in exchange for her testimony, and claims that the prosecution's failure to disclose these benefits or correct Colman's statements that she expected no such benefits, and perhaps even more important Minier's deliberate efforts to mislead the jury and the court as to the existence of an immunity agreement, violated his due process rights under *Napue* and *Brady*. We examine the benefits cited by Phillips, and conclude that they involved violations of both *Napue* and *Brady*."); Blumberg v. Garcia, 687 F.Supp.2d 1074, 1115 (C.D.Cal.2010) ("In sum—and contrary to the state appellate court's determination—the record reflects that [Officer] Hewitt's testimony served both substantive and impeachment purposes other than merely rebutting Petitioner's purported gang status. *Napue* directs that false evidence, whether used substantively or for impeachment purposes, is

material if there is any reasonable likelihood that it could have affected the jury's judgment.").

2.   *Imputed knowledge.* In Giglio v. United States, 405 U.S. 150, 154 (1972), one assistant United States Attorney promised a key government witness that he would not be prosecuted if he cooperated with the government. Another assistant, who tried the case, stated in summation that no promises had been made, after the witness testified to that effect. In reversing defendant's conviction and remanding for a new trial, the Court said:

> In the circumstances shown by this record neither [the first assistant's] authority nor his failure to inform his superiors or his associates is controlling. Moreover, whether the nondisclosure was a result of negligence or design, it is the responsibility of the prosecutor. The prosecutor's office is an entity and as such it is the spokesman for the Government.

3.   *Extent of obligation.* In Commonwealth of N. Mariana Islands v. Bowie, 243 F.3d 1109, 1113 (9th Cir.2001), the police seized the following letter from one of six defendants charged with murder and kidnapping:

> Hey brod I want you to help me please for this problem that were facing right now because if they know that Im the one that did this theyre gonna put me in jail for life. I tried this before. Brah this Is what we gonna do listen carefully okay if we go to court on Thursday and they ask us questions how the murder happens and who kill the philipino just say J.J. because I already talk to John and Brasslley before I was arrested but anyway don't worry about Lucas because I talk to Lucas that don't tell the detectives that Im the one that did this things. You know what brah, don't worry about this case because well win this just imagine four against one I I even lied to my lawyer about the incedent.

The letter was unsigned. Despite the letter, the prosecution went ahead and entered into plea agreements with four of the defendants, which required their testimony against the other two defendants. The court held that turning the letter over to the defense was insufficient—that the prosecutor had an independent constitutional and ethical duty to investigate. The failure to discharge this obligation deprived the defendant of due process. Citing *Napue*, the court wrote: "This duty is not discharged by attempting to finesse the problem by pressing ahead without a diligent and a good faith attempt to resolve it. A prosecutor cannot avoid this obligation by refusing to search for the truth and remaining willfully ignorant of the facts." Id. at 1118. The court elaborated:

> Never has it been more true than it is now that a criminal charged with a serious crime understands that a fast and easy way out of trouble with the law is not only to have the best lawyer money can buy or the court can appoint, but to cut a deal at someone else's expense and to purchase leniency from the government by offering

testimony in return for immunity, or in return for reduced incarceration. * * *

[B]ecause of the perverse and mercurial nature of the devils with whom the criminal justice system has chosen to deal, each contract for testimony is fraught with the real peril that the proffered testimony will not be truthful, but simply factually contrived to "get" a target of sufficient interest to induce concessions from the government. Defendants or suspects with nothing to sell sometimes embark on a methodical journey to manufacture evidence and to create something of value, setting up and betraying friends, relatives, and cellmates alike. Frequently, and because they are aware of the low value of their credibility, criminals will even go so far as to create corroboration for their lies by recruiting others into the plot, a circumstance we appear to confront in this case.

Id. at 1123. The author of *Bowie,* Judge Trott, had previously written on this subject. See Trott, Words of Warning for Prosecutors Using Criminals as Witnesses, 47 Hastings L.J. 1381 (1996).

4.   *Access to witnesses.* See ABA Model Rules 3.4(f) ("A lawyer shall not: * * * (f) request a person other than a client to refrain from voluntarily giving relevant information to another party unless * * * "). See also United States v. Hyatt, 565 F.2d 229, 232 (2d Cir.1977) ("[W]e shall not tolerate the view that the government has some special right or privilege to control access to trial witnesses."); Gregory v. United States, 369 F.2d 185, 188 (D.C.Cir.1966) ("Witnesses, particularly eye witnesses, to a crime are the property of neither the prosecution nor the defense. Both sides have an equal right, and should have an equal opportunity, to interview them. * * * But we know of nothing in the law which gives the prosecutor the right to interfere with the preparation of the defense by effectively denying defense counsel access to the witnesses except in his presence.").

5.   *Defense counsel.* The obligations of defense counsel are discussed in Pye, The Role of Counsel in the Suppression of Truth, 1978 Duke L.J. 921. Should they be coextensive with those of the prosecutor? See Mosteller, Discovery Against the Defense: Tilting the Adversarial Balance, 74 Cal.L.Rev. 1567 (1986) (criticizing tendency to move toward equal disclosure requirements under vague concept of "litigative fairness").

Circumstances that may require defense disclosure of evidence arise in a number of contexts. Many problems center on the perjurious defendant. See Lefstein, Client Perjury in Criminal Cases: Still in Search of an Answer, 1 Geo.J. Legal Ethics 521 (1988); Rutherglen, Dilemmas and Disclosures: A Comment on Client Perjury, 19 Am.J.Crim.L. 267 (1992). See also Nix v. Whiteside, 475 U.S. 157 (1986) (right to effective assistance of counsel not violated when counsel refused to cooperate with defendant's presentation of perjured testimony). Counsel may also be permitted or obligated to disclose information to prevent a client from committing a future crime. See Mosteller, Child Abuse Reporting Laws and Attorney–Client Confidences:

The Reality and the Specter of Lawyer as Informant, 42 Duke L.J. 203, 244–55 (1992). Similar issues face lawyers with civil clients who either commit perjury or plan future frauds. Hazard, Lawyers and Client Fraud: They Still Don't Get It, 6 Geo.J. Legal Ethics 701 (1993).

Possession of potentially incriminating physical evidence also presents difficult issues concerning the obligation of disclosure. See, e.g., People v. Meredith, 631 P.2d 46 (Cal.1981) (statements by defendant concerning location of incriminating physical evidence privileged but privilege waived if defense counsel removes the evidence); Hitch v. Pima County Superior Court, 708 P.2d 72 (Ariz.1985) (where defense attorney receives incriminating physical evidence from source other than client and reasonably believes it may be destroyed if returned, counsel is obligated to give evidence to authorities). See generally Lefstein, Incriminating Physical Evidence, The Defense Attorney's Dilemma, and the Need for Rules, 64 N.C.L.Rev. 897 (1986); Uphoff, Handling Physical Evidence, Crim. Just. 4 (Summer 2011).

UNITED STATES V. BAGLEY
Supreme Court of the United States, 1985.
473 U.S. 667.

JUSTICE BLACKMUN announced the judgment of the Court and delivered an opinion of the Court except as to Part III.

In *Brady v. Maryland,* 373 U.S. 83, 87 (1963), this Court held that "the suppression by the prosecution of evidence favorable to an accused upon request violates due process where the evidence is material either to guilt or punishment." The issue in the present case concerns the standard of materiality to be applied in determining whether a conviction should be reversed because the prosecutor failed to disclose requested evidence that could have been used to impeach Government witnesses.

I

In October 1977, respondent Hughes Anderson Bagley was indicted in the Western District of Washington on 15 charges of violating federal narcotics and firearms statutes. On November 18, 24 days before trial, respondent filed a discovery motion. The sixth paragraph of that motion requested:

> "The names and addresses of witnesses that the government intends to call at trial. Also the prior criminal records of witnesses, and any deals, promises or inducements made to witnesses in exchange for their testimony." App. 18.

The Government's two principal witnesses at the trial were James F. O'Connor and Donald E. Mitchell. O'Connor and Mitchell were state law-enforcement officers employed by the Milwaukee Railroad as private security guards. Between April and June 1977, they assisted the federal

Bureau of Alcohol, Tobacco and Firearms (ATF) in conducting an undercover investigation of respondent.

The Government's response to the discovery motion did not disclose that any "deals, promises or inducements" had been made to O'Connor or Mitchell. In apparent reply to a request in the motion's ninth paragraph for "[c]opies of all Jencks Act material," the Government produced a series of affidavits that O'Connor and Mitchell had signed between April 12 and May 4, 1977, while the undercover investigation was in progress. These affidavits recounted in detail the undercover dealings that O'Connor and Mitchell were having at the time with respondent. Each affidavit concluded with the statement, "I made this statement freely and voluntarily without any threats or rewards, or promises of reward having been made to me in return for it."

Respondent waived his right to a jury trial and was tried before the court in December 1977. At the trial, O'Connor and Mitchell testified about both the firearms and the narcotics charges. On December 23, the court found respondent guilty on the narcotics charges, but not guilty on the firearms charges.

In mid–1980, respondent filed requests for information pursuant to the Freedom of Information Act and to the Privacy Act of 1974, 5 U.S.C. §§ 552 and 552a. He received in response copies of ATF form contracts that O'Connor and Mitchell had signed on May 3, 1977. Each form was entitled "Contract for Purchase of Information and Payment of Lump Sum Therefor." * * * Each form contained the following typewritten description of services:

> "That he will provide information regarding T–I and other violations committed by Hughes A. Bagley, Jr.; that he will purchase evidence for ATF; that he will cut [sic] in an undercover capacity for ATF; that he will assist ATF in gathering of evidence and testify against the violator in federal court." [App. 22 and 23.]

The figure "$300.00" was handwritten in each form on a line entitled "Sum to Be Paid to Vendor."

Because these contracts had not been disclosed to respondent in response to his pretrial discovery motion, respondent moved under 28 U.S.C. § 2255 to vacate his sentence. He alleged that the Government's failure to disclose the contracts, which he could have used to impeach O'Connor and Mitchell, violated his right to due process under *Brady v. Maryland, supra.*

* * *

II

The holding in *Brady v. Maryland* requires disclosure only of evidence that is both favorable to the accused and "material either to guilt or punishment." 373 U.S., at 87. See also *Moore v. Illinois,* 408 U.S. 786, 794–795 (1972). The Court explained in *United States v. Agurs,* 427 U.S. 97, 104 (1976): "A fair analysis of the holding in *Brady* indicates that implicit in the requirement of materiality is a concern that the suppressed evidence might have affected the outcome of the trial." The evidence suppressed in *Brady* would have been admissible only on the issue of punishment and not on the issue of guilt, and therefore could have affected only Brady's sentence and not his conviction. Accordingly, the Court affirmed the lower court's restriction of Brady's new trial to the issue of punishment.

The *Brady* rule is based on the requirement of due process. Its purpose is not to displace the adversary system as the primary means by which truth is uncovered, but to ensure that a miscarriage of justice does not occur.[5] Thus, the prosecutor is not required to deliver his entire file to defense counsel, but only to disclose evidence favorable to the accused that, if suppressed, would deprive the defendant of a fair trial:

> "For unless the omission deprived the defendant of a fair trial, there was no constitutional violation requiring that the verdict be set aside; and absent a constitutional violation, there was no breach of the prosecutor's constitutional duty to disclose. * * *

" * * * But to reiterate a critical point, the prosecutor will not have violated his constitutional duty of disclosure unless his omission is of sufficient significance to result in the denial of the defendant's right to a fair trial." 427 U.S., at 108.

In *Brady* and *Agurs,* the prosecutor failed to disclose exculpatory evidence. In the present case, the prosecutor failed to disclose evidence that the defense might have used to impeach the Government's witnesses by showing bias or interest. Impeachment evidence, however, as well as exculpatory evidence, falls within the *Brady* rule. * * *

---

[5] By requiring the prosecutor to assist the defense in making its case, the *Brady* rule represents a limited departure from a pure adversary model. The Court has recognized, however, that the prosecutor's role transcends that of an adversary: he "is the representative not of an ordinary party to a controversy, but of a sovereignty * * * whose interest * * * in a criminal prosecution is not that it shall win a case, but that justice shall be done." *Berger v. United States,* 295 U.S. 78, 88 (1935). See *Brady v. Maryland,* 373 U.S., at 87–88.

* * *

III

A

It remains to determine the standard of materiality applicable to the nondisclosed evidence at issue in this case. Our starting point is the framework for evaluating the materiality of *Brady* evidence established in *United States v. Agurs.* The Court in *Agurs* distinguished three situations involving the discovery, after trial, of information favorable to the accused that had been known to the prosecution but unknown to the defense. The first situation was the prosecutor's knowing use of perjured testimony or, equivalently, the prosecutor's knowing failure to disclose that testimony used to convict the defendant was false. The Court noted the well-established rule that "a conviction obtained by the knowing use of perjured testimony is fundamentally unfair, and must be set aside if there is any reasonable likelihood that the false testimony could have affected the judgment of the jury." 427 U.S., at 103 (footnote omitted).[6] Although this rule is stated in terms that treat the knowing use of perjured testimony as error subject to harmless-error review,[7] it may as easily be stated as a materiality standard under which the fact that testimony is perjured is considered material unless failure to disclose it would be harmless beyond a reasonable doubt. The Court in *Agurs* justified this standard of materiality on the ground that the knowing use of perjured testimony involves prosecutorial misconduct and, more importantly, involves "a corruption of the truth-seeking function of the trial process." *Id.,* at 104.

---

[6]   In fact, the *Brady* rule has its roots in a series of cases dealing with convictions based on the prosecution's knowing use of perjured testimony. In *Mooney v. Holohan,* 294 U.S. 103 (1935), the Court established the rule that the knowing use by a state prosecutor of perjured testimony to obtain a conviction and the deliberate suppression of evidence that would have impeached and refuted the testimony constitutes a denial of due process. The Court reasoned that "a deliberate deception of court and jury by the presentation of testimony known to be perjured" is inconsistent with "the rudimentary demands of justice." *Id.,* at 112. The Court reaffirmed this principle in broader terms in *Pyle v. Kansas,* 317 U.S. 213 (1942), where it held that allegations that the prosecutor had deliberately suppressed evidence favorable to the accused and had knowingly used perjured testimony were sufficient to charge a due process violation.

The Court again reaffirmed this principle in *Napue v. Illinois,* 360 U.S. 264 (1959). In *Napue,* the principal witness for the prosecution falsely testified that he had been promised no consideration for his testimony. The Court held that the knowing use of false testimony to obtain a conviction violates due process regardless of whether the prosecutor solicited the false testimony or merely allowed it to go uncorrected when it appeared. The Court explained that the principle that a State may not knowingly use false testimony to obtain a conviction—even false testimony that goes only to the credibility of the witness—is "implicit in any concept of ordered liberty." *Id.,* at 269. * * *

[7]   The rule that a conviction obtained by the knowing use of perjured testimony must be set aside if there is any reasonable likelihood that the false testimony could have affected the jury's verdict derives from *Napue v. Illinois,* 360 U.S. at 271. *Napue* antedated *Chapman v. California,* 386 U.S. 18 (1967), where the "harmless beyond a reasonable doubt" standard was established.

It is [clear], that this Court's precedents indicate that the standard of review applicable to the knowing use of perjured testimony is equivalent to the *Chapman* harmless-error standard.

At the other extreme is the situation in *Agurs* itself, where the defendant does not make a *Brady* request and the prosecutor fails to disclose certain evidence favorable to the accused. The Court rejected a harmless-error rule in that situation, because under that rule every nondisclosure is treated as error, thus imposing on the prosecutor a constitutional duty to deliver his entire file to defense counsel. *Id.,* at 111–112. At the same time, the Court rejected a standard that would require the defendant to demonstrate that the evidence if disclosed probably would have resulted in acquittal. *Id.,* at 111. The Court reasoned: "If the standard applied to the usual motion for a new trial based on newly discovered evidence were the same when the evidence was in the State's possession as when it was found in a neutral source, there would be no special significance to the prosecutor's obligation to serve the cause of justice." *Ibid.* The standard of materiality applicable in the absence of a specific *Brady* request is therefore stricter than the harmless-error standard but more lenient to the defense than the newly discovered evidence standard.

The third situation identified by the Court in *Agurs* is where the defense makes a specific request and the prosecutor fails to disclose responsive evidence. The Court did not define the standard of materiality applicable in this situation, but suggested that the standard might be more lenient to the defense than in the situation in which the defense makes no request or only a general request. *Id.,* at 106. The Court also noted: "When the prosecutor receives a specific and relevant request, the failure to make any response is seldom, if ever, excusable." *Ibid.*

The Court has relied on and reformulated the *Agurs* standard for the materiality of undisclosed evidence in * * * subsequent cases arising outside the *Brady* context. * * *

[I]n *Strickland v. Washington,* 466 U.S. 668 (1984), the Court held that a new trial must be granted when evidence is not introduced because of the incompetence of counsel only if "there is a reasonable probability that, but for counsel's unprofessional errors, the result of the proceeding would have been different." *Id.,* at 694. The *Strickland* Court defined a "reasonable probability" as "a probability sufficient to undermine confidence in the outcome." *Ibid.*

We find the *Strickland* formulation of the *Agurs* test for materiality sufficiently flexible to cover the "no request," "general request," and "specific request" cases of prosecutorial failure to disclose evidence favorable to the accused: The evidence is material only if there is a reasonable probability that, had the evidence been disclosed to the defense, the result of the proceeding would have been different. A "reasonable probability" is a probability sufficient to undermine confidence in the outcome.

The Government suggests that a materiality standard more favorable to the defendant reasonably might be adopted in specific request cases. See Brief for United States 31. The Government notes that an incomplete response to a specific request not only deprives the defense of certain evidence, but has the effect of representing to the defense that the evidence does not exist. In reliance on this misleading representation, the defense might abandon lines of independent investigation, defenses, or trial strategies that it otherwise would have pursued. *Ibid.*

We agree that the prosecutor's failure to respond fully to a *Brady* request may impair the adversary process in this manner. And the more specifically the defense requests certain evidence, thus putting the prosecutor on notice of its value, the more reasonable it is for the defense to assume from the nondisclosure that the evidence does not exist, and to make pretrial and trial decisions on the basis of this assumption. This possibility of impairment does not necessitate a different standard of materiality, however, for under the *Strickland* formulation the reviewing court may consider directly any adverse effect that the prosecutor's failure to respond might have had on the preparation or presentation of the defendant's case. The reviewing court should assess the possibility that such effect might have occurred in light of the totality of the circumstances and with an awareness of the difficulty of reconstructing in a post-trial proceeding the course that the defense and the trial would have taken had the defense not been misled by the prosecutor's incomplete response.

B

In the present case, we think that there is a significant likelihood that the prosecutor's response to respondent's discovery motion misleadingly induced defense counsel to believe that O'Connor and Mitchell could not be impeached on the basis of bias or interest arising from inducements offered by the Government. * * * Accordingly, we reverse the judgment of the Court of Appeals and remand the case to that court for a determination whether there is a reasonable probability that, had the inducement offered by the Government to O'Connor and Mitchell been disclosed to the defense, the result of the trial would have been different.

It is so ordered.

JUSTICE POWELL took no part in the decision of this case.

JUSTICE WHITE, with whom THE CHIEF JUSTICE and JUSTICE REHNQUIST join, concurring in part and concurring in the judgment.

I agree with the Court that respondent is not entitled to have his conviction overturned unless he can show that the evidence withheld by the Government was "material," and I therefore join Parts I and II of the Court's opinion. * * * Given the flexibility of the standard and the inherently factbound nature of the cases to which it will be applied, however, I see no reason to attempt to elaborate on the relevance to the inquiry of the specificity of the defense's request for disclosure, either generally or with respect to this case. * * *

JUSTICE MARSHALL, with whom JUSTICE BRENNAN joins, dissenting.

When the Government withholds from a defendant evidence that might impeach the prosecution's *only witnesses,* that failure to disclose cannot be deemed harmless error. Because that is precisely the nature of the undisclosed evidence in this case, I would affirm the judgment of the Court of Appeals and would not remand for further proceedings. * * *

II

Instead of affirming, the Court today chooses to reverse and remand the case for application of its newly stated standard to the facts of this case. While I believe that the evidence at issue here, which remained undisclosed despite a particular request, undoubtedly was material under the Court's standard, I also have serious doubts whether the Court's definition of the constitutional right at issue adequately takes account of the interests this Court sought to protect in its decision in *Brady v. Maryland,* 373 U.S. 83 (1963).

A

* * *

When the State does not disclose information in its possession that might reasonably be considered favorable to the defense, it precludes the trier of fact from gaining access to such information and thereby undermines the reliability of the verdict. Unlike a situation in which exculpatory evidence exists but neither the defense nor the prosecutor has uncovered it, in this situation the State already has, resting in its files, material that would be of assistance to the defendant. With a minimum of effort, the State could improve the real and apparent fairness of the trial enormously, by assuring that the defendant may place before the trier of fact favorable evidence known to the Government. * * *

This recognition no doubt stems in part from the frequently considerable imbalance in resources between most criminal defendants and most prosecutors' offices. Many, perhaps most, criminal defendants in the United States are represented by appointed counsel, who often are paid minimal wages and operate on shoestring budgets. In addition, unlike police, defense counsel generally is not present at the scene of the crime, or at the time of arrest, but instead comes into the case late. Moreover, unlike the Government, defense counsel is not in the position to make deals with witnesses to gain evidence. Thus, an inexperienced, unskilled, or unaggressive attorney often is unable to amass the factual support necessary to a reasonable defense. When favorable evidence is in the hands of the prosecutor but not disclosed, the result may well be that the defendant is deprived of a fair chance before the trier of fact, and the trier of fact is deprived of the ingredients necessary to a fair decision. This grim reality, of course, poses a direct challenge to the traditional model of the adversary criminal process, and perhaps because this reality so directly questions the fairness of our longstanding processes, change has been cautious and halting. Thus, the Court has not gone the full road and expressly required that the State provide to the defendant access to the prosecutor's complete files, or investigators who will assure that the defendant has an opportunity to discover every existing piece of helpful evidence. But cf. *Ake v. Oklahoma,* 470 U.S. 68 (1985) (access to assistance of psychiatrist constitutionally required on proper showing of need). Instead, in acknowledgment of the fact that important interests are served when potentially favorableevidence is disclosed, the Court has fashioned a compromise, requiring that the prosecution identify and disclose to the defendant favorable material that it possesses. This requirement is but a small, albeit important, step toward equality of justice.[8]

B

* * *

Once the prosecutor suspects that certain information might have favorable implications for the defense, either because it is potentially exculpatory or relevant to credibility, I see no reason why he should not be required to disclose it. After all, favorable evidence indisputably enhances the truth-seeking process at trial. And it is the job of the defense, not the prosecution, to decide whether and in what way to use arguably favorable evidence. In addition, to require disclosure of all evidence that might reasonably be considered favorable to the defendant would have the precautionary effect of assuring that no information of potential consequence is mistakenly overlooked. By requiring full disclosure of favorable evidence in this way, courts could begin to assure that a possibly dispositive piece of information is not withheld from the trier of fact by a prosecutor who is torn between the two roles he must play. A clear rule of this kind, coupled with a presumption in favor of disclosure, also would facilitate the prosecutor's admittedly difficult task by removing a substantial amount of unguided discretion. * * *

---

[8] Indeed, this Court's recent decision stating a stringent standard for demonstrating ineffective assistance of counsel makes an effective *Brady* right even more crucial. Without a real guarantee of effective counsel, the relative abilities of the state and the defendant become even more skewed, and the need for a minimal guarantee of access to potentially favorable information becomes significantly greater. See *Strickland v. Washington,* 466 U.S. 668 (1984); *id.,* at 712–15 (Marshall, J., dissenting); Babcock, [Fair Play: Evidence Favorable to an Accused and Effective Assistance of Counsel, 34 Stan.L.Rev. 1133, 1163–1174 (1982)] (discussing the interplay between the right to *Brady* material and the right to effective assistance of counsel).

C

The Court, however, offers a complex alternative. It defines the right not by reference to the possible usefulness of the particular evidence in preparing and presenting the case, but retrospectively, by reference to the likely effect the evidence will have on the outcome of the trial. Thus, the Court holds that due process does not require the prosecutor to turn over evidence unless the evidence is "material," and the Court states that evidence is "material" "only if there is a reasonable probability that, had the evidence been disclosed to the defense, the result of the proceeding would have been different." * * * Although this looks like a post-trial standard of review, see, *e.g., Strickland v. Washington,* 466 U.S. 668 (1984) (adopting this standard of review), it is not. Instead, the Court relies on this review standard to define the contours of the defendant's constitutional right to certain material prior to trial. By adhering to the view articulated in *United States v. Agurs,* 427 U.S. 97 (1976)—that there is no constitutional duty to disclose evidence unless nondisclosure would have a certain impact on the trial—the Court permits prosecutors to withhold with impunity large amounts of undeniably favorable evidence, and it imposes on prosecutors the burden to identify and disclose evidence pursuant to a pretrial standard that virtually defies definition. * * *

JUSTICE STEVENS, dissenting.

* * *

[T]he Court's analysis reduces the significance of deliberate prosecutorial suppression of potentially exculpatory evidence to that merely of one of numerous factors that "may" be considered by a reviewing court. * * * Such suppression is far more serious than mere nondisclosure of evidence in which the defense has expressed no particular interest. * * * Such silence actively misleads in the same way as would an affirmative representation that exculpatory evidence does not exist when, in fact, it does (*i.e.,* perjury) * * *.

NOTES AND QUESTIONS

1. *Later Supreme Court cases.* In Kyles v. Whitley, 514 U.S. 419 (1995), the Court reversed a first degree murder conviction due to a *Brady* violation, noting that in *Bagley* it had "disavowed any difference between exculpatory and impeachment evidence for *Brady* purposes, and it abandoned the distinction between the second and third *Agurs* circumstances, i.e., the 'specific-request' and 'general-or no-request' situations." Id. at 432. The Court went on to explain that *Bagley* had addressed four aspects of the "materiality" requirement. First, that requirement did not mean that the defendant had to show that the undisclosed evidence would have resulted in an acquittal. Second, the *Bagley* materiality requirement is "not a sufficiency of evidence test. A defendant need not demonstrate that after discounting the inculpatory evidence in light of the undisclosed evidence, there would not

have been enough left to convict." Third, once a reviewing court has found constitutional error, "there is no need for further harmless-error review." Id. at 435. Fourth, the materiality standard focuses on the "suppressed evidence considered collectively, not item-by-item." Id. at 436. The Court also observed: "On the one side, showing that the prosecution knew of an item of favorable evidence unknown to the defense does not amount to a *Brady* violation, without more. But the prosecution, which alone can know what is undisclosed, must be assigned the consequent responsibility to gauge the likely net effect of all such evidence and make disclosure when the point of 'reasonable probability' is reached. This in turn means that the individual prosecutor has a duty to learn of any favorable evidence known to the others acting on the government's behalf in the case, including the police." Id. at 437. If in doubt, the prosecutor should disclose: "This means, naturally, that a prosecutor anxious about tacking too close to the wind will disclose a favorable piece of evidence * * *. This is as it should be." Id. at 439. See also Wood v. Bartholomew, 516 U.S. 1, 10 (1995) (per curiam) ("Disclosure of the polygraph results, then, could have had no direct effect on the outcome of trial, because respondent could have made no mention of them either during argument or while questioning witnesses.").

In Strickler v. Greene, 527 U.S. 263 (1999), the Court found that the suppressed evidence was exculpatory. The materials consisted of notes taken by a detective during his interviews with an eyewitness and letters written by the witness to the detective. "They cast serious doubt on [the witness'] confident assertion of her 'exceptionally good memory.' " Id. at 273. The Court added a significant comment: "We certainly do not criticize the prosecution's accused had not satisfied the materiality requirement. Nevertheless, the Court use of the open file policy. We recognize that this practice may increase the efficiency and the fairness of the criminal process. We merely note that, if a prosecutor asserts that he complies with *Brady* through an open file policy, defense counsel may reasonably rely on that file to contain all materials the State is constitutionally obligated to disclose under *Brady*." Id. at 283 n.23.

In Banks v. Dretke, 540 U.S. 668 (2004), the State did not disclose that one of the prosecution's essential witnesses was a paid police informant, nor did it disclose a pretrial transcript revealing that another witness' trial testimony had been intensively coached by prosecutors and law enforcement officers. In addition, the prosecution failed to correct false statements by these witnesses. The Court reversed.

In Connick v. Thompson, 131 S.Ct. 1350 (2011), the prosecution failed to provide to the defense a laboratory report, which stated that the perpetrator had blood type B. The defendant was blood type O. The defendant filed a civil rights action against the prosecutor for failing to adequately train his staff. Although the *Brady* violation was conceded, the defendant did not establish a pattern of violations, which is necessary for § 1983 relief.

In Smith v. Cain, 132 S.Ct. 627 (2012), the Court ruled that an eyewitness's inconsistent statements to police on the night of the murder and five days later were "material" for purposes of *Brady* and reversed.

2. *Preservation of evidence. Brady's* due process disclosure requirement has been extended to encompass the right to have evidence preserved, at least under limited circumstances. If the evidence is not preserved, it cannot be disclosed to the defense. In Arizona v. Youngblood, 488 U.S. 51 (1988), the Supreme Court addressed the issue in a case involving the failure to preserve semen in a sexual assault case. The evidence was critical. While bad faith is not a requirement in the *Brady* suppression cases, the Court nevertheless ruled it determinative in a failure to preserve situation. The Court wrote: "The failure of the police to refrigerate the clothing and to perform tests on the semen samples can at worst be described as negligent." Numerous state courts have rejected the bad-faith test as a matter of state law because the importance of the evidence is not a consideration under that test. As one court observed: "Apparently only Arizona and California * * * have concluded that their state charters offer the same limited degree of protection as the federal constitution." State v. Morales, 657 A.2d 585, 594 n.20 (Conn.1995). The court went on to reject *Youngblood* as a matter of state constitutional law: "Like our sister states, we conclude that the good or bad faith of the police in failing to preserve potentially useful evidence [semen stains that could have been tested for DNA] cannot be dispositive of whether a criminal defendant has been deprived of due process of law. Accordingly, we, too, reject the litmus test of bad faith on the part of the police, which the United States Supreme Court adopted under the federal constitution in *Youngblood*."

The *Youngblood* test provides no incentive for police departments to adopt standard operating procedures that ensure the proper collection and preservation of evidence—procedures that in all likelihood would benefit the prosecution more in the long run. After having spent nine years in prison, Larry Youngblood was exonerated through DNA testing. Dr. Edward Blake, a DNA scientist, told a reporter: "We now have before us a flawed legal precedent that stands on the shoulders of an innocent man * * *. For those organizations that are poorly run or mismanaged or don't give a damn, * * * the Youngblood case was a license to let down their guard and be lazy. The effect that had was generally to lower the standards of evidence collection." Whiteaker, DNA Frees Inmate Years After Justices Rejected Plea, N.Y. Times, Aug. 11, 2000, at A12.

3. *Sources.* For an interesting analysis of the place of the *Brady* doctrine in our adversary system, see Babcock, Fair Play: Evidence Favorable to an Accused and Effective Assistance of Counsel, 34 Stan.L.Rev. 1133 (1982). See also 6 LaFave et al., Criminal Procedure § 24.3(b) (3d ed. 2007); Dewar, Note, A Fair Trial Remedy for *Brady* Violations, 115 Yale L.J. 1450 (2006); Giannelli & McMunigal, Prosecutors, Ethics, and Expert Witnesses, 76 Fordham L.Rev. 1493 (2007); Note, *Brady v. Maryland* and the Search for Truth in Criminal Trials, 63 U.Chi.L.Rev. 1673 (1996).

4. *DNA Exonerations.* Would a prosecutor have an obligation under *Brady* or ethical standards to assist in having post-conviction DNA testing performed at the request of a defendant. The experience of the Cardozo Law School Innocence Project is not encouraging: "[I]n nearly half the sixty-four

[DNA] exonerations, local prosecutors refused to release crime evidence for DNA tests until litigation was threatened or filed." Scheck et al., Actual Innocence: Five Days to Execution, and Other Dispatches From the Wrongly Convicted xvi (2000). In contrast, the San Diego District Attorney adopted a different approach. Sterngold, San Diego District Attorney Offering Free DNA Testing, N.Y. Times, July 28, 2000, at A12. ABA Rule of Professional Conduct 3.8(g) now imposes a duty on prosecutors to act when "new, credible and material evidence creating a reasonable likelihood that a convicted defendant did not commit an offense of which the defendant was convicted."

If DNA evidence undercuts the prosecution's case, is it ethical to oppose a new trial based on theories that were never presented to the jury? See Ritter, Note, It's the Prosecution's Story, But They're Not Sticking to It: Applying Harmless Error and Judicial Estoppel to Exculpatory Post–Conviction DNA Testing, 74 Fordham L.Rev. 825 (2005).

5. *Ethical duty.* Does the prosecution have an ethical duty to disclose exculpatory information to the defense and what sanctions are appropriate for a violation of any such duty? See Zacharias, Structuring the Ethics of Prosecutorial Trial Practice: Can Prosecutors Do Justice?, 44 Vand.L.Rev. 45 (1991) (criticizing the difficulty of enforcing the present "do justice" ethical standard); Rosen, Disciplinary Sanctions Against Prosecutors for *Brady* Violations: A Paper Tiger, 65 N.C.L.Rev. 693 (1987) (sanctions illusory). ABA Rule of Professional Conduct 3.8(d) also imposes a disclosure obligation on prosecutors. The rule does not include a "materiality" requirement.

HOLMES V. SOUTH CAROLINA

United States Supreme Court, 2006.
547 U.S. 319.

JUSTICE ALITO delivered the opinion of the Court.

This case presents the question whether a criminal defendant's federal constitutional rights are violated by an evidence rule under which the defendant may not introduce proof of third-party guilt if the prosecution has introduced forensic evidence that, if believed, strongly supports a guilty verdict.

I

On the morning of December 31, 1989, 86–year–old Mary Stewart was beaten, raped, and robbed in her home. She later died of complications stemming from her injuries. Petitioner was convicted by a South Carolina jury of murder, first-degree criminal sexual conduct, first-degree burglary, and robbery, and he was sentenced to death. * * * Upon state postconviction review * * *, petitioner was granted a new trial. * * *

At the second trial, the prosecution relied heavily on the following forensic evidence:

"(1) [Petitioner's] palm print was found just above the door knob on the interior side of the front door of the victim's house; (2) fibers consistent with a black sweatshirt owned by [petitioner] were found on the victim's bed sheets; (3) matching blue fibers were found on the victim's pink nightgown and on [petitioner's] blue jeans; (4) microscopically consistent fibers were found on the pink nightgown and on [petitioner's] underwear; (5) [petitioner's] underwear contained a mixture of DNA from two individuals, and 99.99% of the population other than [petitioner] and the victim were excluded as contributors to that mixture; and (6) [petitioner's] tank top was found to contain a mixture of [petitioner's] blood and the victim's blood." * * *

In addition, the prosecution introduced evidence that petitioner had been seen near Stewart's home within an hour of the time when, according to the prosecution's evidence, the attack took place. * * *

As a major part of his defense, petitioner attempted to undermine the State's forensic evidence by suggesting that it had been contaminated and that certain law enforcement officers had engaged in a plot to frame him. * * * Petitioner's expert witnesses criticized the procedures used by the police in handling the fiber and DNA evidence and in collecting the fingerprint evidence. * * * Another defense expert provided testimony that petitioner cited as supporting his claim that the palm print had been planted by the police. * * *

Petitioner also sought to introduce proof that another man, Jimmy McCaw White, had attacked Stewart. * * * At a pretrial hearing, petitioner proffered several witnesses who placed White in the victim's neighborhood on the morning of the assault, as well as four other witnesses who testified that White had either acknowledged that petitioner was " 'innocent' " or had actually admitted to committing the crimes. * * * One witness recounted that when he asked White about the "word * * * on the street" that White was responsible for Stewart's murder, White "put his head down and he raised his head back up and he said, well, you know I like older women." * * * According to this witness, White added that "he did what they say he did" and that he had "no regrets about it at all." * * * Another witness, who had been incarcerated with White, testified that White had admitted to assaulting Stewart, that a police officer had asked the witness to testify falsely against petitioner, and that employees of the prosecutor's office, while soliciting the witness' cooperation, had spoken of manufacturing evidence against petitioner. * * * White testified at the pretrial hearing and denied making the incriminating statements. * * * He also provided an alibi for the time of the crime, but another witness refuted his alibi. * * *

The trial court excluded petitioner's third-party guilt evidence citing *State v. Gregory,* 198 S.C. 98, 16 S.E.2d 532 (1941), which held that such evidence is admissible if it " 'raise[s] a reasonable inference or presumption as to [the defendant's] own innocence' " but is not admissible if it merely " 'cast[s] a bare suspicion upon another' " or " 'raise[s] a conjectural inference as to the commission of the crime by another.' " * * * On appeal, the South Carolina Supreme Court found no error in the exclusion of petitioner's third-party guilt evidence. Citing both *Gregory* and its later decision in *State v. Gay,* 343 S.C. 543, 541 S.E.2d 541 (2001), the State Supreme Court held that "where there is strong evidence of an appellant's guilt, especially where there is strong forensic evidence, the proffered evidence about a third party's alleged guilt does not raise a reasonable inference as to the appellant's own innocence." * * * Applying this standard, the court held that petitioner could not "overcome the forensic evidence against him to raise a reasonable inference of his own innocence." * * * We granted certiorari. * * *

II

"[S]tate and federal rulemakers have broad latitude under the Constitution to establish rules excluding evidence from criminal trials." *United States v. Scheffer,* 523 U.S. 303, 308 (1998); see also *Crane v. Kentucky,* 476 U.S. 683, 689–690 (1986); *Marshall v. Lonberger,* 459 U.S. 422, 438, n.6 (1983); *Chambers v. Mississippi,* 410 U.S. 284, 302–303 (1973) * * *. This latitude, however, has limits. "Whether rooted directly in the Due Process Clause of the Fourteenth Amendment or in the Compulsory Process or Confrontation clauses of the Sixth Amendment, the Constitution guarantees criminal defendants 'a meaningful opportunity to present a complete defense.' " * * * This right is abridged by evidence rules that "infring[e] upon a weighty interest of the accused" and are " 'arbitrary' or 'disproportionate to the purposes they are designed to serve.' " *Scheffer, supra,* at 308 (quoting *Rock v. Arkansas,* 483 U.S. 44, 58, 56 (1987)).

This Court's cases contain several illustrations of "arbitrary" rules, *i.e.,* rules that excluded important defense evidence but that did not serve any legitimate interests. In *Washington v. Texas,* 388 U.S. 14 (1967), state statutes barred a person who had been charged as a participant in a crime from testifying in defense of another alleged participant unless the witness had been acquitted. As a result, when the defendant in *Washington* was tried for murder, he was precluded from calling as a witness a person who had been charged and previously convicted of committing the same murder. Holding that the defendant's right to put on a defense had been violated, we noted that the rule embodied in the statutes could not "even be defended on the ground that it rationally sets apart a group of persons who are particularly likely to commit perjury" since the rule allowed an alleged participant to testify if he or she had been acquitted or was called by the prosecution. *Id.,* at 22–23 * * *.

A similar constitutional violation occurred in *Chambers v. Mississippi, supra.* A murder defendant called as a witness a man named McDonald, who had previously confessed to the murder. When McDonald repudiated the confession on the stand, the defendant was denied permission to examine McDonald as an adverse witness based on the State's " 'voucher' rule," which barred parties from impeaching their own witnesses. * * * In addition, because the state hearsay rule did not include an exception for statements against penal interest, the defendant was not permitted to introduce evidence that McDonald had made self-incriminating statements to three other persons. Noting that the State had not even attempted to "defend" or "explain [the] underlying rationale" of the "voucher rule," * * * this Court held that "the exclusion of [the evidence of McDonald's out-of-court statements], coupled with the State's refusal to permit [the defendant] to cross-examine McDonald, denied him a trial in accord with traditional and fundamental standards of due process," *id.*, at 302.

Another arbitrary rule was held unconstitutional in *Crane v. Kentucky, supra.* There, the defendant was prevented from attempting to show at trial that his confession was unreliable because of the circumstances under which it was obtained, and neither the State Supreme Court nor the prosecution "advanced any rational justification for the wholesale exclusion of this body of potentially exculpatory evidence." * * * *Id.*, at 691.

In *Rock v. Arkansas, supra,* this Court held that a rule prohibiting hypnotically refreshed testimony was unconstitutional because "[w]holesale inadmissibility of a defendant's testimony is an arbitrary restriction on the right to testify in the absence of clear evidence by the State repudiating the validity of all post-hypnotic recollections." * * * By contrast, in *United States v. Scheffer, supra,* we held that a rule excluding all polygraph evidence did not abridge the right to present a defense because the rule "serve[d] several legitimate interests in the criminal trial process," was "neither arbitrary nor disproportionate in promoting these ends," and did not "implicate a sufficiently weighty interest of the defendant." *Id.* at 309.

While the Constitution thus prohibits the exclusion of defense evidence under rules that serve no legitimate purpose or that are disproportionate to the ends that they are asserted to promote, well-established rules of evidence permit trial judges to exclude evidence if its probative value is outweighed by certain other factors such as unfair prejudice, confusion of the issues, or potential to mislead the jury. See, *e.g.,* Fed. Rule Evid. 403 * **. Plainly referring to rules of this type, we have stated that the Constitution permits judges "to exclude evidence that is 'repetitive * * *, only marginally relevant' or poses an undue risk of 'harassment, prejudice, [or] confusion of the issues.' " *Crane, supra,* at 689–690 * * *.

A specific application of this principle is found in rules regulating the admission of evidence proffered by criminal defendants to show that someone else committed the crime with which they are charged. See, *e.g.,*41 C.J.S., Homicide § 216, pp. 56–58 (1991) ("Evidence tending to show the commission by another person of the crime charged may be introduced by accused when it is inconsistent with, and raises a reasonable doubt of, his own guilt; but frequently matters offered in evidence for this purpose are so remote and lack such connection with the crime that they are excluded"); 40A Am.Jur.2d, Homicide § 286, pp. 136–138 (1999) * * *.

In *Gregory,* the South Carolina Supreme Court adopted and applied a rule apparently intended to be of this type, given the court's references to the "applicable rule" from Corpus Juris and American Jurisprudence * * *.

In *Gay* and this case, however, the South Carolina Supreme Court radically changed and extended the rule. In *Gay,* after recognizing the standard applied in *Gregory,* the court stated that "[i]n view of the strong evidence of appellant's guilt—especially the forensic evidence—* * * the proffered evidence * * * did not raise 'a reasonable inference' as to appellant's own innocence." *Gay,* 343 S.C., at 550 * * *. Similarly, in the present case, as noted, the State Supreme Court applied the rule that "where there is strong evidence of [a defendant's] guilt, especially where there is strong forensic evidence, the proffered evidence about a third party's alleged guilt" may (or perhaps must) be excluded. * * *

Under this rule, the trial judge does not focus on the probative value or the potential adverse effects of admitting the defense evidence of third-party guilt. Instead, the critical inquiry concerns the strength of the prosecution's case: If the prosecution's case is strong enough, the evidence of third-party guilt is excluded even if that evidence, if viewed independently, would have great probative value and even if it would not pose an undue risk of harassment, prejudice, or confusion of the issues.

Furthermore, as applied in this case, the South Carolina Supreme Court's rule seems to call for little, if any, examination of the credibility of the prosecution's witnesses or the reliability of its evidence. Here, for example, the defense strenuously claimed that the prosecution's forensic evidence was so unreliable (due to mishandling and a deliberate plot to frame petitioner) that the evidence should not have even been admitted. The South Carolina Supreme Court responded that these challenges did not entirely "eviscerate" the forensic evidence and that the defense challenges went to the weight and not to the admissibility of that evidence. * * * Yet, in evaluating the prosecution's forensic evidence and deeming it to be "strong"—and thereby justifying exclusion of petitioner's third-party guilt evidence—the South Carolina Supreme Court made no mention of the defense challenges to the prosecution's evidence.

Interpreted in this way, the rule applied by the State Supreme Court does not rationally serve the end that the *Gregory* rule and its analogues in other jurisdictions were designed to promote, *i.e.,* to focus the trial on the central issues by excluding evidence that has only a very weak logical connection to the central issues. The rule applied in this case appears to be based on the following logic: Where (1) it is clear that only one person was involved in the commission of a particular crime and (2) there is strong evidence that the defendant was the perpetrator, it follows that evidence of third-party guilt must be weak. But this logic depends on an accurate evaluation of the prosecution's proof, and the true strength of the prosecution's proof cannot be assessed without considering challenges to the reliability of the prosecution's evidence. Just because the prosecution's evidence, *if credited,* would provide strong support for a guilty verdict, it does not follow that evidence of third-party guilt has only a weak logical connection to the central issues in the case. And where the credibility of the prosecution's witnesses or the reliability of its evidence is not conceded, the strength of the prosecution's case cannot be assessed without making the sort of factual findings that have traditionally been reserved for the trier of fact and that the South Carolina courts did not purport to make in this case.

The rule applied in this case is no more logical than its converse would be, *i.e.,* a rule barring the prosecution from introducing evidence of a defendant's guilt if the defendant is able to proffer, at a pretrial hearing, evidence that, if believed, strongly supports a verdict of not guilty. In the present case, for example, the petitioner proffered evidence that, if believed, squarely proved that White, not petitioner, was the perpetrator. It would make no sense, however, to hold that this proffer precluded the prosecution from introducing its evidence, including the forensic evidence that, if credited, provided strong proof of the petitioner's guilt.

The point is that, by evaluating the strength of only one party's evidence, no logical conclusion can be reached regarding the strength of contrary evidence offered by the other side to rebut or cast doubt. Because the rule applied by the State Supreme Court in this case did not heed this point, the rule is "arbitrary" in the sense that it does not rationally serve the end that the *Gregory* rule and other similar third-party guilt rules were designed to further. Nor has the State identified any other legitimate end that the rule serves. It follows that the rule applied in this case by the State Supreme Court violates a criminal defendant's right to have " 'a meaningful opportunity to present a complete defense.' " *Crane,* 476 U.S., at 690 * * *.

III

For these reasons, we vacate the judgment of the South Carolina Supreme Court and remand the case for further proceedings not inconsistent with this opinion.

It is so ordered.

NOTES AND QUESTIONS

1. *Right to present a defense. Holmes* is the latest in a line of cases often classified under the rubic "the right to present a defense." In *Washington v. Texas*, Chapter 12 (A), infra, 388 U.S. at 19, the Court first recognized this right:

> The right to offer the testimony of witnesses, and to compel their attendance, if necessary, is in plain terms the right to present a defense, the right to present the defendant's version of the facts as well as the prosecution's to the jury so it may decide where the truth lies. Just as an accused has the right to confront the prosecution's witnesses for the purpose of challenging their testimony, he has the right to present his own witnesses to establish a defense. This right is a fundamental element of due process of law.

Washington rested on the Compulsory Process Clause. The Court's next case, *Chambers v. Mississippi*, was based on due process. See also California v. Trombetta, 467 U.S. 479, 485 (1984) (In finding a qualified right for the preservation of evidence in the government's control, the Court stated: "We have long interpreted [the due process] standard of fairness to require that criminal defendants be afforded a meaningful opportunity to present a complete defense."); note 5 following *Old Chief v. United States*, Chapter 7, Section C, infra. *Crane v. Kentucky*, which is cited in *State v. Sheehan*, Chapter 1(A), supra, cited several different constitutional provisions. Does it matter where among these provisions the right is anchored?

2. *Right to jury trial.* Why didn't the Court base its decision on the right to a jury trial as one amicus brief argued? The Court has recently reinvigorated that right. See Apprendi v. New Jersey, 530 U.S. 466, 490 (2000) ("Other than the fact of a prior conviction, any fact that increases the penalty for a crime beyond the prescribed statutory maximum must be submitted to a jury, and proved beyond a reasonable doubt."). See also Blakely v. Washington, 542 U.S. 296 (2004). Isn't the South Carolina rule a direct invasion of the jury trial right? Does the exclusion of such evidence undercut the prosecution's burden of proof? See Imwinkelried, The Reach of *Winship*: Invalidating Evidentiary Admissibility Standards that Undermine the Prosecution's Obligation to Prove the Defendant's Guilt Beyond a Reasonable Doubt, 70 U.M.K.C.L.Rev. 865 (2002).

3. *Perry Mason?* For a comprehensive treatment of third-party guilt evidence, see McCord, "But Perry Mason Made It Look So Easy!": The Admissibility of Evidence Offered by a Criminal Defendant to Suggest That

Someone Else is Guilty, 63 Tenn.L.Rev. 917, 919 (1996). Professor McCord notes that "the law is much less favorable to criminal defendants than one might expect, given the unassailable logic that a defendant should be able to defend by offering proof that someone else committed the crime." He labels the most prevalent view, cited in *Holmes*, as the "direct connection" doctrine. Does a prosecutor have to satisfy such a burden when introducing evidence? Also, several states permit third-party guilt evidence only if the prosecution's case is entirely circumstantial. Would such a rule survive *Holmes*?

4.   *Polygraph evidence.* In United States v. Scheffer, 523 U.S. 303 (1998), the Supreme Court upheld the military's per se exclusionary rule of polygraph results in face of the same constitutional challenge that was made in *Holmes*. For a discussion of *Scheffer*, see Giannelli, The Supreme Court's "Criminal" *Daubert* Cases, 33 Seton Hall L.Rev. 1071 (2003).

5.   *Other evidence rules.* At least two other evidence rules potentially raise third-party guilt issues. Federal Rule 804(b)(3) recognizes a hearsay exception for statements against penal interest, which may be offered to exculpate the accused. See Chapter 14(J), infra. In addition, evidence of "other acts" may be offered to establish third-party guilt. See Chapter 8(C), infra, after *Robinson*.

LEECH V. PEOPLE
Supreme Court of Colorado, 1944.
146 P.2d 346.

BURKE, JUSTICE. Plaintiff in error, hereinafter referred to as defendant, was convicted of the theft of an automobile and sentenced to the penitentiary for a term of fifteen months to two years. To review that judgment he prosecutes this writ and asks that it be made a supersedeas. He further requests, for good cause appearing, that final disposition be had on this application and in that request the people join. We proceed accordingly. * * *

November 18, 1940, defendant bought a new Pontiac automobile of the Kenyon Company of Cortez. For an unpaid balance on the purchase price he gave his note for approximately $1,000, secured by a mortgage on the car. Title was registered in defendant but in January following (without consideration) it was transferred to his wife. The car carried insurance. The Kenyon Company assigned to the Intermountain Finance Company of Durango. December 12, 1941, with installments on said note delinquent and another in the immediate offing, defendant and one Holman took the car from the former's residence to a place some miles distant where they concealed it out of sight of the main highway. The next morning defendant reported the car stolen and search was begun. December 24, 1941, apparently fearful of discovery, defendant sought the further aid of Holman and together they transferred it to a point near Egnar, concealed it in a clump of trees about 150 feet from the highway, and removing and taking with them the wheels and tires they departed. The automobile was later stripped of almost everything detachable. The insurance company, on the theory of actual theft, paid the policy. Eventually the stripped carcass was discovered, report made to the sheriff and an investigation started which resulted in the filing of an information against defendant and Holman. When the cause came on for trial, Holman entered a plea of guilty, his sentence was postponed, and he testified against defendant. He claimed to have first been hired to help with the concealment of the car, later coerced into assisting in its transfer and a promise to return and burn it, and finally, having quarreled with defendant, apparently over his failure to burn, defendant's failure to pay, and the stripping and disposition of accessories he went to the police. A further detail of evidence is not essential. Suffice it to say that the jurors were entitled to believe the foregoing, and that while this was the theory of the people[,] that of defendant was that most of the testimony of Holman was false, that he was the actual thief, and that his evidence was motivated by the fact that he was unable to extricate himself from the net in which he was caught and determined, as a measure of revenge, to carry defendant down with him. There was evidence to support a verdict to that effect had the jurors elected to accept defendant's theory. * * *

Let it here be borne in mind that Holman's testimony was indispensable to support the verdict, that Holman had been originally informed against jointly with defendant and that he had entered a plea of guilty. Now, called as a witness for the people, Holman was asked by the district attorney, on direct examination:

"Q. You have been charged with the same crime as Mr. Leech is being tried for now, have you? A. Yes, sir.

"Q. Have you entered a plea of guilty to the charge? A. Yes, sir.

"Q. Do you desire to testify now concerning what you know about this case? A. Yes, sir."

This was neither incidental nor accidental. It was no by-product of cross examination. It did not come from the witness as a voluntary statement. It was the fifth question propounded by the prosecution on direct examination and apparently came with the most careful deliberation. We have held this prejudicial error. Paine v. People, 106 Colo. 258, 103 P.2d 686.[9]

But, say the people, no objection was interposed, hence the error need not be noticed. True, but it is equally true that when such an error

---

9 ["Our cases clearly establish that a defendant is entitled to have the question of his guilt determined upon the evidence against him, not on whether a codefendant or government witness has been convicted on the same charge." United States v. Miranda, 593 F.2d 590, 594 (5th Cir.1979). Ed.]

appears and justice requires its consideration this court will not ignore it. Reppin v. People, 95 Colo. 192, 34 P.2d 71.

Is this such a case? We need but call attention to one disclosure of this record to so demonstrate. In addition to the two foregoing errors at least several minor ones appear. Yet here is a record of 230 pages in an important criminal case in which sixteen instructions were given to the jury and from first to last not a single objection on the part of counsel for defendant appears. There was no instruction tendered for defendant and no objection made to any instruction given. Ignoring the failure to object to the Holman testimony, as noted above, it is a test on credulity to believe that defendant's interests called for no faint protest from beginning to end. In the face of such a record justice certainly requires that we note serious prejudicial error and act accordingly. We should here observe that counsel who appear for defendant in this court did not represent him on the trial.

The judgment is reversed and the cause remanded for a new trial.

NOTES AND QUESTIONS

1. *Federal Rule 103.* Important and obvious errors not objected to at trial may be reviewed under the principle of plain error. See Fed.R.Evid. 103(e). See discussion in Chapter 1, Section B, supra.

2. *Sources.* The extent to which courts have been willing to ignore the general rule of the adversary system that issues must be raised in the trial court to be reviewed on appeal is examined in 7 LaFave et al., Criminal Procedure § 27.5(d) (3d ed. 2007); Martineau, Considering New Issues on Appeal: The General Rule and the Gorilla Rule, 40 Vand.L.Rev. 1023 (1987); Vestal, Sua Sponte Consideration in Appellate Review, 27 Fordham L.Rev. 477 (1958–59); Note, 64 Ind.L.J. 985 (1989).

3. *Ineffective assistance of counsel.* Claims of plain error will to some extent overlap with claims of inadequate representation of counsel. If counsel's failure to object is the result of ineffective assistance of counsel, the failure to object will not bar review either in state court or in federal court on collateral attack. See Murray v. Carrier, 477 U.S. 478, 488 (1986). See also Jeffries & Stuntz, Ineffective Assistance and Procedural Default in Federal Habeas Corpus, 57 U.Chi.L.Rev. 679 (1990). However, the showing required to sustain a claim of ineffective assistance of counsel is substantial. See Strickland v. Washington, 466 U.S. 668, 686 (1984) (counsel's conduct must both violate an objective reasonableness standard and also create a reasonable probability that but for counsel's errors the result would have been different). "Surmounting *Strickland*'s high bar is never an easy task." Padilla v. Kentucky, 130 S.Ct. 1473, 1485 (2010). And success in establishing ineffectiveness is relatively infrequent. See Colbert, Thirty–Five Years After *Gideon*: The Illusory Right to Counsel at Bail Proceedings, 1998 U.Ill.L.Rev. 1. The difficulty of establishing ineffectiveness of counsel has received most

attention in capital cases. See Beck & Shumsky, A Comparison of Retained and Appointed Counsel in Cases of Capital Murder, 21 Law & Hum.Behav. 525 (1997); Langfitt & Nolas, Ineffective Assistance of Counsel in Death Penalty Cases, 26 Litigation 6 (Summer 2000); White, Effective Assistance of Counsel in Capital Cases: The Evolving Standard of Care, 1993 U.Ill.L.Rev. 323.

HOUSE V. BELL

United States Supreme Court, 2006.
547 U.S. 518.

JUSTICE KENNEDY delivered the opinion of the Court.

Some 20 years ago in rural Tennessee, Carolyn Muncey was murdered. A jury convicted petitioner Paul Gregory House of the crime and sentenced him to death, but new revelations cast doubt on the jury's verdict. House, protesting his innocence, seeks access to federal court to pursue habeas corpus relief based on constitutional claims that are procedurally barred under state law. Out of respect for the finality of state-court judgments federal habeas courts, as a general rule, are closed to claims that state courts would consider defaulted. In certain exceptional cases involving a compelling claim of actual innocence, however, the state procedural default rule is not a bar to a federal habeas corpus petition. See *Schlup v. Delo,* 513 U.S. 298, 319–322 (1995). After careful review of the full record, we conclude that House has made the stringent showing required by this exception; and we hold that his federal habeas action may proceed.

I

[Mrs. Muncey was last seen the evening before her body was discovered. She told a neighbor (Luttrell) that she was going to make her husband take her fishing the next day. Later her daughter Lora (age 10) said she thought she heard a horn blow, and somebody with a deep voice asked if her father was home and said that he had been in a wreck. She also heard her mother going down the steps crying. Another witness claimed to have seen House, a neighbor, "come out from under a bank, wiping his hands on a black rag" near where the body was later discovered, although when and where he saw House, and how well he could have observed him, were disputed at trial. When questioned by the sheriff, House falsely claimed that he had spent the entire evening with his girlfriend, Donna Turner, at her trailer. After initially supporting House's alibi, Turner informed authorities that House had left her trailer around 10:30 or 10:45 p.m. to go for a walk. According to Turner's trial testimony, House returned later—she was not sure when—"hot and panting, missing his shirt and his shoes." House told her that while he was walking on the road near her home, a vehicle pulled up beside him and somebody inside "called him some names and then they told him he didn't belong here anymore." A fight ensued and House ran away. Turner's trailer was located just under two miles by road, through hilly terrain, from the Muncey residence. FBI testing showed that semen consistent with House's was present on Mrs. Muncey's nightgown and panties, and that small bloodstains consistent with her blood appeared on his jeans.

The Tennessee Supreme Court affirmed House's conviction, finding the evidence "circumstantial" but quite strong. House filed but lost a state postconviction relief application. A second application was then filed. The Tennessee Supreme Court held that House's claims were barred under a state statute providing that claims not raised in prior postconviction proceedings are presumptively waived. House next sought federal habeas relief, asserting numerous claims of ineffective assistance of counsel and prosecutorial misconduct. The district court deemed House's claims procedurally defaulted but held an evidentiary hearing to determine whether House fell within the "actual innocence" exception to the procedural default rule.]

IV

As a general rule, claims forfeited under state law may support federal habeas relief only if the prisoner demonstrates cause for the default and prejudice from the asserted error. * * * The rule is based on the comity and respect that must be accorded to state-court judgments. * * * The bar is not, however, unqualified. In an effort to "balance the societal interests in finality, comity, and conservation of scarce judicial resources with the individual interest in justice that arises in the extraordinary case," *Schlup,* 513 U.S., at 324, the Court has recognized a miscarriage-of-justice exception. * * *

In *Schlup,* the Court adopted a specific rule to implement this general principle. It held that prisoners asserting innocence as a gateway to defaulted claims must establish that, in light of new evidence, "it is more likely than not that no reasonable juror would have found petitioner guilty beyond a reasonable doubt." 513 U.S., at 327. * * *

* * *

With this background in mind we turn to the evidence developed in House's federal habeas proceedings.

DNA Evidence

First, in direct contradiction of evidence presented at trial, DNA testing [not available at the time of trial] has established that the semen on Mrs. Muncey's nightgown and panties came from her husband, Mr. Muncey, not from House. The State, though conceding this point, insists this new evidence is immaterial. At the guilt phase at least, neither sexual contact nor motive were elements of the offense, so in the State's view the evidence, or lack of evidence, of sexual assault or sexual advance is of no consequence. We disagree. In fact we consider the new disclosure of central importance.

From beginning to end the case is about who committed the crime. When identity is in question, motive is key. The point, indeed, was not lost on the prosecution, for it introduced the evidence and relied on it in the final guilt-phase closing argument. Referring to "evidence at the scene," the prosecutor suggested that House committed, or attempted to commit, some "indignity" on Mrs. Muncey that neither she "nor any mother on that road would want to do with Mr. House." * * * Particularly in a case like this where the proof was, as the State Supreme Court observed, circumstantial, * * * we think a jury would have given this evidence great weight. Quite apart from providing proof of motive, it was the only forensic evidence at the scene that would link House to the murder.

Law and society, as they ought to do, demand accountability when a sexual offense has been committed, so not only did this evidence link House to the crime; it likely was a factor in persuading the jury not to let him go free. At sentencing, moreover, the jury came to the unanimous conclusion, beyond a reasonable doubt, that the murder was committed in the course of a rape or kidnaping. The alleged sexual motivation relates to both those determinations. This is particularly so given that, at the sentencing phase, the jury was advised that House had a previous conviction for sexual assault.

A jury informed that fluids on Mrs. Muncey's garments could have come from House might have found that House trekked the nearly two miles to the victim's home and lured her away in order to commit a sexual offense. By contrast a jury acting without the assumption that the semen could have come from House would have found it necessary to establish some different motive, or, if the same motive, an intent far more speculative. When the only direct evidence of sexual assault drops out of the case, so, too, does a central theme in the State's narrative linking House to the crime. In that light, furthermore, House's odd evening walk and his false statements to authorities, while still potentially incriminating, might appear less suspicious.

Bloodstains

The other relevant forensic evidence is the blood on House's pants, which appears in small, even minute, stains in scattered places. As the prosecutor told the jury, they were stains that, due to their small size, "you or I might not detect[,] [m]ight not see, but which the FBI lab was able to find on [House's] jeans." App. 11. The stains appear inside the right pocket, outside that pocket, near the inside button, on the left thigh and outside leg, on the seat of the pants, and on the right bottom cuff, including inside the pants. Due to testing by the FBI, cuttings now appear on the pants in several places where stains evidently were found. (The cuttings were destroyed in the testing process, and defense experts were unable to replicate the tests.) At trial, the government argued "nothing that the defense has introduced in this case explains what blood is doing on his jeans, all over [House's] jeans, that is scientifically, completely different from his blood." *Id.,* at 105. House, though not disputing at this point that the blood is Mrs. Muncey's, now presents an alternative explanation that, if credited, would undermine the probative value of the blood evidence.

During House's habeas proceedings, Dr. Cleland Blake, an Assistant Chief Medical Examiner for the State of Tennessee and a consultant in forensic pathology to the TBI for 22 years, testified that the blood on House's pants was chemically too degraded, and too similar to blood collected during the autopsy, to have come from Mrs. Muncey's body on the night of the crime. The blood samples collected during the autopsy were placed in test tubes without preservative. Under such conditions, according to Dr. Blake, "you will have enzyme degradation. You will have different blood group degradation, blood marker degradation." * * * The problem of decay, moreover, would have been compounded by the body's long exposure to the elements, sitting outside for the better part of a summer day. In contrast, if blood is preserved on cloth, "it will stay there for years," *ibid.;* indeed, Dr. Blake said he deliberately places blood drops on gauze during autopsies to preserve it for later testing. The blood on House's pants, judging by Agent Bigbee's tests, showed "similar deterioration, breakdown of certain of the named numbered enzymes" as in the autopsy samples. *Id.,* at 110. "[I]f the victim's blood had spilled on the jeans while the victim was alive and this blood had dried," Dr. Blake stated, "the deterioration would not have occurred," *ibid.,* and "you would expect [the blood on the jeans] to be different than what was in the tube," *id.,* at 113. Dr. Blake thus concluded the blood on the jeans came from the autopsy samples, not from Mrs. Muncey's live (or recently killed) body.

Other evidence confirms that blood did in fact spill from the vials. It appears the vials passed from Dr. Carabia, who performed the autopsy, into the hands of two local law enforcement officers, who transported it to the FBI, where Agent Bigbee performed the enzyme tests. The blood was contained in four vials, evidently with neither preservative nor a proper seal. The vials, in turn, were stored in a styrofoam box, but nothing indicates the box was kept cool. Rather, in what an evidence protocol expert at the habeas hearing described as a violation of proper procedure, the styrofoam box was packed in the same cardboard box as other evidence including House's pants (apparently in a paper bag) and other clothing (in separate bags). The cardboard box was then carried in the officers' car while they made the 10–hour journey from Tennessee to the FBI lab. Dr. Blake stated that blood vials in hot conditions (such as a car trunk in the summer) could blow open; and in fact, by the time the blood reached the FBI it had hemolyzed, or spoiled, due to heat exposure. By the time the blood passed from the FBI to a defense expert, roughly a vial and a half were empty, though Agent Bigbee testified he used at most a quarter of one vial. Blood, moreover, had seeped onto one corner of the styrofoam box and onto packing gauze inside the box below the vials.

In addition, although the pants apparently were packaged initially in a paper bag and FBI records suggest they arrived at the FBI in one, the record does not contain the paper bag but does contain a plastic bag with a label listing the pants and Agent Scott's name—and the plastic bag has blood on it. The blood appears in a forked streak roughly five inches long and two inches wide running down the bag's outside front. Though testing by House's expert confirmed the stain was blood, the expert could not determine the blood's source. Speculations about when and how the blood got there add to the confusion regarding the origins of the stains on House's pants.

Faced with these indications of, at best, poor evidence control, the State attempted to establish at the habeas hearing that all blood spillage occurred after Agent Bigbee examined the pants. Were that the case, of course, then blood would have been detected on the pants before any spill—which would tend to undermine Dr. Blake's analysis and support using the bloodstains to infer House's guilt. In support of this theory the State put on testimony by a blood spatter expert who believed the "majority" of the stains were "transfer stains," that is, stains resulting from "wip[ing] across the surface of the pants" rather than seeping or spillage. * * * Regarding the spillage in the styrofoam box, the expert noted that yellow "Tennessee Crime Laboratory" tape running around the box and down all four sides did not line up when the bloodstains on the box's corner were aligned. The inference was that the FBI received the box from Tennessee authorities, opened it, and resealed it before the spillage occurred. Reinforcing this theory, Agent Bigbee testified that he observed no blood spillage in the styrofoam box and that had he detected such signs of evidence contamination, FBI policy would have required immediate return of the evidence.

* * *

In sum, considering " 'all the evidence,' " *Schlup,* 513 U.S., at 328 * * * on this issue, we think the evidentiary disarray surrounding the blood, taken together with Dr. Blake's testimony and the limited rebuttal of it in the present record, would prevent reasonable jurors from placing significant reliance on the blood evidence. We now know, though the trial jury did not, that an Assistant Chief Medical Examiner believes the blood on House's jeans must have come from autopsy samples; that a vial and a quarter of autopsy blood is unaccounted for; that the blood was transported to the FBI together with the pants in conditions that could have caused vials to spill; that the blood did indeed spill at least once during its journey from Tennessee authorities through FBI hands to a defense expert; that the pants were stored in a plastic bag bearing both a large blood stain and a label with TBI Agent Scott's name; and that the styrofoam box containing the blood samples may well have been opened before it arrived at the FBI lab. Thus, whereas the bloodstains, emphasized by the prosecution, seemed strong evidence of House's guilt at trial, the record now raises substantial questions about the blood's origin.

A Different Suspect

Were House's challenge to the State's case limited to the questions he has raised about the blood and semen, the other evidence favoring the prosecution might well suffice to bar relief. There is, however, more; for in the post-trial proceedings House presented troubling evidence that Mr. Muncey, the victim's husband, himself could have been the murderer. * * *

[Two weeks before the murder Mrs. Muncey's brother received a frightened phone call from his sister indicating that she and Mr. Muncey had been fighting, that she was scared, and that she wanted to leave him. Moreover, the brother once saw the husband smack her. In addition, multiple sources suggested that Mr. Muncey regularly abused his wife. Another witness (Atkins) saw him hit Mrs. Muncey at a dance on the night of the murder. Still another witness (Lawson) testified that Mr. Muncey visited her the morning after the murder, before the body was found, and asked her to tell anyone who inquired that he had breakfasted at her home at 6 o'clock that morning. Mr. Muncey had not been with her so early. Moreover, Kathy Parker and her sister Penny Letner, testified at the habeas hearing that, around the time of House's trial, Mr. Muncey when intoxicated confessed to the crime, claiming he did not mean to kill her. He said that his wife was "bitching him out," he smacked her, she fell and hit her head. Letner, who was then 19 years old, testified she was scared and kept silent because she thought no one would believe her. Parker claimed she went to the Sherriff's Department, but no one would listen. Other evidence suggested Mr. Muncey had the opportunity to commit the crime.]

In the habeas proceedings, then, two different witnesses (Parker and Letner) described a confession by Mr. Muncey; two more (Atkins and Lawson) described suspicious behavior (a fight and an attempt to construct a false alibi) around the time of the crime; and still other witnesses described a history of abuse.

As to Parker and Letner, the District Court noted that it was "not impressed with the allegations of individuals who wait over ten years to come forward with their evidence," especially considering that "there was no physical evidence in the Munceys' kitchen to corroborate [Mr. Muncey's] alleged confession that he killed [his wife] there." * * * Parker and Letner, however, did attempt to explain their delay coming forward, and the record indicates no reason why these two women, both lifelong acquaintances of Mr. Muncey, would have wanted either to frame him or to help House. Furthermore, the record includes at least some independent support for the statements Parker and Letner attributed to Mr. Muncey. The supposed explanation for the fatal fight—that his wife was complaining about going fishing—fits with Mrs. Muncey's statement to Luttrell earlier that evening that her husband's absence was "all right, because she was going to make him take her fishing the next day" * * *. And Dr. Blake testified, in only partial contradiction of Dr. Carabia, that Mrs. Muncey's head injury resulted from "a surface with an edge" or "a hard surface with a corner," not from a fist. * * * (Dr. Carabia had said either a fist or some other object could have been the cause.)

Mr. Muncey testified at the habeas hearing, and the District Court did not question his credibility. Though Mr. Muncey said he seemed to remember visiting Lawson the day after the murder, he denied either killing his wife or confessing to doing so. Yet Mr. Muncey also claimed, contrary to Constable Wallace's testimony and to his own prior statement, that he left the dance on the night of the crime only when it ended at midnight. Mr. Muncey, moreover, denied ever hitting Mrs. Muncey; the State itself had to impeach him with a prior statement on this point.

It bears emphasis, finally, that Parker's and Letner's testimony is not comparable to the sort of eleventh-hour affidavit vouching for a defendant and incriminating a conveniently absent suspect that Justice O'Connor described in her concurring opinion in [Herrera v. Collins, 506 U.S. 390 (1993)] as "unfortunate" and "not uncommon" in capital cases, 506 U.S., at 423; nor was the confession Parker and Letner described induced under pressure of interrogation. The confession evidence here involves an alleged spontaneous statement recounted by two eyewitnesses with no evident motive to lie. For this reason it has more probative value than, for example, incriminating testimony from inmates, suspects, or friends or relations of the accused.

The evidence pointing to Mr. Muncey is by no means conclusive. If considered in isolation, a reasonable jury might well disregard it. In combination, however, with the challenges to the blood evidence and the lack of motive with respect to House, the evidence pointing to Mr. Muncey likely would reinforce other doubts as to House's guilt.

Other Evidence

Certain other details were presented at the habeas hearing. First, Dr. Blake, in addition to testifying about the blood evidence and the victim's head injury, examined photographs of House's bruises and scratches and concluded, based on 35 years' experience monitoring the development and healing of bruises, that they were too old to have resulted from the crime. In addition Dr. Blake claimed that the injury on House's right knuckle was indicative of "[g]etting mashed"; it was not consistent with striking someone. * * * (That of course would also eliminate the explanation that the injury came from the blow House supposedly told Turner he gave to his unidentified assailant.)

The victim's daughter, Lora Muncey (now Lora Tharp), also testified at the habeas hearing. She repeated her recollection of hearing a man with a deep voice * * * and a statement that her father had had a wreck down by the creek. She also denied seeing any signs of struggle or hearing a fight between her parents, though she also said she could not recall her parents ever fighting physically. The District Court found her credible, and this testimony certainly cuts in favor of the State.

Finally, House himself testified at the habeas proceedings. He essentially repeated the story he allegedly told Turner about getting attacked on the road. The District Court found, however, based on House's demeanor, that he "was not a credible witness." * * *

Conclusion

This is not a case of conclusive exoneration. Some aspects of the State's evidence—Lora Muncey's memory of a deep voice, House's bizarre evening walk, his lie to law enforcement, his appearance near the body, and the blood on his pants—still support an inference of guilt. Yet the central forensic proof connecting House to the crime—the blood and the semen—has been called into question, and House has put forward substantial evidence pointing to a different suspect. Accordingly, and although the issue is close, we conclude that this is the rare case where— had the jury heard all the conflicting testimony—it is more likely than not that no reasonable juror viewing the record as a whole would lack reasonable doubt.

V

In addition to his gateway claim under *Schlup,* House argues that he has shown freestanding innocence and that as a result his imprisonment and planned execution are unconstitutional. In *Herrera,* decided three years before *Schlup,* the Court assumed without deciding that "in a capital case a truly persuasive demonstration of 'actual innocence' made after trial would render the execution of a defendant unconstitutional, and warrant federal habeas relief if there were no state avenue open to process such a claim." 506 U.S., at 417; see also *id.,* at 419 (O'Connor, J., concurring) ("I cannot disagree with the fundamental legal principle that executing the innocent is inconsistent with the Constitution"). "[T]he threshold showing for such an assumed right would necessarily be extraordinarily high," the Court explained, and petitioner's evidence there fell "far short of that which would have to be made in order to trigger the sort of constitutional claim which we have assumed, *arguendo,* to exist." *Id.,* at 417, 418–419 * * *. House urges the Court to answer the question left open in *Herrera* and hold not only that freestanding innocence claims are possible but also that he has established one.

We decline to resolve this issue. We conclude here, much as in *Herrera,* that whatever burden a hypothetical freestanding innocence claim would require, this petitioner has not satisfied it. * * *

[CHIEF JUSTICE ROBERTS, with JUSTICE SCALIA and JUSTICE THOMAS, concurred in the judgment in part and dissented in part on the grounds that House had not met his burden of proof under *Schlup*. JUSTICE ALITO took no part in the decision. The Chief Justice made a number of points, including that the majority essentially disregarded the district court's role in assessing the reliability of House's new evidence. He also pointed out that the jury had been informed that Mrs. Muncey's body was found fully clothed. He stressed that the Munceys' daughter had heard a deep-voiced perpetrator arrive at the Muncey home late at night and tell Mrs. Muncey that her husband had been in a wreck near the creek. He concluded: "Surely a reasonable juror would give the fact that an alibi had been made up and discredited significant weight. People facing a murder charge, who are innocent, do not make up a story out of concern that the truth might somehow disturb their parole officer. And people do not lie to the police about which jeans they were wearing the night of a murder, if they have no reason to believe the jeans would be stained with the blood shed by the victim in her last desperate struggle to live."]

NOTES AND QUESTIONS

1. *Procedural default.* Procedural default is just one aspect of habeas corpus law. See 3 LaFave et al., Criminal Procedure § 28.4 (3d ed. 2007). The changes in federal habeas law that began in the late 1970s have had the effect of dramatically restricting its scope from that enjoyed during the Warren Court era. These changes have generated an extensive body of largely critical commentary. Congress further limited the availability of habeas review.

2. *Innocence.* As *House* suggests, the power of DNA evidence to exonerate convicted prisoners is having a significant impact on the criminal justice system. According to the Innocence Project, DNA analysis has exonerated over 306 convicts, 18 of whom had been on death row. Many states enacted post-conviction DNA testing laws, as did Congress in the Innocence Protection Act of 2004, 18 U.S.C. § 3600, which was part of major crime legislation, the Justice for All Act, Public Law 108–405. As a result of the exonerations, commentators began to examine the causes of these miscarriages of justice. A study of 200 DNA exonerations found that expert testimony (55 percent) was the second leading type of evidence (after

eyewitness identifications, 79 percent) used in the wrongful conviction cases. Brandon L. Garrett, Judging Innocence, 108 Colum.L.Rev. 55, 81 (2008). See also Brandon L. Garrett & Peter J. Neufeld, Invalid Forensic Science Testimony and Wrongful Convictions, 95 Va.L.Rev. 1, 44 (2009); Giannelli, Wrongful Convictions and Forensic Science: The Need to Regulate Crime Labs, 86 N.C.L.Rev. 163 (2007). The ABA House of Delegates passed a number of resolutions addressing these issues, including recommendations for videotaping all interrogations, accrediting crime laboratories, conducting double blind lineups, and requiring corroboration in all cases involving jailhouse snitches. Report of the ABA Criminal Justice Section's Ad Hoc Innocence Committee to Ensure the Integrity of the Criminal Process, Achieving Justice: Freeing the Innocent, Convicting the Guilty (Giannelli & Raeder eds., 2006).

3. *Victim's Rights*. Rape shield laws, which are discussed in Chapter 8(C), infra, can be viewed as privileges that often exclude defense evidence. They are reflective of the growing recognition in modern criminal proceedings of a role for the crime victim, who may have specific interests that differ from those of the party prosecuting the case, the state or federal government. The movement to give recognition to "victim rights" has produced a substantial body of legislation to compensate and protect victims and to give them more say in the conduct of the prosecution. See, e.g., Victim and Witness Protection Act of 1982, 18 U.S.C. §§ 1501 et seq.; Justice for All Act of 2004, Public Law 108–405, with victim's rights provisions codified in 18 U.S.C.A. § 3771. Here too there is a growing body of scholarly commentary. See Cassell, Recognizing Victims in the Federal Rules of Criminal Procedure: Proposed Amendment in Light the Crime Victims' Rights Act, 2005 BYU L.Rev. 835; Henderson, The Wrongs of Victim's Rights, 37 Stan.L.Rev. 937 (1985); Mosteller, Victim's Rights and the Constitution: An Effort to Recast the Battle in Criminal Litigation, 85 Geo.L.J. 1691 (1997); Mosteller, Victim's Rights and the Constitution: Moving from Guaranteeing Participatory Rights to Benefitting the Prosecution, 29 St. Mary's L.J. 1053 (1998); Welling, Victim Participation in Plea Bargains, 65 Wash.U.L.Q. 301 (1987); Symposium, Crime Victims' Rights in the Twenty–First Century, 1999 Utah L.Rev. 285–552; Symposium, Victims' Rights, 11 Pepperdine L.Rev. 1–182 (1984).

4. *Jury Nullification*. This chapter has explored a few of the limitations on our adversary system. Jury nullification, the jury's ability to acquit in the face of law and facts demonstrating guilt, constitutes another theoretically important check upon the "efficient" operation of that system. While the jury is consistently recognized to have the power to nullify, does it have that "right"? With extremely rare exceptions, American courts hold that the jury is not to be instructed regarding its ability to nullify. Why is that position held? See, e.g., United States v. Dougherty, 473 F.2d 1113 (D.C.Cir.1972). See also United States v. Abbell, 271 F.3d 1286, 1302 (11th Cir.2001) ("Because of the danger that a dissenting juror might be excused under the mistaken view that the

juror is engaging in impermissible nullification, we must apply a tough legal standard. In these kind of circumstances, a juror should be excused only when no 'substantial possibility' exists that she is basing her decision on the sufficiency of the evidence."); People v. Williams, 21 P.3d 1209, 1222 (Cal.2001) ("It is striking that the debate over juror nullification remains vigorous after more than a hundred years. But it is equally significant that, during this time, no published authority has restricted a trial court's authority to discharge a juror when the record demonstrates that the juror is unable or unwilling to follow the court's instructions."). See generally Conrad, Jury Nullification: The Evolution of a Doctrine (1998); Bressler, Reconstruction and the Transformation of Jury Nullification, 78 U.Chi.L.Rev. 1133 (2011); Brown, Jury Nullification Within the Rule of Law, 81 Minn.L.Rev. 1149 (1997); Butler, Racially Based Jury Nullification: Black Power in the Criminal Justice System, 105 Yale L.J. 677 (1995); Horowitz & Willging, Changing Views of Jury Power: The Nullification Debate, 1787–1988, 15 Law & Hum.Behav. 165 (1991); Leipold, Rethinking Jury Nullification, 82 Va.L.Rev. 253 (1996); Saks, Judicial Nullification, 68 Ind.L.J. 1281 (1993); Wiener et al., The Social Psychology of Jury Nullification: Predicting When Jurors Disobey the Law, 21 J. Applied Soc.Psychol. 1379 (1991); Note, License to Nullify: The Democratic and Constitutional Deficiencies of Authorized Jury Lawmaking, 106 Yale L.J. 2563 (1997).

CHAPTER 3

ALLOCATING THE CASE

■ ■ ■

CLEARY, PRESUMING AND PLEADING: AN ESSAY ON JURISTIC IMMATURITY[1]
12 Stanford Law Review 5 (1959).

* * *

The Substantive Law

Since all are agreed that procedure exists only for the purpose of putting the substantive law effectively to work, a preliminary look at the nature of substantive law, as viewed procedurally, is appropriate.

Every dog, said the common law, is entitled to one bite. This result was reached from reasoning that man's best friend was not in general dangerous, and hence the owner should not be liable when the dog departed from his normally peaceable pursuits and inflicted injury. Liability should follow only when the owner had reason to know of the dangerous proclivities of his dog, and the one bite afforded notice of those proclivities. So the formula for holding a dog owner liable at common law is: + *ownership + notice of dangerous character + biting.*

This rule of law becomes monotonous to postmen. Hence the postmen cause to be introduced in the legislature a bill making owners of dogs absolutely liable, i.e., eliminating notice from the formula for liability. At the hearing on the bill, however, the dog lovers appear and, while admitting the justness of the postmen's complaint, point out that a dog ought at least to be entitled to defend himself against human aggression. Then the home owners' lobby points out the usefulness of dogs in guarding premises against prowlers. Balancing these factors, there emerges a statute making dog owners liable for bites inflicted except upon persons tormenting the dog or unlawfully on the owner's premises. The formula for liability now becomes: + *ownership + biting — being tormented — unlawful presence on the premises.*

---

[1] Copyright © 1959–1960 by the Trustees of the Leland Stanford Junior University. Reprinted by permission. Some footnotes have been omitted, and the remainder have been renumbered. [Ed.]

So in any given situation, the law recognizes certain elements as material to the case, and the presence or absence of each of them is properly to be considered in deciding the case. Or, to rephrase in somewhat more involved language, rules of substantive law are "statements of the specific factual conditions upon which specific legal consequences depend. * * * Rules of substantive law are conditional imperatives, having the form: *If* such and such *and* so and so, *etc.* is the case, *and unless* such and such *or unless* so and so, *etc.* is the case, *then* the defendant is liable * * *."[2] Now obviously the weighing and balancing required to determine what elements ought to be considered material cannot be accomplished by any of the methodologies of procedure. The result is purely a matter of substantive law, to be decided according to those imponderables which travel under the name of jurisprudence.

This view of the substantive law may seem unduly Euclidean, yet some system of analysis and classification is necessary if the law is to possess a measure of continuity and to be accessible and usable.

Prima Facie Case and Defense

Under our adversary method of litigation a trial is essentially not an inquest or investigation but rather a demonstration conducted by the parties.

Since plaintiff is the party seeking to disturb the existing situation by inducing the court to take some measure in his favor, it seems reasonable to require him to demonstrate his right to relief. How extensive must this demonstration be? Should it include every substantive element, which either by its existence or nonexistence may condition his right to relief? If the answer is "yes," then plaintiff under our dog statute would be required to demonstrate each of the elements in the formula: + *ownership* + *biting* — *tormenting* — *illegal presence on the premises.*

In the ordinary dog case this would not be unduly burdensome, but if the suit is on a contract and we require plaintiff to establish the existence or nonexistence, as may be appropriate, of every concept treated in Corbin and Williston, then the responsibility of plaintiff becomes burdensome indeed and the lawsuit itself may include a large amount of unnecessary territory. Actually, of course, the responsibility for dealing with every element is not placed on plaintiff. Instead we settle for a "prima facie case" or "cause of action," consisting of certain selected elements which are regarded as sufficient to entitle plaintiff to recover, *if* he proves them and *unless* defendant in turn establishes other elements which would offset them. Thus in a simple contract case, by establishing + *offer* + *acceptance* + *consideration* + *breach,* plaintiff is entitled to recover, unless

---

[2]   [Michael & Adler, *The Trial of an Issue of Fact: I,* 34 Colum.L.Rev. 1224, 1241 (1934).]

defendant establishes + *accord and satisfaction* or + *failure of consideration* or + *illegality* or—*capacity to contract,* and so on.

Observe that the plus and minus signs change, in accord with proper mathematical rules, when we shift elements to the defendant's side of the equation as "defenses." For example, if plaintiff were required to deal with capacity to contract, it would become + *capacity to contract* as a part of his case, rather than the—*capacity to contract* of defendant's case.

Defenses, too, may be prima facie only and subject to being offset by further matters produced by plaintiff, as in the case of the defense of release, offset by the further fact of fraud in the inducement for the release. The entire process is the familiar confessing and avoiding of the common law.

Allocating the Elements

The next step to be taken is the determination whether a particular material element is a part of plaintiff's prima facie case or a defense. Or, referring back to the statement that rules of substantive law are "conditional imperatives, having the form: *If* such and such *and* so and so, etc.,* is the case * * * *then* the defendant is liable,"[3] should the element in question be listed as an *if* or as an *unless?*

In some types of situations, the test has been purely mechanical, with the mechanics in turn likely to be accidental and casual. Thus, in causes of action based on statute, if an exception appears in the enacting clause, i.e., the clause creating the right of action, then the party relying on the statute must show that the case is not within the exception; otherwise the responsibility for bringing the case within an exception falls upon the opposite party. The principle is widely recognized, but the vagaries of statutory draftsmanship detract largely from its certainty of application. Returning to our dogs, two statutes will serve as illustrations.

> If any dog shall do any damage to either the body or property of any person, the owner * * * shall be liable for such damage, unless such damage shall have been occasioned to the body or property of a person who, at the time such damage was sustained, was committing a trespass or other tort, or was teasing, tormenting or abusing such dog. Mass.Ann.Laws ch. 140, § 155 (1950).

> Every person owning or harboring a dog shall be liable to the party injured for all damages done by such dog; but no recovery shall be had for personal injuries to any person when they [sic] are upon the premises of the owner of the dog after night, or

---

[3]　Michael & Adler, supra note [2].

upon the owner's premises engaged in some unlawful act in the day time. Ky.Laws 1906, ch. 10, at 25, Ky.Stats.1936, § 68a–5.

The Massachusetts statute was construed as imposing on a two and one quarter year old plaintiff the burden of establishing that he was not teasing, tormenting or abusing the dog,[4] while under the Kentucky statute a plaintiff was held to have stated a prima facie case by alleging only that he was bitten by a dog owned by defendant, leaving questions of presence on the premises at night or unlawful activities in the day time to be brought in as defenses.[5] The difference in result can scarcely be regarded as calculated but is typical. Unfortunately, the statute which states in so many words the procedural effects of its terms is a rarity.

Exceptions in contracts receive similar treatment. If the words of promising are broad, followed by exceptions, the general disposition is to place on defendant the responsibility of invoking the exception. Of course, many of the cases involve insurance policies, with all that implies. In Munro, Brice & Co. v. War Risks Ass'n,[6] during World War I one underwriter insured plaintiffs' ship against loss due to hostilities and another underwriter insured it against perils of the sea except consequences of hostilities. The ship was lost, and plaintiffs sued on both policies. The King's Bench Division held that as regards the first policy plaintiffs must show the loss to have been due to hostilities, but that under the second policy merely establishing the loss was sufficient, leaving it to the underwriter to bring in loss by hostilities as a defense. Since evidence of the cause of loss was wholly lacking, the loss fell on the second underwriter.

Julius Stone commented as follows:

> Every qualification of a class can equally be stated without any change of meaning as an exception to a class not so qualified. Thus the proposition "All animals have four legs except gorillas", and the proposition "all animals which are not gorillas have four legs", are, so far as their meanings are concerned, identical. * * *

> If the distinction between an element of the rule and an exception to it does not represent any distinction in meaning, it may still remain a valid distinction for legal purposes. In that case, however, it must turn upon something other than the meaning of the propositions involved. It may turn, for instance, merely upon their relative form or order.[7]

---

4   Sullivan v. Ward, 304 Mass. 614, 24 N.E.2d 672, 130 A.L.R. 437 (1939).

5   Bush v. Wathen, 104 Ky. 548, 47 S.W. 599 (1898).

6   [1918] 2 K.B. 78.

7   Stone, *Burden of Proof and the Judicial Process,* 60 L.Q.Rev. 262, 280–81 (1944).

So in a few kinds of cases the answer to the question of allocation is found in the structure of a statute or contract, perhaps with some tenuous reference to intent, either of the legislature or of the contracting parties. But what of the great bulk of the cases, involving neither exception in a statute nor limitation upon words of promising? What general considerations should govern the allocation of responsibility for the elements of the case between the parties?

Precedent may settle the manner in a particular jurisdiction, but precedent as such does nothing for the inquiring mind. Thayer was of the view that questions of allocation were to be referred to the principles of pleading, or perhaps to analysis of the substantive law, and "one has no right to look to the law of evidence for a solution of such questions as these. * * * "[8] Books about pleading, however, have not been numerous in recent years, except for the local practice works; and aside from a brief but provocative treatment by Judge Clark[9] they offer slight assistance. The substantive law texts, when they deal with the matter at all, tend to describe results rather than reasons.

Despite Thayer's strictures, his descendants in the field of writing about evidence, by assuming to deal with problems of burden of proof as an aspect of the law of evidence, have found themselves inevitably enmeshed in the problems of allocation and have contributed most of the literature on the subject, although in an introductory and incidental fashion.

Before trying to establish some bench marks for allocation, let us note, though only for the purpose of rejecting them, two which are sometimes suggested. (a) That the burden is on the party having the affirmative; or, conversely stated, that a party is not required to prove a negative. This is no more than a play on words, since practically any proposition may be stated in either affirmative or negative form. Thus a plaintiff's exercise of ordinary care equals absence of contributory negligence, in the minority jurisdictions which place this element in plaintiff's case. In any event, the proposition seems simply not to be so. (b) That the burden is on the party to whose case the element is essential. This does no more than restate the question.

Actually the reported decisions involving problems of allocation rarely contain any satisfying disclosure of the *ratio decidendi*. Implicit, however, seem to be considerations of policy, fairness and probability. None affords a complete working rule. Much overlap is apparent, as sound policy implies not too great a departure from fairness, and probability may constitute an aspect of both policy and fairness. But

---

[8]   Thayer, A Preliminary Treatises on Evidence at the Common Law 371 (1898). * * *

[9]   Clark, Code Pleading § 96, at 606–11 (2d ed. 1947). * * *

despite the vagueness of their generality, it is possible to pour enough content into these concepts to give them some real meaning.

(1) *Policy.* As Judge Clark remarks, "One who must bear the risk of getting the matter properly set before the court, if it is to be considered at all, has to that extent the dice loaded against him."[10] While policy more obviously predominates at the stage of determining what elements are material, its influence may nevertheless extend into the stage of allocating those elements by way of favoring one or the other party to a particular kind of litigation. Thus a court which is willing to permit a recovery for negligence may still choose to exercise restraints by imposing on plaintiff the burden of freedom from contributory negligence, as a theoretical, though perhaps not a practical, handicap. Or the bringing of actions for defamation may in some measure be discouraged by allocating untruth to plaintiff as an element of his prima facie case, rather than by treating truth as an affirmative defense. And it must be apparent that a complete lack of proof as to a particular element moves allocation out of the class of a mere handicap and makes it decisive as to the element, and perhaps as to the case itself. In Summers v. Tice[11] plaintiff was hunting with two defendants and was shot in the eye when both fired simultaneously at the same bird. The court placed on each defendant the burden of proving that his shot did not cause the injury. To discharge this burden was impossible, since each gun was loaded with identical shot. In Munro, Brice & Co. v. War Risks Ass'n[12] the absence of proof of the cause of the ship's loss meant that the party on whom that burden was cast lost the case. In these cases the admonition of Julius Stone is particularly apt: "the Courts should not essay the impossible task of making the bricks of judge-made law without handling the straw of policy."[13]

(2) *Fairness.* The nature of a particular element may indicate that evidence relating to it lies more within the control of one party, which suggests the fairness of allocating that element to him. Examples are payment, discharge in bankruptcy, and license, all of which are commonly treated as affirmative defenses. However, caution in making any extensive generalization is indicated by the classification of contributory

---

[10]   Clark, Code Pleading § 96, at 609 (2d ed. 1947).

[11]   33 Cal.2d 80, 199 P.2d 1, 5 A.L.R.2d 91 (1948). Like presumptions, liberal party joinder provisions appear to be no more than procedural in nature. However, they may encourage courts to impose blanket responsibility upon a group of defendants, leaving each to extricate himself as he can. Thus they may have a significant role in extending the substantive law of liability. See McCoid, *Negligence Actions Against Multiple Defendants,* 7 Stan.L.Rev. 480 (1955).

[12]   [1918] 2 K.B. 78. * * *

[13]   Stone, *Burden of Proof and the Judicial Process,* 60 L.Q.Rev. 262, 283 (1944).

Compare: "where natural logic is insufficient the state is disposed to discard it and to adopt other procedures for arriving at a decision; and so by means of ingenious procedural mechanisms, it creates a kind of 'artificial' or 'official' logic that serves to resolve all questions at issue, even those that common reason would call insoluble." Calamandrei, Procedure and Democracy 6 (1956).

negligence, illegality, and failure of consideration also as affirmative defenses, despite the fact that knowledge more probably lies with plaintiff. Certainly in the usual tort cases, knowledge of his own wrongdoing rests more intimately in defendant, though the accepted general pattern imposes this burden on plaintiff.

(3) *Probability.* A further factor which seems to enter into many decisions as to allocation is a judicial, i.e., wholly nonstatistical, estimate of the probabilities of the situation with the burden being put on the party who will be benefited by a departure from the supposed norm.

The probabilities may relate to the type of situation out of which the litigation arises or they may relate to the type of litigation itself. The standards are quite different and may produce differences in result. To illustrate: If it be assumed that most people pay their bills, the probabilities are that any bill selected at random has been paid; therefore, a plaintiff suing to collect a bill would be responsible for nonpayment as an element of his prima facie case. If, however, attention is limited to bills upon which suit is brought, a contrary conclusion is reached. Plaintiffs are not prone to sue for paid bills, and the probabilities are that the bill is unpaid. Hence payment would be an affirmative defense. Or again, "guest" statutes prohibit nonpaying passengers from recovering for the negligence of the driver. If most passengers are nonpaying, then the element of compensation for the ride would belong in the prima facie case of the passenger-plaintiff. If, however, most passengers in the litigated cases ride for compensation, then absence of compensation would be an affirmative defense. In the payment-of-a-bill situation the probabilities are estimated with regard to the litigated situation, payment being regarded generally as an affirmative defense, while in the guest situation they are estimated with regard to such situations generally and not limited to those which are litigated, status as a nonguest being a part of plaintiff's prima facie case. No reason for the shift is apparent, and it may be unconscious. The litigated cases would seem to furnish the more appropriate basis for estimating probabilities.

Matters occurring after the accrual of the plaintiff's right are almost always placed in the category of affirmative defenses. Examples are payment, release, accord and satisfaction, discharge in bankruptcy, and limitations. A plausible explanation is that a condition once established is likely to continue; hence the burden ought to fall on the party benefited by a change.

In the cases of complete absence of proof, a proper application of the probability factor is calculated to produce a minimum of unjust results, and the same is true, though less impressively, even if proof is available.

The Role of Pleading

Determining what elements are relevant to a case and allocating them between the parties does not of necessity have to be done at any particular stage of litigation. These questions can be left suspended in mid-air like Mohammed's coffin until the very end of the case, when it can be decided what are the responsibilities of each party and whether he has discharged them. This is the practice followed in small claims cases. However, decision prior to trial helps to eliminate uncertainties and lends direction and assurance to preparation and presentation. This is one of the useful functions of pleadings. Unhappily, certain characteristics of the legal mind at times enter in to divorce the pleadings from the realities.

* * *

On the whole, however, the pleadings can and do constitute reasonably accurate blueprints of the trial which is to follow, except as their accuracy may be impaired by the workings of presumptions, which will be treated hereinafter. * * *

* * *

NOTES

1. *More recent articles.* Professor Cleary's classic article has withstood the test of time. In the more than 50 years since its publication, its analysis has essentially gone unchallenged. More recent articles have put forth similar ideas, particularly with regard to the importance of the probability of an event occurring, although the analysis is presented in the language of law and economics. The premises of these writers is that the allocation of the burdens of proof is based or at least ought to be based in substantial measure on minimizing the costs of litigation—a premise with which Professor Cleary would likely have been very comfortable. See Hay, Allocating the Burden of Proof, 72 Ind.L.J. 651 (1997); Hay & Spier, Burdens of Proof in Civil Litigation: An Economic Perspective, 26 J. Legal Stud. 413 (1997); Lee, Pleading and Proof: The Economics of Legal Burdens, 1997 B.Y.U.L.Rev. 1. For a case discussing the various factors in allocating the burdens of proof, *see* Acuity Mut. Ins. Co. v. Olivas, 726 N.W.2d 258, 267–68 (Wis.2007) (burden on insurer to show that workers were employees).

2. *Criminal cases.* The problem of allocating responsibility for proof of the elements of a criminal case between prosecution and defense obviously entails considerations not pertinent in civil litigation. While one or more of the factors noted in the above discussion would clearly tend to support the allocation of certain elements of criminal cases to the defendant, nevertheless it may easily be seen that a wholesale allocation of elements to the defendant would render the time-honored presumption of innocence largely nugatory and radically alter the traditional form of the Anglo–American criminal proceeding. Indeed, as we shall see in the next two chapters, any allocation of

a burden to the defendant, especially the burden of persuasion, will present serious constitutional issues.

CHAPTER 4[1]

BURDEN OF PROOF

■ ■ ■

The preceding chapter sketched briefly the problem of allocating between the respective parties to litigation the responsibility for proof of the various elements in the case. Ordinarily this allocation will be at least preliminarily made at a relatively early stage of the lawsuit and, at the optimum, will be reflected by the pleadings in the case. The next question, then, and the one to be considered in the present section, is the nature of the responsibility, or "burden of proof," so allocated. Of what does this responsibility or burden consist, and how is it to be successfully fulfilled or discharged?

By way of introduction it should be noted that analysis of these and related problems has been plagued by an essentially semantic difficulty. The commonly used phrase "burden of proof," being singular, might suggest that party responsibility for proof is a single, integral responsibility. Analytically, however, as was first pointed out by the great Professor James Bradley Thayer,[2] party responsibility is not single and integral, but instead consists of two interrelated but quite distinguishable responsibilities.

The first of these distinguishable responsibilities or burdens which a party may initially be allocated (or to which he may fall heir during the course of the trial) is that of producing evidence sufficient to enable a jury, acting reasonably, to find the existence or nonexistence of a particular element. The fulfillment or nonfulfillment of this burden by a party possessing it is generally deemed a question for determination by the court, and nonfulfillment is sanctionable, depending upon local practice, by a directed verdict, involuntary nonsuit, or peremptory instruction.

The second burden obliges the party possessing it, in the ordinary civil case, actually to persuade the trier of fact that the existence or nonexistence of a particular element is more probable than not. In certain other types of cases this second burden will be more onerous, requiring persuasion of the trier of fact that the existence or nonexistence of a given

---

[1] In the cases and materials throughout this chapter, some footnotes have been omitted; others have been renumbered. Notes 1–8 are editor's notes. [Ed.]

[2] Thayer, Preliminary Treatise on Evidence 353–89 (1898).

element is much more probable than not, or that it exists or does not exist beyond a reasonable doubt.[3] Whether this second burden has been satisfied by the party possessing it will, as already indicated, be determined by the trier of fact, and imposition of the burden will, in the jury case, be accomplished by an instruction requiring the trier, unless persuaded to the requisite level, to find against the burdened party.

Since the time of Thayer's writing it has become fairly common, in the interest of precision, to denominate the first of the above described burdens as the "burden of going forward," or the "burden of producing evidence," and the second as the "burden of persuasion." Unfortunately terminology has not become standardized, nor has the practice entirely disappeared of referring indiscriminately to either or both of the two burdens as the "burden of proof."[4]

A. THE BURDEN OF GOING FORWARD

According to one definition previously suggested, the burden of producing evidence is the obligation of a party to produce evidence sufficient to enable a jury, acting reasonably, to find the existence or nonexistence of an element of the case. This same burden has also been defined as the obligation of a party to produce evidence when necessary to avoid a directed verdict against her. Taken together, these definitions suggest that recognition of a burden of producing evidence means simply that juries are not to be allowed to render verdicts on grounds which are without reasonable support in the evidence, and that courts will, through use of various devices, see to it that they do not do so.

The basic problem suggested, then, is to articulate a general test by which it may be determined that a jury, in a given situation, would be acting unreasonably in returning a given verdict. Over the years the courts have devoted their best efforts toward the articulation of such a general standard, but with limited success. It is common ground, of course, that a total absence of evidence upon an essential element of the case is fatal to the party assigned the burden of production as to that element. Again, it is at least commonly agreed today, that a "mere scintilla" of evidence on an essential element will not suffice to support a

---

[3] The formulations here adopted for the various burdens of persuasion are substantially those recommended by McBaine, Burden of Proof: Degrees of Belief, 32 Cal.L.Rev. 242 (1944). It should be noted, however, that the device of instructing the trier of fact on the burden of persuasion in terms of probabilities is a relatively recent suggestion, and has been vigorously rejected by a number of courts. See, e.g., Lampe v. Franklin American Trust Co., 339 Mo. 361, 96 S.W.2d 710 (1936). The more traditional formulations are, of course, "by a preponderance of the evidence," "by clear and convincing evidence," and "beyond a reasonable doubt."

[4] Thayer himself viewed as Utopian the possibilities of banishing the phrase "burden of proof" from the language, or of standardizing its usage, and contented himself with an exhortation which remains good advice today: "[A]dopt other terms where it is necessary to mark the discrimination between one meaning and the other." Thayer, Preliminary Treatise on Evidence 386–87 (1898).

verdict for the burdened party. Beyond this point, a plethora of differing formulations, already familiar from readings in other courses, may be found currently in use by appellate courts across the country. Whatever the abstraction used, the rub comes, as is usual in the law, in its concrete application. The materials which follow therefore focus upon the propriety of judicially determined results where the evidence presents one or another of certain commonly recurring patterns.

As a general point of reference throughout this section, consider to what extent the various rules of sufficiency encountered reflect assumptions, explicit or implicit, concerning the relative areas of competence of juries and judges respectively. At the end of the section, you might well ask yourself whether today's juries are given too much or too little to do. There is respectable modern authority for either conclusion you may reach.

NOTES

1.   *History.* The concept of a burden of going forward, owing its very existence to the power of the court to evaluate the sufficiency of evidence by some legal standard, was of relatively recent origin. As late as 1670 Chief Justice Vaughn, in the celebrated decision of Bushell's case, granted habeas corpus to a juror who had been imprisoned for refusing to follow the direction of the trial court to return a verdict against William Penn. As one ground for his decision, Vaughn indicated that the court should not have directed a verdict since:

> Being return'd of the vicinage, where the cause of action ariseth, the law supposeth them [the jury] thence to have sufficient knowledge to try the matter in issue (and so they must) though no evidence were given on either side in Court, but to this evidence the Judge is a stranger.

Vaughn 135, 124 Eng.Rep. 1006 (C.P.1670).

Thus, before the end of the 17th century, no device equivalent to today's directed verdict was available in the English courts.[5] At that time, however, there were at least two devices available by which certain questions concerning the sufficiency of one's opponent's evidence might be raised. These were the demurrer to the evidence and the motion for a new trial. A demurrer to the evidence was substantially similar to a demurrer to the pleadings and, if joined in by the opponent, resulted in a decision of the case by the court. The demurrer to the evidence, however, possessed serious deficiencies from the standpoint of the demurrant. First, the party to whose evidence the demurrer was interposed might avoid a decision by the court by refusing to join in the demurrer. Moreover, the decision of the court on a demurrer to the evidence resulted in a final judgment. Thus where the demurrer was ill-

---

5   For fuller accounts of the history here synopsized, see Blume, Origin and Development of the Directed Verdict, 48 Mich.L.Rev. 555 (1950); Galloway v. United States, 319 U.S. 372 (1943).

founded the case was concluded by a ruling to that effect, and the demurrant was precluded from rebutting the evidence of the proponent with evidence of his own.[6]

The motion for a new trial, on the other hand, possessed quite different but no less significant inadequacies from the standpoint of a party wishing to challenge the sufficiency of his opponent's proof. While the motion for a new trial did not of course entail loss of the challenging party's right to introduce evidence, neither did it serve as a device for obtaining a final adjudication by the court. Then, as now, the only relief obtainable on such a motion was the opportunity to try again before a different jury.

The gradual abandonment, following Bushell's case, of the notion that juries might predicate verdicts upon facts known to them but not established by evidence removed one major conceptual objection to final determinations of litigation by the courts on grounds of insufficiency of the evidence. The English courts seem to have begun to "direct verdicts" in scattered cases shortly before the beginning of the 18th century, and the device appeared in the United States at least as early as 1850.[7] As developed in both England and the United States, the directed verdict allowed challenge of the legal sufficiency of an opponent's evidence without waiver of the right to rebut, and usually permitted such a challenge to be interposed even after rebutting evidence had been introduced.[8] As the preceding materials have suggested, however, no unanimity has been achieved either as to the proper standard for evaluating sufficiency, or as to whether rebutting evidence should or should not be considered in the evaluation. The classic article on the directed verdict in the federal courts is Cooper, Directions for Directed Verdicts: A Compass for Federal Courts, 55 Minn.L.Rev. 903 (1971).

2. *Judgments notwithstanding the verdict.* As its name would suggest, the directed verdict in its original form consisted of an instruction by the court to the jury to return a verdict in favor of one of the parties. Thus, while the directed verdict in substance represented a determination by the court, it was in form a determination by the jury, and of necessity had to be moved for and granted, if at all, prior to the jury's return of its verdict.

The judge may, even after the jury's return of a verdict, set aside that verdict and enter judgment for the opposing party. A judgment of this kind is called, variously, a judgment notwithstanding the verdict, a judgment *non obstante veredicto,* or a judgment n.o.v. Where the judgment n.o.v. or its equivalent is recognized, the standard employed for passing upon motions for judgment of this sort is generally the same as that applied in ruling on motions for directed verdicts. In fact, in the federal courts since 1991, the two motions share the same name, a motion for judgment as matter of law. See 9

---

[6] Conversely, the introduction of evidence waived the right to demur.

[7] Parks v. Ross, 52 U.S. (11 How.) 362 (1850).

[8] The constitutionality of the device, as embodied in Fed.R.Civ.P. 50, was challenged, and upheld, in Galloway v. United States, supra note 5. The essence of the petitioner's argument in *Galloway* was that the device, not having existed at the time of the ratification of the 7th Amendment, offended against that amendment's guarantee of trial by jury.

Moore's Federal Practice ¶ 50.03(3d ed. 2001); 9A Wright & Miller, Federal Practice and Procedure § 2521 (1995). If the identical issue is raised, what justification exists for permitting the court to delay its ruling until after return of the jury verdict? See Hazard, Leubsdorf & Bassett, Civil Procedure § 11.30 (6th ed. 2011).

(1) DIRECT EVIDENCE
CALIFORNIA EVIDENCE CODE

§ 410. Direct Evidence

As used in this chapter, "direct evidence" means evidence that directly proves a fact, without an inference or presumption, and which in itself, if true, conclusively establishes that fact.

§ 411. Evidence of One Witness Sufficient to Prove Fact

Except where additional evidence is required by statute, the direct evidence of one witness who is entitled to full credit is sufficient for proof of any fact.

NOTE

As in California under § 411, throughout the United States, direct evidence by a single witness affirming the existence of an elemental fact in the case will generally be sufficient to satisfy the burden of going forward. A corroboration requirement exists in a few instances, generally in criminal cases. Most notably, corroboration is required in treason and perjury cases. Hazard, Leubsdorf & Bassett, Civil Procedure § 11.19 (6th ed. 2011). In addition to these kinds of cases, it is frequently required that certain types of evidence in a criminal prosecution be corroborated in order to support a conviction. Among the most noteworthy rules of this type are those requiring corroboration of: the extrajudicial confession or admission of a criminal defendant, Annot., 45 A.L.R.2d 1316; the testimony of an accomplice to the crime with which the defendant is charged, 7 Wigmore, Evidence §§ 2056–2060 (Chadbourn rev. 1978); the testimony of the complaining witness in a prosecution for rape, Annot., 31 A.L.R.4th 120 (now abandoned in most jurisdictions).

Of the few analogous requirements enjoying widespread currency in civil cases, perhaps the most common are the requirements of corroboration of the testimony of the petitioner in a divorce or separate maintenance proceeding. See Annots., 15 A.L.R.2d 170, 100 A.L.R.2d 612. The requirement of corroboration will also occasionally be resounded in certain highly specialized contexts. Price v. Symsek, 988 F.2d 1187 (Fed.Cir.1993) (in patent law, uncorroborated testimony of inventor insufficient to prove conception), and finally, some of the so-called "Dead Man's Acts" necessitate corroboration by prohibiting judgment against the personal representative of a deceased person on the uncorroborated testimony of his adversary. Annot., 21 A.L.R.2d 1013.

SCOTT V. HANSEN

Supreme Court of Iowa, 1940.
289 N.W. 710.

[Plaintiff brought suit to recover for personal injuries sustained when defendant's automobile, in which plaintiff was riding as a guest, collided with a cow that was crossing the highway. Defendant's auto was proceeding west at the time of the collision. Plaintiff alleged defendant's operation of the car at the time of the collision was reckless, and that such reckless operation was the proximate cause of plaintiff's injuries. The jury returned a verdict for the plaintiff, and defendant appeals.]

RICHARDS, JUSTICE.

* * *

At the conclusion of the evidence defendant moved for a directed verdict. One of the grounds was that in the record there was no competent evidence to show that defendant was guilty of recklessness in the operation of the car which was the proximate cause of the collision and injuries to plaintiff. Defendant claims that upon this ground the motion should have been sustained and that consequently the court erred in ordering that it be overruled. Plaintiff specified that there was reckless operation in that defendant failed to reduce the speed of the car as he approached the cattle and continued to drive into the cattle at an excessive and reckless rate of speed. Whether there was competent evidence showing that there was such failure and such continued manner of driving into the cattle as plaintiff specified, and if so whether in view of the attendant facts and surrounding circumstances a jury would have been warranted in finding that when the accident happened defendant was driving at a rate of speed that evidenced recklessness of operation of the car, appear to be the questions raised by the above stated ground. In seeking the answers it seems needful that we review the evidence.

* * * [The court here summarized the evidence introduced by the plaintiff relating to the situs of the accident and to the respective conditions of car and cow following the collision.] Plaintiff also adduced from his witnesses the fact that there were black tire marks four or five inches in width having the appearance of brake marks or skid marks that extended east from the point of the collision. One of these witnesses testified that measurements of these marks were taken by him and others, and that the marks extended for a distance of 354 feet east from the point where the cow was struck. All these matters plaintiff fully developed in either his own testimony or upon his quite extended direct examination of the witnesses he produced.

At this point the query obtrudes itself whether, in deciding upon the ruling on the motion, we should eliminate from any consideration on our part, as plaintiff says we should, certain unfavorable portions of the showing plaintiff himself made as a part of his case as set out in the foregoing paragraph. It seems to be plaintiff's thought that in viewing the evidence in a light that is favorable to him it becomes our duty to consign to oblivion the physical facts and some other matters that plaintiff not only conceded but affirmatively and intentionally established, and concerning which there is no contradiction by any witness. Then, according to plaintiff, we should determine the right of the controversy upon certain other testimony in the record the salient features of which are the following. One of plaintiff's witnesses testified he saw the car hit the cow. Then, says this witness, "The cow just spun around and around and around and went up the pavement as it threw her a ways. She flew pretty near up thirty feet without touching the pavement at all; and then she hit the pavement and bounced better than five feet; then she hit the pavement again and bounced again to where she laid." It was like a rubber ball, the witness explained to the jury. The bounce of five feet or more was a bounce of ten or more feet the witness related later in his testimony. He reiterated that preceding this bounce he had seen the cow "fly through the air thirty feet." His testimony was also to the effect that the cow's flying weight when she took off was 1200 pounds. What car velocity and weight would have been required to develop the foot-pounds this witness allegedly saw expended would be a worthwhile if possible calculation. Plaintiff's own testimony was that he was almost sure that defendant at no time applied the brakes and that in his opinion the speed was about seventy or seventy-five miles per hour when the car struck the cow. At another place in his testimony he says it was eighty miles per hour. One of the tenants, as plaintiff's witness, stated "as near as I can say the car was coming down the hill seventy-five to eighty miles per hour and did not slow up so far as I could see." This was the witness to whom it appeared that the cow performed so amazingly like a rubber ball. The other tenant testified that there was an awful roar and that "it never slowed down until they struck the cattle." This was the witness who also testified concerning the measurement of the black tire marks that extended 354 feet. The rate of speed as estimated by plaintiff and his two witnesses together with the manner in which, allegedly, the cow was catapulted, was sufficient and effective, in plaintiff's opinion, to generate jury questions respecting the specifications that (1) defendant failed to reduce his speed and (2) drove into the cattle at seventy to eighty miles per hour. But defendant urges, and it appears to us, that this testimony of plaintiff and his witnesses is so wholly inconsistent with the undisputed and established physical facts, related in the preceding paragraph, that the inevitable conclusion is that plaintiff and his witnesses were mistaken. In connection with what defendant urges, plaintiff was undoubtedly entitled to have his evidence viewed in a light as favorable to his contention as is reasonably possible. But one should not be unmindful of the element of reasonableness that inheres in this rule, or of the fact that the scintilla of evidence doctrine does not obtain in this jurisdiction. The estimates of the rate of speed at the time of the collision as stated by plaintiff and his witnesses, together with the testimony concerning the exhibition of levitation credited to the cow by one witness, were in such conflict with incontestable [sic] facts that plaintiff established as verities, including plaintiff's showing that the brakes were being applied for 354 feet, that we are of the opinion that such testimony of said witnesses was so lacking in probative force or effect that a jury finding that the car's speed as it approached the cattle was not reduced, would be unwarranted. * * *

[The court then considered and rejected, plaintiff's contention that the evidence was sufficient to show that defendant drove into the cattle at an excessive rate of speed.]

* * * The court erred in not sustaining the motion for a directed verdict upon the ground that has been discussed. The judgment is reversed.

Reversed.

STIGER, MILLER, SAGER, and HALE, JJ., concur.

HAMILTON, C.J., dissents.

NOTES AND QUESTIONS

1. *Evidence contradicted by physical facts.* In connection with the principal case, consider the following statement:

> It is generally agreed by all courts that the jury will not be permitted to believe testimony that is contradicted by physical facts. Were a witness to testify that the sun rose at midnight in Chicago, no one would argue that the jury might believe him. This is the sort of "physical fact" that is within the realm of judicial notice. The difficult questions arise when the physical facts must be established in some other way.

Dow, Judicial Determination of Credibility in Jury–Tried Actions, 38 Neb.L.Rev. 835, 854–55 (1959).

In *Scott v. Hansen* were the items of testimony relied upon by the plaintiff to establish unabated speed by the defendant contradicted by physical facts of which the court took judicial notice, or by facts established in some other way? To what extent might it be said that facts of both varieties figured in the court's determination? If "facts" of the latter sort were involved, on what basis were these facts deemed to be established?

2. *Evidence contrary to law of nature.* Cases involving evidence judicially determined to be incredible as contrary to some scientific principle or law of nature are collected in Annot., 21 A.L.R. 141. The doctrine of judicial notice, which is more frequently seen operating to assist rather than to baffle the discharge of the burden of going forward, is treated more fully in Chapter 9, infra.

(2) CIRCUMSTANTIAL EVIDENCE

UNITED STATES V. NELSON

United States Court of Appeals, Ninth Circuit, 1969.
419 F.2d 1237.

BROWNING, CIRCUIT JUDGE: Roy Arthur Nelson and Frank Brewton were indicted for robbery of a federally-insured institution in violation of 18 U.S.C.A. § 2113(a) (1964). Brewton was found incompetent to stand trial. Nelson was tried separately and convicted. He has appealed on three grounds, all of which relate to the use of circumstantial evidence to secure his conviction.

The government offered direct evidence of the following facts. Brewton entered a bank and presented a teller with a written demand for money. The teller handed Brewton $627 in currency, including five marked $20 bills. Meanwhile, an unidentified person was observed sitting in a car in an adjacent parking lot, racing the engine. Brewton fled from the bank to the waiting car and entered on the passenger side. The car immediately sped away. Shortly thereafter, a police officer, alerted to these incidents, observed the car, with two male occupants, at an intersection some blocks away. The car fled. The officer pursued at high speed. After a chase the car slowed down, defendant alighted from the driver's side and ran, and was captured. Currency in the amount of $125 was taken from his person. The car, driverless, crashed into a tree. Brewton emerged from the wreck, and was arrested after attempting to conceal $502 in currency, including the marked bills taken from the bank, under an adjacent building. Ten to fifteen minutes elapsed between the robbery of the bank and defendant's flight from the car.

Defendant asserts that since he was charged as a principal in the bank robbery rather than as an accessory after the fact, the government was required to prove that he had actual knowledge that Brewton intended to rob the bank. We assume, arguendo, that proof of precisely that specific knowledge was required.

Defendant contended below, and in this court, that such proof was lacking. He argued that if such knowledge could be inferred at all, the inference must be based upon the prior inference that he was the man waiting in the car while the robbery occurred—and such an "inference upon an inference" was precluded by l aw. Further, he argued that even if the jury were permitted to infer that he knowingly acted as the "get-away" driver, there was no evidence that he knew Brewton planned to commit a robbery, as distinguished from some other illegal act, or planned to rob the bank, and not one of the several stores and offices in the area, and that circumstantial evidence which does not "exclude every hypothesis but that of guilt" is insufficient as a matter of law.

The court denied a motion for acquittal based on these grounds, and rejected proposed instructions embodying the theories that a conviction could not be based upon inferences drawn from other inferences, or upon circumstances "which while consistent with guilt, are not inconsistent with innocence."

The legal theories upon which defendant relies, although clearly wrong, are repeatedly asserted in the trial courts of this circuit and in fruitless appeals to this court. It would be a boon to both the parties and the courts if they could be laid finally to rest.

I

For at least a third of a century this court has rejected the notion that it is improper to infer a fact at issue from other facts which have been established by circumstantial evidence. E.K. Wood Lumber Co. v. Andersen, 81 F.2d 161, 166 (9th Cir.1936).[9] * * * As Professor Wigmore has said, "[t]here is no such orthodox rule; nor can be. If there were, hardly a single trial could be adequately presented." 1 Wigmore, Evidence, § 41, at 435 (3rd ed. 1940).

The error in this discredited doctrine is clearly reflected in the defendant's formulation:[10] it assumes that a fact established by circumstantial evidence is not a "proven fact." But as we have repeatedly said, circumstantial evidence is not inherently less probative than direct evidence. Under some conditions it may even be more reliable, as this case illustrates.

The intermediate fact at issue here was whether defendant was the driver of the car waiting in the parking lot. That fact was established to a moral certainty by circumstances proven by uncontradicted and unquestioned testimony. Unless defendant was Brewton's accomplice waiting in the get-away car, it is all but inconceivable that he would have been driving that car with Brewton as a passenger a few minutes after Brewton ran from the bank to the car and was driven from the scene; that he would have had part of the stolen currency in his possession, and

---

[9] A significant number of footnotes, primarily those containing citations to cases, have been omitted from this opinion. [Ed.]

[10] The following instruction was requested and refused:

"Permissible inferences from the evidence must be based upon proven facts and one inference may not be based upon another inference to support a conclusion of fact."

Brewton the rest; and that upon seeing the police officer he would have driven away at high speed, and later fled from the office[r] on foot.

If none of this circumstantial evidence had been available and the only evidence offered had been a courtroom identification of the defendant by a witness who had a fleeting glimpse of the driver as the car stood in the parking lot, the truth of the fact that defendant was that man would not have been established with equal certainty.[11]

Of course either direct or circumstantial evidence may fail to prove the fact in issue—direct evidence because the credibility of the witness is destroyed; circumstantial evidence for that reason, or because the inference from the proven circumstances to the fact in issue is too speculative, or remote. Whether such a failure has occurred is an appropriate inquiry in any case—be the evidence direct, circumstantial, or both. But since under some conditions circumstantial evidence may be equally or more reliable than direct evidence, it would be wholly irrational to impose an absolute bar upon the use of circumstantial evidence to prove any fact, including a fact from which another fact is to be inferred.

The trial court therefore properly refused to instruct the jury that "one inference may not be based upon another inference to support a conclusion of fact." It would be error for the jury, the trial court, or this court, to apply such an arbitrary formula in the performance of their respective roles in the fact-finding process.

II

It is also clear that the court properly rejected defendant's proposed instruction embodying a variation on the theme that circumstantial evidence must exclude every hypothesis but that of guilt.[12]

This much, at least, is settled by Holland v. United States, 348 U.S. 121 * * * (1955). * * *

* * *

III

One question remains: Did the district court properly overrule the motion for acquittal?

---

[11] As the Supreme Court pointed out in United States v. Wade, 388 U.S. 218 * * * (1967), "the annals of criminal law are rife with instances of mistaken [eyewitness] identifications." 388 U.S. at 228 * * *. * * *

[12] Defendant proposed the following instruction:

"You may not base a finding of the existence of any fact in issue upon the basis of circumstantial evidence, if the circumstances relied upon are consistent with another conclusion, even if they are consistent with a conclusion of the truth of the fact in issue.

"Proof of circumstances which while consistent with guilt, are not inconsistent with innocence, will not support a conviction."

Defendant contends that whether or not he was entitled to the proposed jury instruction, this court, in reviewing the sufficiency of the evidence, must ask "whether reasonable minds could find that the evidence excludes every hypothesis but that of guilt."

The test to be applied by the trial court in deciding a motion for acquittal in a criminal case, and the test to be applied by this court in reviewing that decision, are, as a practical matter, identical. 8 J. Moore, Federal Practice ¶ 29.06, at 29–19 (1968). It is also undisputed that the evidence must be taken in the light most favorable to the verdict—that it is the exclusive function of the jury to determine the credibility of witnesses, resolve evidentiary conflicts, and draw reasonable inferences from proven facts. Therefore the reviewing court must assume that the jury resolved all such matters in a manner which would support the verdict. 4 Barron, Federal Practice and Procedure, § 2221, at 235 (1951). Beyond this, however, the substance of the standard to be applied is subject to much confusion and dispute.

The opinions of our court dealing with this issue combine various threads of doctrine in such a wide variety of ways that no simple analysis can accurately reflect their content. Nonetheless, it is convenient to deal with the issues as involving two different, though overlapping, questions.

The first is whether the test of the sufficiency of the evidence in a criminal case is the same as that applied in civil cases—namely, whether there is substantial evidence to support a judgment adverse to the moving party—or whether a different test is to be applied in criminal cases reflecting the burden of establishing guilt beyond a reasonable doubt.

Some courts, led by the Court of Appeals for the Second Circuit, apply the substantial evidence test in criminal as well as civil cases. There is language in Supreme Court opinions, and in opinions of this court, supporting this approach.

However, other courts—indeed, most courts—"have included the standard of persuasion as part of their criterion of sufficiency." A. Goldstein, The State and the Accused: Balance of Advantage in Criminal Procedure, 69 Yale L.J. 1149, 1157 (1960). Thus, in American Tobacco Co. v. United States, 328 U.S. 781, 787 n.4 * * * (1946), the Supreme Court stated: "The verdict in a criminal case is sustained only when there is relevant evidence from which the jury could properly find or infer, *beyond a reasonable doubt,* that the accused is guilty. Mortensen v. United States, 322 U.S. 369 * * *." (Emphasis added.) Similar expressions appear in an overwhelming majority of our opinions reviewing the sufficiency of the evidence in criminal cases.

The function which the court performs in passing upon a motion for acquittal suggests that this latter view is correct. That function is to determine whether the jury in arriving at the verdict has acted within the bounds of its authority. Since it is the jury's duty to acquit unless guilt is established beyond a reasonable doubt, the reviewing court may properly inquire whether the evidence, considered most favorably to the government, was such as to permit a rational conclusion by the jury that the accused was guilty beyond a reasonable doubt.

The second question is that specifically raised by the defendant, namely, whether the court is also to inquire whether the evidence "excludes every hypothesis but that of guilt."

Precisely as put, the test is unquestionably wrong. Although we have frequently stated the rule as defendant does, it has never been held that the evidence must exclude "*every* hypothesis," as distinguished from every reasonable hypothesis, of innocence. Furthermore, in applying the test, the question is not whether the court itself would find that every reasonable hypothesis of innocence had been excluded, but rather whether the jurors could reasonably arrive at the conclusion.

Thus, as first stated in this court in Stoppelli v. United States, 183 F.2d 391, 393 (9th Cir.1950), the test was as follows:

> "The testimony * * * was sufficient to go to the jury if its nature was such that reasonable minds could differ as to whether inferences other than guilt could be drawn from it. It is not for us to say that the evidence was insufficient because we, or any of us, believe that inferences inconsistent with guilt may be drawn from it. To say that would make us triers of the fact. We may say that the evidence is insufficient to sustain the verdict only if we can conclude *as a matter of law* that reasonable minds, as triers of the fact, must be in agreement that reasonable hypotheses other than guilt could be drawn from the evidence."

This formulation, commonly condensed to "whether 'reasonable minds could find the evidence excludes every hypothesis but that of guilt,' " appears frequently in our opinions.

Yet this is precisely the standard which was rejected by the Supreme Court in Holland v. United States, supra, 348 U.S. at 139 * * *, as a guide for the jury, on the ground that it was "confusing and incorrect." Id. at 140 * * *. Our opinions demonstrate that it is equally confusing as a guide for the reviewing court. Moreover, if it is "incorrect" as an instruction defining the jury's duty, it must be equally "incorrect" as a test for determining whether the jury has performed its duty within the limits fixed by the instructions. Accordingly, most courts have held that its use as a test of the sufficiency of the evidence on review is inconsistent with *Holland*.

The "reasonable hypothesis" test was formulated for the evaluation of circumstantial evidence; it is often referred to as the "circumstantial evidence test." See, e.g., Comment, *Sufficiency of Circumstantial Evidence in a Criminal Case,* 55 Colum.L.Rev. 549 (1955). * * * [T]he Supreme Court rejected the test in *Holland* on the premise that there is no essential difference in the mental processes required of the jury in weighing direct and circumstantial evidence. As to both, "the jury must use its experience with people and events in weighing the probabilities. If the jury is convinced beyond a reasonable doubt, we can require no more." Holland, 348 U.S. at 140 * * *.

The key word is "probabilities." The jury cannot determine that a proposition is true or false but only that it is more or less probable. Guilt "is proved beyond a reasonable doubt if it proved not only to be more probable than its contradictory but much more probable than its contradictory." Adler & Michael, *The Trial of an Issue of Fact I,* 34 Colum.L.Rev. 1224, 1256 (1934). The required degree of probability is reached if the jury is free of "the kind of doubt that would make a person hesitate to act" in the more serious and important affairs of his own life. Holland v. United States, supra, 348 U.S. at 140 * * *.

It adds only an illusion of certainty, and is both misleading and wrong, to attempt to describe this broad exercise of practical judgment in abstract generalizations borrowed from the terminology of formal logic.

The "reasonable hypothesis" test does not reflect what juries and reviewing courts in reality do. Juries constantly convict, and the convictions are duly affirmed, on evidence upon which none would hesitate to act but which cannot be said to exclude as a matter of inexorable logic, every reasonable hypothetical consistent with innocence.

Moreover, the impression left by appellate court opinions is that the "reasonable hypothesis" standard may lead to serious departures from the proper appellate role in evaluating the sufficiency of evidence. Courts following the rule exhibit a noticeable tendency to divide the evidence into separate lines of proof, and analyze and test each line of proof independently of others rather than considering the evidence as an interrelated whole. The sufficiency of the evidence is often tested against theoretical and speculative possibilities not fairly raised by the record, and inferences are sometimes considered which, though entirely possible or even probable, are drawn from evidence which the jury may have disbelieved.

We affirm the denial of the motion for acquittal in this case because we are satisfied that the jurors reasonably could decide that they would not hesitate to act in their own serious affairs upon factual assumptions as probable as the conclusion that defendant planned and executed the robbery of the bank as a joint venture with Brewton in which each carried out a prearranged role.

Affirmed.

NOTES AND QUESTIONS

1.   *Only reasonable hypothesis test.* The "only reasonable hypothesis" test for determining the sufficiency of circumstantial evidence relied on by the state in a criminal case still commands a following. See, e.g., State v. Nichols, 725 S.W.2d 927 (Mo.Ct.App.1987). A number of jurisdictions, however, while continuing to use the "only reasonable hypothesis" language, have reconstrued the standard as something other than a test for legal sufficiency.

> Whether or not in a given case circumstances are sufficient to exclude every reasonable hypothesis save the guilt of the accused, is primarily a question for determination by the jury. This of necessity is so, for we have no legal yardstick by which we can ordinarily determine what in a given case is a reasonable hypothesis, save the opinion of twelve upright and intelligent jurors.

Townsend v. State, 195 S.E.2d 474, 476 (Ga.Ct.App.1972). How does the view of the Georgia court compare with that expressed in the principal case?

> For an argument for a reinvigorated "only reasonable hypothesis" test as a standard of sufficiency, see Gregory, Whose Reasonable Doubt? Reconsidering the Appropriate Role of the Reviewing Court in the Criminal Decision Making Process, 24 Am.Crim.L.Rev. 911 (1987).

2.   *Standard for sufficiency in criminal cases.* Note the statement of the *Nelson* court, that "the reviewing court may properly inquire whether the evidence, considered most favorably to the government, was such as to permit a rational conclusion by the jury that the accused was guilty beyond a reasonable doubt." In Jackson v. Virginia, 443 U.S. 307 (1979), the Supreme Court held that the articulated standard is not only proper but is the standard constitutionally required to be applied in reviewing the sufficiency of evidence to support state convictions in federal habeas corpus proceedings. The *Jackson* case effectively ended the debate that had raged for decades concerning the desirability and feasibility of differentiating between the standards of sufficiency in criminal as opposed to civil cases. See the classic article, McNaughten, Burden of Production of Evidence: A Function of a Burden of Persuasion, 68 Harv.L.Rev. 1382 (1955) (arguing for differing standards). However, the precise formulation and application of the higher standard remains problematic. See, for example, Newman, Beyond "Reasonable Doubt," 68 N.Y.U.L.Rev. 979 (1993).

3.   *Inference on an inference.* Though the court in the principal case concurs with Dean Wigmore that there is not, and could not be, a rule prohibiting the predication of an inference upon a previous inference, the conception that there is such a rule has proved extremely difficult to eradicate. Decisions variously adopting, rejecting, and discussing the "non-rule" are compendiously collected in Annot., 5 A.L.R.3d 100. Kindred problems are raised by the attempted predication of a presumption on a presumption or a presumption on an inference.

What significance, if any, should be attached to the *Nelson* court's statement that any inference other than that defendant was the driver waiting in the parking lot would be "all but inconceivable?" In Voelker v. Combined Ins. Co., 73 So.2d 403 (Fla.1954), it was held that inferences may be predicated upon prior inferences if every inference other than the last is "inescapable" as the only reasonable theory. Compare Vaccarezza v. Sanguinetti, 163 P.2d 470, 477 (Cal.Ct.App.1945): "In a civil case, if the first inference is a reasonably probable one it may be used as a basis for a succeeding inference."

Consider the bearing of the following mathematical hypothetical on the problem. Suppose that in seven-tenths of the cases in which fact A exists fact B will exist, and further that in seven-tenths of the cases in which fact B exists fact C will exist. Should proof of fact A alone be sufficient to support a finding of the existence of fact C?

For an interesting fictional inquiry into the question of whether a succession of inferences, each reasonable when viewed in isolation, may lead to a false conclusion, see Harry Kemmelman's short detective story, The Nine Mile Walk, reprinted in Barzun, Delights of Detection (1961).

SMITH V. BELL TEL. CO. OF PENNSYLVANIA

Supreme Court of Pennsylvania, 1959.
153 A.2d 477.

MCBRIDE, JUSTICE. This case is here on plaintiff's appeal from the refusal of the court below to take off a compulsory non-suit.

In 1948 defendant, Counties Contracting and Construction Company, under contract to defendant, Bell Telephone Company of Pennsylvania, constructed an underground conduit to carry telephone lines along Baltimore Avenue in Lansdowne, Pennsylvania. In 1950, after an inspection which revealed no structural or other defects, plaintiff purchased a house on Baltimore Avenue. Sometime prior to March 25, 1951, he discovered seepage in his basement, which proved to be sewage backed up from the sewer lateral running from his home to the street. He made efforts several times that summer with varying degrees of success, to find the cause and cure the trouble. These efforts continued from time to time until September 1956, when, in desperation, plaintiff and a friend tunnelled under the sidewalk, found that the telephone conduit had crushed the sewer lateral and was blocking it. Plaintiff brought suit September 19, 1957 and, after presenting evidence, met with a compulsory non-suit which the court later refused to take off. The refusal was based on two grounds:

(1) That plaintiff had not made out a prima facie case,

* * *

In support of the judgment of non-suit the court below applied the standard that where plaintiff's case is based on circumstantial evidence and inferences to be drawn therefrom, such evidence must be so conclusive as to exclude any other reasonable inference inconsistent therewith, and that plaintiff did not produce such evidence. Indeed, he did not, but did he have to?

A variety of formulae for determining the sufficiency of circumstantial evidence to sustain a verdict may be found, including: "such as to satisfy reasonable and well balanced minds". Connor v. Hawk, 1957, 387 Pa. 480, 483, 128 A.2d 566; Rowles v. Evanuik, 1944, 350 Pa. 64, 68, 38 A.2d 255; Ferry v. Philadelphia Rapid Transit Co., 1911, 232 Pa. 403, 406, 81 A. 426. "[The facts and inferences] must so preponderate in favor of the basic proposition he is seeking to establish as to exclude any equally well-supported belief in any inconsistent proposition", Wagner v. Somerset County Memorial Park, 1953, 372 Pa. 338, 342, 93 A.2d 440, 442; Polk v. Steel Workers Organizing Committee, 1949, 360 Pa. 631, 634, 62 A.2d 850. Although some of the formulations appear to be mutually inconsistent, they have sometimes been used together. See Stauffer v. Railway Express Agency, 1946, 355 Pa. 24, 47 A.2d 817. The formula that "the circumstances must be so strong as to preclude the possibility of injury in any other way and provide as the only reasonable inference the conclusion plaintiff advances" is not a correct statement of the rule to be applied by the judge on deciding a motion for either a non-suit or binding instructions. If that were the rule what would be the province of the jury? In no case where there was more than one reasonable inference would the jury be permitted to decide. Insofar as this rule is stated in our cases it is disapproved.

We have said many times that the jury may not be permitted to reach its verdict merely on the basis of speculation or conjecture, but that there must be evidence upon which logically its conclusion may be based. Schofield v. King, 1957, 388 Pa. 132, 136, 130 A.2d 93; Connor v. Hawk, 1957, 387 Pa. 480, 482, 128 A.2d 566; Ebersole v. Beistline, 1951, 368 Pa. 12, 16, 82 A.2d 11. Clearly this does not mean that the jury may not draw inferences based upon all the evidence and the jurors' own knowledge and experiences, for that is, of course, the very heart of the jury's function. It means only that the evidence presented must be such that by reasoning from it, without resort to prejudice or guess, a jury can reach the conclusion sought by plaintiff, and not that conclusion must be the *only* one which logically can be reached.

It is not necessary, under Pennsylvania law, that every fact or circumstance point unerringly to liability; it is enough that there be sufficient facts for the jury to say reasonably that the preponderance favors liability. The judge cannot say as a matter of law which are facts and which are not unless they are admitted or the evidence is inherently incredible. Also, it is beyond the power of the court to say whether two or more reasonable inferences are "equal". True enough the trial judge has to do something like this in deciding a motion for new trial based on the weight of the evidence but no such rule governs him in deciding whether a case is submissible to the jury. The facts are for the jury in any case whether based upon direct or circumstantial evidence where a reasonable conclusion can be arrived at which would place liability on the defendant. It is the duty of plaintiff to produce substantial evidence which, if believed, warrants the verdict he seeks. The right of a litigant to have the jury pass upon the facts is not to be foreclosed just because the judge believes that a reasonable man might properly find either way. A substantial part of the right to trial by jury is taken away when judges withdraw close cases from the jury. Therefore, when a party who has the burden of proof relies upon circumstantial evidence and inferences reasonably deducible therefrom, such evidence, in order to prevail, must be adequate to establish the conclusion sought and must so preponderate in favor of that conclusion as to outweigh in the mind of the fact-finder any other evidence and reasonable inferences therefrom which are inconsistent therewith. This rule has been applied in substance in many cases. See Miller v. Hickey, 368 Pa. 317, 81 A.2d 910, Rockey v. Ernest, 367 Pa. 538, 541, 80 A.2d 783; Turek v. Pennsylvania R. Co., 361 Pa. 512, 64 A.2d 779; Randolph v. Campbell, 360 Pa. 453, 62 A.2d 60.

To the court below it seems that all plaintiff had proved was "the happening of an accident", and that the best that could be said for plaintiff's case was that "the collapse of the conduit may have been the consequence of defendant's negligence." It would seem however, that plaintiff has proved more than that; enough more, in fact, that he should have been permitted to have the jury pass upon the problem. We are not here faced with a case relying on circumstantial evidence to show both the happening of the accident and the defendants' negligence. It is clear that the injury was caused by the conduit crushing the sewer lateral. The question is, did defendants' negligence cause the conduit so to behave?

* * *

Plaintiff has fairly shown that defendants buried a heavy conduit over his sewer lateral, and that after about three years the conduit crushed the lateral. It is hard to see how a plaintiff in these circumstances could prove more.

A likely inference under the conditions described is that the soil was normal and the crushing of the pipe was due to defendants' negligence in not supporting a conduit which passed over plaintiff's lateral with less than six inches clearance. It is also possible, as defendants suggest, though perhaps not as likely, that the clearance was adequate for normal conditions or that piers were installed and that the mischief resulted from abnormal soil conditions, or from subterranean waters. The difficulty with that hypothesis for defendants is that it too presents a strong probability of negligence since it seems unlikely that soil conditions could have changed very much in what was apparently an established community in the short space of three years or less. If the condition of the soil at the time of installation of the conduit was subnormal, defendants were bound to support their conduit accordingly, and not to proceed on the basis of ideal or average soil conditions. To suggest that the collapse which broke the sewer lateral occurred through the undermining action of sewage flowing from the break would be patently absurd.

Under the conditions described, it is entirely reasonable for the jury to find that the accident resulted from the negligence of the defendants. Of course, if the jury is not convinced of that fact by the preponderance of the evidence, they may not conclude that negligence was the cause. But that decision is for the jury, and neither the trial judge nor this Court may assume it. * * *

* * *

Judgment reversed and a new trial ordered.

BELL, JUSTICE (concurring).

I cannot agree with some parts of the Court's opinion, hence this concurring opinion. We agree that mere conjecture or guess do not amount to proof, and a jury's verdict cannot be supported if it is based upon conjecture, guess or sympathy. Whenever a party has the burden of proving certain facts, his evidence tending to prove such facts cannot prevail if, in the opinion of either the Court or of the jury, it is so uncertain, or inadequate, or equivocal, or ambiguous, or contradictory as to make findings or legitimate inferences therefrom a mere conjecture. * * *

Since the Court has decided to change, in cases of circumstantial evidence, "the only reasonable inference rule" which had been reiterated in at least 18 cases in the last few years, we should attempt to make certain that the new test is accurately expressed. In my judgment that has not been done in the majority opinion. The adequacy of the evidence is first of all a matter for the Court and if it passes that test it is then a matter for the jury. In my judgment it would be more accurate if the new rule read as follows:

When a party who has the burden of proof relies—not upon direct evidence, but—upon circumstantial evidence, such evidence, together with all inferences reasonably deducible therefrom, must, in order to prevail, be adequate to establish the conclusion sought and must so *preponderate* in favor of that conclusion as to outweigh any other *reasonable* or possible inference or deduction inconsistent therewith. * * *

Whether the evidence, if believed, is legally sufficient to satisfy this test is in the first instance for the Court's determination; if the Court is of the opinion that the evidence, if believed, is sufficient, then the Court must submit to the jury the determination of what evidence to believe, and whether in its mind the person who relies on the circumstantial evidence has met and satisfied his burden of proof.

* * *

NOTES AND QUESTIONS

1. *Judge or jury?* Note the way in which Justice Bell, concurring, would prefer to have the new rule of sufficiency in civil cases formulated. Is this preference merely a matter of semantics, or does it reflect a view of the respective roles of court and jury in the fact-finding process which differs substantially from that taken by the majority? Formulations such as Justice Bell's have been strongly criticized as suggesting an improper focus for judicial evaluation of questions of sufficiency. See, e.g., Tennant v. Peoria & P. U. Ry. Co., 321 U.S. 29 (1944); McCarty v. National Life & Acc. Ins. Co., 129 S.E.2d 408 (Ga.Ct.App.1962). In considering the legitimacy of this criticism, consider the following statement by one state supreme court in the process of applying a test like that suggested by Justice Bell:

> We cannot support our belief by mathematical proof that the probabilities favor the plaintiff's contention. * * * We have only our own experiences, observations and understanding of what commonly happens from which to judge whether the inferences drawn from the circumstances connect up defendant's conduct to the injury more strongly than the conduct of some other person.

Eitel v. Times, Inc., 352 P.2d 485, 490 (Or.1960).

Whose decision-making qualifications rather than its own might the court appear to be describing? Is the rule of sufficiency enunciated by the majority in *Smith* to be preferred on the ground that it will exert a retarding influence upon the phenomenon observed by Lord Bramwell, that "one-third of a judge is a common-law juror if you get beneath his ermine"?[13]

Judicial recognition that evidence might reasonably convince a jury though it does not convince the court is clearly essential to the preservation of a substantial role for the jury in the fact-finding process. Does the distinction between potentially convincing evidence and evidence actually convincing to the judge have any utility where the court sits without a jury? Stated another way, may the court sitting as trier of fact direct a verdict against a party who has made out a prima facie case? Should it? See Mattoon v. City of Pittsfield, 775 N.E. 2d 770 (Mass.App. 2002) ("[A] trial judge is not limited to that standard of proof required for a directed verdict * * * rather, the judge is free to weigh the evidence and resolve all questions of credibility,

___
[13] Quoted in J. Frank, Courts on Trial 180 (1949).

ambiguity, and contradiction in reaching a decision"); cases are collected in Annot., 55 A.L.R.3d 272.

2. *Expert testimony.* Suppose that the evidence relied upon to establish a material proposition is not only circumstantial but of a sort which may only be interpreted by an "expert witness," a person viewed as having special competency by virtue of special training or experience. Will the expert testimony, if relied upon by the party with the burden of going forward on the proposition, need to assume any particular form if a directed verdict is to be avoided? See 2 Dobbs, Hayden & Bublick, The Law of Torts § 302 (2d ed. 2012). Reconsider this question after reading *Toy v. Mackintosh*, Chapter 12, Section D(1).

COLTHURST V. LAKE VIEW STATE BANK

United States Court of Appeals, Eighth Circuit, 1927.
18 F.2d 875.

OTIS, DISTRICT JUDGE. April 19, 1924, the Lake View State Bank of Chicago, an Illinois corporation, herein referred to as the plaintiff, filed in the District Court for the Southern District of Iowa its petition, thereafter amended, in which, as amended, it alleged it was the holder in due course, for value, and without notice of any defense thereto, of a note in the principal amount of $3,200, with interest at 6 per cent., dated December 16, 1918, due in one year, and signed by the plaintiff in error, herein referred to as the defendant. The answer charged procurement of the note by fraud and denied that the bank held it in due course.

Upon the trial, having heard the testimony offered by the plaintiff to the effect that it had purchased the note February 20, 1919, for $3,234.67 (being the principal plus the interest then due) from the then holder, one W.F. Van Buskirk, to whom the note had been indorsed by a prior indorsee, and that it had no knowledge of any defenses existing in favor of the maker of the note, the District Court directed the defendant to put on his evidence in this order: First, any evidence he had tending to show that the bank was not a holder in due course and without notice; and, second, after such evidence (but not otherwise) any evidence he had tending to show that the note in the first instance was obtained by fraud.

* * * [The trial court excluded the only evidence, referred to in the opinion as the Van Buskirk letters, offered by the defendant to show that the plaintiff was not a holder in due course.]

The District Court directed a verdict for the plaintiff. It is contended that the court erred therein, first, because the Van Buskirk letters showed that the bank did not receive the note before maturity and therefore was not a holder in due course; second, because, even if the Van Buskirk letters properly were excluded, facts and circumstances in evidence tended to show the bank was not a holder in due course; and, third, because, in any event, it was for the jury to pass upon the credibility of the witnesses for the plaintiff.

* * * [The court here held that the Van Buskirk letters were properly excluded by the trial court.]

2.   It is true, of course, that even if there were no direct testimony tending to show that the bank had knowledge of defenses existing against the note when it obtained possession of it, if in the evidence there were facts and circumstances from which such a conclusion reasonably could be inferred then a verdict should not have been directed. In our view, however, there were not in evidence any facts or circumstances which, whether considered separately or together, furnish any basis for such an inference.

3.   The contention of defendant that even in the absence of any disproof of the prima facie case made by the plaintiff it was still the duty of the court to submit the case to the jury solely upon the matter of credibility is not tenable. Even if on that question the decisions of the Iowa Supreme Court were controlling, and it is on them the defendant bases his argument, they do not support the contention. Earlier decisions by that court apparently did. Arnd v. Aylesworth, 136 Iowa 297, 111 N.W. 407; Connelly v. Greenfield, 192 Iowa 876, 185 N.W. 887. But not so its later pronouncements.

In First National Bank of Montour v. Brown, 197 Iowa 1376, 199 N.W. 272, the Supreme Court of Iowa said:

"To sustain the proposition advanced by the appellant in the instant case, we would be compelled to say that the defendant has an inherent right to have a jury pass upon his claim, or that the credibility of an uncontradicted and unimpeached witness in all cases presents a jury question. We cannot make such a pronouncement."

Again in First National Bank v. Dutton, 199 Iowa 468, 202 N.W. 228, the same court said:

"We have intimated, if not decided, in some of our cases, such as Connelly v. Greenfield Sav. Bank, 192 Iowa, 876, 185 N.W. 887, and Arnd v. Aylesworth, 136 Iowa 297, 111 N.W. 407, and kindred cases, that although the officers specifically denied notice, yet at least its credibility is for the jury, hence making a jury question. If these pronouncements were followed to the conclusion contended for by appellant, then, in every case, where prima facie case of fraud is made by defendant, thereby casting the burden on the plaintiff to show that it was an innocent purchaser, it would have to go to the jury on the question of the credibility of witnesses tendered to establish that plaintiff was an innocent purchaser. We refuse to acquiesce in any such construction of that line of cases."

Our conclusion is that the action of the court below in directing a verdict for the plaintiff was right. Accordingly the judgment is affirmed.

NOTES AND QUESTIONS

1. *Shifting burdens.* "In contrast with the accepted view that the burden of persuasion remains on the same party throughout the trial, it is everywhere agreed that the other burden, i.e., the burden of producing evidence * * * may and often does shift back and forth between the parties like a tennis ball in play." Ray, Burden of Proof and Presumptions, 13 Tex.L.Rev. 33, 44 (1934).

In *Colthurst v. Lake View State Bank*, did the plaintiff succeed not only in discharging the burden of going forward but also in shifting that burden to the defendant? If the view were adopted that "the credibility of an uncontradicted and unimpeached witness in all cases presents a jury question" might the burden of going forward ever be shifted? By the introduction of what type of evidence? See Gardner v. Linwedel, 192 S.W.2d 613, 617 (Mo.Ct.App.1946); Sunderland, Directing a Verdict for the Party Having the Burden of Proof, 11 Mich.L.Rev. 198, 203–06 (1912).

2. On the propriety of directing a verdict in favor of the party with the burden of persuasion, see Hazard, Leubsdorf & Bassett, Civil Procedure § 11.19 (6th ed. 2011).

B. THE BURDEN OF PERSUASION

DELAWARE COACH CO. v. SAVAGE
United States District Court, District of Delaware, 1948.
81 F.Supp. 293.

RODNEY, DISTRICT JUDGE. This was an action brought as a result of a collision in the City of Wilmington, Delaware between a trolley coach of the plaintiff and a truck and trailer of the defendants. As a result of the collision the driver of the trolley coach was killed and his widow received from the plaintiff compensation for his death, and this suit is brought pursuant to the subrogation provisions of the Delaware Workmen's Compensation Act. Rev.Code Del.1935, § 6108. Recovery was also sought for the damage sustained to the trolley coach. Jurisdiction is based upon diversity of citizenship. The case was tried to the court without the intervention of a jury, and separate findings of fact and conclusions of law have been filed. This comment is collateral to such findings and conclusions.

The collision was a right angle collision and happened at the intersection of two paved and well-travelled highways. The accident happened in broad daylight when the weather was clear and the roadways dry and in good condition. The intersection was protected by traffic lights upon all four corners operating in unison and controlling traffic in all four directions. The traffic lights were activated by treadles in each street placed at varying distances from the intersection.

It was established that when a green light or "Go" signal is shown, the "traffic facing such signal may proceed except that vehicular traffic and coaches proceeding under such signal shall yield the right of way to pedestrians, vehicles and coaches lawfully within a crosswalk or the intersection at the time such signal was exhibited."

It was also established that when a red light or "Stop" signal is shown the "traffic facing the signal shall stop before entering the nearest crosswalk at the intersection or at such other point as may be plainly and officially designated by authority of the Street and Sewer Department, and remain standing until green or 'Go' is shown alone."

The plaintiff, in support of its allegation of the negligence of the defendants, produced several highly intelligent and entirely disinterested witnesses who were in a position to see the traffic lights just prior to the accident, as well as the collision itself. They testified that the traffic lights were favorable to the trolley coach of the plaintiff and against the truck and trailer of the defendants.

The defendants, in support of their denial of their own negligence and in support of their allegations of contributory negligence of the plaintiff, produced an even greater number of disinterested witnesses who were in an equally favorable position to see and to know the conditions just prior to the accident. These witnesses testified unequivocally that the red or unfavorable traffic signal was shown toward the trolley coach of the plaintiff and that, notwithstanding such adverse signal, the trolley coach entered the intersection and the collision ensued.

The court found that the accident was not an unavoidable accident, but was caused by the negligence of at least one of the drivers of the motor vehicles involved. The evidence was in direct and irreconcilable conflict with witnesses on both sides who were disinterested, intelligent and entitled to credence. The court found that there was no preponderance on behalf of the plaintiff of the evidence of negligence of the defendants, but that such evidence was in equipoise and as a legal consequence the plaintiff had not sustained its burden and judgment must be entered for the defendants.

Jurisdiction being based upon the diversity of citizenship, it is essential that the law of Delaware be ascertained.

* * *

The burden of proof rests upon the party asserting the affirmative of an issue, such as, in this case, the negligence of the defendants. If an allegation, such as the negligence of the defendant, be alleged, the party asserting such fact must prove it by a preponderance of the evidence. The burden of proof of such fact continues throughout the case and this burden of proof never shifts. The burden of going forward with the evidence may shift from time to time during a trial after the establishing of a prima facie case or due to some other development in the case, but the burden of proof of the main fact remains with the party who alleged such main fact.

Upon the establishment of a prima facie case the burden of evidence or the burden of going forward with the evidence shifts to the defensive party. It then becomes incumbent upon such defensive party to meet the prima facie case which has been established. For this purpose the defensive party need not produce evidence which preponderates or outweighs or surpasses the evidence of his adversary, but it is sufficient if such evidence is co-equal, leaving the proof in equilibrium. If the defensive party, either by a preponderance of evidence or evidence sufficient to establish equilibrium, has met and answered the prima facie case, then the burden of going forward with the evidence returns to the original proponent charged with the burden of proof who must in turn, by a preponderance or greater weight of evidence, overcome the equilibrium thus established, or otherwise support his burden of proof by a preponderance of the evidence. This is true whether the original prima facie case is founded upon affirmative evidence or established by the doctrine of res ipsa loquitur or other presumption or inference of law. Sweeney v. Erving, 228 U.S. 233 * * *. As said in Commercial Molasses Corporation v. New York Tank Barge Corporation, 314 U.S. 104, 111 * * *, an inference or presumption "does no more than require the [defensive party,] if he would avoid the inference, to go forward with evidence sufficient to persuade that the nonexistence of the fact, which would otherwise be inferred, is as probable as its existence. It does not cause the burden of proof to shift, and if the [defensive party] does go forward with evidence enough to raise doubts as to the validity of the inference, which the trier of facts is unable to resolve, the [proponent] does not sustain the burden of persuasion which upon the whole evidence remains upon him, where it rested at the start." The court cited, inter alia, the opinion of Judge Woolley in Tomkins Cove Stone Co. v. Bleakley Transp. Co., 3 Cir., 40 F.2d 249. * * *

Wigmore in his elaborate treatise shows the shifting and progressive nature of the burden of producing evidence for the satisfaction of the judge as well as the permanent and non-shifting nature of the burden of proof (the non-persuasion of the jury), which remains at all times with the proponent of the issue, to be established by a preponderance of the evidence. 9 Wigmore on Evidence, 3d Ed., Sec. 2485–2489. See also 2 Chamberlayne, Modern Law of Evidence, Sec. 940, etc.; McKelvey on Evidence, 75.

In Board of Education v. Makely, 139 N.C. 31, 51 S.E. 784, and Shepard v. Western Union Telegraph Co., 143 N.C. 244, 55 S.E. 704, 118 Am.St.Rep. 796, is cited a terse and apt quotation from 1 Elliott on Evidence, as follows: "The burden of the issue, that is, the burden of proof, in the sense of ultimately proving or establishing the issue or case of the party upon which such burden rests, as distinguished from the burden or duty of going forward and producing evidence, never shifts, but the burden or duty of proceeding or going forward often does shift from one party to the other, and sometimes back again. Thus, when the actor has gone forward and made a prima facie case, the other party is compelled in turn to go forward or lose his case, and in this sense the burden shifts to him. So the burden of going forward may, as to some particular matter, shift again to the first party in response to the call of a prima facie case or presumption in favor of the second party. But the party who has not the burden of the issue is not bound to disprove the actor's case by a preponderance of the evidence, for the actor must fail if, upon the whole evidence, he does not have a preponderance, no matter whether it is because the weight of evidence is with the other party, or because the scales are equally balanced."

Because, in this case, the plaintiff did not sustain its burden toward the fact-finding tribunal and show the negligence of the defendants by a preponderance of the evidence, judgment must be entered for the defendants.

On Motion for Reargument

Subsequent to the filing of the court's opinion in this case, plaintiff moved for reargument, grounding such motion upon an alleged failure by the court to apply the principle of law that all facts and circumstances must be weighed by the trier of facts in reaching its decision, especially in determining the credibility of witnesses and the probabilities of a case. The motion is supported by a memorandum in which plaintiff sets forth three cases as authorities for the principle urged by plaintiff. One of the three cases, Le Fevre v. Crossan, 3 Boyce 379, 26 Del. 379, 396, 84 A. 128, was cited by the court in its opinion.

The court is in complete agreement with plaintiff's contention and indicated as much in its opinion. Indeed, the very procedure which plaintiff contends must be followed by the trier of facts was, in fact, followed by the court in the instant case.

It is only necessary to add that courts of Delaware have uniformly set forth to juries certain aids or means of assistance when the testimony presented has been in conflict. Quite uniformly have juries been told that when the testimony is in conflict the juries should consider all the facts of the case and take into consideration the demeanor of the witnesses on the stand, their apparent fairness in giving their testimony, their opportunities for knowing the facts about which they have testified, any bias or interest they may have in the outcome of the litigation, and any other matters appearing from the evidence and having a bearing upon the reliability or unreliability of the testimony.

Where, as in this case, all those means of establishing the burden of proof have been exhausted and the trier of facts is still confronted with an equilibrium of testimony, as is here found, the plaintiff must be adjudged to have failed in its burden of proof.[14]

The motion for reargument is denied.

PROBLEM

If *Delaware Coach Co. v. Savage* had been tried to a jury rather than to the court, how should the jury have been instructed with respect to the burden of persuasion? Prepare a jury instruction which could properly (and helpfully) have been given in the case. With your result, compare O'Malley, Grenig & Lee, Federal Jury Practice & Instructions § 104.01 (2000). See also, the Uniform Jury Instructions cited in the next case.

RILEY HILL GENERAL CONTRACTOR, INC. V. TANDY CORP.

Supreme Court of Oregon, 1987.
737 P.2d 595.

JONES, JUDGE.

Plaintiff, Riley Hill General Contractor, Inc., sought compensatory and punitive damages on claims labeled "fraud," "breach of warranty" and "negligence" against defendant, Tandy Corporation, arising out of plaintiff's purchase of a computer that was manufactured and sold by defendant doing business as Radio Shack. Defendant answered with a general denial of the claims and raised an affirmative defense of contributory fault. The trial court instructed the jury that:

"You are instructed that the law recognizes a presumption against fraud and this presumption against fraud must be overcome by clear and convincing evidence." The Party alleging fraud must thus bring forth evidence to prove it, and may not rely upon mere suspicious circumstances or equivocal conduct. "Thus, there must be a certain quality of evidence to overcome the presumption against fraud even though the burden of proof remains in this case as in all civil cases, proof by a preponderance of the evidence." (Emphasis added.)

---

[14] Model Code of Evidence, p. 3.

Defendant excepted to these instructions. The jury returned a verdict for plaintiff. Defendant appealed, and the Court of Appeals reversed and remanded for a new trial because of the inconsistency in the trial court's jury instructions on the burden of proof. Riley Hill General Contractor v. Tandy Corp., 82 Or.App. 458, 728 P.2d 577 (1986). We allowed review to decide whether the burden of persuasion[15] for common law deceit should be by "clear and convincing evidence," by a "preponderance of the evidence" or by a combination of both concepts. We hold that the burden of persuasion for common law deceit requires the proponent to prove each of the elements of deceit by clear and convincing evidence, but that general or punitive damages arising out of that deceit need be proved only by a preponderance of the evidence. The Court of Appeals is affirmed.

* * *

At the conclusion of the trial, the judge gave the above-quoted instruction to the jury. The Court of Appeals reversed the trial court, holding that the instructions were inconsistent because the jury was told that the burden of proof in "fraud" cases is by both clear and convincing evidence and by a preponderance of the evidence. As mentioned, the Court of Appeals held that the instruction was reversible error, because it was not possible to tell from the verdict whether the jury used the correct clear and convincing evidence standard or the incorrect preponderance of the evidence standard. 82 Or.App. at 461, 728 P.2d 577.

Before we set forth the level of proof required in civil actions for deceit, we address the origins and meanings of the terms "preponderance of evidence" and "clear and convincing evidence."

The Origins and Meanings of "Preponderance" and "Clear and Convincing" Evidence

"Preponderance" derives from the Latin word "praeponderare," which translates to "outweigh, be of greater weight." 8 Oxford English Dictionary 1289 (1933). With regard to the burden of proof or persuasion in civil actions, it is generally accepted to mean the greater weight of evidence. At one time in the history of English law, the translation received a literal interpretation, with heads of witnesses being counted on each side, and each item of testimony receiving a quantitative value or weight. See Millar, in Engelmann, History of Continental Civil Procedure 41–49 (1927); 9 Wigmore, Evidence 424–31, § 2498 (Chadbourn rev 1981); 1 Holdsworth, History of English Law 302–04 (3d ed 1922). The term suggests to the jury that the evidence should be weighed on a scale and, frequently, trial judges will speak of weights and scales in explaining to jurors under this standard that they cannot speculate or guess what

---

[15] OEC [Oregon Evidence Code] 305 provides: "A party has the burden of persuasion as to each fact the existence or nonexistence of which the law declares essential to the claim for relief or defense the party is asserting."

happened but that a party with the burden of persuasion in a civil case must prove what probably occurred. Uniform Jury Instructions (Civil), Nos. 21.01, 21.02 (Oregon CLE 1986), read, respectively:

"A party has the burden of proving by a preponderance of the evidence any claim made in that party's pleadings. In the absence of such proof, the party cannot prevail as to that claim."

" 'Preponderance of the evidence' means the greater weight of evidence. It is such evidence that, when weighed with that opposed to it, has more convincing force and is more probably true and accurate. If, upon any question in the case, the evidence appears to be equally balanced, or if you cannot say upon which side it weighs heavier, you must resolve that question against the party upon whom the burden of proof rests."[16]

Mellinkoff, in his extensive work, The Language of the Law (1963), does not specifically trace the origins of the terms "preponderance of the evidence" or "clear and convincing evidence." However, he asserts that certain words, such as "plaintiff," "defendant," "fee simple" and "lessee," are terms of art with a specific meaning, id. at 17, but that other language of the law is better characterized as equivocal because "there is a deliberate choice of the flexible," id. at 21. Among a sample of words and phrases which are often used "because they are flexible or despite their flexibility," are the words "clear and convincing," id. at 21, and he lists among "the cats and dogs of law language, defined and redefined, but not more precise for all of that," the words "preponderance of the evidence," id. at 385. Thus, he tells us what we already know, that these terms are not precise standards but are words that do no more than characterize evidence. See Byers v. Santiam Ford, Inc., 281 Or. 411, 420, 574 P.2d 1122 n.2 (1978) (Lent, J., specially concurring).

We now examine why there are two somewhat parallel words, "clear" and "convincing," for a separate standard of proof. Mellinkoff traces this repetition of words to the origins of the English language. * * *. He writes:

One of the sources of tautology [that is, a needless repetition of words] is the prolonged presence of two languages side by side. England, for example, is peppered with place names which would read Hill-hill, or worse, except that the first hill is Celtic (bre or cruc or penn) and the other Old English (hyll), for instance, names like Breedon-on-the-Hill, Churchill, Penhill, Pendle Hill. * * *

* * *

---

[16] We note that the uniform jury instruction still refers to the former usage, "burden of proof." Since January 1, 1982, the statutory terminology is "burden of persuasion." OEC 305, set out ante at note [15]. [Was the change warranted? Ed.]

He then comments that, sometimes for clarity, sometimes for emphasis and sometimes in keeping with the bilingual fashion of the day, English lawyers joined synonyms. A sampling of bilingual synonyms coupled in the law are:

fit and proper (OE; F)

free and clear (OE; F)

give, devise, and bequeath (OE; F; OE)

goods and chattels (OE: F)

* * *

peace and quiet (F; L)

* * *

will and testament (OE; L)

Such a combination of languages is found in the "clear and convincing" standard of proof, although this pair of words does not repeat a single concept. Outside the law, a proposition may be very clear but unconvincing, and murky statements may be persuasive in the absence of criticism or contrary assertions. In short, "clear" describes the character of unambiguous evidence, whether true or false; "convincing" describes the effect of evidence on an observer.

"Clear" is a Norman French word which means "of words, statements, explanations, meanings: Easy to understand, fully intelligible, free from obscurity of sense; of a vision, concept, notion, view, memory, etc.; Distinct, unclouded, free from confusion." 2 Oxford English Dictionary, supra at 475. The use of the term "clear" by itself after the Norman Conquest could have created great confusion due to its close association with the native English word "clean," which meant "without anything left or omitted, without any exception that may vitiate the statement, without qualification wholly, entirely, quite absolutely." Id. at 482.

"Convincing" is an English word derived from the Latin "convincere." It means "to overcome, to conquer, convict; to overcome (a person) in argument, to prove wrong, confute; to cause (a person) to admit, as establish to his satisfaction, that which is advanced in argument; that which convinces, that convicts, proves guilty, that which brings conviction to the mind." Id. at 950–51.

The use of similar terms, one Norman French, one English, arose in English history around the time of William the Conqueror and the Norman Conquest in 1066. King William I encouraged and maintained the loyalty and obligations system which had bound subjects to the kings of England. He made great use of certain trusted Norman followers, but these prelates were required to rule within a native English framework of law and custom * * *.

* * * In furtherance of his use of the jury system, and as part of his assimilation policy, William I directed that, where possible, Norman French words be joined with Anglo–Saxon words for purposes of effectuating the law. 1 Pollock & Maitland, The History of English Law, chs 2, 3 (1895).

In trying to understand the Norman French and English terms, of course, we need to examine not only their origins but also the usage given to them by judicial decisions.

The Use of the Terms

Historically, the "clear and convincing" standard of proof

> "was first applied in equity to claims which experience had shown to be inherently subject to fabrication, lapse of memory, or the flexibility of conscience. Conceding the validity of policies which the parol evidence rule and the Statutes of Wills and Frauds were designed to carry out, the chancery courts compromised between becoming a mecca for the trumped-up prayer for relief and refusing altogether to mitigate the stern fulfillment of these policies in the law courts, by granting relief only in cases where the evidence in support of this type of claim was 'clear and convincing.' * * * " Note, Appellate Review in the Federal Courts of Findings Requiring More than a Preponderance of the Evidence, 60 Harv.L.Rev. 111, 112 (1946).

The author of the above-quoted law review article notes that in jury trials of civil actions at law, the clear and convincing rule was applied to actions for fraud or deceit as well as to equitable defenses based on fraud or mistake. He concludes that one method of enforcing the demand for clear and convincing evidence available in appeals from jury verdicts is the approval of a charge to the jury which directs them to apply that level of proof or reversal for error where the charge does not incorporate it. Id. at 116–17, nn.43 & 44 (citing Fidelity & Casualty Co. of N.Y. v. Genova, 90 F.2d 874 (C.C.A.6th.1937); Kuhn v. Chesapeake & Ohio Ry., 118 F.2d 400 (C.C.A.4th.1941)).

Many courts have recognized that the intermediate standard of "clear and convincing" evidence is applicable in appropriate civil cases. Then Chief Justice Warren Burger, in Addington v. Texas, 441 U.S. 418, 424 * * * (1979), wrote that this

> " 'intermediate standard, which usually employs some combination of the words "clear," "cogent," "unequivocal," and "convincing," is less commonly used, but nonetheless is no stranger to the civil law.' One typical use of the standard is in

civil cases involving allegations of fraud or some other quasi-criminal wrongdoing by the defendant. The interests at stake in those cases are deemed to be more substantial than mere loss of money and some jurisdictions accordingly reduce the risk to defendant of having his reputation tarnished erroneously by increasing the plaintiff's burden of proof." Citing Woodby v. INS, 385 U.S. 276, 285 * * * (1966); McCormick Evidence § 320 (1954); 9 Wigmore, Evidence § 2498 (3d ed. 1940).

Application of this intermediate standard permeates a line of United States Supreme Court decisions declaring that "clear and convincing" evidence is required in various quasi-criminal proceedings or where the proceedings threaten the individual involved with a significant deprivation of liberty or with a stigma.

The Levels of Proof in Oregon

Since the time of the first Deady Code, Oregon statutes have set forth the level of proof required in civil and criminal actions. See General Laws of Oregon, ch. 9, § 835, pp. 355–56 (Deady 1845–1864). Those standards are now codified at ORS 10.095(5) and (6), as follows: "The jury, subject to the control of the court, in the cases specified by statute, are the judges of the effect or value of evidence addressed to them, except when it is thereby declared to be conclusive. They are, however, to be instructed by the court on all proper occasions:" * * *

"(5) That in civil cases the affirmative of the issue shall be proved, and when the evidence is contradictory, the finding shall be according to the preponderance of evidence;

(6) That in criminal cases a person is innocent of a crime or wrong until the prosecution proves otherwise, and guilt shall be established beyond reasonable doubt;" (Emphasis added.)

Plaintiff contends that, under ORS 10.095(5), in a civil action, a plaintiff's burden can never be more than a preponderance of the evidence. We disagree.

In Cook v. Michael, 214 Or. 513, 526–27, 330 P.2d 1026 (1958), this court stated that there are three standards of proof: "a preponderance," "clear and convincing" and "beyond a reasonable doubt." Proof by a "preponderance of the evidence" means that the jury must believe that the facts asserted are more probably true than false. To be "clear and convincing," evidence must establish that the truth of the facts asserted is "highly probable." "Beyond a reasonable doubt" means that the facts asserted are almost certainly true. This part of the Cook opinion has been endorsed repeatedly by this court. See, e.g., Mutual of Enumclaw Ins. v. McBride, 295 Or. 398, 405–06, 667 P.2d 494 (1983). * * *

In Mutual of Enumclaw Ins. v. McBride, supra, this court signaled that

> "[t]he time may come when it is proper to address the question of the requirement of a higher level of proof in actions for common law fraud; but we decline to do so here because we disagree that the statutory provisions of fraud and false swearing are sufficiently similar to common law fraud as urged by defendants, nor do we think that to be the proper basis on which to decide this case." 295 Or. at 403, 667 P.2d 494.

Acknowledging that "skepticism [is] often voiced regarding the practical importance of an intermediate measure of proof," this court nonetheless stated that

> "ORS 10.095 requires the court 'on all proper occasions' to instruct the jury '[t]hat in civil cases * * * the finding shall be according to the preponderance of evidence' while 'in criminal cases guilt shall be established beyond reasonable doubt.' ORS 10.095(5), (6). The 'proper occasion' for interpolating an intermediate measure of proof is in cases that are between 'civil' and 'criminal' and where what is to be established is akin to 'guilt.'" Id. at 405, 667 P.2d 494.

One reason for imposing the higher "clear and convincing" standard in a claim based on deceit is that the defendant is branded with something akin to guilt. In Mutual of Enumclaw, after conceding that setting the clear and convincing standard for "fraud" was dictum in Cook v. Michael, an assault case, this court said:

> "So well established is this rule that the commentary to OEC 305 states, '[i]n actions that allege fraud or gift, for example, the trier of fact must be persuaded by "clear and convincing evidence," which means that the truth of the facts asserted must be highly probable,' citing Cook v. Michael, supra. This is repeated in L. Kirkpatrick, Oregon Evidence 51 (1982). The dictum of Cook v. Michael has become the accepted practice in Oregon. Thus, while the preponderance standard is the rule in most civil cases, an exception to the standard is applied in civil cases of common law fraud." Mutual of Enumclaw, 295 Or. at 403, 667 P.2d 494.

* * *

A party who is found "guilty" of deceit is not found merely negligent in deceiving the victim. That party must have intended to deceive the victim or acted in reckless disregard for the truth. The type of interest protected by the law of deceit is the interest in formulating business judgments without being misled by others—in short, in not being cheated. See U.S. National Bank v. Fought, supra, 291 Or. at 220, 630 P.2d 337. A person who has been found "guilty" of deceiving or cheating someone certainly has been found "guilty" of conduct which carries the same stigma of guilt whether the conduct is a criminal or civil act of deceit.

As mentioned in Mutual of Enumclaw v. McBride, supra, ORS 10.095 is not cast in absolute terms. It requires the jury be instructed to apply the "preponderance" standard "on all proper occasions," thus leaving some discretion for this court to decide which cases are proper for such an instruction and which are not.

We conclude that the standard of proof in a civil action for common law deceit must be "clear and convincing." As our discussion above of the origins of the words points out, the evidence must be free from confusion, fully intelligible, distinct and establish to the jury that the defendant intended to deceive the plaintiff or did so with a reckless disregard for the truth. To be both clear and convincing, the truth of the facts asserted must be highly probable. Cook v. Michael, supra, 214 Or. at 527, 330 P.2d 1096. A trial judge should not tell a jury in a deceit case that it must be convinced by clear and convincing evidence. This misuse of parallel words would thrust us back to the dark ages. As Justice O'Connell cautioned in Cook v. Michael, 214 Or. at 528, 330 P.2d 1096.

> "when the proposition to be proved must be established by clear and convincing evidence, we regard it as improper for the trial court to use the word 'preponderance' in any of the instructions relating to that proposition. * * * "

However, as this court held in Dizick v. Umpqua Comm. College, supra, 287 Or. at 311, 599 P.2d 444, even though "fraud" must be proved by "clear and convincing evidence," the extent of damages need only be proved by a preponderance of the evidence. See also Byers v. Santiam Ford, Inc., supra, 218 Or. at 418, 574 P.2d 1122 (Lent, J., specially concurring).

In sum, in a common law deceit action the trial judge, when referring to the basic elements of the claim, should tell the jury that proof by clear and convincing evidence is required, which means that the truth of the facts is highly probable. However, when considering the issue of damages, be they general or punitive, the judge should instruct the jury that the proponent need only prove those damages by a preponderance, or greater weight of the evidence.[17]

---

[17] The court should not instruct the jury that deceit is not presumed or make any reference that a presumption must be overcome by evidence. In a properly tried civil case, the term "presumption" should not be heard by a jury. The legislative commentary to OEC 308 reads in part: "Under ORE 308, once a party invoking a presumption establishes the basic facts giving rise to it, the burden of establishing the nonexistence of the presumed fact shifts to the opposing party. Plaintiff, for example, may raise the presumption that a letter duly addressed and mailed was received in the regular course of the mail. See Rule 311(1)(h). The judge in such a case would determine whether the evidence is sufficient to support a finding of the existence of the basic

We agree with the Court of Appeals' disposition as to defendant's assignment of error in the submission of the jury verdict form, which inferred that punitive damages could be allowed for simple negligence. Other assignments of error raised by defendant are not meritorious.

* * *

NOTE AND QUESTION

While most jurisdictions recognize the existence of a burden of persuasion intermediate between that applicable in an ordinary civil case and a criminal prosecution, unanimity is lacking with respect to the types of issues as to which the burden should be imposed. What types of considerations are suggested by the issues to which the Supreme Court of the United States has held the standard constitutionally required? See Rivera v. Minnich, 483 U.S. 574 (1987) (finding no constitutional requirement of the clear and convincing standard in a state paternity proceeding.)

IN RE WINSHIP

Supreme Court of the United States, 1970.
397 U.S. 358.

MR. JUSTICE BRENNAN delivered the opinion of the Court. Constitutional questions decided by this Court concerning the juvenile process have centered on the adjudicatory stage at "which a determination is made as to whether a juvenile is a 'delinquent' as a result of alleged misconduct on his part, with the consequence that he may be committed to a state institution." In re Gault, 387 U.S. 1, 13 (1967). *Gault* decided that, although the Fourteenth Amendment does not require that the hearing at this stage conform with all the requirements of a criminal trial or even of the usual administrative proceeding, the Due Process Clause does require application during the adjudicatory hearing of " 'the essentials of due process and fair treatment.' " Id., at 30. This case presents the single, narrow question whether proof beyond a reasonable doubt is among the "essentials of due process and fair

---

facts: that the letter was properly addressed, that it was mailed, and that it was not returned. If so, the judge would instruct the jury that if they find the basic facts to be true, then the burden is on defendant to prove by a preponderance of the evidence that the letter was not received. The jury should never hear the word 'presumption' during this instruction. * * * The Legislative Assembly decided to change Oregon practice on presumptions for several reasons. First, it is extremely difficult to phrase a jury instruction without conveying the impression that the presumption itself is evidence. That proposition has long been discredited. Second, under the current approach to presumptions, the jury must weigh the force of the legal conclusion mandated by the presumption against the testimony of witnesses and other direct evidence. That is a difficult or impossible task. Finally, the considerations of fairness, policy and probability, which underlie the creation of presumptions, are not satisfied by giving them any lesser effect. The approach set forth in this rule is simple and workable, and gives due consideration to the policies behind the creation of presumptions. All presumptions, whether legislatively or judicially created, must be treated in the manner prescribed by this section." Evidence 4–8 to 4–9, § 4.13 (Oregon CLE 1986) (emphasis in original; citations omitted).

treatment" required during the adjudicatory stage when a juvenile is charged with an act which would constitute a crime if committed by an adult.

Section 712 of the New York Family Court Act defines a juvenile delinquent as "a person over seven and less than sixteen years of age who does any act which, if done by an adult, would constitute a crime." During a 1967 adjudicatory hearing, conducted pursuant to § 742 of the Act, a judge in New York Family Court found that appellant, then a 12–year–old boy, had entered a locker and stolen $112 from a woman's pocketbook. The petition which charged appellant with delinquency alleged that his act, "if done by an adult, would constitute the crime or crimes of Larceny." The judge acknowledged that the proof might not establish guilt beyond a reasonable doubt, but rejected appellant's contention that such proof was required by the Fourteenth Amendment. The judge relied instead on § 744(b) of the New York Family Court Act which provides that "[a]ny determination at the conclusion of [an adjudicatory] hearing that a [juvenile] did an act or acts must be based on a preponderance of the evidence."[18] During a subsequent dispositional hearing, appellant was ordered placed in a training school for an initial period of 18 months, subject to annual extensions of his commitment until his 18th birthday— six years in appellant's case. The Appellate Division of the New York Supreme Court, First Judicial Department, affirmed without opinion, 30 A.D.2d 781, 291 N.Y.S.2d 1005 (1968). The New York Court of Appeals then affirmed by a four-to-three vote, expressly sustaining the constitutionality of § 744(b), 24 N.Y.2d 196, 299 N.Y.S.2d 414, 247 N.E.2d 253 (1969).[19] We noted probable jurisdiction, 396 U.S. 885 (1969). We reverse.

I

The requirement that guilt of a criminal charge be established by proof beyond a reasonable doubt dates at least from our early years as a Nation. The "demand for a higher degree of persuasion in criminal cases was recurrently expressed from ancient times, [though] its crystallization

---

[18] The ruling appears in the following portion of the hearing transcript:
Counsel: "Your Honor is making a finding by the preponderance of the evidence."
Court: "Well, it convinces me."
Counsel: "It's not beyond a reasonable doubt, Your Honor."
Court: "That is true * * * Our statute says a preponderance and a preponderance it is."

[19] * * * Legislative adoption of the reasonable-doubt standard has been urged by the National Conference of Commissioners on Uniform State Laws and by the Children's Bureau of the Department of Health, Education, and Welfare's Social and Rehabilitation Service. See Uniform Juvenile Court Act § 29(b) (1968); Children's Bureau, Social and Rehabilitation Service, U.S. Department of Health, Education and Welfare, Legislative Guide for Drafting Family and Juvenile Court Acts § 32(c) (1969). Cf. the proposal of the National Council on Crime and Delinquency that a "clear and convincing" standard be adopted. Model Rules for Juvenile Courts, Rule 26, p. 57 (1969). See generally Cohen, The Standard of Proof in Juvenile Proceedings: Gault Beyond a Reasonable Doubt, 68 Mich.L.Rev. 567 (1970).

into the formula 'beyond a reasonable doubt' seems to have occurred as late as 1798. It is now accepted in common law jurisdictions as the measure of persuasion by which the prosecution must convince the trier of all the essential elements of guilt." C. McCormick, Evidence § 321, pp. 681–682 (1954); see also 9 J. Wigmore, Evidence, § 2497 (3d ed. 1940). Although virtually unanimous adherence to the reasonable-doubt standard in common-law jurisdictions may not conclusively establish it as a requirement of due process, such adherence does "reflect a profound judgment about the way in which law should be enforced and justice administered." Duncan v. Louisiana, 391 U.S. 145, 155 (1968).

Expressions in many opinions of this Court indicate that it has long been assumed that proof of a criminal charge beyond a reasonable doubt is constitutionally required. * * * Mr. Justice Frankfurter stated that "[i]t is the duty of the Government to establish * * * guilt beyond a reasonable doubt. This notion—basic in our law and rightly one of the boasts of a free society—is a requirement and a safeguard of due process of law in the historic, procedural content of 'due process.' " Leland v. Oregon, supra, 343 U.S., at 802–803 (dissenting opinion). In a similar vein, the Court said in Brinegar v. United States, supra, 338 U.S., at 174, that "[g]uilt in a criminal case must be proved beyond a reasonable doubt and by evidence confined to that which long experience in the common-law tradition, to some extent embodied in the Constitution, has crystallized into rules of evidence consistent with that standard. These rules are historically grounded rights of our system, developed to safeguard men from dubious and unjust convictions, with resulting forfeitures of life, liberty and property." Davis v. United States, supra, 160 U.S., at 488 stated that the requirement is implicit in "constitutions * * * [which] recognize the fundamental principles that are deemed essential for the protection of life and liberty." In *Davis* a murder conviction was reversed because the trial judge instructed the jury that it was their duty to convict when the evidence was equally balanced regarding the sanity of the accused. This Court said: "On the contrary, he is entitled to an acquittal of the specific crime charged, if upon all the evidence, there is reasonable doubt whether he was capable in law of committing crime. * * * No man should be deprived of his life under the forms of law unless the jurors who try him are able, upon their consciences, to say that the evidence before them * * * is sufficient to show beyond a reasonable doubt the existence of every fact necessary to constitute the crime charged." Id., at 484, 493.

The reasonable-doubt standard plays a vital role in the American scheme of criminal procedure. It is a prime instrument for reducing the risk of convictions resting on factual error. The standard provides concrete substance for the presumption of innocence—that bedrock "axiomatic and elementary" principle whose "enforcement lies at the foundation of the administration of our criminal law." Coffin v. United States, supra, 156 U.S., at 453. As the dissenters in the New York Court of Appeals observed, and we agree, "a person accused of a crime * * * would be at a severe disadvantage, a disadvantage amounting to a lack of fundamental fairness, if he could be adjudged guilty and imprisoned for years on the strength of the same evidence as would suffice in a civil case." 24 N.Y.2d, at 205, 299 N.Y.S.2d, at 422, 247 N.E.2d, at 259.

The requirement of proof beyond a reasonable doubt has this vital role in our criminal procedure for cogent reasons. The accused during a criminal prosecution has at stake interest of immense importance, both because of the possibility that he may lose his liberty upon conviction and because of the certainty that he would be stigmatized by the conviction. Accordingly, a society that values the good name and freedom of every individual should not condemn a man for commission of a crime when there is reasonable doubt about his guilt. As we said in Speiser v. Randall, supra, 357 U.S., at 525–526: "There is always in litigation a margin of error, representing error in factfinding, which both parties must take into account. Where one party has at stake an interest of transcending value—as a criminal defendant his liberty—this margin of error is reduced as to him by the process of placing on the other party the burden of * * * persuading the factfinder at the conclusion of the trial of his guilt beyond a reasonable doubt. Due process commands that no man shall lose his liberty unless the Government has borne the burden of * * * convincing the factfinder of his guilt." To this end, the reasonable-doubt standard is indispensable, for it "impresses on the trier of fact the necessity of reaching a subjective state of certitude of the facts in issue." Dorsen & Rezneck, In Re Gault and the Future of Juvenile Law, 1 Family Law Quarterly, No. 4, pp. 1, 26 (1967).

Moreover, use of the reasonable-doubt standard is indispensable to command the respect and confidence of the community in applications of the criminal law. It is critical that the moral force of the criminal law not be diluted by a standard of proof that leaves people in doubt whether innocent men are being condemned. It is also important in our free society that every individual going about his ordinary affairs have confidence that his government cannot adjudge him guilty of a criminal offense without convincing a proper factfinder of his guilt with utmost certainty.

Lest there remain any doubt about the constitutional stature of the reasonable-doubt standard, we explicitly hold that the Due Process Clause protects the accused against conviction except upon proof beyond a reasonable doubt of every fact necessary to constitute the crime with which he is charged.

II

We turn to the question whether juveniles, like adults, are constitutionally entitled to proof beyond a reasonable doubt when they are charged with violation of a criminal law. The same considerations that demand extreme caution in factfinding to protect the innocent adult apply as well to the innocent child. We do not find convincing the contrary arguments of the New York Court of Appeals. *Gault* rendered untenable much of the reasoning relied upon by that court to sustain the constitutionality of § 744(b). * * *

Nor do we perceive any merit in the argument that to afford juveniles the protection of proof beyond a reasonable doubt would risk destruction of beneficial aspects of the juvenile process.[20]

* * *

We conclude, as we concluded regarding the essential due process safeguards applied in *Gault,* that the observance of the standard of proof beyond a reasonable doubt "will not compel the States to abandon or displace any of the substantive benefits of the juvenile process." *Gault,* supra, at 21.

Finally, we reject the Court of Appeals' suggestion that there is, in any event, only a "tenuous difference" between the reasonable-doubt and preponderance standards. The suggestion is singularly unpersuasive. In this very case, the trial judge's ability to distinguish between the two standards enabled him to make a finding of guilt that he conceded he might not have made under the standard of proof beyond a reasonable doubt. Indeed, the trial judge's action evidences the accuracy of the observation of commentators that "the preponderance test is susceptible to the misinterpretation that it calls on the trier of fact merely to perform an abstract weighing of the evidence in order to determine which side has produced the greater quantum, without regard to its effect in convincing his mind of the truth of the proposition asserted." Dorsen & Rezneck, supra, at 26–27.[21]

---

[20] Appellee, New York City, apparently concedes as much in its Brief, page 8, where it states:

"A determination that the New York law unconstitutionally denies due process because it does not provide for use of the reasonable doubt standard probably would not have a serious impact if all that resulted would be a change in the quantum of proof." * * *

[21] Compare this Court's rejection of the preponderance standard in deportation proceedings, where we ruled that the Government must support its allegations with "clear, unequivocal, and convincing evidence." Woodby v. Immigration and Naturalization Service, 385 U.S. 276, 285 (1966). Although we ruled in *Woodby* that deportation is not tantamount to a criminal conviction, we found that since it could lead to "drastic deprivations," it is impermissible for a person to be "banished from this country upon no higher degree of proof than applies in a negligence case." Ibid.

III

In sum, the constitutional safeguard of proof beyond a reasonable doubt is as much required during the adjudicatory stage of a delinquency proceeding as are those constitutional safeguards applied in *Gault*— notice of charges, right to counsel, the rights of confrontation and examination, and the privilege against self-incrimination. We therefore hold, in agreement with Chief Judge Fuld in dissent in the Court of Appeals, "that, where a 12–year–old child is charged with an act of stealing which renders him liable to confinement for as long as six years, then, as a matter of due process * * * the case against him must be proved beyond a reasonable doubt." 24 N.Y.2d, at 207, 299 N.Y.S.2d, at 423, 247 N.E.2d, at 260.

Reversed.

MR. JUSTICE HARLAN, concurring. No one, I daresay, would contend that state juvenile court trials are subject to *no* federal constitutional limitations. Differences have existed, however, among the members of this Court as to *what* constitutional protections do apply. See In re Gault, 387 U.S. 1 (1967).

The present case draws in question the validity of a New York statute that permits a determination of juvenile delinquency, founded on a charge of criminal conduct, to be made on a standard of proof that is less rigorous than that which would obtain had the accused been tried for the same conduct in an ordinary criminal case. While I am in full agreement that this statutory provision offends the requirement of fundamental fairness embodied in the Due Process Clause of the Fourteenth Amendment, I am constrained to add something to what my Brother Brennan has written for the Court, lest the true nature of the constitutional problem presented become obscured or the impact on state juvenile court systems of what the Court holds today be exaggerated.

I

Professor Wigmore, in discussing the various attempts by courts to define how convinced one must be to be convinced beyond a reasonable doubt, wryly observed: "The truth is that no one has yet invented or discovered a mode of measurement for the intensity of human belief. Hence there can be yet no successful method of communicating intelligibly * * * a sound method of self-analysis for one's belief," 9 J. Wigmore, Evidence 325 (3d ed. 1940).[22]

Notwithstanding Professor Wigmore's skepticism, we have before us a case where the choice of the standard of proof has made a difference: the juvenile court judge below forthrightly acknowledged that he believed by a preponderance of the evidence, but was not convinced beyond a

---

[22] See also Paulsen, *Juvenile Courts and the Legacy of '67*, 43 Ind.L.J. 527, 551–552 (1968).

reasonable doubt, that appellant stole $112 from the complainant's pocketbook. Moreover, even though the labels used for alternative standards of proof are vague and not a very sure guide to decisionmaking, the choice of the standard for a particular variety of adjudication does, I think, reflect a very fundamental assessment of the comparative social costs of erroneous factual determinations.[23]

To explain why I think this so, I begin by stating two propositions, neither of which I believe can be fairly disputed. First, in a judicial proceeding in which there is a dispute about the facts of some earlier event, the factfinder cannot acquire unassailably accurate knowledge of what happened. Instead, all the factfinder can acquire is a belief of what *probably* happened. The intensity of this belief—the degree to which a factfinder is convinced that a given act actually occurred—can, of course, vary. In this regard, a standard of proof represents an attempt to instruct the factfinder concerning the degree of confidence our society thinks he should have in the correctness of factual conclusions for a particular type of adjudication. Although the phrases "preponderance of the evidence" and "proof beyond a reasonable doubt" are quantitatively imprecise, they do communicate to the finder of fact different notions concerning the degree of confidence he is expected to have in the correctness of his factual conclusions.

A second proposition, which is really nothing more than a corollary of the first, is that the trier of fact will sometimes, despite his best efforts, be wrong in his factual conclusions. In a lawsuit between two parties, a factual error can make a difference in one of two ways. First, it can result in a judgment in favor of the plaintiff when the true facts warrant a judgment for the defendant. The analogue in a criminal case would be the conviction of an innocent man. On the other hand, an erroneous factual determination can result in a judgment for the defendant when the true facts justify a judgment in plaintiff's favor. The criminal analogue would be the acquittal of a guilty man.

The standard of proof influences the relative frequency of these two types of erroneous outcomes. If, for example, the standard of proof for a criminal trial were a preponderance of the evidence rather than proof beyond a reasonable doubt, there would be a smaller risk of factual errors that result in freeing guilty persons, but a far greater risk of factual errors that result in convicting the innocent. Because the standard of proof affects the comparative frequency of these two types of erroneous outcomes, the choice of the standard to be applied in a particular kind of litigation should, in a rational world, reflect an assessment of the comparative social disutility of each.

---

[23] For an interesting analysis of standards of proof see Kaplan, *Decision Theory and the Factfinding Process,* 20 Stan.L.Rev. 1065, 1071–1077 (1968).

When one makes such an assessment, the reason for different standards of proof in civil as opposed to criminal litigation becomes apparent. In a civil suit between two private parties for money damages, for example, we view it as no more serious in general for there to be an erroneous verdict in the defendant's favor than for there to be an erroneous verdict in the plaintiff's favor. A preponderance of the evidence standard therefore seems peculiarly appropriate for, as explained most sensibly,[24] it simply requires the trier of fact "to believe that the existence of a fact is more probable than its nonexistence before [he] may find in favor of the party who has the burden to persuade the [judge] of the fact's existence."[25]

In a criminal case, on the other hand, we do not view the social disutility of convicting an innocent man as equivalent to the disutility of acquitting someone who is guilty. As Mr. Justice Brennan wrote for the Court in Speiser v. Randall, 357 U.S. 513, 525–526 (1958):

> "There is always in litigation a margin of error, representing error in factfinding, which both parties must take into account. Where one party has at stake an interest of transcending value—as a criminal defendant his liberty—this margin of error is reduced as to him by the process of placing on the other party the burden * * * of persuading the fact-finder at the conclusion of the trial of his guilt beyond a reasonable doubt."

In this context, I view the requirement of proof beyond a reasonable doubt in a criminal case as bottomed on a fundamental value determination of our society that it is far worse to convict an innocent man than to let a guilty man go free. It is only because of the nearly complete and long-standing acceptance of the reasonable-doubt standard by the States in criminal trials that the Court has not before today had to hold explicitly that due process, as an expression of fundamental procedural fairness, requires a more stringent standard for criminal trials than for ordinary civil litigation.

II

When one assesses the consequences of an erroneous factual determination in a juvenile delinquency proceeding in which a youth is accused of a crime, I think it must be concluded that, while the consequences are not identical to those in a criminal case, the differences will not support a distinction in the standard of proof. * * * I therefore agree that a juvenile court judge should be no less convinced of the

---

[24] The preponderance test has been criticized, justifiably in my view, when it is read as asking the trier of fact to weigh in some objective sense the quantity of evidence submitted by each side rather than asking him to decide what he believes most probably happened. See J. Maguire, Evidence, Common Sense and Common Law 180 (1947).

[25] F. James, Civil Procedure 250–251 (1965); see E. Morgan, Some Problems of Proof Under the Anglo–American System of Litigation 84–85 (1956).

factual conclusion that the accused committed the criminal act with which he is charged than would be required in a criminal trial.

III

I wish to emphasize, as I did in my separate opinion in *Gault,* 387 U.S. 1, that there is no automatic congruence between the procedural requirements imposed by due process in a criminal case, and those imposed by due process in juvenile cases.

* * *

MR. CHIEF JUSTICE BURGER, with whom MR. JUSTICE STEWART joins, dissenting.

[The dissenting opinion of MR. CHIEF JUSTICE BURGER is omitted.]

NOTES AND QUESTIONS

1. *Jury instructions.* How the jury should be instructed as to the "reasonable doubt" standard is a question which has received considerable judicial attention. One definition which has received extensive usage in jury charges is that found in Commonwealth v. Webster,[26] 59 Mass. (5 Cush.) 295, 320 (1850):

It is not a mere possible doubt; because everything relating to human affairs and depending on moral evidence, is open to some possible or imaginary doubt. It is that state of the case, which, after the entire comparison and consideration of all the evidence, leaves the minds of the jurors in that condition that they cannot say they feel an abiding conviction, to a moral certainty, of the truth of the charge.

Charges drawing largely upon *Webster*, including references to "moral certainty," were upheld against constitutional attack in Victor v. Nebraska, 511 U.S. 1 (1994), although the Court made clear its view that such phraseology is less than optimum. What formulation would be preferable? Justice Ginsburg, concurring in *Victor,* characterizes the following as "clean, straight forward, and accurate:"

[T]he government has the burden of proving the defendant guilty beyond a reasonable doubt. Some of you may have served as jurors in civil cases, where you were told that it is only necessary to prove that a fact is more likely true than not true. In criminal cases, the government's proof must be more powerful than that. It must be beyond a reasonable doubt.

---

[26] In addition to its legal significance, the *Webster* case constitutes a fascinating piece of Americana which has been of continuing interest to historians. See Borowitz, The Janitor's Story: An Ethical Dilemma in the Harvard Murder Case, 66 A.B.A.J. 1540 (1980); Thomson, Murder at Harvard (1971). [Ed.]

> Proof beyond a reasonable doubt is proof that leaves you firmly convinced of the defendant's guilt. There are very few things in this world that we know with absolute certainty, and in criminal cases the law does not require proof that overcomes every possible doubt. If, based on your consideration of the evidence, you are firmly convinced that the defendant is guilty of the crime charged, you must find him guilty. If on the other hand, you think there is a real possibility that he is not guilty, you must give him the benefit of the doubt and find him not guilty. Federal Judicial Center, Pattern Criminal Jury Instructions 17–18 (1987) (instruction 21).

511 U.S. at 27.

For a more recent discussion of reasonable doubt instructions, see Sheppard, The Metamorphoses of Reasonable Doubt: How Changes in the Burden of Proof Have Weakened the Presumption of Innocence, 78 Notre Dame L.Rev. 1165 (2003).

2. *Probabilities.* In light of Justice Harlan's comment, concurring *In re Winship*, that all the factfinder can acquire is a belief as to what probably happened, would it be desirable (and constitutional) to define "reasonable doubt" in terms of probabilities? What degree of probability? For a challenging proposal admitted by the author to be somewhat heretical, see Ball, Probability Theory: The Moment of Truth, 14 Vand.L.Rev. 807 (1961).

More recent attempts to utilize probability theory with respect to burdens of persuasion include Cohen, Confidence in Probability: Burdens of Persuasion in a World of Imperfect Knowledge, 60 N.Y.U.L.Rev. 385 (1985); Kaye, Do We Need a Calculus of Weight to Understand Proof Beyond a Reasonable Doubt, 66 B.U.L.Rev. 657 (1986). See also Chambers, Reasonable Certainty and Reasonable Doubt, 81 Marq.L.Rev. 655 (1998). For an argument that the standard of proof under the rubric of reasonable doubt can and should vary with the kind of case, see Lillquist, Recasting Reasonable Doubt: Decision Theory and the Virtues of Variability, 36 U.C. Davis L.Rev. 85 (2002).

3. *Error in instructions.* There is no federal constitutional requirement that the phrase "beyond a reasonable doubt" be defined for the jury, and some authority exists for the proposition that any attempt to do so will constitute reversible error. Note, Defining Reasonable Doubt: To Define or Not to Define, 90 Colum.L.Rev. 1716 (1990). If an instruction is given which misdescribes the standard under federal constitutional law, the Supreme Court has held that the error is "structural" and thus not susceptible to harmless error analysis. Sullivan v. Louisiana, 508 U.S. 275 (1993). See also Note, Reasonable Doubt: An Argument Against Definition, 108 Harv.L.Rev. 1955 (1995).

4. *Circumstantial evidence cases.* Where the state relies upon circumstantial evidence, it is common for the defense to request an instruction in effect equating reasonable doubt with any reasonable

hypothesis consistent with the circumstances and inconsistent with guilt. In Holland v. United States, 348 U.S. 121, 139–40 (1954), discussed by the court in *United States v. Nelson, supra,* in reference to the standard on review, the Supreme Court stated:

> The petitioners assail the refusal of the trial judge to instruct that where the Government's evidence is circumstantial it must be such as to exclude every reasonable hypothesis other than that of guilt. There is some support for this type of instruction in the lower court decisions, * * * but the better rule is that where the jury is properly instructed on the standards for reasonable doubt, such an additional instruction on circumstantial evidence is confusing and incorrect * * *.

> Circumstantial evidence in this respect is intrinsically no different from testimonial evidence. Admittedly, circumstantial evidence may in some cases point to a wholly incorrect result. Yet this is equally true of testimonial evidence. In both instances, a jury is asked to weigh the chances that the evidence correctly points to guilt against the possibility of inaccuracy or ambiguous inference. In both, the jury must use its experience with people and events in weighing the probabilities. If the jury is convinced beyond a reasonable doubt, we can require no more.

But see State v. Ohler, 134 N.W.2d 265 (Neb.1965) (suggesting such an instruction is not only proper but required).

See also Rosenberg & Rosenberg, " 'Perhaps What Ye Say Is Based Only on Conjecture'—Circumstantial Evidence, Then and Now," 31 Hous.L.Rev. 1371 (1995).

5.   *Difference in civil and criminal standards.* In the principal case, the majority "rejects" the suggestion that there is only a "tenuous difference" between the reasonable doubt and preponderance standards, noting in support of its position that the trial judge was clearly cognizant of a distinction. In this connection, see Simon & Mahan, Quantifying Burdens of Proof, 5 Law & Soc.Rev. 319, 329 (1971) (reporting the results of an empirical study of jury and judge behavior): "For the judges a preponderance means a little more than half; for the jurors it means a probability almost indistinguishable from the standard applied in criminal trials." See also Stoffelmayr & Diamond, The Conflict Between Precision and Flexibility in Explaining "Beyond a Reasonable Doubt," 6 Psychol.Pub.Pol'y & L. 769 (2000); Kaplow, Burden of Proof, 121 Yale L. J. 738 (2012).

6.   *Affirmative defenses.* The implications of the *Winship* decision for "affirmative defenses"—particularly rules that assign the burden of persuasion to the defendant—in criminal cases deserve note. Though some states decline to impose the burden of persuasion upon the defendant as to any element of a criminal case, it has long been assumed, in light of Leland v. Oregon, 343 U.S. 790 (1952), that there is no general federal constitutional

barrier to the practice. In *Leland* the Supreme Court upheld an Oregon statute which required an accused pleading insanity to establish that defense beyond a reasonable doubt. See also Martin v. Ohio, 480 U.S. 228 (1987) (constitutional to allocate burden of persuasion on self defense to accused).

But there are some limitations on the placement of the burden of persuasion on the defense although the exact nature of those limitations is not entirely clear. Compare Mullaney v. Wilbur, 421 U.S. 684 (1975) (holding unconstitutional to place burden on defendant to show that he acted in the heat of passion on sudden provocation), with Patterson v. New York, 432 U.S. 197 (1977) (ruling not unconstitutional to require defendant to prove that he acted under the influence of "extreme emotional disturbance" and distinguishing *Mullaney* as dealing with a situation which the defendant was asked to disprove an essential element of the prosecution's case). See discussion in 2 McCormick, Evidence §§ 346–348 (7th ed. 2013). See also Allen, Restructuring Jury Decision Making in Criminal Cases: A Unified Constitutional Approach to Evidentiary Devices, 94 Harv.L.Rev. 321 (1980); Garfield, Back to the Future: Does *Apprendi* Bar a Legislature's Power to Shift the Burden of Proof Away from the Prosecution by Labeling an Element of a Traditional Crime as an Affirmative Defense?, 35 Conn.L.Rev. 1351 (2003); Rosenberg, *Winship* Redux: 1970 to 1990, 69 Tex.L.Rev. 109 (1990); Saltzburg, Burdens of Persuasion in Criminal Cases: Harmonizing the Views of the Justices, 20 Am.Crim.L.Rev. 393 (1983); Sundby, The Reasonable Doubt Rule and the Meaning of Innocence, 40 Hastings L.J. 457 (1989).

CHAPTER 5[1]

PRESUMPTIONS

■ ■ ■

McNULTY V. CUSACK

District Court of Appeal of Florida, 1958.
104 So.2d 785.

ALLEN, ACTING CHIEF JUDGE. This is an appeal from a final judgment in a negligence action, entered after a directed verdict for plaintiff as to liability. Annie B. Cusack sued F. Jerome McNulty as the result of a rear-end collision between a car driven by plaintiff and another driven by defendant. Defendant's car ran into the rear of plaintiff's car at an intersection. The jury brought in a verdict for plaintiff in the amount of $16,000.

* * *

We state the principal question involved here as follows:

"Whether the showing of a rear-end collision and the circumstances under which it occurred, in the absence of explanation, gives rise to a presumption of negligence so as to authorize a directed verdict, or whether it only gives rise to an inference of negligence sufficient for presentation to the jury."

There is a split of authority on whether or not a rear-end collision, coupled with circumstances under which it occurs, gives rise to an inference or a presumption of negligence. [Some] * * * authorities hold that a presumption arises and that the burden of going forward with the evidence is on the person who ran into the preceding car from the rear * * *.

The Rhode Island court, in the case of Douglas v. Silvia, supra, said:

"We agree with the rule established by the cases of O'Donnell v. United Electric Rys. Co., 48 R.I. 18, 134 A. 642 and Riccio v. Ginsberg, 49 R.I. 32, 139 A. 652, 62 A.L.R. 967, that proof of a rear-end collision makes a prima facie case of negligence against the driver of the car in the rear. This does not mean, however,

---

[1]   Throughout the cases and materials in this chapter some footnotes have been omitted; others have been renumbered. [Ed.]

that the driver of an automobile which is following another is to be held liable under all conditions and irrespective of existing circumstances. When a prima facie case is made out by proving that the plaintiff was damaged in a rear-end collision, the duty of going forward with evidence of due care falls upon the defendant. If the testimony then shows a conflict of evidence from which different conclusions may reasonably be drawn by ordinarily prudent persons, then the question becomes one of fact for the jury to determine under proper instructions from the court. The burden of proof[2] in such a case still remains with the plaintiff."

* * *

The case of Harvey v. Borg, 1934, 218 Iowa 1228, 257 N.W. 190, 193, indicates the logic of those cases which hold that only an inference of neglect arises from the fact that a rear-end collision occurred and, therefore, it becomes a matter for the jury.

In Harvey v. Borg, supra, the Supreme Court of Iowa said:

"It is universally agreed that no inference of negligence arises from the mere fact that a collision occurred. A collision of two motor vehicles might result without negligence upon the part of the operator of either of them. The facts and circumstances surrounding the occurrence must be considered. It is certainly the general rule that a truck driven by a careful and prudent driver would not ordinarily crash with the rear of a forward moving vehicle of any kind. The inference recognized in such cases is by no means conclusive and may be readily dissipated by an explanation on the part of the party causing the injuries by evidence in the usual way. Appellant [sic] did not see fit to offer any explanation or to present testimony in their behalf. Appellee made out a prima facie case of negligence, and, in the absence of explanation on the part of defendant or of other evidence, an issue was presented for the jury."

* * *

The record shows that the sole testimony as to negligence in the case was that of the plaintiff. After the plaintiff rested, the defendant also rested, so there was no explanation on the part of the defendant of his actions of crashing his car into the rear-end of plaintiff's car. * * *

We, therefore, have the testimony of the plaintiff that she had stopped her car at a street intersection where the traffic light showed red and was waiting for the light to change to green, that while still sitting there, the defendant's car crashed into the back of her car; and in addition, that the defendant rushed up and apologized to her and when

---

2   [In what sense is the court here using the phrase "burden of proof?" Ed.]

she stated to him that he had wrecked her car, he remarked that that could be fixed.

Was there sufficient evidence before the court to create a presumption of negligence on the part of the defendant so as to require him to go forward with testimony to show that he was not legally at fault in crashing into the back of plaintiff's car? We agree with the circuit judge that the facts above stated created a presumption of negligence and not an inference of negligence and that, in the absence of an explanation from the defendant, a verdict should have been directed by the lower court in favor of the plaintiff. We think the court could take judicial notice of the fact that it was the duty of both the plaintiff and the defendant to stop at the intersecting street when a traffic light was showing red. In this day of heavy motor traffic all over the nation, the youngest or the most careless motorist knows that it is negligence to go through a red light. In addition, the rules of the road would require the defendant, as he approached the intersection, to have his car under control so that he would not drive into the rear-end of a motorist obeying traffic signals by waiting for the red light to turn green. If the defendant had a justifiable reason for not observing traffic rules, then it was his duty to go forward with the evidence to show that he was not negligent and thus, permit the case to go to a jury for the jury's determination on conflicting theories or facts.

* * *

The judgment is affirmed.

SHANNON, J., concurs.

GERALD, LYNN, ASSOCIATE JUDGE, dissents.

NOTES AND QUESTIONS

1. *"Real presumptions."* "[I]t must be kept in mind that the peculiar effect of a presumption 'of law' (that is, the real presumption) is merely to invoke a rule of law compelling the jury to reach the conclusion *in the absence of evidence to the contrary* from the opponent." 9 Wigmore, Evidence § 2491 (Chadbourn rev. 1981).

Under the above classic and widely accepted definition, the dubious distinction of being designated a presumption is denied to a rule of law which declares merely that a party's burden of producing evidence as to fact A is sufficiently met by proof of facts B and C without calling for the further consequence that the trier of fact *must* find A from B and C in the absence of contrary evidence. In light of the multiplicity and importance of rules of this latter sort, however, it would seem expedient to have a name for them. Most of the older decisions, and many recent ones, denominate these rules "presumptions of fact" as distinguished from "presumptions of law" (the latter being Wigmore's "real" presumptions). Somewhat in vogue more recently has been the terminology of Professor McCormick who urged that the term presumption should be considered a generic one, embracing both "permissive" and "mandatory" presumptions which "have in common the most important advantage that a presumption, however defined, could give, namely [that of enabling] the proponent to 'get to the jury.'" McCormick, Evidence § 308, at 640–641 (1st ed. 1954). Compare 2 McCormick, Evidence § 342 (7th ed. 2013).

2. *Res ipsa loquitur.* Should facts sufficient to invoke the doctrine of *res ipsa loquitur* be considered to raise a presumption, or merely a permissible inference? Though the question has been heatedly debated, it currently appears that a large majority of jurisdictions accord the doctrine only the latter effect.1 Dobbs, Hayden & Bublick, The Law of Torts § 170 (2d ed. 2012). Is *McNulty v. Cusack* inconsistent with this majority view? For a criticism of the *McNulty* decision on this basis, see Note, 13 U.Miami L.Rev. 236 (1958).

The Bases of Presumption

What considerations underlie the creation and recognition of presumptions? One of the better judicial statements on the subject is contained in the opinion in Watkins v. Prudential Ins. Co., 173 A. 644, 648 (Pa.1934):

> Presumptions arise as follows: They are either (1) a procedural expedient, or (2) a rule of proof production based upon the comparative availability of material evidence to the respective parties, or (3) a conclusion firmly based upon the generally known results of wide human experience, or (4) a combination of (1) and (3). The presumption as to the survivorship of husband and wife meeting death in a common disaster is a procedural expedient. It is not based upon extensive data arising from human experience. An unexplained absence for seven years raises the presumption of the death of the absentee upon the expiration of the last day of the period. This also is a procedural expedient—an arbitrary but necessary rule for the solution of problems arising from unexplained absences of human beings. An example of (2) is the rule requiring persons on trial for doing certain acts which are illegal if done without a license to produce evidence that they belong to the class privileged by license. See Com. v. Wenzel, 24 Pa.Super.Ct. 467. The following are examples of (3): (a) An envelope properly addressed and stamped will reach the addressee if the latter is alive; (b) a child born during the wedlock of its parents is legitimate; (c) a person who drives across a railroad crossing will show due care. If the driver is killed at such a crossing, the presumption that he showed due care shifts the burden of proof to the party who defends the action on the ground of the victim's want of care. (In this example, the presumption of the victim's due care is merely the

converse of the statement that the burden of proof rests on the asserter of the victim's negligence.) A presumption that a debt is paid after a lapse of a definite long period of time is both a procedural expedient (1) and a conclusion based on the results of wide human experience (3).

To the list of reasons for creating presumptions set forth by the Pennsylvania court, most authorities would make at least one addition, that of social policy.

> [N]otions, usually implicit rather than expressed, of social and economic policy incline the courts to favor one contention by giving it the benefit of a presumption, and correspondingly to handicap the disfavored adversary. A classic instance is the presumption of ownership from possession, which tends to favor the prior possessor and to make for the stability of estates.

2 McCormick, Evidence § 343 (7th ed. 2013). For a more elaborate list of considerations underlying the creation of various presumptions, see Morgan, Presumptions, 12 Wash.L.Rev. 255 (1937).

QUESTIONS

Upon which one or more of the reasons for raising presumptions did the court rely in recognizing a presumption in *McNulty v. Cusack*? Which, if any, of these considerations would you view as supporting the following commonly recognized presumptions? (1) The presumption that the driver of a motor vehicle is the agent of the owner, acting in the scope of his employment. See Malone v. Hanna, 156 So.2d 626 (Ala.1963). Compare Judson v. Bee Hive Auto Serv. Co., 297 P. 1050, 1052 (Or.1931). (2) The presumption that goods bailed in good condition and returned in damaged condition were damaged through the fault of the bailee. See Richmond Sand & Gravel Corp. v. Tidewater Constr. Corp., 170 F.2d 392 (4th Cir.1948). Compare Wyatt v. Baughman, 239 P.2d 193 (Utah 1951). (3) The presumption that a lost will has been revoked. See In re Givens' Estate, 119 N.W.2d 191 (Iowa 1963).

O'BRIEN V. EQUITABLE LIFE ASSUR. SOC'Y

United States Court of Appeals, Eighth Circuit, 1954.
212 F.2d 383.

COLLET, CIRCUIT JUDGE. This is an action to recover double indemnity insurance for the alleged accidental death of plaintiff's husband. From a directed verdict for the defendant insurance company at the close of all the evidence, plaintiff appeals. The sole question for review is whether plaintiff established a prima facie case warranting its submission to the jury. It is conceded that the law of Missouri is controlling.

The policy provided for the payment of $10,000 upon the death of the insured. That has been paid and is not in dispute. In addition, the policy provided for the payment of an additional $10,000 in the event of accidental death, with certain qualifications. Whether those qualifications, only one of which is now involved, constituted an integral part of the definition of coverage for accidental death, or were exceptions to coverage, is given considerable importance by the parties. The definition of coverage and the qualifications appear in the policy in the following language:

> "The Society agrees, subject to the provisions hereinafter stated, to increase the amount payable under said policy by a sum equal to the face amount thereof upon receipt of due proof, as herein required, that

> "(1) the death of the Insured resulted from bodily injuries caused directly and independently of all other causes by external, violent and purely accidental means,

* * *

> "(3) such death was not the result of or caused by * * * (d) committing or attempting to commit an assault or felony * * * "

The insured was shot and instantly killed by Robert Jackson on the evening of October 27, 1951, at the home of Virginia Jackson, his wife, from whom he was temporarily separated. There were no witnesses to the shooting and what transpired immediately theretofore except the Jacksons and the deceased. The Jacksons' testimony constitutes substantial but not clear, positive and unequivocal evidence that the insured was at the time of his death committing an assault or a felony, or both, and that that was the cause and reason for the shooting. The husband, Robert Jackson, testified that he heard an outcry from his father's home some 300 feet away, saw something flit by a window, and got his father's revolver, went to the house, found the insured in bed with his wife, and opened fire. Several shots were fired, one of them taking effect in the hips of Virginia Jackson. She substantiated his testimony and testified that she was forced into the bedroom and onto the bed but does not remember what happened after that until the first shot was fired. There was some uncertainty on the part of both Jacksons concerning the number of times they had been married to each other and divorced, but both were sure that at the time in question they were married. There is no conflict in the evidence on that point.

The plaintiff offered in evidence the policy, made proof of death by gunshot wounds inflicted by another, and rested. A motion for a directed verdict was made and denied. The defendant then offered the evidence heretofore referred to, which is uncontradicted and which, as heretofore stated, showed that death occurred while the insured was committing an assault or felony or both. Plaintiff then offered some evidence tending to create the inference that robbery might have been the motive for the shooting. Whether that evidence, together with the other evidence on plaintiff's behalf, was sufficient to make out a submissible case in plaintiff's favor will be alluded to later. At the close of all of the evidence the trial court sustained defendant's motion for a directed verdict.

As stated, this case is to be determined upon principles of law consonant with the law of Missouri. Before considering the legal principles which, in view of the facts, must govern the propriety or impropriety of the directed verdict, it is necessary to keep in mind those double indemnity provisions of the policy, heretofore quoted, which give rise to the instant litigation. It is plaintiff's contention that her burden of establishing a submissible, prima facie case of accidental death was satisfied upon the mere showing of the insurance agreement and the violent death of the insured at the hands of another. Plaintiff insists that defendant had the burden of proving its "affirmative defense" that the insured was engaged in the commission of a felony at the time of his death. Thus it is argued, not without logic, that plaintiff's prima facie case and defendant's affirmative defense should have been submitted to the trier of the facts.

It is fundamental that in cases involving double indemnity benefits the burden of proving accidental death rests firmly upon the plaintiff seeking recovery. * * *

Just what are the evidentiary demands at trial necessary to meet this initial and never shifting burden is obscured considerably by a broad procedural utilization of legal presumptions. To illustrate more graphically, it is said that the burden of proving accidental death rests unswervingly upon the plaintiff, yet, due to recognized human propensities, we will presume that there is so strong a love of life in the human breast that death by one's own hand or by invitation is lacking, in the absence of evidence to the contrary. Sellars v. John Hancock Mutual Life Ins. Co., Mo.App.1941, 149 S.W.2d 404. In this way a prima facie case of accidental death arises from the presumption against nonaccidental death, thereby satisfying plaintiff's burden of proof. Some courts have said that death by accident is not presumed, but merely follows, so to speak, from the presumption *against* suicide or death by invitation. Perringer v. Metropolitan Life Ins. Co., Mo.App.1951, 244 S.W.2d 607. But whether it is said an unexplained violent death will be presumed accidental, or, instead, a showing of violent death merely raises a presumption *against* suicide or invited injury, we think the difference is one without legal distinction. Suffice it to say, an unexplained death by violence is alone sufficient to make out a prima facie case of "accidental death", whether the presumption utilized is one in *favor* of death by accident or *against* death by suicide. Sellars v. John Hancock Mutual Life

Ins. Co., supra; cf. Perringer v. Metropolitan Life Ins. Co., supra. As stated in the Sellars case, 149 S.W.2d loc. cit. 405:

> " * * * where no more is shown than the fact of the insured's violent death without the benefit of any of the explanatory circumstances, then such fact, considered in the light of the presumption of love of life which obtains in the case of the normal individual, is so repugnant to the idea of death by intention or invitation as to afford the presumption that death was by accident or accidental means, and thereby satisfy the plaintiff's initial burden of proof upon such issue."

In effect, plaintiff argues that once this "prima facie" case is established, the burden thereafter rests with defendant to prove its affirmative defense on the excepted risk which, whatever the testimony, creates a question of fact submissible to the jury. In so arguing, plaintiff ignores the legal import of the procedural presumption utilized which, unlike the substantive presumption in a res ipsa loquitur case, is not indestructably immune from the effects of refutatory testimony. The presumption of accidental death, while accomplishing the function of evidence in so far as plaintiff's initial burden of going forward is concerned, nevertheless is not evidence of the fact presumed and is merely a rule of procedure or "rebuttable legal presumption". It casts upon defendant the burden of going forward with substantial evidence to the contrary which, if adduced, destroys the procedural presumption on which plaintiff had relied as an evidentiary substitute. As so strikingly quoted by Justice Lamm of the Missouri Supreme Court in Mackowik v. Kansas City, St. J. & C.B.R. Co., 1906, 196 Mo. 550, 94 S.W. 256, 262, " 'Presumptions * * * may be looked on as the bats of the law, flitting in the twilight, but disappearing in the sunshine of actual facts'." The significance of the procedural presumption relates then only to the burden of going forward with testimony, not to the burden of proof. Though the burden of going forward may frequently shift during the course of a trial, the burden of proof remains upon the plaintiff to establish his substantive case.

Where a plaintiff's "prima facie" case vitally depends upon a rebuttable presumption, which is destroyed, then, too, must the "prima facie" case collapse with the presumption, thereby placing upon plaintiff the burden of going forward with evidence sufficient to avoid a directed verdict. Once the presumption is destroyed it is no longer a question of plaintiff's prima facie case versus defendant's affirmative defense, but rather has plaintiff made out a continuing prima facie case at all. Where a rebuttable procedural presumption has been utilized, as in the instant case, at most plaintiff makes out but a "rebuttable" prima facie case which is procedurally but not substantively significant.

With this in mind, we can more easily understand plaintiff's contention that the burden is upon defendant to show facts negating accidental death heretofore presumed. The pitfall lies, however, in confusing this burden, which is one of going *forward* procedurally, with the underlying substantive burden of *proof* which lies constantly with the plaintiff throughout the course of trial. In a limited sense, the insured's commission of a felony or even suicide is always a risk excepted from accident coverage, in that it is incumbent upon defendant initially to bring the issue forth. But the burden is one dictated by the presumption against death from misconduct which, when removed by substantial testimony, shifts the burden of going forward back to plaintiff to establish by evidence what had formerly been presumed. This is entirely consistent with the underlying burden of proof cast upon plaintiff to establish recoverable accidental death within the meaning of the policy.

* * *

In the instant case appellee proffered the direct testimony of Robert and Virginia Jackson relating the manner of and circumstances surrounding the death of the insured. In view of the authorities cited herein, we are convinced that such testimony amply destroyed any presumption of "accidental death" theretofore arising from plaintiff's bare showing of death by violence. The only question remaining is whether the state of the evidence, when viewed in light of plaintiff's underlying burden of proof and absent presumptions, justified a directed verdict. The test to be used has been variously stated. In the Sellars case, the court held, 149 F.2d loc. cit. 406:

> "When contrary facts appear, the presumption [of accidental death] disappears; * * * if the plaintiff, in rebuttal, adduces countervailing evidence supporting the conclusion that death resulted from a cause within the coverage of the policy, then the ultimate question is one of fact to be determined by the jury as in the case of any other factual issue."

By the foregoing it is not meant that in an action of this kind *any* rebuttal testimony, however, feeble, will suffice to avoid a directed verdict on behalf of the defending insurance company. The "scintilla of evidence" doctrine is no longer the law of Missouri. Hardwick v. Kansas City Gas Co., 1944, 352 Mo. 986, 180 S.W.2d 670. To hold otherwise would be to ignore a plaintiff's burden to establish his case, no longer aided by presumption. Unless the plaintiff produces some substantial evidence negativing the excepted misconduct and thereby brings the death within the coverage of the policy, a directed verdict will be proper. Ray v. Mutual Life Ins. Co. of New York, Mo.App.1949, 218 S.W.2d 986.

In the instant case the only positive evidence proffered was that at the time of his death the insured was committing an assault or a felony.

It is only by inference and innuendo that plaintiff suggests that the insured may have been the victim of robbery and foul play. Although plaintiff testified that the insured had some $200 on his person the morning of the fatal day, it would be patently improper to assume that the absence of this money from his personal effects proves thievery claimed his life. To do so we would have to infer that not only did O'Brien have this money with him when he called at the Jackson residence many hours later, but we would have to infer further that theft of this purportedly missing money brought about this tragedy. It requires the citation of no authority that such an inference upon an inference is entitled to no evidentiary consideration. The fact, as testified to by plaintiff, that the insured's trousers were missing is of no substantial evidentiary significance in furthering plaintiff's burden of proving accidental death.

Viewing the circumstances surrounding the insured's death most favorably to plaintiff's hypothesis, we have at most inferences arising which are as consistent with a theory of death while in the commission of a felony as with death by accident. Though plaintiff's initial burden of going forward with the evidence was obviated by a procedural presumption of accidental death, this presumption was destroyed, by the positive, substantial testimony of the two Jacksons, thereby casting upon plaintiff the burden, *ab initio,* of going forward with evidence sufficient to sustain her unshifting and underlying burden of proof on the issue. With this in mind, plaintiff offers only the violent death of the insured from gunshot wounds received at the Jackson residence, and the absence of money, eyeglasses, and certain items of clothing from the personal effects of the insured. Can it be reasonably said that such facts, assuming them to be true, even approach to support plaintiff's burden of proof that the insured was not in the commission of an assault or felony? We think not. The inferences to be gleaned from such evidence are as consistent with defendant's theory of death (which is supported by positive testimony) as they are with plaintiff's. As this court said in New York Life Ins. Co. v. King, 93 F.2d 347, 353:

> " * * * evidence which is equally consistent with two hypotheses, under one of which a defendant is liable, and under the other of which it is not liable, supports neither hypothesis."

Cf., Christianson v. Metropolitan Life Ins. Co., Mo.App.1937, 102 S.W.2d 682; Stafford v. New York Life Ins. Co., Mo.App.1952, 248 S.W.2d 76. Consequently we are convinced the trial court below properly directed a verdict for the defendant.

In view of the foregoing considerations and their decisive effect upon the propriety of the trial court's action, it is unnecessary to consider other grounds advanced by defendant in support of the judgment.

Judgment affirmed.

NOTES AND QUESTIONS

1. *The Thayer doctrine.* Of the many difficult questions concerning presumptions, perhaps none has proven so troublesome as the question of what, if any, continuing effect a presumption should be given once evidence contrary to the presumption has been introduced. The view taken by the court in the principal case, i.e., that a presumption once countered disappears like a "bat of the twilight," is commonly called the Thayer or Thayer–Wigmore doctrine of presumptions. It is today applied by many, perhaps a majority, of the American courts. Annot., 5 A.L.R.3d 19.

2. *Disappearing presumptions.* What, properly, should be understood from the statement that a presumption, once met by counter evidence, disappears? What was the consequence of the disappearance of the presumption involved in *O'Brien v. Equitable Life Assur. Soc.*? Should the same consequence flow whenever a presumption is met by counter evidence and irrespective of what particular presumption is involved? With the principal case, compare Schlichting v. Schlichting, 112 N.W.2d 149, 155–56 (Wis.1961), where the court stated:

> In the instant case, a presumption of undue influence arose from the part which John played in the transaction, the confidential relationship in which John stood to his father, and the advanced age of the father. Christian's testimony * * * does have a tendency to rebut the presumption. However, the introduction of such evidence did not remove from the case the inference upon which such presumption was grounded. Therefore, plaintiff father and his conservator were not thereby reduced to the position where, in order to prevail and set aside the conveyance, they were required to adduce further proof of the four constituent elements of undue influence. Without offering further evidence, they were entitled to judgment if the trial court, in weighing the evidence adduced which tended to negative undue influence against the inference of undue influence arising by reason of the presumption, could reasonably conclude that the weight of the evidence was in favor of a finding of undue influence. * * *

> We have no hesitancy in upholding the trial court's finding that the conveyance from Herman to Christian was the result of undue influence exercised by John. The court could reasonably conclude that the evidence adduced to rebut the presumption was too weak to overcome the inference embodied in the presumption.

3. *Life beyond the presumption.* It has been urged that the Thayer doctrine of presumptions, correctly applied, rarely necessitates a result such as that reached in the *O'Brien* case. See Laughlin, In Support of the Thayer Theory of Presumptions, 52 Mich.L.Rev. 195 (1953). Would this thesis seem to be supported by the following statement: "Presumptions in the law are

almost invariably crystallized inferences of fact"? In re Estate of Wood, 132 N.W.2d 35, 42 (Mich.1965). See also Widmayer v. Leonard, 373 N.W.2d 538 (Mich.1985) (*Wood* abandoned as to its holding that the trier of fact must be instructed as to the existence of a presumption; however, court notes that "[a]lmost all presumptions are made up of permissible inferences").

Sample Rules Dealing With the Effect of Presumptions

Model Code of Evidence, Rule 704 (1942). Effect of Presumptions.

(1) * * * when the basic fact of a presumption has been established in an action, the existence of the presumed fact must be assumed unless and until evidence has been introduced which would support a finding of its nonexistence or the basic fact of an inconsistent presumption has been established.

(2) * * * when the basic fact of a presumption has been established in an action and evidence has been introduced which would support a finding of the nonexistence of the presumed fact or the basic fact of an inconsistent presumption has been established, the existence or nonexistence of the presumed fact is to be determined exactly as if no presumption had ever been applicable in the action.

Uniform Rule of Evidence 14 (1953). Effect of Presumptions.

* * * (a) if the facts from which the presumption is derived have any probative value as evidence of the existence of the presumed fact, the presumption continues to exist and the burden of establishing the non-existence of the presumed fact is upon the party against whom the presumption operates, (b) if the facts from which the presumption arises have no probative value as evidence of the presumed fact, the presumption does not exist when evidence is introduced which would support a finding of the non-existence of the presumed fact, and the fact which would otherwise be presumed shall be determined from the evidence exactly as if no presumption was or had ever been involved.

Federal Rule of Evidence 301. Presumptions in General in Civil Actions and Proceedings.

In a civil case, unless a federal statute or these rules provide otherwise, the party against whom a presumption is directed has the burden of producing evidence to rebut the presumption. But this rule does not shift the burden of persuasion, which remains on the party who had it originally.

Uniform Rule of Evidence 302(a) (1999). Effect of Presumptions in Civil Cases.

* * * In a civil action of proceeding, unless otherwise provided by statute, judicial decision, or these rules, a presumption imposes on the

party against whom it is directed the burden of proving that the nonexistence of the presumed fact is more probable than its existence.

California Evidence Code

§ 603. Presumption affecting the burden of producing evidence defined.

A presumption affecting the burden of producing evidence is a presumption established to implement no public policy other than to facilitate the determination of the particular action in which the presumption is applied.

§ 604. Effect of presumption affecting burden of producing evidence.

The effect of a presumption affecting the burden of producing evidence is to require the trier of fact to assume the existence of the presumed fact unless and until evidence is introduced which would support a finding of its nonexistence, in which case the trier of fact shall determine the existence or nonexistence of the presumed fact from the evidence and without regard to the presumption. Nothing in this section shall be construed to prevent the drawing of any inference that may be appropriate.

§ 605. Presumption affecting the burden of proof defined.

A presumption affecting the burden of proof is a presumption established to implement some public policy other than to facilitate the determination of the particular action in which the presumption is applied, such as the policy in favor of establishment of a parent and child relationship, the validity of marriage, the stability of titles to property, or the security of those who entrust themselves or their property to the administration of others.

§ 606. Effect of presumption affecting burden of proof.

The effect of a presumption affecting the burden of proof is to impose upon the party against whom it operates the burden of proof as to the nonexistence of the presumed fact.

North Carolina Rule of Evidence 301(a). Presumptions in General in Civil Actions and Proceedings.

* * * In all civil actions and proceedings when not otherwise provided for by statute, by judicial decision, or by these rules, a presumption imposes on the party against whom it is directed the burden of going forward with evidence to rebut or meet the presumption, but does not shift to such party the burden of proof in the sense of the risk of nonpersuasion, which remains throughout the trial upon the party on whom it was originally cast. The burden of going forward is satisfied by the introduction of evidence sufficient to permit reasonable minds to

conclude that the presumed fact does not exist. If the party against whom a presumption operates fails to meet the burden of producing evidence, the presumed fact shall be deemed proved, and the court shall instruct the jury accordingly. When the burden of producing evidence to meet a presumption is satisfied, the court must instruct the jury that it may, but is not required to, infer the existence of the presumed fact from the proved fact.

NOTES AND QUESTIONS

1. *The academic debate.* The above samples illustrate some of the many approaches to the question of the effect of presumptions. The debate has been a long and heated one in academic circles. Professor Edmund M. Morgan had long been a critic of the Thayer view of presumptions when he was appointed Reporter for the American Law Institute's (ALI) Model Code of Evidence. As Reporter, Professor Morgan to a limited extent incorporated his own views on presumptions into a draft rule submitted for the Institute's consideration at its 1941 meeting. The ALI rejected his views and instead adopted the rule set forth above. Professor Morgan was later successful in having his views incorporated into the Uniform Rules of Evidence promulgated in 1953 by the Commissioners on Uniform State Laws. In 1954, the ALI withdrew its endorsement of the Model Code and recommended adoption of the Uniform Rules of Evidence.

The rule proposed by Professor Morgan to the American Law Institute and ultimately adopted by the drafters of the Uniform Rules distinguished between presumptions the basic facts of which have probative value as evidence of the presumed fact and presumptions the basic facts of which have no such probative value. This distinction was thought by Professor Morgan to be necessitated by constitutional considerations deriving from Western & Atlantic R.R. v. Henderson, 279 U.S. 639 (1929). See ALI, Model Code of Evidence, Foreword by Edmund M. Morgan 69 (1942). For additional interpretations of the *Henderson* decision, see Keeton, Statutory Presumptions—Their Constitutionality and Effect, 10 Tex.L.Rev. 34 (1931); Note, Constitutionality of Rebuttable Statutory Presumptions, 55 Colum.L.Rev. 527 (1955). The draftsmen of recent codifications of Evidence law have concluded that the *Henderson* case would not today impose any restriction upon implementation of the Morgan treatment of presumptions in civil cases. See Fed.R.Evid. 301 advisory committee's note, 56 F.R.D. 183, 209 (1972); Report of the New Jersey Supreme Court Committee on Evidence 50 (1963). See also 2 McCormick, Evidence § 345 (7th ed. 2013). Constitutional limitations on the creation and effect of presumptions clearly continue to persist in the criminal area. See *County Court of Ulster County v. Allen*, set forth later in this chapter.

Proposed Federal Rule 301 as promulgated by the Supreme Court followed Morgan and the Uniform Rule approach for all presumptions, but a Thayer rule was substituted by the Congress and became Rule 301 set forth above. In 1975, however, the Uniform Commissioners adopted the Court's Morgan rule. This adoption was reaffirmed by the Commissioners in their 1999 amendments.

While rules on presumptions are classifiable as Thayer or Morgan depending upon whether or not they operate upon the burden of persuasion, it should be noted that each generic rule comes in several variants. For an exhaustive analysis and comparison of the Thayer and Morgan rules and their respective subspecies, see Mueller, Instructing the Jury Upon Presumptions in Civil Cases: Comparing Federal Rule 301 with Uniform Rule 301, 12 Land & W.L.Rev. 219 (1977). For an assessment of which type of Thayer rule is embodied in Rule 301, see Louisell, Construing Rule 301: Instructing the Jury on Presumptions in Civil Actions and Proceedings, 63 Va.L.Rev. 281 (1977). A general treatment of presumptions is Ladd, Presumptions in Civil Cases, 1977 Ariz.St.L.J. 275.

The states are divided as to whether they adopt the Federal Rules approach allocating only the burden of producing evidence to the party against whom the presumption is directed or the Uniform Rules approach allocating the burden of persuasion to that party. Compare Colo.R.Evid. 301 (burden of producing evidence allocated), with Wis.Stat.Ann. 903.01 (burden of persuasion allocated). As set forth above, California gives a different effect to different kinds of presumptions. Compare the California approach to that of the original Uniform Rules of Evidence. Isn't the approach the exact opposite? Which approach better reflects the policy behind presumptions?

2. *Elimination of the term "presumption."* Some authors have argued for elimination of the term "presumption." One has called for the replacement of the functions which it serves with direct allocations of the burdens of proof and by judicial comment describing the logical implications of certain facts. Allen, Presumptions, Inferences and Burden of Proof in Federal Civil Actions—An Anatomy of Unnecessary Ambiguities and a Proposal for Reform, 76 Nw.U.L.Rev. 892 (1982); Allen, Presumptions in Civil Actions Reconsidered, 66 Iowa L.Rev. 843 (1981). See also Cleary, Presuming and Pleading: An Essay on Juristic Immaturity, 12 Stan.L.Rev. 5 (1959). See discussion in 2 McCormick, Evidence § 344 (7th ed. 2013).

3. *Statutory presumptions.* In addition to the classic debate directed primarily to common law presumptions, there has been considerable controversy over legislative intent, especially congressional intent, in dealing with statutory presumptions. The public policy debate has raged with special fervor in the field of employment discrimination. See Texas Dep't of Community Affairs v. Burdine, 450 U.S. 248 (1981); St. Mary's Honor Ctr. v. Hicks, 509 U.S. 502 (1993); Note, Developments in the Law—Employment Discrimination, 109 Harv.L.Rev. 1579 (1996).

4. *Use of the term "presumption" in jury instructions.* Judge Learned Hand wrote, in Alpine Forwarding Co. v. Pennsylvania R.R., 60 F.2d 734, 736 (2d Cir.1932), that "if the trial is properly conducted the presumption will not be mentioned [to the jury] at all." What, if anything, is objectionable in the

contrary view taken by some courts that a presumption constitutes "evidence" which the jury may be instructed to weigh against other countervailing evidence? Do any difficulties with this approach appear if the presumption involved is not a pure probability presumption but is based, wholly or partially, upon considerations of social policy or procedural convenience? See McBaine, Presumptions, Are They Evidence?, 26 Cal.L.Rev. 519 (1938). Some states have specifically provided for the jury to be told something about the presumption. The Alaska rule is similar to the North Carolina rule set forth above but at the same time prohibits the judge from using the word presumption. See Alaska R.Evid. 301(a). The next principal case raises additional questions with regard to instructions on presumptions.

5. *The Shakespeare authorship debate.* For an interesting application of the law of burdens of proof and presumptions to the debate over who wrote the works attributed to William Shakespeare, see Causey, Burden of Proof and Presumptions in the Shakespeare Authorship Debate, 72 Tenn.L.Rev. 93 (2004).

STATE OF MARYLAND V. BALTIMORE TRANSIT CO.
United States Court of Appeals, Fourth Circuit, 1964.
329 F.2d 738.

J. SPENCER BELL, CIRCUIT JUDGE. The plaintiffs' intestate was killed at a street corner in the city of Baltimore when struck by a bus owned by the defendant Transit Company and driven by the individual defendant. Judgment was entered for the defendants upon a general verdict. Plaintiffs allege that the court erred in charging the jury as follows:

> "I instruct you that ordinarily, a decedent is presumed to have exercised ordinary care for his own safety in accordance with the natural instinct of human beings to guard against danger, but where as here, evidence has been offered to show that the decedent failed to exercise ordinary care in a number of respects, you shall consider the proof which has been offered and determine whether you are persuaded by a preponderance of the evidence that he failed to exercise ordinary care, and you are not to reply upon the presumption."

Both parties to this appeal concede, and we agree, that the federal courts are bound in diversity cases by the applicable state rules with respect to the effect to be given to presumptions, "since the effect accorded these presumptions may substantially affect the rights of the parties and there is nothing in the Federal Rules to the contrary." 5 Moore's Federal Practice § 43.08. The plaintiffs had submitted a written request for an instruction to the jury that they might consider the presumption of due care in connection with the other evidence. The court rejected the request and instructed the jury as above set out. In this we find fatal error.

The principal Maryland case on this point is Grier v. Rosenberg, 213 Md. 248, 131 A.2d 737 (1957). In that case the plaintiff, a passenger, was injured by the sudden stopping of the bus. She sued the bus company, the bus driver, and one Rosenberg, who was the owner of an automobile which, the bus driver testified, cut sharply across his path and caused him to come to a sudden stop. The jury rendered a verdict for all three defendants. The plaintiff appealed from a judgment for the car owner, Rosenberg. The Court of Appeals of Maryland reversed the judgment and remanded the case for a new trial. In doing so the court pointed out that the plaintiff had offered evidence from which the jury could find ownership of the car in the defendant Rosenberg. She had asked for an instruction that from this evidence, if believed, a presumption arose that the car was being driven by the owner or by the owner's agent about the owner's business. The trial court refused to give the instruction because the defendant had offered evidence which conflicted with the presumption. The appellate court held failure to give the instruction was fatal. In a careful review of the Maryland decisions and authorities in the field of Evidence, Judge Prescott said that the presumption prevails and the jury should have been so instructed despite the fact that countervailing evidence was adduced upon the disputed presumption. The court said:

> "In cases of this nature, after the plaintiff has offered proof of the ownership of the automobile in the defendant, if the defendant does not offer any evidence on the issue of agency, the Court should instruct the jury that if they find as a fact that the defendant owned the car, they must find that he is responsible for the negligence (if any) of the driver. If the defendant does present evidence to show that the alleged driver was engaged on business or a purpose of his own, it may be so slight that the Court will rule it is insufficient to be considered by the jury in rebuttal of the presumption, in which case the Court should grant the same instruction it would have granted if the defendant had offered no evidence on the issue. The evidence may be so conclusive that it shifts the burden or duty of going forward with the evidence back to the plaintiff, in which event the defendant would be entitled to a directed verdict, if the plaintiff does not produce evidence in reply, unless there is already evidence in the case tending to contradict defendant's evidence. Erdman v. Horkheimer & Co., supra, 169 Md. [204] 207, 181 A. 221; Fowser Fast Freight v. Simmont, supra, 196 Md. [584] 588, 78 A.2d 178. The evidence, however, may fall between the two categories mentioned above, in which event the issue of agency should be submitted to the jury. Cf. 3 Md.Law Rev. 287, 288. It would be difficult, if not impossible, to lay down a rule, that would apply in all cases, as to when the evidence is

so slight that it is insufficient to be considered by the jury in rebuttal of the presumption of agency, or so conclusive as to require a directed verdict for the defendant. These matters must depend upon, and be decided by, the facts developed in each individual case."

The defendant in this appeal argues that Grier v. Rosenberg is not applicable because the evidence there offered in rebuttal of the presumption was so slight that the trial court would have been justified in holding that it was insufficient to be submitted to the jury in the face of the presumption, but such was not the holding of the court. Indeed, the appellant in the Grier case made the point in an effort to secure a reversal instead of a remand for a new trial, but the argument was rejected. The court expressly held that the conflicting evidence was enough to take the case to the jury.

The defendant here also argues that the presumption in Grier v. Rosenberg is different from the presumption of due care here considered and thus that case may not be taken as a precedent. With this argument we must also disagree, because first, we can find no case in Maryland which makes any such distinction and second, in reaching its decision the court reviewed and cited cases involving the presumption of due care in negligence cases in support of its opinion.

Our dissenting Brother similarly misinterprets Grier v. Rosenberg and would unduly restrict its rule. We perceive no basis in law or in logic for the suggested distinction; but more importantly, Judge Prescott, speaking for the Maryland Court, explicitly pointed out that the precedents in that State recognize no basis for any distinction between the presumption that the decedent exercised due care for his self-preservation and the presumption of agency arising from the fact of ownership. And this observation of Judge Prescott is immediately followed by the very sensible question, "[I]ndeed, if the instruction be not granted, how is the jury to know of the presumption?"

* * *

We are * * * aware that in many states the rule as to presumptions is to the contrary—that is, that the presumption survives only until conflicting evidence is offered. This is the rule suggested in the American Law Institute's Model Code of Evidence, Rule 704. It is the rule attributed to Thayer and suggested by Wigmore. But we are bound by the law of Maryland, and we might add that the Maryland rule is strongly supported by such eminent authorities as McCormick, Evidence §§ 316, 317 (1954), and by the writings of Professor Morgan, who, contrary to his expressed opinions, finally acceded [sic] to the wishes of the committee in drafting the Model Code.

* * *

We are unable to acquiesce in the final suggestion in our colleague's dissenting opinion, that the presumption in Maryland that the decedent acted with due care stands on a parity with the presumption that the defendant was free from negligence and that therefore the district court should tell the jury at the retrial that the presumption as to the disposition to act in self-preservation applies equally to the defendant's driver. The comment is then added that the result would be a radical distortion, and perversion. This comment would indeed be true, if the trial judge were to permit such a confusing double instruction, linking and treating as equal two entirely disparate and unequal ideas. The presumption with which we are concerned in this case may be invoked only where the injured person is unavailable because of the injuries suffered or because of death. Such incapacity is the just reason for the presumption; the premise upon which the presumption rests is lacking in the situation of this defendant.

* * *

Reversed and remanded.

HAYNSWORTH, CIRCUIT JUDGE (dissenting).

I am unpersuaded that Maryland would attribute any such evidentiary effect to the presumption as the majority conclude on the basis of an opinion of the Maryland Court of Appeals dealing with a different presumption in a very dissimilar context.

* * *

The question of the office of the presumption arises in this case under the following circumstances. Witnesses for the plaintiff testified that her decedent was crossing a street in downtown Baltimore at an intersection and in a marked pedestrian crosswalk, with the invitation and the protection of an electric "walk" signal, when he was struck by the bus. Witnesses for the defendant, however, testified that the decedent undertook to cross the street some distance from the intersection and the pedestrian crosswalk and without the invitation or protection of an electric signal. The evidence was sharply conflicting, but there was no dearth of it. Resolution by the jury of the factual question on the contributory negligence issue depended simply upon whether the jurors believed the one set of witnesses or the other. No presumption artificially endowed with evidentiary weight was needful or useful to them in resolving the simple issue of credibility which was presented to them.

The District Court, of course, instructed the jury that the defendant had the burden of proving by a preponderance of the evidence that the decedent was contributorily negligent. On this question of fact, the Court clearly and unequivocally placed the burden of persuasion upon the defendant. If the jury, under its instructions, was unable to decide the issue of credibility upon which its finding of the decedent's conduct depended, if its mind was in equipoise, it was required to find for the plaintiff. If, then, my brothers are correct that under the Maryland law the jury should have been allowed to consider as evidence the presumption of due care, then the office of the presumption was not merely to place upon the defense the burden of producing evidence sufficient to support a finding inconsistent with the presumed fact; it was not merely to place upon the defendant the burden of persuasion on the factual question underlying the contributory negligence issue; it is to require that the defendant carry the burden of persuasion by a measure of proof greater than a mere preponderance of the evidence. How much greater the burden placed upon the defense to prove its contention beyond a preponderance of evidence, the majority does not specify, but it would invite them to apply a standard of proof akin to that applicable in criminal cases, that they must be persuaded beyond all reasonable doubt, for jurors are not unaware of the existence of that standard.

Having in mind the circumstances in which the question now arises and the practical effect of the instruction which my brothers now require, it is appropriate to turn to Grier v. Rosenberg upon which my brothers' hats are hung.

* * *

Maryland's Court of Appeals held in Grier that the jury should have been instructed that a presumption that Rosenberg, or one of his authorized employees, was driving the car arose out of proof of his ownership of it which they might consider along with the defendant's testimony indicating that it was not.

In Grier, of course, unlike the present case, there was a dearth of proof. Beyond proof of the basic fact of Rosenberg's ownership of the offending vehicle, the plaintiff had no source of reliable information. The ultimate fact was peculiarly within the knowledge of her adversary, and the kind of general disclaimer he entered was not susceptible to direct contradiction. There was thus a compelling need for some instruction to inform the jury that it need not accept Rosenberg's self-serving testimony as conclusive of the plaintiff's rights.

The two presumptions are in sharp contrast. That with which the court was concerned in Grier arose out of proof of basic, evidentiary facts which were logically related to it. In the absence of some instruction, there was grave danger that the jury would not appreciate the evidentiary value of the basic, proven facts. The presumption of due care, however, is not dependent upon proof of any basic fact or facts. There is in this case no circumstantial evidence, the utility of which might go unnoticed by the jury in the absence of some instruction which would draw their attention to it.

Grier's formulation may be offensive to Thayerian purists, but clearly the circumstances there called for some instruction which would inform the jurors that they were not bound to accept Rosenberg's self-serving testimony. The jury could have been told that a permissible inference that Rosenberg, or his authorized servant, was driving the offending automobile might be drawn from proof of his ownership of it, and that it was for the jury to determine, after consideration of Rosenberg's denials, whether or not his automobile at the time was being driven by him or one of his employees engaged in Rosenberg's business. An instruction in terms of the presumption would have no other practical effect.

Thus in Grier, reference to the presumption of the identity and authority of the driver arising out of proof of ownership of the vehicle did not place upon Rosenberg a greater burden of persuasion than proof by a preponderance of the evidence. * * *

That a court holds under certain circumstances that a jury should be informed of the existence of a particular presumption, is far from persuasive authority that a different presumption having a wholly different relationship to the basic fact out of which it arises should be mentioned to a jury under different circumstances and with wholly different consequences. Indeed, it is trite now to repeat what everyone addressing himself to the subject has said that so much of the confusion over presumptions springs from failure to distinguish between different presumptions and the different situations out of which the problems regarding their use arise.

The occasion seems inappropriate for entry upon the controversy over the relative merits of any particular theory about the employment of presumptions and their offices. Since my brothers read Grier as taking Maryland out of the main stream of the prevailing current of thought, I may briefly refer to those authorities which my brothers adroitly, but it seems to me inexactly, align on one side or the other, for I can give Grier no such reading.

Thayer thought that presumptions of the sort with which the Maryland Court was concerned in Grier should have no other office than to shift the burden of producing enough evidence to support a finding inconsistent with the fact sought to be presumed. When such evidence comes into the case, the presumption disappears. This is the theory adopted by the American Law Institute's Model Code of Evidence in Rule 704.

Professor Edmund Morgan, when he first began to write about presumptions, expounded a complicated theory which would attribute to some presumptions a larger effect, but he, himself, withdrew from that suggestion long before he began to work as Reporter for the American Law Institute in the formulation of the Model Code of Evidence. When he approached that task, he was firmly of the view that such a presumption should not only shift the burden of production of evidence but should fix the ultimate burden of persuasion. He thought it should have no other office. * * * As we have indicated, the Court in this case clearly placed the burden of persuasion upon the defendant, which is all that Professor Morgan would require. Even his earliest writings ascribed no such undefined and unbounded evidentiary effect to presumptions as the majority would attribute to this one.

Wigmore, in general, supports the Thayerian view, but he clearly recognizes that there are times and circumstances calling for mention to a jury of a presumption, though he would not have that word employed by the court. In the circumstances of Grier v. Rosenberg, Wigmore advocates an instruction to the jury that it is bound by no rule of law in deciding the issue, but it may give special weight, in its discretion, to the fact that in the course of experience automobiles not shown to have been stolen are usually driven by their owners or their authorized servants. This is plainly stated in ¶ 21 under Remedies in § 2498a.[3]

I find in McCormick on Evidence nothing which lends support to what the majority does here. In §§ 316 and 317, to which the majority opinion refers, Professor McCormick is principally concerned with the preservation of the practical utility of circumstantial evidence in the face of inconsistent evidence, however incredible, going directly to the ultimate fact and the mechanics of telling the jury how to resolve the issue when the basic facts upon which the presumption rests are in dispute. In the first mentioned aspect of the problem he is dealing with the Grier v. Rosenberg situation. * * * McCormick may be searched in vain for any hint that a presumption may be used to place a heavier, undefined burden of persuasion on the presumption's opponent, or that a presumption having no evidentiary basis may be given evidentiary value.

* * * What the Maryland Court of Appeals did in Grier v. Rosenberg, and all that it did, was to leave in the case a permissible inference inconsistent with the defendant's weak, self-serving denial of the ultimate fact. If, in the courts of a state whose trial judges are not allowed to comment upon the evidence, this must be done in terms of a presumption rather than in terms of a permissible inference, the effect is the same.

Far from being a departure from the current course of thought about presumptions, Grier v. Rosenberg is a specific application of the affirmatively expressed teachings of Wigmore. That decision is no premise for a conclusion that it is a rejection of what it embraces. What my brothers do is certainly a rejection of Wigmore's theory,[4] as they

---

[3]   IX Wigmore on Evidence, 3d ed., pages 340–341. See, also, ¶ 41 on page 343 and the illuminating comments of others on pages 348–350.

[4]   The presumption of due care, as we have noted, is not dependent upon proof of any basic fact or facts. If it be given no substantive, evidentiary value, it leaves no base of proven facts

recognize, but Grier v. Rosenberg, the platform upon which they stand, was not.

* * *

Finally, it may be observed that in Maryland the presumption that the decedent acted with due care for his own self-protection is no stronger and stands on no higher basis than the presumption that the driver of the bus that killed him acted with due care for the safety of pedestrians and others using the streets. Indeed, Maryland's Court of Appeals has spoken of the two presumptions in the same breath.[5] If, therefore, upon a new trial, the District Court is to be required to inform the jury of the one and permit it to weigh it as evidence, surely it must inform the jury of the other and permit it to weigh that one as evidence, too. The result will be a radical distortion and perversion of the burden of persuasion, but if the burden of persuasion resting on the defendant on the contributory negligence question is to be enlarged to confusing proportions, it cannot logically or fairly be said that the burden of persuasion resting upon the plaintiff as to the primary negligence question is not similarly enlarged to undefined proportions by the identical presumption of due care.

* * *

I thus do not understand that Maryland has held, or even suggested, that the presumption of due care is to be given evidentiary effect if the actor is dead, but not if alive. Though, here, the plaintiff's decedent is unavailable as a witness while the defendant's bus driver presumably is available. I do not think those circumstances warrant disparate treatment of the concomitant presumptions.

Unconvinced that Maryland's Court of Appeals would apply to the presumption of due care the undefined evidentiary weight attributed to it by my brothers, I respectfully dissent.

NOTES AND QUESTIONS

1. *The Maryland aftermath.* In 1994, Maryland sought to codify the approach to presumptions taken in Grier v. Rosenberg, 131 A.2d 737 (Md. 1957), the case upon which the majority in the principal case relies, by enacting Rule of Evidence 5–301. See Note, Court of Appeals Standing Committee on Practice and Procedure to Rule 5–301. The rule provides, with regard to all presumptions that shift the burden of going forward: "If the party introduces evidence tending to disprove the presumed fact, the

---

from which an inference of due care might conceivably be drawn. The presumption is wholly unlike those which Wigmore and McCormick think require some instruction to the jury in some situations, and the difference is critical. We have here no problem of preservation of the practical utility of circumstantial evidence; the jury was here called upon only to resolve, on conflicting, direct evidence, a simple question of credibility.

[5] P.W. & B.R.R. Co. v. Stebbing, 62 Md. 504 (1884); State, for Use of Chenoweth v. Baltimore Contracting Co., 177 Md. 1, 6 A.2d 625 (1939).

presumption will retain the effect of creating a question to be decided by the trier of fact unless the court concludes that such evidence is legally insufficient or is so conclusive that it rebuts the presumption as a matter of law." The Rule has not been construed as mandating an instruction with regard to the presumption of due care in a situation like that in the *Baltimore Transit Co.* case. Indeed the question of whether to instruct or not is more complex than ever. See McQuay v. Schertle, 730 A.2d 714 (Md.Ct.Spec.App.1999) (trial judge had discretion not to instruct the jury on decedent's due care where there was eyewitness testimony about the decedent's conduct immediately before the accident).

Washington, another jurisdiction in which contributory negligence is an affirmative defense, finally abandoned the giving of the presumption instruction discussed in the principal case. For thoughtful analysis and discussion, see Falknor, Notes on Presumptions, 15Wash.L.Rev. 71 (1940), and Comment, Presumption of Due Care by Decedent: An Anomaly Destroyed, 29 Wash.L.Rev. 79 (1954) in Selected Writings on Evidence and Trial 1020, 1032 (Fryer ed. 1957).

2. *One rule for all presumptions?* On what basis does Judge Haynsworth, dissenting in the principal case, refuse to view *Grier v. Rosenberg* as controlling authority? In connection with Judge Haynsworth's discussion consider the following statement: "The theoretically sound view, therefore is that 'the procedural effect of each presumption should depend upon the reasons which induced the courts to create or enforce it, [but it] has met with little favor, principally because of the practical difficulties of applying it at the trial.'" Gausewitz, Presumptions in a One Rule World, 5 Vand.L.Rev. 324, 330 (1952). See also Broun, The Unfulfillable Promise of One Rule for All Presumptions, 62 N.C.L.Rev. 697 (1984); Hjelmaas, Stepping Back from the Thicket: A Proposal for the Treatment of Rebuttable Presumptions and Inferences, 42 Drake L.Rev. 427 (1993). Note that the existence of Federal 301 has not prevented the federal courts from giving some presumptions stronger effects where so desired. See, e.g., Fazio v. Heckler, 760 F.2d 187 (8th Cir.1985) (Social Security Act); ACS Hospital Systems, Inc. v. Montefiore Hosp., 732 F.2d 1572 (Fed.Cir.1984) (validity of a patent). What practical difficulties might be involved in the attempt to attach varying procedural effects to different presumptions depending upon the reasons for their creation? See Maguire, Evidence, Common Sense and Common Law 188 (1947). If these difficulties are critical [and at least one court has intimated that they are not, see O'Dea v. Amodeo, 170 A. 486 (Conn.1934)], are they of such a nature as to be obviated by a legislative rather than a judicial attack on the problem?

3. *Conflicting presumptions.* It will sometimes occur that each of two adverse contentions as to the same fact is supported by a different presumption, raising the problem of what are generally called "conflicting presumptions." Under this definition would it be improper to refer to the two presumptions arguably applicable in the principal case as "conflicting"? How

should a conflict of presumptions, when one exists, be resolved? See Turro v. Turro, 120 A.2d 52 (N.J.Super.Ct.App.Div.1956).

4. The court's decision in the principal case to follow Maryland law with regard to the effect to be given to presumptions is consistent with current law. See Federal Rule 302.

COUNTY COURT OF ULSTER COUNTY v. ALLEN

Supreme Court of the United States, 1979.
442 U.S. 140.

MR. JUSTICE STEVENS delivered the opinion of the Court.

A New York statute provides that, with certain exceptions, the presence of a firearm in an automobile is presumptive evidence of its illegal possession by all persons then occupying the vehicle. The United States Court of Appeals for the Second Circuit held that respondents may challenge the constitutionality of this statute in a federal habeas corpus proceeding and that the statute is "unconstitutional on its face." * * * We granted certiorari to review these holdings and also to consider whether the statute is constitutional in its application to respondents. * * *

Four persons, three adult males (respondents) and a 16–year–old girl (Jane Doe, who is not a respondent here), were jointly tried on charges that they possessed two loaded handguns, a loaded machinegun, and over a pound of heroin found in a Chevrolet in which they were riding when it was stopped for speeding on the New York Thruway shortly after noon on March 28, 1973. The two large-caliber handguns, which together with their ammunition weighed approximately six pounds, were seen through the window of the car by the investigating police officer. They were positioned crosswise in an open handbag on either the front floor or the front seat of the car on the passenger side where Jane Doe was sitting. Jane Doe admitted that the handbag was hers. The machinegun and the heroin were discovered in the trunk after the police pried it open. The car had been borrowed from the driver's brother earlier that day; the key to the trunk could not be found in the car or on the person of any of its occupants, although there was testimony that two of the occupants had placed something in the trunk before embarking in the borrowed car. The jury convicted all four of possession of the handguns and acquitted them of possession of the contents of the trunk.

Counsel for all four defendants objected to the introduction into evidence of the two handguns, the machinegun, and the drugs, arguing that the State had not adequately demonstrated a connection between their clients and the contraband. The trial court overruled the objection, relying on the presumption of possession created by the New York statute. * * * Because that presumption does not apply if a weapon is found "upon the person" of one of the occupants of the car, * * * the three male defendants also moved to dismiss the charges relating to the handguns on the ground that the guns were found on the person of Jane Doe. Respondents made this motion both at the close of the prosecution's case and at the close of all evidence. The trial judge twice denied it, concluding that the applicability of the "on the person" exception was a question of fact for the jury. * * *

At the close of the trial, the judge instructed the jurors that they were entitled to infer possession from the defendants' presence in the car. He did not make any reference to the "upon the person" exception in his explanation of the statutory presumption, nor did any of the defendants object to this omission or request alternative or additional instructions on the subject.

Defendants filed a post-trial motion in which they challenged the constitutionality of the New York statute as applied in this case. The challenge was made in support of their argument that the evidence, apart from the presumption, was insufficient to sustain the convictions. The motion was denied, * * * and the convictions were affirmed by the Appellate Division without opinion. * * *

The New York Court of Appeals also affirmed. It rejected the argument that as a matter of law the guns were on Jane Doe's person because they were in her pocketbook. Although the court recognized that in some circumstances the evidence could only lead to the conclusion that the weapons were in one person's sole possession, it held that this record presented a jury question on that issue. Since the defendants had not asked the trial judge to submit the question to the jury, the Court of Appeals treated the case as though the jury had resolved this fact question in the prosecution's favor. It therefore concluded that the presumption did apply and that there was sufficient evidence to support the convictions. * * * It also summarily rejected the argument that the presumption was unconstitutional as applied in this case. * * *

Respondents filed a petition for a writ of habeas corpus in the United States District Court for the Southern District of New York contending that they were denied due process of law by the application of the statutory presumption of possession. The District Court issued the writ, holding that respondents had not "deliberately bypassed" their federal claim by their actions at trial and that the mere presence of two guns in a woman's handbag in a car could not reasonably give rise to the inference that they were in the possession of three other persons in the car. * * *

The Court of Appeals for the Second Circuit affirmed, but for different reasons. First, the entire panel concluded that the New York Court of Appeals had decided respondents' constitutional claim on its merits rather than on any independent state procedural ground that might have barred collateral relief. Then, the majority of the court, without deciding whether the presumption was constitutional as applied in this case, concluded that the statute is unconstitutional on its face because the "presumption obviously sweeps within its compass (1) many occupants who may not know they are riding with a gun (which may be out of their sight), and (2) many who may be aware of the presence of the gun but not permitted access to it." Concurring separately, Judge Timbers agreed with the District Court that the statute was unconstitutional as applied but considered it improper to reach the issue of the statute's facial constitutionality. * * *

The State's petition for a writ of certiorari presented three questions: (1) whether the District Court had jurisdiction to entertain respondents' claim that the presumption is unconstitutional; (2) whether it was proper for the Court of Appeals to decide the facial constitutionality issue; and (3) whether the application of the presumption in this case is unconstitutional. We answer the first question in the affirmative, the second two in the negative. We accordingly reverse.

I

[In this section of its opinion, the Court concluded that the decisions of the New York courts had not been based upon independent state grounds, and that the case was therefore properly before the federal courts.]

II

Although § 2254 authorizes the federal courts to entertain respondents' claim that they are being held in custody in violation of the Constitution, it is not a grant of power to decide constitutional questions not necessarily subsumed within that claim. * * *

A party has standing to challenge the constitutionality of a statute only insofar as it has an adverse impact on his own rights. As a general rule, if there is no constitutional defect in the application of the statute to a litigant, he does not have standing to argue that it would be unconstitutional if applied to third parties in hypothetical situations. Broadrick v. Oklahoma, 413 U.S. 601, 610 (and cases cited). A limited exception has been recognized for statutes that broadly prohibit speech protected by the First Amendment. Id., at 611–616. This exception has been justified by the overriding interest in removing illegal deterrents to the exercise of the right of free speech. E.g., Gooding v. Wilson, 405 U.S. 518, 520; Dombrowski v. Pfister, 380 U.S. 479, 486. That justification, of course, has no application to a statute that enhances the legal risks associated with riding in vehicles containing dangerous weapons.

In this case the Court of Appeals undertook the task of deciding the constitutionality of the New York statute "on its face." Its conclusion that the statutory presumption was arbitrary rested entirely on its view of the fairness of applying the presumption in hypothetical situations—situations, indeed, in which it is improbable that a jury would return a conviction, or that a prosecution would ever be instituted. We must accordingly inquire whether these respondents had standing to advance the arguments that the Court of Appeals considered decisive. An analysis of our prior cases indicates that the answer to this inquiry depends on the type of presumption that is involved in the case.

Inferences and presumptions are a staple of our adversarial system of factfinding. It is often necessary for the trier of fact to determine the existence of an element of the crime—that is, an "ultimate" or "elemental" fact—from the existence of one or more "evidentiary" or "basic" facts. * * * The value of these evidentiary devices, and their validity under the Due Process Clause, vary from case to case, however, depending on the strength of the connection between the particular basic and elemental facts involved and on the degree to which the device curtails the factfinder's freedom to assess the evidence independently. Nonetheless, in criminal cases, the ultimate test of any device's constitutional validity in a given case remains constant: the device must not undermine the factfinder's responsibility at trial, based on evidence adduced by the State, to find the ultimate facts beyond a reasonable doubt. See In re Winship, 397 U.S. 358, 364; Mullaney v. Wilbur, 421 U.S. 684, 702–703 n.31.

The most common evidentiary device is the entirely permissive inference or presumption, which allows—but does not require—the trier of fact to infer the elemental fact from proof by the prosecutor of the basic one and that places no burden of any kind on the defendant. See, e.g., Barnes v. United States, 412 U.S., at 840 n.3. In that situation the basic fact may constitute prima facie evidence of the elemental fact. See, e.g., Turner v. United States, 396 U.S. 398, 402 n.2. When reviewing this type of device, the Court has required the party challenging it to demonstrate its invalidity as applied to him. * * * Because this permissive presumption leaves the trier of fact free to credit or reject the inference and does not shift the burden of proof, it affects the application of the "beyond a reasonable doubt" standard only if, under the facts of the case, there is no rational way the trier could make the connection permitted by the inference. For only in that situation is there any risk that an explanation of the permissible inference to a jury, or its use by a jury, has caused the presumptively rational factfinder to make an erroneous factual determination.

A mandatory presumption is a far more troublesome evidentiary device. For it may affect not only the strength of the "no reasonable doubt" burden but also the placement of that burden; it tells the trier that he or they *must* find the elemental fact upon proof of the basic fact, at least unless the defendant has come forward with some evidence to rebut the presumed connection between the two facts. * * *[6] In this situation, the Court has generally examined the presumption on its face to determine the extent to which the basic and elemental facts coincide. * * * To the extent that the trier of fact is forced to abide by the presumption, and may not reject it based on an independent evaluation of the particular facts presented by the State, the analysis of the presumption's constitutional validity is logically divorced from those facts and based on the presumption's accuracy in the run of cases.[7] It is for this reason that

---

[6] This class of more or less mandatory presumptions can be subdivided into two parts: presumptions that merely shift the burden of production to the defendant, following the satisfaction of which the ultimate burden of persuasion returns to the prosecution; and presumptions that entirely shift the burden of proof to the defendant. The mandatory presumptions examined by our cases have almost uniformly fit into the former subclass, in that they never totally removed the ultimate burden of proof beyond a reasonable doubt from the prosecution. E.g., Tot v. United States, supra, at 469. See Roviaro v. United States, 353 U.S. 53, 63, describing the operation of the presumption involved in *Turner, Leary,* and *Romano.*

To the extent that a presumption imposes an extremely low burden of production—e.g., being satisfied by "any" evidence—it may well be that its impact is no greater than that of a permissive inference and it may be proper to analyze it as such. See generally Mullaney v. Wilbur, supra, 421 U.S., at 703 n.31.

In deciding what type of inference or presumption is involved in a case, the jury instructions will generally be controlling, although their interpretation may require recourse to the statute involved and the cases decided under it. Turner v. United States, supra, provides a useful illustration of the different types of presumptions. It analyzes the constitutionality of two different presumption statutes (one mandatory and one permissive) as they apply to the basic fact of possession of both heroin and cocaine, and the presumed facts of importation and distribution of narcotic drugs. The jury was charged essentially in the terms of the two statutes.

The importance of focusing attention on the precise presentation of the presumption to the jury and the scope of that presumption is illustrated by a comparison of United States v. Gainey, 380 U.S. 63, with United States v. Romano, 382 U.S. 136. Both cases involved statutory presumptions based on proof that the defendant was present at the site of an illegal still. In *Gainey* the Court sustained a conviction "for carrying on" the business of the distillery in violation of 26 U.S.C. § 5601(a)(4), whereas in *Romano,* the Court set aside a conviction for being in "possession, custody, and * * * control" of such a distillery in violation of § 5601(a)(1). The difference in outcome was attributable to two important differences between the cases. Because the statute involved in *Gainey* was a sweeping prohibition of almost any activity associated with the still, whereas the *Romano* statute involved only one narrow aspect of the total undertaking, there was a much higher probability that mere presence could support an inference of guilt in the former case than in the latter.

Of perhaps greater importance, however, was the difference between the trial judge's instructions to the jury in the two cases. In *Gainey* the judge had explained that the presumption was permissive; it did not require the jury to convict the defendant even if it was convinced that he was present at the site. On the contrary, the instructions made it clear that presence was only "a circumstance to be considered along with all the other circumstances in the case." As we emphasized, the "jury was thus specifically told that the statutory [presumption] was not conclusive." 380 U.S., at 69–70. In *Romano* the trial judge told the jury that the defendant's presence at the still "shall be deemed sufficient evidence to authorize conviction." 382 U.S., at 138. Although there was other evidence of guilt, that instruction authorized conviction even if the jury disbelieved all of the testimony except the proof of presence at the site. This Court's holding that the statutory presumption could not support the *Romano* conviction was thus dependent, in part, on the specific instructions given by the trial judge. Under those instructions it was necessary to decide whether, regardless of the specific circumstances of the particular case, the statutory presumption adequately supported the guilty verdict.

[7] In addition to the discussion of *Romano* in n. [6], supra, this point is illustrated by Leary v. United States, supra. In that case, Dr. Timothy Leary, a professor at Harvard University was stopped by customs inspectors in Laredo, Texas as he was returning from the Mexican side of the

the Court has held it irrelevant in analyzing a mandatory presumption, but not in analyzing a purely permissive one, that there is ample evidence in the record other than the presumption to support a conviction.* * *

Without determining whether the presumption in this case was mandatory, the Court of Appeals analyzed it on its face as if it were. In fact, it was not, as the New York Court of Appeals had earlier pointed out. 40 N.Y.2d, at 510–511, 387 N.Y.S.2d, at 100, 354 N.E.2d, at 840.

The trial judge's instructions make it clear that the presumption was merely a part of the prosecution's case, that it gave rise to a permissive inference available only in certain circumstances, rather than a mandatory conclusion of possession, and that it could be ignored by the jury even if there was no affirmative proof offered by defendants in rebuttal. The judge explained that possession could be actual or constructive, but that constructive possession could not exist without the intent and ability to exercise control or dominion over the weapons. He also carefully instructed the jury that there is a mandatory presumption of innocence in favor of the defendants that controls unless it, as the exclusive trier of fact, is satisfied beyond a reasonable doubt that the defendants possessed the handguns in the manner described by the judge. In short, the instructions plainly directed the jury to consider all the circumstances tending to support or contradict the inference that all four occupants of the car had possession of the two loaded handguns and to decide the matter for itself without regard to how much evidence the defendants introduced.[8]

---

international border. Marihuana seeds and a silver snuff box filled with semirefined marihuana and three partially smoked marihuana cigarettes were discovered in his car. He was convicted of having knowingly transported marihuana which he knew had been illegally imported into this country in violation of 21 U.S.C.A. § 176a. That statute includes a mandatory presumption: "possession shall be deemed sufficient evidence to authorize conviction [for importation] unless the defendant explains his possession to the satisfaction of the jury." Leary admitted possession of the marihuana and claimed that he had carried it from New York to Mexico and then back.

Justice Harlan for the Court noted that under one theory of the case, the jury could have found direct proof of all of the necessary elements of the offense without recourse to the presumption. But he deemed that insufficient reason to affirm the conviction because under another theory the jury might have found knowledge of importation on the basis of either direct evidence or the presumption, and there was accordingly no certainty that the jury had not relied on the presumption. 395 U.S., at 31–32. The Court therefore found it necessary to test the presumption against the Due Process Clause. Its analysis was facial. Despite the fact that the defendant was well educated and had recently traveled to a country that is a major exporter of marihuana to this country, the Court found the presumption of knowledge of importation from possession irrational. It did so not because Dr. Leary was unlikely to know the source of the marihuana but instead because "a majority of possessors" were unlikely to have such knowledge. Id., at 53. Because the jury had been instructed to rely on the presumption even if it did not believe the government's direct evidence of knowledge of importation (unless, of course, the defendant met his burden of "satisfying" the jury to the contrary), the Court reversed the conviction.

[8]   The verdict announced by the jury, clearly indicates that it understood its duty to evaluate the presumption independently and to reject it if it was not supported in the record. Despite receiving almost identical instructions on the applicability of the presumption of

* * *

Our cases considering the validity of permissive statutory presumptions such as the one involved here have rested on an evaluation of the presumption as applied to the record before the Court. None suggests that a court should pass on the constitutionality of this kind of statute "on its face." It was error for the Court of Appeals to make such a determination in this case.

III

As applied to the facts of this case, the presumption of possession is entirely rational. Notwithstanding the Court of Appeals' analysis, respondents were not "hitch-hikers or other casual passengers," and the guns were neither "a few inches in length" nor "out of [respondents'] sight." * * * The argument against possession by any of the respondents was predicated solely on the fact that the guns were in Jane Doe's pocketbook. But several circumstances—which, not surprisingly, her counsel repeatedly emphasized in his questions and his argument, * * * made it highly improbable that she was the sole custodian of those weapons.

Even if it was reasonable to conclude that she had placed the guns in her purse before the car was stopped by police, the facts strongly suggest that Jane Doe was not the only person able to exercise dominion over them. The two guns were too large to be concealed in her handbag. The bag was consequently open, and part of one of the guns was in plain view, within easy access of the driver of the car and even, perhaps, of the other two respondents who were riding in the rear seat.

Moreover, it is highly improbable that the loaded guns belonged to Jane Doe or that she was solely responsible for their being in her purse. As a 16–year–old girl in the company of three adult men she was the least likely of the four to be carrying one, let alone two, heavy handguns. It is far more probable that she relied on the pocketknife found in her brassiere for any necessary self-protection. Under these circumstances, it was not unreasonable for her counsel to argue and for the jury to infer that when the car was halted for speeding, the other passengers in the car anticipated the risk of a search and attempted to conceal their weapons in a pocketbook in the front seat. The inference is surely more likely than the notion that these weapons were the sole property of the 16–year–old girl.

Under these circumstances, the jury would have been entirely reasonable in rejecting the suggestion—which, incidentally, defense counsel did not even advance in their closing arguments to the jury—that

---

possession to the contraband found in the front seat and in the trunk, the jury convicted all four defendants of possession of the former but acquitted all of them of possession of the latter. See n. [8], supra.

the handguns were in the sole possession of Jane Doe. Assuming that the jury did reject it, the case is tantamount to one in which the guns were lying on the floor or the seat of the car in the plain view of the three other occupants of the automobile. In such a case it is surely rational to infer that each of the respondents was fully aware of the presence of the guns and had both the ability and the intent to exercise dominion and control over the weapons. The application of the statutory presumption in this case therefore comports with the standard laid down in Tot v. United States, 319 U.S. 463, 467, and restated in Leary v. United States, supra, 395 U.S., at 36. For there is a "rational connection" between the basic facts that the prosecution proved and the ultimate fact presumed, and the latter is "more likely than not to flow from" the former.

Respondents argue, however, that the validity of the New York presumption must be judged by a "reasonable doubt" test rather than the "more likely than not" standard employed in *Leary*. Under the more stringent test, it is argued that a statutory presumption must be rejected unless the evidence necessary to invoke the inference is sufficient for a rational jury to find the inferred fact beyond a reasonable doubt. See Barnes v. United States, 412 U.S. 837, 842–843. Respondents' argument again overlooks the distinction between a permissive presumption on which the prosecution is entitled to rely as one not-necessarily-sufficient part of its proof and a mandatory presumption which the jury must accept even if it is the sole evidence of an element of the offense.[9]

In the latter situation, since the prosecution bears the burden of establishing guilt, it may not rest its case entirely on a presumption unless the fact proved is sufficient to support the inference of guilt beyond a reasonable doubt. But in the former situation, the prosecution may rely on all of the evidence in the record to meet the reasonable doubt standard. There is no more reason to require a permissive statutory presumption to meet a reasonable doubt standard before it may be permitted to play any part in a trial than there is to require that degree of probative force for other relevant evidence before it may be admitted. As long as it is clear that the presumption is not the sole and sufficient basis for a finding of guilt, it need only satisfy the test described in *Leary*.

The permissive presumption, as used in this case, satisfied the *Leary* test. And, as already noted, the New York Court of Appeals has concluded

---

[9] The dissenting argument rests on the assumption that "the jury [may have] rejected all of the prosecution's evidence concerning the location and origin of the guns." * * * Even if that assumption were plausible, the jury was plainly told that it was free to disregard the presumption. But the dissent's assumption is not plausible; for if the jury rejected the testimony describing where the guns were found, it would necessarily also have rejected the only evidence in the record proving that the guns were found in the car. The conclusion that the jury attached significance to the particular location of the handguns follows inexorably from the acquittal on the charge of possession of the machineguns and heroin in the trunk.

that the record as a whole was sufficient to establish guilt beyond a reasonable doubt.

The judgment is reversed.

[The concurring opinion of MR. CHIEF JUSTICE BURGER is omitted.]

MR. JUSTICE POWELL, with whom MR. JUSTICE BRENNAN, MR. JUSTICE STEWART, and MR. JUSTICE MARSHALL join dissenting.

I agree with the Court that there is no procedural bar to our considering the underlying constitutional question presented by this case. I am not in agreement, however, with the Court's conclusion that the presumption as charged to the jury in this case meets the constitutional requirements of due process as set forth in our prior decisions. On the contrary, an individual's mere presence in an automobile where there is a handgun does not even make it "more likely than not" that the individual possesses the weapon.

I

In the criminal law presumptions are used to encourage the jury to find certain facts, with respect to which no direct evidence is presented, solely because other facts have been proved.[10] See, e.g., Barnes v. United States, 412 U.S. 837, 840 n.3 (1973); United States v. Romano, 382 U.S. 136, 138 (1965). The purpose of such presumptions is plain: Like certain other jury instructions, they provide guidance for jurors' thinking in considering the evidence laid before them. Once in the juryroom, jurors necessarily draw inferences from the evidence—both direct and circumstantial. Through the use of presumptions, certain inferences are commended to the attention of jurors by legislatures or courts.

Legitimate guidance of a jury's deliberations is an indispensible part of our criminal justice system. Nonetheless, the use of presumptions in criminal cases poses at least two distinct perils for defendants' constitutional rights. The Court accurately identifies the first of these as being the danger of interference with "the factfinder's responsibility at trial, based on evidence adduced by the State, to find the ultimate facts beyond a reasonable doubt." * * * If the jury is instructed that it must infer some ultimate fact (that is, some element of the offense) from proof of other facts unless the defendant disproves the ultimate fact by a preponderance of the evidence, then the presumption shifts the burden of proof to the defendant concerning the element thus inferred.[11]

---

[10] Such encouragement can be provided either by statutory presumptions, see, e.g., 18 U.S.C.A. § 1201(b), or by presumptions created in the common law. See, e.g., Barnes v. United States, 412 U.S. 837 (1973). Unless otherwise specified, "presumption" will be used herein to "permissible inferences," as well as to "true" presumptions. See F. James, Civil Procedure § 7.9 (1965).

[11] The Court suggests that presumptions that shift the burden of persuasion to the defendant in this way can be upheld provided that "the fact proved is sufficient to support the

But I do not agree with the Court's conclusion that the only constitutional difficulty with presumptions lies in the danger of lessening the burden of proof the prosecution must bear. As the Court notes, the presumptions thus far reviewed by the Court have not shifted the burden of persuasion * * *; instead they either have required only that the defendant produce some evidence to rebut the inference suggested by the prosecution's evidence, see Tot v. United States, 319 U.S. 463 (1943), or merely have been suggestions to the jury that it would be sensible to draw certain conclusions on the basis of the evidence presented.[12] See Barnes v. United States, supra 412 U.S. at 840 n.3. Evolving from our decisions, therefore, is a second standard for judging the constitutionality of criminal presumptions which is based—not on the constitutional requirement that the State be put to its proof—but rather on the due process rule that when the jury is encouraged to make factual inferences, those inferences must reflect some valid general observation about the natural connection between events as they occur in our society.

This due process rule was first articulated by the Court in Tot v. United States, supra, in which the Court reviewed the constitutionality of § 2(f) of the Federal Firearms Act. That statute provided in part that "possession of a firearm or ammunition by any * * * person [who has been convicted of a crime of violence] shall be presumptive evidence that such firearm or ammunition was shipped or transported [in interstate or foreign commerce]." As the Court interpreted the presumption, it placed upon a defendant only the obligation of presenting some exculpatory evidence concerning the origins of a firearm or ammunition, once the Government proved that the defendant had possessed the weapon and had been convicted of a crime of violence. Noting that juries must be permitted to infer from one fact the existence of another essential to guilt, "if reason and experience support the inference," id., at 467, the Court concluded that under some circumstances juries may be guided in making these inferences by legislative or common-law presumptions, even though they may be based "upon a view of relation broader than that a jury might take in a specific case," 319 U.S., at 468. To provide due process,

---

inference of guilt beyond a reasonable doubt." * * * As the present case involves no shifting of the burden of persuasion, the constitutional restrictions on such presumptions are not before us, and I express no views on them.

It may well be that even those presumptions that do not shift the burden of persuasion cannot be used to prove an element of the offense, if the facts proved would not permit a reasonable mind to find the presumed fact beyond a reasonable doubt. My conclusion in Part II, infra, makes it unnecessary for me to address this concern here.

[12] The Court suggests as the touchstone for its analysis a distinction between "mandatory" and "permissive" presumptions. * * * For general discussions of the various forms of presumptions, see Jeffries & Stephan, Defenses, Presumptions, and Burden of Proof in the Criminal Law, 88 Yale L.J. 1325 (1979); F. James, Civil Procedure § 7.9 (1965). I have found no recognition in the Court's prior decisions that this distinction is important in analyzing presumptions used in criminal cases. Cf. F. James, Civil Procedure, ibid. (distinguishing true "presumptions" from "permissible inferences").

however, there must be at least "a rational connection between the facts proved and the fact presumed"—a connection grounded in "common experience." Id., at 467. In *Tot,* the Court found that connection to be lacking.

Subsequently, in Leary v. United States, 395 U.S. 6 (1969), the Court reaffirmed and refined the due process requirement of *Tot* that inferences specifically commended to the attention of jurors must reflect generally accepted connections between related events. At issue in *Leary* was the constitutionality of a federal statute making it a crime to receive, conceal, buy, or sell marihuana illegally brought into the United States, knowing it to have been illegally imported. The statute provided that mere possession of marihuana "shall be deemed sufficient evidence to authorize conviction unless the defendant explains his possession to the satisfaction of the jury." After reviewing the Court's decisions in Tot v. United States, supra, and other criminal presumption cases, Mr. Justice Harlan, writing for the Court, concluded "that a criminal statutory presumption must be regarded as 'irrational' or 'arbitrary,' and hence unconstitutional, unless it can be said with substantial assurance that the presumed fact is more likely than not to flow from the proved fact on which it is made to depend." 395 U.S., at 36 * * *. The Court invalidated the statute, finding there to be insufficient basis in fact for the conclusion that those who possess marihuana are more likely than not to know that it was imported illegally.[13]

Most recently, in Barnes v. United States, supra, we considered the constitutionality of a quite different sort of presumption—one that suggested to the jury that "[p]ossession of recently stolen property, if not satisfactorily explained, is ordinarily a circumstance from which you may reasonably draw the inference * * * that the person in possession knew the property had been stolen." Id., 412 U.S. at 840 n.3. After reviewing the various formulations used by the Court to articulate the constitutionally required basis for a criminal presumption, we once again found it unnecessary to choose among them. As for the presumption suggested to the jury in *Barnes,* we found that it was well founded in history, common sense, and experience, and therefore upheld it as being "clearly sufficient to enable the jury to find beyond a reasonable doubt" that those in the unexplained possession of recently stolen property know it to have been stolen. Id., at 845.

---

[13] Because the statute in Leary v. United States, 395 U.S. 6 (1969), was found to be unconstitutional under the "more likely than not" standard, the Court explicitly declined to consider whether criminal presumptions also must follow "beyond a reasonable doubt" from their premises, if an essential element of the crime depends upon the presumption's use. Id., at 36 n.64 * * * The Court similarly avoided this question in Turner v. United States, 396 U.S. 398, 416 (1970).

In sum, our decisions uniformly have recognized that due process requires more than merely that the prosecution be put to its proof.[14] In addition, the Constitution restricts the court in its charge to the jury by requiring that, when particular factual inferences are recommended to the jury, those factual inferences be accurate reflections of what history, common sense, and experience tell us about the relations between events in our society. Generally this due process rule has been articulated as requiring that the truth of the inferred fact be more likely than not whenever the premise for the inference is true. Thus, to be constitutional a presumption must be at least more likely than not true.

II

In the present case, the jury was told that,

> "Our Penal Law also provides that the presence in an automobile of any machine gun or of any handgun or firearm which is loaded is presumptive evidence of their unlawful possession. In other words, [under] these presumptions or this latter presumption upon proof of the presence of the machine gun and the hand weapons, you may infer and draw a conclusion that such prohibited weapon was possessed by each of the defendants who occupied the automobile at the time when such instruments were found. The presumption or presumptions is effective only so long as there is no substantial evidence contradicting the conclusion flowing from the presumption, and the presumption is said to disappear when such contradictory evidence is adduced."

Undeniably, the presumption charged in this case encouraged the jury to draw a particular factual inference regardless of any other evidence presented: to infer that respondents possessed the weapons found in the automobile "upon proof of the presence of the machine gun and the hand weapon" and proof that respondents "occupied the automobile at the time such instruments were found." I believe that the presumption thus charged was unconstitutional because it did not fairly reflect what common sense and experience tell us about passengers in automobiles and the possession of handguns. People present in automobiles where there are weapons simply are not "more likely than not" the possessors of those weapons.

Under New York law, "to possess" is "to have physical possession or otherwise to exercise dominion or control over tangible property." N.Y.Penal Law § 10.00(8). Plainly the mere presence of an individual in an automobile—without more—does not indicate that he exercises "dominion or control over" everything within it. As the Court of Appeals

---

[14] The Court apparently disagrees, contending that "the factfinder's responsibility * * * to find the ultimate facts beyond a reasonable doubt" is the only constitutional restraint upon the use of criminal presumptions at trial. * * *

noted, there are countless situations in which individuals are invited as guests into vehicles the contents of which they know nothing about, much less have control over. Similarly, those who invite others into their automobile do not generally search them to determine what they may have on their person; nor do they insist that any handguns be identified and placed within reach of the occupants of the automobile. Indeed, handguns are particularly susceptible to concealment and therefore are less likely than are other objects to be observed by those in an automobile.

In another context, this Court has been particularly hesitant to infer possession from mere presence in a location, noting that "[p]resence is relevant and admissible evidence in a trial on a possession charge; but absent some showing of the defendant's function at [the illegal] still, its connection with possession is too tenuous to permit a reasonable inference of guilt—'the inference of the one from proof of the other is arbitrary * * *.' Tot v. United States, 319 U.S. 463, 467." United States v. Romano, 382 U.S. 136, 141 (1965). We should be even more hesitant to uphold the inference of possession of a handgun from mere presence in an automobile, in light of common experience concerning automobiles and handguns. Because the specific factual inference recommended to the jury in this case is not one that is supported by the general experience of our society. I cannot say that the presumption charged is "more likely than not" to be true. Accordingly, respondents' due process rights were violated by the presumption's use.

As I understand it, the Court today does not contend that in general those who are present in automobiles are more likely than not to possess any gun contained within their vehicles. It argues, however, that the nature of the presumption here involved requires that we look, not only to the immediate facts upon which the jury was encouraged to base its inference, but to the other facts "proved" by the prosecution as well. The Court suggests that this is the proper approach when reviewing what it calls "permissive" presumptions because the jury was urged "to consider all the circumstances tending to support or contradict the inference." * * *

It seems to me that the Court mischaracterizes the function of the presumption charged in this case. As it acknowledges was the case in *Romano,* supra, the "instruction authorized conviction even if the jury disbelieved all of the testimony except the proof of presence" in the automobile.[15] * * * The Court nevertheless relies on all of the evidence

---

[15] In commending the presumption to the jury, the court gave no instruction that would have required a finding of possession to be based on anything more than mere presence in the automobile. Thus, the jury was not instructed that it should infer that respondents possessed the handguns only if it found that the guns were too large to be concealed in Jane Doe's handbag * * *; that the guns accordingly were in the plain view of respondents * * *; that the weapons were within "easy access of the driver of the car and even, perhaps, of the other two respondents who were riding in the rear seat," ibid; that it was unlikely that Jane Doe was solely responsible for the placement of the weapons in her purse, id.; or that the case was "tantamount to one in

introduced by the prosecution and argues that the "permissive" presumption could not have prejudiced defendants. The possibility that the jury disbelieved all of this evidence, and relied on the presumption, is simply ignored.

I agree that the circumstances relied upon by the Court in determining the plausibility of the presumption charged in this case would have made it reasonable for the jury to "infer that each of the respondents was fully aware of the presence of the guns and had both the ability and the intent to exercise dominion and control over the weapons." But the jury was told that it could conclude that respondents possessed the weapons found therein from proof of the mere fact of respondents' presence in the automobile. For all we know, the jury rejected all of the prosecution's evidence concerning the location and origin of the guns, and based its conclusion that respondents possessed the weapons solely upon its belief that respondents had been present in the automobile.[16] For purposes of reviewing the constitutionality of the presumption at issue here, we must assume that this was the case. * * *

The Court's novel approach in this case appears to contradict prior decisions of this Court reviewing such presumptions. Under the Court's analysis, whenever it is determined that an inference is "permissive," the only question is whether, in light of all of the evidence adduced at trial, the inference recommended to the jury is a reasonable one. The Court has never suggested that the inquiry into the rational basis of a permissible inference may be circumvented in this manner. Quite the contrary, the Court has required that the "evidence *necessary to invoke the inference* [be] sufficient for a rational juror to find the inferred fact * * *." Barnes v. United States, 412 U.S. 837 (1973) (emphasis supplied). See Turner v. United States, 396 U.S. 398, 407 (1970). Under the presumption charged in this case, the only evidence necessary to invoke the inference was the presence of the weapons in the automobile with respondents—an inference that is plainly irrational.

In sum, it seems to me that the Court today ignores the teaching of our prior decisions. By speculating about what the jury may have done with the factual inference thrust upon it, the Court in effect assumes

---

which the guns were lying on the floor or the seat of the car in the plain view of the three other occupants of the automobile." * * *.

[16] The Court is therefore mistaken in its conclusion that, because "respondents were not 'hitch-hikers or other casual passengers,' and the guns were neither 'a few inches in length' nor 'out of [respondents'] sight,'" reference to these possibilities is inappropriate in considering the constitutionality of the presumption as charged in this case. * * * To be sure, respondents' challenge is to the presumption as charged to the jury in this case. But in assessing its application here, we are not free, as the Court apparently believes, to disregard the possibility that the jury may have disbelieved all other evidence supporting an inference of possession. The jury may have concluded that respondents—like hitchhikers—had only an incidental relationship to the auto in which they were traveling, or that, contrary to some of the testimony at trial, the weapons were indeed out of respondents' sight.

away the inference altogether, constructing a rule that permits the use of any inference—no matter how irrational in itself—provided that otherwise there is sufficient evidence in the record to support a finding of guilt. Applying this novel analysis to the present case, the Court upholds the use of a presumption that it makes no effort to defend in isolation. In substance, the Court—applying an unarticulated harmless error standard—simply finds that the respondents were guilty as charged. They may well have been but rather than acknowledging this rationale, the Court seems to have made new law with respect to presumptions that could seriously jeopardize a defendant's right to a fair trial. Accordingly, I dissent.

NOTES AND QUESTIONS

1. *Mandatory presumptions.* In the same term as the principal case, the Supreme Court decided Sandstrom v. Montana, 442 U.S. 510 (1979). In *Sandstrom*, the Court found that a jury instruction in a homicide case that the "law presumes that a person intends the ordinary consequences of his voluntary acts" could have been interpreted either as creating a conclusive presumption or as shifting the burden of persuasion with regard to the question of intent to the defendant. The Court held that such a shift of the burden would be constitutionally impermissible, citing, among others, the *Ulster County* case. See also Francis v. Franklin, 471 U.S. 307 (1985), where the Court rejected another "mandatory" presumption. Are "mandatory" presumptions ever constitutionally permissible in a criminal case? What about a "mandatory" presumption which simply shifts the burden of production? The Court in the *Francis* case expressly reserved the question of the treatment of such a presumption. Id. at 314 n.3. For discussions and criticism of the Court's treatment of presumptions in criminal cases, see Allen & De Grazia, The Constitutional Requirement of Proof Beyond a Reasonable Doubt in Criminal Cases: A Comment Upon Incipient Chaos in the Lower Courts, 20 Am.Crim.L.Rev. 1 (1982); Note, The Improper Use of Presumptions in Recent Criminal Law Adjudication, 38 Stan.L.Rev. 423 (1986); 2 McCormick, Evidence §§ 347, 348 (7th ed. 2013).

2. *Presumptions or affirmative defenses?* To what extent is the problem in the principal case related to the question of what elements of a criminal case may be allocated to the accused as affirmative defenses? See Jeffries & Stephan, Defenses, Presumptions and the Burden of Proof in the Criminal Law, 88 Yale L.J. 1325 (1979); 2 McCormick, Evidence § 348 (7th ed. 2013). Related discussions include: Allen, Structuring Jury Decisionmaking in Criminal Cases: A Unified Constitutional Approach to Evidentiary Devices, 94 Harv.L.Rev. 321 (1980); Allen, More on Constitutional Process-of-Proof Problems in Criminal Cases, 94 Harv.L.Rev. 1795 (1981); Ashford & Risinger, Presumptions, Assumptions and Due Process in Criminal Cases: A Theoretical Overview, 79 Yale L.J. 165 (1969); Ranney, Presumptions in Criminal Cases: A New Look at an Old Problem, 41 Mont.L.Rev. 21 (1980).

See also the concurring opinions of Judge Phillips in Rook v. Rice, 783 F.2d 401 (4th Cir.1986), and Davis v. Allsbrooks, 778 F.2d 168 (4th Cir.1985).

3. *Harmless error.* May a jury instruction which puts an impermissible burden of persuasion on the defendant ever be harmless error? If so, is it enough that there is evidence in the record, independent of the presumption, to support the verdict? In Yates v. Evatt, 500 U.S. 391 (1991), the Court held that, in order for the error to be harmless, all of the evidence in the case must have been of such compelling force to show beyond a reasonable doubt that the presumption must have made no difference in reaching the verdict.

CHAPTER 6[1]

THE ORDER OF PROOF

■ ■ ■

LIPTAK V. SECURITY BENEFIT ASS'N

Supreme Court of Illinois, 1932.
183 N.E. 564.

STONE, J. The appellee, as widow of Julius Liptak, brought suit in the circuit court of Madison county against appellant, a fraternal benefit society, on a benefit certificate issued to Liptak on November 26, 1921, in the amount of $1,000. To the declaration appellant filed no plea of general issue but a special plea setting out certain sections of its by-laws and alleging that before his death the insured became suspended for failure to pay premium assessments in accordance with the provisions of those by-laws. There was a trial by jury and a verdict for plaintiff in the sum of $1,000. Judgment entered thereon was affirmed by the Appellate Court.

The special plea relied on was to the effect that under the by-laws of the society Liptak's policy had lapsed by reason of his failure to pay the assessment for June, 1929, before the last day of that month. The appellant asserts that thereafter, in July of that year, Liptak, or some one for him, attempted to reinstate him by payment of assessments for the months of June and July, but that this payment was made to one not authorized by the society to receive it, and as a result Liptak was not reinstated. It further states that he was not in good health at that time and could not have been reinstated. * * *

The dispute in the case arises over the payment during June, 1929, of the assessment and dues for that month. Liptak died on November 13, 1929. He was ill from the spring of that year, and it is conceded that if he became suspended in June his health was such as to prevent his reinstatement. The testimony of appellee and her witnesses is to the effect that one John R. De Bow, an officer of the association, came to the house of appellee, at her request, on the 29th of June and received the payment for that month on the certificate of Julius Liptak and other members of the family who were likewise members of the society. De Bow was an officer of appellant having a sort of supervision over certain

---

[1] Throughout the cases and materials in this chapter some footnotes from the originals have been omitted; others have been renumbered. [Ed.]

lodges, or councils as they were styled, including the one holding Liptak's membership. It does not appear that he was the "financier" of the local council of this society, but that he had at times taken dues and assessments of various members of the council and signed the receipt books therefor. Appellant's evidence is a denial of the presence of De Bow at the house of appellee during the month of June and of his authority to accept dues. That evidence tends to show that De Bow received the June and July assessments from appellee on July 23, with the request that he try and have Julius Liptak reinstated. He testified that he agreed to do what he could in that behalf. This is denied on rebuttal by appellee. Concerning this payment there is sharp dispute in the evidence, and it is on this evidence that the case turns.

When the case was called for trial counsel for appellant stated to the court that under the pleadings in the case they admitted the issuance of the certificate, the relationship of the parties, the correctness of the by-laws referred to in the certificate and declaration, admitted the death of the insured and receipt of proof of death, and moved the court to be permitted to take the lead in the examination of the jury on account of the fact that under the pleadings the burden of proof was upon the defendant. This motion was denied. It was for the same reason renewed before the taking of evidence and again before the arguments to the jury were had. In each case it was denied, and the ruling of the court in that matter is here urged as error. Counsel for appellee argues that it was necessary that she introduce proof in support of her case in chief and that therefore she had a right to open and close, and whether this be so or not, the matter of opening and closing lay in the discretion of the trial court. The right to open and close is a substantial right coexistent with the burden of proof and is corollary thereto. Whenever the plaintiff has anything to prove in order to secure a verdict, the right to open and close belongs to him. It is generally held that the right to open and close is not a matter resting merely in the discretion of the trial judge, but is a substantial right in the person who must introduce proof to prevent judgment against him. The party who asserts the affirmative of an issue is entitled to begin and reply. * * * If appellee was, under the pleadings and admissions of appellant, entitled to judgment, in the absence of proof supporting the special plea, appellant carried the burden to go forward in the offer of proof and was entitled to open and close the evidence and arguments. No plea of general issue was on file. The only controversy in the case was that raised on the affirmative special plea. This threw the burden of proof upon appellant. The issue of fact raised by that plea was sharply controverted. The right of appellant to open and close was a substantial right. In a trial before a jury, where the pivotal fact is in sharp dispute, the advantage of opening and closing the evidence and arguments becomes one controlled by rules of law defining rights, and is not left to the discretion of the judge.

* * *

For the error in denying appellant the right to open and close the case, the judgments of the appellate and circuit courts are reversed, and the cause remanded to the circuit court for a new trial.

Reversed and remanded.

SEGUIN V. BERG

Supreme Court of New York, Appellate Division, 1940.
21 N.Y.S.2d 291.

HEFFERNAN, JUSTICE. On January 2, 1938, the automobiles of plaintiff and defendants collided on the state highway connecting Lake Placid and Saranac Lake as a result of which both cars were damaged. Each of the owners of the respective vehicles charged the other with negligence in causing the collision.

Plaintiff instituted this action to recover a money judgment for the damages to his car. Defendants interposed an answer denying liability and also asserted a counterclaim against plaintiff for the damages to their car. After a trial of the issues the jury rendered a verdict in favor of defendants on their counterclaim and plaintiff has appealed.

Only a question of law relating to practice is presented for our determination. In support of his cause of action plaintiff offered his own testimony and that of the mechanic who repaired his car and rested. At the conclusion of defendants' proof plaintiff called as witnesses three persons—passengers in his car—who saw the collision and sought to obtain their version as to how it occurred. Upon objection of defendants the evidence was excluded on the ground that it was not proper rebuttal.

The proper administration of justice requires some regular method of procedure in the trial of an action. No rule for the conduct of trials is more familiar than that a plaintiff must put in all his evidence before he rests. He must exhaust all of his testimony in support of the issue on his side before the proof of his adversary is heard. The defendant should then produce his evidence, and finally the evidence in rebuttal is received. Marshall et al. v. Davies, 78 N.Y. 414; Richardson on Evidence, Fifth Edition, § 537. Plaintiff cannot put in merely enough evidence to make out a prima facie case and reserve the rest to meet the emergency of later needs. He has no right to reopen his case after defendants have closed theirs although he may introduce proof in rebuttal. He may not however under the guise of rebuttal put in evidence tending to support the allegations of his pleading. Notwithstanding the general rule that a party holding the affirmative is bound to introduce all the evidence on his side before he closes the trial court in the exercise of its discretion and for sufficient reason may allow a departure from the rule and permit a party to reopen and supply defects in the evidence which have inadvertently occurred. The order of proof may be varied as occasion requires being a matter resting in the discretion of the trial court.

If we were not dealing with a case involving a counterclaim we would have no hesitancy in sustaining the ruling of the learned trial justice. We are convinced, however, that the decision under review is erroneous. The Civil Practice Act, § 424, provides that where a defendant interposes a counterclaim and demands an affirmative judgment against the plaintiff the mode of trial of an issue of fact arising thereupon is the same as if it arose in an action brought by defendant against the plaintiff for the cause of action stated in the counterclaim and demanding the same judgment.

In the case before us plaintiff had the right to offer such testimony as he desired in support of his cause of action. It is true that the evidence which he sought to introduce in rebuttal, and which was excluded, would have been competent as part of his affirmative case. He was not obliged however to avail himself of it for that purpose. It seems clear to us that he had the right to offer the proof, not to establish his case, but to defeat the cause of action which defendants were asserting against him. The evidence was clearly admissible in rebuttal for the purpose of contradicting the evidence on the part of defendants to the effect that the collision was due solely to plaintiff's negligence. Evidence which would have been proper as part of plaintiff's affirmative case, and which he has no right to introduce as affirmative evidence after the defendants had rested, may still be offered by the plaintiff if it tends to impeach or discredit the testimony of defendants. Winchell v. Winchell et al., 100 N.Y. 159, 2 N.E. 897; Ankersmit et al. v. Tuch, 114 N.Y. 51, 20 N.E. 819. Rebutting evidence "means, not merely evidence which contradicts the witnesses on the opposite side and corroborates those of the party who began, but evidence in denial of some affirmative fact which the answering party has endeavored to prove." Marshall et al. v. Davis, supra.

For these reasons we think plaintiff is entitled to have the evidence which was excluded considered by the jury and hence the judgment and order appealed from should be reversed on the law and a new trial granted with costs to appellant to abide the event.

Judgment and order reversed on the law, and new trial granted, with costs to appellant to abide the event.

HILL, P.J., and BLISS and FOSTER, JJ., concur.

CRAPSER, J., dissents, and votes to affirm.

QUESTIONS

1.   Would it have been permissible for the plaintiff in *Seguin v. Berg* to begin the presentation of his case in chief by offering the testimony of the mechanic who repaired his car? See 6 Wigmore, Evidence § 1869 (Chadbourn rev. 1976).

2.   P sues D for negligence. In his answer, D denies P's allegations with respect to negligence and further raises the affirmative defense that P had executed a release of his claim. May P, as a part of his case in chief, introduce evidence tending to show that D obtained the release by fraud?

DURAN V. NEFF
District Court of Appeal of Florida, 1979.
366 So.2d 169.

In a medical malpractice action, the plaintiff sought and received the right to have her case presented first on a Monday morning before the trial court. On Monday afternoon, at 5:10 P.M., counsel for the plaintiff suggested that the court take a short recess before permitting him to put on an expert witness, whose examination would be lengthy. The court declined to do this and recessed until the next day. Plaintiff was unable to produce the expert witness on the following day and directed verdict was rendered against the plaintiff.

The plaintiff appeals and urges error in the trial judge's refusal to take her expert's testimony late on the first day. We find no abuse of discretion in the trial court's ruling. It is elementary that a trial judge must be given broad latitude in the control of causes before him, particularly jury cases, and on this record there is certainly no abuse of discretion demonstrated. * * *

Therefore, the final judgment based on the directed verdict is affirmed.

Affirmed.

NOTE

While the trial judge's discretion to control the timing and order of proof is generally held to be very broad, it should not be considered to be totally unfettered. With the principal case, compare Loinaz v. EG & G, Inc., 910 F.2d 1 (1st Cir.1990) (reversible error to refuse defendant's request to present main witness during plaintiff's case, where result was to force defendant to resort to witness' deposition).

ATKINSON V. SMITH

Supreme Court of New Brunswick, 1859.
9 N.B. 309.

Trespass for breaking and entering the plaintiff's close and cutting down a mill-dam. Plea—not guilty; with a notice of defense, that the locus in quo was a branch of the Buctouche river, which was a public navigable river for driving logs and lumber; that it was obstructed by a mill-dam built across it, and that the defendants having occasion to pass down the river with their lumber, were obliged to remove a part of the dam to enable them to pass. There was another notice stating the river to be a public highway and navigable stream, and that the defendants removed the dam to enable their lumber to pass down.

At the trial before Parker, J., at the last Kent circuit, the defendants' counsel proposed on the cross-examination of one of the plaintiff's witnesses, to ask certain questions connected with the justification, which had not been enquired into on the examination in chief, and were not available on the general issue; but the learned Judge ruled that the evidence could not be gone into till the defendants had opened their case. * * * The jury found that the justification was proved, but gave a verdict for the plaintiff for £25, for the excessive damage in cutting the dam.

A rule nisi for a new trial having been granted on the ground of the improper rejection of evidence,

D.S. Kerr shewed cause in Hilary term. He contended that since the case of Browne v. Murray[2], the rule was, that the plaintiff might either go into his whole case in the first instance, or merely prove his prima facie case and leave the defendant to answer it. That case was confirmed in Shaw v. Beck[3], which shewed that the particular period of the cause when evidence should be received, was in the discretion of the Judge. The defendant had no right to prove a justification until the plaintiff's case was closed, unless the plaintiff went into the whole case in the first instance.

A.J. Smith, contra. It was a matter of right for the defendant to extract from the plaintiff's witnesses on cross-examination, all they know about the case. The witness was sworn to tell the whole truth, and he was bound to answer all questions put to him, if when answered they would be legal evidence. It is not a matter in the Judge's discretion at all, but a matter of right. [PARKER, J. I thought the defendants had no right to go into evidence on cross-examination, of any matter that did not constitute a defence under the general issue.] The recent alteration in the law, allowing the parties to give evidence, required that the old practice should

---

[2]   R. & M. 254.
[3]   20 Eng.R. 309; 8 Exch. 392.

be relaxed, and that the defendant should be allowed to prove his case by cross-examination of the plaintiff's witnesses.

PARKER, J., now delivered the judgment of the Court. The only point on which the rule was granted in this case was, the rejection of evidence—the rejection not amounting to an exclusion, but a postponement of the evidence tendered, until a later stage of the trial. No injustice seems to have been done by the ruling, even if wrong, for the defendants, though somewhat irregularly, have had the benefit of their justification of which they went into proof, damages having only been given for the excess; but as the point has now come distinctly up, it is very important for our future guidance that it should be settled, especially as there has not hitherto been an entire uniformity of practice, though the deviations from what we all believe to be the true rule, have not been frequent. The question is, has the defendants' counsel a right on the cross-examination of the plaintiff's witnesses, and before he has opened the defence, to prove a special justification of which notice has been given under the Act of Assembly, and the affirmative of which, if pleaded and traversed, would lie on the defendant—a right not to be controlled by the discretion of the Judge, and where the plaintiff's counsel has carefully and advisedly abstained from leading to it by the examination in chief? It appears to the Judges present (and I should add we have not been able to confer with His Honour the Chief Justice on the point) that the defendant has no such right, and that the ruling at the trial was quite correct; indeed, we think it would be almost impossible fairly to try causes if a right existed to the extent claimed. The difficulties attendant on trials at Nisi Prius by the generality of pleading, and which it has been the policy of the Legislature of the mother country of late years to contract, have been much enhanced by recent legislation in this Province, to compensate for which, whatever the benefits may be in other respects, certainly relief to the Judges is no part of the equivalent. It would be impossible for the Judges to decide on the relevancy of many questions put by the defendant's counsel, and it would be in the power of an ingenious counsel to multiply discussion to almost any extent. It would be most inconvenient, and often positively unjust, to interrupt the course of the examination of the plaintiff's witnesses while constantly recurring arguments were gone into on the admissibility of proof under the notice of defence, to be at once heard and decided on, which would be found afterwards when the real defence, if any, was opened, to be utterly useless, except for the purpose of making difficulties and causing ruinous delay. The Judge's notes would become a mass of confusion; and no better illustration could be given than a case before us at the last term, where, in an action of slander, charging theft and false swearing, the defendant justified under a notice of over a dozen larcenies in different places, and half a dozen perjuries. Until the defendant's case was opened, what question could a Judge say might not be directly or indirectly applicable to some part of such matter? The discretion which is exercised by the Judge would in reality be shifted to the defendant's counsel, who, under the prompting of a crafty client, would find his duty much more arduous than it is at present.

* * *

Rule discharged.

NOTES

1. *Cross-examination for impeachment.* The rule restricting cross-examination to the scope of the direct, recognized in a large majority of American jurisdictions, does not apply to cross-examination for purposes of impeachment. Cross-examination to impeach is treated in Chapter 12, Section E, infra. In England and in a few states the cross-examiner is free to question about any issue relevant to the case. See 1 McCormick, Evidence § 21 (7th ed. 2013).

2. *Trial court discretion.* Cross-examination to impeach possesses considerable potential for injecting confusion of, and distracting attention from, the issues. In Howard v. United States, 389 F.2d 287, 292 (D.C.Cir.1967), the court spoke of the judge's authority to control this aspect of cross-examination:

> Although opportunity to cross-examine is a fundamental right demanding great respect,* * * the courts have also recognized that regulation of the extent and scope of cross-examination must generally lie within the discretion of the trial court, and reversal is warranted only when an abuse of discretion leads to prejudice. * * * We will not reverse the judge for cutting off what he reasonably believed * * * was a fruitless endeavor that would succeed only in needlessly proliferating and confusing the issues. This is all the more so since the questions posed were designed solely to test * * * general credibility. A trial court has much more leeway with respect to cross-examination for that purpose than with cross-examination on subjects raised in direct.

BOLLER V. COFRANCES
Supreme Court of Wisconsin, 1969.
166 N.W.2d 129.

This is an appeal from a judgment of the circuit court for LaCrosse county, which, after a jury verdict assessing the negligence of each driver at 50 percent, dismissed the complaint of Virginia M. Boller, the administratrix of Henry W. Boller, deceased.

The action arose out of an automobile accident that occurred in the city of LaCrosse on May 23, 1965. Henry W. Boller and his passenger, Catherine Case, were both killed in the accident.

* * *

In motions after verdict, the plaintiff, Virginia M. Boller, asked for a new trial because of errors in the instructions, prejudicial conduct on the part of defendant's counsel, and in the interest of justice. These motions were denied, and judgment on the verdict was entered for the defendant. The plaintiff has appealed to this court.

HEFFERNAN, JUSTICE.

Is a new trial warranted because of defendant's counsel's conduct in asking an allegedly improper question that indelibly prejudiced the jury despite the admonitions of the trial judge?

The plaintiff argues that a new trial should be granted because Virginia Boller was asked the following question on cross-examination by defense counsel:

"Q. Were you aware of the affair that your husband was having with Mrs. Case [the passenger in the car]?

"MR. ARNESON: I object to this, Your Honor, as improper cross examination. There's no foundation for any kind of questioning about that. It's beyond the scope of direct examination in every respect.

"THE COURT: *Beyond the scope,* Mr. Crosby. Objection sustained. [Emphasis supplied.]

"MR. ARNESON: And I ask that the jury be instructed to disregard it.

"THE COURT: Jury will be instructed to disregard it.

"MR. CROSBY: That's all."

* * *

In the instant case plaintiff's counsel, although he objected to the question, was at the time satisfied with the judge's order to strike the question and with his direction to the jury to disregard it. It was only after the disappointing verdict that the plaintiff, who could well have been benefitted by the question, claimed it to be prejudicial. His claim is not only without merit, but it is also untimely.

Was it error to exclude the question in regard to Henry Boller's affair with Mrs. Case?

While the trial judge excluded the question, "Were you [Virginia Boller] aware of the affair that your husband was having with Mrs. Case?"—and the plaintiff assumes that such ruling was correct—the defendant on this appeal stoutly contends that the question was proper and Virginia Boller's answer should have been admitted into evidence.

Defendant points out in his brief that the plaintiff on direct examination testified, "that she and her husband had a close relationship and were very happily married."

When defendant's counsel asked his question, it was objected to and that objection was sustained on the grounds that it was *beyond the scope of the direct* examination. We do not agree with the ruling of the trial judge. One of the major issues to be resolved by the jury was the evaluation, to the extent possible, of the loss Virginia Boller sustained by losing the society and companionship of Henry Boller. Certainly, the existence of an "affair" with another woman and Virginia Boller's knowledge of it were probative of the value to be placed upon Virginia Boller's loss. Moreover, the question was directly related to, and in impeachment of, her testimony on direct examination. We are satisfied that the question was relevant to the questions posed on direct examination and was within its scope. Of course, despite its probativeness, it is within the discretion of the trial judge to exclude evidence if its probativeness is offset by possible jury prejudice. * * * Here, however, such discretion was not in fact exercised, and in view of the state of the record, such evidence should not have been excluded. While we find the disputed question to be within the scope of the direct examination, we have grave doubts that such rule of exclusion should be followed, particularly when the witness on the stand is a party and subject to be called, in a civil case at least, by the opponent. * * * The rule against questioning any witness "beyond the scope of direct examination" has no intrinsic merit and does not demonstrably assist in the search for the truth. Rather, by encouraging pettifogging objections that go to form and not substance, the rule is likely to be disruptive of trial procedure and results in appeals that basically have no merit.

The only claimed virtue for the rule is that it ensures the orderly presentation of evidence, i.e., that a plaintiff's witness should not be expected to help make the defendant's case on cross-examination. But why shouldn't he? If the question is relevant and is otherwise admissible and the information solicited is within the knowledge of the witness, it should be within the sound discretion of the trial judge to determine whether or not questions on cross-examination prevent an orderly and cogent presentation of the evidence. They well might, and usually would, contribute to the intelligent search for the truth.[4]

---

[4] In the recent case of Neider v. Spoehr (March 4, 1969), Wis., 165 N.W.2d 171, Mr. Justice Beilfuss, speaking for the Court, pointed out that it is within the discretion of the trial judge to control cross-examination:

"* * * the right of * * * cross-examination * * * can be controlled by the trial court so that the trial proceeds in an orderly and fair manner. The exercise of discretion by the trial court to deny or restrict cross-examination must be dependent upon the circumstances of the trial. This court will not reverse unless it clearly appears that the trial court abused its discretion

This test, which leaves the admission or exclusion to the discretion of the trial judge, is infinitely preferable to the artificial and meaningless rule that excludes all evidence whether it should then logically come into the record or not, simply because it is "beyond the scope." The Model Code of Evidence recommends the following rule to supplant the present practice:

> "Rule 105. Control of Judge over Presentation of Evidence. The judge controls the conduct of the trial to the end that the evidence shall be presented honestly, expeditiously and in such form as to be readily understood, and in his discretion determines, among other things, * * *

> "(h) to what extent and in what circumstances a party cross-examining a witness may be forbidden to examine him concerning material matters not inquired about on a previous examination by the judge or by an adverse party."

Wigmore points out that the present rule, as practiced in Wisconsin, is a recent one, and that the historical or orthodox rule permitted:

> " * * * the opposite party * * * not only [to] cross-examine him in relation to the point which he was called to prove, but he may examine him as to any matter embraced in the issue. He may establish his defence by him without calling any other witnesses. If he is a competent witness to the jury for any purpose, he is so for all purposes." 6 Wigmore, Evidence (3d ed.) sec. 1885, p. 532, quoting Sutherland, J., Fulton Bank v. Stafford, 2 Wend. 483, 485.

Wigmore in that volume, sec. 1885 ff., discusses in detail the shortcomings of the present rule. In his Students' Textbook, Wigmore on Evidence, he summarizes the effect of the present rule:

> "Cross examination is the greatest engine for getting at the truth; * * * and a rule which needlessly hampers its exercise as this one does cannot be a sound one."

McCormick, in his treatise on Evidence (hornbook series), sec. 27, p. 51, points out that, when all relevant factors are considered, "the balance [is] overwhelmingly in favor of the wide-open rule." He points out that:

> "The restrictive practice in all its forms * * * is productive * * * of continual bickering over the choice of the numerous variations of the 'scope of the direct' criterion, and of their application to particular cross-questions. These controversies are often

---

and that the error affected a substantial right of the complaining party and probably affected the result of the trial."

This statement is valid under the rule we herein adopt and expresses the rationale of the Model Code of Evidence that discretion in this respect is properly vested in the trial court.

reventilated on appeal, and reversals for error in their determination are frequent. Observance of these vague and ambiguous restrictions is a matter of constant and hampering concern to the cross-examiner. If these efforts, delays and misprisions were the necessary incidents to the guarding of substantive rights or the fundamentals of fair trial, they might be worth the cost. As the price of the choice of an obviously debatable regulation of the order of evidence, the sacrifice seems misguided."

McCormick also emphasizes the deleterious effect of the present rule in the prosecution of criminals:

" * * * the accused may limit his direct examination to some single aspect of the case, such as age, sanity or alibi, and then invoke the court's ruling that the cross-examination be limited to the matter thus opened. Surely the according of a privilege to the accused to select out a favorable fact and testify to that alone, and thus get credit for testifying but escape a searching inquiry on the whole charge, is a travesty on criminal administration * * * "

"In jurisdictions following the wide-open practice there is of course no obstacle to cross-examining the accused upon any matters relevant to any issue in the entire case." Sec. 26, pp. 49, 50.

While the Wisconsin cases appear to allow greater latitude in the cross-examination of a criminal defendant, they appear to permit examination of all facets of an alleged crime only when the defendant has opened the door on direct by testifying on the merits of the case. Sprague v. State (1925), 188 Wis. 432, 206 N.W. 69.

We are satisfied that the wide-open rule should be adopted by this court. The appeal herein is founded upon the exclusion from the record of relevant evidence on the grounds that it elicited information not covered by, or within, the scope of the direct evidence. The evidence, in reason, ought not to have been excluded. Because the plaintiff, by invoking the spurious "beyond the scope" rule, contends that the jury made use of improper and inadmissible evidence, he has brought a patently specious appeal. The exclusion of the evidence on the basis of the restrictive rule is founded in neither reason nor the interest of justice. It is productive of confusion and super-technical appeals similar to the one brought in this instance.

Had the rule been the one permitting wide-open cross-examination, the answer to the question would have been clearly admissible and the subsequent bickering would have been avoided. Of course, as stated above, otherwise admissible evidence can still be excluded in the discretion of the trial judge if its harmful effects on the legal process *still for em, by place*

outweigh its probative value. In such event, e.g., had it been clearly admissible under the wide-open rule, the question would have hinged upon the question of abuse of discretion by the trial judge and not upon a mechanistic rule of evidence.

We conclude that in the instant case the plaintiff failed to preserve his right to review the judge's instructions to the jury. We also conclude that the disputed question properly should have been allowed as eliciting evidence relevant to the issue or an impeachment. On both scores the answer would be admissible even under the restrictive rule heretofore in use. It would without a doubt have been a proper question under the wide-open rule which we herein adopt. Under this rule the trial judge shall exercise discretion to assure an orderly and intelligible presentation of the facts without the requirement of slavish compliance with the "beyond the scope" rule.

We conclude that the plaintiff was not prejudiced by the proceedings and the apportionment of negligence is supported by substantial evidence. The interest of justice would not be secured by a new trial.

Judgment affirmed.

NOTES AND QUESTIONS

1. *Support for wide-open cross-examination.* Scholarly opinion has long inclined heavily to the views espoused in the principal case. See, e.g., McCormick, The Scope and Art of Cross Examination, 47 Nw.U.L.Rev. 177 (1952); Degnan, Non–Rules Evidence Law: Cross–Examination, 6 Utah L.Rev. 323 (1959); Note, The Limiting Effect of Direct Examination upon the Scope of Cross-examination, 37 Colum.L.Rev. 1373 (1937). And the ABA Committee for the Improvement of the Law of Evidence for 1937–38 commented:

> The rule limiting cross-examination to the precise subject of direct examination is probably the most frequent rule (except the opinion rule) leading in trial practice today to refined and technical quibbles which obstruct the trial, confuse the jury, and give rise to appeal on technical grounds only.

But despite occasional defections such as that in the principal case the restrictive American rule continues as the law in the great majority of jurisdictions.

2. *Broad interpretations of the restrictive view.* Some jurisdictions have interpreted the American rule in a manner that leaves enormous discretion in the trial court judge. See, e.g., Eno v. Adair County Mut. Ins. Ass'n, 294 N.W. 323, 327 (Iowa 1940) ("[W]here the testimony of a witness on direct examination makes a prima facie case, or creates a presumption or inference as to the existence of a fact not directly testified to, the witness may be cross-

examined to rebut such prima facie proof, presumption or inference"). Does such a rule restrict cross-examination in any significant way?

3. *Rule 611(b)*. The history of Federal Rule 611(b) reflects the strenuous disagreement on the subject within the profession. The original Advisory Committee draft embodied the restrictive majority rule. Preliminary Draft of Proposed Rules of Evidence for United States District Courts, 46 F.R.D. 161, 302 (1969). The wide-open rule was substituted in the version of the rules approved by the Supreme Court. Proposed Rule of Evidence 611(b), 56 F.R.D. 183, 273 (1972). The final congressionally enacted version restores the orthodoxy. Arizona, Maine, Michigan, Mississippi, New Hampshire, North Carolina, Ohio, South Carolina, Tennessee, West Virginia, and Wisconsin, though adopting counterparts of the Federal Rules, have opted for wide-open cross-examination.

Although Rule 611(b) adopts the American approach, in operation the Rule leaves a great deal of discretion and flexibility in the trial court judge. The following case is illustrative.

UNITED STATES V. LARA

United States Court of Appeals, First Circuit, 1999.
181 F.3d 183.

SELYA, CIRCUIT JUDGE.

A federal grand jury indicted a coterie of defendants, including the six appellants (Giovanni "King G" Lara, George "King Paradise" Sepulveda, Terrence "King Bullet" Boyd, Shariff "King Biz" Roman, George "King Animal" Perry, and Eryn "King Guy" Vasquez) for a multiplicity of crimes arising out of their involvement in the Providence chapter of the Almighty Latin King Nation. Following a 44–day trial, each appellant was convicted on one or more of the following charges: racketeering, 18 U.S.C. § 1962(c); conspiracy to commit racketeering, *id.* § 1962(d); violent crime in aid of racketeering (including two murders and two attempted murders), *id.* § 1959(a)(1) & (5); carjacking, *id.* § 2119(3); witness intimidation, *id.* § 1512(b); use or carriage of a firearm during a crime of violence, *id.* § 924(c); and being a felon in possession of a firearm, *id.* § 922(g). The district court sentenced five of the appellants to life imprisonment and the sixth, Vasquez, to 100 months in prison. These appeals followed. We affirm.

I. Background

We offer a thumbnail sketch of the interrelationship between the appellants and the Latin Kings, taking the information contained in the record in the light most congenial to the jury's verdict. *See United States v. Houlihan,* 92 F.3d 1271, 1277 (1st Cir.1996). We eschew an exposition of the other evidence, preferring to discuss that evidence in the body of the opinion as it pertains to our consideration of particular points raised by the appellants.

The Latin Kings originated in Chicago in the 1940s. Over time, the street gang's influence spread to other venues. The movement migrated east to Providence in the early 1990s. Though some chapters of the Latin Kings, called Charter Nations, require Hispanic descent as a condition of membership, others (like the Providence chapter) allow persons of all races and ethnicities to join.

Members of the Latin Kings signal their affiliation by sporting beads and other accouterments (including tattoos) in the gang's colors—black and gold. They pay dues, attend weekly meetings, and undertake "missions" (a euphemism that covers an array of activities ranging from running errands to committing violent crimes) when directed by gang leaders. Respect and security rank among the gang's paramount concerns: the Latin Kings routinely discipline members for disrespectful behavior or for discussing Latin King business with outsiders. Discipline runs a lengthy gamut from the "silent treatment" (suspension of all communications with other gang members), to revocation of drug use privileges, to a "bounce" (a time-controlled beating limited to certain areas of the body), to death.

The Almighty Latin King Nation is a hierarchical organization, and each of the appellants held one or more leadership positions within the Providence chapter. Sepulveda served as the group's president (sometimes called "Inca"). Boyd served as the vice-president (sometimes called "Cacique"), and later succeeded Sepulveda as president. Roman served as the chief enforcer (a position previously held by Lara and subsequently held by Perry), and replaced Boyd as vice-president. Vasquez functioned as the group's philosopher and then graduated to the post of investigator.

* * *

C.   Scope of Cross–Examination

Perry, who testified at trial in his own defense, strives to persuade us that the district court gave the government too free rein in cross-examination. We are unconvinced. *Issue*

Perry's thesis is that the challenged cross-examination exceeded the scope of direct examination and, therefore, should have been foreclosed. This thesis rests primarily on the first sentence of Fed.R.Evid. 611(b), which reads: "Cross-examination should be limited to the subject matter of the direct examination and matters affecting the credibility of the witness." Perry notes that his direct examination consisted of only ten questions, restricted to the Vandergroen carjacking and its sequelae. * * * Yet, the trial court allowed the prosecutor, over objection, to cross- *Perry 4s.*

question Perry not only about the carjacking, but also about other crimes of which he and his codefendants were accused (including the Mendez murder and two attempted homicides charged as predicate acts in the RICO conspiracy count), and about a draft of a letter seized from his jail cell in which he accused his former girlfriend of "snitching" and requested that she be silenced.

We review district court rulings anent the scope of cross-examination solely for abuse of discretion. *See United States v. Smith,* 145 F.3d 458, 462 (1st Cir.1998); *United States v. Morla–Trinidad,* 100 F.3d 1, 4 (1st Cir.1996). We find none here. It is standard fare for cross-examiners to inquire into issues not mentioned on direct examination, but related to and made relevant by that examination. *See McGautha v. California,* 402 U.S. 183, 215 * * * (1971). It is equally standard—and equally proper—for a cross-examiner to delve into matters which, although not mentioned on direct examination, bear on the witness's credibility. *See id.* Collectively, these two categories envelop the questions that Perry challenges. We explain briefly.

The indictment charged the Vandergroen carjacking as a predicate act within the RICO conspiracy and as a violent crime in aid of racketeering. At trial, the government asserted that Vandergroen's disrespect of Perry offended the Latin King code and led Perry to target him. During the government's case in chief, at least two witnesses testified in support of this theory. Because Perry's direct examination included a denial that the Vandergroen incident had anything to do with the Latin Kings, the government was entitled to test the veracity of this denial. One way of doing so was to interrogate Perry about other crimes that he had committed under the organization's auspices.

In his direct testimony, Perry also endeavored to exonerate Lara, portraying him on direct examination as unaware—until it was too late—that either the carjacking or the killing would transpire. On cross-examination, the government sought to show that this version of events conflicted with Perry's earlier statement to the police and to suggest that he was covering for Lara as part of his perceived duty as a Latin King not to "rat" on fellow gang members. It was in this context that the prosecutor asked about the correspondence in which Perry solicited punishment for his loose-lipped girlfriend. Thus, we detect no abuse of discretion in Judge Lisi's determination that these lines of cross-questioning were not beyond the scope of Perry's direct examination.

We hasten to add that, even were we to conclude that the challenged questions exceeded the scope of direct examination, we nonetheless would uphold the judge's rulings. Perry's animadversions largely overlook the second sentence of Rule 611(b), which empowers trial courts, "in the exercise of discretion, [to] permit inquiry into additional matters as if on direct examination." Fed.R.Evid. 611(b). [This authorization confers discretion on trial judges to disregard the first sentence of Rule 611(b) and allow cross-examination to extend into areas not explored on direct.] *See Losacco v. F.D. Rich Constr. Co.,* 992 F.2d 382, 385 (1st Cir.1993); *United States v. Arnott,* 704 F.2d 322, 324 (6th Cir.1983); *United States v. Raper,* 676 F.2d 841, 846–47 (D.C.Cir.1982). *But cf. Lis v. Robert Packer Hosp.,* 579 F.2d 819, 823 (3d Cir.1978) (confining the exercise of a district court's discretion under the second sentence of Rule 611(b) to "special circumstances"). In this instance, the challenged questions occupied only a fraction of the cross-examination and bore a close relationship to major trial issues. Thus, whether or not the questions fell within the scope of the direct examination, we could not say that the trial judge's overruling of Perry's objections constituted an abuse of discretion.

* * *

Affirmed.

NOTES AND QUESTIONS

1.   *Liberal construction of Rule 611(b).* The liberal construction of Rule 611(b) is further illustrated by statements such as the widely quoted one from United States v. Arnott, 704 F.2d 322, 324 (6th Cir.1983), "[Rule 611(b)] has been liberally construed to include all inferences and implications arising from [direct examination] testimony." Based upon such statements, as well as the application of the rule in *Lara,* is there much left of the American rule in the federal courts? See also United States v. Chance, 306 F.3d 356 (6th Cir.2002) (no abuse of discretion to permit testimony on recross examination about the competency of all employees where redirect examination had elicited testimony about four specific employees).

2.   *Limiting cross-examination.* Despite the broad discretion in the trial judge to open cross-examination to matters only remotely related to those covered on direct examination, discretion is perhaps not as broad when the decision has been to limit the examination, particularly on questions of credibility. See, e.g., Harbor Ins. Co. v. Schnabel Foundation Co., 946 F.2d 930 (D.C.Cir.1991). But see United States v. Route, 104 F.3d 59 (5th Cir.1997) (trial judge properly exercised discretion in limiting defendant's cross-examination of government witness); United States v. Mikutowicz, 365 F.3d 65 (1st Cir.2004) (court did not abuse its discretion in limiting cross-examination of IRS agent with regard to tax court opinions).

3.   *The accused as witness.* Particularly troublesome questions are raised when the witness being cross-examined is the accused in a criminal case who has elected to testify on the merits. With the dictum in the principal case, compare Tucker v. United States, 5 F.2d 818 (8th Cir.1925). See also Carlson, Cross–Examination of the Accused, 52 Cornell L.Q. 705 (1967); 1 McCormick, Evidence § 26 (7th ed. 2013). It is to be noted that the problem does not arise where the accused testifies solely on a preliminary matter,

such testimony having been held not to open the witness to cross-examination on the entire case. Simmons v. United States, 390 U.S. 377 (1968).

BOMMER V. STEDELIN

St. Louis Court of Appeals, Missouri, 1951.
237 S.W.2d 225.

HOUSER, COMMISSIONER. This is a bailment case involving a claim for damages to an automobile delivered to a public parking lot for storage and parking.

This appeal involves the propriety of the action of the trial court in directing a verdict for defendants at the close of plaintiff's evidence and in refusing plaintiff's request to reopen the case to present additional evidence.

* * *

The testimony showed that plaintiff's wife, intending to shop in downtown St. Louis, took plaintiff's automobile to the parking lot at 8th and Delmar, turned the car over to an attendant, received "a little stub", paid "a quarter" and the attendant drove the car "away"; that the parking lot was "two or three stories high and it has no sides". Plaintiff testified that it was "a three story steel affair". Upon returning for the car later in the day plaintiff's wife went to the office on the premises, gave the stub "to the boy, and he went and rang it out on a time card and went and got it for me"; that he went upstairs; that "he got on some kind of a little elevator and went on some kind of a lift." She was standing about 30 or 40 feet from the ramp down which the automobile was driven. She heard and saw the car coming down the ramp. She testified "It sounded like wheels squeaking, and the brakes squeaking and whistling."

> "Q. What happened to your car? A. It come on down and hit into a parked car and part of the building, one of those big girders.
>
> "Q. A steel girder? A. Yes, sir.
>
> "Q. Did it stop against the girder or this other automobile? A. Oh, yes."

She testified that "some young fellow" was driving the car down the ramp. She could not say whether or not he was the one to whom she had given the ticket or with whom she had left the car.

The "whole front end" of the automobile was damaged. It looked like the engine was pushed back under the seat. Plaintiff was called to the scene and when he arrived his car was "laying against a big, new car and the balance of it was against the steel girder."

Plaintiff's wife testified that a gentleman who identified himself as Mr. Stedelin came to the parking lot after the occurrence; that he was "in charge there"; that after her husband arrived Stedelin said he did not own the parking lot; that it was owned by the Glueck Realty Company. "Q.—Did he indicate to you or to your husband what capacity he held, if any? A. Well, I don't know whether he was in charge or vice-president or president of it."

Plaintiff testified that he had a conversation with Jerome Stedelin; that plaintiff wanted to know "who was in charge"; that Stedelin said "he was the manager of the parking lot under the Glueck Realty Company at 1103 North Third Street, were the owners of the lot"; that Stedelin did not disclose to plaintiff his capacity with the company.

Plaintiff's proof of damages is not challenged.

When defendants' counsel requested a directed verdict at the close of the plaintiff's evidence, the trial judge indicated he would direct a verdict, whereupon plaintiff's counsel requested leave to reopen the case "in order to bring in additional witnesses to testify with respect to ownership and operation of the parking lot * * * by bringing in the officers of the Glueck Realty Company" stating he could "within an hour" produce evidence to "further show to the court the ownership of this parking lot by the defendants." Leave to reopen was denied.

* * *

Defendants moved for a directed verdict "for the reason that plaintiff wholly failed to identify the ownership and management of the parking lot mentioned in evidence, with either or both the said defendants." Since that motion was sustained the court must have based its action on failure of proof in this connection. Since as we shall see the case must be retried we will not weigh the sufficiency of the proof in this regard, but will consider now the question whether the trial court abused its discretion.

Although a trial judge is vested with a wide latitude and broad discretion in the allowance or denial of leave to reopen a case for additional testimony, that discretion must be a sound judicial discretion. It cannot be exercised in an arbitrary manner. The record shows that the request was made at 6 minutes before 1:00 o'clock P.M.; that the jury was recessed until 2:00 o'clock; that counsel assured the court that he could produce the required evidence "within an hour". There was no showing of surprise to defendants or of inconvenience to the court, parties, counsel, or jury or that the adverse party would have been deceived or prejudiced in any manner by granting the leave. The ruling on the motion for a directed verdict had not yet been made. The court denied plaintiff the opportunity to offer evidence to prove that defendants owned and operated the parking facility, while at the same time directing a verdict against plaintiff for failure to prove such fact. This constituted an abuse of discretion. * * *

For the reasons stated the Commissioner recommends that the judgment of the circuit court be reversed and the cause remanded.

PER CURIAM.

The foregoing opinion of HOUSER, C., is adopted as the opinion of the court.

The judgment of the circuit court is, accordingly, reversed and the cause remanded.

NOTE

It is commonly held that the trial court may, in its sound discretion, permit reopening of the evidence after both parties have formally rested. At what stage of the proceedings should the court's discretion to permit reopening expire? See United States v. Nunez, 432 F.3d 573 (4th Cir.2005) (district court abused its discretion in permitting the government to reopen its case after summation and after jury deliberations began to present report summarizing interview with defendant; by admitting the report at that point, the report "gained distorted importance, prejudiced the appellants' case," and precluded an adequate opportunity to meet the additional evidence offered). See also 6 Wigmore, Evidence §§ 1876–81 (Chadbourn rev. 1976); Annot., 87 A.L.R.2d 849.

CHAPTER 7

THE CONCEPT OF RELEVANCY

■ ■ ■

A. INTRODUCTION

JAMES, RELEVANCY, PROBABILITY AND THE LAW[1]
29 California Law Review 689, 690–91 (1941).

Relevancy, as the word itself indicates, is not an inherent characteristic of any item of evidence but exists as a relation between an item of evidence and a proposition sought to be proved. If an item of evidence tends to prove or to disprove any proposition, it is relevant to that proposition. If the proposition itself is one provable in the case at bar, or if it in turn forms a further link in a chain of proof the final proposition of which is provable in the case at bar, then the offered item of evidence has probative value in the case. Whether the immediate or ultimate proposition sought to be proved is provable in the case at bar is determined by the pleadings, by the procedural rules applicable thereto, and by the substantive law governing the case. Whether the offered item of evidence tends to prove the proposition at which it is ultimately aimed depends upon other factors, shortly to be considered. But because relevancy, as used by Thayer and in the Code, means tendency to prove a proposition properly provable in the case, an offered item of evidence may be excluded as "irrelevant" for either of these two quite distinct reasons: because it is not probative of the proposition at which it is directed, or because that proposition is not provable in the case.[2]

NOTES AND QUESTIONS

1. *Discussions.* Other helpful treatments of the nature of relevancy include: Crump, On the Uses of Irrelevant Evidence, 34 Hous.L.Rev. 1 (1997); Ladd, Determination of Relevancy, 31 Tul.L.Rev. 81 (1956); Lempert, Modeling Relevance, 75 Mich.L.Rev. 1021 (1977); Lyon & Koehler, The Relevance Ratio: Evaluating the Probative Value of Expert Testimony in

---

[1] Copyright by Fred B. Rothman & Co. Reprinted by permission. Throughout the cases and materials in this chapter some footnotes from the originals have been omitted; others have been renumbered. [Ed.]

[2] Henceforth, for brevity, propositions of ultimate fact properly provable in a case under the pleadings and substantive law will be referred to as "material propositions"; the characterization "relevant" will be reserved for propositions of evidence which, whether or not material themselves, tend to prove other propositions which are material. "Irrelevant" and "immaterial" are of course the contraries of the two first terms, as defined. * * *

Child Abuse Cases, 82 Cornell L.Rev. 43 (1996); Trautman, Logical or Legal Relevancy—A Conflict in Theory, 5 Vand.L.Rev. 385 (1952).

2. *Materiality.* As indicated in the quotation from James, the admissibility of evidence often depends upon the substantive law, which governs whether a proposition is properly in the case. Thus an allegation in a complaint that a promissory note was given for "a valuable consideration" would not be provable by evidence that it was given for an antecedent debt in a jurisdiction where that did not constitute a valuable consideration. The evidence is immaterial under that classic but seldom observed concept and irrelevant under the looser definition in Federal Rule 401. Accordingly, in diversity cases the admissibility of evidence in federal courts may depend upon state substantive law.

3. *Standard.* By what standard should the probative value of offered evidence be judged in determining whether to admit it? At least two possibilities will come to mind: (1) evidence to be relevant must render the fact sought to be proved more probable than not, and (2) evidence to be relevant must help to render the fact sought to be proved more probable than would be so in the absence of the evidence. The first standard, which, as suggested by the materials of Topic II, is commonly used in evaluating the sufficiency of evidence, has also sometimes been employed by courts in the present context. These applications would appear unfortunate. Not only will the standard, if rigorously applied, exclude a great deal of helpful evidence, but it also entirely fails to take into account the fact that it is frequently possible to establish a material proposition by a conjunction of evidentiary items, none of which would alone suffice. To extend Professor McCormick's metaphor, a brick is not a wall, but many bricks may make one.

The second standard noted above is most commonly applied. See Rule 401. It allows the legal mind to display a tremendous sweep of ingenuity in attacking problems of proof, but it also entails problems of its own. The cases of the present section, all dealing with the same generic type of evidence, will serve to illustrate both facets of the standard, and also to suggest the relative nature of relevancy itself.

4. *Federal Rules of Evidence.* Rules 401–403 deal with the general question of relevancy and the exclusion of relevant evidence on grounds of prejudice, confusion, or waste of time. For discussion of these rules see Dolan, Rule 403: The Prejudice Rule in Evidence, 49 S.Cal.L.Rev. 220 (1976); Gold, Federal Rule of Evidence 403: Observations on the Nature of Unfairly Prejudicial Evidence, 58 Wash.L.Rev. 497 (1983); Travers, An Essay on the Determination of Relevancy Under the Federal Rules of Evidence, 1977 Ariz.St.L.J. 327; Weinstein & Berger, Basic Rules of Relevancy in the Proposed Federal Rules of Evidence, 4 Ga.L.Rev. 43 (1969).

5. *Rule 403.* Rule 403 recognizes the problems which arise from taking the broad view of relevancy reflected by Rule 401. Should identical effect be given to each of the various factors which may weigh against the admissibility of relevant evidence? If Justice Holmes was correct in saying

that the exclusion of evidence which would unduly consume time is "a concession to the shortness of life," Reeve v. Dennett, 11 N.E. 938, 944 (Mass.1887), then the admission of such evidence can scarcely be more than harmless error. Is this true of evidence which may involve the other factors enumerated by the Rule?

B. AN ILLUSTRATION OF RELEVANCY RULES: EVIDENCE OF FINANCIAL WORTH

CITY OF CLEVELAND V. PETER KIEWIT SONS' CO.

United States Court of Appeals, Sixth Circuit, 1980.
624 F.2d 749.

WEICK, CIRCUIT JUDGE.

* * *

I

Dock 34, the dock in question, was originally constructed in the year 1908. In recent years, because of its deterioration and lack of repair, it was no longer used for its original purpose and only a small portion of which was being used chiefly as a parking lot for nearby sporting events, and for the mooring of a schoolship and a pleasure boat. In 1973, Peter Kiewit Sons' Co., a contracting firm headquartered in Omaha, Nebraska (and incorporated in that state), was engaged in performing dike construction and dike modification at another place in the Cleveland Harbor, pursuant to a contract with the Corps of Engineers. Kiewit entered into the permit agreement with the City whereby Kiewit was permitted to use a portion of the dock to load blast furnace slag on barges to be transported to the dike project. Under the agreement, Kiewit was permitted to occupy and use a 100–400 foot portion of the southwest corner of the dock from July 9, 1973, to and including October 12, 1973 (except for six days in late July when the area would be occupied by a carnival). Kiewit agreed to pay the City therefor $2,000 a month.

Kiewit actually occupied the dock site from July 16 to and including October 6 (except for the period from July 21 through July 30 when it was used by the carnival); the dock was used for the slag loading operation from August 1 to October 6. The slag loading operation consisted of trucking slag to the dock, where the slag was piled and then loaded onto barges for transportation to the breakwall some distance away. The operations were concluded, and Kiewit vacated the dock on October 8, 1973.

On October 24, 1973, after Kiewit had surrendered possession to the City, portions of the dock collapsed. The portion that collapsed included only a small section of the area which had been leased to Kiewit; the major portion of the area which collapsed was not within the section that had been leased to and used by Kiewit.

The City of Cleveland filed suit against Kiewit in the Court of Common Pleas of Cuyahoga County in a three-count complaint. The three causes of action alleged reflected different theories of law under which the plaintiff sought to impose liability on defendant for the collapses of the dock. The action was removed on the basis of diversity of citizenship to the United States District Court for the Northern District of Ohio on August 28, 1974. The City sought recovery of $350,000 in compensatory damages plus interest. Following a November 1976 trial which lasted six days, the jury[3] returned a general verdict in favor of the City and against Kiewit in the amount of $350,000. Judgment was entered thereon plus costs. Kiewit then filed a timely motion for judgment notwithstanding the verdict, or, in the alternative, for a new trial, alleging misconduct of counsel for the City as one of the three grounds that "the remarks, argument and questioning of witnesses by plaintiff's counsel regarding liability insurance and defendant's financial resources, considered in total, were prejudicial." *—kews crs.*

The District Judge ordered a remittitur of $175,000, and stated that, if the remittitur were not accepted within thirty days, he would grant a new trial on the issue of damages. * * * The City thereafter advised the District Court that it would decline to accept the remittitur, and would instead proceed to a new trial on the issue of damages. The court then ordered a new trial solely on the issue of damages, with the trial date to be set following this appeal.

The comments which are at issue here began early in the City's opening statement to the jury, when Nick DeVito, an Assistant Law Director of the City, stated that "the defendant is Peter Kiewit and Sons, a corporation whose headquarters are in Omaha, Nebraska * * * Peter Kiewit is one of the largest construction corporations." Counsel for Kiewit promptly objected; the Court explained that "if they (plaintiff) can prove that in their evidence, I will overrule the objection, but if they can't, I will then admonish the jury to disregard it." Mr. DeVito then proceeded to tell the jury that "Peter Kiewit Co. is one of the largest construction corporations in the United States * * * it has international operations throughout the world. Its marine division is headquartered in New Jersey, and * * * you will have * * * testimony * * * from some of its executives from that part of the country." Mr. DeVito then stated that Kiewit, in 1973, "was awarded approximately a $9 million contract with the United States Corps of Army Engineers." Kiewit's attorney objected, but was overruled by the Court. Counsel for the City then repeated his statement about the $9 million contract. At the conclusion of the

---

[3]   Of the six members of the jury, three were residents of the City of Cleveland, and the other three resided in Cuyahoga County.

plaintiff's opening statement, the court admonished the jury as to Mr. DeVito's remarks that Kiewit was one of the nation's largest construction companies, and that the defendant had a $9 million contract with the Corps. The court instructed the jury that "these two statements standing by themselves are not be considered in your deliberations * * * the fact that they were large or that they had a large monetary contract with the United States government has no bearing on the case whatsoever."

During direct examination of Robert Jones, a witness for the City, Mr. DeVito, referring to Kiewit, inquired "How big a company is that?" Counsel for Kiewit promptly objected, but the Court permitted Jones to answer that defendant had "a rather large, good credit rating" and was a large corporation. Mr. DeVito asked where Kiewit was headquartered, and Jones responded "Omaha, Nebraska." Mr. DeVito also inquired whether Kiewit had a marine division, and where it was headquartered; Jones replied that defendant's marine division headquarters was located in Tenafly, New Jersey. Counsel for the City then asked: "Do you know the size of the contract that they had with the federal government?" Kiewit's attorney objected immediately, and was sustained.

During cross-examination of William Bogas, a witness for the City, the attorney representing Kiewit asked several questions concerning a provision of the permit agreement, under the terms of which Kiewit was obligated to take out a general public liability insurance policy in the amount of $300,000 and $100,000. The witness acknowledged that the City was named as an additional insured, so that the insurance protected the City as well as Kiewit from liability to third persons. The witness testified that he did not know whether the City had made any claims under the policy for damage to the dock.

Later, on redirect, the following exchange between Mr. DeVito and witness Bogas transpired:

Q. Are you aware of the contract between Peter Kiewit and the Corps of Engineers?

A. Yes.

Q. Do you know approximately the amount of that contract?

Counsel for Kiewit immediately objected, and the court sustained the objection.

Jack Frakes, a Kiewit employee who testified on behalf of the defendant, was asked on direct examination about the permit agreement's insurance provisions. Frakes acknowledged that the City had drafted the provisions, calling for a general public liability insurance policy with $100,000 and $300,000 limits, and, further, that Kiewit complied with the provisions and obtained said insurance which, as required by the contract, named the City as an additional insured.

On cross-examination, DeVito asked Frakes whether Kiewit "is a pretty big corporation?" Frakes answered: "It is a fair-sized corporation." DeVito then inquired "how large" Kiewit was in the field of marine engineering. The trial court permitted the witness to answer over objection. DeVito persisted in asking "how big" the defendant was, and finally the court interrupted: "I have already admonished the jury that the largeness of the company doesn't make any difference as far as the verdict is concerned in this case."

Subsequently during the cross-examination of Frakes, the following exchange occurred:

Q. You talked about insurance. You did take out insurance?

A. Yes, sir.

Q. And you did have the City of Cleveland as an additional insured?

A. Yes, sir.

Q. And wasn't that in relation to claims from third parties?

A. Yes, sir, liability insurance.

Keenen (counsel for Kiewit): Objection, your Honor.

Court: Are you talking about liability insurance?

DeVito: Yes. I mean, Mr. Keenen represents an insurance company, doesn't he?

Keenen: Objection, your Honor.

Court: Objection sustained.

DeVito: Well, you tell me: Is there insurance involved in this particular case?

Keenen: Objection, your Honor.

Court: Objection sustained.

Keenen: I think that is highly prejudicial, your Honor, He asked three times.

Court: I will ask the jury to disregard that. Whether there is or not has no bearing on this lawsuit.

DeVito: Now, Peter Kiewit has many claims against it in various places throughout the world?

A. No.

Keenen: Objection.

Court: Objection sustained.

DeVito: Are you familiar with various claims and lawsuits against Peter Kiewit Co.?

Keenen: Objection.

Court: Sustained.

During cross-examination of defense witness Saada, the following transpired:

DeVito: Now, you talked about insurance just briefly. You said that you can only get insurance—

Court: Just one minute.

Denny (counsel for Kiewit): Objection.

Court: I don't recall anything about insurance.

Keenen: I can't recall anything about it. It is prejudicial at this point anyway. This is the third or fourth time he has done that.

Court: I am going to sustain the objection, and I am going to admonish counsel that he is not to talk about it.

DeVito: I would like to approach the bench.

Court: No. You can take exception.

DeVito: I am not talking about insurance in this case.

Court: I am not going to permit you to ask these questions.

Q.   You have talked about buildings and you talked about buildings having a useful life; is that correct?

A.   Yes, sir.

Q.   And you also talked about the limit to which someone could acquire insurance on a building, is that correct?

A.   The limits. My statement went something like that. I doubt very much anybody would give you insurance for something built for more than 50 years.

DeVito: Your Honor, if I may and I do not mean to be disrespectful to the Court, this is something he testified to earlier, and this is what I was going to ask him about.

Court: That you may do.

During his closing argument, Mr. DeVito again mentioned that Kiewit had undertaken a "seven or eight million dollar job, whatever it was that they were doing for the Corps of Engineers." Counsel for Kiewit promptly objected to the mention of said contract, which had not been admitted into evidence, and the Court admonished Mr. DeVito "not to comment on it."

During his summation, Mr. Keenen, representing Kiewit, said:

As far as the insurance permit that opposing counsel says is in the contract, read it for yourself. You will find that the City is the named insured, so that if there is any coverage under that contract for Peter Kiewit, the same coverage belongs to the City, and they could collect fully the limit in that policy.

The following colloquy ensued:

DeVito: Your Honor, I am going to object. That insurance was for third—

Court: I will sustain the objection. The insurance in the contract, so there will be no misunderstanding, is with reference to third party liability, and not as between the parties.

DeVito: That insurance does not extend between Peter Kiewit and the City, your Honor.

Court: They can read the contract for themselves.

In his rebuttal, Mr. DeVito stated that Kiewit was "a $75 million corporation in the marine engineering field." Mr. Keenen objected, and the Court, in sustaining the objection, admonished DeVito: "Now, you have done this before, Mr. DeVito, and I am going to have to reprimand you. I have said the size of the corporation makes no difference."

Finally, in concluding his summation, Mr. DeVito told the Jury:

I respectfully request that you discharge your responsibility in your own conscience as best you can and that you find for the City of Cleveland and that you make us whole and hold Peter Kiewit responsible for the damage that they have caused to the taxpayers of the City of Cleveland.

In his charge to the jury, Judge Green instructed:

This case should be considered and decided by you as an action between persons of equal standing in the community, of equal worth, and holding the same or similar stations in life. Both the plaintiff, a municipal corporation, and the defendant, a private corporation, stand equal before the law, and are to be dealt with as equals in a court of justice.

II

Kiewit was entitled to a fair trial but, as we have pointed out, did not receive it because of the pervasive misconduct of counsel for the City.

* * *

In the case at bar, counsel for the City almost continuously sought to plant the seed in the minds of the jurors that Kiewit was a very large corporation with international operations. In addition to the comments recounted above, Mr. DeVito made several other remarks, and asked other questions designed to convey to the jury the image of the defendant as a giant in the field of marine engineering. For example, plaintiff's trial counsel managed to inform the jury that defendant's headquarters was located at "1000 Kiewit Plaza" leaving it for the jurors to draw the inevitable inference that defendant was a huge corporation. Similarly, Mr. DeVito suggested that Kiewit employed several attorneys at its headquarters. Since the Kiewit name is not, among the general public, synonymous with a "corporate giant," as, for example, IBM or General Motors would be, it is unlikely that the jurors would have been aware of defendant's size had Mr. DeVito not strived to so inform them at every opportunity. It was obviously an appeal to passion and prejudice.

The City has advanced the contention that its comments about Kiewit's stature were intended to show that defendant's ability and experience would enable it to determine the condition of the dock in advance of entering the agreement and beginning operations. Indeed, the court below noted that "there was a tenable argument that defendant's size was relevant to the question of its expertise which in turn could be relevant to its knowledge of conditions pertaining to the dock." Yet, the trial court emphasized that "it was not necessary to make mention of defendant's status as a leader in the field of marine engineering in the manner and with the frequency that plaintiff's counsel did." It seems clear that plaintiff could have demonstrated defendant's knowledge and expertise in a much less prejudicial (and perhaps an even more direct and effective) manner.

This court has said, in a diversity case governed by Ohio law, that "evidence as to the poverty or wealth of a party to an action is inadmissible in a negligence action." Eisenhauer v. Burger, 431 F.2d 833, 837 (6th Cir.1970). "Appealing to the sympathy of jurors through references to financial disparity is improper." Draper v. Airco, Inc., 580 F.2d 91, 95 (3d Cir.1978). The Third Circuit in *Draper* explained that:

> The cumulative thrust of plaintiff's counsel's argument * * * was that because the defendants were rich (giants of the industrial world) and because the plaintiff was poor, the jury should base its verdict in favor of plaintiff on this financial disparity. But justice is not dependent upon the wealth or poverty of the parties and a jury should not be urged to predicate its verdict on a prejudice against bigness or wealth.

In *Draper,* plaintiff's counsel repeatedly referred to a $7 million contract between defendant Airco and U.S. Steel.

In Ohio, a "great number of cases * * * have condemned arguments of counsel contrasting the wealth and poverty or strength and weakness, of the opposing litigants, appealing to prejudice against a party to an action because it is a corporation, or corporation of a particular class * * * " 53 Ohio Jur.2d Section 270, pp. 185–186. The Supreme Court of Ohio articulated the general rule in Hudock v. Ry. Co., 164 Ohio St. 493, 498–499, 132 N.E.2d 108 (1956):

> * * * in damage actions in which compensatory damages only are recoverable, evidence is not admissible, directly or indirectly, to show the wealth or financial standing of either the plaintiff or the defendant, except in those exceptional cases, such as actions for defamation or injury to reputation, where the position or wealth of the parties is necessarily involved in determining the damages sustained. It has ever been the theory of our government and a cardinal principle of our jurisprudence that the rich and poor stand alike in courts of justice and that neither the wealth of one nor the poverty of the other shall be permitted to affect the administration of law.

See Book v. Erskine & Sons, Inc., 154 Ohio St. 391, 399–401, 96 N.E.2d 289, 293 (1951) (statements relating to the poverty of one of the parties or the wealth of the other "are clearly calculated to direct the jury's attention to the need of an injured party for compensation rather than the real issues in the case" and have been held to be prejudicial error).

Counsel for the City, as noted above, also made several comments, and asked several questions, which were intended to inform and emphasize that Kiewit had its corporate "residence in another state." Smith v. Travelers Insurance Company, 438 F.2d 373, 375 (6th Cir.1971). Here, as in *Smith,* "[T]he remarks were * * * obviously designed to prejudice the jurors. Taken alone the statements may well have been prejudicial." Id.

The other topic about which counsel for the City made improper and prejudicial references was insurance. Although it is true that it was counsel for Kiewit who first brought up the subject of insurance, the insurance to which he referred was the general public liability insurance policy required under the permit agreement with the City, which protected both Kiewit and the City from claims by third parties. The Court below correctly observed that this "mention of insurance was inevitable in the course of the trial by reason of the fact that matters of insurance coverage were included in the contracts between the parties." However, it was counsel for the plaintiff who interjected the subject of *another* insurance policy—one covering Kiewit in the instant litigation, and one under which Mr. Keenen was allegedly representing Kiewit at trial. * * * As the Court in Radinsky v. Ellis, 167 F.2d 745, 746 (D.C.Cir.1948), stated:

> In a case such as this, when the existence of insurance protection in favor of the defendant is shown to the jury, a mistrial should be declared forthwith. * * *

In light of the foregoing, the curative instructions which the trial court eventually chose to give were plainly, "not sufficient to remove the probability of prejudice." *Draper,* supra at 97. As the Fifth Circuit has so accurately observed:

> * * * the bench and bar are both aware that cautionary instructions are effective only up to a certain point. There must be a line drawn in any trial where, after repeated exposure of a jury to prejudicial information, * * * cautionary instructions will have little, if any, effect in eliminating the prejudicial harm. O'Rear v. Fruehauf Corp., 554 F.2d 1304, 1309 (5th Cir.1977).

Furthermore, the excessive size of the verdict demonstrates the prejudicial effect of counsel's comments. * * * This Court is likewise of the opinion that the remittitur ordered below does not, and cannot, erase the prejudicial error deliberately injected by plaintiff's counsel. In *Draper,* supra * * * at 97, the Court explained:

> A jury which is prejudiced with respect to its finding of liability is not likely to be free from prejudice in awarding damages. Because there is a substantial probability that the error which affected the liability verdict also affected the determination of damages, the new trial must deal with both liability and damages.

This Court believes that the spillover of prejudice discussed in *Draper* may also occur in a case such as this: since the jury was prejudiced with respect to its award of damages, it cannot be said that its finding of liability was free from prejudice. Thus, on remand, "the new trial must deal with both liability and damages." * * *

* * * Since the prejudicial error here cannot be corrected by remittitur, this Court reverses and remands for a new trial on all issues.

NOTES AND QUESTIONS

1. *Basis of the objection?* What was the court's basis for condemning the injection into the case of defendant's financial condition? Of the existence of liability insurance covering the claim? What arguments can be made in support of the relevance of each of them? In a negligence case?

2. *More colorful statements.* At an earlier day, forays into the financial condition of the parties tended to be more colorful. E.g., Louisville & N.R. Co. v. Hull, 68 S.W. 433, 436 (Ky.1902), an action for delay in shipment of the corpse of plaintiff's wife. Plaintiff's lawyer in final argument declared, "We were in the magnificent depot of defendant in Nashville * * * which is more magnificent than Soloman's [sic] Temple. The ticket office there cost more than this court house, I reckon; and the doors of that station, more than plaintiff asked for his damages in this case, I imagine."

3. *Determining prejudice.* How does a court determine what is prejudicial? Under rules such as Rule 403, how does a court compare the probative value of evidence against its danger of unfair prejudice, etc.? See Teitelbaum, Sutton–Barbere & Johnson, Evaluating the Prejudicial Effect of Evidence: Can Judges Identify the Impact of Improper Evidence on Juries? 1983 Wis.L.Rev. 1147, and Gold, Federal Rule of Evidence 403: Observations on the Nature of Unfairly Prejudicial Evidence, 58 Wash.L.Rev. 497 (1983).

4. *Cases in this section.* The cases in the present section of the casebook develop the concept of relevancy by considering varying aspects of the financial condition of parties as evidence. Liability insurance is considered following *Reed v. General Motors Corp.,* which appears later in this section.

5. *Annotations.* See Annots., 122 A.L.R. 1408 and 65 A.L.R.2d 945, as to admissibility of evidence of a party's financial condition.

PLUMB V. CURTIS

Supreme Court of Errors of Connecticut, 1895.
33 A. 998.

[Plaintiff, Hanford C. Plumb, sued Lewis F. Curtis for building materials allegedly purchased by the latter through his agent Simeon Plumb. Plaintiff had furnished materials for three houses, on Simeon Plumb's order, and defendant admitted responsibility therefor. Thereafter plaintiff furnished materials for an additional five houses, also on Simeon Plumb's order, and defendant denied liability, claiming the materials had been sold to Simeon Plumb. The jury returned a verdict for plaintiff, and defendant appeals from the judgment entered thereon.]

BALDWIN, J. * * * The plaintiff was allowed, against the defendant's objection, to testify that Simeon Plumb was a man of no property, so far as he knew. It was not disputed that all the goods charged to the defendant had been ordered by Simeon Plumb, and sold on credit. The plaintiff claimed that he had extended this credit to the defendant, and was justified by the circumstances in so doing. The defendant denied that Simeon Plumb had any authority to buy on his credit the goods charged in 1891; and the main controversy was as to this point.

Unless excluded by some rule or principle of law, any fact may be proved which logically tends to aid the trier in the determination of the issue. Evidence is admitted not because it is shown to be competent, but because it is not shown to be incompetent. No precise and universal test of relevancy is furnished by the law. The question must be determined in each case according to the teachings of reason and judicial experience. Thayer's Cases on Evidence, 2, 3. "If the evidence offered conduces in any reasonable degree to establish the probability or improbability of the fact in controversy, it should go to the jury." Insurance Company v. Weide, 78 U.S. 438, 20 L.Ed. 197, 11 Wall. 438, 440. The question as to its admission or rejection addresses itself to the court as one to be answered with a view to practical rather than theoretical considerations. The guiding principle is well stated in Stephen's Digest of the Law of Evidence (Chap. 1, p. 36) in these words: "The word 'relevant' means that any two facts to which it is applied are so related to each other, that according to the common course of events one either taken by itself or in connection with other facts proves or renders probable the past, present, or future existence or non-existence of the other."

The jury, in the case at bar, were to determine whether it was probable that the plaintiff, after charging all the materials furnished on the order of Simeon Plumb, for the construction of three houses in Bridgeport, to the defendant as the principal for whom Plumb acted, and for whom it was not denied that he had authority to act, proceeded to furnish like materials for the construction of five other houses in Bridgeport on the order of Plumb, and to charge them to the defendant, when he really gave credit to Plumb and dealt with him as the only party to the transaction. According to the common course of human conduct, a merchant is not likely to continue for several months to make almost daily sales on credit, of goods worth in the aggregate several hundred dollars, to a man who, so far as he knows, is destitute of any means to pay for them. Inglis v. Usherwood, 1 East, 515, 524; O'Brien v. Norris, 16 Md. 122, 77 Am.Dec. 284. If he has been selling to him the same line of goods previously, as an agent for a responsible principal, and claims that the sales in question were made in the same way, and under the same circumstances, any evidence which renders a change of credit improbable, is relevant to an inquiry as to whether such a change was made. We think the plaintiff's testimony, taken in connection with the other evidence already in the case, fairly tended to throw light on the matter in controversy, and was properly received. * * *

There was no error in the judgment of the trial court.

NOTES AND QUESTIONS

1. *How many definitions?* If plaintiff had not introduced evidence that Simeon was without means, should defendant have been allowed to introduce evidence that Simeon was a man of means? How many definitions of relevancy does the opinion contain?

2. *Payment defense.* If the defense of payment were raised, would evidence of the financial condition of the parties be admissible? See Horicon v. Langlois' Estate, 66 A.2d 16 (Vt.1949).

3. *Will contest.* In a will contest on grounds of testamentary incapacity, should evidence be admitted of the financial condition of the various "natural objects of the testator's bounty"? See Norris v. Bristow, 236 S.W.2d 316 (Mo.1951).

STATE V. MATHIS
Supreme Court of New Jersey, 1966.
221 A.2d 529.

WEINTRAUB, C.J.

F*h*1*st*

Defendant was convicted of murder in the first degree, and the jury not having recommended life imprisonment, he was sentenced to die. He appeals directly to this Court. R.R. 1:2–1(c).

The deceased, Stanley Caswell, had an insurance debit route which took him to North Ninth Street in Kenilworth. The residents there knew him as "the insurance man."

There are two houses at 218–220 North Ninth Street, one behind the other. Defendant's father occupied an apartment in the rear house. On February 12, 1965 Mr. Caswell was at the premises. Defendant, too, was there, to see his father on some matter. One State's witness placed defendant outside the house at about 6:00 P.M. on a course on which defendant and Mr. Caswell would have met. Moments later, one occupant heard two reports, like those of exploding firecrackers.

James Faines, who also lived at 220 North Ninth Street, testified that he and his friend, Lewis Clark, were working in the driveway on Faines' automobile; that he saw defendant pushing a man into the back seat of a red Renault which belonged to the insurance man; that he looked into the car and saw that it was the insurance man; that blood was coming from the victim's forehead and he was moaning; and that defendant struck Faines with his arm, saying "Get away from here, boy." Faines left, remarking to Clark that "It looks like Marvin was rolling the guy." Clark testified substantially to the same effect, although he did not look into the Renault and could not say who the victim was.

The testimony shows the Renault was then driven a short distance to a wooded area; that two further shots were fired; and the car then set afire. When the blaze was extinguished, the badly charred body of the deceased was found.

The autopsy revealed that death was due to four shots fired from a .22 caliber gun. There was testimony that late on the day of the murder or early the next morning, defendant tried to sell a small gun and a box of shells.

Defendant admitted being at his father's home at the time of the murder, but denied all knowledge of it. He said he did not know Mr. Caswell and did not see the red Renault. He denied trying to sell a gun. He said that on the 13th, the day after the crime, he heard his wife was in police custody and that he was wanted as a "material witness." He said his brother-in-law advised him to lose himself in Harlem for a while, in the hope that the culprit would meanwhile be found, and this because defendant had a criminal record. Defendant did go to New York City, but on the 15th he called the F.B.I., identified himself, and was taken into custody.

I

* * *

* * * Mrs. Caswell testified the deceased wore a wristwatch, a wedding ring, and a Masonic lapel pin, none of which were recovered. Mr. Brady, a chemist, testified that his analysis of the charred remnants revealed no evidence of gold beyond that usually found in ordinary dirt or debris. There was no direct proof of the loss of money, for the deceased had apparently secreted his wallet in the car where it was found by the police, and some change, totaling less than two dollars, was still in his trousers. But the debit book was found, and an audit of it indicated a shortage of $3.93. There was also testimony that the right rear pocket of deceased's trousers was turned inside out.

* * *

V

The prosecutor cross-examined defendant as to how much money he had and when he last worked. The examination suggested strongly that the State might be urging that defendant was in financial need, and hence was likely to commit a robbery. The trial court interrupted to say it would not permit proof of a financial need, unless the State was in a position to show also that things of value were stolen and that thereafter the defendant was affluent. Cf. State v. Schuck, 96 N.J.L. 154, 114 A. 562 (E. & A.1921). This the State could not do.

Prior to that ruling the prosecutor had asked defendant when he last worked and in response defendant said he had from time to time assisted his father in the repair of automobiles at his father's home. The prosecutor wished to pursue that matter, and in order to take it outside the trial court's ban against inquiry into financial need, the prosecutor said his inquiry was directed solely at "credibility," that the inquiry

> " * * * was intended for purposes of testing the validity of the defendant's testimony and his credibility in that, if I recall correctly, he said that he never saw the insurance man, for one thing. Now, if he was working with any degree of regularity at 220 North Ninth Street, he may have seen the insurance man on one or more occasions. That is an element of testing the credibility of this witness. And also the other element that may arise out of such testimony involving pure and simple credibility."

The court permitted the inquiry on "your representation that the question goes to the credibility of the defendant and is not a part of a designed attempt to picture as one critically in need of funds. The prosecutor then drew from defendant a statement of the number of times he had worked with his father on the repair of automobiles. 2 .

If the State's purpose remained only to show defendant was there with such frequency as to make it likely he knew the deceased, defendant's testimony that he was thus at his father's home would not have been challenged. But the State proceeded to call two neighbors of the father to testify they never saw defendant working there; and in summation the prosecutor asked why defendant had not called his father or his sister-in-law, who also lived there, to support his testimony. Thus instead of proving defendant was at the premises, the State in essence undertook to prove that he was not. The State was no longer trying to show that defendant visited his father's home so often that he probably knew the deceased. Rather the State's rebuttal testimony had to mean that defendant lied when he said he had worked with his father, *ergo,* his financial needs must have been met in some other way. 3

* * *

Whether defendant did or did not work with his father was of course not an issue in the case. Nor would it directly bear upon credibility, for surely there is nothing about working with one's father, or not working with one's father, which suggests a man cannot be a trustworthy witness. Thus the rebuttal evidence was not germane to the case, either with respect to the triable issues or as to defendant's reliability as a witness. His testimony therefore could not be contradicted. If no more were involved than an infraction of the rules relating to collateral issues, the irregularity might be of no moment. But what emerged was something more than a mere trial of something extraneous. The point the State in truth made by its rebuttal witnesses was that defendant lied when he said he worked for his father, and hence he did not earn money that way, and being otherwise essentially unemployed, he must have been destitute and therefore he likely would rob. Thus, in ultimate effect, the State made the very point which the trial court said was impermissible.

Undoubtedly a lack of money is logically connected with a crime involving financial gain. The trouble is that it would prove too much against too many. As said in 2 Wigmore, Evidence (3d ed. 1940), § 392, p. 341:

> "The *lack of money* by A might be relevant enough to show the probability of A's desiring to *commit a crime* in order to obtain money. But the practical result of such a doctrine would be to put a poor person under so much unfair suspicion and at such a relative disadvantage that for reasons of fairness this argument has seldom been countenanced as evidence of the graver crimes, particularly of violence."

The relationship between the deceased and defendant of creditor and debtor may be competent as to motive, see State v. Rogers, 19 N.J. 218, 116 A.2d 37 (1955), but, in general terms, there must be something more than poverty to tie a defendant into a criminal milieu. [Hence we are satisfied the trial court was correct in its approach to this subject.] The State, however, transgressed that ruling when by its cross-examination of defendant and its rebuttal testimony it again projected before the jury the forbidden theme that defendant had no apparent means of income and hence was likely to commit a crime for dollar gain. This was improper and injurious.

The judgment is reversed [on this and other grounds] and the matter remanded for a new trial.

For reversal: CHIEF JUSTICE WEINTRAUB and JUSTICES JACOBS, FRANCIS, PROCTOR, HALL and SCHETTINO—6.

For affirmance: None.

NOTES AND QUESTIONS

1.   *Affluence after a crime.* Would the principle of *Mathis* foreclose the prosecution in a bank robbery case from introducing evidence that the accused had been without means prior to the robbery and exhibited affluence after the robbery? See United States v. Weller, 238 F.3d 1215 (10th Cir.2001); State v. Kane, 492 N.W.2d 209 (Iowa Ct.App.1992).

2.   *Evidence of poverty.* [Evidence that an accused person is poor is generally excluded when offered to prove motive for a crime involving financial gain.] See United States v. Reed, 700 F.2d 638 (11th Cir.1983); Vitek v. State, 453 A.2d 514 (Md.1982); 2 Wigmore, Evidence § 392 (Chadbourn rev. 1979). However, note the following: United States v. Hawkins, 360 F.Supp.2d 689 (E.D.Pa. 2005) (evidence of financial condition admitted in fraud and perjury case where it bore directly on transaction relevant to the indictment); State v. Delahoussaye, 534 So.2d 76 (La.Ct.App.1988) (couple's financial condition and insurance policies on husband admissible in case where wife claimed shooting of husband was accidental); United States v. Reed, 639 F.2d 896 (2d Cir.1981) (securities fraud trial, letter threatening foreclosure of defendant's home held admissible); United States v. Hernandez, 588 F.2d 346 (2d Cir.1978) (unlawful importation of cocaine by airline steward; not error to admit evidence that accused was having problems with alimony and debts; court noted absence of evidence that he was a poor person); Commonwealth v. Johnson, 225 N.E.2d 360 (Mass.1967) (robbery murder; not error to admit evidence that accused needed but did not have money for down payment on automobile); State v. Schieving, 535 P.2d 1232 (Utah 1975) (embezzlement; not error to admit evidence of heavy indebtedness and poor financial condition). In addition, compare United States v. Saniti, 604 F.2d 603 (9th Cir.1979) (bank robbery; proper to admit evidence of $250–a–day heroin habit to show motive), with State v. LeFever, 690 P.2d 574 (Wash.1984) (robbery;

prejudicial effect of evidence of $125–a–day heroin habit overwhelmed any probative value to show motive).

HALL v. MONTGOMERY WARD & CO.

Supreme Court of Iowa, 1977.
252 N.W.2d 421.

UHLENHOPP, JUSTICE.

This appeal involves a jury award of damages in an action by plaintiff Thomas C. Hall against defendant Montgomery Ward & Company for mental anguish caused by threatening language by Wards' representatives. We view the evidence in the light most favorable to the verdict. Jacobson v. Benson Motors, Inc., 216 N.W.2d 396 (Iowa).

Hall, a borderline mental retardate with an intelligence quotient of 69, worked as a maintenance man in Wards' store at Cedar Falls, Iowa. He "borrowed" Wards' floor scrubber to moonlight by cleaning tavern floors, and also took cleaning material for the scrubber. He testified he did not take other items.

A security officer of Wards came from Chicago and, with the local store manager, interrogated Hall in the manager's office. The officer threatened Hall with jail, among other statements, and emerged from the interrogation with four documents signed by Hall. A clinical psychologist testified that some of the words in the documents were beyond Hall's comprehension and that Hall would probably sign anything in a stressful situation to extricate himself. Hall testified he signed the documents because of the threats of jail. The documents were a consent that Wards' representatives could detain and interview Hall on company business as long as they deemed necessary, a list of items Hall allegedly took from the store (such as shorts, knife, belt, brush), a confession to the theft of store merchandise worth $5000, and a promissory note to Wards for $5000. The store manager testified the items listed in the second document as stolen would come to $25 to $35 but the list did not cover everything and the figure $5000 was Hall's estimate.

Hall testified to his mental anguish from the incident. He stated several times that he had recurring dreams from the incident and that the incident affected his relationship with his family. The psychologist testified that Hall reacted as though the incident was "the end of the world," and Wards' officer testified he had to assure Hall at the conclusion of the interrogation that the situation was not the end of the world. Hall did not introduce evidence of physical injury or of financial loss or expense.

Hall testified regarding the pitifully small amount of property possessed by himself and his wife, as tending to show he did not have the property Wards contended he stole. Over Wards' objection of irrelevant, immaterial, and prejudicial, overruled by the trial court, Hall also introduced Wards' balance sheet and operating statement showing inter alia assets of $1,964,822,000 and net annual sales of $2,640,122,000.

The trial court overruled a motion for directed verdict by Wards. The jury found for Hall and awarded him $12,500 actual and $50,000 exemplary damages.

Wards moved for judgment notwithstanding verdict and alternatively for a new trial. The trial court overruled the former motion but sustained the latter one on the ground that the court erred in overruling Wards' objection to admission of the exhibit containing the balance sheet and operating statement which, according to the court, Hall's attorney used to make a "devastating" jury argument.

Hall appealed from the new trial award. Wards cross appealed from the court's failure to sustain its motions for directed verdict and for judgment notwithstanding verdict. The appeal and cross appeal present several issues.

* * *

III. Hall contends that the trial court erred in granting a new trial for admitting Wards' balance sheet and operating statement into evidence. The rule in this jurisdiction has been that with certain exceptions not involved here, a defendant's pecuniary condition may not be shown although the plaintiff asks smart money. Guengerech v. Smith, 34 Iowa 348; Bailey v. Bailey, 94 Iowa 598, 63 N.W. 341. This view has the support of a few courts, which state that if pecuniary condition is shown the fact finder will tend to get off on the relative poverty or affluence of the parties; despite trial-court instructions to juries, the issues of liability and damages will become intermixed. Wilson v. McLendon, 225 Ga. 119, 166 S.E.2d 345; Givens v. Berkley, 108 Ky. 236, 56 S.W. 158; Texas Public Utilities Corp. v. Edwards, 99 S.W.2d 420 (Tex.Civ.App.).

The great weight of authority today, however, holds the other way where the plaintiff seeks and the evidence supports exemplary damages. Many of the decisions are gathered in Annotations, 16 A.L.R. 838 and 123 A.L.R. 1136. See also Jones on Evidence, § 4:50 at 486 (6th ed.); 22 Am.Jur.2d Damages § 322 at 422; 25 C.J.S. Damages § 126 at 1168–1170. The rationale employed in these decisions is that the jury needs to know the extent of the defendant's holdings in order to know how large an award of damages is necessary to make him smart. E.g. Suzore v. Rutherford, 35 Tenn.App. 678, 684, 251 S.W.2d 129, 131 ("what would be 'smart money' to a poor man would not be, and would not serve as a deterrent, to a rich man").

We are impressed by the large number of courts which have arrived at the conclusion that generally the rule of admissibility is the better one.

We are more impressed by the actual need of jurors, in connection with exemplary damages, to have evidence about the defendant's poverty or wealth. We thus overrule the *Guengerech* and *Bailey* decisions and hold that the [trial court properly admitted the exhibit and erroneously sustained Wards' motion for new trial.] In adopting the rule of admissibility, we caution trial courts to confine plaintiffs carefully to the proper use of such evidence—to the issue of the amount of exemplary damages which is necessary to punish the particular defendant.

* * *

The trial court should have overruled Wards' motion for new trial and it properly overruled Wards' motion for judgment notwithstanding verdict. Its rulings at trial were correct in the first instance. We thus return the case to district court for reinstatement of the verdict and judgment thereon.

Reversed and Remanded.

NOTES AND QUESTIONS

1. *Nature of financial worth evidence.* Should the evidence be of actual or reputed wealth? Should it make any difference that the action is for slander or breach of promise to marry? Is there an effective control against excessive awards? Should the financial condition be that at the time of the injury or that at the time of trial? May defendant introduce evidence of his own poverty? Only in rebuttal?

2. *Timing of admissibility.* Some jurisdictions provide that evidence of a defendant's financial means is not admissible until there has been both a finding of liability and a finding that punitive damages are supportable under the facts. See, e.g., Md.Code C.J. § 10–913(a); Montgomery Ward Stores v. Wilson, 647 A.2d 1218, 1225 (Md. App.1994). Some other states require that evidence of financial worth be withheld until a *prima facie* case for punitive damages is made out. See, e.g., Arthur v. Davis, 178 Cal. Rptr 920, 925–26 (Cal.App.1981). The question of whether discovery of financial worth is permitted before trial is a separate issue and may be permitted even in a state in which such evidence is not admissible until at least a *prima facie* case for punitive damages has been made out. See cases collected at Annot., 32 A.L.R. 4th 432.

3. *Absence of evidence of financial condition.* May the jury consider and award exemplary damages in the absence of evidence of defendant's financial condition? Compare Rinaldi v. Aaron, 314 So.2d 762 (Fla.1975) (yes), with City of El Monte v. Superior Court, 34 Cal.Rptr.2d 490 (Ct.App.1994) (no). See also Annot., 87 A.L.R. 4th 141.

REED V. GENERAL MOTORS CORP.

United States Court of Appeals, Fifth Circuit, 1985.
773 F.2d 660.

ALVIN B. RUBIN, CIRCUIT JUDGE:

This personal injury suit arising out of an automobile accident was prosecuted against two individual defendants and their insurers. Because the district court admitted evidence of the amount of liability insurance carried by the defendants and because we are unable to conclude that this was not prejudicial both on the question of the defendants' liability and the amount of damages awarded, we reverse the judgment in favor of the plaintiffs. We conclude that there was, however, sufficient evidence to warrant a verdict that both defendants were negligent even though the plaintiffs' car was struck only by the vehicle driven by one of the defendant drivers and affirm the district court's denial of a directed verdict. We, therefore, remand the case for a new trial.

One Saturday night in May, 1982, David Reed, his wife, Patricia Loretta, his mother, Ardell, and his fifteen-year-old brother, Keith, were traveling west on Interstate Highway 10 in David Reed's Chevrolet Monza. They had left their home in Alabama earlier that day and were traveling to Texas. Near Lafayette, Louisiana, Ardell Reed began to suffer from cramps so David stopped the car to adjust her seat and thus ease her discomfort. David parked the car, with its emergency lights flashing, on the right shoulder of the highway, when it was violently struck in the rear by a Pontiac Trans Am driven by Brent Boudreaux. All of the passengers in the Reed auto were seriously injured.

At the time of the accident, Boudreaux and his friend, John Fontenot, were returning home to Kaplan, Louisiana from the Breaux Bridge Crawfish Festival. Some of their friends had left earlier, en route through Lafayette to Kaplan, and Boudreaux was trying to catch up with them. Soon after he left Breaux Bridge, Boudreaux's vehicle was passed on the right shoulder of the road by a 1981 Chevrolet ¾–ton pick-up truck, driven at a high rate of speed by Gerard Meche. With encouragement from Fontenot, Boudreaux followed Meche onto the shoulder of the highway, driving equally fast and passing vehicles proceeding in the same direction. The two vehicles at times speeded to over ninety miles an hour. There was testimony that Boudreaux merely followed Meche but there was also testimony that at times Boudreaux passed Meche and took the lead. The evidence warranted, although it certainly did not compel, the inference that Meche knew what Boudreaux was doing and that the two were engaged in racing or some other sort of rivalry.

As the two vehicles approached the Reed vehicle, Meche passed an automobile by traveling on the right shoulder of the road and returned to the right lane of the highway. Boudreaux attempted to follow Meche's example. As his car moved onto the shoulder it struck the rear of the Reed vehicle.

Invoking diversity jurisdiction, the four Reeds sued Boudreaux and Meche, and, as the Louisiana Direct Action Statute permits, their insurers, Insured Lloyds and Casualty Reciprocal Exchange. After trial on the merits, the jury returned a verdict in favor of each of the plaintiffs and against all of the defendants jointly.

In response to special interrogatories, the jury found that (1) both drivers had been negligent; and (2) Meche had caused, assisted, or encouraged Boudreaux in the commission of an unlawful act that had proximately caused the plaintiffs' injuries. The jury attributed fault under the Louisiana Comparative Negligence Act 70% to Boudreaux and 30% to Meche. It awarded damages totalling $450,000. Under Louisiana law, Meche and his insurer are solidarily liable with Boudreaux and his insurer for the full award. The determination that Boudreaux was 70% negligent does not reduce Meche's exposure to the plaintiffs, but serves only to fix the liability for contribution between the codefendants. Only Meche and his insurer, Casualty Reciprocal Exchange, appeal.

At the time this case was tried, Louisiana courts permitted a defendant to try to mitigate the damages that might be assessed against him by introducing evidence of his poverty and inability to pay a large verdict. For this purpose, Boudreaux sought to introduce evidence of the limits of his insurance coverage, $5,000 per person and $10,000 per accident, amounts clearly inadequate to compensate any of the plaintiffs. To accord the plaintiffs supposed equal treatment, the district court permitted them to introduce evidence of Meche's coverage, $500,000.

The Louisiana inability-to-pay doctrine originated in an 1886 Louisiana Supreme Court decision, *Williams v. McManus*.[4] In that case, the court reduced an award for slander, in part because the defendant was "a laborer of general good demeanor and of limited means."[5] Twelve years later, in *Loyacano v. Jurgens*,[6] the Louisiana court held: "A party's circumstances may not improperly be considered to a reasonable extent in estimating damages to be awarded in a case like this, where defendant personally was not at fault."

The inability-to-pay rule was founded on equitable considerations explained by a Louisiana Court of Appeal a half century later:

> It has never been considered good policy to bankrupt one to pay another even though the award granted is not in line with other cases involving the same injuries and might not fully

---

[4] 38 La.Ann. 161 (1886).
[5] *Id.* at 164.
[6] 50 La.Ann. 441, 23 So. 717, 718 (1898).

compensate the plaintiff for the injuries he received. Fair justice between both parties must be arrived at.

The propriety of the rule, however, had been questioned by some Louisiana appellate judges, and the Louisiana Supreme Court had held the doctrine inapplicable in suits involving solvent and insolvent joint tortfeasors.

After this case was tried, the Louisiana Supreme Court reversed entirely the jurisprudential line that admitted evidence of inability to pay. In *Rodriguez v. Taylor,*[7] the court stated: "[T]he wealth or poverty of a party to a lawsuit is not a proper consideration in the determination of compensatory damages."[8] The defendants argue that *Rodriguez* should be given retroactive effect and applied here, but we need not decide that issue. There is a more fundamental reason why Louisiana's inability-to-pay doctrine should not have been applied in this federal action.

The inability-to-pay doctrine was not a defense. It did not bar recovery; it merely allowed evidence concerning the defendant's pecuniary condition to be considered in arriving at the measure of damages. Although the *Erie* rule requires federal courts sitting in diversity to follow substantive state law, they apply federal procedural rules. Because the inability-to-pay doctrine was evidentiary in nature, it was not applicable in federal actions. The Federal Rules of Evidence, rather than state rules, therefore govern the admissibility of evidence in diversity cases, including questions of the admissibility of evidence of insurance.

Rule 411 of the Federal Rules of Evidence proscribes the admission of evidence that a person was or was not insured against liability "upon the issue whether he acted negligently or otherwise wrongfully." However, "[e]vidence of insurance against liability" is not barred, it continues, "when offered for another purpose, such as proof of agency, ownership, or control, or bias or prejudice of a witness."

The jury knew, of course, that Casualty Reciprocal Exchange insured Meche because it was named as a defendant. The fact that each party was insured had "independent, substantive evidentiary relevance," as we held in *Dicks v. Cleaver.*[9] But the fact that the existence of insurance was admissible, did not mean that the court was bound, or even permitted, to admit the amount of coverage. There was no issue to which the amount of either Meche's or Boudreaux's insurance was relevant. Therefore, the limits of coverage should have been excluded pursuant to the dictates of Rule 411. As the Ninth Circuit observed in *Geddes v. United Financial Group,*[10] consideration of "the ability of a defendant to pay the necessary

---

[7]   468 So.2d 1186 (La.1985).
[8]   *Id.* at 1188.
[9]   433 F.2d 248, 254 (5th Cir.1970).
[10] 559 F.2d 557, 560 (9th Cir.1977).

damages injects into the damage determination a foreign, diverting, and distracting issue which may effectuate a prejudicial result."

The parties had stipulated that Boudreaux and Meche were both insured and the names of their insurers; this established the predicate for a judgment against the insurers, as named defendants, if judgment were rendered against their respective insureds. However, even in a Louisiana court, it would have been error to admit evidence of the amount of Meche's insurance, for as a Louisiana appellate court held in *Ponder v. Groendyke Transport, Inc.*[11] "[t]he financial status of a defendant is irrelevant unless he places it at issue by claiming inability to pay." Even under the now discarded Louisiana rule, when there were solvent and insolvent joint tortfeasors, evidence of the insolvent defendant's inability to pay was inadmissible, and might not be considered in determining the amount of damages to be awarded or in apportioning the damages.

The parties' stipulation in the pretrial order that Meche's policy was the best evidence of its contents did not make the amount of insurance relevant or make the entire policy admissible. The failure of the insurance company to object to admissibility at some time before the day of trial does not constitute a waiver of its objections in the absence of pretrial proceedings that required it to take a position.

The trial court's admonitions to the jurors at the trial's conclusion that they were not to consider the liability limits of the parties' insurance policies in determining who, if anyone, was negligent, did not suffice to cure the error. The jury could not be expected to ignore the fact that, if it found only Boudreaux liable, the seriously injured plaintiffs would share only $10,000 but, if it found both Boudreaux and Meche liable, a deeper pocket would be available. We may speculate that the evidence of Meche's negligence was so overwhelming that the liability verdict was not tainted, but we cannot be sure. The wisdom of experience is embodied in the aphorism that the scent of a skunk thrown into the jury box cannot be wiped out by a trial court's admonition to ignore the smell. The reference to insurance coverage was not accidental or fleeting. The plaintiffs' counsel argued for admissibility of the limits in Meche's policy, persuaded the district court, and made a deliberate effort to inform the jury of the amount. Considering how important the matter was considered to be, we cannot overlook it now as harmless even as to the issue of Meche's liability.

* * *

[Reversed and remanded.]

---

[11] 454 So.2d 823, 831 (La.App. 3d Cir.1984).

NOTES AND QUESTIONS

1. *Application of Rule 411.* For what purpose did Louisiana permit evidence of inability to pay? If admitted on the issue of damages, is not the evidence relevant under Rule 401 and not precluded under Rule 411? Is there another basis, other than by application of Rule 411, for excluding this evidence?

2. *Direct action statutes.* Statutes permitting direct action against a liability insurer are extremely rare. In addition to the Louisiana procedure, see also Wis.Ann.Stat. § 803.04. For an analysis of evidentiary problems under the Louisiana statute, see Comment, Admissibility of Insurance Policy Limits, 45 La.L.Rev. 1299 (1985).

3. *Common law rulings.* The courts at common law generally agreed that evidence that the defendant carried liability insurance is not admissible for the purpose of proving that he acted negligently. Annot., 4 A.L.R.2d 761, 767; Annot., 71 A.L.R. 4th 1025 (medical malpractice cases); for federal cases, see Annot., 40 A.L.R.Fed. 541. Correspondingly, evidence that a defendant is not insured against liability has been excluded. Koonce ex rel. Koonce v. Pacilio, 718 N.E.2d 628 (Ill. App. 1999); King v. Starr, 260 P.2d 351 (Wash.1953); Annot., 68 A.L.R. 4th 954. In general, see Calnan, The Insurance Exclusionary Rule Revisited: Are Reports of its Demise Exaggerated, 52 Ohio St.L.J. 1177 (1991); 1 McCormick, Evidence § 201 (7th ed. 2013); Leonard, The New Wigmore: Selected Rules of Limited Admissibility § 6.1 to 6.13 (2002).

4. *Exceptions.* The similarity to evidence of financial condition is readily apparent, and a similar set of exceptions has evolved. See Rule 411. Illustrative cases are: Oliveira v. Jacobson, 846 A.2d 822, 828 (R.I.2004) (proper to ask expert testifying as to absence of medical malpractice about his payments as a board member of medical malpractice insurance company and his omission of that position from his curriculum vitae); Maggard Truck Line, Inc. v. Deaton, Inc., 573 F.Supp. 1388 (N.D.Ga.1983) (action between shipping broker and motor carrier; evidence of insurance admissible as tending to prove the existence of agreement to shift liability for loss of goods); People v. Steele, 37 N.Y.S.2d 199 (Erie County Ct.1942) (error to exclude evidence that defendant had liability insurance when offered to prove lack of motivation to commit the offense of leaving the scene of an accident); Filloon v. Stenseth, 498 N.W.2d 353 (N.D.1993) (error to exclude evidence that witness who testified that plaintiff was out of the cross-walk had become adjuster for defendant's insurance carrier); Pinckard v. Dunnavant, 206 So.2d 340 (Ala.1968) (admissible to prove who had management and maintenance of premises, which was disputed).

5. *Modern applications.* In general, the tendency now is to take a less serious view of the disclosure of the existence of liability insurance of the plaintiff, or conversely the absence of coverage of defendant, than formerly, and reversals are rare unless the disclosure is viewed as a deliberate invitation to the jury to base its decision on the presence or absence of

insurance. E.g., Ouachita Nat'l Bank v. Tosco Corp., 686 F.2d 1291 (8th Cir.1982), aff'd on rehearing, 716 F.2d 485 (8th Cir.1983) (mention of insurance harmless error); Carpinet v. Mitchell, 853 A.2d 366,376 (Pa. Super. 2004) (law requires more than the mere mention fo the word "insurance" to establish prejudice warranting the extreme remedy of a mistrial). But see Calnan, supra note 3. In ruling on questions involving the admissibility of insurance, should weight be accorded the consideration that jurors, like other people, today know that carrying liability insurance is common practice? See Bott v. Wendler, 453 P.2d 100 (Kan.1969); Notman, Insurance Nondisclosure: The "Hush, Hush" Game, 53 Ill.B.J. 896 (1965). What if the particular jurisdiction involved makes the carrying of certain types of liability insurance mandatory? See Uy v. Shapmor, Inc., 257 N.Y.S.2d 208 (Sup.App.Term 1965).

6. *Punitive damages.* Questions that arise as to the admissibility of liability insurance in cases where punitive damages are sought are discussed in King, The Insurability of Punitive Damages: A New Solution to an Old Dilemma, 16 Wake Forest L.Rev. 345 (1980); Powell & Leiferman, Results Most Embarrassing: Discovery and Admissibility of Net Worth of the Defendant, 40 Baylor L.Rev. 527 (1988). Contrast Fleegel v. Estate of Boyles, 61 P.3d 1267 (Alaska 2002) (evidence of insurance relevant to defendant's financial condition as it related to punitive damages), with City of West Allis v. Wisconsin Elec. Power Co., 635 N.W.2d 873 (Wis.Ct.App.2001) (evidence of insurance inadmissible as a factor in assessing punitive damages).

7. *Jury selection.* In jury selection, should a plaintiff be allowed to ask a prospective juror about his or her connection either with the defendant's liability insurer or with the insurance industry generally? Compare Langley v. Turner's Exp., Inc., 375 F.2d 296 (4th Cir.1967), with Kiernan v. Van Schaik, 347 F.2d 775 (3d Cir.1965). Is not the more sensible practice to require prospective jurors to furnish information concerning any connections with the insurance industry prior to being called for duty in a particular case? See Calnan, supra note 3; Vetter, Voir Dire II: Liability Insurance, 29 Mo.L.Rev. 305 (1964).

C. SPECIAL APPLICATIONS OF RULE 403

Since the balance between the probative value of a given type of evidence and its capacity for raising the countervailing considerations cited by Rule 403 will vary with the nature of the case, the issue sought to be proved, and the specific evidentiary item offered, might all questions of relevancy best be left for ad hoc determination by the trial judge under the guidance of the general propositions embodied in Rules 401 and 403? See James, Relevancy, Probability and the Law, 29 Cal.L.Rev. 689 (1941).

While any attempt to strike the balance suggested by Rule 403 a priori for every conceivable type of evidence which may be offered to prove a material fact would obviously be doomed to failure, certain questions of relevancy have occurred with sufficient frequency for more or less specific rules to evolve. For example, the drafters of the Federal Rules did not leave the admissibility of evidence of liability insurance to prove negligence for ad hoc resolution, but specifically declared such evidence inadmissible by Rule 411. Is this treatment of the question justified? Which factor enumerated by Rule 403 would the admission of such evidence preeminently entail?

OLD CHIEF v. UNITED STATES

Supreme Court of the United States, 1997.
519 U.S. 172.

[Defendant was prosecuted under 18 U.S.C. § 922(g)(1), possession of a firearm by a person with a prior felony conviction. The defendant offered to stipulate to the prior-conviction element of the crime and argued that such a stipulation meant that the probative value of evidence of the prior conviction (for assault causing serious bodily injury) was necessarily substantially outweighed by the danger of unfair prejudice under Rule 403. The Government refused to join in the stipulation and was permitted to introduce the judgment record for the prior conviction. The court of appeals affirmed defendant's conviction.]

JUSTICE SOUTER delivered the opinion of the Court.

* * *

II

A

Issue I

As a threshold matter, there is Old Chief's erroneous argument that the name of his prior offense as contained in the record of conviction is irrelevant to the prior-conviction element, and for that reason inadmissible under Rule 402 of the Federal Rules of Evidence. Rule 401 defines relevant evidence as having "any tendency to make the existence of any fact that is of consequence to the determination of the action more probable or less probable than it would be without the evidence." Fed. Rule Evid. 401. To be sure, the fact that Old Chief's prior conviction was for assault resulting in serious bodily injury rather than, say, for theft was not itself an ultimate fact, as if the statute had specifically required proof of injurious assault. But its demonstration was a step on one evidentiary route to the ultimate fact, since it served to place Old Chief within a particular sub-class of offenders for whom firearms possession is outlawed by § 922(g)(1). A documentary record of the conviction for that named offense was thus relevant evidence in making Old Chief's § 922(g)(1) status more probable than it would have been without the evidence. *A*

Nor was its evidentiary relevance under Rule 401 affected by the availability of alternative proofs of the element to which it went, such as an admission by Old Chief that he had been convicted of a crime "punishable by imprisonment for a term exceeding one year" within the meaning of the statute. The 1972 Advisory Committee Notes to Rule 401 make this point directly:

> "The fact to which the evidence is directed need not be in dispute. While situations will arise which call for the exclusion of evidence offered to prove a point conceded by the opponent, the ruling should be made on the basis of such considerations as waste of time and undue prejudice (see Rule 403), rather than under any general requirement that evidence is admissible only if directed to matters in dispute." Advisory Committee's Notes on Fed. Rule Evid. 401, 28 U.S.C.App., p. 859.

If, then, relevant evidence is inadmissible in the presence of other evidence related to it, its exclusion must rest not on the ground that the other evidence has rendered it "irrelevant," but on its character as unfairly prejudicial, cumulative or the like, its relevance notwithstanding.

B

The principal issue is the scope of a trial judge's discretion under Rule 403, which authorizes exclusion of relevant evidence when its "probative value is substantially outweighed by the danger of unfair prejudice, confusion of the issues, or misleading the jury, or by considerations of undue delay, waste of time, or needless presentation of cumulative evidence." Fed. Rule Evid. 403. Old Chief relies on the danger of unfair prejudice.

1

The term "unfair prejudice," as to a criminal defendant, speaks to the capacity of some concededly relevant evidence to lure the factfinder into declaring guilt on a ground different from proof specific to the offense charged. See generally 1 J. Weinstein, M. Berger, & J. McLaughlin, Weinstein's Evidence ¶ 403[03] (1996) (discussing the meaning of "unfair prejudice" under Rule 403). So, the Committee Notes to Rule 403 explain, " 'Unfair prejudice' within its context means an undue tendency to suggest decision on an improper basis, commonly, though not necessarily, an emotional one." Advisory Committee's Notes on Fed. Rule Evid. 403, 28 U.S.C.App., p. 860.

Such improper grounds certainly include the one that Old Chief points to here: generalizing a defendant's earlier bad act into bad character and taking that as raising the odds that he did the later bad act now charged (or, worse, as calling for preventive conviction even if he should happen to be innocent momentarily). As then-Judge Breyer put it, "Although * * * 'propensity evidence' is relevant, the risk that a jury will convict for crimes other than those charged—or that, uncertain of guilt, it will convict anyway because a bad person deserves punishment—creates a prejudicial effect that outweighs ordinary relevance." *United States v.*

Moccia, 681 F.2d 61, 63 (C.A.1 1982). Justice Jackson described how the law has handled this risk:

> "Courts that follow the common-law tradition almost unanimously have come to disallow resort by the prosecution to any kind of evidence of a defendant's evil character to establish a probability of his guilt. Not that the law invests the defendant with a presumption of good character, *Greer v. United States,* 245 U.S. 559 * * *, but it simply closes the whole matter of character, disposition and reputation on the prosecution's case-in-chief. The state may not show defendant's prior trouble with the law, specific criminal acts, or ill name among his neighbors, even though such facts might logically be persuasive that he is by propensity a probable perpetrator of the crime. The inquiry is not rejected because character is irrelevant; on the contrary, it is said to weigh too much with the jury and to so overpersuade them as to prejudge one with a bad general record and deny him a fair opportunity to defend against a particular charge. The overriding policy of excluding such evidence, despite its admitted probative value, is the practical experience that its disallowance tends to prevent confusion of issues, unfair surprise and undue prejudice." *Michelson v. United States,* 335 U.S. 469, 475–476 * * * (1948) (footnotes omitted).

Rule of Evidence 404(b) reflects this common-law tradition by addressing propensity reasoning directly: "Evidence of other crimes, wrongs, or acts is not admissible to prove the character of a person in order to show action in conformity therewith." Fed. Rule Evid. 404(b). There is, accordingly, no question that propensity would be an "improper basis" for conviction and that evidence of a prior conviction is subject to analysis under Rule 403 for relative probative value and for prejudicial risk of misuse as propensity evidence. Cf. 1 J. Strong, McCormick on Evidence 780 (4th ed. 1992) (hereinafter McCormick) (Rule 403 prejudice may occur, for example, when "evidence of convictions for prior, unrelated crimes may lead a juror to think that since the defendant already has a criminal record, an erroneous conviction would not be quite as serious as would otherwise be the case").

As for the analytical method to be used in Rule 403 balancing, two basic possibilities present themselves. An item of evidence might be viewed as an island, with estimates of its own probative value and unfairly prejudicial risk the sole reference points in deciding whether the danger substantially outweighs the value and whether the evidence ought to be excluded. Or the question of admissibility might be seen as inviting further comparisons to take account of the full evidentiary context of the case as the court understands it when the ruling must be made. This second approach would start out like the first but be ready to go further.

On objection, the court would decide whether a particular item of evidence raised a danger of unfair prejudice. If it did, the judge would go on to evaluate the degrees of probative value and unfair prejudice not only for the item in question but for any actually available substitutes as well. If an alternative were found to have substantially the same or greater probative value but a lower danger of unfair prejudice, sound judicial discretion would discount the value of the item first offered and exclude it if its discounted probative value were substantially outweighed by unfairly prejudicial risk. As we will explain later on, the judge would have to make these calculations with an appreciation of the offering party's need for evidentiary richness and narrative integrity in presenting a case, and the mere fact that two pieces of evidence might go to the same point would not, of course, necessarily mean that only one of them might come in. It would only mean that a judge applying Rule 403 could reasonably apply some discount to the probative value of an item of evidence when faced with less risky alternative proof going to the same point. Even under this second approach, as we explain below, a defendant's Rule 403 objection offering to concede a point generally cannot prevail over the Government's choice to offer evidence showing guilt and all the circumstances surrounding the offense. * * *

The first understanding of the Rule is open to a very telling objection. That reading would leave the party offering evidence with the option to structure a trial in whatever way would produce the maximum unfair prejudice consistent with relevance. He could choose the available alternative carrying the greatest threat of improper influence, despite the availability of less prejudicial but equally probative evidence. The worst he would have to fear would be a ruling sustaining a Rule 403 objection, and if that occurred, he could simply fall back to offering substitute evidence. This would be a strange rule. It would be very odd for the law of evidence to recognize the danger of unfair prejudice only to confer such a degree of autonomy on the party subject to temptation, and the Rules of Evidence are not so odd.

Rather, a reading of the companions to Rule 403, and of the commentaries that went with them to Congress, makes it clear that what counts as the Rule 403 "probative value" of an item of evidence, as distinct from its Rule 401 "relevance," may be calculated by comparing evidentiary alternatives. The Committee Notes to Rule 401 explicitly say that a party's concession is pertinent to the court's discretion to exclude evidence on the point conceded. Such a concession, according to the Notes, will sometimes "call for the exclusion of evidence offered to prove [the] point conceded by the opponent * * *." Advisory Committee's Notes on Fed. Rule Evid. 401, 28 U.S.C.App., p. 859. As already mentioned, the Notes make it clear that such rulings should be made not on the basis of Rule 401 relevance but on "such considerations as waste of time and undue prejudice (see Rule 403) * * *." *Ibid.* The Notes to Rule 403 then take up the point by stating that when a court considers "whether to exclude on grounds of unfair prejudice," the "availability of other means of proof may * * * be an appropriate factor." Advisory Committee's Notes on Fed. Rule Evid. 403, 28 U.S.C.App., p. 860. The point gets a reprise in the Notes to Rule 404(b), dealing with admissibility when a given evidentiary item has the dual nature of legitimate evidence of an element and illegitimate evidence of character: "No mechanical solution is offered. The determination must be made whether the danger of undue prejudice outweighs the probative value of the evidence in view of the availability of other means of proof and other facts appropriate for making decision of this kind under 403." Advisory Committee's Notes on Fed. Rule Evid. 404, 28 U.S.C.App., p. 861. Thus the notes leave no question that when Rule 403 confers discretion by providing that evidence "may" be excluded, the discretionary judgment may be informed not only by assessing an evidentiary item's twin tendencies, but by placing the result of that assessment alongside similar assessments of evidentiary alternatives. See 1 McCormick 782, and n.41 (suggesting that Rule 403's "probative value" signifies the "marginal probative value" of the evidence relative to the other evidence in the case); 22 C. Wright & K. Graham, Federal Practice and Procedure § 5250, pp. 546–547 (1978) ("The probative worth of any particular bit of evidence is obviously affected by the scarcity or abundance of other evidence on the same point").

2

In dealing with the specific problem raised by § 922(g)(1) and its prior-conviction element, there can be no question that evidence of the name or nature of the prior offense generally carries a risk of unfair prejudice to the defendant. That risk will vary from case to case, for the reasons already given, but will be substantial whenever the official record offered by the Government would be arresting enough to lure a juror into a sequence of bad character reasoning. Where a prior conviction was for a gun crime or one similar to other charges in a pending case the risk of unfair prejudice would be especially obvious, and Old Chief sensibly worried that the prejudicial effect of his prior assault conviction, significant enough with respect to the current gun charges alone, would take on added weight from the related assault charge against him.

The District Court was also presented with alternative, relevant, admissible evidence of the prior conviction by Old Chief's offer to stipulate, evidence necessarily subject to the District Court's consideration on the motion to exclude the record offered by the Government. Although Old Chief's formal offer to stipulate was, strictly, to enter a formal agreement with the Government to be given to the jury, even without the Government's acceptance his proposal amounted to an offer to admit that the prior-conviction element was satisfied, and a defendant's admission is, of course, good evidence. See Fed. Rule Evid. 801(d)(2)(A).

Old Chief's proffered admission would, in fact, have been not merely relevant but seemingly conclusive evidence of the element. The statutory language in which the prior-conviction requirement is couched shows no congressional concern with the specific name or nature of the prior offense beyond what is necessary to place it within the broad category of qualifying felonies, and Old Chief clearly meant to admit that his felony did qualify, by stipulating "that the Government has proven one of the essential elements of the offense." App. 7. As a consequence, although the name of the prior offense may have been technically relevant, it addressed no detail in the definition of the prior-conviction element that would not have been covered by the stipulation or admission. Logic, then, seems to side with Old Chief.

3   IV

There is, however, one more question to be considered before deciding whether Old Chief's offer was to supply evidentiary value at least equivalent to what the Government's own evidence carried. In arguing that the stipulation or admission would not have carried equivalent value, the Government invokes the familiar, standard rule that the prosecution is entitled to prove its case by evidence of its own choice, or, more exactly, that a criminal defendant may not stipulate or admit his way out of the full evidentiary force of the case as the Government chooses to present it. The authority usually cited for this rule is *Parr v. United States,* 255 F.2d 86 (CA5 1958), in which the Fifth Circuit explained that the "reason for the rule is to permit a party 'to present to the jury a picture of the events relied upon. To substitute for such a picture a naked admission might have the effect to rob the evidence of much of its fair and legitimate weight.'" 255 F.2d, at 88 (quoting *Dunning v. Maine Central R. Co.,* 91 Me. 87, 39 A. 352, 356 (1897)).

This is unquestionably true as a general matter. The "fair and legitimate weight" of conventional evidence showing individual thoughts and acts amounting to a crime reflects the fact that making a case with testimony and tangible things not only satisfies the formal definition of an offense, but tells a colorful story with descriptive richness. Unlike an abstract premise, whose force depends on going precisely to a particular step in a course of reasoning, a piece of evidence may address any number of separate elements, striking hard just because it shows so much at once; the account of a shooting that establishes capacity and causation may tell just as much about the triggerman's motive and intent. Evidence thus has force beyond any linear scheme of reasoning, and as its pieces come together a narrative gains momentum, with power not only to support conclusions but to sustain the willingness of jurors to draw the inferences, whatever they may be, necessary to reach an honest verdict. This persuasive power of the concrete and particular is often essential to the capacity of jurors to satisfy the obligations that the law places on them. Jury duty is usually unsought and sometimes resisted, and it may be as difficult for one juror suddenly to face the findings that can send another human being to prison, as it is for another to hold out conscientiously for acquittal. When a juror's duty does seem hard, the evidentiary account of what a defendant has thought and done can accomplish what no set of abstract statements ever could, not just to prove a fact but to establish its human significance, and so to implicate the law's moral underpinnings and a juror's obligation to sit in judgment. Thus, the prosecution may fairly seek to place its evidence before the jurors, as much to tell a story of guiltiness as to support an inference of guilt, to convince the jurors that a guilty verdict would be morally reasonable as much as to point to the discrete elements of a defendant's legal fault. Cf. *United States v. Gilliam,* 994 F.2d 97, 100–102 (CA2 1993).

But there is something even more to the prosecution's interest in resisting efforts to replace the evidence of its choice with admissions and stipulations, for beyond the power of conventional evidence to support allegations and give life to the moral underpinnings of law's claims, there lies the need for evidence in all its particularity to satisfy the jurors' expectations about what proper proof should be. Some such demands they bring with them to the courthouse, assuming, for example, that a charge of using a firearm to commit an offense will be proven by introducing a gun in evidence. A prosecutor who fails to produce one, or some good reason for his failure, has something to be concerned about. "If [jurors'] expectations are not satisfied, triers of fact may penalize the party who disappoints them by drawing a negative inference against that party." Saltzburg, A Special Aspect of Relevance: Countering Negative Inferences Associated with the Absence of Evidence, 66 Calif. L.Rev. 1011, 1019 (1978) (footnotes omitted). Expectations may also arise in jurors' minds simply from the experience of a trial itself. The use of witnesses to describe a train of events naturally related can raise the prospect of learning about every ingredient of that natural sequence the same way. If suddenly the prosecution presents some occurrence in the series differently, as by announcing a stipulation or admission, the effect may be like saying, "never mind what's behind the door," and jurors may well wonder what they are being kept from knowing. A party seemingly responsible for cloaking something has reason for apprehension, and the prosecution with its burden of proof may prudently demur at a defense request to interrupt the flow of evidence telling the story in the usual way.

In sum, the accepted rule that the prosecution is entitled to prove its case free from any defendant's option to stipulate the evidence away rests on good sense. A syllogism is not a story, and a naked proposition in a courtroom may be no match for the robust evidence that would be used to prove it. People who hear a story interrupted by gaps of abstraction may be puzzled at the missing chapters, and jurors asked to rest a momentous decision on the story's truth can feel put upon at being asked to take responsibility knowing that more could be said than they have heard. A convincing tale can be told with economy, but when economy becomes a break in the natural sequence of narrative evidence, an assurance that the missing link is really there is never more than second best.

* * *

This recognition that the prosecution with its burden of persuasion needs evidentiary depth to tell a continuous story has, however, virtually no application when the point at issue is a defendant's legal status, dependent on some judgment rendered wholly independently of the concrete events of later criminal behavior charged against him. As in this case, the choice of evidence for such an element is usually not between eventful narrative and abstract proposition, but between propositions of slightly varying abstraction, either a record saying that conviction for some crime occurred at a certain time or a statement admitting the same thing without naming the particular offense. The issue of substituting one statement for the other normally arises only when the record of conviction would not be admissible for any purpose beyond proving status, so that excluding it would not deprive the prosecution of evidence with multiple utility; if, indeed, there were a justification for receiving evidence of the nature of prior acts on some issue other than status (*i.e.,* to prove "motive, opportunity, intent, preparation, plan, knowledge, identity, or absence of mistake or accident," Fed. Rule Evid. 404(b)), Rule 404(b) guarantees the opportunity to seek its admission. Nor can it be argued that the events behind the prior conviction are proper nourishment for the jurors' sense of obligation to vindicate the public interest.

The issue is not whether concrete details of the prior crime should come to the jurors' attention but whether the name or general character of that crime is to be disclosed. Congress, however, has made it plain that distinctions among generic felonies do not count for this purpose; the fact of the qualifying conviction is alone what matters under the statute. * * * The most the jury needs to know is that the conviction admitted by the defendant falls within the class of crimes that Congress thought should bar a convict from possessing a gun, and this point may be made readily in a defendant's admission and underscored in the court's jury instructions. Finally, the most obvious reason that the general presumption that the prosecution may choose its evidence is so remote from application here is that proof of the defendant's status goes to an element entirely outside the natural sequence of what the defendant is charged with thinking and doing to commit the current offense. Proving status without telling exactly why that status was imposed leaves no gap in the story of a defendant's subsequent criminality, and its demonstration by stipulation or admission neither displaces a chapter from a continuous sequence of conventional evidence nor comes across as an officious substitution, to confuse or offend or provoke reproach.

Given these peculiarities of the element of felony-convict status and of admissions and the like when used to prove it, there is no cognizable difference between the evidentiary significance of an admission and of the legitimately probative component of the official record the prosecution would prefer to place in evidence. For purposes of the Rule 403 weighing of the probative against the prejudicial, the functions of the competing evidence are distinguishable only by the risk inherent in the one and wholly absent from the other. In this case, as in any other in which the prior conviction is for an offense likely to support conviction on some improper ground, the only reasonable conclusion was that the risk of unfair prejudice did substantially outweigh the discounted probative value of the record of conviction, and it was an abuse of discretion to admit the record when an admission was available. What we have said shows why this will be the general rule when proof of convict status is at issue, just as the prosecutor's choice will generally survive a Rule 403 analysis when a defendant seeks to force the substitution of an admission for evidence creating a coherent narrative of his thoughts and actions in perpetrating the offense for which he is being tried.

The judgment is reversed, and the case is remanded to the Ninth Circuit for further proceedings consistent with this opinion.

It is so ordered.

JUSTICE O'CONNOR, with whom THE CHIEF JUSTICE, JUSTICE SCALIA, and JUSTICE THOMAS join, dissenting.

The Court today announces a rule that misapplies Federal Rule of Evidence 403 and upsets, without explanation, longstanding precedent regarding criminal prosecutions. I do not agree that the Government's introduction of evidence that reveals the name and basic nature of a defendant's prior felony conviction in a prosecution brought under 18 U.S.C. § 922(g)(1) "unfairly" prejudices the defendant within the meaning of Rule 403. Nor do I agree with the Court's newly minted rule that a defendant charged with violating § 922(g)(1) can force the Government to accept his concession to the prior conviction element of that offense, thereby precluding the Government from offering evidence on this point. I therefore dissent.

I

Rule 403 provides that a district court may exclude relevant evidence if, among other things, "its probative value is substantially outweighed by the danger of unfair prejudice." Certainly, Rule 403 does not permit the court to exclude the Government's evidence simply because it may hurt the defendant. As a threshold matter, evidence is excludable only if it is "unfairly" prejudicial, in that it has "an undue tendency to suggest decision on an improper basis." * * * The evidence tendered by the Government in this case—the order reflecting petitioner's prior conviction and sentence for assault resulting in serious bodily injury, in violation of 18 U.S.C. § 1153 and 18 U.S.C. § 113(f) (1988 ed.)—directly proved a necessary element of the § 922(g)(1) offense, that is, that petitioner had committed a crime covered by § 921(a)(20). Perhaps petitioner's case was damaged when the jury discovered that he previously had committed a felony and heard the name of his crime. But I cannot agree with the Court that it was *unfairly* prejudicial for the Government to establish an essential element of its case against petitioner with direct proof of his prior conviction.

The structure of § 922(g)(1) itself shows that Congress envisioned jurors' learning the name and basic nature of the defendant's prior offense. Congress enacted § 922(g)(1) to prohibit the possession of a firearm by any person convicted of "a crime punishable by imprisonment for a term exceeding one year." Section 922(g)(1) does not merely prohibit the possession of firearms by "felons," nor does it apply to all prior felony convictions. Rather, the statute excludes from § 922(g)(1)'s coverage certain business crimes and state misdemeanors punishable by imprisonment of two years or less. § 921(a)(20). Within the meaning of § 922(g)(1), then, "a crime" is not an abstract or metaphysical concept. Rather, the Government must prove that the defendant committed a *particular* crime. In short, under § 922(g)(1), a defendant's prior felony conviction connotes not only that he is a prior felon, but also that he has engaged in specific past criminal conduct.

Even more fundamentally, in our system of justice, a person is not simply convicted of "a crime" or "a felony." Rather, he is found guilty of a specified offense, almost always because he violated a specific statutory prohibition. For example, in the words of the order that the Government offered to prove petitioner's prior conviction in this case, petitioner "did knowingly and unlawfully assault Rory Dean Fenner, said assault resulting in serious bodily injury, in violation of Title 18 U.S.C. §§ 1153 and 113(f)." App. 18. That a variety of crimes would have satisfied the prior conviction element of the § 922(g)(1) offense does not detract from the fact that petitioner committed a specific offense. The name and basic nature of petitioner's crime are inseparable from the fact of his earlier conviction and were therefore admissible to prove petitioner's guilt.

The principle is illustrated by the evidence that was admitted at petitioner's trial to prove the other element of the § 922(g)(1) offense— possession of a "firearm." The Government submitted evidence showing that petitioner possessed a 9–mm. semiautomatic pistol. Although petitioner's possession of any number of weapons would have satisfied the requirements of § 922(g)(1), obviously the Government was entitled to prove with specific evidence that petitioner possessed the weapon he did. In the same vein, consider a murder case. Surely the Government can submit proof establishing the victim's identity, even though, strictly speaking, the jury has no "need" to know the victim's name, and even though the victim might be a particularly well loved public figure. The same logic should govern proof of the prior conviction element of the § 922(g)(1) offense. That is, the Government ought to be able to prove, with specific evidence, that petitioner committed a crime that came within § 922(g)(1)'s coverage.

* * *

Any incremental harm resulting from proving the name or basic nature of the prior felony can be properly mitigated by limiting jury instructions. Federal Rule of Evidence 105 provides that when evidence is admissible for one purpose, but not another, "the court, upon request, shall restrict the evidence to its proper scope and instruct the jury accordingly."

Indeed, on petitioner's own motion in this case, the District Court instructed the jury that it was not to " 'consider a prior conviction as evidence of guilt of the crime for which the defendant is now on trial.' " * * * The jury is presumed to have followed this cautionary instruction, see *Shannon v. United States,* 512 U.S. 573, 585 (1994) * * *.

* * *

III

The Court manufactures a new rule that, in a § 922(g)(1) case, a defendant can force the Government to accept his admission to the prior felony conviction element of the offense, thereby precluding the Government from offering evidence to directly prove a necessary element of its case. I cannot agree that it "unfairly" prejudices a defendant for the Government to prove his prior conviction with evidence that reveals the name or basic nature of his past crime. Like it or not, Congress chose to make a defendant's prior criminal conviction one of the two elements of the § 922(g)(1) offense. Moreover, crimes have names; a defendant is not convicted of some indeterminate, unspecified "crime." Nor do I think that Federal Rule of Evidence 403 can be read to obviate the well accepted principle, grounded in both the Constitution and in our precedent, that the Government may not be forced to accept a defendant's concession to an element of a charged offense as proof of that element. I respectfully dissent.

NOTES AND QUESTIONS

1.   *The defense perspective.* In excluding evidence as to defendant's "status" in light of the defendant's offer to stipulate, while still emphasizing the prosecution's entitlement in most cases to "prove its case by evidence of

its own choice," has the Court made it more or less difficult for a defendant to invoke Rule 403 to limit prosecution proof in the ordinary case? See Note, The Supreme Court—Leading Cases, 111 Harv.L.Rev. 197, 360 (1997). See also Risinger, John Henry Wigmore, Johnny Lynn Old Chief, and "Legitimate Moral Force"—Keeping the Courtroom Safe for Heartstrings and Gore, 49 Hastings L.J. 403 (1998).

2.   *Photographs.* The Court in *Old Chief* distinguishes "status" evidence from evidence of "what the defendant is charged with thinking and doing to commit the current offense." Would photographs of a victim's body be evidence going to "what the defendant is charged with thinking and doing to commit the current offense?" Most courts admit such photographs despite defendant's attempts to stipulate to the ultimate facts to which they may be relevant. See, e.g., State v. Fisher, 445 S.E.2d 866 (N.C.1994) (autopsy photographs properly admitted despite defendant's offer to stipulate as to the identity of the victim, that the cause of death was multiple stab wounds, and that defendant was the individual who inflicted the wounds).

3.   *Limitations of Old Chief holding.* Federal courts have been reluctant to extend the holding in *Old Chief* beyond its facts. See, e.g., United States v. Jandreau, 611 F.3d 922 (8th Cir. 2010) (DNA paternity evidence properly admitted despite defendant's offer to stipulate that a ssexual encounter occurred); United States v. Becht, 267 F.3d 767 (8th Cir.2001) (defendant's stipulation that images seized from his computer depicted child pornography did not negate probative value of images on issue of defendant's knowledge of the images); United States v. Crowder, 141 F.3d 1202 (D.C.Cir.1998) (defendant's offer of a stipulation with regard to intent insufficient to preclude admission of prior crimes evidence). The issue of a stipulation tendered to preclude an aspect of prosecution proof occurs with some frequency in connection with prosecution efforts to introduce evidence of prior crimes to prove intent. Some courts have held that a stipulation as to the existence of intent is effective under Rule 403 to preclude the admission of prior crimes; most have said not. The issue is revisited in connection with evidence admitted under Rule 404(b). See *United States v. Miller*, Chapter 8, Section C, infra.

4.   *Judicial discretion.* How much discretion does a trial judge have under Rule 403 to exclude relevant evidence? See Gold, Limiting Judicial Discretion to Exclude Prejudicial Evidence, 18 U.C.Davis L.Rev. 59 (1984); Waltz, Judicial Discretion in the Admission of Evidence Under the Federal Rules of Evidence, 79 Nw.U.L.Rev. 1097 (1985).

5.   *Constitutional limitations on the exclusion of defense evidence.* The exclusion of evidence offered by the defense for reasons other than the absence of logical relevance or the possibility of undue prejudice may raise constitutional issues. In Holmes v. South Carolina, 547 U.S. 319 (2006), the Court overturned a conviction under a state rule that precluded the defendant from introducing evidence that another person had committed the crime in the face of "strong forensic evidence" of defendant's guilt. The Court noted (547 U.S. at 329):

Under this rule, the trial judge does not focus on the probative value or the potential adverse effects of admitting the defense evidence of third-party guilt. Instead, the critical inquiry concerns the strength of the prosecution's case: If the prosecution's case is strong enough, the evidence of third-party guilt is excluded even if that evidence, if viewed independently, would have great probative value and even if it would not pose an undue risk of harassment, prejudice, or confusion of the issues.

Viewed this way, the South Carolina rule resulted in a denial of defendant's right to present a complete defense. The *Holmes* decision is found in Chapter 2 with further discussion of constitutional limitations on the defendant's right to introduce evidence.

6.   The succeeding chapter deals with other frequently occurring questions of relevancy. In reading about them, attempt not only to extract those more or less specific rules which the courts have evolved but also to gain the ability to predict the probable application of the doctrine embodied in Rule 403 to more unusual methods of proof.

CHAPTER 8

FORMALIZED APPLICATIONS OF THE RELEVANCY CONCEPT

■ ■ ■

A. OTHER HAPPENINGS

CITY OF BLOOMINGTON V. LEGG
Supreme Court of Illinois, 1894.
37 N.E. 696.

This was an action on the case to recover damages for the death of Silas M. Legg, son of appellee. The declaration charges that the City of Bloomington erected a fountain on North Main street, to be used for drinking purposes and for watering horses. That around the fountain was a basin, into which water was conducted by two spouts; that the spouts were placed where the heads and bridles of the horses would come when drinking. That the spouts projected out several inches over the basin, and then bent, forming a hook, so that horses in drinking and after drinking, in lifting their heads, were liable to catch or break their bridles, of which the city had notice.

Silas M. Legg, on September 10, 1889, was driving a team of horses, hitched to an oil wagon, on which he was riding, on said street, and while exercising due care and diligence for his own safety, and permitting the horses to drink from the basin of the fountain, the bridle of one of the horses caught upon a curved or bent spout and was pulled off, and the horses ran away without his fault, threw him off, and the wagon on to him, thereby causing his death. * * *

A trial by jury resulted in a verdict for plaintiff, and damages assessed at the sum of $1,000, on which judgment was rendered. That judgment was affirmed by the Appellate Court, and this appeal is prosecuted by the city, it assigning error in allowing evidence to go to the jury that other accidents had occurred on account of the fountain spouts, and that it was error to allow evidence to show other accidents when the spouts were not in the same condition as at the time of the accident, and that instructions for plaintiff were erroneous.

MR. JUSTICE PHILLIPS delivered the opinion of the Court:

The declaration contained several counts, some of which alleged that the spouts of the fountain turned downward at an angle at the end, whilst other counts charged the spouts as projecting straight out.

Evidence was admitted, over the defendant's objection, that other accidents had occurred of a similar character to that which resulted in injury to the deceased. Evidence of other accidents occurring from the same cause is by many courts held incompetent.

This court has held such evidence competent, not for the purpose of showing independent acts of negligence, but as tending to show the common cause of these accidents is a dangerous, unsafe thing. Where an issue is made as to the safety of any machinery or work of man's construction which is for practical use, the manner in which it has served that purpose, when put to that use, would be a matter material to the issue, and ordinary experience of that practical use, and the effect of such use, bear directly upon such issue. It no more presents a collateral issue than any other evidence that calls for a reply which bears on the main issue. Such evidence is held competent by the weight of authority. * * * The same rule is adopted in Georgia, Alabama, Connecticut, Minnesota, Michigan, and other States. In addition to being evidence material to the issue to show a dangerous condition, it is also evidence material as tending to show notice. City of Chicago v. Powers, Admx., supra. The frequency of such accidents would create a presumption of knowledge, and would be material to the question of diligence used to obviate the cause of injury.

The further point is made that plaintiff was permitted to show, over the objection of defendant, that other accidents occurred on account of the fountain spouts, when they were not in the same condition as they were at the time of injury to the deceased. The rule is clear, that to render evidence of similar accidents, resulting from the same cause, competent, it must appear, or the evidence must reasonably tend to show that the instrument or agency which caused the injury was in substantially the same condition at the time such other accidents occurred, as at the time the accident complained of was caused. The fountain spouts, when the fountain was first erected, projected two or three inches from the standard, and an elbow was screwed on to the outer end, which, in position, was perpendicular to the end of the spout, and projected downward. That elbow was removed, and that was the changed condition. It is not possible for a trial court to know the fact to be testified to by a particular witness, and whenever a witness was inquired of as to other accidents, the court, when the question was objected to, ruled in the presence of the jury that such evidence, if there were changed conditions, could not be considered to the prejudice of the city. And on the trial the court instructed the jury that they were not "to consider any testimony regarding accidents or trouble with horses, occurring at the fountain in question, at a time or times when you believe from the evidence the spouts complained of were in a materially different condition from what they were at the time of the injury complained of in this case."

Considering the instruction, and what was said by the court in ruling on the objection, we are not disposed to hold there was such error in the admission of that evidence that this judgment should be reversed. * * *

Judgment affirmed.

NOTES AND QUESTIONS

1. *Early less tolerant approach.* The principal case is in accord with modern treatments of evidence of other happenings. The courts were not always so tolerant of such of evidence. Compare Diamond Rubber Co. v. Harryman, 92 P. 922, 924 (Colo.1907), which involved a claim that plaintiff had tripped on a "goose-neck" placed in the sidewalk by defendant and used to inflate bicycle and automobile tires. The court held that the evidence had been improperly admitted, stating:

> Testimony that other persons had tripped upon this "goose-neck" was clearly not admissible for the purpose of establishing negligence of the defendants, or that the "goose-neck" was dangerous. If the fact that others had tripped upon the obstruction could be shown for the purpose of establishing negligence, then there would necessarily be as many distinct issues injected into the case as there were persons called as witnesses who had passed over the sidewalk in the vicinity of the "goose-neck." The care they had exercised and the conditions under which they had tripped upon the obstruction would be a subject of inquiry. If such evidence was admissible, then it would be proper to show that persons had passed along the sidewalk and had not tripped upon the obstruction; and again, the care they had exercised and the conditions under which they had passed by the "goose-neck" could be gone into, and thus the case would be confused by a great number of collateral issues, which would not aid in determining whether or not the obstruction was dangerous. * * *

2. *Cases of inadmissibility.* Despite the generally more tolerant recent attitude toward this kind of evidence, it is not always admitted. See, e.g., Coate v. State, 306 S.W.2d 727 (Tex.Crim.App.1957), commented upon in 36 Tex.L.Rev. 664 (1958), and Smith v. City of Rock Island, 161 N.E.2d 369 (Ill.App.Ct.1959). In the former, a negligent homicide case, the accused offered evidence of prior collisions at the same intersection. In the latter, defendant city, being sued for failure to maintain a proper stop sign at the intersection where plaintiff was injured, offered evidence of collisions at other intersections having proper stop signs. In both cases the evidence was ruled inadmissible.

3. *Rebutting extreme claims.* The court of appeals opted for admissibility of testimony of three one-eyed marine carpenters that they were successfully employed at their trade, offered to rebut plaintiff-marine

carpenter's claim in admiralty that loss of an eye had rendered him unemployable. Rapisardi v. United Fruit Co., 441 F.2d 1308 (2d Cir.1971).

4. *Degree of similarity.* The degree of similarity of circumstances required may depend upon the purpose for which the evidence is offered. Strict similarity is likely to be required where the evidence is offered to show the dangerousness of the condition; a lesser showing of similarity may be required where the evidence is offered to show notice. Why? Compare Kelsay v. Consolidated Rail Corp., 749 F.2d 437 (7th Cir.1984) (evidence of prior railroad crossing accidents excluded as too remote and dissimilar), with Young v. Illinois Cent. Gulf R. Co., 618 F.2d 332 (5th Cir.1980) (evidence of recent prior accidents admissible to show notice of an arguably dangerous railroad crossing without a "trial of the details and circumstances of those prior accidents").

5. *Examples of treatments of other happenings.* For treatments of other happenings in a variety of situations, see Annots., 15 A.L.R.6th 1, prior accidents at same place; 26 A.L.R.2d 136, prior escapes of gas; 45 A.L.R.2d 1121, explosion damage to other properties; 46 A.L.R.2d 935, other failures of railroad crossing devices; 42 A.L.R.3d 780, other accidents to prove dangerous nature of product. See generally 2 Imwinkelried, Uncharged Misconduct Evidence §§ 7:14–7:19 (2012).

6. *Federal Rule 404(b).* A strong argument can be made that evidence of other happenings in civil cases should be considered under Rule 404(b) as evidence of "other crimes, wrongs, or acts." See, e.g., Imwinkelried, note 5, supra, §§ 7:13, 7:24, 7:27. Many courts considering the question under the Federal Rules have ignored Rule 404(b) and relied instead either on common law principles or on Rule 403. See, e.g., *Kelsay v. Consolidated Rail Corp.,* note 4, supra (trial court properly excluded evidence of two prior accidents at railroad crossing, one 30 years and one 12 years before, on grounds of remoteness and dissimilarity of conditions). Might the application of Rule 404(b) make any difference in such cases?

JONES V. PAK–MOR MANUFACTURING CO.

Supreme Court of Arizona, En Banc, 1985.
700 P.2d 819.

FELDMAN, JUSTICE.

Jerry Jones (plaintiff) was injured on January 27, 1979, while working on a machine manufactured by Pak–Mor Manufacturing Company (defendant). In the product liability action which followed, plaintiff alleged improper design and sought recovery on theories of negligence and strict liability. Before trial, plaintiff moved to exclude all evidence of the absence of prior, similar accidents. The trial court granted plaintiff's motion, ruling that such evidence was inadmissible under Arizona law. After verdict and judgment for plaintiff, defendant appealed, claiming, *inter alia,* that the exclusion ruling was in error. The court of appeals affirmed. *Jones v. Pak–Mor Manufacturing Co.,* 145 Ariz. 132,

700 P.2d 830 (1984). * * * We accepted review only on the issue pertaining to admissibility of evidence of the absence of prior accidents.

* * *

Plaintiff was employed by SCA Services of Arizona, Inc. On January 27, 1979, plaintiff was injured while working on a side-loading refuse compaction and collection machine on a route serviced by SCA.

[Plaintiff, a worker on the machine, seriously injured his leg when he was caught between the vehicle and a fence. The trial involved his claims of negligence and strict liability against the manufacturer of the vehicle based upon its design of the standing space on the machine.]

* * *

[T]he evidence indicates that no material change in the design occurred and that the compactor on which plaintiff was riding was a model which had been used without relevant change for a period of twenty-six years.

At the beginning of trial, plaintiff moved to exclude any evidence that the machine had been in use for twenty-six years without report of similar accidents. In opposing the motion, defendant offered to prove that the product had been designed and put into use in 1947, that the relevant portion of the design had not been changed, that thousands of machines with the same design had been sold, that they had been used under widely varying conditions, and that there had been no report of claims to or against defendant based on any injury sustained in a manner similar to that alleged by plaintiff. Defendant was prepared to offer this evidence through the testimony of its president. It argued that the evidence was relevant to show that the design was not defective, that the product was not unreasonably dangerous, and that the defendant had no notice of any defect or danger.

While recognizing that there is authority from other jurisdictions supporting the admission of evidence relating to the absence of prior accidents in both negligence and strict liability actions, both the trial judge and the court of appeals correctly noted the existence of Arizona decisions "admit[ting] evidence of prior accidents, but exclud[ing] evidence of the absence of prior accidents." (*Jones v. Pak–Mor,* at 123, 700 P.2d at 821.) As the court of appeals further noted, in Arizona the rule is "applied mechanically." (*Id.*) Although the trial court has discretion to admit evidence of prior accidents, the rule relating to inadmissibility of evidence of the absence of prior accidents is a *per se* rule. *Hlavaty v. Song,* 107 Ariz. 606, 491 P.2d 460 (1971). Evidence of the absence of prior accidents under similar conditions is inadmissible to prove lack of defect, lack of danger, or similar issues. * * *

The rule of *per se* inadmissibility was first adopted by this court in *Fox Tucson Theaters Corp. v. Lindsay,* 47 Ariz. 388, 56 P.2d 183 (1936). * * *

1.   The Basis for Rejection

The reason given in *Lindsay* for the rule of inadmissibility was that

> * * * it is apparent that such testimony, could the parties be prepared to meet it, might introduce into the case numerous collateral issues bearing only remotely on the main issue, which would tend to greatly protract the trial, distract the attention of the jury from the issues involved in the suit, and impose great and unnecessary expense on the parties.

Fox Tucson Theaters Corp. v. Lindsay, 47 Ariz. at 395, 56 P.2d at 186, quoting from the seminal case of *Anderson v. Taft,* 20 R.I. 362, 39 A. 191, 192 (1898). A second reason sometimes given for the *per se* rule of inadmissibility in some of the earlier literature was that

> Litigants should be protected against surprise * * *. [S]afety-history evidence is not closely confined in time, and sometimes not in space. Therefore, opposing counsel may be unprepared to meet fraudulent, partial, or mistaken testimony about accidents other than the principal one, or about long periods of safe use.

Morris, *Proof of Safety History in Negligence Cases,* 61 Harv.L.Rev. 205, 210 (1948). A final consideration was that jurors would be misled or prejudiced by such evidence. Thus, jurors impressed by the defendant's good record might be swayed in his favor and fail to see that he had lowered his standards. Id. at 210–11.

While some of these objections may still be viable, recent cases indicate that the rule of *per se* inadmissibility is "manifestly incompatible with modern principles of evidence." *Simon v. Town of Kennebunkport,* 417 A.2d 982, 985 (Me.1980). In *Simon* the court rejected a *per se* rule of inadmissibility of evidence of other accidents and stated:

> Whatever the continued vitality * * * of an absolute prohibition against other-accident evidence, it is clear that such a rule did not survive the adoption of our new Rules of Evidence * * *.

Id. at 986; see also *Sturm v. Clark Equipment Co.,* 547 F.Supp. 144, 145 (W.D.Mo.1982), aff'd, 732 F.2d 161 (8th Cir.1984) (noting that under the Federal Rules of Evidence the absence of prior accidents is "relevant and admissible, assuming an adequate foundation is established regarding comparability of circumstances").

We note also that the rule of *per se* inadmissibility, adopted in *Fox Tucson Theaters Corp. v. Lindsay* and followed in other cases, has been criticized by most, if not all, evidence scholars. *See McCormick on Evidence* § 200 at 590–92 (E. Cleary ed.1984); M. Udall & J. Livermore,

Arizona Law of Evidence § 85 at 190 (2d ed.1982); 2 Wigmore, *Evidence* § 443–44 at 528–32 (Chadbourn rev.1979). Observing that few recent decisions have applied a general rule of exclusion, McCormick has criticized the lack of symmetry in the rule allowing a judge discretion to admit proof of other accidents but not proof of the absence of other accidents:

> One might think that if proof of similar accidents is admissible in the judge's discretion to show that a particular condition or defect exists, or that the injury sued for was caused in a certain way, or that a situation is dangerous, or that defendant knew or should have known of the danger, then evidence of the absence of accidents during a period of similar exposure and experience likewise would be receivable to show that these facts do not exist in the case at bar. Indeed, it would seem perverse to tell a jury that one or two persons besides the plaintiff tripped on defendant's stairwell while withholding from them the further information that another thousand persons descended the same stairs without incident.

McCormick, supra, § 200 at 590. Similarly, Wigmore has rejected as unsound a fixed rule of admissibility or inadmissibility, favoring instead a general rule of judicial discretion:

> It is much wiser and more practical to leave the possible inconvenience to be determined by the tribunal best fitted to determine it, the trial court, and to sanction the reception of all such relevant evidence subject to this exclusionary discretion based on inconvenience.

2 Wigmore, supra, § 444 at 532.

Whatever the debate waged in the courts and by the authors of articles and treatises, we believe that our position should be compatible with the rules of evidence which we adopted in 1977. A blanket rule of inadmissibility is essentially a rule of relevancy. As a matter of law it declares the evidence inadmissible either because it lacks probative value with regard to the issues presented or because its probative value is outweighed by the danger of prejudice and the problems associated with inquiry into collateral matters, such as time wasted, expense, and the like. *See Simon v. Town of Kennebunkport,* 417 A.2d at 986.

2.   The Rules of Evidence

We turn, then, to an examination of the rules of evidence. Rule 401 defines "relevant evidence" as that "having any tendency to make the existence of any fact that is of consequence to the determination of the action more probable or less probable than it would be without the evidence." The essence of a negligence action based on defective design is that defendant distributed a product when it was reasonably foreseeable that its design presented an unreasonable risk of harm. W. Prosser & W. Keeton, *The Law of Torts* §§ 96, 99 at 688–89, 698–702 (5th ed.1984). In a strict liability action, the plaintiff must prove that the product was defective and unreasonably dangerous. Restatement (Second) of Torts § 402A. The factors which bear upon this determination in a defective design case were considered by us in *Byrns v. Riddell, Inc.,* 113 Ariz. 264, 550 P.2d 1065 (1976). One of those factors is the likelihood that the product, as designed, will cause serious injury. *Id.* at 267, 550 P.2d at 1068. Thus, in product liability actions based on defective design, relevant issues may include whether defendant should have foreseen the potential for danger from use of the product as designed, whether a defect existed, and whether a particular danger was unreasonable—including the likelihood of its causing serious injury. Safety-history, including the presence or absence of prior accidents under similar use, is evidence which may make these ultimate facts "more probable or less probable than [they] would be without the evidence." Rule 401, Ariz.R.Evid., 17A A.R.S. * * * There can be no doubt that evidence of safety-history is relevant.

Once evidence is shown to be relevant, Rule 402 provides that it is admissible unless "otherwise provided" by constitutional provision, statute, or rule. Several rules of evidence provide for *per se* inadmissibility, subject to enumerated exceptions. *See* Rules 404 and 407–411. No specific rule of evidence mandates rejection of evidence of safety-history. The one rule that applies to safety-history evidence is Rule 403, which covers the concerns expressed by this court in *Fox Tucson Theaters Corp. v. Lindsay, supra,* and described by Wigmore as "considerations of auxiliary probative policy." 2 Wigmore, *supra,* § 443 at 528. Rule 403 permits exclusion of evidence when

> [a]lthough relevant, * * * its probative value is substantially outweighed by the danger of unfair prejudice, confusion of the issues, or misleading the jury, or by considerations of undue delay, waste of time, or needless presentation of cumulative evidence.

Rule 403 is not a rule of per se inadmissibility, but one which gives the court discretion to reject relevant evidence upon the grounds stated. 1 Weinstein's Evidence § 403[01] (1982). It is essentially a rule which requires the court to weigh and balance the benefit to be gained by admission against the harm which may result from admission. It is the rule applicable to evidence showing the existence of prior accidents. Simon v. Town of Kennebunkport, 417 A.2d at 986. It is the rule which defendant claims logically should apply to evidence of the absence of prior accidents in cases involving alleged negligent or defective design. For this proposition defendant cites a number of recent cases holding that the trial court has discretion under Rule 403 to admit evidence of the absence of prior accidents. * * *

3. Characterization of Evidence of the Absence of Prior Accidents

There is little logic in the proposition that the trial court may admit evidence of other accidents but may never admit evidence of their absence. *See* McCormick, *supra,* § 200 at 590. Nevertheless, experience teaches us that the problems of prejudice, inability of the opposing party to meet the evidence, and the danger of misleading the jury are substantial. We are aware, also, that defendant's "lack of notice" of injury does not establish the fact that no injuries had occurred, and that a "long history of good fortune" may not preclude the conclusion that the product was defective and unreasonably dangerous. *Tucson Industries, Inc. v. Schwartz,* 108 Ariz. 464, 468, 501 P.2d 936, 940 (1972).

We believe that the true problem underlying the rejection of evidence of the lack of prior accidents is more evidentiary than substantive in nature. The essential nature of evidence of the absence of prior accidents is different from evidence of the existence of prior accidents. It is harder to prove that something did not happen than to prove that it did happen. When a witness testifies that he knows of no prior accidents, there are two possible explanations. The first is that there have been no prior accidents; the second is that there have been prior accidents but the witness does not know about them. This problem, however, is not peculiar to safety-history evidence in product liability cases. It is, we believe, a variant of the "negative evidence" problem. *See* M. Udall & J. Livermore, *supra,* § 65 at 120; 2 Wigmore, *supra,* § 664. The response of most courts to this problem has been that testimony that a witness did not see an event (knows of no prior accident) "has, in and of itself no probative force sufficient to prove that the event did not occur." *Byars v. Arizona Public Service Co.,* 24 Ariz.App. 420, 424, 539 P.2d 534, 538 (1975). *See also State v. Jeffers,* 135 Ariz. 404, 661 P.2d 1105 (1983). Generally, courts hold that such negative evidence is inadmissible, unless testimony that the witness did not see the event or does not know of it is coupled with further evidence that the witness was in such a position or has such sources of knowledge that if the event had occurred, he would have seen it or would have known about it. M. Udall & J. Livermore, *supra,* § 65 at 120; 2 Wigmore, *supra,* § 664 at 907.

All of these factors indicate the path that should be taken. If the *per se* rule is rejected, the trial court will apply Rule 403, weigh the auxiliary probative problems, and balance them against the value of the evidence. The trial judge should be aware of the difficulty of meeting an allegation that there have been no prior accidents. If a product is very widely distributed, it will be almost impossible for the plaintiff to rebut such a contention when the real issue is simply whether, among millions of users, a few each year may have used the product in a way which produced serious injuries. The trial judge must remember that where plaintiff alleges that a particular use of the product has produced a prior injury, he is put to his proof of the specific instance. The existence of a specific prior occurrence, the question of similarity, and other questions of specific proof are all much easier to meet than the general assertion that there have been no prior accidents. These factors, then, should weigh in the trial judge's determination of admissibility under Rule 403.

Other matters also should be considered. One of these is the plain nature of the danger. An open hole in a sidewalk poses a patent, unreasonable danger to pedestrians. Evidence of the lack of prior accidents is no more than evidence that the plaintiff was the first to fall in the hole. It creates a considerable risk of misleading the jury with respect to the purpose for which the evidence is admitted. Further considerations are similarity of use and length of exposure to the particular danger. *See Darrough v. White Motor Co.,* 74 Ill.App.3d at 565, 30 Ill.Dec. at 472, 393 N.E.2d at 125. The foundation should include evidence that the product experience which the proponent seeks to prove "is so extensive as to be sure to include an adequate number of similar situations." McCormick, *supra,* § 200 at 591.

We come, then, to the important consideration of the characterization of the evidence. The character of the evidence which might be admissible is determined by the issue on which it is offered. The ultimate issue is not whether lawsuits have been filed, nor whether claims have been made, nor whether the witness is aware of any accidents. The relevance of safety-history evidence is to establish evidentiary facts from which it may be inferred that there have been no prior accidents, thus warranting the ultimate inference that the product was neither defective and unreasonably dangerous nor the cause of the injury. Thus, the proponent of the evidence must establish that if there had been prior accidents, the witness probably would have known about them. This portion of the evidentiary predicate will, in most cases, be formidable. It is not, however, insurmountable. The defendant may have established a department or division to check on the safety of its products and may have a system for ascertaining whether accidents have occurred from the use of its products. The defendant or its insurers may have made a survey of its customers and the users of its product to determine whether particular uses of the product have produced particular types of injuries. Information may have been compiled by and obtained from governmental agencies such as the Consumer Product Safety Commission, the FAA, the FDA, or the FTC. Defendant may have established a system with its insurers, distributors, or retailers whereby retail customers are encouraged to report accidents, accidents are investigated, and data is compiled. Any of these methods, or others, may produce facts with which the proponent of the evidence may establish that if there had been accidents or near-accidents when the product was used in a relevant manner, defendant probably would have learned of the information and would have it available. Thus, if the import of the evidence is no more than testimony that no lawsuits have been filed, no claims have been made, or "we have never heard of any accidents," the trial judge generally should refuse the offered evidence since it has very little probative value and carries much danger of prejudice.

We are cognizant, also, that in the ordinary case (*see Fox Tucson Theaters Corp. v. Lindsay, supra*) involving the design or construction of buildings or intersections, the evidentiary predicate which we have described will militate strongly against admission of the evidence. Where, for instance, plaintiff alleges that premises were negligently designed or maintained, the mere fact that no prior accidents have been reported is incomplete. It does not tell us how many near-accidents, nor how many fortuitous escapes from injury, may have occurred, and it leaves the opponent of the evidence no method to ascertain and identify those who may have passed by the area, under what conditions, and with what risks or experience. In such a case, the scales tip strongly in favor of rejection of the evidence. However, in product design defect cases, the focus is on the inherent nature and quality of all products of similar design. If the design is "defective," then all units have the same defect. *See* R. Hursh & H. Bailey, 1 *American Law of Products Liability* § 1.21 at 66–67 (2d ed.1974). In such cases, the accumulation of relevant data is possible if the defendant, its insurers, distributors, customers, or some governmental agency has undertaken appropriate steps to acquire and compile information on safety-history. Under such circumstances, we believe that the problem of trial preparation is manageable. Once either party learns, through appropriate discovery, of the other's intent to offer evidence of safety-history, the opponent usually will be in a position to undertake some type of discovery or investigation to meet the assertion, so long as the offer is specific and not merely "we know of no claims." In these cases, the balancing test required by Rule 403 may well tip toward admission.

One further consideration must be examined. Plaintiff argues that the policy of product liability law should be to foster the manufacture and distribution of safe products and to discourage the distribution of unsafe products. Therefore, plaintiff maintains that we should continue to follow a policy of admission of proof of prior accidents under similar circumstances and *per se* exclusion of relevant evidence of lack of prior accidents, even though this rule has been criticized. We agree with the premise but not with the conclusion. We have recognized safety incentive as a factor in the evolution of Arizona law of product liability. *Salt River Project v. Westinghouse,* 143 Ariz. 368, 694 P.2d 198 (1984). We disagree, however, with the assumption made by the plaintiff. Safety is not promoted by giving manufacturers, sellers, and distributors an incentive to refrain from learning about their products. The present rule, providing for discretionary admission of evidence of prior accidents and automatic exclusion of evidence of the lack of prior accidents, does just that. We believe the law is better served by a rule which gives manufacturers and distributors the utmost incentive to acquire, record, and maintain information regarding the performance of their products.

We hold, therefore, that in product liability cases involving a claim of defective design, whether based on negligence, strict liability, or both, the trial court has discretion under Rule 403 to admit evidence of safety-history concerning both the existence and the nonexistence of prior accidents, provided that the proponent establishes the necessary predicate for the evidence.[1] The evidence of safety-history is admissible on issues pertaining to whether the design caused the product to be defective, whether the defect was unreasonably dangerous, whether it was a cause of the accident, or—in negligence cases—whether the defendant should have foreseen that the design of the product was not reasonably safe for its contemplated uses.

In the case at bench, the trial court held that evidence of the lack of prior accidents was *per se* inadmissible. The court of appeals affirmed that holding. We turn, then, to determine whether that ruling constituted reversible error.

[Despite its rejection of the *per se* rule, the court affirmed the lower court decision. It found that the defendant's offer of proof was insufficient to establish that its evidence would have been admissible. The defendant had simply stated that, over the past 26 years, it had had no reports of injuries like those to the plaintiff. The court responded:

> * * * the absence of claims and reports is not the relevant fact, nor even one which justifies an inference of the relevant fact (that there have been no accidents), absent a showing that if there had been accidents the witness would have known of them either from the system utilized to track safety-history or from the investigation made at the sources of such information. There may have been no lawsuits filed against defendant, but we have no way of knowing what workers' compensation claims were filed with appropriate administrative bodies nor any way of knowing what injuries were sustained but not pursued. * * *]

NOTE

For a more recent case adopting an approach similar to that in the *Pak–Mor* case see Forrest v. Beloit Corp., 424 F.3d 344 (3d Cir.2005) (evidence not

---

[1] We emphasize that this is a rule applicable to defective design cases and not those involving a manufacturing flaw. Cases involving a manufacturing flaw do not implicate the inherent design or quality of the entire line of products in question, but only the quality of a particular unit or number of units of that product. In such cases, the fact that the product as a whole has a demonstrated safety-history is irrelevant.

admitted where no records of injuries or accidents involving same model were kept; thorough discussion of problems that may exist where proof of absence of åccidents is offered). See also Evans v. State, 18 P.3d 227 (Idaho Ct.App.2001) (evidence of infrequency of accidents resulting from dives from platform properly admitted); Spino v. John S. Tilley Ladder Co., 696 A.2d 1169 (Pa.1997) (evidence of prior claims properly admitted in design defect product liability case); Bazzano v. Killington Country Village, Inc., 830 A.2d 24 (Vt. 2003) (evidence of no prior falls down stairs properly admitted to show absence of defect). See generally Morris, Proof of Safety History in Negligence Cases, 61 Harv.L.Rev. 205 (1948); 1 McCormick, Evidence § 200 (7th ed. 2013); Annots., 10 A.L.R.5th 371; 42 A.L.R.2d 1055.

REDFIELD V. IOWA STATE HIGHWAY COMM'N

Supreme Court of Iowa, 1959.
99 N.W.2d 413.

GARRETT, JUSTICE. In February, 1956 plaintiffs-appellants purchased 97.2 acres of land near the north edge of Des Moines for contemplated development as a residential sub-division. In November, 1957 the State Highway Commission filed notice of proceedings to condemn the north 77.2 acres of said land in connection with the construction of limited access interstate highway number 80. On December 10, 1958 the condemnation commission filed its report fixing plaintiffs' damages at $70,000. On December 26, 1957 the highway commission took possession of said condemned property and proceeded to complete the construction of said highway.

Within the proper time plaintiffs filed suit in the district court seeking damages in the amount of $198,925. The case was tried to a jury which gave plaintiffs a verdict for $60,000. They, being dissatisfied, have appealed to this court. * * *

Appellants' four witnesses testified to values as follows:

	Before	After	Difference
Redfield	$195,000.	$20,000.	$175,000.
Ashby	179,500.	20,000.	159,500.
Holden	143,000.	20,000.	123,000.
Neal	169,750.	20,000.	149,750.

Appellee's witnesses testified to values as follows:

	Before	After	Difference
Froning	66,000.	10,000.	56,000.
Donahoe	80,000.	8,000.	72,000.
Brandt	76,050.	11,550.	64,500.

It is enlightening to observe the extreme differences between the values placed on the subject property by the witnesses for the respective sides. All witnesses on value showed outstanding training and experience but when experts differ so widely on a proposition they profess to know all about, it lends force to appellants' claim that the actual records of sales of comparable properties from which the witnesses gained their knowledge are more reliable evidence than mere opinions of the experts. * * *

Appellants assign as error the striking of the testimony of their witness Ashby on direct examination regarding the price paid in a sale he used in arriving at his opinion of the value of appellants' property. This assignment has reference to a tract referred to as follows: "Also the piece inside the city limits on Merle Hay purchased by the water works, 360 by 360 for $15,000.00". On motion the amount of the purchase price was stricken. The witness had testified this was a comparable sale which he took into consideration in fixing the value of plaintiffs' property. After describing other sales he said, "All of these sales, I have informed myself as to the sales price and can give accurate details. Most of the properties were raw land and most of it sub-division land."

It appeared at that stage the court would continue to rule against the admission on direct examination of evidence of the prices paid for other similar properties. * * *

Under the rule heretofore prevailing in Iowa, such evidence would not be admissible. We have been asked by appellants to review our former decisions and to change the rule in this state to conform with the majority rule. * * *

We do not hold the view that the majority is always right but in this instance, after considering the advantages and disadvantages of each rule, being aided by well considered opinions of learned courts on both sides of the question, we feel it is advisable now to join those who adhere to the Massachusetts rule and we now adopt that rule. We quote from the Annotation, 118 A.L.R. 869, 870 * * * "The view is taken in a majority of jurisdictions that evidence of the sale price of other real property is admissible upon the issue of the value of other real property where the conditions with respect to the other land and the sale thereof are similar to those involved in the case at bar." Cases from many states following the above rule are cited as are also cases from states holding contra. At page 387 of 174 A.L.R. will be found an extensive annotation listing additional cases sustaining both views. It is stated this annotation supplements the one above from which we quoted. For the evidence to be admitted it must be shown that the conditions are similar. "Similar does not mean identical, but having a resemblance; and property may be similar in the sense in which the word is here used though each possess various points of difference." Forest Preserve Dist. of Cook County v. Lehmann Estate, Inc., 388 Ill. 416, 58 N.E.2d 538, 544. Size, use, location and character of the land, time, mode and nature of the sale all have a bearing on the admissibility of such evidence.

The futility, if not the absurdity of the rule under which we now operate is well described in an opinion in a California case before that court adopted the majority rule. "Everyone recognizes that the first thing a prospective buyer of any kind of property wants to know is what other people have paid for like property in the recent past. * * * But when the valuation of realty is the problem, court and jury are suddenly cut off from informative sources and forced to rely (theoretically) upon opinions based principally upon undisclosed prices of other sales. * * * The main objective of the rule—avoidance of collateral issues—has proved abortive and the procedural aspect of the trial has changed for the worse. * * * Ever since adoption of the rule excluding other sales on direct it has been stated repeatedly that such sales, though the prices are given on cross-examination, are not evidence of value, are to be considered only upon the imputation of lack of information or trustworthiness of the witness. The jurors are so instructed. They know that sales are the basis on which mankind universally values properties; they have many of the pertinent sales before them; when they hear the judge instruct that those sales are not any evidence of value the jurors who are still listening begin to wonder what is the matter with the judge; * * * That such an instruction must be given is well settled in the law of this state." County of Los Angeles v. Faus, Cal.App., 304 P.2d 257, 269.

On appeal of the above case to the Supreme Court of California the decision was reversed and California in 1957 adopted the majority rule. In County of Los Angeles v. Faus, (Decided June 21, 1957) 48 Cal.2d 672, 312 P.2d 680, 684 the court said: "In taking this position it is recognized that we are overruling a line of decisions in this state that announce a contrary rule. The former rule was contrary to logic, unrealistic, and followed in only a few other states. It was merely a rule of procedure. Therefore, it becomes our duty not to follow decisions that we are convinced are erroneous and obsolete." * * * That court then taking the view that neither contract nor property rights had vested in either party by reason of its prior decision, stated: "The rule now announced is available to both parties upon a retrial." We make the same pronouncement in this case.

New York, formerly on uncertain ground, is now aligned with those states which hold evidence of sales of comparable properties admissible as substantive proof of the value of the property under condemnation. Village of Lawrence v. Greenwood, 300 N.Y. 231, 90 N.E.2d 53. Utah and Nebraska are among the large number of states now following this rule. State, By and Through Its Engineering Comm. v. Peek, 1 Utah 2d 263, 265 P.2d 630; City of Lincoln v. Marshall, 161 Neb. 680, 74 N.W.2d 470; 2 Wigmore on Evidence, 3rd Edition, 503 to 507, Section 463.

Much must necessarily be left to the sound discretion of the trial court as to whether or not the conditions are met which make the admissibility rule applicable. * * *

Reversed and remanded.

LARSON, C.J., and THORNTON, PETERSON, HAYS, BLISS and GARFIELD, JJ., concur.

THOMPSON and OLIVER, JJ., dissent.

NOTES AND QUESTIONS

1. *Another example.* In Hays v. State, 342 S.W.2d 167 (Tex.Civ.App.1960), a discrepancy of as much as eight to one between values given by experts for the landowners and those for the condemnor was emphasized as influencing the court to adopt the rule admitting evidence of similar sales.

2. *Discussions.* Broad discussions of valuation evidence are found in Note, Methods of Proving Land Value, 43 Iowa L.Rev. 270 (1958), and Note, Valuation Evidence in California Condemnation Cases, 12 Stan.L.Rev. 766 (1960). Cases on similar sales are collected in Annot., 85 A.L.R.2d 110. With regard to the requirement of similarity see County of Dakota v. Cameron, 812 N.W.2d 851 (Minn. App. 2012); Patterson v. City of Lincoln, 550 N.W.2d 650 (Neb.1996);.

3. *Forced sales and offers.* Consider the admissibility of foreclosure sales, sales to a body having the power of eminent domain, and partition sales. Should offers to buy or sell be admitted? See, e.g., Arkansas State Highway Comm'n v. Barker, 931 S.W.2d 138 (Ark.1996) (condemnation sale improperly admitted); Samonek v. Norvell Township, 527 N.W.2d 24 (Mich.Ct.App.1994) (evidence of forced sales inadmissible).

CARPENTER V. KURN
Supreme Court of Missouri, 1941.
157 S.W.2d 213.

TIPTON, P.J.—Respondent brought this action as widow of Reuben Carpenter, deceased, to recover damages for alleged wrongful death of her husband, which occurred on May 25, 1937, near Henryetta, Oklahoma. She brought this action for the benefit of herself and deceased's four minor children. This action was first tried in the Circuit Court of Barry County, Missouri, where respondent obtained a judgment for $18,000. We reversed that judgment for error in respondent's instruction; our opinion is reported in 345 Mo. 877, 136 S.W.2d 997, where a full statement of the facts may be found. Thereafter, the case was sent to Henry County, Missouri, on a change of venue, where a judgment of $20,000 was obtained by respondent. The appellants have duly appealed from that judgment. * * *

The appellants assigned as error the testimony of witnesses Sherman Gipson and Luther Houk, who testified that on two occasions following the accident, they, with others, made certain tests for the purpose of ascertaining the distance one standing on the track could tell that a person sitting in the same position and dressed the same as deceased was a human being. The conditions under which these tests were made were the same as existed when deceased was struck by appellants' train, except that persons making the observation were on foot instead of being in the cab of a moving engine.

The appellants contend this testimony is inadmissible; first, for the reason that these witnesses knew in advance the object on the track when the tests were made was a man and just how he was dressed, and second, that these witnesses were on foot, while the engineer was in a moving engine attended with much vibration and lateral motion.

> " ' * * * But, if the evidence shows that the experiment was made under circumstances similar, or approximately similar, to those which surround the original transaction, and such experiment would serve to shed any light upon that transaction, we can see no reason for the exclusion of such experiment, although it might not have been made under exactly similar conditions as attended the original transaction. The dissimilarity would not exclude, but would go to, its weight before the jury. * * * ' " [Amsbary v. Grays Harbor Ry. & Light Co., 78 Wash. 379, 139 Pac. 46, l. c. 51, 8 A.L.R. 1.]

The above quotation was approved by this court in the case of Griggs v. Kansas City Rys. Co. (Mo.), 228 S.W. 508, l. c. 512. In that case, we held: "The difference in the conduct of such an experiment arising from the fact that the experimenter looks for what he is expected to see, while the engineer or motorman is expected only to watch for any object that might appear upon the track, and has his attention more or less engaged in operating his car or engine, is not a difference of condition sufficient to warrant the exclusion of the evidence. Its weight is a matter for the jury." To the same effect is the case of Norfolk & W. Ry. Co. v. Henderson, 132 Va. 297, 111 S.E. 277. We, therefore, overrule appellants' first objection to this testimony.

The question next arises, were the conditions when the witnesses were standing on the track making the experiments substantially the same as those when the engineer was in the cab of his engine, when the accident occurred resulting in deceased's death? Respondent's witness Ruskoski testified that an engineer could not see as far when the engine was running as when it was standing still, but he did testify that the engineer on a moving engine could see as well as a man standing on the ground and that the lateral motion of the cab impairs the view of an engineer looking down the track "very little, if any," and is not noticeable. Respondent's witness Wilson testified that side-sway "didn't have any material effect on your vision, and that you could see as far looking through one of those plate glasses as you could if you were standing on the ground."

The Supreme Court of Arkansas, in ruling almost the same question in the case of St. Louis, I.M. & S. Ry. Co. v. McMichael, 115 Ark. 101, 171 S.W. 115, l. c. 121, said:

> "We are of the opinion that the court did not err in holding that the conditions under which the experiments were made by the witnesses on behalf of the appellee were substantially the same. It is true that the witnesses who made these observations were not on an engine moving at a speed of 35 or 40 miles an hour, but there was testimony of expert passenger engineers to the effect that one accustomed to the movements of an engine could see a man as plainly from an engine going 35 or 40 miles per hour as one standing or walking on the track. This testimony, although contradicted by expert passenger engineers testifying for appellant, was nevertheless sufficient to render the testimony of the witnesses for appellee competent, so far as the essential similarity of viewpoints was concerned." * * *

[Affirmed, subject to remittitur of excessive damages.]

NOTES AND QUESTIONS

1. *Purpose of offer.* In the experiment cases, as in cases involving other happenings generally, a fair amount of confusion may be engendered by failure to make clear the exact purpose for which the evidence is offered. In the visibility cases, is the experiment calculated to determine a "normal" human reaction under the circumstances, what actually happened, or merely to establish some physical fact or facts? With the principal case, compare Handley v. Erb, 41 N.E.2d 222 (Ill.App.Ct.1941), upholding exclusion of evidence of experiments to determine the visibility of a rope stretched across a street because the subject of the experiment knew that the rope was there while defendant at the time of the occurrence did not.

2. *The human factor.* When an experiment involving human participants is probative of some material fact despite dissimilarities between the persons involved in the experiment and those involved in the actual occurrence in litigation, may admission of evidence of the experiment nevertheless constitute error? In Spurlin v. Nardo, 114 S.E.2d 913 (W.Va.1960), the plaintiff was injured when defendant's car, in which plaintiff was riding, descended a hill out of control as a result of failure of the foot brake. Plaintiff offered evidence of experiments by an expert automotive mechanic with thirty-five years driving experience, conducted in a like-model car on the same hill, to prove that the car could have been stopped by alternative means. The evidence was admitted by the trial court. On appeal, held: *Reversed.* While the evidence was proper to show "what the machine could do," nevertheless "where a human element is involved [in an experiment], such experiments should be excluded or the human element separated." Id. at 920. What did the court mean by "separating the human element"? How do you suppose the court felt this might have been

accomplished in the *Spurlin* case? Are there problems even where the same driver is involved in the experiment? See First Midwest Trust Co. v. Rogers, 701 N.E.2d 1107 (Ill.App.Ct.1998) (experiment improperly admitted).

3. *Danger.* Situations involving disastrous or fatal consequences to human beings may present practical problems of securing a suitable subject for experimentation. However, in Louisville Gas and Elec. Co. v. Duncan, 31 S.W.2d 915 (Ky.1930), involving the electrocution of a miner, the superintendent induced another employee to assume the same position as the deceased.

4. *Other cases.* Experiment cases are collected in Annots., 26 A.L.R.2d 892, ballistics; 54 A.L.R.2d 922, damages from electricity; 76 A.L.R.2d 354, chemical or physical qualities; 76 A.L.R.2d 402, explosions; 78 A.L.R.2d 152, visibility; 78 A.L.R.2d 218, skidding of vehicles; 64 A.L.R.4th 125, defect in motor vehicle; 11 A.L.R.5th 497, distance of gun fired at victim. Absence of the accused from the site does not generally render the results of experiments inadmissible. Annot., 17 A.L.R.2d 1078.

FOSTER v. AGRI–CHEM, INC.

Supreme Court of Oregon, 1963.
385 P.2d 184.

DENECKE, JUSTICE.

[One of] the primary problems in this case involve[s] the admissibility of evidence of out-of-the-courtroom experiments. * * *

The defendant contracted to sell and apply liquid nitrogen fertilizer on the plaintiffs' wheatlands. The defendant agreed to apply not more than 50 pounds of fertilizer per acre. Plaintiffs contend that 64 pounds per acre were applied and the application was performed in an unhusbandlike manner. They allege that because of this negligence the land yielded 10,550 bushels of wheat less than it would have yielded had the fertilizer been performed according to the contract.

The defendant denied excessive or improper application; alleged plaintiffs were contributorily negligent in improperly applying the fertilizer; and contended plaintiffs waived any claim for damages by paying for the entire amount of fertilizer. The jury returned a verdict for the defendant.

A crucial question was whether or not the application of 64 pounds of fertilizer per acre caused the yield to decrease 10,550 bushels or in any substantial amount. The claimed loss was approximately 11 bushels of wheat per acre. Plaintiffs' evidence was that in the crop year involved, 1959, their wheatland produced an average of 46 bushels per acre. (The crop year of 1959 means the crop is harvested in the summer of 1959, but seeded and fertilized in the fall of 1958.) To prove that the application of 64 pounds of fertilizer adversely affected their yield, the plaintiffs introduced evidence of the amount of fertilizer used by their neighbors and the crop yield of their neighbors. The evidence was that plaintiffs' neighbors used a maximum of 45 pounds per acre and had yields of no less than 58 bushels per acre.

To counteract this testimony defendant offered the testimony of two experts, Mr. Oveson, superintendent of the Pendleton Branch, Oregon Agricultural Experiment Station, and Mr. Gassett, supervisor of the research laboratory of Pendleton Grain Growers, a large farmers cooperative. Both of these witnesses testified that in the course of their work they had conducted various tests to determine the effect of nitrogen fertilizer upon wheat. They testified these tests indicated that the application of 60, 90, and 120 pounds of liquid nitrogen fertilizer had not substantially reduced the yield of wheat. Evidence of specific test results was admitted. Plaintiffs objected to the introduction of these test results upon the ground that the results of experiments cannot be introduced without evidence that they were made under conditions substantially similar to those present in the matter in dispute.

As a general proposition an experiment is admissible only if the experiment is performed under conditions substantially similar to those existing in the case being tried. See Western Feed Co. v. Heidloff, 230 Or. 324, 347, 370 P.2d 612 (1962). It is also a general principle that the trial court has wide discretion in the admission of the results of experiments. Loibl v. Niemi, 214 Or. 172, 181, 327 P.2d 786 (1958).

There was testimony that the type of soil and the amount and time of rainfall on the test plots were the same as those on the Foster ranch. The time when seeding was done is unknown as to either plaintiffs' land or the test crops. Mr. Oveson, one of the testers, stated this was immaterial. He also stated it was immaterial whether or not the land had been fallow or had a previous crop of peas or grain.

The tests conducted by these two witnesses are not the usual kind of "experiments" as that term is used in decisions on the admissibility of evidence. The usual "experiment" consists of the arranging of conditions approximating those attendant upon the fact in issue and observing data emanating from such arranged conditions. The sole purpose of such an "experiment" is to obtain information for use in a particular lawsuit. The tests here had no relation to any lawsuit and were for the sole purpose of obtaining scientific knowledge. No decisions have been found pointing up this distinction. However, because this type of evidence is free from the taint of interest or bias that might accompany the usual "experiment" evidence, we believe greater latitude should be shown in admitting such evidence.[2]

___

[2] The same kind of evidence may have been visualized in the statement at 361, § 169, McCormick, Evidence (1954): "It seems also that experiments designed to show the general traits and capacities of materials involved in the controversy might often reasonably be admitted in

Therefore, for these two reasons, that it is within the discretion of the trial court to admit the usual "experiment" if as much similarity of conditions is shown as was here, and that these were not "experiments for trial," the trial court's admission of the evidence is approved. * * *

[Reversed on other grounds.]

NOTES AND QUESTIONS

1. *Other decisions.* Other decisions illustrative of the distinction between experiments calculated to show what happened in the particular case and experiments to develop principles, physical or chemical characteristics and the like, include: Pandit v. American Honda Motor Co., 82 F.3d 376 (10th Cir.1996) (operation of charge warning light system on automobile); Osborne v. United States, 542 F.2d 1015 (8th Cir.1976) (time required to drive automobile between two points); Gardner v. Q.H.S., Inc., 448 F.2d 238 (4th Cir.1971) (flammability test of hair rollers); Millers' Nat'l Ins. Co. v. Wichita Flour Mills Co., 257 F.2d 93 (10th Cir.1958) (principles of dust explosions); Walden v. Dep't of Transp., 27 P.3d 297, 306 (Alaska 2001) (traits and capacities of "Willow sand" on the coefficient of friction on a road). Would relaxation of the similar condition requirement appear warranted with respect to experiments of the latter sort even when they are conducted at the request of one of the parties and in contemplation of use in litigation? See discussion in Gladhill v. General Motors Corp., 743 F.2d 1049 (4th Cir.1984) (court held that test of braking went beyond demonstrating general principles so as to constitute a re-enactment of the accident). But see Van Steemburg v. General Aviation, Inc., 611 N.E.2d 1144 (Ill.App.Ct.1993) (evidence of test flight admissible; lower standard for similarity of conditions where no attempt to re-enact accident, even where test conducted by party in contemplation of use in litigation).

2. *Ex parte experiments.* Despite the obvious preferability of experimental evidence free from the taint of interest or bias, ready-made evidence of this sort will usually be unavailable. Thus, it is generally held that whatever bias inheres in the pure ex parte experiment does not in and of itself require exclusion of the experiment. Might any benefit nevertheless accrue from inviting participation by the adversary? See United States v. Love, 482 F.2d 213 (5th Cir.1973).

3. *Physical facts.* Under the "physical facts" rule, evidence contrary to unquestionably established physical facts will be disregarded. A very high degree of accuracy and neutrality in testing has been indicated when test results are sought to be qualified as "physical facts." Fortunato v. Ford Motor Co., 464 F.2d 962 (2d Cir.1972).

---

evidence without confining such experiments to the conditions surrounding the litigated situation."

B. PERSONALITY TRAITS AND BEHAVIOR PATTERNS—CIVIL CASES

RUMBAUGH v. McCORMICK

Supreme Court of Ohio, 1909.
88 N.E. 410.

[McCormick and Blair filed separate actions against Rumbaugh for injuries allegedly inflicted upon their respective sheep by a dog owned by Rumbaugh. Each plaintiff recovered judgment, and defendant appeals, assigning errors which include admitting evidence "as to the propensity of the dog to attack sheep."]

PRICE, J. * * * In the Blair case the following questions and answers appear on page 28 of the record: "What do you know about that dog as to having a habit of running and killing sheep?" An objection to the question was sustained. Later, on page 33, the following was propounded to the same witness: "Do you know whether or not this dog is in the habit of attacking sheep?" Objection was overruled and witness answered: "Yes, sir." Again, he was asked: "Do you know whether or not in the fall of 1903 and spring of 1904 this dog was in the habit of attacking sheep?" Answer: "Yes, sir, he was." But the witness was not permitted to tell what or whose sheep had been attacked.

In each case evidence was given that this dog had been driven away from plaintiff's sheep on several occasions prior to the time of the particular injuries sued for. The above covers all we can find in the Blair case as to prior assaults, and as to the habits of the dog. No evidence of reputation was offered and none given. Hence the wasted time spent in the brief, discussing the question of dog reputation.

It is well to state a fact or two before considering the legal question said to be involved. Defendant Rumbaugh urged in each case an *alibi* for the canine; that he was at home either tied up, or under close surveillance of the family. Again, defendant gave some evidence tending to prove that McCormick owned a dog bearing a strong resemblance to the other, and that witnesses might be mistaken about the animal which perpetrated the mischief—a case of mistaken identity. Intimate acquaintance with the accused animal could be properly shown—such as seeing him frequently about defendant's premises, at his house and in his company and under his control. And if the plaintiff's familiarity was partly made up of having seen the dog at his sheep on former occasions, when he was driven away to prevent injury, that would aid in the matter of identification, and for that reason evidence of such former assaults was competent. In both cases there is direct and positive evidence of the several forays made by the dog including those in which the damages were inflicted. No better means of qualification as to the identity of the guilty animal can be suggested than frequently seeing him upon the sheep of the two plaintiffs from which it was necessary to drive him away. He was a close neighbor's dog and the means of establishing his identity were entirely legitimate. It was the same dog still after the same sheep, in both cases. Whether the knowledge of these former raids was the foundation for the answer made to the foregoing questions as to the habits of the dog, we are not able to say, but we think the answers were competent evidence, when considered in their relation to the other testimony. It tended to prove that this particular canine was viciously disposed towards the neighbor's sheep, and had a propensity to chase, worry and kill them. Such a disposition in an animal moved by instinct and not by reason, may be shown in corroboration of direct testimony where there is conflict as to his identity. We have examined such authorities as can be found on this subject, and are satisfied they justify the preceding questions. Some of these authorities are text-books, among which is Wigmore on Evidence. In Section 201, Volume 1, and the appended notes, we find the view taken by that author, and several illustrations of the application of the rule are given as well as a reference to the decided cases. In Section 68 of the same volume, the author says, "The character or disposition of an animal is no less relevant than that of a human being, as indicating his probable conduct on a particular occasion, and it is open to none of the objections of auxiliary policy which affect the use of a party's character. It is therefore commonly conceded to be admissible. The hesitation sometimes observed in the rulings has been due to the *time* at which the disposition is predicated in the offer; but here, as with human character, the existence of a trait at a given time is evidence that it existed also for a reasonable time before and afterwards, and within liberal limits should therefore be received." See also footnotes on same page. In Maggi v. Cutts, 123 Mass. 535, it is held "that in an action for personal injuries, caused by an obstruction in the highway, where the evidence is conflicting as to the cause of the accident and the character of the horse which plaintiff was driving at the time of the accident, evidence of the character and habits of the horse, as well after as before the accident, is admissible." In Broderick v. Higginson, 169 Mass. 482, it is held that "it is competent to prove that a dog has a habit of attacking passing teams, in support of a disputed allegation that he attacked a passing team on a particular occasion."

Without quoting from other authorities, we have concluded that no error was committed in admitting evidence of habit of the animal, and his vicious propensity towards sheep at and preceding the time when the injuries complained of were inflicted.

Finally, we observe that this sheep loving dog has had "his day in court"—yea, in four courts—although uniformly condemned.

We will let the judgment stand.

Judgments affirmed.

SUMMERS, SPEAR and SHAUCK, JJ., concur.

NOTES AND QUESTIONS

1.   Compare Kelly v. Alderson, 37 A. 12, 13 (R.I.1896), a dog-bite action under a statute imposing strict liability:

> It is further argued that testimony as to the character of the dog was admissible to show that it was improbable that the dog would have attacked the plaintiff without being first assaulted by the plaintiff himself. This would set up the character of the dog against the plaintiff's oath. We think that the inference of probability is too remote and inconclusive. Dogs have often bitten persons when they have not been known to bite before, and the statute takes account of this fact by giving a remedy in such a case, if it be upon a highway.

2.   *Bloodhounds.* In a criminal prosecution, should it be admissible for the state to introduce evidence that bloodhounds brought to the scene of the crime shortly after its commission led their handlers to the home of the defendant? If defendant testifies that he was not at the scene, is the evidence objectionable as setting up the character of the dogs against the oath of the defendant? See Blair v. Commonwealth, 204 S.W. 67, 68 (Ky.1918), upholding the admission of the evidence and citing Sir Walter Scott's Talisman in which Richard I is represented as preferring the mute testimony of Roswell the hound to the knightly word of Conrade, Marquis of Montserrat. For a more recent discussion of the admission of canine scent evidence see Brooks v. People, 975 P.2d 1105 (Colo.1999). See also Rex v. Trupedo, 1920 A.D. 58 (S.Af.1920) (prejudicial error to admit evidence that dog identified accused based on scent left in room). Cases dealing with the admissibility of evidence of trailing by dogs are collected in Annot., 81 A.L.R.5th 563.

3.   *Recent case.* For a more recent case involving animal character, see Durst v. Newby, 685 F.Supp. 250, 252 n.2 (S.D.Ga.1988) ("the wanderlust of cows is simply a relevant fact not relating to the character of a party or witness").

4.   *Sniffer dogs.* The issue of the reliability of dogs also occurs in another context—the reliability of a dog's signal that contraband is present in order to establish probable cause for a police search. See the discussion in Myers, Detector Dogs and Probable Cause, 14 George Mason L. Rev. 1 (2006).

BEACH V. RICHTMYER

Supreme Court of New York, Appellate Division, 1949.
90 N.Y.S.2d 332.

HEFFERNAN, JUSTICE. At about nine o'clock in the evening of October 11, 1947, a collision occurred on the state highway near Cobleskill between an automobile truck owned and operated by defendant Richtmyer and an automobile owned by defendant Carpenter and operated by Glenn W. Harris, her chauffeur.

At the time of the accident the plaintiffs, Mr. and Mrs. Beach, the latter a sister of Harris, were passengers in the Carpenter car as were also Ethel E. Morrison, the mother of Harris and a Mrs. Smith. As a result of the collision Harris and Mrs. Smith lost their lives and the other occupants of the car were seriously injured.

Thereafter these plaintiffs instituted actions against defendants Richtmyer, Carpenter and Wildove as administrator of the estate of Harris, for the recovery of the damages which they sustained on the theory that the operators of both vehicles were negligent.

The actions were tried together and the jury found a verdict in favor of Mrs. Beach in the sum of $20,000 against defendants Carpenter and Wildove as administrator and a verdict in her husband's favor in the sum of $8000, against the same defendants. The jury's verdicts exonerated defendant Richtmyer.

From judgments entered on these verdicts and from orders denying their motions to vacate them defendants Carpenter and Wildove have come to this court. * * *

After a careful review of the record before us we cannot escape the conviction that the negligence of Harris is the sole cause of this tragic occurrence. Neither defendant contends otherwise and no claim is made by either of them that the plaintiffs were at fault in any respect. It should also be noted that neither defendant asserts that the verdicts are excessive.

The interests of these two defendants are adverse.

Two points are urged by defendant Carpenter to be relieved of liability. She asserts that Harris had no permission, either express or implied, to use her car on the night of the accident and that the admission of evidence on behalf of defendant Wildove pertaining to the good character of Harris was prejudicial and constitutes reversible error.

Although defendant Wildove has appealed from the judgments against him in his representative capacity his brief is devoted to a justification of the good character evidence of his decedent and he is asking us to affirm both judgments and orders.

We now come to the only remaining questions in these cases—the contentions of defendant Carpenter. In her testimony she emphatically denied that her chauffeur had any authority to use her car on the night in question. She was a vitally interested witness. Her testimony is uncorroborated. Death has sealed the lips of Harris and he could not contradict her. Although uncontradicted her credibility was exclusively for the jury. The question before us is whether this defendant produced substantial evidence to rebut the statutory presumption that the car was in use with her consent. It would serve no useful purpose to discuss in detail the evidence relating to this question. There is ample evidence in this record from which the triers of the facts might conclude that Harris' use of the car at the time of the accident was not unlawful. Either he had defendant's permission to use it then, as he had frequently used it theretofore, or he was guilty of larceny. Defendant's evidence, when read in connection with the other evidence in the case, and with all the surrounding circumstances, is not sufficient in law to destroy the presumption of responsibility.

Mr. Kniffen, a lawyer of repute in Schoharie County, and the president of a local bank, was sworn as a witness on behalf of plaintiffs. On his cross-examination by counsel for defendant, Wildove, he was interrogated as to the general moral character of Harris. He was asked the following questions and made the following answers:

> "Q. You may answer this question yes or no. Did you know his general reputation from the speech of people in the community in which he resided as to his general moral character? A. Why, I would say that I did.

> "Q. And was it good or bad? A. I would say that it was good."

Like testimony was given by the police justice of Cobleskill, by the pastor of the Methodist Church and by the mayor of the village.

All this evidence was received over the objection and exception of defendant Carpenter.

In our opinion this evidence should have been excluded by the trial judge. The credibility of Harris had not been impeached. He was neither a party nor a witness and for obvious reasons could not be.

In civil actions the character or reputation of a party is not a proper subject of inquiry. The courts of this State are committed to the doctrine that evidence of the character or reputation of a party to a civil action, where character is not at issue, is generally irrelevant and inadmissible, * * *

Mr. Ford in his excellent work on Evidence, Volume 3, § 244–a states the rule as follows:

> "In a civil action the general rule is that evidence of character is inadmissible as a probative fact to show that a party did or did not do an act which is the subject of the issue."

In 32 C.J.S., Evidence, § 423, it is said:

> "As a general rule the character of a party to a civil action is not a proper subject of inquiry, for, while it is recognized that ground for an inference of some logically probative force as to whether or not a person did a certain act may be furnished by the fact that his character is such as might reasonably be expected to

predispose him toward or against such an act, this consideration is outweighed by the practical objections to opening the door to this class of evidence."

We may not say as a matter of law that the reception of this testimony did not prejudice the rights of defendant Carpenter. It is presumptively injurious. To justify this court in disregarding the erroneous admission of this evidence it is not enough to say that possibly the result would have been the same if the improper evidence had been excluded, nor even that it is probable that defendant sustained no injury by the error. It must appear that the evidence could not by any possibility have affected the result.

The plaintiffs had no part in the introduction of the incompetent testimony. It is unfortunate that they should suffer because of the act of one of the defendants.

The judgments and orders in favor of defendant Richtmyer are affirmed without costs. The judgments and orders in favor of plaintiffs against the codefendants are reversed on the law and new trials granted in each action with costs to abide the event. The findings of fact implicit in the judgments are affirmed.

NOTES AND QUESTIONS

1. *Discussions.* See generally Ladd, Techniques and Theory of Character Testimony, 24 Iowa L.Rev. 498 (1939); Leonard, In Defense of the Character Evidence Prohibition: Foundations of the Rule Against Trial by Character, 73 Ind.L.J. 1161 (1998); Reed, The Pushy Ox: Character Evidence in Pennsylvania Civil Actions, 58 Temple L.Q. 623 (1985); Slough, Relevancy Unraveled—Character and Habit, 5 U.Kan.L.Rev. 404 (1957); 1 McCormick, Evidence ch. 17 (7th ed. 2013); 1 Wigmore, Evidence § 64 (Tillers rev. 1983).

2. *When alleged acts are crimes.* Evidence of character to prove conduct, as will be seen in the next section, is quite freely admitted in criminal prosecutions where offered by the defendant. Would the fact, noted by the court in the principal case, that if Harris was not driving the car with permission he was guilty of larceny, have provided a rationale for admitting the evidence of character? Courts have generally rejected the suggestion. In Greenberg v. Aetna Ins. Co., 235 A.2d 582 (Pa.1967), an action to recover on a policy of fire insurance to which the defense of arson by the insured was raised, plaintiff offered testimony of his exemplary service record during World War II. Admission of the testimony was held improper, the court noting that "the fact that the act in question is indictable if proved, or that fraud is charged in the pleadings is not sufficient" as a basis for admitting character evidence. Occasional cases, however, notably involving civil assault, have held in favor of admission, particularly where punitive damages have been sought. See Annot., 154 A.L.R. 121.

3. *Federal Rule 404.* Rule 404(a)(1) was amended in 2006 to make certain what most federal courts had held—evidence of character is inadmissible in civil cases to prove a propensity to act in a particular way. See 1 Saltzburg, Martin & Capra, Federal Rules of Evidence Manual, Rule § 404.02 [3] (10th ed. 2011). Rule 404(a)(2), providing that the accused may introduce evidence of a pertinent character trait of the victim of a crime and that, in a homicide case, the prosecutor may introduce evidence of the peacefulness of the victim in order to rebut evidence that the victim was the first aggressor, was amended at the same time to clarify that its provisions do not apply in civil cases. Some federal and state cases have held to the contrary. See Perrin v. Anderson, 784 F.2d 1040 (10th Cir.1986) (police officer charged in civil case with shooting victim entitled to protection of Rule 404(a)(2)); Feliciano v. City and County of Honolulu, 611 P.2d 989 (Haw.1980) (character of both victim and assailant admissible on issue of who was the first aggressor). But see Palmquist v. Selvik, 111 F.3d 1332 (7th Cir.1997) (victim's death wish inadmissible in civil rights action against police for shooting him).

Rule 404(b), which provides for admissibility of other crimes, wrongs, or acts if probative of something other than the character of a person to show that he acted in conformity therewith, is applicable to civil as well as criminal cases. E.g., Macsenti v. Becker, 237 F.3d 1223 (10th Cir.2001) (evidence of dentist's erratic behavior admissible in malpractice case). See generally 2 Imwinkelried, Uncharged Misconduct Evidence ch. 7 (2012); Annot., 171 A.L.R.Fed. 483.

SCHAFER V. TIME, INC.

United States Court of Appeals, Eleventh Circuit, 1998.
142 F.3d 1361.

BIRCH, CIRCUIT JUDGE:

* * *

This appeal * * * presents a number of evidentiary questions, most notably whether specific instances of misconduct are admissible to prove character under Federal Rule of Evidence 405(b) in an action for libel under Georgia law. The plaintiff-appellant challenges the district court's decision to admit character evidence pursuant to Rule 405(b) * * *. Although these evidentiary issues are not dispositive given our decision to reverse the district court on the grounds mentioned above, they may well arise at a second trial.

* * *

On December 21, 1988, Pan Am Flight 103 exploded in mid-flight over Lockerbie, Scotland, causing the death of everyone on board. A terrorist's bomb was then, and is now, widely suspected to be the source of that explosion. On April 20, 1992, defendant-appellee, Time, Inc. ("Time"), published a cover story entitled "The Untold Story of Pan Am

103." The article purported to debunk the then-prevailing theory that the government of Lybia [sic] had sponsored the attack on Pan Am 103. Instead, the article posited that a Palestinian group, with connections to Syrian drug traffickers, had targeted Pan Am 103 to eliminate several of the passengers who were members of a United States counter terrorism team attempting to rescue United States hostages in Lebanon. The article claims that these passengers had discovered an unsavory, covert relationship between the Syrian drug traffickers and a unit of the United States Central Intelligence Agency and intended to expose it upon their return to the United States.

The article further stated that an American agent, David Lovejoy, had become a double agent and had leaked information regarding the team's travel plans to forces hostile to the United States. The article included a photograph of a man identified by the following caption:

> David Lovejoy, a reported double agent for the U.S. and Iran, is alleged to have told Iranian officials that McKee [one of the U.S. agents] was booked on Flight 103.

* * * The article went on to imply that the information Lovejoy disclosed to hostile forces led to the attack on Pan Am 103.

The photograph in question apparently became associated with the Pam Am 103 bombing in connection with a civil case filed by the families of the Pan Am 103 victims. The families' law suit claimed that Pan Am had failed to take adequate security precautions to prevent the bombing. One of Pan Am's lawyers in that case, James Shaughnessy, filed a sworn affidavit that contained a variety of assertions about the attack that he hoped to explore through discovery in the Pan Am litigation. Shaughnessy's affidavit alleged that unnamed sources had identified Lovejoy, the double agent whose treachery facilitated the attack on Pan Am 103, as the man in an attached photograph. The man in the photograph, however, is Michael Schafer, the plaintiff-appellant in this case.

Time's article, therefore, erroneously identified Schafer, then working in his family's janitorial business in Austell, Georgia, both as a traitor to the United States government and a player in the bombing of Pan Am 103.

Upon discovering his picture in the magazine, Schafer demanded and eventually received a retraction from Time. Schafer filed suit against Time, making claims under Georgia's libel laws. A jury returned a verdict in Time's favor, finding no liability for the error. After filing a motion for a new trial, which the district court denied, Schafer filed this timely appeal. Schafer challenges a number of the district court's evidentiary rulings as well as the court's recharge to the jury on the definition of "malicious" under Georgia's libel statute. He also challenges both the district court's refusal to instruct the jury that the republication of a libelous depiction constitutes libel under Georgia law and the court's decision not to charge the jury on Georgia's retraction statute.

* * *

Schafer also argues that the district court committed reversible error by permitting Time's counsel to question Schafer regarding a number of "specific acts of misconduct" during cross-examination and by excluding from evidence a memorandum discussing the credibility of Time's sources for the Pan Am 103 article. We review the district court's legal decision to apply a particular rule of evidence *de novo* but its decision to admit or exclude particular evidence under that rule for an abuse of discretion. *Cf.* Carmichael v. Samyang Tire, Inc., 131 F.3d 1433, 1435 (11th Cir.1997). We will not overturn an evidentiary ruling unless the complaining party has shown a "substantial prejudicial effect." *See* Judd v. Rodman, 105 F.3d 1339, 1341 (11th Cir.1997).

* * *

Evidence of a person's character is viewed with some suspicion under the law and generally is disfavored in the Federal Rules of Evidence. *See* Fed.R.Evid. 404 (character evidence generally inadmissible to prove conforming conduct). In an action for defamation or libel, however, the issue of the plaintiff's reputation and character scarcely can be avoided because the plaintiff typically seeks to recover compensation for damage to his or her reputation. Even in such cases, however, the rules of evidence prescribe particular methods for broaching the issue of character. *See* Fed.R.Evid. 405 ("Methods of Proving Character").

Before trial, the district court instructed the parties that Time would not be permitted to introduce and explore a number of specific acts and events in Schafer's life as they were irrelevant to the issues before the jury. At that time, however, the district court warned both parties that the court would revisit the character issue to the extent that particular acts and events were shown to be relevant to the question of damages or how Schafer's picture might have become associated with the Pan Am case. During the course of the trial, the district court made a preliminary ruling permitting Time to explore selective incidents and acts in Schafer's background but excluding evidence of others. Specifically, the district court ruled that Time would be permitted to question Schafer about a felony conviction, a possible violation of his subsequent parole, convictions for driving under the influence, an arrest for writing a bad check, failure to file tax returns, failure to pay alimony and child support, and evidence concerning Schafer's efforts to change his name and social security number. Schafer attacks the district court's ruling and argues that these specific acts were inadmissible.

The Federal Rules of Evidence detail the circumstances under which character evidence is admissible and the methods available for presenting such evidence. In all cases in which character evidence is admissible a party may offer reputation or opinion testimony on the issue of a person's character. *See* Fed. R. Evid. 405(a). Only in cases in which a person's character is "an essential element of a charge, claim or defense," however, may a party offer evidence of specific instances of conduct. *See* Fed.R.Evid. 405(b).[3]

Character evidence does not constitute an "essential element" of a claim or charge unless it alters the rights and liabilities of the parties under the substantive law. *See* United States v. Keiser, 57 F.3d 847, 856 & n.20 (9th Cir.1995); Perrin v. Anderson, 784 F.2d 1040, 1045 (10th Cir.1986) (citing McCormick on Evidence § 187 at 551 (3d ed.1984)). Our determination of whether character constitutes an essential element requires us to examine the "authoritative statutory or common law statement of the elements of the prima facie case and defenses." *Keiser*, 57 F.3d at 856 n.20. The advisory committee's notes to the Federal Rules of Evidence provide two examples in which character evidence constitutes such an essential element: "[1] the chastity of a victim under a statute specifying her chastity as an element of the crime of seduction, or [2] the competency of the driver in an action for negligently entrusting a motor vehicle to an incompetent driver." Fed.R.Evid. 404(a) adv. comm. note (explaining that Rule 404 does not exclude such evidence because it is not offered to prove conduct consistent with character). In addition to these examples, a charge of defamation or libel commonly makes damage to the victim's reputation or character an essential element of the case. *See e.g.*, Johnson v. Pistilli, No. 95 C 6424, 1996 WL 587554 (N.D.Ill. Oct. 8, 1996) ("It is rare that character is an essential element. The typical example of such a case is defamation where injury to reputation must be proven."); *see also* Michael H. Graham, Handbook of Federal Evidence § 405.2 (4th ed.1996). Georgia law confirms that an assertion of damage to reputation in a libel case makes the plaintiff's character an issue under the substantive law. *See* Ajouelo v. Auto–Soler Co., 61 Ga.App. 216, 6 S.E.2d 415, 419 (1939) ("It is generally held that the foundation of an action for defamation is the injury done to the reputation, that is, injury to character in the opinion of others arising from publication * * *."); Redfearn v. Thompson, 10 Ga.App. 550, 555, 73 S.E. 949 (1912) (permitting the jury to consider plaintiff's bad reputation in mitigation of damages). (Since the plaintiff's character is substantively at issue in a

---

[3] The advisory committee notes to Rule 405 provide some insight as to the rule's limitations on the use of specific acts to prove character:

Of the three methods of proving character provided by the rule, evidence of specific instances of conduct is the most convincing. At the same time it possesses the greatest capacity to arouse prejudice, to confuse, to surprise, and to consume time. Consequently the rule confines the use of evidence of this kind to cases in which character is, in the strict sense, in issue and hence deserving of a searching inquiry. Fed.R.Evid. 405, adv. comm. note.

libel case under Georgia law, Rule 405(b) permits the admission of evidence regarding specific instances of the plaintiff's conduct on that issue.[4] See Perrin, 784 F.2d at 1045; Government of the Virgin Islands v. Grant, 775 F.2d 508, 511 n.4 (3d Cir.1985); cf. Longmire v. Alabama State Univ., 151 F.R.D. 414, 419 (M.D.Al.1992) (permitting discovery regarding specific incidents because the libel plaintiff put his character in issue); accord Ex Parte Healthsouth Corp., Nos. 1961758, 1970010, 2–3, 1997 WL 778837 (Ala.1997) (permitting discovery of such evidence in a libel case under a state rule of evidence identical to Fed.R.Evid. 405(b)); Daniels v. Wal–Mart Stores, Inc., 634 So.2d 88, 93 (Miss.1993) (making a similar observation in dicta). Given the plain language of Rule 405(b), Schafer's arguments that specific acts remain inadmissible to prove character in an action for libel are unpersuasive.[5]

Accordingly, we find no error in Time's exploration of these and other issues of character during its cross-examination of Schafer. To the extent that Time strayed from the specific issues of character enumerated in the district court's preliminary ruling, including Time's questions regarding Schafer's work for *Soldier of Fortune* magazine, Time's questions fell within the scope of Federal Rules of Evidence 405(a) and 608(b). We cannot say that the district court's decisions on these matters rose to the level of an abuse of discretion, nor can we say that Schafer suffered a "substantial prejudicial effect." See Rodman, 105 F.3d at 1341. * * *

[The court reversed and remanded the case based on its holding with regard to an error in jury instructions.]

---

[4]   Schafer's argument that this analysis puts "the horse before the cart" because Rule 404 governs the question of whether character evidence is admissible is unavailing. Rule 404 forbids the use of character evidence to prove "action in conformity therewith on a particular occasion," or as the advisory committee's notes describe it, the "circumstantial" use of character evidence. See Fed.R.Evid. 404(a) adv. comm. notes. Rule 404 does not bar the admission of character evidence when character or a particular character trait is actually at issue. Id. Rule 404 permits the character evidence in dispute here, and Rule 405 governs the acceptable methods for introducing it. For the sake of completing the analysis, however, we note that even though evidence of specific acts is admissible to prove character in a libel case under Rule 405(b), a district court must still determine whether such acts pass muster under Federal Rule of Evidence 401 (relevance) and Federal Rule of Evidence 403 (prejudice). See United States v. Barry, 814 F.2d 1400, 1403–04 & n.6 (9th Cir.1987). The district court's decision to admit the evidence at issue here cannot be said to constitute an abuse of discretion under these rules.

[5]   Schafer cites Butts v. Curtis Publ'g Co., 225 F.Supp. 916 (N.D.Ga.1964) aff'd, 351 F.2d 702 (5th Cir.1965), 388 U.S. 130 * * * (1967), a case decided before the Federal Rules of Evidence entered into effect on July 1, 1973, for the proposition that specific incidents of prior conduct are not admissible to prove character in a libel case. Although the district court in that case confirmed that character was an essential issue in a libel case under Georgia law and that a defendant could demonstrate that the "plaintiff's general character is bad," it held that both federal and state case law prevented the defendant from relying on specific acts or general rumors to do so. Id. at 921. The plain language of Rule 405(b), however, contradicts Butts by expressly permitting the admission of specific acts when character is an essential element of the case. Schafer's citation to Sharon v. Time, Inc., 103 F.R.D. 86 (S.D.N.Y.1984), a case that does not refer to Rule 405(b), does not require a different result.

NOTES AND QUESTIONS

1. *Instances in which character is an essential element.* The instances in which character will actually be an essential element of a charge, claim, or defense are very limited. The court in the principal case refers to the examples of seduction and negligent entrustment cases. Seduction cases are now rare to nonexistent. Negligent entrustment is somewhat more common. For an example of the application of the rule in such a case see Guedon v. Rooney, 87 P.2d 209 (Or.1939). Are there other instances in which character is an essential element of a claim or defense? Could character be an essential element of a criminal charge? See Robinson v. California, 370 U.S. 660 (1962) (statute criminalizing addiction unconstitutional).

2. *Federal Rule 405.* Under Rule 405(b), when character is an essential element, it may be shown by specific acts. The court in *Schafer* notes that it can also be proved by reputation or opinion proof. Is the rule as clear as it could be on that point?

3. *Character or reputation?* Are the terms character and reputation as used in the principal case synonymous? Is reputation simply one of the ways by which character can be shown? Is evidence going solely to character without reference to reputation relevant to the issue of damages in a defamation case?

MISSOURI–KANSAS–TEXAS R.R. v. McFERRIN

Supreme Court of Texas, 1956.
291 S.W.2d 931.

CALVERT, JUSTICE. This is a suit for damages for wrongful death brought against the petitioner Railroad by respondent, Ruth Adele McFerrin, for herself and as next friend for the minor children of herself and her deceased husband, R.T. McFerrin, who was killed in a crossing accident. * * * [The fireman testified that decedent failed to stop, but merely slowed down and drove onto the crossing.]

Mrs. McFerrin testified, over the objection of petitioner, that on occasions when she was in the car with him her husband never crossed the crossing in question without first stopping the car and looking and listening for trains. The objection was that what the deceased did on other occasions or what his habit and custom was with respect to stopping before proceeding over the crossing would not be evidence as to whether he stopped on this particular occasion. The question briefed here is whether evidence of habit and custom is admissible to prove care or negligence on a particular occasion. The sufficiency of the predicate laid for the testimony of habit is not questioned.

On the question presented the decided cases in this state, like those in some of the other states, are conflicting. * * *

With respect to the state of the decided cases in other jurisdictions, the following definite statements, as drawn from the authorities listed, may be made. 1. Where there are eyewitnesses to the accident, the overwhelming weight of authority is that evidence of habit or custom of care or negligence is not admissible. 2. Where there is no eyewitness to the accident, the weight of authority is that evidence of habit or custom is admissible. 3. In a few jurisdictions habit and custom evidence is admitted in all cases, even those in which there is an eyewitness to the accident, and in a few it is not admitted in any case, even those in which there is no eyewitness. * * * In the few cases in which the question has been considered, it is held that the fact that the only witness may be an employee of the opposite party or that his veracity is under attack does not let in habit or custom evidence. * * *

With the exception of the writer and Associate Justice Smith, all members of the Court are in agreement that this Court should adopt and follow the majority rule that habit evidence should not be admitted where there is an eyewitness to the accident, even though the eyewitness be an employee of the opposite party. What is now to be said on the subject is said in support of the writer's position that such evidence has probative force and therefore should be admitted under circumstances to be noted.

Habit evidence to prove care or negligence is not usually excluded because wholly lacking in probative value, but for reasons such as those given by the court in Zucker v. Whitridge, 205 N.Y. 50, 98 N.E. 209, 213, 41 L.R.A., N.S., 683, where it is said:

> " * * * Habit is an inference from many acts, each of which presents an issue to be tried, and necessarily involves direct, and naturally invites, cross examination. The circumstances surrounding each act present another issue, and thus many collateral issues would be involved which would not only consume much time, but would tend to distract the jury and lead them away from the main issue to be decided. From the want of previous notice, the other party would not be prepared to meet such evidence; and after all the testimony of this character was in the fact would remain that, as no one is always careful, the subject of inquiry, although careful on many occasions, might have been careless on the occasion in question."

Wigmore suggests that "there is no reason why such a habit should not be used as evidential,—either a habit of negligent action or a habit of careful action", and states that "such evidence often is of probative value and is not attended by the inconveniences of character evidence." 1 Wigmore on Evidence, Third Edition, § 97, pp. 530 and 532.

The American Law Institute's Model Code of Evidence has not been adopted in this state and of course does not control our decisions. On the other hand, the Model Code was prepared by and with the advice of many of this country's outstanding lawyers, judges and teachers in the field of evidence, and the rules suggested in the Model Code are entitled to serious consideration in deciding any evidence question which is still open in this state. By Rule 307(2) of the Model Code it is stated: "Evidence of a habit of a person is admissible as tending to prove that his behavior on a specified occasion conformed to the habit." It is then suggested, by way of example, that if in an action for the wrongful death of X at a railway crossing "W offers to testify for P that he had on numerous occasions been with X when X crossed the track in question and that on such occasions X had stopped and looked in both directions before entering the crossing" the testimony should be admitted; whereas, if the offer is that each of ten witnesses will testify that he was with X on one separate occasion and that on that occasion X stopped and looked in both directions before entering the crossing, the testimony should be excluded. No doubt the basis of the distinction is that in the first example the probative value of the evidence is thought to outweigh the slight inconvenience that would be caused by the examination and cross-examination of one witness on a somewhat collateral matter, while in the second example the inconvenience to the court of examining and cross-examining ten witnesses as to ten different incidents would outweigh the value of the evidence.

If it be conceded that habit evidence has any probative value (and most courts concede that it has) and it can be obtained from one witness, it is my opinion that it should be admitted even though there was an eyewitness to the accident. * * *

[Reversed and remanded.]

The writer and Associate Justice Smith dissent from the judgment. * * * We * * * believe the judgment of the courts below should be affirmed. * * *

NOTES AND QUESTIONS

1. *Eyewitnesses.* The principal case is commented upon in 10 Vand.L.Rev. 447 (1957). See also Snell, Eying the Iowa No Eyewitness Rule, 43 Iowa L.Rev. 57 (1957); Annot., 28 A.L.R.3d 1293. Federal Rule 406 specifically makes the presence of eyewitnesses an irrelevant consideration in dealing with the admissibility of habit evidence. Although the number of states requiring that there be no eyewitnesses in order for habit evidence to be introduced has dropped significantly with state adoptions of Rule 406, the concept is not entirely dead. Compare Isbell v. Union Pac. R.R., 745 N.E.2d 53 (Ill.App.Ct.2001) (habit testimony inadmissible where there are eyewitnesses), with Alvarado v. Goepp, 663 N.E.2d 63 (Ill.App.Ct.1996) (admissibility of habit testimony not dependent on absence of eyewitnesses).

2. *Sources.* Concerning the use of habit evidence generally, see Duffield, Distorting the Limits of FRE 406, A Tough Habit to Break, 38

Rutgers L.J. 897 (2007); Lewan, The Rationale of Habit Evidence, 16 Syracuse L.Rev. 39 (1964); Schroeder, Evidence of Habit and Routine Practice, 29 Loy.U.Chi.L.J. 385 (1998).

3. *Business habit.* Can evidence that a person has done business in a particular way in the past constitute habit proof? Compare Hollingham v. Head, 4 C.B.(N.S.) 388, 140 Eng.Rep. 1135 (1858) (terms of other sales contracts inadmissible), and Turpin v. Branaman, 58 S.E.2d 63 (Va.1950) (past business dealings inadmissible), with Whittemore v. Lockheed Aircraft Corp., 151 P.2d 670 (Cal.Ct.App.1944) (evidence that plaintiff's intestate had on other occasions flown planes from the factory for delivery to his employer, admissible to prove that he, rather than a factory pilot, was flying plane when it crashed en route for delivery).

REYES v. MISSOURI PACIFIC R.R.
United States Court of Appeals, Fifth Circuit, 1979.
589 F.2d 791.

JAMES C. HILL, CIRCUIT JUDGE:

In this diversity case plaintiff-appellant challenges the admission into evidence of his four prior misdemeanor convictions for public intoxication, introduced for the purpose of showing that he was intoxicated on the night that he was run over by defendant-appellee's train. We agree with appellant, finding the evidence of his prior convictions to be inadmissible under Rule 404(a) of the Federal Rules of Evidence; therefore, we reverse and remand the case for a new trial.

I.

Shortly after midnight on June 17, 1974, appellant Reyes was run over by appellee-railroad's train as he lay on the railroad tracks near a crossing in Brownsville, Texas. Reyes brought this diversity suit against the railroad, alleging negligence on the part of the railroad's employees in failing to discover plaintiff as he lay on the tracks and stop the train in time to avoid the accident. The railroad answered by claiming that Reyes, dressed in dark clothing that night, was not visible from the approaching train until it was too late for its employees to avert the accident. Moreover, the railroad alleged that Reyes was contributorily negligent because he was intoxicated on the night of the accident and passed out on the tracks before the train arrived. Reyes explained his presence on the railroad tracks by claiming that he was knocked unconscious by an unknown assailant as he walked along the tracks.

Reyes made a motion *in limine* to exclude the evidence relating to his prior misdemeanor convictions for public intoxication. The railroad opposed this motion, arguing that the convictions were admissible to show that Reyes was intoxicated on the night of the accident. The district court agreed and refused to grant Reyes' motion.

In an attempt to minimize the damaging effects of his prior convictions, Reyes brought them out on direct examination. In answering a special interrogatory submitted to them, the jury found the plaintiff more negligent than the defendant; under Texas law, this finding precluded Reyes from recovering against the railroad. *See* 7 Tex.Civ.Code Ann. Art. 2212a, § 1 (Vernon).

II.

Rule 404 of the Federal Rules of Evidence embodies the well-settled principle that evidence of a person's character is usually not admissible for the purpose of proving that the person acted in conformity with his character on a particular occasion. Fed.R.Evid. 404, 28 U.S.C.A. *See also McCormick on Evidence* § 188 (2d ed. 1972). This general rule of exclusion, applicable to both civil and criminal proceedings, is based upon the assumption that such evidence is of slight probative value yet very prejudicial.

An analysis of the admissibility of character evidence necessarily begins, then, with an examination of the purposes for which the evidence is proffered. If the evidence is introduced for the purpose of showing that a person acted in accordance with his character on a given occasion, then the evidence is inadmissible unless it falls within one of the exceptions noted in Rule 404.

The record in this case makes clear that the railroad intended for Reyes' prior convictions to show that he was intoxicated on the night of the accident. Indeed, that purpose was the only possible one for which the evidence could be offered. Moreover, the trial judge specifically noted in the motion *in limine* hearing that evidence of the prior convictions would be relevant to the issue of whether Reyes was intoxicated on the night of the accident. Because the evidence of Reyes' prior convictions was admitted for the sole purpose of showing that he had a character trait of drinking to excess and that he acted in conformity with his character on the night of the accident by becoming intoxicated, we conclude that the prior convictions were inadmissible character evidence under Rule 404.

III.

The suggestion that the prior convictions constituted evidence of Reyes' "habit" of excessive drinking is equally unpersuasive. Rule 406 allows the introduction of evidence of the habit of a person for the purpose of proving that the person acted in conformity with his habit on a particular occasion. Fed.R.Evid. 406, 28 U.S.C.A. *See generally McCormick on Evidence* § 195 (2d ed. 1972); 1 *Wigmore on Evidence* § 92 (3d ed. 1940). Habit evidence is considered to be highly probative and therefore superior to character evidence because "the uniformity of one's response to habit is far greater than the consistency with which one's

conduct conforms to character or disposition." *McCormick on Evidence*
§ 195 at 463 (2d ed. 1972).

Perhaps the chief difficulty in deciding questions of admissibility
under Rule 406 arises in trying to draw the line between inadmissible
character evidence and admissible habit evidence. Quite often the line
between the two may become blurred.

Character and habit are close akin. (Character is a generalized
description of one's disposition, or one's disposition in respect to a general
trait, such as honesty, temperance, or peacefulness.) ("Habit," in modern
usage, both lay and psychological, is more specific. It describes one's
regular response to a repeated specific situation.)If we speak of character
for care, we think of the person's tendency to act prudently in all the
varying situations of life, in business, family life, in handling automobiles
and in walking across the street. A habit, on the other hand, is the
person's regular practice of meeting a particular kind of situation with a
specific type of conduct, such as the habit of going down a particular
stairway two stairs at a time, or of giving the hand-signal for a left turn,
or of alighting from railway cars while they are moving. The doing of the
habitual acts may become semi-automatic. *McCormick on Evidence* § 195
at 462–63 (2d ed. 1972). Although a precise formula cannot be proposed
for determining when the behavior may become so consistent as to rise to
the level of habit, "adequacy of sampling and uniformity of response" are
controlling considerations. *Notes of Advisory Committee on Proposed
Rules,* Fed.R.Evid. 406, 28 U.S.C.A. at p. 153. *See also Wilson v.
Volkswagen of America,* 561 F.2d 494 (4th Cir.1977). Thus, the probative
force of habit evidence to prove intoxication on a given occasion depends
on the "degree of regularity of the practice and its coincidence with the
occasion." *McCormick on Evidence* § 195 n.16 (2d ed. 1972).

We do not undertake here to prescribe the precise quantum of proof
necessary to transform a general disposition for excessive drinking into a
"habit" of intemperance; (we simply find that four prior convictions for
public intoxication spanning a three and one-half year period are of
insufficient regularity to rise to the level of "habit" evidence.) Consequently, we hold the evidence to be inadmissible under Rule 406 as
well.

IV.

A principle purpose behind the exclusion of character evidence, as we
have said, is the prejudicial effect that it can have on the trier of fact.
This concern is especially compelling here where the character evidence
relates to one of the critical issues in the case, *i.e.,* the contributory
negligence of Reyes. Finding the introduction of the prior convictions to be
extremely prejudicial, we feel that the error affected the substantial
rights of Reyes, thus requiring a new trial. Fed.R.Civ.P. 61, 28 U.S.C.A.
* * *

Reversed and Remanded.

NOTE

Contrast the holding in *Reyes* with those in Loughan v. Firestone Tire & Rubber Co., 749 F.2d 1519 (11th Cir.1985) (evidence of extensive drinking over a 6–year period, including proof that plaintiff regularly carried a cooler of beer on his truck, sufficient to establish habit under Rule 406), and Keltner v. Ford Motor Co., 748 F.2d 1265 (8th Cir.1984) (court permitted cross-examination of plaintiff under Rule 406 to the effect that he drank a six pack of beer four nights a week). Cases on evidence of intemperate habits in accident litigation are collected in Annot., 46 A.L.R.2d 103; for federal cases, see Annot., 53 A.L.R.Fed. 703. See also Tillers, The Death of a Youth and of a Drunkard: A Remarkable Story of Habit and Character in New Jersey, in Evidence Stories 29 (Lempert ed., 2006).

EATON V. BASS

United States Court of Appeals, Sixth Circuit, 1954.
214 F.2d 896.

[Wrongful death action in which defendant trucking company was charged with operating a truck with defective brakes. Plaintiffs appeal from a judgment rendered on a verdict in favor of the trucking company.]

MILLER, CIRCUIT JUDGE. * * *

Hunter Mir, shop foreman for Hoover Motor Express Company, testified for the appellees, over objection of appellants, that he was in charge of safety checking the trucks before they went out on the highway; that it was the custom of the company to check every unit that went out to see that it was safe to put on the road; that the trucks were driven through three lanes in the shop; that the mechanics tried the brakes and the safety equipment, lights, horn and anything pertaining to the safety of the operation of the equipment; that if any defect is found it is repaired or the unit is cut out and replaced by another; and that no equipment went out on the road without it having been checked through his department. He had no records or personal knowledge about the check which was given the particular truck involved in the accident.

Appellants contend that evidence of custom or usage is not admissible to prove the exercise of due care by one charged with negligence, in that what ought to be done is fixed by a standard of reasonable prudence, whether it usually is complied with or not, and that in any event such custom must be a general custom among others acting under similar circumstances, rather than the usage or custom of a single person. Texas & Pacific Ry. Co. v. Behymer, 189 U.S. 468, 470 * * *; Standard Oil Co. v. Swan, 89 Tenn. 434, 15 S.W. 1068, 10 L.R.A. 366. The rule is not an unqualified one, Brigham Young University v. Lillywhite,

10 Cir., 118 F.2d 836, Annotation, 137 A.L.R. 611, and in any event is not applicable to the present case.

The evidence was not received for the purpose of proving that appellees were not negligent because they followed a custom generally in use in the particular industry. It was offered and received for the purpose of proving the existence of a particular fact, namely, that the truck was inspected in a certain way, leaving open the question whether such inspection, if it did take place, was sufficient to constitute due care. No evidence was offered or received pertaining to the custom of other truck operators, with which the particular inspection by the appellees would be compared. We think the District Judge ruled correctly in admitting the evidence on the ground that it had probative value on the issue of what, if any, inspection the truck received before being sent out on the highway, but at the same time pointing out that it was not conclusive that the particular truck was so inspected, and that whether it was or was not so inspected was still a question for the jury. Knickerbocker Life Ins. Co. v. Pendleton, 115 U.S. 339, 344–347 * * *; Thorn v. Aler, 92 W.Va. 290, 114 S.E. 741, 28 A.L.R. 536, 542. See Atlanta Coco–Cola [sic] Bottling Co. v. Shipp, 170 Ga. 817, 154 S.E. 243, 71 A.L.R. 1295. * * *

The judgments are affirmed.

NOTES AND QUESTIONS

1. *Sufficiency.* Was the testimony of the shop foreman in *Eaton* sufficient to establish that the inspection was in fact made? See also United States v. Cornett, 484 F.2d 1365 (6th Cir.1973), where a clerk who sold defendant a gun and filled in the answers on a required form that he signed testified that she always read the questions "word by word" to the purchaser. Cases on a notary's usual practice are collected in Annot., 59 A.L.R.3d 1327.

2. *Establishing habit.* Federal Rule 406 contains no guidance as to how a habit or routine practice is to be established. An earlier version of the Rule had a subsection (b) which provided that proof could be "in the form of an opinion or by specific instances of conduct sufficient in number to warrant a finding that the habit existed or that the practice was routine." The House Committee on the Judiciary deleted the section, stating that the method of proof should be dealt with on a "case-by-case" basis. H.R.Rep. No. 650, 93d Cong., 1st Sess. 5 (1973). One witness' testimony in the form of an opinion has been held sufficient under Rule 406 to establish a routine practice. See, e.g., Envirex, Inc. v. Ecological Recovery Assoc., Inc., 454 F.Supp. 1329 (M.D.Pa.1978), aff'd, 601 F.2d 574 (3d Cir.1979) (single witness established routine business practice of sending complete proposals to all general contractors with whom business contracted).

3. *Mailing.* Many of the cases of evidence of the practice or routine of a business organization involve proving mailing. Some courts at common law hold that, in addition to proving a routine of mailing, there must be a

showing that a "part of the routine was followed." Others find proof of a routine mailing sufficient in itself. Compare Consolidated Motors v. Skousen, 109 P.2d 41 (Ariz.1941) (need to show that part of routine followed), with General Mills, Inc. v. Zerbe Bros., Inc., 672 P.2d 1109 (Mont.1983) (routine sufficient). See cases cited in Annot., 45 A.L.R.4th 476. Does Federal Rule 406 do away with the need for proof in addition to the routine by its elimination of the requirement of corroboration?

C. PERSONALITY TRAITS AND BEHAVIOR PATTERNS—CRIMINAL CASES

(1) ACCUSED'S CHARACTER: FEDERAL RULE 404(a)(2)(A)

STATE v. RENNEBERG

Supreme Court of Washington, En Banc, 1974.
522 P.2d 835.

BRACHTENBACH, ASSOCIATE JUSTICE.

Virginia Sue [Renneberg] LaVanway was charged with and convicted of grand larceny. Her codefendant, Milton V. LaVanway, whom she married after they were charged with these crimes, was charged with and convicted of aiding and abetting grand larceny. The Court of Appeals affirmed the convictions and we granted review.

The defendant wife had been employed by a restaurant but had been discharged from that employment. In the early evening of June 24, 1970, the defendants visited the restaurant to obtain her final paycheck. The defendants went to the rest rooms in the rear of the restaurant and then returned to the front where defendant wife used the telephone which was located next to the cash register. Defendant husband stood near the restaurant door where he paced back and forth, looked about and kept moving around, according to the witnesses. The restaurant employee who was the only one operating the cash register that evening heard the register bell, indicating the register was being opened, and went toward the cash register. He saw defendant wife facing the cash register, then the defendants left the restaurant. A witness reported to the employee that his son had seen a young woman at the register with a stack of money bills in her hand. An immediate tally of the register disclosed a shortage of approximately $250.

The first issue arises from the following testimony elicited by the prosecutor:

Q. Mrs. LaVanway, is it true that in June of this year you were addicted to or were using a narcotic drug? A. Yes. Q. Mrs.

LaVanway, is it true that on July 14th, you went onto a methadone program to cure a narcotic addiction or use? A. Yes.

It appears that the question of admissibility of this testimony was discussed in chambers before the trial started. Apparently, although it is not clear from the record, the court indicated that testimony as to drug addiction would be inadmissible in the state's case. Only after defendant wife took the stand and testified as to her character, as described later, did the court allow this testimony. Admissibility of evidence of prior drug addiction can be considered on at least two distinctly different grounds. First, that it relates to the witness' credibility and second, that it is an unrelated act of misconduct, admissible to contradict character evidence. It is obvious that there is an immense difference between the practical effect of the two theories of admissibility. If it is admissible to attack credibility, it will come in whenever a defendant testifies while, if it is restricted to countering character evidence, it will only be used against that defendant who chooses to put his or her character into evidence. As to admissibility relating to credibility, there is a division of authority. *See* 3A J. Wigmore, Evidence § 934 (J. Chadbourn rev. 1970); 52 A.L.R.2d 848 (1957).

We note that we are not confronted with a situation where it is contended that the witness was under the influence of drugs at the time of the events to which he testifies as in Doe v. State, 487 P.2d 47 (Alaska 1971), or that the witness is under the influence at the time of testifying such as in State v. Reyes, 99 Ariz. 257, 408 P.2d 400 (1965).

The Court of Appeals recognized the division in the authorities but felt bound by our decision in Lankford v. Tombari, 35 Wash.2d 412, 213 P.2d 627 (1950), wherein a terse holding concluded that drug use or addiction is relevant to veracity. In view of society's deep concern today with drug usage and its consequent condemnation by many if not most, evidence of drug addiction is necessarily prejudicial in the minds of the average juror. Additionally there is no proof before the court connecting addiction to a lack of veracity. If such medical or scientific proof were made, it might well be admissible as relevant to credibility. Absent such proof its relevance on credibility or veracity is an unknown factor while its prejudice is within common knowledge. The Lankford v. Tombari decision is limited accordingly by our view herein.

However, the alternate and more restrictive ground of character impeachment dictates admissibility here. The defendant wife voluntarily put her character before the jury. She testified to her work experience, that she had attended college, that she had been a candidate in the Miss Yakima pageant, that she had participated in a glee club, drill team, pep club and was the treasurer of a science club. Implicit in such testimony is the painting of a picture of a person most unlikely to commit grand larceny. While the character of defendant husband was not so clearly put into evidence, it was introduced sufficiently to subject the defendant husband to the same questions as recited above which were asked of the wife. There was testimony as to his occupation as a professional photographer, as to his physical dress on the day in question, as to his somewhat lengthy engagement and subsequent marriage to the defendant wife whose character had been so vividly pictured, as to his working in his garden at home and as to the planned attendance at a family barbecue on the day of the alleged crime. The state was entitled to complete the tapestry with his admitted drug addiction.

This court has consistently followed the rule stated in State v. Emmanuel, 42 Wash.2d 1, 14, 253 P.2d 386, 393 (1953), that: "[I]f a defendant puts his prior conduct into issue by testifying as to his own past good behavior, he may be cross-examined as to specific acts of misconduct unrelated to the crime charged." * * *

The court instructed the jury that evidence of prior misconduct was to be considered only as bearing on credibility and on the weight to be given to the witness' testimony. That instruction was proposed by the defendants. The record discloses that the defendants felt the instruction was necessary to lessen the impact of the evidence. Defendants had a choice to propose no instruction, to propose one relating to credibility or one relating to character. The choice was made and cannot now be urged as error. * * *

NOTES AND QUESTIONS

1. *Relevance.* What was defendant wife's purpose in testifying to her work experience, that she had attended college, that she had been a candidate in the Miss Yakima pageant, etc., or of comparable testimony from the defendant husband?

2. *"Opening the door" by the defense.* A number of cases have held that a defendant may put his or her character "in issue" by door-opening testimony, which the prosecution is then entitled to rebut. For example, in United States v. Castillo, 181 F.3d 1129, 1132 (9th Cir.1999), a drug prosecution, the trial court initially ruled that the defendant's prior arrest for cocaine possession was inadmissible:

> On direct examination, Castillo testified that he worked with disadvantaged children, and would not have smuggled drugs "for a million dollars." Castillo portrayed himself as an anti-drug counselor who taught kids to "stay away from drugs." He added that he had never used drugs and would not touch them. Castillo's sweeping denial of any association with drugs was volunteered and often not responsive to questions posed by his lawyer. After hearing Castillo's testimony, the district court advised the parties it was reconsidering its earlier ruling excluding evidence of the 1997 arrest for cocaine possession. * * * Explaining that Castillo had portrayed

himself as a "paragon of virtue" and "quintessential model citizen" who would never have anything to do with drugs, the district court concluded that the 1997 cocaine arrest "bears directly on [Castillo's] credibility" and admitted extrinsic evidence concerning the earlier arrest to impeach Castillo.

See also United States v. Allen, 630 F.3d 762, 766 (8th Cir.2011) ("Based on the numerous times Allen mentioned his military service, the district court did not abuse its discretion by permitting the government to question him about the nature of his service, revealing arrests, charges, and his discharge ('general under less than honorable')."); United States v. Chance, 306 F.3d 356, 387 (6th Cir.2002) ("The phrase 'competent hard-working people' suggests that the persons identified were wholesomely industrious citizens. We do not think that wholesomely industrious law enforcement officers plant evidence, mistake flour for cocaine, or swear out false affidavits in support of search and arrest warrants."); Hattaway v. United States, 416 F.2d 1178, 1180 (5th Cir.1969) (defendant in Mann Act prosecution (transporting a female in interstate commerce for immoral purposes) testified that "she had been raised in a very Christian home and had always been concerned about the children's welfare").

3. *"Opening the door" by the prosecution.* While the courts have been sensitive to attempts by prosecutors themselves to open up character on cross-examination, United States v. Gilliland, 586 F.2d 1384 (10th Cir.1978) (prosecution could not convert defense eyewitness into character witness by asking what kind of man defendant was), and Martin v. People, 162 P.2d 597 (Colo.1945) (improper cross-examination of defendant challenging him to put his character in issue), the risk that a defendant may volunteer a "good character" statement on cross-examination is graphically illustrated in United States ex rel. Johnson v. Johnson, 531 F.2d 169, 175 n.17 (3d Cir.1976). See also *Castillo*, note 2, supra, 181 F.3d at 1133–34 ("Courts are more willing to permit, and commentators more willing to endorse, impeachment by contradiction where * * * testimony is volunteered on direct examination. The distinction between direct and cross-examination recognizes that opposing counsel may manipulate questions to trap an unwary witness into 'volunteering' statements on cross-examination. * * * The distinction also recognizes that, as a practical matter, it is often difficult to determine whether testimony is invited or whether it is volunteered on cross-examination.").

4. *Other ways to insinuate character into a trial.* E.g., United States v. Phaknikone, 605 F.3d 1099, 1109 (11th Cir.2010) ("The government wanted the jury to infer that, because Phaknikone is willing to publish these kinds of photographs online, under an incendiary alias, he is a gangster who is likely to rob banks. The district court abused its discretion by admitting the MySpace evidence."); Belmar v. State, 621 S.E.2d 441 (Ga.2005) (photograph of appellant's right upper back displaying a tattoo reading "12 gauge" where a 12–gauge shotgun was the murder weapon); State v. Breedlove, 271 N.E.2d 238, 241 (Ohio 1971) ("[W]e believe it unjustifiable for the state, on direct

examination, to present police mug shots, bearing police identification numbers, from which a reasonable inference can be drawn that the defendant, at some indefinite time in the past had had trouble with the law."); State v. McMillan, 590 N.E.2d 23, 26 (Ohio Ct.App.1990) (profile of sex abusers improper "group character evidence").

5. *Character on issue of credibility.* The question of the introduction of evidence with regard to the credibility of a witness, the accused or any other witness, is considered more completely in Chapter 12, Section E, infra.

6. *What is character?* The law obviously assumes there is something called "character"? But is there such a thing? See Sanchirico, Character Evidence and the Object of Trial, 101 Colum.L.Rev. 1227, 1233, 1240–41 (2001) ("Personality psychologists are now in general agreement that individuals do have identifiable cross situational attributes that, along with situation specific factors, help to determine individual behavior. * * * Current research suggests that a defendant's cross situation attributes, as evidence by past acts, may be quite probative of conduct in the case at hand. * * * Several influential studies specifically maintain that the stability of criminal and tortious behavior is due to the stability of certain personality features, such as 'low empathy' or lack of 'self-control.' "). Professor Sanchirico further argues that the character rules only make sense when viewed as a mechanism to regulate behavior outside the courtroom. See also Anderson, Note, Recognizing Character: A New Perspective on Character Evidence, 121 Yale L.J. 1912 (2012).

EDGINGTON v. UNITED STATES

Supreme Court of the United States, 1896.
164 U.S. 361.

At the March term, 1895, in the District Court of the United States for the Southern District of Iowa, Avington A. Edgington was tried and found guilty of the crime of making a false deposition on April 13, 1894, in aid of a fraudulent pension claim on behalf of his mother, Jennie M. Edgington, claiming to be the widow of Francis M. Edgington. * * *

MR. JUSTICE SHIRAS, after stating the case, delivered the opinion of the court. * * *

We are constrained to sustain the assignments which complain of the exclusion of testimony offered to show defendant's general reputation for truth and veracity. It is not necessary to cite authorities to show that, in criminal prosecutions, the accused will be allowed to call witnesses to show that his character was such as would make it unlikely that he would be guilty of the particular crime with which he is charged. And as here the defendant was charged with a species of the *crimen falsi,* the rejected evidence was material and competent. This, indeed, is conceded in the brief for the government; but it is argued that, as the learned judge, in overruling the offer of the evidence, observed that the testimony might "become proper later on," he was merely passing on the order of proof, his discretion in respect to which is not reversible. It is possible, as suggested, that the judge thought that such evidence should not be offered until it appeared that the defendant had himself testified. But this would show a misconception of the reason why the evidence was competent. It was not intended to give weight to the defendant's personal testimony in the case, but to establish a general character inconsistent with guilt of the crime with which he stood charged; and the evidence was admissible whether or not the defendant himself testified. When testimony, competent and material, has been offered and erroneously rejected, the error is not cured by a conjecture that if offered at a subsequent period in the trial the evidence might have been admitted. It should also be observed that when a subsequent offer to the same effect was made the judge rejected it without qualification. * * *

Whatever may have been said in some of the earlier cases, to the effect that evidence of the good character of the defendant is not to be considered unless the other evidence leaves the mind in doubt, the decided weight of authority now is that good character, when considered in connection with the other evidence in the case, may generate a reasonable doubt. The circumstances may be such that an established reputation for good character, if it is relevant to the issue, would alone create a reasonable doubt, although, without it, the other evidence would be convincing.

The judgment of the court below is reversed and the cause remanded with directions to set aside the verdict and award a new trial.

MR. JUSTICE BREWER concurred in the judgment.

MR. JUSTICE BROWN dissented.

NOTES AND QUESTIONS

1.   *Pertinent trait.* If the accused was tried for assault or murder, what would be the pertinent trait? For larceny? For perjury? Both the common law and the Federal Rules limit character evidence to traits pertinent to the crime in question. See, e.g., State v. Howland, 138 P.2d 424 (Kan.1943) (proper to exclude evidence of character of accused for truth and veracity to meet a charge of statutory rape). What about law-abiding character? E.g., United States v. Kellogg, 510 F.3d 188, 1932 (3d Cir.2007) (Witness "testified that he knows people who know the defendant, and that the defendant's reputation among others for being a law abiding citizen is excellent."); United States v. Angelini, 678 F.2d 380 (1st Cir.1982) (accused's character as law-abiding citizen always admissible).

2.   *Prosecution rebuttal.* The "pertinence" requirement is particularly significant when the prosecution seeks to rebut the accused's evidence of good character. See United States v. Reed, 700 F.2d 638 (11th Cir.1983) (introduction of character evidence on truth and veracity did not open the

door for questions to the accused with regard to marijuana use); State v. Kramp, 651 P.2d 614 (Mont.1982) (character evidence as to truth, integrity, honesty and veracity did not open door to evidence of traffic or drinking offenses). But see United States v. Diaz, 961 F.2d 1417, 1419 (9th Cir.1992) ("Diaz's proneness to criminal activity is an admissible character trait encompassed under [the] general definition of 'law-abidingness.'").

3. *Reputation testimony.* The bulk of the common law decisions limited proof of character as proof of conduct to reputation evidence. Several problems may arise in connection with this method of proof. For example, should a reputation witness be required to be a resident of the same community? Should an investigator be allowed to testify to the results of his inquiries? See United States v. Lewin, 467 F.2d 1132 (7th Cir.1972). What geographical and social factors should be considered in determining the "community" in which a reputation exists? See United States v. Oliver, 492 F.2d 943 (8th Cir.1974) (college roommates of seven weeks' acquaintance); People v. Bouton, 405 N.E.2d 699, 704 (N.Y.1980) ("A reputation may grow wherever an individual's associations are of such quantity and quality as to permit him to be personally observed by a sufficient number of individuals to give reasonable assurance of reliability."). In United States v. Straughan, 453 F.2d 422 (8th Cir.1972), allowing a police officer to testify that defendant had two reputations, a good one in the community where he lived and a bad one in state law-enforcement circles, was held error. Should a witness who has not heard the person's reputation discussed nevertheless be allowed to testify concerning it? See People v. Van Gaasbeck, 82 N.E. 718, 722 (N.Y.1907) (ruling that a witness could testify to the good reputation of the defendant without ever hearing anything said of his character if the witness has lived a considerable time in the defendant's community since "one's character does not get talked about until there is some fault to be found with it").

4. *Opinion testimony.* The rationale for rejecting opinion testimony at common law was typically expressed in language such as the following:

> An opinion as to reputation, however, (although composed of numerous individual subjective opinions) is essentially an objective fact about a defendant, thus subject to reasonably limited cross-examination. A witness can be accurate or inaccurate as to reputation, but his opinion as to character is essentially his own personal estimate.

United States v. White, 225 F.Supp. 514, 522 (D.D.C.1963).

Wigmore argued strongly in favor of enlarging the scope of character proof to include opinion, contrasting such proof with "the secondhand, irresponsible product of multiplied guesses and gossip which we term 'reputation.'" 7 Wigmore, Evidence § 1986 (Chadbourn rev. 1978). Federal Rule 405(a) specifically permits opinion evidence. What about the problems with opinion suggested by the language in the *White* case?

5. *Expert testimony.* The removal of the prohibition against opinion evidence gave rise to the possibility that expert testimony with regard to

character might be introduced. See United States v. Roberts, 887 F.2d 534, 536 (5th Cir.1989) (expert testimony that defendant's "naive and autocratic" personality traits were consistent with his claimed activity as a self-appointed vigilante should not have been excluded); United States v. Hill, 655 F.2d 512 (3d Cir.1981) (psychologist's testimony as to defendant's susceptibility was relevant to defense of entrapment and should not have been excluded); United States v. Staggs, 553 F.2d 1073 (7th Cir.1977) (psychologist's testimony that defendant's impulsive acts are more likely to be directed inwardly than outwardly should not have been excluded); State v. Hood, 346 N.W.2d 481 (Iowa 1984) (expert testimony that co-defendant in homicide prosecution was a "passive-dependent" individual who will allow others to assume responsibility was properly admitted). But cf. United States v. MacDonald, 688 F.2d 224, 227 (4th Cir.1982) (upholding trial judge's discretion under Rule 403 to exclude psychiatric evidence that the defendant had "a personality configuration inconsistent with the outrageous and senseless murder of his family"). At least one state adopting rules based upon the Federal Rules has attempted specifically to exclude expert testimony of this kind. See N.C.R.Evid. 405(a).

6. *Specific acts.* Even under modern practice, the accused may not attempt to prove his good character by evidence of specific instances, United States v. Benedetto, 571 F.2d 1246 (2d Cir.1978) (honesty of meat inspector charged with taking bribes not provable by testimony of other packers that he did not solicit bribes from them), or by religious beliefs, Government of the Virgin Islands v. Petersen, 553 F.2d 324 (3d Cir.1977) (proper to exclude evidence of membership in Rastafarians, who believe in nonviolence). Is this position justifiable? See Uviller, Evidence of Character to Prove Conduct: Illusion, Illogic, and Injustice in the Courtroom, 130 U.Pa.L.Rev. 845 (1982).

7. *Character instruction.* The *Edgington* opinion contains the following statement: "The circumstances may be such that an established reputation for good character, if it is relevant to the issue, would alone create a reasonable doubt, although, without it, the other evidence would be convincing." See also Michelson v. United States, 335 U.S. 469, 476 (1948) ("Such testimony alone, in some circumstances, may be enough to raise a reasonable doubt of guilt."). Defense attorneys frequently request that these sentiments be incorporated into a jury instruction. However, most federal courts hold that the "standing alone-reasonable doubt" instruction need not be given. E.g., United States v. Pujana–Mena, 949 F.2d 24, 28 n.2 (2d Cir.1991) ("Seven circuits have held that a defendant is not entitled to a 'standing alone' charge. In addition, the Seventh Circuit has held that the 'standing alone' instruction is improper in a case where the defendant testifies, but has left open the question whether the charge should be forbidden in all cases. The Fourth and Tenth Circuits similarly have held that the 'standing alone' charge need not always be given, but may be necessary when defendant relies solely on evidence of good character. The District of Columbia Circuit is the only circuit still requiring a 'standing alone' instruction in all cases in which a defendant offers character evidence."). Should trial counsel request such an instruction? See also State

v. Surbaugh, 737 S.E.2d 240, 257 (W.Va.2012) ("[I]f evidence of the good character of the defendant is properly admitted, the jury should be instructed that this good character evidence may be considered in connection with all the other evidence to generate reasonable doubt. An instruction which states or suggests that good character, standing alone, may generate reasonable doubt is erroneous.").

BROYLES V. COMMONWEALTH

Kentucky Court of Appeals, 1954.
267 S.W.2d 73.

COMBS, JUSTICE. George Richard Broyles appeals from a sentence of life imprisonment imposed after a jury found him guilty of the murder of Billy D. Smithers. He urges as grounds for reversal: (1) Improper cross-examination of defense witnesses by the Assistant Commonwealth's Attorney * * *.

The appellant introduced several witnesses who testified that his reputation for peace and quietue was good. These witnesses were asked on cross-examination if they knew appellant had been arrested and convicted on separate occasions for drunken driving, for reckless driving, and for disorderly conduct. One witness admitted to having knowledge of these convictions; the others disavowed such knowledge. Appellant contends the questions were improper because they related to a trait of character not involved in the crime with which he was charged.

Broadly speaking, it is the rule in this state that where the defendant introduces evidence of his good reputation, the witness so testifying may be asked on cross-examination whether he has heard reports of particular acts of misconduct by the defendant. * * * But the rule is not absolute. When there is an objection to such evidence or a motion to limit its effect, the court is required to admonish the jury that it is admitted only for the purpose of testing the accuracy and credibility of the witness' testimony and not as substantive evidence of defendant's guilt. * * * Moreover, inquiry may be made only about those acts of misconduct having some relation to the particular trait of character which the defendant has put in issue. * * *

Another limitation to the rule, but one with which we are not here concerned, is that the attorney for the Commonwealth may not deliberately inject into the case the issue of previous acts of misconduct by the defendant without some basis for his questions. * * *

The question here is whether one who is guilty of drunken driving, reckless driving, and disorderly conduct thereby evinces a trait of character inconsistent with a good reputation for peace and quietude. Courts in other jurisdictions have answered the question in the affirmative and have permitted questions designed to test the witness' knowledge of the other offenses. * * *

We find no Kentucky case directly in point, but an examination of related cases reveals that this court has taken a cautious attitude toward the introduction of such testimony. In Smith v. Commonwealth, 206 Ky. 728, 268 S.W. 328, the defendant, being tried for murder, introduced witnesses who testified that his reputation for peace and quietude was good. The witnesses were asked on cross-examination if they had heard that defendant had an illegitimate child by his sister-in-law; that he had taken another man's wife to Tennessee and lived with her, and that he had been convicted for the illegal sale of whisky. It was held that the questions should not have been permitted because responsive answers would have thrown no light on defendant's reputation for peace and quietude.

In Albertson v. Commonwealth, 312 Ky. 68, 226 S.W.2d 523, the defendant, under charge of murder, introduced witnesses who testified to his good reputation for peace and quietude. The witnesses were asked on cross-examination if they knew the defendant had engaged in the illegal traffic of whisky. This was held to be reversible error on the ground that a responsive answer to the question would have had no bearing on defendant's reputation for peace and quietude.

 Although we are of the opinion the practice should be indulged in cautiously and that the rule should be kept within strict limitations, it seems to us that a conviction for drunken driving, or reckless driving, or disorderly conduct has some reasonable connection with a man's reputation for peace and quietude. In the legal sense, peace and quietude signify obedience to law, public quiet, good order and tranquility. A jury might reasonably infer that a propensity to drunken driving, reckless driving, or disorderly conduct is evidence of an attitude of disrespect for the law inconsistent with a good reputation for peace and quietude. It should be kept in mind that such evidence is never competent unless the defendant himself puts his reputation in issue; and even then it is competent only for the purpose of testing the witness' credibility, and not as substantive evidence. It is noted that proper admonition to this effect was given by the trial judge in this case. We conclude that the court properly permitted the attorney for the state to ask the defendant's character witnesses whether they had heard reports of his previous conviction for drunken driving, reckless driving, or disorderly conduct.
* * *

The judgment is reversed because of the improper argument of the attorney for the Commonwealth.

NOTES AND QUESTIONS

1. *Purpose of cross-examination.* See Michelson v. United States, 335 U.S. 469, 479 n.16 (1948) ("A classic example in the books is a character witness in a trial for murder. She testified she grew up with defendant, knew

his reputation for peace and quiet, and that it was good. On cross-examination she was asked if she had heard that the defendant had shot anybody and, if so, how many. She answered, 'Three or four,' and gave the names of two but could not recall the names of the others. She still insisted, however, that he was of 'good character.' The jury seems to have valued her information more highly than her judgment and convicted."). See also Mueller, Of Misshapen Stones and Compromises: *Michelson* and the Modern Law of Character Evidence, in Evidence Stories 75 (Lempert ed., 2006).

2. *Form of question.* Observe that the court at the beginning of *Broyles* describes the cross-examination as inquiring into whether the witness *knew* of the arrests and convictions, while at the conclusion the questions are described as inquiring into whether the witness has *heard*. The opinion in *Michelson*, note 1, supra, says that with respect to reputation witnesses "the form of inquiry, 'Have you heard?' has general approval, and 'Do you know?' is not allowed." 335 U.S. at 482. Since Federal Rule 405(a) now permits opinion evidence to prove character, the restriction in *Michelson*, which flowed from only reputation being admissible, is not applicable to such a character witness. Moreover, the Advisory Committee note indicates that the second sentence of the rule was designed to eliminate this distinction—hear/know—in formulating questions for either reputation or opinion.

3. *Good faith requirement.* As Wigmore observed: "This method of inquiry or cross-examination is frequently resorted to by counsel for the very purpose of injuring by indirection a character which they are forbidden directly to attack in that way; they rely upon the mere putting of the question (not caring that it is answered negatively) to convey their covert insinuation." 3A Wigmore, Evidence § 988, at 921 (Chadbourn rev. 1970).

4. *Guilt assuming hypotheticals.* Should a cross-examiner be permitted to ask a reputation or opinion character witness questions that refer to the crime on trial or some element of it? E.g., United States v. Candelaria–Gonzalez, 547 F.2d 291, 293 n.2 (5th Cir.1977) ("Would his reputation with your firm be affected if he were convicted of trafficking in narcotics [the charged crimes]?"). See also United States v. Shwayder, 312 F.3d 1109, 1121 (9th Cir.2002) ("Following almost every other circuit that has addressed the question, we now hold that the use of guilt assuming hypotheticals undermines the presumption of innocence and thus violates a defendant's right to due process."). But see United States v. Kellogg, 510 F.3d 188, 196 (3d Cir.2007) ("Because a reputation character witness, by definition, can only provide testimony about the defendant's reputation in the community, a person testifying regarding the defendant's reputation at the time of the crime can only speculate about how information regarding the crime would affect the community's assessment of the defendant, and a witness's speculation in that regard is of no probative value at all. * * * [T]here is nothing inherent in guilt-assuming hypotheticals, in the abstract, that makes them unfairly prejudicial, let alone so prejudicial as to constitute a *per se* violation of due process. * * * Generally speaking, a person testifying

regarding a present opinion should be open to cross-examination on how additional facts would affect that opinion.") (citation omitted).

(2) VICTIM'S CHARACTER: FEDERAL RULE 404(a)(2)(B)

EVANS v. UNITED STATES

United States Court of Appeals, District of Columbia, 1960.
277 F.2d 354.

BAZELON, CIRCUIT JUDGE.

Appellant was convicted of second-degree murder. The homicide occurred on the sidewalk of a street in Washington about 5:30 a.m., on May 1, 1955. The Government called three disinterested eyewitnesses, none of whom observed all the events surrounding the homicide. When pieced together, however, their testimony showed that appellant was in the company of two other women and a man; that they hailed the deceased, who was walking on the other side of the street, and he joined the group; and that a few moments later, tussling and fighting began in the group, in the course of which appellant inflicted mortal wounds with a knife. There was also strong evidence that the deceased was drunk. The Government advanced no motive for the killing and none appears. Since appellant and the deceased were total strangers and money on his person was undisturbed, there is no basis for imputing a personal or a robbery motive.

Appellant took the stand and testified that she killed the deceased in defending herself from a sexual assault. She said that she was returning home alone; that the decedent came up from behind and asked whether she was "out for some sporting"; that when she rebuffed this and other obscenities, he grabbed her, ripping some of her clothing. Appellant admitted that in the course of the ensuing struggle she stabbed the decedent with a knife which she carried for protection.

Able counsel appointed by this court urge only one ground for reversal. It is that the trial court erred in rejecting the defendant's proffer of testimony by the deceased's wife that he

> "was ill mentally, not insane * * * a lost soul who wanted to be with people, get along with the rest, and did not know how to do it; that at times, that he would like to drink and at times on drinking and otherwise he would even go to the extent of being psychotic, perhaps, and with her at least she would know—acted belligerent and in a really bellicose type of manner."

Appellant's counsel contend that upon a plea of self-defense, evidence of the deceased's "character and belligerency," though unknown to the defendant, is admissible in corroboration of the defendant's testimony that the deceased was the aggressor. They say this is but a logical extension of the rule of Griffin v. United States, 1950 [183 F.2d 990, 992], that "evidence of uncommunicated threats of the deceased against the defendant is admissible." We agree. The reasons for our view are well summarized by Professor Wigmore:

> "When the issue of self-defense is made in a trial for homicide, and thus a controversy arises *whether the deceased was the aggressor,* one's persuasion will be more or less affected by the character of the deceased; it may throw much light on the probabilities of the deceased's action:

> * * *

> "[The] additional element of communication is unnecessary; for the question is what the deceased probably did, not what the defendant probably thought the deceased was going to do. The inquiry is one of objective occurrence, not of subjective belief." I Wigmore, Evidence § 63, at 467, 470–471 (3d ed. 1940). See also 2 id. § 246, at 54.

Although the proffer in this case was inartful, we think that, at the very least, it adequately apprised the trial judge that the evidence would show that the deceased was aggressive when drunk. Since it is clear that the deceased was drunk, such testimony was relevant in corroborating appellant's contention that she was attacked. Moreover, the proffer, broadly construed, purported to explain the deceased's general character and reputation. We think that, in the circumstances of this case, almost any evidence showing what kind of man the decedent was would be highly relevant in helping the jury to determine whether appellant's story of a sexual assault was truthful, and would therefore serve the interests of justice.

2. We cannot say that the error in excluding this testimony was harmless. It is true that three disinterested prosecution witnesses testified that appellant was not alone at the time of the incident, and that this adversely affected her credibility. But none of the Government's witnesses could say who instigated the fight. Consequently even if the jury believed all that the Government's witnesses said, it still could have found that appellant acted in self-defense if it believed her uncontradicted statement that the deceased was the aggressor. We think the proffered evidence might have led the jury to believe that statement, notwithstanding its apparent doubts as to appellant's credibility on other phases of her testimony.

Finally, but equally important, even if it convincingly appeared that the excluded testimony could not induce the jury to acquit, evidence suggesting that he was the aggressor might well have induced the jury to convict appellant for the lesser included offense of manslaughter, instead of second-degree murder.

Reversed and remanded.

FAHY, CIRCUIT JUDGE (dissenting).

The defense offered was the need to kill deceased in resisting a sexual assault. In my view the proffered testimony was too tenuous in corroborative relationship to this particular defense to justify reversal because of rejection of the proffer, especially when all the evidence as to the manner in which the homicide occurred is considered. It follows from this view that I attach no significance to the circumstance that the jury could convict of manslaughter.

NOTES AND QUESTIONS

1. *Method of proof.* See United States v. Bautista, 145 F.3d 1140, 1152 (10th Cir.1998) ("evidence of the victim's aggressive character may be admissible * * * to establish that the victim was the aggressor. * * * However, Fed. R. Evid. 405 limits the type of character evidence to reputation or opinion evidence * * *. Therefore, Bautista could have introduced evidence of Carrillo's reputation for aggressiveness, but he could not introduce specific instances of aggressive conduct.").

2. *Homicide cases.* Rule 404(a)(2)(C) contains a special rule in homicide cases. Any evidence that the victim was the first aggressor in a homicide case triggers the prosecution's right to introduce rebuttal evidence of the victim's peaceful character. For example, if the accused testifies that the victim was the first aggressor, but does not introduce character evidence on this issue, the prosecution may nevertheless introduce evidence of the victim's peaceful character in rebuttal. This rule does not apply in assault cases in which self-defense is raised. Why not?

3. *Accused's character.* A 2000 amendment permits the prosecutor to introduce evidence of the accused's character if the accused offers evidence of the victim's character. Rule 404(a)(2)(B)(ii). One state adopted a comparable rule as a matter of common law. See Commonwealth v. Morales, 982 N.E.2d 1105, 1111 (Mass.2013) ("[W]here the judge has determined that the jury may hear evidence of violent acts on the part of the victim to assist in their assessment of who initiated the fight or confrontation * * *, the jury also should be able to hear evidence (if it exists) of specific violent acts of the defendant."; however, admissibility is subject to the trial court's discretion and the prosecution must provide the defendant with notice).

4. *Communicated character.* "Whether evidence concerning the victim is admissible to prove self-defense depends upon the type of evidence being offered. Typically, such evidence falls into two general categories: (1) testimony concerning the victim offered to demonstrate the defendant's state of mind at the time of the incident, and (2) testimony about the victim's character offered to prove that the victim was more likely the aggressor." State v. Baker, 623 N.E.2d 672, 674 (Ohio Ct.App.1993). The first use does not involve character-as-proof-of-conduct, and hence, the restriction on

methods of proof found in Rule 405(a) is not applicable. In reversing petitioner's conviction on the basis that exclusion of evidence violated due process, the court in DePetris v. Kuykendall, 239 F.3d 1057, 1058–59 (9th Cir.2001), stated:

> Petitioner Kelly DePetris shot and killed her husband Dana DePetris while he was asleep in bed. At trial, she claimed 'imperfect self-defense'—that is, she claimed to have had an actual, honest belief that she was in imminent danger even if such a belief was objectively unreasonable. Under California law, imperfect self-defense is not a complete defense to homicide; however, if established, it negates malice and reduces murder to voluntary manslaughter. To prove her claim that she acted out of an actual fear that her husband would make good on his threats to kill her and their baby that night, petitioner attempted (1) to offer into evidence Dana's handwritten journal and (2) to testify herself about how having read the journal contributed to her belief that Dana's threats were to be taken seriously. The journal contained Dana's chilling account of his violent behavior toward his first wife and others. The trial court excluded as irrelevant the journal and petitioner's testimony about having read it.

(3) VICTIM'S CHARACTER: FEDERAL RULE 412

DOE v. UNITED STATES

United States Court of Appeals, Fourth Circuit, 1981.
666 F.2d 43.

BUTZNER, CIRCUIT JUDGE:

These appeals concern the district court's evidentiary ruling in a pre-trial proceeding held pursuant to rule 412 of the Federal Rules of Evidence. The court held that evidence concerning the past sexual behavior and habits of the prosecutrix was admissible in the rape trial of Donald Robert Black. We conclude that we have jurisdiction to hear her appeal, and we affirm in part and reverse in part the order of the district court.

I

The appellant is the alleged victim and chief government witness in the impending rape trial of Black. Pursuant to rule 412 of the Federal Rules of Evidence, Black made a pre-trial motion to admit evidence and permit cross-examination concerning the victim's past sexual behavior. After a hearing, the district court ruled that Black could introduce the evidence which he proffered.

Several days later, the district court granted Black's motion for the issuance of subpoenas for individuals who were to testify about the victim's sexual history. These included the victim's former landlord, a social worker who had previously investigated the victim, a sexual partner of the victim, and two people who claimed to be aware of the victim's reputation for promiscuity.

Thereafter, the victim instituted a civil action seeking the permanent sealing of the record of the rule 412 proceedings and other relief. During the course of this civil action, the court learned that the rape victim had not received notice of the earlier proceeding as mandated by subsection (c) (1) of rule 412. Consequently, it reopened the rule 412 hearing. The court then reaffirmed its prior ruling in the criminal case and entered summary judgment in favor of the defendants in the civil action. The victim appeals from the orders in both the civil and criminal actions.

II

Black asserts that this court lacks jurisdiction to entertain the victim's appeal from the district court's order in the rule 412 proceeding. Resolution of this issue requires an examination of the procedural provisions of the rule.

Rule 412 places significant limitations on the admissibility of evidence concerning the past sexual behavior of a rape victim. The rule provides the additional safeguard of a hearing in chambers to determine the admissibility of such evidence. These provisions were adopted "to protect rape victims from the degrading and embarrassing disclosure of intimate details about their private lives." 124 Cong.Rec. at H 11945 (1978). To effectuate this purpose, subsections (c) (1) and (2) of the rule require that rape victims receive notice of the evidentiary hearing and a copy of the defendant's motion and offer of proof. Additionally, subsection (c) (2) makes provision for the victim's testimony at the evidentiary hearing.

The text, purpose, and legislative history of rule 412 clearly indicate that Congress enacted the rule for the special benefit of the victims of rape. The rule makes no reference to the right of a victim to appeal an adverse ruling. Nevertheless, this remedy is implicit as a necessary corollary of the rule's explicit protection of the privacy interests Congress sought to safeguard. *Cf. Cort v. Ash,* 422 U.S. 66 (1975). No other party in the evidentiary proceeding shares these interests to the extent that they might be viewed as a champion of the victim's rights. Therefore, the congressional intent embodied in rule 412 will be frustrated if rape victims are not allowed to appeal an erroneous evidentiary ruling made at a pre-trial hearing conducted pursuant to the rule.

Section 1291 of title 28 U.S.C. confers on courts of appeals jurisdiction to review final decisions of the district courts. The Supreme Court has held that this finality requirement should be "given a 'practical rather than a technical construction.' " *Gillespie v. U.S. Steel Corp.,* 379 U.S. 148, 152 (1964). The Court also has instructed that the most important considerations for determining whether an order is final are "the inconvenience and costs of piecemeal review on the one hand and the danger of denying justice by delay on the other." *Dickinson v. Petroleum Corp.,* 338 U.S. 507, 511(1950).

In this case the balancing of these factors weighs heavily in favor of a conclusion of finality. The inconvenience and costs associated with permitting the victim to appeal are minimal. Certainly, they are no greater than those resulting from government appeals of suppression orders that are authorized by 18 U.S.C. § 3731. Because the rule provides for pre-trial evidentiary hearings, appeals are unlikely to involve significant postponements of criminal trials. Indeed, in this case, we heard the appeal and filed an order resolving the issues without any delay of the criminal trial.

On the other hand, the injustice to rape victims in delaying an appeal until after the conclusion of the criminal trial is manifest. Without the right to immediate appeal, victims aggrieved by the court's order will have no opportunity to protect their privacy from invasions forbidden by the rule. Appeal following the defendant's acquittal or conviction is no remedy, for the harm that the rule seeks to prevent already will have occurred. Consequently, we conclude that with respect to the victim the district court's order meets *Gillespie*'s test of practical finality, and we have jurisdiction to hear this appeal.

III

At the pre-trial rule 412 evidentiary hearing, Black presented several witnesses who told about the victim's past sexual behavior and reputation. Black testified that although he had talked on the phone with the victim several times, he did not meet her until the night of the alleged crime. Several men previously had told him the victim was promiscuous, and he had read a love letter she had written to another man.

At the conclusion of the hearing, the district court ruled that the following evidence was admissible:

(1) evidence of the victim's "general reputation in and around the Army post * * * where Mr. Black resided;"

(2) evidence of the victim's "habit of calling out to the barracks to speak to various and sundry soldiers;"

(3) evidence of the victim's "habit of coming to the post to meet people and of her habit of being at the barracks at the snack bar;"

(4) evidence from the victim's former landlord regarding "his experience with her" alleged promiscuous behavior;

(5) evidence of what a social worker learned of the victim;

(6) telephone conversations that Black had with the victim;

(7) evidence of the defendant's "state of mind as a result of what he knew of her reputation * * * and what she had said to him."

Black argues that all of the evidence delineated in items 1–7 is admissible to support his claim that the victim consented, to show the reasonableness of his belief that she consented, and to corroborate his testimony. He relies on the rule's provision for the admission of constitutionally required evidence. Exclusion of the evidence, he maintains, will deprive him of the rights secured by the due process clause of the fifth amendment and the right of confrontation and compulsory process guaranteed by the sixth amendment.

Rule 412 restricts the admission of evidence in several respects. Subsection (a) excludes reputation or opinion evidence of the past sexual behavior of the victim. Subsection (b) provides that evidence of past sexual behavior, other than reputation and opinion, is only admissible in three circumstances: first, the defendant may introduce this evidence when it is constitutionally required; second, when the defendant claims that he was not the source of semen or injury, he may introduce evidence of the victim's relations with other men; and third, when the defendant claims the victim consented, he may testify about his prior relations with the victim. [Citations omitted.]

The evidence delineated in items 1–5 of the district court's order clearly falls within the proscription of subsection (a) of the rule. Though sometimes couched in terms of habit, this evidence is essentially opinion or reputation evidence. Consequently, the exceptions set forth in subsection (b) do not render it admissible.

The constitutional justification for excluding reputation and opinion evidence rests on a dual premise. First, an accused is not constitutionally entitled to present irrelevant evidence. Second, reputation and opinion concerning a victim's past sexual behavior are not relevant indicators of the likelihood of her consent to a specific sexual act or of her veracity. *Privacy of Rape Victims: Hearings on H.R. 14666 and Other Bills Before the Subcomm. on Criminal Justice of the Committee on the Judiciary,* 94th Cong., 2d Sess. 14–15 (1976). Indeed, even before Congress enacted rule 412, the leading federal case on the subject, *United States v. Kasto,* 584 F.2d 268, 271–72 (8th Cir.1978), stated that in the absence of extraordinary circumstances:

> evidence of a rape victim's unchastity, whether in the form of testimony concerning her general reputation or direct or cross-examination testimony concerning specific acts with persons other than the defendant, is ordinarily insufficiently probative either of her general credibility as a witness or of her consent to

intercourse with the defendant on the particular occasion * * * to outweigh its highly prejudicial effect.

State legislatures and courts have generally reached the same conclusion. We are not prepared to state that extraordinary circumstances will never justify admission of such evidence to preserve a defendant's constitutional rights. The record of the rule 412 hearing in this case, however, discloses no circumstances for deeming that the rule's exclusion of the evidence classified in items 1–5 is unconstitutional.

[The evidence described in items 6 and 7 of the district court's ruling is admissible.] Certainly, the victim's conversations with Black are relevant, and they are not the type of evidence that the rule excludes. Black's knowledge, acquired before the alleged crime, of the victim's past sexual behavior is relevant on the issue of Black's intent. * * * Moreover, the rule does not exclude the production of the victim's letter or testimony of the men with whom Black talked if this evidence is introduced to corroborate the existence of the conversations and the letter.

The legislative history discloses that reputation and opinion evidence of the past sexual behavior of an alleged victim was excluded because Congress considered that this evidence was not relevant to the issues of the victim's consent or her veracity. * * * There is no indication, however, that this evidence was intended to be excluded when offered solely to show the accused's state of mind. Therefore, its admission is governed by the Rules of Evidence dealing with relevancy in general. Knowledge that Black acquired after the incident is irrelevant to this issue. * * *

NOTES AND QUESTIONS

1. *Rape shield laws.* Rule 412 is known as the federal rape shield law. It was adopted in 1978, after many states had already enacted such laws. See 1 McCormick, Evidence § 193 (7th ed. 2013) ("In the 1970s, however, nearly all jurisdictions enacted criminal 'rape shield' laws * * *."). The federal rule was amended in 1994 to extend the rule (1) to all criminal cases (e.g., kidnaping), (2) impeachment, and (3) to civil cases (such as sexual harassment).

Why should the evidence precluded under the rape shield act be inadmissible generally in criminal cases, except for some narrowly prescribed circumstances, and, in civil cases, admissible whenever its "probative value substantially outweighs the danger of harm to any victim and of unfair prejudice to any party"? Given the protections afforded defendants in criminal cases, should it not be easier for an accused to have such evidence admitted than a party in a civil case?

2. *Common law approach.* In the not-too-distant past, evidence of prior sexual activity was offered either for substantive purposes, i.e., as evidence going to a defense of consent, or as evidence going to the credibility of the complaining witness. Given the fact that the victim of a sexual assault is

usually the principal witness for the prosecution, it was most frequently offered for both purposes. In the absence of a rape shield statute, would the evidence excluded by the court in the principal case be admitted? For substantive purposes? For credibility? See Rule 608(b), discussed in Chapter 12, Section E(7), infra.

The following statement was written long before the adoption of rape shield laws, but is still contained in 3A Wigmore, Evidence § 924a, at 736 (Chadbourn rev. 1970):

> There is, however, at least one situation in which chastity may have a direct connection with veracity, viz. when a woman or young girl testifies as complainant against a man charged with a sexual crime. * * * Modern psychiatrists have amply studied the behavior of errant young girls and women coming before the courts in all sorts of cases. Their psychic complexes are multifarious, distorted partly by inherent defects, partly by diseased derangements or abnormal instincts, partly by bad social environment, partly by temporary physiological or emotional conditions. One form taken by these complexes is that of contriving false charges of sexual offenses by men. The unchaste (let us call it) mentality finds incidental but direct expression in the narration of imaginary sex incidents of which the narrator is the heroine or the victim. The real victim, however, too often in such cases is the innocent man; for the respect and sympathy naturally felt by any tribunal for a wronged female helps to give easy credit to such a plausible tale.

Does this statement accurately reflect the attitudes of the past? Does it reflect current attitudes? For a criticism of Wigmore's scientific methodology see Bienen, A Question of Credibility: John Henry Wigmore's Use of Scientific Authority in Section 924(a) of the Treatise on Evidence, 19 Cal.W.L.Rev. 235 (1983). For an interesting account of a defense lawyer's struggle with the issues involved in attacking the credibility of a complaining witness in a rape case by use of prior sexual activity, see Mortimer, Rumpole of the Bailey, "Rumpole and the Honourable Member" 79–105 (Penguin Books 1986).

3.   *Mens rea issue.* The principal case is strongly criticized in Spector & Foster, Rule 412 and the Doe Case: The Fourth Circuit Turns Back the Clock, 35 Okla.L.Rev. 87 (1982), for admitting evidence going to the reasonableness of the defendant's belief. The authors argue that such an exception violates congressional intent. The case receives somewhat more favorable treatment in Galvin, Shielding Rape Victims in the State and Federal Courts: A Proposal for the Second Decade, 70 Minn.L.Rev. 763 (1986). See also United States v. Saunders, 943 F.2d 388, 392 (4th Cir.1991) ("The rule manifests the policy that it is unreasonable for a defendant to base his belief of consent on the victim's past sexual experiences with third persons, since it is intolerable to suggest that because the victim is a prostitute, she automatically is assumed to have consented with anyone at any time. If we were to require admission of Smith's testimony about his affair with Duckett, we would eviscerate the clear intent of the rule to protect victims of rape from being

exposed at trial to harassing or irrelevant inquiry into their past sexual behavior, an inquiry that, prior to the adoption of the rule, had the tendency to shield defendants from their illegal conduct by discouraging victims from testifying.").

4. *Prostitution.* Courts have differed on the admissibility of evidence that an alleged victim engaged in prostitution. Compare State v. DeJesus, 856 A.2d 345, 355 (Conn.2004) ("[E]vidence of the victim's prior history of prostitution and the defendant's knowledge of that history was sufficiently material to the issue of consent that its exclusion violated the defendant's constitutional rights."), with Commonwealth v. Jones, 826 A.2d 900, 909 (Pa.Super.Ct.2003) (en banc) ("[T]he Rape Shield Law's purpose would not be served in the instant case by permitting Appellee to explore any of the complainant's prostitution convictions solely to show she has a propensity to engage in sexual activity for hire."). When should such evidence be admissible? See also Commonwealth v. Harris, 825 N.E.2d 58, 63 (Mass.2005) (defendant argued that he was accused of rape because the complainant was angry because she had not been paid for sex as agreed; "[A] judge has discretion to allow impeachment of a sexual assault complainant by prior convictions [for prostitution], but that in exercising that discretion, the purposes of the rape-shield statute should be considered.").

5. *Texting.* See State v. J.A.C., 44 A.3d 1085, 1097 (N.J.2012) (Twelve-year old's "instant messages—evidently intended to convey the impression that she was sexually experienced—included references to purported activity and sexual advances to her adult correspondents. The child's apparent invention of most or all of the content of her messages does not deprive her of the protection of N.J.S.A. 2C:14–7. Sexual conduct that is a matter of fantasy rather than fact has frequently been protected in federal and state courts.").

6. *Demise of instruction recommending skepticism in rape cases.* A related rule was based on Sir Matthew Hale's text—i.e., rape "is an accusation easily made and hard to be proved, and harder to be defended by the party accused, tho never so innocent." 1 Hale, History of the Pleas of the Crown 634 (1st Am. ed. 1847). Why aren't similar instructions given in one-on-one robbery cases? See Hardin v. State, 840 A.2d 1217, 1223 (Del.2003) ("Lord Hale's caution has grown increasingly out of favor in other jurisdictions. The major movement to abandon the caution began in 1975 with California, closely followed by Iowa and Arizona. Several other courts have subsequently held that the instruction is improper. Additionally, in the 1980s, Colorado, Minnesota, Nevada and Pennsylvania all enacted statutes abolishing Lord Hale's caution as an instruction to the jury."). See also Baker, Once a Rapist? Motivational Evidence and Relevancy in Rape Law, 110 Harv.L.Rev. 563, 584 (1997) ("Lord Hale had it precisely backwards: rape allegations are not easily made, and they are very easy to defend against.").

UNITED STATES V. AZURE

United States Court of Appeals, Eighth Circuit, 1988.
845 F.2d 1503.

LARSON, SENIOR DISTRICT JUDGE.

Defendant Anthony Damian Azure was convicted by a jury of carnal knowledge of a female under the age of sixteen, in violation of 18 U.S.C. §§ 1153 and 2032. This Court reversed defendant's initial conviction because we found the district court had improperly admitted expert opinion testimony on the credibility of the victim. *United States v. Azure,* 801 F.2d 336, 341 (8th Cir.1986). On retrial, a jury again found the defendant guilty as charged. Defendant has again appealed to this Court, arguing his subsequent conviction must be reversed because the district court erred in (1) excluding evidence of the victim's past sexual behavior under Fed.R.Evid. 412. * * * We affirm.

I.   Background

Azure was charged with having had sexual intercourse on or about December 8, 1984, with Wendy Lozensky, one of the daughters of Azure's common law wife, Patty Lozensky. Wendy was ten years old at the time. She testified at trial concerning the events surrounding the December 8th incident, and also testified that Azure had been abusing her since she was eight years old. Wendy's sisters, Melissa Lozensky and Michelle Faine, testified that they had seen Azure take Wendy into his bedroom alone when their mother Patty was gone. They also corroborated Wendy's testimony concerning the events on the evening of December 8th.

According to the girls' testimony, Wendy, Melissa, and Michelle were staying with their two younger siblings at Mary Lou Caine's house on December 8, 1984, while Azure and their mother went out drinking. Azure and Patty had a fight and Patty went to her mother's house. Later that evening, Azure returned alone to Mary Lou Caine's house to pick up the children. He was angry and drunk and Caine did not want the children to leave with him. Azure hit Wendy and gave her a bloody nose. When Wendy went outside to put some snow on her nose, Azure grabbed her and took her back to their house. He attempted to have sexual intercourse with her in his pickup truck on the way home and again when they got home. He also forced her to have oral sex. In the morning, Wendy called Mary Lou Caine and asked if she would pick her up and take her with the rest of the children to their grandmother's house. Caine agreed, and met Wendy across the road from Azure's home. Azure was still sleeping when Wendy left, and she asked Bill Berceir, who also lived with them, not to tell Azure where she was going.

When Wendy and Melissa went to stay with their father for Christmas, he brought them to social services personnel because he suspected they were being physically abused. Social worker Linda

Heilman interviewed Wendy in late December, 1984, and Wendy told her about the episodes of sexual abuse. At Heilman's request, Wendy was examined by Dr. Warren Keene on December 31, 1984. The examination revealed that Wendy had a three centimeter healing laceration on the side wall of her vagina, which Dr. Keene testified would have resulted from some recent, painful penetration to the vaginal wall; a vaginal opening of two centimeters, which Dr. Keene stated was twice the size one would anticipate in a child of Wendy's age; and a stretched hymenal ring. Wendy also tested positive for gonorrhea.[6] Wendy told Dr. Keene that Azure had sexually abused her and that "the last time Damian did that to me was 2 or 4 weeks ago." Keene offered his opinion, based on his medical examination, that Wendy was in fact a victim of sexual abuse.

II. Discussion

A. Exclusion of Wendy's Alleged Past Sexual Activities

Prior to trial, defendant sought to introduce evidence of past sexual relations between Wendy and a boy named David Malterre under Fed.R.Evid. 412. Rule 412 provides that evidence of a victim's past sexual behavior is not admissible except in certain narrow situations. The relevant exception in this case states that, subject to the procedural and relevancy requirements of subdivision (c), evidence of specific instances of an alleged victim's past sexual behavior is admissible if offered "upon the issue of whether the accused was or was not, with respect to the alleged victim, the source of semen or injury." Fed.R.Evid. 412(b) ([1]) (A).

We have previously applied Rule 412 in the context of child abuse cases. *See United States v. Shaw*, 824 F.2d 601, 602–04 (8th Cir.1987). In *Shaw*, we affirmed the district court's exclusion of evidence of prior sexual behavior on the ground that the victim's stretched hymen did not constitute an "injury" within the meaning of Rule 412(b) ([1]) (A). *Id.* at 605. In this case, the victim suffered from a healing laceration on her vaginal wall; an "injury" sufficient to trigger subdivision (b) ([1]) (A)'s exception. The district court nonetheless excluded defendant's proffered evidence of Wendy's past sexual behavior on the ground that it was not relevant to the source of this injury. We agree.

Following defendant's Rule 412 motion, the district court held an in camera hearing at which Malterre and Patty Lozensky testified. Malterre's testimony was vague and at times contradictory. He stated that he had had consensual sexual intercourse with Wendy, but could not remember how many times. He testified it could have been between one

---

[6] Dr. Robert ten Bensel, a pediatrician and an expert on child abuse, also interviewed Wendy and reviewed the medical records in the case. He testified that in his opinion Wendy was the victim of sexual abuse, and confirmed Dr. Keene's testimony that only repeated or chronic penetration would cause the stretched hymenal ring and the two centimeter vaginal opening which was observed in Wendy. Ten Bensel also confirmed that the laceration on Wendy's vaginal wall would have been very painful; something a child would not have submitted to voluntarily.

and four times over a one and one half year period. He also could not remember any specific dates; he could only recall that the first time was when he was thirteen years old. He denied having sex with Melissa and then minutes later stated that he had had sex with Melissa. He nonetheless clearly testified that he never forced or hurt Wendy, and she never cried. At the time of trial, Malterre was living with Rose Azure, defendant's mother. Malterre had previously denied any sexual contact with Wendy and admitted at the hearing that he would like to help the defendant if he could. Lozensky testified only that Malterre had recently told her of his alleged past sexual contact with Wendy.

We believe the district court properly excluded this evidence as irrelevant to the source of the three centimeter laceration on Wendy's vaginal wall. Malterre testified that all contacts he had had with Wendy were consensual; that he never hurt her. Both Dr. Keene and Dr. ten Bensel unequivocally testified that the laceration Dr. Keene observed would be very painful; that it was an indication of force. Moreover, Malterre was unable to testify that his contact with Wendy occurred during the time the laceration was received. Under these circumstances, we cannot say the district court abused its discretion in excluding evidence of Wendy's alleged prior sexual activities.

Defendant also claims the evidence of Wendy's alleged contact with Malterre should have been admitted for "impeachment purposes," since Wendy had previously denied any contact with Malterre, and to demonstrate Wendy's capability to fabricate a story. These are not recognized exceptions under Rule 412. As we have previously stated, the effect of Rule 412 is "to preclude the routine use of evidence of specific instances of a rape victim's prior sexual behavior." *United States v. Shaw,* 824 F.2d at 607 (citing 124 Cong.Rec. 34913 (1978) (statement of Rep. Mann)). Defendant's arguments to the contrary must be rejected. * * *

III. Conclusion

For all of the foregoing reasons, the judgment of the district court is affirmed.

NOTES

1. *Statutory exceptions.* Where rape shield laws enumerate exceptions, the most frequent are those specifically set forth in Rule 412: (1) prior sexual activity with the accused and (2) evidence going to the source of semen or injury. Yet, the possibilities for exceptions are seemingly endless. See Galvin, Shielding Rape Victims in the State and Federal Courts: A Proposal for the Second Decade, 70 Minn.L.Rev. 763 (1986). Cases in which the defense seeks to set up a pattern of prior conduct are perhaps the most frequent. See, e.g., People v. Hackett, 365 N.W.2d 120 (Mich.1985). Attempts to show that the victim was likely to have fantasized the event (as suggested by Wigmore) also are frequent. See, e.g., State v. Clarke, 343 N.W.2d 158 (Iowa 1984). North

Carolina specifically makes such evidence an exception to the rule if offered as the basis of expert opinion. N.C.Evid.R. 412(b)(4).

2. *Exception for accused-complaint conduct.* The courts have not always admitted evidence of prior sexual conduct with the defendant. See, e.g., United States v. Ramone, 218 F.3d 1229, 1238 (10th Cir.2000) (In a case involving armed aggravated assault and sexual abuse, the court stated: "[I]t is difficult to discern what relevance the testimony could have to Ramone's consent defense. We can not agree with the defendant that evidence of prior consensual use of inanimate objects during sex is probative of whether sex after a brutal beating was consensual."); State v. Hopkins, 377 N.W.2d 110, 116–17 (Neb.1985) (ruling that evidence of the victim's prior sexual conduct with the defendant was not admissible where the defendant failed at the in camera hearing to introduce any evidence that the victim had consented to the sexual act at issue in the case).

REDMOND V. KINGSTON

United States Court of Appeals, Seventh Circuit, 2001.
240 F.3d 590.

POSNER, CIRCUIT JUDGE.

* * * The petitioner, Redmond, a counselor at an institution for drug- and alcohol-abusing minors, was convicted of statutory rape of Heather, a 15–year–old resident of the institution. The specific charge was that he had traded cocaine to her for sex. The state acknowledged at argument that the principal evidence of the offense was Heather's testimony and that of another resident, Michelle, who, however, merely repeated what Heather had told her had happened. There was also evidence that Heather had tested positive for cocaine after the alleged offense but that she had a long history of using cocaine and might have gotten it from someone other than Redmond or for something other than sex.

Eleven months before the alleged offense, Heather had told her mother that she had been forcibly raped, and she had offered her torn clothes as evidence. She had repeated the story of the rape, with many circumstantial details, to a hospital nurse and to a police officer investigating the incident, but later had admitted making up the story (and ripping her clothes herself) in order to get her mother's attention. Her new story was that she had had sex with the man she had accused of forcible rape, but that it had been with her consent. Since she was underage, the police continued to investigate the incident as a crime. The man was never found, and there is no evidence other than Heather's say-so that the incident actually occurred. There is no serious doubt that her recantation of the forcible-rape story was truthful. Redmond offered more than thirty police reports of the investigation of Heather's claim that she had been forcibly raped, convincingly demonstrating its falsity, and in addition the district attorney had instituted contempt charges against Heather. * * *

Redmond wanted to bring out her lie on cross-examination in order to show that Heather would lie about a sexual assault in order to get attention, and thus had a motive to accuse him falsely. The trial judge, seconded by the Wisconsin court of appeals, refused to permit this cross-examination. The court of appeals held that although the state's rape-shield law makes an exception for a prior false charge of sexual assault, Wis. Stat. § 972.11(2) (b)3, Heather's false charge did not have "sufficient probative value to outweigh its inflammatory and prejudicial nature," and therefore, under another section of the statute, § 971.31(11), it was inadmissible. The court thought the false charge merely "cumulative of other evidence which went to Heather's credibility," namely that she had begun using drugs at the age of 12, had stolen and occasionally danced (!) to obtain money for cocaine, had run away from the institution, had skipped school, and had told lies in the past. Furthermore, the court thought the evidence of the false charge might have "confused the issue" since "the initial recantation involved consent which was not an element of the current charges," and also that it might have misled the jury "into focusing on Heather's willingness to have sexual intercourse with a complete stranger, instead of on the charges against Redmond." State v. Redmond, 1996 WL 485095, at *10 (Wis.App.1996).

With all due respect, we believe that the court of appeals' analysis and conclusion cannot be considered a reasonable application of the Supreme Court's confrontation doctrine. * * * The evidence of the false charge of forcible rape was not cumulative of other evidence bearing on Heather's credibility, because none of the other evidence either involved a false charge of being sexually assaulted or furnished a motive for such a charge. The fact that a teenage girl has a disordered past and lies a lot (who doesn't?) does not predict that she will make up stories about having sex. To indulge such an assumption would be to place such persons largely beyond the protection of the law. But the fact that the girl had led her mother, a nurse, and the police on a wild goose chase for a rapist merely to get her mother's attention supplied a powerful reason for disbelieving her testimony eleven months later about having sex with another man, by showing that she had a motive for what would otherwise be an unusual fabrication. * * *

The evidence thus was not cumulative, or otherwise peripheral, considering that testimony by Heather was virtually the only evidence of Redmond's guilt that the prosecution had. Nor was the evidence of her previous false charge of rape prejudicial to the state, except insofar as its prejudicial effect was a function of its probative weight, which of course is not the relevant meaning of prejudice. * * * The prejudice that offsets probative weight has to inhere in some extraneous fact, such as embarrassing but irrelevant details or, as the court believed, in the potential of the evidence to confuse the trier of fact. But in concluding that there was a danger of confusion the court committed a fatal analytical mistake. It assumed that Heather would be required or permitted to testify that she had had consensual sex with the alleged rapist, evidence barred by the rape-shield law. The only evidence that was relevant to her credibility in Redmond's case, however, the only evidence she would or should have been permitted to give on that subject, was that within the preceding year she had made up a story about being forcibly raped. Whether or not she had had sex with the alleged rapist was irrelevant, since Redmond was not prepared to try to prove that she had not. For unexplained reasons the Wisconsin court of appeals thought that if Redmond's lawyer had been permitted to ask Heather whether she had ever made a false charge of forcible sexual assault, the door would have been opened to an inquiry into whether she had had sex on that occasion at all. We cannot think of any reason why. The state could not have used the "fact" that Heather had had sex with the alleged forcible rapist to show that she fabricates only tales of being *forcibly* raped, because, all objections based on the rape-shield statute to one side, the state can no more show that Heather had sex with the alleged rapist than Redmond can show the contrary.

And thus the court's ruling, though ostensibly based on the rape-shield statute, derives no support from that statute. The statute protects complaining witnesses in rape cases (including statutory-rape cases) from being questioned about their sexual conduct, but a false charge of rape is not sexual conduct. See Wis. Stat. § 972.11(2) (a) (defining such conduct); * * *. The false-charge "exception" to the rape-shield statute is not really an exception, but rather a reminder of the limited meaning of "sexual conduct" as defined in the statute. The only basis for the court's ruling was the general principle of the law of evidence, which is codified for federal trials in Fed.R.Evid. 403 but is equally a principle of Wisconsin's law of evidence, see Wis. Stat. § 904.03, that relevant evidence may be excluded if its probative value is substantially outweighed by its prejudicial (confusing, or cumulative) effect. When that unexceptionable rule is applied as it was here to exclude highly probative, noncumulative, nonconfusing, nonprejudicial evidence tendered by a criminal defendant that is vital to the central issue in the case (Heather's credibility), the defendant's constitutional right of confrontation has been infringed. Olden v. Kentucky, 488 U.S. 227, 232 (1988) (per curiam) * * *.

Olden is factually very similar to the present case, which eliminates any question about the scope of the applicable federal doctrine declared by the Supreme Court, while cases such as Hogan v. Hanks, 97 F.3d 189, 191 (7th Cir.1996), and United States v. Bartlett, 856 F.2d 1071, 1087–89 (8th Cir.1988), which upheld the exclusion from evidence of false rape charges, are readily distinguishable. They are cases in which the defendant wanted to use the falsity of the charges to demonstrate that the complaining witness was a liar, rather than to demonstrate that she had a motive to lodge a false accusation against the defendant. The use of evidence that a person has lied in the past to show that she is lying now is questionable, quite apart from rape-shield laws, since very few people, other than the occasional saint, go through life without ever lying, unless they are under oath. Cf. Fed.R.Evid. 404(b), 608(b); Hogan v. Hanks, supra, 97 F.3d at 191; * * *. The probative value of such evidence when used for such a purpose is small and may be outweighed by the prejudicial effect of revealing that the witness had made such a serious charge falsely. United States v. Bartlett, supra, 856 F.2d at 1088–89. But while "generally applicable evidentiary rules limit inquiry into specific instances of conduct through the use of extrinsic evidence and through cross-examination with respect to general credibility attacks, * * * no such limit applies to credibility attacks based upon motive or bias," Quinn v. Haynes, 234 F.3d 837, 845 (4th Cir.2000)—as in this case. * * *

H

Reversed.

NOTES

1. *Constitutional issues.* The limitations placed by rape shield statutes on the accused's ability to cross-examine the prosecution's principal witness have given rise to constitutional challenges. The language of Rule 412 is obviously an attempt to circumvent such attacks. For a discussion of the constitutional problems generally, see Tanford & Bocchino, Rape Victim Shield Laws and the Sixth Amendment, 128 U.Pa.L.Rev. 544 (1980). Most courts have upheld the constitutionality of the statutes when challenged facially. Challenges in particular cases are different. See State v. Jalo, 557 P.2d 1359 (Or.Ct.App.1976) (en banc); State v. Jones, 230 P.3d 576, 580 (Wash.2010) ("Jones was prepared to testify that K.D. consented to sex during an all-night drug-induced sex party. The trial court refused to let Jones present this testimony or cross-examine K.D. about the testimony. This is not marginally relevant evidence that a court should balance against the State's interest in excluding the evidence. Instead, it is evidence of extremely high probative value; it is Jones's entire defense * * *."; "Jones's evidence refers not to past sexual conduct but to conduct on the night of the alleged rape.").

2. *Olden v. Kentucky.* In Olden v. Kentucky, 488 U.S. 227 (1988) (per curiam), an alleged rape victim testified that Olden had tricked her into leaving a bar, raped her, and then drove her to the house of Bill Russell, where she was released. Russell, also a prosecution witness, testified that he had seen the victim leave Olden's car and that she had immediately complained of rape. The defense claimed consent, arguing that the victim and Russell were involved in an extramarital relationship and that the victim fabricated the rape story to explain to Russell why she was in the defendant's car. By the time of trial, the victim and Russell were living together, but the

trial judge refused to permit cross-examination on this fact. The judge believed that this information would prejudice the jury against the victim because she was white and Russell was African American. The Supreme Court reversed. Olden had consistently maintained that the alleged victim lied because she feared jeopardizing her relationship with Russell. Thus, her current living arrangement with Russell was relevant to impeachment, and foreclosure of this line of inquiry violated the right of confrontation.

3. *False accusations of rape.* Several courts have taken the position that evidence of past accusations of sexual assault is not protected under rape shield rules. See, e.g., Miller v. State, 779 P.2d 87 (Nev.1989). The Advisory Committee note to amended Federal Rule 412 states: "Evidence offered to prove allegedly false prior claims by the victim is not barred by Rule 412. However, this evidence is subject to the requirements of Rule 404." A rape accusation could be false for either of two reasons: first, there was never any sexual intercourse, or second, there was intercourse but it was consensual. The latter situation involves sexual history and could come within a rape shield law depending the law's scope. If such evidence is admissible, most courts hold that the prior allegation must have been demonstrably false. See State v. Manning, 973 A.2d 524, 535 (R.I.2009) ("[D]efendant made no effort to demonstrate the falsity of Sandy's prior accusation other than a third-hand statement that 'no criminal charges ever resulted.' We cannot view the state's apparent decision not to prosecute as evidence that the allegation was false. * * * The fact that the state did not undertake a criminal prosecution could mean nothing more than that the attorney general decided he lacked sufficient evidence to obtain a conviction."); Dennis v. Commonwealth, 306 S.W.3d 466, 472 (Ky. 2010) (noting that courts use different standards of proof for the preliminary showing of falsity: a preponderance of the evidence, clear and convincing evidence, a reasonable probability of falsity, strong and substantial proof of actual falsity, and demonstrably false); Perry v. Commonwealth, 390 S.W.3d 122, 132 (Ky.2012) ("This case provides a good example of the situation where the sheer number and variety of allegations, even when it cannot be proven that each claim is demonstrably false standing alone due to the impossibility of substantiating some of the claims, nonetheless can create a distinct and substantial probability that they are demonstrably false when considered together.").

4. *Bias v. untruthful character.* In Boggs v. Collins, 226 F.3d 728, 739–40 (6th Cir.2000), the court drew a distinction between evidence of bias, which is often admissible under the Confrontation Clause, and a more general attack on character, which is not. It stated:

> [W]e must reject Boggs's primary argument because it improperly blurs the precise distinctions drawn in Confrontation Clause jurisprudence. Not having articulated an argument sounding in motive, bias or prejudice, Boggs instead seeks to elevate his purpose—attacking Berman's general credibility—into a constitutionally mandated right. * * * No matter how central an

accuser's credibility is to a case—indeed, her credibility will almost always be the cornerstone of a rape or sexual assault case, even if there is physical evidence—the Constitution does not *require* that a defendant be given the opportunity to wage a general attack on credibility by pointing to individual instances of past conduct.

5. *Alternate sources of knowledge.* See LaJoie v. Thompson, 217 F.3d 663, 673 (9th Cir.2000) (Constitution required admissibility of evidence of prior rape to show that victim could have learned about sexual acts and male genitalia from source other than defendant accused of rape); State v. Rolon, 777 A.2d 604 (Conn.2001) (exclusion violated right of confrontation); State v. Grovenstein, 530 S.E.2d 406, 410 (S.C.Ct.App.2000) ("Other jurisdictions have concluded that evidence of a young victim's sexual history is relevant where the defendant seeks to admit the evidence to show a source for the victim's sexual knowledge. Specifically, these courts found the evidence relevant to rebut the inference that a child victim could not describe the sexual acts unless the defendant had committed the alleged acts."). See also State v. Bass, 465 S.E.2d 334 (N.C.Ct.App.1996) (upholding trial court's exclusion of evidence of a child/victim's past sexual abuse but reversing because state had argued to the jury that child would have had no prior knowledge of the types of conduct she had testified about).

6. *Notice requirement.* See United States v. Rouse, 111 F.3d 561, 569 (8th Cir.1997) ("The Rule has strict procedural requirements, including a timely offer of proof delineating what evidence will be offered and for what purpose, and an *in camera* hearing at which the victim may respond. Defendants' vague notice fell far short of complying with the Rule, and the district court properly excluded this evidence.").

7. *Sanctions.* In Michigan v. Lucas, 500 U.S. 145 (1991), the United States Supreme Court ruled that the exclusion of defense evidence for failing to comply with the notice provision of a rape shield statute was not per se unconstitutional. The Court indicated, however, that exclusion in a particular case may be unconstitutional.

(4) ACCUSED'S CHARACTER: FEDERAL RULES 413–415

UNITED STATES V. LEMAY
United States Court of Appeals, Ninth Circuit, 2001.
260 F.3d 1018.

TROTT, CIRCUIT JUDGE:

Fred LeMay appeals his convictions for two counts of child molestation * * *. LeMay lived on the Fort Peck Reservation from 1991 to 1998, and intermittently resided at the home of his sister, Justine Shields, and her husband, Daniel Renz. Shields and Renz had several young children, for whom LeMay often babysat. One such instance occurred during the summer of 1997. Shields and Renz had gone out for the evening, leaving LeMay to watch their children D.R. and A.R., two boys ages five and seven.

LeMay made both children orally copulate with him while their parents were away and threatened to beat them up if they told anyone. Undeterred, the boys informed their mother of the abuse the next morning. Although Shields refused to let LeMay babysit for her children after that, she did not report the incident, look for evidence, or take the boys to a doctor or a counselor. Two years later, however, law enforcement authorities got wind of LeMay's abuse of the children and investigated the allegations. LeMay was eventually arrested and charged with child molestation.

Before trial, the prosecutor gave notice of her intent to introduce evidence of LeMay's prior acts of sexual misconduct under Rule 414 of the Federal Rules of Evidence. * * *

As in the 1997 incident for which LeMay was charged, LeMay sexually abused the children while babysitting for them [in 1989]. Francine LeMay returned from the grocery store to find her two-year old daughter upset and bruised. Upon confrontation, Francine LeMay extracted an admission from LeMay that he had "put his penis in" the older child's mouth. Francine LeMay also found a cream-like substance in her infant's vagina when she changed her diaper, and implied that this substance was semen. In a subsequent juvenile adjudication, LeMay was found guilty of rape. * * *

At trial, the prosecution called both A.R. and D.R., who by that time were seven and nine years old. Both boys remembered the incidents and testified consistently. The prosecution also called the boys' mother, Justine Shields. Because Shields had not informed anyone that LeMay had molested her children, the prosecution was unable to offer any forensic, medical, or psychological evidence that the boys had been abused, and the case therefore rested on their testimony.

LeMay took advantage of this lack of evidence in his opening statement, arguing that no eyewitnesses or medical or scientific experts would corroborate the testimony of A.R. and D.R. Further, in cross-examining the boys, LeMay's counsel attempted to call into question their ability to remember events accurately. He also suggested that the boys might have a motive to lie because they were currently in foster care, and that they might have thought that accusing LeMay of molesting them would be a way to be reunited with their parents. * * *

[The prosecutor] first called Francine LeMay, who testified about the defendant's abuse of her children in Oregon in 1989. Ms. LeMay, who began her testimony in tears, described generally how she had discovered that LeMay had abused her daughters and how she had gotten him to admit to that abuse. The prosecution's final witness established that

---

LeMay had been found guilty of rape in a juvenile adjudication. After these witnesses, the prosecution closed its case.

* * *

The jury found LeMay guilty of both counts of molestation, and the district judge sentenced him to 405 months in prison.* * *

B.   Due Process

Prior to 1994, when Rules 413 through 415 were passed, admission of a defendant's prior crimes or acts was governed by Rule 404(b), which disallows such evidence when used to prove "the character of a person in order to show action in conformity therewith." * * *

The Supreme Court has held that the primary guide for determining whether a rule is so "fundamental" as to be embodied in the Constitution is historical practice. * * * In this case, however, evidence of historical practice does not lead to a clear conclusion. On the one hand, it seems clear that the general ban on propensity evidence has the requisite historical pedigree to qualify for constitutional status. *See, e.g.,* McKinney v. Rees, 993 F.2d 1378, 1384–85 (9th Cir.1993) (holding in the context of a murder prosecution that "[t]he character rule is based on * * * a 'fundamental conception of justice' and the 'community's sense of fair play and decency' "); Old Chief v. United States, 519 U.S. 172, 182 (1997) (stating in dicta that "[t]here is * * * no question that propensity would be an 'improper basis' for conviction"); Michelson v. United States, 335 U.S. 469, 475–76 (1948) (noting in dicta that "[c]ourts that follow the common-law tradition almost unanimously have come to disallow resort by the prosecution to any kind of evidence of a defendant's evil character to establish a probability of his guilt").

On the other hand, courts have routinely allowed propensity evidence in sex-offense cases, even while disallowing it in other criminal prosecutions. In many American jurisdictions, evidence of a defendant's prior acts of sexual misconduct is commonly admitted in prosecutions for offenses such as rape, incest, adultery, and child molestation. *See, e.g.,* 2 JOHN H. WIGMORE, WIGMORE ON EVIDENCE, §§ 398–402. As early as 1858, the Michigan Supreme Court noted that "courts in several of the States have shown a disposition to relax the rule [against propensity evidence] in cases where the offense consists of illicit intercourse between the sexes." People v. Jenness, 5 Mich. 305, 319–20, 1858 WL 2321 at *8 (Mich.1858) Today, state courts that do not have evidentiary rules comparable to Federal Rules 414 through 415 allow this evidence either by stretching traditional 404(b) exceptions to the ban on character evidence or by resorting to the so-called "lustful disposition" exception, which, in its purest form, is a rule allowing for propensity inferences in sex crime cases. * * * Thus, "the history of evidentiary rules regarding a criminal defendant's sexual propensities is ambiguous at best, particularly with regard to sexual abuse of children." United States v. Castillo, 140 F.3d 874, 881 (10th Cir.1998). * * *

The historical evidence in this case thus leads to no clear conclusion. In holding that Rule 414 is constitutional, we therefore do not rely solely on the fact that courts have historically allowed propensity evidence to reach the jury in sex offense cases. Because LeMay has the burden of proving that the ban on propensity evidence is a matter of fundamental fairness, the divergence in historical evidence does cut against his position. * * * Yet while we recognize the importance of historical practice in determining whether an evidentiary rule is embodied in the Due Process Clause, in this case, we find it necessary to conduct an independent inquiry into whether allowing propensity inferences violates fundamental ideas of fairness. * * *

With the protections of the Rule 403 balancing test still in place, LeMay's due-process challenge to Rule 414 loses much of its force. The evidence that he had sexually molested his cousins in 1989 was indisputably relevant to the issue of whether he had done the same thing to his nephews in 1997. *See, e.g.,* Michelson, 335 U.S. at 475 (noting that defendant's prior crimes or ill name "might logically be persuasive that he is by propensity a probable perpetrator of the crime"). The introduction of relevant evidence, by itself, cannot amount to a constitutional violation. * * *

The introduction of such evidence can amount to a constitutional violation only if its prejudicial effect far outweighs its probative value. In *McKinney*, we granted a writ of habeas corpus and overturned a murder conviction where the petitioner's trial had been infused with highly inflammatory evidence of almost no relevance. *See* McKinney, 993 F.2d at 1384–85. LeMay, of course, emphasizes that *McKinney* held that the ban on propensity evidence is of constitutional magnitude. What he misses, however, is the fact that we held that such evidence will only *sometimes* violate the constitutional right to a fair trial, if it is of no relevance, or if its potential for prejudice far outweighs what little relevance it might have. Potentially devastating evidence of little or no relevance would have to be excluded under Rule 403. Indeed, this is exactly what Rule 403 was designed to do. We therefore conclude that as long as the protections of Rule 403 remain in place so that district judges retain the authority to exclude potentially devastating evidence, Rule 414 is constitutional. * * *

C.   Rule 403

* * * Rule 403 provides that relevant evidence may be excluded, among other reasons, if "its probative value is substantially outweighed by the danger of unfair prejudice." FED. R. EVID. 403. In *Glanzer*, we stated that "[b]ecause of the inherent strength of the evidence that is covered by [Rule 414], when putting this type of evidence through the [Rule 403] microscope, a court should pay 'careful attention to both the

significant probative value and the strong prejudicial qualities' of that evidence." [United States v.] Glanzer, 232 F.3d at 1268 (quoting United States v. Guardia, 135 F.3d 1326, 1330 (10th Cir.1998)). We also articulated several factors that district judges must evaluate in determining whether to admit evidence of a defendant's prior acts of sexual misconduct. These factors are: (1) "the similarity of the prior acts to the acts charged," (2) the "closeness in time of the prior acts to the acts charged," (3) "the frequency of the prior acts," (4) the "presence or lack of intervening circumstances," and (5) "the necessity of the evidence beyond the testimonies already offered at trial." Id. We also stated that this list of factors is not exclusive, and that district judges should consider other factors relevant to individual cases. Id.

* * *

We also conclude that admitting LeMay's prior acts of molestation was proper in light of the factors we discussed in *Glanzer* and others relevant to this particular case. We begin by noting, as the district judge did, that the evidence of LeMay's prior acts of child molestation was highly relevant. The 1989 molestations were very similar to the charged crimes. Each case involved forced oral copulation. In each case the victims were young relatives of LeMay, and each instance occurred while LeMay was babysitting them.

Moreover, as the district judge suggested, the prior acts evidence was relevant to bolster the credibility of the victims after LeMay suggested they could be fabricating the accusations. The evidence also countered LeMay's claim that there was no evidence corroborating the testimony of D.R. and A.R.

We recognize that this characterization of the evidence is essentially a veiled propensity inference. *See, e.g.,* Wright & Graham, 22 FEDERAL PRACTICE AND PROCEDURE § 5248 (noting that use of prior act evidence to "corroborate" testimony of victims is propensity evidence if it "depends upon an inference to the defendant's character"). However, it is also exactly the sort of use of prior acts evidence that Congress had in mind when enacting Rule 414. *See* 140 Cong. Rec. H8991–92 (August 21, 1994) (statement of Rep. Molinari) (noting that child molestation cases "require reliance on child victims whose credibility can readily be attacked in the absence of substantial corroboration"). The case against LeMay rested on testimony of D.R. and A.R. Both children were very young at the time of the incidents, and two years had passed before LeMay was tried. LeMay attacked their credibility and suggested that there was not enough evidence to prove their allegations. That this case made use of the prior acts evidence in precisely the manner Congress contemplated strongly indicates that its admission was not an abuse of discretion.

Additionally, the evidence of LeMay's prior abuse of his cousins was also highly reliable. LeMay had been convicted of at least one of the rape charges arising from the incidents in Oregon. Because LeMay had admitted to abusing his cousins, Francine LeMay's testimony fell within a well-established exception to the hearsay rule. To the extent that allowing the evidence permitted a propensity inference, it was an inference based on proven facts and LeMay's own admissions, not rumor, innuendo, or prior uncharged acts capable of multiple characterizations. Thus, although we do not suggest that district courts may *only* introduce prior acts of molestation for which a defendant has been tried and found guilty, we hold that the extent to which an act has been proved is a factor that district courts may consider in conducting the Rule 403 inquiry.

We must also consider the remoteness in time of LeMay's prior acts of molestation, the frequency of prior similar acts, and whether any intervening events bear on the relevance of the prior similar acts. *See* Glanzer, 232 F.3d at 1268. The "intervening events" factor seems to have little relevance in the present case, and the other two cut in favor of the government. About eleven years had passed between LeMay's abuse of his nieces and his trial for the abuse of D.R. and A.R. We have held, in the context of Rule 404(b), that the lapse of twelve years does not render the decision to admit relevant evidence of similar prior acts an abuse of discretion. *See* United States v. Rude, 88 F.3d 1538, 1550 (9th Cir.1996). The "frequency of events" factor discussed in *Glanzer* also cuts in favor of the government. Although it was not introduced at trial, the government also had evidence of a third incident in which LeMay had sexually abused his young relatives. True, this incident occurred even before the 1989 abuse of his cousins when LeMay himself was extremely young, and, as the prosecutor noted, was "triple hearsay." However, that there was evidence of a third similar incident suggests that LeMay's abuse of his cousins in 1989 was not an isolated occurrence.

Glanzer also instructs that courts must consider whether the prior acts evidence was necessary to prove the case. This factor also supports the government's position and indicates that the district judge did not abuse his discretion in admitting the evidence. The prosecution's case rested on the testimony of A.R. and D.R. No other scientific, forensic, medical, or psychological witness was available. LeMay had attacked the credibility of the boys and capitalized on the lack of eyewitness and expert testimony. That the prosecutor claimed that she could get a conviction without introducing LeMay's prior acts of molestation does not suggest that the evidence was not "necessary." Prior acts evidence need not be *absolutely necessary* to the prosecution's case in order to be introduced; it must simply be helpful or *practically necessary.*

Finally, Francine LeMay's testimony was necessary to establish that LeMay's 1989 molestations were very similar, and thus relevant, to the charged crimes. We reject the idea that the district court should have limited the prosecution to merely proving that LeMay had been convicted of rape eleven years before. The relevance of the prior act evidence was in the details. Establishing the simple fact of conviction would leave out the information that LeMay had been convicted of sexually abusing his young relatives, by forced oral copulation, while they were in his care. Francine LeMay's testimony was necessary to fill in the details that made the prior rape conviction relevant. Therefore, the "necessity" factor favors the government in all respects.

Several factors do admittedly favor LeMay. LeMay himself was only twelve years old at the time of the 1989 molestations. And foremost, of course, is the emotional and highly charged nature of Francine LeMay's testimony. Although we, as an appellate court, are not in a position to evaluate how great an effect Francine LeMay's testimony had on the jury, we do not doubt that it was powerful. Francine LeMay began her testimony in tears, and certainly, her suggestion that LeMay had raped her infant daughter would have been particularly shocking. However, evidence of a defendant's prior acts of molestation will always be emotionally charged and inflammatory, as is the evidence that he committed the charged crimes. Thus, that prior acts evidence is inflammatory is not dispositive in and of itself. Rather, district judges must carefully evaluate the potential inflammatory nature of the proffered testimony, and balance it with that which the jury has already heard, the relevance of the evidence, the necessity of introducing it, and all the other relevant factors discussed above. The record here shows that the district judge did just that. Therefore, admitting LeMay's prior acts of molestation was not an abuse of discretion.

All in all, the record shows that the district judge struck a careful balance between LeMay's rights and the clear intent of Congress that evidence of prior similar acts be admitted in child molestation prosecutions.

* * * [The court also rejected equal protection and other arguments.]

Affirmed.

PAEZ, CIRCUIT JUDGE, concurring in part and dissenting in part:

I concur in all but Discussion § C of the majority's decision. I respectfully dissent from the majority's holding that the district court did not abuse its discretion in admitting the evidence under Fed.R.Evid. 403. I would reverse the district court's Rule 403 ruling and remand for reconsideration in light of our decision in Doe by Rudy–Glanzer v. Glanzer, 232 F.3d 1258 (9th Cir.2000) (hereinafter *Glanzer*). * * *

Rules 413, 414, and 415 were extraordinarily controversial at the time of their passage. The Judicial Conference Advisory Committee on Evidence Rules and the Judicial Conference Committee on Rules of

Practice and Procedure both voted overwhelmingly to oppose the rules because they "would permit the introduction of unreliable but highly prejudicial evidence * * *." Fed.R.Evid. 413 hist. notes. The report submitted by the Judicial Conference to Congress expressed "significant concern" about the "danger of convicting a criminal defendant for past, as opposed to charged, behavior or for being a bad person." *Id.*

Nevertheless, there are benefits to these rules. As members of Congress repeatedly recognized, "[i]n most rape or molestation cases, it is the word of the defendant against the word of the victim. If the defendant has committed similar acts in the past, the claims of the victim are more likely to be considered truthful if there is substantiation of other assaults." 140 Cong. Rec. H5437–03, *H5439 (daily ed. June 29, 1994) (statement of Rep. Kyl). This case, with two child victims and no other witnesses, is precisely the type of case for which Fed.R.Evid. 414 was designed.

As courts, we are left to balance the public's interest in convicting those charged with sexual abuse crimes, as expressed in these evidentiary rules, with the right of the accused to be convicted only for the crime charged, and not his previous acts. LeMay served his sentence for his previous criminal acts, and he may not be punished again, unless the government can prove that he committed new crimes as well. The best way for district courts to balance these competing interests is to conduct the Rule 403 analysis on the record, carefully considering each of the factors, and others as necessary, identified by this court in *Glanzer.* * * *

In this case, the district court made no record of its Rule 403 analysis at all. Unlike *Glanzer*, there was much more the district court could—and should—have done. In fact, the district court did not even identify the probative value of the evidence, only describing it as "relevant." There is a marked difference between describing evidence as relevant and describing it as having probative value significant enough to outweigh any unfair prejudicial effect. * * *

In this case, the district court found that evidence of LeMay's prior conviction was "relevant" to bolstering the child witnesses' credibility and to rebutting the suggestion that there was no proof that a crime actually occurred. But the district court later made an explicit factual finding that the two victims were "extremely credible," that their testimony was clear, and that they testified with certitude and impressive demeanor. This, combined with the prosecution's own assertion that the children's testimony alone was sufficient for a conviction, suggests that the prior acts evidence had minimal probative value. That minimal probative value should have been weighed against the risk of unfair prejudice to LeMay.

Because the district court did not conduct the 403 balancing on the record and consider the *Glanzer* factors, I would find that it abused its discretion. * * *

NOTES AND QUESTIONS

1. *Legislative history.* The congressional enactment of Rules 413–415 was delayed for 150 days in order to permit the Judicial Conference to submit recommendations with regard to the admissibility of such evidence. The Conference urged Congress to reconsider these rules: "[T]he new rules, which are not supported by empirical evidence, could diminish significantly the protections that have safeguarded persons accused in criminal cases and parties in civil cases against undue prejudice. These protections form a fundamental part of American jurisprudence and have evolved under long-standing rules and case law. A significant concern identified by the [Standing] committee was the danger of convicting a criminal defendant for past, as opposed to charged, behavior or for being a bad person. In addition, * * * because prior bad acts would be admissible even though not the subject of a conviction, mini-trials within trials concerning those acts would result when a defendant seeks to rebut such evidence." Report of the Judicial Conference on the Admission of Character Evidence in Certain Sexual Misconduct Cases, 159 F.R.D. 51, 53 (1995). Congress enacted the rules without change.

2. *Change in law.* See United States v. LeCompte, 131 F.3d 767, 768 (8th Cir.1997) ("The admissibility of T.T.'s testimony has been considered by this Court once before. In LeCompte's first trial, the government offered the evidence under Rule 404(b). It was not then able to offer the evidence under Rule 414 because of its failure to provide timely notice of the offer, as required by Rule 414. The District Court admitted the evidence, and the jury convicted LeCompte. On appeal, this Court held that the District Court's admission of the evidence under Rule 404(b) was improper, and reversed LeCompte's conviction. United States v. LeCompte, 99 F.3d 274 (8th Cir.1996). We now consider the admissibility of T.T.'s testimony in LeCompte's retrial, under Rule 414, the government having given timely notice the second time around." The court ruled the evidence admissible.).

3. *Recidivism rationale.* Is recidivism a convincing rationale for treating character evidence differently in sexual assault or child molestation cases than in other cases? See Baker, Once a Rapist? Motivational Evidence and Relevancy in Rape Law, 110 Harv.L.Rev. 563, 578 (1997) ("A 1989 Bureau of Justice Statistics recidivism study found that only 7.7% of released rapists were rearrested for rape. In contrast, 33.5% of released larcenists were rearrested for larceny; 31.9% of released burglars were rearrested for burglary; and 24.8% of drug offenders were rearrested for drug offenses."). Are molestation cases different? See Prentky et al., Recidivism Rates Among Child Molesters and Rapists: A Methodological Analysis, 21 Law & Hum.Behav. 635 (1997).

4. *Equal Protection.* See United States v. Mound, 149 F.3d 799, 801 (8th Cir.1998) ("Promoting the effective prosecution of sex offenses is a legitimate end. The legislative history of Rule 413 indicates good reasons why Congress believed that the rule was 'justified by the distinctive characteristics of the cases it will affect.' 140 Cong. Rec. H8991 (daily ed.

Aug. 21, 1994) (statement of Rep. Molinari). These characteristics included the reliance of sex offense cases on difficult credibility determinations that 'would otherwise become unresolvable swearing matches,' as well as, in the case of child sexual abuse, the 'exceptionally probative' value of a defendant's sexual interest in children.").

5. *Due process and Rule 403.* See United States v. Enjady, 134 F.3d 1427, 1433 (10th Cir.1998) ("Considering the safeguards of Rule 403, we conclude that Rule 413 is not unconstitutional on its face as a violation of the Due Process Clause."). But see State v. Cox, 781 N.W.2d 757, 762 (Iowa 2010) ("[T]he Iowa Constitution prohibits admission of prior bad acts evidence involving a different victim when admitted solely for the purpose of demonstrating propensity. Instead, the evidence must be relevant to a 'legitimate issue.' "); State v. Ellison, 239 S.W.3d 603, 607–08 (Mo.2007) (Missouri statute allowing admission of evidence of prior sexual crimes unconstitutional under the Missouri Constitution even though the statute contained a balancing clause similar to Federal Rule 403).

6. *Rule 403 balancing.* Compare United States v. Loughry, 660 F.3d 965, 970 (7th Cir.2011) ("[A]lthough evidence cannot be excluded under Rule 403 simply because it tends to show that the defendant has a propensity to commit a sex offense, Rule 403 continues to rigorously apply to Rule 414 evidence."), with United States v. Meacham, 115 F.3d 1488, 1492 (10th Cir.1997) ("Rule 403 balancing is still applicable, * * * but clearly under Rule 414 the courts are to 'liberally' admit evidence of prior uncharged sex offenses."). See also Orenstein, Deviance, Due Process, and the False Promise of Federal Rule of Evidence 403, 90 Cornell L.Rev. 1487, 1519, 1520 (2005) ("Propensity shifted from being the quintessential example of unfair prejudice to being a permissible—and indeed officially endorsed—method of proving guilt. * * * In practice, despite their dicta to the contrary, the courts have weakened Rule 403 by tending to admit evidence of prior sexual offenses automatically under a pro forma approach to Rule 403 ['403–lite'].").

7. *Relevant factors.* Other courts have proposed different factors. See United States v. Enjady, 134 F.3d 1427, 1433 (10th Cir.1998) ("1) how clearly the prior act has been proved; 2) how probative the evidence is of the material fact it is admitted to prove; 3) how seriously disputed the material fact is; [4]] whether the government can avail itself of any less prejudicial evidence[;] * * * [5]] how likely it is such evidence will contribute to an improperly-based jury verdict; [6]] the extent to which such evidence will distract the jury from the central issues of the trial; and [7]] how time consuming it will be to prove the prior conduct.").

8. *Remoteness.* See United States v. O'Connor, 650 F.3d 839, 853, 854 (2d Cir.2011) ("At trial [for child sex trafficking], the government offered in evidence eight passages from Sacco's [2000] autobiography, in which Sacco had written of his sexual attraction to children and described, inter alia, his sexual acts against '[his] little sister' and her girlfriends while they were asleep [30 years prior to trial].", "[A]lthough Sacco suggests that his predilections as a teenager should be discounted, pointing out that the acts

described in his autobiography occurred more than 30 years before his conduct with S.O. * * *, that argument rings hollow in light of the evident relish with which he wrote the passages just seven years before his molestation of S.O."); United States v. Larson, 112 F.3d 600, 605 (2d Cir.1997) ("[T]he Stevens testimony covered events 16–20 years prior to trial. Those events closely paralleled the events complained of by Furs, taking place in the same geographic locations, with Larson using the same enticements for both boys, plying both with alcohol, and engaging both in similar progressions of sexual acts. The similarity of the events clearly demonstrated the Stevens testimony's relevance. The court was entitled to view both the traumatic nature of the events and their repetition over a span of four years as strong indicators of the reliability of the witness's memory. We see no abuse of discretion in the admission of this testimony.").

9. *Record.* See United States v. Castillo, 140 F.3d 874, 884 (10th Cir.1998) ("As we said in a similar case: '[T]he district court's summary disposition of this issue renders it impossible for us to review the propriety of its decision * * *. Without any reasoned elaboration by the district court we have no way of understanding the basis of its decision * * *.").

10. *"Consent" cases.* Should Rules 413–415 be limited to the issue of consent in rape cases? See Bryden & Park, Other Crimes Evidence in Sex Offense Cases, 78 Minn.L.Rev. 529 (1994). What is the difference between "consent" and "identity" cases?

11. *Method of proof.* See United States v. Enjady, 134 F.3d 1427, 1434 (10th Cir.1998) ("But here the government established that B had filed a contemporaneous police report and it presented the investigating officer's testimony about why the alleged rape of B was not prosecuted."). Should these Rules be limited to situations where there is a prior conviction? See Orenstein, note 6, supra, at 1541–42 ("By allowing propensity evidence only where there is a prior conviction, we significantly enhance the likelihood that the prior offense occurred * * * [and avoid mini-trials]. * * * Because the accused has already been punished, the jury is less likely to want to punish him again.").

12. *State cases and rules.* See Alaska Evid.R. 404(b)(3) ("In a prosecution for a crime of sexual assault in any degree, evidence of other sexual assaults or attempted sexual assaults by the defendant against the same or another person is admissible if the defendant relies on a defense of consent. In a prosecution for a crime of attempt to commit sexual assault in any degree, evidence of other sexual assaults or attempted sexual assaults by the defendant against the same or another person is admissible."); Ariz.R.Evid. 404(c). Other jurisdictions have created similar rules by court decision. Some states limit this "lustful disposition" exception to cases involving the same victim, to cases in which the victim is a minor, or to incest cases. See People v. Donoho, 788 N.E.2d 707, 717–18 (Ill.2003) (discussing various positions); State v. Kennedy, 803 So.2d 916, 921 (La.2001) ("[W]e have consistently restricted this judicially-recognized 'lustful disposition' exception to Article 404(B) to evidence of other sexual crimes committed by

the defendant against the same prosecuting victim, whether child or adult."); Craigg v. State, 2012 WL 4829813 (Ark.2012) ("For the pedophile exception [to Rule 404(b)] to apply, there must be a sufficient degree of similarity between the evidence to be introduced and the charged sexual conduct. We also require that there be an 'intimate relationship' between the defendant and the victim of the prior act. Although our early jurisprudence on the pedophile exception required that the alleged victim of a prior bad act be a member of the defendant's family or household, modernly the State need only demonstrate a relationship close in friendship or acquaintance, familiar, near, or confidential.") (citation omitted).

13. *Sources.* Baker, Once a Rapist? Motivational Evidence and Relevancy in Rape Law, 110 Harv.L.Rev. 563 (1997) (arguing that there are different motivations for different types of rape (e.g., date rape, gang rape, spousal rape, opportunistic rape during the course of a robbery, etc.), and this should affect admissibility decisions); Ojala, Propensity Evidence Under Rule 413: The Need for Balance, 77 Wash.U.L.Q. 947 (1999); Symposium, Perspectives on Proposed Federal Rules of Evidence 413–15, 22 Fordham Urban L.J. 265 (1995).

(5) "OTHER ACTS" EVIDENCE: FEDERAL RULE 404(b)

UNITED STATES V. ROBINSON

United States Court of Appeals, Seventh Circuit, 1998.
161 F.3d 463.

KANNE, CIRCUIT JUDGE.

* * *

I.   History

A federal grand jury returned a four-count indictment against Richard Robinson on charges stemming from two armed bank robberies. Counts one and two of the indictment alleged that on April 8, 1997, Robinson robbed the Americana Bank in Anderson, Indiana, and that he used a firearm during the commission of this offense. Counts three and four of this same indictment alleged that ten days later, on April 18, 1997, Robinson committed another armed robbery with a firearm, this time robbing Harrington Bank in Fishers, Indiana. The cities of Anderson and Fishers are separated by approximately twenty-five miles. Robinson pleaded guilty to the later armed robbery of Harrington Bank and went to trial on the charges stemming from the earlier Americana Bank robbery. Because the government offered evidence of the April 18 Fishers robbery at Robinson's trial, it is necessary to review the facts of both robberies when considering the issues before us. * * *

[Following the April 18th robbery, a high speed pursuit of Robinson ensued, at times exceeding speeds of 100 miles per hour. Evidence indicated that he disregarded traffic signals, operated his vehicle on the wrong side of the road, nearly caused numerous traffic accidents, and evaded a road block that had been set up by police before his Chevrolet Cavalier was eventually disabled. In addition, numerous local police officers were required to subdue him after a prolonged struggle. Robinson assaulted one and drove his car into a sheriff.]

II. Analysis

A. Admission of Evidence of the Harrington Bank Robbery and the Subsequent Chase

Robinson contends that the District Court abused its discretion by allowing the government to admit evidence of his plea of guilty to the charges stemming from the April 18 armed bank robbery at his trial for the April 8 armed bank robbery. The evidence of the April 18 armed bank robbery included evidence tending to demonstrate the similarities between the two robberies, evidence of the high speed chase and Robinson's struggle with police subsequent to the chase, and the materials recovered from Robinson's vehicle following his apprehension, including the orange ski mask, the distinctive duffle bag ["Louis Vuitton"-brand] containing money from the April 18 armed bank robbery, and the handgun used in both robberies. Prior to trial, the District Court conducted an evidentiary hearing on the admissibility of this evidence and, over Robinson's objections, ruled that the admission of this evidence was not prohibited by Rule 404(b) of the Federal Rules of Evidence. The admission of evidence under Rule 404(b) by a district court is reviewed only for an abuse of discretion. * * *

* * *

The categories that appear in the text of Rule 404(b) are not exclusive. Indeed, Rule 404(b) does not require the party offering the evidence to force the evidence into a particular listed category, but simply to show *any* relevant purpose other than proving conduct by means of a general propensity inference. We have held that evidence may be admissible under Rule 404(b) to demonstrate *modus operandi*. * * * Evidence of *modus operandi* is evidence that shows a defendant's distinctive method of operation. Such evidence may be properly admitted pursuant to Rule 404(b) to prove identity. Id. In addition, some courts have interpreted the admission of evidence establishing consciousness of guilt as coming within the identity exception to Rule 404(b). *See, e.g.,* United States v. Sims, 617 F.2d 1371, 1378 (9th Cir.1980) ("Flight immediately after the commission of a crime, especially where the person learns that he may be a suspect * * * supports an inference of guilt * * *. It was therefore relevant under the identity exception to Rule 404(b)."). Irrespective of whether such evidence may be admitted specifically to show identity, we have held that evidence demonstrating consciousness of guilt may be properly admitted under Rule 404(b). *See* United States v. Acevedo, 28 F.3d 686, 688 (7th Cir.1994) * * *.

We have fashioned a four-prong test to determine the appropriateness of admitting evidence of other crimes, wrongs, or acts. Under this test, the admissibility of the evidence is dependant [sic] upon whether: (1) the evidence is directed toward establishing a matter in issue other than the defendant's propensity to commit the crime charged; (2) the evidence shows that the other act is similar enough and close enough in time to be relevant to the matter in issue; (3) the evidence is sufficient to support a jury finding that the defendant committed the similar act; and (4) the evidence has probative value that is not substantially outweighed by the danger of unfair prejudice. * * * The fourth prong of this test incorporates Rule 403, which provides for the exclusion of relevant evidence on grounds of prejudice, confusion, or waste of time. Though not specifically stated as such, the primary thrust of Robinson's argument, both before the District Court during the evidentiary hearing and before this Court on appeal, is that the second and fourth prongs of this test were not met with respect to the District Court's admission of evidence relating to the April 18 armed bank robbery.

* * *

When considering the second and fourth prongs—whether the evidence shows that the other act is similar enough and close enough in time to be relevant to the matter in issue and whether the evidence has a probative value that is not substantially outweighed by the danger of unfair prejudice—it is helpful to consider the evidence of the similarities between the two armed bank robberies first and then to turn our attention to the evidence of flight and Robinson's struggle with the police.

As stated, the evidence demonstrating the similarities between the two crimes amounts, in essence, to evidence demonstrating *modus operandi*. We have cautioned that "[i]f defined broadly enough, *modus operandi* evidence can easily become nothing more than the character evidence that Rule 404(b) prohibits." Smith, 103 F.3d at 603. To ensure that the evidence at issue is not merely offered to establish the defendant's propensity to commit certain conduct, we require that *modus operandi* evidence bear "a singular strong resemblance to the pattern of the offense charged." United States v. Shackleford, 738 F.2d 776, 783 (7th Cir.1984) * * *, and that the similarities between the crimes be "sufficiently idiosyncratic to permit an inference of pattern for purposes of truth." United States v. Hudson, 884 F.2d 1016, 1021 (7th Cir.1989) (quoting Shackleford, 738 F.2d at 783 * * *)). "Thus, we must first determine whether there are sufficient similarities between the other crime evidence and the charged crime that clearly distinguish the defendant from other criminals committing bank robberies." Moore, 115 F.3d at 1355.

There are numerous similarities between the armed bank robberies of April 8 and April 18 that make them "clearly distinctive from the thousands of other bank robberies committed each year." Moore, 115 F.3d at 1355 (quoting Smith, 103 F.3d at 603). In both cases, the robber donned an orange ski mask prior to entering the bank, and he entered the bank carrying a distinctive duffle bag in one hand and brandishing a handgun in the other. Once inside the banks, the robber vaulted over the teller counter and demanded money. The robber emptied the teller drawers at each bank by himself, but only after placing the handgun down. The getaway vehicle in both cases was identified as a blue Chevrolet Cavalier. Furthermore, the robberies occurred within ten days and twenty-five miles of each other. This proximity in both time and location has significant bearing on the determination of whether the robberies are sufficiently idiosyncratic so as to permit an inference of pattern when considered in conjunction with the distinctive characteristics of each robbery. *See* Smith, 103 F.3d at 603 (noting the one month interval and 40 mile distance between two bank robberies when viewed in light of the rural locations of the banks in Wisconsin was relevant to demonstrating *modus operandi*). It is clear that sufficient similarities exist with respect to the April 8 and the April 18 robberies to identify Robinson as the individual responsible for committing these robberies.

Given the similarities between the two robberies, it cannot be said that the probative value of evidence demonstrating these similarities is substantially outweighed by the danger of unfair prejudice. Moreover, any risk of unfair prejudice was lessened by the jury instruction given by the District Court that the evidence offered by the government relating to the April 18 bank robbery was relevant only to the purposes contemplated by Rule 404(b). * * *

The government's theory for the admission of evidence of the chase and Robinson's struggle with the police following the April 18 armed bank robbery, however, is somewhat more troublesome. During the evidentiary hearing before the District Court, the government argued that the evidence of the chase and subsequent struggle demonstrated Robinson's consciousness of guilt with respect to the April 8 armed bank robbery. The government explained that the motivation prompting flight and struggle on April 18 was twofold—Robinson was fleeing from the most recent armed bank robbery and he also knew that he possessed evidence connecting him to the April 8 armed bank robbery. Thus, he had a dual purpose in fleeing from law enforcement after the April 18 armed bank robbery. The government argued that the fervor with which he attempted to escape from the police was proportional to Robinson's consciousness of guilt, and, therefore, the magnitude of Robinson's resistance was directly related to Robinson's consciousness that he possessed evidence connecting him with not one, but two armed bank robberies. In short, the government asserted that Robinson was fleeing, in effect, from both armed bank robberies. * * *

In the instant case, Robinson's conduct in attempting to elude police after the April 18 armed bank robbery certainly constituted flight. It cannot be seriously disputed that this flight was the result of consciousness of guilt. The degree of confidence with which the jury could reasonably draw inferences from Robinson's flight to an ultimate finding of his guilt with respect to the April 8 armed bank robbery is also substantial. The relative proximity in time between the crime charged and Robinson's flight and the fact that at the time he fled from police he possessed considerable evidence linking him to the April 8 armed bank robbery are sufficient to establish a reasonable inference that he fled because of consciousness of guilt stemming from both the April 8 and the April 18 armed bank robberies.

Despite Robinson's arguments to the contrary, evidence of flight from the April 18 bank robbery is not merely generalized evidence offered to establish Robinson's character or his propensity to commit criminal acts. By establishing that Robinson fled from the April 18 armed bank robbery and struggled with police while in possession of evidence linking him to both that robbery and an armed bank robbery occurring a mere ten days before that date, the government was able to offer proof that Robinson possessed a culpable state of mind. As we have explained, "[t]his is a legitimate use of such evidence, whether one conceives of it as outside the scope of Rule 404(b) because of the evidence's 'intrinsic' value deriving from its specific relationship to the facts of the offense or as countenanced by Rule 404(b) because of its relevance in proving a non-character-related consequential fact—consciousness of guilt." Acevedo, 28 F.3d at 688. Under either theory, the evidence is probative of Robinson's state of mind in a manner entirely separate from how it reflects upon his character.

While it may be tempting to conclude Robinson's flight from the April 18 armed bank robbery has no bearing on his consciousness of guilt with respect to the April 8 armed bank robbery, and, indeed, Robinson argues as much, this position can be dispensed with if one considers two scenarios not far removed from the instant case. Under Rule 404(b), evidence of flight certainly would be admissible to show consciousness of guilt of a defendant who knew he was in possession of evidence demonstrating his involvement in an armed bank robbery if that defendant fled from or struggled with police even if the police were attempting to stop him for a mere routine traffic violation, such as a broken taillight, shortly after the commission of the bank robbery. *Cf.* United States v. Dierling, 131 F.3d 722, 731 (8th Cir.1997) (concluding that evidence of a defendant's flight and struggle with a police officer attempting to arrest the defendant for violation of a domestic protection order was admissible as evidence of consciousness of guilt with respect to a conviction for conspiracy to distribute narcotics and stating that "[t]he intended purpose of the attempted stop need not be related to the conspiracy * * *. The real question is what is in the mind of the person who flees and whether there is sufficient evidence to allow the inference that the flight was prompted by consciousness of guilt."). Similarly, if a defendant committed a string of five armed bank robberies and was pursued by police after robbing a sixth, it can hardly be said that evidence of flight could not be admitted to show consciousness of guilt with respect to the other five robberies based on the contention that he was merely fleeing from his latest endeavor to plunder a bank. *Cf.* United States v. Clark, 45 F.3d 1247, 1251 (8th Cir.1995) ("The existence of other possible reasons for flight does not render the inference [of guilt] impermissible or irrational."). And so it is with this case. Robinson had knowledge that he committed acts proscribed by law on both April 8 and April 18. This knowledge was manifested in his efforts to evade police after the robbery on April 18. In such a case, it is not the role of the District Court to parse the mind of a defendant to determine which act may have created a higher consciousness of guilt on a given occasion when the defendant is in possession of evidence linking him to both robberies and when the underlying crimes are virtually identical and separated by a mere ten days.

To the extent that the evidence at issue falls outside the scope of Rule 404(b), we will not deprive a party from presenting evidence when its exclusion leaves a conceptual or chronological void. *See* United States v. Lahey, 55 F.3d 1289, 1295–96 (7th Cir.1995); *see also* United States v. King, 126 F.3d 987, 995 (7th Cir.1997) ("[A] court may admit evidence of other criminal conduct that is inextricably intertwined with a charged offense or that completes the story of the charged offense."). The government needed the evidence of the chase and Robinson's struggle to present a complete picture of the events transpiring between the short time separating the April 8 armed bank robbery and Robinson's capture on April 18. Beyond merely establishing consciousness of guilt, this evidence explains the circumstances surrounding Robinson's arrest and how the government came into possession of the orange ski mask, the distinctive duffle bag, and the handgun—three pieces of evidence of paramount importance to the government's case. "While prosecutorial need alone does not mean probative value outweighs prejudice, the more essential the evidence, the greater its probative value, and the less likely that a trial court should order the evidence excluded." Jackson, 886 F.2d at 847. * * *

NOTES AND QUESTIONS

1.   *"Signature" quality.* What features make the two robberies similar? See United States v. Luna, 21 F.3d 874, 881 (9th Cir.1994) (generic "takeover" bank robberies not sufficiently distinctive); State v. Bey, 709 N.E.2d 484, 491 (Ohio 1999) ("[T]he 'other act' evidence established a 'behavioral fingerprint' linking [the defendant] to the [other] crime due to the common features shared by the [prior] homicide and the [present] homicide.

The deaths of [the two victims] occurred under practically identical circumstances.").

2. *Subsequent acts admissible.* See United States v. Dickerson, 248 F.3d 1036, 1046 (11th Cir.2001) (As to cocaine distribution almost two years after the last overt act in the alleged conspiracy, the court stated: "It is well-settled in this circuit that 'the principles governing what is commonly referred to as other crimes evidence are the same whether the conduct occurs before or after the offense charged, and regardless of whether the activity might give rise to criminal liability.").

3. *Defense use of Rule 404(b).* See United States v. Wilson, 307 F.3d 596, 601 (7th Cir.2002) ("Under what has come to be known as 'reverse 404(b) evidence,' a defendant can introduce evidence of someone else's conduct if it tends to negate the defendant's guilt. The trial court is entitled to exclude this kind of evidence if, upon a balancing of the evidence's probative value against considerations such as prejudice, undue waste of time, and confusion of the issues under Rules 401 and 403 * * *, it concludes that the evidence would not be beneficial."); Watkins v. State, 23 A.3d 151, 155 (Del. 2011) (trial court abused its discretion by precluding evidence of a similar robbery to which another person plead guilty); People v. Primo, 753 N.E.2d 164, 168 (N.Y.2001) (As to evidence that a person who had been present at the shooting had used the same gun in an unrelated crime two months later, the court stated: "The better approach, we hold, is to review the admissibility of third-party culpability evidence under the general balancing analysis that governs the admissibility of all evidence."); Broderick, Reverse 404(b) Evidence: Exploring the Standards When Defendants Want to Introduce Other Bad Act of Third Parties, 79 U.Colo.L.Rev. 587 (2008).

4. *Noncriminal conduct.* See United States v. Rubio–Gonzalez, 674 F.2d 1067, 1075 (5th Cir.1982) ("The fact that the records did not show that appellant's prior conduct was criminal is immaterial. Rule 404(b) authorizes the admission of prior 'acts' as well as 'crimes' and 'wrongs.' ").

5. *Civil cases.* See Udemba v. Nicoli, 237 F.3d 8, 14 (1st Cir.2001) ("The appellant himself set the stage for the admission of the evidence that he now seeks to challenge. In elaboration of his claimed damages, he told on direct examination about his humiliation when news of his arrest appeared in the local newspaper and emphasized the mental anguish that followed. Since the appellant did not testify to a closed period of emotional distress, defense counsel sought to minimize this open-ended claim by inquiring about a subsequent arrest that evoked the same sort of newspaper publicity. The district court allowed this cross-examination for the limited purpose of assisting the jury in determining the extent of damages suffered for mental anguish and emotional distress."); Turley v. State Farm Mut. Auto. Ins. Co., 944 F.2d 669, 672–75 (10th Cir.1991) (evidence of prior insurance scams admissible); Cole, "Bad Acts" Evidence in Civil Cases under Rule 404(b): It's Not Just for Prosecutors Anymore, 37 Litigation 47 (Spring 2011).

6.   *Inextricably intertwined.* See United States v. Bowie, 232 F.3d 923, 927 (D.C.Cir.2000) ("Courts have denominated evidence of the same crime 'intrinsic' and evidence of 'other' crimes 'extrinsic.' * * * So far as we can tell, the only consequences of labeling evidence 'intrinsic' are to relieve the prosecution of Rule 404(b)'s notice requirement and the court of its obligation to give an appropriate limiting instruction upon defense counsel's request"). See also United States v. Green, 617 F.3d 233, 248–49 (3d Cir.2010) ("[W]e will reserve the 'intrinsic' label for two narrow categories of evidence. First, evidence is intrinsic if it 'directly proves' the charged offense. * * * Second, 'uncharged acts performed contemporaneously with the charged crime may be termed intrinsic if they facilitate the commission of the charged crime.' But all else must be analyzed under Rule 404(b).") (citations and internal quotation marks omitted); United States v. Gorman, 613 F.3d 711, 719 (7th Cir.2010) ("the inextricable intertwinement doctrine has since become overused, vague, and quite unhelpful"); State v. Nelson, 791 N.W.2d 414, 423 (Iowa 2010) ("the inextricably intertwined doctrine should be used infrequently and as a narrow exception").

7.   *Flight evidence.* See United States v. Levine, 5 F.3d 1100, 1107 (7th Cir.1993) ("The probative value of flight as evidence of a defendant's guilt depends on the degree of confidence with which four inferences can be drawn: (1) from behavior to flight; (2) from flight to consciousness of guilt; (3) from consciousness of guilt to consciousness of guilt concerning the crime charged; and (4) from consciousness of guilt concerning the crime charged to actual guilt of the crime charged.").

8.   *Rule 403.* The mere fact that the prosecutor states that other crimes evidence is offered for one of the purposes listed in Rule 404(b) does not guarantee admissibility. The evidence must also meet the test of relevancy. Under Rule 403, relevant evidence is admissible so long as its probative value is not "substantially outweighed" by the danger of unfair prejudice, etc. The Rule places the burden of showing unfair prejudice on the opponent of the evidence. Should a different test be applied when considering other crimes evidence? See discussion in Kuhns, The Propensity to Misunderstand the Character of Specific Acts Evidence, 66 Iowa L.Rev. 777 (1981). What other factors should be considered by the judge? See Gleason v. State, 57 P.3d 332, 342 (Wyo.2002) (One factor is the "comparative enormity of the charged crime and the prior bad act. When the prior act is a more serious offense than the charged crime, the introduction of that act will tend to place the defendant in a different and unfavorable light.").

9.   A classic example of other acts evidence is Whitty v. State, 149 N.W.2d 557 (Wis.1967). In *Whitty*, the defendant was charged with taking indecent liberties with a 10–year–old girl. The state's evidence showed that the accused approached the victim and asked for help in finding a black and white rabbit which he had lost. She went with him to a house where the indecent liberties were taken. The Wisconsin Supreme Court held that evidence had been properly admitted that the accused had approached an 8–year–old girl on the evening before the incident in question and told her he

was looking for a black and white rabbit and was about to take indecent liberties with her when he was frightened off. For what purpose or purposes might such evidence have been admitted? How much proof of the earlier occurrence should have been required?

UNITED STATES V. MILLER

United States Court of Appeals, Seventh Circuit, 2012.
673 F.3d 688.

HAMILTON, CIRCUIT JUDGE.

In April 2008, acting on a tip from a confidential informant, police obtained a search warrant and then raided a home where defendant Shariff Miller and several other people were staying. After apprehending Miller on his way out the side door, police searched the house and found several guns and a quantity of crack cocaine. The cocaine and a pistol were found close to some of Miller's personal effects in a room where he was alleged to be staying. Miller was tried and convicted of three offenses: possessing more than five grams of crack cocaine with intent to distribute * * *, possession of a firearm in furtherance of a drug crime * * *, and possession of a firearm by a convicted felon * * *. He was sentenced to a total of twenty years in prison.

* * *

III. *Evidence of Prior Intent to Distribute Cocaine*

The government's use of Miller's eight-year-old conviction for possession of cocaine with intent to distribute was far more problematic, and the admission of that evidence here requires reversal of his conviction on the two drug-related charges. Miller was caught in 2000 with crack cocaine and pled guilty to felony possession with intent to distribute. At that time, the cocaine was also packaged in small plastic bags inside larger plastic bags—though Miller was of course not unusual in packaging drugs for sale in this way. When officers searched the house on April 21, 2008, they found crack cocaine packaged in plastic bags on the bed in Miller's alleged room. They also found a scale and similarly packaged cocaine in shoe boxes that also contained some of Miller's personal papers. Miller has never argued that the bags of drugs—some of which had price tags attached—were not intended for distribution. His defense at trial was instead that, despite the proximity to his personal effects, the drugs were not in fact his and he was not staying in the room where the drugs and pistol were found.

Because felon status is an element of the felon-in-possession charge, the government needed to prove that Miller was a convicted felon. The fact of his prior conviction of an *unspecified* felony was admissible for that purpose. E.g., Old Chief v. United States, 519 U.S. 172 (1997).[7] The

---

7   [*Old Chief* is discussed at Chapter 7, Section C, supra. Ed.]

Z.   nature and underlying story of that prior conviction, however, were not
necessary or admissible merely to prove felon status—although they
might have been admissible for another purpose under Rule 404(b). Id.
The jury would learn that Miller was a convicted felon, but the
government also wanted to use the details of the prior conviction for
possessing cocaine with intent to distribute. The district court wisely
waited until after opening statements and cross-examination of a key
witness to learn the defense theory before deciding whether to admit the
details under Rule 404(b). * * *

& 3.   Miller contends, and we agree, that the drug crime evidence from
2000 was substantially more prejudicial than it was probative. The only
purpose for which it could have been used by the jury here was to draw an
a.   impermissible propensity inference. The arguments presented in this case
suggest that admission of prior drug crimes to prove intent to commit
present drug crimes has become too routine. Closer attention needs to be
paid to the reasons for using prior drug convictions—to lessen the danger
that defendants like Miller will be convicted because the prosecution
invited, and the jury likely made, an improper assumption about
propensity to commit drug crimes.

B.   Rule 404(b) does not provide a rule of automatic admission whenever
bad acts evidence can be plausibly linked to "another purpose," such as
knowledge or intent, listed in the rule. The Rule 402 requirement of
relevance and the unfair prejudice balancing inquiries of Rule 403 still
apply with full force. United States v. Beasley, 809 F.2d 1273, 1279–80
(7th Cir.1987); * * * This must be so because the "list of exceptions in
Rule 404(b), if applied mechanically, would overwhelm the central
principle. Almost *any* bad act evidence simultaneously condemns by
besmirching character and by showing one or more of 'motive,
opportunity, intent, preparation, plan, knowledge, identity, or absence of
mistake or accident', not to mention the 'other purposes' of which this list
is meant to be illustrative." *Beasley*, 809 F.2d at 1279 (emphasis in
original). Rule 404(b) requires a case-by-case determination, not a
categorical one. The trial judge must balance the relevance of the
proposed use of the evidence to the case—and the evidence's relevance to
that proof—against the high risk that the evidence will also tend to
establish bad character and propensity to commit the charged crime.
When, as was true here, intent is not meaningfully disputed by the
defense, and the bad acts evidence is relevant to intent only because it
implies a pattern or propensity to so intend, the trial court abuses its
discretion by admitting it.

The parties debate whether intent is always at issue, and whether
the answer to that question depends on the "general intent" or "specific
intent" nature of the crimes charged. We explained in United States v.
Hicks, 635 F.3d 1063, 1071 (7th Cir.2011) * * *, that if a mere claim of

innocence were enough to automatically put intent at issue, the resulting exception would swallow the general rule against admission of prior bad acts. * * * Identification of an at-issue, non-propensity Rule 404(b) exception is a necessary condition for admitting the evidence, but not a sufficient condition. Whether the intent element is specific or general for the charged crimes, all bad acts evidence must be balanced for probative value and unfair prejudice. * * *

It is helpful to distinguish between two aspects of the relevance inquiry. The first aspect concerns whether a Rule 404(b) exception, like intent, is "at issue"—that is, whether the issue is relevant to the case. For example, knowledge may not be at issue at all where the charge is a strict liability offense, so that knowledge is not even an element of the crime. Similarly, while intent is at least formally relevant to all specific intent crimes, intent becomes more relevant, and evidence tending to prove intent becomes more probative, when the defense actually works to deny intent, joining the issue by contesting it. When, as in this case, the drugs in question were clearly a distribution quantity, the packages had price tags, and the defendant did not deny they were intended for distribution by someone, intent was "at issue" in only the most attenuated sense.

The second aspect of relevance is not concerned with whether the government must prove intent or how difficult that proof might be. This second inquiry assumes intent is relevant to the case and asks whether the bad acts evidence offered is relevant to and probative of intent, without being too unfairly prejudicial by invoking a propensity inference. In other words, can the government fairly use this evidence to meet its burden of proof on this issue? Intent can be "automatically at issue" because it is an element of a specific intent crime, but the prior bad acts evidence offered to prove intent can still be completely irrelevant to that issue, or relevant only in an impermissible way. Here, even though the purpose of proving "intent" was invoked, the bad acts evidence was not probative of intent except through an improper propensity inference.

* * *

The government argues that Miller's prior conviction is relevant to prove intent here, but has not satisfactorily explained why this is true. Miller's defense, that the drugs were not his, has nothing to do with whether he intended to distribute them. He did not argue that he intended to consume rather than sell the drugs, or that he lacked knowledge of cocaine or how to sell it. Either argument would have better joined a genuine issue of intent or knowledge. Rather, the only conceivable link between the defense and intent here would also be true of almost any defense Miller might raise; by pleading not guilty, Miller necessarily contradicted the government's belief that he intended to distribute the drugs. But as we said in *Hicks*, if merely denying guilt opens the door wide to prior convictions for the same crime, nothing is left of the Rule 404(b) prohibition.

We recognize that many of our cases approve the admission of prior drug-dealing crimes to show intent in drug-dealing prosecutions, despite the fact that, of the Rule 404(b) other purpose exceptions, intent is the exception most likely to blend with improper propensity uses. E.g., United States v. Perkins, 548 F.3d 510, 514–15 (7th Cir.2008) (admitting three prior convictions for possession or delivery of small amounts of cocaine to show knowledge and intent with regard to small amounts of cocaine); United States v. Hearn, 534 F.3d 706, 712–13 (7th Cir.2008) (admitting prior drug conviction to rebut defendant's assertion that the quantity of drugs was too small to indicate intent to distribute); United States v. Hurn, 496 F.3d 784, 787–88 (7th Cir.2007) (admitting prior drug conviction to rebut an innocent bystander defense); United States v. Best, 250 F.3d 1084, 1091–93 (7th Cir.2001) (admitting prior conviction for possession in a rented house to show intent, knowledge, and absence of mistake with regard to a crack house). But in each of these cases, after discussing relevance of the evidence to intent, the court balanced the asserted probative value of the evidence against its potential for unfair prejudice. We have never approved admission of bad acts evidence solely because it was formally relevant to intent and intent was "at issue."

There may be enough cases affirming such admissions, however, that in cases charging specific-intent drug crimes, the admission of prior drug convictions may have come to seem almost automatic. It is not. * * *

Confusion and misuse of Rule 404(b) can be avoided by asking the prosecution exactly how the proffered evidence should work in the mind of a juror to establish the fact the government claims to be trying to prove. Here, Miller claimed that the drugs found in the shoe box and on the bed were not his, that he was in effect an innocent bystander. Witnesses told the jury about Miller's arrest and conviction for dealing drugs in 2000. The government defends use of that evidence on the ground that it showed his intent to distribute drugs in 2008. How, exactly, does Miller's prior drug dealing conviction in 2000 suggest that he intended to deal drugs in 2008? When the question is framed this way, the answer becomes obvious, even though implicit: "He intended to do it before, ladies and gentlemen, so he must have intended to do it again." That is precisely the forbidden propensity inference.

* * *

Later, in addressing Miller's post-trial motions, the district court also suggested that the prior conviction was probative of intent because of the identical packaging of the drugs at issue. Miller's prior conviction cannot be admissible merely because it was for the same crime or because it also involved drugs in small plastic bags. Pattern evidence is propensity evidence, and it is inadmissible unless the pattern shows some meaningful specificity or other feature that suggests identity or some other fact at issue. *Beasley*, 809 F.2d at 1278 ("Unless something more than a pattern and temporal proximity is required, the fundamental rule is gone. This is why 'pattern' is not listed in Rule 404(b) as an exception."). Crack cocaine in small plastic bags is far too generic in drug cases to make a pattern of two acts over eight years probative of anything beyond propensity. * * *

The danger that the jury would unfairly rely on Miller's prior drug dealing to suggest his current guilt was not cured in this case by the court's limiting instruction to the jury: "You may consider this evidence only on the questions of knowledge, intent and in deciding whether the defendant's testimony is truthful in whole, in part, or not at all." A considerable literature argues for and against, and attempts to measure empirically, the effectiveness of this sort of pattern jury instruction. Some have suggested that such instructions are incoherent even to bright laypeople. We leave the broader questions for another day. For this case, it is enough to note that when the government cannot explain how the prior conviction relates to the question of intent without resorting to a propensity inference, it would be unfair to expect the jury to do so based only on this instruction.[8]

This reasoning requires us to reverse Miller's convictions for possession of cocaine with intent to distribute and the closely related possession of a firearm in furtherance of a drug trafficking crime. Miller's conviction for being a felon in possession of a firearm, however, stands on sufficiently independent evidence that we are satisfied, with "fair assurance," that the government's case on that charge was not substantially affected by the improper Rule 404(b) evidence. There was undisputed evidence that Miller's fingerprint was on one of the rifles, and he admitted handling it. Propensity evidence may be harmless with regard to unrelated counts while requiring reversal of others. * * *

NOTES AND QUESTIONS

1. *Pattern, Plan, and Scheme.* The principal case discusses "pattern" evidence. Rule 404(b) mentions "plan." How does this differ from propensity? See State v. Verde, 296 P.3d 673, 682–83 (Utah 2012) ("Evidence of a general plan to commit crimes with common features is perilously close to evidence of a general disposition to commit crime. Any difference between the two concepts 'is extremely subtle and quite likely to be lost on a jury.' * * * There is no suggestion of a prior, conscious resolve on Verde's part to formulate an

---

[8] Rather than leaving juries to decode for themselves how they may properly consider admissible bad acts evidence "on the questions of knowledge and intent," we encourage district judges to add to the pattern instruction a case-specific explanation of the permissible inference— with the requisite care not to affirmatively credit that inference. * * * If a suitable explanation cannot be drafted without invoking a propensity inference, the evidence may not in fact be admissible.

overarching grand design encompassing both the charged and uncharged offenses.") (emphasis added).

2. *Disputed issues.* The principal case requires a disputed issue. See also United States v. Williams, 577 F.2d 188, 191 (2d Cir.1978) ("other crimes evidence is inadmissible to prove intent when that issue is not really in dispute"); Robbins v. State, 88 S.W.3d 256, 260 (Tex.Crim.App.2002) ("[I]n Texas a simple plea of not guilty usually does not make issues such as intent a relevant issue of consequence for purposes of determining the admissibility of relationship evidence under Rule 404(b)."). Other courts, however, reject this approach. See United States v. Matthews, 431 F.3d 1296, 1311–12 (11th Cir.2005) ("Matthews's 1991 arrest for distribution of cocaine was relevant to the intent at issue in the charged conspiracy to distribute cocaine."; The "precise difficulty of proving intent in conspiracies is what creates the presumption that intent is always at issue."); United States v. Miller, 725 F.2d 462, 466 (8th Cir.1984) (prosecution need not await the defendant's denial of intent before offering evidence of similar acts). See Leonard, The Use of Uncharged Misconduct Evidence to Prove Knowledge, 81 Neb.L.Rev. 115, 148 (2002) ("Though weak judicial analysis of the admissibility of uncharged misconduct to prove knowledge can be found in many types of cases, it is perhaps most commonly represented in drug-related prosecutions, particularly those charging possession of illegal drugs with intent to distribute.").

3. *Stipulations.* See United States v. Jemal, 26 F.3d 1267, 1274 (3d Cir.1994) ("District courts should generally deem prior bad acts evidence inadmissible to prove an issue that the defendant makes clear he is not contesting. * * * [H]owever, * * * to succeed, the defendant's proffer to stipulate must be comprehensive and unreserved, completely eliminating the government's need to prove the point it would otherwise try to establish using 404(b) evidence.").

4. *Stipulations revisited.* In *Old Chief v. United States*, discussed in Chapter 7, Section C, *supra*, the Supreme Court wrote: "[If] there were a justification for receiving evidence of the nature of prior acts on some issue other than status (i.e., to prove motive, opportunity, intent, preparation, plan, knowledge, identity, or absence of mistake or accident), Rule 404(b) guarantees the opportunity to seek its admission." 519 U.S. at 190. See also United States v. Williams, 238 F.3d 871, 876 (7th Cir.2001) (In a case involving intent to distribute cocaine, the court stated: "[A]s the other circuits to consider this issue after *Old Chief* have held, we believe that *Old Chief* counsels that a defendant's offer to stipulate unequivocally to an element of an offense, such as those demonstrating knowledge or intent, does not render the Government's evidence of prior crimes that are relevant to those elements inadmissible under Rule 404(b)."). But see State v. Verde, 296 P.3d 673, 681 (Utah 2012) ("Absent any legitimate explanation for the prosecution's rejection of the defendant's offer to stipulate, we view this rejection to reinforce the conclusion that the prosecution's purpose was not to tell a legitimate narrative to the jury but instead to present an improper one. So,

while the state was free to reject Verde's offer to stipulate, it was not free to distance itself from the probative implications of that decision, which in our view thoroughly undermine the State's position on appeal.").

5. *Instructions.* One federal appellate court stated that the trial judge "must carefully identify, in its instructions to the jury, the specific factor named in the rule that is relied upon to justify admission of the other acts evidence, explain why that factor is material, and warn the jurors against using the evidence to draw the inferences expressly forbidden in the first sentence of Rule 404(b)." United States v. Spikes, 158 F.3d 913, 929 (6th Cir.1998). Can a jury follow such an instruction? Is the proposed instruction in the principal case effective?

6. *Malice (drunk driving).* See United States v. Tan, 254 F.3d 1204, 1209 (10th Cir.2001) ("[I]ntent is at issue here. In fact, it appears to be *the* issue. In addition, there is no evidence in this case from which Defendant's malice can be readily inferred other than his numerous prior drunk driving convictions."); United States v. Fleming, 739 F.2d 945, 949 (4th Cir.1984) ("[T]he driving record was relevant to establish that defendant had grounds to be aware of the risk his drinking and driving while intoxicated presented to others. It thus was properly admitted."). What about lesser offenses? See United States v. Leonard, 439 F.3d 648 (10th Cir.2006) (in a vehicular homicide case, court upheld use of 15 traffic citations, including 9 for driving with a suspended license, 2 for failing to appear for traffic citation hearings, and 2 for moving violations); People v. Caban, 927 N.E.2d 1050, 1053 (N.Y.2010) (Negligent homicide: "When the issue is criminal negligence, a prior similar act for which defendant has been punished shows more than propensity; a defendant who is repeatedly negligent in the same way may be found to be unable or unwilling to learn from her mistakes—and thus to be guilty not just of deviation, but of 'gross deviation,' from reasonable care. The prior conduct is thus directly relevant to the extent of defendant's negligence in the case on trial—to her mens rea.").

7. *Lack of mistake or accident.* See United States v. Knope, 655 F.3d 647, 657 (7th Cir.2011) ("The [online] chats show that Knope had expressed interest in having sex with minors in the past, that he had attempted to meet with at least one minor (Alyssa) for this purpose, and that he attempted to distinguish between actual minors and others who might pose as minors on the internet. These facts undermined Knope's defense that his chats with Maria were harmless fantasy and that he believed that she was over eighteen years old. Therefore, the evidence was relevant to establishing Knope's knowledge, intent, and lack of mistake."); United States v. Bowie, 232 F.3d 923, 930 (D.C.Cir.2000) ("Evidence that Bowie possessed and passed counterfeit notes on a prior occasion was relevant because it decreased the likelihood that Bowie accidentally or innocently possessed the counterfeit notes on May 16."); State v. Kuehn, 728 N.W.2d 589, 602 (Neb.2007) ("When a defendant asserts that a child's injuries were accidental, the defendant has placed in issue whether the injuries were indeed the result of an accident. * * * The evidence of prior incidents in which Cameron [10 months old] was

injured or ill while in Kuehn's care was properly admitted.") (citation omitted).

8. *Inconsistent results?* In United States v. Curtin, 443 F.3d 1084 (9th Cir.2006), the accused was convicted of traveling across state lines with intent to have sex with a minor (14–year–old girl) and use of the Internet to attempt to persuade a minor to have sex. When he was arrested approaching a police decoy, his PDA contained over 140 stories about adults having sex with children. The court held the evidence inadmissible because possession of lawful reading material is not the type of conduct contemplated by Rule 404(b) and possession of lawful reading material was not similar to the actual criminal conduct charged. The court distinguished an earlier case, United States v. Allen, 341 F.3d 870 (9th Cir.2003), in which the defendants were charged with violating federally protected rights on the basis of race and religion. The court upheld the admissibility of "skinhead and white supremacist evidence," including color photographs of the defendant's tattoos (e.g., swastikas), Nazi-related literature, group photographs including some of the defendants (e.g., in "Heil Hitler" poses and standing before a swastika that they later set on fire), and other skinhead paraphernalia. Are there meaningful differences between *Curtin* and *Allen*?

UNITED STATES V. WOODS

United States Court of Appeals, Fourth Circuit, 1973.
484 F.2d 127.

WINTER, CIRCUIT JUDGE:

Martha L. Woods was found guilty by a jury of murder in the first degree and seven other charges of assault with intent to murder, attempt to murder, and mistreatment of her eight-month-old pre-adoptive foster son, Paul David Woods. [Federal jurisdiction was based on the claim that the alleged crimes took place on an army base.]

* * *

Beginning August 4, 1969, a bizarre series of events occurred. Twice on that date, and once again on August 8, August 13, and August 20, Paul suffered instances of gasping for breath and turning blue from lack of oxygen. Each time he responded to mouth-to-mouth resuscitation, except on August 20, when he went into a coma which persisted until September 21, when he died at an age of slightly more than seven months. On each of these occasions the evidence indicated that Paul had been in Mrs. Woods' custody, and only Mrs. Woods had had access to him. On each occasion prior to August 20, Paul was taken to the hospital. On the first occasion, he was immediately released because an examination disclosed that he was apparently well. On the other occasions, even after several days' observation, no reason for his cyanosis or respiratory difficulties could be discovered.

To prove that Paul's death was neither accidental nor the result of natural causes, the government presented the testimony of a forensic pathologist, Dr. DiMaio, who, based upon Paul's medical history, the records of his various hospitalizations, and the results of an autopsy which the pathologist had performed after Paul's death stated that Paul's death was not suicide or accident and that he found no evidence of natural death. Dr. DiMaio expressed his opinion as one of seventy-five percent certainty that Paul's death was homicide caused by smothering. Dr. DiMaio explained his twenty-five percent degree of doubt as being the possibility that Paul died naturally from a disease currently unknown to medical science, and he agreed that his doubt was a "reasonable doubt" within the standard definition given by the court.

Next, the government showed that beginning in 1945 Mrs. Woods had had custody of, or access to, nine children who suffered a minimum of twenty episodes of cyanosis. Seven children died, while five had multiple episodes of cyanosis. * * *

Defendant's contention that the government failed to prove the corpus delicti beyond a reasonable doubt rests upon the three propositions that (a) proof of the corpus delicti for culpable homicide requires proof of death of the alleged victim _and_ proof that that death occurred by means other than suicide, accident or natural causes, in short, that death occurred by a criminal act, (b) evidence of other crimes is not admissible to show that the death of the alleged victim occurred by homicide, but (c) even if admissible, the proof of other crimes presented by the government in the instant case was not so clear and convincing as to permit the jury to find that Paul's death was homicide.

* * *

* * * [W]e proceed directly to discuss whether proof of the prior events concerning the other children was legally admissible to prove that (a) Paul's death was the result of culpable homicide and not of natural causes, and (b) defendant was the perpetrator of the crime.

We state, at the outset, that if otherwise legally admissible, we have no doubt about the relevance of the proof and its probative effect to establish both propositions. The evidence of what happened to the other children was not, strictly speaking, evidence of other crimes. There was no evidence that defendant was an accused with respect to the deaths or respiratory difficulties of the other children, except for Judy. Simultaneously with her trial for crimes alleged against Paul, defendant was being tried for crimes alleged against Judy, but there was no direct proof of defendant's guilt and the district court ruled that the circumstantial evidence was insufficient for the government to have proved its case. Thus, with regard to no single child was there any legally sufficient proof that defendant had done any act which the law forbids. Only when all of the evidence concerning the nine other children and Paul is considered collectively is the conclusion impelled that the probability that some or all of the other deaths, cyanotic seizures, and respiratory deficiencies were accidental or attributable to natural causes was so remote, the truth must be that Paul and some or all of the other children died at the hands of the defendant. We think also that when the crime is one of infanticide or child abuse, evidence of repeated incidents is especially relevant because it may be the only evidence to prove the crime. A child of the age of Paul and of the others about whom evidence was received is a helpless, defenseless unit of human life. Such a child is too young, if he survives, to relate the facts concerning the attempt on his life, and too young, if he does not survive, to have exerted enough resistance that the marks of his cause of death will survive him. Absent the fortuitous presence of an eyewitness, infanticide or child abuse by suffocation would largely go unpunished. See Minnesota v. Loss, 295 Minn. 271, 204 N.W.2d 404 (1973).

B. *Admissibility of Evidence Generally.* The government and the defendant agree that evidence of other crimes is not admissible to prove that an accused is a bad person and therefore likely to have committed the crime in question. Indeed, the rule is beyond dispute: Michelson v. United States, 335 U.S. 469, 475–476 (1948) * * *. Defendant argues that while there are certain recognized exceptions to this rule, the instant case cannot be fitted into any of them, emphasizing that corpus delicti is not an exception. McCormick on Evidence § 190 (Cleary Ed.1972). The government, in meeting this approach, contends that the evidence was admissible on the theory that it tended to prove (a) the existence of a continuing plan,[9] (b) the handiwork or signature exception,[10] (c) that the acts alleged in the indictment were not inadvertent, accidental, or unintentional, and (d) the defendant's identity as the perpetrator of the crime. We are inclined to agree with the defendant that the evidence was not admissible under the scheme or continuing plan exception because there was no evidence that defendant engaged in any scheme or plan, or, if so, the objective or motive. The evidence may have been admissible under the lack of accident exception, although ordinarily that exception is invoked only where an accused admits that he did the acts charged but denies the intent necessary to constitute a crime, or contends that he did the acts accidentally. McCormick, p. 450. However, in State v. Lapage, 57 N.H. 245, 294 (1876), there was dictum that under certain circumstances where several children of the same mother had died, evidence of the

---

[9]   Makin v. Attorney General of New South Wales, [1894] A.C. 57 (P.C.1893) (N.S.Wales) and Regina v. Roden, 12 Cox Cr. 630 (1874) support this view. *Makin* was a prosecution for infanticide by a professional foster parent. Evidence that the bodies of twelve other infants, who had been entrusted to him with inadequate payment for their support, was held admissible. In *Roden,* a prosecution for infanticide by suffocation, evidence that three of defendant's other children died in her lap, was held admissible.

[10]   Rex. v. George Joseph Smith, [1914–15] All.E.R.Rep. 262 ("Brides of Bath" case) and People v. Peete, 28 Cal.2d 306, 169 P.2d 924 (1946) permitted proof of unique methods of previous homicides to establish guilt of the accused.

previous deaths ought to be admissible because of the unlikelihood of such deaths being accidental. Finally, the identity exception is not really an exception in its own right, but rather is spoken of as a supplementary purpose of another exception. McCormick, p. 451.

The handiwork or signature exception is the one which appears most applicable, although defendant's argument that cyanosis among infants is too common to constitute an unusual and distinctive device unerringly pointing to guilt on her part would not be without force, were it not for the fact that so many children at defendant's mercy experienced this condition. In the defendant's case, the "commonness" of the condition is outweighed by its frequency under circumstances where only defendant could have been the precipitating factor.

While we conclude that the evidence was admissible generally under the accident and signature exceptions, we prefer to place our decision upon a broader ground. Simply fitting evidence of this nature into an exception heretofore recognized is, to our minds, too mechanistic an approach.

McCormick, in listing the instances in which evidence of other crimes may be admissible, cautions "that the list is not complete, for the range of relevancy outside the ban is almost infinite * * *." Id. 448. And then, McCormick states:

> [S]ome of the wiser opinions (especially recent ones) recognize that the problem is not merely one of pigeon-holing, but one of balancing, on the one side, the actual need for the other crimes evidence in the light of the issues and other evidence available to the prosecution, the convincingness of the evidence that the other crimes were committed and that the accused was the actor, and the strength or weakness of the other crimes evidence in supporting the issue, and on the other, the degree to which the jury will probably be roused by the evidence to overmastering hostility.

Id. p. 453. This approach is one which finds support in [numerous cases including Dirring v. United States, 328 F.2d 512 (1 Cir.1964)]. These cases stand for the proposition that evidence of other offenses may be received, if relevant, for any purpose other than to show a mere propensity or disposition on the part of the defendant to commit the crime, provided that the trial judge may exclude the evidence if its probative value is outweighed by the risk that its admission will create a substantial danger of undue prejudice to the accused.

As we stated at the outset, we think that the evidence would prove that a crime had been committed because of the remoteness of the possibility that so many infants in the care and custody of defendant would suffer cyanotic episodes and respiratory difficulties if they were not induced by the defendant's wrongdoing, and at the same time, would prove the identity of defendant as the wrongdoer. Indeed, the evidence is so persuasive and so necessary in case of infanticide or other child abuse by suffocation if the wrongdoer is to be apprehended, that we think that its relevance clearly outweighs its prejudicial effect on the jury. We reject defendant's argument that the proof was not so clear and convincing that its admissibility should not be sustained. As we stated at the outset, if the evidence with regard to each child is considered separately, it is true that some of the incidents are less conclusive than others; but we think the incidents must be considered collectively, and when they are, an unmistakable pattern emerges. That pattern overwhelmingly establishes defendant's guilt.

C. *Admissibility of Evidence to Prove Corpus Delicti.* For the reasons stated, the sufficiency of the evidence of (a) what happened to the other children, (b) proof of the fact of Paul's death, and (c) the government's expert testimony of the probable cause of death, to prove the corpus delicti was apparent. Defendant argues strenuously, however, that even if admissible for other purposes, the law does not permit evidence of prior acts to be employed to prove the corpus delicti * * *.

Counsel have not cited, nor have we found, any case which considers whether or not prior acts can be used to establish the corpus delicti of murder, but the law seems clear that prior acts can be proved to establish the corpus delicti of arson,[11] and also that a confession may be relied upon to prove the corpus delicti if there is other corroborating evidence, short of independent proof of the corpus delicti, to prove the reliability of the confession. The rule in cases of arson would seem equally applicable in cases of murder, and the rule with regard to confessions bears a close analogy to the use of other acts to prove murder. We therefore hold that in the instant case proof of the incidents involving other children was admissible to prove the corpus delicti of murder and other acts of child abuse. * * *

Affirmed.

WIDENER, CIRCUIT JUDGE (dissenting):

I respectfully dissent from the majority opinion as it relates to evidence of incidents concerning other children, and especially as it holds

[11] State v. Schleigh, 210 Or. 155, 310 P.2d 341, 348 (1957) (repeated fires by spontaneous combustion unlikely; eight fires along one country road immediately after defendant, his father and others drove by show "a deliberate plan to set them"); State v. Smith, 221 S.W.2d 158 (Mo.1949) (proof of prior fire was admissible to show that fire charged in indictment was incendiary); People v. Wolf, 334 Ill. 218, 165 N.E. 619 (1929) (proof of separate fires admissible to prove corpus delicti); State v. Ritter, 288 Mo. 381, 231 S.W. 606 (1921) (proof of prior fires admissible to prove the corpus delicti); People v. Jones, 123 Cal. 65, 55 P. 698 (1898) (proof of burning of other buildings admissible to prove corpus delicti). Contra: Kahn v. State, 182 Ind. 1, 105 N.E. 385 (1914).

such evidence may be considered proof of the *corpus delicti* (which may include the criminal agency of the accused). * * *

While I do not agree with the majority that the evidence of prior occurrences was admissible under either the signature exception or to show lack of accident, since the majority gives no reason for its holding, the reason for my dissent will not be further mentioned here. * * *

I am convinced that the defendant here did not receive a fair trial because the evidence of prior occurrences, fitting no recognized exception to the general rule, was so highly inflammatory and prejudicial, as well as being neither plain, nor clear, nor convincing, that it should not have been admitted for any purpose, much less for all purposes. * * *

In applying a balancing test, the considerations confronting the district court may be summarized succinctly: assuming an exception to the rule is applicable, before admitting evidence of prior acts or crimes, the court should determine, first, whether the evidence is relevant; secondly, whether the evidence is unduly prejudicial notwithstanding its relevancy; and, thirdly, having met both prior tests, whether the evidence is truly needed by the prosecution.[12] * * *

NOTES AND QUESTIONS

1. *Doctrine of chances.* How many other incidents is sufficient? In the "Brides in the Bath" case, cited in a footnote in *Woods*, two other wives had drowned while taking baths. Compare the principal case with Tucker v. State, 412 P.2d 970 (Nev.1966):

> On May 7, 1957, Horace Tucker telephoned the police station and asked a detective to come to the Tucker home in North Las Vegas. Upon arrival the detective observed that Tucker had been drinking, was unshaven, and looked tired. Tucker led the detective to the dining room where one, Earl Kaylor, was dead on the floor. Kaylor had been shot several times. When asked [what] had happened, Tucker said that he (Tucker) had been sleeping in the bedroom,

---

[12] The majority alters the balance by weighing the relevance of the evidence plus the need for the evidence against the prejudice resulting to the defendant. It also applies the test without first finding an exception to gain admissibility. The infirmity in this formulation is that as the need for the evidence increases, the probative value may decrease and still the evidence will be admissible. This new test given effect by today's ruling, elevates need, if accompanied by the slightest probative value, to the status of an exception in compelling cases. This, of course, coupled with the absence of a limiting instruction, gives no protection to the defendant in a case already clouded with emotional issues.

Indeed, I find that such emphasis on need comes perilously close to a rule in the law of evidence that the end may justify the means, and my inhibition at such a departure from the common law tradition is at the root of my dissent. While the executive branch of government must frequently, of necessity, make the decision as to need as against consequences in securing evidence, such a balance should not be given dignity by the courts in ascertaining admissibility absent an exception to the general rule. The use of need in any balancing test properly ought to be limited to applying, in a negative sense, an exclusionary rule, not to bolstering admissibility. McCormick on Evidence, 1954 Ed. § 157, clearly points this out, and advocates that the test be used as a further limit on admissibility, not as an extension of it.

awakened, and walked to the dining room where he noticed Kaylor lying on the floor. Upon ascertaining that Kaylor was dead, Tucker telephoned the police station. He denied having killed Kaylor. A grand jury conducted an extensive investigation. Fifty-three witnesses were examined. However, an indictment was not returned as the grand jury deemed the evidence inconclusive. No one, including Tucker, has ever been charged with that killing.

On October 8, 1963, Horace Tucker telephoned the police and asked a sergeant to come to the Tucker home in North Las Vegas; that there was an old man dead there. Upon arrival the sergeant noticed that Tucker had been drinking. The body of Omar Evans was dead on the couch in the living room. Evans had been shot. Tucker stated that he (Tucker) had been asleep, awakened, and found Evans dead on the couch. Subsequently Tucker was charged with the murder of Evans. * * *

See also State v. Verde, 296 P.3d 673, 685–86 (Utah 2012) ("Many courts, in Utah and elsewhere, have employed this 'doctrine of chances' reasoning to analyze the relevance of uncharged misconduct evidence when a defense of fabrication [in a child sexual abuse case] has been raised. * * * A charge of fabrication is insufficient by itself to open the door to evidence of any and all prior bad acts. As with other questions arising under rule 404(b), care and precision are necessary to distinguish permissible and impermissible uses of evidence of prior bad acts, and to limit the factfinder's use of the evidence to the uses allowed by rule."); Imwinkelried, *United States v. Woods*: A Story of the Triumph of Traditions, in Evidence Stories 59 (Lempert ed., 2006).

2. *Unenumerated purposes.* Should evidence of other acts be admitted which purportedly is not offered for the purpose of proving that the accused acted in accordance with his character, but is not within any of the purposes listed in Rule 404(b)? Judge Widener in his dissent in *Woods* used the term "exclusionary" rule. Is that still good law? See United States v. Tan, 254 F.3d 1204, 1208 (10th Cir.2001) ("The list of proper purposes is illustrative, not exhaustive, and Rule 404(b) is considered to be 'an inclusive rule, admitting all evidence of other crimes or acts except that which tends to prove *only* criminal disposition.' "). For examples of cases in which evidence has been admitted other than for an enumerated purpose, see United States v. Verduzco, 373 F.3d 1022, 1029 (9th Cir.2004) ("Other circuits agree with us that Rule 404(b) evidence may be admitted to refute a duress defense."); United States v. Tafoya, 757 F.2d 1522 (5th Cir.1985) (tax evasion prosecution; evidence of three attempted killings for hire admitted to show that the accused "did something to earn the income * * * he failed to report"); State v. Jeffers, 661 P.2d 1105 (Ariz.1983) (prior murder attempt upon victim offered in homicide prosecution to rebut opening statement claim by counsel that the accused had an "abiding love" for the victim which would not allow him to cause her harm).

There are a few crimes, such as domestic violence, that make the victim's state of mind an essential element of the offense and prior other acts may be relevant for this purpose. E.g., State v. Drake, 734 N.E.2d 865, 868 (Ohio Ct.App.1999) ("The act of previously putting Eva Drake's arm in a cast is admissible to show Eva Drake's state of mind when appellant made the threats in this case. The second statement also goes to Eva Drake's state of mind. The third statement is directly relevant to the threat to put Eva Drake in the river. These two previous threatening statements and one prior act are not generalized bad acts from appellant's past.").

3.   *Defendant's involvement in the other act.* In Huddleston v. United States, 485 U.S. 681 (1988), the Supreme Court held that proof that the accused participated in the other act is governed by Rule 104(b) (conditional relevance). In other words, only a prima facie case need be shown. The Court rejected cases that had required the "preponderance of evidence" or "clear and convincing evidence" standard. *Huddleston* is in Chapter 1, Section A, supra. *Huddleston* adopts a lax standard. See United States v. Bergrin, 682 F.3d 261, 279 (3d Cir.2012) (holding that under *Huddleston*, trial judge does not assessing credibility of witness testifying about other act; "By discounting Pozo's testimony based on a lack of corroboration and questions about credibility, the Court usurped the jury's role."); United States v. Dickerson, 248 F.3d 1036, 1047 (11th Cir.2001) (" 'the uncorroborated word of an accomplice * * * provides a sufficient basis for concluding that the defendant committed extrinsic acts admissible under Rule 404(b)' "). Some states have rejected *Huddleston*. See Minn.R.Evid. 404(b) ("the other crime, wrong, or act and the participation in it by a relevant person are proven by clear and convincing evidence"); James v. State, 152 P.3d 255, 257 (Okla.Crim.App.2007) (clear and convincing evidence); Bigpond v. State, 270 P.3d 1244, 1250 (Nev.2012) (clear and convincing evidence).

4.   *Acquittal.* May the prosecution introduce evidence of an alleged past crime where the defendant has been acquitted of that crime? While the United States Supreme Court has held there is no constitutional impediment to the use of such evidence, Dowling v. United States, 493 U.S. 342 (1990), some courts have nevertheless refused to permit its admission. See, e.g., State v. Scott, 413 S.E.2d 787 (N.C.1992). If there is no constitutional impediment, on what grounds might such evidence be excluded? Rule 403? Collateral estoppel? With regard to the application of collateral estoppel, see State v. Aparo, 614 A.2d 401 (Conn.1992).

If the evidence is admitted, does the defendant have the right to introduced the fact of acquittal? See People v. Ward, 952 N.E.2d 601, 611 (Ill.2011) ("[B]arring the admission of the acquittal evidence was an abuse of the trial court's discretion."). Moreover, an acquittal instruction may be required by some state (but not federal) courts. See Kinney v. People, 187 P.3d 548, 555–56 (Colo.2008) ("Generally, federal circuits have found no abuse of discretion when trial courts have not given the requested instruction. * * * State courts, on the other hand, have generally ruled that under the facts of a particular case, a defendant was entitled to an acquittal instruction such that it was an abuse of discretion when no instruction was given. These state courts have ruled that fairness requires that an acquittal instruction be given when the jury is likely to have learned that the defendant was charged criminally for the prior act * * *.").

5. *Notice.* A notice requirement was added to Federal Rule 404(b) in 1991. See also Ky.R.Evid. 404(c) (notice required in criminal cases). Compare United States v. Blount, 502 F.3d 674, 678 (7th Cir.2007) ("The real question, though, is whether the notice was adequate. Mindful of Rule 404(b)'s requirement that the government provide the 'general nature' of the evidence, courts have not been stringent in this regard."), with United States v. Carrillo, 660 F.3d 914, 927 (5th Cir.2011) (The "document only gives notice of the government's intent to introduce evidence of Carrillo's 'repeated distribution of methamphetamine * * * over a period of 12 to 18 months up until the time of [Carrillo's and Rodriguez's] arrest.' The document does not give any notice about evidence of prior incidents of Carrillo's *personal use* of methamphetamine, as opposed to *distribution.* Therefore, the record establishes that the government did not comply with Rule 404(b)'s notice requirement.").

6. *Reform proposal.* Ross, "He Looks Guilty": Reforming Good Character Evidence to Undercut the Presumption of Guilt, 65 U.Pitt.L.Rev. 227 (2004) (arguing for both the reduction of Rule 404(b) evidence and the expansion of good character evidence by the defense).

D. THE INTERSECTION OF RELEVANCY AND ANCILLARY POLICY CONSIDERATIONS

Introductory Note

Two rationales generally support Rules 407–410. Take, as an example, offers of compromise under Rule 408. One rationale is that the evidence is of marginal relevancy. See 4 Wigmore, Evidence § 1061, at 36 (Chadbourn rev. 1972) ("The true reason for excluding an offer of compromise is that it does not ordinarily proceed from and *imply a specific belief that the adversary's claim is well-founded,* but rather a belief that the further prosecution of that claim, whether well-founded or not, would in any event cause such annoyance as is preferably avoided by the sum offered.") But see Advisory Committee Note to Rule 408 ("The validity of this position will vary as the amount of the offer varies in relation to the claim and may also be influenced by other circumstances."). The second is that the admission of the evidence would contravene some important ancillary policy—here the promotion of settlement of suits short of trial that would be discouraged if offers of compromise were freely admissible. See 2 McCormick, Evidence § 266 (7th ed. 2013). What are the ancillary policy considerations behind Rules 407, 409 and 410?

A hearsay issue arises regarding evidence covered by Rules 407–410, although it is typically easily resolved. Often the evidence is nonhearsay because the actor or declarant had no intention to make an assertion (see Rule 801(a)). In other circumstances, where an intention to assert may be found, the evidence is treated as an admission (see Rule 801(d)(2)). In both situations, the hearsay objection is overcome, see Chapter 13, infra, and admissibility depends upon relevancy and ancillary policy questions. Nevertheless, the status of such evidence as admissions has caused some legal scholars to treat the questions raised in this section as part of the study of hearsay. See 2 McCormick, Evidence ch. 25 (7th ed. 2013).

IN RE AIR CRASH DISASTER

United States Court of Appeals, Sixth Circuit, 1996.
86 F.3d 498.

[In August 1987, a Northwest Airlines flight crashed during takeoff from the airport in Detroit, Michigan killing all passengers and crew and two bystanders. Plaintiffs sued Northwest Airlines and McDonnell Douglas, the plane's manufacturer. The airline and manufacturer filed claims against each other for contribution and indemnity. A jury found Northwest one hundred percent liable, and the trial court permitted McDonnell Douglas to recover money it paid to settle certain claims. Northwest appealed, and the Sixth Circuit affirmed.]

BOGGS, CIRCUIT JUDGE.

* * *

We now address Northwest's claims that it is entitled to a new trial because the district court erred by excluding various items of evidence from the jury's consideration.

Excluding Evidence of Northwest's Post–Accident Rewiring of the Central Aural Warning System

Northwest claims that the district court erred in excluding evidence relating to its post-accident rewiring of the plane's Central Aural Warning System ("CAWS"). After the accident, Northwest rewired all of its fleet of MD–80 aircraft (the model that crashed) so that the CAWS Fail Light would illuminate upon loss of input power. Northwest sought to introduce the fact of this rewiring as circumstantial evidence that the system had been unsafe.

The district court granted McDonnell Douglas's Motion *in Limine* No. 3 and excluded the evidence. The court reasoned that Northwest's post-accident rewiring of the CAWS was inadmissible under Fed.R.Evid. 407 as a subsequent remedial measure offered to prove culpable conduct of a tortfeasor. Order, October 30, 1989, at 11.

According to Northwest, the court erred in excluding the evidence of the rewiring because it was relevant and not excludable under Rule 407. Northwest contends that its rewiring evidence was not precluded under

Rule 407 "because [the Rule] does not apply to subsequent measures taken by a third party." Northwest Br. at 51. Inasmuch as Northwest is not a third party to this suit, its claim appears to be that Rule 407 does not bar evidence of subsequent remedial measures taken by a party other than the one with primary responsibility for the subject of the remedial measures (a "non-responsible party"). Northwest also argues that even if the court's Rule 407 ruling was correct, later developments at trial opened the door to admission of the CAWS rewiring.

We agree with Northwest that its rewiring of the CAWS fell within the federal rules' broad definition of relevance. Fed.R.Evid. 401. Under Rule 401, evidence is relevant if it has "any tendency to make the existence of any fact that is of consequence to the determination of the action more probable or less probable than it would be without the evidence." Whether the CAWS was improperly wired was an issue of consequence in this case. Northwest's rewiring of the CAWS is circumstantial evidence, if only of a weak and suspect sort, that the CAWS as it existed at the time of the accident was not foolproof.

However, it is not clear that the court erred by excluding the fact of the rewiring under Rule 407 as a subsequent remedial measure. There is nothing in the text of Rule 407 that limits its application to measures by a "responsible" party—i.e., measures by a party against whom the evidence is offered. The Rule provides,

> When, after an event, measures are taken which, if taken previously, would have made the event less likely to occur, evidence of the subsequent measures is not admissible to prove negligence or culpable conduct in connection with the event. This rule does not require the exclusion of evidence of subsequent measures when offered for another purpose, such as proving ownership, control, or feasibility of precautionary measures, if controverted, or impeachment.

Fed.R.Evid. 407. Although the Rule specifically removes from its reach evidence of remedial measures offered for purposes other than to prove negligence or culpable conduct, it nowhere embraces the limitation Northwest urges. By its terms, the Rule seems to exclude evidence of remedial measures regardless of who undertook them.

It is true that exceptions to the Rule have developed. *E.g., Werner v. Upjohn Co., Inc.,* 628 F.2d 848, 855 (4th Cir.1980). Northwest cites several cases in which courts declined to exclude evidence of subsequent remedial measures. Some cases contain language saying that "Rule 407 applies only to subsequent remedial measures taken voluntarily *by the defendant." Raymond v. Raymond Corp.,* 938 F.2d 1518, 1524 (1st Cir.1991). *Accord Middleton v. Harris Press & Shear, Inc.,* 796 F.2d 747, 751 (5th Cir.1986). In each of these cases, however, the remedial measure was taken, not by a plaintiff, but by someone who was not a party to the suit. * * * There is no direct support for Northwest's argument that it should have been able to introduce evidence of its own voluntary remedial measures to prove the culpability of an adversary.

Courts have been wary to restrict the scope of Rule 407. "[W]e should not be too quick to read new exceptions into the rule because by doing so there is a danger of subverting the policy underlying the rule." *Werner,* 628 F.2d at 856. In this case, there is neither clear textual authority nor legislative history supporting an exception. *See Bradley v. Austin,* 841 F.2d 1288, 1293 (6th Cir.1988) (unambiguous language in a statute is conclusive of its meaning).

One might argue that the purpose of Rule 407, at least as that purpose is commonly understood, is not directly served by the application of the rule to the present circumstances. Allowing evidence of subsequent remedial measures by someone suing the manufacturer of an allegedly faulty product does not *deter* subsequent safety precautions. In fact, allowing such evidence might *encourage* subsequent precautions, as the value of a subsequent remedial measure to the buyer of the faulty product would include its safety effect *and* its tactical advantage during litigation.

However, it would be wrong to construe the function of Rule 407 so narrowly. Independent of its effect on safety upgrades by alleged tortfeasors, the rule bars a class of evidence that is very poor proof of negligence or defectiveness. 2 Weinstein's Evidence § 407, 13–14 (finding in the unreliability of such evidence a primary purpose of the rule). There is nothing that makes evidence of a subsequent remedial measure by a plaintiff (or someone in the position of a plaintiff, like Northwest) better proof of culpable conduct than evidence of a remedial measure by a defendant. Indeed, measures taken by a plaintiff—especially one contemplating litigation—strike us as *more* dubious because of the possibility that the plaintiff is only "repairing" an item in order to create helpful evidence.

We believe that the district court's interpretation of Rule 407 was correct and that the rule can encompass situations like the one presented here. The text of the rule is unqualified, and there is precedent cautioning us from creating exceptions. Furthermore, although applying the rule to measures taken by plaintiffs does not serve the rule's purpose to encourage safety precautions, it does serve the rule's purpose of excluding inherently unreliable evidence. Therefore, we hold that the district court did not err by excluding the evidence of the CAWS rewiring.

Northwest's argument that later developments at trial opened the door to admission of the CAWS rewiring evidence is also unpersuasive. Northwest contends that MDC opened the door in its cross-examination of Northwest witness Rodney Peters. Our review of the record indicates that while McDonnell Douglas examined Peters about Northwest's "fleet campaign" to remove and replace all CAWS circuit breakers from its MD–

80s, it did not question Peters about the rewiring of the CAWS. Northwest argues that the replacement of the circuit breakers was nonetheless sufficiently related to the rewiring of the CAWS to open the door to the use of the CAWS rewiring evidence. In our view, however, the replacement of the breakers and the rewiring of the CAWS to warn the crew when the system is not receiving any power are not so related that McDonnell Douglas's examination of Peters on the former opens the door to Northwest's examination of him on the latter. Therefore, we agree with the district court that McDonnell Douglas did not open the door to admission of Northwest's rewiring of the CAWS.[13]

We note that, even if the exclusion of the rewiring evidence was an error, the error was harmless. The parties stipulated into evidence the feasibility of rewiring the CAWS Fail Light. 199 Transcript 130–32 (jury instructions). Furthermore, the court permitted Northwest to introduce factual and expert opinion testimony critical of McDonnell Douglas's wiring scheme. *See* Northwest Br. at 10 (summarizing).

Excluding Evidence that the Flight Director Was Defective

Northwest claims that the court erred in excluding from evidence Exhibits 1106, 1107, 1123–29, and 1138, which related to the Honeywell flight directors used on MD–83, MD–87, and MD–88 aircraft. According to Northwest, the court erred in excluding these exhibits because they were relevant to its case and not otherwise inadmissible.

The court granted in part MDC's Motion *in Limine* No. 8 and excluded the exhibits as irrelevant, unduly prejudicial, and, except as to Exhibit 1126, concerned with subsequent remedial measures. Order, October 30, 1990, at 12–13. The court held that the exhibits were irrelevant under Rule 401, because they related to different model flight directors used on heavier planes with different engines. For much the same reason, the court excluded the exhibits on grounds that they would confuse the jury and result in an unwarranted expenditure of time, under Rule 403. Furthermore, the court held that the exhibits (except for Exhibit 1126) were inadmissible under Rule 407 on grounds that "remedial measures taken before an accident are excludable for the same policy considerations involved in a standard Rule 407 ruling." *Ibid.*

In disagreement with the district court's holding, we believe that the exhibits at issue have at least minimal relevance. Although many of the

---

[13] Although the court did not exclude the evidence of Northwest's rewiring the CAWS under Rule 403, we believe that exclusion of this evidence may alternatively be affirmed under that Rule. Rule 403 provides that "evidence may be excluded if its probative value is substantially outweighed by the danger of unfair prejudice, confusion of the issues, or misleading the jury * * *." In our view, the danger of unfair prejudice from this evidence was great—especially because the repairs in question were made by a non-responsible party in whose interest it was to minimize its liability and maximize the liability of its codefendant—and substantially outweighed the minimal probative worth of the evidence. *See Bauman v. Volkswagenwerk Aktiengesellschaft,* 621 F.2d 230, 233 (6th Cir.1980) (noting extent of prejudice caused by evidence of remedial measures).

exhibits related to different and newer models of flight directors than the model aboard flight 255, what the parties call the "control laws," or computer program, for the takeoff mode of all the flight directors were identical. 177 Transcript at 57. The exhibits lent at least some support to Northwest's claim that the flight director was defective.

Nor do we agree with the district court that Rule 407 bars the exhibits' admission. Rule 407 bars the admission of evidence of remedial measures taken after an event that would have made the event less likely to occur. Fed.R.Evid. 407. Here, however, the evidence was of measures taken *after* the design of a product but *before* the accident. Inasmuch as the exhibits related to pre-accident changes to the flight director, they fell outside the reach of Rule 407. * * *

Moreover, Rule 407 does not preclude evidence of subsequent measures offered for purposes of impeachment. Fed.R.Evid. 407; *see Patrick v. South Cent. Bell Tel. Co.,* 641 F.2d 1192, 1196–97 (6th Cir.1980). McDonnell Douglas's flight director expert, Jean–Jacques LeBlond, testified that the flight director was not defective and represented the state of the art, 76 Transcript at 56–57, and that there was no reason for McDonnell Douglas to advise operators about any "error" in the control laws operating immediately after takeoff, 79 Transcript at 72. In our view, Northwest was entitled to impeach LeBlond's testimony by showing that McDonnell Douglas, in later models, modified the design of the flight director aboard Flight 255 to correct deficiencies. *See Muzyka v. Remington Arms Co., Inc.,* 774 F.2d 1309, 1313–14 (5th Cir.1985) (originally excluded evidence of post-accident design change should have been admitted for impeachment purposes once the nature of the evidence presented by defendant manufacturer became apparent).

In the final analysis, however, we cannot conclude that the district court abused its discretion in excluding the exhibits under Rule 403 because their probative value was substantially outweighed by the danger of unfair prejudice, confusion of the issues, or misleading the jury. Though not irrelevant, the exhibits in question were of marginal probative value, because they related to different model flight directors used on heavier planes with different engines. The exhibits would have complicated the proceedings, and could easily have confused the jury.[14]

Excluding an Internal Memorandum from McDonnell Douglas

Northwest claims that the court erred in excluding Exhibit 297, an internal memorandum from McDonnell Douglas dated two months after the crash. The short memorandum says that McDonnell Douglas recommended to the buyers of DC–10 planes that they should perform a

---

[14] [The court also ruled that if exclusion under Rule 403 was erroneous, it was harmless. Ed.]

"takeoff warning system check" prior to takeoff. The memorandum says that this recommendation was made in response to "the Chicago Accident"—a reference to the crash on takeoff of an American Airlines DC–10 in Chicago in 1979. The memorandum also says that a "takeoff warning system check" was not recommended to buyers of MD–80 planes because the CAWS Fail Light should catch similar problems.

The district court excluded the exhibit on two grounds. We agree with Northwest that one reason given by the court—that the memorandum, because it mentioned the Chicago accident, was more prejudicial than probative under Fed.R.Evid. 403—was improper. It may be true that the jury would have been swayed unfairly by the fact that another McDonnell Douglas plane crashed on takeoff. It may also be true that the fact that a "takeoff warning systems check" was not recommended is of little probative value—both because other systems checks were recommended and not performed by the Crew, and because there was evidence that the Crew pulled the circuit breaker connected to the CAWS. However, the district court did not consider the possibility that the memorandum could be redacted. We find this a minor error.

The error made no difference in the case, however. First, the court's other reason for excluding the exhibit is legitimate: Rule 407. The memorandum, written shortly after the crash, explains why the additional check was not recommended for the MD–80 model. It is obvious that the memorandum is part of a discussion about whether McDonnell Douglas should recommend the check in the future—and such a change in policy is a subsequent remedial measure within the meaning of Fed.R.Evid. 407. *Hall v. American Steamship Co.,* 688 F.2d 1062, 1066 (6th Cir.1982) (steamship's choice to follow new safety policy after an accident not admissible evidence of negligence under Rule 407). Second, the probative value of the memorandum, as mentioned above, is minimal. Even if one of the precautions neglected by the flight crew was not necessary, others certainly were. Our review of the record indicates that the neglect of these other, far more important, precautions constituted the heart of McDonnell Douglas's case, and the crux of the jury's verdict.

* * *

It is impossible to summarize completely in a concluding paragraph the results of the legal system's effort to cope with a tragedy of this magnitude. The deaths of 156 people resulted in five years of proceedings below, nineteen months of trial, 199 volumes of trial transcript, over 4000 evidentiary exhibits, and more than 3000 record entries reproduced in 77 volumes of Joint Appendix in our court, comprising 18,922 pages and eight videocassettes.

At the end of the day, however, we are firmly convinced that Chief Judge Cook and the jury provided a fair trial based on permissible rulings of law. In the words of Justice Minton, "There must be an end to litigation

someday * * *." *Ackermann v. United States,* 340 U.S. 193, 198 * * *
(1950). The judgment of the district court is AFFIRMED.

NOTES AND QUESTIONS

1. *Applicability of rule to actions of others or involuntary remedial measures by defendant.* The first issue examined by *Air Crash Disaster* is whether Rule 407 excludes subsequent remedial measures other than those done voluntarily by the defendant. The conduct by another party to the suit, Northwestern, presented the issue in an unusual situation. More commonly the action is taken by an entity that is not party to the suit, where courts often find the Rule inapplicable. See Diehl v. Blaw–Knox, 360 F.3d 426, 429–30 (3d Cir.2004) (finding policy argument and therefore Rule inapplicable to conduct of non-parties); Buchanna v. Diehl Mach., Inc., 98 F.3d 366, 370–71 (8th Cir.1996) (same); Stevens v. Novartis Pharm. Corp., 247 P.3d 244, 266 (Mont.2010) (same). Also, when the change is made by the defendant but done involuntarily, such as when ordered by a "superior authority," such as a government agency, courts sometimes also find Rule 407 inapplicable. See State v. Elementis Chem., Inc., 887 A.2d 1133, 1139 (N.H.2005) (observing that for identical state rule to apply the act must be voluntarily undertaken by the defendant). The law is in some conflict. Compare O'Dell v. Hercules, 904 F.2d 1194, 1204 (8th Cir.1990) (adopting exception), with Werner v. Upjohn, 628 F.2d 848, 859–60 (4th Cir.1980) (rejecting exception). Finally, as *Air Crash Disaster* illustrates, when the conduct at issue is that of a third party, its relevance may be more problematic, and it may be excluded for that reason. See, e.g., Raymond v. Raymond Corp., 938 F.2d 1518, 1524–25 (1st Cir.1991).

2. *Meaning of "event."* In *Air Crash Disaster*, which was decided in 1996, the court was construing a Rule that stated "[w]hen, after an event, [remedial] measures are taken * * *." It concluded that a remedial measure taken after the design of the product but before the accident was not covered by Rule 407 as a "subsequent" remedial measure. It defined the critical "event" as the accident, not the design. In 1997, Rule 407 was amended consistent with this ruling. It now begins, "[w]hen measures are taken that would have made an earlier injury or harm less likely to occur * * *." The Advisory Committee Note explains: "Evidence of measures taken by the defendant prior to the 'event' do not fall within the exclusionary scope of Rule 407 even if they occurred after the manufacture or design of the product."

3. *Scope of "impeachment" exception. Air Crash Disaster* acknowledges that Rule 407 lists impeachment among the purposes for which evidence of subsequent remedial measures may be received. Given the broad potential scope of impeachment, including the right of parties to impeach their own witnesses, the impeachment exception, if construed liberally, could constitute a particularly effective means of circumventing the protections of the Rule. Commentators and courts, as a consequence, argue for a narrow application of this exception. As distinguished from simple contradiction where the limited probative value is typically outweighed by the risk of prejudice and

confusion, testimony in terms of "superlatives—e.g., 'this is the safest product on the market—' * * * provides a more direct and probative form of impeachment, which justifies a limited exception to the Rule." 2 Saltzburg, Martin & Capra, Federal Rules of Evidence Manual § 407.02[8], at 407–12 (10th ed. 2011). Compare Doe v. Wal–Mart Stores, Inc., 558 S.E.2d 663, 677 (W.Va.2001) (recognizing the danger in permitting impeachment, but holding it proper under the circumstances because of the extreme claim that no greater care was possible), with United Tool Rental, Inc. v. Riverside Contracting, Inc., 260 P.3d 156, 160–61 (Mont.2011) (narrowly applying impeachment exception where party made no exaggerated claim and simply denied negligence).

4. *Practices admitted under common law.* Under common law development, the general rule excluding evidence of subsequent remedial measures was subject to numerous exceptions, e.g., evidence of subsequent installation of crossing flasher admitted to rebut defendant's contention that wigwag signal was safest, Daggett v. Atchison, T. & S.F.Ry., 313 P.2d 557 (Cal.1957); evidence of design modification admitted to show feasibility of using safeguard or changing design, Boeing Airplane Co. v. Brown, 291 F.2d 310 (9th Cir.1961); evidence admitted that defendant road contractor put out warning signs after accident to show defendant was in control of locus, Powers v. J.B. Michael & Co., 329 F.2d 674 (6th Cir.1964). Exceptions of these types are continued by the final sentence of the Rule. Indeed, as Professor Michael Graham put it, "In practice the exception to Rule 407 may fairly be said to come close to swallowing up the rule—evidence as to the subsequent remedial repair is very frequently brought to the attention of the jury for a purpose other than to establish negligence or culpable conduct. Since the efficiency of * * * a limiting instruction, Rule 105, is extremely suspect, policy considerations underlying Rule 407 are greatly compromised." 3 Graham, Handbook of Federal Evidence § 407.1, at 609 n.9 (7th ed. 2012).

5. *"When disputed."* Rule 407 after restyling states that evidence of subsequent remedial measures may be admitted to prove feasibility "if disputed" ("controverted" formerly use). The federal courts are divided on when exactly a claim is "disputed." Compare In re Joint Eastern District & Southern District Asbestos Litigation, 995 F.2d 343, 345–46 (2d Cir.1993) (defendant did not affirmatively contest feasibility issue so it was not controverted), with Meller v. Heil Co., 745 F.2d 1297, 1300 n.7 (10th Cir.1984) (absent stipulation as to feasibility, it was controverted).

6. *Self-critical analysis.* In *Air Crash Disaster*, a memorandum that the court described as "part of a discussion about whether McDonnell Douglas should recommend the [takeoff warning check] in the future" was excluded because such a change in policy is a protected remedial measure. Protecting this memorandum resembles protection sometimes given by courts to an organization's post-accident internal investigative report, labeled self-critical analysis. The Massachusetts Supreme Court ruled that such reports should not be treated differently than the remedial measures they help bring about because "[t]o do so would discourage potential defendants from

conducting such investigations, and so preclude safety improvements, and frustrate the salutary public policy under the rule." Martel v. Massachusetts Bay Transp. Auth., 525 N.E.2d 662, 664 (Mass.1988). Whether such investigatory reports should be protected by the Rule is the subject of lively debate in federal and state courts, although the weight of authority appears to oppose such an extension of the Rule. See, e.g., Granberry v. Jet Blue Airways, 228 F.R.D. 647, 650–51 (N.D.Cal.2005); City of Bethel v. Peters, 97 P.3d 822, 825–27 (Alaska 2004); Fox v. Kramer, 994 P.2d 343, 355–61 (Cal.2000). For discussion of self-critical analysis "privilege," see generally 2 Imwinkelried, The New Wigmore: Evidentiary Privileges § 7.8 (2d ed. 2010) (noting three schools of thought on the scope of a self-critical analysis privilege: first, a broad privilege to be invoked by any entity (§ 7.8.1), second, a more limited privilege for medical peer review (§ 7.8.2), and third, a more limited privilege for environmental audits (§ 7.8.3)).

7. *Broad construction of "remedial measure."* Other situations comparable to subsequent remedial measures, in that either it is unclear whether the conduct or statement may fairly be construed as an admission or their evidentiary use may discourage desirable conduct, are fairly numerous. This is probably the true rationale of cases excluding evidence of the discharge of an employee after an accident. See, e.g., Rynar v. Lincoln Transit Co., 30 A.2d 406 (N.J.1943). Indeed, the broad language of Rule 407 protects not only subsequent repairs but also installation of safety devices, changes in company rules, and the discharge of employees. 2 McCormick, Evidence § 267 (7th ed. 2013). By contrast, company rules in effect at the time of the occurrence have generally been held admissible against the company. Most of the cases involve railroad companies, and the quasi-public nature of their rules likely affected the decisions. Danbois v. New York Central R.R., 189 N.E.2d 468 (N.Y.1963); Winters, The Evidentiary Value of Defendant's Safety Rules in a Negligence Action, 38 Neb.L.Rev. 906 (1959).

8. *Application to product liability cases.* In 1997, Federal Rule 407 was amended to make clear that it applied to product liability cases in addition to those based on negligence. Where the Rule had previously excluded evidence to prove "negligence" or "culpable conduct," it now also excludes evidence that proves "a defect in a product or its design" and "a need for a warning or instruction." Prior to the amendment, most of the federal circuit courts had already adopted this position. By contrast, a number of state courts, although apparently a dwindling number, follow the lead of the California Supreme Court in Ault v. International Harvester Co., 528 P.2d 1148 (Cal.1974), and do not extend the protection of their version of Rule 407 to product liability cases. See Scott v. Dutton–Lainson–Co., 774 N.W.2d 501, 507 (Iowa 2009) (applying statute that incorporates *Ault*'s rationale); but see First Premier Bank v. Kolcraft Enters., Inc., 686 N.W.2d 430, 449–52 (S.D.2004) (applying the Rule to products liability case and describing the shift in the states against the result in *Ault*).

In Forma Scientific, Inc. v. Biosera, Inc., 960 P.2d 108, 115–16 (Colo.1998), the Colorado Supreme Court articulates the rationales for non-application to strict liability cases:

> We agree with the reasoning expressed in *Ault* as well as in pre-amendment decisions of the Eighth and Tenth Circuits. We decline to follow the newly amended Rule 407 which is now in direct opposition to our reading of CRE 407 and the Colorado Committee Comment following that rule.
>
> The explicit language of CRE 407—that "evidence of the subsequent measures is not admissible to prove negligence or culpable conduct"—does not permit the exclusion of evidence of remedial actions in strict liability claims premised on design defect. This is true because the manufacturer's conduct, whether culpable or negligent, is not germane in a strict liability action. *See Camacho v. Honda Motor Co.,* 741 P.2d 1240, 1246 n.7 (Colo.1987) ("[I]n accordance with one of the underlying goals of strict liability of easing the burden of proof for a plaintiff injured by a defective product, the plaintiff is relieved of the requirement of proving the manufacturer's negligence."). What is germane in such a case is the nature of the manufactured product itself. *See id.* at 1246. ("The primary focus must remain upon the nature of the product under all relevant circumstances rather than upon the conduct of either the consumer or the manufacturer."). Thus, any attempt to stretch the meaning of "culpable conduct" or negligence to include design defect products liability claims would be disingenuous at best.
>
> Next, we agree with *Ault* and its progeny that the public policy rationale underlying CRE 407—not to discourage entities from taking safety precautions—is largely inapplicable in the context of today's mass manufacturers. It is unreasonable to presume that a mass manufacturer of goods takes its cue from evidentiary rules rather than considerations of consumer safety and/or the safety of consumer property. Even taking a less rosy view, recognizing that not all manufacturers necessarily place the best interests of their consumers at the forefront, market forces generally operate to compel manufacturers to improve their products. This is amply demonstrated by the actions taken here by Forma to protect its consumers' property interests by lessening the risk of inadvertent shut offs of its ultra-cold temperature freezers.

See generally Carver, Subsequent Remedial Measures 2000 and Beyond, 27 Wm. Mitchell L.Rev. 583 (2000).

MCINNIS V. A.M.F., INC.

United States Court of Appeals, First Circuit, 1985.
765 F.2d 240.

PETTINE, SENIOR DISTRICT JUDGE.

The plaintiff * * * claims that the trial judge erred in admitting evidence that Patricia McInnis had released Florence Poirier from liability for the accident prior to instituting suit against the defendants. She argues that the release was offered to show that Mrs. Poirier, not the defendants, had in fact caused the amputating injury to her leg. Such evidence, she urges, is barred by Federal Rule of Evidence 408, which precludes admission of settlement agreements to prove the validity or invalidity of a claim or its amount. The defendants counter that the admission of the release does not prove the "invalidity" of the plaintiff's claim against them, but rather "narrows the issues" to allow the jury to determine what injuries were actually caused by the defendants. * * * We concur with the plaintiff/appellant and hold that the trial court erred in admitting the release. We further find that this error was prejudicial, and therefore necessitates a new trial.

* * *

[McInnis] asserted that the defendants were liable for her injuries on theories of negligent design of the motorcycle's clutch housing, negligent failure to warn, and strict products liability. Specifically, plaintiff claimed that when Poirier struck her motorcycle, it fell on its left side where the clutch housing is located. When it fell, she argued, the clutch housing shattered, exposing her leg to the sharp jagged edges and whirring gears which caused the almost complete severance of her limb. A.M.F. * * * defended the action in part on the theory that the plaintiff's severe injury was actually and immediately caused by the impact with the bumper of the Poirier vehicle, and had already occurred before the motorcycle fell.

* * *

The Trial Court Erred in Admitting the Release

Rule 408 of the Federal Rules of Evidence governs the admissibility of evidence of compromise offers or agreements in federal trials. * * * The exclusion of evidence of settlement offers is justifiable on two grounds. First, the rule illustrates Congress' desire to promote a public policy favoring the compromise and settlement of claims by insulating potential litigants from later being penalized in court for their attempts to first resolve their dispute out of court. Second, such evidence is of questionable relevance on the issue of liability or the value of a claim, since settlement may well reflect a desire for peaceful dispute resolution, rather than the litigants' perceptions of the strength or weakness of their relative positions. *See* Fed.Rule of Evid. 408, advisory committee note.

In analyzing the impact of Rule 408 on the admissibility of the Poirier release, we shall initially allay any doubts that the Rule applies to cases which are posturally like the one now before us. The settlement agreement at issue here was entered into between a litigant and a third party, rather than between the two litigants themselves. The Advisory Committee Note clearly acknowledges that the policies underlying the exclusionary rule are equally applicable to such a situation. The note states that:

> While the rule is ordinarily phrased in terms of offers of compromise, it is apparent that a similar attitude must be taken with respect to completed compromises when offered against a party thereto. *The latter situation will not, of course, ordinarily occur except when a party to the present litigation has compromised with a third person.* * * * (emphasis added).

In the context of settlements between a litigant and a third party, it is true that Rule 408 is more commonly invoked to bar the admission of agreements between a defendant and a third party to compromise a claim arising out of the same transaction as the one being litigated. * * * If the policies underlying Rule 408 mandate that settlements may not be admitted against a defendant who has recognized and settled a third party's claim against him, it is axiomatic that those policies likewise prohibit the admission of settlement evidence against a plaintiff who has accepted payment from a third party against whom he has a claim. The admission of such evidence would discourage settlements in either case. In addition, the relevance of the settlement to the validity of the claim cannot logically be considered stronger in the former instance than in the latter. * * * A number of recent federal cases have adopted this position, holding that Rule 408 bars evidence of settlements between plaintiffs and third party joint tortfeasors or former co-defendants. *See Quad/Graphics, Inc. v. Fass,* 724 F.2d 1230, 1235 (7th Cir.1983) (evidence of plaintiff's settlement with two defendants in contract action not admissible at trial of remaining defendants) * * *.

Although Rule 408 bars the admission of evidence of settlement to prove liability or the validity of a claim, it expressly allows such evidence offered for other purposes. * * * A critical inquiry in the instant case, therefore, is for what purpose the Poirier release was admitted at trial. We think it evident from a reading of the trial transcript that the district judge admitted the evidence as tending to prove that it was Mrs. Poirier's collision with the plaintiff, not the shattering of the motorcycle clutch housing, that in fact severed the plaintiff's leg.

The defendants began their case in chief at trial by calling Patricia McInnis to the stand. Their attorney, over strenuous objection by the plaintiff, entered the release into evidence and questioned McInnis at length about its significance. The objective of his line of questioning was manifest—he was attempting to elicit an admission from McInnis that she received $60,000 from Florence Poirier because it was Mrs. Poirier alone who caused her injury. While McInnis persistently maintained that she had received the money because Mrs. Poirier had been responsible for setting the accident in motion, defense counsel repeatedly suggested that the $60,000 represented compensation for the full extent of her injuries. * * *

The trial judge's comments in overruling the plaintiff's objection to the admission of the release further illuminate the purpose of that evidence. The judge stated:

> It seems to me that there's an issue in this case which relates to the question of who caused what, what injuries were sustained as a result of the contact with the Poirier vehicle, and what injuries the plaintiff had were the responsibilities of the defendants in this case; and it may well be that the reliance [sic] represents an admission on the part of the plaintiff. I don't see that it comes within 408 because it's not offered to prove liability or invalidity of the claims or its amount. I'm going to allow it. You may have an exception. * * *

From this record it is apparent that the release was admitted as relevant to the issue of causation in fact.

* * *

Having concluded that the Poirier release was offered as relevant to the issue of causation, we have no difficulty in ruling that the evidence of causation or non-causation is fully subsumed under Rule 408's meaning of validity or invalidity of a claim. Causation in fact is an integral component of a tort claim; without causation there can be no liability. In the instant case, it is obvious that the defendants wanted the jury to infer that Mrs. Poirier would not have paid the significant sum of $60,000 to the plaintiff unless it was she, *and not the defendants,* who had caused the plaintiff's injury. Whether cast in terms of "causation", "responsibility", or the "validity of the claim", the defendants wanted the jury to conclude from the fact of settlement that the defendants could not be held liable for the amputation of the plaintiff's leg. This clearly flouts the most basic policies underlying Rule 408.

Other federal courts have held in closely analogous situations that this type of jury inference is unquestionably improper under the Federal Rule. In *McHann v. Firestone Tire and Rubber Co.,* 713 F.2d 161 (5th Cir.1983), for example, the Fifth Circuit reversed the trial court's admission of a covenant not to sue given by a plaintiff in a products liability action to a third party service station owner. The plaintiff had sued the defendant Firestone Tire for injuries he sustained when a tire on his vehicle exploded, alleging that the defendant had negligently designed and manufactured the tire. *Id.* at 162–3. Firestone introduced evidence at trial that the plaintiff had previously given a covenant not to sue to a service station owner whose employee had mounted the tire. The Fifth Circuit held the covenant inadmissible under Rule 408, since the evidence "might lead the jury to deny [plaintiff's] claim against Firestone on the perception that Green Oaks Exxon would not have paid the substantial sum of $27,000 if it * * * were not the party at fault." *Id.* at 166.

The *McHann* case illustrates the applicability of the policies underlying rule 408 to a situation such as the one now before us. Certainly, the admission of settlement evidence to prove or disprove causation would discourage a plaintiff from settling with one of several potential defendants. In addition, the fact of settlement, as the Advisory Committee has observed, is of questionable relevance to the issue. An innocent third party may settle, even for a large amount, merely to avoid the burdens of litigation. In the instant case, in fact, the Poirier release is even more doubtfully relevant to the causation issue than was the covenant not to sue in *McHann*. Since neither of the parties contests the fact that the Poirier vehicle negligently struck the plaintiff's motorcycle, Mrs. Poirier is liable for the ultimate injury to the plaintiff, whether or not the collision itself was the immediate cause. Under elementary principles of proximate cause, Mrs. Poirier is legally responsible for any harm that could foreseeably result from her tortious act. * * * We think it obvious that it is reasonably foreseeable that once struck by a car, a motorcycle may crash, causing serious bodily injury to its driver. * * * The fact that Poirier settled or the amount she paid, therefore, cannot reasonably be indicative of the harm that was in fact caused by the collision between her car and the motorcycle as opposed to that which was in fact caused by the shattering of the clutch housing.

* * *

The defendants also suggest that they introduced the Poirier release for a purpose other than proving causation—to impeach McInnis' testimony. Specifically, they sought to undermine her assertion that the injury to her leg occurred only after the clutch housing shattered. They wanted the jury to infer that if Patricia McInnis accepted $60,000 from Mrs. Poirier, it was because she believed her to be responsible for the injury. The introduction of the release, then, would allegedly discredit her present claim against the defendants.

Even if the record were not clear, as it is, that the release was admitted to prove causation, the defendants' deft paralogism would still fail. The use of the settlement for this purpose implicitly requires the jury to infer some indicia of causation in fact from the existence of the release; otherwise it would be of no logical relevance to the issue of McInnis' credibility. We cannot permit the defendants to avoid the policies of rule

408 by merely recasting the issue of who caused the injury as an issue of who the plaintiff believed caused it.[15] * * *

NOTES AND QUESTIONS

1.   *Bias. McInnis* excluded a settlement by the plaintiff with a third party, which the court concluded was being used as evidence of the validity of the plaintiff's claim against the remaining defendant. Such settlements with third parties are more frequently encountered when offered "for another purpose" allowed under the Rule—bias. The argument is typically that a witness who is testifying "for" the party with whom the settlement was made was influenced to give favorable testimony by a generous settlement. See Miller v. Marymount Med. Ctr., 125 S.W.3d 274, 278–82 (Ky.2004) (ruling that settlement could be admitted to show bias where expert witnesses changed opinion regarding defendant's liability after settlement). However, while using settlements for this purpose is not prohibited by the Rule, admission is not always permitted. See Graber v. City of Ankeny, 616 N.W.2d 633, 638–41 (Iowa 2000) (use of evidence to show witness' bias held improper based on analysis of circumstances of settlement, effect on testimony, and potential for prejudice). Admissibility is determined by the balancing process of Rule 403.

2.   *Protection for statement of facts beyond the offer.* One of the most significant differences between the protection offered under Rule 408 and its common law antecedents is the treatment of admissions of fact made during settlement efforts. Under common law doctrine, statements of fact, unless either made hypothetically or inseparably connected with the offer, were admissible. Federal Rule 408 excludes evidence of "conduct or a statement made during compromise negotiations" because lack of protection for statements of facts had the tendency to discourage open communications important to successful settlement efforts. See 2 McCormick, Evidence § 266 (7th ed. 2013). *Affiliated Manufacturers*, which follows, reflects a liberal application of such protection by shielding internal documents related to settlement negotiations. Is such an extension warranted or wise?

AFFILIATED MANUFACTURERS, INC. V. ALUMINUM CO. OF AMERICA

United States Court of Appeals, Third Circuit, 1995.
56 F.3d 521.

RESTANI, JUDGE.

Following a trial in this action brought by plaintiff-appellant Affiliated Manufacturers, Inc. ("AMI") alleging additional money was due

---

[15] We also note that the existence of the Poirier release could not have been legally relevant to the issue of McInnis' credibility. As we have already discussed, Mrs. Poirier, by colliding with the motorcycle and instigating the crash, was a proximate, legal cause of the plaintiff's ultimate injury. Since she was jointly liable for the harm, if any, that was caused by the shattering of the clutch housing, the fact that the plaintiff settled with her is hardly inconsistent with a claim that the motorcycle crash in fact caused the amputating injury.

on a contract, the jury returned a verdict in favor of defendant-appellee Aluminum Company of America ("Alcoa") on its counterclaim for failure to satisfy contract specifications and breach of warranties. AMI appeals from the district court's grant of a motion *in limine* brought by Alcoa to exclude certain documents and deposition testimony as evidence of settlement negotiations under Fed.R.Evid. 408. For the reasons set forth herein, we affirm the judgment of the district court.

I.

* * *

The dispute between AMI and Alcoa arose from a contract for design and fabrication of an automated greenline handling system ("the system"). The system built under this contract was never put into production. During the construction of the system, AMI submitted to Alcoa invoices for work not included in the contract. Upon receipt, Alcoa processed the invoices for payment. The parties disagree concerning one unpaid invoice for hardware costs (four screen printers) totalling $280,000, and another unpaid invoice for $208,130 in software costs. These two invoices were submitted by AMI at the end of the project, on April 5, 1990, to the attention of Thomas Pollak ("Pollak"), Alcoa's procurement manager.

Pollak consulted with Alcoa employees Earle Lockwood ("Lockwood") and Phil Kasprzyk ("Kasprzyk") concerning the invoices, because both were closely involved with the project. In memoranda, Lockwood and Kasprzyk each evaluated one of the two invoices from AMI. At a meeting between Pollak, Lockwood and AMI's president, Benson Austin ("Austin"), on May 2, 1990, one topic of discussion was the issue of unpaid invoices, as reflected in handwritten contemporaneous notes.

Alcoa's original motion *in limine* sought exclusion of portions of the Lockwood and Kasprzyk memoranda and a letter from Austin dated June 26, 1990, as well as portions of the meeting notes from May 2, deposition exhibits and transcripts that were not specifically described. At the request of the district court, Alcoa supplied an additional submission detailing twelve items (meeting notes, deposition testimony and letters) for which Alcoa also sought portions excluded from admission at trial. * * *

[The district court ruled portions of thirteen items inadmissible. AMI challenges these rulings.]

II.

* * *

A district court's ruling as to admissibility of evidence is reviewed under an abuse of discretion standard, where the question presented involves the application of the Federal Rules of Evidence. *See In re Paoli*

R.R. Yard PCB Litig., 35 F.3d 717, 749 (3d Cir.1994). To the extent the district court's ruling turns upon an interpretation of Rule 408, it is subject to plenary review. *Id.* Where the trial court has made a factual finding in determining admissibility of evidence, the clearly erroneous standard is applied. *United States v. 68.94 Acres of Land,* 918 F.2d 389, 392 (3d Cir.1990) * * *.

III.

A.   Fed.R.Evid. 408

1.   Evidence of negotiations to settle a disputed claim

AMI contends that the district court erred in its interpretation and application of Rule 408. AMI alleges that the court took an extreme view of the meaning of "settlement negotiations" as contemplated within the rule. AMI asserts that the district court incorrectly found that even an "apparent difference of opinion between the parties" could trigger an exclusion under the rule. *See [Affiliated Mfrs., Inc. v. Aluminum Co. of America, Civ. No. 91–2877, at 7 (D.N.J. Dec. 23, 1993) ("AMI I")]* at 6 * * *. Further, AMI argues that the district court erred in its factual finding that a dispute existed between the parties.

* * * The application of [Rule 408] is limited to evidence concerning settlement or compromise of a claim, where the evidence is offered to establish liability, or the validity or amount of the claim. Additionally, Rule 408 has been interpreted as applicable to an actual dispute, or at least an apparent difference of view between the parties concerning the validity or amount of a claim. 2 Jack B. Weinstein & Margaret A. Berger, *Weinstein's Evidence* ¶ 408[01] at 408–12 (1994); Kenneth S. Brown et al., *McCormick on Evidence* § 266, at 466 (John William Strong ed., 4th ed. 1992). The policy behind Rule 408 is to encourage freedom of discussion with regard to compromise. *See Weinstein's Evidence, supra,* ¶ 408[01] at 408–10.

AMI argues that the case law clearly delineates distinctions as to what constitutes "a claim which was disputed," and characterizes the excluded documents at issue as merely evidencing discussions that had not yet reached the "dispute" stage for Rule 408 purposes. Thus, AMI maintains that Rule 408 is inapplicable here, arguing that the intended construction of Rule 408 is that there must be a threat or contemplation of litigation, that goes beyond conduct or statements made to resolve differences of opinion as to the validity or amount of a claim. AMI relies chiefly upon the holdings from other circuits to support its view that the district court misinterpreted the term "dispute" and misapplied the rule. Alcoa responds that AMI has mischaracterized these decisions, as well as the district court's reasoning, in its discussion of relevant precedent.

In reaching its conclusion to apply the Rule 408 exclusion, the district court reasoned that the Tenth Circuit's application of Rule 408, in

Big O Tire Dealers, Inc. v. Goodyear Tire & Rubber Co., 561 F.2d 1365 (10th Cir.1977), was too restrictive in its establishment of "the point of threatened litigation [as] a clear cut-off point" for application. *AMI I* at 5 (quoting *Big O Tire,* 561 F.2d at 1373). Instead, the district court adopted the view articulated by the court in *Alpex,* 770 F.Supp. at 164–65, finding that the *Alpex* court "considered factors apart from any indicia of threatened litigation." *AMI I* at 5–6. * * *

In *Big O Tire,* a small tire manufacturer that had used the term "Big Foot" in its business was approached by Goodyear Tire, who wished to use the same term for a national ad campaign for a new product. 561 F.2d at 1368. Both parties participated in a series of discussions about how to proceed, and Goodyear sought assurance from Big O Tire that it would not object to such use. *Id.* * * * The district court in *Big O Tire* determined that phone and letter communications between the parties prior to litigation concerning use of the trademark did not fall within the Rule 408 exclusion, as the calls and letters were merely "business communications." *See id.* at 1368, 1372–73. The Court of Appeals for the Tenth Circuit concluded that the district court did not commit manifest error in finding the disputed statements were business communications because the discussions at issue "had not crystallized to the point of threatened litigation." *Id.* at 1373.

To the extent *Big O Tire* establishes a strict standard for application of Rule 408, it was rejected by *Alpex. See* 770 F.Supp. at 164. The plaintiff in *Alpex* held certain rights relating to a patent for video games and pursued a program to combat infringement by sending letters from counsel offering certain alleged infringers the opportunity to settle what plaintiff viewed as meritorious infringement claims. *Id.* at 162. * * * The *Alpex* court determined that certain license agreements reached in the absence of litigation fell within the purview of the Rule 408 exclusion. *Id.* at 165. In its analysis, the *Alpex* court examined various factors in addition to indicia of threat of litigation, that might call for application of the exclusion. *Id.* at 164–65.

We believe that AMI has oversimplified the *Big O Tire* and *Alpex* holdings. Regarding the issue of when a "dispute" between parties exists, the *Alpex* court acknowledged that litigation need not have commenced for Rule 408 to apply. 770 F.Supp. at 164*; see North Am. Biologicals, Inc. v. Illinois Employers Ins.,* 931 F.2d 839, 841 (11th Cir.1991) (finding letter written prior to suit excludable under Rule 408 as offer of settlement). * * * Furthermore, the *Alpex* court did not, as AMI asserts, adopt *in toto* the view that a dispute must "crystallize [ ] to the point of threatened litigation" before evidence of settlement negotiations are excludable. Rather, *Alpex* and other courts make clear that the Rule 408 exclusion applies where an actual dispute or a difference of opinion exists, rather than when discussions crystallize to the point of threatened litigation. *See Alpex,* 770 F.Supp. at 163; *Dallis v. Aetna Life Ins. Co.,* 768 F.2d 1303, 1307 (11th Cir.1985) (citing *Weinstein's Evidence, supra,* ¶ 408[01]) (affirming admission of testimony involving settlement of similar claim between party to action and third party, where no evidence that validity or amount of payment had been in dispute).

Accordingly, we hold that the district court's construction of Rule 408 did not constitute legal error. As a matter of interpretation, the meaning of "dispute" as employed in the rule includes both litigation and less formal stages of a dispute, and this meaning "is unchanged by the broader scope of Rule 408." *Weinstein's Evidence, supra,* ¶ 408[01] at 408–12. The district court properly interpreted the scope of the term "dispute" to include a clear difference of opinion between the parties here concerning payment of two invoices.

The facts of each case bear upon the trial court's exercise of discretion to apply the exclusion. *See Alpex,* 770 F.Supp. at 164–65; *Bradbury v. Phillips Petroleum Co.,* 815 F.2d 1356, 1364 (10th Cir.1987) (holding if application of Rule 408 exclusion doubtful, better practice is to exclude evidence of compromise negotiations). Admittedly, it can be difficult to discern whether an "offer" was made to attempt to "compromise a claim." The existence of a disputed claim as well as the timing of the offer are relevant to making this determination. *Pierce v. F.R. Tripler & Co.,* 955 F.2d 820, 827 (2d Cir.1992). The district court here found that inherent in each of the documents presented for exclusion was the parties' disagreement or dispute as to the amount and the validity of the invoice presented for payment. *AMI I* at 6–14.

The district court found that when viewed in context, the April 5, 1990 letter from Austin at AMI was evidence of a dispute concerning the printer design and software programming. *See id.* at 2–3, 6. As this letter was not among the disputed documents, we need not consider whether a dispute arose as early as April 5. Following receipt of the April 5 letter and invoices, Kasprzyk described to Pollak in his May 1, 1990 memorandum his evaluation of the amount billed by AMI for software and his assessment of the merits of AMI's claim. This is the earliest document in dispute. In this memorandum, Kasprzyk concluded that

> [s]ince the original purchase order for the line did not thoroughly specify the capability of the line, I feel that AMI has a legitimate claim to some software compensation. I feel that AMI should only be compensated for 1/3 of the requested amount since the line does not meet [certain specifications]. I also feel that this is appropriate due to the AMI's overall inferior performance on system software.

AMI characterizes this memorandum as an "evaluation," implying that it did not evidence a dispute under Rule 408. * * * We also need not reach the question of whether the mere existence of an internal evaluation such as this memorandum provides evidence of a dispute. In his deposition Pollak stated that "[i]n preparation for [a May 2 settlement] meeting, I asked Phil Kasprzyk, an Alcoa engineer familiar with the project, his view of the disputed invoices."[16] That Kasprzyk's evaluation was written in order to prepare Pollak for a meeting to discuss a possible compromise necessarily demonstrates that at least as of May 1 there was a dispute. We cannot say that the district court erred in concluding that a dispute existed as of May 1 and that the documents at issue evidenced attempts to compromise the dispute.

2.   *Exclusion of internal memoranda*

AMI's second argument is that the district court erred in applying the Rule 408 exclusion to internal memoranda that were a part of the fifteen items offered for exclusion under Rule 408. AMI argues that the rule only protects conduct and statements during negotiations, and does not protect internal memoranda, or deposition testimony concerning these memoranda. Alcoa responds that such an interpretation and application of Rule 408 would contradict the rule's purpose, serving instead to discourage open settlement discussions.

The district court found both the Lockwood and Kasprzyk memoranda, and testimony concerning these documents, to be eligible for exclusion under Rule 408. *AMI I* at 8–9. The district court declined to adopt the reasoning in *Blue Circle Atl., Inc. v. Falcon Materials, Inc.,* 760 F.Supp. 516, 522 (D.Md.1991), *aff'd without op.,* 960 F.2d 145 (4th Cir.1992), which interpreted Rule 408 to require communication of internal memoranda to an opposing party, and instead relied upon the holding in *Ramada Dev. Co. v. Rauch,* 644 F.2d 1097 (5th Cir.1981). The Court of Appeals for the Fifth Circuit in *Ramada* upheld the district court's exclusion of an internal report "made in the course of an effort to compromise." *Id.* at 1106–07. The Fifth Circuit quoted the text of Rule 408, that *"[e]vidence of conduct or statements made in compromise negotiations is likewise not admissible." Id.* at 1106. In construing this language, the district court here determined that the

> failure of Alcoa to communicate the internal memoranda to AMI is not dispositive in the context of a Rule 408 analysis; rather, any statements prepared by Alcoa representatives that function as the basis for compromise negotiations demonstrate 'evidence of conduct' in compromise negotiations.

AMI I at 8–9. The district court further found that the memoranda served as a basis for calculation of compromise figures. Thus, the court concluded that the Rule 408 exclusion applied. *Id.* at 9.

---

[16] In an affidavit, Austin denied Pollak's statement that one purpose of the May 2 meeting was to attempt settlement of the dispute. As we previously indicated, however, the notes of the May 2 meeting contained mathematical calculations, as well as the terms "software proposal" and "above settlement proposal by Alcoa unacceptable."

First, AMI argues that the legislative history of Rule 408 suggests a different result and that the district court has incorrectly broadened the language of the rule. Second, AMI asserts that the district court should have followed *Blue Circle,* and that the court disregarded an important fact in *Ramada* that narrows its application.

Under the common law, offers of compromise were excluded from evidence, but the exclusion did not extend to "admissions of fact, even though made in the course of compromise negotiations, unless hypothetical, stated to be 'without prejudice,' or so connected with the offer as to be inseparable from it." 10 James Wm. Moore, *Moore's Federal Practice* § 408.01[9] (Daniel R. Coquillette et al. eds., 2d ed. 1995) (Advisory Committee's Note on Proposed Rule 408). Thus, AMI argues, Rule 408 was intended to remedy the common law rule by expanding it merely to include evidence of conduct or statements, but not internal memoranda. *Id.* While Rule 408 was specifically designed to cover admissions of fact, its language is considerably broader than that necessary to accomplish this change.

Next, in *Ramada,* the report sought to be excluded was generated by an architect hired for the purpose of preparing an analysis of defects in the construction of a motel that plaintiff had contracted to have built. 644 F.2d at 1099, 1106. Testimony in *Ramada* indicated that the architect was "commissioned by Ramada to prepare a report that would function as a basis of settlement negotiations regarding the alleged defects in the motel." *Id.* at 1107. Thus, the Fifth Circuit determined that because the report had been prepared as a tool for settlement negotiations, it fell within the scope of Rule 408. *Id.*

In contrast to *Ramada,* the District Court of Maryland in *Blue Circle* interpreted Rule 408 as inapplicable to internal memoranda, unless they were communicated to the other side in an attempt at settlement. 760 F.Supp. at 523, citing 23 Charles Alan Wright & Kenneth W. Graham, Jr., *Federal Practice and Procedure* § 5303 (1980). We reject this interpretation of Rule 408 as too broad, and find that the district court in *Blue Circle* overstated the meaning of the treatise citation.[17]

---

[17] The treatise states that "[o]f course, the mere fact that information may be useful in compromise negotiations does not mean that it is privileged where it was never communicated to the opponent." *Federal Practice and Procedure, supra,* § 5303, at 179 n.26 (citing *United States v. Reserve Mining Co.,* 412 F.Supp. 705, 711–12 (D.C.Minn.1976)). * * *

Reserve Mining does not define clearly a rule for treatment of internal memoranda, as *Blue Circle* implies. Rather, the *Reserve Mining* court noted that the party's request for Rule 408 exclusion, if granted, would permit the exclusion of studies done long before any dispute arose. See 412 F.Supp. at 711–12. Such is not the case here, as the Kasprzyk memorandum was written immediately before, and in preparation for, the first meeting in which the settlement of the dispute over invoices was discussed. The Lockwood memorandum was formulated after a number of correspondence concerning settlement figures.

* * *

The court notes that the Eleventh Circuit's decision in *Blu–J, Inc. v. Kemper C.P.A. Group,* 916 F.2d 637, 642 (11th Cir.1990), reinforces the reasoning in *Ramada.* In *Blu–J,* the Eleventh Circuit upheld the exclusion of evidence of an accountant's evaluation "prepared by mutual agreement of [the parties] as part of their settlement negotiations." *Id.* at 641. This independent evaluation in *Blu–J* was found to fall within the Rule 408 exception, and the holding in *Ramada,* because although the parties disagreed as to whether "an offer was on the table" during "negotiations," both parties agreed that the evaluation was done to promote settlement of a dispute. *Id.* at 642. Here, the district court found the Alcoa memoranda was prepared as a basis for compromise negotiations, particularly because the memoranda appeared to be intended to assist in calculation of compromise figures discussed subsequently. *AMI I* at 9. The district court's analysis is consistent with the view of Rule 408 expressed in the *Ramada* and *Blu–J* decisions of our sister circuits, which we find persuasive. Thus, we hold that the district court did not abuse its discretion in excluding internal memoranda prepared for use in discussion of settlement of AMI invoice amounts.

IV.

The district court properly interpreted and applied the Rule 408 exclusion to suppress portions of the documents and testimony discussed herein. Further, the court's factual finding as to the existence of a dispute between the parties was not clearly erroneous. Thus, the district court did not err in its denial of the motion for new trial on the basis of its rulings as to evidentiary exclusions. The judgment of the district court is affirmed.

NOTES AND QUESTIONS

1. *Dispute as to either validity or amount.* Rule 408 protects statements made regarding disputed claim as to either "validity or amount." However, as the Advisory Committee's Note makes clear, it does not protect efforts to settle an admitted debt for a lesser sum. Judge Weinstein provides an interesting example of the type of delicate judgments still required under the Rule:

> [A] careful distinction [must be made] between a frank disclosure during the course of negotiations—such as "All right, I was negligent. Let's talk about damages" (inadmissible)—and the less frequent situation in which the validity of the claim and the amount of damages are admitted—"Of course, I owe you the money, but unless you're willing to settle for less, you'll have to sue me for it" (admissible).

2 Weinstein's Federal Evidence § 408.06 (2d ed. 2013).

2. *Existence of dispute and beginning of negotiations.* As *Affiliated Manufacturers* discusses, major issues under Rule 408 are whether a dispute exists and whether and when compromise negotiations have commenced. See Johnson v. Land O' Lakes, Inc., 181 F.R.D. 388, 390–93 (N.D.Iowa 1998) (discussing different approaches to the applicability of Rule 408). For the Rule to have full effectiveness, a dispute must be considered to exist prior to the filing of a formal complaint. Should it operate to protect an unsolicited partial payment? Judge Weinstein argues that it should because such initial efforts create a favorable atmosphere for successful compromise negotiations. 2 Weinstein & Berger, Weinstein's Evidence ¶ 408[01], at 16 (1994). But see Deere & Co. v. International Harvester Co., 710 F.2d 1551, 1557–58 (Fed.Cir.1983) (finding Rule 408 inapplicable to offer to license a patent since there was not at the time of the offer any dispute or contest concerning the patent); Wal–Mart Stores, Inc. v. Londagin, 37 S.W.3d 620, 625 (Ark.2001) (treating Rule inapplicable where store apologized and took full responsibility for paying the entire claim).

3. *Impeachment not a permitted other purpose.* In 2006, Rule 408 was amended to make explicit that offers of compromise or statements made during such negotiations could not be used to impeach as a prior inconsistent statement or contradiction. As the Advisory Committee noted, " 'Use of statements made in compromise negotiations to impeach the testimony of a party * * * is fraught with danger of misuse of the statement to prove liability, threatens frank interchange of information during negotiations * * *.' 2 McCormick, Evidence § 266, at 186 & n.25 (5th ed. 1999)." This amendment eliminates what was sometimes a difficult matter of legislative interpretation for the courts. In contrast, Rule 407 specifically lists "impeachment" as one of those other purposes not excluded by that Rule.

4. *Obstruction of justice not protected.* Compromise negotiations that constitute an effort to obstruct a criminal investigation or prosecution, such as buying off the complaining witness, are not protected under the explicit terms of the Rule 408. Another element of the 2006 amendment to Rule 408 was intended to clarify that as a general matter Rule 408's exclusion is applicable when the evidence is offered in a criminal case outside the obstruction-of-justice area. Prior to the revision, courts disagreed as to whether Rule 408 should be applicable at all in criminal cases. Some found Rule 408 applicable in criminal cases to bar admission of civil compromise efforts. See, e.g., United States v. Arias, 431 F.3d 1327, 1336–38 (11th Cir.2005); United States v. Bailey, 327 F.3d 1131, 1144–46 (10th Cir.2003); State v. Gano, 988 P.2d 1153, 1160 (Haw.1999). Others found the Rule applicable only to civil proceedings. See, e.g., Manko v. United States, 87 F.3d 50, 54–55 (2d Cir.1996); United States v. Logan, 250 F.3d 350, 367 (6th Cir.2001); State v. O'Connor, 119 P.3d 806, 809–813 (Wash.2005) (construing identical state provision). The revision to Rule 408, however, means that in federal court the evidence is clearly excluded in most criminal cases, the exception applying only when the defendant negotiated in a related civil case with a public office or agency.

5.   *Interaction with mediation proceedings and emerging debate on privilege.* The protections of Rule 408 sometimes intersect with the developing privilege for mediation proceedings. See Folb v. Motion Picture Indus. Pension & Health Plans, 16 F.Supp.2d 1164, 1180 (C.D.Cal.1998) (defining the boundary between and interaction of mediation privilege and Rule 408 protections). Whether outside the formal mediation context there is a privilege that would prevent third party discovery of settlement negotiations is in dispute. Compare Goodyear Tire & Rubber Co. v. Chiles Power Supply, Inc., 332 F.3d 976, 979–82 (6th Cir.2003) (recognizing privilege), with In re Subpoena Issued to Commodity Futures Trading Commission, 370 F.Supp.2d 201 (D.D.C.2005) (rejecting privilege).

Rule 409

1.   *Contrast to Rule 408.* Two differences should be noted between Rule 409, which excludes payments of or offers to pay medical expenses, and Rule 408, examined above. First, Rule 409 requires no dispute concerning the validity of any claim in order to be applicable. On this dimension, Rule 409 is less demanding than Rule 408, which requires a dispute as to either the claim's validity or its amount. Second, Rule 409 provides no protection to "conduct or statements not a part of the act of furnishing or offering or promising to pay." Advisory Committee Note on Rule 409. Such communications are protected under Rule 408. Under Rule 409, communications are not considered essential to the provision of medical services to an injured party. In contrast, a full and frank exchange of information is seen as critical to the negotiation of settlements under Rule 408. Id.

2.   *Statements that go beyond protections of rule.* The meager case law construing Federal Rule 409 and its counterparts in the states disagree as to when statements are not a part of the act of "furnishing, promising to pay, or offering to pay." Compare Port Neches Indep. Sch. Dist. v. Soignier, 702 S.W.2d 756, 757 (Tex.Ct.App.1986) (letter stating that future bills should be submitted to insurance company and acknowledging insurance coverage was admissible under Texas Rule 409 in that it admitted coverage), with Holguin v. Smith's Food King Properties, Inc., 737 P.2d 96, 100 (N.M.Ct.App.1987) (statement on insurance form that defendant would "take full responsibility" was inadmissible as part of offer to pay medical bills).

3.   *Other (unstated) purposes.* Although it does not list other purposes for which the evidence remains admissible, Rule 409, like the other rules considered in this section, does not exclude statements or conduct offered for a purpose other than proving liability. See Savoie v. Otto Candies, Inc., 692 F.2d 363, 370 n.7 (5th Cir.1982) (evidence of maintenance payments after injury admissible as circumstantial evidence to prove plaintiff's employment status as seaman); Passaro v. Wal–Mart Stores, Inc., 4 So. 3d 158, 161 (La.App.2009) (ruling statement that medical bill should be sent to company was admissible on credibility issue as to whether offer made).

Rule 410

1. *Prohibition of impeachment by rule but not by agreement.* While the final sentence of Rule 410 specifies certain circumstances where statements made in connection with plea discussions may be introduced, impeachment of the subsequent testimony of the defendant is not one of them. United States v. Lawson, 683 F.2d 688, 693 (2d Cir.1982) (legislative history demonstrates "Congress' explicit intention to preclude use of statements made in plea negotiations for impeachment purposes"). However, in United States v. Mezzanatto, 513 U.S. 196 (1995), the Supreme Court held that the general prohibition in Rule 410 and Federal Rule of Criminal Procedure 11(e)(6) against use for impeachment of statements made in the course of unsuccessful plea negotiations could be waived by the defendant and that waiver required by the prosecutor as a condition of entering into plea negotiations was valid. Justice Souter in dissent, id. at 215–16, argued that allowing waiver would largely eliminate this general restriction because most defendants lack the bargaining power to refuse the condition. Lower courts have interpreted *Mezzanatto* agreements quite broadly. See 2 McCormick, Evidence § 266 (7th ed. 2013). For example, the agreements may apply even to evidence offered by the government in its case in chief. *See* United States v. Mitchell, 633 F.3d 997, 1003–04 (10th Cir.2011) (ruling that agreement permits use in government's case in chief); United States v. Sylvester, 583 F.3d 285, 289–93 (5th Cir.2009) (reaching same conclusion as to an agreement that was a precondition to any negotiation with the government). See generally Naftalis, "Queen For A Day" Agreements and the Proper Scope of Permissible Waiver of the Federal Plea–Statement Rules, 37 Colum.J.L. & Soc.Probs. 1 (2003); Slobogin, The Story of Rule 410 and United States v. Mezzanatto, in Evidence Stories 103 (Lempert ed., 2006).

2. *Protecting only negotiations with prosecuting attorney.* In 1980, Rule 410 was amended to make explicit that, in order to fall within the protections of the Rule, plea negotiations must be made with an *attorney* for the prosecution. The original language of the Rule had been interpreted to cover statements made by suspects to law enforcement officers who might be incapable of reaching a plea agreement where the defendant "made the statements during the course of a conversation in which he sought concessions from the government in return for a guilty plea." United States v. Herman, 544 F.2d 791, 798 (5th Cir.1977). Such statements to law enforcement officials are now clearly outside the potential protection of modified Rule 410. See People v. Hart, 828 N.E.2d 260, 266–72 (Ill.2005) (giving state law provision similar interpretation).

3. *Permitted use of valid guilty and nolo contendere pleas.* Rule 410 protects statements made in connection with unsuccessful guilty plea negotiations and withdrawn guilty pleas. However, an unwithdrawn plea constitutes a binding admission in the case in which it is made and would also be admissible in other litigation. By contrast, Rule 410 generally prohibits use of an extant, still valid, nolo contendere plea when offered in relevant civil litigation. Convictions based on nolo contendere pleas have,

however, been held admissible under Rule 609 for impeachment, see, e.g., Brewer v. City of Napa, 210 F.3d 1093, 1096 (9th Cir.2000), and occasionally for very limited substantive purposes. See Olsen v. Correiro, 189 F.3d 52 (1st Cir.1999) (admissible to show valid conviction and sentence).

CHAPTER 9[1]

JUDICIAL NOTICE

∎ ∎ ∎

STATE V. MANN

New Mexico Supreme Court, 2002.
39 P.3d 124.

SERNA, CHIEF JUSTICE.

Defendant William Mark Mann appeals his conviction for intentional child abuse resulting in death. * * * Defendant argues that he is entitled to a new trial based on juror misconduct during deliberations. We affirm Defendant's conviction.

I.   Facts and Background

* * *

The victim was the six-year-old son of Defendant and Rita Yancher. Yancher had primary custody of the victim, and the victim usually spent every other weekend with Defendant and Patricia St. Jeor Mann, at the time, Defendant's girlfriend. On August 29, 1996, the victim was present at Defendant's house. At about 11:00 p.m., Defendant and Yancher argued during a telephone conversation regarding the victim staying with him through Saturday as well as late child support payments. At approximately 1 a.m., on August 30th, St. Jeor awoke and saw Defendant going to the victim's room to take him to the bathroom. She heard a noise from the victim, followed by a loud crash and a scream. She ran to the bathroom and saw the victim, apparently having a seizure, on the floor with Defendant cushioning his head. St. Jeor called 911 and reported that the victim was injured. She returned to the bathroom and saw the victim on his back with a screwdriver protruding from his chest. St. Jeor testified that the victim was trying to move himself and Defendant was cupping the screwdriver. St. Jeor, a nurse, attempted to attend the victim, but Defendant punched her in the eye, grabbed her by her hair and by the back of the neck and "slammed" her through the door into the opposite wall. She again called 911, telling them that Defendant attacked her.

* * *

---

[1]   Throughout this chapter some footnotes from the cases and materials have been omitted; others have been renumbered. [Ed.]

The victim's cause of death was the stab wound in his chest. Almost the entire screwdriver's blade, approximately four inches, was embedded in his chest; an autopsy revealed that the screwdriver was wedged between the sternum and the second and third ribs. * * *

Defendant was also charged with child abuse for a head injury the victim suffered in 1994. The State's pathologist testified regarding the victim's earlier skull fracture. He concluded that the brain injuries he observed were inconsistent with a simple fall from a bar stool as described by Defendant.

Defendant testified that he got up around 1 a.m. and realized that he had not taken the victim to the bathroom, a routine occurrence. He woke up the victim and walked him into the bathroom. Defendant testified that he was standing in the bathroom doorway when he saw the victim trip on a rug, put out his arms and knock the items on the hamper, and then fall to the floor. Defendant testified that he turned the victim over and saw the screwdriver. Defendant said he grabbed the screwdriver to prevent the victim from pulling it out in order to minimize the injuries. Defendant testified that St. Jeor came back in and that he thought that she would try to move him, so he pushed her from him and told her to get away. He testified that he did not remember hurting her.

Defendant presented the testimony of Dr. Alan Watts, a physicist, regarding the possibility of the victim impaling himself on the screwdriver consistent with Defendant's explanation of events. He performed several calculations in the courtroom relating to the angle at which the screwdriver may have landed and the amount of force which the victim's body would have exerted upon it on impact, as well as videotaped and live demonstrations for the jury. The videotape consisted of Dr. Watts performing experiments in which he dropped a metal rod, which simulated the victim's body, and a screwdriver onto the concrete floor of his garage. Dr. Watts analogized how a screwdriver might bounce if it hits a solid object with the randomness of throwing dice. Dr. Watts testified that the occurrence of an impalement such as that described by Defendant has "a relatively small overall probability." He stated that, based on the "probability aspects of this," it would be a "freakish accident." Dr. Watts said that "[i]t is a probability calculation" and he offered an example for comparison to "Monte Carlo [codes] because basically you roll the dice."

The State did not present rebuttal testimony, but instead cross-examined Defendant's expert. * * * The prosecutor asked if Dr. Watts could calculate "the probability of [Defendant's] explanation of the stab wound." Dr. Watts testified that he did not calculate the probability of impaling oneself on a screwdriver because "the whole issue that [he] was asked to address was can this happen, and the answer is, yes, it can." He said that the probability would be "finite," but "never zero." Dr. Watts testified that if he "were to run every option possible, [he'd] come to the conclusion that on average you won't stab yourself by falling on a screwdriver, but there is nevertheless a finite possibility it can happen."

* * *

Defendant filed a motion for a new trial, arguing that the verdict was tainted by juror misconduct. Defense counsel interviewed several jurors and was told that Juror 7 [an engineer] presented probability calculations to the other members of the jury regarding the chances of a child and a screwdriver falling in such a manner as to result in impalement. Defendant identified several jurors who he believed had information regarding Juror 7.

* * *

Juror 7 told the trial court that he did not do any calculations or experiments at home. He contended that he did not dispute or discredit Dr. Watts' testimony but believed that Dr. Watts' testimony consisted of "fine calculations and [he] would agree with the calculations." Juror 7 thought that the testimony did not "[answer] the right question" because he did not accept the "logical tie" between the testimony and Defendant's story. Juror 7 completed a probability calculation to "verify [his] own gut feeling," beginning with Dr. Watts' calculations which were presented during the trial. He stated that he used his "professional judgment" and a "fairly simple five-step probability" calculation with five events from Defendant's description of the event: first, whether "the screwdriver land[ed] in the correct orientation" or "solid angle" perpendicular to the victim's falling body; second, whether the screwdriver landed with the blade facing up; third, whether the screwdriver separated itself, as it fell, from other items that had been knocked off the hamper; fourth, where it landed on the floor; and fifth, whether its orientation caused the wound path. He recounted, "I simply multiplied the numbers, one over 10 times one over two times 1 over 100 three times, and the number you get is basically five times ten to minus 8 or in what most of us think about, one in a 20 million chance."

* * *

II. Discussion

As discussed below, we conclude that Juror 7's statements constituted proper deliberations based upon his professional and educational experience. Defendant argues that Juror 7 injected new evidentiary facts which contradicted defense testimony rather than expressing opinions, views or beliefs about the evidence. We disagree. Defendant concedes that Juror 7 began with Dr. Watts' testimony, but he asserts that Juror 7 "added his own testimony of probability and physics."

* * * Juror 7, albeit with greater understanding than the average person, was engaging in deliberation of the evidence presented at trial. * * *

In order to provide expert testimony supporting Defendant's version of events, Dr. Watts described basic physics principles, completed extensive calculations, and performed both in-court and videotaped demonstrations with a screwdriver and other materials. Dr. Watts testified that the occurrence of an accidental impalement consistent with Defendant's theory has "a relatively small overall probability." * * * Defendant himself placed probability calculations regarding his accidental impalement theory in evidence before the jury.

Juror 7 articulated his own thought process as to what this "finite" probability calculation would be, based on the evidence presented in court and based on Dr. Watts' testimony. * * * Juror 7's deliberations properly took their content from the evidence and testimony presented at trial. His calculation, as well as several other jurors' calculations, expressed the probability, introduced into evidence by Defendant, as one in several million. The jury's deliberation was an attempt to review and evaluate Defendant's expert testimony. Juror 9 rejected the conclusion of Defendant's expert, and decided that "Not in a zillion billion years did that happen." Juror 4 estimated the probability of Defendant's accident occurring as "one in 10 million." Defendant concedes that this type of opinion is proper. * * * Juror 7, because of his life experience, occupation, and education, verbalized a similar opinion as other jurors based on evidence and testimony presented at trial in a more complex manner, explaining the basis behind the conclusion that Defendant finds permissible. Concluding that Defendant's theory has a less than one in twenty million chance, rather than Dr. Watts' characterization of a "freak accident," is not a new evidentiary fact. The jury, including Juror 7, carefully considered Defendant's theory but was ultimately persuaded that the State demonstrated that Defendant was guilty beyond a reasonable doubt; thus, the jury performed its duty. * * * Defendant wishes to be allowed, and in fact, was properly allowed, to present expert physics testimony regarding the ultimate conclusion of the probability of impalement to the jury (possible but extremely unlikely), but now strenuously objects to the jury actually deliberating on this very issue. It would be inordinately bad policy to single out a juror who thoughtfully and conscientiously engaged in deliberation and presented his conclusion to the jury because he was able to express exactly why he came to that conclusion based on the evidence at trial, rather than more simply state the theory as one in a million.

* * *

"In deciding every case, jurors must necessarily take into consideration their knowledge and impressions founded upon experience in their everyday walks of life, and the fact that these things affect them in reaching their verdict cannot be reversible error, because, indeed, jurors without possessing such knowledge and impressions could not be had." *State v. Dascenzo,* 30 N.M. 34, 37, 226 P. 1099, 1100 (1924). The trial court did not abuse its discretion by denying Defendant's motion for a new trial under New Mexico precedent. Cases from other jurisdictions also support this conclusion. *See, e.g., Wagner v. Doulton,* 112 Cal.App.3d 945, 169 Cal.Rptr. 550, 552–53 (1980) (concluding that an engineer juror's map, drawn based on his understanding of the testimony and used during deliberations, did not constitute extraneous evidence); *State v. Heitkemper,* 196 Wis.2d 218, 538 N.W.2d 561, 563–64 (App.1995) (concluding that a pharmacist juror's remark that he disbelieved a witness regarding drugs she ingested because the quantities should have knocked her out did not constitute extraneous information). "A juror's common sense and experience, including expertise in particular subjects, is not extrinsic information warranting relief if used during deliberations." *State v. Dickens,* 187 Ariz. 1, 926 P.2d 468, 483 (1996) (en banc) (holding that a mechanic juror's statement that he did not believe the defendant's claim that his truck overheated based on his expertise did not constitute extraneous information).

Remarks made by the jurors in the present case illustrate the problematic application of a broad definition that communication of specific knowledge from a particular juror to others constitutes extraneous prejudicial information. Juror 9 described how another juror discussed that juror's experience with his own child falling from a tree and how that experience related to his understanding of the child abuse charge stemming from the victim's 1994 head injury. Both Juror 9 and Juror 7 mentioned that two jurors who were nurses discussed their opinion regarding the expert medical testimony, based on their educational and professional experience. Finally, Juror 7 described another juror recounting a previous experience in which the juror fell straight forward and sustained an injury to her chin. All of this information was not subject to cross-examination regarding the similarity or dissimilarity to the charges in the present case; it could be considered extraneous under this definition. * * *

Defendant argues that the Court of Appeals opinion will result in the "dumbing down" of juries because attorneys will remove individuals such as Juror 7. We disagree. We do not believe that because an individual has particular professional experience or is well-educated one can assume that he or she is biased in favor of any particular party. As discussed above, venire members who express experiences which would affect their ability to be unbiased can be dismissed through cause challenges during voir dire. * * *

NOTES AND QUESTIONS

1.   *"Jury notice."* Obviously it is not feasible for every judicial inquiry to begin from the Cartesian postulate *cogito, ergo sum.* In order for the trial of factual issues to proceed with anything like dispatch, indeed for them to proceed at all, it must be assumed that the trier of fact comes to his or her task already apprised of the multitude of nonevidence or background facts which will enable him or her to comprehend and utilize the additional data communicated to him or her by the formal introduction of evidence. Thus, as one writer has stated, "[i]t is considered appropriate that a judge or juror be permitted to employ, inconspicuously and interstitially in his elementary process of understanding and reasoning, his beliefs (though they are not in evidence) which he reasonably thinks he shares with other intelligent persons as to the general nature of things—the meanings of ordinary words, typical modes of human behavior, causal relations between commonplace events, and the like. * * * [T]his category of judicial notice is often referred to by the somewhat misleading name 'jury notice.' " McNaughton, Judicial Notice—Excerpts Relating to the Morgan–Wigmore Controversy, 14 Vand.L.Rev. 779, 789–90 (1961). See also Davis, A System of Judicial Notice Based on Fairness and Convenience, in Perspectives of Law 69 (1964); Thayer, A Preliminary Treatise on Evidence at the Common Law 279–80 (1898). Lest the jury feel any hesitancy in this regard, the notion is commonly conveyed to it by instruction.

2.   *Jury special knowledge.* In *Mann*, is there a difference between Jurors 4 and 9's colloquial expressions and Juror 7's calculations? Do these calculations differ from comments of the nurse jurors concerning the expert medical testimony? Compare Hunt v. State, 603 S.W.2d 865 (Tex.Crim.App.1980), in which a juror enlightened his fellow jurors concerning the use of ligatures to cause death, based upon his Marine training years previously. The court held this incident to be "improper" and to entitle defendant to a new trial.

3.   *The imprecise line between background facts and adjudicatory facts.* In Palestroni v. Jacobs, 73 A.2d 89 (Bergen County Ct.1950), the jurors used a standard dictionary, during their deliberations, in order to determine the meaning of the word "wainscot", which was used in the evidence. The trial court found no error: "Since jurors may take judicial notice of the commonly accepted meaning of all English words used in the evidence, they are entitled to have the use of a standard English dictionary to aid their understanding by refreshing their recollection of the meaning of any English word used in the evidence, where no unusual, special, or legal significance of its use is involved. Therefore, it is not improper for a jury to have the use of a standard English dictionary during its deliberations." On review, the appellate court reversed, 77 A.2d 183 (N.J.App.Div.1950). Judge Brennan (later a Supreme Court Justice) stated that "even if the word was employed in the specification with its ordinary meaning, defendant was denied the chance to challenge the completeness of the definition given in the dictionary used. Here counsel might have properly suggested that another dictionary containing a more

comprehensive definition was appropriate * * *." Id. at 185. Does the specific meaning of a word like "wainscot" that is ordinarily outside the concern of judicial notice of adjudicative facts take on a more sensitive status in a contract case where the issue involves the adequacy of wainscoting? Was the problem the specific definition of the term or a procedural defect in failing to provide an opportunity to contest the definition provided?

4. *The theory of the dividing line.* At what points other than during jury deliberations are "background facts" inevitably going to be assumed and used by various participants in the trial process? Should jury notice of background facts for one or more of these purposes be regulated in some way? How? For a discussion of these questions suggesting the imposition of some strictures on jury notice, see Mansfield, Jury Notice, 74 Geo.L.J. 395 (1985). Professor Mansfield's thesis is strenuously criticized by Fraher, Adjudicative Facts, Non–Evidence Facts, and Permissible Jury Background Information, 62 Ind.L.J. 333 (1987), in part on the ground that such strictures are not feasible. Among the points discussed by Mansfield is the extent to which the jury notice principle applies to argument by counsel which draws upon facts or propositions which have not been supported by evidence. For an excellent earlier discussion of this question, see Levin & Levy, Persuading the Jury with Facts Not in Evidence: The Fiction–Science Spectrum, 105 U.Pa.L.Rev. 139 (1956).

STATE V. CANADY

Court of Appeals of North Carolina, 1993.
431 S.E.2d 500.

GREENE, JUDGE.

Appeal by defendant from judgment and commitment to fourteen years imprisonment entered 3 March 1992, after jury verdict convicting him of voluntary manslaughter. N.C.G.S. § 14–18 (1986). *PH*

The State's evidence tends to show, *inter alia,* that defendant stabbed George Bullard (Bullard), who was romantically involved with defendant's estranged wife, to death on the evening of 24 May 1990 at the mobile home where defendant's estranged wife was living. One of the State's witnesses, Mrs. Nunnery, testified that her house was approximately 150 feet from Mrs. Canady's mobile home and that she could see Mrs. Canady's mobile home and front yard from her porch. On the evening Bullard was killed, Mrs. Nunnery received a telephone call from Mrs. Canady. Mrs. Nunnery heard a "scuffle" on the phone, and Mrs. Canady asked her to "call the law," which Mrs. Nunnery did. As she hung up the telephone, Mrs. Canady came into her house. *FF*

Mrs. Nunnery then went out onto the front porch and observed Bullard and defendant. She saw Bullard standing beside defendant's car with no weapon in his hand. Defendant was inside the car at the time, but the driver's door was open and defendant's leg was outside the door.

Mrs. Nunnery observed that Bullard was attempting to get defendant into his car, and heard Bullard say "[g]et your leg in and go on. I don't want to fight you." Mrs. Nunnery then went back inside her house. She returned to the front porch minutes later and observed both Bullard and defendant standing outside the car, neither one armed. Mrs. Nunnery returned inside, and then heard defendant call out that an ambulance should be called. Mrs. Nunnery was the only witness, other than defendant, to the altercation. Mrs. Nunnery testified that when she was watching defendant and Bullard "[i]t was still daylight. It was getting toward dusk * * *. [T]here was good light."

Defendant's evidence, consisting primarily of statements made to officers at the scene, tended to establish that he killed Bullard in self-defense, and conflicted with the testimony of Mrs. Nunnery. Defendant did not testify, but claimed in statements made to the police that it was dark when he arrived at the mobile home. Defendant's counsel moved in writing that the trial court take judicial notice of the fact that the sunset on 24 May 1990 occurred at 8:19 p.m., and that there was a new moon on that date. Defendant offered verification of these facts in the form of the reports published daily in *The Fayetteville Observer*. The trial court refused defendant's request. The jury returned a verdict finding defendant guilty of voluntary manslaughter.

Defendant contends that the evidence of the time of sunset and presence of a new moon was critical to his case because such information casts doubt on Mrs. Nunnery's testimony that there was sufficient daylight by which to see the exchanges between defendant and Bullard. Thus, defendant claims, he was prejudiced when the trial court wrongfully refused to take judicial notice of the information offered. The State contends that the information in *The Fayetteville Observer* is not official, and therefore not the proper subject for judicial notice.

———

The dispositive issue is whether the trial court is required to take judicial notice of the time of the sunset and the phase of the moon as reported in *The Fayetteville Observer*.

The Rules of Evidence provide that the trial "court shall take judicial notice [of adjudicative facts] if requested by a party and supplied with the necessary information." N.C.G.S. § 8C-1, Rule 201(d) (1992). Once a request to take judicial notice is made and accompanied by supporting data, the trial court "is entitled to pass upon the sufficiency of the data." 1 Henry Brandis, Jr., *Brandis on North Carolina Evidence* § 11 (3d ed. 1988) (footnote omitted). The trial court weighs the sufficiency of the data by determining whether the fact put forth for judicial notice is one not subject to reasonable dispute in that it is either (1) generally known within the territorial jurisdiction of the trial court or (2) capable of accurate and ready determination by resort to sources whose accuracy cannot reasonably be questioned.

N.C.G.S. § 8C–1, Rule 201(b) (1992). To warrant judicial notice under the second part of this test, the source from which the data is drawn must be "a document of such indisputable accuracy as [would] justif[y] judicial reliance." State v. Dancy, 297 N.C. 40, 42, 252 S.E.2d 514, 515 (1979). It is the responsibility of counsel seeking to have a fact judicially noticed to supply the trial court with such information, and "[t]he trial judge is not required to make an independent search for data of which he may take judicial notice." Id.

The exact time of sunset and the current phase of the moon on a particular date are not facts "generally known." They are, however, facts which are "capable of accurate and ready determination by resort to sources whose accuracy cannot reasonably be questioned." Thus, it was the responsibility of defendant's counsel, upon his request that the trial court take judicial notice of the moon phase and time of sunset, to provide that information to the trial court in "a document of such indisputable accuracy as [would] justif[y] judicial reliance." Dancy, 297 N.C. at 42, 252 S.E.2d at 515. The Fayetteville Observer is not such a document. We note that the newspaper excerpt does not even identify the source of its data. We believe that, in the case of facts such as the time of sunset and the phase of the moon, a document of "indisputable accuracy" contemplates material from a primary source in whose hands the gathering of such information rests. Our Supreme Court has approved this view in Dancy, refusing to find error in the trial court's failure to take judicial notice of the phase of the moon when the source was The Ladies Birthday Almanac, but taking judicial notice on its own initiative of the same fact as found in the records of the U.S. Naval Observatory. Id.

Accordingly, the trial court did not err in failing to take judicial notice of the facts put forth by defendant.

NOTES AND QUESTIONS

1. *Morgan–Wigmore Debate.* Guidice & Kraft, Comment, The Presently Expanding Concept of Judicial Notice, 13 Villanova L.Rev. 528, 534–36 (1968)[2]:

> The scope of judicial notice of fact has been traditionally considered in the context of the Morgan–Wigmore, indisputable-disputable controversy. On the one side, Professors Morgan and McNaughton contend that the primary purpose of judicial notice is to prevent

---

[2] Copyright © 1968 by Villanova University. Reprinted by permission. [Ed.]

wasteful litigation of moot questions of fact. Therefore, they maintain that judicial notice should be confined to indisputables, that is, those facts which are so notorious or so universally known or so easily and accurately verifiable that they cannot reasonably be disputed. They reason that since judicial notice, by their definition, applies only to indisputables, once such an indisputable proposition is properly noticed, it should not be allowed to be controverted. In other words, judicial notice is conclusive, so that in a jury trial, once a judge judicially notices a fact, he should give the jury binding instructions to find the fact as noticed, and no evidence may be introduced in an effort to persuade the jury to make a finding contrary to the noticed fact. The parties may, however, present informal 'information' to the judge, before or after his ruling, in an effort to convince him that the fact is not indisputable.

On the other side of the dispute, Professors Wigmore and Thayer contend that a judge may notice facts unlikely to be challenged as well as those considered to be absolutely indisputable. Under their definition, judicial notice operates in the way of a presumption. Says Thayer:

> Taking judicial notice does not import that the matter is indisputable. It is not necessarily anything more than a *prima facie* recognition, leaving the matter still open to controversy. * * * In very many cases * * * taking judicial notice of a fact is merely presuming it, i.e., assuming it until there shall be reason to think otherwise.

Under the Wigmore–Thayer approach, as under the Morgan approach, the parties may initially present information to the court to help it decide whether or not it should take judicial notice of the particular fact in question. If the judge decides to notice the fact, he will instruct the jury that they *may find the noticed fact to be true* even though no evidence has been introduced in its support. The opponent of the fact, at this point, has the option of producing material in an effort to convince the *judge* that he has decided incorrectly—that he should not have noticed the fact because the fact was not unlikely to be challenged. Having failed to dissuade the judge as to the propriety of taking notice, or not having attempted to do so, the opponent of the fact may yet introduce evidence directed at rebutting the presumption and persuading the *jury* to find that the noticed fact is not true.

Which theory does Federal Rule 201 adopt?

2. *Indisputability requirement.* In Jespersen v. Harrah's Operating Co., Inc., 444 F.3d 1104 (9th Cir.2006), a sex discrimination suit based on a requirement that female bar tenders wear makeup ("face powder, blush and mascara must be worn and applied neatly in complimentary colors, and lip color must be worn at all times"), the appellate court refused to take judicial

notice of the fact that it costs more money and takes more time for a woman to comply with the makeup requirement than it takes for a man to comply with the requirement that he keep his hair short because such facts lack a high degree of indisputability. The dissent rejoined:

> Harrah's policy requires women to apply face powder, blush, mascara and lipstick. You don't need an expert witness to figure out that such items don't grow on trees. Nor is there any rational doubt that application of makeup is an intricate and painstaking process that requires considerable time and care. Even those of us who don't wear makeup know how long it can take from the hundreds of hours we've spent over the years frantically tapping our toes and pointing to our wrists. It's hard to imagine that a woman could "put on her face," as they say, in the time it would take a man to shave—certainly not if she were to do the careful and thorough job Harrah's expects. Makeup, moreover, must be applied and removed every day; the policy burdens men with no such daily ritual. While a man could jog to the casino, slip into his uniform, and get right to work, a woman must travel to work so as to avoid smearing her makeup, or arrive early to put on her makeup there.

Is there another basis for the majority opinion? See also Johnson v. State, 969 A.2d 262, 271 (Md.2009) (defense requested court to take judicial notice that currency contamination is so widespread as to require the exclusion of the canine scan evidence in cocaine distribution case; "We decline to take judicial notice in this instance because we do not believe that such a fact is either commonly known or readily determinable through unquestionably reliable sources.").

3.   *Types of facts.* Courts have often taken judicial notice of historical and geographical facts. In addition, the identity of the principal officers of the national government and the incumbents of principal state offices are also subject to judicial notice. 2 McCormick, Evidence § 330 (7th ed. 2013). See also Disabled Rights Action Committee v. Las Vegas Events, Inc., 375 F.3d 861, 866 n.1 (9th Cir.2004) ("Under Federal Rule of Evidence 201, we may take judicial notice of the records of state agencies and other undisputed matters of public record."); Dippin' Dots, Inc. v. Frosty Bites Distribution, LLC, 369 F.3d 1197, 1205 (11th Cir.2004) ("[T]he district court took judicial notice of the fact that color is indicative of flavor in ice cream. This fact is adjudicative in nature and is generally known among consumers."); Denius v. Dunlap, 330 F.3d 919, 926 (7th Cir.2003) ("[T]he fact that the [National Personnel Records Center] maintains medical records of military personnel is appropriate for judicial notice because it is not subject to reasonable dispute.").

4.   *Political facts.* See Namo v. Gonzales, 401 F.3d 453, 458 (6th Cir.2005) ("[W]e recognize that the situation in Iraq has changed due to the demise of the regime of Saddam Hussein. This court may take judicial notice of changed circumstances."); Singh v. Ashcroft, 393 F.3d 903, 905 (9th

Cir.2004) ("We can notice that the government of India exists. We can notice that the office of the Prime Minister of India exists. We can notice that a part of the Prime Minister of India's office is the RAW [Research and Analysis Wing]."); Gafoor v. Immigration and Naturalization Serv., 231 F.3d 645, 656 (9th Cir.2000) ("We do not exceed our authority by taking judicial notice of dramatic foreign developments * * *."); Ivezaj v. INS, 84 F.3d 215, 219 (6th Cir.1996) (taking judicial notice of persecution of Albanians by Serbs).

5. *Scientific facts.* As the Supreme Court has noted: "[T]heories that are so firmly established as to have attained the status of scientific law, such as the laws of thermodynamics, properly are subject to judicial notice under Fed. Rule Evid. 201." Daubert v. Merrell Dow Pharms., Inc., 509 U.S. 579, 593 n.11 (1993). See also Izer v. State, 511 S.E.2d 625, 627 (Ga. App.1999) ("[O]nce a procedure or technology has been recognized in a substantial number of courts, or has been utilized for a significant period of time and expert testimony has been received thereon in case after case, a trial court may take judicial notice of the devices's reliability and acceptance. The trial court does not have to keep reinventing the wheel; a once novel technology can and does become commonplace.") (citations omitted). The principles underlying many scientific techniques, including radar, intoxication tests, fingerprints, palm prints, firearms identification, bite mark examinations, handwriting comparisons, DNA profiling, blood-spatter evidence, as well as other procedures have all been judicially recognized in this fashion. See Giannelli, Imwinkelried, Roth & Moriarty, Scientific Evidence ch. 1 (5th ed. 2012).

6. *Authoritative sources.* See Morgan, Basic Problems in Evidence 10 (1962) ("If the issue is whether a matter falls within the scope of judicial notice, neither judge nor counsel will be hampered by the rules of evidence."); 9 Wigmore, Evidence § 2568a, at 538 (3d ed. 1940) ("any source whatever that suffices to satisfy [the judge's] mind in making a ruling" is acceptable; listing "official records, encyclopedias, any books or articles" as examples); Cal.Evid.Code § 454(a)(1) ("Any source of pertinent information, including the advice of persons learned in the subject matter, may be consulted or used."). In the principal case, what was wrong with the *Fayetteville Observer*? Would the newspaper have been admissible? See Federal Rules 803(17) and 902(6).

7. *Internet as an authoritative source.* "It is not uncommon for courts to take judicial notice of factual information found on the world wide web." O'Toole v. Northrop Grumman Corp., 499 F.3d 1218, 1225 (10th Cir.2007) (Northrop Grumman has failed to explain "why its own website's posting of historical retirement fund earnings is unreliable. Moreover, Northrop Grumman could have asked the district court for a hearing under Rule 201(e), but did not do so. In short, Northrop Grumman's failure to dispute its own information, contributes to its indisputability."). But see Victaulic Co. v. Tieman, 499 F.3d 227, 236 (3d Cir.2007) ("[A] company's website is a marketing tool. Often, marketing material is full of imprecise puffery that no one should take at face value. Thus courts should be wary of finding judicially noticeable facts amongst all the fluff; private corporate websites, particularly

when describing their own business, generally are not the sorts of 'sources whose accuracy cannot reasonably be questioned,' Fed.R.Evid. 201(b), that our judicial notice rule contemplates."). Other courts have taken judicial notice of facts derived from internet mapping tools when deciding questions concerning child custody, proper venue in a civil action, proof of venue in a criminal action, discovery disputes and compensation for travel expenses. See United States v. Kelly, 535 F.3d 1229, 1236–37 (10th Cir.2008); Saco v. Tug Tucana Corp., 483 F. Supp. 2d 88, 93 (D.Mass.2007); Gordon v. Lewistown Hospital, 272 F. Supp. 2d 393, 429 (M.D.Pa.2003); Coppola v. Ferrellgas, Inc., 250 F.R.D. 195, 199 (E.D.Pa.2008).

8. *Timing of judicial notice.* Rule 201(d) authorizes the taking of judicial notice at any stage of the proceeding. See Dippin' Dots, Inc. v. Frosty Bites Distribution, LLC, 369 F.3d 1197, 1204 (11th Cir.2004) ("A court may take judicial notice * * * at the summary judgment stage."). This would include appeals. Is it fair to permit a party to do through judicial notice on appeal what that party should have done at trial? See Colonial Leasing Co. v. Logistics Control Group Int'l, 762 F.2d 454, 461 (5th Cir.1985) ("[W]hen Logistics declined to produce evidence, it relied on Colonial's failure to establish its prima facie case. When the district court subsequently took notice of the only fact necessary to complete Colonial's prima facie proof, Logistics was deprived of the opportunity to adduce evidence on a critical fact.").

Sᴛᴀᴛᴇ ᴠ. Vᴇᴊᴠᴏᴅᴀ
Supreme Court of Nebraska, 1989.
438 N.W.2d 461.

Sʜᴀɴᴀʜᴀɴ, Jᴜsᴛɪᴄᴇ.

In a bench trial in the county court for Hall County, Mark Vejvoda was convicted of drunk driving and received an enhanced sentence as the result of his second conviction for drunk driving. * * * On appeal, the district court affirmed Vejvoda's conviction and sentence. Vejvoda contends that the evidence is insufficient to sustain his conviction for drunk driving and that the State failed to prove that Hall County was the venue for his trial because the court improperly took judicial notice that locations mentioned in Vejvoda's trial were within Hall County.

* * *

The only testimony regarding venue was that of Edwards', a Grand Island police officer, who observed Vejvoda's car at "7th and Vine Streets" and later apprehended Vejvoda on a street called "Oak." Edwards never identified the city or county where he observed and apprehended Vejvoda. As this court noted in *State v. Bouwens*, 167 Neb. 244, 247, 92 N.W.2d 564, 566 (1958), the fact that a defendant was arrested by policemen to a particular city "is not proof that the offense was committed within the jurisdiction * * * of the city * * *." When the judicial notice in question is disregarded, the evidence offered in Vejvoda's case fails to establish that either a Vine Street or an Oak Street exists in Grand Island or Hall County.

Judicial Notice

Neb.Evid.R. 201(2), Neb.Rev.Stat. § 27–201(2) (Reissue 1985), pertains to judicial notice of adjudicative facts and states: "A judicially noticed fact must be one not subject to reasonable dispute in that it is either (a) generally known within the territorial jurisdiction of the trial court or (b) capable of accurate and ready determination by resort to sources whose accuracy cannot reasonably be questioned."

A fact is adjudicative if the fact affects the determination of a controverted issue in litigation, or, as one author has characterized adjudicative facts:

> When a court or an agency finds facts concerning the immediate parties—who did what, where, when, how, and with what motive or intent—the court or agency is performing an adjudicative function, and the facts so determined are conveniently called adjudicative facts * * *.

> Stated in other terms, the adjudicative facts are those to which the law is applied in the process of adjudication. They are the facts that normally go to the jury in a jury case. They relate to the parties, their activities, their properties, their businesses.

Davis, *Judicial Notice*, 55 Colum.L.Rev. 945, 952 (1955).

* * *

Judicial Notice: A Species of Evidence

Judicial notice of an adjudicative fact is a species of evidence, which, if relevant as an ultimate fact or a fact from which an ultimate fact may be inferred, is received without adherence to the Nebraska Evidence Rules otherwise applicable to admissibility of evidence and established a fact without formal evidentiary proof. * * * *National Aircraft Leasing v. American Airlines*, 74 Ill.App. 3d 1014, 1017, 31 Ill.Dec. 268, 394 N.E.2d 470, 474 (1979): "Judicial notice is an evidentiary concept which operates to admit matters into evidence without formal proof * * *." * * *

Judicial Notice v. A Judge's Personal Knowledge

Judicial notice, however, is not the same as extrajudicial or personal knowledge of a judge. "What a judge knows and what facts a judge may judicially notice are not identical data banks * * *. [A]ctual private knowledge by the judge is no sufficient ground for taking judicial notice of a fact as a basis for a finding or a final judgment * * *." McCormick on Evidence § 329 at 922–23 (E. Cleary 3d ed. 1984). As Wigmore observes:

There is a real but elusive line between the judge's *personal knowledge* as a private man and these matters of which he takes judicial notice as a judge. The latter does not necessarily include the former; as a judge, indeed, he may have to ignore what he knows as a man and contrariwise.

* * *

It is therefore plainly accepted that the judge is not to use from the bench, under the guise of judicial knowledge, that which he knows *only as an individual* observer outside of court. The former is in truth "known" to him merely in the fictional sense that it is known and notorious to all men, and the dilemma is only the result of using the term "knowledge" in two senses. Where to draw the line between knowledge by notoriety and knowledge by personal observation may sometimes be difficulty but the principle is plain.

(Emphasis in original.) 9 J. Wigmore, Evidence in Trials at Common Law § 2569(a) at 722–23 (J. Chadbourn rev. 1981). * * *

Judicial Notice in Criminal Cases

In function and effect, judicial notice in a civil action is fundamentally different from judicial notice in a criminal case. "In a civil action or proceeding, the judge shall instruct the jury to accept as conclusive any fact judicially noticed. In a criminal case, the judge shall instruct the jury that it may, but is not required to, accept as conclusive any fact judicially noticed." Neb.Evid.R. 201(7). In a civil action, the adjudicative fact judicially noticed is conclusively established and binds the jury, whereas in a criminal case a jury ultimately has the freedom to find that an adjudicative fact has not been established notwithstanding judicial notice by the trial court. If the conclusive effect of judicial notice in a civil action were transposed to the trial of a criminal case, judicial notice might supply proof of an element in the charge against an accused and thereby have the practical effect of a directed verdict on the issue of the defendants guilt * * *.

* * *

In *U.S. v. Mentz*, 840 F.2d 315 (6th Cir.1988), the government prosecuted Mentz in a jury trial on charges of bank robbery. To convict Mentz, the government had to prove that Mentz robbed a financial institution insured by the federal Deposit Insurance Corporation. * * * When Mentz moved for dismissal of the charges at the close of the government's case, claiming that evidence failed to establish that the banks were FDIC-insured at the time of the robberies, the court overruled Mentz' motion and, although there was no evidence of FDIC insurance, instructed the jury that each of the banks, which Mentz was accused of robbing, was "insured by the Federal Deposit Insurance Corporation at the time of the offense alleged in the indictment." * * * In reversing Mentz' conviction, the court stated:

> Regardless of how overwhelming the evidence may be, the Constitution delegates to the jury, not to the trial judge, the important task of deciding guilt or innocence. "[The jury's] overriding responsibility is to stand between the accused and a potentially arbitrary or abusive Government that is in command of the criminal sanction. For this reason, a trial judge is prohibited from entering a judgment of conviction or directing the jury to come forward with such a verdict, regardless of how overwhelming the evidence may point in that direction. The trial judge is thereby barred from attempting to override or interfere with the jurors' independent judgment in a manner contrary to the interests of the accused." *United States v. Martin Linen Supply Co.* [430 U.S. 564 (1977)] * * *.

* * *

Specifically referring to judicial notice under Fed.R.Evid. 201([f]), the counterpart to Neb.Evid.R. 201(7), the court concluded in *Mentz*:

> In a criminal case, a trial court that takes judicial notice of an adjudicative fact must "instruct the jury that it may, but is not required to, accept as conclusive any fact judicially noticed." Rule 201([f]), Fed.R.Evid. This provision "contemplates that the jury in a criminal case [will] pass upon facts which are judicially noticed." *United States v. Jones*, 580 F.2d 219, 224 (6th Cir.1978). As so construed, Rule 201([f]) preserves the jury's "traditional prerogative to ignore even uncontroverted facts in reaching a verdict," and thereby prevents the trial court from transgressing the spirit, if not the letter, of the Sixth Amendment right to a jury trial by directing a partial verdict as to the facts. * * *

As one commentator has remarked concerning judicial notice and Fed.R.Evid. 201([f]), which remark is equally applicable to Neb.Evid.R. 201(7):

> With respect to criminal cases, Rule 201([f]) apparently contemplates that contrary evidence is admissible, which of course means that evidence, if any, in support of the fact judicially noticed may also be admitted. Problems arising with respect to the court considering inadmissible evidence in determining the propriety of taking judicial notice coupled with the confusion that naturally would be expected to rise in the jury's mind when presented with judicial notice accompanied by conflicting evidence, makes resort to judicial notice in criminal

cases where the opposing party is prepared to introduce contrary evidence highly undesirable.

M. Graham, Handbook of Federal Evidence § 201.7 at 83 (2d ed. 1986).

Judicial Notice in A Bench Trial

Potential problems from judicial notice in a bench trial are discussed in 21 C. Wright & K. Graham, Federal Practice and Procedure § 5104 at 488 (1977):

> [T]he high degree of indisputability required before a fact can be judicially noticed applies to both forms of litigation [jury trials and court or bench trials]. However, the procedural context in which notice is taken makes the process quite different in court trials. Since the judge is not insulated, as the jury is, from the material consulted in deciding whether or not to take notice, it may make little difference whether he takes formal judicial notice based on the material or whether he is simply convinced of the fact as a result of having examined the sources. Technically, the source material is not in evidence, and thus a finding that was without other support in the record could not stand unless the matter was properly noticeable; but otherwise, the line between judicial notice and proof-taking is blurred in court trials.

From all the foregoing observations, we believe, and for that reason suggest, that judicial notice should be sparingly used in a criminal case lest prejudicial error result from denial of a defendant's constitutional or statutory rights in the trial of a criminal case.

Judicial Notice in Vejvoda's Case

Under the Nebraska Evidence Rules, the trial court's sua sponte judicial notice was permissible at the point in Vejvoda's trial where adduction of evidence has been concluded and the case was ready for submission to the factfinding process. See Neb.Evid.R. 201(4): "A judge or court shall take judicial notice if requested by a party and supplied with the necessary information." See, also, Neb.Evid.R. 201(6): "Judicial notice may be taken at any stage of the proceeding."

However, from the record in Vejvoda's case, one cannot conclude that the location of the municipal microcosm known as Vine Street or 8th and Oak Streets was known throughout the length and breadth of Hall County and, therefore, a fact "known within the territorial jurisdiction of the trial court." Neb.Evid.R. 201(2)(a). Consequently, we must focus on the alternative expressed in Neb.Evid.R. 201(2)(b), that is, whether the location of Vine and Oak streets in Grand Island and the site of Vejvoda's arrest are adjudicative facts "capable of accurate and ready determination by resort to sources whose accuracy cannot reasonably be questioned."

For resolution of Vejvoda's claim regarding the impropriety of the trial court's judicial notice, we must first identify and characterize the scope of the trial court's "judicial notice," which actually has two components: (1) Vine, Oak, 7th, and 8th Streets exist in Grand Island, which is located in Hall County, and (2) Vejvoda's drunk driving occurred at 8th and Oak in Grand Island. Thus, existence of Grand Island streets is inferentially correlated with Edwards' testimony, producing a conclusion judicially noticed by the trial court, namely, the judicially noticed streets are the same streets mentioned in Edwards' testimony, and, therefore, Vejvoda was arrested in Grand Island.

An inference may be entirely reasonable, yet nevertheless an improper subject for judicial notice. * * *

* * *

In Vejvoda's case, the trial court could properly take judicial notice that Grand Island, which is wholly within Hall Country, has streets named "Vine" and "Oak." Furthermore, by simply referring to a map of Grand Island, the court could properly take judicial notice that the intersection of 7th and Vine Streets is within two blocks of the intersection of 8th and Oak Streets. At that point the site of the offense was an issue submissible to the trier of fact.

Although the location of streets within Grand Island is readily verifiable by reference to a city map, a source capable of ready certification and a cartographic source of information which cannot reasonably be questioned, the county court took another and impermissible step by judicially noticing the inference that Vejvoda was driving in Grand Island. The court's locational inference necessary for venue was not an adjudicative fact "capable of accurate and ready determination by resort to sources whose accuracy cannot reasonably be questioned." The county court erred in taking judicial notice of the inference that Vejvoda was driving in Grand Island and, therefore, that Vejvoda's drunk driving occurred in Grand Island.

If Vejvoda had been convicted in a jury trial, we would reverse Vejvoda's conviction on account of the trial court's invasion of the factfinding process within a jury's province in the trial of a criminal case. However, as mentioned, Vejvoda's case was tried to the court. Although Vejvoda's arrest by Edwards, a Grand Island police officer, does not establish venue, Edwards' official affiliation as a Grand Island police officer was a circumstance bearing on the issue of venue. When combined with other evidence, namely, the trial court's judicial notice of "Vine" and "Oak" as street in Grand Island, Edwards' testimony supplied a sufficient evidentiary basis for a fact finder's determination that Vejvoda's drunk driving occurred in Grand Island, Hall County, Nebraska. "Harmless error exists in a jury trial of a criminal case when there is some incorrect conduct by the trial court which, on review of the entire record, did not materially influence the jury in a verdict adverse to a substantial right of the defendant." *State v. Watkins*, 227 Neb. 677, 686, 419 N.W.2d 660, 666 (1988). The preceding principle applicable in a jury trial of a criminal case is equally applicable to a judgment embodying factfinding in the bench trial of a criminal case.

Therefore, the trial court's error in judicially noticing the inferential location of Vejvoda's conduct, namely, drunk driving, is harmless error beyond a reasonable doubt. Vejvoda's conviction is affirmed.

Affirmed.

NOTES AND QUESTIONS

1. *Criminal cases.* In United States v. Dior, 671 F.2d 351, 358 n.11 (9th Cir.1982), the prosecution failed to enter the Canadian–American exchange rate into evidence to establish the value of transported property. The court declined to take judicial notice on appeal:

> [T]o take judicial notice of an adjudicative fact after a jury's discharge in a criminal case would cast the court in the role of a fact-finder and violate defendant's Sixth Amendment right to trial by jury * * * Indeed, for a trial court (in a post-verdict motion) or an appellate court to take judicial notice of an adjudicative fact in a criminal case would frustrate the policies Congress sought to achieve in providing in F.R. Evid. 201([f]) that a jury is not required to accept as conclusive a judicially noticed fact. These policies are to preserve the jury's traditional prerogative, in a criminal case, to ignore even uncontroverted facts in reaching a verdict and to prevent the trial court from violating the spirit of the Sixth Amendment * * * by directing a partial verdict as to facts.

See also United States v. Herrera–Ochoa, 245 F.3d 495, 501 (5th Cir.2001) ("Taking judicial notice in this case of an essential element of the crime * * * potentially infringes on Herrera's right to have each element proved beyond a reasonable doubt."); United States v. Jones, 580 F.2d 219, 224 (6th Cir.1978) ("As enacted by Congress, Rule 201([f]) plainly contemplates that the jury in a criminal case shall pass upon facts which are judicially noticed. This it could not do if this notice were taken for the first time * * * on appeal.") (status of phone company as "common carrier" not established at trial).

For a survey and analysis of federal results under Rule 201(f), see Turner, Judicial Notice and Federal Rule of Evidence 201—A Rule Ready for Change, 45 U.Pitt.L.Rev. 181 (1983). Professor Turner concludes that the congressional effort to vindicate the right to trial by jury through Rule 201(f) is ineffective, unnecessary, and should be rescinded.

Nevertheless, the Supreme Court's reinvigoration of the right to jury trial suggests that caution is in order when taking any issue away from the jury. See Apprendi v. New Jersey, 530 U.S. 466, 490 (2000) ("Other than the fact of a prior conviction, any fact that increases the penalty for a crime beyond the prescribed statutory maximum must be submitted to a jury, and proved beyond a reasonable doubt."). See also Blakely v. Washington, 542 U.S. 296 (2004). One commentator has argued that taking judicial notice of jurisdictional facts in federal trials in unconstitutional. See Carter, "Trust Me, I'm a Judge": Why Binding Judicial Notice of Jurisdictional Facts Violates the Right to Jury Trial, 68 Mo.L.Rev. 649 (2003). See also Comment, Proper Venue as a Jury Issue in Federal Criminal Cases: The "in issue" Approach to When Venue Presents a Fact Question for the Jury as Opposed to a Question of Law for the Court, 76 Temp.L.Rev. 883 (2003).

2. *Ambiguous status of generalized knowledge.* Central to the application of rules patterned upon Fed.R.Evid. 201 is the question of what types of facts are "adjudicative facts" subject to the strictures of the rule. For example, are the principles underlying X-rays, fingerprinting, various tests for intoxication, radar, and ballistics adjudicative facts? These and other scientific principles are frequently "noticed" by courts[3] with the consequence that the foundation necessary for the introduction of evidence obtained through their application can be abbreviated somewhat. But does judicial notice taken for such a purpose fall within Rule 201? Clearly the advisory committee originally charged with drafting the Federal Rules did not consider such "facts" as adjudicative facts.

> While judges use judicial notice of "propositions of generalized knowledge" in a variety of situations: determining the validity and meaning of statutes, formulating common law rules, deciding whether evidence should be admitted, assessing the sufficiency and effect of evidence, all are essentially nonadjudicative in nature. * * * It is not believed that judges now instruct juries as to "propositions of generalized knowledge" derived from encyclopedias or other sources, or that they are likely to do so, or indeed, that it is desirable that they do so. There is a vast difference between ruling on the basis of judicial notice that radar evidence of speed is admissible and explaining to the jury its principles and degree of accuracy, or between using a table of stopping distances of automobiles at various speeds in a judicial evaluation of testimony and telling the jury its precise application in the case.

Fed.R.Evid. 201 advisory committee's note.

Concerning the judicial use of "background facts" in passing on questions of relevancy and sufficiency, see Mansfield, Jury Notice, 74 Geo.L.J. 395 (1985).

---

[3] See Daubert v. Merrell Dow Pharm., Inc., 509 U.S. 579, 593 n.11 (1993) ("[T]heories that are so firmly established as to have attained the status of scientific law, such as the laws of thermodynamics, properly are subject to judicial notice under Fed. Rule Evid. 201.").

POTTS V. COE

United States Court of Appeals, District of Columbia, 1944.
145 F.2d 27.

ARNOLD, ASSOCIATE JUSTICE. This is a motion to vacate our decision in the case of *Louis M. Potts and Teletype Corporation v. Conway P. Coe, Commissioner of Patents*,[4] and to withdraw the opinion filed in support of that decision. The moving parties had appealed from a judgment dismissing their complaint brought under Section 4915, R.S., 35 U.S.C.A. § 63, to require the Patent Office to grant patents on certain claims relating to an automatic stock quotation board capable of giving nationwide service. Our decision affirmed the order of the court below dismissing the complaint. The ground for the present motion to vacate is that in affirming the District Court we raised and decided a question not presented by the record and based our opinion on facts found in investigations authorized by Congress.

* * *

We will restate the principle on which our decision rests and which appellants claim was improperly injected into the case. Where a corporation, as assignee of one of its employees, seeks a patent on a discovery made in the course of its organized technical research it must assume a different burden of proof from that imposed where the discovery is the product of independent inventive genius. The corporation, which in substance is seeking the patent, must show that (1) the employee is the real inventor, and (2) the discovery is above the level of the art current in its own corporate laboratory and other corporate laboratories with which it has connections and affiliations. Such a burden is not met merely by showing that the discovery is an advance over the art shown in technical literature outside the laboratory or in previous patent application by others.

We believe this result is compelled if we apply the fundamental principles of the patent law to the actual facts of the complex modern technology of corporate research laboratories. These principles are (1) that a discovery which is the result of step-by-step experimentation does not rise to the level of invention; (2) that invention must rise above the level of accomplishment of the ordinary skilled technicians engaged in the art; (3) that the patent law must be so administered as to promote science and the useful arts. These three somewhat overlapping principles are questioned by no one.

Our opinion holds that in applying these principles to discoveries which arise out of the experimentation of modern organized corporate research we must take judicial notice of the character of that kind of

---

[4] [140 F.2d 470 (D.C.Cir.1944)].

enterprise. Unless we do so the patent law may become a cloak under which a corporate group may prevent the independent use of modern technical information by obtaining patents on the step-by-step progress of scientific knowledge. The methods employed by successful corporate research are well known. It has become a device by which a corporation may get a patent on what has been called "know how", which means the technical skill which large groups of men acquire through extensively financed experimentation and cooperation. By taking an assignment in advance from each employee the corporation appears to satisfy the requirement that there be an individual inventor. But the corporation is the real applicant, and the man whose name appears on the patent is only a nominal party. Furthermore, though the discovery may appear to be a startling innovation, actually it is frequently the product of years of research by many men who come and go, who consult each other and the employees of other corporations with which their own employer has affiliations and agreements. The result is a gradual advance in scientific knowledge made possible because large funds have been spent on research—not an invention. The use of this accumulating body of technical information is denied to the public and to new enterprise whenever a patent is granted on this kind of "discovery". Corporate patenting of this character gives the first private group that trains its employees in a modern industrial technique the right to prevent others from using the same knowledge which they may obtain by similar methods. For that reason acquisition of control over technical education acquired by years of routine experimentation has become a major patent policy of domestic and international cartels.

* * *

Today, when the strangling effects on industrial progress and the promotion of patent cartels, through the growth of the fiction under which corporate patenting has been inadvertently approved, are written large in the investigations authorized by Congress, appellants argue that we have no right to consider such public hearings in applying the principles of the patent law to corporate research. This argument is not worthy of serious consideration. The purpose of economic investigations by Congress is not only to promote sensible legislation; it is also to aid in the intelligent interpretation and administration of the law. Facts brought out by such investigations are particularly important in construing the patent law since it must effectuate the broad economic purpose defined in the Constitution as the promotion of science and the useful arts. Furthermore, we have used Congressional investigations only to illustrate characteristics of organized research that are obvious without their support. The patent law is designed to encourage competition among inventors by giving a patent to the ingenious individual who wins in a race for discovery. The modern corporate research laboratory is a negation of this principle because it is compelled to suppress competition between individuals. Instead the race is between the financial interests that organize the laboratories. The result is that a corporation, by successfully eliminating competition for prior discovery between individuals, receives the statutory reward offered to encourage the individual effort which it has suppressed. A court which grants patents on an assumption contrary to these facts[5] is guilty of affirmatively promoting a fiction which inevitably leads to the monopoly grants to corporations on the technical education of our time.

We suspect that the underlying reason for appellants' objection to our opinion is not that it is based on judicial notice of the facts of industrial research. It is rather that it lays down a principle of law which is not acceptable to appellants. Leaders in corporate research have argued that corporate patenting of technical information is in the public interest. Their contention is that corporate research is so expensive that the financing of research would stop if corporations were not offered a monopoly on the information for which they spend their funds. Independent innovators like Henry Kaiser and Edsel Ford repudiate this notion. The argument justifying corporate control of technical information is simply a variation of the larger argument justifying the protection of the investments and dominating position of cartels to insure orderly production and full employment. To those who believe in the economics of free enterprise this position is both unsound and dangerous. But a debate on these opposing economic philosophies is not relevant here because our legislative policy is clearly committed to the proposition that public interest can only be protected through freedom of competitive enterprise to use the technology of our time. It is sufficient, therefore, to say that the policy of the patent law gives no support whatever to monopolies on step-by-step experimentation however expensive that process may be.

* * *

The motion is denied.

---

[5] What we believe to be the view of the Supreme Court has been adequately summarized by Mr. Justice Brandeis as follows:

"The judge came to the bench unequipped with the necessary knowledge of social and economic science, and his judgment suffered likewise through lack of equipment in the lawyers who presented the cases to him. For a judge rarely performs his functions adequately unless the case before him is adequately presented. Thus were the blind led by the blind. It is not surprising that under such conditions the laws as administered failed to meet contemporary economic and social demands. * * * The court reawakened to the truth of the old maxim of the civilians, Ex factor jus oritur. It realized that no law, written or unwritten, can be understood without a full knowledge of the facts out of which it arises and to which it is to be applied. * * * "Address before the Chicago Bar Association January 3, 1916, in The Brandeis Guide to the Modern World, edited by Alfred Lief (1941), pp. 100–101.

NOTES AND QUESTIONS

1. *Legislative facts.* For what purpose does the court utilize judicial notice in *Potts v. Coe*? Due primarily to the ideas advanced by Professor Kenneth Culp Davis, first set out in Davis, An Approach to Problems of Evidence in the Administrative Process, 55 Harv.L.Rev. 364 (1942), it has become common among commentators, and more recently among courts, to distinguish between "adjudicative" and "legislative" facts.

> * * * [A]djudicative facts are those to which the law is applied in the process of adjudication. They are the facts that normally go to the jury in a jury case. They relate to the parties, their activities, their properties, their businesses. Legislative facts are those which help the tribunal to determine the content of law and policy and to exercise its judgment or discretion in determining what course of action to take. Legislative facts are ordinarily general and do not concern the immediate parties. In the great mass of cases decided by courts and by agencies, the legislative aspect is either absent, unimportant, or interstitial, because in most cases the applicable law and policy have been previously established. But whenever a tribunal is engaged in the creation of law or of policy, it may need to resort to legislative facts, whether or not those facts have been developed on the record.

Davis, Judicial Notice, 55 Colum.L.Rev. 945, 952 (1955).

Note that the term "legislative" facts is not restricted to facts developed and relied upon by a legislature in the process of formulating statutory law, but extends to all facts utilized by the courts in determining what the law, either statutory or decisional, is or should be. See Rogers v. Tennessee, 532 U.S. 451, 461 (2001) ("In the context of common law doctrines (such as the year and a day rule), there often arises a need to clarify or even to reevaluate prior opinions as new circumstances and fact patterns present themselves. Such judicial acts, whether they be characterized as 'making' or 'finding' the law, are a necessary part of the judicial business in States in which the criminal law retains some of its common law elements.").

2. *Criticism.* Professor Davis vigorously criticized both the Model Code and the original Uniform Rules of Evidence, neither of which drew any distinction between "legislative" and "adjudicative" facts, on the ground that judicial notice of "legislative" facts should not be, and is not in fact, confined to facts which are indisputable. Davis, Judicial Notice, 55 Colum.L.Rev. 945 (1955). Federal Rule 201 does draw such a distinction since it purports to regulate only judicial notice of "adjudicative facts." Professor Davis proved almost equally critical of the federal rule, however, on the ground that it left legislative facts out of account. For Davis' criticisms and the rule which he would prefer, see Davis, Judicial Notice, 1969 Law & Soc.Ord. 513.

3. *Sources for judicial notice of legislative facts.* Assuming, as implied by Rule 201, notice of legislative facts is not to be regulated by the same

strictures and standards applicable to adjudicative facts, by what means may a court apprise itself of the pertinent facts? In Chastleton Corp. v. Sinclair, 264 U.S. 543, 548 (1924), Justice Holmes stated that "the Court may ascertain as it sees fit any fact that is merely a ground for laying down a rule of law * * *." In *Chastleton*, the appropriate mode of ascertainment was deemed to be a remand of the case to the district court, apparently for the reception of further evidence. Adopting the same expedient, see Borden's Farm Products Co. v. Baldwin, 293 U.S. 194 (1934). Are legislative facts always susceptible to satisfactory development through traditional evidentiary channels? See Roberts, Preliminary Notes Toward a Study of Judicial Notice, 52 Cornell L.Q. 210, 225 (1967). One commentator proposed that the Supreme Court ask the National Academy of Sciences to develop legislative facts. Auerbach, Legislative Facts in Grutter v. Bollinger, 45 San Diego L.Rev. 33 (2008).

4. *Brandeis Brief.* A method by which a party may undertake to apprise the court of "legislative" facts is that of the so-called "Brandeis Brief," the prototype of which was authored by Louis Brandeis, in the case of Muller v. Oregon, 208 U.S. 412 (1908), before his elevation to the Supreme Court. In attempting to support the constitutionality of an Oregon statute regulating the employment of women, Brandeis devoted virtually his entire brief to a monumental collection of social and economic data tending to demonstrate the factual realities of the problem at which the statute was directed. The Brandeis Brief was originally conceived as a method of supporting the constitutionality of legislation, usually social legislation, attacked as having no reasonable basis in fact and therefore arbitrary and capricious. When used for this purpose is it necessary that the court take judicial notice of the "truth" of the data adduced, or only of the fact that the data exist? See the dissenting opinion of Justice Brandeis in Jay Burns Baking Co. v. Bryan, 264 U.S. 504, 519–20 (1924).

5. *Social authority.* Where the proposed use of legislative facts logically requires not only that the data exist but that they be accurate, troublesome questions arise concerning how the reliability of the data should be assessed. A novel and potentially valuable approach to this problem is suggested by Monahan & Walker, Social Authority: Obtaining, Evaluating, and Establishing Social Science in Law, 134 U.Pa.L.Rev. 477 (1986). The authors of this article argue that much of the product of social science research might more appropriately and usefully be analogized to legal precedent than to evidentiary fact. What assessment methodologies are suggested by this new analogy?

6. *Sources.* More traditional treatments of the same problem include: Roberts, Preliminary Notes Toward a Study of Judicial Notice, 52 Cornell L.Q. 210 (1967); Currie, Appellate Courts Use of Facts Outside the Record by Resort to Judicial Notice and Independent Investigation, 1960 Wis.L.Rev. 39; Laughlin, Judicial Notice, 40 Minn.L.Rev. 365 (1956); Morgan, Judicial Notice, 57 Harv.L.Rev. 269 (1944).

CHAPTER 10[1]

REAL AND DEMONSTRATIVE EVIDENCE

■ ■ ■

SMITH V. OHIO OIL CO.

Appellate Court of Illinois, 1956.
134 N.E.2d 526.

SCHEINEMAN, JUSTICE. Plaintiff, W.R. Smith, suffered personal injuries when his truck was run into by a truck of the Ohio Oil Company, driven by its employee, Maurice M. Smedley. In a suit against these parties, plaintiff recovered a judgment on a verdict of $50,000 and the defendants have appealed.

* * *

During the testimony of a medical witness for plaintiff, the court permitted the use of a plastic model of a human skeleton to assist the explanations. This is assigned as error on the ground that it was unnecessary to an understanding of the issues, was gruesome, and tended only to arouse emotion rather than explain anything.

The use of physical objects before a jury falls into two categories: 1, real evidence, which Wigmore calls "adoptive," and 2, demonstrative evidence. The tests for the proper use of either are substantially similar, i.e., the object must be relevant to some issue in the case, and it must also be actually explanatory of something which it is important for the jury to understand. If these tests are met, the courts do not seem to be greatly concerned with the question whether the object is gruesome.

Real evidence involves the production of some object which had a direct part in the incident, and includes the exhibition of injured parts of the body. * * *

Demonstrative evidence (a model, map, photograph, X-ray, etc.) is distinguished from real evidence in that it has no probative value in itself, but serves merely as a visual aid to the jury in comprehending the verbal testimony of a witness. Wigmore, Evid. Sec. 790 et seq. It is said its great value lies in the human factor of understanding better what is seen than what is heard. Wigmore favors the use of any aid modern science may provide, to the end that the jury may have the best possible

---

[1] Throughout this chapter some footnotes from the original cases and materials have been omitted; others have been renumbered. [Ed.]

understanding of matters it must decide. The limitations are that the evidence must be relevant and the use of the object actually explanatory. Sometimes the question of accuracy of an exhibit is pertinent, but this seems to be a phase of its explanatory function, since it may be misleading if inaccurate.

Similar views have been expressed by the courts. Reinke v. Sanitary District, 260 Ill. 380, 103 N.E. 236; 20 Am.Jur.Evid. § 740; 9 A.L.R.2d 1044, note. The skeleton of a human foot was held properly used by physicians in explanation of their testimony. Chicago & A. Ry. Co. v. Walker, 217 Ill. 605, 75 N.E. 520. It was proper to use a model skeleton where it was of assistance to the jury. Carnine v. Tibbetts, 158 Or. 21, 74 P.2d 974. But where its use would not aid a jury, trial court properly excluded it. Dameron v. Ansbro, 39 Cal.App. 289, 178 P. 874.

Articles by law professors and trial attorneys in various law reviews have pointed out that the very fact people learn and understand better with the eyes than with the ears, makes it possible to abuse demonstrative evidence by giving a dramatic effect, or undue emphasis to some issue at the expense of others. There is obvious merit in these criticisms and the courts must be alert to eliminate such abuse. Apparently the enthusiasm of Wigmore, Greenleaf, and other writers for demonstrative evidence is shared by the courts, and the desirability of giving the jury the best possible understanding of the subject on which they are to pass seems to have outweighed other factors.

As a result, the use of such evidence is usually left to the discretion of the trial court, and expressions of disapproval are generally based on irrelevance, or that the model, picture, etc., was misleading or not explanatory. Therefore, this court will not announce any flat rule that a skeletal model may never be used, but holds that its use must be actually explanatory of some relevant issue in the case.

This court holds that the determination of relevancy and explanatory value of demonstrative evidence is primarily within the discretion of the trial court, but, to curtail abuses, is subject to review as to the actual use made of the object. If it appears that the exhibit was used for dramatic effect, or emotional appeal, rather than factual explanation useful to the reasoning of the jury, this should be regarded as reversible error, not because of abuse of discretion, but because actual use proved to be an abuse of the ruling.

Applying these tests to the actual use in the case at bar, it appears that the model was not used at all during the physician's testimony as to injuries he found, operations performed, methods of treatment, etc. Not until he proceeded to describe the present condition of plaintiff was the model exhibited. This involved the pelvic area, which is probably the part of the body most difficult for the average person to visualize.

In reply to questions by the court, the witness stated the model would assist his explanation, and that it was an excellent reproduction of a normal human skeleton. Permission was given to use the model. The witness then pointed to displacement of bones of the pelvis in a recent X-ray of plaintiff, and pointed to the model to illustrate normal alignment. Witness also explained the muscular arrangement and how the weight of the upper torso is transmitted to the lower extremities. He pointed out where excess strain would occur because of damaged ligaments and bone displacement, and how this would affect the ability to balance, or to stoop over. This was important as an explanation of the doctor's statement that a built-up shoe would not remedy the condition.

From consideration of testimony of the witness, this court concludes that the explanation was relevant, legitimate and helpful, and contained nothing emotional or dramatic in character. The rulings of the court thereon were correct. * * *

Judgment affirmed.

BARDENS, P.J., and CULBERTSON, J., concur.

NOTES AND QUESTIONS

1.   *Sources.* The increased interest in recent years in real and demonstrative evidence has produced a wealth of periodical literature on the subject. Some classic articles dealing basically with the efficacy of tangible evidence as a vehicle of persuasion and the range of possibilities for its use include: Belli, Demonstrative Evidence and the Adequate Award, 22 Miss.L.J. 284 (1951); Dooley, Demonstrative Evidence—Nothing New, 42 Ill.B.J. 136 (1953); Hinshaw, Use and Abuse of Demonstrative Evidence: The Art of Jury Persuasion, 40 A.B.A.J. 479 (1954); Spangenberg, The Use of Demonstrative Evidence, 21 Ohio St.L.J. 178 (1960). For more recent treatments see Imwinkelried, Evidentiary Foundations (8th ed. 2012); Lubet, Modern Trial Advocacy ch. 10 (4th ed. 2009); Mauet, Trial Techniques ch. VI (8th ed. 2010).

2.   *Directly involved exhibits.* The court in the principal case follows Wigmore in citing models, maps and photographs as examples of demonstrative, rather than real, evidence. No great effort, however, is required to imagine numerous possible situations in which, e.g., a map or photograph will have "had a direct part in the incident." The problems of classifying and labeling types of evidence other than oral testimony are treated in Michael & Adler, Real Proof, 5 Vand.L.Rev. 344 (1952); Nokes, Real Evidence, 65 L.Q.Rev. 57 (1949), reprinted in Selected Writings on Evidence and Trial 668 (Fryer ed. 1957).

3.   *Classification as "real" or "demonstrative."* What practical difference will it make whether a particular item is properly classified as "real" or merely "demonstrative" evidence? In contrast to the principal case, one Texas trial judge is said to have excluded a proffered skeleton on the ground that it

did not comprise the "very bones" of the plaintiff. See Cady, Objections to Demonstrative Evidence, 32 Mo.L.Rev. 333, 338 (1967). Where, as is generally the case, the admissibility of both real and demonstrative evidence is viewed as depending upon whether it will assist the understanding of the jury, one importance of classification may be to determine the foundation which will be required for introduction of the item. For other practical differences in consequence, see 1 Giannelli, Imwinkelried, Roth & Moriarty, Scientific Evidence ch. 7 (5th ed. 2012); Graham, Relevancy and Exclusion of Relevant Evidence—Real Evidence, 18 Crim.L.Bull. 333 (1982); 2 McCormick, Evidence § 212 (7th ed. 2013). For a discussion of the theoretical basis for the admissibility of demonstrative evidence, see Brain & Broderick, The Derivative Relevance of Demonstrative Evidence: Charting Its Proper Evidentiary Status, 25 U.C. Davis L. Rev. 957 (1992).

Sometimes a physical object will be offered as demonstrative evidence because the actual item involved in the incident is no longer available. See United States v. Aldaco, 201 F.3d 979, 986 (7th Cir.2000) (replica of destroyed shotgun properly admitted as demonstrative evidence).

Had you represented the plaintiff in *Smith v. Ohio Oil Co.*, what foundation would you have sought to lay through the testimony of your expert medical witness prior to offering the skeleton in evidence? Prepare a series of questions calculated to elicit such foundation testimony. With your result, compare that suggested in Lay, Use of Real Evidence, 37 Neb.L.Rev. 501, 513 (1958).

4.   *Which federal rule?* Which, if any, of the Federal Rules deals with the issues involved in the admission of real or demonstrative evidence?

GALLAGHER V. PEQUOT SPRING WATER CO.

Circuit Court of Connecticut, Appellate Division, 1963.
199 A.2d 172.

KOSICKI, JUDGE. The plaintiff sued the defendant, a bottler and vendor of grape soda, for injuries sustained by her after consuming soda sold by the defendant, because of the presence in it of a foreign substance. The complaint was in two counts, one sounding in negligence and the other for breach of an implied warranty as to the merchantability of the soda and as to its fitness for the intended use. The jury returned a general plaintiff's verdict for $2500. On motion to set aside the verdict, the court ordered a remitter of $1000, which was filed, and judgment was entered on the verdict as modified. * * *

The following facts are not in dispute. The plaintiff was married on August 26, 1961, and a wedding reception was held at the Mount Carmel Hall. There were approximately 150 guests present, of whom about thirty were children. At the wedding dinner, the plaintiff's father poured for her some of the soda sold by the defendant. There were approximately fifteen people seated at the bride's table. The plaintiff consumed the soda as her father poured the remaining contents of the bottle for others at the table. While he was pouring, some of those at the table, other than the plaintiff and her mother, who were the only witnesses to testify for the plaintiff, exclaimed excitedly over a foreign substance which they variously described, within hearing of the plaintiff, as a "bloodsucker" or "cockroach." Neither the plaintiff nor her mother saw what was in the bottle. On trial, there was no identification of the substance other than a characterization of it by a defendant's witness as a "mold." The plaintiff became ill and retired to the ladies' room, where she vomited. She was unable to eat her dinner and left before the grand march took place. According to custom, the guests are expected to make gifts of money to the bride and groom in the course of the grand march, but because of the early departure of the plaintiff many of the guests also left and consequently some of the expected gifts failed to materialize. Because of her illness, the plaintiff abstained from the joyous incidents of the nuptial night, abandoned the plans for her honeymoon, and a few days later returned to work.

Among the errors assigned by the defendant is error in the ruling of the court admitting in evidence, as exhibit 1 a soda bottle containing some unidentified substance. If the exhibit was admitted improperly, the error would be material because the jury then would have been permitted to accept as true the very fact which the plaintiff needed in order to establish the defendant's liability on either count. The exhibit was offered through Mrs. Alaimo, the plaintiff's mother, who, in the course of her direct examination, testified that the bottle was the one opened by her husband at the table where she sat about twelve feet from him. The defendant objected, stating as reasons that the substance in the bottle had not been identified, that there was no proof that the substance was in the bottle at the time of the alleged occurrence, that custody and care of the bottle until the date of trial had not been accounted for, and that a proper foundation had not been laid for admitting this item of evidence. The objection was overruled and the bottle admitted as a full exhibit. Upon further questioning, the witness testified as follows: "Q.—Now, did anything unusual happen while he was pouring from the bottle? A.—Yes, everybody—well, as he was pouring, they noticed this object in the bottle was moving around and they got up and there was quite a commotion. They was wondering what was in the bottle. The court: And while he was pouring this, some people noticed something? A.—Well, yes—you know— they were facing her table and as he was pouring it, someone nearby said something about a cockroach being in the bottle, or something, and they named other bugs and then the people sitting in back walked up. They wanted to see what was in the bottle. Q.—Now, Mrs. Alaimo, can you tell me what actually this object in the bottle was? A. I don't know, I mean— Q.—Did you know at that time? A.—Everybody was saying different things—Mr. Higgins: Objection, Your Honor. She is just not answering the question. The court: She doesn't know. Q.—Do you know at this time? A.—Well, I don't know—do you mean do I know what's in the bottle? Q.—Yes. A.—No, I don't know. I know something is in the bottle, but I don't know what it is. Q.—But this is the bottle as you saw it there? A.—Yes it is." On cross-examination, the witness stated that after the wedding reception her husband took the bottle home and later turned it over to a lawyer. Her husband had died some time before the trial.

The plaintiff, during her testimony, identified the bottle as being the one from which she had consumed soda poured by her father. "Q.—What did you do with the soda when you got it? A.—I drank it. Q.—Right away? A.—Yes. Q.—Now, did any incident occur while your father was pouring the soda in other people's cups? A.—Yes, it started an uproar. They saw something shaking around in the bottle, they said there was a bloodsucker, cockroaches, there was a lot of comments about what was in the bottom of the bottle. Q.—Now it's true that you don't know what is in that bottle now, isn't it? A.—No. Q.—Is that right? A.—Yes. Q.—And you didn't know what was in it—supposedly in it—at the reception, is that right? A.—No, that's right. Q.—And you consumed a cup of grape soda at the reception? A.—Yes. Q.—And thereafter, didn't you testify that some people around there saw something in the bottle? A.—Splashing around in the bottle. Q.—And they started making remarks? A.—Yes. Q.—And isn't that what upset you? A.—No, that wasn't what upset me, no."

We have set down the testimony verbatim and at considerable length so that all of the evidence material to the issue raised by the defendant's objection may be examined in the light most favorable to the plaintiff. In laying a foundation for the receipt in evidence of the thing claimed to have caused the injury, it is ordinarily sufficient for the witness having knowledge of the object to identify it. See Lestico v. Kuehner, 204 Minn. 125, 283 N.W. 122, Exhibit 1 was admitted on identification of the bottle. It was not introduced to prove the identity of the bottle which had contained the beverage consumed but as real evidence of the purported substance which allegedly the beverage contained and which caused the plaintiff's illness and suffering. See 1 Wigmore, Evidence (3d Ed.) § 24. In order to justify its admission for that purpose, it was necessary first to show that it was the substance it purported to be, that is, that it was present in the bottle at the time of the occurrence, in a condition reasonably the same as that viewed at the trial, eighteen months later. The plaintiff had the burden of proving as a preliminary matter that the substance allegedly contained in the bottle at the time it was first opened was the same substance, without any material change, as that found in the bottle when it was offered as an exhibit. See Wieland v. C.A. Swanson & Sons, 223 F.2d 26 (2d Cir.). This is usually accomplished by showing original apperception of the object and then its care and custody under circumstances which would reasonably exclude any tampering with or material alteration in it so as to render the exhibit misleading—or, as in this case, the probability of chemical changes or organic growth resulting from environmental factors such as air, moisture and temperature. See Jasper Coca Cola Bottling Co. v. Breed, 40 Ala.App. 449, 452, 115 So.2d 126; 32 C.J.S. Evidence §§ 601, 602, 607. The rule, however, is not so rigid as to render things sometimes called unique inadmissible unless absolute continuity of possession and the absence of tampering are first established. Pasadena Research Laboratories, Inc. v. United States, 169 F.2d 375, 380 (9th Cir.); Anheuser–Busch, Inc. v. Southard, 191 Ark. 107, 84 S.W.2d 89; Coca–Cola Bottling Co. of Arkansas v. Adcox, 189 Ark. 610, 74 S.W.2d 771. It is enough if the object offered in evidence has been reasonably identified as that sought to be proved, by someone who can testify of his own knowledge that the object proffered is the one claimed to have caused the result.

The questioned exhibit consists of a dark green quart bottle with a roughened surface, some liquid therein, and a substance described by one witness as a "mold." To see this substance at all requires observation at very close range in good light. It is plain that neither witness who identified the bottle had any knowledge of what was in it, other than soda, at the time the plaintiff partook of the contents. Neither of them examined the bottle at that time; they relied on what they heard, not on what they saw; no testimony was offered as to care and custody of the bottle and its contents; and no evidence supports the conclusion, obviously reached by the jury, that the substance they observed was the same as that which was allegedly present in the bottle when the soda was consumed by the plaintiff. * * *

The objection of the defendant was well taken; a sufficient foundation had not been laid for the admission of exhibit 1 and its examination by the jury; and the error was harmful and prejudicial to the defendant.

* * *

There is error, the judgment is set aside and a new trial is ordered.

In this opinion DEARINGTON and KINMONTH, JJ., concurred.

NOTES AND QUESTIONS

1. *Differences in testimony.* Would you expect the holding of the principal case to have been different: (a) had either the plaintiff or her mother been able to testify as to the contents of the bottle at the time of the wedding supper, or (b) if the attorney to whom the bottle was subsequently delivered had been called to testify as to what he did with it?

2. *Chain of custody.* The exactitude with which the "chain of custody" of a tangible object must be traced as a precondition to its admission will frequently vary with the nature of the object. Thus, an object which is more or less readily identifiable by observation and relatively impervious to change

or alteration will frequently be admitted without perfect tracing of the chain. See, e.g., State v. Sugimoto, 614 P.2d 386 (Haw.1980) (check held properly admitted without complete chain because identifiable and relatively impervious to change); Brown v. State, 518 P.2d 898 (Okla.Crim.App.1974) (jack properly admitted despite broken chain of custody which would have been of "grave concern" had evidence been a specimen for chemical analysis). And some courts expressly consider "identification" testimony a complete alternative to establishing a chain of custody, at least where identifiable objects are concerned. Cooper v. Eagle River Mem. Hosp., 270 F.3d 456 (7th Cir. 2001) (authentication sufficient without chain of custody where reference number on pathology slide matched the specimen number in pathology report); State v. Emery, 688 P.2d 175 (Ariz.1984) (linen taken from victim's bed properly authenticated without chain of custody by police officer's tags). For a clear statement of the relativity of foundation requirements, see Loza v. State, 325 N.E.2d 173 (Ind.1975).

3. *Strictness of showing chain.* A showing sufficient to preclude the possibilities of tampering or unintentional interchange or contamination is frequently said to be necessary to the introduction of more fungible items, particularly in criminal cases. One authority, however, has contended that such standards are not always applied with the strictness with which they are enunciated. See 1 Giannelli, Imwinkelried, Roth & Moriarty, Scientific Evidence ch. 7 (5th ed. 2012) (a thorough treatment of the subject). See also People v. Smith, 949 N.Y.S.2d 190 (A.D. 2012) (as long as there is reasonable assurance, doubts about chain of custody go to the weight of the evidence, not admissibility).

SEMET V. ANDORRA NURSERIES, INC.

Supreme Court of Pennsylvania, 1966.
219 A.2d 357.

BELL, CHIEF JUSTICE. * * *

On May 22, 1962, plaintiff was sent by his employer Milton Sugerman (an electric contractor) to a construction site owned by defendant, Andorra Nurseries, Inc. Plaintiff was to string a temporary line from an electric service box in the basement of a sample home to the chimney of the sample home and then to poles for the purpose of carrying electric current to the job site. Plaintiff instructed an employee of Andorra Nurseries to place an aluminum 34–foot extension ladder against the left side of the chimney of the sample home. This employee went to the top of the ladder and came down without any unusual incident occurring. Plaintiff made certain that the ladder was straight and settled. He then climbed to the top of the ladder and took some wire off his shoulder. While on the upper portion of the ladder it began to slip downward, and telescoping into the lower portion, as a result of which plaintiff fell and was severely injured. The lower Court entered a compulsory nonsuit which the Court en banc refused to take off. Plaintiff thereafter appealed to this Court.

* * *

52 days after this accident Martin Alkon, a registered Engineer, went to the scene and examined a ladder to which he had been directed by *unnamed* employees of defendant Andorra Nurseries, Inc. Photographs were taken of this ladder. Plaintiff offered Alkon's testimony and the photographs for the purposes of explaining the mechanical function of the ladder and the reasons for the ladder's collapse. The lower Court properly held that this testimony and the accompanying photographs were inadmissible. There was no legally admissible testimony that the ladder examined by Alkon and the ladder photographed was the ladder from which plaintiff fell. Moreover, even if this were proven to be the same ladder, the proffered evidence would still be inadmissible. 52 days passed before the ladder was examined. There was no testimony that the condition of the ladder had not changed from the time of the accident. In Brandon v. Peoples Natural Gas Co., 417 Pa. 128, at pages 133–134, 207 A.2d 843, at page 846, the Court said:

> " * * * 'Whenever the condition of a particular place or thing at a certain time is in question, evidence of its condition at a prior or subsequent time is admissible if accompanied by proof that it has not changed in the meanwhile.' "

Plaintiff attempted to have the photograph admitted into evidence on the ground that it was authenticated by him. Plaintiff was not present when the photograph was taken. A photograph may be proven at the trial of a case without calling the person who took it. Commonwealth v. White, 160 Pa.Super. 522, 52 A.2d 360 (1947). Nevertheless, the photograph must be shown to be a faithful and accurate reproduction of the object in question. Puskarich v. Trustees of Zembo Temple, 412 Pa. 313, 194 A.2d 208. There is nothing in the record which indicates plaintiff had the kind of familiarity with the ladder in question which would enable him to examine a picture of a common two-part metal ladder and verify it as a faithful and accurate reproduction of the ladder which caused his injuries. Plaintiff was injured on or prior to May 22, 1962. The time of his injury was the only instance he saw the ladder. His recollection of the ladder at the time of the trial, over three years from the time of the accident, was extremely dim. We therefore must conclude that plaintiff's vague knowledge and recollection makes it impossible for him to establish that the photographs offered in evidence by him accurately depicted the ladder from which he fell.

In Puskarich v. Trustees of Zembo Temple, 412 Pa. 313, 194 A.2d 208, supra, the Court said (at page 317, 194 A.2d at page 211) quoting from Nyce v. Muffley, 384 Pa. 107, 119 A.2d 530 (1956):

"The admission of photographs is a matter largely within the discretion of the trial Judge. A photograph must be verified either by the testimony of the person who took it or by another person with sufficient knowledge to state that it fairly and accurately represents the object or place reproduced as it existed at the time of the accident, or if there is a difference or change, the difference or change is specifically pointed out and is readily capable of being clearly understood and appreciated by the jury: Taylor v. Modena Borough, 370 Pa. 100, 87 A.2d 195; Beardslee v. Columbia Township, 188 Pa. 496, 41 A. 617." The lower Court correctly excluded this evidence.

The Order of the lower Court refusing to take off the nonsuit is affirmed.

MUSMANNO, J., dissents.

EAGEN and ROBERTS, JJ., concur in the result.

NOTES AND QUESTIONS

1.   *Purpose of offer.* The theory upon which photographs are usually offered, i.e., that they serve "to illustrate or explain" oral testimony, makes for rather liberal admission of this type of evidence. Why did the theory not suffice in the principal case? Would the following rule have provided ancillary support to the plaintiff's argument for admissibility? "Where only the generic characteristics of the item are significant no objection would appear to exist to the introduction of a substantially similar 'duplicate'." 2 McCormick, Evidence § 213 (7th ed. 2013), citing several cases including United States v. Weeks, 919 F.2d 248 (5th Cir.1990) (pistol similar to one used in crime showed by witness but jury instructed it was a model for demonstrative purposes).

2.   *Modern technology.* For discussions of some of the problems that arise as a result of modern technology see Madison, Seeing Can be Deceiving: Photographic Evidence in a Visual Age—How Much Weight Does It Deserve?, 25 Wm. & Mary L.Rev. 705 (1984); Note, A Picture is Worth a Thousand Lies: Electronic Imaging and the Future of the Admissibility of Photographs into Evidence, 18 Rutgers Computer & Tech.L.J. 365 (1992); Witkowski, Can Juries Really Believe What They See? New Foundational Requirements for the Authentication of Digital Images, 10 Wash. U.J.L. & Pol'y 267 (2002). For cases dealing with specific problems related to photographic evidence, see Annots., 9 A.L.R.2d 899 (photos generally); 72 A.L.R.2d 308 (enlargements); 53 A.L.R.2d 1102 (colored slide projection); 85 A.L.R.5th 671(aerial photographs); 19 A.L.R.2d 877 (posed photographs).

CLARK V. ST. THOMAS HOSPITAL

Court of Appeals of Tennessee, 1984.
676 S.W.2d 347.

Opinion

TODD, PRESIDING JUDGE (Middle Section).

Plaintiff has appealed from a jury verdict and judgment dismissing his suit for injuries sustained in a fall in defendant's hospital. The sole issue presented on appeal is the admission in evidence of a video tape of a reenactment of the occasion of his injury.

The background facts are undisputed.

Plaintiff entered the defendant hospital as a patient on October 7, 1977, and was discharged on November 12, 1977. On October 25, 1977, plaintiff's left kidney and spleen were surgically removed. On November 12, 1977, plaintiff was taken to the x-ray room where an x-ray picture was to be taken in a standing position. While standing for the picture, plaintiff fell and was injured.

The principal issue of fact relates to whether plaintiff was attended at the time of his fall. Plaintiff asserted that the x-ray technician was some distance away when she ordered him to move slightly; and, when he endeavored to do so without assistance, he fell. The technician testified that she went to plaintiff and was assisting him in a slight change of position when his knees began to buckle and she lowered him to the floor.

The video tape depicts a reenactment of the events just stated in which the technician performs her version of her actions and a third party performs the movements of plaintiff as described by the technician in her testimony. The technician testified that the movie was a fair representation of the events narrated in her testimony.

Appellant argues:

Appellant contends that it is grossly unfair, inappropriate, judicially unsound and factually inaccurate to allow either party to a lawsuit to make an obviously rehearsed out of court movie of that party's version of how the alleged negligent act occurred for presentation to the jury. Should such a procedure be approved, the obvious next step in every major lawsuit would be to have a theatrical production shown for the jury. The convincing effect of such a production would be in excess of credibility ordinary testimony concerning the matter would be given and jury verdicts would be based, not on the true facts but, on a party's ability to glamorize their versions of the facts.

This Court respectfully disagrees with the foregoing argument as applied to the present case.

First, the admission of the questionable evidence was not grossly unfair. Frequently witnesses are permitted to reenact before the jury the actions of the witness described in the testimony. Sometimes the reenactment requires a second person to represent the other participant in the actions. Such evidence is not original evidence, but is illustrative evidence and is valid for consideration only to the extent that it illustrates facts otherwise shown by sworn testimony. Of such character was the evidence in question. The fundamental evidence to be considered by the jury was the sworn oral testimony of the witness who also swore that the reenactment was the same as her testimony. See *McCormick on Evidence* 2nd Edition, § 212, p. 527.

There is no unfairness in the fact that defendant's witness was supported by illustrative evidence, while plaintiff's testimony was not. There was no reason why plaintiff could not have reenacted the events by videotape or in person during his testimony. He did not see fit to do so. Actually, it would have been even simpler for plaintiff to illustrate his testimony. His version of the incident was that he was alone.

Appellant's fears about the ultimate result of allowing reenactments are unfounded, because the sound discretion of trial judges will prevent the abuse of the device in specific cases and in limiting the subject matter to facts stated in the sworn testimony being illustrated.

Appellant cites *Mize v. Skeen,* 63 Tenn.App. 37, 468 S.W.2d 733 (1971) which involved a motion picture depicting the static condition of an intersection and a vehicle moving in the manner in which testimony had shown the defendant's vehicle was moving at the time of the accident. In that opinion, this Court said:

> The general rule is that the admissibility of photographs is to be determined by the trial judge in the exercise of his sound discretion. *Monday v. Millsaps,* 37 Tenn.App. 371, 264 S.W.2d 6 [1953]; *Strickland Transp. Co. v. Douglas,* 37 Tenn.App. 421, 264 S.W.2d 233 [1953] We know of no reason for a different rule to be applied to motion pictures. Generally the courts in other jurisdictions have held motion pictures to be admissible in the discretion of the trial court when they are shown to be relevant and properly authenticated. See annotation in 62 A.L.R.2d 688. (at 46)

Appellant is largely but not completely correct in stating that the moving picture was confined to static conditions in *Lampley v. Waygood* 57 Tenn.App. 610, 422 S.W.2d 708 (1967). One of the issues in that case was the visibility of a vehicle as it rounded a curve and traversed a crest as it approached an intersection. The moving pictures were made from the position of the eyes of the driver of a vehicle about to enter the intersection from a side street and showed another vehicle approaching over the crest. The movement of the vehicle did illustrate the manner in which the approaching vehicle came into the view of the driver waiting at the intersection. In the cited opinion, this Court said:

> The question whether a photograph is helpful or instructive to the jury on any material issue in the case, is generally a preliminary question to be determined by the Trial Judge, and the fact that a photograph is incorrect in some particulars does not render it inadmissible as evidence but merely affects the weight thereof.

> Considering the specific instructions of the Trial Judge to the jury regarding the introduction of these motion pictures, and considering all the other matters hereinabove referred to, we are of opinion that there is no reversible error shown in this record, * * * (at 620, 422 S.W.2d 708).

Appellant cites *Summit County Development Corporation v. Bagnoli,* 1968, 166 Colo. 27, 441 P.2d 658, which is distinguishable on its facts. One of the issues in that case was the safety of the speed of the movement of a ski lift, and there was no evidence that the speed shown in the movie was the same as the speed at the time of the injury. Speed of movement has no such relation to the present issues which involve manner of fall, i.e. unassisted or assisted. Also, in the cited case it was held that the trial court did not abuse its discretion in excluding the evidence.

Appellant's textual quotations from *Wigmore, McCormick* and Am Jur are reasonable and correct, but not applicable, for they appear to refer to original evidence as to which the rules of accuracy are more strict. As previously pointed out, in the present case the exhibit was illustrative and its admissibility was based upon its conformity to sworn testimony.

Appellant complains that the movie was not subject to cross examination. The witness whose testimony was illustrated was present for cross examination, and this was sufficient.

As early as 1912, the Tennessee Supreme Court recognized the value and admissibility of posed still pictures to illustrate the testimony of an eyewitness to the facts depicted. *Hughes v. State*, 126 Tenn. 40, 148 S.W. 543 (1912). In the present case, no reason is seen for applying a different standard to a movie which did not distort or embellish sworn testimony.

For an extensive collection of authorities from other jurisdictions, see 32 C.J.S., Evidence, § 715, pp. 1016–1018 notes 76 and 76.5.

The admission of the challenged evidence was clearly within the proper scope of the discretionary powers of the Trial Judge. Any fears of the plaintiff as to prejudicial effect might have been readily relieved by a proper request for instructions to the jury as to the consideration of the evidence.

Appellant's sole issue is found to be without merit. The judgment of the Trial Court is affirmed. Costs of this appeal are taxed against appellant. The cause is remanded for such further proceedings as may be necessary and proper.

Affirmed & Remanded.

LEWIS and CANTRELL, JJ.

NOTES AND QUESTIONS

1. *Motion pictures and videotapes.* The theory of admissibility utilized by the court in the principal case was first advanced to facilitate the introduction of motion pictures. See Paradis, The Celluloid Witness, 37 Colo.L.Rev. 235 (1965). That theory, now widely accepted by the courts, is readily applicable to videotapes despite the fact that the latter are created through a different technology. For a comprehensive collection of authorities relating to the use of videotapes, see Joseph, Modern Visual Evidence (2013)

2. *Reconstructions or reenactments.* Note the distinction drawn in *Clark* between videotapes (or motion pictures) of the actual event in litigation and those of reconstructions or reenactments. To what extent is the court justified in stating that "the rules of accuracy are more strict" with respect to the former? If exact accuracy is not to be required of the latter are any other precautions appropriate? See Balian v. General Motors, 296 A.2d 317 (N.J.Super.1972); Note, Videotaped Reenactments in Civil Trials: Protecting Probative Evidence from the Trial Judge's Unbridled Discretion, 24 J. Marshall L.Rev. 433 (1991).

COMMONWEALTH V. SERGE
Supreme Court of Pennsylvania, 2006.
896 A.2d 1170.

JUSTICE NEWMAN. Michael Serge (Appellant) appeals the sentence of life imprisonment entered by the Court of Common Pleas of Lackawanna County (trial court) following his conviction for first-degree murder * * * . We granted allowance of appeal in this case to consider the admissibility of a computer-generated animation (CGA) illustrating the Commonwealth's theory of the homicide. For the reasons discussed herein, we hold that the trial court properly admitted the CGA as demonstrative evidence. * * *

On the morning of January 15, 2001, Appellant shot his wife, Jennifer Serge (Victim), three times, killing her inside their home in Scott Township, Lackawanna County. Appellant was arrested that morning and charged with one count of first-degree murder, * * * and one count of third-degree murder * * *.

On June 18, 2001, prior to trial, the Commonwealth filed a Motion *in limine,* seeking to present the prosecution's theory of the fatal shooting through a CGA based on both forensic and physical evidence.[2] On September 14, 2001, following an evidentiary hearing, the trial court granted the Commonwealth's Motion in limine provided that certain evidentiary foundations were established at trial.[3] * * * The trial court required the Commonwealth to authenticate the animation as both a fair and accurate depiction of expert reconstructive testimony and exclude any inflammatory features that may cause unfair prejudice. To safeguard against potential prejudice, the trial court required the pre-trial disclosure of the CGA.

At his jury trial held January 29, 2002 to February 12, 2002, Appellant alleged that he had acted in self-defense as his wife attacked him with a knife. He further asserted that he should be acquitted on the grounds of justifiable self-defense. Alternatively, Appellant argued that

---

[2] A CGA is a drawing, or drawings, created by a computer that, when assembled frame-by frame, produce the image of motion. The image is merely a graphic representation depicting the previously formed opinion of a witness or witnesses, in this case the Commonwealth experts. F. Galves, *Where the Not So Wild Things Are: Computers in the Courtroom, the Federal Rules of Evidence, and the Need for Institutional Reform and More Judicial Acceptance,* 13 Harv. J.L. & Tech. 161, 227–30 (2000). Presently, the CGA is akin to the traditionally permitted drawings used by crime scene reconstructionists to show bullet path trajectory. Accordingly, a CGA is only as credible as the underlying testimony that it represents and the computer plays no part in calculating an outcome or presenting its own conclusions. Conversely, computer-generated simulations do not depict witness opinion; rather, the computer program, based upon the data entered, draws a conclusion. As such, a computer simulation presents not only the testimony of an expert regarding the programming and data input but also a conclusion of the computer based upon the formulas programmed to use the raw data entered. For example, scientists use computer simulations to predict the effects of earthquakes on a building's structure by inputting factors such as: (1) wind; (2) magnitude of earthquake; (3) proximity of earthquake; (4) building materials; (5) building height; (6) amplitude of the earthquakes waves; and so forth. However, the simulation creates a result that nobody can testify to with personal knowledge nor is it the representation of an individual's opinion. Rather it is the outcome of the program's mathematical formulas based on the various inputted data and the laws of physics as entered by the programmers. As noted by Justice Castille in his concurring Opinion, the program used for either a CGA or a simulation is a human product and may be subjected to scrutiny regarding its programming bias and soundness in principles of both math and physics. At that point, a proper determination of the appropriate weight to be assigned to its output can occur. Further, as discussed *infra,* jury instructions may help in reducing or eliminating the potential for a jury to assign undue weight to a CGA by clarifying that it is, in actuality, a graphic representation of biased testimony of one party and not a product of neutral infallible artificial intelligence. Today, we address only the admissibility of CGA evidence as defined above and not that of computer simulations.

[3] Chief Justice Cappy urges this Court to adopt a standard in which the Commonwealth would be required to file a pre-trial motion *in limine* whenever CGA evidence is involved. Although this is a recommended procedure to reduce potential prejudice, we hold that the moving party, be it the Commonwealth or a defendant, should file a motion *in limine* and seek permission of the trial court to admit the evidence as soon as possible, even if after the start of trial. It is conceivable that a party may find, after the start of trial, that a CGA would be helpful to rebut evidence or new testimony set forth by the opposing party. Should a party discover that a CGA would be helpful at that point in time that party should not be precluded from asking the trial court to admit a CGA into evidence. The timing of the request must be weighed along with the various other factors involved in determining if the prejudicial effect of the CGA outweighs its probative value. * * *

his extreme intoxication at the time of the shooting rendered him incapable of formulating the specific intent to kill.

The Commonwealth countered that the killing was intentional, and that Appellant, a former Lieutenant of Detectives with the Scranton Police Department, "used his decades of experience as a police officer to tamper with the crime scene to stage a self-defense setting." * * * In particular, the Commonwealth asserted that Appellant had moved his wife's body and strategically positioned her near a knife that he had placed on the floor, as depicted in the CGA.

On February 7, 2002, during its case-in-chief, the Commonwealth presented a CGA as demonstrative evidence to illustrate the expert opinions of its forensic pathologist, Gary W. Ross, M.D. (Dr. Ross), and crime scene reconstructionist, Trooper Brad R. Beach (Trooper Beach). The CGA showed the theory of the Commonwealth based upon the forensic and physical evidence, of how Appellant shot his wife first in the lower back and then through the heart as she knelt on the living room floor of their home. More importantly, the animation showed the location of Appellant and his wife within the living room, the positioning of their bodies, and the sequence, path, trajectory, and impact sites of the bullets fired from the handgun.

The trial court thoroughly instructed the jury of the purely demonstrative nature of the CGA both before the animation was presented and during the jury charge prior to deliberation. In particular, the court noted that the CGA was a demonstrative exhibit, not substantive evidence, and it was being offered solely as an illustration of the Commonwealth's version of the events as recreated by Dr. Ross and Trooper Beach. Finally, the court informed the jury that they should not confuse art with reality and should not view the CGA as a definitive recreation of the actual incident.

On February 12, 2002, the jury found Appellant guilty of first-degree murder and the trial court immediately sentenced him to life imprisonment. Appellant filed a timely appeal, challenging several of the jury instructions and evidentiary rulings of the trial court. * * * On August 25, 2004, we granted allowance of appeal limited solely to the issue of whether the admission of the CGA depicting the Commonwealth's theory of the case was proper. The admissibility of a CGA is an issue of first impression in the Commonwealth. * * *

We determine that, for the reasons below, a CGA is admissible evidence in this Commonwealth. In particular, CGA evidence must be weighed by the same criteria of admissibility; namely, probative value versus prejudicial effect to which all other evidence is subject. Notably, certain concerns prior to admission carry more weight and deserve closer scrutiny when admitting CGA evidence than more traditional forms of evidence.

Appellant argues that the trial court erred in allowing the Commonwealth to present a CGA, which was used to introduce evidence of the Commonwealth's theory of the killing. Appellant alleges that the Commonwealth's use of the CGA: (1) lacked proper authentication; (2) lacked proper foundation; and (3) was, essentially, cumulative and unfairly prejudicial. The Commonwealth counters this argument and posits that the trial court properly admitted the CGA as demonstrative evidence used to explain or illustrate the testimony of its expert witnesses and should be subject to the same rules of admissibility as any other demonstrative evidence.

Society has become increasingly dependent upon computers in business and in our personal lives. With each technological advancement, the practice of law becomes more sophisticated and, commensurate with this progress, the legal system must adapt. Courts are facing the need to shed any technophobia and become more willing to embrace the advances that have the ability to enhance the efficacy of the legal system. However, before we are too quick to differentiate CGA's or create a special test for their admission, it must be noted that the rules for analyzing the admission of such evidence have been previously established. In particular, a CGA should be treated equivalently to any other demonstrative exhibit or graphic representation and, thus, a CGA should be admissible if it satisfies the requirements of Pa.R.E. 401, 402, 403, and 901.[4] See *State v. Tollardo*, 134 N.M. 430, 77 P.3d 1023, 1029 (Ct.App.2003) (opining that, "[w]hen the [CGA] is used to illustrate an opinion that an expert has arrived at without using the computer, the fact that the visual aid was generated by a computer * * * does not matter because the witness can be questioned and cross-examined concerning the perceptions or opinions to which the witness testifies. In that situation, the computer is no more or less than a drafting device."); *People v. McHugh*, 124 Misc.2d 559, 476 N.Y.S.2d 721, 722 (N.Y.Sup. Gen. Term 1984) ("Whether a diagram is hand drawn or mechanically drawn by means of a computer is of no importance.").

There are three basic types of evidence that are admitted into court: (1) testimonial evidence; (2) documentary evidence; and (3) demonstrative

---

[4] Because a CGA is a graphic illustration of an expert's reconstruction rather than a simulation based upon scientific principles and computerized calculations, it is not subject to the *Frye* test governing the admissibility of scientific evidence in Pennsylvania. *See Frye v. United States*, 293 F. 1013 (D.C.Cir.1923). Of course, the underlying expert opinion that the animation seeks to illustrate must satisfy Pa.R.E. 702 and be premised upon principles and methodology that are generally accepted in the relevant scientific community. Moreover, in accordance with Pa.R.E. 703, the facts or data on which the expert has relied in forming the opinion, which is illustrated by the computer animation, must be "of a type reasonably relied upon by experts in the particular field." *Id.* However, the issue of applying the *Frye* test to a computer simulation must await another day.

evidence. 2 McCormick on Evidence § 212 (5th ed. 1999). Presently, at issue is demonstrative evidence, which is "tendered for the purpose of rendering other evidence more comprehensible to the trier of fact." *Id.* As in the admission of any other evidence, a trial court may admit demonstrative evidence whose relevance outweighs any potential prejudicial effect. *Commonwealth v. Reid*, 571 Pa. 1, 811 A.2d 530, 552 (2002), *cert. denied*, 540 U.S. 850 * * * (2003). The offering party must authenticate such evidence. "The requirement of authentication or identification as a condition precedent to admissibility is satisfied by evidence sufficient to support a finding that the matter in question is what its proponent claims." Pa.R.E. 901(a). Demonstrative evidence may be authenticated by testimony from a witness who has knowledge "that a matter is what it is claimed to be." Pa.R.E. 901(b)(1). Demonstrative evidence such as photographs, motion pictures, diagrams, and models have long been permitted to be entered into evidence provided that the demonstrative evidence fairly and accurately represents that which it purports to depict. *See Nyce v. Muffley*, 384 Pa. 107, 119 A.2d 530, 532 (1956).

The overriding principle in determining if any evidence, including demonstrative, should be admitted involves a weighing of the probative value versus prejudicial effect. We have held that the trial court must decide first if the evidence is relevant and, if so, whether its probative value outweighs its prejudicial effect. *Commonwealth v. Hawk*, 551 Pa. 71, 709 A.2d 373, 376 (1998). This Commonwealth defines relevant evidence as "having any tendency to make the existence of any fact that is of consequence to the determination of the action more probable or less probable than it would be without the evidence." Pa.R.E. 401. Relevant evidence may nevertheless be excluded "if its probative value is outweighed by the danger of unfair prejudice, confusion of the issues, or misleading the jury, or by considerations of undue delay, waste of time, or needless presentation of cumulative evidence." Pa.R.E. 403.

At issue is both the basis and form of the demonstrative evidence offered. An expert witness may offer testimony other than opinions. Pa.R.E. 702 provides that an expert witness may testify "in the form of an opinion **or otherwise.**" (Emphasis added). An important function of an expert witness is to educate the jury on a subject about which the witness has specialized knowledge but the jury does not. * * * To help perform the function of educating a jury, an expert witness may use various forms of demonstrative evidence.

Demonstrative evidence continues to evolve as society advances technologically. Medical witnesses use computerized axial tomography, i.e. CAT scans, and magnetic resonance imaging instead of, or with, traditional x-rays. Forensic pathologists previously used only blood types in an attempt to bolster their testimony and implicate a defendant, but now use specific DNA matches to prove the statistical probability that a defendant was, by virtue of biological evidence at the scene of a crime, present at some point in time. *See Commonwealth v. Blasioli,* 552 Pa. 149, 713 A.2d 1117 (1998) (accepting the use of DNA matching of blood and semen to prove the statistical probability that the blood and semen found on the victim after an alleged rape was that of the defendant).

The law has been flexible enough to accommodate scientific progress and technological advances in all fields, and should continue to do so.[5] Pa.R.E. 702 permits expert testimony if it "will assist the trier of fact to understand the evidence or to determine a fact in issue [.]" Such expert testimony is not limited to that which is purely verbal; rather, it includes pertinent illustrative adjuncts that help explain the testimony of one or more expert witnesses.

Presently, had the Commonwealth's experts, a crime scene reconstructionist and a pathologist, used traditional methods, they may have drawn chalk diagrams or sketches on a blackboard to help explain the basis for their opinions. Instead, they used a CGA to more concisely and more clearly present their opinion. The difference is one of mode, not meaning. The law does not, and should not, prohibit proficient, professional employment of new technology in the courtroom. This is, after all, the twenty-first century. As such, we must turn to the traditional factors considered in determining if a particular CGA is admissible.

Therefore, despite the relative novelty of CGA evidence, the evaluation of its admissibility relates back to this longstanding evaluation of probative value versus prejudicial value. G. Joseph, *A Simplified Approach to Computer–Generated Evidence and Animations,* 43 N.Y.L. Sch. L.Rev. 875 (1999–2000) (stating that, "[a]t its simplest, an animation is merely a sequence of illustrations that, when filmed, videotaped or computer-generated, creates the illusion that the illustrated objects are in motion. Traditionally—because they are drawings—animations have been subjected to the fair-and-accurate-portrayal test and have been admitted, within the trial judge's discretion, generally for illustrative purposes.") As a preliminary matter, a CGA should be deemed admissible as demonstrative evidence if it (1) is properly authenticated pursuant to Pa.R.E. 901 as a fair and accurate representation of the evidence it purports to portray; (2) is relevant pursuant to Pa.R.E. 401 and 402; and

---

[5] CGA evidence has been admitted in most states that have considered the matter, including in the criminal context. *See Pierce v. State,* 718 So.2d 806 (Fla.App.1997) (holding that a CGA of an automobile accident was admissible when the testimony of three accident-reconstruction experts established that the: (1) computer program used was accepted in engineering field as one of the leading computer-aided design programs in the world; (2) CGA fairly and accurately reflected expert opinion of how accident occurred; (3) CGA was fair and accurate representation of what it purported to depict; and (4) data, information, and evidence utilized was of type reasonably relied upon by experts in field of forensic animation) * * * .

(3) has a probative value that is not outweighed by the danger of unfair prejudice pursuant to Pa.R.E. 403. However, new factors must be considered when evaluating a CGA. In particular, in determining the admissibility of a CGA the courts must address the additional dangers and benefits this particular type of demonstrative evidence presents as compared with more traditional demonstrative evidence.[6] As a result, the court must, as discussed *infra,* issue limiting instructions to the jury explaining the nature of the specific CGA.

It should be noted that conspicuously absent among the factors to be considered in determining the relevancy and prejudice of evidence is the potency of the evidence. Thus, although the use of illustrative demonstrative evidence by an expert, such as a CGA, may help explain his or her opinion and make the testimony more persuasive than it otherwise might have been, it is not proper grounds for excluding this relevant evidence.

Here, both the trial court and the Superior Court determined that the Commonwealth had satisfied all foundational requirements for admitting the animation and therefore it was properly admitted as demonstrative evidence. After applying the three-prong test noted above, we agree.

Appellant initially argues that the Commonwealth did not properly authenticate the CGA. Pa.R.E. 901(a) provides, "The requirement of authentication or identification as a condition precedent to admissibility is satisfied by evidence sufficient to support a finding that the matter in question is what its proponent claims." *See also* A. Albrecht, *Laying a Proper Foundation for Computer–Generated Demonstrative Evidence,* 90 Ill. B.J. 261 (2002) (stating that "courts have said that computer-generated demonstrative evidence must be relevant and authenticated by testimony that (a) the witness has personal knowledge of the exhibit's subject matter and (b) the exhibit is accurate. * * * To lay a proper foundation for computer-generated visual evidence, the proponent must first establish through witness testimony the accuracy of the exhibit's portrayal of the substantive information in question.")

In authenticating the CGA, the Commonwealth presented the testimony of multiple individuals, including: (1) Randy Matzkanin

---

[6] Appellant argues that a CGA or computer simulation has the potential to influence unduly a jury due to its visual impact. However, at least one controlled study suggests that a CGA, although helpful, has a negligible measurable impact upon a jury when the CGA does not present new information. R. Bennett, Jr., J. Leibman, R. Fetter, *Seeing is Believing; or is it? An Empirical Study of Computer Simulations as Evidence,* 34 Wake Forest L.Rev. 257, 285 (1999) ("[T]he extraordinary possibilities inherent in computer animations and computer simulations raised hopes—and fears—that juries would find computer-generated displays more persuasive or convincing than other forms of evidence. These hopes and fears seem to be unwarranted, at least within the context of the empirical results of this study. In other words, computer-generated evidence is not a "silver bullet" which guarantees victory.").

(Matzkanin), the Director of Operations for 21st Century Forensic Animations; (2) Trooper Beach; and (3) Dr. Ross. Additionally, Patrolman Jared Ganz, Patrolman Joseph Zegalia, Trooper George Scochin, Trooper Connie Devens, and Trooper Gustas testified at trial concerning the physical evidence and the measurements taken at the crime scene, both of which were used in creating the CGA. Further, the creator of the CGA testified at the Motion *in limine* hearing that the CGA was a graphical presentation of another expert's opinion, not the conclusions or calculations of a computer or himself. * * *

Matzkanin described the process employed in making the animation and testified that it was a strict depiction of the Commonwealth's forensic evidence and expert opinions. Matzkanin stated that he used the expert opinions provided by Trooper Beach and Dr. Ross as well as the measurements gathered at the crime scene. * * * Moreover, Matzkanin discussed both the computer software and hardware that created the three dimensional CGA drawings and their general use in the field. * * * Matzkanin, at the questioning of the Commonwealth, carefully explained the differences between a CGA and a simulation. * * * Matzkanin stated that he began working on the project at the end of January 2001, or beginning of February 2001, and continued until December 20, 2001. * * * During his testimony, Matzkanin explained that photos are used to reconstruct the room, including color and the like, but the major factor in recreation is the measurements.* * * However, Matzkanin explained that the character depictions are more difficult because of the stock models used by the company to represent people. * * * He further testified that the models do not represent the defendants. * * * Next, the CGA is created in a rough draft and sent to the Commonwealth for further input. Matzkanin could not recall the exact number of versions created but specified that many changes were made to ensure that the CGA conformed to the opinions of Trooper Beach and Dr. Ross. Matzkanin further explained that drawings are recorded in time intervals of thirty frames per second and thereafter transferred onto a DVD or video tape to create the image of motion. * * *

The court analyzed the record and found that the depictions within the CGA were supported by the evidence. Defendant had the opportunity in cross examination of the experts to bring the credibility of the animation and the opinions of the experts to the attention of the jury.

The CGA is not meant to represent the theories of both parties; rather, as noted by both the trial court and Matzkanin, the sole purpose of the CGA and role of Matzkanin was to represent the findings of Trooper Beach and Dr. Ross. Matzkanin made no active decisions, rather, he merely interpreted the data and made corrections to the CGA based on the recommendations given to him by the two experts. The CGA is, ultimately, a representation of the expert opinions and demonstrative evidence. The line of questions presented by Appellant highlighted the alleged uncertainty regarding specific facts within the CGA and alerted the jury to the possible lack of credibility of Trooper Beach, Dr. Ross, and, by extension, the CGA. However, the jury ultimately found the testimony of the Commonwealth experts, and the CGA, to be credible. As such, the foundation was properly laid and the CGA was, in fact, what the Commonwealth purported it to be, a depiction of the various testimonies of the Commonwealth witnesses concerning their theory about the chain of events. * * *

Prong 2   Because the CGA was properly authenticated, we must turn to the second prong of the three-part test, which involves a question of its relevancy. The CGA was relevant because it clearly, concisely, and accurately depicted the Commonwealth's theory of the case and aided the jury in the comprehension of the collective testimonies of the witnesses without use of extraneous graphics or information.   *A.*

Appellant argues that, in the alternative, even if the CGA is relevant, it is cumulative. However, as noted by the Superior Court, although the evidence did not offer anything inherently original, it presented a clear and precise depiction of the Commonwealth's theory and evidence as presented by its experts. Pursuant to * * * demonstrative depictions of the testimony of an expert have long been allowed into evidence, including drawings or depictions of bullet trajectories as here. Therefore, the cumulative argument carries no weight. Rather, the question is whether the evidence presented by the CGA is relevant and whether its probative value outweighs its prejudicial effect. Pa.R.E. 401, 403.

Prong 3   Accordingly, we must turn to the third and final prong, prejudice. It is within this prong that a CGA has the potential danger due to the visual nature of the presentation. Various jurisdictions that have been faced with the issue of CGA-evidence have noted the potentially powerful impact based upon its visual nature, but, nonetheless, have permitted CGA evidence. * * * Despite this potential power,[7] even inflammatory evidence may be admissible if it is relevant and helpful to a jury's understanding of the facts and the probative value outweighs the prejudicial effect. * * *   *A.*

Presently, the content of the CGA was neither inflammatory nor unfairly prejudicial. Any prejudice derived from viewing the CGA resulted not from the on-screen depiction of the Commonwealth's theory, but rather was inherent to the reprehensible act of murder. The possible unnecessary and prejudicial aspects of a CGA were not present. In

---

[7] At least one empirical study * * * has shown that the use of CGA evidence is not the deciding factor for a jury. Rather, the evidence and opinions underlying the CGA are the ultimate determinants of the jury's decision. The CGA merely facilitates the jury's understanding of the evidence and opinions without shifting the weight a jury assigns to the presenting side's testimony.

particular, the CGA did not include (1) sounds; (2) facial expressions; (3) evocative or even life-like movements; (4) transition between the scenes to suggest a story line or add a subconscious prejudicial effect; or (5) evidence of injury such as blood or other wounds. Instead, much like a two-dimensional hand drawing of bullet trajectories, the CGA merely highlighted the trajectory of the three bullets fired, concluding from ballistics and blood splatter that the body had been moved after the victim died as part of Appellant's attempt to stage his self-defense. The CGA was devoid of drama so as to prevent the jury from improperly relying on an emotional basis. *See People v. Hood,* 53 Cal.App.4th 965, 972, 62 Cal.Rptr.2d 137 (1997) (permitting a CGA in a murder trial, in part because "[t]he animation was clinical and emotionless. This, combined with the instruction given the jurors about how they were to utilize both animations, persuades us that the trial court did not [err in permitting the CGA].") The major difference between a traditional chart or drawing of bullet trajectories and the instant presentation lays in the three-dimensional nature that enabled the Commonwealth experts to present their exact theory and the underlying mathematics used in formulating its case. In particular, the ability to rotate the view allowed the Commonwealth's experts to explain the exact path of the bullets and show why the evidence suggested that it was not a killing in self-defense. As such, it was a clearly relevant and helpful tool for an expert to present an informed opinion to the jury. *See* Pa.R.E. 703.

Within his argument concerning prejudice, Appellant, in this appeal, additionally raises the issue that public policy should prevent the presentation of a CGA, which, allegedly, costs between $10,000.00 and $20,000.00 to make.[8] He notes that his entire defense fund, provided by the Commonwealth due to his *in forma pauperis* status, was limited to $10,000.00. (Brief of Appellant, p. 44). Any additional expenditure would then come from Appellant.[9]

This argument is waived because it was not raised at the trial court level. * * * (stating that issues not raised in the lower court are waived and cannot be raised for the first time on appeal). However, Appellant argues that we should consider this factor because of the implications of permitting the Commonwealth to present expensive CGA productions at

---

[8] As noted previously, Appellant did not raise the issue of cost in the courts below and, therefore, it is waived. Pa.R.A.P. 302(a). As a result, the record was not developed on this issue and does not contain the exact final cost. However, both Appellant's brief and the Commonwealth during oral argument before this Court indicated the cost to be between $10,000.00 and $20,000.00. * * *

[9] However, although cost is a consideration, this issue will lessen over time because of the inevitable reduction in cost as technology advances. This fact has been acknowledged from the inception of CGA usage. *See* R. Sherman, *Moving Graphics: Computer Animation Enters Criminal Cases,* Nat'l L.J., p. 32 (Apr. 6, 1992) (noting that, in 1992, the overall cost of computer animations had already dropped dramatically, thereby increasing their usage, including in criminal trials).

trial against an indigent defendant. * * * [The court cited United States Supreme Court and Pennsylvania decisions it characterized as holding that the defense is entitled to access to expert testimony only in limited situations and that the decision is ordinarily within the discretion of the trial court.]

Similarly, there can be no obligation to provide the defendant the finances necessary to create a CGA of his or her own. Chief Justice Cappy's concurring Opinion accurately summarizes the ultimate concerns regarding the economic disparity between the Commonwealth and an indigent defendant. * * * Thus, we ultimately conclude that the relative monetary positions of the parties are relevant for the trial court to consider when ruling on whether or not to admit a CGA into evidence. Such a question and determination are within the province of the trial court and should not be overturned absent an abuse of discretion. In particular, the trial court sitting with all facts before it, including the monetary disparity of the parties, must determine if the potentially powerful effect of the CGA and the inability of a defendant to counter with his or her own CGA should lead to its preclusion. Nevertheless, as noted above, this specific argument is waived in the instant matter.

It is argued that the uniquely dangerous aspect of a CGA is in its visual appeal to a jury resulting in an acceptance of the CGA as fact. However, such a danger is vitiated by thorough cautionary instructions that educate the jury on the exact nature and role of a CGA. Presently, the trial court safeguarded against the possibility of jury confusion over the animation or potential prejudice by supplying a thorough and extensive cautionary instruction before playing the CGA. * * *

Although limiting instructions may not be necessary, such cautionary instructions limit the prejudice or confusion that could surround a CGA. See Harris, 13 P.3d at 495 (requiring cautionary jury instructions when using a CGA and noting South Carolina's requirement of the same in Clark, supra). Additionally, the trial court reiterated the same concerns and instructions during its closing jury charge. In so doing, the trial court duly minimized any possible prejudice by insisting that the jury not make more of the CGA than what it was—an illustration of expert witness testimony. The repetition of the instructions in the case sub judice ensured that the jury comprehended the nature of the CGA and would not mistake it for fact, but could only rely upon it to the extent they credited the underlying testimony. * * *

In a question of first impression in this Commonwealth, we hold that a CGA is potentially admissible as demonstrative evidence, as long as the animation is properly authenticated, it is relevant, and its probative value outweighs the danger of unfair prejudice or confusion. Therefore, because in the instant matter: (1) the Commonwealth satisfied all of the foundational requirements for admitting the CGA as demonstrative evidence; (2) the CGA was relevant evidence that enabled the Commonwealth experts to illustrate their opinions and educate the jury on the forensic and physical data; and (3) the alleged prejudicial effect of the CGA does not outweigh its relevance, we conclude that the admission of this evidence was proper. Hence, the admission of a CGA depicting the theory of the Commonwealth in this case was proper. Accordingly, we affirm the decision of the Superior Court.

[The concurring opinions of CHIEF JUSTICE CAPPY and JUSTICES CASTILLE and EAKIN are omitted.]

NOTES AND QUESTIONS

1. *Computer generated simulations distinguished.* The court distinguishes the kind of exhibit involved in *Serge*, a computer generated animation, from a computer generated simulation. It notes that simulations would be subject to the rules governing scientific evidence. See Chapter 12, Section D. For a case rejecting a computer generated simulation for failure to meet the requirements for admission of scientific evidence, see State v. Sipin, 123 P.3d 862 (Wash.Ct.App.2005) (court rejected a simulation of automobile crash "inputting" variables from the scene and the vehicle, such as steering, braking, and speed, to create a predictive image of the vehicle movement). Why should there be a difference between the two types of computer generated exhibits? For a further discussion of the differences and the policy behind the different treatment, see 2 McCormick, Evidence § 218 (7th ed. 2013).

2. *The foundation for admission of computer generated animations.* Might it be useful to require a more significant analysis of the scientific basis for the creation of computer generated animations than was required by the court in *Serge?* Certainly, there are possibilities for jury misuse of the exhibits, including inadequate sophistication of software to accurately depict technical data input and the injection of programmer creativity or personal assumptions about the evidence. See Fiedler, Note, Are Your Eyes Deceiving You?: The Evidentiary Crisis Regarding the Admissibility of Computer Generated Evidence, 48 N.Y.L.Sch.L.Rev. 295 (2003); Morande, A Class of Their Own: Model Procedural Rules and Evidentiary Evaluation of Computer–Generated "Animations", 61 U. Miami L. Rev. 1069 (2007); Weinreb, Note, "Counselor, Proceed With Caution": The Use of Integrated Evidence Presentation System and Computer–Generated Evidence in the Courtroom, 23 Cardozo L.Rev. 393 (2001). Is it sufficient simply to leave such matters to for cross-examination of the expert presenting the animation?

3. *Requiring pretrial motions.* The court in *Serge* rejected the requirement of a pre-trial motion *in limine* in favor of a more flexible approach. For an example of a rule governing the procedure for admission of computer generated evidence, including a requirement of pre-trial disclosure, see Md. Rule 2–504.3.

FISHER V. STATE

Court of Appeals of Arkansas, 1982.
643 S.W.2d 571.

COOPER, JUDGE.

This is a criminal case in which the appellant was charged with theft of property having a value of over $100.00, but less than $2,500.00. After a trial by jury, she was found guilty.* * * On appeal, the appellant challenges the sufficiency of the evidence, and alleges that the trial court erred in ruling that certain portions of a video tape recording were properly admitted into evidence. We find no merit to either contention, and therefore we affirm.

The Facts

The appellant and her two daughters were employed by M & W Thriftway in Nashville, Arkansas to clean the store. On August 12, 1981, the appellant and her daughters arrived at the store for the purpose of cleaning it. The manager and owner of the store had installed a video tape camera on the premises, prior to the time that the appellant and her daughters arrived. He testified that he adjusted the camera, started it, and then left the building, leaving the camera unattended. He testified that he started the video tape camera at approximately 9:15 p.m. and that he returned at approximately midnight. He testified that he replaced the tape in the camera, since the first tape was about to run out. The manager testified that at approximately 1:30 to 2:00 a.m., he returned to get the tapes. When he arrived at the store, he found law enforcement officers on the scene, and, pursuant to their instructions, he removed the video tapes. He testified that he had safeguarded those tapes until the time of trial.

The sheriff of Howard County, Dick Wakefield, testified that he observed the appellant's daughters removing groceries in paper sacks from the back door of the store. The sheriff had the individuals arrested. * * *

The Admissibility of the Video Tape Recording

The appellant argues that the trial court erred in admitting in evidence a video tape recording[10], since no witness testified that the photographic evidence was a fair and accurate representation of the subject matter.

Immediately prior to the trial, the trial court conducted a hearing on the appellant's motion *in limine* which sought to preclude the State from

---

[10] A video tape recording is an electronic means of recording sound and action on tape for subsequent playback in the form of a sound motion picture. 1 C. Scott, Photographic Evidence § 87 (2d ed. 1969). Video tape recordings are admissible in evidence on the same basis as sound motion picture films. 3 C. Scott, Photographic Evidence § 1294 (2d ed. Supp.1980).

introducing the video tapes The trial court required the State to present the foundational facts which would support its claim that the video tapes were admissible. The manager of the store, Mr. Moore, testified that he had positioned the video tape camera on a tripod on top of an ice machine, so as to provide a view of the back door. He testified that he loaded the tape into the camera, started it, and checked to make sure that it was operating properly, prior to the time that he left the store. He testified that at the time he left the store, no one else was present in the store. He further testified that he changed the tape approximately two hours later and that he had continuous custody of the tapes, since the date of the alleged theft.

Mr. Moore further testified regarding the contents of the tapes, that the camera worked properly at all times, and that there were no gaps in the tapes. He testified that, when he returned to the store, the camera had not been moved or tampered with in any way, and that that fact could be verified, since the tapes would have shown movement had the camera been moved. He testified that in order to turn the camera off or to change the tapes, he had to pose in front of the camera and that his image appeared on the video tapes. He also testified that, once the camera had been turned on, the controls could not be approached, without a picture of that approach being made.

The trial court held that a proper foundation had been presented, and that the video tape was admissible. He found that the video tape fairly represented the situation that existed at the store, and he further noted that any question regarding the tapes went more to their credibility, rather than to admissibility. He noted it was for the jury to determine whether any criminal activity was taking place by virtue of the events which were shown on the video tape. The tape showed appellant and her daughters sacking groceries, and removing them.

The admissibility of photographic evidence is based on two different theories. One theory is the "pictorial testimony" theory. Under this theory, the photographic evidence is merely illustrative of a witness' testimony and it only becomes admissible when a sponsoring witness can testify that it is a fair and accurate representation of the subject matter, based on that witness' personal observation. Obviously, the photographic evidence in this case is not admissible under such a theory, since no person could verify that the video tape accurately represented what occurred at the store, based on personal observation. A second theory under which photographic evidence may be admissible is the "silent witness" theory. Under that theory, the photographic evidence is a "silent witness" which speaks for itself, and is substantive evidence of what it portrays independent of a sponsoring witness. *See,* 2 C. Scott, Photographic Evidence § 1021 (2d ed. Supp.1980); 3 J. Wigmore, Evidence § 790 (Chadbourn rev. 1970).

In Arkansas, photographic evidence is admissible under the "pictorial testimony" theory, when a sponsoring witness testifies that it is a fair and accurate representation of the subject matter. *Martin v. State,* 258 Ark. 529, 527 S.W.2d 903 (1975) * * * .

The question presented on this appeal has never been answered in Arkansas. A video tape recording and a film produced by an automatic camera have been admitted into evidence in two cases. However, the precise objection made in the case at bar was not raised in either case. *See, French v. State,* 271 Ark. 445, 609 S.W.2d 42 (1980); *Lunon v. State,* 264 Ark. 188, 569 S.W.2d 663 (1978).

This case presents the question of whether photographic evidence may be admitted as substantive evidence under the "silent witness" theory. We hold that the trial court correctly ruled that the video tape recording was admissible.

The Uniform Rules of Evidence, Rule 901(a), Ark.Stat.Ann. § 28–1001 (Repl.1979), provides that authentication is a condition precedent to the admissibility of evidence and that this requirement is met by a showing of evidence sufficient to support a finding that the matter in question is what its proponent claims. Section (b) lists various illustrations, showing methods of authentication or identification. The Uniform Rules of Evidence, Rule 1001(2), Ark.Stat.Ann. § 28–1001 (Repl.1979), provides that "photographs" includes photographs, x-ray films, video tapes, and motion pictures.

X-ray films are admissible in Arkansas, subject to proper authentication. *Oxford v. Villines,* 232 Ark. 103, 334 S.W.2d 660 (1960); *Arkansas Amusement Corporation v. Ward,* 204 Ark. 130, 161 S.W.2d 178 (1942); *Prescott & N.W.R. Co. v. Franks,* 111 Ark. 83, 163 S.W. 180 (1914); *Miller v. Minturn,* 73 Ark. 183, 83 S.W. 918 (1904). Obviously, it is impossible for a witness to testify that an x-ray film is a fair and accurate representation of the subject matter, based on that witness' personal observation. Therefore, x-rays could never be admissible under the "pictorial testimony" theory. 3 C. Scott, Photographic Evidence § 1262 (2d ed. 1969). Every jurisdiction admits x-ray films as substantive evidence upon a sufficient showing of authentication, thus utilizing the "silent witness" theory, even if unintentionally.[11] We note that Rule 1001(2) treats x-rays, photographs, video tapes, and motion pictures, as one and the same.

Photographic evidence is the best available means of preserving the appearance of a scene at a given time. It is superior to eyewitness

---

[11] Some jurisdictions treat x-rays as scientific evidence, and not photographic evidence. *See, Howard v. State,* 264 Ind. 275, 342 N.E.2d 604 (1976). Professor Wigmore treats the admissibility of x-rays as scientific evidence, even though admitting that the "silent witness" theory may be a "more satisfactory rationale." 3 J. Wigmore, Evidence § 795 n.1 (Chadbourn rev. 1970).

testimony in certain respects. Eyewitness testimony is subject to errors in perception, memory lapse, and a witness' problem of adequately expressing what he observed in language so that the trier of fact can understand. *See,* 1 C. Scott, Photographic Evidence § 41–54 (2d ed. 1969). Photographic evidence can observe a scene in detail without interpreting it, preserve the scene in a permanent manner, and transmit its message more clearly than the spoken word.

We hold that photographic evidence is admissible where its authenticity can be sufficiently established in view of the context in which it is sought to be admitted.[12] Obviously, the foundational requirements for the admissibility of photographic evidence under the "silent witness" theory are fundamentally different from the foundational requirements under the "pictorial testimony" theory. It is neither possible nor wise to establish specific foundational requirements for the admissibility of photographic evidence under the "silent witness" theory, since the context in which the photographic evidence was obtained and its intended use at trial will be different in virtually every case. It is enough to say, that adequate foundational facts must be presented to the trial court, so that the trial court can determine that the trier of fact can reasonably infer that the subject matter is what its proponent claims. The trial court determines the preliminary questions regarding the admissibility of evidence, and the appellate court reviews those determinations only for an abuse of discretion. Uniform Rules of Evidence, Rule 104(a), (b), Ark.Stat.Ann. § 28–1001 (Repl.1979); *Wilson v. City of Pine Bluff,* 6 Ark.App. 286, 641 S.W.2d 33 (1982). Our holding in this case in no way affects the admissibility of, or the foundational requirements for, photographic evidence used as demonstrative evidence under the "pictorial testimony" theory.

In adopting the "silent witness" theory, we join the overwhelming majority of other jurisdictions that have decided this issue. [Citations from 20 states and three federal circuits omitted.]

[The court here held that the state's evidence was sufficient to prove appellant guilty of theft.]

Affirmed.

NOTES AND QUESTIONS

1. *Other silent witness evidence.* Several modern photographic techniques, infrared photography, surveillance cameras, and self-timing mechanisms, are calculated to produce products which cannot be said to

---

[12] Photographic evidence is subject to the same rules as other evidence. Thus, even if photographic evidence is properly authenticated, it may still be excluded because it is not relevant or because its probative value is substantially outweighed by the danger of unfair prejudice, confusion of the issues, or misleading the jury. Uniform Rules of Evidence, Rules 401, 402, 403, Ark.Stat.Ann. § 28–1001 (Repl.1979).

"illustrate" the testimony of anyone and are therefore impossible to introduce under conventional doctrine. Comment, Photographic Evidence—Is There a Recognized Basis for Admissibility?, 8 Hast.L.J. 310 (1957).

2. *Silent witness or scientific evidence?* What practical difference does it make whether a jurisdiction admits X–rays under the "silent witness" theory or as scientific evidence? Are these two theories mutually exclusive, as the court's discussion in *Fisher* might seem to suggest, or is a scientific foundation only one of several possible avenues to the introduction of "silent witness" photographic evidence? See McNeal, Silent Witness Evidence in Relation to the Illustrative Evidence Foundation, 37 Okla.L.Rev. 219 (1984). What is the characteristic which distinguishes illustrative from "silent witness" photographs? For a case applying the Federal Rules in a silent witness situation and reaching a result similar to that in *Fisher*, see United States v. Rembert, 863 F.2d 1023 (D.C.Cir.1988).

NOTES ON REAL AND DEMONSTRATIVE EVIDENCE APPEALING TO NONVISUAL SENSES

1. *Evidence involving other senses.* Though the great bulk of real and demonstrative evidence introduced in litigation is of a visual nature, it should not be assumed that the senses other than sight cannot or should not be appealed to when occasion presents itself. Thus, jurors have not infrequently been permitted to hear, taste, feel, and smell evidence in appropriate cases. See, e.g., Dowling v. Peyroux, 126 So. 270 (La.Ct.App.1930) (children's band known as "The Kiddies" whose practice sessions were alleged to constitute a nuisance allowed to perform in court); People v. Kinney, 83 N.W. 147 (Mich.1900) (jury allowed to taste cider to determine whether it was "hard" or "soft"); McAndrews v. Leonard, 134 A. 710 (Vt.1926) (jurors allowed to feel plaintiff's skull).

2. *Sound recordings.* Next to evidence appealing to the visual sense, probably the most frequently encountered type of real or demonstrative evidence today is the sound recording. Is a sound recording, given its nature and possible points of relevancy, more likely to be offered as illustrative or as substantive evidence? When offered as the latter, sound recordings will present foundational problems analogous to "silent witness" photographs. See United States v. McKeever, 169 F.Supp. 426 (S.D.N.Y.1958), which lays down a set of foundational requirements that has been widely followed. But compare State v. Lavers, 814 P.2d 333 (Ariz.1991) (upholding admission of tape recording apparently made by homicide victim on basis of "flexible" test which requires only that trial judge be satisfied that the recording is accurate, authentic, and generally trustworthy). Cases concerning the admissibility of sound recordings generally are collected in Annot., 58 A.L.R.2d 1024. For cases involving taped 911 calls, see Annot., 3 A.L.R.5th 784. Where the recording is of human speech as opposed to mere sounds or noise, the recording may raise problems traditionally associated with written evidence. Such questions are treated in the next chapter.

3. *Juror squeamishness.* Jurors today are generally given little choice with respect to what they are required to see and hear even when the evidence is extremely unpleasant. Should the juror have an option as to what he or she is required to touch? See Curry v. American Enka, Inc., 452 F.Supp. 178 (E.D.Tenn.1977).

EVANSVILLE SCHOOL CORP. V. PRICE

Appellate Court of Indiana, 1965.
208 N.E.2d 689.

PRIME, PRESIDING JUSTICE. This action was commenced by Alfred Price, father of Alfred Lee Price (deceased), against the Evansville School Corporation, to recover damages for wrongful death allegedly sustained as the result of the decedent, Alfred Lee Price, being injured while a spectator attending a baseball game at Bosse Field in the City of Evansville, Indiana. The boy, age 11, was struck on the head with a baseball on May 27, 1960, and died as a result of said injuries on May 29, 1960.

The case was originally filed in the Vanderburgh Probate Court and subsequently venued to the Warrick Circuit Court where it was tried by a jury on the issues as formed by the appellee's amended complaint and the amended answer of the appellant thereto. The jury returned a verdict favorable to the plaintiff-appellee, awarding him the sum of $14,500.00, and the court rendered judgment on the verdict. The appellant filed its motion for a new trial, said motion was overruled by the trial court, and appellant appeals from this adverse ruling.

At the trial the appellee offered in evidence a color photograph designated Plaintiff's Exhibit No. 5. It depicted the deceased youth lying in his casket, after preparation by a mortician, and prior to interment. The photograph shows the white satin interior of the casket and that portion of the body exposed to public view. The decedent's face bears a deep tan, and he is clothed in a white sport coat and a blue shirt open at the neck. The photograph is not gruesome, nor does it depict any physical markings, wounds, defects or other bodily abnormalities. The appellant objected to the admission of Exhibit No. 5 for a number of reasons. First, appellant objected on the ground that the pleadings admitted the fact that the decedent died as a result of injuries sustained on May 27, 1960, and therefore, no issue was presented to the jury concerning the fact or cause of death. Second, that Exhibit No. 5 could only serve to inflame the minds of the jury or excite their feelings rather than to enlighten them as to any of the facts in issue. Third, Exhibit No. 5 is not material to any issue involved in the case.

Appellee alleged that the photograph was being offered into evidence to show the physical characteristics of the boy, and to corroborate testimony that the boy was a "nice looking and healthy chap." It was also offered into evidence to establish the fact that the parents incurred funeral expenses for the boy, and "that he was properly interred."

Appellant further objected to the admission of Exhibit No. 5 into evidence on the grounds that there was testimony in the record of two witnesses concerning the boy's health prior to his death, and that a picture of a person after death could not establish the person's condition of health prior to death, especially in light of the fact that the body had been prepared for burial by a mortician. Appellant also objected on the ground that the fact that the boy was "nice looking" or handsome does not constitute an admissible item of evidence because the measure of damages is limited to the pecuniary loss sustained by the parent.

Appellant's objections were overruled and the photograph was admitted into evidence. The appellant predicates error on this ruling by the trial court, for the reasons stated in the objections.

It is the rule in Indiana that the admission or rejection of photographs in evidence lies largely within the discretion of the trial court, and will not be disturbed unless an abuse of discretion is shown to have occurred. Dill v. Dill (1949), 120 Ind.App. 61, 65, 88 N.E.2d 396 (Transfer denied). It is also the law in this state that in order for a photograph to be admissible in evidence, it must first be accepted by the trial court as *material and relevant,* and must tend to prove or disprove some material fact in issue. Kiefer v. State (1958), 239 Ind. 103, 153 N.E.2d 899. See also: St. Lukes Hospital Asso. v. Long (1952), 125 Colo. 25, 240 P.2d 917, 31 A.L.R.2d 1120; 3 Wigmore, Evidence 3d ed. § 792.

Relevancy is determined by an inquiry into whether or not a witness would be permitted to describe the objects photographed. Hawkins v. State (1942), 219 Ind. 116, 37 N.E.2d 79. Photographs should assist and enlighten the members of the jury, and not confuse or unduly prejudice them. Kiefer v. State, supra.

The fact that a photograph might arouse the passions of the jury and prejudice them against one of the parties is not a sufficient ground to justify its exclusion if the photograph is *material and relevant.* Kiefer v. State, supra.

The above stated rules are applicable, whether the judicial proceedings involved are criminal or civil in nature, and whether the photograph of the deceased is taken during his lifetime, or after death. State of New Jersey v. Bucanis, 26 N.J. 45, 138 A.2d 739, 73 A.L.R.2d 760, 769; Elliott v. Black River Electric Cooperative, 233 S.C. 233, 104 S.E.2d 357, 74 A.L.R.2d 907, 928.

In the case at bar appellee argues primarily that Exhibit No. 5 was offered to corroborate the testimony of certain witnesses with respect to the decedent's physical characteristics prior to his death. This testimony was to the effect that the decedent was in excellent health, practically never sick, and was a good looking boy with a husky build. Further, that the boy was about 5 feet tall, weighed about 115 pounds, blond haired and blue eyed. Appellee asserts that the photograph accurately depicted the decedent's appearance before his death as well as after his death. It is difficult for us to see how Exhibit No. 5 could possibly be construed to establish the physical conditions and characteristics of this boy during his lifetime. This picture was not only taken after death, but also after the boy's body had been prepared for burial by a mortician.

Appellee also argued that Exhibit No. 5 was being offered into evidence to prove that the parents incurred funeral expenses for the boy, and "that he was properly interred." Again, we fail to see how this photograph of the decedent, lying in his casket, showing only a part of the interior of the casket, could aid the jury in deciding the question of funeral expenses. There was testimony concerning the amount of expenses incurred, and a copy of the funeral bill was introduced into evidence without objection as Plaintiff's Exhibit No. 19.

It appears to us that the only legitimate purpose for admitting this photograph would have been to establish the fact of death, and this fact was admitted by virtue of the pleadings.

Therefore, we are of the opinion that Plaintiff's Exhibit No. 5 should not have been admitted into evidence, and the trial court abused its discretion in permitting it to be admitted and exhibited to the jury. In the Kiefer case at page 107, of 239 Ind. at page 900, of 153 N.E.2d our Supreme Court said:

"As a general rule a photograph that is 'entirely irrelevant and immaterial to any issue in the cause and which is of such a character as to divert the minds of the jury to improper or irrelevant considerations should be excluded from evidence.' 20 Am.Jur., Evidence, § 729, p. 609; Underhill's Cr. Evidence, 5th Ed., § 117, p. 16 (1958 Supp.)."

In our opinion Exhibit No. 5 was immaterial and irrelevant to any of the material facts in issue, and was prejudicial to the defendant.

Again we refer to the *Kiefer* case, wherein it is stated at pages 117 and 118, at page 905, of 153 N.E.2d:

" * * * [T]o introduce evidence only for the purpose of arousing the passions and prejudices of the jury, in such a manner as to cause them to abandon any serious consideration of the facts of the case and give expression only to their emotions, is clearly outside the scope of such duty * * *." (Referring to a duty of counsel to present relevant and material facts to the jury.)

Judgment reversed with instructions to sustain appellant's motion for a new trial.

NOTES AND QUESTIONS

1. *Wrongful death cases.* It has sometimes been held that an ante mortem picture of the deceased is relevant to the issue of damages in an action for wrongful death. Drinon v. Wilson, 113 F.2d 654 (2d Cir.1940). Compare Roberts v. Stevens Clinic Hosp., Inc., 345 S.E.2d 791 (W.Va.1986), a medical malpractice case brought to recover damages for the death of a 2 ½ year old child. Plaintiff was allowed to introduce a professionally prepared videotape which combined home videos and still pictures of the deceased with his family, combined with a sound track of child's singing and mother and child talking. The tape was said by the court to demonstrate that the deceased was a healthy, intelligent, enthusiastic, and well-loved child; admission was held discretionary. The jury award was $10,000,000, although the West Virginia Supreme Court of Appeals required a remittitur of $7,000,000 of that amount.

2. *Admissions in pleadings.* Did the admission by pleading of decedent's death in the principal case render the offered photograph irrelevant? The traditional answer has been in the negative. Dunning v. Maine Central R.R., 39 A. 352 (Me.1897). It has been argued, however, that admission of the fact sought to be proved alters the balance required by Rule 403. Dolan, Rule 403: The Prejudice Rule in Evidence, 49 S.Cal.L.Rev. 220 (1976). The potential value of such an approach to the defendant in a criminal case is discussed in Fortune, Judicial Admissions in Criminal Cases: Blocking the Introduction of Prejudicial Evidence, 17 Crim.L.Bull. 101 (1981). But many courts continue to discern points of relevancy for such evidence beyond those which have been stipulated or otherwise admitted. See, e.g., State v. Clabourne, 690 P.2d 54 (Ariz.1984); State v. Schneider, 736 S.W.2d 392 (Mo.1987); State v. Broberg, 677 A.2d 602 (Md.1996). See also Note, North Carolina's "Test for Excess": The Prejudicial Use of Photographic Evidence in Criminal Prosecutions After *State v. Hennis,* 67 N.C.L.Rev. 1367 (1989).

3. *Paternity cases.* Should the prosecution in a paternity proceeding be allowed to exhibit the illegitimate child to the jury for the purpose of showing its resemblance to the defendant? See Annot., 55 A.L.R.3d 1087. To what extent is the problem analogous to that in the principal case? To what extent does it raise additional difficulties?

ENSOR V. WILSON

Supreme Court of Alabama, 1987.
519 So.2d 1244.

BEATTY, JUSTICE

Appeal by Herman Ensor, M.D. and Ensor, Baccus & Williamson, P.A., from a judgement for plaintiff, Misty Wilson, a minor suing by her next friend, based upon a jury verdict that awarded plaintiff $2.5 million. The action was based upon allegations of malpractice.

Plaintiff is a child who was born prematurely, suffering a degree of brain damage and retardation * * * .

II.

Did the trial court err in permitting an in-court demonstration between Misty and a special education therapist? We quote from defendants' brief for an understanding of this issue:

> "Over the numerous and vigorous objections of defendant's counsel * * *, the court permitted a demonstration of Misty's *physical and mental abilities* and limitations to be conducted by Ms. Holland, a special education therapist, in the presence of the jury. During the course of that demonstration, Misty cried out, laughed, and called for her mother * * * . Ms. Holland repeatedly admonished her not to fall over as she walked and moved about on the mat which Ms. Holland admitted was not stable for walking on by anyone * * * . Presenting an adorable six-year-old child to the jury in this manner served no useful purpose other than to win the sympathy of the jurors for Misty and to substantially prejudice the defendants. Further, Ms. Holland testified on cross-examination that the demonstration was not necessary to explain Misty's physical and mental limitations to the jury—only that it would make it 'easier' or more 'graphic.' * * *

> "As noted in the objections raised prior and subsequent to the demonstration * * *, the exhibition of Misty in this fashion put the defendants at an unwarranted and unjust disadvantage. There was no opportunity during the demonstration to cross-examine Misty, she was not placed under oath, she was not competent to testify, and there were no adequate means for preserving for appeal purposes the effect of such a demonstration upon the jury. Indeed, to fully comprehend the impact of this demonstration upon the jury and all present in the courtroom, one had to have been there. All of these reasons justify the reversal of this case." (Emphasis added.)

In considering this issue, we note that the therapist, Dr. Francine Holland, the holder of a Ph.D. in education, was sworn as a witness and was subjected to a searching cross-examination. The trial court, moreover, required her examination to be previewed outside the jury's presence. It is clear, also, that the plaintiff's cognitive, as well as physical, ability was in issue on the matter of damages.

In his order denying the defendants' post-trial motions, the trial court made the following observations:

> "The defendants also contend that the in-court demonstration of the child by plaintiff's expert, Dr. Holland, was highly prejudicial and inflammatory. Undersigned Judge observed the witnesses and the child on a preliminary run-through outside the presence of the jury and again observed all concerned when the jury was present. In the court's view the demonstration fully comported with due process and modern standard personal injury lawsuit procedure. The minor plaintiff sat with her parents in the courtroom during an all-day voir dire, in the full presence of the jury, with no objection of any kind from the defendant's attorneys. In the court's opinion, the child appeared more animated in the Dr. Holland demonstration than she did while simply lying, almost comatose, with the parents during the voir dire."

The exhibition of injuries, usually by photograph or like means, see *Occidental Life Ins. Co. of California v. Nichols,* 266 Ala. 521, 97 So.2d 879 (1957); C. Gamble, *McElroy's Alabama Evidence,* § 207.01(5) at 461–2 (3d ed. 1977), is permissible in the measurable discretion of the trial court. While we have been unable to find a case directly on point, an Ohio case, *Heidbreder v. Northhampton Township Trustees,* 64 Ohio App.2d 95, 411 N.E.2d 825, 829 (1979), approved the demonstration in open court of an infant who allegedly had suffered brain damage:

> "The infant, Jonathan Heidbreder, remained outside the courtroom during the entire trial except for the period of demonstration. He was brought before the jury to demonstrate the extent of his motor paralysis and *ability to communicate and do simple tasks.* This evidence was relevant to the issue of damages and peripherally so to the liability issue. Prior to this demonstration, an in-camera hearing was held and the proposed demonstration enacted for the trial court. The trial court specifically found that the evidentiary value of the appearance would not be outweighed by its prejudicial effect. We find no error in permitting the jury to see the demonstration and view the infant * * *." (Emphasis added.)

It is not clear from *Heidbreder* that the demonstration held in that case contained questions and answers between the demonstrator and the demonstratee, or that, as here, the demonstration was conducted by a testifying witness or by counsel. Nevertheless, under the control of the trial judge, the demonstration in the present case was not different in theory and practice from the relevant exhibition of wounds, movement, articulation, and the like, whether by the witness himself or through the use of the medium of photography, which, after all, is in effect another witness. Indeed, it would be difficult to exhibit cognition without a demonstration of vocal expression, physical response, or a combination of both, and thus it would not be, as a matter of law, erroneous to have such a demonstration guided by a witness skilled in ascertaining such relevant responses and explaining their meaning. The accuracy of such a demonstration, of course, is to be tested by the requirements of relevancy, and such a demonstration is to be disallowed when its probative worth is exceeded by its capacity for prejudice. In this case, we find no abuse in the trial court's permitting the demonstration.

* * *

Let the judgment be affirmed.

NOTES AND QUESTIONS

1.   *Presence in the courtroom.* In the principal case the plaintiff was allowed to sit with her parents all day without objection. What if objection had been made? What would be the bearing of a rule such as Rule 615 on the question? See Bremner v. Charles, 821 P.2d 1080 (Or.1991).

2.   *Day in the life films.* An evidentiary development of recent years now encountered is the so-called "day in the life" film or videotape, in which a substantially incapacitated plaintiff is pictured carrying out his or her daily routine. To what extent are the evidentiary questions raised by such films similar to those in the principal case? To what extent do such films raise additional questions? See Bannister v. Town of Noble, 812 F.2d 1265 (10th Cir.1987), for a discussion of the frequently raised concerns with regard to such films or videotapes. See also 2 McCormick, Evidence § 216 (7th ed. 2013); Note, Beyond Words: The Evidentiary Status of Day in the Life Films, 66 B.U.L.Rev. 133 (1986).

3.   *Effect of injury.* Cases involving demonstrations to show the effect of injury are collected in Annot., 82 A.L.R.4th 980.

McDowell v. Schuette

Missouri Court of Appeals, 1980.
610 S.W.2d 29.

STEWART, JUDGE.

Plaintiffs, David and Donna McDowell, who are in the construction business, brought an action in two counts against defendants. In the first count they sought to recover the balance due under a contract for construction of a house for defendants. The second count was in quantum meruit for labor and materials furnished defendants that were not within the terms of the contract. Defendants filed a counterclaim in two counts alleging inter alia that they had been damaged because the house was not completed in "a good and workmanlike manner" and because the work was not timely completed. Judgment was entered upon a jury verdict for plaintiffs on both counts of their petition that assessed damages at $14,150 on Count I and $5,280 on Count II. Defendants were awarded $2,600 on Count I of their counterclaim. Defendants appeal from the judgment.

We affirm. * * *

As we understand defendants' next point they contend that the court erred when it told the jury that it had decided to allow the jury to view the home of defendants, how they were to be transported and who would be present, and then admonished them not to discuss the case or their view of the premises with anyone. Defendants claim that this was an oral instruction which should have been reduced to writing and given to the jury before they viewed the building.

The statement made by the court reads as follows:

"Ladies and gentlemen of the Jury, it's my determination that after hearing evidence for two days that a view of the premises involved would not be inappropriate and therefore I am going to rule that you be allowed to view the house in question. However, I want to do this with some very strict guidelines, within some strict guidelines.

You will be taken to the, to the home in a van, with a chauffeured driver. Eleven of you can go with that driver. I'm going to order the Bailiff to accompany you to the home. The Bailiff will take the twelfth juror to the home.

I will allow any of the parties, Mr. and Mrs. Schuette or Mr. and Mrs. McDowell, to go in their own separate vehicles. I will not allow the attorneys to accompany either the Jury, the parties or the Bailiff.

When you get to the home I want you to remember the caution that we have given you before. Do not discuss this case among yourselves or with anyone. If any of the parties, the Bailiff, the driver, if anyone, or a member of your own Jury, attempts to emphasize some portion of the house or to point something out to you, I want to know about it immediately.

You are to go to the home, view the home, and then return to the jury room; you are to do no more, no less.

Now, I hope we understand one another."

While it is true that Rule 70.02(a) requires that "all instructions shall be submitted in writing and shall be given or refused by the court according to the law and the evidence in the case" not every statement of the court to the jury is an instruction within the meaning of the rule. An oral direction or cautionary remark not a part of the law of the case need not be in writing. *State v. Jordan,* 506 S.W.2d 74, 78 (Mo.App.1974).

The first three paragraphs of the statement made by the court contain no instruction to the jury. In this portion of the statement the court announced its ruling upon plaintiffs' request that the jury be permitted to view the house and explained the manner in which this would be accomplished.

* * *

In any event the court was not required to give any written instructions to the jury before they viewed the premises. Written instructions are given to the jury only at the close of the case. Rule 70.02(a).

The defendants contend that the court erred when it did not grant a new trial because most of the jurors were transported to view the house in a bus owned by plaintiffs and driven by one of their employees. Defendants' counsel made an affidavit that he had learned of this alleged impropriety after the jury returned its verdict. In this case the jurors were cautioned not to speak with anyone including the driver of the vehicle and to report any attempt by anyone to emphasize any portion of the house.

Defendants made no attempt to produce any evidence which might show any impropriety on the part of the driver or the jurors. There is no evidence that the jurors even knew that the vehicle had been furnished by plaintiffs or that the driver was Mr. Cook, an employee of plaintiffs.

The action of the trial court in matters such as this requires the exercise of sound discretion on the part of the trial court. We find no abuse of discretion in this instance. *Kelley v. Prince,* 379 S.W.2d 508, 513 (Mo.1964).

We consider defendants' next two subpoints together because they are premised upon defendants' contention that the jury's view of the premises constituted evidence.

II - issue   Defendants argue that it was error to bar counsel for the parties and the court reporter from the inspection of the house because their absence prevented objections to and preservation of evidence presented by the jury view. Defendants also claim that plaintiffs' introduction of expert testimony was an admission that laymen (the jury) could not understand the defects in the house. Thus, defendants believe the jury view improperly allowed evidence of lay opinion.

These subpoints are answered by the court's holding in *Koplar v. State Tax Comm'n,* 321 S.W.2d 686, 696 (Mo.1959):

> "While a view may be taken by the triers of the fact to enable them to understand the evidence, such view cannot be substituted for evidence, nor can it constitute evidence in the case. We think its purpose is well stated in *Cowan v. Bunting Glider Co.,* 159 Pa.Super. 573, 49 A.2d 270, 271, as follows: 'Triers of fact, be they judges, jurors, viewers, board or commissions, may always visit and inspect the locus in quo to secure a better understanding of the evidence and to enable them to determine the relative weight of conflicting testimony. But a view cannot replace testimony; the visual observations of the trier cannot be substituted for testimony; and the only legitimate purpose of an inspection is to illustrate the evidence and provide a base for understanding and comprehending testimony upon the record.' "

A .   The record indicates the court's comments to the jury regarding the disparity of the testimony served as the basis for the jury view of the house. The court allowed the view in order to determine the relative weight of the conflicting testimony as suggested in the *Koplar* case. Because the jury view did not constitute evidence, defendants' argument that the view was evidence of lay opinion fails.

2 .   The question of whether to permit an inspection of the premises is a matter within the discretion of the trial court. We find no abuse of discretion in this case. *State ex inf. McKittrick v. Jones,* 353 Mo. 900, 185 S.W.2d 17, 22 (1945).

Other issues sought to be raised with respect to the inspection of the premises have not been preserved for our review because the defendants did not raise them at the time the court made its ruling. *Germann v. City of Kansas City,* 577 S.W.2d 54, 55[1] (Mo.App.1978). * * *

Finding no reversible error, the judgment of the trial court is affirmed.

KELLY, P.J., and SNYDER, J., concur.

NOTES AND QUESTIONS

1.   *Views as evidence.* The position taken by the court in the principal case, that a jury view does not constitute evidence, has generally been criticized by the commentators. See, e.g., Hardman, The Evidentiary Effect of a View: Stare Decisis or Stare Dictis, 53 W.Va.L.Rev. 103 (1951); Wendorf, Some Views on Jury Views, 15 Baylor L.Rev. 379 (1963); 2 McCormick, Evidence § 219 (7th ed. 2013). Some courts have been moved to promote the view to evidentiary status. In an especially thoughtful opinion, the court in State v. Pauline, 60 P.3d 306, 322–30 (Haw.2002), rejected the former Hawaii rule that a view was not evidence, noting, among other things, that technological advances permit the view to be recorded and included in the record. See also United States v. Gray, 199 F.3d 547, 549 (1st Cir.1999); Moore, Kelly & Reddish, Inc. v. Shannondale, Inc., 165 S.E.2d 113 (W.Va.1968). Other recent decisions have persisted in finding that a view is not evidence. See, e.g., Stephenson v. State, 742 N.E.2d 463 (Ind.2001). Should the practice of treating the view as evidence be subject to any restrictions or limitations? In light of its ruling that the view would be considered evidence, the court in *Pauline* suggested a number of procedural safeguards including the presence of counsel and the judge, a full and accurate recording of the view and the presence of the defendant. See generally Keele, Note, When Mohamed Goes to the Mountain: The Evidentiary Value of a View, 80 Ind.L.J. 1091 (2005).

2.   *Attendance by accused.* Does the suggestion in *Pauline* that the defendant be present rise to a constitutional level? In Snyder v. Massachusetts, 291 U.S. 97 (1934), the Supreme Court held, four Justices dissenting, that due process had not been denied a defendant who was refused the opportunity to be present at a view. The Court, however, carefully limited its holding in *Snyder* to the facts of the case. These included the fact that a view is not deemed evidence in Massachusetts, that no oral testimony was taken at the view, and that the judge, court reporter, and also defendant's counsel were present.

Despite the trend toward recognizing the view as itself evidence, the defendant's right to be present is frequently seen as dependent upon whether testimony was taken. See 2 McCormick, Evidence § 219 (7th ed. 2013). In the various states, the question is commonly treated by statute. E.g., N.Y. Crim. Pro. § 270.50; N.C. Gen. Stat. § 15A–1229.

3.   To what extent should demonstrations be permitted at a view? See discussion in Commonwealth v. Gomes, 944 N.E. 2d 1007, 1012–14 (Mass.2011) (prosecutor's unauthorized demonstration at view was error, but harmless in light of other evidence and the court's instructions to the jury).

4.   *Eminent domain proceedings.* In some jurisdictions a jury view is a matter of right in an eminent domain proceeding. Assume that in such a proceeding both the condemnor and the condemnee present expert testimony

as to the value of the land taken, the highest expert valuation being $25,000 and the lowest $19,000. The jury is also allowed to view the premises. If the jury thereafter returns a verdict in favor of the condemnee for $28,000 should such a verdict be allowed to stand? Would you expect the answer to turn upon whether or not the particular jurisdiction holds that a jury view constitutes "evidence?" What significance, if any, should be accorded the fact that in virtually every American jurisdiction only a qualified "expert" may give testimony as to the monetary value of real property? See Annot., 1 A.L.R.3d 1397.

GEO. C. CHRISTOPHER & SON, INC. v. KANSAS PAINT & COLOR CO.

Supreme Court of Kansas, 1974.
523 P.2d 709.

OWSLEY, JUSTICE: This action was based on the breach of an implied warranty to furnish a suitable paint to prime steel. In a jury trial the plaintiff prevailed, resulting in an appeal by defendant.

* * *

In support of its motion for a new trial, defendant filed the affidavit of one of its attorneys stating he had conferred with several jury members following the verdict and that the foreman of the jury had performed certain tests on a paint sample panel submitted as evidence. The foreman scraped paint from plaintiff's exhibit with a pocket knife and discussed these results with the jury; no such tests were performed on defendant's exhibits. The affidavit contends jurors admitted these tests were influential factors in their decision for plaintiff. The trial court denied the motion for new trial saying the facts stated in the affidavit were insufficient grounds upon which to order a new trial. There was no questioning of the jurors themselves, but the facts in the affidavit were not disputed and were accepted as true although held insufficient.

Misconduct of jurors *per se* does not necessitate a new trial, but misconduct which results in prejudice to a litigant and impairs his right to a fair and impartial trial requires a new trial. (Baker v. Western Casualty & Surety Co., 196 Kan. 345, 411 P.2d 711; Furstenberg v. Wesley Medical Center, 200 Kan. 277, 436 P.2d 369.) It is for the trial court to determine in the first instance whether misconduct on the part of the jury has resulted in prejudice to a litigant, and its judgment thereon will not be overturned unless abuse of discretion is manifest. (Walker v. Holiday Lanes, 196 Kan. 513, 413 P.2d 63; Furstenberg v. Wesley Medical Center, supra.) Defendant contends the action of the jury in independently testing only plaintiff's paint panel exhibit was prejudicial to it and cites several Kansas cases in support of its argument. The cases are not relevant because they involve jury gathering of evidence either outside the physical surroundings of the courtroom or outside the scope of the evidence and issues presented for jury consideration. In Kaminski v. Kansas City Public Service Co., 175 Kan. 137, 259 P.2d 207, several jurors visited the scene of the collision and measured distances; in Kincaid v. Wade, 196 Kan. 174, 410 P.2d 333, jurors followed the woman defendant in a motor accident and reported to other jurors on her driving habits; in Barajas v. Sonders, 193 Kan. 273, 392 P.2d 849, one juror used a slide rule to determine the point of impact and other computations; in Walker v. Holiday Lanes, supra, a juror went to the bowling alley, the scene of a slip and fall incident, and reported the results of his independent investigation. These were instances of prejudicial jury conduct because, as the court said in *Kaminski:*

> " * * * Litigants have a right to expect that with respect to evidence juries will confine themselves to the evidence introduced, and that members of a jury will not engage in any 'extra curricular' activities such as were indulged in here." (175 Kan. p. 140, 259 P.2d p. 210.)

In the case at bar, the jurors duplicated tests performed in the courtroom on exhibits sent with them to the jury room. This instance more closely resembles or parallels the circumstances in State v. Levin, 117 Kan. 739, 232 P. 1020, where the jury's thorough examination of a still produced half a pint of the forbidden product. When defendant claimed he was prejudiced, the court said:

> "Obviously the object of sending exhibits to the jury is to enable the jurors to make a more thorough examination of them than it was possible to make when the exhibits were offered in evidence. * * * " (p. 741, 232 P. p. 1022.)

An even closer parallel is presented by Taylor v. Reo Motors, Inc., 275 F.2d 699 (10th Cir.1960). A poorly manufactured heat exchanger was the alleged cause of a fire. The device was admitted into evidence and went with the jury to the jury room. During their deliberations, members of the jury took the device apart and put it back together, using pocket knives, nail clippers, and other pocket tools. Defendant claimed this was jury misconduct prejudicial to it and moved for a new trial. The court commented on the action of the jurors as follows:

> "The salient question is whether the experiment or investigation made by the jury out of the presence of the parties, and while they were deliberating, can be said to be within the scope or purview of the evidence introduced at the trial, or whether it amounts to the taking of evidence outside the presence of the parties. See Annotation 80 A.L.R. 108. If the experiment or demonstration was conducted by the jury for the purpose of testing the truth of the statements made concerning the functioning of the heat exchanger, it was proper. The heat

exchanger was offered in evidence. It had been disassembled and reassembled in open court by experts for the purpose of demonstrating negligence or lack of negligence in its manufacture or assemblage. The exhibit was before the jury, and it was permissible to take it to the jury room and examine it for the purpose of testing the validity of statements made in open court in respect thereto. If it had been a written document in fine print, we do not suppose that it would have been improper for the jury to use a magnifying glass in possession of one of them for the purpose of scrutinizing critical language. It therefore does not seem improper for the jury to disassemble this exhibit for the purpose of deciding the issues presented to them." (pp. 705, 706.)

The conduct of the jurors in this case passes the test of *Kaminski* in that they did not stray beyond the confines of the evidence presented to them with their tests, and it also passes the test of *Taylor* because the purpose of the test was to check the validity of evidence presented in open court. An experiment or demonstration is proper when conducted by the jury with the use of exhibits properly submitted to it for the purpose of testing the truth of statements made by witnesses or duplicating tests made by witnesses in open court.

The trial court correctly denied defendant's motion for a new trial based on alleged jury misconduct.

Affirmed.

NOTES AND QUESTIONS

1.   *Exhibits in the jury room.* American authority generally supports the sending of formally offered and admitted tangible exhibits with the jury upon its retirement, subject in some jurisdictions to discretionary control of the practice by the court. See 2 McCormick, Evidence § 220 (7th ed. 2013). Federal criminal cases are collected in Annot., 62 A.L.R.Fed. 950. Cases relating to jury acquisition of items not formally admitted are collected in Annot., 37 A.L.R.2d 662.

2.   *Juror testimony.* If the attorney's affidavit as to the jury conduct had been disputed, would it have been proper to question the jurors themselves as to what they did? The long-standing rule is that "a juror may not impeach his own verdict," but jurisdictions are divided on the application of this rule to facts such as those in the principal case. As to the effect of Rule 606(b) on the question, see Note, The Room Without a View: Inquiries Into Jury Misconduct After the Adoption of Texas Rule of Evidence 606(b), 38 Baylor L.Rev. 965 (1986). Federal Rule 606(b) was amended in 2006 to deal with instances of mistakes in filling out a verdict form, but with no effect on this question. See also Chapter 16, Section B. Cases involving experimentation by jurors are collected in Annot., 31 A.L.R.4th 566.

Unauthorized jury views raise similar questions. See Annot., 11 A.L.R.3d 918.

CHAPTER 11[1]

WRITINGS AND RELATED MATTERS

■ ■ ■

A. AUTHENTICATION

UNITED STATES V. SKIPPER

United States Court of Appeals, Fifth Circuit, 1996.
74 F.3d 608.

DUHÉ, CIRCUIT JUDGE:

John Derrick Skipper appeals his conviction for possession of crack cocaine with intent to distribute, in violation of 21 U.S.C. § 841(a)(1). Finding insufficient evidence to support the jury's verdict, we reverse, vacate the sentence and remand for sentencing on the lesser included offense of simple possession. * * *

While patrolling Interstate Highway 10, Deputy Sheriff Todd Richards and criminal justice student Benny Soileau observed a Nissan automobile changing lanes erratically. Officer Richards closed on the Nissan and activated the lights of his patrol car. As the Nissan moved to the right lane, Richards and Soileau observed a small plastic bag fly from the driver's side of the car.

After pulling over to the shoulder, John Derrick Skipper, the driver and owner of the Nissan, exited his car and approached the police car. Officer Richards immediately placed Skipper under arrest. Richards then went to the Nissan, where he found a passenger, Jerome Cutright, seated in the car. Officer Richards next placed Skipper in the patrol car and drove to retrieve the bag from the side of the road. The bag contained 2.89 grams of crack cocaine. Richards also searched the Nissan and found one straight-edge razor between the front two seats.

At trial, pursuant to Federal Rule of Evidence 404(b), the district court admitted into evidence two state-court convictions for crimes allegedly committed by Skipper. Government Exhibit #3 was a certified copy of a judgment against "John Derrick Skipper" indicating that Appellant pled guilty to possession of a controlled substance. An expert testified that the fingerprints on this conviction matched Appellant's

---

[1] Throughout this chapter some footnotes from the original cases and materials have been omitted; others have been renumbered. [Ed.]

fingerprints. Government Exhibit #2 was a certified copy of a deferred adjudication order indicating that "John D. Skipper" was placed on ten years probation for possession of a controlled substance. However, this order did not bear any fingerprints, and the government did not otherwise identify Appellant as the person named in the order.

The jury convicted Skipper of possession of crack cocaine with intent to distribute, in violation of 21 U.S.C. § 841(a)(1). On appeal, Skipper challenges the sufficiency of the evidence and also argues that the district court erred by admitting the deferred adjudication order. * * *

We review the admission of evidence only for an abuse of discretion. United States v. Eakes, 783 F.2d 499, 506–07 (5th Cir.1986). Furthermore, even if we find an abuse of discretion in the admission or exclusion of evidence, we review the error under the harmless error doctrine. United States v. Scott, 678 F.2d 606, 612 (5th Cir.1982). Finally, we must affirm evidentiary rulings unless they affect a substantial right of the complaining party. Fed.R.Evid. 103(a); *Foster v. Ford Motor Co.*, 621 F.2d 715, 721 (5th Cir.1980).

The district court admitted into evidence a deferred adjudication order indicating that a "John D. Skipper" was placed on ten years probation for possession of a controlled substance. However, the court erred in admitting this evidence because the government should have been required to produce evidence proving that Appellant was the actual "John D. Skipper" named in the deferred adjudication order. Rule 901(a) of the Federal Rules of Evidence provides: "The requirement of authentication or identification as a condition precedent to admissibility is satisfied by evidence sufficient to support a finding that the matter in question is what its proponent claims." We hold that the mere similarity in name between a criminal defendant and a person named in a prior conviction alone does not satisfy Rule 901's identification requirement.

[The court found the error to be harmless.]

NOTE AND QUESTION

Is the fact that there was a John D. Skipper placed on probation logically relevant to this prosecution? Is the authentication rule simply a specific application of Rule 403 guarding against the admission of evidence that may be logically relevant where admission of that evidence runs the danger of unfair prejudice? Why should there be an additional rule? Are there specific considerations involved in the requirement of authentication that make a separate rule a good idea? See generally Imwinkelried, Evidentiary Foundations (8th ed. 2012); 2 McCormick, Evidence § 221 (7th ed. 2013).

BUCKINGHAM CORP. V. EWING LIQUORS CO.
Appellate Court of Illinois, 1973.
305 N.E.2d 278.

STAMOS, PRESIDING JUSTICE. Defendant, Ewing Liquors Co., appeals from an order granting plaintiff a permanent injunction. The trial court found that plaintiff's Cutty Sark scotch whiskey is sold in Illinois pursuant to a valid fair trade agreement, and that on December 13, 1971, defendant knowingly sold Cutty Sark scotch whiskey at a price below plaintiff's fair trade price in contravention of the Illinois Fair Trade Act.[2] The order permanently enjoined defendant from advertising, offering for sale or selling plaintiff's products in Illinois at prices less than those stipulated by plaintiff from time to time pursuant to the fair trade agreement. Plaintiff's fair traded products and their current prices were also set forth in the order.

On appeal defendant contends that:

1. Plaintiff failed to prove the execution of the fair trade agreement;

2. Plaintiff failed to prove knowledge by defendant of its fair trade prices;

* * *

Plaintiff filed a verified complaint alleging that Cutty Sark scotch whiskey is in free and open competition in Illinois; that plaintiff imports and distributes this product to wholesale distributors in Illinois; that plaintiff has entered into fair trade contracts in Illinois wherein it is provided that Cutty Sark shall not be sold, advertised or offered for sale at prices below the prices stipulated by plaintiff; that defendant had due notice of the stipulated prices; that on December 13, 1971 defendant sold a fifth of Cutty Sark scotch whiskey at a price of $5.99 whereas the fair trade price was $6.59; and that defendant is continuing knowingly to sell Cutty Sark scotch whiskey at prices below the fair trade prices.[3]

Defendant filed a verified answer denying plaintiff's material allegations, and raising various affirmative defenses. Plaintiff then filed a reply to defendant's answer, and attached an affidavit of Ted Herbik, an employee of Buckingham Distributors, a letter from plaintiff to all Illinois liquor retailers informing them of amended fair trade prices effective

---

[2] Ill.Rev.Stat.1971, ch. 121½, par. 188 et seq.

[3] Defendant did not contract with plaintiff to sell plaintiff's products at fair trade prices. However, under the Illinois Fair Trade Act, defendant is a "non-signer" (one who is not a party to a fair trade agreement), and is also prohibited from "wilfully and knowingly advertising, offering for sale or selling" plaintiff's products at less than plaintiff's stipulated prices. Ill.Rev.Stat.1971, ch. 121½, par. 189; Kinsey Distilling Sales Co. v. Foremost Liquor Stores, Inc., 15 Ill.2d 182, 154 N.E.2d 290.

December 1, 1969, and a page from the December, 1969 issue of the *Illinois Beverage Journal* reproducing plaintiff's letter to Illinois retailers.

At the hearing for a temporary injunction, the parties stipulated that they would proceed with a hearing for a permanent injunction. A private detective testified that on December 13, 1971 he entered defendant's store and purchased a fifth of Cutty Sark scotch whiskey at a price of $5.99. He testified that the fair trade price schedule which he received from plaintiff's attorney listed the fair trade price as $6.59 per fifth. His report was introduced into evidence.

The managing editor of the *Illinois Beverage Journal* testified that the *Journal* is a trade publication which advertises, lists trade prices and publishes news of interest in the industry. He stated that the *Journal* conducted a mailing of price schedules for Buckingham Corporation in November, 1969, and that defendant was on that mailing list. The witness admitted on cross-examination that he had no personal knowledge of whether defendant received the letter, or indeed of whether in fact the letter had actually been mailed to defendant, because the mailing was handled by the *Journal's* mailing service. However, the witness did receive an attestation from the mailing service that the mailing was being conducted. On redirect examination the witness stated that the mailing service handled 4 or 5 mailings per month other than the *Journal,* and had been reliable for 17 years. In addition, defendant was a subscriber to the *Journal* in December, 1969, and plaintiff's price schedule was reproduced in that issue of the *Journal.* Reproductions of the price list as it was mailed, and as it was reproduced in the *Journal,* were introduced into evidence.

Evidence of the fair trade agreement was then adduced. A Chicago liquor retailer acknowledged his signature on a fair trade agreement dated July 30, 1969 between himself and Buckingham Corporation. Ted Herbik, a marketing director of Buckingham Distributors, testified that he recognized the signature of William Gallagan, plaintiff's vice-president, and he identified Gallagan's signature on the July 30, 1969 agreement. He stated that he was familiar with Gallagan's signature because he had received correspondence from him in the past; he admitted that he had never seen Gallagan sign his name. The fair trade agreement was then introduced into evidence.

* * *

Defendant contends that plaintiff failed to adequately prove an essential element of its cause of action—the existence of a fair trade agreement. Defendant's answer demanded strict proof of all allegations of plaintiff's complaint, and one of defendant's affirmative defenses stated that defendant had no knowledge of plaintiff's alleged fair trade agreement. Plaintiff was therefore required to prove the execution, existence and authenticity of the agreement before it was admitted into evidence. Dick v. Halun, 344 Ill. 163, 176 N.E. 440; Crosier v. Crosier, 201 Ill.App. 406; 18 I.L.P. Evidence, §§ 234, 235.

It has long been the rule in Illinois that handwriting may be proved by a witness's show of familiarity with it. This familiarity may be gained from having seen the party actually write, or from having been acquainted with the handwriting in the course of business dealings. (Riggs v. Powell, 142 Ill. 453, 32 N.E. 482; Gard, Illinois Evidence Manual, Rule 316; Cleary, Evidence (2d Ed.) § 11.14.) The extent of the knowledge of the witness goes to the weight to be given his opinion.

The evidence adduced as to the execution and authenticity of the fair trade agreement was the testimony of the liquor retailer and plaintiff's employee, Herbik. The retailer identified his signature on the agreement dated July 30, 1969; he was not asked whether he saw plaintiff's vice-president, William Gallagan, sign the agreement. Herbik testified on direct examination that he had personal knowledge of Gallagan's signature from having seen it on documents sent to him in the regular course of business. Upon the objection of defendant's counsel, his testimony that Gallagan also had told him that he had signed the agreement was stricken from the record as hearsay. On cross-examination, however, the following colloquy occurred:

> Defendant's Counsel: So, your testimony as to Mr. Gallagan's signature is the result of what he said in Siegel's office while you were present, is that right?
>
> Witness: That is right.
>
> Defendant's Counsel: Which I objected to. You heard me object to that, didn't you?
>
> Witness: I have no objection of your objections.

It is clear that, although Herbik's hearsay testimony was stricken from the record on direct examination, counsel for defendant allowed the same testimony to be entered into the record on his cross-examination of the witness. It is elementary that hearsay evidence is competent if not objected to (Town of Cicero v. Industrial Commission, 404 Ill. 487, 89 N.E.2d 354; Potato Growers' Exchange v. Wignall–Moore Co., 249 Ill.App. 34). Therefore, this testimony was competent evidence of Herbik's knowledge of Gallagan's signature in addition to the testimony regarding Herbik having seen the signature on correspondence in the regular course of business. In any event, the trial court was in a superior position to observe and hear the witness and determine the weight to be given this testimony. (First National Bank of Elgin v. Dierking, 87 Ill.App.2d 4, 230 N.E.2d 520.) Therefore, we will not disturb the trial court's finding that plaintiff adequately proved the execution of the fair trade agreement.

[The court nevertheless reversed on the basis that the plaintiff failed to prove an essential element of its case in failing adequately to prove notice of the fair trade price to defendant. It noted that the plaintiff had not established that the *Illinois Beverage Journal* was commonly relied upon by retailers for notice of fair trade prices, nor had plaintiff adequately proved that a copy of the *Journal* was actually mailed to the defendant.]

NOTES AND QUESTIONS

1. *Lay witness authentications.* In accord with the principal case, identification of signature by a lay witness is generally held sufficient to authenticate. 2 McCormick, Evidence § 223 (7th ed. 2013). While the courts have varied as to the degree of familiarity which the authenticating witness must be shown to have with the purported author's writing, the requirements in this regard have tended to be minimal. See, e.g., State v. Freshwater, 85 P. 447 (Utah 1906) (single observation of writing sufficient to confer familiarity); Morgan v. First Pennsylvania Bank, 541 A.2d 380 (Pa.Super.1988) (familiarity through correspondence). See also the authenticating testimony of the witness set out in footnote 5 of the next principal case, *United States v. American Radiator & Standard Sanitary Corp.* As to the inherent unreliability of lay witness handwriting identification, see Inbau, Lay Witness Identification of Handwriting (An Experiment), 34 Ill.L.Rev. 433 (1939). What purpose, if any, is served by the exaction of such testimony?

2. *Familiarity not acquired for litigation.* Under Rule 901(b)(2) nonexpert opinion of the genuineness of handwriting cannot be based on familiarity acquired for purposes of the litigation. What should constitute the "litigation"? See United States v. Scott, 270 F.3d 30 (1st Cir.2001) (IRS agent properly permitted to authenticate handwriting based upon knowledge of defendant's handwriting over the course of several years of investigating his activities).

3. *Authenticating relationships.* Authentication most commonly involves the introduction of evidence tending to show authorship. The substantive law, however, frequently declares many other types of relationship between individuals and things to be legally significant. The prima facie establishment of relationships such as ownership, publication, manufacture, and distribution may also constitute authentication.

4. *Trademarked items.* Was the testimony of the private detective that he purchased a bottle of "Cutty Sark" potentially objectionable for lack of sufficient authentication? Authentication of trademarked items has traditionally been required, usually with untoward results. See, e.g., Keegan v. Green Giant Co., 110 A.2d 599 (Me.1954) (directed verdict against plaintiff who testified that she suffered injury to teeth while eating peas (and a stone) from a can bearing Green Giant label). Compare, however, State v. Rines, 269 A.2d 9 (Me.1970). The problem is now resolved in those jurisdictions adopting Federal Rule 902(7), which renders trademarked items self-authenticating.

5. *Newspapers and periodicals.* Consider also the copy of the Illinois Beverage Journal admitted in the principal case. Was the copy itself authenticated? If so, what of the plaintiff's listed fair trade price? See the comment of Wigmore, a zealot for authentication: "There is usually available as much evidence of the act of * * * handing to a printer as there would be of any other act, such as chopping a tree or building a fence." 7 Wigmore, Evidence § 2150, at 608 (Chadbourn rev. 1978). Are either or both of these problems resolved by the provisions of Rule 902(6) applying the principle of self-authentication to "newspapers and periodicals?" For an interesting application of Rule 902(6), see Boim v. Quranic Literacy Inst., 340 F.Supp.2d 885 (N.D.Ill.2004) (interview published in well-known Arabic language newspaper was self-authenticating).

UNITED STATES V. AMERICAN RADIATOR & STANDARD SANITARY CORP.

United States Court of Appeals, Third Circuit, 1970.
433 F.2d 174.

[Appellants were convicted by a jury of certain violations of section 1 of the Sherman Act. The indictment charged, among other things, that the appellants and other indicted and non-indicted co-conspirators had met at various "official" conventions of the Plumbing Fixtures Manufacturers Association (hereinafter PFMA) and entered into various specified illegal agreements, including one to discontinue the manufacture of regular enameled cast iron plumbing fixtures which were lower-priced than acid-resistant enameled cast iron plumbing fixtures. One of the alleged meetings was held at the Palm Beach Biltmore Hotel. The Crane Company, referred to in the opinion, was indicted as a defendant in the action, but was not a party to the present appeal.]

SEITZ, CIRCUIT JUDGE:

* * *

Evidentiary Rulings

Appellants argue they were prejudiced by certain rulings on government evidence. They first challenge the propriety of the admission of Government Exhibits 551 through 556 (HCA notes). As we have noted, the elimination of regular enamel products and the fixing of acid resistant enamel prices was the fourth alleged event in the criminal conspiracy charged by the government. A part of the government's evidence on this aspect of the conspiracy concerned events at an informal session after the PFMA meeting at the Palm Beach Biltmore on March 28, 1963. As evidence of the agreement to eliminate regular enamel and to fix acid resistant fixture prices, the government offered two documents. One was an American Standard worksheet entitled "Acid–Resisting Enamel Prices" dated March 1, 1963. The other consisted of six pages of undated and unsigned handwritten notes on the stationery of the Hotel Corporation of America (HCA notes), which echoed figures and statements on the American Standard price worksheet. The appellants claim the admission of the HCA notes was reversible error.

They first argue that the notes were inadequately identified in that there was insufficient evidence concerning their author for them to be admitted in evidence. The government's contention is that Raymond Pape, a Crane official, wrote the notes at the Palm Beach meeting. In support of their position, government counsel introduced a stipulation by all counsel that the HCA notes were found in Crane's files and were stapled together. The government also called a former secretary in Pape's department to make a lay handwriting identification of the notes.[4] She testified that she had done work for Pape and had been familiar with his handwriting "at times." She identified the handwriting on four of the six pages as resembling Pape's. She could not identify the writing on the two remaining pages.[5]

Appellants contend that since a substantial danger of a wrongful attribution of guilt existed if these documents were erroneously identified, no less than a "positive, unequivocal identification of the handwriting must be required." In fact the weight of authority requires only that a prima facie case of the alleged author's identity be established for the documents to be admitted. See generally 3 Wigmore, Evidence § 693 et seq. (1940); McCormick, Evidence § 189 (1954). The ultimate issue of their authorship and the probative weight to be afforded them is for the jury. We conclude upon a reading of the record that the requisite prima facie case as to the four pages identified by the secretary was established. Thus, we hold that the trial judge did not abuse his discretion in admitting them.

Two of the pages were admitted without any handwriting identification. The jury was instructed that these pages might be

---

[4]   The government represents in its brief that although Pape himself was technically available to be called as a witness, he was not called to identify the HCA notes because of the precarious state of his health. Indeed, Pape filed a motion to quash the government's subpoena to him on this ground. Although his motion was denied, the trial judge indicated his intention to take all possible measures short of granting Pape's motion to protect him. Moreover, the government represented to the trial judge that it would avoid calling Pape if at all possible. Pape died of heart failure shortly after the trial ended.

[5]   The witness testified as follows concerning each of the six pages:

(1) GX–551: "As I remember, it looks as if it could be Mr. Pape's but I can't be sure right now."

(2) GX–552: "[I]t resembles Mr. Pape's."

(3) GX–553: "It looks like it could be Mr. Pape's."

(4) GX–554: "There really isn't too much handwriting on here to say too much about it." * * * "I can't really say."

(5) GX–555: "That appears to be Mr. Pape's."

(6) GX–556: "I can't be sure about this one."

compared with the other four pages for handwriting similarities should the other four be determined to be Pape's. Appellants challenge the propriety of allowing the jury to make such a comparison. They assert that the standard for comparison—the four pages—must be "admitted or proved" to be genuine before they may be used for comparison purposes. They further assert that the evidence was insufficient for the trial judge to properly determine the genuineness of the handwriting on the four pages so that they could be used as a standard of comparison.

Where documents are admitted for purposes other than handwriting comparison, they may be used by the jury as a standard for handwriting comparison if the handwriting is admitted or proved to be that of the alleged author. Williams v. Conger, 125 U.S. 397, 411–415 * * * (1888); cf. 28 U.S.C.A. § 1731. The vast weight of authority requires that the trial judge determine whether the genuineness of the handwriting on the documents to be used as the standard is sufficiently proved. E.g., United States v. Swan, 396 F.2d 883 (2d Cir.1968); Citizens' Bank & Trust Co. of Middlesboro, Ky. v. Allen, 43 F.2d 549 (4th Cir.1930); 7 Wigmore, Evidence § 2020 (1940). In those jurisdictions where the trial judge is required to make the initial determination of genuineness the courts have adopted differing standards of proof. We believe the proper standard requires that there be sufficient evidence so that a jury finding of genuineness would not be subject to reversal as against the weight of the evidence. See United States v. Swan, supra.

In view of the present state of the law as developed above, we are convinced that the trial judge, had he considered this question directly, could only have properly held that the four pages were appropriate for jury use as a handwriting standard.[6] We say this because the evidence supplied by the lay handwriting witness, a former Crane employee, in conjunction with the fact that the HCA notes were subpoenaed from Crane's PFMA file, were stapled together, and were internally consistent in content convince us that a jury finding that the four pages were in Pape's hand would be fairly supported by the evidence. Thus, we conclude the four pages were properly before the jury for use as a handwriting standard.

The appellants challenge the judge's instruction on the HCA notes in this connection as well. They contend that the instruction assumed that the four pages to be used as a handwriting standard were in Pape's hand

---

[6] In view of our disposition of this issue, we need not decide at this time whether the requirement of an initial determination of genuineness by the trial judge ought to be eliminated and the question of genuineness both as to the standard and the other documents be left solely to the jury. Such a course has been suggested by some commentators. See Committee on Rules of Practice and Procedure of the Judicial Conference of the United States, Preliminary Draft of Proposed Rules of Evidence for the United States District Courts and Magistrates, Article IX, Rule 9–01 (March 1969).

when in fact that very issue was in dispute. We have read the instruction and do not find that it contains such an assumption.

* * *

[Affirmed.]

NOTES AND QUESTIONS

1. *Exemplars.* Authentication by comparison of handwriting may be made by experts or, as the principal case indicates, by the trier of fact, but not by lay witnesses. The early cases limited the use of specimens (exemplars) for comparison purposes to those already in the case for some other purpose. That rule was modified by statutes and decisions so as to permit use of exemplars admitted to be genuine or proved to be genuine to the satisfaction of the court. For an excellent opinion tracing the evolution of the law in one state, see State v. LeDuc, 291 S.E.2d 607 (N.C.1982) (holding *inter alia* that jury may compare exemplars and contested writings even in absence of expert testimony.) Rule 901(b)(3) adopts the same standard for authentication of handwriting exemplars as for documents generally. See United States v. Mangan, 575 F.2d 32 (2d Cir.1978) (income tax returns in government files admitted as exemplars on basis of presumption of genuineness under statute). Cases dealing with the establishment of exemplars as genuine are collected in Annot., 41 A.L.R.2d 575. Should any distinction be made between exemplars prepared for use in the case and those preexisting? Between those prepared to demonstrate similarity and those prepared to demonstrate dissimilarity? See United States v. Pastore, 537 F.2d 675 (2d Cir.1976).

2. *Court or jury?* As to the respective roles of court and jury in the process of authentication, see United States v. Goichman, 547 F.2d 778 (3d Cir.1976).

3. *Required attesting witnesses.* While most writings may be authenticated by the testimony of any witness having the requisite familiarity with the handwriting of the signatory, different rules were evolved by the courts for writings whose execution is required to be attested by witnesses. Thus, the attesting witnesses must be called or shown to be unavailable before other evidence of authenticity could be resorted to. 2 McCormick, Evidence § 222 (7th ed. 2013). But compare Rule 903.

4. *Expert testimony.* The sufficiency, based upon a comparison of the offered item with an authenticated sample, of expert testimony to authenticate handwritten evidence has long been accepted doctrine. It is embodied in Rule 901(b)(3). The reliability of the "science," however, is seriously questioned by Risinger, Denbeaux & Saks, Exorcism of Ignorance as a Proxy for Rational Knowledge: The Lessons of Handwriting Identification "Expertise," 137 U.Pa.L.Rev. 731 (1989). This article and another by two of the same authors, Risinger & Saks, Science and Nonscience in the Courts: *Daubert* Meets Handwriting Identification Expertise, 82 Iowa L.Rev. 21

(1996), sparked a lively debate. See also Mnookin, Scripting Expertise: The History of Handwriting Identification Evidence and the Judicial Construction of Reliability, 87 Va.L.Rev. 1723 (2001); Moenssens, Handwriting Identification Evidence in the Post–*Daubert* World, 66 U.M.K.C.L.Rev. 251 (1997); Risinger, Denbeaux & Saks, Brave New "Post–*Daubert* World"—A Reply to Professor Moenssens, 29 Seton Hall L.Rev. 405 (1998). Another species of expert testimony bearing on the authenticity *vel non* of writings seems to be emerging. This is expert testimony based upon the comparison of linguistic patterns exhibited by exemplars of known authorship and the disputed document. See Estate of Ciaffoni, 446 A.2d 225 (Pa.1982). The case is the subject of Annot., 36 A.L.R.4th 598. See also Comment, Stylistics Evidence in the Trial of Patricia Hearst, 1977 Ariz.St.L.J. 387.

UNITED STATES V. SUTTON

United States Court of Appeals, District of Columbia Circuit, 1969.
426 F.2d 1202.

SPOTTSWOOD W. ROBINSON, III, CIRCUIT JUDGE. This appeal, from convictions by a jury of first degree murder and the unlicensed carrying of a dangerous weapon, presents [the question] whether four writings, three purportedly authored by appellant, were sufficiently authenticated by their interrelated contents, the circumstances under which they were discovered, and a connecting note found on appellant's person to qualify them for admission into evidence at his trial. * * *

[The government's evidence included the testimony of two eyewitnesses to the effect that they observed the appellant and the victim, Mrs. Matilda Glass, emerge from an automobile and embrace momentarily, after which appellant fired a shot and Mrs. Glass fled. Appellant pursued her and, when she fell to the ground, turned her over and fired two or three shots at her at point-blank range. These witnesses rushed to obtain assistance.] When they returned once more, police officers were there, and an assessment of the gruesome details was begun.

Mrs. Glass, struck by three bullets, either then was dead or died very shortly thereafter. Lying wounded nearby was appellant, a revolver under his right hand containing five expended cartridges and one that was live. Appellant was removed to a hospital, where seven more live cartridges were discovered in a pocket of his trousers.

Found also, beside Mrs. Glass' body, was an envelope bearing these notations:[7]

---

[7] These quotations, as well as others from the documentary evidence, are as they appear in the trial transcript. The original exhibits were not transmitted with the record on appeal. Slight variations respecting names may perhaps be accounted for by Government counsel's explanation to the court and the jury that he experienced some difficulty in deciphering the handwriting when he undertook to read the documents into the record.

From Alexander Sutton to daughter, Frances D. Sutton, JA 26671. Wife, Birdie Mal Sutton, 587–2456. Call them at once. Fort Launderdale, Florida. My mother JA 22779.

Inside the envelope were four notes, three of which were received in evidence.[8] The lengthiest of the three notes mentioned difficulties between the writer and "Matilda,"[9] and indicated plainly enough that an ominous event was about to occur.[10] This note also detailed dispositions of personal estate the writer desired to make, and designated relatives of the writer by names and telephone numbers identical to those appearing on the envelope.[11] These features pointed to appellant as the penman, in a degree which was later to be judicially gauged. Another writing placed in evidence, also purportedly written by appellant, began with the words "[r]ead this other note," and identified one "Arthur" as the party who had "carr[ied] her home Sunday night."[12] The third writing received, clearly not appellant's creation, was an amorous note ostensibly from "Arthur" to an unnamed addressee.[13]

---

[8] One of the enclosures was not introduced into evidence because its sole significance lay in its reference to a note stationed in appellant's locker at his place of work. The latter note also remained outside the evidence, and all references to it in other Government exhibits were deleted.

[9] As stated in the text, this was the deceased's forename.

[10] This note read as follows:

> To my daughter. Call her at Florida, JA 26671 587–2456. Frances D. Sutton, Fort Lauderdale Florida.
>
> The car note is paid until April 12. It is paid until then until it paid for March 12. Send it on the 13th Frances, don't worry about what happened. You all just keep the car. I am sick. Let me say this. I might not get a chance to paid, but it might be in my pocket and the card where I send the money over to you all I have the most of the thing fix up.
>
> I have some money on my job. I would not have done this but Matilda made me do this. Now we will both are in bad shape. I have no other choice at all. I have something pack. All of the lamps of mine, two floor lamps, one table lamp, Frances, the car may be paid for. These are the people that owe me where I work at the Shoreham West. These are the number.
>
> Mr. Mazor, L614, $25. Mrs. Sherling or Sherring, L2517, $125. Mr. Birch, L312.
>
> Just a few days there are two snow tires put in the receiving room. One way or the other, it will be two of some kind left in there. The diamond ring, give it to Jal on my finger. The watch for Lloyd, my son. I have spent hundred of dollars on this woman. But the Judge will not believe it of the jury.
>
> There are some checks to show and the rest in cash. Hub Furniture Store and we will put a hundred on the house which was my money. I have live with her for at least five or five and a half months. She were treated better than my wife or any other woman. There is $40 of $47 in my pocket.
>
> Bessie Sutton, mother, Fort Lauderdale Florida, Ja 22779. Birdie Sutton, wife, Fort Lauderdale, Florida 587–2456. My daughter, Frances Sutton, JA 26671.

[11] See note [10], supra.

[12] March 13, 1967, the day of the alleged homicide, was a Monday.

[13] In overall tone, this note, dated August 30, 1966, was something of a temporary farewell to the addressee. In it, "Arthur" stated, among other things, "that I will always cherish the moments and time that I have spent with you and even today I have the same feeling in respect for you that I had the day I stopped you in the Shoreham driveway." Later, he said that "[i]f this comes out okay someday later, I hope I can make you real happy like we used to be, at least for

There was, at the hospital to which appellant had been removed, another discovery which was to assume special importance at the trial. In the pocket of appellant's trousers was still another note, also let into evidence, which, as read into the trial transcript,[14] was as follows:

> Call Fort Lauderdale, Florida, JA 22779. Mother, Bessie Sutton, 587–2456. Wife, Birdie Neal Sutton. Daughter, Frances Sutton [more numbers].[15]

The Government's proffer of the envelope and the notes in evidence was strenuously resisted on the ground, inter alia, that they were not properly authenticated. The trial judge, after entertaining extensive argument by counsel, overruled the objection and allowed the prosecutor to read the envelope's inscription and three of the notes to the jury.[16] The judge also denied appellant's motion for a judgment of acquittal, presented at the conclusion of the Government's case in chief, and appellant then proceeded with his defense.

* * *

The jury, as we have stated, returned verdicts finding appellant guilty of murder in the first degree and carrying a dangerous weapon. The jury could not, however, agree on the punishment to be imposed on the murder conviction. The trial judge sentenced appellant to life imprisonment on that conviction, and to a concurrent one-year term of imprisonment on the other. This appeal followed.

II

Ordinarily, documentary evidence possesses no self-authenticating powers; unaided by an operable presumption, its reliability is not automatically assumed. The legal requirement obtaining in normal contexts is that its genuineness be shown independently before it is accepted as proof. The contention is vigorously pressed upon us that the communications purportedly written by appellant and "Arthur" were not sufficiently authenticated prior to their submission for consideration by the jury. Our scrutiny of the record in the light of the authorities leads us to conclude that the writings were properly received in evidence.

Indubitably, the sufficiency of a showing of authenticity of a document sought to be introduced into evidence is a matter residing in the sound discretion of the trial judge. As is always true with

---

one day, anyhow." He concluded: "But always remember I do love you regardless of what or who. Please be careful and don't do anything to get yourself in trouble."

[14] See note [7], supra.

[15] We are not benefited by information respecting the other numbers. Government counsel, reading this note to the jury, stated simply that "there are some numbers appearing at the bottom which seem to have no relevancy."

[16] The notes read were those quoted, wholly or partially in text supra following notes [7] and [15], and in notes [10] and [13], supra.

discretionary exercises there are discernible limits which judges must not transcend, but the judge's assessment of admissibility is vulnerable only if the error is clear. The applicable test to determine error is not whether the evidence of genuineness induces a belief beyond a reasonable doubt that the document is the handiwork of its alleged drafter, but whether, if it is uncontradicted, a reasonable mind might—though not necessarily would—fairly conclude favorably to the fact of authorship. In the case at bar, the contents of the questioned notes, conjoined with the circumstances surrounding their discovery, fashioned an adequate basis for the ruling admitting them in evidence.

We abide fully the usual judicial concession "that the mere *contents of a written communication,* purporting to be a particular person's, are of themselves not sufficient evidence of genuineness."[17] Such a rule serves meaningfully as a protective device minimizing the occasion for fraud on the innocent and imposition on the courts. At the same time, we recognize the general proposition that authorship of writings may be shown by circumstantial evidence, among the components of which the contents of the writing may play a significant role. Circumstances beyond the four corners of a document may point with sufficient certitude to the person whose pen created it. Moreover, "in special circumstances, where the contents reveal a *knowledge* or other trait peculiarly referable to a single person, * * * the contents alone [may] suffice,"[18] and where a document, purportedly that of a particular person, makes reference to facts peculiarly known to him, the "manifest probabilities" that the document is his permit a logical conclusion that in actuality he is in fact the composer. The receipt of otherwise unauthenticated writings in evidence under such conditions adequately safeguards the policy considerations underlying the broad rule disfavoring authentication of writings solely on the basis of what they contain.

III

The situation before us is interlaced with artifacts pointing to appellant's hand in the generation and placement of the questioned writings.[19] The envelope and the notes inside it were found beside the body of the deceased at the site of the macabre events that gave birth to the prosecution. The envelope bore the name of appellant as the addressor, and designated three persons, all described as close relatives, as the intended addressees. Full names, including the surname "Sutton," were supplied for two of the latter, as were telephone numbers for each of

---

[17] 7 J. Wigmore, Evidence § 2148 (3d ed. 1940) (emphasis in original).

[18] 7 J. Wigmore, Evidence § 2148 (3d ed. 1940) (emphasis in original).

[19] We test the trial judge's ruling accepting the envelope and notes in evidence without regard to appellant's subsequent testimonial admissions, which alone might have warranted the conclusion that he had previously possessed the note from "Arthur" and had himself written the others. Compare Harrison v. United States, 392 U.S. 219 * * * (1968).

the three. Inscribed on the face of the envelope was the single entreaty "[c]all them at once."

One of the envelope's enclosures, beginning "[r]ead this other note," named "Arthur" as the man who had taken "her" home on a Sunday night, which could have been the night before the homicide. Another, signed "Arthur," contained enough to explain why someone—perhaps our appellant—might have become upset over "Arthur's" affair with "her." A third note gave the names and telephone numbers of three persons, each with the surname "Sutton" and otherwise denominated kinfolk, and requested that they be contacted. In names, telephone numbers and specifications of kinship, these designations matched exactly those appearing on the covering envelope.

Additionally, the latter note discussed intimate business and personal affairs which, if true, would have been peculiarly within the writer's knowledge. Included were references to the author's difficulties with "Matilda," and expressions of despondency over the deterioration of his own relationship with her. Included, too, were a summary statement of the status of the writer's financial affairs, and the dispositions he desired of his worldly estate. We do not suggest that appellant's authorship of this note was sufficiently denoted to qualify it for admission simply on the basis that such matters would normally reside solely within appellant's knowledge, for here there was no attempt by the Government to prove their accuracy.[20] This shortcoming is overcome, however, by its other evidentiary virtues, particularly its clairvoyant qualities in terms of personal history that was yet to be made.

The writer forecasted portentous events. His words clearly contemplated suicide and probably murder as well. This latter thought is revealed not merely by the statement that "[n]ow we will both are in bad shape," but is bolstered by the moribund mood permeating the note. Its tenor indicates an author who expected that his life would soon be terminated. It also suggests that the deceased's conduct was the driving force to that end, and intimates that she too was doomed. These are

---

[20] It is obvious that one's authorship of a document is not connoted simply by its reference to what supposedly is a fact known only to him unless the so-called fact is shown to be actually true. A note giving the combination of a safe exclusively within A's knowledge indicates that A wrote it. The indication is lacking if the safe defies opening when the dial is spun strictly in accordance with the information in the note, however much that information had seemed to be the combination.

While some of the matters discussed in the note in suit, if factually accurate, tended to earmark appellant as the author, there is little or nothing to show that they were accurate. The record does not explain why no effort was made in that direction at trial, or why there was no resort to a handwriting analysis. Nonetheless, if the Government's demonstration on authenticity sufficed legally for the purpose, it is immaterial that the authenticity requirement might have been better met by another method. "It is not ground for complaint that the Government chose instead to stake the prosecution on evidence that appellant regards as proof of a distinctly lower order." Powell v. United States, 135 U.S.App.D.C. 254, 258, 418 F.2d 470, 474 (1969) (footnote omitted).

thoughts uniquely within the mind of the one planning a murder-suicide, a deed which, as things eventuated, seemingly was partially accomplished. Appellant came to the death scene with a loaded gun and seven more live cartridges in his pocket. He fired several shots at the deceased at close range, and then wounded himself. These were facts of record at the time introduction of the note was sought. A jury could reasonably feel that only by irrationally defying the probabilities could one say that the author of the note was not describing the events later witnessed by Hall and Brock.

Not only were there these indicia of a connection between appellant and the interrelated documents at the scene, but further indication of such a nexus was supplied by another note found in appellant's pocket after his admittance to the hospital. The probability of genuineness of that note is enhanced by its discovery in appellant's possession, an unchallenged factor increasing the prospect that he was the scrivener.[21] And the note listed the same persons—by the same names, the same familial relationships, and in two instances the same telephone numbers—as were furnished by the writings beside the deceased's body. The documents found in the two locations bore obvious similarities in subject matter and style, and in common pled that the named relatives be called. While the interrelation of all of the documents was such that each tended to afford reassurance of the authenticity of the others, the most important single welding agent was perhaps the in-pocket note. For it strengthened both the already close integration of the on-scene writings and their tie to appellant; indeed, the trial judge considered it to be the clinching item.

In our view, the aggregated circumstances forged such links between the questioned writings and appellant as reasonably to enable findings by the jury that he was a prior possessor of the note from "Arthur" and the author of the remainder. By the same token, we conclude that the trial judge did not exceed his authority in letting the writings in. Indeed, we applaud his identification and synthesis of the relevant factors, his sensitivity to the need for a firm circumstantial foundation for admission, and the caution with which he proceeded to his ruling. We hold that the disputed exhibits were properly accepted in evidence, and were entitled to such consideration as the jury was inclined to give them. * * *

---

[21] We find a close analogy in cases permitting the introduction into evidence of writings found in the possession of an accused as exemplars for purposes of expert comparison with the handwriting in a disputed document. The courts have frequently sanctioned receipt of the exemplar when there were additional circumstances supporting its authenticity. See Dean v. United States, 246 F. 568 (5th Cir.1917) (handwriting taken from defendant's memorandum book); People v. Davis, 65 Cal.App.2d 255, 150 P.2d 474 (1944) (application for bank loan taken from defendant's wallet); Little v. Rogers, 99 Ga. 95, 24 S.E. 856 (1896) (possession of notes coupled with fact that the deceased paid them). In at least a few cases, possession alone was deemed sufficient. * * *

[Affirmed.]

NOTES AND QUESTIONS

1. *Location as authenticating circumstance.* The location in which writings were found, plus contents reflecting peculiar knowledge on the part of the scrivener, has been held to authenticate even where the circumstances do not point to any particular individual as the author. United States v. Helmel, 769 F.2d 1306 (8th Cir.1985) (illegal gambling; ledgers reflecting intimate acquaintance with organization found at one of defendants' homes held authenticated); United States v. De Gudino, 722 F.2d 1351 (7th Cir.1983) ("pollo" lists of smuggled aliens with dates and payment records found at headquarters of operation); United States v. Wilson, 532 F.2d 641 (8th Cir.1976) (notebooks revealing familiarity with drug operations found at apartment frequented by defendants). What was the "connection" which constituted authentication in these cases?

2. *Standardized rulings.* Obviously, as pointed out in the principal case, circumstantial evidence to authenticate may vary extensively and must, in many cases, be evaluated for sufficiency on an ad hoc basis. Like the field of relevancy of which it is analytically a subpart, however, authentication has a double aspect. While a broad general rule is required to accommodate the wide variety of questions which may arise, it has also proved true that certain specific problems recur with great frequency. The next case deals with one of the most significant of the crystallized applications of the general rule that have been developed to deal with these recurrent problems.

PEOPLE V. LYNES

Court of Appeals of New York, 1980.
401 N.E.2d 405.

FUCHSBERG, JUDGE.

Defendant Julius Lynes was convicted, after a jury trial, of rape in the first degree, sodomy in the first degree, robbery in the first degree and burglary in the first degree. His conviction was affirmed by the Appellate Division. The issues on which the present appeal turns are the admissibility at trial of (1) a telephone conversation between a police detective and a caller who identified himself as the defendant * * *

Police attention in this case was directed at defendant after the complainant, happening to observe him with a group of young men on a congested street in the Harlem section of Manhattan, recognized him as her assailant. When the defendant ran into a nearby tenement house, other people who had been standing with him told the complainant that the man was nicknamed Speedy. Acting on her relay of this information to the police, a detective, Donald Longo, repaired to the building into which the man had disappeared, where, in the course of his inquiries of tenants, he came upon a man who identified himself as Speedy's brother and provided the information that defendant's formal name was Julius Lynes. However, the man denied knowing where Speedy was at the time and, when he asked why the detective was seeking his brother, was advised that it was in connection with the investigation of an old warrant. Before departing, Longo requested that Speedy telephone him and, for that purpose, left with the brother a slip of paper bearing the detective's name and telephone number at the Manhattan Sex Crimes Squad. This sets the stage for the call which gives rise to the first of the two evidentiary points with which we treat here.

For, only hours later, Longo picked up a telephone receiver at the other end of which was an unfamiliar male voice that asked for him by name. According to the record, the detective, having then inquired who was calling, received the response, "Speedy—Julius Lynes" and then, "What are you looking for me for?" In reply, the detective said, "Your knife was found in an apartment", to which the voice was then heard to say "Oh no, oh no". When the detective thereupon asked if the man who had identified himself as Julius Lynes would come in and talk to the police, the caller refused, saying "you are going to have to find me" and then hung up. It is this conversation which was introduced at trial over the defense's vigorous objection that Longo admittedly was unfamiliar with the voice and therefore could not personally identify it as that of the defendant. The trial court's ruling was based generally on the rationale that other circumstances provided sufficient corroboration of the identity of the caller.

Prefatory to focusing on the question so raised, we note that the problem was fundamentally one of authentication, i.e., not merely whether the sound of the voice was recognizable as that of the defendant, but, more broadly, whether a sufficient foundation had been laid to permit a finding that the conversation was one with the party against whom it was offered. Putting the issue another way, in this case was the proof such that a jury could find that defendant was indeed the caller? (See *People v. Dunbar Contr. Co.,* 215 N.Y. 416, 422, 109 N.E. 554, 555 [Cardozo, J.]; *Carbo v. United States,* 9 Cir., 314 F.2d 718, 743.)

The question of authentication, of course, presents no great legal difficulty when the witness testifies that he recognizes the voice of the caller, and that is irrespective of whether the familiarity was acquired before or after the conversation (*People v. Dunbar Contr. Co., supra,* p. 422, 109 N.E. p. 555; *People v. Strollo,* 191 N.Y. 42, 61, 83 N.E. 573, 580). At the opposite end, it goes without saying that, without more, a mere self-serving statement of identity by a caller whose voice is unknown to the listener is not enough to permit it to go in (*Murphy v. Jack,* 142 N.Y. 215, 36 N.E. 882; 7 Wigmore, Evidence [Chadbourn rev. ed.], § 2155, p. 760). But that defect need not be fatal where alternative indices of

reliability are to be found in surrounding facts and circumstances (see
People v. McKane, 143 N.Y. 455, 38 N.E. 950; *Van Riper v. United States,*
2 Cir., 13 F.2d 961, 968).

Thus, in part on the theory that the customary mode of operation of
telephone users provides some assurance of reliability, in some instances
the placing of a call to a number listed in a directory or other similarly
responsible index of subscribers, coupled with an unforced
acknowledgment by the one answering that he or she is the one so listed,
has been held to constitute an adequate showing (see, e.g., *Mankes v.
Fishman,* 163 App.Div. 789, 149 N.Y.S. 228; *Van Riper v. United States,
supra*). In other cases, the substance of the conversation itself has
furnished confirmation of the caller's identity, as, for example, when
subsequent events indicated that the party whose identity is sought to be
established had to have been a conversant in the telephone talk (see
Ottida, Inc. v. Harriman Nat. Bank & Trust Co. of City of N.Y., 260
App.Div. 1008, 24 N.Y.S.2d 63; *United States v. Frankel,* 2 Cir., 65 F.2d
285, 286–287) or when the caller makes reference to facts of which he
alone is likely to have knowledge (see *Levine & Co. v. Wolf's Package
Depot,* 29 Misc.2d 1085, 1088, 138 N.Y.S.2d 427, 431; *Dege v. United
States,* 308 F.2d 534; *State v. Bassano,* 67 N.J.Super. 526, 171 A.2d 108).
From all this emerges the rule that, while in each case the issue is one to
be decided upon its own peculiar facts, in the first instance the Judge who
presides over the trial must determine that the proffered proof permits
the drawing of inferences which make it improbable that the caller's voice
belongs to anyone other than the purported caller (see *United States v. Lo
Bue,* 180 F.Supp. 955, 956–957; see, generally, Comment, 11 N.C.L.Rev.
344).

So measured, it was not error for the court to overrule the objection.
The call was made to the detective after he had made a specific request
that the defendant call and had left his name and telephone number for
that very purpose with a man purporting to be defendant's brother. The
promptness of the call—within a few hours of this invitation—can be said
to impart a quality of reflexiveness that tends to undermine the chance
that the invitation and the response are connected by only a *post hoc ergo
propter hoc* rationalization (see *People v. Conway,* 3 Ill.App.3d 69, 278
N.E.2d 852; *People v. Kroeger,* 61 Cal.2d 236, 37 Cal.Rptr. 593, 390 P.2d
369). Moreover, aside from the immediacy of the response, the court could
weigh such factors as the caller's seeming ability to track the message left
for the defendant, specifically in asking to speak to Detective Longo and
in using his own formal name as provided by the brother as well as the
more informal appellation "Speedy". And, since the record reveals no
attempt by Detective Longo to communicate with Lynes other than on the
occasion when he left the request to call, the court also was entitled to
view defendant's subsequent admission, made to another police officer,

that he knew the detective was looking for him as additional confirmation that the message was delivered intact to its intended recipient. Beyond this, the substance of the conversation supplies further criteria of reliability. Not only did the caller indicate that he knew the detective had been searching for him, but, perhaps above all, what could be found to be his dismayed and spontaneous reaction to the information that the complainant's attacker had left a knife behind—a fact which Longo had not communicated to the brother—could be taken as telltale evidence that the caller indeed was Speedy.

2   Moreover, the question here was whether the conversation was admissible and not whether, standing alone, it would suffice to support a finding of guilt beyond a reasonable doubt. In that connection, it is well to remember that the complainant directly described the details of the criminal event and identified the defendant as its perpetrator on the basis of her personal observations at the time of its commission.

In sum, taking these facts and inferences in various combinations or in concert, it cannot be said as a matter of law that the Trial Judge erred in leaving it to the jury—aided as it could be by the instruments of cross-examination, counsels' arguments and other fact-finding tools available at the trial level—to decide whether, as Learned Hand put it, "The chance that these circumstances should unite in the case of some one [other than the defendant] seems * * * so improbable that the speaker was sufficiently identified" (*Van Riper v. United States,* 13 F.2d 961, 968, *supra*). * * *

NOTES AND QUESTIONS

1.   *Reply letter doctrine.* The rule applied in the principal case has an analogue in the area of written evidence known as the "reply letter doctrine." Under the latter, if it is proved that a communication was properly dispatched to a certain addressee and a response duly received by the sender purporting to be from the addressee, the authenticity of the latter communication will be considered as sufficiently established to permit admission. See Whelton v. Daly, 37 A.2d 1 (N.H.1944).

2.   *Subsequent voice familiarity.* Voice familiarity for purposes of identifying a telephoner may be acquired subsequently to the conversation in question. McGuire v. State, 92 A.2d 582 (Md.1952); State v. McGee, 83 S.W.2d 98 (Mo.1935); Annot., 79 A.L.R.3d 79. See Rule 901(b)(5).

3.   *Outgoing telephone calls.* The identity of a speaker, answering the telephone and giving his first name, has been held sufficiently established as that of the person with the same first name, in whose name the number called was listed. United States v. Scully, 546 F.2d 255 (9th Cir.1976). When the listed number is that of a business, the person answering is generally presumed to have authority to speak for the enterprise. 2 McCormick, Evidence § 228 (7th ed. 2013). See also Rule 901(b)(6).

4. *Caller identification.* Should evidence that a number appeared on a caller identification device be sufficient to authenticate the call as coming from that number? The courts have found such information to be "reliable." See, e.g., State v. Lucier, 887 A.2d 129 (N.H.2005); Tatum v. Commonwealth, 440 S.E.2d 133 (Va.Ct.App.1994). Would the evidence be sufficient to authenticate the call as coming from a particular person?

5. *Sound recordings.* The issues involving the introduction of sound recordings generally were discussed in Chapter 10. If such recordings are of the human voice, additional questions are raised similar to those involving telephone calls. Under most circumstances, in addition to the other foundational requirements, there must also be an identification of the voice on the recording, either through a witness who can identify the voice or by circumstantial evidence. See Williams v. Butler, 746 F.2d 431, 441 (8th Cir.1984) (identification of voices by person with knowledge and by circumstantial evidence); State v. Stager, 406 S.E.2d 876 (N.C.1991) (audiotape of murder victim's statements expressing concerns about accused's conduct admissible based upon voice identification and circumstances of finding of tape). Cases are collected in Annot., 58 A.L.R.2d 1024.

UNITED STATES V. SIDDIQUI

United States Court of Appeals, Eleventh Circuit, 2000.
235 F.3d 1318.

GEORGE, DISTRICT JUDGE: Mohamed Siddiqui appeals his convictions for fraud and false statements to a federal agency, and obstruction in connection with a federal investigation. Siddiqui challenges the district court's admission into evidence of e-mail and foreign depositions.

I. Background

The National Science Foundation ("NSF") is a congressionally established federal agency. The NSF presents the Waterman Award annually to an outstanding scientist or engineer, and consists of a $500,000 research grant. To become eligible for the Waterman Award, candidates are nominated by a nominator who completes and submits a form to the NSF, and recruits four outside references to support the candidate. The nominator identifies the references on the form, and sends forms to the references for letters to be submitted on behalf of the nominee.

On December 15, 1996, Susan Fannoney, Executive Secretary of the Waterman Award, received a form indicating that Dr. Hamuri Yamada was nominating Mohamed Siddiqui, an Indian citizen, and at that time a visiting professor at the University of South Alabama, for the award. The nomination form listed three references, Dr. von Gunten, James Westrick and Dr. Mysore. Along with the nomination form, Ms. Fannoney received a reference form apparently signed by von Gunten, recommending

Siddiqui for the Waterman Award. In addition, Fannoney received by fax a letter of reference from James Westrick.

On January 14, 1997, Fannoney received a letter from von Gunten addressed to the Waterman Awards Committee. The letter stated that von Gunten had received confirmation for a letter of recommendation in support of Siddiqui, but that he had never sent such a letter. Fannoney alerted the Inspector General's office, which began an investigation. On February 7, 1997, Fannoney received a fax from Siddiqui stating that he was withdrawing his name from consideration for the award.

On February 18, 1997, Jodi Saltzman, a special agent with the NSF interviewed Siddiqui at Siddiqui's office at the University of South Alabama. During the interview, Siddiqui signed a statement admitting that he had nominated himself for the Waterman Award, but that he had permission from Yamada and von Gunten to submit forms on their behalf. Siddiqui also acknowledged in the statement that Westrick had recommended Siddiqui for a different award, the PECASE Award, but that Siddiqui had changed the wording of the letter to apply to the Waterman Award. Siddiqui was indicted on April 29, 1997.

* * *

Yamada's deposition was taken in Japan on March 6, 1998. At government expense, Siddiqui's counsel attended the deposition and cross-examined the witness, but was not in telephonic contact with Siddiqui during the deposition. Yamada testified that on February 1, 1997, she received an e-mail stating that if she received a phone call from the NSF to "please tell good words about me." Yamada testified that she knew the e-mail was from Siddiqui because the name on the e-mail had Siddiqui's sender address, and it ended with the name "Mo" which Siddiqui had previously told her was his nickname, and which he had used in previous e-mail.

Yamada further testified that she never signed or submitted a Waterman Award form on behalf of Siddiqui, nor had she given Siddiqui permission to sign her name to the form. On February 22, 1997, Yamada received another e-mail from Siddiqui requesting that she prepare a letter indicating that she had permitted Siddiqui to sign the nomination form on her behalf. Yamada testified that during that time period Siddiqui had also contacted her by phone making the same request, and that she recognized his voice. On February 28, 1997, Yamada sent an e-mail to Agent Saltzman stating that she had permitted Siddiqui to sign on her behalf. Yamada later admitted to Saltzman that she had not given Siddiqui permission to sign, but had made the earlier representation because she thought Siddiqui would go to jail.

During cross-examination of Yamada at the deposition, Siddiqui's counsel introduced an e-mail from Yamada to Siddiqui. This e-mail contained the same e-mail address for Siddiqui as the e-mail received by Yamada and von Gunten apparently from Siddiqui.

Von Gunten's video deposition was taken in Switzerland. At government expense, Siddiqui's counsel attended the deposition and cross-examined von Gunten. During the deposition, Siddiqui was in communication with his counsel by telephone. Von Gunten testified at the deposition that he had not submitted a letter of recommendation in favor of Siddiqui for the Waterman Award, and that he had not given Siddiqui permission to submit such a letter in his name.

Von Gunten further testified that on February 24, 1997, he received an e-mail from what appeared to be Siddiqui's e-mail address asking him to tell the NSF that Siddiqui had permission to use von Gunten's name. Von Gunten replied by e-mail to the address that he could not tell the NSF anything but the truth. Von Gunten also testified that during the same time period as the exchange of e-mail he spoke with Siddiqui by phone two or three times. In those conversations, in which Siddiqui identified himself and von Gunten recognized his voice, Siddiqui urged von Gunten to change the statements that he had made to the NSF that Siddiqui did not have permission to use von Gunten's name. Von Gunten refused those requests.

During trial, the district court allowed the depositions to be read into evidence, and admitted the e-mail into evidence.

II. Discussion

Siddiqui * * * claims that the district court abused its discretion by allowing the government to offer the e-mail into evidence without proper authentication * * *.

* * *

A. Authentication of the E-mail

Under Fed.R.Evid. 901(a), documents must be properly authenticated as a condition precedent to their admissibility "by evidence sufficient to support a finding that the matter in question is what its proponent claims." A document may be authenticated by "[a]ppearance, contents, substance, internal patterns, or other distinctive characteristics, taken in conjunction with circumstances." Fed.R.Evid. 901(b)(4); *United States v. Smith,* 918 F.2d 1501, 1510 (11th Cir.1990) ("[t]he government may authenticate a document solely through the use of circumstantial evidence, including the document's own distinctive characteristics and the circumstances surrounding its discovery"). A district court has discretion to determine authenticity, and that determination should not be disturbed on appeal absent a showing that there is no competent evidence in the record to support it. *United States v. Munoz,* 16 F.3d 1116, 1120–21 (11th Cir.1994).

In this case, a number of factors support the authenticity of the e-mail. The e-mail sent to Yamada and von Gunten each bore Siddiqui's e-mail address *"msiddiquo@jajuar1.usouthal.edu"* at the University of South Alabama. This address was the same as the e-mail sent to Siddiqui from Yamada as introduced by Siddiqui's counsel in his deposition cross-examination of Yamada. Von Gunten testified that when he replied to the e-mail apparently sent by Siddiqui, the "reply-function" on von Gunten's e-mail system automatically dialed Siddiqui's e-mail address as the sender.

The context of the e-mail sent to Yamada and von Gunten shows the author of the e-mail to have been someone who would have known the very details of Siddiqui's conduct with respect to the Waterman Award and the NSF's subsequent investigation. In addition, in one e-mail sent to von Gunten, the author makes apologies for cutting short his visit to EAWAG, the Swiss Federal Institute for Environmental Science and Technology. In his deposition, von Gunten testified that in 1994 Siddiqui had gone to Switzerland to begin a collaboration with EAWAG for three or four months, but had left after only three weeks to take a teaching job.

Moreover, the e-mail sent to Yamada and von Gunten referred to the author as "Mo." Both Yamada and von Gunten recognized this as Siddiqui's nickname. Finally, both Yamada and von Gunten testified that they spoke by phone with Siddiqui soon after the receipt of the e-mail, and that Siddiqui made the same requests that had been made in the e-mail. Considering these circumstances, the district court did not abuse its discretion in ruling that the documents were adequately authenticated.

* * *

Affirmed.

NOTES AND QUESTIONS

1.   *E-mail.* Despite vast technological differences between various computer aided communications and what has become known as snail-mail, the courts have had little trouble applying long established authentication principles to the age of the internet. For examples of other such applications, see the annotated cases collected in 5 Saltzburg, Martin & Capra, Federal Rules of Evidence Manual § 901.03[1][i], at 901–52 (10th ed. 2011). The paucity of cases dealing with authentication problems in connection with e-mails is some indication of the general comfort level with such exhibits. As in *Siddiqui*, the courts may look to the content of the e-mail to bolster authentication. See Commonwealth v. Purdy, 945 N.E.2d 372 (Mass. 2011); Massimo v. State, 144 S.W.3d 210 (Tex.App.2004). For a comprehensive treatment of the evidentiary issues involving e-mail, see Robins, Evidence at the Electronic Frontier: Introducing E–Mail at Trial in Commercial Litigation, 29 Rutgers Computer & Tech.L.J. 219 (2003).

2. *Text messages.* As in the case of e-mail, the courts have usually been receptive to the authentication of text messages by circumstantial evidence. See, e.g., State v. Damper, 225 P.3d 1148 (Ariz.2010) (text message authenticated where the recipient's phone displayed sender's nickname and victim/sender's cell phone was found on bed beside her body). See also discussion in 2 McCormick, Evidence § 227 (7th ed. 2013).

3. *Ancient documents.* On the other side of the modernity spectrum, Rule 901(b)(8) codifies the common law doctrine authenticating "ancient documents," i.e., those that have been in existence 20 years or more. For an application of the common law rule, see Town of Ninety Six v. Southern Ry. Co., 267 F.2d 579 (4th Cir.1959). As illustrated by that case, mere authentication of such a document does not necessarily guarantee admissibility. Other rules of evidence, especially the hearsay rule, may come into play.

4. *Public documents.* Among those documents that are self-authenticating under the Federal Rules are various types of public documents and certified copies of public records. See Rule 902(1), (2), (3) and (4). What is the relationship between authentication and certification? Compare Rule 901(b)(7) and Rule 902(4). Why are both rules necessary?

5. *Records of regularly conducted activities.* The Federal Rules of Evidence were amended in 2000 to provide for self-authentication of domestic or foreign records of regularly conducted activities certified as such by the custodian. See Rules 902(11) & (12). For the hearsay implications of such authentication, see Chapter 14, Section E. Does such self-authentication expand dramatically the kinds of documents as to which there need be no supporting testimony from a witness? See 2 McCormick, Evidence § 229.1 (7th ed. 2013).

6. *Computerized records.* As to proving computerized public records, see Annot., 71 A.L.R.3d 232. Higher standards in the authentication of computer records generally are advocated in Peritz, Computer Data and Reliability: A Call for Authentication of Business Records Under the Federal Rules of Evidence, 80 Nw.U.L.Rev. 956 (1986).

GRIFFIN V. STATE

Court of Appeals of Maryland, 2011.
19 A.3d 415

BATTAGLIA, J.

In this case, we are tasked with determining the appropriate way to authenticate, for evidential purposes, electronically stored information printed from a social networking website, in particular, MySpace.[22]

---

[22] "MySpace is a 'social networking' website where members can create 'profiles' and interact with other members. Anyone with Internet access can go onto the MySpace website and view content which is open to the general public such as a music area, video section, and members' profiles which are not set as 'private.' However, to create a profile, upload and display

Pet'r
avs

Antoine Levar Griffin, Petitioner, seeks reversal of his convictions in the Circuit Court for Cecil County, contending that the trial judge abused his discretion in admitting, without proper authentication, what the State alleged were several pages printed from Griffin's girlfriend's MySpace profile.[23] The Court of Special Appeals determined that the trial judge did not abuse his discretion, * * * and we granted Griffin's Petition for Writ of Certiorari, * * * to consider the two questions, which we have rephrased:

PH

Issue I.

1. Did the trial court err in admitting a page printed from a MySpace profile alleged to be that of Petitioner's girlfriend?

* * *

I.

We shall hold that the pages allegedly printed from Griffin's girlfriend's MySpace profile were not properly authenticated pursuant to Maryland Rule 5–901, and shall, therefore, reverse the judgment of the Court of Special Appeals and remand the case for a new trial.

Griffin was charged in numerous counts with the shooting death, on April 24, 2005, of Darvell Guest at Ferrari's Bar in Perryville, in Cecil County. During his trial, the State sought to introduce Griffin's girlfriend's, Jessica Barber's, MySpace profile to demonstrate that, prior to trial, Ms. Barber had allegedly threatened another witness called by the State. The printed pages contained a MySpace profile in the name of "Sistasouljah," describing a 23 year-old female from Port Deposit, listing her birthday as "10/02/1983" and containing a photograph of an embracing couple. The printed pages also contained the following blurb:

F

FREE BOOZY!!!! JUST REMEMBER SNITCHES GET STITCHES!! U KNOW WHO YOU ARE!!

f

When Ms. Barber had taken the stand after being called by the State, she was not questioned about the pages allegedly printed from her MySpace profile.

Instead, the State attempted to authenticate the pages, as belonging to Ms. Barber, through the testimony of Sergeant John Cook, the lead investigator in the case. Defense counsel objected to the admission of the pages allegedly printed from Ms. Barber's MySpace profile, because the State could not sufficiently establish a "connection" between the profile and posting and Ms. Barber * * * *

F

Defense counsel was permitted to voir dire Sergeant Cook, outside of the presence of the jury, as follows:

---

photographs, communicate with persons on the site, write 'blogs,' and/or utilize other services or applications on the MySpace website, one must be a 'member.' Anyone can become a member of MySpace at no charge so long as they meet a minimum age requirement and register." *United States v. Drew,* 259 F.R.D. 449, 453 (D.C.D.Cal.2009).

[23] To establish a "profile," a user needs only a valid email account * * *

[Defense Counsel]: How do you know that this is her [MySpace] page? * * *

[Sergeant Cook]: Through the photograph of her and Boozy on the front, through the reference to Boozy, [ ] the reference [to] the children, and [ ] her birth date indicated on the form.

[Defense Counsel]: How do you know she sent it?

[Sergeant Cook]: I can't say that.

[The Court]: I failed—I am sorry. I misrepresented. I failed to realize there is a photograph there. It's in the block that says "Sistasouljah," and then there's a photograph of a person that looks like Jessica Barber to me.

[Defense Counsel]: When was it sent?

[Sergeant Cook]: That is a MySpace page. That wasn't particularly sent. That is on the web, and it's accessible to whoever views MySpace. It is open to the public.

[Defense Counsel]: I understand that. When did it get posted?

[Sergeant Cook]: The print date on the form, printed on 12/05/06.

[The Court]: You can tell by looking at it because that's when he went to it.

[Defense Counsel]: So that would have been after the first trial. So how could that possibly affect [the witness]? He said it was before the first trial.

[The Court]: On its face, there is no way that you can conclude that on its face this establishes anything in regard to [the witness]. What it's being offered for, as I understand it, is corroboration, consistency that she's making a statement in a public forum, "snitches get stitches." And I guess the argument is going to be made that that's consistent with what [the witness] said, that she threatened him.

[Assistant State's Attorney]: That's correct.

[The Court]: It's weak. I mean, there is no question it's weak, but that's what it is offered for.

The trial judge, thereafter, indicated that he would permit Sergeant Cook to testify in support of authentication of the redacted portion of the pages printed from MySpace, containing the photograph "of a person that looks like Jessica Barber" and the Petitioner, allegedly known as "Boozy," adjacent to a description of the woman as a 23 year-old from Port Deposit, and the blurb, stating "FREE BOOZY!!!! JUST REMEMBER SNITCHES GET STITCHES!! U KNOW WHO YOU ARE!!"

In lieu of Sergeant Cook's testimony, while maintaining his objection to the admissibility of the redacted MySpace page, defense counsel agreed to the following stipulation:

> If asked, Sergeant Cook would testify that he went onto the Internet to the website known as MySpace * * * * [F]rom that site he downloaded some information of a posting that someone had put there.
>
> That posting contains a photograph which the witness would say he recognizes as a photograph of Jessica * * * Barber, who testified, * * * that she is the defendant's live-in fiance; and that it also contains a date of birth, to wit October 2nd, 1983, which the witness would testify is the date of birth that Jessica Barber gave as her date of birth.
>
> When the exhibit, the download, comes to you, you are going to see that it has a great—that most of its content has been redacted; that is, blacked out. That's because some of it, in my judgment, might tend to be inflammatory without proving anything one way or the other. There is one portion of it that will not be redacted when it comes to you, and this is the only portion of it which you should consider. And you certainly should not speculate as to what any of the redacted portions may be.
>
> The portion that will not be redacted says, just remember snitches get stitches. You will see that. The phrase is, just remember snitches get stitches * * * * And * * * the witness would testify that the date it was retrieved was * * * December 5, 2006.

Whether the MySpace printout represents that which it purports to be, not only a MySpace profile created by Ms. Barber, but also upon which she had posted, "FREE BOOZY!!!! JUST REMEMBER SNITCHES GET STITCHES!! U KNOW WHO YOU ARE!!," is the issue before us.

With respect to social networking websites in general, we have already had occasion, in *Independent Newspapers, Inc. v. Brodie,* 407 Md. 415, 424 n. 3, 966 A.2d 432, 438 n. 3 (2009), to describe those sites as "sophisticated tools of communication where the user voluntarily provides information that the user wants to share with others." A number of social networking websites, such as MySpace, enable members "to create online 'profiles,' which are individual web pages on which members [can] post photographs, videos, and information about their lives and interests." *Doe v. MySpace, Inc.,* 474 F.Supp.2d 843, 845 (W.D.Tex.2007).

Anyone can create a MySpace profile at no cost, as long as that person has an email address and claims to be over the age of fourteen:

MySpace users create profiles by filling out questionnaire-like web forms. Users are then able to connect their profiles to those of other users and thereby form communities. MySpace profiles contain several informational sections, known as "blurbs." These include two standard blurbs: "About Me" and "Who I'd Like to Meet." Users may supplement those blurbs with additional sections about their interests, general additional details, and other personal information. MySpace profiles also incorporate several multimedia features. For instance, users may post photos, music, videos, and web logs to their pages.

Richard M. Guo, *Stranger Danger and the Online Social Network,* 23 Berkeley Tech. L.J. 617, 621 (2008) (footnotes omitted). After a profile is established, the user may invite others to access her profile, as a "friend," who if the user accepts the befriending, can access her profile pages without further ado:

Users establish virtual communities by linking their profiles in a process known as "friending" or "connecting." One user requests to add another as a friend, and the recipient may either accept or reject the invitation. If the recipient accepts, the profiles are linked and the connected members are generally able to view one another's online content without restriction. The network created by the linking process allows a user to chat with friends, display support for particular causes, "join interest groups dedicated to virtually any topic," and otherwise "hang out."

Nathan Petrashek, Comment, *The Fourth Amendment and the Brave New World of Online Social Networking,* 93 Marq. L.Rev. 1495, 1499–1500 (2009–2010) (footnotes omitted). Although a social networking site generally requires a unique username and password for the user to both establish a profile and access it, posting on the site by those that befriend the user does not. [citations omitted]

The identity of who generated the profile may be confounding, because "a person observing the online profile of a user with whom the observer is unacquainted has no idea whether the profile is legitimate." Petrashek, 93 Marq. L.Rev. at 1499 n. 16. The concern arises because anyone can create a fictitious account and masquerade under another person's name or can gain access to another's account by obtaining the user's username and password:

Although it may seem that, as creators of our own online social networking profiles, we are able to construct our own online persona, this is not always the case. There is no law that prevents someone from establishing a fake account under another person's name, so long as the purpose for doing so is not to deceive others and gain some advantage. Moreover, fragments of information, either crafted under our authority or fabricated by others, are available by performing a Google search * * * forever. Thus, online social networking poses two threats: that information may be (1) available because of one's own role as the creator of the content, or (2) generated by a third party, whether or not it is accurate.

David Hector Montes, *Living Our Lives Online: The Privacy Implications of Online Social Networking,* Journal of Law and Policy for the Information Society, Spring 2009, at 507, 508. For instance, in one circumstance, Sophos, a Boston-based Internet security company, created a profile for a toy frog named "Freddi Staur," and nearly 200 Facebook[24] users chose to add the frog as a "friend." Miller, 97 Ky. L.J. at 542.

2. The possibility for user abuse also exists on MySpace, as illustrated by *United States v. Drew,* 259 F.R.D. 449 (D.C.D.Cal.2009), in which Lori Drew, a mother, was prosecuted under the Computer Fraud and Abuse Act, 18 U.S.C. § 1030, for creating a MySpace profile for a fictitious 16 year-old male named "Josh Evans." Drew had contacted a former friend of her daughter's, Megan Meier, through the MySpace network, using the Josh Evans screen name or pseudonym, and began to "flirt with her over a number of days." *Id.* at 452. Drew then had "Josh" inform Megan that he no longer "liked her" and that "the world would be a better place without her in it," after which Megan killed herself. *Id.* Thus, the relative ease with which anyone can create fictional personas or gain unauthorized access to another user's profile, with deleterious consequences, is the *Drew* lesson.

The potential for fabricating or tampering with electronically stored information on a social networking site, thus poses significant challenges from the standpoint of authentication of printouts of the site, as in the present case. Authentication, nevertheless, is generally governed by Maryland Rule 5–901.

[Maryland rule 5–901 is substantively identical to Fed.R.Evid. 901.]

* * *

We and our colleagues on the Court of Special Appeals have had the opportunity to apply the tenets of Rule 5–901(b)(4) to a toxicology report, *State v. Bryant,* 361 Md. 420, 761 A.2d 925 (2000), to recordings from 911 emergency calls, *Clark v. State,* 188 Md.App. 110, 981 A.2d 666 (2009), and to text messages received on the victim's cellular phone, *Dickens v. State,* 175 Md.App. 231, 927 A.2d 32 (2007), but neither we nor our

---

[24] Facebook, the behemoth of the social networking world, allows users to build a profile and interact with "friends" in much the same way as MySpace.

appellate brethren heretofore has considered the Rule's application to authenticate pages printed from a social networking site.

Rather, we turn for assistance to the discussion in *Lorraine v. Markel* A. *American Insurance Co.,* 241 F.R.D. 534 (D.Md.2007), wherein Maryland's own Magistrate Judge Paul W. Grimm, a recognized authority on evidentiary issues concerning electronic evidence, outlined issues regarding authentication of electronically stored information, in e-mail, websites, digital photographs, computer-generated documents, and internet postings, etc. with respect to Rule 901 of the Federal Rules of Evidence.

* * *

Regarding Rule 901(a), Judge Grimm iterated in *Lorraine* that the "requirement of authentication or identification as a condition precedent to admissibility is satisfied by evidence sufficient to support a finding that 1. the matter in question is what its proponent claims," to insure trustworthiness. *Id.* at 541–42. Judge Grimm recognized that authenticating electronically stored information presents a myriad of concerns because "technology changes so rapidly" and is "often new to many judges." *Id.* at 544. Moreover, the "complexity" or "novelty" of electronically stored information, with its potential for manipulation, requires greater scrutiny of "the foundational requirements" than letters or other paper records, to bolster reliability. *Id.* at 543–44, quoting Jack B. Weinstein & Margaret A. Berger, *Weinstein's Federal Evidence* § 900.06[3] (Joseph M. McLaughlin ed., Matthew Bender 2d ed.1997).

In the present case, Griffin argues that the State did not appropriately, for evidentiary purposes, authenticate the pages allegedly printed from Jessica Barber's MySpace profile, because the State failed to offer any extrinsic evidence describing MySpace, as well as indicating how Sergeant Cook obtained the pages in question and adequately linking both the profile and the "snitches get stitches" posting to Ms. Barber. The State counters that the photograph, personal information, and references to freeing "Boozy" were sufficient to enable the finder of fact to believe that the pages printed from MySpace were indeed Ms. Barber's.

We agree with Griffin and disagree with the State regarding whether the trial judge abused his discretion in admitting the MySpace profile as appropriately authenticated, with Jessica Barber as its creator and user, as well as the author of the "snitches get stitches" posting, based upon the inadequate foundation laid. We differ from our colleagues on the Court of Special Appeals, who gave short shrift to the concern that "someone other than the alleged author may have accessed the account and posted the message in question." [citation omitted] While the intermediate appellate court determined that the pages allegedly printed from Ms. Barber's MySpace profile contained sufficient indicia of reliability, because the printout "featured a photograph of Ms. Barber and [Petitioner] in an embrace," and also contained the "user's birth date and identified her boyfriend as 'Boozy,' " the court failed to acknowledge the possibility or likelihood that another user could have created the profile in issue or authored the "snitches get stitches" posting. [citation omitted]

We agree with Griffin that the trial judge abused his discretion in admitting the MySpace evidence pursuant to Rule 5–901(b)(4), because the picture of Ms. Barber, coupled with her birth date and location, were not sufficient "distinctive characteristics" on a MySpace profile to authenticate its printout, given the prospect that someone other than Ms. Barber could have not only created the site, but also posted the "snitches get stitches" comment. The potential for abuse and manipulation of a social networking site by someone other than its purported creator and/or user leads to our conclusion that a printout of an image from such a site requires a greater degree of authentication than merely identifying the date of birth of the creator and her visage in a photograph on the site in order to reflect that Ms. Barber was its creator and the author of the "snitches get stitches" language.

In so holding, we recognize that other courts, called upon to consider authentication of electronically stored information on social networking sites, have suggested greater scrutiny because of the heightened possibility for manipulation by other than the true user or poster. In *Commonwealth v. Williams,* 456 Mass. 857, 926 N.E.2d 1162 (2010), the Supreme Judicial Court of Massachusetts considered the admission, over the defendant's objection, of instant messages a witness had received "at her account at MySpace." * * * In the case, the defendant was convicted of the shooting death of Izaah Tucker, as well as other offenses. The witness, Ashlei Noyes, testified that she had spent the evening of the murder socializing with the defendant and that he had been carrying a handgun. She further testified that the defendant's brother had contacted her "four times on her MySpace account between February 9, 2007, and February 12, 2007," urging her "not to testify or to claim a lack of memory regarding the events of the night of the murder." * * * At trial, Noyes testified that the defendant's brother, Jesse Williams, had a picture of himself on his MySpace account and that his MySpace screen name or pseudonym was "doit4it." She testified that she had received the messages from Williams, and the document printed from her MySpace account indicated that the messages were in fact sent by a user with the screen name "doit4it," depicting a picture of Williams * * * *

The Supreme Judicial Court of Massachusetts determined that there was an inadequate foundation laid to authenticate the MySpace messages, because the State failed to offer any evidence regarding who had access to the MySpace page and whether another author, other than Williams, could have virtually-penned the messages.

* * *

Similarly, in *People v. Lenihan,* 30 Misc.3d 289, 911 N.Y.S.2d 588 (N.Y.Sup.Ct.2010), Lenihan challenged his second degree murder conviction because he was not permitted to cross-examine two witnesses called by the State on the basis of photographs his mother had printed from MySpace, allegedly depicting the witnesses and the victim making hand gestures and wearing clothing that suggested an affiliation with the "Crips" gang. The trial judge precluded Lenihan from confronting the witnesses with the MySpace photographs, reasoning that "[i]n light of the ability to 'photo shop,' edit photographs on the computer," Lenihan could not adequately authenticate the photographs. *Id.* at 592.

In *United States v. Jackson,* 208 F.3d 633 (7th Cir.2000), Jackson was charged with mail and wire fraud and obstruction of justice after making false claims of racial harassment against the United Parcel Service in connection with an elaborate scheme in which she sent packages containing racial epithets to herself and to several prominent African–Americans purportedly from "racist elements" within UPS * * * * At trial, Jackson sought to introduce website postings from "the Euro– American Student Union and Storm Front," in which the white supremacist groups gloated about Jackson's case and took credit for the UPS mailings * * * * The court determined that the trial judge was justified in excluding the evidence because it lacked an appropriate foundation, namely that Jackson had failed to show that the web postings by the white supremacist groups who took responsibility for the racist mailings "actually were posted by the groups, as opposed to being slipped onto the groups' websites by Jackson herself, who was a skilled computer user." * * *

The State refers us, however, to *In the Interest of F.P.,* 878 A.2d 91 (Pa.Super.Ct.2005), in which the Pennsylvania intermediate appellate court considered whether instant messages were properly authenticated pursuant to Pennsylvania Rule of Evidence 901(b)(4), providing that a document may be authenticated by distinctive characteristics or circumstantial evidence. In the case, involving an assault, the victim, Z.G., testified that the defendant had attacked him because he believed that Z.G. had stolen a DVD from him. The hearing judge, over defendant's objection, admitted instant messages from a user with the screen name "Icp4Life30" to and between "WHITEBOY Z 404." * * * Z.G. testified that his screen name was "WHITEBOY Z 404" and that he had printed the instant messages from his computer. In the transcript of the instant messages, moreover, Z.G. asked "who is this," and the defendant replied, using his first name. Throughout the transcripts, the defendant threatened Z.G. with physical violence because Z.G. "stole off [him]." *Id.* On appeal, the court determined that the instant messages were properly authenticated through the testimony of Z.G. and also because

"Icp4Life30" had referred to himself by first name, repeatedly accused Z.G. of stealing from him, and referenced the fact that Z.G. had told high school administrators about the threats, such that the instant messages contained distinctive characteristics and content linking them to the defendant. *In the Interest of F.P.* is unpersuasive in the context of a social networking site, because the authentication of instant messages by the recipient who identifies his own "distinctive characteristics" and his having received the messages, is distinguishable from the authentication of a profile and posting printed from MySpace, by one who is neither a creator nor user of the specific profile.[25]

* * *

In the case sub judice, the MySpace printout was used to show that Ms. Barber had threatened a key witness, who the State had characterized as "probably the most important witness in this case;" the State highlighted the importance of the "snitches get stitches" posting during closing argument, as follows:

> Sergeant Cook told you that he went online and went to a website called MySpace and found a posting that had been placed there by the defendant's girlfriend, Jessica Barber, recognized her picture, able to match up the date of birth on the posting with her date of birth, and the posting included these words, "Free Boozy. Just remember, snitches get stitches. You know who you are."

In addition, during rebuttal argument, the State again referenced the pages printed from MySpace, asserting that Ms. Barber had employed MySpace as a tool of intimidation against a witness for the State. It is clear, then, that the MySpace printout was a key component of the State's case; the error in the admission of its printout requires reversal.

In so doing, we should not be heard to suggest that printouts from social networking sites should never be admitted. Possible avenues to explore to properly authenticate a profile or posting printed from a social networking site, will, in all probability, continue to develop as the efforts to evidentially utilize information from the sites increases. *See, e.g.,* Katherine Minotti, Comment, *The Advent of Digital Diaries: Implications of Social Networking Web Sites for the Legal Profession,* 60 S.C.L.Rev. 1057 (2009). A number of authentication opportunities come to mind, however.

The first, and perhaps most obvious method would be to ask the purported creator if she indeed created the profile and also if she added

---

[25] We further note that authentication concerns attendant to e-mails, instant messaging correspondence, and text messages differ significantly from those involving a MySpace profile and posting printout, because such correspondences is sent directly from one party to an intended recipient or recipients, rather than published for all to see. * * *

the posting in question, i.e. "[t]estimony of a witness with knowledge that the offered evidence is what it is claimed to be." Rule 5–901(b)(1). The second option may be to search the computer of the person who allegedly created the profile and posting and examine the computer's internet history and hard drive to determine whether that computer was used to originate the social networking profile and posting in question. One commentator, who serves as Managing Director and Deputy General Counsel of Stroz Friedberg, a computer forensics firm, notes that, "[s]ince a user unwittingly leaves an evidentiary trail on her computer simply by using it, her computer will provide evidence of her web usage." Seth P. Berman, et al., *Web 2. 0: What's Evidence Between "Friends"?,* Boston Bar J., Jan.–Feb.2009, at 5, 7.

A third method may be to obtain information directly from the social networking website that links the establishment of the profile to the person who allegedly created it and also links the posting sought to be introduced to the person who initiated it. This method was apparently successfully employed to authenticate a MySpace site in *People v. Clevenstine,* 68 A.D.3d 1448, 891 N.Y.S.2d 511 (2009). In the case, Richard Clevenstine was convicted of raping two teenage girls and challenged his convictions by asserting that the computer disk admitted into evidence, containing instant messages between him and the victims, sent via MySpace, was not properly authenticated. Specifically, Clevenstine argued that "someone else accessed his MySpace account and sent messages under his username." * * * The Supreme Court of New York, Appellate Division, agreed with the trial judge that the MySpace messages were properly authenticated, because both victims testified that they had engaged in instant messaging conversations about sexual activities with Clevenstine through MySpace. In addition, an investigator from the computer crime unit of the State Police testified that "he had retrieved such conversations from the hard drive of the computer used by the victims." Finally, the prosecution was able to attribute the messages to Clevenstine, because a legal compliance officer for MySpace explained at trial that "the messages on the computer disk had been exchanged by users of accounts created by [Clevenstine] and the victims." * * * The court concluded that such testimony provided ample authentication linking the MySpace messages in question to Clevenstine himself.

[Reversed and remanded for a new trial]

HARRELL, J., dissenting in which MURPHY, J., joins.

I dissent from the Majority Opinion's holding that "the picture of Ms. Barber, coupled with her birth date and location, were not sufficient 'distinctive characteristics' on a MySpace profile to authenticate its [redacted] printout * * * * " [citation omitted]

Maryland Rule 5–901 ("Requirement of authentication or identification") derives from and is similar materially to Federal Rule of Evidence 901. * * * In construing and applying Federal Rule 901, federal courts have held almost unanimously that "a document is properly authenticated if a *reasonable juror could find in favor of authenticity.*" *United States v. Gagliardi,* 506 F.3d 140, 151 (2d Cir.2007) (emphasis added); [citations omitted] Although, to date, we have not enunciated such a standard, because I think that the "reasonable juror" standard is consistent with Maryland Rule 5–901—requiring only "evidence *sufficient to support a finding* that the matter in question is what its proponent claims" (emphasis added)—I would adopt it. [citations omitted]

Applying that standard to the present case, a reasonable juror could conclude, based on the presence on the MySpace profile of (1) a picture of a person appearing to Sergeant Cook to be Ms. Barber posing with the defendant, her boyfriend; (2) a birth date matching Ms. Barber's; (3) a description of the purported creator of the MySpace profile as being a twenty-three year old from Port Deposit; and (4) references to freeing "Boozy" (a nickname for the defendant), that the redacted printed pages of the MySpace profile contained information posted by Ms. Barber.

I am not unmindful of the Majority Opinion's analysis relating to the concern that someone other than Ms. Barber could access or create the account and post the threatening message. The record, however, suggests no motive to do so. The technological heebie jeebies discussed in the Majority Opinion go, in my opinion, however, not to the admissibility of the print-outs under Rule 5–901, but rather to the weight to be given the evidence by the trier of fact. *See Hays v. State,* 40 Md. 633, 648 (1874) (holding that where there was evidence that a paper was what it purported to be, it was not error for the trial court to instruct the jury that "if they were not satisfied of the identity of the paper * * *, then they should not consider it all"); LYNN MCLAIN, MARYLAND EVIDENCE—STATE AND FEDERAL § 901:1 (2001) (stating that "authentication of an item is only the first step").

It has been said that the "purpose of authentication is to * * * filter untrustworthy evidence." *Phillip M. Adams & Assocs., L.L.C. v. Dell, Inc.,* 621 F.Supp.2d 1173, 1184 (D.Utah 2009). Like many filters that are unable to remove completely all impurities, Rule 5–901 does not act to disallow any and all evidence that may have "impurities" (i.e., in this case, evidence that could have come, conceivably, from a source other than the purported source). As long as a reasonable juror could conclude that the proffered evidence is what its proponent purports it to be, the evidence should be admitted. *See Gerald v. State,* 137 Md.App. 295, 304, 768 A.2d 140, 145 (2001) (stating that, after a trial court admits a document as being authenticated properly, "the ultimate question of authenticity is left to the jury"). The potentialities that are of concern to the Majority Opinion are fit subjects for cross-examination or rebuttal testimony and go properly to the weight the fact-finder may give the print-outs. Accordingly, I dissent.

NOTES AND QUESTIONS

1. *Social networks.* For a discussion of social networks, how they function, and what documents they generate, see Guo, Stranger Danger and the Online Social Network 23 Berkeley Tech.L.J. 617 (2008).

2. *Chat rooms.* Are the issues involved in authentication of chat room conversations different from authentication of social network matters? See United States v. Tank, 200 F.3d 627, 630–31 (9th Cir.2000) (chat room log printouts sufficiently authenticated where defendant admitted use of screen name and evidence introduced that, when meetings arranged by chat room messages, defendant showed up).

3. *Electronic and computer generated material generally.* For a discussion of the issues involved in most types of electronic and computer generated material see 2 McCormick, Evidence § 227 (7th ed. 2013).

NOTE ON ALTERNATIVES TO AUTHENTICATION

Given the inconvenience and expense frequently entailed in authenticating items of evidence in the ways suggested by the foregoing materials, it will obviously be desirable whenever possible to utilize alternative methods to the same end. One clearly available method which is in fact commonly used with reference to questions of authentication is the stipulation. In addition, the Federal Rules of Civil Procedure and their state counterparts afford additional options which may prove effective even where the opponent initially refuses to stipulate. Federal Rules of Civil Procedure of particular utility in this regard include Fed.R.Civ.P. 10(c), 16(c)(3), 26(a)(1)(B), 26 (a)(3)(C), 33, 36, and 37(c). The general subject of alternatives to authentication is discussed in 2 McCormick, Evidence § 229 (7th ed. 2013).

NOTE ON THE RULE OF COMPLETENESS

The so-called rule of completeness allows the opposite party to introduce other parts of a recorded conversation or document or series thereof insofar as pertinent to a part already introduced by her adversary. Sometimes this result is reached on the broad ground that statements ought to be considered in context. At other times principles governing the scope of cross-examination are invoked. In either event, the original authentication is an incidental benefit to the party calling for the additional matter.

The rule of completeness does not ordinarily extend to bringing out matters in violation of a positive rule of exclusion when no inseparable connection appears. Illustrative are Derrick v. Rock, 236 S.W.2d 726 (Ark.1951), and Jeddeloh v. Hockenhull, 18 N.W.2d 582 (Minn.1945) (references to liability insurance in conversations following automobile collision). But see Nance, A Theory of Verbal Completeness, 80 Iowa L.Rev. 825 (1995).

The longer the time which intervenes between the introduction of the original portion and the introduction of the remainder, the less the impact of the latter. Hence rather than requiring a wait until cross-examination or even until the party is putting in the party's own case, Federal Rule of Civil Procedure 32(a)(4) provides:

> If only part of a deposition is offered in evidence by a party, an adverse party may require the offeror to introduce any other part which ought in fairness to be considered with the part introduced, and any party may introduce any other parts.

See also Rule 106.

B. PROOF OF CONTENTS (THE "BEST EVIDENCE" RULE)

UNITED STATES V. DUFFY

United States Court of Appeals, Fifth Circuit, 1972.
454 F.2d 809.

WISDOM, CIRCUIT JUDGE: The defendant-appellant James H. Duffy was convicted by a jury of transporting a motor vehicle in interstate commerce from Florida to California knowing it to have been stolen in violation of 18 U.S.C.A. § 2312. He was sentenced to imprisonment for a term of two years and six months. On this appeal, Duffy complains of error in the admission of certain evidence and of prejudice resulting from members of the jury having been present during a sentencing in an unrelated case. We affirm.

At the trial, the Government established that Duffy was employed in the body shop of an automobile dealership in Homestead, Florida; that the stolen vehicle was taken by the dealership as a trade-in on the purchase of a new car; that the vehicle was sent to the body shop for repair; and that the vehicle and the defendant disappeared over the same weekend. The Government also presented testimony as to the discovery of the car in California including the testimony of (1) a witness who was found in possession of the vehicle and arrested and who testified he had received the vehicle from the defendant, (2) a San Fernando, California police officer who made the arrest and recovered the automobile, and (3) an F.B.I. agent who examined the vehicle, its contents, and the vehicle identification number. The defense stipulated to the authenticity of fingerprints, identified as Duffy's found on the rear-view mirror of the vehicle. The defense sought, through the testimony of three witnesses including the defendant, to establish that Duffy had hitchhiked to California and that, although he had worked on the stolen vehicle in the automobile dealership in Florida, he had not stolen it and had not transported it to California.

Both the local police officer and the F.B.I. agent testified that the trunk of the stolen car contained two suitcases. Found inside one of the suitcases, according to the witnesses, was a white shirt imprinted with a laundry mark reading "D–U–F". The defendant objected to the admission of testimony about the shirt and asked that the government be required to produce the shirt.[26] The trial judge overruled the objection and admitted the testimony. This ruling is assigned as error.

The appellant argues that the admission of the testimony violated the "Best Evidence Rule". According to his conception of the "Rule", the Government should have been required to produce the shirt itself rather than testimony about the shirt. This contention misses the import of the "Best Evidence Rule." The "Rule", as it exists today, may be stated as follows:

> [I]n proving the terms of *a writing*, where such terms are material, the original writing must be produced, unless it is shown to be unavailable for some reason other than the serious fault of the proponent. (Emphasis supplied.)

McCormick, Evidence 409 (1954).[27] See also United States v. Wood, 1840, 10 L.Ed. 527, 14 Pet. 430; 4 Wigmore, Evidence §§ 1173–1282 (3rd ed. 1940). Although the phrase "Best Evidence Rule" is frequently used in general terms, the "Rule" itself is applicable only to the proof of the contents of a writing. See 2 Wharton's Criminal Evidence 476 (1955) and cases cited therein; McCormick, Evidence 408–410 (1954); United States v. Waldin, 3 Cir.1958, 253 F.2d 551; Dicks v. United States, 5 Cir.1958, 253 F.2d 713; Burney v. United States, 5 Cir.1964, 339 F.2d 91.[28] McCormick summarizes the policy-justifications for the rule preferring the original writing:

> (1) * * * precision in presenting to the court the exact words of the writing is of more than average importance, particularly as respects operative or dispositive instruments, such as deeds, wills and contracts, since a slight variation in words may mean a great difference in rights, (2) * * * there is a substantial hazard of inaccuracy in the human process of making a copy by

---

[26] It is undisputed that the shirt was available to be produced and that there was no reason for failure to produce the shirt.

[27] Wharton states the "Rule" as follows:

[I]f the primary evidence of a fact is a writing, that writing must be produced in evidence as the best evidence of that fact, and * * * secondary evidence may only be produced when the nonproduction of the primary writing is explained and excused.

2 Wharton's Criminal Evidence 475–476 (1955).

[28] For a discussion of the other uses of the phrase, see 4 Wigmore, Evidence 302–303 (3rd ed. 1940).

handwriting or typewriting, and (3) as respects oral testimony purporting to give from memory the terms of a writing, there is a special risk of error, greater than in the case of attempts at describing other situations generally. In the light of these dangers of mistransmission, accompanying the use of written copies or of recollection, largely avoided through proving the terms by presenting the writing itself, the preference for the original writing is justified.

McCormick, Evidence 410 (1954).

The "Rule" is not, by its terms or because of the policies underlying it, applicable to the instant case. The shirt with a laundry mark would not, under ordinary understanding, be considered a writing and would not, therefore, be covered by the "Best Evidence Rule". When the disputed evidence, such as the shirt in this case, is an object bearing a mark or inscription, and is, therefore, a chattel *and* a writing, the trial judge has discretion to treat the evidence as a chattel or as a writing. See 4 Wigmore, Evidence § 1182 and cases cited therein; McCormick, Evidence 411–412 and cases cited therein. In reaching his decision, the trial judge should consider the policy-consideration behind the "Rule". In the instant case, the trial judge was correct in allowing testimony about the shirt without requiring the production of the shirt. Because the writing involved in this case was simple, the inscription "D–U–F", there was little danger that the witness would inaccurately remember the terms of the "writing". Also, the terms of the "writing" were by no means central or critical to the case against Duffy. The crime charged was not possession of a certain article, where the failure to produce the article might prejudice the defense. The shirt was collateral evidence of the crime. Furthermore, it was only one piece of evidence in a substantial case against Duffy.

The appellant relies on Watson v. United States, 5 Cir.1955, 224 F.2d 910 for his contention that the testimony was inadmissible without production of the shirt. *Watson* involved a prosecution for possession of liquor without internal revenue stamps affixed to the containers in violation of what was then 26 U.S.C.A. § 2803(a). This Court held that admission of testimony that there were no revenue stamps on seized containers without requiring production of the containers was erroneous. This case, however, does not provide support for appellant's assertion. First, the only case cited in *Watson* in support of application of the "Best Evidence Rule" to an object was a 1917 Ninth Circuit case involving a writing and not an object. See Simpson v. United States, 9 Cir.1917, 245 F. 278. Second, the containers in *Watson* were critical to the proof of the crime. Possession of the containers was an element of the crime. As mentioned above, the shirt in the instant case, was not critical and possession of the shirt was not an element of the crime. Finally, *Watson,* although it has never been specifically overruled, has been distinguished into oblivion by this and other courts. [citations omitted] Where *Watson* has been followed, a writing has been involved. See Daniel v. United States, 5 Cir.1956, 234 F.2d 102; United States v. Maxwell, 2 Cir.1967, 383 F.2d 437. In [Burney v. United States, 339 F.2d 91 (5th Cir. 1964)], we held that oral testimony describing the contents of two containers as distilled spirits was admissible without producing the containers or their contents.

> The Watson decision is a minority decision on this point. As far as we are able to ascertain, the Watson case is the only case in all of the Circuits which does not confine the scope of the best evidence rule to the production of original documents or writings whenever feasible.

339 F.2d at 93.

In sum, the admission of the testimony in the instant case did not violate the "Best Evidence Rule".

* * *

Affirmed.

NOTES AND QUESTIONS

1. *Inscribed chattels.* There is almost universal agreement that the rule applies only to writings and not to chattels generally. 4 Wigmore, Evidence § 1181 (Chadbourn rev. 1972). The proper treatment of inscribed chattels within this dichotomy is further discussed in 2 McCormick, Evidence § 233 (7th ed. 2013). The *Duffy* case was decided before the adoption of the Federal Rules of Evidence. Would the result in the case have been different had the Rules been in effect? *Compare* United States v. Marcantoni, 590 F.2d 1324 (5th Cir.1979) (the court treated two $10 bills, found but not seized during a search of the defendants' residence and bearing the serial numbers included in the list of "bait money" taken in the robbery in question, as within the best evidence rule) *with* United States v. Buchanan, 604 F.3d 517, 524 (8th Cir. 2010) (safe treated as a chattel and not as a writing within the best evidence rule despite the fact that it bore the number "2010").

2. *"Proving the terms of" or "identifying" a writing.* How legitimate is the distinction sometimes drawn between proving the terms of a writing and identifying it? Can one "identify" a license to sell liquor or firearms without proving its terms? See Reyna v. State, 477 S.W.2d 564 (Tex.Crim.App.1972). Can one "identify" identification cards as the property of a given individual without proving terms? See People v. Prince, 275 N.E.2d 181 (Ill.App.Ct.1971).

3. *Sound recordings.* Issues involved in the admission of sound recordings have already been discussed in connection with the Chapter 10 material on real and demonstrative evidence and the material earlier in this chapter dealing with authentication. Such recordings also present best

evidence rule problems. See United States v. Workinger, 90 F.3d 1409 (9th Cir.1996), where the court applied the rule to a transcript of a tape recording but indicated that it would not have applied the rule to testimony from someone who had heard the conversation recorded. Why this difference? Consider this question in light of the next case. On the subject of sound recordings and the best evidence rule generally, see cases collected in Annot., 58 A.L.R.3d 598.

4. *Applications to modern technology.* For an example of the application of the rule to readings from a global positioning satellite (GPS), see United States v. Bennett, 363 F.3d 947, 952–53 (9th Cir.2004). The court held that testimony about what a custom's officer had found on the "backtrack" feature of the GPS concerning the route of defendant's boat violated the best evidence rule. The testimony "was analogous to proffering testimony describing security camera footage of an event instead of introducing the footage itself."

MEYERS v. UNITED STATES

United States Court of Appeals, District of Columbia Circuit, 1948.
171 F.2d 800.

[Defendant Lamarre testified before a committee of the United States Senate investigating fraud and corruption in the conduct of World War II that he, and not General Bennett Meyers, was the actual owner of Aviation Electric Corporation. The Corporation had held numerous lucrative contracts with the Army Air Force. Meyers was deputy chief procurement officer for the Army Air Force. Lamarre was indicted for perjury, and Meyers was indicted for suborning the perjury of Lamarre. Lamarre pleaded guilty, and Meyers was found guilty after trial.]

WILBUR K. MILLER, CIRCUIT JUDGE. * * *

At the opening of the dissent it is said, "The testimony given by Lamarre before the Senate Committee was presented to the jury upon the trial in so unfair and prejudicial a fashion as to constitute reversible error."

The reference is to the fact that the William P. Rogers, chief counsel to the senatorial committee, who had examined Lamarre before the subcommittee and consequently had heard all the testimony given by him before that body, was permitted to testify as to what Lamarre had sworn to the subcommittee. Later in the trial the government introduced in evidence a stenographic transcript of Lamarre's testimony at the senatorial hearing.

In his brief here the appellant characterizes this as a "bizarre procedure" but does not assign as error the reception of Rogers' testimony. The dissenting opinion, however, asserts it was reversible error to allow Rogers to testify at all as to what Lamarre had said to the subcommittee, on the theory that the transcript itself was the best evidence of Lamarre's testimony before the subcommittee.

That theory is, in our view, based upon a misconception of the best evidence rule. As applied generally in federal courts, the rule is limited to cases where the contents of a writing are to be proved. Here there was no attempt to prove the contents of a writing; the issue was what Lamarre had said, not what the transcript contained. The transcript made from shorthand notes of his testimony was, to be sure, evidence of what he had said, but it was not the only admissible evidence concerning it. Rogers' testimony was equally competent, and was admissible whether given before or after the transcript was received in evidence. Statements alleged to be perjurious may be proved by any person who heard them, as well as by a reporter who recorded them in shorthand.

A somewhat similar situation was presented in Herzig v. Swift & Co., 146 F.2d 444, decided by the United States Court of Appeals for the Second Circuit in 1945. In that case the trial court had excluded oral testimony concerning the earnings of a partnership on the ground that the books of account were the best evidence. After pointing out the real nature and scope of the best evidence rule, the court said, 146 F.2d at page 446: " * * * Here there was no attempt to prove the contents of a writing; the issue was the earnings of a partnership, which for convenience were recorded in books of account after the relevant facts occurred. Generally, this differentiation has been adopted by the courts. On the precise question of admitting oral testimony to prove matters that are contained in books of account, the courts have divided, some holding the oral testimony admissible, others excluding it. The federal courts have generally adopted the rationale limiting the 'best evidence rule' to cases where the contents of the writing are to be proved. We hold, therefore, that the district judge erred in excluding the oral testimony as to the earnings of the partnership." * * *

As we have pointed out, there was no issue as to the contents of the transcript, and the government was not attempting to prove what it contained; the issue was what Lamarre actually had said. Rogers was not asked what the transcript contained but what Lamarre's testimony had been.

After remarking, " * * * there is a line of cases which holds that a stenographic transcript is not the best evidence of what was said. There is also a legal cliche that the best evidence rule applies only to documentary evidence", the dissenting opinion asserts that the rule is outmoded and that "the courts ought to establish a new and correct rule." We regard the principle set forth in the cases which we have cited as being, not a legal cliche, but an established and sound doctrine which we are not prepared to renounce.

With the best evidence rule shown to be inapplicable, it is clearly seen that it was neither "preposterously unfair", as the appellant asserts, nor unfair at all, to permit the transcript of Lamarre's evidence to be introduced after Rogers had testified. Since both methods of proving the perjury were permissible, the prosecution could present its proof in any order it chose.

There is no substance in the criticism, voiced by the appellant and in the dissent, of the fact that Rogers testified early in the unduly protracted trial and the transcript was introduced near its close. Appellant's counsel had a copy of the transcript from the second day of the trial, and had full opportunity to study it and to cross-examine Rogers in the light of that study. The mistaken notion that, had the transcript been first put in evidence, Rogers' testimony would have been incompetent is, of course, based on the erroneous idea that the best evidence rule had application.

* * *

Affirmed.

PRETTYMAN, CIRCUIT JUDGE (dissenting).

I am of strong opinion that the judgment in this case should be reversed. I think so for two reasons.

I.   The testimony given by Lamarre before the Senate Committee was presented to the jury upon the trial in so unfair and prejudicial a fashion as to constitute reversible error.

Lamarre testified before the Committee in executive session, only Senators, Mr. William P. Rogers, who was counsel to the Committee, the clerk, the reporter, and the witness being present. An official stenographic record was made of the proceedings. The testimony continued for two days, and the transcript is 315 typewritten pages. * * *

The notable characteristics of this testimony of Rogers are important. In each instance, the "substance" was a short summation, about half a printed page in length. The witness did not purport to be absolute in his reproduction but merely recited his unrefreshed recollection, and his recollection on each of the three matters bears a striking resemblance to the succinct summations of the indictment. It is obvious that what the witness gave as "substance" was an essence of his own distillation and not an attempt to reproduce the whole of Lamarre's testimony. * * *

In my view, the court iterates an error when it says that the best evidence rule is limited to cases where the contents of a writing are to be proved. The purpose of offering in evidence a "written contract" is not to prove the contents of the writing. The writing is not the contract; it is merely evidence of the contract. The contract itself is the agreement between the parties. Statutes such as the statute of frauds do not provide that a contract be in writing; they provide that the contract be evidenced by a writing, or that a written memorandum of it be made. The writing is offered as evidence of an agreement, not for the purpose of proving its own contents. A deed to real estate is different, being actually the instrument of conveyance, although there is authority that it too is merely evidence of the agreement between the parties. * * *

From the theoretical point of view, the case poses this question: Given both (1) an accurate stenographic transcription of a witness' testimony during a two-day hearing and (2) the recollection of one of the complainants as to the substance of that testimony, is the latter admissible as evidence in a trial of the witness for perjury? I think not. To say that it is, is to apply a meaningless formula and ignore crystal-clear actualities. The transcript is, as a matter of simple, indisputable fact, the best evidence. The principle and not the rote of the law ought to be applied.

I do not suggest that a stenographer's report is unimpeachable; that question is not here. * * *

NOTES AND QUESTIONS

1. *Coincidental recordings.* For another example of the distinction made by the majority in the principal case, see Forrester v. State, 167 A.2d 878 (Md.1961) (disallowing testimony of what was contained in a "dictabelt" recording of conversation as not the best evidence), with United States v. Rose, 590 F.2d 232 (7th Cir.1978), and People v. Sica, 247 P.2d 72 (Cal.Ct.App.1952) (proper to allow officers to testify to telephone conversations overheard by them though conversations had been recorded). An alternative approach to the problem is found in 2 McCormick, Evidence § 234 (7th ed. 2013), where the author suggests a rule based upon the centrality of the writing to the litigation. Despite such criticism, the orthodoxy is well entrenched. See, e.g., R & R Associates, Inc. v. Visual Scene, Inc., 726 F.2d 36 (1st Cir.1984) (testimony as to cost of items admissible without necessity for records); Jackson v. State, 411 N.E.2d 609 (Ind.1980) (semble; videotape); State v. Hill, 505 P.2d 704 (Kan.1973) (testimony of witness to contents of oral statement by defendant admissible though transcript was taken); Naranjo v. Paull, 803 P.2d 254 (N.M.Ct.App.1990) (IRS forms did not necessitate exclusion of other evidence of partnership income).

2. *Writings that become the act.* From the situation in the principal case, distinguish cases in which an act may be done only in writing, and the writing in effect becomes the act, e.g., the judgment of a court of record. 9 Wigmore, Evidence § 2453 (Chadbourn Rev. 1981). What about corporate minutes. See Annot., 48 A.L.R.2d 1259, 1260. What writings would Judge Prettyman place in this category?

3. *Collateral writings.* Another escape from the rule is via a holding that, [although a writing is concerned, its contents are not of sufficient importance or likely enough to be controverted as to require application of the rule.]Judicial language commonly describes these situations as involving the writing only "collaterally." See also Rule 1004(d). Illustrative cases are: United States v. Beebe, 467 F.2d 222 (10th Cir.1972) (prosecution for making false statement to obtain a firearm from a licensed dealer; dealers allowed to testify as to licensing without producing licenses); Farr v. Zoning Bd. of Appeals, 95 A.2d 792 (Conn.1953) (parties to zoning appeal allowed to testify they were town landowners without producing documentary evidence of titles); Chicago City Ry. v. Carroll, 68 N.E. 1087 (Ill.1903) (testimony of plaintiff that he was a passenger admissible without production of or accounting for streetcar transfer).

4. *Admissions.* The possibility of proving the contents of a document by the admission of a party-opponent should also be noted. Slatterie v. Pooley, 6 M. & W. 664, 151 Eng.Rep. 579 (Exch.1840), held in favor of proof by an oral admission without production of the original. The Federal Rules restrict the principle to admissions made by testimony or deposition, or in writing. Rule 1007.

UNITED STATES v. DIAZ–LOPEZ

United States Court of Appeals, Ninth Circuit, 2010.
625 F.3d 1198.

GOULD, CIRCUIT JUDGE:

At a bench trial, Luis Diaz–Lopez ("Diaz") was convicted of being a removed alien found in the United States in violation of 8 U.S.C. § 1326(a). Diaz contends that the district court erred in admitting testimony about the results of a database search introduced to show that Diaz had no permission to return, urging theories that the testimony lacked foundation and that it violated the best evidence rule. We have jurisdiction under 28 U.S.C. § 1291, and we affirm.

I

Diaz was born in and is a citizen of Mexico. On February 13, 2009, a Border Patrol agent found and arrested Diaz on a road in California, north of the United States–Mexico border. The government charged Diaz under 8 U.S.C. § 1326(a) with being a removed alien found in the United States without permission. At a bench trial, the government introduced testimony from a Border Patrol agent stating that he had performed a search of the Computer Linked Application Information Management System ("CLAIMS") database using Diaz's name, alien number, and date of birth, and had found no record of Diaz having filed a Form I–212, which is the required application for permission to reapply for admission to the United States after having been previously removed.

The district court found Diaz guilty and sentenced him to twenty-one months in prison and three years of supervised release. This appeal followed.

II

Diaz appeals the district court judge's decision to admit the Border Patrol agent's testimony about the database search. He contends that the testimony lacked foundation and that it violated Federal Rule of Evidence 1002 (the "best evidence rule"). We review the district court's decision to admit this testimony for abuse of discretion. *United States v. Hernandez*, 109 F.3d 1450, 1452 (9th Cir.1997).

We reject Diaz's claim that the agent's testimony lacked foundation. At the bench trial, the agent testified that he had performed a search of the CLAIMS database using Diaz's name, alien number, and date of birth, and found no record of Diaz having filed a Form I–212. Diaz concedes that this testimony is governed by Federal Rule of Evidence 803(10), an exception to the hearsay rule allowing testimony to prove the absence of a public record. However, Diaz argues that this testimony lacked foundation because the agent did not establish the trustworthiness of the CLAIMS database by describing the processes by which database entries are made or deleted and errors are identified. *See United States v. Rich*, 580 F.2d 929, 938 (9th Cir.1978) ("To merit judicial reliance on the contents of records, it is necessary that the proponent of particular records establish the trustworthiness of those records.").

The agent testified about his experience with and personal use of the CLAIMS database and his knowledge of its maintenance. The government need not produce a computer programmer or expert witness to testify as to the accuracy of the database. *See U–Haul Intern., Inc. v. Lumbermens Mut. Cas. Co.*, 576 F.3d 1040, 1045 (9th Cir.2009). For purposes of establishing foundation, it was sufficient that the agent testified that he was familiar with both the process of searching the records and the government's recordkeeping practices with regard to the database. *See id.* The testimony established that the government relied on the CLAIMS database in conducting its business. *See id.* The agent was not required to explicitly state that his search was "diligent." *See United States v. Neff*, 615 F.2d 1235, 1241–42 (9th Cir.1980) (holding that testimony of a government agent that his search of an IRS database revealed no records was sufficient for purposes of Rule 803(10)). Diaz has not seriously challenged the accuracy of the CLAIMS database, "and nothing in the record on appeal reveals a lack of trustworthiness." *Rich*, 580 F.2d at 939 (holding that it is necessary that "there be some evidence suggesting the unreliability of the [challenged] records"). Diaz's attack on the extent of the agent's knowledge regarding particular database policies and procedures was a fair subject for a reasonable cross-examination, but goes to the weight accorded to the agent's testimony by the factfinder rather than to its admissibility. The agent's testimony laid a sufficient foundation for this relevant evidence to be admissible. The district court did not abuse its discretion by admitting testimony about the results of the database search.

III

Diaz next argues that the agent's testimony regarding the results of the CLAIMS database search violated Federal Rule of Evidence 1002, which codifies a principle long referred to at common law as the "best evidence rule." *See* Fed.R.Evid. 1001–1008. Diaz's assertion challenging the testimony under the best evidence rule presents a question of first impression in our circuit. We must decide if testimony that a search of a computer database revealed no record of a matter violates the best evidence rule when it is offered without the production of an "original" printout showing the search results. We hold that it does not.

As we previously have observed, the best evidence rule "requires not, as its common name implies, the best evidence in every case but rather the production of an original document instead of a copy." *Seiler v. Lucasfilm, Ltd.,* 808 F.2d 1316, 1318 (9th Cir.1986). Federal Rule of Evidence 1002, on its face, is simple and clear in its statement: "To prove the content of a writing, recording, or photograph, the original writing, recording, or photograph is required, except as otherwise provided in these rules or by Act of Congress." Fed.R.Evid. 1002. For purposes of this rule, " '[w]ritings' and 'recordings' consist of letters, words, or numbers, or their equivalent, set down by handwriting, typewriting, printing, photostating, photographing, magnetic impulse, mechanical or electronic recording, or other form of data compilation." Fed.R.Evid. 1001. But despite its simple name and concise definition, experience has shown that application of this principle, as with other difficult questions of the law of evidence, may not "safely be handled in slap-dash fashion." John MacArthur Maguire, *Evidence: Common Sense and Common Law,* at v (1947).

The scope, application, and relevance of the best evidence doctrine have been debated by treatise-writers for centuries. Professor Thayer thought it would "help to clear the subject, and keep our heads clear, if we drop the name and the notion of any specific rule of the Best Evidence." James Bradley Thayer, *A Preliminary Treatise on Evidence at the Common Law* 507 (Boston, Little, Brown, and Co. 1898). A century later, however, the name is still with us. Although the best evidence doctrine in the federal courts has since been refined to encompass only the requirement for originals set out in the Federal Rules of Evidence (and in no way involves comparing evidence to determine which is "the best"), it has also been enlarged to include not just writings, but also recordings and photographs. The modern doctrine appears to be a rule of evolving scope (applying to ever-increasing varieties of media) with less-frequent application (owing to the easy availability of exact duplicates, modern discovery procedures, and exceptions to the federal version of the best evidence rule).

The animating purpose of the best evidence rule has been persuasively summarized as follows:

> [P]resenting to a court the exact words of a writing is of more than average importance, particularly in the case of operative or dispositive instruments such as deeds, wills or contracts, where a slight variation of words may mean a great difference in rights. In addition, it is to be considered (1) that there has been substantial hazard of inaccuracy in some of the commonly utilized methods of making copies of writings, and (2) oral testimony purporting to give the terms of a writing from memory is probably subject to a greater risk of error than oral testimony concerning other situations generally. The danger of mistransmitting critical facts which accompanies the use of written copies or recollection, but which is largely avoided when an original writing is presented to prove its terms, justifies preference for original documents.

George E. Dix et al., *McCormick on Evidence* § 232 (Kenneth S. Broun, ed., 6th ed. 2009). Professor Wigmore offered a similar explanation of the "fundamental notion" of the best evidence rule:

> [I]n writings the smallest variation in words may be of importance * * * * Thus the rule applies only to the *terms of the document,* and not to any *other facts about the document.* In other words, the rule * * * does not apply to exclude testimony which concerns the document without aiming to establish its terms * * * *

4 John Henry Wigmore, *Evidence in Trials at Common Law,* § 1242 at 574 (James H. Chadbourn rev. 1972).

We turn now to the issue presented by Diaz on this appeal. Diaz contends that, under Federal Rule of Evidence 1002, the government was required to produce an "original" to show that the CLAIMS database did not contain any record of Diaz having filed an I–212. When records or data are stored "in a computer or similar device, any printout or other output readable by sight, shown to reflect the data accurately, is an 'original.'" Fed.R.Evid. 1001(3). Diaz argues that the government should have introduced a printout of the search results from the CLAIMS database rather than testimony from the agent performing the search.

Diaz is correct that the CLAIMS database falls within the scope of the best evidence rule, because the database is a "[w]riting[ ] or recording[ ] * * * set down by * * * magnetic impulse * * * or electronic recording, or other form of data compilation." Fed.R.Evid. 1001. The next question is whether the evidence was introduced "[t]o prove the content of a writing, recording, or photograph." Fed.R.Evid. 1002. We conclude that it was not. The agent's testimony that he searched the database and found no record of Diaz having filed an I–212 is similar to testimony "that an event did *not* occur because relevant records contain no mention of it. This negative type of testimony is usually held not to constitute proof of contents and thus not to require production of records." Dix et al., *supra,* at § 234 (emphasis in original). Indeed, the advisory committee's note to Rule 1002 states that the best evidence rule does not apply to "testimony that books or records have been examined and found not to contain any reference to a designated matter." Fed.R.Evid. 1002, advisory committee's note.[29]

Diaz concedes that if no record were found pursuant to an agent's physical search of an A-file, testimony to that effect would be admissible under Federal Rule of Evidence 1002. However, Diaz asserts that, although the Rule applies to computer databases, the advisory committee note's limitation on the Rule applies only to searches of "physical" records. We decline to adopt such a position. First, we do not see any meaningful difference between a search of a physical file and a search of a database. Databases contain "physical" records, too, even if those records are not printed on paper. Second, the best evidence rule, like us, now survives in the twenty-first century. It is common sense, and not mere symmetry, to say that because the rule applies to computer databases, the rule's limitations must also apply to such databases. It is reasonable to apply the best evidence rule to new circumstances as technology evolves, but when the rule is extended, courts will necessarily be required to decide if the limits on the rule extend as well. When, by virtue of new technology, the best evidence rule can be applied to testimony about databases, the traditional limits on the rule should be properly extended as well.

Our decision here does not conflict with our holding in *United States v. Bennett,* 363 F.3d 947 (9th Cir.2004). There, we held that testimony about data retrieved from a boat's global positioning system ("GPS") was

---

[29] We have not passed explicitly on this issue, but other jurisdictions are in accord. *See United States v. Jewett,* 438 F.2d 495, 497–98 (8th Cir.1971) (holding that there was no error in admitting testimony that a search of books and records revealed no transfer of title to a property); *Aiuppa v. United States,* 393 F.2d 597, 602 (10th Cir.1968) (finding no error in allowing two employees to testify that they searched government records in their regions and found no record that defendant had applied for permission to possess more than the statutory limit of mourning doves), *vacated on other grounds by Giordano v. United States,* 394 U.S. 310, 89 S.Ct. 1163, 22 L.Ed.2d 297 (1969); *McDonald v. United States,* 200 F.2d 502, 504 (5th Cir.1953) (finding no error where a witness testified that he examined the books and records of the company and there was no record of payment by the defendant); *Allen v. Wells Fargo Bank Minn., N.A.,* 334 B.R. 746, 750 n. 7 (D.D.C.2005) (holding that the best evidence rule did not apply to testimony that voicemail logs did not contain a record of a message).

barred by the best evidence rule because the testimony had been introduced to prove the "content" of the GPS, which, in turn, was evidence that the defendant had come from Mexico. *Id.* at 953. But *Bennett* concerned testimony about the *contents* of the GPS data, not testimony about the *absence* of data. In that case, we concluded that "the GPS itself—or a printout or other representation of such data—* * * would have been the best evidence of the data showing [the defendant's] travels." *Id.* at 954 (citations omitted). We reached that decision because the testimony about the GPS data was introduced to prove its content (i.e., the location and travels of a boat). In Diaz's case, the government did not introduce testimony to prove the content of a writing; rather, the government introduced testimony to prove that a particular record was *not* part of the contents of a database. Moreover, the testimony about the search of the database was not testimony in which "the smallest variation in words may be of importance." Wigmore, *supra; see also State v. Nano,* 273 Or. 366, 543 P.2d 660, 662 (1975) ("In the present case the witness testified to what the document did not contain; that is, the sales records did not show any sales of the calculators * * * * [T]his is not testimony in which 'the smallest variation in words may be of importance.' " (quoting Wigmore, *supra*)).

It might be contended that, while the "smallest variation in words" is not of importance in the case of testimony regarding the negative results of a database search, such variations may well be significant if the testimony is offered to prove what particular search terms were used to search a database. However, even if Diaz had raised this argument, it would not aid his case. Any dispute about the particular search terms used by the agent for searching the CLAIMS database is not a dispute about the contents of the database, or about the contents of any records in the database, but rather a dispute about the specific actions performed by the agent. As a result, the best evidence rule would not apply because it applies only to writings, recordings, and photographs (as defined by Federal Rule of Evidence 1001), and not to actions. Moreover, even if the search terms used to search the database were genuinely in dispute, Diaz was free to cross-examine the agent who performed the search. Any doubts that might be raised by Diaz regarding the completeness of the search or the search terms used are a proper subject for a reasonable cross-examination, and go to the weight accorded to the testimony, not its admissibility under the best evidence rule.

We hold that Federal Rule of Evidence 1002 is inapplicable to the agent's testimony that his search of the CLAIMS database revealed no record of a Form I–212 filed by Diaz. The district court did not abuse its discretion by admitting the agent's testimony.

AFFIRMED.

NOTE AND QUESTIONS

The weight of authority supports the holding of the principal case that a witness may testify to the absence of a particular entry based on his examination of records without producing the records themselves. See, e.g., State v. Phillips, 259 P.2d 185 (Kan.1953); State v. Nano, 543 P.2d 660, 662 (Or.1975). Given the rationale supporting the best evidence rule, how supportable is this non-application of it? Might such testimony better be considered as a "summary" of documents and subjected to the requirements for admission of such a summary? See *United States v. Stephens*, infra. See also 2 McCormick, Evidence § 234 (7th ed. 2013).

WILSON V. STATE

Court of Appeals of Indiana, 1976.
348 N.E.2d 90.

GARRARD, JUDGE.

Appellant Wilson was charged with robbery and was subsequently convicted of theft. His appeal challenges the introduction of certain evidence at trial and asserts the prosecution was barred because he was subjected to double jeopardy. We affirm the conviction.

* * *

[Charges against Wilson had stemmed from an incident occurring in a township poor relief office. While Wilson was discussing a problem with a township employee, the employee's paycheck was delivered to her. Shortly thereafter Wilson allegedly knocked the employee from her chair, took the paycheck, and attempted to flee. He was subdued by other employees.]

Wilson next claims error over the introduction into evidence of a Xerox copy of the payroll check. The objection was that no proper foundation had been laid to excuse the requirement that the state produce the original.

It is suggested that the copy was capable of introduction pursuant to IC 1971, 34–1–17–7 which provides:

> "Exemplifications or copies of records, and records of deeds and other instruments, or of office books or parts thereof, and official bonds which are kept in any public office in this state, shall be proved or admitted as legal evidence in any court or office in this state, by the attestation of the keeper of said records, or books, deeds or other instruments, or official bonds, that the same are true and complete copies of the records, bonds, instruments or books, or parts thereof, in his custody, and the seal of office of said keeper thereto annexed if there be a seal, and if there be no official seal, there shall be attached to such attestation, the

certificate of the clerk, and the seal of the circuit or superior court of the proper county where such keeper resides, that such attestation is made by the proper officer."

While we doubt that the paycheck in question qualifies as a public record within the purview of this statute, we need not so decide. The statute requires an attestation and it is undisputed that none was appended to the exhibit in question. The copy was not allowable under this statute.

We are also aware of IC 1971, 34–3–15–1, 2 and 3 which provide:

"Any business may cause any or all records kept by such business to be recorded, copied or reproduced by any photographic, photostatic or miniature photographic process which correctly, accurately and permanently copies, reproduces or forms a medium for copying or reproducing the original record on a film or other durable material, and such business may thereafter dispose of the original record."

"Any such photographic, photostatic or miniature photographic copy or reproduction shall be deemed to be an original record for all purposes and shall be treated as an original record in all courts or administrative agencies for the purpose of its admissibility in evidence. A facsimile, exemplification or certified copy of any such photographic copy or reproduction shall, for all purposes, be deemed a facsimile, exemplification or certified copy of the original record."

"For purposes of this act [34–3–15–1—34–3–15–3] 'business' shall mean and include such business, bank, industry, profession, occupation and calling of every kind."

The primary thrust of this statute is to permit businesses to substitute copies for original records. Such copies may then be used as originals. There was no evidence in the case before us qualifying the exhibit as a photographic, etc., copy maintained by the business under this statute.

We return then to the objection made. As commonly stated, the rule prohibits introduction in evidence of a copy of a document or writing unless and until the absence of the original is accounted for on some reason other than the serious fault of the proponent. The purpose of the rule is to ensure trustworthiness. In earlier times a "copy" was a handmade reproduction. It was amenable not only to deliberate falsification but to scrivener's error and, in some instances, a "sure" recollection which was in fact not sure at all. That the rule has been so premised and has had sufficient flexibility to respond to circumstances where its application is uncalled for, may be readily determined from our prior decisions.

In *Federal Union Surety Co. v. Indiana, etc., Mfg. Co.* (1911), 176 Ind. 328, 95 N.E. 1104, the Court considered the admissibility of one of three copies of an order prepared on an "autographic register." Holding the document admissible without the others having been accounted for, the Court stated:

> "Each of the three slips was printed by a single mechanical impression. There is a distinction between letterpress copies of writing, and triplicate writings produced as was the slip in controversy. The law does not require the doing of unnecessary things. The slip delivered to the contractor was of necessity exactly like the slip admitted, and may be regarded as a triplicate original and no useful purpose would be subserved by requiring a notice for the production of the slip delivered to the contractor." 176 Ind. 328, 331, 95 N.E. 1104, 1106.

The Court similarly ruled in *Pittsburgh, C.C. & St. L. Ry. Co. v. Brown* (1912), 178 Ind. 11, 98 N.E. 625, that a copy of a bill of lading was admissible without accounting for a duplicate original. (The offering party's original was shown to have been lost.) While the facts of the case are not as strong, the language chosen by the Court is:

> "Where duplicates are produced by mechanical means, all are duplicate originals and any of them may be introduced in evidence without accounting for the nonproduction of the other." 178 Ind. 11, 30, 98 N.E. 625.

In *Watts v. Geisel* (1935), 100 Ind.App. 92, 194 N.E. 502, the Appellate Court approved the introduction in evidence of an apparently unsigned carbon copy of a letter. The court stated that in absence of proof that it was not a true copy, it was primary evidence and admissible.

The court again allowed admission of a carbon copy in *Town of Frankton v. Closer* (1939), 107 Ind.App. 193, 202, 20 N.E.2d 216, 220. Significantly, the court stated:

> "No objection was made (nor was there any effort to show) that the copy offered in evidence was not a carbon copy of the original. In the absence of such showing we may fairly infer that the type-written copies prepared by the attorney were carbon copies or duplicate originals and as such they may be introduced in evidence without accounting for any other impressions of the writing." [Citations omitted. Parentheses added for clarification.]

While it may be noted that these decisions all involved copies produced simultaneously, the importance of that fact is not the time of

production. Under the technology of the times, it was the assurance of
trustworthiness. *See, e.g.,* McCormick On Evidence (2nd Ed.) §§ 231, 236.

Thus, McCormick points out that with the advent of modern
technology in the production of facsimiles, no good reason exists for
excluding such copies under the rule unless there is raised some issue of
authenticity which might be resolved by requiring presentation of the
original. McCormick, *supra,* p. 569.[30] In this connection, it should also be
noted that modern ability to secure discovery of documents greatly
reduces the opportunity for surprise or injustice through the production
at trial of a thitherto undisclosed written exhibit.

Similarly, the Federal Rules of Evidence now permit use of duplicates
without accounting for the "original" unless authenticity is in issue or it
would be unfair under the circumstances to permit use of a duplicate.
Federal Rules of Evidence, Rules 1001–1003.

We think the position taken by McCormick and the federal rules is
proper and clearly supported by the decisions of the Supreme and
Appellate Court of this state.

We therefore hold that a "duplicate" of a document or other writing is
a counterpart produced by the same impression as the original, or from
the same matrix, or by means of photography, including enlargements
and miniatures, or by mechanical, electronic or chemical reproduction or
other equivalent technique which accurately reproduces the original.[31]
Such duplicates are admissible in evidence to the same extent as an
original unless a genuine issue is raised as to the authenticity of the
original, or under the circumstances existing it would be unfair to admit
the duplicate as an original. By this latter qualification, we refer
primarily to circumstances affecting the trustworthiness of the duplicate
for the purpose for which it is offered. Such circumstances might occur
where the duplicate is not fully legible or where only a portion of the total
original document is offered and the remainder would be useful for cross
examination, or might qualify the portion offered, or otherwise be useful
to the opposing party.

In the case before us no question was presented regarding
authenticity of the original check or its contents, nor was any other
reason advanced for rejection of the duplicate, except that it was not the
original. There was no error in admitting the duplicate.

---

[30] For example, identification of watermarks, types of paper and inks used in the document
may aid in determining its genuineness. On the other hand, we also take note of the common
practice of the parties in moving the court for permission to substitute copies for the record once
the original has been produced. While this practice retains whatever guarantee of
trustworthiness use of the original provides, it appears to be a useless formality when
genuineness or completeness are not in issue.

[31] This tracks the language of the federal rule applicable to writings. F.R.E. § 1001(4) [now
Fed.R.Evid. 1001(d)].

* * *

The judgment is affirmed.

STATON, P.J., concurs.

HOFFMAN, J., concurs in result with opinion.

HOFFMAN, JUDGE (concurring).

I concur in result since I do not agree with the reasoning permitting the admission of a photograph of a check into evidence.

The photograph of the check was admissible since it was proved to be a true representation of that which it purports to represent and it was competent evidence because the witness could testify to give a verbal description of the check.

The check was the object stolen and it could have been verbally described by a witness. *Hawkins v. State* (1941), 219 Ind. 116, 37 N.E.2d 79; *Highshew v. Kushto* (1956), 126 Ind.App. 584, 131 N.E.2d 652 (transfer denied, 235 Ind. 505, 134 N.E.2d 555).

NOTES AND QUESTIONS

1. *Duplicates and duplicate originals.* Consider the distinction between a duplicate and a duplicate original. See Rules 1001(c) & (d). See Thompson v. State, 488 A.2d 995 (Md.Ct.Spec.App.1985) (discussing the distinction and holding that a search warrant created by filling in blanks on a mass produced form, then photocopying the form and having it signed in multiple copies by the issuing magistrate qualified for admission both as an original and as a duplicate).

2. *Raising a question of authenticity or unfairness.* What is required to raise a question of authenticity under Rule 1003? When would unfairness result from admission of a duplicate? On both questions, see Equitable Life Assur. Soc. v. Starr, 489 N.W.2d 857 (Neb.1992). On the question of authenticity, see United States v. Mulinelli–Navas, 111 F.3d 983 (1st Cir.1997) (objection as to authenticity insufficient). On the question of fairness, see United States v. Sinclair, 74 F.3d 753 (7th Cir.1996) (no abuse of discretion in admitting duplicates). See also a case predating the Federal Rules, Toho Bussan Kaisha, Ltd. v. American President Lines, Ltd., 265 F.2d 418 (2d Cir.1959) (photostats of parts of records properly excluded).

3. *Computer printouts.* A similar pattern has very recently emerged with respect to the admissibility of computer printouts. See Annot., 7 A.L.R.4th 8. As to the admissibility of computer maintained public records, see Annot., 71 A.L.R.3d 232. Rule 1001(c) resolves the question by defining printouts as originals, but the adequacy of the solution is questioned in Peritz, Computer Data and Reliability: A Call for Authentication of Business Records Under the Federal Rules of Evidence, 80 Nw.U.L.Rev. 956 (1986).

4. *Digitally enhanced copies* [Special problems may exist where copies have been digitally enhanced.] See United States v. Seifert, 351 F.Supp.2d 926 (D.Minn.2005) (enhanced version changed from analog to digital format and made other changes; court found enhanced version to be fair and accurate and admitted as a duplicate).

5. *Copies as originals.* [Although an item may appear to be a "copy" from the point of view of the means used to produce it, is there any reason why a person may not by his treatment of it constitute it an original?] United States v. Gerhart, 538 F.2d 807 (8th Cir.1976) (in support of allegedly false loan application defendant submitted to bank photocopies of checks claimed to be due him from other sources); United States v. Manton, 107 F.2d 834 (2d Cir.1939) (copies of items passing through bank, kept as record); Chicago & E.I.R. Co. v. Zapp, 70 N.E. 623 (Ill.1904) (letterpress copies of reports, retained by local weather bureau).

UNITED STATES V. STEPHENS

United States Court of Appeals, Fifth Circuit, 1985.
779 F.2d 232.

Before RUBIN, RANDALL and WILLIAMS, CIRCUIT JUDGES.

JERRE S. WILLIAMS, CIRCUIT JUDGE.

Columbus Schalah Stephens, Jr. appeals his conviction on one count of falsifying information on a Farmers' Home Administration (FmHA) loan application, 18 U.S.C. § 1014, and five counts of mail fraud, 18 U.S.C. § 1341. He contends on appeal: * * * (4) government summary exhibits were erroneously admitted into evidence, * * * We reject the defendant's arguments and affirm his convictions.

Stephens complains that the district court erred in admitting into evidence on the government's proffer certain charts which constituted summaries of evidence already received. He asserts the charts did not qualify for admission under Fed.R.Evid. 1006 and that he was further severely prejudiced when the court allowed the charts to accompany the jury into the jury room.

This contention involves six summary charts which the government introduced in evidence through a witness who was a special agent with the office of the Inspector General of the United States Department of Agriculture. The witness had prepared them. A separate chart illustrated each of the five counts of mail fraud, and the sixth chart summarized the disposition of the entire loan funds. The charts were approximately three feet by five feet in size and consisted of simple flow charts tracing Stephens' use of the loan proceeds. The sixth chart categorized Stephens' expenditures as either "questioned" or "not questioned." The witness defined "questioned" to mean that as an investigator he questioned the particular use of the loan funds. It is clear that all the records upon which the charts were based were also in evidence.

The trial court overruled Stephens' objections to the admission of the charts in evidence. The court expressly found that the charts were summaries of "voluminous writings and records which have been introduced into evidence and which cannot be conveniently examined in court by this jury" and thus were properly admitted under Rule 1006. As each chart was introduced, the court instructed the jury that the summary charts did not in themselves constitute evidence in the case, the real evidence was the underlying documents. The judge repeated this instruction in his general charge to the jury, and then the court allowed the summary charts to go into the jury room with the jury. The defendant also had introduced a summary chart, and it as well accompanied the jury into the jury room.

Stephens attacks on two fronts the introduction of the charts into evidence under Fed.R.Evid. 1006. First, he argues that the charts were merely pedagogical devices, not proper Rule 1006 summaries, and second, the charts were argumentative. This Court has noted the importance of distinguishing between charts or summaries as evidence pursuant to Rule 1006, *United States v. Smyth,* 556 F.2d 1179, 1184 (5th Cir.1977) (summaries admitted pursuant to Rule 1006 are evidence) and charts or summaries as pedagogical devices. In *Pierce v. Ramsey Winch Co.,* 753 F.2d 416, 431 (5th Cir.1985), we recognized that pedagogical charts are not themselves evidence, and, absent the consent of all parties, they should not be sent to the jury room with the other exhibits. Relying on *Pierce,* Stephens argues that the charts were pedagogical because they summarize and organize data already in evidence. It is his contention that Rule 1006 is restricted to summaries of writings that cannot feasibly be admitted into evidence.

We reject Stephens' reading of Rule 1006. The language of Rule 1006 is not so restrictive. Rule 1006 does not require that "it be literally impossible to examine the underlying records" before a summary chart may be introduced. *United States v. Scales,* 594 F.2d 558, 562 (6th Cir.1978). The fact that the underlying documents are already in evidence does not mean that they can be "conveniently examined in court." *United States v. Lemire,* 720 F.2d 1327, 1347 (D.C.Cir.1983). Stephens' reading of Rule 1006 is also clearly inconsistent with one proper method of laying a foundation for admission of summary charts—admitting the documentation on which the summary is based. 5 J. Weinstein & M. Berger, Weinstein's Evidence ¶ 1006[03], p. 1006–7 (1983).

Stephens' reliance on *Pierce* is misplaced. *Pierce* did not hold that charts based upon documents already in evidence are always pedagogical charts and ineligible under Rule 1006. The party in *Pierce* seeking to admit the charts into evidence did not offer the charts pursuant to Rule 1006, so Rule 1006 was not even an issue in the case. Stephens' position runs counter to our decisions that do deal with Rule 1006 charts. In *United States v. Means,* 695 F.2d 811 (5th Cir.1983), we held that a chart based on documents in evidence was properly admitted under Rule 1006. To the same effect are *United States v. Evans,* 572 F.2d 455 (5th Cir.1978) and *United States v. Smyth,* 556 F.2d 1179 (5th Cir.1977).

Rule 1006 requires (1) the underlying writings be voluminous and (2) in-court examination not be convenient. *Scales,* 594 F.2d at 562. The decision of the trial judge to admit the charts is subject only to an abuse of discretion standard of review. *United States v. Means,* 695 F.2d 811, 817 (5th Cir.1983). There is no abuse of discretion in this case. The evidence was undisputably complex as it involved hundreds of exhibits. Stephens does not question that the underlying documentation was voluminous. Examination of the underlying materials would have been inconvenient without the charts utilized by the government. *See United States v. Evans,* 572 F.2d at 491; *United States v. Howard,* 774 F.2d 838, 844 (7th Cir.1985).

We also find no merit to Stephens' contention that the charts were argumentative. Stephens objects to the "questioned" and "unquestioned" characterization used in the sixth chart. He claims that the word "questioned" appeared to establish conclusively that the use of the loan funds was questioned. The use of the term, he maintains, improperly shifted the burden of proof to him.

This case is similar to *United States v. Smyth,* 556 F.2d 1179 (5th Cir.1977). The government introduced computer printout summaries that contained "original data", "classified data", "falsified data summarized" and "difference between original/false" headings to illustrate how the defendant used forged time cards to overbill the government. The trial court admitted the computer printout into evidence and instructed the jury that the underlying documents were the evidence and that the computer printout summaries were not evidence. We stated, "[I]n light of appellants' objections to the characterizations the Government utilized in the summary headings the cautionary instruction given by the trial judge was entirely appropriate, if not necessary, for it neutralized their possible prejudicial effect." 556 F.2d at 1184.

Like the court in *Smyth,* the court admitted the summary charts into evidence and instructed the jury that the charts were not to be considered as the evidence in the case,[32] and thus, neutralized the possible prejudicial effect of the headings. Moreover, "questioned" falls far short of being as argumentative as "falsified". The use of the term "questioned" is

---

[32] This practice is consistent with our other cases. *See, e.g., United States v. Evans,* 572 F.2d 455, 495 (5th Cir.1978).

no more than accurate in a case dealing with alleged conversion of loan proceeds. In sum, we find that the judge properly admitted the summary charts into evidence under Rule 1006, and consequently there was no error in allowing the charts to go into the jury room with the jury. * * *

Affirmed.

NOTE

Given the increasingly complex nature of the business world and, consequently, business litigation, the use of summaries in such trials has become routine. See cases collected in 5 Saltzburg, Martin & Capra, Federal Rules of Evidence Manual § 1006.03, at 1006–8—1006–31 (10th ed. 2011).

SEILER V. LUCASFILM, LTD.

United States Court of Appeals, Ninth Circuit, 1986.
808 F.2d 1316.

FARRIS, CIRCUIT JUDGE:

Lee Seiler, a graphic artist and creator of science fiction creatures, alleged copyright infringement by George Lucas and others who created and produced the science fiction movie "The Empire Strikes Back." Seiler claimed that creatures known as "Imperial Walkers" which appeared in The Empire Strikes Back infringed Seiler's copyright on his own creatures called "Garthian Striders." The Empire Strikes Back appeared in 1980; Seiler did not obtain his copyright until 1981.

Because Seiler wished to show blown-up comparisons of his creatures and Lucas' Imperial Walkers to the jury at opening statement, the district judge held a pre-trial evidentiary hearing. At the hearing, Seiler could produce no originals of his Garthian Striders nor any documentary evidence that they existed before The Empire Strikes Back appeared in 1980. The district judge, applying the best evidence rule, found that Seiler had lost or destroyed the originals in bad faith under Fed.R.Evid. 1004(1) and denied admissibility of any secondary evidence, even the copies that Seiler had deposited with the Copyright Office. With no admissible evidence, Seiler then lost at summary judgment, 613 F.Supp. 1253.

Facts

Seiler contends that he created and published in 1976 and 1977 science fiction creatures called Garthian Striders. In 1980, George Lucas released The Empire Strikes Back, a motion picture that contains a battle sequence depicting giant machines called Imperial Walkers. In 1981 Seiler obtained a copyright on his Striders, depositing with the Copyright Office "reconstructions" of the originals as they had appeared in 1976 and 1977.

Seiler contends that Lucas' Walkers were copied from Seiler's Striders which were allegedly published in 1976 and 1977. Lucas responds that Seiler did not obtain his copyright until one year after the release of The Empire Strikes Back and that Seiler can produce no documents that antedate The Empire Strikes Back.

Because Seiler proposed to exhibit his Striders in a blow-up comparison to Lucas' Walkers at opening statement, the district judge held an evidentiary hearing on the admissibility of the "reconstructions" of Seiler's Striders. Applying the "best evidence rule," Fed.R.Evid. 1001–1008, the district court found at the end of a seven-day hearing that Seiler lost or destroyed the originals in bad faith under Rule 1004(1) and that consequently no secondary evidence, such as the post-Empire Strikes Back reconstructions, was admissible. In its opinion the court found specifically that Seiler testified falsely, purposefully destroyed or withheld in bad faith the originals, and fabricated and misrepresented the nature of his reconstructions. The district court granted summary judgment to Lucas after the evidentiary hearing.

On appeal, Seiler contends 1) that the best evidence rule does not apply to his works, 2) that if the best evidence rule does apply, Rule 1008 requires a jury determination of the existence and authenticity of his originals, and 3) that 17 U.S.C. § 410(c) of the copyright laws overrides the Federal Rules of Evidence and mandates admission of his secondary evidence.

* * *

Discussion

1. *Application of the best evidence rule.*

The best evidence rule embodied in Rules 1001–1008 represented a codification of longstanding common law doctrine. Dating back to 1700, the rule requires not, as its common name implies, the best evidence in every case but rather the production of an original document instead of a copy. Many commentators refer to the rule not as the best evidence rule but as the original document rule.

Rule 1002 states: "To prove the content of a writing, recording, or photograph, the original writing, recording, or photograph is required, except as otherwise provided in these rules or by Act of Congress." Writings and recordings are defined in Rule 1001 as "letters, words, or numbers, or their equivalent, set down by handwriting, typewriting, printing, photostating, photographing, magnetic impulse, mechanical or electronic recording, or other form of data compilation."

The Advisory Committee Note supplies the following gloss:

Traditionally the rule requiring the original centered upon accumulations of data and expressions affecting legal relations set forth in words and figures. This meant that the rule was one essentially related to writings. Present day techniques have expanded methods of storing data, yet the essential form which the information ultimately assumes for usable purposes is words and figures. Hence the considerations underlying the rule dictate its expansion to include computers, photographic systems, and other modern developments.

Some treatises, whose approach seems more historical than rigorously analytic, opine without support from any cases that the rule is limited to words and figures. 5 *Weinstein's Evidence* (1983), ¶ 1001(1)[01] at 1001–11; 5 Louisell & Mueller, § 550 at 285.

We hold that Seiler's drawings were "writings" within the meaning of Rule 1001(1); they consist not of "letters, words, or numbers" but of "their equivalent." To hold otherwise would frustrate the policies underlying the rule and introduce undesirable inconsistencies into the application of the rule.

In the days before liberal rules of discovery and modern techniques of electronic copying, the rule guarded against incomplete or fraudulent proof. By requiring the possessor of the original to produce it, the rule prevented the introduction of altered copies and the withholding of originals. The purpose of the rule was thus long thought to be one of fraud prevention, but Wigmore pointed out that the rule operated even in cases where fraud was not at issue, such as where secondary evidence is not admitted even though its proponent acts in utmost good faith. Wigmore also noted that if prevention of fraud were the foundation of the rule, it should apply to objects as well as writings, which it does not. 4 Wigmore, *Evidence* § 1180 (Chadbourn rev. 1972).

The modern justification for the rule has expanded from prevention of fraud to a recognition that writings occupy a central position in the law. When the contents of a writing are at issue, oral testimony as to the terms of the writing is subject to a greater risk of error than oral testimony as to events or other situations. The human memory is not often capable of reciting the precise terms of a writing, and when the terms are in dispute only the writing itself, or a true copy, provides reliable evidence. To summarize then, we observe that the importance of the precise terms of writings in the world of legal relations, the fallibility of the human memory as reliable evidence of the terms, and the hazards of inaccurate or incomplete duplication are the concerns addressed by the best evidence rule. *See* 5 Louisell & Mueller, *Federal Evidence,* § 550 at 283; *McCormick on Evidence* (3d ed. 1984) § 231 at 704; Cleary & Strong,

The Best Evidence Rule: An Evaluation in Context, 51 Iowa L.Rev. 825, 828 (1966).

Viewing the dispute in the context of the concerns underlying the best evidence rule, we conclude that the rule applies. McCormick summarizes the rule as follows:

> [I]n proving the terms of a writing, where the terms are material, the original writing must be produced unless it is shown to be unavailable for some reason other than the serious fault of the proponent.

McCormick on Evidence § 230, at 704.

The contents of Seiler's work are at issue. There can be no proof of "substantial similarity" and thus of copyright infringement unless Seiler's works are juxtaposed with Lucas' and their contents compared. Since the contents are material and must be proved, Seiler must either produce the original or show that it is unavailable through no fault of his own. Rule 1004(1). This he could not do.

The facts of this case implicate the very concerns that justify the best evidence rule. Seiler alleges infringement by The Empire Strikes Back, but he can produce no documentary evidence of any originals existing before the release of the movie. His secondary evidence does not consist of true copies or exact duplicates but of "reconstructions" made after The Empire Strikes Back. In short, Seiler claims that the movie infringed his originals, yet he has no proof of those originals.

The dangers of fraud in this situation are clear. The rule would ensure that proof of the infringement claim consists of the works alleged to be infringed. Otherwise, "reconstructions" which might have no resemblance to the purported original would suffice as proof for infringement of the original. Furthermore, application of the rule here defers to the rule's special concern for the contents of writings. Seiler's claim depends on the content of the originals, and the rule would exclude reconstituted proof of the originals' content. Under the circumstances here, no "reconstruction" can substitute for the original.

Seiler argues that the best evidence rule does not apply to his work, in that it is artwork rather than "writings, recordings, or photographs." He contends that the rule both historically and currently embraces only words or numbers. Neither party has cited us to cases which discuss the applicability of the rule to drawings.[33]

---

[33] Lucas argues that Seiler's work, involving painting and photographic processes, is photography and therefore under the explicit reach of rule 1001. But the pleadings, Lucas' memoranda in opposition to summary judgment, and the district judge's initial references all characterize Seiler's work as drawings.

To recognize Seiler's works as writings does not, as Seiler argues, run counter to the rule's preoccupation with the centrality of the written word in the world of legal relations. Just as a contract objectively manifests the subjective intent of the makers, so Seiler's drawings are objective manifestations of the creative mind. The copyright laws give legal protection to the objective manifestations of an artist's ideas, just as the law of contract protects through its multifarious principles the meeting of minds evidenced in the contract. Comparing Seiler's drawings with Lucas' drawings is no different in principle than evaluating a contract and the intent behind it. Seiler's "reconstructions" are "writings" that affect legal relations; their copyrightability attests to that.

A creative literary work, which is artwork, and a photograph whose contents are sought to be proved, as in copyright, defamation, or invasion of privacy, are both covered by the best evidence rule. *See* McCormick, § 232 at 706 n. 9; Advisory Committee's Note to Rule 1002; 5 Louisell & Mueller, § 550 at 285 n. 27. We would be inconsistent to apply the rule to artwork which is literary or photographic but not to artwork of other forms. Furthermore, blueprints, engineering drawings, architectural designs may all lack words or numbers yet still be capable of copyright and susceptible to fraudulent alteration. In short, Seiler's argument would have us restrict the definitions of Rule 1001(1) to "words" and "numbers" but ignore "or their equivalent." We will not do so in the circumstances of this case.

Our holding is also supported by the policy served by the best evidence rule in protecting against faulty memory. Seiler's reconstructions were made four to seven years after the alleged originals; his memory as to specifications and dimensions may have dimmed significantly. Furthermore, reconstructions made after the release of the Empire Strikes Back may be tainted, even if unintentionally, by exposure to the movie. Our holding guards against these problems.

2. *Rule 1008.*

As we hold that the district court correctly concluded that the best evidence rule applies to Seiler's drawings, Seiler was required to produce his original drawings unless excused by the exceptions set forth in Rule 1004. The pertinent subsection is 1004(1), which provides:

> The original is not required, and other evidence of the contents of a writing, recording, or photograph is admissible if—
>
> (1) Originals lost or destroyed. All originals are lost or have been destroyed, unless the proponent lost or destroyed them in bad faith;

In the instant case, prior to opening statement, Seiler indicated he planned to show to the jury reconstructions of his "Garthian Striders" during the opening statement. The trial judge would not allow items to be shown to the jury until they were admitted in evidence. Seiler's counsel reiterated that he needed to show the reconstructions to the jury during his opening statement. Hence, the court excused the jury and held a seven-day hearing on their admissibility. At the conclusion of the hearing, the trial judge found that the reconstructions were inadmissible under the best evidence rule as the originals were lost or destroyed in bad faith. This finding is amply supported by the record.

Seiler argues on appeal that regardless of Rule 1004(1), Rule 1008 requires a trial because a key issue would be whether the reconstructions correctly reflect the content of the originals. Rule 1008 provides: A.

> When the admissibility of other evidence of contents of writings, recordings, or photographs under these rules depends upon the fulfillment of a condition of fact, the question whether the condition has been fulfilled is ordinarily for the court to determine in accordance with the provisions of rule 104. However, when an issue is raised (a) whether the asserted writing ever existed, or (b) whether another writing, recording, or photograph produced at the trial is the original, or (c) whether other evidence of contents correctly reflects the contents, the issue is for the trier of fact to determine as in the case of other issues of fact.[34]

Seiler's position confuses admissibility of the reconstructions with the weight, if any, the trier of fact should give them, after the judge has ruled that they are admissible. Rule 1008 states, in essence, that when the *admissibility* of evidence other than the original depends upon the fulfillment of a condition of fact, the trial judge generally makes the determination of that condition of fact. The notes of the Advisory Committee are consistent with this interpretation in stating: "Most preliminary questions of fact in connection with applying the rule preferring the original as evidence of contents are for the judge * * * [t]hus the question of * * * fulfillment of other conditions specified in Rule 1004 * * * is for the judge." In the instant case, the condition of fact which Seiler needed to prove was that the originals were not lost or destroyed in bad faith. Had he been able to prove this, his reconstructions would have been admissible and then their accuracy would have been a question for the jury. In sum, since admissibility of the reconstructions was dependent upon a finding that the originals were not lost or destroyed in bad faith, the trial judge properly held the hearing to determine their admissibility.

---

[34] Lucas conceded the originals existed and Seiler conceded the items he sought to introduce were not the originals. Hence, as subsections (a) and (b) are not in issue, Seiler is arguing that 1008(c) requires that the case be submitted to the jury.

[The court then held that § 410(c)[35] of the Copyright Act does not mandate the admissibility of copies of a work deposited at the Copyright Office.]

Affirmed.

NOTES AND QUESTIONS

1. *Excuses for non-production.* The "best evidence" rule, it is said, is a rule of preference only. In Thompson v. State, 488 A.2d 995, 1006 (Md.Ct.Spec.App.1985), the essence of the rule is said to be captured in the statement, "You always have to produce the original document * * * unless you can't."[36] In Hernandez v. Pino, 482 So.2d 450 (Fla.Dist.Ct.App.1986), a malpractice plaintiff was unable to produce dental x-rays which had been lost after their release to plaintiff's attorney. The x-rays had already been reviewed by defendant's expert prior to their release. Should plaintiff be allowed to present expert testimony as to what they showed? Other circumstances in addition to inadvertent loss or destruction which have traditionally been accepted as excuses for failing to produce the original of a document include possession by a third person beyond the reach of the court's process, and failure of an adversary having possession to produce after being given notice. See 2 McCormick, Evidence § 237 (7th ed. 2013). These excuses are recognized by Rule 1004.

2. *Notice.* How is notice to an adversary to produce to be proved? "Every written notice is, for the best of all reasons, to be proved by a duplicate original; for if it were otherwise, the notice to produce the original could be proved only in the same way as the original notice itself; and thus a fresh necessity would be constantly arising, *ad infinitum,* to prove notice of the preceding notice; so that the party would, at every step, be receding instead of advancing." Eisenhart v. Slaymaker, 14 Serg. & R. 153, 156 (Pa.1826), allowing a notice to quit to be proved by a "duplicate original" without proof of service of notice to produce the original. Is the reasoning suggested in the quotation valid except as to proving notice to produce the original? Compare McDonald v. Hanks, 113 S.W. 604 (Tex.Civ.App.1908), holding carbons of letters written by attorneys to relatives of alleged grantor in order to lay foundation for proof of contents of lost deed not admissible without accounting for nonproduction of the original letters.

---

[35] Section 410(c) of the act provides as follows:

In any judicial proceedings the certificate of a registration made before or within five years after first publication of the work shall constitute prima facie evidence of the validity of the copyright and of the facts stated in the certificate. The evidentiary weight to be accorded the certificate of a registration made thereafter shall be within the discretion of the court. [Ed.]

[36] The statement is attributed by the court to the late Professor Irving Younger. [Ed.]

DOE D. GILBERT V. ROSS

7 M. & W. 102, 151 Eng.Rep. 696 (Exch. of Pleas 1840).

EJECTMENT by the lessors of the plaintiff, who claimed as co-heiresses-at-law of Arthur Gramer Miller. At the trial before Lord Denman, Ch. J., at the Warwickshire Spring Assizes, 1840, it appeared that, in 1779, the father of A.G. Miller had devised the property to A.G. Miller for life, with remainder as he should by deed or will appoint, with remainder, in default of and until appointment, to the heirs of his body, with remainders over. A.G. Miller died in 1832 without issue, and it therefore became necessary for the lessors of the plaintiff, who claimed as his collateral heirs, to prove that he had acquired the fee-simple of the property before the time of his death. For this purpose they sought to give evidence of the marriage settlement of A.G. Miller, executed by him in 1789, after his father's death, in order to show that he had acquired the fee by exercising the power of appointment. This settlement was in the possession of Mr. Baxter, the defendant's attorney, who had been subpoenaed to produce it: and upon his examination, he stated that he had received it from a Mr. Weetman, who was in possession of another part of the property, and against whom the lessors of the plaintiff had previously brought an ejectment, which was tried at the Summer Assizes of 1838, before Lord Abinger, C.B., and in which the lessors of the plaintiff were nonsuited. Mr. Baxter stated that he claimed a lien on the deeds for professional business done for Mr. Weetman, and he declined to produce it on this ground. Mr. Weetman himself was in Court, but was not examined, or called on to produce the deed.

Upon Mr. Baxter's refusal to produce the deed, the lessors of the plaintiff proposed to give secondary evidence of its contents. This was objected to on the part of the defendants, but Lord Denman ruled that such evidence was admissible. The lessors of the plaintiff then tendered in evidence a copy of the deed; but upon examination it appeared that this had been made an attested copy, and was unstamped, and it was consequently rejected. It was then proposed to read, as secondary evidence of the contents of the deed, a short-hand writer's notes of the proceedings of the trial in the former action, when the settlement had been produced and proved by the then defendant Weetman. This evidence was objected to, but Lord Denman allowed it to be admitted, and the short-hand writer's notes were read; but it appeared from them that the deed had not been actually read by the officer of the Court, but that its contents were stated by the defendant's junior counsel. It was objected that this statement could not be received, but Lord Denman considered that it was substantially the same as if the deed had been read by the officer, and accordingly the note of this statement was read, and it thereby appeared that A.G. Miller had exercised the appointment in favour of himself and his heirs in fee, subject to a life interest in part of the estate to his wife, who died before him. * * *

Adams, Serjt., in Easter Term last, moved for a nonsuit or a new trial, on several grounds:

> 1st, that secondary evidence of the settlement was altogether inadmissible. 2ndly, that even if secondary evidence was receivable, the short-hand writer's notes were not admissible evidence. 3rdly, that at all events they were not receivable, when it appeared that a copy of the settlement was in existence. * * * The Court granted a rule on all the points except the third, which was disposed of on the application. Adams, Serjt., urged in support of this point, that, assuming that the short-hand writer's notes might have been evidence if no better evidence had been in existence, it appeared here that better evidence did exist, viz. the attested copy, which the lessors of the plaintiff might have produced if they had procured it to be stamped. The short-hand writer's notes, at best, amount to nothing more than mere parol evidence. * * *

PARKE, B.: You must contend then, that there is to be primary, secondary, and tertiary evidence. If an attested copy is to be one degree of secondary evidence, the next will be a copy not attested; and then an abstract: then would come an inquiry, whether one man has a better memory than another, and we should never know where to stop.

LORD ABINGER, C.B.: There can be no rule upon this point. Upon examination of the cases, and upon principle, we think there are no degrees of secondary evidence. The rule is, that if you cannot produce the original, you may give parol evidence of its contents. If indeed the party giving such parol evidence appears to have better secondary evidence in his power, which he does not produce, that is a fact to go to the jury, from which they might sometimes presume that the evidence kept back would be adverse to the party withholding it. But the law makes no distinction between one class of secondary evidence and another. In cases where the contents of public records and documents are to be proved, examined copies are allowed as primary evidence; but this is upon public grounds; for in these cases, the law, for public convenience, gives credit to the sworn testimony of any witness who examines the entry, and produces the copy.

NOTE

A majority of American jurisdictions at one time rejected the "English" view espoused in the principal case in favor of a hierarchical system of preference between types of secondary evidence. See 4 Wigmore, Evidence § 1275 (Chadbourn rev. 1972). However, the Federal and Revised Uniform

Rules of Evidence contain no provision for "degrees" of secondary evidence. Rule 1004. See also United States v. Gerhart, 538 F.2d 807 (8th Cir.1976).

CHAPTER 12[1]

TESTIMONIAL EVIDENCE

∎ ∎ ∎

A. COMPETENCY OF WITNESSES

The term "competent," with reference to witnesses, is generally used to describe a person who is free of personal characteristics which would disable him from giving testimony before a court of law. In times gone by, questions relating to the competency of witnesses bulked extremely large in the law of Evidence. "Under the English common law, at various times and in various instances, a person might be disqualified to be a witness because of race, color, sex, relationship by blood or marriage [to a party or interested person], infancy, interest, mental derangement, conviction of crime, or self-confessed moral turpitude."[2] By a gradual process of judicial decision and legislative enactment, however, early begun and greatly accelerated during the 19th century, this extensive list of incompetencies was greatly constricted, so that Thayer, writing in 1898, could state with some justification that "as to rules for the exclusion of witnesses, they have nearly disappeared. Little remains except what reason requires, namely, the exclusion of persons too young to be trusted, or too deficient in intelligence."[3] The materials which follow will deal briefly with the present significance of those characteristics which formerly served to render a witness incompetent, and with certain vestigial remnants of the rules of incompetency themselves.

(1) GENERAL REQUIREMENT: FEDERAL RULE 601

WASHINGTON V. TEXAS
Supreme Court of the United States, 1967.
388 U.S. 14.

MR. CHIEF JUSTICE WARREN delivered the opinion of the Court.

We granted certiorari in this case to determine whether the right of a defendant in a criminal case under the Sixth Amendment to have compulsory process for obtaining witnesses in his favor is applicable to

---

[1] Throughout this chapter some footnotes from cases and materials have been omitted; others have been renumbered. [Ed.]

[2] American Law Institute, Model Code of Evidence Rule 101, Comment (1942).

[3] Thayer, Preliminary Treatise on Evidence 526 (1898).

the States through the Fourteenth Amendment, and whether that right was violated by a state procedural statute providing that persons charged as principals, accomplices, or accessories in the same crime cannot be introduced as witnesses for each other.

[At his trial, petitioner sought to introduce the testimony of one Fuller, which was excluded. However, for purposes of the record, petitioner established that if allowed to testify Fuller would have substantiated petitioner's version of the facts leading up to the homicide.]

It is undisputed that Fuller's testimony would have been relevant and material, and that it was vital to the defense. Fuller was the only person other than petitioner who knew exactly who had fired the shotgun and whether petitioner had at the last minute attempted to prevent the shooting. Fuller, however, had been previously convicted of the same murder and sentenced to 50 years in prison, and he was confined in the Dallas County jail. Two Texas statutes provided at the time of the trial in this case that persons charged or convicted as co-participants in the same crime could not testify for one another, although there was no bar to their testifying for the State. On the basis of these statutes the trial judge sustained the State's objection and refused to allow Fuller to testify. Petitioner's conviction followed, and it was upheld on appeal by the Texas Court of Criminal Appeals. 400 S.W.2d 756. * * * We reverse.

I.

We have not previously been called upon to decide whether the right of an accused to have compulsory process for obtaining witnesses in his favor, guaranteed in federal trials by the Sixth Amendment, is so fundamental and essential to a fair trial that it is incorporated in the Due Process Clause of the Fourteenth Amendment. At one time, it was thought that the Sixth Amendment had no application to state criminal trials. That view no longer prevails, and in recent years we have increasingly looked to the specific guaranties of the Sixth Amendment to determine whether a state criminal trial was conducted with due process of law. We have held that due process requires that the accused have the assistance of counsel for his defense,[4] that he be confronted with the witnesses against him,[5] and that he have the right to a speedy[6] and public[7] trial.

The right of an accused to have compulsory process for obtaining witnesses in his favor stands on no lesser footing than the other Sixth Amendment rights that we have previously held applicable to the States. * * *

---

[4] Gideon v. Wainwright, 372 U.S. 335 (1963).
[5] Pointer v. State of Texas, 380 U.S. 400 (1965).
[6] Klopfer v. North Carolina, 386 U.S. 213 (1967).
[7] In re Oliver, 333 U.S. 257 (1948).

The right to offer the testimony of witnesses, and to compel their attendance, if necessary, is in plain terms the right to present a defense, the right to present the defendant's version of the facts as well as the prosecution's to the jury so it may decide where the truth lies. Just as an accused has the right to confront the prosecution's witnesses for the purpose of challenging their testimony, he has the right to present his own witnesses to establish a defense. This right is a fundamental element of due process of law.

II.

Since the right to compulsory process is applicable in this state proceeding, the question remains whether it was violated in the circumstances of this case. The testimony of Charles Fuller was denied to the defense not because the State refused to compel his attendance, but because a state statute made his testimony inadmissible whether he was present in the courtroom or not. We are thus called upon to decide whether the Sixth Amendment guarantees a defendant the right under any circumstances to put his witnesses on the stand, as well as the right to compel their attendance in court. The resolution of this question requires some discussion of the common-law context in which the Sixth Amendment was adopted.

Joseph Story, in his famous Commentaries on the Constitution of the United States, observed that the right to compulsory process was included in the Bill of Rights in reaction to the notorious common-law rule that in cases of treason or felony the accused was not allowed to introduce witnesses in his defense at all.[8] Although the absolute prohibition of witnesses for the defense had been abolished in England by statute before 1787,[9] the Framers of the Constitution felt it necessary specifically to provide that defendants in criminal cases should be provided the means of obtaining witnesses so that their own evidence, as well as the prosecution's, might be evaluated by the jury.

Despite the abolition of the rule generally disqualifying defense witnesses, the common law retained a number of restrictions on witnesses who were physically and mentally capable of testifying. To the extent that they were applicable, they had the same effect of suppressing the truth that the general proscription had had. Defendants and codefendants were among the large class of witnesses disqualified from testifying on the ground of interest.[10] A party to a civil or criminal case was not allowed to

---

[8]   3 Story, Commentaries on the Constitution of the United States §§ 1786–1788 (1st ed. 1833).

[9]   By 1701 the accused in both treason and felony cases was allowed to produce witnesses who could testify under oath. See 2 Wigmore, Evidence § 575, at 685–686 (3d ed. 1940).

[10]   See generally 2 Wigmore §§ 575–576. We have discussed elsewhere the gradual demise of the common-law rule prohibiting defendants from testifying in their own behalf. See Ferguson v. State of Georgia, 365 U.S. 570 (1961).

testify on his own behalf for fear that he might be tempted to lie. Although originally the disqualification of a codefendant appears to have been based only on his status as a party to the action, and in some jurisdictions coindictees were allowed to testify for or against each other if granted separate trials, other jurisdictions came to the view that accomplices or coindictees were incompetent to testify at least in favor of each other even at separate trials, and in spite of statutes making a defendant competent to testify in his own behalf. It was thought that if two persons charged with the same crime were allowed to testify on behalf of each other, "each would try to swear the other out of the charge."[11] This rule, as well as the other disqualifications for interest, rested on the unstated premises that the right to present witnesses was subordinate to the courts' interest in preventing perjury, and that erroneous decisions were best avoided by preventing the jury from hearing any testimony that might be perjured, even if it were the only testimony available on a crucial issue.[12]

The federal courts followed the common-law restrictions for a time, despite the Sixth Amendment. In United States v. Reid, 53 U.S. 361 (1852), the question was whether one of two defendants jointly indicted for murder on the high seas could call the other as a witness. Although this Court expressly recognized that the Sixth Amendment was designed to abolish some of the harsh rules of the common law, particularly including the refusal to allow the defendant in a serious criminal case to present witnesses in his defense, it held that the rules of evidence in the federal courts were those in force in the various States at the time of the passage of the Judiciary Act of 1789, including the disqualification of defendants indicted together. The holding in United States v. Reid was not satisfactory to later generations, however, and in 1918 this Court expressly overruled it, refusing to be bound by "the dead hand of the common law rule of 1789," and taking note of "the conviction of our time that the truth is more likely to be arrived at by hearing the testimony of all persons of competent understanding who may seem to have knowledge of the facts involved in a case, leaving the credit and weight of such testimony to be determined by the jury or by the court * * *." Rosen v. United States, 245 U.S. 467, 471 (1918).

Although Rosen v. United States rested on nonconstitutional grounds, we believe that its reasoning was required by the Sixth Amendment. * * *

---

[11] Benson v. United States, 146 U.S. 325, 335 (1892).

[12] "Indeed, the theory of the common law was to admit to the witness stand only those presumably honest, appreciating the sanctity of an oath, unaffected as a party by the result, and free from any of the temptations of interest. The courts were afraid to trust the intelligence of jurors." Benson v. United States, 146 U.S. 325, 336 (1892).

The rule disqualifying an alleged accomplice from testifying on behalf of the defendant cannot even be defended on the ground that it rationally sets apart a group of persons who are particularly likely to commit perjury. The absurdity of the rule is amply demonstrated by the exceptions that have been made to it. For example, the accused accomplice may be called by the prosecution to testify against the defendant. Common sense would suggest that he often has a greater interest in lying in favor of the prosecution rather than against it, especially if he is still awaiting his own trial or sentencing. To think that criminals will lie to save their fellows but not to obtain favors from the prosecution for themselves is indeed to clothe the criminal class with more nobility than one might expect to find in the public at large. Moreover, under the Texas statutes, the accused accomplice is no longer disqualified if he is acquitted at his own trial. Presumably, he would then be free to testify on behalf of his comrade, secure in the knowledge that he could incriminate himself as freely as he liked in his testimony, since he could not again be prosecuted for the same offense. The Texas law leaves him free to testify when he has a great incentive to perjury, and bars his testimony in situations when he has a lesser motive to lie.

We hold that the petitioner in this case was denied his right to have compulsory process for obtaining witnesses in his favor because the State arbitrarily denied him the right to put on the stand a witness who was physically and mentally capable of testifying to events that he had personally observed, and whose testimony would have been relevant and material to the defense.[13] The Framers of the Constitution did not intend to commit the futile act of giving to a defendant the right to secure the attendance of witnesses whose testimony he had no right to use. The judgment of conviction must be reversed. It is so ordered.

Reversed.

[The opinion of JUSTICE HARLAN, concurring in the result, is omitted.]

NOTES AND QUESTIONS

1. *Common law.* In the absence of specific legislative abrogation, many of the common law incompetencies have shown surprising hardiness. For example, the common law rule prohibiting the defendant in a criminal prosecution from testifying in his own behalf continued to be enforced in most jurisdictions until legislatively abolished. To the credit of the bench, however,

---

[13] Nothing in this opinion should be construed as disapproving testimonial privileges, such as the privilege against self-incrimination or the lawyer-client or husband-wife privileges, which are based on entirely different considerations from those underlying the common-law disqualifications for interest. Nor do we deal in this case with nonarbitrary state rules that disqualify as witnesses persons who, because of mental infirmity or infancy, are incapable of observing events or testifying about them.

it can be noted that judicial patience with the rule sometimes snapped somewhat earlier, as witness the following anecdote concerning Charles Doe, one-time Chief Justice of the Supreme Court of New Hampshire:

> As a trial judge, Doe broke with the established common law rule that a party was incompetent to testify in his own behalf. This rule provided the basis for numerous eloquent lamentations by counsel for clients clearly guilty that innocence could easily be shown but for the fact that the clients' lips were sealed. Eventually Doe lost his patience with such orations and interrupted one lawyer to tell him he could put his clients on the stand.

> The astonished lawyer at first couldn't believe his ears. Finally, after Doe repeated himself, the lawyer sensing that the jig was up, turned to his colleague and whispered, "Well, John, we shall have to put the rascals on * * * "

Geisler, Book Review, Harvard Law Record, Oct. 19, 1967, at 11. The incompetency of the criminally accused has now been abolished in all states, Georgia being the last in 1962.

2.   *Right to present a defense. Washington* is the seminal case in establishing a right to present a defense. In Holmes v. South Carolina, 547 U.S. 319 (2006), the Court held that a defendant's constitutional rights were violated by an evidence rule that precluded the defendant from introducing proof of third-party guilt if the prosecution had introduced forensic evidence that, if believed, strongly supports a guilty verdict. See Chapter 2, supra. See also Chambers v. Mississippi, 410 U.S. 284, 313 (1973) (Mississippi's "voucher rule" and hearsay rule prevented the defendant from introducing out-of-court admissions by a third party admitting to the murder that Chambers was charged with committing. The Court concluded that, "[i]n these circumstances, where constitutional rights directly affecting the ascertainment of guilt are implicated, the hearsay rule may not be applied mechanistically to defeat the ends of justice.").

3.   *Recent example.* See Harris v. Thompson, 698 F.3d 609, 628, 639 (7th Cir.2012) ("It is undisputed that [six-year old] Diante was in the room when Jaquari died and that his account was entirely exculpatory to Harris."; "If the Compulsory Process Clause is to be more than a 'dead letter,' it demands that courts recognize that the exclusion of defense evidence can have constitutional consequences beyond the rules of evidence. * * * By disqualifying Diante from taking the stand, the trial court deprived Harris of evidence that was favorable and material to her defense, and on the evidence before it, the exclusion was 'arbitrary or disproportionate' to the interests served by the competency rule.") (citation omitted).

(2) OATH REQUIREMENT: FEDERAL RULE 603

GORDON V. IDAHO

United States Court of Appeals, Ninth Circuit, 1985.
778 F.2d 1397.

PREGERSON, CIRCUIT JUDGE:

* * *

George K. Gordon filed a *pro se* complaint alleging constitutional violations under 42 U.S.C. § 1983 against the State of Idaho, Ada County, several state and county officials, and other individuals. In his federal civil rights complaint, Gordon asserts that the defendants violated his First Amendment rights during the course of state civil proceedings by imprisoning him for twelve days for civil contempt for refusal to take an oath or affirmation.

The defendants in the instant federal civil rights action served Gordon with a Notice of Taking Deposition Duces Tecum and an Amended Notice of Taking Deposition Duces Tecum requiring him to appear at a deposition and testify under oath. Gordon appeared at the deposition but, because of his religious beliefs, refused to swear under oath or make an alternative affirmation. The defendants thereafter moved the district court to compel discovery. The district court granted that motion and specifically ordered Gordon either to swear or affirm before testifying at the rescheduled deposition. At the second deposition, Gordon again refused both to swear under oath or to affirm before testifying. The defendants thereafter filed a motion to dismiss pursuant to Fed.R.Civ.P. 37(b)(2)(C) for failure to comply with the court's order. Following a hearing on the motion, the district court dismissed Gordon's federal civil rights action with prejudice. Gordon timely filed this appeal.
* * *

We review the district court's imposition of sanctions under Fed.R.Civ.P. 37(b)(2)(C) for abuse of discretion. * * *

* * *

In this case, the district court ordered Gordon to take an oath or to make an alternative affirmation before giving his deposition. The court's order specified the precise language that such an oath or alternative affirmation was to take, despite Gordon's religious objection to taking an oath or using the word "affirmation." The court abused its discretion in insisting that Gordon use either the word "swear" or "affirm" in light of Gordon's sincere religious objections.

The First Amendment's guarantee of the free exercise of religion requires that our procedural rules be interpreted flexibly to protect sincerely-held religious beliefs and practices. In *Callahan v. Woods,* 736 F.2d 1269, 1273 (9th Cir.1984), we set forth factors that courts must consider in determining whether a neutrally based statute violates the First Amendment guarantee of the free exercise of religion. We stated that the "government must shoulder a heavy burden to defend a regulation affecting religious actions." *Id.* at 1272. And we emphasized that it is "the 'least restrictive means' inquiry which is the critical aspect of the free exercise analysis." *Id.* The specific verbal formula offered by the district court was not the least restrictive means of assuring that Gordon testify truthfully at his deposition.

Courts that have considered issues involving oaths and affirmations have interpreted procedural rules flexibly to accommodate religious objections. In *Moore v. United States,* 348 U.S. 966 (1955) (per curiam), for example, the Supreme Court ruled that the trial court erred by refusing to allow a witness to testify because of his refusal to use the word "solemnly" in his affirmation. The Court held that there "is no requirement that the word 'solemnly' be used in the affirmation." *Id.* at 966. The Fourth Circuit has also noted that "all that the common law requires [of a criminal defendant testifying at trial on his own behalf] is a form of statement which impresses upon the mind and conscience of a witness the necessity for telling the truth." *United States v. Looper,* 419 F.2d 1405, 1407 (4th Cir.1969). *See also Baynes v. Ossakow,* 336 F.Supp. 386, 388 (E.D.N.Y.1972) (plaintiff's handwritten "affirmation" made expressly under penalty of perjury deemed a sufficient affidavit for purposes of defeating summary judgment motion).

Fed.R.Civ.P. 30(c) requires that deponents be placed under oath, and Fed.R.Civ.P. 43(d) allows the substitution of a "solemn affirmation" in lieu of an oath. We have found no authority insisting on the use of the word "affirm" in such alternative affirmations.

The Federal Rules of Evidence, which contain a provision parallel to Fed.R.Civ.P. 43(d), are also instructive on the need of the courts to protect minority religious views about oaths and affirmations. Fed.R.Evid. 603 states that every witness "shall be required to declare that he will testify truthfully, by oath or affirmation administered in a form calculated to awaken his conscience and impress his mind with his duty to do so." The advisory committee notes to Rule 603 illustrate that an affirmation need take no particular form: "The rule is designed to afford the flexibility required in dealing with religious adults, atheists, conscientious objectors, mental defectives, and children. Affirmation is simply a solemn undertaking to tell the truth; no special verbal formula is required." Fed.R.Evid. 603 advisory committee note.

This reasoning should also apply to affirmations at depositions under the Federal Rules of Civil Procedure. We therefore conclude that any statement indicating that the deponent is impressed with the duty to tell the truth and understands that he or she can be prosecuted for perjury for failure to do so satisfies the requirement for an oath or affirmation under Fed.R.Civ.P. 30(c) and 43(d). Deponents, furthermore, need not raise their hand when they state the words necessary to satisfy Fed.R.Civ.P. 30(c) and 43(d) if to do so impinges on sincerely-held religious beliefs. This flexible approach is consistent with the constitutional obligation to protect the free exercise of religious beliefs by using the least restrictive means to further compelling state interests that impinge on such free exercise. * * *

Gordon has demonstrated that raising his right hand and swearing an oath or making an affirmation violates his sincerely-held religious beliefs. The district court, therefore, should have explored the least restrictive means of assuring that Gordon would testify truthfully at his deposition. At oral argument before our court, Gordon said that before his deposition is taken he is willing to state: "I understand that I must tell the truth. I agree to testify under penalty of perjury. I understand that if I testify falsely I may be subject to criminal prosecution."[14] This statement, we believe, would satisfy Fed.R.Civ.P. 30(c) and 43(d). By failing to explore less restrictive means of assuring truthful deposition testimony, the district court abused its discretion when it dismissed Gordon's federal civil rights action. The court, therefore, erred in dismissing the action with prejudice for failure to comply with the discovery order directing Gordon to take an oath or make an affirmation.

Reversed.

WEIGEL, DISTRICT JUDGE, dissenting:

I respectfully dissent.

The alternative of affirming testimony (as distinguished from swearing to it) has been provided for all witnesses who, for religious or other reasons, object to oath taking. * * *

Appellant seeks to assert claimed rights in the federal courts. He should not be permitted to disregard reasonable Federal Rules of Procedure because of his insistence, however sincere, that his esoteric interpretation of one of those rules must prevail over the interpretation established by the federal courts.[15]

---

[14] Because of his religious beliefs, Gordon also stated at oral argument that he would prefer to say: "I understand that I must accurately state the facts" in place of "I understand that I must tell the truth." That would also suffice, so long as Gordon acknowledges that he understands he is testifying under penalty of perjury.

[15] Neither of the statements approved by the majority satisfies an important purpose of requiring oath or affirmation, i.e., to insure that the witness makes a conscious commitment to tell the truth. (See Looper, supra; * * * ; A Reconsideration of the Sworn Testimony Requirement: Securing Truth in the Twentieth Century, 75 Mich.L.R. 1681 (1977).) To say that "I understand that I must tell the truth" or that "I understand I must accurately state the facts" is not a

Dissent
Reasoning

Appellant's demand trivializes the vital purposes of the free exercise clause. Moreover, yielding to appellant's demand in this case tends to invite demands for special formulations in future cases and thus cause needless delay in the administration of justice.

The trial court's dismissal of appellant's action should be affirmed.

NOTES AND QUESTIONS

1. *Common law.* The common law's rigid insistence upon definite religious belief is parodied in Charles Dickens' *Bleak House,* a work more commonly cited as a biting indictment of the delays of the 19th century Courts of Chancery. At an inquest into the death of a personage known as the "law-writer" it transpires that the only person having any knowledge concerning the victim is the boy, Jo, who is summoned with the following results:

"Here he is, very muddy, very hoarse, very ragged. Now, boy!—But stop a minute. Caution. This boy must be put through a few preliminary paces.

"Name, Jo. Nothing else he knows on * * * Knows a broom's a broom, and knows it's wicked to tell a lie. Don't recollect who told him about the broom, or about the lie, but knows both. Can't exactly say what'll be done to him after he's dead if he tells a lie to the gentlemen here, but believes it'll be something very bad to punish him, and serve him right—and so he'll tell the truth.

" 'This won't do, gentlemen!,' says the Coroner, with a melancholy shake of his head.

" 'Don't you think you can receive his evidence, sir?' asks an attentive Juryman.

" 'Out of the question,' says the Coroner. 'You have heard the boy. "Can't exactly say" won't do, you know. We can't take *that,* in a Court of Justice, gentlemen. It's terrible depravity. Put the boy aside!' "

2. *Rule 603.* Despite flexibility in the form of the oath, "testimony taken from a witness who has not given an oath or affirmation to testify truthfully is inadmissible." United States v. Hawkins, 76 F.3d 545, 551 (4th Cir.1996). See also United States v. Odom, 736 F.2d 104, 116 (4th Cir.1984) (holding that right to object on appeal to the failure to swear witnesses is

---

promise to tell the truth nor accurately to state the facts. Appellant was aware of this as shown by his statements at oral argument that

" * * * Now the scripture says 'Let God be true though every man be a liar.' I'm simply saying that since we've all lied in the past and we've lied once or twice today and we're going to lie in the future, why kid ourselves by saying we tell the truth when in fact we do not. It's my position I would be guilty of perjury the moment I said 'Do you swear to tell the truth, the whole truth and nothing but the truth so help you God' and I say 'I do' I'm committing a lie."

waived when the objecting party voluntarily and knowingly refused to object at trial); State v. Ward, 242 S.W.3d 698, 704 (Mo.2008) ("He would not state that his testimony was subject to the pains and penalties of perjury as required * * *. The trial court then asked if there was any form of an oath or affirmance that he would take, and Ward replied there was none. Under the facts of this case, the trial court did not err in denying Ward's request to testify.").

(3) CHILD WITNESSES

EVANS V. STATE
Supreme Court of Nevada, 2001.
28 P.3d 498.

BECKER, J.:

In 1994 appellant Vernell Ray Evans was convicted of burglary and four counts of first-degree murder and sentenced to death. * * *

Around 1:00 a.m. on May 1, 1992, officers of the Las Vegas Metropolitan Police Department responded to a report of a shooting at a Wardelle Street apartment. They discovered four people shot to death: Jermaine Woods, Steven Walker, Lisa Boyer, and Samantha Scotti. Scotti and her eighteen-month-old son, Francois, were residents of the apartment.

Four-year-old Adriana Ventura (Adriana) and her mother and infant sister also resided at the apartment. Adriana witnessed the murders and testified at trial to the following. Two men entered the apartment carrying guns. Adriana referred to the men as "Scary Eyes" and "Little Ray." The intruders first shot the two men already in the apartment, Woods and Walker. They then shot Scotti, who was in the bathroom, and Boyer, who was in the bedroom. Adriana could not remember how many times the two women were shot or which one of the intruders fired the shots, and she did not see how the men left the apartment. Sometime thereafter, Adriana's mother, Alicia Ventura (Ventura), called the apartment. Adriana answered and told her mother that Scotti was dead. After that, Adriana went to the apartment next door and told the neighbor that everyone had been killed.

Adriana testified that she did not know "Scary Eyes," but she had seen "Little Ray" before at the apartment. Adriana was unable to identify Evans as "Little Ray" either in court or in a lineup at the jail. However, [Alicia] Ventura testified that Adriana usually referred to Evans as either "Little Ray" or "Uncle Ray."

* * *

Adriana Ventura was four at the time of the murders and six when she testified. At trial, the prosecutor first questioned Adriana about her family, the difference between the truth and lies, and the need to tell the truth. Adriana then testified regarding the murders.

According to Evans, before her trial testimony Adriana testified at a preliminary hearing, a grand jury hearing, and a federal sentencing hearing and was questioned repeatedly about the crimes by her mother, neighbors, a detective, a child psychologist, and the media. Her grandfather allowed reporters to tape her telling her story on several occasions. Evans argues that there was great potential that the child's testimony was contaminated, particularly by her mother.

Evans also asserts that Adriana's testimony shows that she was not competent to testify. For example, she was unable to remember whether she lived in a house or an apartment at the time of the murders or the name of the other child who was present. Evans also claims that Adriana could not remember whether the murderers left through the door or jumped out of a window, but this claim is mistaken. Adriana actually said they could have done either, but she did not know because she did not watch them leave. Our review of Adriana's trial testimony shows that she readily admitted whenever she did not know or could not remember something and did not appear to make up information just to answer a question. For example, she had apparently told defense counsel before trial that each killer had shot a specific victim. She acknowledged this on cross-examination but maintained, as she had on direct examination, that she actually did not know who shot whom. The material facts which Adriana did remember and provide, such as where each victim was when shot, were consistent with the evidence at the crime scene.

A child is competent to testify if he or she is able to receive just impressions and relate them truthfully. Courts must evaluate a child's competency on a case-by-case basis, but relevant considerations include:

> (1) the child's ability to receive and communicate information; (2) the spontaneity of the child's statements; (3) indications of "coaching" and "rehearsing;" (4) the child's ability to remember; (5) the child's ability to distinguish between truth and falsehood; and (6) the likelihood that the child will give inherently improbable or incoherent testimony.[16]

This court will not disturb a finding of competency absent a clear abuse of discretion. A child's testimony supports a finding of competency if it is clear, relevant, and coherent. Inconsistencies in the testimony go to the weight of the evidence.

---

[16] [Felix v. State, 849 P.2d 220, 235 (Nev.1993). Ed.]

[handwritten margin note: Conclusion to arg 2]

We conclude that Adriana's testimony indicates that she was competent. Her basic account of the crimes remained coherent and consistent, even under cross-examination. Her testimony reflected none of the serious problems—inability to differentiate between fact and fantasy, confusion between truth and falsehood, inherently improbable testimony, suggestions of coaching, inability to recall recent events—which in other cases have prompted this court to overturn the district court's finding of competency.

[handwritten margin note: Argument 3]

Evans also contends that the district court violated this court's directive requiring trial courts to examine a child under ten years of age before permitting her to testify. He cites this court's decision in *Felix v. State*, which stands for this rule. However, at least part of the foundation for the rule no longer exists. *Felix* followed a line of authority that relied on former NRS 48.030(2), which provided that children under ten years of age could not be witnesses if they appeared "incapable of receiving just impressions of the facts * * * or of relating them truly." Nevada's statutes no longer treat the competency of witnesses younger than ten as a special case. Even assuming the rule still retains its full force, the district court's failure to examine Adriana before she testified was prejudicial only if she indeed lacked competency. We conclude that her testimony shows she was competent.

[handwritten margin note: STATUTE no longer APPLICABLE]

Nevertheless, Evans's allegations regarding possible contamination of Adriana's testimony arguably warranted an evidentiary hearing. Roughly two years had passed since the crimes occurred, and she had apparently talked with a number of people about the murders. On the other hand, the mere fact that Adriana spoke with people about her experience does not establish that her testimony was improperly influenced. Evans has not pointed to any particular behavior by Adriana or to inconsistencies in her statements—or to any words or conduct by anyone else—that indicate her testimony was deliberately or inadvertently tainted. Evans stresses that a detective suspected that Adriana's mother, Ventura, knew that Scotti was going to be murdered, but he does not explain why this suggests that Ventura manipulated her daughter's account of the crimes. We conclude that the district court could have reasonably found that Evans's allegations on this issue were insufficient to warrant an evidentiary hearing.

Adriana was competent to testify * * *.

NOTES AND QUESTIONS

1. *Rule 601.* Most states provide that a witness is incompetent to testify if she does not have the intelligence to make it worthwhile to hear her or if she does not feel a duty to tell the truth. See 1 McCormick, Evidence § 62 (7th ed. 2013). In contrast, Federal Rule 601 provides that every person is "competent to be a witness," with exceptions for the application of other rules

and instances in which state law governs. The Advisory Committee Note emphasizes that "no mental or moral qualifications for testifying as a witness are specified." Yet, several federal cases decided since the enactment of the Rules have suggested that a witness may be disqualified if he "does not have the capacity to recall, or that he does not understand the duty to testify truthfully." United States v. Lightly, 677 F.2d 1027 (4th Cir.1982). The matter is left in the discretion of the trial judge. What basis is there for such a statement? Does Rule 403 come into play?

2. *Presumption of competency.* As the principal case indicates, in some jurisdictions children of ten years of age or older are made "presumptively competent" by statute. Under such statutes children under the statutory age may still be found competent by the trial court in its discretion, but generally a voir dire examination of the child will be conducted. See Ohio R. Evid. 601 ("Every person is competent to be a witness except: (A) * * * children under ten years of age, who appear incapable of receiving just impressions of the facts and transactions respecting which they are examined, or of relating them truly."); State v. Clark, 644 N.E.2d 331, 334 (Ohio 1994) (A child witness under ten years of age "is not presumed incompetent, but rather, the proponent of the witness's testimony bears the burden of proving that the witness" is competent.); State v. Frazier, 574 N.E.2d 483, 487 (Ohio 1991) (During the voir dire examination, the "trial judge has the opportunity to observe the child's appearance, his or her manner of responding to the questions, general demeanor and any indicia of ability to relate the facts accurately and truthfully. Thus, the responsibility of the trial judge is to determine through questioning whether the child of tender years is capable of receiving just impressions of facts and events and to accurately relate them."). See also State v. Woods, 114 P.3d 1174, 1178 (Wash.2005) (in a molestation case against a father, children ages 3 and 5 at time of abuse were competent because they "were able to provide details of contemporaneous events and circumstances which demonstrated that they had the mental capacity to receive accurate impressions"); 1 McCormick, Evidence § 62 (7th ed. 2013) ("Children as young as three years old have been ruled competent as witnesses.").

3. *Competency hearings.* See Ex parte Brown, 74 So.3d 1039, 1044–45 (Ala.2011) ("[W]e decline to establish a per se rule requiring a trial court's examination of a child witness to determine the child's understanding of the duty to testify truthfully to be conducted outside the presence of the jury."); People v. Wittrein, 221 P.3d 1076, 1080 (Colo.2009) ("[T]here is no per se rule against conducting child competency proceedings in front of the jury, but by far the better practice is to excuse the jury."). What are the advantages of a hearing? Disadvantages?

4. *Child abuse cases.* More recent statutes have focused on child sexual abuse cases. See Utah Code Ann. § 76–5–410 ("A child victim of sexual abuse under the age of ten is a competent witness and shall be allowed to testify without prior qualification in any judicial proceeding. The trier of fact shall determine the weight and credibility of the testimony."). See also State v.

Webb, 779 P.2d 1108, 1113–14 (Utah 1989) (holding that trial court erred by assuming that an 18–month old child was unavailable due to immaturity without interviewing the child or taking expert testimony regarding the capability of the child, then two years old, to testify in court).

5. *Oath requirement.* Many courts have undertaken to evaluate the competency of witnesses, particularly children of tender years, by whether the witness "understands the nature and obligation of an oath." Does this constitute a viable standard? For an excellent judicial discussion, see State v. Walton, 179 A.2d 78 (N.J.Super.Ct.Law Div.1962) (holding competent a ten-year-old girl who stated she did not believe in God). See also Del.Code Ann. tit. 10, § 4302 ("No child under the age of 10 years may be excluded from giving testimony for the sole reason that such child does not understand the obligation of an oath. Such child's age and degree of understanding of the obligation of an oath may be considered by the trier of fact in judging the child's credibility."); N.Y.Crim.Proc.Law § 60.20(2) ("A witness less than nine years old may not testify under oath unless the court is satisfied that he or she understands the nature of an oath. * * * [T]he witness may nevertheless be permitted to give unsworn evidence if the court is satisfied that the witness possesses sufficient intelligence and capacity to justify the reception thereof. A witness understands the nature of an oath if he or she appreciates the difference between truth and falsehood, the necessity for telling the truth, and the fact that a witness who testifies falsely may be punished."); Id. § 60.20(3) ("A defendant may not be convicted of an offense solely upon unsworn evidence given pursuant to subdivision two.").

6. *Interviewing techniques.* "An emerging consensus in the case law relies upon scientific studies to conclude that suggestibility and improper interviewing techniques are serious issues with child witnesses, and that expert testimony on these subjects is admissible * * *." Washington v. Schriver, 255 F.3d 45, 57 (2d Cir.2001). See also Porter et al., The Nature of Real, Implanted, and Fabricated Memories for Emotional Childhood Events: Implications for the Recovered Memory Debate, 23 Law & Hum.Behav. 517, 529 (1999) ("Over repeated interviews, one fourth of participants came to report that they experienced a stressful emotional childhood incident which actually had been contrived by the researchers. The 'recovered' memories included a serious medical procedure, getting lost, getting seriously harmed by another child, a serious animal attack, and serious outdoor accident. These findings cast doubt on the argument against false memories for highly emotional events.").

Some courts use "taint" hearings to determine competency. *See* Commonwealth v. Delbridge, 859 A.2d 1254, 1256 (Pa.2004) ("[A]n allegation of taint raises a legitimate question of witness competency in cases involving complaints of sexual abuse by young children. Because taint implicates the ability of a child to distinguish real memories of an event from falsely implanted suggestions, we found that taint could infect the mental capacity of the child witness to independently recall the event and truthfully testify."). For a discussion of the problems raised by offers of the testimony of children, see Ceci & Friedman, The Suggestibility of Children: Scientific Research and Legal Implications, 86 Cornell L.Rev. 33 (2000).

7. *Parental objection.* What if the parents object to having the child testify? See State v. Iban C., 881 A.2d 1005, 1031 (Conn.2005) (in a prosecution of an uncle for sexual abuse, trial court appointed a guardian ad litem for a 5 year old child when parents resisted having child testify; court held parents were entitled to a hearing, notice, and representation by counsel at the appointment hearing).

UNITED STATES V. SNYDER

United States Court of Appeals, Seventh Circuit, 1999.
189 F.3d 640.

BAUER, CIRCUIT JUDGE.

James W. Snyder was convicted of producing, receiving, and distributing child pornography, as well as possessing child pornography with intent to sell. On appeal, he argues that: (1) the district court should have granted his request for a psychological examination to determine the competency of the victim * * *. [The victim, referred to as Michael Doe, was an eleven-year-old boy who had engaged in sex with Snyder and another man. Pornographic images of Doe were projected over the Internet.]

A.   Competency Examination

Children are presumed to be competent to testify. 18 U.S.C. § 3509(c)(2). Accordingly, a "competency examination regarding a child may be conducted only if the court determines, on the record, that compelling reasons exist," 18 U.S.C. § 3509(c)(4), and "only upon written motion and offer of proof of incompetency by a party," 18 U.S.C. § 3509(c)(3). Furthermore, "[p]sychological and psychiatric examinations to assess the competency of a child witness shall not be ordered without a showing of compelling need." 18 U.S.C. § 3509(c)(9). As long as a witness has the capacity to testify truthfully, it is best left to the fact-finder to determine whether he in fact did so. See Fed.R.Evid. 601, Advisory Notes (noting that unless witness is wholly without capacity, the question is one of credibility and weight) * * *.

Snyder's motion for a psychological examination stated simply that Doe's prior statements demonstrated that he could not differentiate between truth and fantasy, and that "[u]pon information and belief," Doe was being treated with anti-depressants that "can have extreme side effects on individuals which could make the witness incompetent to testify at trial." These assertions, even if true, did not establish a compelling reason or need for a competency examination. First, the fact that some of Doe's statements were unfounded does not show that he was unable to differentiate between reality and fantasy. Second, Snyder stated only that Doe was taking medication that could render him incompetent to testify; he did not assert that the medication had in fact made Doe incompetent. Finally, the reliability of Doe's testimony was predictably (and effectively) called into question on cross examination, when Snyder's attorney elicited detailed descriptions of imaginary events from Doe. Under these circumstances, the district court was safely within its discretion when it refused to order a psychological evaluation of Doe. Indeed, we have found no abuse of discretion in situations where the competency of a witness was much more questionable. *See e.g. United States v. Gutman*, 725 F.2d 417, 420 (7th Cir.1984) (witness had "bouts of serious mental illness in the year before the trial"). * * *

For the foregoing reasons, we AFFIRM Snyder's conviction and sentence.

UNITED STATES V. ROUSE

United States Court of Appeals, Eighth Circuit, 1997.
111 F.3d 561.

LOKEN, CIRCUIT JUDGE.

[The defendants, the victims' uncles, appealed their convictions for sexual abuse of young children.] * * *

B.   Victim Testimony by Closed Circuit Television.

Prior to trial, the government filed a motion to permit all child witnesses to testify by closed circuit television. At a hearing on this motion, therapist Kelson testified that the victims were afraid of defendants—"They still believe if they walked in the courtroom today that their uncles would attack them." The district court denied the motion without prejudice, concluding there had not been a sufficient showing that the children could not testify due to fear of the defendants.

At trial, when three of the victims were called as witnesses and appeared to be emotionally unable to testify in open court, the district court questioned each child in chambers, in the presence of defense counsel, one prosecutor, the child's guardian ad litem, and a court reporter. *See* 18 U.S.C. § 3509(b)(1)(C). Five-year-old J.R. was unable to speak when called to testify and stated in chambers that she was afraid to speak in front of her uncles. Considering this statement along with Kelson's pretrial testimony, the court found that defendants' presence in the courtroom would "more than anything else prevent her from testifying." The court made similar findings after questioning six-year-old R. R., who was found sobbing outside the courtroom and affirmed in chambers that she was crying out of fear of her uncles; and nine-year-old T. R., who became so fearful before testifying that "the guardian ad litem would have had to physically pull her into the courtroom." Defendants argue that the district court erred in permitting these three victims to testify by closed circuit television. (The other two child witnesses were able to testify in open court.)

The Sixth Amendment's Confrontation Clause "guarantees the defendant a face-to-face meeting with the witnesses appearing before the trier of fact." *Coy v. Iowa,* 487 U.S. 1012, 1016 (1988). However, this right is not absolute and must accommodate the State's "compelling" interest in "the protection of minor victims of sex crimes from further trauma and embarrassment." *Globe Newspaper Co. v. Superior Court,* 457 U.S. 596, 607 (1982). Accordingly, "where necessary to protect a child witness from trauma that would be caused by testifying in the physical presence of the defendant, at least where such trauma would impair the child's ability to communicate, the Confrontation Clause does not prohibit use of a procedure" which preserves "the essence of effective confrontation"— testimony by a competent witness, under oath, subject to contemporaneous cross-examination, and observable by the judge, jury, and defendant. *Maryland v. Craig,* 497 U.S. 836, 851, 857 (1990). Testimony by closed circuit television is a procedure now authorized by statute. *See* 18 U.S.C. § 3509(b).

Before invoking such a procedure, the district court must find that the child "would be traumatized, not by the courtroom generally, but by the presence of the defendant." *Hoversten v. Iowa,* 998 F.2d 614, 616 (8th Cir.1993), quoting *Craig,* 497 U.S. at 856. *See* 18 U.S.C. § 3509(b)(1)(B)(i) (child may testify by closed circuit television "if the court finds that the child is unable to testify in open court in the presence of the defendant * * * because of fear"). In this case, the district court made specific "because of fear" findings for three victims. Our review of the children's responses to the court's questions in chambers and the prior testimony by therapist Kelson persuades us these findings are not clearly erroneous. * * *

Defendants argue that the district court's findings are inadequate because they were not based upon the expert testimony required by § 3509(b)(1)(B)(ii). However, the statute does not require an expert to support a "because of fear" finding. That finding may be based upon the court's own observation and questioning of a severely frightened child. "[O]nce the trial has begun, the court may judge with its own eyes whether the child is suffering the trauma required to grant the requested order." H.R.Rep. No. 101–681(I), 101st Cong., 2nd Sess. (1990), *reprinted in* 1990 U.S.C.C.A.N. 6472, 6574. We also reject defendants' contention that the closed circuit television system infringed their Sixth Amendment rights because defense counsel could not see the jury while cross examining the sequestered witnesses.[17] * * *

The judgments of the district court are affirmed.

NOTES AND QUESTIONS

1. *Fair trial.* The protective procedures in *Rouse* have the potential to prejudice the right of the defendant to have his guilt fairly assessed by suggesting that even in court he threatens to do the victim harm. Are the protective mechanism used in the child sexual abuse cases based on the assumption of the defendant's guilt? Do they shift the balance of advantage by altering evidentiary rules that normally would control the admission of probative evidence and govern attacks on the credibility of witnesses? Are they justified by important social policies that overcome legitimate objections to altering the balance? Cf. Coy v. Iowa, 487 U.S. 1012 (1988) (in child sex abuse case, screen blocking complaining witnesses' view of defendant during their testimony violated Sixth Amendment confrontation rights in absence of individualized showing that screen necessary to protect them from trauma; claim not reached that screen violated due process by creating appearance of defendant's guilt).

2. *Reason for closed-circuit procedure.* Fear of testifying in front of a jury or in a large room is not sufficient to permit closed-circuit television. See United States v. Bordeaux, 400 F.3d 548, 555 (8th Cir.2005) ("The district court's findings did not satisfy the *Craig* standard. The district court found that AWH's fear of the defendant was only one reason why she could not testify in open court; it did not find that AWH's fear of the defendant was the dominant reason.").

3. *Placement of monitors.* See United States v. Etimani, 328 F.3d 493, 501 (9th Cir.2003) ("§ 3509 does not require that the television monitor in the witness room be located directly in the child's field of vision while she testifies. Rather, it is sufficient (1) if the presence of the monitor has been called to the child's attention, (2) if the child can see the monitor, if she wishes, with little effort from where she is seated while testifying, and (3) if the jury is able to observe whether or not the child looks at the monitor during her testimony.").

4. *Other special procedures.* See State v. Reeves, 448 S.E.2d 802 (N.C.1994) (finding no error where child was permitted to testify from step-mother's lap where trial court made findings as to the need for the special procedure and gave cautionary instruction to step-mother not to influence child's testimony); State v. Johnson, 528 N.E.2d 567 (Ohio Ct.App.1986) (court permitted child to testify while sitting on a relative's lap). But see Czech v. State, 945 A.2d 1088, 1094 (Del.2008) ("In the absence of

---

[17] The system included five monitors in the courtroom for the judge, jury, defense expert, and defendants to view the child testifying in chambers; a monitor for the child witness to view defendants as she testified; and separate communication lines permitting each defendant to confer with his attorney.

extraordinary circumstances, * * * a trial judge should not make special accommodations *sua sponte* [mother sat behind 5–year child complainant]. * * * [S]uch special accommodations should only be made if it has been determined, upon motion, that the requesting party has demonstrated a 'substantial need' for their implementation."). See generally ABA Criminal Justice Section's Task Force, Child Witnesses in Criminal Cases (2002).

5.   *Videotape.* In United States v. Miguel, 111 F.3d 666 (9th Cir.1997), the victim was allowed to give testimony via a videotaped deposition, while the defendant watched from another room via closed circuit television. The judge did not allow the defendant to communicate by telephone with counsel during the deposition, but only during breaks. After viewing the complete tape, defense counsel had the opportunity to make additional objections before trial. However, the federal statute provides that the defendant be allowed "contemporaneous communication" with his counsel "during the deposition." The court found that, under the statute, a defendant must be allowed to communicate instantly during the deposition. Although counsel could request a recess to communicate with the defendant, the right to communicate belongs to the defendant. It may distress the victim if the defense counsel talks to the defendant during the deposition; however, "section 3509 represents a careful compromise of highly important rights." Id. at 670. While the defendant loses the right to face to face confrontation, he retains "some of the protections inherent in the confrontation of witnesses." Id. In this case, however, the error was harmless.

6.   *Hearsay exceptions.* Child abuse cases have caused several jurisdictions to adopt new exceptions to the hearsay rule permitting out-of-court statements of children to be introduced. See Mosteller, Remaking Confrontation Clause and Hearsay Doctrine Under the Challenge of Child Sexual Abuse Prosecutions, 1993 U.Ill.L.Rev. 691. For further discussion, see Chapter 13, Section C, infra.

(4) ABILITY TO COMMUNICATE

BYNDOM V. STATE

Supreme Court of Arkansas, 2001.
39 S.W.3d 781.

HANNAH, JUSTICE.

Appellant Gregory Charles Byndom appeals his rape conviction, arguing that the trial court erred in finding the victim, Shaneani Mason, competent to testify at trial. * * *

Mason is a twenty-five-year-old woman with cerebral palsy and mental retardation caused by suffering strokes as a child due to Sickle Cell disease. Mason lived with Byndom's girlfriend, Rita Bealer, who was paid a stipend by the State to help care for Mason because Mason cannot care for herself, stand or move without assistance, or speak without the assistance of a Dynavox computer, an augmented speaking device.

* * *

* * * [T]he focus in such a case is on the witness's ability to communicate thoughts, impressions, feelings, and beliefs, and here Mason was able to do all of that by virtue of her gestures, facial expressions, ability to sign "yes" and "no," and by the limited use of the yes/no function key on her Dynavox computer. To hold otherwise would render a segment of society incompetent merely because they cannot communicate as effectively and in the same manner as those who can speak through oral, written, or signed language. Furthermore, * * * the trial court actually allowed Mason to return to using the Dynavox computer during cross-examination as long as the icons did not appear on the projection screen set up behind her for the jury to see. This ruling properly recognized that the Dynavox computer did not constitute hearsay evidence where the user, Mason, could directly answer a question with an answer only she could choose from thousands of words and phrases programmed into the computer. As such, the defendant's assertion that Mason could not communicate effectively suffers a devastating blow when it is apparent that the defense had the opportunity to elicit more detailed responses from Mason through the Dynavox computer. However, the defense continued to mostly ask yes/no questions of Mason even after the trial court allowed Mason to utilize her computer to render more thorough responses.

NOTES AND QUESTIONS

1. *Other cases.* What are the problems associated with this method of communication? See United States v. Bell, 367 F.3d 452, 463 (5th Cir.2004) ("George Cotton is deaf and mute. He is able to effectively communicate through a form of sign language, a system of grunts and gestures, that is understood by family and friends familiar with him. The district court held a competency hearing before Bell's trial to determine whether George would be able to testify and who should serve as interpreter when George testified."); People v. White, 238 N.E.2d 389 (Ill.1968) (a partially paralyzed and bed-ridden mute person could communicate by raising the right knee to answer affirmatively and remaining still to answer negatively; reversed); People v. Spencer, 457 N.E.2d 473 (Ill.App.Ct.1983) (thirty-one-year-old deaf-mute woman rape victim who was mildly to moderately retarded could communicate through gestures and references to anatomically-correct dolls, picture symbols, numbers, colors, and the alphabet; defense objection on confrontation grounds rejected).

2. *Interpreters.* If the witness does not speak English, the obvious expedient is to appoint an interpreter. The competency of interpreters is covered by Federal Rule 604. See also Court Interpreters Act, 28 U.S.C 1827.

Federal Civil Rule 43 and Criminal Rule 28 authorize appointment and compensation for interpreters.

3. *Accuracy of translation.* Ensuring that the interpreter provides a literal translation of testimony and does not embellish upon the testimony is a significant problem. E.g., United States v. Gomez, 908 F.2d 809, 811 (11th Cir.1990) (improper embellishment); Valladares v. United States, 871 F.2d 1564, 1566 (11th Cir.1989) (perfect translation not required).

4. *Accused's right to an interpreter.* What about the defendant? See United States v. Carrion, 488 F.2d 12, 14 (1st Cir.1973) ("Clearly, the right to confront witnesses would be meaningless if the accused could not understand their testimony, and the effectiveness of cross-examination would be severely hampered. * * * If the defendant takes the stand in his own behalf, but has an imperfect command of English, there exists the additional danger that he will either misunderstand crucial questions or that the jury will misconstrue crucial responses. The right to an interpreter rests most fundamentally, however, on the notion that no defendant should face the Kafkaesque spectre of an incomprehensible ritual which may terminate in punishment."). Accord United States ex rel. Negron v. New York, 434 F.2d 386, 389 (2d Cir.1970).

5. *Transcripts of tape recordings.* See United States v. Rrapi, 175 F.3d 742, 746 (9th Cir.1999) ("Generally, the Court reviews the following steps taken to ensure the accuracy of the transcripts: (1) whether the court reviewed the transcripts for accuracy, (2) whether defense counsel was allowed to highlight alleged inaccuracies and to introduce alternative versions, (3) whether the jury was instructed that the tape, rather than the transcript, was evidence, and (4) whether the jury was allowed to compare the transcript to the tape and hear counsel's arguments as to the meaning of the conversations. The third factor (instruction that the tape, not the transcript, is evidence) does not apply with foreign language tapes."); United States v. Fuentes–Montijo, 68 F.3d 352, 355 (9th Cir.1995) ("[W]hen faced with a taped conversation in a language other than English and a disputed English translation transcript, the usual admonition that the tape is the evidence and the transcript only a guide is not only nonsensical, it has the potential for harm").

(5) MENTAL COMPETENCY

UNITED STATES V. HEINLEIN
United States Court of Appeals, District of Columbia Circuit, 1973.
490 F.2d 725.

McGOWAN, CIRCUIT JUDGE: [Defendants were convicted of felony-murder and assault with intent to rape while armed.] * * *

All of the participants in the events giving rise to these appeals appear to have lived in the nether world of chronic alcoholism, and the events themselves are of a singularly squalid nature. Because of this, as well as the difficulties of reconstructing—through the imperfect instrument of a chronic alcoholic—what happened in this instance in that confused and cloudy environment, this was obviously a difficult and distasteful case to try, both for judge and jury. * * *

I

Appellants chose not to testify at trial. Accordingly, the only purportedly eyewitness version of the events in question was given by Mr. James Harding, a chronic alcoholic. On the morning of April 13, 1968, so Harding testified, he and Marie McQueen, the murder victim, were released after overnight incarceration for drunkenness. After buying some wine, they met Bernard Heinlein and the Walker brothers, David and Frank, on the street. The five of them then went to an apartment occupied by the Walkers to drink the wine. Heinlein told McQueen that he wanted to have sexual relations with her, and the Walkers both voiced support of this proposal. When McQueen refused, the three appellants seized her, held her down, and began to remove her clothing. During the struggle, McQueen slapped Heinlein in the face. His response was to take a knife from his pocket and stab her, inflicting what proved to be a fatal wound. McQueen was then carried down into the basement by her assailants, and Harding last saw her lying on the floor there, apparently just barely alive.

Harding testified that he was a friend of the deceased, but that paralysis of the left side of his body prevented him from helping her during the brutal assault. Harding was arrested for drunkenness again a few hours later but made no report of the incident. Appellants were also arrested for drunkenness later that day. The body of the deceased was discovered two days later by a neighbor. One day after that, Harding made a statement to the police which implicated appellants.

[The court here reviewed the circumstantial evidence presented by the prosecution which tended to corroborate the testimony of the witness Harding.]

The defense put forward at trial was an effort to demolish Harding's credibility. This was based upon asserted inconsistencies between his testimony at trial and prior statements made by him to the police, at the preliminary hearing, and to the grand jury. A witness was produced in the person of Dr. Prochazka, a psychiatric resident at St. Elizabeths, who testified that she examined Harding in October of 1967 and made a diagnosis then of chronic brain syndrome associated with alcoholic intoxication, with moderate to severe memory defect. The District Court also permitted Harding's credibility to be impeached by prior convictions consisting of 42 prior drunk convictions, a 1950 conviction of assault with intent to commit rape, two 1953 convictions for forgery and uttering, and a 1968 larceny conviction.

II

A principal claim of error advanced on behalf of all the appellants is that Harding was not a competent witness. In particular, it is urged that the District Court erred in failing to grant appellants' motion that Harding be subjected to a psychiatric examination with respect to his competency.

The trial began on April 28, 1969. On the second day Harding completed his direct examination, and was cross-examined at great length by counsel for Heinlein. At the beginning of the third day of trial, appellants' motion was made. In support of it, it was argued that Harding had displayed confusion in his testimony on the previous day. Counsel also reported that, at the end of the preceding day, St. Elizabeths' records had been subpoenaed which indicated a medical basis for Harding's allegedly inadequate performance on the stand. It was also said that an expert examination would take into account the fact that Harding had been drinking at the time of the events described by him. The court's ruling was couched in these terms:

> "THE COURT: As far as this witness is concerned, he has shown confusion and he has shown different statements at different times, primarily about matters that really don't go to the crux of this case, and that is as to where he went and what order immediately after this thing went on.
>
> He may have been inexpertly questioned. We have seen from the stand that he has to be questioned very carefully; otherwise he gets the wrong impression of the question and gives an answer that might be considered at variance with another answer he has given.
>
> But his testimony is primarily important, as I see it, to put these people at the scene of this crime, and in this he has never varied, never varied.
>
> The jury is perfectly competent to weigh the testimony of this witness.
>
> As a matter of fact, that is one of the two chief functions of a jury. One is to weigh the testimony of witnesses, the other of course is to decide the facts.
>
> And the jury is perfectly competent to do this.
>
> I have observed nothing in this man to indicate other than that he is an alcoholic, that his memory is clouded as to certain events, it doesn't appear to have been clouded as to others as far as putting these people at the scene of the crime. That he has never been shaken in by any statement that I know of.

I don't believe that the interest of justice demands such a psychiatric examination, which I don't believe would be the slightest help.

I think the jury in this matter is altogether competent to judge the effect of this man's testimony, and I will deny your motion."

It is apparent from the foregoing that the trial court did not regard Harding as a particularly impressive witness, as indeed he was not—a fact upon which appellants presumably relied when they decided not to take the witness stand, and which was argued vigorously by their counsel to the jury as a reason for rejecting his story *in toto*. In this jurisdiction as elsewhere, however, the "competency of the witness to testify before the jury is a threshold question of law committed to the trial court's discretion;" and the decision as to whether a court should order a psychiatric examination in order to aid it in resolving the issue of competency "must be entrusted to the sound discretion of the trial judge in light of the particular facts (footnote omitted)." United States v. Benn & Hunt, 155 U.S.App.D.C. 180, 476 F.2d 1127 (1973).

In United States v. Butler, 156 U.S.App.D.C. 356, 481 F.2d 531 (1973), this court has quite recently said:

> The question of when a trial judge should order a physical and psychiatric examination of a prosecution witness was directly considered by this court in United States v. Benn & Hunt. * * * We there explained that such an examination "may seriously impinge on a witness' right to privacy; * * * the examination itself could serve as a tool of harassment;" and the likelihood of an examination could deter witnesses from coming forward. * * * The resultant presumption against ordering an examination must be overcome by a showing of need.

In both *Benn* and *Butler,* this court, speaking through Chief Judge Bazelon, sustained the action of the District Court in failing to order a psychiatric examination of a key Government witness.

* * *

The scope of our review of that ruling is limited—and necessarily so—by the fact that it was the trial court, in contrast to ourselves, which had the opportunity to observe Harding at first hand. * * *

The arguments urged upon the trial court in support of the motion stressed (1) what was said to be the highly confusing character of Harding's testimony as given, and (2) the suggestion in the St. Elizabeths' records that Harding had a clinical history which rendered him wholly unreliable. As to the former, the trial court, as we have seen, readily recognized that there had been elements of confusion in Harding's story. A prominent one of these had been his apparent inability to differentiate between the Walker brothers by name, which resulted in the court's fashioning the expedient of having Harding refer to one brother as "the tall one" and the other as the "heavy-set one;" and it is by no means certain from the transcript that even this device was uniformly successful. * * *

Cross-examination on the first day of trial had also exposed discrepancies and gaps in Harding's statements to the police, his appearance at the preliminary hearing, and his testimony before the grand jury. But the court, noting that Harding's various statements, despite some differences, related essentially to the same event and described all three appellants as active participants, concluded that these differences were not such as to shake significantly Harding's all-important account of what happened to Marie McQueen. Although subjected to severe defense challenge, as the only prosecution witness purporting to have direct knowledge of what went on in the Walkers' apartment, Harding's story in that regard held together in a way not indicative of incompetency.

The second aspect of the defense argument was that Harding was essentially lacking in capacity to recall past events accurately, and that any effort on his part at historical reconstruction could only be pure confabulation. At the time the motion was argued, the defense had two things to go on in this regard. One was the St. Elizabeths' records.[18] The other was the fact that Harding's account of his movements during the several hours immediately succeeding the alleged slaying was plainly untrue, as the official records showed that he had again been arrested and detained for intoxication during the afternoon of the day in question. It was argued that, if this latter account was a fabrication, then so must be the tale of the Walkers' apartment.

The difference, however, is that Harding's friend, McQueen, was subsequently found dead under circumstances corroborative of Harding's version of the events culminating in her death. This hard fact stands against any claim that, because Harding may, although with no apparent

---

[18] Counsel pressed upon the trial court certain entries made in 1961 and 1967. In the former year a clinical report characterized Harding in these terms:

"The patient drank excessively, had domestic problems and had a feeling that when he walked down the streets people were looking at him and wanted to harm him."

In 1967 one clinical report said of Harding that he "was only fairly well oriented." Two others referred to memory difficulties; and the eventual diagnosis was couched in these terms:

"Acute brain syndrome associated with alcohol intoxication and chronic brain syndrome associated with alcohol intoxication without qualifying phase."

One of the examining physicians in 1967, Dr. Martha Prochazka, testified later in the trial for the defense. Her testimony was generally to the effect that Harding's mental problems were caused by excessive use of alcohol. She suggested that Harding might be suffering from something known as Korsakoff's Psychosis—a condition in which a person conceals his inability to remember by fabrication. She could not make a positive diagnosis of such a condition without further neurological examination. The motion for psychiatric examination was not, however, renewed during or at the close of the defense testimony.

incentive to do so, have lied about where he was and what he did later in the fatal day, he also lied about the events of the morning. In any event, it leaves us unable to say that the trial court abused its discretion in refusing to treat Harding as a witness of actual or potential incompetency.

* * *

NOTES AND QUESTIONS

1.   *Another example.* In United States v. Hicks, 389 F.2d 49 (3d Cir.1968), the defendant asserted as error the admission against him of the testimony of a witness alleged to be incompetent by virtue of a combination of factors, specifically, *inter alia*, that the witness used narcotics, that she heard voices telling her that "they" would take her to Hell, that she was scheduled for a mental examination in a state hospital, that she was a prostitute, and that she was being supported by a burglar who had shot the defendant. *Held:* The trial court did not err in admitting the witness' testimony in light of the lucidity of the testimony and the witness' expression of an appreciation of the obligation to tell the truth.

2.   *Trial court discretion.* The discretion of the trial court to admit the testimony of a witness alleged to be incompetent is very broad. Compare, however, People v. McCaughan, 317 P.2d 974, 981–82 (Cal.1957), where the testimony of certain inmates of a mental institution was admitted by the trial court in a prosecution of a hospital attendant for manslaughter. The witnesses were shown to have histories of delusions relating to mistreatment by hospital personnel. Reversing on other grounds, the Supreme Court of California stated: "It is universally recognized that the competency of a witness is to be determined by the trial court in the exercise of its discretion * * *. Manifestly, however, sound discretion demands the exercise of great caution in qualifying as competent a witness who has a history of insane delusions relating to the very subject of inquiry in a case in which the question is not simply whether or not an act was done but, rather, the manner in which it was done and in which testimony as to details may mean the difference between conviction and acquittal."

3.   *Intoxicated at trial.* In People v. Alley, 232 P.3d 272, 275 (Colo.App.2010), an assault trial, a witness showed up intoxicated. After learning that the witness' BAC [blood-alcohol concentration] measured over 0.2, the trial judge delayed putting him on the stand for nearly 5 hours. By then, the witness' BAC had dropped. "When N.H. was tested again approximately five hours later, his BAC was 0.084. Over defendant's objection that N.H. was not competent to testify, the trial court permitted him to take the stand. The court informed the jury of N.H.'s BAC level, and permitted defendant to cross-examine him regarding his intoxication. At the end of N.H.'s testimony, he was again tested, and the jury was told that his BAC was then 0.049. * * * The record indicates that N.H. abused alcohol and was customarily intoxicated. The prosecution expressed concern that, if his

testimony were unduly delayed, he might begin to exhibit symptoms of alcohol withdrawal, possibly resulting in a mistrial. The trial court stated it would 'make an evaluation to see if [N.H. is] competent to testify.'"

4. *Psychiatric examinations.* The determination of a witness' competency will generally be made by the trial judge solely on the basis of his or her own observation of the witness on the stand. However, "the judge has discretion to admit extrinsic evidence on the question [of competency], to use mental and psychological tests, and to hear opinion evidence of psychiatric experts." Weihofen, Testimonial Competence and Credibility, 34 Geo.Wash.L.Rev. 53, 55 (1964). See also Conrad, Mental Examination of Witnesses, 11 Syracuse L.Rev. 149, 153–56 (1960). And discretion, it would seem, is most frequently exercised against compelling the examination. See United States v. Jackson, 576 F.2d 46 (5th Cir.1978); United States v. Gutman, 725 F.2d 417 (7th Cir.1984). What if the trial court orders an examination but the witness refuses to cooperate? Compare State v. Franklin, 229 A.2d 657 (N.J.1967), with State v. Miller, 151 N.W.2d 157 (Wis.1967).

For historical interest, see Hutchins & Slesinger, Some Observations on the Law of Evidence—The Competency of Witnesses, 37 Yale L.J. 1017 (1928). In this article, the authors advocate the employment of simple intelligence tests in determining competency. They also note, to support the growing acceptance of intelligence testing in 1928: "Even the law schools are becoming interested. One of the leading law schools in the East has just announced that it will base its system of entrance henceforth partly on a 'capacity test.'"

5. *Attorney competence.* There is no express provision in the Federal Rules of Evidence governing the competency of attorneys as witnesses. Therefore, the language of Rule 601 would seem to permit their testimony. However, some judges have refused to permit such testimony, presumably based on the court's inherent power to control attorneys and the trial. In addition, an attorney should also be aware of the provisions of Model Rule of Professional Conduct 3.7, which provides, with limited exceptions, that a "lawyer shall not act as advocate at a trial in which the lawyer is likely to be a necessary witness." See Gonzalez v. State, 117 S.W.3d 831, 837–38 (Tex.Crim.App.2003) ("Counsel may be disqualified under the disciplinary rules when the opposing party can demonstrate actual prejudice resulting from opposing counsel's service in the dual role of advocate-witness. Allegations of one or more violations of the disciplinary rules or evidence showing only a possible future violation are not sufficient.").

6. *Hypnotically-refreshed testimony.* Some courts have held that the testimony of a witness who has been hypnotized is incompetent, at least with regard to matters not contained in statements given prior to the hypnotic session. The question is discussed in connection with refreshing the recollection of witnesses, Section B(4), infra.

(6) DEAD MAN'S STATUTES

RAY, DEAD MAN'S STATUTES
24 Ohio State Law Journal 89 (1963).[19]

At common law in England and the United States, parties to a lawsuit and all other persons having a direct pecuniary or proprietary interest in the outcome of the action were excluded from testifying in the case. A party could not testify in his own behalf nor could he be required to testify if called by his adversary. The rule was thus a combination of disqualification and privilege. The theory of the disqualification was that self-interest would probably cause such persons to perjure themselves; therefore, they should be prevented from giving testimony.[20] Defenders of the rule of exclusion realized, of course, that perjury would not always result from self-interest and that by silencing truthful persons the rule threatened honest litigants with injustice, but they argued that the rule did more good than harm.[21] No justification was advanced for the privilege. Jeremy Bentham, the great English Reformer, made a determined attack upon the rule in his Treatise on Evidence published in 1827 and, in the words of Wigmore, "first furnished the arsenal of arguments for transforming public opinion."[22] The unanswerable arguments that pecuniary interest did not make it probable that parties and witnesses would commit perjury, that the rule underestimated the ability of the judge and jurors to detect perjury, and that it created intolerable injustice, were taken up by such reformers as Denman and Brougham who led the assault on the disqualification. Through their efforts and those of others, professional opinion was gradually brought to the realization that the disqualification created more injustice than it prevented. In 1843 a statute was enacted by Parliament abolishing the disqualification of interested persons. And in 1851 another statute swept away the disqualification of parties and those on whose behalf a suit was brought or defended. These reforms spread to the United States, and the English statutes served as models for legislation here. As in England the change was brought about in two steps: the first qualifying interested nonparties and the second qualifying parties.

Unfortunately most of the states which enacted similar statutes departed from the English model in a most significant respect. They retained a portion of the old disqualification as an exception to the new

---

[19] Copyright © 1963 by The Ohio State University. Reprinted by permission. [Ed.]

[20] Gilbert, Evidence 119 (1727). Baron Gilbert's words were: "The law removes them from testimony to prevent their sliding into perjury."

[21] Starkie, Evidence 83 (1832): "The law must prescribe general rules; and experience proves that more mischief would result from the general reception of interested witnesses than is occasioned by their exclusion."

[22] 2 Wigmore § 576. Bentham's attack is found in his Rationale of Judicial Evidence, book IX, pt. III, ch. III and pt. V, ch. I.

rule of qualification. At the time when the first statutes abolishing the interest disqualification were offered to the state legislatures in this country, the objection was made that if parties and interested persons were allowed to testify in cases involving contracts and transactions where one party had died and the other survived, this would work a hardship on the estate of the deceased. Since the lips of one party to the transaction were sealed by death, the suggestion was that the living party's lips should be sealed by excluding his testimony.[23] This compromise was accepted in most of the early statutes and became the pattern of legislation in this country. Today in most jurisdictions the statutes contain a general statement to the effect that no person shall be disqualified because he is a party to a suit or proceeding or interested in the issue to be tried. But they add a provision to the effect that in suits brought or defended by an executor or administrator, such persons shall remain incompetent to testify concerning a communication with the testator or intestate. While this is the most common type of statute, there are many which vary substantially from this in certain respects * * * The statutes usually provide that the surviving party or interested person may testify if called by the opposite party, thus doing away with the privilege feature of the common-law rule. These statutes which retain the common-law interest disqualification of parties and interested persons with respect to testimony as to transactions with decedents are popularly known as "Dead Man's Statutes" * * *.[24] They vary greatly in their wording and coverage, and the attitudes of the courts differ as to their interpretation, even where similar provisions are involved. Consequently, precedents from one state may be of little value in another jurisdiction. * * *

NOTES

1.   *Choice of law issues.* The language in Rule 601, providing for the application of state competency rules when state substantive law governs, may have a significant impact in a case in which the state law would apply a Dead Man's Act.

2.   *Sources.* See Barnard, The Dead Man's Act Rears its Ugly Head Again, 72 Ill.Bar J. 420 (1984); Johnson & Hanzman, Construing Florida's Dead Man Statute: Let the Dead Speak in Will Contests, 60 Fla.Bar J. 35 (1986); Paige, Dead Man Talking: A Historical Analysis of West Virginia's Dead Man's Statute and a Recommendation for Reform, 109 W.Va.L.Rev. 897

---

[23] Owens v. Owen's Adm'r, 14 W.Va. 88, 95 (1878): "The temptation to falsehood and concealment in such cases is considered too great, to allow the surviving party to testify in his own behalf. Any other view of this subject, I think, would place in great peril the estates of the dead, and would in fact make them an easy prey for the dishonest and unscrupulous, which with due deference to the views and opinions of others, it seems to me, the Legislature never intended."

[24] [Professor Ray cited 34 states as having "Dead Man's Acts" at the time his article appeared in 1963. By 2013, the number had shrunk to less than a dozen. Ed.].

(2007); Wallis, An Outdated Form of Evidentiary Law: A Survey of Dead Man's Statutes and a Proposal for Change, 53 Clev.St.L.Rev. 75 (2005); Yeager, The Pennsylvania Dead Man's Satute, 18 Widener L.Rev. 53 (2012); Comment, The Deadman's Statutes—Who is an Interested Party in Wisconsin?, 87 Marq.L.Rev. 1025 (2004).

B. ELICITATION OF TESTIMONY

(1) EXCLUSION OF WITNESSES: FEDERAL RULE 615

UNITED STATES V. RHYNES

United States Court of Appeals, Fourth Circuit, En Banc, 2000.
218 F.3d 310.

KING, CIRCUIT JUDGE:

Michael Rhynes and several co-defendants were tried before a jury in the Western District of North Carolina on a number of drug-related charges. * * *

* * *

On September 24, 1996, at the commencement of the trial in Charlotte, North Carolina, a lawyer for one of Rhynes's co-defendants moved for sequestration of the Government's witnesses. In response, the district court entered its sequestration order from the bench. The Government then noted that its "case agent" and a "summary witness" were in the courtroom and intended to "sit[ ] in on the testimony prepared to testify at the end of the trial [.]" * * * The district court granted the Government's request that two of its witnesses be excepted from the sequestration order and another motion that the defense witnesses be sequestered. Thereafter, the lawyer for one of Rhynes's co-defendants sought to have his investigator excepted from the sequestration order, and the court granted the exception "[s]o long as your investigator observes Rule 615 and does not talk to the witnesses about testimony that has just concluded or testimony that has concluded." * * *

During the Government's case-in-chief, it presented the testimony of witness D.S. Davis. Davis is a convicted felon and was, at the time of trial, serving a seven-year sentence for participating in a drug conspiracy. Davis testified, *inter alia,* that he first met [Corwin] Alexander in 1990, when he (Davis) asked Alexander to serve as an intermediary in a drug transaction between Davis and Michael Rhynes.

* * *

During Rhynes's defense, he testified on his own behalf; then, he called a single witness to corroborate his testimony: Corwin Alexander. Alexander testified on a number of subjects * * * before he was asked about the Government's earlier witness, Davis. Alexander explained that, at a meeting between the two, Davis told Alexander that the Government had offered Davis a deal in exchange for information about Rhynes. Alexander then stated, "And he [(Davis)] went off to do his time, and I hear from Tuesday he got up and said—," whereupon the Government objected and requested a bench conference. * * *

At the bench, Mr. Scofield [defense counsel] advised the district court that he had discussed Davis's testimony with Alexander: "I specifically told him about that testimony and told him I was going to ask him about that, Your Honor. And I don't think that violates the sequestration order." * * * The district court indicated its belief that the sequestration order had been violated. Mr. Scofield then responded, "I'm sorry then, Your Honor. I've done wrong then because I don't know how else I can prepare him to testify. I told him that that guy told him that he was a drug dealer." * * *

The district court nonetheless granted the Government's motion to strike Alexander's testimony and to exclude him as a witness. * * *

* * * It is clear from the plain and unambiguous language of Rule 615 that lawyers are simply not subject to the Rule. This Rule's plain language relates only to "witnesses," and it serves only to exclude witnesses from the courtroom. Thus, Rule 615 did not prohibit Mr. Scofield from discussing D.S. Davis's testimony with Corwin Alexander.

The district court's bald Rule 615 order was then extended by the statement that "the witnesses shall not discuss one with the other their testimony." Of course, nothing on the face of this extending language addresses the conduct of lawyers in any way. Moreover, the relevant authorities interpreting Rule 615, including court decisions and the leading commentators, agree that sequestration orders prohibiting discussions between witnesses should, and do, permit witnesses to discuss the case with counsel for either party: "Sequestration requires that witnesses not discuss the case among themselves or anyone else, *other than the counsel for the parties.*" United States v. Walker, 613 F.2d 1349, 1354 (5th Cir.1980) * * *.

D.

The Government has conceded that neither the plain language of the district court's order, nor the provisions of Rule 615, prohibit any conduct by lawyers * * *. Nonetheless, the Government asserts that the "purpose and spirit" of the sequestration order were compromised by Mr. Scofield's discussion with Alexander. Specifically, the Government contends that the "truth-seeking" process would be hindered if lawyers were permitted to reveal testimony in the manner exercised by Mr. Scofield. This is basically an argument that Rule 615, the extending language, or the policies underlying sequestration implicitly proscribed Mr. Scofield's conduct; we reject the argument for several reasons.

We have properly recognized the purpose and spirit underlying witness sequestration: it is "designed to discourage and expose fabrication, inaccuracy, and collusion." Opus 3 Ltd. v. Heritage Park, Inc., 91 F.3d 625, 628 (4th Cir.1996). Put differently, sequestration helps to smoke out lying witnesses: "It is now well recognized that sequestering witnesses 'is (next to cross-examination) one of the greatest engines that the skill of man has ever invented for the detection of liars in a court of justice.' " Id. (citing 6 *Wigmore on Evidence* § 1838, at 463).

To the extent that the Government asserts that Mr. Scofield frustrated the purpose and spirit of sequestration, we disagree. The Government asserts that Mr. Scofield's actions undermined the truthfulness of Alexander's testimony, which, in the Government's view, is surely an act that runs afoul of the sequestration order. On the contrary, lawyers are not like witnesses, and there are critical differences between them that are dispositive in this case. Unlike witnesses, lawyers are officers of the court, and, as such, they owe the court a duty of candor, *Model Rules of Professional Conduct* Rule 3.3 (1995) ("Model Rules"). Of paramount importance here, that duty both forbids an attorney from knowingly presenting perjured testimony and permits the attorney to refuse to offer evidence he or she reasonably believes is false. *Id.* Rule 3.3(a)(4), (c). Similarly, an attorney may not "counsel or assist a witness to testify falsely." *Id.* Rule 3.4(b). And, if an attorney believes that a non-client witness is lying on the witness stand about a material issue, he is obliged to "promptly reveal the fraud to the court." *Id.* Rule 3.3, cmt. 4. The Supreme Court has emphasized the importance of attorneys' duty of candor: "Any violation of these strictures would constitute a most serious breach of the attorney's duty to the court, to be treated accordingly." Geders v. United States, 425 U.S. 80, 90 n.3 (1976) (citing to parallel provisions of *Model Code of Professional Responsibility*). Consequently, lawyers' ethical obligations to the court distinguish them from trial witnesses.

Moreover, the purpose and spirit underlying sequestration are not absolute; indeed, we have aptly recognized that even the "powerful policies behind sequestration" must bend to the dictates of the Constitution. Opus 3 Ltd., 91 F.3d at 628.[25] Thus, to the extent that they

---

[25] It is important to note that the language of Rule 615 does not require exclusion of *all* witnesses from the courtroom. While an absolute rule might further promote the truth-seeking policy behind Rule 615, constitutional considerations have required that exceptions be built into the Rule itself. Opus 3 Ltd., 91 F.3d at 628 ("confrontation and due process considerations" drive Rule 615's exceptions). Parties or their representatives, as well as expert witnesses, are authorized by Rule 615 to remain in the courtroom, hear testimony, and subsequently testify. Fed.R.Evid. 615(1)–(3). In criminal cases these exceptions are applied to allow the prosecution's case agent to remain at counsel table with the prosecutor, hear the other witnesses testify, and nevertheless testify on behalf of the prosecution. In this very case, moreover, the district court's

are implicated in this case, the policies and spirit of sequestration must yield to the constitutional and ethical duties Mr. Scofield sought to effectuate here.[26] That is, in the context of a criminal trial like this one, a defense attorney's duty to his client assumes constitutional stature: "In all criminal prosecutions, the accused shall * * * have the Assistance of Counsel for his defence." U.S. Const. amend. VI. To all clients, an attorney owes competence. *Model Rules* Rule 1.1. To fulfill this basic duty, the attorney must prepare carefully for the task at hand: "Competent representation requires * * * thoroughness and preparation reasonably necessary for the representation." *Id.* Rule 1.1(a).

Thorough preparation demands that an attorney interview and prepare witnesses before they testify. No competent lawyer would call a witness without appropriate and thorough pre-trial interviews and discussion. In fact, more than one lawyer has been punished, found ineffective, or even disbarred for incompetent representation that included failure to prepare or interview witnesses. United States v. Tucker, 716 F.2d 576 (9th Cir.1983) (defense counsel ineffective for failing to interview witnesses); McQueen v. Swenson, 498 F.2d 207 (8th Cir.1974) (same); In re Warmington, 212 Wis.2d 657, 668, 568 N.W.2d 641 (1997) (lawyer disbarred for, among other things, "failing to supervise the preparation of an expert witness"); In re Wolfram, 174 Ariz. 49, 847 P.2d 94, 96 (1993) (failure to interview witnesses cited among reasons for suspending attorney).

In this context, Mr. Scofield's actions were necessary in the exercise of his duties, both constitutional and ethical, as a lawyer. First, when the Government called Davis as a witness and began asking him questions about Alexander, Mr. Scofield made clear that he was unaware that Alexander had been implicated as a co-conspirator. * * * Although Davis's subsequent testimony did not implicate Alexander in any specific drug deal, the import of Davis's allegation was clear: Alexander was serving as an intermediary between drug buyers and Rhynes. Faced with an allegation that his prime supporting witness, Alexander, had been assisting, or participating in, a drug conspiracy with Rhynes, Mr. Scofield

---

sequestration order specifically exempted the Government's FBI case agent as well as its summary witness. * * *

[26] While it is unnecessary for us to reach the issue in this case, we observe that sequestration orders that prevent attorneys from performing their duties as counsel, including discussing trial proceedings with future witnesses, may well violate a criminal defendant's Sixth Amendment rights. The Supreme Court has explicitly forbidden some sequestration orders that prohibit a defendant-witness from conferring with counsel. Geders v. United States, 425 U.S. [at 91]. And at least one court has extended this reasoning to sequestration orders preventing counsel from discussing prior testimony with non-defendant witnesses:

> It has been held that to deprive a party * * * of the right to consult with counsel as the trial proceeds is to infringe its right to due process of law. This court believes that similar considerations apply to the right of a party to have his counsel free to discuss with prospective witnesses developments in the case, *including the testimony of other witnesses.*

United States v. Scharstein, 531 F.Supp. 460, 463–64 (E.D.Ky.1982) (emphasis added).

had ethical (and possibly constitutional) duties to investigate these allegations with Alexander before he put Alexander on the stand. Mr. Scofield was thus compelled to ascertain, if possible: (1) whether Davis's allegations were untrue (or, if true, whether Alexander intended to invoke his Fifth Amendment rights); (2) whether Alexander's denials were credible; and (3) why Davis would make potentially false allegations against Alexander. Put simply, Mr. Scofield needed to fully assess his decision to call Alexander as a witness, and, to fulfill his obligations to his client, Scofield was compelled to discuss Davis's testimony with Alexander. *See Chandler v. Jones,* 813 F.2d 773 (6th Cir.1987) (finding counsel's performance deficient for (1) failing to prepare witness for trial; (2) improperly using leading questions; and (3) calling witness who was expected to invoke the Fifth Amendment).

In response, the Government claims that Mr. Scofield did not violate the sequestration order by merely speaking with Alexander; instead, it was Mr. Scofield's informing Alexander of Davis's testimony that violated the order. Based on this view, the Government asserts that counsel had ample room to interview and prepare witnesses without running afoul of the sequestration order. But this conclusion begs the question, "How was counsel to discern the limits of the sequestration order?" Those limits—as declared after the fact by the district court—did not appear on the face of the order, in Rule 615, in controlling precedent, or even in persuasive authorities. In fact, adoption of the Government's position would make it virtually impossible for counsel to know whether they have "ample room" to perform essential tasks without violating an order. This argument thus fails to persuade us.

Further, sequestration is not the only technique utilized to ensure the pursuit of truth at trial. Indeed, if an attorney has inappropriately "coached" a witness, thorough cross-examination of that witness violates no privilege and is entirely appropriate and sufficient to address the issue. * * *

In short, the Government's position requires the implication that by discussing prior trial testimony with Corwin Alexander, Mr. Scofield necessarily coached Alexander or made it likely that Alexander would commit perjury.[27] To the contrary, we must trust and rely on lawyers' abilities to discharge their ethical obligations, including their duty of candor to the court, without being policed by overbroad sequestration orders. Furthermore, we are confident that, if an attorney is lax in his duty of candor, that laxness will normally be exposed—even exploited—by skillful cross-examination. * * *

---

[27] For the sake of clarification, we note that nothing in the record even remotely suggests that Mr. Scofield improperly coached Alexander or encouraged him to commit perjury.

III.

Even if Mr. Scofield had violated a sequestration rule or order, we would still hold, in the context of this case, that the sanction imposed—exclusion of Alexander's testimony—constituted reversible error. "Because exclusion of a defense witness impinges upon the right to present a defense, we are quite hesitant to endorse the use of such an extreme remedy." United States v. Cropp, 127 F.3d 354, 363 (4th Cir.1997). Under these circumstances, we conclude that exclusion of Alexander's testimony in its entirety was unduly severe.

At the outset, sanction analysis must encompass proportionality, and sanctions as extreme as witness exclusion must be proportional to the offense. * * * In this case, when the district court excluded Alexander's testimony, it was aware, through Mr. Scofield's representations, that Alexander had been exposed to Davis's accusation that Alexander was involved in drug deals. However, the district court conducted no examination of Alexander to determine exactly what he had been told; neither did the court attempt to ascertain through Mr. Scofield what he had revealed to Alexander.

More importantly, the proffer of Alexander's testimony covered at least six other Government witnesses and a number of other topics that were crucial to Rhynes's defense. Mr. Scofield specifically represented that, "Your Honor, I do not believe, as I stand here and think about it, that I mentioned anybody else's testimony other than D.S. Davis." * * * Notwithstanding this representation, the district court determined that Alexander's testimony relating to each of the other Government witnesses and other subjects was tainted by the same "coaching" as the testimony relating to D.S. Davis. * * *

* * *

We are also cognizant that although the alleged violation of the sequestration order was effected by Mr. Scofield, the sanction imposed inured to the defendant.[28] There was, of course, no requirement that Rhynes be sanctioned for his lawyer's conduct; indeed, a lawyer may be personally sanctioned for violations of court orders. If, however, a defendant is being sanctioned for his lawyer's conduct, courts should impose the least severe sanction justified under the circumstances. The district court had alternative sanctions at its disposal; we have endorsed at least two others: "sanction of the witness; [and] instructions to the jury that they may consider the violation toward the issue of credibility." Cropp, 127 F.3d at 363. Further, there were many other possible corrective measures that could have been taken, including: limiting the scope of the witness's testimony, see English, 92 F.3d at 913 (endorsing

---

[28] There has been no allegation that Rhynes participated in this alleged violation in any way.

limitation of witness's testimony following violation of sequestration order); permitting broad cross-examination into the alleged "coaching," * * *; or any other sanction appropriate under the circumstances. There is no doubt that, under facts like these, the district court could have imposed a less severe sanction.

* * *

Vacated and Remanded.

[WILKINS, CIRCUIT JUDGE concurred in part and concurred in the judgment.]

WILKINSON, CHIEF JUDGE, dissenting:

* * * The district court should be commended, not chastised, for refusing to recognize an exception to Rule 615 that does not exist and for acting to preserve trial proceedings as a means of ascertaining truth.

* * *

Scofield's conduct * * * utterly thwarted the sequestration order. * * * It has no conceivable object other than to prevent prospective witnesses from knowing the testimony of prior witnesses before taking the stand themselves. * * * Yet Scofield's actions accomplished this prohibited end as surely as if Alexander had heard Davis' testimony in the courtroom himself. This was a matter of no small concern to the district court. Davis' testimony was extremely problematic for Alexander, because Davis had linked Alexander to Rhynes' drug-dealing activities. Foreknowledge of Davis' testimony would enable Alexander to counter these allegations with greater credibility, specificity, and force. The district court was understandably troubled when it learned that Scofield had related Davis' testimony to Alexander. The court was not compelled to countenance Scofield's conduct any more than it was required to permit Alexander to hire a courtroom scribe to record prior testimony, *see McMahon,* 104 F.3d 638, or read trial transcripts of what earlier witnesses said, *see Miller v. Universal City Studios, Inc.,* 650 F.2d 1365 (5th Cir.1981).

Nor did the district court's ruling impair Scofield's ability to discharge his professional obligations to thoroughly prepare his witnesses. * * * To argue that the district court's ruling impermissibly ties attorneys' hands is both gross overstatement and a red herring. Indeed, Scofield himself commendably acknowledged to the district court that attorneys may fully prepare witnesses without revealing the details of prior testimony in contravention of a sequestration order * * *.

[NIEMEYER, CIRCUIT JUDGE, dissenting opinion omitted.]

NOTES AND QUESTIONS

1. *Recent example.* In the prosecution for the 9/11 terrorist attacks, the trial judge barred the testimony of government aviation officials because a Transportation Security Administration official, who was assisting prosecutors, sent e-mails coaching these officials, including transcripts of the opening statements and the testimony of an FBI agent. Lewis, Judge Penalizes Moussaoui Prosecutors by Barring Major Witnesses, N.Y.Times, Mar. 15, 2006, at A23. See also Carter, Note, Court Order Violations, Witness Coaching, and Obstructing Access to Witnesses: An Examination of the Unethical Attorney Conduct that Nearly Derailed the Moussaoui Trial, 20 Geo.J.Legal Ethics 463 (2007).

2. *Scope of rule.* See United States v. Hargrove, 929 F.2d 316, 320–21 (7th Cir.1991) ("The testimony of Baker did not contravene [Rule 615's] purpose. Baker was a surprise witness whom the government did not intend to call until Michael Beckett testified that the police pressured him to falsely identify Hargrove as his source for cocaine. The government called Baker solely to testify to the lack of police coercion and not to the substance of what Michael Beckett had said about Hargrove.").

3. *Exception: Parties.* In Portuondo v. Agard, 529 U.S. 61 (2000), the prosecutor, in her summation, called the jury's attention to the fact that the defendant had the opportunity to hear all other witnesses testify and to tailor his testimony accordingly. The defendant argued that these comments burdened his Sixth Amendment right to be present at trial and to be confronted with the witnesses against him, as well as his Fifth and Sixth Amendment rights to testify on his own behalf. The Court rejected these arguments. Some courts distinguish between different types of comments, permitting comment only when there is specific evidence of tailoring. Generic accusations are prohibited. See State v. Daniels, 861 A.2d 808, 819 (N.J.2004) (The latter "occur when the prosecutor, despite no specific evidentiary basis that defendant has tailored his testimony, nonetheless attacks the defendant's credibility by drawing the jury's attention to the defendant's presence during trial and his concomitant opportunity to tailor his testimony."). See also State v. Martin, 252 P.3d 872, 879 (Wash.2011) (prohibiting comment on defendant's presence in closing argument as a matter of state constitutional law).

4. *Exception: Designated representatives.* The Senate Judiciary Committee construed this exception to permit an "investigative agent" to remain during trial notwithstanding the possibility that the agent may be called as a witness. "The investigative agent's presence may be extremely important to government counsel, especially when the case is complex or involves some specialized subject matter. The agent, too, having lived with the case for a long time, may be able to assist in meeting trial surprises where the best-prepared counsel would otherwise have difficulty." S. Rep. No. 1277, 93d Cong., 2d Sess., reprinted in 1974 U.S.C.C.A.N. 7051, 7072. But see In re United States, 584 F.2d 666, 667 (5th Cir.1978) (trial court has

authority under Rule 611(a) to require the investigative agent to testify "at an early stage of the government's case if he remains the government's designated representative under Rule 615"); Carter v. State, 610 S.E.2d 181, 183–84 (Ga.Ct.App.2005) ("We have reached a point where the prosecution acts as though it has an absolute right to have its witness present for the duration of trial. An empty assertion that the prosecution simply 'needs' a witness during trial to assist in the orderly presentation of its case, without more, should not be the kind of assertion upon which discretion can be granted.").

5. *Exception: Essential persons.* This exception "contemplates such persons as an agent who handled the transaction being litigated or an expert needed to advise counsel in the management of the litigation." Fed.R.Evid. 615 advisory committee's note.

6. *Exception: Statutes.* Federal statutes recognize a crime victim's right to be present unless the victim's testimony would be materially affected by attendance. 42 U.S.C. § 10606(b)(4). Many state provisions are more specific. See Ala.R.Evid. 615 ("This rule does not authorize exclusion of * * * (4) a victim of a criminal offense or the representative of a victim who is unable to attend, when the representative has been selected by the victim, the victim's guardian, or the victim's family."); Fla.Stat.Ann. § 90.616(d) (recognizing an exception: "In a criminal case, the victim of the crime, the victim's next of kin, the parent or guardian of a minor child victim, or a lawful representative of such person, unless, upon motion, the court determines such person's presence to be prejudicial."). See also Mosteller, The Unnecessary Victims' Rights Amendment, 1999 Utah L.Rev. 443, 457–62 (discussing Rule 615 issues and victims' rights).

7. *Separation of attorney and client.* In Geders v. United States, 425 U.S. 80 (1976), a sequestration order so broad that it prohibited the accused from consulting with his counsel during a 17–hour overnight recess violated the Sixth Amendment. But see Perry v. Leeke, 488 U.S. 272 (1989) (proper for trial court to order accused not to talk to anyone, including counsel, during a 15–minute recess between direct and cross-examination). At what point is an order not to confer with counsel too broad? See also State v. Mundon, 219 P.3d 1126, 1153–54 (Haw.2009) (rejecting *Perry* under state constitution: "[A]criminal defendant's well-settled constitutional right to the assistance of counsel does not—and should not—turn on the length of time that a trial court chooses to recess or what the defendant and his attorney choose to discuss. To the contrary, a criminal defendant has a constitutional right to confer with counsel at all stages of his case, including recesses taken during his testimony.").

8. *Sanctions.* "Sanctions for violations of sequestration orders fall into three general categories: (1) citing the witness for contempt; (2) permitting counsel or the court to comment to the jury on the witness's non-compliance as a reflection on his or her credibility; and (3) precluding the witness's testimony." People v. Melendez, 102 P.3d 315, 319 (Colo.2004). May an

accused who has failed to list a witness prior to trial, as required by applicable discovery rules, be prevented from calling that witness at trial? See Taylor v. Illinois, 484 U.S. 400 (1988) (preclusion of testimony proper under certain circumstances).

9. *"Coaching."* Where the issue is what constitutes improper coaching and tailoring of testimony, the answer may not be as easily answered as would first appear. Can a lawyer practice cross-examination with the witness? Suggest the language to be used by the witness in testimony? Can the lawyer bring to the witness' attention facts not initially mentioned by the witness but instead learned from another witness, and if upon hearing the fact the witness wishes to include it in his or her testimony, may the lawyer ethically elicit such testimony? See Opinion 79, Legal Ethics Committee of the District of Columbia Bar, 108 Daily Washington L.Rptr. 285 (1980); Ibarra v. Baker, 338 Fed.Appx. 457, 465–66 (5th Cir.2009) ("An attorney enjoys extensive leeway in preparing a witness to testify truthfully, but the attorney crosses a line when she influences the witness to alter testimony in a false or misleading way. The district court sanctioned Baker and Sanders in part for using Rodriguez to alter the officers' deposition testimony substantively.") (citation omitted); Flowers, Witness Preparation: Regulating the Profession's "Dirty Little Secret," 38 Hastings Const.L.Q. 1007 (2011); Lewis, Witness Preparation: What Is Ethical, and What Is Not, 36 Litigation 41 (Winter 2010).

(2) NARRATIVE TESTIMONY: FEDERAL RULE 611(a)

NORTHERN PAC. R.R. v. CHARLESS
United States Court of Appeals, Ninth Circuit, 1892.
51 Fed. 562.

MORROW, DISTRICT JUDGE. This action was brought by Hugh Charless, defendant in error, the plaintiff below, to recover the sum of $25,000 for damages for personal injuries alleged to have been received by him while in the employ of the Northern Pacific Railroad Company, defendant in error, as a section hand engaged at work on the line of the road at a point near Cheney, then in the territory, now in the state, of Washington. The case was tried before a jury, and the plaintiff had a verdict and judgment for $18,250 and costs. A motion for a new trial was made and denied, and thereupon the company sued out this writ of error.
* * *

* * *

It is next claimed as error that the plaintiff was allowed on the trial to make a statement in narrative form, as a witness in his own behalf, without being specially interrogated by his counsel in reference to the particular matters involved in the case; that the statement was made in such a way as to afford the defendant no opportunity of making any objection to any particular portion, and was allowed to be made over the general objection that it contained matters immaterial to the issues, and incompetent as being hearsay and not the best evidence. It appears from the record that after a few preliminary questions the plaintiff was asked the following question by his counsel: "Turn to the jury, and tell them the facts in this case, commencing at the time of your employment with the Northern Pacific Railroad Company, and tell them the complete story." To this question no objection was made. The plaintiff therefore proceeded to relate the facts in the case requested. After stating the particulars of his employment, the use of a hand car, the method of stopping it, and the breaking of one of its wheels, counsel for defendant objected to the course in which the taking of the testimony was proceeding, claiming that the witness was making a statement of matters immaterial to the issues involved in the case, and incompetent as being hearsay, and not the best evidence, and that he desired to interpose such objections, but that, owing to the fact that the testimony was being given in a narrative form, no opportunity was given counsel to properly interpose such objection. The court replied to this objection that the taking of the witness' testimony in the narrative form would be the best way of getting at what he knew or could state concerning the matter at issue; that it would save time to proceed in that way, and would perhaps furnish to the jury a more connected statement of the matter to be told as it occurred and took place. It was within the discretion of the court to allow the witness to give his testimony in a narrative form. Thomp. Trials, § 354. In general, this practice is commended by text writers. Mr. Chitty, in speaking of this method of examining witnesses, says:

> "It is certainly the practice, when the time and place of the scene of action have once been fixed, to desire the witness *to give his own account of the matter,* directing him, when not a professional person to omit, as he proceeds, account of what he has only heard from others and not seen or heard himself, and which he is apt to suppose is quite as material as that which he himself has seen."

* * *

But if, in the giving of such testimony, the witness states matters irrelevant or immaterial or incompetent as being hearsay, it is the right and duty of counsel objecting to such testimony to interpose and arrest the narrative by calling the attention of the court particularly to the objectionable matter, and by a motion to strike it out obtain a ruling of the court excluding such testimony from the case. * * * It does not appear that counsel for defendant was deprived of an opportunity to make such a motion, and the proceedings cannot be considered as error.

* * *

Judgment affirmed.

NOTES

1. *Policy.* It has long been assumed that narrative testimony is likely to result in a more complete presentation of the facts, a consideration which, if true, would go far to outweigh the objections to such testimony noted in the principal case. See Wigmore, The Science of Judicial Proof § 264 (3d ed. 1937). The traditional assumption, however, may be a questionable one. See Marshall, Marquis & Oskamp, Effects of Kind of Question and Atmosphere of Interrogation in Accuracy and Completeness of Testimony, 84 Harv.L.Rev. 1620 (1971); Tanford, An Introduction to Trial Law, 51 Mo.L.Rev. 623 (1986).

2. *Federal cases.* See United States v. Pless, 982 F.2d 1118, 1123 (7th Cir.1992) ("Fed. R. Evid. 611(a) provides district judges with authority to allow testimony in narrative form rather than as answers to specific questions."); United States v. Garcia, 625 F.2d 162, 169 (7th Cir.1980) ("[T]here is * * * nothing particularly unusual, or incorrect, in a procedure of letting a witness relate pertinent information in a narrative form as long as it stays within the bounds of pertinency and materiality."). Despite this discretion, many judges require that counsel ask specific questions because of the opportunity that such a format gives to the opposing party to object. See discussion in Tanford, The Trial Process 336 (1983). An objection to narrative testimony is likely to be effective only where counsel can suggest some real prospect of harm that cannot be cured by striking testimony and instructing the jury to disregard or where testimony may concern a matter inadmissible on constitutional grounds. See 1 McCormick, Evidence § 5 (7th ed. 2013); Tanford, note 1, supra, at 665.

3. *Other "objections."* Numerous common objections are not based on any Federal Rule: (1) argumentative questions, (2) asked and answered, (3) assuming facts not in evidence, (4) misleading questions, (5) compound questions, and (6) nonresponsive answers. The entire catalog of possible objections to the form of questions is discussed in Denbeaux & Risinger, Questioning Questions: Objections to Form in the Interrogation of Witnesses, 33 Ark.L.Rev. 439 (1980).

(3) LEADING QUESTIONS: FEDERAL RULE 611(C)

STATE V. DIAR
Supreme Court of Ohio, 2008.
900 N.E.2d 565.

O'CONNOR, J.

On the morning of August 27, 2003, a fire seriously damaged the Lorain, Ohio home of defendant-appellant, Nicole Diar. The body of her four-year-old son, Jacob Diar, was found in the bedroom. Subsequent investigation determined that gasoline was used to start the fire and that Jacob had been killed before the fire began.

Diar was convicted of the aggravated murder of Jacob and was sentenced to death. For the following reasons, we affirm Diar's convictions but reverse the death sentence and remand the cause for a new mitigation hearing.

* * *

The prosecutor also asked [Detective] Garcia a series of leading questions in establishing a possible reason that Diar had moved her car across the street on the night before the fire:

"Q: All right. Now, the fire was in the house, correct?

"A: That is correct.

"Q: And the person, Nicole Diar, who started that fire, wouldn't know how far—

"Mr. Bradley (defense counsel): Objection.

"Q:—the fire might—

"The Court: Sustained.

"Q: I'm, sorry. The person who started the fire wouldn't know, number one, how long it would take the fire department to get there; would that be a fair statement?

"A: Yes.

"Q: And therefore, wouldn't know how far that fire might spread; would that be a fair statement?

"A: Yes.

"Q: And wouldn't know that that fire might leapfrog into the garage and destroy her prize possession of the car, correct?

"Mr. Bradley: Objection, leading.

"The Court: Well, leading, correct.

"Q: Right?

"The Court: Sustained.

"Q: At any rate, there's no predictability to what a fire might do until it's put out * * *, correct?

"A: Yes.

"Q: Could have gone into the garage, correct?

"A: It could have.

"Q: And if her car had been in there, her prize possession, it would have been destroyed, correct?

"A: Yes.

"Q: So very conveniently, she just happened to hide it someplace else the night * * * before this particular fire, correct?

"A: Correct."

The prosecutor's leading questions suggested that Diar moved her car across the street so that it would not be destroyed after she started the fire. The prosecutor committed misconduct by continuing to ask leading questions after the trial court had sustained objections to such questioning. See State v. LaMar, 95 Ohio St.3d 181, 2002–Ohio–2128, 767 N.E.2d 166, ¶ 149. However, such misconduct did not pervade the trial to such a degree that there was a denial of due process. Compare State v. Keenan (1993), 66 Ohio St.3d 402, 410, 613 N.E.2d 203. Other compelling evidence was presented at trial that established Diar's guilt, and there is no reason to believe that the outcome of the trial was affected by the prosecutor's improper questioning.

* * *

NOTES AND QUESTIONS

1. *Rationale.* See Stine v. Marathon Oil, 976 F.2d 254, 266 (5th Cir.1992) ("We urge the trial court * * * to limit the use of leading questions to non-controversial or background areas—leading questions must not be allowed in controverted substantive areas where the jury must weigh the evidence and make credibility determinations. As we all are fully aware, any good trial advocate who is allowed leading questions can both testify for the witness and argue the client's case by the use of leading questions. This practice must not be allowed."); Fed.R.Evid. 611 advisory committee's note ("The rule continues the traditional view that the suggestive powers of the leading question are as a general proposition undesirable.").

2. *Exceptions.* Rule 611(c) contains a general prohibition against leading questions "except as necessary to develop the witness's testimony." As was the case at common law, the issue is left clearly within the discretion of the trial judge. Leading questions are permitted in a variety of circumstances. See United States v. Grassrope, 342 F.3d 866, 869 (8th Cir.2003) ("It is not uncommon that the precise physiological details of sexual assault must be elicited by focused questioning. We have repeatedly upheld the use of leading questions to develop the testimony of sexual assault victims, particularly children."); United States v. Salameh, 152 F.3d 88, 128 (2d Cir.1998) ("The challenged question was necessary to develop Igiri's testimony and elicit information from a nervous witness."); United States v. Goodlow, 105 F.3d 1203, 1207 (8th Cir.1997) (witness suffering from mental

retardation); United States v. Ajmal, 67 F.3d 12, 16 (2d Cir.1995) ("a non-English speaking witness testifying through a translator").

3. *Sanction.* At the trial level the prohibition against leading questions may preclude the admission of evidence. A good attorney, however, will often merely rephrase the question and the witness, now alerted by the suggestion, will provide the desired information. Is the purpose of the rule adequately served by sustaining an objection to the suggestive question?

What if counsel does not stop? United States v. Gant, 487 F.2d 30, 35 (10th Cir.1973), had occasion to rule on the question:

> Counsel for Gant also argues that the trial court should have prevented the attorney for codefendant Doyle from asking excessive leading questions. From the record it appears that a genuine effort was made by the trial court to prevent this and the judge finally gave up, apparently being of the opinion that counsel for Doyle was unable to ask a question which was not leading.[29] We are at a loss to know what a trial court can do when faced with this condition. The judge sought to prevent it and to help the attorney, and he did everything short of taking over the examination himself. We fail to see this as a source of error on the judge's part, and we fail also to see that there was any prejudice to the appellant arising from this.

See also United States v. Meza–Urtado, 351 F.3d 301, 303 (7th Cir.2003) ("[A]n objection to a question as 'leading' is only an objection to the 'form' of the question. If an objection is offered and sustained, the examiner simply rephrases the question and draws the desired information from the witness. Any reasonably good lawyer worth his salt can accomplish this little trick. Without a sustained objection, an examiner would never have a chance to rephrase his question. For this reason, we think error, plain or otherwise, could never be identified in a case where only the form of a question to which no objection is made is challenged on appeal.").

Is it fair to conclude that the rule is lacking in substance? See Cleary, Evidence as a Problem in Communicating, 5 Vand.L.Rev. 277, 287 (1952).

---

[29] The trial court reproached counsel for Rebecca Doyle as follows:

> Well look, you are just completely leading this witness, and for a day and a half I have been trying to tell you how you should do it, and, please, please, this is a sensitive area, now, don't lead the witness. Let the witness testify.

He further commented:

> I am criticizing you because you are asking her leading questions. You are testifying in effect, counsel. Let the witness testify.

Again he explained:

> Well now you are leading her. Do you know what a leading question is?

And again:

> * * * you don't put words in her mouth. I have told you and told you and told you.

Finally, in response to an objection by counsel, for defendant-appellant, that the questions were still leading, the trial judge acknowledged:

> I know it, but he can't do it any differently. Go on.

TYPES OF LEADING QUESTIONS

1. *Leading questions defined.* Leading questions are ones that suggest the answer, and they are often less obvious than the ones in the principal case. For instance, the inflection of the voice could turn a neutral question into a leading question.

2. *Yes or no answer.* A question that calls for a "yes" or "no" answer "may or may not be leading." See 3 Wigmore, Evidence § 772(1), at 164 (Chadbourn rev. 1970); State v. Scott, 149 P.2d 152, 153 (Wash.1944) ("Even though the question may call for a yes or a no answer, it is not leading for that reason, unless it is so worded that, by permitting the witness to answer yes or no, he would be testifying in the language of the interrogator rather than in his own.").

3. *Alternative forms.* A question put in the alternative form may nevertheless be leading. See Wigmore, note 2, supra, § 772(2), at 164 ("The alternative form of question ('State whether or not you said that you refused,' 'Did you or did you not refuse?') is free from this defect of form, because both affirmative and negative answers are presented for the witness' choice. Nevertheless, such a question may become leading, in so far as it rehearses lengthy details which the witness might not otherwise have mentioned, and thus supplies him with full suggestions which he incorporates without any effort, by the simple answer, 'I did,' or 'I did not.' Accordingly, the sound view is that such a question may or may not be improper, according to the amount of palpably suggestive detail which it embodies.").

4. *Conduct.* Accompanying conduct may make a question leading. See United States v. Warf, 529 F.2d 1170, 1173–74 (5th Cir.1976) ("[W]ithout Hartman's testimony it was * * * a very dubious identification * * *. The prosecutor assisted Hartman both verbally and by pointing. The explanation made to the District Court that he was pointing at the table where Warf was seated rather than at Warf individually is no explanation at all. The trial judge's statement that Hartman would have picked out Warf eventually was speculative, and, in any event, delay or indecision by Hartman in making an identification might have diminished the effect of his testimony.").

UNITED STATES V. BROWN
United States Court of Appeals, First Circuit, 1979.
603 F.2d 1022.

BOWNES, CIRCUIT JUDGE.

Defendant-appellant, John T. Brown, appeals from a jury conviction of stealing sixteen birds in violation of 18 U.S.C.A. § 659 and 18 U.S.C.A. § 2. [Appellant assigned several errors on appeal, among them the District Court's permitting one Jerome Proulx to be examined as a hostile witness.] * * *

* * * The government here had to prove beyond a reasonable doubt that on or about April 27, 1977, the defendant stole sixteen birds worth more than $100 from the Delta Airlines air freight terminal at Logan Airport which had been shipped from Virginia to Massachusetts. The evidence, which has a Damon Runyon flavor, viewed from the government's vantage, was as follows. Nancy Pancoast who, along with her husband, operates Blue Ridge Aviaries in Lowesville, Virginia, received an order from a pet store in Somerville, Massachusetts, called Big Fish Little Fish for eight male and four female cockatiels and one yellow headed Amazon parrot. A cockatiel is a small Australian parrot. The value of the birds was in excess of $100.

Appellant and two friends, Roland Coyne and Jerome Proulx, went to Big Fish Little Fish sometime during the evening of April 27, 1977. Proulx was a frequent visitor to the store and was called Gerry the Canary. While at the store, appellant was in a position to hear a clerk, Lester Thomson, acknowledge a telephone message from Delta Airlines that a shipment of birds addressed to the store had arrived at the airport. The clerk put the information down on paper and then called the owner of the store and repeated the message. Appellant was also in a position to hear this. The message could be understood to state that the birds were cockatoos, a variety of parrot, described accurately, if not scientifically, at the trial as the kind that sits on Baretta's shoulder in the TV show of the same name. A cockatoo is much larger and more expensive than a cockatiel. Appellant sometime later asked Proulx if he would be interested in some cockatoos and said that he would have no trouble picking them up.

After leaving the store, the three men, accompanied by Proulx's wife, went to appellant's home from where he made a phone call. Appellant then suggested to Proulx and his wife that they take a ride with him and his wife to the airport. On the way, appellant borrowed $20 from Proulx. Coyne did not go to the airport. At the airport, appellant, his wife, and Proulx's wife got out of the station wagon and went into one of the buildings. When they returned, appellant had a box with him that he put in the back of the station wagon. Appellant laughed all the way home. Proulx testified that he did not see what was in the box or hear any chirping.

* * *

Based on the evidence, the jury could find beyond a reasonable doubt that appellant overheard at least one of the telephone conversations relative to the arrival of the birds at Delta's air freight terminal. There was evidence from which it could find that appellant decided to steal the birds and that he called Delta to confirm the shipment and ascertain the shipping charges. There is little question that appellant went to the airport and picked up a box there. The jury was not bound to believe Proulx's testimony that he did not see what was in the box or hear any chirping; * * * Proulx, the chief witness for the government, was a hesitant, confused and very reluctant witness, but the jury had the right to pick and choose from what he said, and he said enough to make the picking and choosing easy. * * *

* * *

3.   Whether the District Court Abused Its Discretion in Ruling That Jerome Proulx Should Be Treated As Hostile Pursuant to Federal Rule of Evidence 611(c).

It has long been established that in the use of leading questions "much must be left to the sound discretion of the trial judge who sees the witness and can, therefore, determine in the interest of truth and justice whether the circumstances justify leading questions to be propounded to a witness by the party producing him." St. Clair v. United States, 154 U.S. 134, 150 (1894). * * *

The record does not bear out appellant's contention that witness Proulx was not adverse, evasive or hostile. Proulx and appellant were close friends. The evidence strongly suggests that Proulx was a participant in the crime. His testimony is replete with lapses of memory attributed to alcohol and drugs. He stressed several times his susceptibility to suggestion by the last person who talks to him. Appellant talked to Proulx at length about the case right up to the trial. While Proulx was not hostile in the sense of being contemptuous or surly, he was both evasive and adverse to the government.

It is true that the prosecutor did not move to have Proulx declared a hostile witness. This was a decision made by the court on its own initiative, but only after a lengthy direct examination (twenty-five transcript pages) during which all leading questions were excluded. It had become painfully clear that the district court was faced with a witness whose apparent lapses of memory, failure to understand what he had said or written on prior occasions, as well as the questions asked and his general air of confusion, made his testimony prolix and difficult to comprehend. The trial judge had a duty to see to it that the case be tried with reasonable dispatch and that the testimony of Proulx be presented as coherently as possible. We find no abuse of discretion in the ruling by the district judge that the prosecutor be allowed to use leading questions in his remaining direct examination of Proulx. * * *

Affirmed.

NOTES

1.   *Another example.* United States v. Meza–Urtado, 351 F.3d 301, 303 (7th Cir.2003) (The leading questions "all were necessary as Farias obviously became conveniently 'forgetful' despite his agreement to help the government. In this situation, had the government asked, he could have been treated as a hostile witness and asked leading questions until the cows came home.").

2.   *Witnesses identified with adverse parties.* Leading questions are also permitted in examining a "witness identified with an adverse party." See Chonich v. Wayne County Community College, 874 F.2d 359, 368 (6th Cir.1989) ("court designated Drs. Waters and Callaghan [employees], as witnesses identified with an adverse party under F.R.E. 611(c) and allowed plaintiffs' counsel to use leading questions on direct examination"); United States v. Hicks, 748 F.2d 854, 859 (4th Cir.1984) ("permitting government to ask two leading questions of girlfriend, who was called as a government witness"); United States v. Tsui, 646 F.2d 365, 368 (9th Cir.1981) ("Tsui argues that he should have been allowed to ask leading questions of [IRS] investigator Ono as an adverse witness. There is some merit to this contention.").

(4) REFRESHING RECOLLECTION: FEDERAL RULE 612

WARD v. MORR TRANSFER & STORAGE CO.

Kansas City Court of Appeals, Missouri, 1906.
95 S.W. 964.

ELLISON, J. The defendant is a general storage and warehouse company in Kansas City, Mo., and the plaintiff, then residing at that place, on March 11, 1903, stored with it a lot of household goods, which she charged it with converting, and brought this action for conversion. She prevailed in the trial court by a judgment for $434.75.

[The court here concluded that certain errors in the instructions of the trial court to the jury necessitated a new trial of the action.]

There were a number of objections to evidence made by the defendant during the trial. * * * There was one much insisted upon, which arose in different forms. It involved the right of the plaintiff to refer to a list of the articles which she claimed were stored with defendant. Her receipt from defendant named, among other things, boxes, barrels, and tubs. These were filled with a great variety of articles of household goods and kitchen ware. The list was not made at the time she packed them, nor at the time she delivered them to defendant. It was made on separate pieces of paper at different times, when the article or articles would come into her memory as being a part of the goods stored. She said, "Just as I would remember things I would jot them down." Before the trial she arranged these various memoranda, thus made, in an orderly way, and had them copied into one list on a typewriter. It made a list of two or three pages of printed matter. It was from the list thus made she proposed using, not as evidence to be read to the jury, but to look at in the course of her testimony in order to bring different articles to her memory. On objection to the typewritten list, she was permitted by the court to use the original slips made by her. These were also objected to.

We think it was proper for her to use either the typewritten list or the slips for that purpose. Either reminded her of things to which and about which she testified, just as anything else may bring to the mind of an individual a fact, distinctly remembered as a fact, when once the mind was brought to bear upon it. The memoranda, in such case, are not evidence; but the memory of the witness is. * * * It is a case of testimony from knowledge and present memory, and it is of no consequence, so far as being admissible is concerned, what circumstance or train of circumstances brought about a recollection. Every one knows what trivial incidents will cause immediate consciousness of matters of which one was temporarily unconscious. It is the right of the opposite party to cross-examine as to how a witness comes to remember anything to which he has testified. * * *

The judgment will be reversed and cause remanded. All concur.

NOTES AND QUESTIONS

1.   *What may be used to refresh memory?* One court said "a song, a face, or a newspaper item," Jewett v. United States, 15 F.2d 955, 956 (9th Cir.1926), may be the source of the awakened memory, while another court pointed out that it "may be a line from Kipling or the dolorous strain of the 'Tennessee Waltz'; a whiff of hickory smoke; the running of the fingers across a swatch of corduroy; the sweet carbonation of a chocolate soda; [or] the sight of a faded snapshot in a long-neglected album." Baker v. State, 371 A.2d 699, 705 (Md.Ct.Spec.App.1977). See also Kenai Chrysler Center, Inc. v. Denison, 167 P.3d 1240, 1253 (Alaska 2007) ("Under this rule, a document need not be admissible to be used to refresh a witness's memory.").

2.   *Problematic procedure.* In N.L.R.B. v. Federal Dairy Co., 297 F.2d 487, 489 (1st Cir.1962), the court took strong exception to the proposition that any writing whatsoever may be used for the purpose of refreshing recollection:

>[W]e must express disapproval of the advocated practice of preparing a written account for the purpose of testifying under the principle that "anything" may be used to refresh recollection. This is, of course, not to say that when recollection is exhausted a witness may not be shown a paper. But he should not bring into court specially prepared extensive testimonial notes to use over objection instead of the original records. One may well ask why

there should be strictures against leading questions if a witness is free to have a prepared answer before him in any event.

But see United States v. Church, 970 F.2d 401, 409 (7th Cir.1992) (approving district court's decision to permit a government informant to testify while referring to notes prepared by government agent who interviewed him after his undercover drug buys).

3. *What is the evidence?* As noted in the principal case, "[t]he memoranda, in such case, are not evidence; but the memory of the witness is." Thus, the writing is not admissible if offered by the proponent. See Aponte–Rivera v. DHL Solutions (USA), Inc., 650 F.3d 803, 812 (1st Cir.2011) ("Aponte's counsel instructed her, 'Don't read the documents. Just read the documents for yourself, and if that refreshes your recollection, tell the jury what * * * did you do to receive the commendations?' Aponte then described what she did to receive a commendation in each instance.").

4. *Cross-examination.* Rule 612(b) provides that "an adverse party is entitled to have the writing produced at the hearing, to inspect it, to cross-examine the witness about it, and to introduce in evidence any portion that relates to the witness's testimony." See also Kenai Chrysler Center, Inc. v. Denison, 167 P.3d 1240, 1253 (Alaska 2007) ("Kenai Chrysler had the opportunity to inspect the rate quote and to use it as a basis for impeaching Goodman during cross-examination.").

NOTES ON RIGHT OF INSPECTION

1. *Policy.* What is the rationale for a right of inspection?

2. *Pretrial refreshment.* Few trial attorneys will call a crucial witness to the stand for direct examination without first having had the witness "refresh her recollection" by reading over her previous statements as the attorney possesses. The version of Rule 612 originally proposed by the drafting committee adopted the growing minority state view that such writings, even though used for refreshment only out of court, should be available to the cross-examiner as of right. The final version of the rule makes the matter one for judicial discretion. Even so limited, the rule has demonstrated a potential for invasion of the traditionally protected "work product" area. See 1 McCormick, Evidence § 9 (7th ed. 2013) ("[T]he clear trend in the federal cases has been to hold that Rule 612 overrides all privileges claims, at least when the witness consulted the passage in the writing pretrial for the precise purpose of freshening his memory in order to testify.").

3. *Verbal refreshment.* What if the form of the matter used to refresh is not susceptible to inspection by anyone, court or adversary? See State v. Schmelz, 111 A.2d 50 (N.J.1955) (witness refreshing recollection by speaking on the telephone during trial recess).

4. *Jencks Act.* 18 U.S.C.A. § 3500, referenced in Federal Rule 612, is known as the Jencks Act. Generally, it provides that the pretrial statement of

a prosecution witness need not be disclosed to the defense until after direct examination. Federal Criminal Rules 26.2 and 17(h) have supplanted the statute.

RUSH V. ILLINOIS CENT. R. CO.

United States Court of Appeals, Sixth Circuit, 2005.
399 F.3d 705.

ECONOMUS, DISTRICT JUDGE.

* * *

This appeal arises from a diversity action brought by the plaintiff-appellant, Annette Rush, following her nine-year-old son's fall from a railcar owned and operated by the defendant-appellee, Illinois Central Railroad Company ("CN–IC"). * * *

[Nine-years-old Johnathan Rush and several friends, including Doyle Lockett (age 10) and Justin Moore (age 8) began playing near a CN–IC train. At some point Rush fell under the train and sustained injuries that ultimately required a below-the-knee amputation of his left leg. Within several hours of the accident, a Risk Manager and Railroad Police Officer for CN–IC, interviewed Lockett and Moore. Each purportedly stated that Rush fell while attempting to jump onto a moving train. These statements were audio-recorded and later transcribed.]

* * *

The plaintiff-appellant contends that the district court erroneously permitted defense counsel to cross-examine Lockett and Moore with the interview transcripts. CN–IC counters that it utilized the interview transcripts to refresh the witnesses' memory pursuant to Rule 612 of the Federal Rules of Evidence.

Rule 612 of the Federal Rules of Evidence authorizes a party to refresh a witness's memory with a writing so long as the "adverse party is entitled to have the writing produced at the hearing, to inspect it, to cross-examine the witness thereon, and to introduce in evidence those portions which relate to the testimony of the witness." Fed. R. Evid. 612.
* * *

* * * While we have authorized the use of leading questions to establish a witness's lack of memory as to a particular event, we have cautioned that the trial court may abuse its discretion when otherwise inadmissible evidence is introduced to the jury through the guise of refreshing a witness's recollection. * * * Defense counsel's question demonstrated that he failed to understand the impropriety of attempting to refresh Lockett's recollection by incorporating into his question the otherwise inadmissible contents of the writing—i.e, that "Johnathan was running alongside the train to get on."

Lockett's subsequent testimony exacerbated the potential evidentiary error caused by defense counsel's improper question. After silently reading the interview transcript,[30] Lockett testified that his memory was refreshed and that the writing accurately reflected his prior statements. See (Tr., Vol. I at 52). He then read aloud from the interview transcript whereby the jury heard his prior statement that "Johnathan was running alongside the train trying to get on." See (Tr., Vol. I at 53); (Tr. Ex. #1). However, Rule 612 requires a witness whose memory has been refreshed to testify from his present recollection, rather than to merely restate the contents of the writing.[31] * * * Faulkner, 538 F.2d at 727 ("[C]aution must be exercised to insure that the document is not used to put words into the mouth of the witness."). See also 4 Weinstein's Federal Evidence § 612.02[2] ("Rule 612 is intended to curb the false memory that might occur when a witness who purports to testify based on a refreshed recollection merely parrots the contents of the writing.") (citing Hall v. American Bakeries Co., 873 F.2d 1133, 1136 (8th Cir. 1989)).

It is the witness's present refreshed recollection—as opposed to the contents of the writing used to refresh memory—that is the substantive evidence of the matter at issue. * * *

It follows that defense counsel's attempt to use Lockett's out of court statements as substantive evidence of the manner in which the accident occurred is governed by the rules of evidence addressing the use of hearsay. * * * CN–IC contends on appeal that Lockett's prior, out of court statements were admissible pursuant to the recorded recollection hearsay exception of Rule 803(5). * * *

CN–IC misplaces its reliance on the recollection recorded exception to the hearsay rule. Rule 803(5) allows a document to be read to the jury as a past recollection recorded if "(1) the witness once had knowledge about the facts in the document; (2) the witness now has insufficient memory to testify about the matters in the document; and (3) the document was recorded at a time when the matters were fresh in the witness's mind and the document correctly reflects the witness's knowledge of the matters." United States v. Smith, 197 F.3d 225, 231 (6th Cir. 1999) * * *. Under CN–IC's application of the recorded recollection exception, the interview transcript served to stand in the place of Lockett's "insufficient memory" of the accident. However, Lockett provided detailed and lengthy

---

[30] Defense counsel immediately requested Lockett to read the transcript in front of the jury. The district court intervened and instructed: "No, I don't want him to read anything out loud just yet. I want him to look at that and determine whether or not he recalls being asked those questions and giving those answers." (Tr., Vol. I at 51.)

[31] We recognize that there are limited circumstances in which the witness may refer to the writing used to refresh recollection while testifying, such as where the witness "is asked to testify about detailed or lengthy matters," 4 Weinstein's Federal Evidence § 612.04[4][a] (citations omitted), or where the testimony pertains to matters that occurred during the relatively distant past.

testimony at trial regarding the events prior to, during, and immediately following the accident. It therefore would be erroneous to conclude that Lockett had "insufficient memory to testify about the matters" in the interview transcript. * * * Accordingly, the past recollection recorded exception to the hearsay rule is wholly inapplicable to Lockett's prior statements regarding the accident.

NOTES AND QUESTIONS

1. *Lack of memory requirement.* Courts often state that a witness' recollection must be totally exhausted before she is to be permitted to look at a writing to refresh her recollection. Furthermore, many courts similarly state that a witness, once having stated that her recollection is refreshed by a writing, must testify independently of it. See 1 McCormick, Evidence § 9 (7th ed. 2013). What about the witness who can remember some portions of a long list of events but not the details without reference to notes? Courts in fact exercise considerable flexibility with regard to such testimony. See, e.g., United States v. Rinke, 778 F.2d 581 (10th Cir.1985) (permissible to use notes even though witness had some recollection of events); Bankers Trust Co. v. Publicker Industries, Inc., 641 F.2d 1361 (2d Cir.1981) (permissible to refer to chronology of events as long as not used as script). What latitude should be given expert witnesses such as physicians who may have to recall a large number of patients with complex histories? What about police officers?

2. *Recorded recollection distinguished.* The principal case discusses the distinction between refreshing recollectioin (Rule 612) and the hearsay exception for recorded recollection (Rule 803(5)), which is treated in Chapter 14, Section D, infra. For an able opinion distinguishing the two doctrines, see United States v. Riccardi, 174 F.3d 883 (3d Cir.1949).

BORAWICK V. SHAY

United States Court of Appeals, Second Circuit, 1995.
68 F.3d 597.

WALKER, CIRCUIT JUDGE:

* * *

Borawick, who is currently thirty-eight years old and a citizen of California, brought a diversity tort action alleging that her aunt and uncle, Christine and Morrie Shay, Connecticut citizens, sexually abused her in the summers of 1961 and 1964, when she visited them at their home at the ages of four and seven, respectively. At the time, she lived in Seattle. Borawick had no memory of the alleged abuse for more than twenty years.

During the fall of 1984, Borawick began to experience panic attacks. [When they continued, she received psychological treatment. She also received treatment] for chronic physical illness with Dr. Ronald Peters, a medical doctor and part owner of the Pacific Medical Center ("PMC") in Santa Monica, California. PMC's clientele was largely composed of people from the entertainment industry.

After reviewing Borawick's medical history of chronic illness, Dr. Peters referred Borawick to Valerian St. Regis, a hypnotist who worked under Peters's supervision, since "problems in childhood" sometimes cause chronic illness and are susceptible to recall through hypnosis. Borawick underwent twelve to fourteen hypnotic sessions with St. Regis from the summer of 1987 through the fall of 1988. Before and immediately following these sessions, she had no recollection of abuse, much less of any abuse by these defendants.

When deposed in 1993, St. Regis testified that he had no permanent records relating to the hypnosis of Borawick; however, prior to his deposition, he had read a portion of Borawick's deposition. St. Regis maintained that, before hypnotizing Borawick, he had no expectation of the type of information that the hypnosis would reveal. He explained that he used "regression therapy" to take Borawick back to the age of between three and five years old. St. Regis also testified that, in general, instead of using hypnotic suggestion with Borawick, he asked broad questions such as "what happened?," "what do you remember?," or "what do you recall?."

St. Regis testified that Borawick revealed under hypnosis that her aunt, defendant Christine Shay, persuaded Borawick, at age four, to strip and engage in "ritual dancing." St. Regis further stated that during hypnosis Borawick described anal object penetration by Christine Shay, as well as another incident in which her aunt inserted a "cap pistol in [Borawick's] vagina." St. Regis also testified that during hypnotic sessions, Borawick disclosed that her uncle, defendant Morrie Shay, anally raped her. St. Regis did not know whether the alleged anal rape involved penile insertion or object insertion.

St. Regis testified that he did not reveal to Borawick what she had described during the sessions, because, in his opinion, such revelations would have been "devastating" and would probably surface in time. Borawick attended her last session with St. Regis in the fall of 1988.

Borawick testified in her deposition that during the second week of February, 1989, several months after her final hypnotic session, she experienced her first non-hypnotic memory of sexual abuse by her father, who is not a defendant in this case. Following this initial recollection, according to Borawick, subsequent memories surfaced in "bits and pieces." Her first memory concerning defendant Christine Shay allegedly occurred on February 10, 1989. On that date, Borawick first recalled her aunt vaginally raping her with a pistol. In late 1990 or early 1991, she first remembered an incident when Christine Shay forced "a broomstick into [Borawick's] vagina." Borawick also stated that she regained memory of being naked in the presence of her aunt and "having to dance around."

Borawick testified that her memory of being anally raped by defendant Morrie Shay surfaced in 1990. In addition to recalling sexual abuse by her father, aunt, and uncle, Borawick also claims sexual abuse by numerous others, including family members and her father's friends. More detailed references to these individuals and their various "rituals" and other alleged abusive conduct are described in the sealed portion of the appendix.

* * * On November 4, 1992, defendants filed a motion in limine seeking to exclude the plaintiff's testimony. [The motion was subsequently granted.]

* * *

I.   Admissibility of Post–Hypnotic Testimony

This circuit has yet to address the admissibility of post-hypnotic testimony of memories elicited as a result of hypnosis. While numerous state and federal courts have considered this issue, nearly all of them dealt with recall in the context of hypnosis that was specifically intended to enhance a memory of a particular known or suspected occurrence. The parties have not cited, nor are we aware of, any case concerning the specific issue before us: the admissibility of testimony about memories of childhood sexual abuse that are recalled for the first time in adulthood following the use of hypnosis as part of psychotherapy.

* * *

D.   What is Hypnosis?

While "[t]here is no single, generally accepted theory of hypnosis, [or] consensus about a single definition," Council on Scientific Affairs, "Scientific Status of Refreshing Recollection by the Use of Hypnosis," 253 JAMA 1918, 1919 (1985) [hereinafter, Scientific Affairs], " 'there is considerable consensus at the descriptive level' as to how the [phenomenon] manifests itself in the hypnotized individual," 27 Charles A. Wright & Victor J. Gold, Federal Practice and Procedure: Evidence § 6011, at 116 (1990) * * * The American Medical Association has described hypnosis as a

> temporary condition of altered attention in the subject which may be induced by another person and in which a variety of phenomena may appear spontaneously or in response to [verbal] or other stimuli. These phenomena include alterations in consciousness and memory, increased susceptibility to suggestion, and the production in the subject of responses and ideas unfamiliar to him in his usual state of mind.

People v. Zayas, 131 Ill.2d 284, 137 Ill.Dec. 568, 546 N.E.2d 513, 515–16 (1989) (alteration in original) (quotations omitted).

As early as 1958, the American Medical Association recognized hypnosis as a valid therapeutic technique. Council on Medical Health of the American Medical Association, "Medical Uses of Hypnosis," 168 JAMA 186, 187 (1958). It has been found useful in psychotherapy, in the treatment of psychosomatic illness, to alleviate pain or as a substitute for anesthesia, and for memory recall. * * * It has sometimes been useful in developing leads in criminal investigations. *See Harker v. Maryland,* 800 F.2d 437, 440 (4th Cir.1986) * * * Despite these successes, many in the field remain skeptical of the reliability of hypnosis as a technique for refreshing or restoring memory. * * * Empirical studies calling into question the ability of hypnosis to restore memory effectively have engendered "considerable controversy" concerning the validity of using hypnosis for that purpose. Scientific Affairs, *supra,* at 1918. Thus, "[t]he popular belief that hypnosis guarantees the accuracy of recall is as yet without established foundation," *Rock v. Arkansas,* 483 U.S. 44, 59 (1987), and no consensus has been reached regarding the ability of hypnosis to enhance memory, Scientific Affairs, *supra,* at 1918.

The controversy over the effectiveness of hypnosis in memory enhancement centers in large part on disagreements concerning theories of memory. Those scientists who are most optimistic about the role of hypnosis in memory recall conceptualize a process whereby the brain records and stores sensory input accurately, much like a videotape. Recall is the ability to "play back" that tape, and loss of memory is the inability to retrieve that information. [Citations omitted.] Under this theory, hypnosis simply enhances the retrieval process.

Many scientists reject this theory, however. They view memory recall as "much more complex and much less accurate than previously thought." *State v. Tuttle,* 780 P.2d 1203, 1210 (Utah 1989) * * * Instead, they espouse a "construction theory" of memory, which holds that a memory is formed and influenced by numerous factors when the mind creates and integrates the information from an event "into the memory representation of that event." *Valdez,* 722 F.2d at 1200. The composite created by this process is malleable and evolves over time as additional input is received. In fact, a leading proponent of this theory has written that memory is " 'being continually remade [and] reconstructed in the interest of the present.' " F. Bartlett, Remembering 213 (reprint 1964) (1932) * * *.

The "constructivists" are highly skeptical of any view that hypnosis can effectively and accurately enhance memory. They believe that because hypnosis has the power to contribute to memory reconstruction, it can create inaccurate memories. In other words, if present events can contribute to a construction of a memory that differs from that which was originally perceived and if the process of hypnosis is such an event, then hypnosis may distort memory.

The courts have identified several problems with the reliability of hypnotically-refreshed recall. First, a person undergoing hypnosis becomes more susceptible to suggestion. The subject may be influenced by verbal and nonverbal cues, intentionally or unintentionally planted by the hypnotist. This suggestibility may be enhanced by the perception that hypnosis will refresh one's memory and by a wish to please the hypnotist. * * *

In addition, a hypnotized person may "confabulate," that is, fill in the gaps in her memory to make it comprehensible. The added details may be derived from irrelevant or unrelated facts or from pure fantasy. * * * Like suggestibility, confabulation can occur as a result of the subject's desire to please the hypnotist by coming up with complete and coherent memories. * * *

A third problem with hypnotically-refreshed recall is "memory hardening," a phenomenon which gives the subject enhanced confidence in the facts remembered, whether they be true or false. * * * Even as inaccurate recollections increase, the subject's confidence is likely to remain constant or even to increase. * * * The lack of correlation between the accuracy of recall and the subject's confidence in the accuracy makes it more difficult for a jury or even an expert to judge the credibility of hypnotically-enhanced testimony, * * * and makes cross-examination difficult * * *.

Finally, after undergoing hypnosis to refresh memory, individuals may lose the ability to assess their memory critically and be more prone to speculation than if they had relied only on normal memory recall. * * * The subject becomes less able "to discriminate between accurate and inaccurate recollections." Scientific Affairs, *supra,* at 1921. He or she may also experience "source amnesia," believing that a statement heard prior to hypnosis was a product of his or her own memory. * * *

As a result of the foregoing phenomena, the "hypnotically recalled memory is apt to be a mosaic of (1) appropriate actual events, (2) entirely irrelevant actual events, (3) pure fantasy, and (4) fantasized details supplied to make a logical whole." Bernard L. Diamond, "Inherent Problems in the Use of Pretrial Hypnosis on a Prospective Witness," 68 Cal.L.Rev. 313, 335 (1980); *see* Scientific Affairs, *supra,* at 1921. In the worst case, someone who has undergone hypnosis might "inaccurately reconstruct the memory * * * and * * * then become convinced of the absolute accuracy of the reconstruction through memory hardening." *Harker,* 800 F.2d at 441. The "constructionist" views, supported as they are in the scientific community, have considerable force. * * *

E. Various Approaches to the Admissibility Question

The state and federal courts that have been faced with the admissibility of hypnotically-refreshed testimony have followed four different approaches. Some courts treat all such testimony as per se admissible under the theory that hypnosis does not render the witness incompetent, but goes to the question of credibility. * * * This position depends in considerable part on one's faith in the jury's ability to evaluate the testimony accurately in light of cross-examination, expert testimony relating to hypnosis, and jury instructions. * * * Such an approach was particularly favored when courts were just beginning to address the admissibility of hypnotically-refreshed testimony, *see Tuttle,* 780 P.2d at 1208, but it "has sparsely been followed since 1980," *Zayas,* 137 Ill.Dec. at 571, 546 N.E.2d at 516.

Courts at the other end of the spectrum have found that post-hypnotic testimony is per se inadmissible because the witness is incompetent to testify regarding such matters. * * * The common thread running through these cases is that the possible distorting effects of hypnosis on memory are impossible to circumvent and are so substantial that "the game is not worth the candle." *Shirley,* 181 Cal.Rptr. at 256, 723 P.2d at 1366. * * * Reasoning that no safeguard can adequately ensure reliability, these courts deem the evidence inadmissible. * * * A number of courts apply a modified version of the rule by confirming the witness's testimony to matters recalled before undergoing hypnosis. * * *

In *Rock v. Arkansas,* * * * the Supreme Court reviewed Arkansas's rule that a criminal defendant's hypnotically-refreshed testimony was per se inadmissible. While the Court recognized the problems with hypnosis, it concluded that certain procedural safeguards could reduce the potential inaccuracies of post-hypnotic testimony. * * * Focusing on the due process right of criminal defendants to testify in their own defense, * * * the Sixth Amendment right to call witnesses in the defendant's favor, * * * and the Fifth Amendment guarantee against compelled testimony, * * * the Court concluded that the rule of per se inadmissibility was an "arbitrary restriction on the [criminal defendant's] right to testify in the absence of clear evidence by the State repudiating the validity of all post-hypnosis recollections," *id.* at 61 * * *. Consequently, the Court deemed Arkansas's prohibition unconstitutional. The Court, however, explicitly limited the reach of its holding by refusing to express an opinion as to the appropriate rule of admissibility "of testimony of previously hypnotized witnesses other than criminal defendants." *Id.* at 58 n.15 * * *.

The third and fourth approaches occupy a middle ground. These attempt to balance the competing concerns that animate the per se positions. The third approach, articulated by the New Jersey Supreme Court in the oft-cited *State v. Hurd,* 86 N.J. 525, 432 A.2d 86 (1981), requires adherence to a list of prescribed safeguards intended to ensure the reliability of hypnotically-refreshed testimony. The court concluded that "a rule of per se inadmissibility is unnecessarily broad and will result in the exclusion of evidence that is as trustworthy as other eyewitness testimony." *Id.,* 432 A.2d at 94.

In light of recommendations offered by a frequent expert witness, Dr. Martin Orne, the court adopted the following procedural requirements:

> First, a psychiatrist or psychologist experienced in the use of hypnosis must conduct the session. This professional should also be able to qualify as an expert in order to aid the court in evaluating the procedures followed * * *.

> Second, the professional conducting the hypnotic session should be independent of and not regularly employed by the prosecutor, investigator or defense * * *.

> Third, any information given to the hypnotist by law enforcement personnel or the defense prior to the hypnotic session must be recorded, either in writing or another suitable form * * *.

> Fourth, before inducing hypnosis the hypnotist should obtain from the subject a detailed description of the facts as the subject remembers them [without] * * * asking structured questions or adding new details.

> Fifth, all contacts between the hypnotist and the subject must be recorded * * *.

> Sixth, only the hypnotist and the subject should be present during any phase of the hypnotic session, including the pre-hypnotic testing and the post-hypnotic interview.

Id., 432 A.2d at 96–97 (footnote omitted).

* * *

Finally, the approach most frequently taken by the federal courts, Federal Practice, *supra,* § 6011, at 173, is a so-called case-by-case or totality-of-the-circumstances approach, *see, e.g., McQueen v. Garrison,* 814 F.2d 951, 958 (4th Cir.1987) * * *. While recognizing the benefits of the *Hurd* guidelines, these courts conclude that the district court should be given discretion to balance all of the factors to determine the reliability of the evidence and the probative versus prejudicial effect of the testimony. They note that even though the safeguards required by other courts

> represent[ ] the type of general reliability inquiry that must be made[,] * * * a court cannot necessarily rest solely on the reliability *vel non* of the hypnosis procedures in ruling on the

admissibility of the proffered testimony. Even though all of the *Hurd* safeguards might be employed, the defendant may still be able to demonstrate by expert testimony that a witness' memory has been irreparably distorted by hypnosis. On the other hand, even if the hypnosis procedures are flawed, a trial or appellate court might discern that a witness' testimony was nonetheless independent of the dangers associated with hypnosis.

McQueen, 814 F.2d at 958 (citations omitted). As the foregoing summary indicates, the law continues to be in a state of flux regarding the reception of hypnotically-enhanced testimony. *See* Federal Practice, *supra,* § 6011, at 123.

F.   Hypnosis as a Therap*eutic Tool*

The existing caselaw concerning the admissibility of post-hypnotic testimony, while helpful to our analysis, is grounded in fact situations where the hypnosis is specifically directed to the witness's recollections of known events, rather than where repressed memories of past traumas previously unknown simply emerge following hypnosis. Borawick, relying heavily on a law review article, Kanovitz, *supra,* at 1213,[32] argues that hypnosis functions differently and more reliably when it results in the retrieval of repressed memories of traumatic events than when it is used to refresh one's memory of eye-witnessed events and therefore testimony relating to the former should be admitted on a per se basis.

The research on hypnosis only uses subjects with normal memory function who are exposed to simulations of real-life events to "replicate eyewitness situations," *id.* at 1212, 1223, since for practical and ethical reasons, it is impossible to design effective controlled studies to test the ability of hypnosis to retrieve accurate, suppressed memories of childhood trauma, *id.* at 1221–22. The Kanovitz article sets forth some arguments in support of the view that hypnosis may be better able to retrieve memories "kept out of conscious awareness by ego-defenses that protect the psyche from trauma," *id.* at 1194, than hypnosis used for normal memory recall. In the clinical setting, hypnosis may overcome the psychological barriers to remembering past traumas because it induces profound relaxation and calmness, intensifies concentration, and focuses the subject's attention inward. *Id.* at 1213. In addition, the clinical literature "abounds with case histories of spectacular memory successes." *Id.* at 1225. Finally, repressed memories of events that have a traumatic impact upon the witness may, even if unconscious, tend to remain fixed and survive longer than memories of events witnessed quickly, in the context of a great deal of other sensory information. *Id.* at 1231–32.

---

[32] [Kanovitz, Hypnotic Memories and Civil Sexual Abuse Trials, 45 Vand.L.Rev. 1185 (1992). Ed.]

* * *

While we appreciate the force of many of these arguments, the fact remains that the literature has not yet conclusively demonstrated that hypnosis is a consistently effective means to retrieve repressed memories of traumatic, past experiences accurately. For example, the Council on Scientific Affairs has pointed out that the case histories of "spectacular memory successes" are anecdotal and difficult to verify independently and there are no controlled studies confirming these reports. Scientific Affairs, *supra,* at 1919. In addition, some in the clinical community express reservations concerning the theory of memory repression, or at least the phenomenon's prevalence. *See* Julie M. Murray, "Repression, Memory, and Suggestibility," 66 U.Colo.L.Rev. 477, 505–08 (1995). Furthermore, we are highly skeptical of the belief in the clinician's ability to "weed out most patently groundless claims" because childhood sexual abuse often "fits like a tailor-made glove" to certain psychiatric disorders. Kanovitz, *supra,* at 1242. Some therapists may be too eager to find patterns of behavior demonstrative of childhood sexual abuse. *See* Murray, 66 U.Colo.L.Rev. at 507–08. *But cf.* Colette M. Smith, "Recovered Memories of Alleged Sexual Abuse," 18 Seattle Univ.L.Rev. 51, 61 (1994) (noting that Harvard Medical School psychiatrist Judith Herman "believes that therapists rarely wield enough power over patients to impose false memories on them"). Therefore, even though there may be important distinctions between the use of hypnosis to enhance memories of witnessed events and the use of hypnosis to retrieve repressed memories, given the lack of empirical studies as to the latter and the complicated nature of hypnotically-induced recall, we are not willing to assume that the risks of suggestibility, confabulation, and memory hardening are significantly reduced when the hypnosis that triggers the testimony is used for therapeutic purposes.

G.   Totality-of-the-Circumstances Approach

Based on our review of the literature and the caselaw, we conclude that the district court was correct to reject a per se rule of admissibility or inadmissibility. A per se rule of exclusion or inclusion is too blunt a tool with which to address the concerns regarding the reliability of post-hypnotic testimony or the concerns that people who have been sexually abused may lose an opportunity to bring suit against their abusers.

To be sure, the exclusion of such testimony in every case avoids the problems of unreliability, but it ignores Federal Rule of Evidence 601, which "abolished almost all grounds for witness disqualification based on new assumptions that took a more optimistic view of witness reliability and jury perceptiveness." Federal Practice, *supra,* § 6011, at 124, 129. In addition, we believe that it risks the elimination of reliable testimony. *See State v. Iwakiri,* 106 Idaho 618, 624, 682 P.2d 571, 577 (1984).

On the other hand, to admit all such testimony without pause, even if the jury is informed of the risks of the potential problems of hypnotically-enhanced testimony, creates the danger of having a lay jury speculate as to the effects of the hypnosis in the case before it. As a result, such an approach seems to us inadequate to protect defendants from unfounded charges in either criminal or civil suits. * * * While we appreciate the care and sensitivity with which the district court chose its methodology, we nevertheless find its approach too rigid and restrictive and prefer a "totality-of-the-circumstances" approach. * * *

In conducting a case-by-case analysis, the district court should consider the following non-exclusive list of factors. First, it should evaluate the purpose of the hypnosis: whether it was to refresh a witness's memory of an accident or crime or whether it was conducted as part of therapy. In the former instance, the subject may feel pressured to remember details, to aid the criminal investigation, whereas when the subject has undergone therapy to explore the sources of her psychological ailments, she may be less inclined to confabulate or describe a complete coherent story. In the latter case, however, the court should be mindful of the possibility that the subject may have received subtle suggestions from her therapist that abuse or other traumas could be at the root of her problems. Thus, a second important consideration is whether the witness received any suggestions from the hypnotist or others prior to or during hypnosis such as a theory of the cause of the subject's ailments or key information relevant to the investigation for which she underwent hypnosis. A third and related factor is the presence or absence of a permanent record, which can help the court ascertain whether suggestive procedures were used. Ideally, the session should be videotaped or audiotaped. Fourth, a court should consider whether the hypnotist was appropriately qualified by training in psychology or psychiatry. A fifth factor is whether corroborating evidence exists to support the reliability of the hypnotically-refreshed memories. Sixth, evidence of the subject's hypnotizability may also be relevant. A highly hypnotizable subject may be more prone to confabulate and more susceptible to suggestion. Seventh, the court should consider any expert evidence offered by the parties as to the reliability of the procedures used in the case. Finally, a pretrial evidentiary hearing is highly desirable to enable the parties to present expert evidence and to test credibility through cross-examination.

After consideration of all of the relevant circumstances, the trial court should weigh the factors in favor and against the reliability of the hypnosis procedure in the exercise of its discretion whether to admit the post-hypnotic testimony. Finally, we add that the party attempting to admit the hypnotically-enhanced testimony bears the burden of persuading the district court that the balance tips in favor of admissibility. *Hurd,* 432 A.2d at 97.

H. Application of Admissibility Approach to this Case

* * * Since in our view the factors before the district court weighed decisively against the admissibility of Borawick's testimony, we are convinced that if the district court had followed our test, it would have necessarily reached the same conclusion. We see no point in remanding the case so that the district court can reach the same finding.

First, Borawick's assertions notwithstanding, it is beyond question that St. Regis lacked adequate professional qualifications as a hypnotist. While a panoply of academic qualifications is not necessary in all circumstances for one to qualify as an expert, there should be a general presumption in favor of appropriate academic credentials. The district court's finding that St. Regis was not properly qualified finds ample support in the record: his formal education ended with a high school diploma; he had no formal training in psychiatry or psychotherapy; his hypnotic technique used an experimental cranial electronic stimulator; he did not read the professional literature; and his work experience prior to being a hypnotist at Pacific Medical Center was intermittent. The fact that Dr. Peters, a medical doctor, self-servingly stated that he considered St. Regis to be qualified is not enough to disturb the district court's determination.

There was also no permanent record of the procedures that St. Regis used; no videotapes, audiotapes, or even contemporaneously-drafted medical reports existed. * * * As a result, the district court was not provided with any means, independent of St. Regis's testimony, to determine whether or not he was inadvertently suggestive in his approach or otherwise used suspect techniques in conducting the hypnosis. Without such a record, expert testimony would have been of little value, since experts similarly would have had no basis on which to evaluate the actual procedures St. Regis used.

Finally, we receive no comfort from the fact that St. Regis read excerpts from Borawick's deposition transcript prior to testifying himself. Given that he is not qualified and that the record lacks any basis on which to assess the reliability of the procedures he used, this circumstance further undermines the value, if any, of his testimony.

Our conclusion is reinforced by the inherent incredibility of Borawick's allegations. In this case, Borawick has levelled fanciful accusations of sexual abuse against numerous persons other than the defendants in this matter that include persons both familiar and unfamiliar to her. For example, Borawick allegedly recalls being raped and sexually abused at the age of three during rituals by men whom she believed to be members of the Masons. She also purports to recollect several incidents in which she was drugged by injection as well as an incident in which she was forced to drink blood at a ritual involving a dead pig, incense, chanting, and people dressed in black gowns. Several additional incidents of a similarly unlikely nature involving sexual abuse by others are included in the sealed record. That Borawick has made these far-fetched, uncorroborated accusations against others, in addition to the defendants, erodes our confidence in the allegations against Morrie and Christine Shay and properly weighs against the admissibility of her hypnotically-induced memories.

* * *

NOTES AND QUESTIONS

1. *Various approaches.* While the federal courts and some states follow the "totality of the circumstances" approach as indicated in the principal case, the majority of courts have adopted the per se exclusion rule, at least in criminal cases. See 1 Giannelli, Imwinkelried, Roth & Moriarty, Scientific Evidence ch. 12 (5th ed. 2012); Webert, Are The Courts in a Trance? Approaches To The Admissibility of Hypnotically Enhanced Witness Testimony in Light of Empirical Evidence, 40 Am.Crim.L.Rev. 1301 (2003). However, these jurisdictions recognize two exceptions. See notes 2 and 3 infra. In State v. Moore, 902 A.2d 1212 (N.J.2006), the N.J. Supreme Court rejected its earlier position in *Hurd* (cited in the principal case) and adopted the per se exclusion approach, which the court stated was followed by 26 other states.

2. *Exception for prehypnotic testimony.* In State ex rel. Collins v. Superior Court, 644 P.2d 1266, 1295 (Ariz.1982), several rape victims were hypnotized in an attempt to discover more information about the identity of their assailant. Although no new information developed from this process, the defendant was later apprehended as he approached a police decoy. The defense moved to disqualify the victims as witnesses. On appeal, the Arizona Supreme Court reaffirmed its earlier position, ruling that the testimony of a hypnotized witness is inadmissible. On a motion for rehearing, however, the court modified this ruling:

> [A] witness will be permitted to testify with regard to those matters which he or she was able to recall *and* relate prior to hypnosis. Thus, for example, the rape victim would be free to testify to the occurrence of the crime, the lack of consent, the injury inflicted and the like, assuming that such matters were remembered and related to the authorities prior to use of hypnosis.

Collins represents the prevailing view on this issue. Are there problems with this approach?

3. *Exception for the accused.* In Rock v. Arkansas, 483 U.S. 44 (1987), cited in the principal case, the Court held that an accused who has been hypnotized cannot be barred from testifying under a rule making hypnotically enhanced testimony per se inadmissible. What about other defense witnesses? See Giuliana, Between *Rock* and a *Hurd* Place: Protecting

the Criminal Defendant's Right to Testify After Her Testimony Has Been Hypnotically Refreshed, 65 Fordham L.Rev. 2151 (1997).

4. *Right of confrontation.* Compare State v. Mena, 624 P.2d 1274, 1280 (Ariz.1981) ("[T]here is a strong belief among several authorities that hypnotism of a witness renders subsequent cross-examination ineffective * * *. Until the general scientific reliability of hypnotism * * * [is] established and/or the barriers which it raises to effective cross-examination are somehow overcome, we think the confrontation clause of the Sixth Amendment * * * requires [exclusion]."), with Bundy v. Dugger, 850 F.2d 1402, 1415 (11th Cir.1988) (*Rock* "teaches that, although hypnosis may make effective cross-examination more difficult, it does not always make it impossible, thereby preserving the opportunity for effective cross-examination safeguarded by the Sixth Amendment.").

5. *Nonforensic hypnosis.* In McGlauflin v. State, 857 P.2d 366, 378 (Alaska Ct.App.1993), the court considered the admissibility of a child abuse victim's testimony. The hypnotic session was intended to focus on her weight problem. The court ruled that there is no presumption of unreliability in this type of case because "the circumstances and results of the hypnosis session make it likely that the witness's memories have not been enhanced or altered by hypnosis." See also Franklin v. Duncan, 884 F.Supp. 1435, 1441 (N.D.Cal.1995) (defendant's daughter recalled murder 20 years later; reversed on other grounds), aff'd, 70 F.3d 75, 78 (9th Cir.1995).

6. *Nonhypnotic recall.* In Commonwealth v. Crawford, 718 A.2d 768 (Pa.1998), an arrest for a murder was not made until 20 years after the victim's body had been found. The witness claimed that his "flashback" occurred when he saw a person who resembled the victim while shopping. The Pennsylvania Supreme Court upheld the exclusion of a defense expert's testimony on the grounds that it would have invaded the jury's province in evaluating credibility. The expert would have testified that the witness' memory was inaccurate. The Court also noted that the prosecution had not introduced expert testimony on revived memory and had not sought to establish the scientific validity of repressed memory.

7. *Repressed memories.* A related issue concerns "repressed memories." The issue remains controversial. Compare Clark v. Edison, 881 F.Supp.2d 192, 215, 217 (D.Mass.2012) ("In sum, notwithstanding the methodological criticisms raised by Dr. Pope, the court finds that memory repression is a sufficiently testable and tested hypothesis to permit it to be submitted to the jury."; "However, neither expert will be permitted to opine as to whether Clark suffered from the alleged abuse, whether he actually repressed any memories of the experience, or whether he is a credible witness or his claimed memory is more credible than it otherwise might appear."), with Doe v. Archdiocese of St. Paul, 817 N.W.2d 150, 169–70 (Minn.2012) (holding statute of limitations not tolled; "Because there is ample evidence in the record supporting a conclusion that the theory of repressed and recovered memory lacks foundational reliability when offered for the purpose of proving

that Doe had a disability delaying the accrual of his causes of action, the district court did not abuse its discretion when it excluded Doe's expert testimony.").

For further discussion, see Fletcher, Repressed Memories: Do Triggering Methods Contribute to Witness Testimony Reliability?, 13 Wash.U.J.L. & Pol'y 335 (2003).

C. LAY WITNESSES

(1) FIRSTHAND KNOWLEDGE: FEDERAL RULE 602

KEMP V. BALBOA

United States Court of Appeals, Eighth Circuit, 1994.
23 F.3d 211.

FRIEDMAN, SENIOR CIRCUIT JUDGE.

In this case, a state prisoner filed suit under 42 U.S.C. § 1983 (1988), accusing a prison guard of improperly confiscating his medication used to control his epilepsy, resulting in the prisoner's having epileptic fits, which injured him. The jury found for the prisoner, but awarded him only nominal damages of $1.00 and punitive damages of the same amount. The prisoner challenges the award of only nominal damages as based upon inadmissible evidence, and the guard appeals from the award of attorney fees against him. We hold that the district court improperly admitted testimony by a lay witness who lacked personal knowledge of the matter about which she testified, in violation of Fed.R.Evid. 602, and remand for a new trial on the issue of damages only. We vacate the attorney fee award.

* * *

Vicki Maness, a licensed practical nurse at the Center, testified that Kemp failed to pick up his medication from the prison infirmary on seven separate occasions. She testified that she had reviewed portions of Kemp's medical file relating to the dispensing of medication. * * * Maness read from the records three dates during June and July, 1989 on which Kemp allegedly failed to pick up his epilepsy medication from the prison infirmary.

Kemp objected repeatedly to Maness' reading of these records while she was testifying on direct examination. * * * Maness then testified that Kemp failed to procure his medication on three occasions in September 1989, and one time in October 1989.

On cross examination, Maness stated she was not on duty on the days that Kemp allegedly failed to obtain his medication, and that her only knowledge of the subject came from her reviewing the medical charts, which someone else had prepared. Upon completion of the cross examination, Kemp moved to strike Maness' testimony on the ground that Maness' had no personal knowledge of Kemp's failure to pick up his medication, since her testimony was based solely on her review of Kemp's medical file. The district court denied the motion to strike. * * *

Unlike an expert witness, who may give his or her opinion about a matter within the witness' expertise (Fed.R.Evid. 703), a lay witness may testify only about matters within his or her personal knowledge. * * * Rule 602 prohibits a lay witness from testifying about matters that are not within the personal knowledge of the witness. * * *

Maness was not tendered and did not testify as an expert witness. She testified only as a lay witness to present factual evidence that Kemp had failed to pick up his medication from the Center infirmary. As her testimony on cross examination brought out, however, she had no personal knowledge of these facts, since she was not on duty on the days on which she stated Kemp failed to pick up his medication. Her testimony was based not upon her personal knowledge of the facts about which she testified, but solely upon what she had read in the medical records prepared by others.

Those medical records themselves were not introduced in evidence. According to the district court and Balboa, however, the records were properly used to refresh Maness' recollection. Since Maness had no personal knowledge of the facts, however, she had no recollection that was capable of being refreshed. * * *

[The court held the error was not harmless.] Maness' testimony that Kemp had failed to pick up his medication might have lead the jury to conclude that it was Kemp's own indifference to his medical needs rather than Balboa's confiscation of his medication that was primarily the cause of Kemp's increased seizures. Indeed, based on Maness' testimony, the jury might have believed that Kemp, himself, sometimes failed to take his own medication. The probable impact of Maness' testimony on the jury is further suggested by the jury's request to see the medical files Maness read from during her testimony. The court denied the request, but instructed the jury to use its "collective recollection" of Maness' testimony regarding the contents of the medical logs.

* * *

NOTES AND QUESTIONS

1. *Time of acquiring firsthand knowledge.* It is the witness' knowledge at the time of trial, not necessarily at the time of the event, that is determinative; a witness could gained new personal knowledge after an accident or crime. See Cleveland Terminal & Valley R.R. v. Marsh, 58 N.E. 821, 822 (Ohio 1900); Strickland Transp. Co. v. Ingram, 403 S.W.2d 192, 195

(Tex.Ct.App.1966) ("A witness may testify in accordance with his knowledge at the time his testimony is offered; he is not restricted to his knowledge at the time the event occurred.").

2. *Hearsay overlap.* As *Kemp* illustrates, there is an overlap between the lack of firsthand knowledge and the hearsay rule. Although hearsay, the records may have been admissible under the public records or business records exceptions to the hearsay rule. See Chapter 14, infra.

3. *Basis of knowledge.* See United States v. Doe, 960 F.2d 221, 223 (1st Cir.1992) (In a case involving possession of a firearm shipped interstate, the court stated: "Doe claims that the district court should have excluded the sports shop owner's testimony that he 'knows' Taurus pistols are 'manufactured in Brazil,' on the ground that the witness did not have 'personal knowledge' of that fact. Evidence proving personal knowledge may, however, 'consist of the witness' own testimony,' and that knowledge includes inferences and opinions, so long as they are grounded in personal observation and experience. * * * A reasonable trier of fact could believe that the sports shop owner had firsthand knowledge from which he could infer that the pistol was made outside of Massachusetts, indeed in Brazil, particularly since his testimony to this effect was unchallenged."). Is the basis sufficient or is the lack of objection determinative?

4. *Controlled drug buy.* A lack of firsthand knowledge on the part of police officers, combined with the suspect credibility of drug informants, sometimes make proof in drug buys tricky. The police have developed procedures for dealing with these issues. See United States v. Beal, 279 F.3d 567, 571–72 (8th Cir.2002) ("The officers testified that they searched Booker's person prior to the controlled buy, though they did not conduct a body cavity search. The officers further testified that the transaction occurred in Beal's car on a public street, that it was monitored by audiotape, and that it lasted less than one minute. Most notably, Booker was under constant surveillance by several officers * * *. The government further demonstrated that the cocaine went from Booker to Officer Troy Smith (who had searched Booker before the buy and provided money for the purchase) to Officer Randy McDowell, who forwarded it to the DEA laboratory where it was received and analyzed by Khrishna James.").

JACKSON V. LEACH
Court of Appeals of Maryland, 1931.
152 A. 813.

ADKINS, J. This is a suit for damages for injuries to the plaintiff resulting from a collision between the automobile of the plaintiff and that of Howard W. Jackson, one of the defendants, while being driven by Riall Jackson, the other defendant. The accident occurred at the intersection of Ellamont street and Clifton avenue in Baltimore city. The plaintiff was driving northerly on Ellamont street and Riall Jackson westwardly on Clifton avenue.

* * *

* * * This appeal is from a judgment on a verdict in favor of the plaintiff.

There was no evidence of negligence on the part of the defendants except as to excessive speed; and the only direct testimony as to that was given by the witness, Hall. It is contended by the appellants that his testimony should have been stricken out on motion duly made, because, according to his own statement, he did not see defendants' car except at the moment of the collision, when he was walking north on the east side of Ellamont street half a block away, and therefore his opinion as to the speed was merely an inference, as in Dashiell v. Jacoby, 142 Md. 330, 336, 120 A. 751, and was not based on his actual observation of the car while running. Hall's testimony on this point was substantially as follows:

"Q. Did you see the other car (referring to the Jackson car)? Ans. I saw it when it hit it.

"Q. You saw it coming up the street then? Ans. At a terrific speed.

"Q. Did you see Mr. Jackson's car at any time before the collision? Ans. I saw the car when it hit.

"Q. Of course you couldn't see around the corner? Ans. No, Oh, no.

"Q. You didn't see around the corner, but when you first saw Mr. Jackson's car how far was it away from the east side of Ellamont street? Ans. You see, I was going extreme north and it was just fortunately my eyes were looking straight ahead, and all of a sudden, right smack off, like that (snapping fingers), just like a shot out of a cannon.

"Q. What attracted your attention, the crash? Ans. No, my eyes just happened to catch the accident.

"Q. Well, you just caught a flashing glance of the machines as they came together, that's right, isn't it? Ans. I got the full view when they came together.

"Q. But you didn't see Mr. Jackson's machine when it was any distance away from Mr. Leach's machine, did you? Ans. It was impossible, on account of the speed.

"Q. You mean it was going so fast you couldn't see it? Ans. Well, you see, the corner covers your view.

"Q. You couldn't see around the corner? Ans. No, sir, And it was on an incline.

"Q. And you didn't see the Jackson car at any time before the accident? Just when they came together, you saw it? Ans. That's right."

The witness further testified as to the position of the car before and after the collision.

And then he was asked:

"All you remember about this accident is that you saw two machines when they came together? Ans. Yes, sir.

"Q. An instantaneous appearance, that is what you saw, isn't it? Ans. Well, the excitement was so great the first thing I thought of was the people in the automobile."

Can we say from all this as a matter of law that the testimony of the witness as to speed was without probative force? It is not like the case of Dashiell v. Jacoby [142 Md. 330, 120 A. 751], relied on by the appellants, where the testimony excluded was an inference merely. Nor is it like the case of Taxicab Co. v. Ottenritter, 151 Md. 525, 135 A. 587, cited by appellee, where the court was asked to exclude testimony on the ground of its incredibility. Here the question is, Was the observation of the car which the witness had immediately before the collision sufficient to give him any information as to the speed of the car? In this connection it should be noted that there was a clear space of twenty-six feet from the building line on the east side of Ellamont street to the gutter in which there was at least a momentary view of the car before the collision. While under the circumstances it might be well argued that the weight to be given to the testimony was slight, we are unable to say that, as a matter of law, it was without any probative force, and that it should have been stricken out. * * *

Finding no error in the rulings presented for review the judgment must be affirmed.

Judgment affirmed, with costs to appellee.

NOTES AND QUESTIONS

1. *Basis of knowledge.* Virtually all courts will today admit testimony concerning the speed of vehicles given by a lay witness demonstrated to have had a sufficient opportunity to observe the vehicle in motion. Holdings concerning what opportunity is to be deemed "sufficient," however, have varied. See, e.g., Hicks v. Reavis, 337 S.E.2d 121 (N.C.Ct.App.1985), where the court held that witnesses who heard, but did not see, vehicles before the accident could testify in relative terms as to speed (for example, "fast," "high rate of speed," etc.) but could not give an opinion of speed in miles per hour,

and Keyes v. Amundson, 391 N.W.2d 602 (N.D.1986), where the court permitted testimony as to speed (40 to 45 mph) by witnesses who saw and heard a motorcycle for three seconds before an accident, noting that noise of a vehicle may be a factor is assessing speed. See also cases collected in Note, Lay Opinion in Civil Cases—Speed of Motor Vehicles, 4 Vill.L.Rev. 245 (1959).

2. *Uncertainty.* Many witnesses, even those testifying as to phenomena observed by them under relatively favorable conditions, will feel obliged to qualify their testimonial assertions by such prefatory statements as, "I believe," "my impression was," or "as nearly as I could tell." Should qualifications of this sort preclude admissibility of the statements so qualified? It is generally held that absolute certainty is not required and that admissibility will not be affected unless, judging from the witness' testimony as a whole, the uncertainty appears to stem from a basic lack of opportunity to observe the matter related. See State v. Thorp, 72 N.C. 186 (1875); 1 McCormick, Evidence § 10 (7th ed. 2013).

3. *Negative testimony.* It is sometimes broadly asserted that testimony that a particular event did not occur ("negative" testimony) is of a relatively weak and unsatisfactory character, and further that as between negative and positive evidence the latter should control. Does this rule have any relevance when a witness shown to have been in a position to observe an event if it had occurred testifies that it did not occur? Should the foundation required for the introduction of negative testimony differ from that required when the witness proposes to testify positively that the event did occur? See South v. National R.R. Passenger Corp., 290 N.W.2d 819 (N.D.1980). The positive-negative rule is discussed in Dow, Judicial Determination of Credibility in Jury Tried Actions, 38 Neb.L.Rev. 835 (1959).

(2) OPINION RULE: FEDERAL RULE 701

PARKER V. HOEFER

Supreme Court of Vermont, 1953.
100 A.2d 434.

SHERBURNE, CHIEF JUSTICE. This is an action for alienation of affections by enticement and criminal conversation. It comes here upon the defendant's exceptions after a verdict and judgment for the plaintiff.

* * *

We next have exceptions to the admission of evidence, and to the refusal of the court to strike out answers to questions, mainly relating to opinion testimony. * * * [The plaintiff] testified that Parker stayed out many nights very late, and came in from four to eight in the morning, and sometimes didn't come in until a day later. That this caused her concern and the effect upon her was such that she became very tired waiting up all night and very lonely and unhappy. That the further effect of his not coming home regularly was that she lost weight, had no sleep, became very nervous and she had a doctor's care. That she noticed the defendant's actions in regard to her husband, noticed her interest, her taking him aside and that there was great intimacy between them. That she noticed that the defendant was absorbed in him. That she noticed that her husband's appearance was abnormal, he was exhausted and had lipstick on his collar, he smelled as though he had been drinking and he looked very haggard. That the plaintiff visited her husband's room in the Gibson Hotel and noticed pictures of the defendant and Tina Thomson,[33] women's gloves, perfume, cigarettes with lipstick on them, flowers. The defendant argues that this evidence relative to what the plaintiff noticed about how the defendant appeared and acted and about how Parker appeared were inadmissible as opinions and conclusions, and that no proper foundation had been laid for its admission.

As a general rule witnesses are to state facts and not give their inferences or opinions; but this rule is subject to the exception that "where the facts are of such a character as to be incapable of being presented with their proper force to anyone but the observer himself so as to enable the triers to draw a correct or intelligent conclusion from them without the aid of the judgment or opinion of the witness who had the benefit of personal observation, he is allowed to a certain extent, to add his conclusion, judgment or opinion." Bates v. Town of Sharon, 45 Vt. 474, 481.

Under this exception to the rule, it is permissible for a witness to testify that a horse appeared tired; that a man appeared worried; that two persons were very intimate; that a person was domineering; that there was nothing peculiar in one's talk or action; the expression of the respondent's face and eyes; that the respondent was under the influence of intoxicating liquor; that cattle were not strong [Citations omitted.]. In this connection we quote State v. Felch, [105 A. 27]: "So, too, it is held that a witness may testify that one spoke affectionately of another * * *; that a respondent acted 'sneaky' * * *; and that one was affectionate toward another * * *. And speaking generally, an ordinary observer may be allowed to state that one appeared pleased, angry, excited, friendly, insulting, affectionate, or the like. * * * The raising of an eyebrow, the wave of a handkerchief, or the flash of an eye may give character to an act otherwise too trivial to notice."

As to laying a foundation for the admission of this evidence it is not pointed out in what respect the witness could have stated more facts than she did. * * *

---

[33] [Defendant had been married successively to one Thomson, to Parker whose affections were the subject of the instant litigation, and to one Hoefer. Ed.]

The defendant also excepted to questions calling for similar testimony from Mr. and Mrs. Grant Titsworth, long time friends and acquaintances of the plaintiff and Parker. * * *

On an earlier occasion before the plaintiff and Parker had first separated Mrs. Titsworth, with the plaintiff and Parker and five other guests, attended a dinner at the home of the defendant * * *. She was asked: "Can you describe for us the attitude of Mrs. Thomson toward Mr. Parker?" to which was added "during the course of that evening?", and she answered: "Well, they kept cozying off into the corners. I don't know how to say it." She was then asked what she observed of her conduct toward Parker, and how she acted, and she answered: "She was attracted by him." She was then asked: "Tell us what she did if you observed anything. If you didn't just tell us that?" and she answered: "She would separate herself and him from the rest of the group and talk together off in either a corner of one room or go into one of the other living rooms and be alone with him rather than with the rest of the guests". Having testified that she had known the plaintiff since their marriage, and that on the occasion of her visit at the Parkers' at the time of this dinner she had noticed a change in their relations toward one another, she was asked: "What change, if any, did you note?", and she answered: "Mr. Parker wasn't as kind and considerate as he had been before."

The exceptions along these lines are not sustained.

Exceptions were taken to questions asked witnesses who were acquainted with the plaintiff and her husband as to their observation of the physical and mental condition of the plaintiff before and after her husband became acquainted with the defendant. Exceptions were also taken to questions asked the plaintiff about the family life, the affection of her husband and the kind of provider he had been. Considerable testimony is set out in the brief and it is claimed generally that the evidence was inadmissible because calling for conclusions. These exceptions are not sustained. The rule stated in Bates v. Town of Sharon, supra, applies.

* * *

Judgment affirmed.

NOTES AND QUESTIONS

1.   *Firsthand knowledge.* The term "opinion" has numerous meanings, many of which are not governed by Rule 701. Suppose "that as the witness was leaving a room in which A, B and others remained, he saw A advance toward B with clenched fist, and on his return to the room later, he saw B wiping blood from his nose and lips and A with skinned knuckles, his statement that A struck B would be the result of a conscious deduction from what he saw to what had happened." Morgan, Basic Problems in Evidence

216 (1962). What evidence rule governs this type of "conscious deduction," opinion, inference, or conclusion? Rule 602 or Rule 701?

2. *Fact-opinion dichotomy.* Is it valid to assume that a clear-cut distinction exists between facts perceived by the witness' senses and opinions, inferences and conclusions drawn from such facts?

> Suppose, for instance, that the witness says that he saw John Jones on the street. No court would reject his testimony on the ground that it is opinion, but, of course, it is just that. To require a minute description of the real John Jones and then to require the witness to describe the man whom he saw in order that the jury could form the opinion as to whether the man was John Jones or not, would be complete nonsense. And so it is with many of the objections to opinion testimony as experience will demonstrate.

Gard, Illinois Evidence Manual 246 (1963). For discussion and illustrations of the relativity of what constitutes fact as opposed to opinion, see King and Pillinger, Opinion Evidence in Illinois (1942); see also 7 Wigmore, Evidence § 1919 (Chadbourn rev. 1978); 1 McCormick, Evidence § 11 (7th ed. 2013). Are the difficulties attendant upon determining what shadings of grays are too gray justified by the considerations supporting the rule? See Ladd, Expert Testimony, 5 Vand.L.Rev. 414, 415–16 (1952).

3. *Shorthand rendition exception.* The rule applied in the principal case, variously called the "collective facts," "congeries of circumstances," or "shorthand rendition" doctrine, clearly constitutes a limited recognition of the extent to which "opinion" or "inference" pervades all human thought and communication. Where liberally applied, the exception has frequently made substantial inroads on the opinion rule itself. See Tyree, The Opinion Rule, 10 Rutgers L.Rev. 601, 604–05 (1956). However, some courts have limited the operation of the rule to instances where the expression of an opinion by the witness is necessarily due to the "impossibility" of expressing the matter in any other form. See, e.g., People v. Manoogian, 75 P. 177, 179 (Cal.1904). Where the rule has been too narrowly applied, the result has been like that described by Judge Learned Hand in Central R.R. v. Monahan, 11 F.2d 212, 213 (2d Cir.1926): "Every judge of experience in the trial of causes has again and again seen the whole story garbled, because of insistence upon a form with which the witness cannot comply, since, like most men, he is unaware of the extent to which inference enters into his perceptions. He is telling the 'facts' in the only way that he knows how, and the result of nagging and checking him is often to choke him altogether, which is, indeed, usually its purpose."

4. *Further inferences.* What if the question posed calls not only for the witness' "shorthand rendition" of his or her own perceptions but for an additional inference concerning what might have been or was perceived by another under the same or similar circumstances? In McVay v. State, 14 So. 862 (Ala.1894), a prosecution for using obscene language, the witness was held properly to have been allowed to state that in his opinion certain females

standing nearby could have heard the defendant's cursing. [The collective facts doctrine is frequently, but not invariably, held applicable to such opinion.] See cases collected in Annot., 10 A.L.R.3d 258.

KRUEGER V. STATE FARM MUT. AUTO. INS. CO.
United States Court of Appeals, Eighth Circuit, 1983.
707 F.2d 312.

* * *

On April 16, 1979, in the early afternoon, Florence and Joseph Krueger were driving in a westerly direction on Missouri State Highway 50, at a point near Union, Missouri. As they approached their home, located on the south side of Highway 50, Mrs. Krueger, who was driving the automobile, noticed that a pick-up truck was parked in their driveway. She therefore pulled her car off the roadway and onto the north shoulder of the highway, just west of the driveway.

The pick-up truck in the driveway was occupied by Anthony Castelli, who had stopped by the Krueger house to discuss the purchase of hay with Mr. Krueger.

Once Florence Krueger had stopped her vehicle, Joseph Krueger exited and walked around the back of the car in order to proceed across Highway 50 to speak to Mr. Castelli.

At that particular location, Highway 50 consists of two, twelve-foot wide travel lanes running east and west. There is also a center left-turn lane and two ten-foot wide shoulders.

At this same time, Gladys Batchman was driving her car in an easterly direction on Highway 50 at a rate of speed of approximately 50 to 55 miles-per-hour. Miss Batchman first noticed Mr. Krueger on the opposite shoulder of the road standing behind his car. At this point, she was approximately 439 feet from him.

Soon after seeing Mr. Krueger, Gladys Batchman took her foot off of her vehicle's accelerator. At about the same time, Mr. Krueger began to proceed, on foot, across the westbound lane, stopping in the center turn lane. He then began to run across the eastbound lane after looking straight at Miss Batchman's vehicle. At the time he started across the eastbound lane, the Batchman vehicle was approximately 150 feet away. Mr. Krueger ran into the path of the Batchman vehicle and was impinged thereby. Miss Batchman applied her brakes either simultaneously with, or immediately after the impact. Mr. Krueger died soon thereafter as a result of the injuries he sustained.

* * *

The second issue raised by appellant deals with the trial court's exclusion of a portion of the testimony of Anthony Castelli, a witness to the collision. Mr. Castelli testified as to his estimate of the distances and speeds involved, but was not allowed to testify as to whether Miss Batchman had enough time to avoid hitting Joseph Krueger once he ran into her lane of traffic. Appellant argues that the Magistrate erred in sustaining appellee's objection to the following question propounded at trial by plaintiff-appellant's counsel: "After you saw Mr. Krueger start to run, did the operator of the car have enough time to stop?" Transcript at 95.[34]

Appellant contends that Mr. Castelli was qualified, pursuant to [Rule] 701, to render such an opinion, and should have been allowed to testify as to his perception of Miss Batchman's ability to avoid hitting Mr. Krueger. Rule 701 provides:

> If the witness is not testifying as an expert, his testimony in the form of opinions or inferences is limited to those opinions or inferences which are (a) rationally based on the perception of the witness and (b) helpful to a clear understanding of his testimony or the determination of a fact in issue.

The trial court sustained the defendant's objection to the question and to the subsequent offer of proof.

We decline to reverse here for three reasons. First, although it appears that Mr. Castelli's opinion might have been rationally based on his perceptions, it would not have been helpful to a clear understanding of his testimony or the determination of a fact in issue. The jury had before it evidence, including testimony by Mr. Castelli, as to the distances, speeds, and conditions which set the stage for the collision.

The Seventh Circuit has held that:

> in order to conclude that such testimony is admissible, the court must find that the witness' testimony is based upon his or her personal observation and recollection of concrete facts * * *, and that those facts cannot be described in sufficient detail to adequately convey to the jury the substance of the testimony.

United States v. Jackson, 688 F.2d 1121, 1124 (7th Cir.1982) (citations omitted). We find that Mr. Castelli could and did describe the facts of which he was aware to the jury in sufficient detail to adequately convey what he perceived on the afternoon of April 16, 1979. There was no need to provide the jury with a "short-hand rendition" of the total situation,

---

[34] Thereafter, the plaintiff's attorney made an offer of proof that, if allowed to testify, Mr. Castelli would have opined that Gladys Batchman could have stopped, slowed, or swerved in such a way as to avoid the accident. Transcript at 95–96.

when he could describe the entire situation. * * * His further conclusions would have been superfluous at best.

(2)   Second, we note that Rule 701 is designed to give the trial court wide latitude in determining the admissibility of lay opinion testimony. "[H]ow far a witness may go in stating an opinion or conclusion is for the practical discretion of the trial court." *United States v. Freeman,* 514 F.2d 1184, 1191 (10th Cir.1975) (citations omitted). "'[T]he decision as to the admissibility [of a lay opinion] is within the sound discretion of the trial judge and the issues involved are peculiarly suited to his determination.' *Bohannon v. Pegelow,* 652 F.2d 729, 732 (7th Cir.1981). There must be a clear abuse of discretion to justify reversal of the trial court's decision. *Id.*" *United States v. Ness,* 665 F.2d 248, 250 (8th Cir.1981). No such abuse of discretion is apparent here.

(3)   Finally, even if we were to find that the exclusion of Mr. Castelli's opinions was error, we would not reverse here, since it is clear that no prejudice has befallen plaintiff. "Taken together, there was sufficient evidence upon which the jury could make an informed decision." *Scheib v. Williams–McWilliams Co.,* 628 F.2d 509, 511 (5th Cir.1980).

Since the trial court's ruling was obviously based upon *Fed.R.Evid.* 701, it is unnecessary to deal with appellant's arguments under *Fed.R.Evid.* 704.

* * *

Affirmed.

NOTES AND QUESTIONS

1. *Rule 701.* The movement for substantial modification of the opinion rule culminated in the adoption of Rule 701. The rule has been described as a rule of "preference" rather than admissibility. 1 McCormick, Evidence § 11 (7th ed. 2013). Why?

2. *Helpfulness standard.* Despite the limitations on the application of Rule 701 noted in the principal case, the federal courts have generally been flexible in its application. See, e.g., United States v. Espino, 317 F.3d 788, 798 (8th Cir.2003) ("[T]he jury heard specific testimony from witnesses, who all had substantial experience in the use and trade of illegal drugs, regarding the weight of the methamphetamine Espino sold."); United States v. Vega–Figueroa, 234 F.3d 744, 755 (1st Cir.2000) (no abuse of discretion "in allowing Gotay to state her opinion as to why her sister was killed"); United States v. Figueroa–Lopez, 125 F.3d 1241, 1246 (9th Cir.1997) (testimony "that the movements of the Monte Carlo were 'suspicious' "); Government of the Virgin Islands v. Knight, 989 F.2d 619, 630 (3d Cir.1993) ("[A]n eyewitness' testimony that Knight fired the gun accidentally would be helpful to the jury. The eyewitness described the circumstances that led to his opinion. It is difficult, however, to articulate all of the factors that lead one to conclude a

person did not intend to fire a gun. Therefore, the witness' opinion that the gunshot was accidental would have permitted him to relate the facts with greater clarity, and hence would have aided the jury."); United States v. De Peri, 778 F.2d 963 (3d Cir.1985) (interpretation of a conversation); United States v. McCullah, 745 F.2d 350 (6th Cir.1984) (stolen tractor was "hidden" under some trees); United States v. Johnson, 805 F.2d 753 (7th Cir.1986) (value of stolen property).

3. _State cases._ See Markgraf v. State, 12 P.3d 197, 200 (Alaska Ct.App.2000) ("lay witness may testify that another person seemed scared"); Marks v. State, 289 S.W.3d 923, 928 (Ark.2008) ("Howard saw the fight, heard the threat, saw Marks get into the car and start driving toward Walker, and then heard the sound of the car running over the body. Based on this, he could certainly form his opinion based on perception that Marks, in fact, ran over Walker."); State v. McKee, 744 N.E.2d 737, 742 (Ohio 2001) ("[M]any courts have used an Evid.R. 701 analysis and have allowed lay witnesses to testify about the identity of a drug. * * * [However, the] evidence was insufficient to show that the girls were qualified to testify as lay witnesses. Their testimony [about marijuana] was sketchy and conclusory."); State v. Davis, 261 P.3d 1197, 1209 (Or.2011) ("In fact, if the requirements of OEC 701 are met, lay opinion on subjects well outside the purview of most people is admissible. For example, in _Lerch_, a witness who had served in an infantry unit with the United States Army for 13 months during the Korean conflict was allowed to testify that he recognized the smell of decomposing human flesh in a dumpster, notwithstanding that that smell would be a 'rare experience to the average person,' because the witness's opinion was 'rationally based on his perception in that he had previously experienced and recognized' that smell."); Osbourn v. State, 92 S.W.3d 531, 537 (Tex.Crim.App.2002) ("It does not take an expert to identify the smell of marihuana smoke. * * * While smelling the odor of marihuana smoke may not be an event normally encountered in daily life, it requires limited, if any, expertise to identify.").

4. _Speech_. See United States v. Jankowski, 194 F.3d 878, 881 (8th Cir.1999) (person spoke Polish on the telephone); United States v. Bostic, 713 F.2d 401, 404 (8th Cir.1983) (robbery witnesses testify that, based on manner and content of speech, robbers were African American); United States v. Card, 86 F.Supp.2d 1115, 1117 (D.Utah 2000) (ethnic identity based on speech admissible). See also Clifford v. Chandler, 333 F.3d 724 (6th Cir.2003) (ruling that racial identification of voice did not violate due process); Purnell et al., Perceptual and Phonetic Experiments on American English Dialect Identification, 18 J.Language & Soc.Psychol. 10 (1999) (In a study involving 421 graduate and undergraduate students at Stanford University, the participants were asked to identify the racial or ethnic background of twenty different speakers. They correctly identified the African–American males' voices approximately 88% of the time.).

RUPERT V. PEOPLE
Supreme Court of Colorado, 1967.
429 P.2d 276.

McWILLIAMS, JUSTICE. Rupert was charged with the crime of kidnapping, to which charge he first entered a plea of not guilty by reason of insanity. Upon trial of this particular issue a jury determined that Rupert was sane at the time the alleged offense was committed.

Rupert thereafter entered a general plea of not guilty. Upon trial of the issues raised by this plea the trial court, sitting without a jury, adjudged Rupert guilty of the crime of kidnapping and sentenced him to a term in the state penitentiary of from fifteen to twenty years. By this writ of error Rupert now seeks reversal of the judgment and sentence thus imposed.

* * *

Rupert contends that the judgment and sentence must be reversed upon any one of the following grounds:

1.   that during the course of the sanity trial the trial court erred when it permitted Durham, a lay witness, to express an opinion as to Rupert's sanity;

* * *

3.   that in the sanity trial the trial court also erred in its refusal to direct the jury to return a verdict finding Rupert insane at the time of the alleged commission of the crime; and

* * *

As concerns the propriety of permitting a lay witness to express an opinion as to the sanity of another, in Turley v. People, 73 Colo. 518, 216 P. 536, we declared as follows:

> "A nonexpert witness may never, in response to purely hypothetical questions stating the facts, be permitted to give an opinion on the question of sanity. But by the great weight of authority one who, in the opinion of the trial court, shows adequate means of becoming acquainted with the person whose mental condition is in issue, after detailing the facts and circumstances concerning his acquaintance and the acts, conduct, and conversation upon which his conclusion is based, may give his opinion on the question of sanity. The weight of that opinion is for the jury. * * *

> "This rule, supported by the weight of authority and better reasoning, has been adopted by the courts in this jurisdiction. * * * "

Application of the foregoing rule compels the conclusion that the trial court committed no error in permitting Durham to express his opinion as to Rupert's sanity. Durham did relate in considerable detail the facts and circumstances concerning his acquaintance with Rupert, as well as the "acts, conduct and conversation" upon which his opinion was based. Under these circumstances, then, his opinion as to Rupert's sanity was admissible, with the weight to be accorded his opinion being a matter to be determined by the jury. * * *

* * *

The contention that at the conclusion of the sanity trial the trial court committed error when it refused to direct the jury to return a verdict of insanity is without merit. There is, at the outset, a presumption of sanity. The People then introduced the testimony of the lay witness, Durham, to the effect that Rupert was sane. It is quite true that thereafter, by way of defense, a psychiatrist did testify that in his opinion Rupert was insane as of the date of the alleged commission of the crime. But all this did was pose a disputed issue of fact to be resolved by the trier of the facts. The instant factual situation is somewhat akin to that found in Arridy v. People, 103 Colo. 29, 82 P.2d 757. In that case we held that there was sufficient evidence to support a jury's determination that Arridy was sane, even though the medical testimony was to the contrary. And in the *Arridy* case, as in the instant one, the supporting evidence came from lay witnesses, as opposed to expert testimony.

* * *

The judgment is affirmed.

NOTES AND QUESTIONS

1. *Difference between expert and lay opinion testimony.* See Ladd, Expert Testimony, 5 Vand.L.Rev. 414, 419 (1952) ("The lay witness is using his opinion as a composite expression of his observations otherwise difficult to state, whereas the expert is expressing his scientific knowledge through his opinions.").

2. *Procedural differences.* The 2000 amendment added the following requirement to Rule 701: "not based on scientific, technical, or other specialized knowledge within the scope of Rule 702." Rule 702 governs expert testimony. See United States v. Peoples, 250 F.3d 630, 641 (8th Cir.2001) ("What is essentially expert testimony, however, may not be admitted under the guise of lay opinions. Such a substitution subverts the disclosure and discovery requirements of Federal Rules of Criminal Procedure 26 and 16 and the reliability requirements for expert testimony as set forth in [*Daubert* and *Kumho*]."). Also Rule 704(b), prohibiting opinion testimony on mental states, applies only to expert testimony. See discussion of Rule 704 in Section D(4), infra.

3.   *Legal terms.* See United States v. Locke, 643 F.3d 235, 241–42 (7th Cir.2011) ("[T]he prosecutors' questions here did not invoke any of the wire fraud statute's language, and they did not call for opinions on whether its elements were fulfilled. The witnesses' responses likewise neither approached the statutory language nor commented on Locke's specific intent in any way. Rather, each witness explained why the loan in question would have been disapproved by using 'fraud' or 'misrepresentation' in a colloquial sense, employing the vernacular of their financial professions."); Torres v. County of Oakland, 758 F.2d 147, 151 (6th Cir.1985) (exclusion of lay opinion testimony containing terms which have "a separate, distinct, and specialized meaning in the law different from that present in the vernacular," such as "fiduciary relationship," "unreasonably dangerous," and "discriminated against because of * * * national origin"; employment discrimination case; witness improperly asked whether plaintiff had been discriminated against; question asking whether national origin "motivated" hiring decision would have been proper). What other legal terms may prove troublesome?

4.   *Mental condition.* Lay opinion concerning mental condition is currently admitted in virtually all American jurisdictions. See, e.g., L. Richardson Mem'l Hosp., Inc. v. Allen, 325 S.E.2d 40 (N.C.Ct.App.1985) (intensive care nurses who watched decedent through video monitor could testify as to her mental competency), and In re Belanger's Estate, 433 N.E.2d 39 (Ind.Ct.App.1982) (nurses could not testify as to mental capacity based upon only 20 minutes contact). Admissibility is generally subject to the requirement that where the opinion is of insanity it must be preceded by a recitation of the "facts" giving rise to the opinion. Cases are collected in 7 Wigmore, Evidence; § 1938 (Chadbourn rev. 1978).

While a lay person's opinion that the accused was insane (a legal concept) would not be helpful under Rule 701, testimony regarding mental condition may be admitted. See United States v. Goodman, 633 F.3d 963, 968 (10th Cir.2011) (insanity defense: "The Federal Rules of Evidence do not * * * categorically prohibit lay witnesses from offering opinion testimony regarding the defendant's mental state. * * * In sum, the district court should have allowed Goodman's witnesses to testify about their observations of his behavior in the three years leading up to the crimes."); Diestel v. Hines, 506 F.3d 1249, 1271 (10th Cir.2007) ("[T]he lay witnesses were not testifying to their opinions of Mr. Diestel's sanity, but were providing observations from which others (the experts and the jury) could draw inferences. To be sure, lay witnesses *alone* may be insufficient in some cases to rebut a particularly strong insanity defense. But the general rule is that lay testimony can suffice.") (citation omitted).

5.   *Sufficiency of evidence.* The view that a verdict of sanity is sufficiently supported by lay testimony even where expert testimony to the contrary is offered continues to be followed by many American courts. See Bowker v. State, 373 P.2d 500 (Alaska 1962) (noting that defendant bore the burden of persuasion on the insanity issue in this jurisdiction); Yates v. State, 703 P.2d 197 (Okla.Crim.1985) (relying on Oklahoma evidence rule

based on Federal Rule 701). At the same time, a large number of courts, while unwilling to lay down a rule that expert must be countered by expert, have reversed cases where such rebuttal was not forthcoming. See, e.g., Brock v. United States, 387 F.2d 254 (5th Cir.1967) (citing a number of federal cases).

D. EXPERT TESTIMONY

(1) SUBJECT MATTER REQUIREMENT: FEDERAL RULE 702

In his 1947 book, *Evidence: Common Sense and Common Law* 30 (1947), Professor Maguire commented on the subject matter of expert testimony:

> The field of expertness is bounded on one side by the great area of the *commonplace*, supposedly within the ken of every person of moderate intelligence, and on the other by the even greater area of the *speculative and uncertain*. Of course both these boundaries constantly shift, as the former area enlarges and the latter diminishes. Only a few years ago it would have been necessary to take expert evidence on issues with respect to the operation of motor cars, airplanes, or radio which are now so completely inside the domain of popular understanding that such evidence would be rejected as superfluous. A century ago purportedly expert evidence on these topics would have been rejected as visionary.

A chart illustrates these two aspects of the subject matter requirement:

speculative-uncertain		expert testimony		commonplace
	A		B	

Boundaries A and B raise distinct issues, and thus the evidentiary standards for these two boundaries are different.

TOY v. MACKINTOSH
Supreme Judicial Court of Massachusetts, 1916.
110 N.E. 1034.

CROSBY, J. This is an action to recover damages for the alleged negligence of the defendant in allowing a tooth to fall into the plaintiff's throat during an operation performed on January 7, 1913, for the extraction of several teeth by the defendant which was performed while the plaintiff was under an anaesthetic. The plaintiff contended that the tooth which fell into his throat ultimately lodged in his lung. There was evidence to show that the plaintiff was in good health before the teeth were extracted and that soon afterwards he had a cough accompanied by a severe pain in his side; that later he became dizzy and felt a numbness in his right arm and leg and was affected by partial loss of speech, and that this condition continued up to the time of the trial except that the condition of his speech had slightly improved.

It appeared that nine weeks after the operation the plaintiff coughed up a tooth which he produced in evidence. He testified that "his coughing was relieved immediately thereafter."

The record recites that the plaintiff offered no dental or medical evidence, nor any further evidence to show "whether the symptoms which it appeared he had were or could have been caused by the tooth."

The defendant's evidence tended to show that he was a dentist of experience and skill. He also offered expert testimony to show that under the conditions attending the extraction of the plaintiff's teeth, it was not carelessness on his part if a tooth was inhaled by the plaintiff during the operation, but was entirely consistent with due care. Four medical experts called by the defendant testified that in their opinion the plaintiff had two shocks soon after his teeth were extracted; that the symptoms from that time on were consistent with hemiplegia[35]; and that the tooth, wherever it had lodged during the nine weeks, had nothing to do with his condition.

1.   The jury properly could not have been instructed that upon the evidence their verdict must be for the defendant. Accordingly the defendant's first request was refused rightly. The jury were not obliged to believe the expert testimony, offered by the defendant, that to allow the tooth to fall into the plaintiff's throat was consistent with due care, although such testimony was not contradicted. * * * We are of opinion that the question whether the defendant was negligent in permitting the tooth to be inhaled by the plaintiff when he was in an unconscious condition was for the jury.

2.   The defendant's second request was that "There is no evidence justifying the jury in finding that the plaintiff's loss of speech, weakened condition of body, partial paralysis and inability to work were in any way caused by the inhaling of his tooth."

We are of opinion that this instruction, in substance at least, should have been given. The connection between the negligent act of the defendant and the plaintiff's condition afterwards was necessary to be established by a fair preponderance of the evidence in order that he might recover. The burden of proof rested upon the plaintiff to show by competent evidence that his condition after the negligent act of the defendant, if that was established, was the effect in part at least of such

---

[35] [Hemiplegia is the paralysis of one side of the body. Ed.]

negligence. Whether such causal connection existed depended upon proof and could not be left to conjecture or speculation. * * * The burden was upon the plaintiff to satisfy the jury that the illness and disabilities from which he has suffered since he was operated upon by the defendant were caused either wholly or in part by the defendant's negligence. Whether these diseases and disabilities could have been the result of inhaling a tooth was not a matter of common knowledge and observation but depended upon affirmative proof. The jury were not bound to believe the expert evidence coming from the defendant's witnesses that the tooth had nothing to do with the plaintiff's condition afterwards; and while this testimony could have been disregarded, still proof was wanting to support the contention that hemiplegia, aphasia,[36] and the plaintiff's weakened condition and inability to work were due to the inhaling of the tooth. In the absence of such evidence, the jury were not warranted in finding that the tooth caused the disabilities with which the plaintiff afterwards was afflicted and for that reason we think that the defendant's second request in substance should have been given. [Citations omitted.]

Under the instructions of the presiding judge the jury were allowed to determine whether the physical ailments from which they found the plaintiff suffered after the operation, and his present condition, were due to the inhaling of the tooth.

We are of opinion that this instruction was wrong, and that the jury were not justified in finding that the plaintiff's condition after the operation was due to the alleged negligence of the defendant in the absence of any proof to that effect. * * *

Exceptions sustained.

NOTES AND QUESTIONS

1. *Causation.* On what element of the plaintiff's case did the court hold that specialized information was indispensable? Had the plaintiff offered the testimony of an expert witness on this element what form would that testimony be required to take in order to preserve the plaintiff from suffering a directed verdict? See note 2, following *Smith v. Bell Tel. Co. of Pennsylvania*, Chapter 4, supra.

2. *Standard of care.* In malpractice actions generally, the great weight of authority requires expert testimony for the purpose of establishing the appropriate standard by which the defendant's actions are to be measured. Dobbs, The Law of Torts § 242 (2d ed.2012). Relaxations of the general rule, such as that in the principal case, are frequently, though perhaps somewhat inaptly, explained with the label res ipsa loquitur. As to the problems of proof

---

[36] [Aphasia is the loss of the capacity to speak or understand speech due to brain injury. Ed.]

in malpractice actions generally, see Selected Writings on the Law of Evidence and Trial 529–42 (Fryer ed. 1957).

3.   *Jury's role.* As the principal case indicates, the jury does not have to accept expert testimony. The "general rule is that juries are not bound to believe opinions of witnesses, even if they are qualified as experts." Diestel v. Hines, 506 F.3d 1249, 1268 (10th Cir.2007). How is the jury to decide whether to credit an expert's testimony? What if the other side also presents expert testimony ("battle of the experts")?

PEOPLE V. KELLY
Supreme Court of California, 1976.
549 P.2d 1240.

RICHARDSON, JUSTICE.

* * *

Defendant was convicted of extortion (Pen.Code, §§ 518–520) arising out of a series of anonymous, threatening telephone calls to Terry Waskin. The police, acting with Waskin's consent, tape recorded two of these calls (the extortion tapes). An informant familiar with defendant's voice subsequently listened to these tapes and tentatively identified defendant as the caller. Thereafter, the officers obtained a tape recording of defendant's voice during a telephone call (the control tape). Copies of the extortion tapes and the control tape were then sent to Lieutenant Ernest Nash of the Michigan State Police for spectrographic analysis. On the basis of his examination, Nash concluded that the voices on these tapes were those of the same person.

Nash * * * testified that among those who were familiar with and used voice identification analysis the technique was considered reliable. No other expert testimony was presented by either side.

* * *

Defendant attacks his conviction arguing that (1) the People failed to establish that voiceprint techniques have reached the requisite degree of general acceptance in the scientific community, (2) Nash was not qualified to express an expert opinion regarding the judgment of scholars and experts and (3) the testing procedures employed in identifying defendant's voice were not conducted in a fair and impartial manner. Finding ourselves in general agreement with defendant's first two contentions, we do not reach the third.

1.   The Voiceprint Technique

Voiceprint analysis is a method of identification based on the comparison of graphic representations or "spectrograms" made of human voices. The method utilizes a machine known as a spectrograph which separates the sounds of human voices into the three component elements of time, frequency and intensity. Using a series of lines or bars, the machine plots these variables across electronically sensitive paper. The result is a spectrogram of the acoustical signal of the speaker, with the horizontal axis representing time lapse, the vertical axis indicating frequency, and the thickness of the lines disclosing the intensity of the voice. * * * Spectrograms are taken of certain cue words, such as "the," "me," "on," "is," "I," and "it," spoken by a known voice and an unknown voice. An examiner then visually compares the spectrograms of the same words, as spoken, and also listens to the two voices. Based upon these visual and aural comparisons, the examiner states his opinion whether or not the voices, known and unknown, are the same. * * * Since the identification process is essentially an exercise in pattern matching, the examiner's opinion is to a large extent a subjective one based upon the relative aural similarity or dissimilarity of the two voices and visual comparison of their spectrograms. * * * In some instances, the examiner is unable to declare positively either that there is a match or nonmatch of the sample tests, in which event no opinion is rendered. * * *

2. General Principles of Admissibility

* * *

The test for determining the underlying reliability of a new scientific technique was described in the germinal case of Frye v. United States (1923) 54 App.D.C. 46, 293 F. 1013, 1014, involving the admissibility of polygraph tests: "Just when a scientific principle or discovery crosses the line between the experimental and demonstrable stages is difficult to define. Somewhere in this twilight zone the evidential force of the principle must be recognized, and while courts will go a long way in admitting expert testimony deduced from a well-recognized scientific principle or discovery, the thing from which the deduction is made must be *sufficiently established to have gained general acceptance in the particular field in which it belongs.*" (Italics added.)

We have expressly adopted the foregoing *Frye* test and California courts, when faced with a novel method of proof, have required a preliminary showing of general acceptance of the new technique in the relevant scientific community. * * * Some criticism has been directed at the *Frye* standard, primarily on the ground that the test is too conservative, often resulting in the prevention of the admission of relevant evidence (see United States v. Sample (E.D.Pa.1974) 378 F.Supp. 43, 53 [voiceprints admissible in probation revocation proceeding]; McCormick, Evidence (2d ed. 1972) § 203, pp. 490–491). * * *

Arguably, the admission of such evidence could be left, in the first instance, to the sound discretion of the trial court, in which event objections, if any, to the reliability of the evidence (or of the underlying scientific technique on which it is based) might lessen the weight of the evidence but would not necessarily prevent its admissibility. This has not been the direction taken by the California courts or by those of most states. *Frye,* and the decisions which have followed it, rather than turning to the trial judge have assigned the task of determining reliability of the evolving technique to members of the scientific community from which the new method emerges. As stated in a recent voiceprint case, United States v. Addison, supra, 498 F.2d 741, 743–744: "The requirement of general acceptance in the scientific community assures that *those most qualified to assess the general validity of a scientific method will have the determinative voice.* Additionally, the *Frye* test protects prosecution and defense alike by assuring that a minimal reserve of experts exists who can critically examine the validity of a scientific determination in a particular case." (Italics added.)

Moreover, a beneficial consequence of the *Frye* test is that it may well promote a degree of uniformity of decision. Individual judges whose particular conclusions may differ regarding the reliability of particular scientific evidence, may discover substantial agreement and consensus in the scientific community. * * *

The primary advantage, however, of the *Frye* test lies in its essentially conservative nature. For a variety of reasons, *Frye* was deliberately intended to interpose a substantial obstacle to the unrestrained admission of evidence based upon new scientific principles. "There has always existed a considerable lag between advances and discoveries in scientific fields and their acceptance as evidence in a court proceeding." (People v. Spigno, [156 Cal.App.2d at p. 289]) Several reasons founded in logic and common sense support a posture of judicial caution in this area. Lay jurors tend to give considerable weight to "scientific" evidence when presented by "experts" with impressive credentials. We have acknowledged the existence of a " * * * misleading aura of certainty which often envelops a new scientific process, obscuring its currently experimental nature." (Huntingdon v. Crowley, supra, 64 Cal.2d at p. 656] * * * As stated in *Addison,* supra, in the course of rejecting the admissibility of voiceprint testimony, "scientific proof may in some instances assume a posture of mystic infallibility in the eyes of a jury * * *." (United States v. Addison, supra, 498 F.2d at p. 744.) * * *

* * * [W]e are persuaded by the wisdom of, and reaffirm our allegiance to, the *Frye* decision and the "general acceptance" rule which that case mandates. In the matter before us, the People attempted to satisfy the *Frye* test by reliance upon prior decisions of the courts of this state and sister states, and upon Lieutenant Nash's testimony. Yet, as discussed below, none of these sources provide satisfactory proof of the reliability of voiceprint evidence.

3. The Voiceprint Cases

Our review of the applicable authorities reveals no uniform or established trend either for or against the admissibility of voiceprint evidence. * * *

4. Lieutenant Nash's Testimony

* * *

As indicated, Lieutenant Nash was *the sole witness* testifying on the reliability issue. The record discloses that Nash has been associated with the voiceprint technique since 1967, having been trained in voiceprint analysis by Kersta, the pioneer in this field. At the time of trial, Nash was employed by the Michigan State Police as head of its voice identification unit. Nash studied audiology and speech sciences at Michigan State University, and completed courses in anatomy and the physiology of speech. Although Nash had received approximately 50 hours of college credit in these subjects, he had not attained a formal degree.

Lieutenant Nash testified that since 1967 he has prepared or reviewed 180,000 voice spectrograms. As noted above, he worked with Dr. Tosi in preparing the design for the 1968–1970 Michigan State University study which Dr. Tosi conducted, and he assisted Tosi in drafting the final report of the study. According to Nash, the Tosi study demonstrated a high degree of reliability. It was a "controlled experimental situation" based on examination and identification of the voices of students and other nonsuspect persons, rather than a forensic, in-the-field, study of the reliability of voiceprint analysis in identifying criminals.

Lieutenant Nash stated that among members of the scientific community involved in voiceprint analysis there is general acceptance of the technique as "extremely" reliable. Nash admitted, however, that those persons who are actually involved in voiceprint work are primarily voiceprint examiners "connected with a government agency of some kind," i.e., law enforcement officers such as Nash himself.

Our analysis of Nash's testimony discloses at least three infirmities which, in combination, are fatal to the People's claim that they established that voiceprint analysis is generally accepted as reliable by the scientific community. First, we think it questionable whether the testimony of a single witness alone is ever sufficient to represent, or attest to, the views of an entire scientific community regarding the reliability of a new technique. Ideally, resolution of the general acceptance issue would require consideration of the views of a typical cross-section of the scientific community, including representatives, if there are such, of those who oppose or question the new technique. * * *

* * *

We are troubled by a second feature of the evidentiary record before us. In addition to the trial court's reliance solely upon Nash's testimony to the exclusion of other, possibly adverse, expert witnesses, a serious question existed regarding Nash's ability fairly and impartially to assess the position of the scientific community. Nash has had a long association with the development and promotion of voiceprint analysis. His qualifications in this somewhat limited area cannot be doubted. In addition to his work with Dr. Tosi, Nash was the chief of the Michigan State Police Voice Identification Unit, a position which led him to testify as a voiceprint expert in numerous cases throughout the country. Further, Nash is either a founder or member of four other organizations which promote the use of voiceprint analysis.

Nash's background thus discloses that he is one of the leading proponents of voiceprint analysis; he has virtually built his career on the reliability of the technique. This situation is closely akin to that in People v. King, [266 Cal.App.2d 437] in which Kersta, a pioneer in the field, was the chief prosecution witness supporting the admissibility of voiceprint evidence. The court in *King* rejected Kersta's testimony regarding the scientific basis of voiceprint analysis and warned that "[b]efore a technique or process is generally accepted in the scientific community, self-serving opinions should not be received which invade the province of the trier of fact." (Id., at p. 458 * * *) Likewise, Nash, a strong advocate of the voiceprint technique, may be too closely identified with the endorsement of voiceprint analysis to assess fairly and impartially the nature and extent of any opposing scientific views. A more detached and neutral observer might more fairly do so. In the absence of additional and impartial evidence regarding general acceptance, the trial court was in a similar position to that presented in *King,* in which "a court could only receive Kersta's opinion on faith." (People v. King, supra, 266 Cal.App.2d at p. 456, 72 Cal.Rptr. at p. 490.)

A third objection to Nash's testimony pertains to his qualifications as an expert in the field of voiceprint analysis. Substantial doubt exists whether Nash possessed the necessary academic qualifications which would have enabled him to express a competent opinion on the issue of the general acceptance of the voiceprint technique in the scientific community.

* * *

The record in the instant case reveals that Nash has an impressive list of credentials in the field of voiceprint analysis. However, these qualifications are those of *a technician and law enforcement officer, not a scientist.* Neither his training under Kersta, his association with the Tosi study, his limited college study in certain speech sciences, his membership in organizations promoting the use of voiceprints, nor his former position as head of the Michigan State Police Voice Identification Unit, necessarily qualifies Nash to express an informed opinion on the view of the scientific community toward voiceprint analysis. This area may be one in which only another scientist, in regular communication with other colleagues in the field, is competent to express such an opinion.

Nash was allowed to testify in a dual role, both as a technician and a scientist, in order to show both that the voiceprint technique is reliable and that it has gained general acceptance in the scientific community. From the demonstrably wide technical experience of Nash, it does not necessarily follow that academic and scientific knowledge are present as well. * * * In considering the position of the scientific community, a court is found to let scientists speak for themselves. Nash's undoubted qualifications as a technician, like Kersta's, do not necessarily qualify him as a scientist to express an opinion on the question of general scientific acceptance. * * *

6.   Conclusion

We conclude that the People failed to carry their burden of establishing the reliability of voiceprint evidence. We emphasize, however, that our decision is not intended in any way to foreclose the introduction of voiceprint evidence in future cases. * * * Although the present record is insufficient to justify the admissibility of voiceprint evidence, the future proponent of such evidence may well be able to demonstrate in a satisfactory manner that the voiceprint technique has achieved that required general acceptance in the scientific community.

The judgment is reversed.

NOTES AND QUESTIONS

1.   *Identifying the issue.* The reliability of evidence derived from a scientific theory or principle depends upon three factors: (1) the validity of the underlying theory, (2) the validity of the technique applying that theory, and (3) the proper application of the technique on a particular occasion. In short, neither an invalid technique nor a valid technique improperly applied will produce reliable results. The first two factors—the validity of the underlying theory and validity of the technique—are distinct issues. One could accept, for example, the validity of the premise underlying "voiceprint" identification—voice uniqueness—but still question whether the voiceprint technique can identify that uniqueness. Similarly, the underlying psychological and physiological principles of polygraph testing could be acknowledged without endorsing the proposition that a polygraph examiner can detect deception by means of the polygraph technique. The validity of a scientific principle and the validity of the technique applying that principle

may be established through judicial notice, legislative recognition, stipulation, or the presentation of evidence, including expert testimony.

The third requirement—the proper application of a scientific technique on a particular occasion—raises a number of additional issues: (a) the condition of any instrumentation used in the technique, (b) adherence to proper procedures, and (c) the qualifications of both the person conducting the procedure and the person interpreting the results. See Giannelli, The Admissibility of Novel Scientific Evidence: *Frye v. United States*, a Half–Century Later, 80 Colum.L.Rev. 1197 (1980).

2.   *Frye survives.* The *Frye* test was the majority rule until 1993, when the United States Supreme Court rejected it. Nevertheless, it is still followed in a dozen or so jurisdictions, including California, Florida, Maryland, Minnesota, New Jersey, New York, Pennsylvania, and Washington. See 1 Giannelli, Imwinkelried, Roth & Moriarty, Scientific Evidence § 1–15 (5th ed. 2012). These populous states try a large number of criminal and civil cases.

3.   *Voiceprint report.* In 1976, the FBI requested the National Academy of Sciences (NAS) to evaluate the validity of voiceprint evidence. The Academy appointed a Committee on Evaluation of Sound Spectrograms, which published its report in 1979. The Report concluded:

> The practice of voice identification rests on the assumption that intraspeaker variability is less than or different from interspeaker variability. However, at present the assumption is not adequately supported by scientific theory and data. Viewpoints about probable errors in identification decisions at present result mainly from various professional judgments and fragmentary experimental results rather than from objective data representative of results in forensic applications.

> The Committee concludes that the technical uncertainties concerning the present practice of voice identification are so great as to require that forensic applications be approached with great caution.

National Research Council, On the Theory and Practice of Voice Identification 2 (1979). In another passage the Committee wrote: "Estimates of error rates now available pertain to only a few of the many combinations of conditions encountered in real-life situations. These estimates do not constitute a generally adequate basis for a judicial or legislative body to use in making judgments concerning the reliability and acceptability of aural-visual voice identification in forensic applications." Id. at 60.

4.   *Later cases.* Prior to this report, many courts had admitted voiceprint evidence. Even after the report, some courts continued to admit voiceprint evidence. See State v. Williams, 446 N.E.2d 444 (Ohio 1983) (did not mention report); State v. Wheeler, 496 A.2d 1382, 1389 (R.I.1985) (same).

In United States v. Smith, 869 F.2d 348 (7th Cir.1989), the court found that the voiceprint technique had been generally accepted by the scientific community, despite the NAS report. The court discounted the report by pointing out that the report had taken no position on the admissibility issue. In United States v. Maivia, 728 F.Supp. 1471, 1478 (D.Haw.1990), the court also admitted voiceprint evidence. In this case, an FBI examiner testified (against FBI policy, but required by subpoena) for the prosecution after the court ruled that the defense could introduce voiceprint evidence through its expert. The court wrote: "Thus it would appear that inasmuch as the admissibility of spectrographic evidence to identify voices has received general judicial recognition, it is no longer considered novel within the *Frye* test and consequently the test is inapplicable." On what scientific basis could these opinions be based?

In *Smith*, the federal prosecutor argued that voiceprint evidence was reliable. The court found that the "government presented ample evidence of the reliability of spectrographic voice identification at trial." 869 F.2d at 353. In *Maivia*, a different federal prosecutor moved to exclude voiceprint evidence "because spectrographic analysis is a novel scientific technique which has not gained sufficient acceptance in its field." 728 F.Supp. at 1473. The only difference between the two cases was the offering party—the defendant proffered the evidence in *Maivia*. In sum, Assistant U.S. Attorneys, both representing the Department of Justice, argued both for and against admissibility in these cases. Compare United States v. Bahena, 223 F.3d 797, 810 (8th Cir.2000) (voiceprint analysis rejected); United States v. Angleton, 269 F.Supp.2d 892, 902 (S.D.Tex.2003) (same); State v. Morrison, 871 So.2d 1086, 1086–87 (La.2004) (same), with State v. Coon, 974 P.2d 386 (Alaska 1999) (admitting voiceprint evidence).

5.   *Defense experts.* One court noted that in 80% of the voiceprint cases no opposing expert had testified on the issue of reliability and general acceptability of the technique. People v. Chapter, 13 Crim.L.Rptr. (BNA) 2479 (Cal.Super.1973). The NAS Report also took note of this fact: "A striking fact about the trials involving voicegram evidence to date is the very large proportion in which the only experts testifying were those called by the state." NAS Report, note 3, supra, at 49.

DAUBERT V. MERRELL DOW PHARMACEUTICALS, INC.
Supreme Court of the United States, 1993.
509 U.S. 579.

JUSTICE BLACKMUN delivered the opinion of the Court.

In this case we are called upon to determine the standard for admitting expert scientific testimony in a federal trial.

I

Petitioners Jason Daubert and Eric Schuller are minor children born with serious birth defects. They and their parents sued respondent in California state court, alleging that the birth defects had been caused by the mothers' ingestion of Bendectin, a prescription anti-nausea drug marketed by respondent. Respondent removed the suits to federal court on diversity grounds.

After extensive discovery, respondent moved for summary judgment, contending that Bendectin does not cause birth defects in humans and that petitioners would be unable to come forward with any admissible evidence that it does. In support of its motion, respondent submitted an affidavit of Steven H. Lamm, physician and epidemiologist, who is a well-credentialed expert on the risks from exposure to various chemical substances. Doctor Lamm stated that he had reviewed all the literature on Bendectin and human birth defects—more than 30 published studies involving over 130,000 patients. No study had found Bendectin to be a human teratogen (*i.e.,* a substance capable of causing malformations in fetuses). On the basis of this review, Doctor Lamm concluded that maternal use of Bendectin during the first trimester of pregnancy has not been shown to be a risk factor for human birth defects.

Petitioners did not (and do not) contest this characterization of the published record regarding Bendectin. Instead, they responded to respondent's motion with the testimony of eight experts of their own, each of whom also possessed impressive credentials. These experts had concluded that Bendectin can cause birth defects. Their conclusions were based upon "in vitro" (test tube) and "in vivo" (live) animal studies that found a link between Bendectin and malformations; pharmacological studies of the chemical structure of Bendectin that purported to show similarities between the structure of the drug and that of other substances known to cause birth defects; and the "reanalysis" of previously published epidemiological (human statistical) studies.

[The District Court granted respondent's motion for summary judgment. Given the vast body of epidemiological data concerning Bendectin, the court held, expert opinion which is not based on epidemiological evidence is not admissible to establish causation. Thus, the animal-cell studies, live-animal studies, and chemical-structure analyses on which petitioners had relied could not raise by themselves a reasonably disputable jury issue regarding causation. Petitioners' epidemiological analyses, based as they were on recalculations of data in previously published studies that had found no causal link between the drug and birth defects, were ruled to be inadmissible because they had not been published or subjected to peer review. The court of appeals affirmed, citing the *Frye* general acceptance test.]

We granted certiorari * * * in light of sharp divisions among the courts regarding the proper standard for the admission of expert testimony. * * *

II

A

In the 70 years since its formulation in the *Frye* case, the "general acceptance" test has been the dominant standard for determining the admissibility of novel scientific evidence at trial. * * * Although under increasing attack of late, the rule continues to be followed by a majority of courts, including the Ninth Circuit.

The *Frye* test has its origin in a short and citation-free 1923 decision concerning the admissibility of evidence derived from a systolic blood pressure deception test, a crude precursor to the polygraph machine.

* * *

The merits of the *Frye* test have been much debated, and scholarship on its proper scope and application is legion.[37] Petitioners' primary attack, however, is not on the content but on the continuing authority of the rule. They contend that the *Frye* test was superseded by the adoption of the Federal Rules of Evidence.[38] We agree. * * *

Frye, of course, predated the Rules by half a century. * * *

* * *

Nothing in the text of this Rule[39] establishes "general acceptance" as an absolute prerequisite to admissibility. Nor does respondent present any clear indication that Rule 702 or the Rules as a whole were intended to incorporate a "general acceptance" standard. The drafting history makes no mention of *Frye,* and a rigid "general acceptance" requirement would be at odds with the "liberal thrust" of the Federal Rules and their "general approach of relaxing the traditional barriers to 'opinion' testimony." * * * See also Weinstein, Rule 702 of the Federal Rules of Evidence is Sound; It Should Not Be Amended, 138 F.R.D. 631, 631 (1991) ("The Rules were designed to depend primarily upon lawyer-

---

[37] *See, e.g.,* Green, Expert Witnesses and Sufficiency of Evidence in Toxic Substances Litigation: The Legacy of *Agent Orange* and Bendectin Litigation, 86 Nw.U.L.Rev. 643 (1992); * * * Giannelli, The Admissibility of Novel Scientific Evidence: *Frye v. United States,* a Half-Century Later, 80 Colum.L.Rev. 1197 (1980); * * * Indeed, the debates over *Frye* are such a well-established part of the academic landscape that a distinct term—"*Frye*-ologist"—has been advanced to describe those who take part. See Behringer, Introduction, Proposals for a Model Rule on the Admissibility of Scientific Evidence, 26 Jurimetrics J., at 239, quoting Lacey, Scientific Evidence, 24 Jurimetrics J. 254, 264 (1984).

[38] Like the question of *Frye*'s merit, the dispute over its survival has divided courts and commentators. Compare, *e.g., United States v. Williams,* 583 F.2d 1194 (C.A.2 1978) (*Frye* is superseded by the Rules of Evidence), with *Christopherson v. Allied–Signal Corp.,* 939 F.2d 1106, 1111, 1115–1116 (C.A.5 1991) (en banc) (*Frye* and the Rules coexist), 3 J. Weinstein & M. Berger, Weinstein's Evidence ¶ 702[03], pp. 702–36 to 702–37 (1988) (hereinafter Weinstein & Berger) (*Frye* is dead), and M. Graham, Handbook of Federal Evidence § 703.2 (2d ed. 1991) (*Frye* lives). See generally P. Gianelli & E. Imwinkelried, Scientific Evidence § 1–5, pp. 28–29 (1986 & Supp.1991) (citing authorities).

[39] [The Court quoted Rule 702, as it existed before 2001. Ed.]

adversaries and sensible triers of fact to evaluate conflicts"). Given the Rules' permissive backdrop and their inclusion of a specific rule on expert testimony that does not mention "general acceptance," the assertion that the Rules somehow assimilated *Frye* is unconvincing. *Frye* made "general acceptance" the exclusive test for admitting expert scientific testimony. That austere standard, absent from and incompatible with the Federal Rules of Evidence, should not be applied in federal trials.

B

That the *Frye* test was displaced by the Rules of Evidence does not mean, however, that the Rules themselves place no limits on the admissibility of purportedly scientific evidence.[40] Nor is the trial judge disabled from screening such evidence. To the contrary, under the Rules the trial judge must ensure that any and all scientific testimony or evidence admitted is not only relevant, but reliable.

The primary locus of this obligation is Rule 702, which clearly contemplates some degree of regulation of the subjects and theories about which an expert may testify. "*If scientific,* technical, or other specialized *knowledge will assist the trier of fact* to understand the evidence or to determine a fact in issue" an expert "may testify *thereto.*" The subject of an expert's testimony must be "scientific * * * knowledge." The adjective "scientific" implies a grounding in the methods and procedures of science. Similarly, the word "knowledge" connotes more than subjective belief or unsupported speculation. The term "applies to any body of known facts or to any body of ideas inferred from such facts or accepted as truths on good grounds." Webster's Third New International Dictionary 1252 (1986). Of course, it would be unreasonable to conclude that the subject of scientific testimony must be "known" to a certainty; arguably, there are no certainties in science. See, *e.g.,* Brief for Nicolaas Bloembergen et al. as *Amici Curiae* 9 ("Indeed, scientists do not assert that they know what is immutably 'true'—they are committed to searching for new, temporary theories to explain, as best they can, phenomena"); Brief for American Association for the Advancement of Science and the National Academy of Sciences as *Amici Curiae* 7–8 ("Science is not an encyclopedic body of knowledge about the universe. Instead, it represents a *process* for proposing and refiningtheoretical explanations about the world that are subject to further testing and refinement") (emphasis in original). But, in order to qualify as "scientific knowledge," an inference or assertion must be derived by the scientific method. Proposed testimony must be supported by appropriate validation—*i.e.,* "good grounds," based on what

---

[40] THE CHIEF JUSTICE "do[es] not doubt that Rule 702 confides to the judge some gatekeeping responsibility," * * * but would neither say how it does so, nor explain what that role entails. We believe the better course is to note the nature and source of the duty.

is known. In short, the requirement that an expert's testimony pertain to "scientific knowledge" establishes a standard of evidentiary reliability.[41]

Rule 702 further requires that the evidence or testimony "assist the trier of fact to understand the evidence or to determine a fact in issue." This condition goes primarily to relevance. "Expert testimony which does not relate to any issue in the case is not relevant and, ergo, nonhelpful." 3 Weinstein & Berger ¶ 702[02], p. 702–18. See also *United States v. Downing,* 753 F.2d 1224, 1242 (C.A.3 1985) ("An additional consideration under Rule 702—and another aspect of relevancy—is whether expert testimony proffered in the case is sufficiently tied to the facts of the case that it will aid the jury in resolving a factual dispute"). The consideration has been aptly described by Judge Becker as one of "fit." *Ibid.* "Fit" is not always obvious, and scientific validity for one purpose is not necessarily scientific validity for other, unrelated purposes. * * * The study of the phases of the moon, for example, may provide valid scientific "knowledge" about whether a certain night was dark, and if darkness is a fact in issue, the knowledge will assist the trier of fact. However (absent creditable grounds supporting such a link), evidence that the moon was full on a certain night will not assist the trier of fact in determining whether an individual was unusually likely to have behaved irrationally on that night. Rule 702's "helpfulness" standard requires a valid scientific connection to the pertinent inquiry as a precondition to admissibility.

That these requirements are embodied in Rule 702 is not surprising. Unlike an ordinary witness, see Rule 701, an expert is permitted wide latitude to offer opinions, including those that are not based on first-hand knowledge or observation. See Rules 702 and 703. Presumably, this relaxation of the usual requirement of first-hand knowledge—a rule which represents "a 'most pervasive manifestation' of the common law insistence upon 'the most reliable sources of information,' " Advisory Committee's Notes on Fed.Rule Evid. 602 (citation omitted)—is premised on an assumption that the expert's opinion will have a reliable basis in the knowledge and experience of his discipline.

C

Faced with a proffer of expert scientific testimony, then, the trial judge must determine at the outset, pursuant to Rule 104(a), whether the expert is proposing to testify to (1) scientific knowledge that (2) will assist the trier of fact to understand or determine a fact in issue.[42] This entails a

---

[41] We note that scientists typically distinguish between "validity" (does the principle support what it purports to show?) and "reliability" (does application of the principle produce consistent results?). * * * In a case involving scientific evidence, *evidentiary reliability* will be based upon *scientific validity.*

[42] Although the *Frye* decision itself focused exclusively on "novel" scientific techniques, we do not read the requirements of Rule 702 to apply specially or exclusively to unconventional evidence. Of course, well-established propositions are less likely to be challenged than those that are novel, and they are more handily defended. Indeed, theories that are so firmly established as

preliminary assessment of whether the reasoning or methodology underlying the testimony is scientifically valid and of whether that reasoning or methodology properly can be applied to the facts in issue. We are confident that federal judges possess the capacity to undertake this review. Many factors will bear on the inquiry, and we do not presume to set out a definitive checklist or test. But some general observations are appropriate.

Ordinarily, a key question to be answered in determining whether a theory or technique is scientific knowledge that will assist the trier of fact will be whether it can be (and has been) tested. "Scientific methodology today is based on generating hypotheses and testing them to see if they can be falsified; indeed, this methodology is what distinguishes science from other fields of human inquiry." Green, at 645. See also C. Hempel, Philosophy of Natural Science 49 (1966) ("[T]he statements constituting a scientific explanation must be capable of empirical test"); K. Popper, Conjectures and Refutations: The Growth of Scientific Knowledge 37 (5th ed. 1989) ("[T]he criterion of the scientific status of a theory is its falsifiability, or refutability, or testability").

Another pertinent consideration is whether the theory or technique has been subjected to peer review and publication. Publication (which is but one element of peer review) is not a *sine qua non* of admissibility; it does not necessarily correlate with reliability, see S. Jasanoff, The Fifth Branch: Science Advisors as Policymakers 61–76 (1990), and in some instances well-grounded but innovative theories will not have been published, see Horrobin, The Philosophical Basis of Peer Review and the Suppression of Innovation, 263 J.Am.Med.Assn. 1438 (1990). Some propositions, moreover, are too particular, too new, or of too limited interest to be published. But submission to the scrutiny of the scientific community is a component of "good science," in part because it increases the likelihood that substantive flaws in methodology will be detected. See J. Ziman, Reliable Knowledge: An Exploration of the Grounds for Belief in Science 130–133 (1978); Relman and Angell, How Good Is Peer Review?, 321 New Eng.J.Med. 827 (1989). The fact of publication (or lack thereof) in a peer-reviewed journal thus will be a relevant, though not dispositive, consideration in assessing the scientific validity of a particular technique or methodology on which an opinion is premised.

Additionally, in the case of a particular scientific technique, the court ordinarily should consider the known or potential rate of error, see, *e.g.*, *United States v. Smith,* 869 F.2d 348, 353–354 (C.A.7 1989) (surveying studies of the error rate of spectrographic voice identification technique), and the existence and maintenance of standards controlling the technique's operation. See *United States v. Williams,* 583 F.2d 1194, 1198

---

to have attained the status of scientific law, such as the laws of thermodynamics, properly are subject to judicial notice under Fed.Rule Evid. 201.

(C.A.2 1978) (noting professional organization's standard governing spectrographic analysis).

Finally, "general acceptance" can yet have a bearing on the inquiry. A "reliability assessment does not require, although it does permit, explicit identification of a relevant scientific community and an express determination of a particular degree of acceptance within that community." *United States v. Downing,* 753 F.2d, at 1238. See also 3 Weinstein & Berger ¶ 702[03], pp. 702–41 to 702–42. Widespread acceptance can be an important factor in ruling particular evidence admissible, and "a known technique that has been able to attract only minimal support within the community," *Downing, supra,* at 1238, may properly be viewed with skepticism.

The inquiry envisioned by Rule 702 is, we emphasize, a flexible one. Its overarching subject is the scientific validity—and thus the evidentiary relevance and reliability—of the principles that underlie a proposed submission. The focus, of course, must be solely on principles and methodology, not on the conclusions that they generate.

Throughout, a judge assessing a proffer of expert scientific testimony under Rule 702 should also be mindful of other applicable rules. Rule 703 provides that expert opinions based on otherwise inadmissible hearsay are to be admitted only if the facts or data are "of a type reasonably relied upon by experts in the particular field in forming opinions or inferences upon the subject." Rule 706 allows the court at its discretion to procure the assistance of an expert of its own choosing. Finally, Rule 403 permits the exclusion of relevant evidence "if its probative value is substantially outweighed by the danger of unfair prejudice, confusion of the issues, or misleading the jury* * *." Judge Weinstein has explained: "Expert evidence can be both powerful and quite misleading because of the difficulty in evaluating it. Because of this risk, the judge in weighing possible prejudice against probative force under Rule 403 of the present rules exercises more control over experts than over lay witnesses." Weinstein, 138 F.R.D., at 632.

III

We conclude by briefly addressing what appear to be two underlying concerns of the parties and *amici* in this case. Respondent expresses apprehension that abandonment of "general acceptance" as the exclusive requirement for admission will result in a "free-for-all" in which befuddled juries are confounded by absurd and irrational pseudoscientific assertions. In this regard respondent seems to us to be overly pessimistic about the capabilities of the jury, and of the adversary system generally. Vigorous cross-examination, presentation of contrary evidence, and careful instruction on the burden of proof are the traditional and appropriate means of attacking shaky but admissible evidence. See *Rock* *v. Arkansas,* 483 U.S. 44, 61 (1987). Additionally, in the event the trial court concludes that the scintilla of evidence presented supporting a position is insufficient to allow a reasonable juror to conclude that the position more likely than not is true, the court remains free to direct a judgment, Fed.Rule Civ.Proc. 50(a), and likewise to grant summary judgment, Fed.Rule Civ.Proc. 56. Cf., *e.g., Turpin v. Merrell Dow Pharmaceuticals,* to find it more probable than not that defendant caused plaintiff's injury); *Brock v. Merrell Dow Pharmaceuticals, Inc.,* 874 F.2d 307 (C.A.5 1989) (reversing judgment entered on jury verdict for plaintiffs because evidence regarding causation was insufficient) * * *. These conventional devices, rather than wholesale exclusion under an uncompromising "general acceptance" test, are the appropriate safeguards where the basis of scientific testimony meets the standards of Rule 702.

Petitioners and, to a greater extent, their *amici* exhibit a different concern. They suggest that recognition of a screening role for the judge that allows for the exclusion of "invalid" evidence will sanction a stifling and repressive scientific orthodoxy and will be inimical to the search for truth. See, *e.g.,* Brief for Ronald Bayer et al. as *Amici Curiae.* It is true that open debate is an essential part of both legal and scientific analyses. Yet there are important differences between the quest for truth in the courtroom and the quest for truth in the laboratory. Scientific conclusions are subject to perpetual revision. Law, on the other hand, must resolve disputes finally and quickly. The scientific project is advanced by broad and wide-ranging consideration of a multitude of hypotheses, for those that are incorrect will eventually be shown to be so, and that in itself is an advance. Conjectures that are probably wrong are of little use, however, in the project of reaching a quick, final, and binding legal judgment—often of great consequence—about a particular set of events in the past. We recognize that in practice, a gatekeeping role for the judge, no matter how flexible, inevitably on occasion will prevent the jury from learning of authentic insights and innovations. That, nevertheless, is the balance that is struck by Rules of Evidence designed not for the exhaustive search for cosmic understanding but for the particularized resolution of legal disputes.[43]

IV

To summarize: "general acceptance" is not a necessary precondition to the admissibility of scientific evidence under the Federal Rules of Evidence, but the Rules of Evidence—especially Rule 702—do assign to

---

[43] This is not to say that judicial interpretation, as opposed to adjudicative factfinding, does not share basic characteristics of the scientific endeavor: "The work of a judge is in one sense enduring and in another ephemeral* * *. In the endless process of testing and retesting, there is a constant rejection of the dross and a constant retention of whatever is pure and sound and fine." B. Cardozo, The Nature of the Judicial Process 178, 179 (1921).

the trial judge the task of ensuring that an expert's testimony both rests on a reliable foundation and is relevant to the task at hand. Pertinent evidence based on scientifically valid principles will satisfy those demands.

The inquiries of the District Court and the Court of Appeals focused almost exclusively on "general acceptance," as gauged by publication and the decisions of other courts. Accordingly, the judgment of the Court of Appeals is vacated and the case is remanded for further proceedings consistent with this opinion.

It is so ordered.

CHIEF JUSTICE REHNQUIST, with whom JUSTICE STEVENS joins, concurring in part and dissenting in part.

* * * The Court concludes, correctly in my view, that the *Frye* rule did not survive the enactment of the Federal Rules of Evidence, and I therefore join Parts I and II–A of its opinion. The second question presented in the petition for certiorari necessarily is mooted by this holding, but the Court nonetheless proceeds to construe Rules 702 and 703 very much in the abstract, and then offers some "general observations." * * *

"General observations" by this Court customarily carry great weight with lower federal courts, but the ones offered here suffer from the flaw common to most such observations—they are not applied to deciding whether or not particular testimony was or was not admissible, and therefore they tend to be not only general, but vague and abstract. This is particularly unfortunate in a case such as this, where the ultimate legal question depends on an appreciation of one or more bodies of knowledge not judicially noticeable, and subject to different interpretations in the briefs of the parties and their *amici*. Twenty-two *amicus* briefs have been filed in the case, and indeed the Court's opinion contains no less than 37 citations to *amicus* briefs and other secondary sources.

* * *

I defer to no one in my confidence in federal judges; but I am at a loss to know what is meant when it is said that the scientific status of a theory depends on its "falsifiability," and I suspect some of them will be, too.

I do not doubt that Rule 702 confides to the judge some gatekeeping responsibility in deciding questions of the admissibility of proffered expert testimony. But I do not think it imposes on them either the obligation or the authority to become amateur scientists in order to perform that role. I think the Court would be far better advised in this case to decide only the questions presented, and to leave the further development of this important area of the law to future cases.

NOTES AND QUESTIONS

1. *Legislative history.* The *Frye* issue was not addressed in the Advisory Committee's Notes, the congressional committee reports, or the hearings on the Federal Rules. Giannelli, *Daubert*: Interpreting the Federal Rules of Evidence, 15 Cardozo L.Rev. 1999 (1994). See also Caudill & LaRue, No Magic Wand: The Idealization of Science in Law (2006); Giannelli, The *Daubert* Trilogy and the Law of Expert Testimony, in Evidence Stories 181 (Lempert ed., 2006).

2. *Relevancy approach.* In addition to the *Frye* general acceptance test and the *Daubert* reliability test, a third test, known as the relevancy test, is followed in some jurisdictions. In his 1954 text, Professor McCormick rejected the *Frye* test, stating: "Any relevant conclusions which are supported by a qualified expert witness should be received unless there are other reasons for exclusion. Particularly, its probative value may be overborne by the familiar dangers of prejudicing or misleading the jury, unfair surprise and undue consumption of time." McCormick, Evidence 363–64 (1954). Few, if any, states follow this approach today.

3. *Death penalty cases.* In Barefoot v. Estelle, 463 U.S. 880 (1983), a capital murder case, the prosecution offered psychiatric testimony concerning Barefoot's future dangerousness in the penalty phase. One psychiatrist, Dr. James Grigson, without ever examining Barefoot, testified that there was a "'one hundred percent and absolute' chance that Barefoot would commit future acts of criminal violence." In an amicus brief, the American Psychiatric Association (APA) stated that the "large body of research in this area indicates that, even under the best of conditions, psychiatric predictions of long-term dangerousness are wrong in at least two out of every three cases." In a later passage, the brief notes that the "unreliability of [these] predictions is by now an established fact within the profession." A substantial body of research supported the APA position.

Nevertheless, the Court rejected Barefoot's challenge to the expert testimony. According to the Court, "[n]either petitioner nor the [APA] suggests that psychiatrists are always wrong with respect to future dangerousness, only most of the time." In one passage the Court set forth the relevancy approach:

> [T]he rules of evidence generally extant at the federal and state levels anticipate that relevant, unprivileged evidence should be admitted and its weight left to the factfinder, who would have the benefit of cross-examination and contrary evidence by the opposing party.
>
> * * * We are not persuaded that such testimony is almost entirely unreliable and that the factfinder and the adversary system will not be competent to uncover, recognize, and take due account of its shortcomings.

See Dix, The Death Penalty, "Dangerousness," Psychiatric Testimony, and Professional Ethics, 5 Am.J.Crim.L. 151, 172 (1977) (Court admitted evidence "at the brink of quackery"); Huber, Galileo's Revenge: Junk Science in the Courtroom 220 (1991) (One could favor the death penalty and "yet still recoil at the thought that a junk science fringe of psychiatry * * * could decide who will be sent to the gallows."). Why would a higher standard (*Daubert*) apply in a civil case than in a capital case?

4.   *Which is the better approach: Frye or Daubert?* In State v. Copeland, 922 P.2d 1304, 1314 (Wash.1996) (en banc), the court commented: "The State maintains that this court should abandon *Frye* and adopt *Daubert*. The State argues that *Frye* is difficult to apply. While *Frye* may be difficult to apply in some contexts, this is a result of the complexity of the particular science at issue, the extent to which the scientific community has made its view known, and the extent of any dispute in the scientific community. The same, or similar problems, arise under *Daubert*, including questions of testability, the extent to which the scientific technique or method is accepted by the scientific community, and drawing the line between legitimate science and 'junk' science, along with other questions. Questions of admissibility of complex, controversial scientific techniques or methods, like those involving DNA evidence, are going to be difficult under either standard."

5.   *Peer review.* An amici brief in *Daubert*, filed on behalf of several scientists, questioned the peer review system. Brief of Amici Curiae Daryl E. Chubin et al., Daubert v. Merrell Dow Pharmaceuticals, Inc., 509 U.S. 579 (1993), at 28 ("[T]he peer review system should not be regarded as more rigorous and reliable than the jury system's use of cross-examination.") In their view, the peer review system is not intended to yield "the truth" and publication does not mean that an article's content is "generally accepted" or represents a "consensus" position of the relevant academic community. In addition, they noted that peer review journals do not replicate or verify experiments; nor do they warrant that the information contained in an article is valid or otherwise amounts to "good science." They also pointed out that often only two referees are selected and that these individuals spend on average "2.4 hours" reviewing each manuscript. Is cross-examination really as good?

6.   *Error rates.* The *Daubert* Court cited United States v. Williams, 583 F.2d 1194 (2d Cir.1978), for specifying the "rate of error." In that case, the Second Circuit had rejected the *Frye* rule and admitted voiceprint evidence. The court recognized "the potential rate of error" as "[o]ne indicator of evidential reliability." Citing a Michigan State study, the court noted that the false identification error rate was 6.3%, a rate reduced to 2.4% when doubtful comparisons are eliminated. However, in note 3 following *People v. Kelly*, supra, a subsequent National Academy of Sciences Report on voiceprints undermined these error rates.

7.   *Litigation science.* On remand, the Ninth Circuit again excluded the plaintiff's evidence; this time on the ground that the underlying research had

been conducted in anticipation of litigation, which undercut its validity. The court saw an important difference where experts were "proposing to testify about matters naturally and directly out of research they have conducted independent of the litigation, or whether they have developed their opinions expressly for purposes of testifying." Daubert v. Merrell Dow Pharmaceuticals, Inc., 43 F.3d 1311, 1317 (9th Cir.1995).

8. *Appellate review.* In General Elec. Co. v. Joiner, 522 U.S. 136 (1997), a city electrician, who suffered from lung cancer, brought action against the manufacturer of polychlorinated biphenyls (PCBs) and manufacturers of electrical transformers and dielectric fluid, alleging strict liability, negligence, fraud, and battery. The district court ruled that Joiner's experts had failed to show that there was a link between exposure to PCBs and small-cell lung cancer. The Eleventh Circuit reversed, holding that "[b]ecause the Federal Rules of Evidence governing expert testimony display a preference for admissibility, we apply a particularly stringent standard of review to the trial judge's exclusion of expert testimony."

In an opinion by Chief Justice Rehnquist, the Court reversed, holding that a stringent standard of review was not required: "Thus, while the Federal Rules of Evidence allow district courts to admit a somewhat broader range of scientific testimony than would have been admissible under *Frye*, they leave in place the 'gatekeeper' role of the trial judge in screening such evidence. A court of appeals applying 'abuse-of-discretion' review to such rulings may not categorically distinguish between rulings allowing expert testimony and rulings disallowing it." Unlike *Daubert*, the Court's analysis involved a close scrutiny of the scientific evidence offered at the trial level. The Court found significant problems with both the animal[44] and epidemiological studies.[45]

The Court also addressed the "methodology/conclusion" dichotomy that had been cited in *Daubert*: "Respondent points to *Daubert's* language that the 'focus, of course, must be solely on principles and methodology, not on the

---

[44] The Court wrote: "The infant mice in the studies had had massive doses of PCB's injected directly into their peritoneums or stomachs. Joiner was an adult human being whose alleged exposure to PCB's was far less than the exposure in the animal studies. The PCB's were injected into the mice in a highly concentrated form. The fluid with which Joiner had come into contact generally had a much smaller PCB concentration of between 0–to–500 parts per million. The cancer that these mice developed was alveologenic adenomas; Joiner had developed small-cell carcinomas. No study demonstrated that adult mice developed cancer after being exposed to PCB's. One of the experts admitted that no study had demonstrated that PCB's lead to cancer in any other species."

[45] The Court commented that the "authors [of one study] noted that lung cancer deaths among ex-employees at the plant were higher than might have been expected, but concluded that 'there were apparently no grounds for associating lung cancer deaths (although increased above expectations) and exposure in the plant.' * * * Given that [the authors] were unwilling to say that PCB exposure had caused cancer among the workers they examined, their study did not support the experts' conclusion that Joiner's exposure to PCB's caused his cancer." Similarly, another a second study was also problematic: "The authors of [a second study] found that the incidence of lung cancer deaths among these workers was somewhat higher than would ordinarily be expected. The increase, however, was not statistically significant and the authors of the study did not suggest a link between the increase in lung cancer deaths and the exposure to PCB's." The Court also found drawbacks in two more studies.

conclusions that they generate.' * * * He claims that because the District Court's disagreement was with the conclusion that the experts drew from the studies, the District Court committed legal error and was properly reversed by the Court of Appeals. But conclusions and methodology are not entirely distinct from one another. Trained experts commonly extrapolate from existing data. But nothing in either *Daubert* or the Federal Rules of Evidence requires a district court to admit opinion evidence that is connected to existing data only by the *ipse dixit* of the expert. A court may conclude that there is simply too great an analytical gap between the data and the opinion proffered. * * * That is what the District Court did here, and we hold that it did not abuse its discretion in so doing."

Other courts have taken a different approach to the standard of review issue. For example, the Massachusetts Supreme Judicial Court has stated that "[i]n considering the issue of scientific validity, our review is de novo because a trial judge's conclusion will have applicability beyond the facts of the case before him." Commonwealth v. Vao Sok, 683 N.E.2d 671, 677 (Mass.1997). Does an abuse-of-discretion standard mean one trial court could find polygraph evidence reliable and another court find the same evidence unreliable?

KUMHO TIRE CO. V. CARMICHAEL

Supreme Court of the United States, 1999.
526 U.S. 137.

JUSTICE BREYER delivered the opinion of the Court.

* * *

[This case requires us to decide how *Daubert* applies to the testimony of engineers and other experts who are not scientists.] We conclude that *Daubert's* general holding—setting forth the trial judge's general "gatekeeping" obligation—applies not only to testimony based on "scientific" knowledge, but also to testimony based on "technical" and "other specialized" knowledge. See Fed. Rule Evid. 702. We also conclude that a trial court *may* consider one or more of the more specific factors that *Daubert* mentioned when doing so will help determine that testimony's reliability. * * *

I

On July 6, 1993, the right rear tire of a minivan driven by Patrick Carmichael blew out. In the accident that followed, one of the passengers died, and others were severely injured. In October 1993, the Carmichaels brought this diversity suit against the tire's maker and its distributor, whom we refer to collectively as Kumho Tire, claiming that the tire was defective. The plaintiffs rested their case in significant part upon deposition testimony provided by an expert in tire failure analysis, Dennis Carlson, Jr., who intended to testify in support of their conclusion.

Carlson's depositions relied upon certain features of tire technology that are not in dispute. A steel-belted radial tire like the Carmichaels' is made up of a "carcass" containing many layers of flexible cords, called "plies," along which (between the cords and the outer tread) are laid steel strips called "belts." Steel wire loops, called "beads," hold the cords together at the plies' bottom edges. An outer layer, called the "tread," encases the carcass, and the entire tire is bound together in rubber, through the application of heat and various chemicals. * * * The bead of the tire sits upon a "bead seat," which is part of the wheel assembly. That assembly contains a "rim flange," which extends over the bead and rests against the side of the tire. See M. Mavrigian, Performance Wheels & Tires 81, 83 (1998) (illustrations).

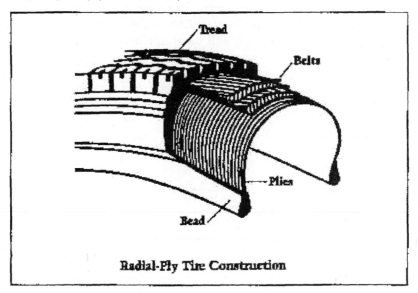

Radial-Ply Tire Construction

Carlson's testimony also accepted certain background facts about the tire in question. He assumed that before the blowout the tire had traveled far. (The tire was made in 1988 and had been installed some time before the Carmichaels bought the used minivan in March 1993; the Carmichaels had driven the van approximately 7,000 additional miles in the two months they had owned it.) Carlson noted that the tire's tread depth, which was 11/32 of an inch when new, * * * had been worn down to depths that ranged from 3/32 of an inch along some parts of the tire, to nothing at all along others. * * * He conceded that the tire tread had at least two punctures which had been inadequately repaired. * * *

Despite the tire's age and history, Carlson concluded that a defect in its manufacture or design caused the blowout. He rested this conclusion in part upon three premises which, for present purposes, we must assume are not in dispute: First, a tire's carcass should stay bound to the inner side of the tread for a significant period of time after its tread depth has worn away. * * * Second, the tread of the tire at issue had separated from its inner steel-belted carcass prior to the accident. * * * Third, this "separation" caused the blowout. * * *

Carlson's conclusion that a defect caused the separation, however, rested upon certain other propositions, several of which the defendants strongly dispute. First, Carlson said that if a separation is *not* caused by a certain kind of tire misuse called "overdeflection" (which consists of underinflating the tire or causing it to carry too much weight, thereby generating heat that can undo the chemical tread/carcass bond), then, ordinarily, its cause is a tire defect. * * * Second, he said that if a tire has been subject to sufficient overdeflection to cause a separation, it should reveal certain physical symptoms. These symptoms include (a) tread wear on the tire's shoulder that is greater than the tread wear along the tire's center, * * *; (b) signs of a "bead groove," where the beads have been pushed too hard against the bead seat on the inside of the tire's rim, * * * (c) sidewalls of the tire with physical signs of deterioration, such as discoloration, * * *; and/or (d) marks on the tire's rim flange * * *. Third, Carlson said that where he does not find *at least two* of the four physical signs just mentioned (and presumably where there is no reason to suspect a less common cause of separation), he concludes that a manufacturing or design defect caused the separation. * * *

Carlson added that he had inspected the tire in question. He conceded that the tire to a limited degree showed greater wear on the shoulder than in the center, some signs of "bead groove," some discoloration, a few marks on the rim flange, and inadequately filled puncture holes (which can also cause heat that might lead to separation). * * * But, in each instance, he testified that the symptoms were not significant, and he explained why he believed that they did not reveal overdeflection. For example, the extra shoulder wear, he said, appeared primarily on one shoulder, whereas an overdeflected tire would reveal equally abnormal wear on both shoulders. * * * Carlson concluded that the tire did not bear at least two of the four overdeflection symptoms, nor was there any less obvious cause of separation; and since neither overdeflection nor the punctures caused the blowout, a defect must have done so.

Kumho Tire moved the District Court to exclude Carlson's testimony on the ground that his methodology failed Rule 702's reliability requirement. [The district court granted the motion on the ground that the evidence did not meet the *Daubert* reliability standard. The Eleventh Circuit reversed, holding that *Daubert* did not apply to non-scientific evidence.]

II

A

In *Daubert*, this Court held that Federal Rule of Evidence 702 imposes a special obligation upon a trial judge to "ensure that any and all scientific testimony * * * is not only relevant, but reliable." 509 U.S. [at 589]. The initial question before us is whether this basic gatekeeping obligation applies only to "scientific" testimony or to all expert testimony. * * *

* * *

[Rule 702] makes no relevant distinction between "scientific" knowledge and "technical" or "other specialized" knowledge. It makes clear that any such knowledge might become the subject of expert testimony. In *Daubert*, the Court specified that it is the Rule's word "knowledge," not the words (like "scientific") that modify that word, that "establishes a standard of evidentiary reliability." 509 U.S. [at 589–590]. Hence, as a matter of language, the Rule applies its reliability standard to all "scientific," "technical," or "other specialized" matters within its scope. We concede that the Court in *Daubert* referred only to "scientific" knowledge. But as the Court there said, it referred to "scientific" testimony "because that [wa]s the nature of the expertise" at issue. Id. [at 590 n.8]

Neither is the evidentiary rationale that underlay the Court's basic *Daubert* "gatekeeping" determination limited to "scientific" knowledge. *Daubert* pointed out that Federal Rules 702 and 703 grant expert witnesses testimonial latitude unavailable to other witnesses on the "assumption that the expert's opinion will have a reliable basis in the knowledge and experience of his discipline." Id. [at 592] (pointing out that experts may testify to opinions, including those that are not based on firsthand knowledge or observation). The Rules grant that latitude to all experts, not just to "scientific" ones.

Finally, it would prove difficult, if not impossible, for judges to administer evidentiary rules under which a gatekeeping obligation depended upon a distinction between "scientific" knowledge and "technical" or "other specialized" knowledge. There is no clear line that divides the one from the others. Disciplines such as engineering rest upon scientific knowledge. Pure scientific theory itself may depend for its development upon observation and properly engineered machinery. And conceptual efforts to distinguish the two are unlikely to produce clear legal lines capable of application in particular cases. * * *

Neither is there a convincing need to make such distinctions. Experts of all kinds tie observations to conclusions through the use of what Judge Learned Hand called "general truths derived from * * * specialized experience." Hand, Historical and Practical Considerations Regarding Expert Testimony, 15 Harv. L.Rev. 40, 54 (1901). And whether the specific expert testimony focuses upon specialized observations, the specialized translation of those observations into theory, a specialized theory itself, or the application of such a theory in a particular case, the expert's testimony often will rest "upon an experience confessedly foreign in kind to [the jury's] own." *Ibid.* * * *

We conclude that *Daubert's* general principles apply to the expert matters described in Rule 702. * * *

B

Petitioners ask more specifically whether a trial judge determining the "admissibility of an engineering expert's testimony" may consider several more specific factors that *Daubert* said might "bear on" a judge's gatekeeping determination. [listing *Daubert* factors] Emphasizing the word "may" in the question, we answer that question yes.

Engineering testimony rests upon scientific foundations, the reliability of which will be at issue in some cases. * * * In other cases, the relevant reliability concerns may focus upon personal knowledge or experience. As the Solicitor General points out, there are many different kinds of experts, and many different kinds of expertise. See Brief for United States as *Amicus Curiae* 18–19, and n.5 (citing cases involving experts in drug terms, handwriting analysis, criminal *modus operandi,* land valuation, agricultural practices, railroad procedures, attorney's fee valuation, and others). Our emphasis on the word "may" thus reflects *Daubert's* description of the Rule 702 inquiry as "a flexible one." 509 U.S. [at 594]. *Daubert* makes clear that the factors it mentions do *not* constitute a "definitive checklist or test." Id. [at 593]. And *Daubert* adds that the gatekeeping inquiry must be " 'tied to the facts' " of a particular "case." Id. [at 591]. We agree with the Solicitor General that "[t]he factors identified in *Daubert* may or may not be pertinent in assessing reliability, depending on the nature of the issue, the expert's particular expertise, and the subject of his testimony." Brief for United States as *Amicus Curiae* 19. The conclusion, in our view, is that we can neither rule out, nor rule in, for all cases and for all time the applicability of the factors mentioned in *Daubert*, nor can we now do so for subsets of cases categorized by category of expert or by kind of evidence. Too much depends upon the particular circumstances of the particular case at issue.

Daubert itself is not to the contrary. It made clear that its list of factors was meant to be helpful, not definitive. Indeed, those factors do not all necessarily apply even in every instance in which the reliability of scientific testimony is challenged. It might not be surprising in a particular case, for example, that a claim made by a scientific witness has never been the subject of peer review, for the particular application at issue may never previously have interested any scientist. Nor, on the other hand, does the presence of *Daubert's* general acceptance factor help show that an expert's testimony is reliable where the discipline itself lacks reliability, as, for example, do theories grounded in any so-called generally accepted principles of astrology or necromancy.

At the same time, and contrary to the Court of Appeals' view, some of *Daubert's* questions can help to evaluate the reliability even of experience-based testimony. In certain cases, it will be appropriate for the trial judge to ask, for example, how often an engineering expert's experience-based methodology has produced erroneous results, or whether such a method is generally accepted in the relevant engineering community. Likewise, it will at times be useful to ask even of a witness whose expertise is based purely on experience, say, a perfume tester able to distinguish among 140 odors at a sniff, whether his preparation is of a kind that others in the field would recognize as acceptable.

We must therefore disagree with the Eleventh Circuit's holding that a trial judge may ask questions of the sort *Daubert* mentioned only where an expert "relies on the application of scientific principles," but not where an expert relies "on skill-or experience-based observation." 131 F.3d, at 1435. We do not believe that Rule 702 creates a schematism that segregates expertise by type while mapping certain kinds of questions to certain kinds of experts. Life and the legal cases that it generates are too complex to warrant so definitive a match.

To say this is not to deny the importance of *Daubert's* gatekeeping requirement. The objective of that requirement is to ensure the reliability and relevancy of expert testimony. It is to make certain that an expert, whether basing testimony upon professional studies or personal experience, employs in the courtroom the same level of intellectual rigor that characterizes the practice of an expert in the relevant field. Nor do we deny that, as stated in *Daubert*, the particular questions that it mentioned will often be appropriate for use in determining the reliability of challenged expert testimony. Rather, we conclude that the trial judge must have considerable leeway in deciding in a particular case how to go about determining whether particular expert testimony is reliable. That is to say, a trial court should consider the specific factors identified in *Daubert* where they are reasonable measures of the reliability of expert testimony.

C

The trial court must have the same kind of latitude in deciding *how* to test an expert's reliability, and to decide whether or when special briefing or other proceedings are needed to investigate reliability, as it enjoys when it decides *whether or not* that expert's relevant testimony is reliable. Our opinion in *Joiner* makes clear that a court of appeals is to apply an abuse-of-discretion standard when it "review[s] a trial court's decision to admit or exclude expert testimony." 522 U.S. [at 138–39]. That standard applies as much to the trial court's decisions about how to determine reliability as to its ultimate conclusion. Otherwise, the trial judge would lack the discretionary authority needed both to avoid unnecessary "reliability" proceedings in ordinary cases where the reliability of an expert's methods is properly taken for granted, and to require appropriate proceedings in the less usual or more complex cases where cause for questioning the expert's reliability arises. Indeed, the Rules seek to avoid "unjustifiable expense and delay" as part of their search for "truth" and the "jus[t] determin[ation]" of proceedings. Fed. Rule Evid. 102. Thus, whether *Daubert's* specific factors are, or are not, reasonable measures of reliability in a particular case is a matter that the law grants the trial judge broad latitude to determine. See *Joiner,* [at 143]. And the Eleventh Circuit erred insofar as it held to the contrary.

III

We further explain the way in which a trial judge "may" consider *Daubert's* factors by applying these considerations to the case at hand, a matter that has been briefed exhaustively by the parties and their 19 *amici.* The District Court did not doubt Carlson's qualifications, which included a masters degree in mechanical engineering, 10 years' work at Michelin America, Inc., and testimony as a tire failure consultant in other tort cases. Rather, it excluded the testimony because, despite those qualifications, it initially doubted, and then found unreliable, "the methodology employed by the expert in analyzing the data obtained in the visual inspection, and the scientific basis, if any, for such an analysis." * * * In our view, the doubts that triggered the District Court's initial inquiry here were reasonable, as was the court's ultimate conclusion.

For one thing, and contrary to respondents' suggestion, the specific issue before the court was not the reasonableness *in general* of a tire expert's use of a visual and tactile inspection to determine whether overdeflection had caused the tire's tread to separate from its steel-belted carcass. Rather, it was the reasonableness of using such an approach, along with Carlson's particular method of analyzing the data thereby obtained, to draw a conclusion regarding *the particular matter to which the expert testimony was directly relevant.* That matter concerned the likelihood that a defect in the tire at issue caused its tread to separate from its carcass. The tire in question, the expert conceded, had traveled far enough so that some of the tread had been worn bald; it should have been taken out of service; it had been repaired (inadequately) for punctures; and it bore some of the very marks that the expert said indicated, not a defect, but abuse through overdeflection. * * * The relevant issue was whether the expert could reliably determine the cause of *this* tire's separation.

Nor was the basis for Carlson's conclusion simply the general theory that, in the absence of evidence of abuse, a defect will normally have caused a tire's separation. Rather, the expert employed a more specific theory to establish the existence (or absence) of such abuse. Carlson testified precisely that in the absence of *at least two* of four signs of abuse (proportionately greater tread wear on the shoulder; signs of grooves caused by the beads; discolored sidewalls; marks on the rim flange), he concludes that a defect caused the separation. And his analysis depended upon acceptance of a further implicit proposition, namely, that his visual and tactile inspection could determine that the tire before him had not been abused despite some evidence of the presence of the very signs for which he looked (and two punctures).

For another thing, the transcripts of Carlson's depositions support both the trial court's initial uncertainty and its final conclusion. Those transcripts cast considerable doubt upon the reliability of both the explicit theory (about the need for two signs of abuse) and the implicit proposition (about the significance of visual inspection in this case). Among other things, the expert could not say whether the tire had traveled more than 10, or 20, or 30, or 40, or 50 thousand miles, adding that 6,000 miles was "about how far" he could "say with any certainty." * * * The court could reasonably have wondered about the reliability of a method of visual and tactile inspection sufficiently precise to ascertain with some certainty the abuse-related significance of minute shoulder/center relative tread wear differences, but insufficiently precise to tell "with any certainty" from the tread wear whether a tire had traveled less than 10,000 or more than 50,000 miles. And these concerns might have been augmented by Carlson's repeated reliance on the "subjective[ness]" of his mode of analysis in response to questions seeking specific information regarding how he could differentiate between a tire that actually had been overdeflected and a tire that merely looked as though it had been. * * * They would have been further augmented by the fact that Carlson said he had inspected the tire itself for the first time the morning of his first deposition, and then only for a few hours. (His initial conclusions were based on photographs.) * * *

Moreover, prior to his first deposition, Carlson had issued a signed report in which he concluded that the tire had "not been * * * overloaded or underinflated," not because of the absence of "two of four" signs of abuse, but simply because "the rim flange impressions * * * were normal." * * * That report also said that the "tread depth remaining was 3/32 inch," * * * though the opposing expert's (apparently undisputed) measurements indicate that the tread depth taken at various positions around the tire actually ranged from .5/32 of an inch to 4/32 of an inch, with the tire apparently showing greater wear along *both* shoulders than along the center * * *.

Further, in respect to one sign of abuse, bead grooving, the expert seemed to deny the sufficiency of his own simple visual-inspection methodology. He testified that most tires have some bead groove pattern, that where there is reason to suspect an abnormal bead groove he would ideally "look at a lot of [similar] tires" to know the grooving's significance, and that he had not looked at many tires similar to the one at issue. * * *

Finally, the court, after looking for a defense of Carlson's methodology as applied in these circumstances, found no convincing defense. Rather, it found (1) that "none" of the *Daubert* factors, including that of "general acceptance" in the relevant expert community, indicated that Carlson's testimony was reliable * * *; (2) that its own analysis "revealed no countervailing factors operating in favor of admissibility which could outweigh those identified in *Daubert*" * * *; and (3) that the "parties identified no such factors in their briefs" * * *. For these three reasons *taken together*, it concluded that Carlson's testimony was unreliable.

Respondents now argue to us, as they did to the District Court, that a method of tire failure analysis that employs a visual/tactile inspection is a reliable method, and they point both to its use by other experts and to Carlson's long experience working for Michelin as sufficient indication that that is so. But no one denies that an expert might draw a conclusion from a set of observations based on extensive and specialized experience. Nor does anyone deny that, as a general matter, tire abuse may often be identified by qualified experts through visual or tactile inspection of the tire. * * * As we said before, * * * the question before the trial court was specific, not general. * * *

The particular issue in this case concerned the use of Carlson's two-factor test and his related use of visual/tactile inspection to draw conclusions on the basis of what seemed small observational differences. We have found no indication in the record that other experts in the industry use Carlson's two-factor test or that tire experts such as Carlson normally make the very fine distinctions about, say, the symmetry of comparatively greater shoulder tread wear that were necessary, on Carlson's own theory, to support his conclusions. Nor, despite the prevalence of tire testing, does anyone refer to any articles or papers that validate Carlson's approach. * * * Indeed, no one has argued that Carlson himself, were he still working for Michelin, would have concluded in a report to his employer that a similar tire was similarly defective on grounds identical to those upon which he rested his conclusion here. Of course, Carlson himself claimed that his method was accurate, but, as we pointed out in *Joiner*, "nothing in either *Daubert* or the Federal Rules of Evidence requires a district court to admit opinion evidence that is connected to existing data only by the *ipse dixit* of the expert." 522 U.S. [at 146].

* * *

In sum, Rule 702 grants the district judge the discretionary authority, reviewable for its abuse, to determine reliability in light of the particular facts and circumstances of the particular case. The District Court did not abuse its discretionary authority in this case. Hence, the judgment of the Court of Appeals is *Reversed.*

JUSTICE SCALIA, with whom JUSTICE O'CONNOR and JUSTICE THOMAS join, concurring.

I join the opinion of the Court, which makes clear that the discretion it endorses—trial-court discretion in choosing the manner of testing expert reliability—is not discretion to abandon the gatekeeping function. I think it worth adding that it is not discretion to perform the function inadequately. Rather, it is discretion to choose among *reasonable* means of excluding expertise that is *fausse* and science that is junky. Though, as the Court makes clear today, the *Daubert* factors are not holy writ, in a particular case the failure to apply one or another of them may be unreasonable, and hence an abuse of discretion.

[JUSTICE STEVENS, concurring in part and dissenting in part, argued that whether the trial judge had abused his discretion required a study of the record that could be performed more efficiently by the court of appeals.]

NOTES AND QUESTIONS

1. *Indication of "exacting standards."* Is the *Daubert* standard less stringent than *Frye*? See Weisgram v. Marley Co., 528 U.S. 440, 455 (2000) (In ruling on summary judgment motion in wrongful death action against the manufacturer of allegedly defective baseboard heater, the Court stated: "Since *Daubert*, moreover, parties relying on expert evidence have had notice of the exacting standards of reliability such evidence must meet.").

2. *Civil v. criminal cases.* A Rand Institute study of civil cases concluded that since *Daubert*, judges have examined the reliability of expert evidence more closely and have found more evidence unreliable as a result. See Dixon & Gill, Changes in the Standards of Admitting Expert Evidence in Federal Civil Cases Since the *Daubert* Decision, 8 Psychol., Pub.Pol'y & L. 251, 298 (2002). Some federal courts have demanded stringent epidemiological studies in toxic tort cases. See Rider v. Sandoz Pharm. Corp., 295 F.3d 1194, 1202 (11th Cir.2002) ("The district court, after finding that the plaintiffs' evidence was unreliable, noted that certain types of other evidence may have been considered reliable, including peer-reviewed epidemiological literature, a predictable chemical mechanism, general acceptance in learned treatises, or a very large number of case reports."). Many cases do not even survive summary judgment, and some commentators have argued that the standards are too strict. See Kassirer & Cecil,

Inconsistency in Evidentiary Standards for Medical Testimony: Disorder in the Courts, 288 J.Am.Med.Ass'n 1382, 1382 (2002) ("In some instances, judges have excluded medical testimony on cause-and-effect relationships unless it is based on published, peer-reviewed, epidemiologically sound studies, even though practitioners rely on other evidence of causality in making clinical decisions, when such studies are not available.").

In contrast, admissibility standards in criminal litigation appear unchanged. An extensive study of reported criminal cases found that "the *Daubert* decision did not impact on the admission rates of expert testimony at either the trial or appellate court levels." Groscup et al., The Effects of *Daubert* on the Admissibility of Expert Testimony in State and Federal Criminal Cases, 8 Pyschol., Pub.Pol'y & L. 339, 364 (2002). A 2009 National Academy of Sciences report on forensic science noted the disparate judicial treatment of expert testimony in civil and criminal cases, commenting that "the appellate courts appear to be more willing to second-guess trial court judgments on the admissibility of purported scientific evidence in civil cases than in criminal cases." National Research Council, Strengthening Forensic Science in the United States: A Path Forward 11 (2009). What would justify such unequal treatment? The report also observed: "In a number of forensic science disciplines, forensic science professionals have yet to establish either the validity of their approach or the accuracy of their conclusions, *and the courts have been utterly ineffective in addressing this problem.*" Id. at 53 (emphasis added).

3. *Jury mistrust.* Are stringent admissibility standards needed because jurors are incapable of dealing with expert testimony? The petitioners in *Kumho* stressed the jury's deficiencies in their briefs. An amicus brief, filed by experts in jury research, attempted to educate the Court on this issue, advising that the Court should *not* decide the case "based on the Petitioners' unsupported or flawed assertions that juries fail to critically evaluate expert testimony, that they are overawed by experts, that they have a 'natural tendency' to defer to experts, and that they have pro-plaintiff and anti-business biases. The heavy preponderance of data from more than a quarter century of empirical jury research points to just the opposite view of jury behavior." Brief Amici Curiae of Neil Vidmar et al., Kumho Tire Co. v. Carmichael, 526 U.S. 137 (1999).

4. *Amended Rule 702.* Rule 702 was amended in 2000. The following requirements were added: "(b) the testimony is based upon sufficient facts or data; (c) the testimony is the product of reliable principles and methods; and (d) the witness has applied the principles and methods reliably to the facts of the case." In Rudd v. General Motors Corp., 127 F.Supp.2d 1330, 1336–37 (M.D.Ala.2001), the court wrote that "the new Rule 702 appears to require a trial judge to make an evaluation that delves more into the facts than was recommended in *Daubert*, including as the rule does an inquiry into the sufficiency of the testimony's basis ('the testimony is based upon sufficient facts or data') and an inquiry into the application of a methodology to the facts ('the witness has applied the principles and methods reliably to the facts

of the case'). Neither of these two latter questions that are now *mandatory* under the new rule * * * were expressly part of the former admissibility analysis under *Daubert*."

The Advisory Committee Note to amended Rule 702 listed a number of additional reliability factors: (1) whether the underlying research was conducted independently of litigation, (2) whether the expert unjustifiably extrapolated from an accepted premise to an unfounded conclusion, (3) whether the expert has adequately accounted for obvious alternative explanations, (4) whether the expert was as careful as she would be in her professional work outside of paid litigation, and (5) whether the field of expertise claimed by the expert is known to reach reliable results.

5. *Findings.* See United States v. Roach, 582 F.3d 1192, 1207 (10th Cir.2009) ("[B]efore admitting expert testimony, the district court is required to make specific, on-the-record findings that the testimony is reliable under *Daubert*.").

6. *Pretrial hearings.* See United States v. Williams, 506 F.3d 151, 161 (2d Cir.2007) ("While the gatekeeping function requires the district court to ascertain the reliability of Kuehner's methodology, it does not necessarily require that a separate hearing be held in order to do so.").

NOTE ON *DAUBERT* AND *KUMHO* IN THE STATES

Tracing the effects of *Daubert* in the states is somewhat complex. First, although many states rejected *Frye* in favor of *Daubert,* they did not necessarily adopt *Joiner* or *Kumho*. See Bernstein & Jackson, The *Daubert* Trilogy in the States, 44 Jurimetrics J. 351, 365 (Spring 2004).

Second, *Daubert's* impact on the *Frye* test has clouded the distinction between the two standards. Terms such as gatekeeper, testability, and peer review have crept into the *Frye* lexicon. Indeed, some *Frye* cases look like *Daubert* in disguise. For instance, in Ramirez v. State, 810 So.2d 836, 844 (Fla.2001), the Florida Supreme Court rejected the testimony of five experts who claimed general acceptance for a process of matching a knife with a cartilage wound in a murder victim—a type of "toolmark" comparison. The court emphasized the lack of testing, the paucity of "meaningful peer review", the absence of a quantified error rate, and the failure to develop objective standards.

Third, *Frye*, which had generally been limited to criminal cases, has been extended to toxic tort litigation, see Bernstein, *Frye, Frye*, Again: The Past, Present, and Future of the General Acceptance Test, 41 Jurimetrics J. 385, 394 (Spring 2001).

Fourth, *Daubert's* effect on the third approach to scientific evidence, the relevancy approach, may have been the most profound development. A number of courts had rejected *Frye* before *Daubert* was decided. Many of these courts now claim that *Daubert* is consistent with their former approach. This is true in some instances but not in others. Many of these jurisdictions had, in practice, adopted the relevancy approach, and their movement toward *Daubert* raises their standard of admissibility.

Fifth, in addition to *Daubert*, there are several other "reliability" tests. Maine rejected the *Frye* test long before *Daubert* was decided. State v. Williams, 388 A.2d 500 (Me.1978). In State v. Bickart, 963 A.2d 183, 189 (Me.2009), the Supreme Judicial Court noted that "we have not adopted the *Daubert* standard applied by federal courts." Instead, a number of factors are considered:

> (1) whether any studies tendered in support of the testimony are based on facts similar to those at issue; (2) whether the hypothesis of the testimony has been subject to peer review; (3) whether an expert's conclusion has been tailored to the facts of the case; (4) whether any other experts attest to the reliability of the testimony; (5) the nature of the expert's qualifications; and (6), if a causal relationship is asserted, whether there is a scientific basis for determining that such a relationship exists.

Searles v. Fleetwood Homes of Pa., Inc., 878 A.2d 509, 516 (Me.2005) (quotation marks and citations omitted, numbers added).

Finally, there has always been strict and lax *Frye* jurisdictions. Well-reasoned *Frye* decisions manifest far more than a superficial "nose-counting"—these cases demonstrate an understanding of the underlying science. See *Kelly*, supra. In contrast, an Illinois court admitted "lip print" comparisons, somehow finding them generally accepted. People v. Davis, 710 N.E.2d 1251 (Ill.App.Ct.1999). The same dichotomy can now be observed with *Daubert*. Compare the majority opinion (lax application) in United States v. Crisp, 324 F.3d 261 (4th Cir.2003) (admitting fingerprint and handwriting comparisons), with the dissent (strict application). See also Lee v. Martinez, 96 P.3d 291, 297 (N.M.2004) (admitting polygraph results under *Daubert*). As a British scholar commented, "The choice is not between easy *Frye* and difficult *Daubert*; it is between strict and lax scrutiny." Redmayne, Expert Evidence and Criminal Justice 113 (2001).

UNITED STATES V. HINES

United States District Court, D. Massachusetts, 1999.
55 F.Supp.2d 62.

GERTNER, DISTRICT JUDGE.

This case raises questions concerning the application of Daubert v. Merrell Dow Pharmaceuticals, Inc., * * * and Kumho Tire Co. v. Carmichael * * * to technical fields, that are not, strictly speaking, science. Two fields are involved: The first is an "old" field, handwriting analysis, which has been the subject of expert testimony for countless years. The second is a comparatively "new" field, the psychology of eyewitness identification. The government maintained that handwriting analysis is "science," meeting the *Daubert* and *Kumho* tests, while the psychology of eyewitness identification is not. Not surprisingly, the defendant insisted that the opposite is true.

Johannes Hines ("Hines") is charged under 18 U.S.C. § 2113 for allegedly robbing the Broadway National Bank in Chelsea, Massachusetts on January 27, 1997. The government's principal evidence consisted of the eyewitness identification of the teller who was robbed, Ms. Jeanne Dunne, and the handwriting analysis of the robbery note. In connection with the latter, the government offered Diana Harrison ("Harrison"), a document examiner with the Federal Bureau of Investigations, to testify as to the authorship of a "stick-up" note found at the scene of the crime.

Hines sought to exclude the handwriting analysis. This testimony, defense claims, notwithstanding its venerable history, does not meet the standards of *Daubert* and *Kumho*. In the alternative, if the court permitted the jury to hear the handwriting testimony, Hines sought to have his expert—Professor Mark Denbeaux ("Denbeaux")—testify as to the weaknesses of the methodology and the basis of Harrison's conclusions. The government, on the other hand, argued for its handwriting expert under the applicable tests, and rejects Denbeaux.

* * *

This trial ended in a hung jury (as did the first). Since the issues noted in this memorandum will recur in the next trial, I outline my reasoning * * *

Kumho extended *Daubert* to non-scientific fields. * * *

Again, a mixed message[Apply *Daubert* to technical fields, even though the scientific method may not *really* fit, but be flexible. Moreover, in this setting, because few technical fields are as firmly established as traditional scientific ones, the new science/old science comparison is less clear. The court is plainly inviting a reexamination even of "generally accepted" venerable, technical fields.

A. Handwriting

Handwriting analysis is one such field. The Harrison testimony may be divided into two parts: Part 1 is Harrison's testimony with respect to similarities between the known handwriting of Hines, and the robbery note. Part 2 is Harrison's testimony with respect to the author of the note, that the author of the robbery note was indeed Hines. I concluded that Harrison could testify only as to the former. * * *

Hines challenges Harrison's testimony under *Daubert/Kumho*. If I were to give special emphasis to "general acceptance" or to treat *Daubert/Kumho* as calling for a rigorous analysis only of new technical fields, not traditional ones, then handwriting analysis would largely pass muster.

Handwriting analysis is perhaps the prototype of a technical field regularly admitted into evidence. But, if I were to apply the *Daubert/ Kumho* standards rigorously, looking for such things as empirical testing, rate of error, etc., the testimony would have serious problems. *See* U.S. v. Starzecpyzel, 880 F.Supp. 1027, 1036 (S.D.N.Y.1995) (finding that if the court had to apply *Daubert* to the preferred handwriting testimony, it would have to be excluded).

According to Denbeaux, handwriting analysis by experts suffers in two respects. It has never been subject to meaningful reliability or validity testing, comparing the results of the handwriting examiners' conclusions with actual outcomes. There is no peer review by a "competitive, unbiased community of practitioners and academics." Starzecpyzel, 880 F.Supp. at 1038. To the extent that it has been "generally accepted," it is not by a "financially disinterested independent community, like an academic community," Id.; only other handwriting analysts have weighed in. It has never been shown to be more reliable than the results obtained by lay people. Some tests have been done, but all lacked a control or comparison group of lay persons. Thus, Denbeaux concludes, there is no need for expert testimony on handwriting analysis. Lay people can do as well. In this regard, I accept Denbeaux's testimony, and the article supporting it.

I do not believe that the government's expert, Kam, and the studies he has cited suggest otherwise. While Kam has conducted several interesting and important tests, purporting to validate handwriting analysis, they are not without criticism. They cannot be said to have "established" the validity of the field to any meaningful degree.

There is no question that lay witnesses are permitted to draw inferences of authorship from handwriting. Where the lay witness is familiar with the handwriting, he or she can testify about it. No expert testimony is necessary. But just because lay witnesses can evaluate handwriting in some circumstances, does not necessarily mean that they can do it as well as an expert can in all.

Handwriting analysis typically involves reviewing two samples, a known sample and an unknown one, to determine if they are similar. Both defense and government experts agree that unlike DNA or even fingerprints, one's handwriting is not at all unique in the sense that it remains the same over time, or uniquely separates one individual from another. Everyone's handwriting changes from minute to minute, day to day. At the same time, our handwriting is sufficiently similar to one another so that people can read each other's writing. Given that variability, the "expert" is obliged to make judgments—these squiggles look more like these, these lines are shaped more like these, etc. And those judgments are, as Harrison conceded, subjective.

When a lay witness, the girlfriend of the defendant for example, says "this is my boyfriend's writing," her conclusion is based on having been exposed to her paramour's handwriting countless times. Without a lay witness with that kind of expertise, the government is obliged to offer the testimony of "experts" who have looked at, and studied handwriting for years. These are, essentially, "observational" experts, taxonomists—arguably qualified because they have seen so many examples over so long. It is not traditional, experimental science, to be sure, but *Kumho's* gloss on *Daubert* suggests this is not necessary. I conclude that Harrison can testify to the ways in which she has found Hines' known handwriting similar to or dissimilar from the handwriting of the robbery note; part 1 of her testimony.

Part 2 of the Harrison testimony is, however, problematic. There is no data that suggests that handwriting analysts can say, like DNA experts, that this person is "the" author of the document. There are no meaningful, and accepted validity studies in the field.[46] No one has shown me Harrison's error rate, the times she has been right, and the times she has been wrong. There is no academic field known as handwriting analysis. This is a "field" that has little efficacy outside of a courtroom. There are no peer reviews of it. Nor can one compare the opinion reached by an examiner with a standard protocol subject to validity testing, since there are no recognized standards. There is no agreement as to how many similarities it takes to declare a match, or how many differences it takes to rule it out. * * *

Moreover, the issue here is not only the validity and reliability of the expert testimony, but its validity and reliability in the context of this lay proceeding. Harrison's account of what is similar or not similar in the handwriting of Hines and the robber can be understood and evaluated by the jury. The witness can be cross examined, as she was, about why this difference was not considered consequential, while this difference was, and the jury can draw their own conclusions. This is not rocket science, or higher math.[47]

---

[46] Kam, the government's proposed expert agrees that "[s]urprisingly, there are only a few studies that examine the reliability of writer screening by document examiners." Kam, et al., *Proficiency of Document Examiners in Writer Identification,* 39 J. Forensic Sci. at 5 * * *). Kam also concluded that "[i]t is very likely that many examiner decisions and associations are difficult to verbalize, and that some verbal explanations are post factum re-creations of the reasoning process." *Id.* at 12.

[47] In United States v. Buck, 1987 WL 19300 (S.D.N.Y.1987), an opinion predating both *Kumho* and *Daubert,* the court observed that "the ability of jurors to perform the crucial visual comparisons relied upon by handwriting experts cuts against the danger of undue prejudice from the mystique attached to 'experts.' " Id. at *3. Denbeaux suggests that it is precisely because the jury can so easily draw their own conclusions that expert testimony even in this limited area is not at all necessary. I am not willing to come to that conclusion—on this record at this time. I am persuaded for now that the testimony involves more than just identifying what is similar and what is different in the same way a lay person would. It involves taking the next step—that this or that similarity matters, that it equals a general pattern. Presumably, the expert is helped in

Her conclusion of authorship, however, has a difference resonance: "Out of all of my experience, and training, I am saying that he is the one, the very author." That leap may not at all be justified by the underlying data; and in the context of this case, is extraordinarily prejudicial.

The Court faced a similar issue in *United States v. McVeigh*, (D.Colo.Trans.) [Oklahoma City bombing case] (citing to *Starzecpyzel*, supra):

> [T]here is a great difference between a witness who has the requisite training and skill saying, 'Look, I've compared this handwriting on this exhibit with this exemplar and I've used the techniques of microscoping (sic) and, you know, all of those things that are often involved in that kind of comparison, and these are the things I find,' and 'I see these similarities and these dissimilarities and so forth' but does not go on to reach any sort of ultimate conclusion that this was written by the same person or expresses some probability or degree of confidence.
>
> The problem with * * * handwriting is that there is no testing of the—no verification-type testing of these opinion results; and in addition, there has never been within the discipline of people who practice this skill—there has never been any agreement on how to express the results. There is no standardized nomenclature, you know. Therefore, it seems to me that we should draw the distinction between somebody getting on the stand and saying 'Yeah, written by the same person,' or 'no, not written by the same person,' vs. 'these are the similarities or these are the dissimilarities'; and the jury can decide.

I find Harrison's testimony meets Fed.R.Evid. 702's requirements to the extent that she restricts her testimony to similarities or dissimilarities between the known exemplars and the robbery note. However, she may not render an ultimate conclusion on who penned the unknown writing. * * *

B. Eyewitness Identification

The government offered the testimony of Jeanne Dunne ("Dunne"), the teller. Dunne, a white woman, gave the following identification moments after the robbery occurred: She identified the man as black with dark skin, a wide nose, and a medium build.[48] Her description was as close to a generic identification of an African American man as one can imagine. Dunne was unable to identify Hines from a book of photographs of African American men shortly after the robbery.[49] She picked out a few

---

drawing general patterns by the numbers of exemplars she has seen, just like the spouse identifies the husband's handwriting because she has seen it numbers of times.

[48] She also noted that he had on a blue jacket, and a baseball cap.

[49] Another witness, a customer at the bank, was unable to effect any identification.

photographs, but none of them were as "dark black" as the robber. Working with a police artist, she helped construct a sketch of the robber. Immediately following, she was shown eight photographs, including one of Hines, and indicated that the Hines photograph "resembled" the robber, that it "looked like him," but she was still not sure. (Since the robber was wearing a hat, she tried to envision the man in the photograph with a baseball cap.) Months later Dunne picked Hines out of a lineup.

Hines offered the testimony of Kassin, a psychologist studying human perception at Williams College with substantial credentials, and trial experience. The government offered a similarly credentialed expert, Ebbesen. I allowed the testimony of both.

The Kassin testimony was offered to show, inter alia, the following: the decreased accuracy of cross-racial identification relative to same-race identification, the effect of stress on identification, the effect of time on memory as it relates to identification, the "confidence-accuracy" phenomenon which suggests the absence of any correlation between the amount of confidence expressed by an eyewitness in his or her memory and the accuracy of that witness' identification, the suggestiveness of subtle aspects of the identification process, such as the darkness of a particular photo as compared to others in the array, the fact that the eyewitness knows there is a suspect in the mix, the transference phenomenon by which a witness may believe that a face looks familiar but is unable to say whether her familiarity comes from seeing a previous mug shot, or from the robbery, etc.

On direct examination, Kassin identified those factors in the Dunne identification that were implicated in the studies with which he was familiar, and could undermine accuracy—the cross racial issues, the differences between the photographs of the other men and Hines' in the photo array,[50] the differences between Hines and the other men in the lineup.[51] He noted problems with what he called relative, comparative judgments: The witness would like to resolve the case and so compares the photographs of one man to another in the array, rather than attempting to compare the photographs to the man she saw. On cross, the government brought up the factors that enhanced accuracy, the nature of the lighting, the distance from the robber, the instructions that were given to the witness, especially at the lineup. The government questioned

---

[50] Kassin testified that Hines' photograph was the darkest of the eight in the array. Moreover, the numbering for his photograph was different from the others. All the others were 6 numbers, beginning with 96, Hines' number was 1234.

[51] The defense pointed out that in the photograph taken of the lineup, which Dunne had indicated was a fair and accurate representation of it, Hines was the darkest man. Furthermore, Dunne could have inferred from the presence of a defense attorney that one of the men in the lineup was a suspect.

Kassin about the instructions given to Dunne at the lineup. Kassin agreed that those instructions were "ideal."

Unlike handwriting analysis, there is no question as to the scientific underpinnings of Kassin's testimony. They are based on experimental psychological studies, testing the acquisition of memory, retention, and retrieval of memory under different conditions. Indeed, the central debate before the jury, eloquently articulated by Ebbesen, the government's expert, is the polar opposite of the debate in the handwriting field— whether conclusions obtained in an experimental, academic, setting with college students should be applied to a real life setting. * * * Kassin and others believe that these conclusions are appropriately applied to eyewitness identifications in court. Ebbesen disagreed.

The government claimed that the jury did not need this testimony at all, that it was not necessary under Fed.R.Evid. 702 to assist the trier of fact. I disagree. While jurors may well be confident that they can draw the appropriate inferences about eyewitness identification directly from their life experiences, their confidence may be misplaced, especially where cross-racial identification is concerned. See *id.* at 1137; *United States v. Smith,* 736 F.2d, 1103, 1106 (6th Cir.1984) (such testimony would "not only 'surpass' common-sense evaluation, it would question common-sense evaluation.") Indeed, in this respect the rationale for the testimony tracks that for battered women syndrome experts. The jury, for example, may fault the victim for not leaving an abusive spouse, believing that they are fully capable of putting themselves in the shoes of the defendant. In fact, psychological evidence suggests that the "ordinary" response of an "ordinary" woman are not in play in situations of domestic violence where the victim suffers from "battered women syndrome." *See e.g., People v. Day,* 2 Cal.App.4th 405, 2 Cal.Rptr.2d 916, 924 (1992). Common sense inferences thus may well be way off the mark.

Nor do I agree that this testimony somehow usurps the function of the jury. The function of the expert here is not to say to the jury—"you should believe or not believe the eyewitness." (Indeed, it has far fewer pretensions to conclusions than does handwriting analysis, with far more science attached to it.) All that the expert does is provide the jury with more information with which the jury can then make a more informed decision.[52] And only the expert can do so. In the absence of an expert, a

---

[52]　In this respect, it is analogous to expert testimony on Rape Trauma Syndrome, *see* Roger B. Handberg, *Expert Testimony on Eyewitness Identification: A New Pair of Glasses for the Jury,* 32 Am.Crim.L.Rev. 1013, 1017 (1995), or pseudologia fantastica. *See United States v. Thomas Shay,* 57 F.3d 126, 129–35 (1st Cir.1995). Pseudologia fantastica is categorized as a factitious disorder in the Diagnostic and Statistical Manual of Mental Disorders and is sometimes referred to as Munchausen's Disease. *See id.* at 129 n.1. This disorder is a variant of lying, often characterized as an extreme form of pathological lying. *See id.* (citing R. Sharrock and M. Cresswell, *Pseudologia Fanastica: A Case Study of a Man Charged with Murder,* 29 Med.Sci.Law. 323, 323 (1989)). People who suffer from this condition present falsifications that

defense lawyer, for example, may try to argue that cross racial identifications are more problematic than identifications between members of the same race, or that stress may undermine accuracy, but his voice necessarily lacks the authority of the scientific studies Kassin cited.

Finally, the fact that the expert has not interviewed the particular eyewitness makes it less likely that the jury will merely accept the expert testimony and more likely that the testimony will be appropriately cabined. The witness can only be providing the jury with the tools to analyze the eyewitness; he has no more specific information. The science makes no pretensions that it can predict whether a particular witness is accurate or mistaken.

In my judgment, the accuracy of these proceedings was enormously enhanced by treating the jury to all sides of the eyewitness debate, rather than assuming there was no controversy, that the issue, notwithstanding this literature is clear. * * *

NOTES AND QUESTIONS

1. *Handwriting.* Several trial courts have excluded handwriting testimony. United States v. Lewis, 220 F.Supp.2d 548, 554 (S.D.W.Va.2002) ("[Expert's] bald assertion that the 'basic principle of handwriting identification has been proven time and time again through research in [his] field,' without more specific substance, is inadequate to demonstrate testability and error rate."); United States v. Fujii, 152 F.Supp.2d 939, 940 (N.D.Ill.2000) (expert testimony concerning Japanese handprinting inadmissible; "Handwriting analysis does not stand up well under the *Daubert* standards. Despite its long history of use and acceptance, validation studies supporting its reliability are few, and the few that exist have been criticized for methodological flaws."). However, most appellate court have not even imposed the limitation found in *Hines.* See United States v. Prime, 363 F.3d 1028, 1033 (9th Cir.2004); United States v. Crisp, 324 F.3d 261 (4th Cir.2003). See also Mnookin, Scripting Expertise: The History of Handwriting Identification Evidence and the Judicial Construction of Reliability, 87 Va.L.Rev. 1723 (2001); Risinger et al., Exorcism of Ignorance as a Proxy for Rational Knowledge: The Lessons of Handwriting Identification "Expertise," 137 U.Pa.L.Rev. 731 (1989).

2. *Fingerprints.* In United States v. Havvard, 117 F.Supp.2d 848 (S.D.Ind.2000), aff'd, 260 F.3d 597 (7th Cir.2001), the court ruled that fingerprint identification satisfied the standards announced in *Daubert* and *Kumho* without citing any scientific research: "First, the methods of latent print identification can be and have been tested. They have been tested for roughly 100 years. They have been tested in adversarial proceedings with the

---

are "disproportionate to any discernable end." *Id.* Pseudologues represent fantasies as real occurrences. *See id.*

highest possible stakes—liberty and sometimes life. * * * Next, the methods of identification are subject to peer review. As just stated, any other qualified examiner can compare the objective information upon which the opinion is based and may render a different opinion if warranted. In fact, peer review is the standard operating procedure among latent print examiners." Is this a proper application of the *Daubert* factors? See also United States v. John, 597 F.3d 263, 274 (5th Cir.2010) ("[I]n most cases, absent novel challenges, fingerprint evidence is sufficiently reliable to satisfy Rule 702 and *Daubert.*"); United States v. Pena, 586 F.3d 105, 110 (1st Cir.2009) (admitting evidence).

Assuming that every finger is unique does not mean that this uniqueness is transferred to a surface in a particular case. Typically, only a partial impression is transferred (often only a fifth of the record print), and distortion due to pressure inevitably affects the impression. The examination, although based on physical characteristics, is basically subjective. There is no minimum number of points of similarity required before a conclusion of identity may be reached. Moreover, because there are frequently "dissimilarities" between the crime scene and record prints, the examiner must decide whether there is a *true* dissimilarity, in which case there is an exclusion ("no match"), or whether the dissimilarity is due to distortion or an artifact.

In the terrorist bombing of a train in Madrid on March 11, 2004, which killed 191 and injured 2,000, the FBI misidentified Brandon Mayfield, a Portland lawyer, as the source of the crime scene prints. See Kershaw, Spain and U.S. at Odds on Mistaken Terror Arrest, N.Y.Times, June 5, 2004, at A1 (Spanish authorities cleared Mayfield and matched the fingerprints to an Algerian national); Stacey, A Report on the Erroneous Fingerprint Individualization in the Madrid Train Bombing Case, 54 J. Forensic Identification 707 (2004). For other misidentifications, see Cole, More Than Zero: Accounting for Error in Latent Fingerprint Identification, 95 J.Crim.L. & Criminology 985 (2005) (discussing 22 misidentifications).

3.   *NAS Forensic Science Report.* In a riveting passage, a 2009 National Academy of Science report on forensic science concluded: "Among existing forensic methods, only nuclear DNA analysis has been rigorously shown to have the capacity to consistently, and with a high degree of certainty, demonstrate a connection between an evidentiary sample and a specific individual or source." National Research Council, Strengthening Forensic Science in the United States: A Path Forward 100 (2009). The report also observed that "some forensic science disciplines are supported by little rigorous systematic research to validate the discipline's basic premises and techniques. There is no evident reason why such research cannot be conducted." Id. at 22. The report identified such common forensic techniques as fingerprint examinations, firearms (ballistics) and toolmark identifications, questioned document comparisons, hair analysis, and bite mark examinations as falling into this category. See Giannelli, *Daubert* and Forensic Science: The Pitfalls of Law Enforcement Control of Scientific Research, 2011 U.Ill.L.Rev. 53.

4. *Rape trauma syndrome.* In People v. Bledsoe, 681 P.2d 291, 300 (Cal.1984), the court noted that "rape trauma syndrome was not devised to determine the 'truth' or 'accuracy' of a particular past event—i.e., whether, in fact, a rape in the legal sense occurred—but rather was developed by professional rape counselors as a therapeutic tool, to help identify, predict and treat emotional problems experienced by the counselors' clients or patients." Thus, although generally accepted by the scientific community for a therapeutic purpose, expert testimony on RTS was not generally accepted "to prove that a rape, in fact, occurred." The court commented:

> [A]s a rule, rape counselors do not probe inconsistencies in their clients' descriptions of the facts of the incident, nor do they conduct independent investigations to determine whether other evidence corroborates or contradicts their clients' renditions. Because their function is to help their clients deal with the trauma they are experiencing, the historical accuracy of the client's descriptions of the details of the traumatizing events is not vital in their task.

The court, however, approved the admissibility of RTS evidence where the defendant suggests to the jury that the conduct of the victim after the incident is inconsistent with the claim of rape. In this situation, the court wrote, "expert testimony on rape trauma syndrome may play a particularly useful role by disabusing the jury of some widely held misconceptions about rape and rape victims, so that it may evaluate the evidence free of popular myths." Id. at 299. Most courts accept this position. For example, expert testimony has been admitted to explain a victim's (1) passive resistance during a rape, (2) delay in reporting the crime, (3) failure to attempt to escape, and (4) calm demeanor after an attack.

Should the same result apply to Child Sexual Abuse Accommodation Syndrome? See United States v. Bighead, 128 F.3d 1329, 1330 (9th Cir.1997) (In rebuttal, an expert "testified about 'delayed disclosure' and 'script memory,' which are typical characteristics she has observed among the more than 1300 persons she has interviewed who say they are victims of child abuse.").

5. *Battered women syndrome.* See Smith v. State, 486 S.E.2d 819, 822 (Ga.1997) ("[T]he battered person syndrome is not a separate defense, but * * * evidence of battered person syndrome is relevant in a proper case as a component of justifiable homicide by self-defense. * * * [E]vidence that a defendant suffered from battered person syndrome is only another circumstance which, if believed by the jury, would authorize a finding that a reasonable person, who had experienced prior physical abuse such as was endured by the defendant, would reasonably believe that the use of force against the victim was necessary, even though that belief may have been, in fact, erroneous.").

If the legal context is not self-defense, should BWS evidence be admissible? See Dunn v. Roberts, 963 F.2d 308 (10th Cir.1992) (accused entitled to expert assistance to raise duress defense); Arcoren v. United

States, 929 F.2d 1235 (8th Cir.1991) (defendant charged with aggravated sexual abuse; his estranged wife reported the assault but then recanted her grand jury testimony at trial; BWS evidence admissible); Barrett v. State, 675 N.E.2d 1112 (Ind.Ct.App.1996) (BWS evidence relevant to a neglect-of-dependent charge).

6. *Modus operandi experts.* The courts have been receptive to expert testimony concerning criminal operations. E.g., United States v. Burchfield, 719 F.2d 356, 358 (11th Cir.1983) (counterfeiting); United States v. Scavo, 593 F.2d 837, 843–44 (8th Cir.1979) (bookmaking); United States v. Jackson, 425 F.2d 574, 576–77 (D.C.Cir.1970) (pickpocketing); United States v. Locascio, 6 F.3d 924, 936 (2d Cir.1993) ("inner workings of the Gambino Family" in the John Gotti trial); United States v. Pungitore, 910 F.2d 1084, 1148–49 (3d Cir.1990) (structure and organization of La Cosa Nostra); Gutierrez v. State, 32 A.3d 2 (Md.2011) (history, hierarchy, and common practices of a street gang).

The most frequent use of this type of testimony involves drug trafficking. Expert testimony has been admitted about the operation of clandestine laboratories, the street value of drugs, the amount of drugs consistent with distribution rather than personal use, strategies of deception, as well as other aspects of the drug trade. In addition, expert testimony on various "tools of the drug trade," including the use of beepers, code words, weapons, duct tape, and the like has been admitted. See United States v. Sepulveda–Barraza, 645 F.3d 1066, 1072 (9th Cir.2011) (expert testimony on drug trafficking organizations and the behavior of unknowing couriers is admissible).

Are there problems with this type of testimony? In United States v. Cruz, 981 F.2d 659 (2d Cir.1992), the expert testified about the use of intermediaries or brokers in the drug trade. The court questioned whether such testimony was useful: "That drug traffickers may seek to conceal their identities by using intermediaries would seem evident to the average juror from movies, television crime dramas, and news stories." Id. at 662. Moreover, the court believed that the expert's testimony was directed at another purpose: "[T]he credibility of a fact-witness may not be bolstered by arguing that the witness's version of events is consistent with an expert's description of patterns of criminal conduct, at least where the witness's version is not attacked as improbable or ambiguous evidence of such conduct." Id. at 663.

7. *Innocence.* A study of 200 DNA exonerations found that expert testimony (55 percent) was the second leading type of evidence (after eyewitness identifications, 79 percent) used in wrongful conviction cases. Of the types of forensic evidence introduced at trial, "serological analysis of blood or semen [was] the most common (79 cases), followed by expert comparison of hair evidence (43 cases), soil comparison (5 cases), DNA tests (3 cases), bite mark evidence (3 cases), fingerprint evidence (2 cases), dog scent identification (2 cases), spectrographic voice evidence (1 case), shoe prints (1 case) and fiber comparison (1 case)." Garrett, Judging Innocence,

108 Colum.L.Rev. 55, 81 (2008). See also Garrett & Neufeld, Invalid Forensic Science Testimony and Wrongful Convictions, 95 Va.L.Rev. 1, 14–15 (2009) ("Of the 100 cases involving serology in which transcripts were located, 57 cases, or 57%, had invalid forensic science testimony. Of the 65 cases involving microscopic hair comparison in which transcripts were located, 25 cases, or 38%, had invalid forensic science testimony."); Giannelli, Wrongful Convictions and Forensic Science: The Need to Regulate Crime Labs, 86 N.C.L.Rev. 163 (2007) (discussing lab scandals in West Virginia, Oklahoma City, Chicago, Houston, Virginia, Montana, and the FBI Lab).

8. *CSI Effect—Expectations of definitive proof?* Scholars, practitioners, and judges have raised the possibility that the recent expansion and popularization of powerful types of forensic proof is having an effect on how jurors perceive and evaluate evidence, particularly in criminal cases. This phenomenon is termed the "CSI effect." CSI stands for *Crime Scene Investigation*, a popular set of television shows. The theory is that jurors learn through popular media about the power of such proof to definitively establish guilt or innocence and come to expect it in all cases, becoming skeptical of a claim where it is not supported by such proof.

Clearly, advances in science and technology have made it possible to extract usable physical trace evidence when it was previously unavailable and to link those physical traces to a particular individual. For example, only a few decades ago tests in rape cases on semen samples could often say no more than that the suspect, the perpetrator, and 20% of the population share a genetic characteristic; now the chances of a random match with a DNA profile may be 1 in a million. Similarly, increases in computing capacity and the growth of databases has allowed identification of the source of that evidence where previously matches were practical only when particular individuals were recognized as suspects. In addition, the ubiquitousness of older technologies, such as photography, in the form of surveillance cameras and camera phones carried by a growing percentage of the population is making another type of "trace" evidence—electronic trace evidence—available in a growing number of prosecutions. These advances can have profound effects on cases where such proof is available. On the other hand, in the huge volume of criminal cases, limits on law enforcement investigative resources, ordinary human failures of imagination and technique, and the fact that trace evidence is often not left, preserved, or collected mean that evidence of this type is frequently unavailable even in prosecutions with clear merit. See Mosteller, Evidence History, the New Trace Evidence, and Rumblings in the Future of Proof, 3 Ohio St.Crim.L.J. 523 (2006).

However, beyond noting that much has changed in recent decades in the quality of forensic proof, that these changes are occurring with increasing speed, and that they have caught popular attention, not much can be said about the reality of the CSI effect on jurors, or if there is such a phenomenon precisely what effect it has on the evaluation of evidence. See Tyler, Viewing CSI and the Threshold of Guilt: Managing Truth and Justice in Reality and Fiction, 115 Yale L.J. 1050 (2006) (noting uncertainty of phenomenon and questioning who benefits if it exists). See also Stabb v. State, 31 A.3d 922, 933 (Md.2011) ("The 'anti-CSI effect' jury instruction given, in the circumstances of this case, was improper because it relieved the State of its burden to prove Stabb was guilty beyond a reasonable doubt, invaded the province of the jury, and, thus, violated Stabb's constitutional right to a fair trial."); Commonwealth v. Perez, 954 N.E.2d 1, 9, 10 (Mass.2011) ("Although anecdotal reports and media coverage have fueled concerns within the legal community about the so-called 'CSI effect,' there is little empirical evidence supporting its existence."; "We conclude that the trial judge did not abuse his discretion questioning the venire about their views on scientific evidence. The questions were tailored to ensure that seated jurors were capable of deciding the case without bias and based on the evidence. The questions did not suggest to potential jurors that a lack of scientific evidence could not be considered in determining whether a reasonable doubt existed as to the defendant's guilt.").

NOTE ON EYEWITNESS IDENTIFICATIONS

As the Supreme Court noted nearly 50 years ago: "The vagaries of eyewitness identification are well-known; the annals of criminal law are rife with instances of mistaken identification." United States v. Wade, 388 U.S. 218, 228 (1967). Decades earlier, before serving on the Supreme Court, Justice Frankfurter questioned the identifications in the Sacco and Vanzetti case. See Frankfurter, The Case of Sacco and Vanzetti 30 (1927) ("What is the worth of identification testimony even when uncontradicted? The identification of strangers is proverbially untrustworthy."). The DNA exoneration cases have vividly documented the problem. Eyewitness misidentifications are the greatest cause of wrongful convictions. See Garrett, Convicting the Innocent: Where Criminal Prosecutions Go Wrong 9 (2011) (76% of 250 exonerations investigated involved misidentifications).

> Research has identified a number of causes for these misidentifications. Many eyewitnesses believe, at least subconsciously, that their assailant "must be" in the lineup or photo spread. Accordingly, they often guess at a choice rather than truly recognize that person as the perpetrator. They make their guess using "relative judgment processes," that is, by selecting the person in the lineup or photo spread who looks most like the wrongdoer, rather than picking someone whom they are convinced is an exact match. Moreover, the detective administering an identification procedure can unwittingly encourage a guess, for example, by smiling or nodding the head slightly or even just widening the eyes as the witness focuses attention toward the suspect. Further, cross-racial identifications are also more likely than intraracial ones to be mistaken. In addition, if "foils"—those persons other than the suspect appearing in the lineup or photo spread—are selected to look more like one another than like the witness's description of the attacker, or if their appearance is significantly different from the

suspect's, an additional risk of error is introduced. Witness certainty likewise tends to rise over time. Thus, witnesses making a tentative identification at a lineup but told that they selected the "right man" become supremely confident of their identification at trial. Finally, juries tend to give great weight to confident identifications, even though the research shows that there is often little, if any, correlation between eyewitness confidence and eyewitness accuracy. Indeed, the research suggests juries, because of their unawareness of the sources of error and the limited evidence enabling them fairly to recreate the circumstances of the lineup or photo spread, find it hard to judge when well-meaning eyewitnesses are just plain wrong.

Report of the ABA Criminal Justice Section's Ad Hoc Innocence Committee to Ensure the Integrity of the Criminal Process, Achieving Justice: Freeing the Innocent, Convicting the Guilty xvii-xviii (Giannelli & Raeder eds., 2006).

Expert testimony. As shown by *Hines,* the use of expert testimony is one approach to the problem. See United States v. Langan, 263 F.3d 613, 621 (6th Cir.2001):

> The use of expert testimony in regard to eyewitness identification is a recurring and controversial subject. Trial courts have traditionally hesitated to admit expert testimony purporting to identify flaws in eyewitness identification. Among the reasons given to exclude such testimony are that the jury can decide the credibility issues itself; that experts in this area are not much help and largely offer rather obvious generalities; that trials would be prolonged by a battle of experts; and that such testimony creates undue opportunity for confusing and misleading the jury.

> Several courts, however, including our own, have suggested that such evidence warrants a more hospitable reception. *See United States v. Smithers,* 212 F.3d 306, 314 (6th Cir.2000) (holding that "the district court abused its discretion in excluding [the eyewitness identification expert's] testimony, without first conducting a hearing pursuant to *Daubert*") * * *. Moreover, such testimony has been allowed in with increasing frequency where the circumstances include "cross-racial identification, identification after a long delay, identification after observation under stress, and [such] psychological phenomena as * * * unconscious transference." *See United States v. Harris,* 995 F.2d 532, 535 (4th Cir.1993). Nonetheless, each court to examine this issue has held that the district court has broad discretion in, first, determining the reliability of the particular testimony, and, second, balancing its probative value against its prejudicial effect.

See also United States v. Lester, 254 F.Supp.2d 602, 612 (E.D.Va.2003) ("[T]he problem of cross-race recognition, the phenomenon of weapon focus, the relationship of different levels of stress on eyewitness perception, and the correlation (or lack thereof) between confidence and accuracy * * * do seem to fall outside the common sense of the average juror."); People v. Santiago, 958 N.E.2d 874, 883 (N.Y. 2011) (Trial court "abused its discretion when it refused to allow testimony on studies showing that eyewitness confidence is a poor predictor of identification accuracy and on studies regarding confidence malleability"); Johnson, Cross–Racial Identification Errors in Criminal Cases, 69 Cornell L.Rev. 934, 938–39 (1984) ("The impairment in ability to recognize black faces is substantial."); Wells & Murray, "Eyewitness Confidence," in Eyewitness Testimony: Psychological Perspectives 155, 165 (Wells & Loftus eds., 1984) ("the eyewitness accuracy-confidence relationship is weak under good laboratory conditions and functionally useless in forensically representative settings").

"Today, a majority of federal circuit courts continues to disfavor the admission of eyewitness identification expert testimony. Given the years of social science evidence emphasizing the reliability problems inherent in eyewitness identifications and the statistics tracking the growing number of exonerations based on erroneous eyewitness identifications, it is no longer tolerable to accept this trend." Tallent, Note, Through the Lens of Federal Evidence Rule 403: An Examination of Eyewitness Identification Expert Testimony Admissibility in the Federal Circuit Courts, 68 Wash. & Lee L.Rev. 765, 808 (2011).

Jury instructions. Some courts have attempted to deal with eyewitness identification problems by requiring special cautionary jury instructions. The leading case is United States v. Telfaire, 469 F.2d 552 (D.C.Cir.1972), which sets forth a recommended instruction. There are three different approaches in the cases: (1) courts requiring the *Telfaire* instruction; (2) courts leaving the decision on whether to instruct to the discretion of the trial court; and (3) courts rejecting *Telfaire*-like instructions and holding that the general instructions on credibility are sufficient. However, the effectiveness of special instructions is debatable. See Penrod & Cutler, Eyewitness Expert Testimony and Jury Decisionmaking, 52 Law & Contemp.Probs. 43, 82 (Aut.1989); Ramirez et al., Judge's Cautionary Instructions on Eyewitness Testimony, 14 Am.J. Forensic Psych. 31 (1996). Indeed, some instructions may mislead. In Brodes v. State, 614 S.E.2d 766, 771 (Ga.2005), the court ruled that, in light of the documented lack of correlation between a witness' certainty in his or her identification, it could "no longer endorse an instruction authorizing jurors to consider the witness's certainty in his/her identification as a factor to be used in deciding the reliability of that identification."

Lineup and photo spread procedures. Several proposed reforms focus on the police procedures used to produce an identification. These include the use of double-blind procedures, increasing the number of foils, and employing sequential (rather than simultaneous) procedures. How do these proposals address the concerns mentioned above? Are there other possible reforms? See Wells et al., Eyewitness Identification Procedures: Recommendations for Lineups and Photospreads, 22 Law & Hum.Behav. 603 (1998).

A field study involving 497 actual lineups showed that "the rates of identifying the suspect were largely the same for the simultaneous versus sequential lineup procedures, with the simultaneous yielding 25.5% suspect identifications and the sequential yielding 27.3% suspect identifications. * * * The rates of filler identifications, however, yielded a larger difference, with 18.1% filler identifications for the simultaneous and 12.2% filler identifications for the sequential." The report goes on to conclude that "to the extent that filler identification rates are a reasonable proxy for mistaken identifications of innocent suspects, the sequential procedure should catch fewer innocent suspects in its net. At the same time, there is no evidence from these data that the sequential lineup produces fewer identifications of suspects, at least when the sequential procedure is operationalized the way it was here (doubleblind administration of the lineup; witness sees all photos even if an identification is made; second lap permitted if the witness requests it; a clear 'not sure' option)." Wells et al., A Test of the Simultaneous vs. Sequential Lineup Methods: An Initial Report of the AJS National Eyewitness Identification Field Studies 13 (Am. Judicature Soc'y 2011).

UNITED STATES V. VEYSEY
United States Court of Appeals, Seventh Circuit, 2003.
334 F.3d 600.

POSNER, CIRCUIT JUDGE.

John Veysey appeals from his conviction, after a jury trial, and sentence of 110 years in prison for mail and wire fraud, arson, and the related offense of felony by fire. The facts are amazing, but we shall resist the temptation to recount them at length. In 1991 Veysey set fire to his house and inflated the claim that he then filed with his insurer. The insurer paid, and the house was rebuilt. The following year Veysey married a woman named Kemp, increased the insurance on the house, removed the valuable contents of the house, along with himself and his wife, and then cut the natural-gas line inside the house, causing the house to fill up with gas and explode spectacularly, utterly destroying it. He grossly exaggerated the value of the property allegedly lost in the explosion—some did not exist and some he had removed before the explosion. The insurance company (a different one) paid, and he used part of the proceeds to buy another house. The next year he tried to kill his wife by driving his van with her in it into a river. When that failed he killed her by poisoning her, and collected $200,000 in the proceeds of insurance policies on her life. He placed personal ads in newspapers, seeking to meet women. He became engaged to one of the women he met through his ads, named Donner, but broke his engagement after failing to procure a $1 million policy on her life. He then took up with a Ms. Beetle. This was in 1996 and the same year he burned down his house, again submitting an inflated estimate of the loss and receiving substantial proceeds from the insurance company (a different one, again). He then married Beetle, and they moved into a rented house. She insured her life for $500,000 with him as beneficiary. One night in 1998, after drugging her, he set fire to the house, hoping to kill both her and their infant son, on whom he had also taken out a life insurance policy and who was in the house with her. They were rescued, and soon afterwards Veysey and Beetle divorced. The house was rebuilt and Veysey persuaded a woman named Hilkin to move in with him after she had accumulated some $700,000 in life insurance and named him as the primary beneficiary. He apparently intended to murder her, but he was arrested before his plans matured. There is more, but these are the highlights.

* * *

The last issue we consider is Veysey's objection to testimony by an actuary, Charles L. McClenahan, that the probability of four residential fires occurring by chance during the 106 months between April 1989 (when Veysey bought the first house that he is known to have set fire to) and January 1998 (when he set fire to his last house) was only one in 1.773 trillion; he described this as a conservative estimate. We can imagine two distinct grounds for Veysey's objection to the actuary's evidence. The first, which, though the stronger, Veysey's lawyer has not made—and in fact expressly disclaimed, when pressed, at argument—is that the calculation was based on implicit assumptions that are untenable.

A simplified version of what the actuary did is that he first determined the number of serious residential fires in the United States over the interval in which houses occupied by Veysey caught fire four times (with "serious" defined as a fire that caused a loss equal to or greater than 20 percent of the amount of fire insurance on the house, and so defined serious fires are 5.3 percent of all residential fires), then divided that number by the number of houses in the United States, and finally multiplied the resulting probability by itself four times. Suppose (we are using hypothetical figures for the sake of simplicity) the probability that a specific house would have caught fire during the 106–month interval were one in 1,000. Then, on the assumption of independence (an important qualification, discussed next), the probability that two specific houses would have caught fire during the interval would be one in a million (1/1,000 x 1/1,000), the probability that three specific houses would have caught fire would be one in a billion, and the probability that four would have caught fire would be one in a trillion.

This simplified calculation does modest violence to the actuary's method, as the mathematics of repeatable events is somewhat complex. When the actuary divided the number of fires by the number of houses, the resulting quotient was not really the probability of a fire happening to a specific house, but an input into a formula designed to assess the probability of a repeated event, in this case a serious fire in a series of Veysey's dwellings. But as with our simple version, the actuary's actual computation assumed that the probabilities of each of a person's multiple fires are independent of each other—that the fact that you had a fire at one time or in one of your houses would not affect the probability that you would have a second fire in that house or a fire in your next house. The assumption was not defended by the actuary, and is unrealistic. Compare Branion v. Gramly, 855 F.2d 1256, 1265 (7th Cir.1988). A fire in a house or in an apartment is likely to be the result, at least in part, of carelessness on the part of the occupant, implying that he is more likely to have another fire than a person who has never had a fire (though against this it can be argued that someone who has experienced a fire will be more careful to avoid a repetition—once burned is twice shy). Moreover, even if the assumption of independence were defensible, the actuary's calculation would be flawed by his failure to limit the reference group to residences comparable in design, materials, age, value, region, and other factors relevant to the likelihood of a fire in Veysey's residences.

But Veysey as we have said does not object to the actuary's methodology. His objection is that the actuary usurped the jury's function by testifying in effect that Veysey was guilty of the crimes with which he was charged way beyond a reasonable doubt, as the probability of his innocence was not 1 or 2 or 5 percent or whatever might be thought the implicit probability of innocence sufficient to prevent a finding of guilt beyond a reasonable doubt, but, if the actuary was believed, a mere .0000000000564 percent. Veysey's counsel goes so far as to argue that statistical evidence should never be admissible to establish an element of a crime. Fingerprint or DNA evidence is admissible, he acknowledges, but the jury must not be told what the probability is that such evidence actually establishes the proposition for which it is introduced, such as that the defendant's fingerprints were on the murder weapon.

In making this argument Veysey's counsel is gesturing toward an academic literature (well summarized in Ronald J. Allen, "On the Significance of Batting Averages and Strikeout Totals: A Clarification of the 'Naked Statistical Evidence' Debate, the Meaning of 'Evidence,' and the Requirement of Proof Beyond A Reasonable Doubt," 65 Tul.L.Rev. 1093 (1991)) that argues that judges and jurors, because they lack knowledge of statistical theory, are both overawed and easily deceived by statistical evidence, see, e.g., Laurence H. Tribe, "Trial by Mathematics: Precision and Ritual in the Legal Process," 84 Harv.L.Rev. 1329 (1971); Charles Nesson, "The Evidence or the Event? On Judicial Proof and the Acceptability of Verdicts," 98 Harv.L.Rev. 1357, 1378–85 (1985); Craig R. Callen, "Adjudication and the Appearance of Statistical Evidence," 65 Tul.L.Rev. 457 (1991), and toward decisions, such as Smith v. Rapid

Transit, 317 Mass. 469, 58 N.E.2d 754 (1945), that refuse to permit a case to go to a jury on purely statistical evidence. In *Smith* the court held that it "was not enough" "that mathematically the chances somewhat favor the proposition that a bus of the defendant caused the accident." *Id.* at 755.

Suppose, to consider a well-known hypothetical variant of *Smith*, that a person is hit by a bus, and it is known that 51 percent of the buses on the road where he was hit are owned by Bus Company A and 49 percent by Bus Company B. He sues A and asks for judgment on the basis of this statistic alone; he presents no other evidence. If the defendant also presents no evidence, should a jury be permitted to award judgment for the plaintiff? See, e.g., Gary L. Wells, "Naked Statistical Evidence of Liability: Is Subjective Probability Enough?" 62 J. Personality & Soc. Psych. 739 (1992). The law answers "no." Richard W. Wright, "Causation, Responsibility, Risk, Probability, Naked Statistics, and Proof: Pruning the Bramble Bush by Clarifying the Concepts," 73 Ia. L. Rev. 1001, 1050–51 (1988). But this is not because of doubt about the evidentiary value of statistical evidence. The true source of disquiet in the example, we believe, is the tacit assumption that the statistic concerning the ownership of the buses is the only evidence the plaintiff can obtain. Howard v. Wal–Mart Stores, Inc., 160 F.3d 358, 360 (7th Cir.1998). If it is his only evidence, the inference to be drawn is not that there is a 51 percent probability that it was a bus owned by A that hit him but that he either investigated and discovered that it was actually a bus owned by B (which might be judgment-proof and so not worth suing), or that he has simply not bothered to conduct an investigation. In either event he should lose, in the first case obviously and in the second because a court should not be required to expend any of its scarce resources of time and effort on a case until the plaintiff has conducted a sufficient search to indicate that an expenditure of public resources is reasonably likely to yield a social benefit.

But if both bus companies had been determined to be negligent, so that the only issue was which had hit the plaintiff, then in many states the 51/49 ratio of A's to B's buses would be enough for a judgment against A—indeed against A and B. See Sindell v. Abbott Laboratories, 26 Cal.3d 588, 163 Cal.Rptr. 132, 607 P.2d 924 (1980); Summers v. Tice, 33 Cal.2d 80, 199 P.2d 1 (1948), Krist v. Eli Lilly & Co., 897 F.2d 293, 300 (7th Cir.1990). Or if the ratio of buses owned by A to those owned by B were much higher than 51/49, the case against allowing "naked" statistical evidence to carry the plaintiff's burden of production on the issue of liability (rather than only causation) would be weakened. The law recognizes this not only in the obvious cases of fingerprint and DNA evidence, the admissibility of which depends on the improbability that two different people would have the same fingerprint or DNA signature, *Branion v. Gramly*, supra, 855 F.2d at 1265, but also in the law's adoption of such presumptions as that a properly addressed, stamped, and mailed letter will reach the addressee. This is a purely statistical presumption because it is applied without regard to the particulars of the case beyond those required to satisfy the conditions of the presumption; and yet it can determine the outcome.

"All evidence is probabilistic—statistical evidence merely explicitly so," Riordan v. Kempiners, 831 F.2d 690, 698 (7th Cir.1987) * * *, because nothing with which the law deals is metaphysically certain. Statistical evidence is merely probabilistic evidence coded in numbers rather than words. "Nothing about the nature of litigation in general, or the criminal process in particular, makes anathema of additional information, whether or not that knowledge has numbers attached. After all, even eyewitnesses are testifying only to probabilities (though they obscure the methods by which they generate those probabilities)—often rather lower probabilities than statistical work insists on." *Branion v. Gramly*, supra, 855 F.2d at 1264. An eyewitness does not usurp the jury's function if he testifies that he is positive that he saw the defendant strike a match, and it would make no difference if he said that he is "99 percent" positive. The significant question would be the accuracy of the estimate. The actuary's one in 1.7 trillion estimate in this case probably was inaccurate, but not because it was a statistic. The issue of its accuracy has been waived, however, and in any event the error in its introduction was harmless; the other evidence against the defendant was overwhelming.

Affirmed.

Notes and Questions

1.   *Probability of guilt.* What is the difference between the probability of a random match and the probability of guilt? In the ABO blood system, the probability of someone in the general population having type O is 45%, A is 42%, B is 10%, and AB is 3%. If blood at a murder scene is AB and this "matches" the defendant's type (and assuming the victim's blood in not AB), is there a 97% probability of guilt? In a community of one million people? See Broun & Kelly, Playing the Percentages and the Law of Evidence, 1970 U.Ill.L.Rev. 23.

2.   *Minnesota rule.* One jurisdiction has concluded that admitting probability calculations, even when based upon a proper foundation, is so prejudicial as to outweigh any probative value. See State v. Boyd, 331 N.W.2d 480 (Minn.1983); State v. Carlson, 267 N.W.2d 170 (Minn.1978). What will the jury do with evidence of a "match" without an accompanying statistic?

3.   *Independence.* In People v. Collins, 438 P.2d 33 (1968), a mathematician testified in effect that the chances were one in twelve million that a robbery had been committed by a couple other than the two defendants: woman with a pony tail (1 in 10); woman with blond hair (1 in 3); yellow car (1 in 10); man with mustache (1 in 4); African American man

wearing a beard (1 in 10); and interracial couple (1 in 1000). Does the product rule work here? See generally Fisher, Green Felt Jungle: The Story of *People v. Collins*, in Evidence Stories 7 (Lempert ed., 2006).

There may also be an independence problem in Sudden Infant Death (SID) cases. See Wilson v. State, 803 A.2d 1034, 1044 (Md.2002) ("[T]he trial court erred in admitting expert testimony based on the product rule because a condition necessary to the proper application of the product rule was lacking: there was inadequate proof of the independence of [siblings] Brandi and Garrett's deaths. As evidenced by the authorities above cited, there is not general agreement in the scientific community as to the relationship between SIDS deaths within a single family. Stated another way, there is not general agreement in the medical community that multiple SIDS deaths in a single family are genetically unrelated.").

4. *Bayes' theorem.* Through a mathematical rule of unquestioned validity known as Bayes' theorem, experts are able to show how data showing the frequency of an occurrence in the population should increase a previously established probability that the defendant is the person who left an incriminating trace. For example, if the jury believed that there was a 25% probability of guilt and then heard new evidence that a trace left at the crime scene was found in only 1% of the population and that the defendant was part of that population, Bayes' rule would provide that there should now be a 97% chance of guilt. See Finkelstein & Fairley, A Bayesian Approach to Identification Evidence, 83 Harv.L.Rev. 489, 500 (1970). Should the jury be told about Bayes' rule so that they can make their own determinations of guilt in a more scientific way? What problems would such evidence present for the accused?

COMMONWEALTH V. ROSIER

Supreme Judicial Court of Massachusetts, 1997.
685 N.E.2d 739.

GREANEY, JUSTICE.

A jury in the Superior Court convicted the defendant, Adam Rosier, of murder in the first degree (by reason of deliberate premeditation and extreme atrocity or cruelty) of sixteen year old Kristal Hopkins. [The defendant challenged the admissibility of DNA test results.[53]]

---

[53] [DNA (deoxyribonucleic acid) is a chemical messenger of genetic information, a code that gives both common and individual characteristics to people. DNA is found in packages called chromosomes. Humans have 23 pairs of chromosomes, half of which are inherited from each parent. DNA is composed of a chain of nucleotide bases twisted into a double helix structure, resembling a twisted ladder. Each rung of the helix is a "base pair." The order of the base pairs on the DNA ladder is known as the DNA sequence; it constitutes the "genetic code." Except for identical twins, no two individuals share the same DNA profile.

DNA is found in every body cell with a nucleus. With few exceptions, DNA does not vary from cell to cell. Each cell contains the entire genetic code, although each cell reads only the part of the code that it needs to perform its job. Thus, blood obtained from a suspect can be compared with semen, sweat, saliva, or hair cells from a crime scene.

* * *

* * * The Commonwealth engaged Cellmark Diagnostics (Cellmark), a recognized forensic laboratory located in Germantown, Maryland, to perform DNA testing on two blood stains taken from the undercarriage of the automobile, one blood stain from the front tire on the passenger side, one blood stain taken from the passenger side quarter panel, the threadlike substance that appeared to be human tissue found on the undercarriage, a blood sample taken from the victim, and one taken from the defendant. Cellmark completed the testing using the polymerase chain reaction (PCR) method, and submitted a written report to the State police. The report concluded that PCR-based testing disclosed * * * that the approximate frequencies in the Caucasian and African–American populations between the genotypes analyzed in the sample, when compared with the same genotypes obtained from the victim's blood sample, were 1 in 770,000 for the Caucasian population and 1 in 7.5 million for the African–American population.

* * *

We turn now to the issues involving the DNA evidence. As has been indicated, the samples submitted by the State police for DNA analysis were examined by the PCR method,[54] and Cellmark performed DQA1, PM, and STR testing, using three commercial kits.[55] We have explained the PCR method and the process of testing at the DQA1 and PM loci in Commonwealth v. Vao Sok, 425 Mass. 787, 683 N.E.2d 671 (1997). We need to explain STR testing.[56] STR is an acronym for short tandem repeat. A tandem repeat involves multiple copies of identical DNA sequence arranged in direct succession in a particular region of a chromosome. A short tandem repeat is a tandem repeat in which the repeat units are three, four, or five base pairs (a base pair has two

---

Approximately 99% of the base pairs found in humans are the same. A single DNA molecule contains roughly three billion base pairs. It is the area of base pair variation that is used in DNA analysis. These base pairs are called "polymorphisms." Approximately three million base pairs are thought to be polymorphic. Examining every polymorphic site on the DNA molecule is not practical. In other words, DNA analysis does not examine an individual's entire genome, but rather a snapshot of a specific area. The analysis focuses on a number of sites (loci) that are highly polymorphic, which are examined to determine whether the evidence and suspect samples contain matching alleles. The more loci used, the more significant the "matches." Note that a non-match at any loci excludes the subject as the source. Ed.]

[54] The PCR method was utilized because the samples were too small to be tested by the Restriction Fragment Length Polymorphism (RFLP) method, which requires larger samples of investigatory materials before profiling can be satisfactorily done. See Commonwealth v. Vao Sok, 425 Mass. 787, 683 N.E.2d 671 (1997)

[55] The AmpliType HLA DQa Forensic DNA Amplification and Typing Kit, the AmpliType PM PCR Amplification and Typing Kit, and GenePrint STR Systems. The DQA1 and PM kits appear to be the same kits that were used by the Center for Blood Research, the laboratory that did the DNA testing in Commonwealth v. Vao Sok, supra at 790–94, 683 N.E.2d at 674–75.

[56] All the information that follows as to STR testing is taken from the 1996 report of the National Research Council entitled, The Evaluation of Forensic DNA Evidence (1996 NRC Report).

complementary nucleotides). Loci containing STRs are scattered throughout the chromosomes in enormous numbers. Such loci have a fairly large number of alleles and are usually capable of unique identification. Cellmark tested at three STR loci,[57] which, in combination with the testing at the DQA1 and PM loci, gave results from nine different loci. The STR testing became important in the case because Cellmark had done prior DNA testing on the samples submitted examining only the DQA1 and PM loci and had concluded, based on results from those loci, that the population frequencies between the victim and the Caucasian and African–American population were 1 in 5,500 and 1 in 11,000 respectively. The additional testing of the STR loci, when considered with the results of the DQA1 and PM testing, increased the probabilities to 1 in 770,000 (Caucasian) and 1 in 7.5 million (African–American). As Dr. Basten agreed, STR analysis made a "significant difference" in terms of the frequency in which the genetic markers would be expected to be seen within a population. As the judge found: "At the CSF1PO locus, scientists have observed nine different alleles, giving rise to 45 possible genotypes. At the TPOX locus, seven different alleles have been observed, giving rise to 28 possible genotypes. At the TH01 locus, eight different alleles have been observed, giving rise to 36 possible genotypes."

At the hearing on the motion in limine, the defendant did not specifically challenge the collection and preservation of the samples submitted to Cellmark for DNA testing, the quality control and assurance standards at the laboratory,[58] the use of the PCR method, the reliability of the three test procedures or the accuracy of the test results obtained from the use of the typing kits. * * *

The PCR method is scientifically valid, and testing at the DQA1 and PM loci is scientifically reliable, if properly done. Commonwealth v. Vao Sok, supra at 799, 683 N.E.2d at 679. The defendant's appellate counsel appears to suggest that STR testing is unreliable because it is too new. No specific scientific or forensic evidence or literature is offered to support that suggestion. The judge heard testimony that, in 1991, several years before the STR kit became commercially available, Cellmark, working under contract to the United States government, used STR testing to identify the remains of soldiers killed in Operation Desert Storm, and that, by the time of the hearing, Cellmark had performed STR analysis in

---

[57] The STR loci tested were at chromosomes identified as CSF1PO, TPOX, and TH01 using GenePrint STR systems.

[58] Cellmark is accredited for forensic work by the American Society of Crime Laboratory Directors and for paternity testing by the American Association of Blood Banks. The accreditations are the result of audits of Cellmark's work by these accrediting groups and regular proficiency and quality assurance testing. The testing and other safeguards adhered to by Cellmark comply with the guidelines set out by the Technical Working Group on DNA Analysis Methods (TWGDAM), a group of forensic DNA analysts from government and private laboratories who are considered authoritative in the field.

approximately fifty cases and had been permitted to testify as to its test results in at least five cases.[59] While we have not been directed to any decisional law approving STR testing, an authoritative scientific study, the 1996 report of the National Research Council entitled, The Evaluation of Forensic DNA Evidence (1996 NRC Report), has concluded (*id.* at 71) that STR testing is "coming into wide use," that "STR loci appear to be particularly appropriate for forensic use" (*id.* at 117), and that "STRs can take their place along with VNTRs as forensic tools" (*id.* at 35). The latter comment appears to recognize that STR testing is similar in principle to the RFLP (or VNTR) method, which has been found to be reliable. See Commonwealth v. Daggett, 416 Mass. 347, 350 n.1, 622 N.E.2d 272 (1993). Based on the evidence before him and his careful analysis of the subject, the judge properly concluded that the methodology underlying the PCR-based tests in this case, including the STR testing, was scientifically valid and relevant to a fact at trial. * * *

The defendant's principal attack on the DNA results is focused on the evidence pertaining to the statistical significance of the match found by the three tests between the DNA in the blood stains and tissue taken from the automobile and the victim's DNA. Evidence of a match based on correctly used testing systems is of little or no value without reliable evidence indicating the "significance of the match, that is, evidence of the probability of a random match of [the victim's or] the defendant's DNA in the general population." Commonwealth v. Lanigan, supra at 20, 641 N.E.2d 1342. To obtain the relevant statistical results in this case, Cellmark used a database it had developed using samples taken from paternity studies done at Cellmark.[60] At the time of the hearing, Cellmark's database was the only one that used samples from the same persons for all of the nine loci analyzed under the DQA1, PM, and STR tests used by Cellmark. The statistical results were calculated by means of the product rule. "Under the product rule, the frequency in the population base of each allele disclosed in the DNA test is multiplied to produce the frequency of the combination of all the alleles found." Commonwealth v. Lanigan, supra at 21, 641 N.E.2d 1342, citing Commonwealth v. Curnin, 409 Mass. 218, 224 n.10, 225 n.11, 565 N.E.2d 440 (1991). The defendant argues that Cellmark's database is too small and, for various other reasons, unreliable.

The judge acted properly in rejecting the defendant's arguments. He accepted the expert testimony that the Cellmark database was adequate and common within the field and that a database larger than Cellmark's

---

[59] Dr. Word testified that, prior to using STR testing in forensic cases, Cellmark had conducted extensive validation tests to evaluate the reliability and sensitivity of STR testing, as well as how much DNA was needed to get results and the development of other "testing parameters."

[60] The database consisted of one hundred blood samples from Caucasian persons and one hundred blood samples from African–American persons.

would produce "no significant difference in the result." There was expert and scientific evidence that the Cellmark database met two factors critical to the reliability of a database. The first factor, "linkage equilibrium" (LE), establishes that the various chromosomal loci identified in a database occur randomly in proportion to one another, thus assuring that results related to one locus are not affected by, nor predictive of, the results related to another.[61] The second factor is "Hardy–Weinberg equilibrium" (HW). A database is considered to be "in HW" when the predicted values for the various loci within the database actually correspond to those found in the population, assuming mates are randomly chosen. Thus, it was properly found that the Cellmark database was both in LE and in HW. The database and statistical results reached by Cellmark were also independently verified by Dr. Basten through calculations of "confidence intervals"[62] and a comparison of Cellmark's results with other databases that achieved statistically comparable results.[63] Dr. Basten also concluded that the methods used by Cellmark to generate statistical results are "generally accepted" within the field of population genetics, and that the statistical results they produce are reliable and accurate.

At the motion hearing, the defendant did not make any argument that Cellmark's use of the product rule to reach its conclusions about population frequencies was wrong. We think it is appropriate, however, to discuss the product rule to assure completeness in the examination of this phase of the case. In Commonwealth v. Lanigan, supra at 21, 641 N.E.2d 1342, we stated that "[t]he product or multiplication rule is based on the assumption that the population does not contain subpopulations with distinct allele frequencies, and, therefore, each person's alleles constitute statistically independent random selections from a common gene pool." We went on to state that "[t]he validity of the use of the multiplication rule thus depends on the absence of population substructure. If there is population substructure, the assumption of complete statistical

[61] There was evidence that the Cellmark database, better than any combination of available databases, allowed for proper testing for LE to determine whether the identified alleles are genetically independent, because it used the same persons for testing results in each of its systems.

[62] Dr. Basten's process of "confidence intervals" involved the selection of individuals at random from Cellmark's database to create a new database and then utilizing a computer to repeat the procedure 1,000 times so that 1,000 new databases of one hundred individuals each were produced. A complicated statistical analysis then followed (which is set forth in the judge's memorandum and need not be described here) to arrive at a statistical result that, according to Dr. Basten, verified Cellmark's results and frequency conclusions. The fact that the proportions derived by Dr. Basten from the confidence intervals differed from Cellmark's proportions did not throw the latter into doubt, because, as the judge noted, Dr. Basten was conducting a verification test and not a test designed to express an opinion as to the actual frequency of genotypes derived from the crime scene samples in the population at large.

[63] Three other databases were consulted by Dr. Basten: one developed by the Federal Bureau of Investigation (FBI) and published in the Journal of Forensic Science; and two others as reported at the Fifth International Symposium on Human Identification.

independence of alleles is not valid." Id. To ameliorate this problem, we accepted the recommendation that population frequencies be calculated by use of "the ceiling principle," which was "adopted to make irrelevant the dispute among population geneticists over the question whether the product rule may properly be used to express numerically the probability of finding a DNA match in a random selection of the appropriate population." Id. at 26, 641 N.E.2d 1342. The ceiling principle was recommended by the National Research Council in its 1992 Report on The Evaluation of Forensic DNA Evidence to help quiet the significant debate over potential problems arising out of population substructuring.[64]

It is fair to say that the controversy has been resolved in large part. The 1996 NRC Report notes (*id.* at 53) that "information is now available from a number of relevant populations, so that experts can usually base estimates on an appropriate database." In considering the same question, the admissibility of statistical evidence calculated under the product rule, the Supreme Court of Washington cited a major Federal Bureau of Investigation (FBI) study of VNTR frequency data from around the world entitled, VNTR Population Data: A Worldwide Study (Feb.1993) (Worldwide Study), which concluded that the product rule is reliable and valid.[65] State v. Copeland, 130 Wash.2d 244, 267–268, 922 P.2d 1304 (1996), quoting Worldwide Study, *supra* at 2. That report has been supported by other studies that have similarly concluded that differences of allelic distribution are not forensically significant, and courts that have

---

[64] The 1996 NRC Report describes the "ceiling principle" and the "interim ceiling principle" as follows:

"The 1992 report * * * recommended the use of an ad hoc approach for the calculation of an upper bound on the frequencies that would be found in any real population; this approach used what was termed the 'ceiling principle.' The report recommended that population frequency data be collected on homogeneous populations from 15–20 racial and ethnic groups. The highest frequency of a marker in any population, or 5%—whichever was higher, was to be used for calculation. Until the highest frequencies were available an 'interim ceiling principle' was to be used. That would assign to each marker the highest frequency value found in any population database (adjusted upward to allow for statistical uncertainty) or 10%—whichever was higher. The result would be a composite profile frequency that did not depend on a specific racial or ethnic database and would practically always exceed the frequency calculated from the database of the reference populations."

Id. at 52.

[65] The Worldwide Study study, *supra* at 2, concluded as follows:

"(1) that there are sufficient population data available to determine whether or not forensically significant differences might occur when using different population databases; (2) that subdivision, either by ethnic group or by U.S. geographic region, within a major population group does not substantially affect forensic estimates of the likelihood of occurrence of a DNA profile; (3) that estimates of the likelihood of occurrence of a DNA profile using major population group databases (e.g., Caucasian, Black, and Hispanic) provide a greater range of frequencies than would estimates from subgroups of a major population category; therefore, the estimate of the likelihood of occurrence of a DNA profile derived by the current practice of employing the multiplication rule and using general population databases for allele frequencies is reliable, valid, and meaningful, without forensically significant consequences; and (4) that the data do not support the need for alternate procedures, such as the ceiling principle approach."

examined the question have agreed that challenges to the use of the product rule have been sufficiently resolved. [Citations omitted.]

It is important to note as well: "The ceiling principles were intended for VNTRs with many alleles, no one of which has a very high frequency [and t]hey are not applicable to PCR-based systems." 1996 NRC Report at 158. We agree with the conclusions of the 1996 NRC Report that "both the ceiling principle and the interim ceiling principle are unnecessary," (*id.* at 162) and that "[i]n general, the calculation of a profile frequency should be made with the product rule," (*id.* at 5) both for VNTR and PCR-based systems.[66] Thus, the use of the product rule by Cellmark in connection with its PCR-based testing in this case was scientifically acceptable.

* * *

Judgment affirmed.

NOTES AND QUESTIONS

1.   *The science.* As the principal case indicates, DNA profiling involves two fields: molecular biology and population genetics. Thus, the process involves two corresponding steps—first, determining whether the genetic markers at different loci "match." If there is a "no match" at any locus, the suspect is excluded.

If there are "matches" at all the tested loci, the significance of these matches must be determined. Once a match is declared, a probability is computed that estimates the chances that someone randomly selected from the population would have the same genetic marker (allele) as the forensic sample. Because a number of people will have the same genetic markers at one locus, more than one locus is tested. The frequencies of the individual alleles are multiplied together (according to the "product rule"), and an aggregate probability estimate is computed. For the calculations to be reliable, all the loci tested must be independent. For this assumption to be true, individuals must reproduce randomly so that distinct subgroups (population substructure) are absent.

2.   *The procedures.* There have been three generations of DNA tests. The first type was based on Restriction Fragment Length Polymorphism (RFLP). The second was polymerase chain reaction (PCR) for specific alleles. PCR permits amplification of DNA ("molecular photocopying"). Thus, it requires far less biological material than RFLP technologies. In many

---

[66] The 1996 NRC Report also recommends that "[i]f the race of the person who left the evidence sample DNA is known, the database for the person's race should be used; if the race is not known, calculations for all the racial groups to which possible suspects belong should be made." 1996 NRC Report at 5 (Recommendation 4.1 of the Recommendations for Estimating Random–Match Probabilities). Recommendations 4.2, 4.3, and 4.4 suggest calculation methodologies for cases where a subpopulation is involved (4.2), where the source of the DNA sample is from a subpopulation for which no database exists (4.3), and where all possible contributors of the sample include relatives of the subject (4.4), situations that complicate the application of the product rule. 1996 NRC Report at 5–6.

instances, the forensic sample may be too small, or too damaged by environmental conditions, for RFLP testing. Also, unlike RFLP, this procedure focused on the presence or absence of alleles at a specific locus, such as the DQ alpha locus. In the beginning, this procedure was far less discriminating than RLFP. The third technique is Short Tandem Repeats (STR).

STR testing is typically based on thirteen to sixteen loci. See People v. Shreck, 22 P.3d 68, 72 (Colo.2001) (probability that the contributor was not the defendant but a random third person was 1 in 5.3 quadrillion); State v. Butterfield, 27 P.3d 1133, 1137 (Utah 2001) (probability of a random individual other than the victim matching the blood on Butterfield's under-shirt was 215 billion to 1). See also Imwinkelried & Kaye, DNA Typing: Emerging or Neglected Issues, 76 Wash.L.Rev. 413 (2001).

3. *Mitochondrial DNA.* In addition to nuclear DNA, mitochondrial DNA testing may be used when nuclear DNA is unavailable (e.g., hair without a root or bone without marrow). See United States v. Beverly, 369 F.3d 516, 531 (6th Cir.2004); State v. Underwood, 518 S.E.2d 231 (N.C.Ct.App.1999); State v. Council, 515 S.E.2d 508, 518 (S.C.1999). It is not as discriminating as nuclear DNA.

4. *Nonhuman DNA evidence.* DNA is found in all living organisms. See United States v. Boswell, 270 F.3d 1200 (8th Cir.2001) (in a false statement prosecution, DNA used to compare swine blood); State v. Bogan, 905 P.2d 515 (Ariz.Ct.App.1995) (in murder case, DNA of seed pods from palo verde trees at scene compared to those found in Bogan's truck); State v. Schmidt, 699 So.2d 448 (La.Ct.App.1997) (in attempted murder by injection of HIV virus, expert testified that HIV from two persons were "closely related"). But see State v. Leuluaialii, 77 P.3d 1192 (Wash.Ct.App.2003) (canine DNA match between sample obtained from defendant and murder victim's dog not generally accepted).

5. *Presenting DNA Evidence.* How should trial counsel offer DNA Evidence before a jury? One experienced DNA prosecutor recommends the K.I.S.S. principle: "Keep it short and simple." Wooley, Presentation of DNA Evidence at Trial: The K.I.S.S. Principle, 1 Profiles in DNA 3 (May 1997). See also Schklar & Diamond, Juror Reactions to DNA Evidence: Errors and Expectancies, 23 Law & Hum.Behav. 159 (1999).

6. *DNA Wars.* DNA evidence was the subject of fierce debates when first introduced. See People v. Castro, 545 N.Y.S.2d 985, 996 (Sup.Ct.1989) ("In a piercing attack upon each molecule of evidence presented, the defense was successful in demonstrating to this court that the testing laboratory failed in its responsibility to perform the accepted scientific techniques and experiments."). The FBI's top DNA expert, Dr. Budowle, later acknowledged the early deficiencies. Lander & Budowle, DNA Fingerprinting Dispute Laid to Rest, 371 Nature 735, 735 (Oct. 27, 1994) ("The initial outcry over DNA typing standards concerned laboratory problems: poorly defined rules for declaring a match; experiments without controls; contaminated probes and

samples; and sloppy interpretation of autoradiograms. Although there is no evidence that these technical failings resulted in any wrongful convictions, the lack of standards seemed to be a recipe for trouble."). See generally Kaye, The Double Helix and the Law of Evidence (2010); Mnookin, *People v. Castro*: Challenging the Forensic Use of DNA Evidence, in Evidence Stories 207 (Lempert ed., 2006).

7. *Lab errors.* Despite the power of DNA evidence, some problems have been exposed in its use. See Madigan, Houston's Troubled DNA Crime Lab Faces Growing Scrutiny, N.Y.Times, Feb. 9, 2003 (operations suspended after an audit found numerous problems including poor calibration and maintenance of equipment, improper record keeping, and a lack of safeguards against contamination; "Among other problems, a leak in the roof was found to be a potential contaminant of samples on tables below."); Liptak & Blumenthal, New Doubt Cast on Crime Testing in Houston Cases, N.Y.Times, Aug. 5, 2004 ("[P]rosecutors in Mr. Sutton's case had used [DNA] to convict him, submitting false scientific evidence asserting that there was a solid match between Mr. Sutton's DNA and that found at the crime scene. In fact, 1 of every 8 black people, including Mr. Sutton, shared the relevant DNA profile. More refined retesting cleared him.").

8. *Testimony without statistics?* Young v. State, 879 A.2d 44, 56–57 (Md.2005) ("[T]here exist methods of DNA analysis employing certain markers that, when tested along a minimum number of loci, yield DNA profiles with an astonishingly small random match probability. When the random match probability is sufficiently minuscule, the DNA profile may be deemed unique. In such circumstances, testimony of a match is admissible without accompanying contextual statistics. In place of the statistics, the expert may inform the jury of the meaning of the match by identifying the person whose profile matched the profile of the DNA evidence as the source of that evidence; *i.e.* the expert may testify that in the absence of identical twins, it can be concluded to a reasonable scientific certainty that the evidence sample and the defendant sample came from the same person.").

9. *DNA evidence without corroboration.* In State v. Toomes, 191 S.W.3d 122, 131 n.4 (Tenn.Crim.App.2005), the court upheld a conviction based on DNA alone but with a caution: "By our holding, we are not announcing an iron-clad princip[le] that DNA evidence, without corroboration, is always sufficient to support a conviction. Practically infinite factual variations can arise, and we do not intend by our opinion to prejudge other factual scenarios. For instance, this case has an unusual feature in that two separate DNA comparisons were performed. The first comparison identified the twin's DNA, and the second comparison identified the twin's and the defendant's DNA, which were identical, thereby reinforcing the integrity of the comparisons. In our opinion, it is quite sufficient in this case to recognize and respect the admissibility of DNA evidence and to conclude that the evidence was sufficient to support the defendant's aggravated rape conviction."

10. *Databases.* A national system of computer databases is run by the FBI: CODIS (Combined DNA Index System). Most states require convicted sex offenders to provide samples for this system. A majority require all felons. Should everyone be a contributor? See Kaye & Imwinkelried, Is a DNA Identification Database in Your Future?, 16 Crim. Just. 4 (Fall 2001).

11. *Cold hits.* Matches produced by DNA databases are called "cold hits" because the police have no suspects. There is a major debate about how to calculate the statistics in such cases. See People v. Johnson, 43 Cal.Rptr.3d 587, 600 (Cal.Ct.App.2006) ("[T]he fact that many profiles have been searched increases the probability of finding a match, so that conceptually, the more populated the database, the less impressive the match. Appellant contends that there is broad scientific consensus concerning the need to determine differently the statistical significance of profile matches in a cold hit case versus a confirmation case, but says that the means of determining the statistical value of a cold hit 'is a matter of continuing and strident debate.' ").

(2) QUALIFICATION REQUIREMENT

ELCOCK V. KMART CORP.
United States Court of Appeals, Third Circuit, 2000.
233 F.3d 734.

BECKER, CHIEF JUDGE.

This is an appeal by defendant Kmart from a judgment entered on a $650,000 jury verdict in favor of plaintiff Carmelita Elcock ("Elcock") for personal injuries [lower back injuries] and economic loss that she suffered as the result of a slip and fall at a Kmart store in Frederiksted, U.S. Virgin Islands. Kmart concedes its liability and acknowledges that Elcock's fall caused her some quantum of harm. However, Kmart challenges several evidentiary rulings that relate to the proof of Elcock's damages, and contends that the $650,000 award, which consisted of $300,000 for pain and suffering and $350,000 for loss of future earnings and earning capacity, was excessive. [Elcock was fifty-one years old and self-employed as a salesperson for Mary Kay Cosmetics.]

The most important questions on appeal relate to the testimony of Dr. Chester Copemann, who was proffered by Elcock, *inter alia*, as an expert in vocational rehabilitation,[67] and whose vocational rehabilitation presentation substantially informed the large award for loss of future earnings and earning capacity. [Copermann opined that she was 50–60% vocationally disabled.] * * *

---

[67] [Elsewhere in the opinion, the court wrote: "A vocational rehabilitationist assesses the extent of an individual's disability, evaluates how the disability affects the individual's employment opportunities, and assists the individual's re-entry into the labor market." Ed.]

II. The Evidentiary Issues Relating to Copemann's Qualifications

Before trial and again during trial, Kmart sought to exclude Copemann's vocational rehabilitation testimony on the grounds that he was not qualified as an expert in the field. The District Court conducted a *voir dire* on Copemann's qualifications, during which Copemann testified regarding his credentials, and Kmart's vocational rehabilitation expert gave testimony that called those credentials into question. The District Court considered the qualifications issue raised by Kmart a "close call," but ultimately found that Copemann was qualified to testify about vocational rehabilitation. Kmart challenges this decision. We review the District Court's decision to qualify Copemann for abuse of discretion. *See* Waldorf v. Shuta, 142 F.3d 601, 627 (3d Cir.1998).

* * * Before an expert witness may offer an opinion pursuant to Rule 702, he must first be qualified by virtue of specialized expertise. * * * In *Waldorf v. Shuta*, * * *, we articulated the standard for qualifying an expert:

> Rule 702 requires the witness to have "specialized knowledge" regarding the area of testimony. The basis of this specialized knowledge "can be practical experience as well as academic training and credentials." We have interpreted the specialized knowledge requirement liberally, and have stated that this policy of liberal admissibility of expert testimony "extends to the substantive as well as the formal qualification of experts." However, "at a minimum, a proffered expert witness * * * must possess skill or knowledge greater than the average layman * * *."

Id. at 625 (citations omitted).

Even under the liberal standard described in *Waldorf*, Copemann's qualifications as a vocational rehabilitationist are thin. In contending that Copemann possessed skill or knowledge "greater than the average layman," Elcock focuses primarily on Copemann's experience. Specifically, Elcock points to (1) Copemann's general training in "assessing" individuals, which he received while earning his Ph.D. in psychology; (2) his experience, twenty years previous, helping drug addicts reenter the workforce; (3) his experience primarily in the last two years dealing with the Virgin Islands Division of Workers' Compensation, which he had advised regarding the ability of approximately fifty to sixty-five disabled employees to return to their previous jobs; (4) his past experience as an expert witness making lost earning capacity assessments; (5) his attendance at two seminars regarding vocational rehabilitation, and his stated familiarity with the literature in the area; (6) his membership in two vocational rehabilitation organizations, both of which place no restrictions on membership; and (7) the fact that when Copemann was in school, a degree in vocational rehabilitation therapy was not available, but that he received similar training nonetheless. This last fact, Elcock argues, explains why Copemann did not possess the degrees or formal training one would ordinarily associate with an expert.

In response, Kmart emphasizes several factors that significantly undermine Copemann's purported qualifications. First, during Kmart's *voir dire*, Copemann admitted that he had neither the academic training nor the standard credentials that would ordinarily qualify one as an expert in vocational rehabilitation. Moreover, Kmart argues that nothing prevented Copemann from either receiving formal training in vocational rehabilitation after he left school or from earning a related degree or certificate while he was in school. Second, Copemann conceded that his experience dealing with the workers' compensation board consisted primarily of diagnosing whether patients were so disabled that they could not return to a particular job; this experience did not include assessing what range of jobs those injured individuals were capable of performing. Third, Kmart adduced evidence suggesting that not only was Copemann's experience as a counselor for drug addicts dated, but that it did not include performing assessments of which jobs the recovered addicts would be able to perform. Fourth, although Copemann maintained that there was no difference between a psychologist and a vocational rehabilitationist, Kmart's vocational rehabilitation therapist testified that despite a common psychological diagnostic component in both jobs, the vocational rehabilitationist's expertise entails a distinct speciality: the capacity to "translate" psychological *and* physical impairments into the "ability to work, earn income, [and] get a job * * *."

Kmart's forceful argument all but persuaded the District Court. Given Copemann's lack of credentials and limited experience, the District Court twice expressed its reluctance to qualify Copemann as an expert in vocational rehabilitation. However, after two attempts by Elcock's counsel to qualify him, the Court eventually admitted Copemann's testimony. The Court relied heavily on the fact that a formal degree in vocational rehabilitation therapy was not available when Copemann attended school, and the fact that the training of psychologists was functionally similar to that of vocational rehabilitationists at the time. The Court also relied on Copemann's practical experience evaluating the ability of injured employees to return to work.

B.

This court has had, for some time, a generally liberal standard of qualifying experts. * * * However, we have also set a floor with respect to an expert witness's qualifications. For example, in Aloe Coal Co. v. Clark Equipment Co., 816 F.2d 110 (3d Cir.1987), we held that a district court abused its discretion in allowing a tractor sales representative to testify as an expert regarding the cause of a tractor fire. *See* id. at 114. In making this determination we stated:

> Drewnoski [the expert witness] was not an engineer. He had no experience in designing construction machinery. He had no knowledge or experience in determining the cause of equipment fire. He had no training as a mechanic. He had never operated construction machinery in the course of business. He was a salesman, who at times prepared damage estimates.

Id. (citations omitted); *see also Waldorf*, 142 F.3d at 625 ("Even though we apply Rule 702 liberally, we have not pursued a policy of qualifying *any* proffered witness as an expert.").

Our decision in *Waldorf* provides guidance for our assessment of Copemann's qualifications. In *Waldorf*, the district court qualified an expert [Rizzo] with credentials similar to Copemann's * * *.

What drove the *Waldorf* panel's decision to affirm on this issue was not the impressiveness of Rizzo's credentials or experience, but the standard of review governing our review of Rule 702 qualification rulings:

> Waldorf has a heavy burden in challenging this decision because, absent an abuse of discretion, we will not substitute our own judgment for that of the trial court regarding the admission or exclusion of expert testimony. Of course, an abuse of discretion means much more than that the appellate court disagrees with the trial court. Rather, a trial court's determination whether to admit or exclude expert testimony will be upheld "unless manifestly erroneous."

* * *

Copemann, like Rizzo, has no formal training in vocational rehabilitation and Elcock must therefore rely on Copemann's practical experience to demonstrate that he "possessed the minimum qualifications necessary to testify as an expert." Id. at 627. In support of Copemann's qualifications, Elcock points to Copemann's experience in helping drug addicts return to employment and to his work with the Virgin Islands Division of Workers' Compensation. Based on this background, one can presume that Copemann has learned about the difficulties disabled individuals face in employment, and has accumulated some experience in evaluating whether they can return to a particular job. Nonetheless, the most fundamental problem with Copemann's experience in this area is that he seems most qualified to testify on a micro-level regarding the ability of a disabled individual to return to a specific job; he does not appear particularly qualified to testify on the macro-level regarding the number of jobs in the national or local economy that the disabled individual is able to perform.

On the other hand, Copemann claims to have kept abreast of the relevant literature in his field, and to have consulted the Dictionary of Occupational Titles, a standard tool of the vocational rehabilitationist. In addition, Copemann possesses a degree in a field tangentially related to the one about which he testified, and he has also attended conferences regarding vocational rehabilitation. Finally, in the process of testifying as an expert in similar matters, Copemann has no doubt performed his brand of vocational rehabilitation assessments.[68] Though his efforts in this regard are not grounded in formal training, when taken together with his review of the literature in the field and his attendance at conferences, we must acknowledge that he has "substantially more knowledge than an average lay person regarding employment opportunities for disabled individuals." Id. at 627.

We consider *Waldorf* to be at the outer limit of this court's generally liberal approach to reviewing the qualifications of experts. We also suspect that, had the district court in *Waldorf* ruled the witness unqualified, the panel would have affirmed. While Copemann seems but marginally qualified to perform a vocational rehabilitation assessment, and a district judge would be free to decline to qualify him, we recognize that Copemann's qualifications fall within Waldorf's outer bounds. Despite misgivings, because we are not prepared to say that the District Court, acting "on the spot" and exercising considerable care in its approach to this question, abused its discretion, we will affirm the Court's decision to qualify Copemann as an expert. * * *

NOTES AND QUESTIONS

1. *Standard.* Does Rule 702 comport with Wigmore's view? He wrote that the witness' expertise "may have been attained, so far as legal rules go, in any way whatever; all the law requires is that it should have been attained." 2 J. Wigmore, Evidence § 556, at 751 (Chadbourn rev. 1979). The federal drafters wrote: "[T]he expert is viewed, not in a narrow sense, but as a person qualified by 'knowledge, skill, experience, training or education.' Thus within the scope of the rule are not only experts in the strictest sense of the word, e.g. physicians, physicists, and architects, but also the large group sometimes called 'skilled' witnesses, such as bankers or landowners testifying to land values." Fed.R.Evid. 702 advisory committee's note.

---

[68] We note that the mere fact that Copemann was previously admitted as an expert witness qualified to give testimony on vocational rehabilitation is irrelevant to the determination whether he is qualified to give such testimony in this case. *See* Thomas J. Kline, Inc. v. Lorillard, Inc., 878 F.2d 791, 800 (4th Cir.1989) ("[I]t would be absurd to conclude that one can become an expert simply by accumulating experience in testifying."). Moreover, while any expertise he may have gained in performing vocational rehabilitation assessments in these cases would be relevant, the crucible of litigation makes for a poor classroom.

2. *Examples.* United States v. Kunzman, 54 F.3d 1522, 1530 (10th Cir.1995) ("Experience alone can qualify a witness to give expert testimony"; banker for 20 years interpreting numbers and bank stamps on checks to show they cleared interstate banking system); Davis v. United States, 865 F.2d 164, 168 (8th Cir.1988) ("Rule 702 does not state a preference for academic training over demonstrated practical experience."); United States v. Barker, 553 F.2d 1013, 1024 (6th Cir.1977) ("An expert need not have certificates of training, nor memberships in professional organizations * * *. Nor need he be, as the trial court apparently required, an outstanding practitioner in the field in which he professes expertise."); United States v. Madoch, 935 F.Supp. 965, 972 (N.D.Ill.1996) ("[O]ne expert need not hold the exact same set of qualifications to rebut another expert's testimony. * * * This Court need not analyze, as Defendant contends it should, whether a psychologist or psychiatrist is more qualified to testify as to the psychological condition of a patient at the time of the offense.").

See also McConnell v. Budget Inns, 718 N.E.2d 948, 955 (Ohio Ct.App.1998) (In receiving expert testimony of a woodworker on chair construction, the court stated: "The witness, a long-time owner of a woodworking company in New York, testified that he had approximately thirty-six years of woodworking experience that included the design, repair, manufacture, and construction of wood furniture, including wood chairs used in commercial settings and chairs of the type involved in the accident herein. These qualifications gave [the witness] knowledge of chair construction and mechanical failure therein superior to that possessed by the average juror.").

3. *Hired guns?* Is the qualification standard set forth in the principal case too low? See the footnote in the principal case. See also In re Air Crash Disaster at New Orleans, 795 F.2d 1230, 1234 (5th Cir.1986) ("experts whose opinions are available to the highest bidder have no place testifying in a court of law"); Chaulk v. Volkswagen of Am., Inc., 808 F.2d 639, 644 (7th Cir.1986) ("There is hardly anything, not palpably absurd on its face, that cannot now be proved by some so-called 'experts.' "). For an insightful discussion of the "hired gun" problem, see Gross, Expert Evidence, 1991 Wis.L.Rev. 1113 (proposing several changes to ensure the appointment of neutral experts).

4. *Criminal cases.* See United States v. Johnson, 575 F.2d 1347, 1360 (5th Cir.1978) (An experienced user, who "had smoked marijuana over a thousand times," was permitted to testify that certain marijuana came from Colombia. "He based his identification upon the plant's appearance, its leaf, buds, stems, and other physical characteristics, as well as upon the smell and the effect of smoking it."); State v. Barnes, 597 So.2d 1109, 1112 (La.Ct.App.1992) (defense expert concerning a pellet dispersion pattern test excluded; He "became a gunsmith after completing a correspondence course. He had never received training in forensic science, firearms identification or ballistics. He had never testified as an expert in any area. He worked as a sales clerk at a hardware store and in his own gun repair business."); Hooten v. State, 492 So.2d 948, 958 (Miss.1986) (dissenting opinion) ("If this witness has indeed testified over 300 times as an *expert* on discovering spurious

handwriting as she claimed, it is an astonishing indictment on the gullibility of lawyers and judges.").

5. *Certification.* See United States v. Bourgeois, 950 F.2d 980, 986 (5th Cir.1992) (upholding exclusion of the testimony of an "expert" who was not a member of the American Board of Forensic Document Examiners, who practiced graphotherapy in addition to handwriting comparison, and who acquired a masters degree in graphoanalysis and a Ph.D. in metaphysics and religion by correspondence). See also MacDonald, The Making of an Expert Witness: It's in the Credentials, Wall Street J., Feb. 8, 1999, at B1 (Article discussing the American College of Forensic Examiners (ACFE), which makes $2.2 million a year certifying experts. The roots of this organization, according to its founder, can be traced to the *Daubert* decision, which was intended to tighten the standards for expert testimony.); Hansen, Expertise to Go, 86 A.B.A.J. 44, 45 (Feb. 2000) ("certification" mill; cost $350 to be certified, dial 1–800–4A–Expert; "ACFE is the biggest credentialing body in forensic science and the only one that credentials experts in many specialties. It has 13,000 members and nearly 17,000 board-certified diplomates.").

6. *Stipulations.* In State v. Colwell, 790 P.2d 430, 434 (Kan.1990), the trial court required defense counsel to accept the prosecution's offer to stipulate to the qualifications of the defense pathologist. Consequently, the jury was deprived of learning the credentials of the expert, who had a "national reputation" in the field of forensic pathology. In contrast, eleven pages of the transcript were needed to record the qualifications of the prosecution's expert. The court reversed: "We conclude that an offer by the State to stipulate to the qualifications of an expert witness called by the defendant is merely an offer unless accepted by the defendant. Absent such acceptance, the defendant has the right to present the witness' qualifications to the jury."

7. *Judicial declaration of expertise.* After the recitation of a witness' credentials, the proponent often tenders the witness to the court as an "expert", and the court then declares the witness an expert. Why? See United States v. Laurienti, 611 F.3d 530, 547 (9th Cir.2010) ("To the extent that Defendants argue that the district court abused its discretion by failing to describe Meyer as an 'expert' in front of the jury, we disagree. The determination that a witness is an expert is not an express imprimatur of special credence; rather, it is simply a decision that the witness may testify to matters concerning 'scientific, technical, or other specialized knowledge.' Fed.R.Evid. 702."); Luttrell v. Commonwealth, 952 S.W.2d 216, 218 (Ky.1997) ("Great care should be exercised by a trial judge when the determination has been made that the witness is an expert. If the jury is so informed such a conclusion obviously enhances the credibility of that witness in the eyes of the jury. All such rulings should be made outside the hearing of the jury and there should be no declaration that the witness is an expert."); Richey, Proposals to Eliminate the Prejudicial Effect of the Use of the Word "Expert" Under the Federal Rules of Evidence in Civil and Criminal Jury Trials, 154 F.R.D. 537, 554 (1994); ABA Civil Trial Practice Standard 14 (2007) ("The

court should not, in the presence of the jury, declare that a witness is qualified as an expert or to render an expert opinion, and counsel should not ask the court to do so.").

WHEELING PITTSBURGH STEEL CORP. V. BEELMAN RIVER TERMINALS, INC.

United States Court of Appeals, Eighth Circuit, 2001.
254 F.3d 706.

HANSEN, CIRCUIT JUDGE.

In this breach of a bailment contract action brought by Wheeling Pittsburgh Steel Corporation (a manufacturer of steel coils and sheet steel) (Wheeling) against Beelman River Terminals, Inc., (a warehouseman) (Beelman) for damages to approximately 3,000 tons of Wheeling's steel held in Beelman's warehouse during the Mississippi River flood of 1993 * * *.

* * *

To begin with, we agree with the district court that Dr. Curtis, a hydrologist specializing in flood risk management [who testified for Beelman], easily qualifies as an expert under Federal Rule of Evidence 702. The real question is, what is he an expert about? Though eminently qualified to testify as an expert hydrologist regarding matters of flood risk management, Dr. Curtis sorely lacked the education, employment, or other practical personal experiences to testify as an expert specifically regarding safe warehousing practices. Dr. Curtis did not study warehousing practices during his formal education, he has not written about warehousing practices in any of his sixty-plus published articles, and he has never been employed by a warehouseman during any of the twenty-one projects on which he has worked. Although he has worked with entire communities and shopping centers, he has never prepared emergency response plans specifically for storage facilities or warehouses. Furthermore, he did not compensate for his lack of education or experience about warehousing by, for example, determining or studying the actions of other warehousemen along the Mississippi River in response to this or any other flood.

* * *

There is no doubt that Dr. Curtis was qualified to testify that Beelman was diligent and reasonable in assessing available river data in historical context, in making judgments about reasonably foreseeable river levels and the risks they posed to the warehouse in light of the available information. But that does not make Dr. Curtis qualified to testify as an expert regarding what specific efforts and specific levels of protection are consistent with good warehousing practices, which he repeatedly did during the trial. * * * Furthermore, Dr. Curtis's improper opinions went to the primary issue upon which the jury had to make a judgment. We are convinced that the district court abused its discretion in allowing Dr. Curtis to give opinions specifically about warehousing practices and that Wheeling was prejudiced as a result. *See* * * * Robertson, 148 F.3d at 907–08 (ordering new trial after manufacturing/ceramics/materials expert offered opinions as to the adequacy of grinding wheel warnings because the opinion was not sufficiently reliable under *Daubert* due to the expert's lack of training, research, practical knowledge, or experience with respect to warning labels); *see also* Redman v. John D. Brush & Co., 111 F.3d 1174, 1179 (4th Cir.1997) (holding it was error for metallurgical engineer to give opinion testimony that a particular safe met industry standards for burglar deterrence when no industry standard for burglar deterrent safes was ever established and the expert had no personal knowledge about or experience with the industry).

NOTES

1. *Technicians.* See People v. King, 72 Cal.Rptr. 478, 491 (Cal.Ct.App.1968) (courts must "differentiate between ability to operate an instrument or perform a test and the ability to make an interpretation drawn from use of the instrument"). Compare People v. Williams, 5 Cal.Rptr.2d 130, 135 (Cal.Ct.App.1992) ("[The officer's] opinion that appellant was under the influence of alcohol, to the extent it was based on the nystagmus test, rests on scientific principles well beyond his knowledge, training, or education. Without some understanding of the processes by which alcohol ingestion produces nystagmus, how strong the correlation is, how other possible causes might be masked, what margin of error has been shown in statistical surveys, and a host of other relevant factors, [the officer's] opinion on causation, notwithstanding his ability to recognize the symptom, was unfounded."), with People v. Ojeda, 275 Cal.Rptr. 472, 474 (Cal.Ct.App.1990) ("The gaze nystagmus test, as do other commonly used field sobriety tests, requires only the personal observation of the officer administering it.").

2. *False credentials.* In United States v. Williams, 233 F.3d 592, 593 (D.C.Cir.2000), the prosecution called an expert on drug distribution to testify that the heroin in the defendant's possession was intended for more than personal use. The witness told the jury he was "a Board-certified pharmacist. I receive, maintain [,] compound and dispense narcotic as well as non-narcotic substances per prescription." After conviction, the defense attorney learned that the expert "was not a pharmacist and had no degree in pharmacology, facts unknown to the prosecution during the trial." In fact, this expert reportedly testified in thousands of cases, misrepresenting his credentials for at least 16 years. See Groner, Your Expert Lied—for 16 Years * * *, Legal Times, July 3, 2000, at 8. Many defense attorneys had stipulated to this expert's qualifications, thus erecting another barrier to obtaining a

new trial. See also Starrs, Mountebanks Among Forensic Scientists, in 2 Forensic Science Handbook 1, 7, 20–29 (Saferstein ed., 1988) (noting that one firearms expert took some credit for "the development of penicillin, the 'Pap' smear, and to top it all off, the atomic bomb").

(3)   BASIS OF EXPERT OPINION: FEDERAL RULES 703 & 705

ICONCO V. JENSEN CONSTRUCTION CO.
United States Court of Appeals, Eighth Circuit, 1980.
622 F.2d 1291.

ARNOLD, CIRCUIT JUDGE.

This is a diversity case. Iconco, the plaintiff below, was the second lowest bidder on a small-business "set aside" construction contract let by the [Army] Corps of Engineers.[69] Jensen Construction Company, the low bidder, was awarded the contract. Iconco filed suit in the United States District Court for the Southern District of Iowa claiming that Jensen, in making its bid, falsely certified that it was a small business under federal law and was awarded the contract based upon that certification. Iconco claimed damages and lost profits based upon fraud and unjust-enrichment theories under Iowa law. The jury awarded Iconco $61,503 on its unjust-enrichment claim, and $10,000 actual damages and $30,000 punitive damages for fraud. The District Court, the Hon. Donald E. O'Brien, entered judgment in the amount of $61,503, but set aside the award for fraud, finding insufficient evidence to support the verdict. We affirm.

* * *

Jensen next argues that Iconco is not entitled to recover because, as a matter of law, it cannot prove that it was entitled to be awarded the contract. Under the provisions of the Armed Services Procurement Act, 10 U.S.C. § 2301 et seq., the award of the contract to the low bidder, or to any bidder, is not automatic * * *.

* * * Jensen argues that since the contracting officer can award the contract only to a "responsible" bidder whose bid is most advantageous to the government, and may reject all bids, no bidder, even the lowest one, has the right to expect that it will be awarded the contract. Jensen argues, in essence, that a claim for lost profits under these circumstances is speculative and improper.

The more logical approach, in our view, is to put the unsuccessful bidder to its proof; if it proves by a preponderance of the evidence that it

---

[69] [The bid invitation was for the removal of structures and the building of barricades in connection with the construction of the Saylorville Reservoir in central Iowa. Ed.]

would have received the contract award absent the successful bidder's wrongdoing, we find no persuasive reasons why recovery should be denied.

Here, Colonel Walter H. Johnson, the Corps of Engineers contracting officer for the Saylorville project, testified on Iconco's behalf. He was ultimately responsible for the awarding of the contract, and if it had not been awarded to Jensen, he would have been the one to decide to whom the award would be made.

According to Colonel Johnson, the standard procedure at bid opening, which was followed on the Saylorville contract, is to rank the bidders by amount of bid and then announce the apparent low bidder. Contractors are required as a matter of course to submit a bid bond along with their bid. If the low bidder submitted the appropriate bid bond, the contracting officer would declare it the apparent low bidder and then direct an investigation known as a "pre-award survey." The purpose of the survey is to determine whether the low bidder is "responsible," in other words, whether it has the financial resources, physical capacity, and skill to perform the contract in a competent and timely fashion. The survey is conducted in accordance with the provisions of 32 C.F.R. §§ 1.903, 1.904, and 1.905 (1974).

Colonel Johnson testified that the overriding consideration in determining contractor responsibility is whether it can provide a performance bond; other important factors regarding responsibility, in his view, are the prior record of the contractor on similar jobs and apparent ability to concentrate sufficient resources on the job to perform the contract competently and in a timely fashion, factors which would require an evaluation of office organization, financial resources, organizational capability, and adequacy of equipment. The Saylorville job, according to Colonel Johnson, was not technically difficult, mostly "mule work" by his characterization. In his view, any contractor who had responsibly performed heavy work of any kind, including the demolition of heavy structures, could have done the job.

* * *

At trial, Iconco propounded a lengthy hypothetical question to Colonel Johnson. Colonel Johnson was asked to assume that the low bidder on the Saylorville contract was not a small business, that the second low bidder was and submitted a bid which was reasonable in amount (roughly 50% of the amount estimated by the Corps as necessary to perform the contract), that the second low bidder could obtain a performance bond and had successfully completed in its ten years experience several other similar contracts, and that it met other requirements of the pre-award survey in terms of financial ability, licensing, organization, experience, equipment, integrity, and reputation.

Assuming these facts, Colonel Johnson was asked for an opinion about whether the contract would have been awarded to the second low bidder. His answer was yes. * * *

The standards by which a hypothetical question is to be judged are well-settled in this Circuit. The form of the question "must be left largely to the discretion of the trial court." United States v. Kiliyan, 456 F.2d 555, 561 (8th Cir.1972). The question need not include all facts shown by the evidence or pertinent to the ultimate issue, but it should be in such a form as not to mislead or confuse the jury. Id. A hypothetical should include only such facts as are supported by the evidence, and "*[o]nly* the basic facts need be assumed in the hypothesis," Twin City Plaza, Inc. v. Central Surety & Ins. Corp., 409 F.2d 1195, 1200 (8th Cir.1969), but "a question which omits any material fact essential to the formation of a rational opinion is * * * incompetent." Harris v. Smith, 372 F.2d 806, 812 (8th Cir.1967). Accord, Fed.R.Evid. 705, which eliminates the mandatory preliminary statement of all the facts underlying an expert's opinion. Jensen argues that the hypothetical omitted some of the findings material to the determination of responsibility by the contracting officer, but we think the question fairly characterized the material considerations. Colonel Johnson's testimony in response to other questions made clear his opinion that any experienced contractor could have performed the Saylorville job, and we evaluate the hypothetical in that context.

Jensen also argues that the hypothetical asked Colonel Johnson to assume facts which were not in evidence. We cannot agree. Iconco's first witness at trial was Richard Joseph Diven, Iconco's president since 1973. He testified to a number of contracts involving the demolition of bridges performed by Iconco satisfactorily before the Saylorville bid was submitted. Diven stated further that the company had obtained hundreds of bid bonds without difficulty. John E. Weber, Iconco's secretary, testified after Colonel Johnson. Mr. Weber described several of the other contracts which Iconco had performed adequately, some of which were more sophisticated and difficult than the Saylorville job. According to Weber, Iconco had never been denied a performance bond, and no one had ever questioned the integrity of the company or its financial capacity. At the time of the award of the Saylorville contract, Iconco had a qualified superintendent and the equipment necessary to do the job. In Weber's view, Iconco complied with the requirements of the pre-award survey in all respects.

* * *

The judgment of the District Court is affirmed in all respects.

NOTES AND QUESTIONS

1.   *Value of hypothetical questions.* If the jury does not accept the facts on which the expert's opinion is based, it should reject the opinion. Does the hypothetical question assist the jury in this regard? The principal case cites *Harris v. Smith* for the proposition that the omission of "any material fact" from the hypothetical question makes the opinion "incompetent." Should such defects in the hypothetical question be left to cross-examination?

2.   *Criticisms.* The hypothetical question as a vehicle for eliciting the expert's opinion upon facts as to which the expert has no personal knowledge has received extensive criticism from every quarter—judges, attorneys, commentators, and the experts themselves. Dieden & Gasparich, Psychiatric Evidence and Full Disclosure in the Criminal Trial, 52 Cal.L.Rev. 543, 556 (1964), contains the following observations:

> Unfortunately the hypothetical question has been the traditionally accepted method of adducing expert testimony. It even has been characterized as one of the truly scientific features of the rules of evidence in that it is designed to reveal all of the pertinent facts in the most logical order to support the expert opinion. In fact, its objectives have never been realized and the method has been uniformly criticized by the authorities, as well as the California courts which have commented on the undue length and complexity of hypothetical questions and the slanting of their hypotheses. Medical men have also been outspoken in expressing their disdain for the technique.

3.   *Optional use.* Mandatory use of the hypothetical question has now been abandoned in virtually all jurisdictions, often by the adoption of rules based upon Federal Rules 703 and 705. What language in those rules frees the examiner from the need to phrase questions to experts in the form of hypothetical questions? Is use of the hypothetical question still permitted? If so, might trial counsel ever elect to use such a question? Might a trial court, in its discretion, require use of a hypothetical question? At least one state has specifically provided, in its version of Rule 705, that the trial judge cannot require the use of a hypothetical question. N.C.R.Evid. 705. With regard to the use of hypothetical questions under the Federal Rules, see McElhaney, Expert Witnesses and the Federal Rules of Evidence, 28 Mercer L.Rev. 463 (1977).

4.   *Misuse of hypothetical questions.* See United States v. Stinson, 647 F.3d 1196, 1214 (9th Cir.2011) ("prosecutorial misconduct to pose questions or hypotheticals" concerning matters not admitted in evidence); People v. Xue Vang, 262 P.3d 581, 585–86 (Cal.2011) ("A hypothetical question need not encompass all of the evidence. * * * But, however much latitude a party has to frame hypothetical questions, the questions must be rooted in the evidence of the case being tried, not some other case. * * * A hypothetical question not based on the evidence is irrelevant and of no help to the jury.").

5. *Problems?* In United States v. Mancillas, 183 F.3d 682, 705 (7th Cir.1999), the prosecution presented a hypothetical to a testifying DEA agent, regarding a person possessing a plastic bag containing 400 grams of marijuana, a slip of paper bearing the notation '420 g,' a handgun, a scale, two pagers, a cellular phone and $2440 in cash. After setting forth these hypothetical facts, the government asked the agent whether, in his opinion, the marijuana was being held for distribution or personal consumption. The agent testified that, in his opinion, the marijuana was being held for distribution. Is there a problem with this type of testimony? What if the hypothetical facts "mirror" the facts in the case?

THOMAS V. METZ

Supreme Court of Wyoming, 1986.
714 P.2d 1205.

BROWN, JUSTICE.

This is a medical malpractice action brought by appellant Phyllis Thomas against appellee Albert Metz, Jr., M.D. Appellant claimed she was damaged as a result of improper back surgery performed by appellee. Trial to a jury resulted in a verdict for appellee. Appellant presents the following issues:

"It was reversible error for the trial court to admit expert opinions of defendant's witnesses which were based upon defendant doctor's deposition and the opinions of other experts when this type of facts or data is not of the type reasonably relied upon by experts in the field.

"It was reversible error for the trial court to refuse to require disclosure of the underlying facts or data upon which the opinions of the defendant's experts were based prior to the giving of the opinions, or once having allowed the opinions, refusing to strike the opinions when it was disclosed that the facts or data was not of that type reasonably relied upon by experts in the field."

We will affirm.

The facts show that on April 17, 1982, appellant rolled over in bed and experienced pain in her back between her shoulder blades. She was admitted to the hospital that same day, complaining of pain between her shoulder blades, pain in her left arm, and numbness in the left thumb, index finger and middle finger. After consultation and testing by Dr. James Maddy and Dr. Malvin Cole, it was concluded that appellant was suffering a disc herniation at the Cervical 6/Cervical 7 (C–6/C–7) level, primarily on the left side. Neurosurgical consultation was then sought from appellee, who, after evaluation, confirmed the findings of Drs. Maddy and Cole, and recommended that surgery be performed to remove disc fragments that were pressing on the spinal cord and the left C–7 nerve root.

After obtaining appellant's consent, appellee performed surgery to remove the disc fragments. A bone plug was then removed from appellant's hip and placed in the spine to fuse the two vertebral bodies. After surgery, appellant experienced pain on her right side, similar to that previously experienced on the left side. Further testing revealed the bone plug was encroaching upon the C–7 nerve root on the right side. Additional surgery was performed to alleviate the condition on April 27, 1982.

When appellant continued to experience pain, she consulted several physicians in Denver during the months of May and June, 1982. In June of 1982, appellant underwent further surgery in Denver. This surgery was performed by another physician, and consisted of removal of the first right thoracic rib.

The pain persisted. An expert witness for appellant, Dr. John Williams, testified appellant now suffers from a condition known as "hysterical conversion"—where pain is a stress reaction and has no medical, anatomical or physiological basis. Dr. Robert Kelso, a clinical psychologist, examined and evaluated appellant and concluded that he believed "this disorder should show significant improvement within a 12–month period."

Appellant filed the present action on January 25, 1983. As noted above, trial to the jury resulted in a verdict for appellee.

We will consider both of appellant's issues together. Basically, appellant claims the trial court erred by admitting the testimony of appellee's expert witnesses, alleging such witnesses improperly based their testimony upon appellee's apparent discovery deposition and previous opinions given by other physicians.

We have heretofore recognized the need for expert testimony in medical malpractice actions. * * *

The two expert witnesses who testified on behalf of appellee were Drs. Federico Mora and Philip Gordy. * * *

* * * Appellant's main objection to the testimony of both expert witnesses is that such testimony was improperly based on material not reasonably relied upon by experts. Specifically, appellant claims it was improper for Dr. Mora to rely upon appellee's discovery deposition in giving his opinion at trial. Appellant further claims it was also error for Dr. Gordy to base his opinion upon appellee's discovery deposition, as well as Dr. Mora's deposition.

Rules 702 and 703, Wyoming Rules of Evidence, are pertinent to this case * * *

It is significant to note that appellee's deposition was only one of several sources of information Dr. Mora relied upon to base his opinion. When asked what materials he had reviewed to form his opinion, Dr. Mora testified:

"Basically what I examined is I looked over the hospital records of Ms. Thomas here when she was treated in Casper. I have also looked at hospital records and personal notes of physicians who treated her when she went to Denver later on. Furthermore, I have read the depositions that were given by Dr. Metz, by Ms. Thomas, and by Dr. Williams, two that come to mind."

And when asked if he felt the surgery performed by appellee was appropriate, Dr. Mora answered:

"Well, basing myself on the hospital record and the review of the X rays, the operation was appropriate."

Dr. Gordy based his opinion upon a review of hospital records, as well as appellee's deposition and depositions from the other physicians. He was then asked:

"Q. Doctor, based upon the information you have reviewed, have you an opinion as to whether or not the surgery performed on April 23, 1982, upon Plaintiff here by Dr. Metz was necessary? Answer yes or no.

"A. Yes, I have an opinion.

"Q. And what is that opinion?

"A. It was absolutely necessary."

Trial counsel for appellant made an objection to the basis for Dr. Mora's expert testimony. After a conference at bench, the trial court ruled that counsel's objection was in the nature of impeachment and counsel would be allowed to thoroughly cross-examine the witness. * * *

* * *

Appellant's trial counsel was allowed to thoroughly cross-examine both expert witnesses, and attack the bases of their opinions for impeachment purposes. [quoting Rule 705]

Appellant contends the court erred in refusing to require disclosure of facts upon which the experts based their opinions. But as we have already pointed out, the experts did state what records they had reviewed in making their conclusions. Therefore, the experts did disclose the basis of their opinions. * * *

It is then within the province of the trier of fact to give whatever credence they may to the expert testimony as well as all the evidence in reaching a verdict.

> " * * * The trier of fact must decide what weight is to be given to expert testimony, and it still remains the duty of the trier of the factual issues, whether jury or judge, to determine the credibility of all witnesses, including expert witnesses, and to evaluate the testimony of each in reaching its verdict. [Citations.]" *Reed v. Hunter,* supra, at 518.

We are not able to find prejudicial error inasmuch as appellee's two expert witnesses based their opinions *in part* upon the deposition of appellee. Appellant has failed to show how such prejudiced her or how such affected the jury's verdict. Both of the witnesses were qualified as experts and possessed a great deal of expertise in the area of neurosurgery.

> "It is common practice for a prospective witness, in preparing himself to express an expert opinion, to pursue pretrial studies and investigations of one kind or another. Frequently, the information so gained is hearsay or double hearsay, insofar as the trier of the facts is concerned. This, however, does not necessarily stand in the way of receiving such expert opinion in evidence. It is for the trial court to determine, in the exercise of its discretion, whether the expert's sources of information are sufficiently reliable to warrant reception of the opinion. If the court so finds, the opinion may be expressed. If the opinion is received, the court may, in its discretion, allow the expert to reveal to the jury the information gained during such investigations and studies. Wide latitude in cross-examination should be allowed." *Standard Oil Co. of California v. Moore,* 251 F.2d 188, 222 (9th Cir.1957).

* * *

We have carefully reviewed the issues raised by appellant and are unable to find the trial court committed reversible error in allowing the testimony of appellee's expert witnesses.

Affirmed.

NOTES AND QUESTIONS

1. *Hearsay.* When an expert witness testifies to facts upon which she based her opinion that are not otherwise admissible in evidence, are such facts admissible for all purposes or only as the basis of the expert's opinion? Does Rule 703 in effect create a new exception to the hearsay rule? See Chapters 13 and 14, infra. A 2000 amendment to Rule 703 made exclusion

the default position. "But if the facts or data would otherwise be inadmissible, the proponent of the opinion may disclose them to the jury only if their probative value in helping the jury evaluate the opinion substantially outweighs their prejudicial effect." See Carlson, Is Revised Expert Witness Rule 703 a Critical Modernization for the New Century?, 52 Fla.L.Rev. 715 (2000).

2. *Background hearsay*. What was the basis of Dr. Mora's opinion in the principal case? Are these sources used differently than the "pretrial studies and investigations" in the quotation from *Standard Oil*, which is cited in the principal case? In Wells v. Miami Valley Hosp., 631 N.E.2d 642, 654 (Ohio Ct.App.1993), a physician testified that Wells "probably died of a cardiac tamponade." This expert "indicated that the factual basis of his testimony was his review of the medical records and the autopsy report." He also read scholarly medical articles on cardiac tamponade risks from CVP catheter placement. Are the medical records and autopsy report the "facts or data in the case" within the meaning of Rule 703? Are the scholarly articles read during the expert's research? See Maguire, Evidence: Common Sense and Common Law 29 (1947) ("Progress of expert knowledge demands reliance upon the learning of the past. Almost invariably this learning is recorded in hearsay form. No individual can ever make himself into an expert without absorbing much hearsay—lectures by his teachers, statements in textbooks, reports of experiments and experiences of others in the same field.").

3. *Other cases*. See United States v. Bramlet, 820 F.2d 851 (7th Cir.1987) (notes and reports of non-professional staff at mental institution); United States v. Lundy, 809 F.2d 392, 395 (7th Cir.1987) (Arson expert based his opinion on his firsthand inspection of the scene and on interviews with witnesses at the scene. "[H]earsay and third-party observations that are of a type normally relied upon by an expert in the field are properly utilized by such an expert in developing an expert opinion * * *. [The expert] presented uncontroverted evidence that interviews with many witnesses to a fire are a standard investigatory technique in cause and origin inquiries."); United States v. 1,014.16 Acres of Land, 558 F.Supp. 1238 (W.D.Mo.1983) (opinion of other real estate appraisers as to the value of land), aff'd, 739 F.2d 1371 (8th Cir.1984).

4. *Admissibility decision*. If an expert testifies that her opinion is based on facts not within her own perception or in evidence at the trial, how much of an inquiry into either the general use of such information by similar experts or the reasonableness of such reliance should the court conduct? There are two different approaches to the judge's role. One approach requires the court to make an independent assessment of the reasonableness of the expert's reliance: "[T]he court may not abdicate its independent responsibilities to decide if the bases meet minimum standards of reliability as a condition of admissibility * * *. If the underlying data are so lacking in probative force and reliability that no reasonable expert could base an opinion on them, an opinion which rests entirely upon them must be

excluded." In re "Agent Orange" Product Liability Litigation, 611 F.Supp. 1223, 1245 (E.D.N.Y.1985), aff'd, 818 F.2d 187 (2d Cir.1987).

The other approach limits the judge's role to determining what experts in the field consider reasonable. The "proper inquiry is not what the court deems reliable, but what experts in the relevant discipline deem it to be." Zenith Radio Corp. v. Matsushita Elec. Indus. Co., 723 F.2d 238, 276 (3d Cir.1983), rev'd on other grounds, 475 U.S. 574 (1986). The Third Circuit added: "In substituting its own opinion as to what constitutes reasonable reliance for that of the experts in the relevant fields the trial court misinterpreted Rule 703." Id. at 277. However, the Third Circuit changed positions after the Supreme Court decided the *Daubert* case. The court noted that its "former view is no longer tenable in light of *Daubert*." In re Paoli R.R. Yard PCB Litigation, 35 F.3d 717, 748 (3d Cir.1994). The court wrote:

> [I]t is the judge who makes the determination of reasonable reliance, and that for the judge to make the factual determination under Rule 104(a) that an expert is basing his or her opinion on a type of data *reasonably* relied upon by experts, the judge must conduct an independent evaluation into reasonableness. The judge can of course take into account the particular expert's opinion that experts reasonably rely on that type of data, as well as the opinions of other experts as to its reliability, but the judge can also take into account other factors he or she deems relevant.

See also Imwinkelried, The Meaning of "Facts or Data" in Federal Rule of Evidence 703: The Significance of the Supreme Court's Decision to Rely on Federal Rule 702 in *Daubert v. Merrell Dow Pharmaceuticals, Inc.*, 54 Md.L.Rev. 352 (1995).

5.   *Confrontation.* In Williams v. Illinois, 132 S.Ct. 2221 (2012), a rape prosecution, Sandra Lambatos, a state crime laboratory expert, testified regarding a "DNA match." Her testimony was based on two DNA profiles, one produced by the state police lab and one by Cellmark, a private company. Cellmark analyzed the crime scene DNA, but its report was not admitted into evidence. Rather, Lambatos testified to the DNA match based upon her own judgment after comparing the Cellmark and state police lab DNA profiles.

In a badly fractured decision, the Court upheld the admissibility of Lambatos's testimony. There was no majority opinion. Part of the opinion focused on Illinois Rule 703. According to the plurality, the expert testimony did not violate the Confrontation Clause because that Clause does not apply to out-of-court statements that are not offered to prove the truth of the matter asserted—i.e., they are offered for a nonhearsay purpose. The plurality concluded that the Cellmark report had not been offered in evidence for its truth content and thus it was not a testimonial statement. Justice Kagan, writing for the dissent, rejected the argument that the Cellmark report was not offered for the truth: "Lambatos's statements about Cellmark's report went to its truth, and the State could not rely on her status as an expert to circumvent the Confrontation Clause's requirements." Id. at

2268. On this issue, Justice Thomas agreed with the dissenters. Thus, five justices rejected the nonhearsay argument in this context.

See also Giannelli, Confrontation, Experts, and Rule 703, 20 J.L. & Policy 443 (2012) (arguing that the lack of discovery in criminal cases (e.g., no discovery depositions) compared to civil litigation undermines the fairness of Rule 703). For a discussion of the Confrontation Clause, see Chapter 13, Section C infra.

6. *Liberalization.* Has the liberalization of the common law rules governing expert testimony gone too far? Is adequate trustworthiness insured by the new rules? See Huber, Galileo's Revenge: Junk Science in the Courtroom (1991); Giannelli, "Junk Science": The Criminal Cases, 84 J.Crim.L. & Criminology 105 (1993); Graham, Expert Witness Testimony and the Federal Rules of Evidence: Insuring Adequate Assurance of Trustworthiness, 1986 U.Ill.L.Rev. 43.

(4) ULTIMATE ISSUE RULE: FEDERAL RULE 704

CARR V. RADKEY
Supreme Court of Texas, 1965.
393 S.W.2d 806.

GREENHILL, JUSTICE. This is a will contest. Upon a finding by the jury that Miss Hattie Hewlett did not have testamentary capacity, the trial court denied probate to her holographic wills of April 17 and December 28, 1936. The only serious contest was and is over the instrument of December 28, 1936. Except for procedural problems later noticed, this opinion will deal only with the December 28 will.

The State[70] appealed on the ground that it (and those aligned with it in support of the will) had not been given a fair trial because of the exclusion of what they regarded as their most important evidence, the testimony of Dr. Sam Hoerster, an expert in mental illnesses. The evidence which was excluded was Dr. Hoerster's opinion, in answer to a hypothetical question, as to whether Miss Hewlett, when she wrote her will, had sufficient ability to understand the business in which she was engaged, the effect of her acts in making the will, realized what she was doing, knew her people and relatives, and knew the property she owned. Also excluded was his answer to a question as to whether Miss Hewlett wrote the will during a lucid interval. Outside the hearing of the jury, in completing a bill of exceptions, Dr. Hoerster answered both questions in such a way as to support the probate of the will.

---

[70] [The State was involved in the case in defense of the will because, as noted in an omitted portion of the opinion, the will contained a residuary bequest to establish scholarships for worthy students in certain disciplines (including law) at the University of Texas. Ed.]

* * *

Miss Hewlett wrote the will when she was 62 years of age, while in the Brown Rest Home in Austin. Before she became mentally ill, she had supported herself and had been in charge of the safety deposit boxes at the American National Bank in Austin. She lived close to the university's campus. She had made investments in Austin real estate, some of them relatively close to the time of her mental illness, which proved to be profitable. Her estate was appraised at $240,000 upon her death in 1960.

* * *

After being * * * qualified [as an expert in mental illnesses], Dr. Hoerster was asked a hypothetical question. As a predicate to the question, counsel reviewed the evidence about Miss Hewlett, including the fact that she had been taken to a rest home in the latter part of 1936. He was told of her periods of excitement and depression. He was told that her brother, David Hewlett, had died, and that she was informed of his death on December 28, 1936, the same day on which her will is dated; she showed no emotion. Her will was read to Dr. Hoerster. Assuming these facts, he was asked whether Miss Hewlett, when she wrote the will, "had sufficient ability to understand the business in which she was engaged, the effects of her acts in making the will, realized what she was doing, knew her people and her relatives, and knew the property she owned." He was not permitted to answer. The court also sustained objections to other questions breaking down the larger question into various elements.

* * *

The question of a witness, lay or expert, being allowed to answer questions regarding the capacity of a testator has been given considerable attention by persons regarded as authorities in the field. They have considered and discussed the objections to the admission of the testimony which fall into these general categories: (1) it invades the province of the jury; (2) the witness is asked to answer a question the jury must answer, or the ultimate issue; and (3) the witness, lay or expert, may not have in mind the same definition of capacity to execute an instrument as is contained in the legal definition of capacity. These textwriters and authorities are almost uniform in their criticism of using "invasion of the province of the jury" as a reason for excluding testimony in this area. The function of the witness is to give information which will be helpful to the jury. The province of the jury is to believe or disbelieve, weigh evidence, and to evaluate it. The witness could not invade that province if he wanted to. Wigmore says the phrase "is so misleading, as well as so unsound, that it should be entirely repudiated. It is a mere bit of empty rhetoric." 7 Wigmore, Evidence 17 (3d ed. 1940). McCormick says the phrase if taken literally is absurd. It suggests that the jury may forego independent analysis and bow too readily to the opinion of an expert or otherwise influential witness. * * * This indicates a mistrust of the mentality and capacity of jurors to decide matters for themselves.* * *

Regarding the second objection, that the juror is asked the ultimate question the jury must answer, Mr. Justice Smedley held for this Court in Federal Underwriters Exchange v. Cost, 132 Tex. 299, 123 S.W.2d 332 (1938), discussed above, that there are many occasions on which a witness may be asked the same question the jury must answer. For example as in *Cost*, a doctor was permitted to give his opinion as to whether an incapacity of a workman would be permanent. Again, an automobile intersection case may turn on whether a party ran a red light, failed to stop at a sign, gave a particular signal, and the like. In all of these, witnesses may testify, if they know, that the person did or did not do these things; and the jury is then asked the same question. Many authorities would permit questions even on an ultimate issue. * * * It is when the question involves a legal definition and a conclusion based on the definition that Brown v. Mitchell and Lindley v. Lindley, 384 S.W.2d 676 (Tex.1964) are offended.

It is the third objection listed above which is the basis for the holdings of Brown v. Mitchell [88 Tex. 350, 31 S.W. 621 (1895)] and Lindley v. Lindley [384 S.W.2d 676 (Tex.Sup.1964)]. A witness may not be asked whether a person had the [legal] capacity to execute a deed, or was acting under an insane delusion when he executed his will, because these concepts involve legal definitions. As stated in Lindley, the doctor's or lay witness's definition or understanding of capacity to perform the act in a legal manner may be different from the legal standard.[71] * * *

It is our conclusion that the jury in cases such as these should be given all relevant and competent testimony with regard to the mental condition of the testatrix; and in our opinion, competent evidence about her mental condition and mental ability or lack of it which does not involve legal definitions, legal tests, or pure questions of law should be admitted. This is in accord with the modern trend in this field. * * *

This has also been the trend of the better cases in Texas. In Chambers v. Winn, 137 Tex. 444, 154 S.W.2d 454 (1941), several witnesses were asked if they thought the testator was of sound or unsound mind. Objection was sustained. This Court reversed, saying that "[t]he courts below failed * * * to observe the distinction between evidence bearing on the mental condition of the testator and that bearing on his legal capacity to make a will." * * *

---

[71] It has been argued by many of the authorities set out above that any difference of definition could be brought out by proper cross examination; and so the question and answer should be allowed if it would be helpful to the jury. Nevertheless, this Court's position is stated in Brown v. Mitchell and followed in Lindley.

* * * Our holding is that a witness may not be asked whether a testator had the mental capacity to make and publish a will because, under Brown v. Mitchell, whether a person has mental capacity to execute a will involves a legal definition and a legal test. A witness may be asked, assuming he knows or is a properly qualified expert, whether the testator knew or had the capacity to know the objects of his bounty, the nature of the transaction in which he was engaged, the nature and extent of his estate, and similar questions.

The particular question here was whether Miss Hewlett, when she wrote her will, had sufficient ability to understand the business in which she was engaged, the effect of her acts in making a will, realized what she was doing, and knew the property she owned. The trial court erred in excluding the question and the answer thereto.

We are also of the opinion that the error was harmful. While Dr. Hoerster, the only medically trained expert tendered by either party, did get in bits of testimony here and there, he was never permitted to develop his testimony, the Petitioner's side of the lawsuit * * *. At least three of Respondents' witnesses were permitted to testify that in their opinion Miss Hewlett was of unsound mind, giving their reasons. Mrs. Radkey had been permitted to testify that in her opinion the testatrix was not mentally capable of knowing or understanding her acts. Similarly, Mrs. Brown was permitted to testify that Miss Hewlett was not mentally capable of knowing the nature and effect of her acts. The Petitioner was entitled to meet that evidence with Dr. Hoerster's testimony.

* * *

The judgments of the courts below are reversed and the case is remanded to the district court for a new trial.

NOTES AND QUESTIONS

1. *Ultimate issues.* Rule 704(a) provides: "An opinion is not objectionable just because it embraces an ultimate issue." A common example illustrates the problem of excluding expert testimony on ultimate issues: In a drug case, a chemist may be called to the witness stand to identify the substance seized by the police as cocaine, which, of course, is an element of the crime. In such a case, an opinion on the "ultimate issue" is both desirable and necessary. (Note that Rule 704(a) also applies to lay witnesses.) Yet, not all opinions are admissible. The Advisory Committee note reads: "The abolition of the ultimate issue rule does not lower the bars so as to admit all opinions. Under Rules 701 and 702, opinions must be helpful to the trier of fact, and Rule 403 provides for exclusion of evidence which wastes time. These provisions afford ample assurances against the admission of opinions which would merely tell the jury what result to reach * * *.".

2. *Legal terms.* Are the court's reservations in the principal case regarding an opinion expressed in legal terms valid? "[C]onclusory testimony that a company engaged in 'discrimination,' that a landlord was 'negligent,' or that an investment house engaged in a 'fraudulent and manipulative scheme' involves the use of terms with considerable legal baggage; such testimony nearly always invades the province of the jury." In contrast, "the legal meaning of some terms is not so distinctive from the colloquial meaning, if a distinction exists at all, making it difficult to gauge the helpfulness, and thus admissibility, of the testimony under Rule 704." United States v. Perkins, 470 F.3d 150, 158 (4th Cir.2006). See also United States v. Sheffey, 57 F.3d 1419, 1426 (6th Cir.1995) (testimony that the defendant had driven "recklessly, in extreme disregard for human life" did not state a legal conclusion because the terms "recklessly" and "extreme disregard for human life" do not have a legal meaning distinct from everyday usage).

3. *Mental states.* Although Rule 704(a) abrogated the ultimate issue rule, Congress took a major step back from this position in 1984 by the enactment of Rule 704(b), which specifically applies the ultimate issue rule to testimony concerning the mental state of a defendant in a criminal case. See California Penal Code § 29 for a state provision with the same effect. The amendment to the Federal Rule arose out of the national concern over the prosecution of John Hinckley for attempting to assassinate President Reagan. The amendment was part of a package of legislation intended to make it more difficult for an accused successfully to assert the insanity defense.

> The purpose of this amendment is to eliminate the confusing spectacle of competing expert witnesses testifying to directly contradictory conclusions as to the ultimate legal issue to be found by the trier of fact. Under this proposal, expert psychiatric testimony would be limited to presenting and explaining their diagnosis, such as whether the defendant had a severe mental disease or defect and what the characteristics of such a disease or defect, if any, may have been.

H.Rep.No. 98–1030, 98th Cong., 2d Sess. 224, 232, U.S.C.C.A.N. 1984, at 1.

Another portion of the legislative history gives further insight into congressional thinking:

> When, however, "ultimate issue" questions are formulated by the law and put to the expert witness who must then say "yea" or "nay" then the expert witness is required to make a leap in logic. He no longer addresses himself to medical concepts but instead must infer or intuit what is in fact unspeakable, namely, the probable relationship between medical concepts and legal or moral constructs such as free will. These impermissible leaps in logic made by expert witnesses confuse the jury.

S.Rep.No. 225, 98th Cong., 1st Sess. 231, quoting American Psychiatric Association Statement on the Insanity Defense, Dec. 1982, at 18.

Are there likely to be problems with this congressional resurrection of the ultimate issue rule? Some have already arisen, such as the difficulty of distinguishing between testimony concerning diagnosis and testimony concerning the ultimate decision. See United States v. Edwards, 819 F.2d 262 (11th Cir.1987) (psychiatrist's testimony that the defendant was "frantic" over financial situation held not to violate Rule 704(b)). See generally Note, Resurrection of the Ultimate Issue Rule: Federal Rule of Evidence 704(b) and the Insanity Defense, 72 Cornell L.Rev. 620 (1987).

To what extent does Rule 704(b) apply in cases other than those involving the insanity defense? See United States v. Campos, 217 F.3d 707, 711 (9th Cir.2000) ("While Congress primarily targeted subdivision (b) towards limiting the use of psychiatric expert testimony on whether a defendant is sane or insane, * * * Rule 704(b) is not limited in 'its reach to psychiatrists and other mental health experts,' but rather, extends to all expert witnesses. * * * Rule 704(b) clearly applies to expert polygraph testimony on ultimate issues. * * * The polygraph examiner's testimony that Campos was truthful in stating that she did not know that she was transporting marijuana leaves no room for inference, but rather, compels the conclusion that she did not possess the requisite knowledge."); United States v. Morales, 108 F.3d 1031, 1036, 1037 (9th Cir.1997) ("The language of Rule 704(b) is perfectly plain. It does not limit its reach to psychiatrists and other mental health experts. Its reach extends to all expert witnesses. * * * [The accountant] was not going to state an opinion or draw an inference that Morales did not intend to make false entries [the ultimate issue]. Rather, she was going to state her opinion as to a predicate matter—that Morales had a weak grasp of bookkeeping principles.").

(5) RIGHT TO EXPERT ASSISTANCE

In Ake v. Oklahoma, 470 U.S. 68 (1985), the accused was charged with capital murder. At arraignment, his conduct was "so bizarre" that the trial judge ordered, sua sponte, a mental evaluation. Ake was found incompetent to stand trial but later recovered due to antipsychotic drugs. When the prosecution resumed, Ake's attorney requested a psychiatric evaluation at state expense to prepare an insanity defense. The trial court refused. Thus, although insanity was the only contested issue at trial, no psychiatrists testified on this issue, and Ake was convicted. In the penalty stage, the prosecution relied on state psychiatrists, who testified that Ake was "dangerous to society," in seeking the death sentence. This testimony stood unrebutted because Ake could not afford an expert.

The Supreme Court overturned Ake's conviction on due process grounds, commenting that "when a State brings its judicial power to bear on an indigent in a criminal proceeding, it must take steps to assure that the defendant has a fair opportunity to present his defense." Id. at 76. This fair opportunity mandates that an accused be provided with the "basic tools of an adequate defense." In another passage, the Court elaborated on what it meant by a "fair opportunity" and "basic tools" for an adequate defense: "We hold that when a defendant has made a preliminary showing that his sanity at the time of the offense is likely to be a significant factor at trial, the Constitution requires that a State provide access to a psychiatrist's assistance on this issue, if the defendant cannot otherwise afford one." Id. at 74. See generally Giannelli, *Ake v. Oklahoma*: The Right to Expert Assistance in a Post–*Daubert*, Post–DNA World, 89 Cornell L.Rev. 1305 (2004).

While the *Ake* decision settled the core issue by recognizing a right to expert assistance, it left a number of important issues unresolved:

Noncapital cases. Compare Isom v. State, 488 So.2d 12, 13 (Ala.Crim.App.1986) ("*Ake* does not reach noncapital cases."), with Taylor v. State, 939 S.W.2d 148, 152 (Tex.Crim.App.1996) ("[W]e have also extended—at least implicitly—the due process protections recognized in *Ake* beyond the capital context.").

Nonpsychiatric experts. Compare Ex parte Grayson, 479 So.2d 76, 82 (Ala.1985) ("[T]here is nothing contained in the *Ake* decision to suggest that the United States Supreme Court was addressing anything other than psychiatrists and the insanity defense."), with Little v. Armontrout, 835 F.2d 1240, 1243 (8th Cir.1987) (en banc) (In finding error in failure to appoint an expert on hypnotism, the court stated: "[T]here is no principled way to distinguish between psychiatric and nonpsychiatric experts. The question in each case must be not what field of science or expert knowledge is involved, but rather how important the scientific issue is in the case, and how much help a defense expert could have given.").

Role of expert. Compare Granviel v. Lynaugh, 881 F.2d 185, 191 (5th Cir.1989) (a "court-appointed psychiatrist, whose opinion and testimony is available to both sides, satisfies [the accused's] rights. * * * The state is not required to permit defendants to shop around for a favorable expert. * * * He has no right to the appointment of a psychiatrist who will reach biased or only favorable conclusions."), with United States v. Sloan, 776 F.2d 926, 929 (10th Cir.1985) ("That duty [to appoint a psychiatrist] cannot be satisfied with the appointment of an expert who ultimately testifies contrary to the defense on the issue of competence. The essential benefit of having an expert in the first place is denied the defendant when the services of the doctor must be shared with the prosecution.").

Standard for appointment. In Volson v. Blackburn, 794 F.2d 173, 176 (5th Cir.1986), the court noted that "the *Ake* decision fails to establish a bright line test for determining when a defendant has demonstrated that sanity at the time of the offense will be a significant factor at the time of trial." Some reasonable threshold showing is necessary because the system cannot afford defense experts on "demand." For example, in State

v. Mason, 694 N.E.2d 932 (Ohio 1998), a capital case, the defendant received state funds for the services of a private investigator, a forensic psychiatrist, a forensic pathologist, and for DNA and blood testing services. He requested, but did not receive, funds to hire a soils and trace evidence expert, a shoeprint expert, an eyewitness identification expert, a homicide investigation expert, a mass media expert, a forensic psychologist, a statistical DNA expert, and a firearms expert. However, if the threshold standard is set too high, the defendant is placed in a "Catch–22" situation, in which the standard "demand[s] that the defendant possess already the expertise of the witness sought." State v. Moore, 364 S.E.2d 648, 657 (N.C.1988).

Statutory provisions. Under 18 U.S.C. § 3006A, an indigent person may obtain expert assistance. The Act limits expenses for expert services to $2,400.00 unless the court certifies that a greater amount is "necessary to provide fair compensation for services of an unusual character or duration." Many states have comparable provisions. See Minn.Stat.Ann. § 611.21 ($1,000 maximum).

Court-appointed experts. Although not frequently used, Rule 706 has been employed in a variety of situations. See, e.g., Students of Cal. Sch. for Blind v. Honig, 736 F.2d 538 (9th Cir.1984) (in case involving seismic safety of new campus of school for blind, after lengthy and conflicting evidence, court appointed expert under Rule 706). The question of the appointment of an impartial expert is within the discretion of the trial court judge. See Quiet Technology DC–8, Inc. v. Hurel–Dubois UK Ltd., 326 F.3d 1333, 1348–49 (11th Cir.2003) ("[W]e are unfamiliar with any set of circumstances under which a district court bears an affirmative obligation to appoint an independent expert. Quite the contrary, as long as the district court thoroughly considers a request for the appointment of such an expert and reasonably explains its ultimate decision thereon, that decision is vested in the sound discretion of the trial court."). See also Nemir v. Mitsubishi Motors Corp., 381 F.3d 540, 556 (6th Cir.2004) ("The rule simply does not condition a party's [right to call a court-appointed expert] on the district court's approval, nor does it maintain merely that the district court 'may allow either party to call the witness.' "). Might frequent use of Rule 706 present problems for the adversary system? See Choy, Judicial Education After *Markman v. Westview Instruments, Inc.*: The Use of Court-appointed Experts, 47 UCLA L.Rev. 1423 (2000); Thorpe, Oelhafen & Arnold, Court–Appointed Experts and Technical Advisors, 26 Litigation 31 (Summer 2000); Note, Improving Judicial Gatekeeping: Technical Advisors and Scientific Evidence, 110 Harv.L.Rev. 941 (1997).

Civil litigation. May the impecunious civil party plaintiff (who unlike the criminal defendant may improve his financial situation by the litigation) obtain expert testimony by means of an agreement with the expert under which the expert's right to receive a fee is conditioned upon success in the litigation? See, e.g., Barnes v. Boatmen's Nat'l Bank, 156 S.W.2d 597 (Mo.1941) (contract upheld against contention that it was against public policy). But see also Model Rule of Prof'l Conduct R. 3.4 cmt. ("The common law rule in most jurisdictions is * * * that it is improper to pay an expert witness a contingent fee.").

E. CREDIBILITY: BOLSTERING, IMPEACHMENT AND REHABILITATION

The credibility of a witness is a quintessential jury issue. For present purposes, credibility may be defined as a witness' worthiness of belief. The evidentiary rules governing credibility can be viewed in three stages: (1) bolstering of credibility, (2) impeachment of credibility, and (3) rehabilitation of credibility. Impeachment is the elicitation or presentation of any matter *for the purpose* of impairing or destroying the credibility of a witness in the estimation of the trier of fact. Note that bolstering and rehabilitation both involve attempts to support the credibility of a witness. The difference is one of timing: Bolstering involves attempts to support credibility before it has been attacked or impeached. In contrast, rehabilitation comes after impeachment. Different rules apply to bolstering and rehabilitation.

Credibility issues cover matters for which there may not be a specific Federal Rule. How many methods are in the following statute?

Cal. Evid. Code § 780

General rule as to credibility. Except as otherwise provided by statute, the court or jury may consider in determining the credibility of a witness any matter that has any tendency in reason to prove or disprove the truthfulness of his testimony at the hearing, including but not limited to any of the following:

(a) His demeanor while testifying and the manner in which he testifies.

(b) The character of his testimony.

(c) The extent of his capacity to perceive, to recollect, or to communicate any matter about which he testifies.

(d) The extent of his opportunity to perceive any matter about which he testifies.

(e) His character for honesty or veracity or their opposites.

(f) The existence or nonexistence of a bias, interest, or other motive.

(g) A statement previously made by him that is consistent with his testimony at the hearing.

(h) A statement made by him that is inconsistent with any part of his testimony at the hearing.

(i) The existence or nonexistence of any fact testified to by him.

(j) His attitude toward the action in which he testifies or toward the giving of testimony.

(k) His admission of untruthfulness.

(1) BOLSTERING

It is not unusual to find statements stating that bolstering the credibility of witnesses is impermissible: United States v. Cosentino, 844 F.2d 30, 32–33 (2d Cir.1988) ("It is well settled that absent an attack, no evidence may be admitted to support a witness' credibility."). Consumption of time and confusion of issues are the principal reasons for this rule. See United States v. LeFevour, 798 F.2d 977, 983 (7th Cir.1986) ("To bolster a witness's credibility in advance is improper. It not only has the potential for extending the length of trials enormously, but asks the jury to take the witness's testimony on faith; it may therefore reduce the care with which jurors listen for inconsistencies and other signs of falsehood or inaccuracy.").

Prominent examples of this rule are (1) the prohibition on the admissibility of evidence of a witness' truthful character prior to attack, Rule 608(a), and (2) the prohibition on the admissibility of prior consistent statements prior to attack. See also Rule 801(d)(1)(B) (altering the common law rule to admit as substantive evidence). See Chapter 13, Section B(1), infra.

UNITED STATES V. THORNTON
United States Court of Appeals, Seventh Circuit, 1999.
197 F.3d 241.

TERENCE T. EVANS, CIRCUIT JUDGE.

Major federal drug cases these days follow a fairly familiar pattern. They are centered in big cities, and they usually involve a wide-ranging drug distribution network that has been operating for several years. The drug of choice is invariably cocaine, often in its most addictive form as crack. * * * The typical case has a dozen or more defendants (many with multiple and often creative nicknames), and other counts in the indictment specifically charge some of them with individual acts of possession of cocaine with intent to distribute at various times and places. * * *

When these cases arrive in court they follow a predictable pattern. Some of the defendants jump ship, make deals with the government, and become principal witnesses against those defendants who do not elect "to cooperate." "Cooperating" defendants usually do not receive a complete pass; instead they are permitted to wrap up their cases on more favorable terms based on their acceptance of responsibility under the federal sentencing guidelines and a motion for a downward departure based on the assistance given to the government. * * *

The facts in this case and the issues raised on appeal are typical of the usual federal drug conspiracy prosecution we have just described. The case involves a 20–count indictment against 14 defendants which grew out of a conspiracy to distribute cocaine in the cities of Indianapolis and Chicago. Today we consider the appeals of three defendants who went to trial and were convicted * * *.

* * *

Third, Harris, Jackson, and Reynolds all fault the trial court for allowing into evidence the government's proffer letters to cooperating witnesses and for not allowing cross-examination of these witnesses to delve into polygraph testing. The admission of proffer letters is an evidentiary decision reviewed for abuse of discretion. United States v. Lewis, 110 F.3d 417, 422 (7th Cir. * * * 1997). * * *

The government introduced into evidence plea agreements for the nine cooperating witnesses, as well as proffer letters for most of those witnesses. Each of the proffer letters makes three references[72] to truthfulness and each of the plea agreements makes five references[73] to truthfulness. Just as defense counsel have every right to attack the credibility of witnesses who get deals, the prosecution is entitled to get into evidence the fact that the deals are conditioned upon truthful testimony. "[O]n direct examination, the prosecutor may elicit testimony regarding the witness' plea agreement and actually introduce the plea agreement into evidence." Lewis, 110 F.3d at 421 (internal quotations and

---

[72] The three references to truthful testimony in the proffer letters pertained to the following topics: (1) providing "false" information could result in prosecution for perjury or giving a false statement; (2) the grant of use immunity is conditioned on the indictee's "complete and candid compliance" with the terms of the agreement and any violation could result in prosecution for perjury, false statements, or obstruction of justice; (3) after the indictee provides the proffer the government "will assess the value of the information provided, your honesty, candor and special circumstances."

[73] The five references to truthful testimony in the plea agreements pertained to the following topics: (1) the codefendant agreed to provide "complete, total and truthful debriefings" regarding criminal activity to the government; (2) the codefendant agreed to provide "complete, total and truthful" testimony before grand juries and at trials; (3) the government agreed not to bring criminal charges against the codefendant for the "full, complete and truthful information and testimony" the codefendant provided; (4) the government reserved the right to prosecute for perjury or false statements if the codefendant testified "falsely"; (5) breach of the agreement, such as the failure to provide "full, complete and truthful information and testimony," could result in the agreement being withdrawn.

citations omitted). Contrary to the defendants' claims, the admission of these agreements does not constitute government vouching for the credibility of the witnesses. Two types of "vouching" are forbidden: a prosecutor may not express her personal belief in the truthfulness of a witness, and a prosecutor may not imply that facts not before the jury lend a witness credibility. United States v. Renteria, 106 F.3d 765, 767 (7th Cir.1997). Neither sin was committed here. The proffer letters and plea agreements merely laid out the terms and conditions of the agreements. * * * Each side could urge competing inferences—as indeed the defendants' did—but the jury's role as independent fact finder was not undermined. Renteria, 106 F.3d at 767.

The documents in this case closely track the language of the proffer letters and plea agreements that were allowed in Lewis, 110 F.3d at 421. Likewise, the judge's jury instructions here[74] resemble the judge's instructions in that case. *Lewis* said that the admission of proffer letters and plea agreements was not an attempt to enhance the credibility of the witnesses and that the judge's instructions should have dispelled any harmful effects. Id. at 421–22. The same logic applies here, and we reach the same result.

However, some words of wisdom to the wise: This decision should not be read as an enthusiastic endorsement for the admission of all proffer letters and all plea agreements at all times and in all places. We approve the admission in this case in light of the judge's jury instructions and in light of the overwhelming evidence that would render any erroneous admission harmless. But for more than a decade we have been warning prosecutors to "avoid unnecessarily repetitive references to truthfulness if it wishes to introduce the agreements into evidence." Id. at 421; * * *. Three references to truthfulness in the proffer letters and five references in the plea agreements comes perilously close to being unnecessarily repetitive. * * *

The admission of the proffer letters, in particular, strikes us as overkill. The plea agreements' references to truthfulness were repetitive enough—admitting the proffer letters, with their own repetitive references to truthfulness, compounded the problem. The government confidently states that "while the immunity letters and plea agreements contained similar language concerning truthfulness, they were executed

---

[74] The judge told the jury that "[y]ou are the sole judges of the credibility—that is, the believability—of the witnesses." The judge said the jury "should draw no inferences" based on the government's exercise of its discretion to enter into plea bargains and emphasized that "[y]ou may give this testimony such weight as you feel it deserves, keeping in mind that such testimony is always to be received with caution and weighed with great care." The judge noted that "[y]ou have heard testimony from witnesses who received immunity, that is a promise from the government that any testimony or other information he or she provided would not be used against him or her in a criminal case. You may give this testimony such weight as you feel it deserves, keeping in mind that it must be considered with caution and great care."

at different times and fulfilled distinct purposes." But this does not explain what distinct evidentiary purpose the admission of the proffer letters served at trial. The plea agreements explained the conditions under which the cooperating codefendants were testifying. The proffer letters, which memorialize the framework under which the codefendants agreed to talk in the first place, seem of scant relevance at trial when a subsequent, superseding plea agreement has been reached. * * *

At the defendants' request, the district judge redacted from all of the cooperating witnesses' plea agreements a sentence in which the witness consented to submit to a polygraph examination upon the government's request. (The government never made any requests and none of the cooperating witnesses ever took a polygraph test.) However, proffer letters to two witnesses, Renee Yvette Booker and Valarie Sanders, also mentioned the possibility of a polygraph test. While cross-examining Sanders, Reynolds' counsel exhibited to the jury the proffer letter containing the polygraph test reference. The judge cut off this line of cross-examination. Later, the judge decided to admit into evidence Booker's proffer letter without redacting the polygraph reference. Admitting the polygraph reference was a mistake. Unlike in United States v. Bursten, 560 F.2d 779, 785 (7th Cir.1977), defense counsel were not permitted to cross-examine the witness on this subject. Unlike in Lewis, 110 F.3d at 421 n.2, defense counsel were not responsible for the admission of the polygraph reference as to Booker. However, the judge cured any problem by instructing the jury not to pay attention to whether Booker might have taken a polygraph test.[75] Furthermore, two passing references to the possibility of polygraph tests for two witnesses was harmless in a jury trial that lasted 19 days, involved 60 witnesses and contained strong evidence of the defendants' guilt.

On a related note, the defendants claim their Sixth Amendment right to confrontation was violated because the district judge prohibited them from bringing out in cross-examination the fact that none of the government's witnesses took lie detector tests. Since the polygraph test statement in Booker's proffer letter was admitted, defense counsel should have been permitted to cross-examine her on this subject. * * *

* * *

For these reasons, the judgments of conviction of Harris, Jackson and Reynolds—as well as of Thornton—are affirmed.

---

[75] The judge told the jury: "[O]ne of the things that you may have heard, or picked up somewhere, is that there are references now and again in these proffer agreements, and sometimes even in plea agreements, to lie detector tests. Now, you are not to draw any inference from that as to whether a particular individual either took or didn't take a lie detector test or passed or didn't pass a lie detector test. Everybody understand that? No speculation about that, no inferences to be drawn from that."

NOTES AND QUESTIONS

1. *The issue.* What is the problem with introducing the plea agreements and proffer letters during the direct examination if they could be introduced during redirect examination after the witnesses have been impeached for bias on cross-examination?

2. *Permissive approach.* In United States v. Spriggs, 996 F.2d 320, 323 (D.C.Cir.1993), the D.C. Circuit explained:

> We think the majority position is the better reasoned. Simply put, we are not persuaded that evidence of the contents of a cooperation agreement unduly bolsters the credibility of a Government witness. First, insofar as the agreement provides that if the witness lies the agreement is revocable, that the witness is liable to prosecution for perjury, and that his perjurious testimony may be used against him, it adds nothing to the law—as the defense is free to bring out upon cross-examination. Therefore, the agreement provides no special incentive for the Government witness to testify truthfully; hence, the jury is not likely to place special credence in the witness merely because of the terms of the agreement. Furthermore, that the Government may (obviously) impose a sanction upon the witness if he lies does nothing to enhance the Government's ability to detect whether he is in fact lying; again the terms of the cooperation agreement should do nothing to enhance the witness's credibility. Finally, at least in the present case there is nothing in the agreement or in the prosecutor's direct examination on that subject to "imply that the government had special knowledge" of the witness's veracity.

See also Woods v. United States, 987 A.2d 451, 454 (D.C.2010) (elicitation during direct examination of a plea agreement containing a promise to testify truthfully does not constitute impermissible bolstering of the witness' credibility even where the defense has stipulated that it will refrain from cross-examination regarding bias relating to that plea agreement).

3. *Restrictive approach.* In State v. Ish, 241 P.3d 389, 393–94 (Wash.2010), the court wrote:

> Presumably, prosecutors know that the contents of an agreement made in exchange for testimony may become an exhibit or the subject of testimony at trial, and there is a natural temptation to insert self-serving language into these agreements. Evidence that a witness has promised to give 'truthful testimony' in exchange for reduced charges may indicate to a jury that the prosecution has some independent means of ensuring that the witness complies with the terms of the agreement. While such evidence may help bolster the credibility of the witness among some jurors, it is generally self-serving, irrelevant, and may amount to vouching, particularly if admitted during the State's case in chief.

See also United States v. Cosentino, 844 F.2d 30, 33 (2d Cir.1988) ("Because of the bolstering potential of cooperation agreements, * * * we have permitted such agreements to be admitted in their entirety only after the credibility of the witness has been attacked. This restriction proceeds from our view that 'the *entire* cooperation agreement bolsters more than it impeaches.' ") (citations omitted).

4.   *Plea reduction motions.* In United States v. Harlow, 444 F.3d 1255, 1263 (10th Cir.2006), the prosecution introduced Criminal Rule 35(b) motions and sentence reduction orders in addition to the plea agreement. The court reversed: "[One] provision [of the agreement] coupled with the introduction of the government's Rule 35(b) motion implies that the government has verified the truthfulness of the witness and believes that his ongoing testimony is truthful, which is why it made a motion for a sentence reduction. The jury could reasonably infer that the government would not have recommended such a downward departure if it had not independently verified the truthfulness of the testimony. * * * [These documents] amount[ ] to prosecutorial vouching. Section 13 only compounds the matter. Not only does it reiterate the role of the government in recommending sentence reductions for truthful testimony, it also implicates the judge in the verification process."

5.   *Polygraph evidence.* A majority of states still follow the traditional rule, holding polygraph evidence per se inadmissible. This exclusionary rule extends to evidence that a person was willing to take, took, or refused to take an examination. A substantial minority of jurisdictions admit polygraph results upon stipulation. A third group leaves the admissibility issue to the trial judge. At one time most federal circuit courts followed the per se approach. However, the *Daubert* decision changed this result. See United States v. Posado, 57 F.3d 428, 429 (5th Cir.1995) ("[T]he rationale underlying this circuit's per se rule against admitting polygraph evidence did not survive *Daubert* * * *."). Most federal courts, however, have exercised their discretion to exclude polygraph evidence. See 1 Giannelli, Imwinkelried, Roth & Moriarty, Scientific Evidence ch. 8 (5th ed. 2012) (polygraph evidence).

6.   *Fresh complaint.* Many jurisdictions recognize an exception to the rule against bolstering in rape cases, where evidence of an alleged victim's "fresh complaint" is admissible to corroborate or bolster her testimony. See State v. Rolon, 777 A.2d 604, 625 (Conn.2001) ("The constancy of accusation doctrine is well established in Connecticut and recently has been reaffirmed by this court. * * * [W]e restricted the doctrine so that a constancy of accusation witness could testify only to the fact and the timing of the victim's complaint. Even so limited, the evidence would be admissible solely for corroboration of the victim's testimony, and not for substantive purposes."); State v. W.B., 17 A.3d 187, 205 (N.J.2011) (requirement of reporting a sexual assault within a reasonable time must be applied more flexibly in cases involving children than in cases involving adults; "D.L. was fourteen years old when the attacks by defendant occurred, and sixteen when she confided in J.C. * * * D.L., as defendant's stepdaughter, appears to have lived with defendant at least some of the time during that interval and also indicated to

J.C. that she was afraid to report the abuse. Both are factors that impact the determination of 'reasonableness.' "). In Commonwealth v. King, 834 N.E.2d 1175, 1197 (Mass.2005), the court changed the rule from the "fresh complaint" to the "first complaint" rule. Why? See generally Stanchi, The Paradox of the Fresh Complaint Rule, 37 B.C.L.Rev. 441 (1996).

7. *Pretrial identifications.* Another exception to the rule against bolstering involved testimony concerning a pretrial identification (e.g., lineup, showup, or photographic display) once an in-court identification had been made. See also Rule 801(d)(1)(C) (altering the common law rule to admit as substantive evidence). See Chapter 13, Section B(1), infra.

(2) IMPEACHMENT: WHO MAY IMPEACH[76]

STATE V. GREEN
Supreme Court of Washington, 1967.
428 P.2d 540.

[Defendant was charged with burglary after having been apprehended by police officers while fleeing from the scene of the crime. Defendant contended that the burglary had been undertaken by two companions of defendant's, Gaither and Wilkerson, while defendant, ignorant of the others' purpose, waited in a car. He further asserted that he subsequently left the car and was protesting against his friends' activities when the police arrived. Defendant was convicted by a jury and appealed.]

HALE, JUDGE.

* * *

Defendant claims reversible error when the prosecution impeached state's witness Gaither, an admitted participant in the burglary. It came about in this way: Charles Gaither, called by the state in its case in chief, testified at the outset that he had participated in the Medical Center Pharmacy burglary on the night of March 10th; then he testified:

Q. All right. I will ask you whether or not the Defendant Nathaniel Leon Green participated with you and aided you in the commission of that burglary? A. No.

He repeated this negative answer after a lengthy colloquy in the jury's absence, and the state, claiming that Gaither had made earlier statements inconsistent with the exonerating testimony, sought to impeach him.

---

[76] Remember that in the majority of American jurisdictions, cross-examination is limited to the subject matter of the direct. All jurisdictions permit cross-examination on matters of impeachment regardless of the scope of the direct examination. Review the materials in Chapter 6, Order of Proof, particularly *Atkinson v. Smith*, *Boller v. Cofrances*, and *United States v. Lara*, supra.

The prosecuting attorney had not interviewed Gaither before trial, nor otherwise ascertained if he intended to contradict the statement. On receiving from the state's witness the exculpatory answer that the defendant was innocent, the state claimed surprise and unexpected hostility from the witness, and laid a foundation for impeachment by establishing that the witness had earlier made a written statement describing the crime and incriminating defendant as an accomplice. When shown this confession on the stand, Gaither denied that the written statement referred to the defendant, Nathaniel Leon Green, asserting that it referred to another man variously mentioned in the statement as Green, Nathaniel, or Nat.

Having thus laid a proper predicate for impeachment by first showing that Gaither denied having incriminated defendant in his confession and meant a different person, the state then impeached the witness through the testimony of a police officer who testified that, throughout the entire statement-taking process, both orally and when reducing it to writing, the witness, in referring to a Nat, Nathaniel or Green at all times identified and referred to the defendant, Nathaniel Leon Green * * *.

* * * [T]he assignment of error focuses directly on the questions of surprise and hostility. Could the prosecuting attorney legitimately claim surprise when he had not interviewed Gaither, nor otherwise made inquiries as to whether he would adhere to his statement concerning the defendant?

* * *

One of the basic obligations resting on everyone living under the protection of our constitutions is that, when called upon to give evidence in court he will, without reservation, speak the truth; that he will not avoid or evade this duty through fear, malice, or hope or promise of reward. The court and every party to a judicial proceedings—indeed, society itself—has a right to assume that the duty to give truthful evidence will be discharged and it need not be anticipated that that duty will be betrayed. Thus, the law—with several notable exceptions, of course—assumes that a party calling one as a witness not only believes the witness to be truthful, but represents him to be truthful. One is thus held to vouch for the credibility of the witnesses he presents. Having called the witness to testify and thereby vouching for his truthfulness—although he may present other evidence of a contradictory nature through other witnesses—a party may not impeach his own witness unless without warning the witness tells a story different than the one the party calling him had a reasonable right to expect of him.

But what if the party's faith in his witness is betrayed?

The law has a protective device for this betrayal through a corollary rule which allows a party to impeach his own witness in event of genuine surprise and hostility. Both the rule as to credibility and impeachment are essential to elicit the truth. If one were not held to vouch for the credibility of witnesses called by him, he could present one lying witness after another in the hope of establishing facts favorable to his cause. Contrarily, if there were no exception or corollary to this rule, a party to a judicial proceedings would be left in a position of hopeless betrayal by a witness upon whom he had good reason to rely and for whose credibility he had vouched.

At the time the state called Gaither, the prosecuting attorney had in hand a detailed statement of the crime signed by Gaither and describing defendant as one of two accomplices. Made by the witness without duress, coercion or fear, the statement recited at firsthand Gaither's and his accomplices' step-by-step participation in the burglary, and corroborated in detail the mass of other evidence which the prosecuting attorney intended to offer in the state's case in chief. Gaither had never, to the prosecuting attorney's knowledge, repudiated the statement nor had he ever intimated to the prosecuting attorney at any time before being put on the witness stand that he intended to do so.

* * *

Gaither's acknowledged guilt did not absolve him from his duty to give truthful evidence. * * * The prosecution had a right to undo this damage by attempting to impeach the witness and thus cancel the effect of this surprisingly hostile testimony. The court properly allowed the impeachment.

* * *

Affirmed.

NOTES AND QUESTIONS

1. *Voucher rule.* The two most commonly cited bases for the rule against impeaching one's own witness are (a) the "vouching" theory expounded in the principal case, and (b) the contention that a party "should not have the power to coerce his own witness." Does either of these theories have modern validity?

2. *Bound by testimony.* Another aspect of the voucher rule concerned whether a party was bound by the testimony of its own witnesses. For example, in Becker v. Eisenstodt, 158 A.2d 706, 708 (N.J.Super.Ct.App.Div.1960), a malpractice case, the plaintiff called the defendant-doctor in its case-in-chief and asked him the following questions:

"Q. Doctor, on December 27, 1957, when Arlene Becker came to your office, you inserted into her nose, the right nostril of her nose, a pledget or a piece of cotton saturated with a ten percent solution of cocaine? A. That's right, sir.

"Q. And nothing else? A. That's right."

There was no cross-examination. On appeal, the defendant stressed the fact that plaintiff called defendant as his own witness, and argued that he was therefore bound by his testimony. The appellate court disagreed, writing

> Such a rule, so broadly stated, ill serves the cause of justice. It is a relic of the earliest system of trial, where those who attended on behalf of the parties were not witnesses, as we understand the word, but "oath-helpers," whose mere oath, when taken by the prescribed number of persons and in the proper form, determined the issue. Ordinarily, these persons were relatives and adherents of either party, clearly partisan. As Wigmore observes, so long as this traditional notion of a witness persisted, it was inconceivable that a party should gainsay his own witness. If a witness failed to swear for him, it was his loss—he should have chosen a better person for his purpose. Accordingly, a party was not allowed to dispute what his witness said. This "primitive" concept of the role of witnesses persisted long after the time when their function had ceased to be that of mere oath-taker and had become that of a testifier to the facts. 3 Wigmore on Evidence (3d ed. 1940), § 896, p. 383.

3. *Exception: Surprise.* The exception to the voucher rule where the calling party is "surprised" by the witness' testimony has received varying interpretations by the courts. May surprise within the meaning of the exception exist if the calling party, in possession of a prior statement of the witness, receives notice that the witness does not intend to testify in accord with the statement? Compare Hooks v. United States, 375 F.2d 212 (5th Cir.1967), with Wheeler v. United States, 211 F.2d 19 (D.C.Cir.1953).

4. *Exception: Affirmative damage.* Should more than surprise, however defined, be required? For example, in the principal case would impeachment of the witness Gaither by the state have been allowed if Gaither had testified that he did not recall what the defendant's activities had been while the robbery was in progress? See United States v. Coppola, 479 F.2d 1153 (10th Cir.1973) (surprise not lacking simply by virtue of prior notice of changed story, but impeachment not allowable where calling party's case not affirmatively damaged); Commonwealth v. Strunk, 293 S.W.2d 629, 630 (Ky.1956) (damage defined as "where the witness testifies positively to the existence of a fact prejudicial to the party, or to a fact clearly favorable to the adverse party").

5. *Exception: Court witnesses.* An alternative escape from the common law voucher rule is potentially afforded by the power of the trial court to call its own witnesses. 3A Wigmore, Evidence § 918 (Chadbourn rev. 1970). The witness is not then in theory that of either party. The utility of this escape has been considerably limited by appellate reminders that the trial courts

should use the power sparingly, although United States v. Karnes, 531 F.2d 214 (4th Cir.1976), seems to stand alone in holding that the calling by the judge of two essential prosecution witnesses was a denial of due process.

6. *Due process.* In Chambers v. Mississippi, 410 U.S. 284 (1973), the defendant sought in vain to have the court call a witness who had repeatedly confessed out of court to the murder with which defendant was charged. The Supreme Court reversed, concluding that the combined effect of Mississippi's voucher rule and its hearsay rule served to deny petitioner due process of law.

7. *New approach.* The law in Washington has now moved away from the traditional common law view illustrated in the principal case by the adoption of that state's Rule 607, based upon Federal Rule 607, which abolishes the voucher rule. See State v. Lavaris, 721 P.2d 515 (Wash.1986).

UNITED STATES V. WEBSTER

United States Court of Appeals, Seventh Circuit, 1984.
734 F.2d 1191.

POSNER, CIRCUIT JUDGE.

The defendant, Webster, was convicted of aiding and abetting the robbery of a federally insured bank and receiving stolen bank funds, was sentenced to nine years in prison, and appeals. Only one issue need be discussed. The government called the bank robber, King (who had pleaded guilty and been given a long prison term), as a witness against Webster. King gave testimony that if believed would have exculpated the defendant, whereupon the government introduced prior inconsistent statements that King had given the FBI inculpating Webster. Although the court instructed the jury that it could consider the statements only for purposes of impeachment, Webster argues that this was not good enough, that the government should not be allowed to get inadmissible evidence before the jury by calling a hostile witness and then using his out-of-court statements, which would otherwise be inadmissible hearsay, to impeach him.

Rule 607 of the Federal Rules of Evidence provides: "The credibility of a witness may be attacked by any party, including the party calling him." But it would be an abuse of the rule, in a criminal case, for the prosecution to call a witness that it knew would not give it useful evidence, just so it could introduce hearsay evidence against the defendant in the hope that the jury would miss the subtle distinction between impeachment and substantive evidence—or, if it didn't miss it, would ignore it. The purpose would not be to impeach the witness but to put in hearsay as substantive evidence against the defendant, which Rule 607 does not contemplate or authorize. We thus agree that "impeachment by prior inconsistent statement may not be permitted where employed as a mere subterfuge to get before the jury evidence not otherwise admissible." *United States v. Morlang,* 531 F.2d 183, 190 (4th Cir.1975). Although *Morlang* was decided before the Federal Rules of Evidence became effective, the limitation that we have quoted on the prosecutor's rights under Rule 607 has been accepted in all circuits that have considered the issue. * * *

But it is quite plain that there was no bad faith here. Before the prosecutor called King to the stand she asked the judge to allow her to examine him outside the presence of the jury, because she didn't know what he would say. The defendant's counsel objected and the voir dire was not held. We do not see how in these circumstances it can be thought that the prosecutor put King on the stand knowing he would give no useful evidence. If she had known that, she would not have offered to voir dire him, as the voir dire would have provided a foundation for defense counsel to object, under *Morlang,* to the admission of King's prior inconsistent statements.

Webster urges us, on the authority of Graham, Handbook of Federal Evidence § 607.3 (1981 and Supp.1983), to go beyond the good-faith standard and hold that the government may not impeach a witness with his prior inconsistent statements unless it is surprised and harmed by the witness's testimony. But we think it would be a mistake to graft such a requirement to Rule 607, even if such a graft would be within the power of judicial interpretation of the rule. Suppose the government called an adverse witness that it thought would give evidence both helpful and harmful to it, but it also thought that the harmful aspect could be nullified by introducing the witness's prior inconsistent statement. As there would be no element of surprise, Professor Graham would forbid the introduction of the prior statements; yet we are at a loss to understand why the government should be put to the choice between the Scylla of forgoing impeachment and the Charybdis of not calling at all a witness from whom it expects to elicit genuinely helpful evidence. The good-faith standard strikes a better balance; and it is always open to the defendant to argue that the probative value of the evidence offered to impeach the witness is clearly outweighed by the prejudicial impact it might have on the jury, because the jury would have difficulty confining use of the evidence to impeachment. See Fed.R.Evid. 403.

The judgment of conviction is

Affirmed.

NOTES AND QUESTIONS

1. *Criticism.* The approach rejected in the *Webster* case is set forth in 4 Graham, Handbook of Federal Evidence § 607.3 (7th ed. 2012). Graham notes that under Federal Rule 801(d)(1)(A), statements made by a person testifying

as a witness, which are inconsistent with his testimony at trial and which were given under oath, subject to the penalty of perjury, at a trial, hearing, or other proceeding or in a deposition, are admissible as nonhearsay. He argues that it was the congressional intent to have such statements admitted without satisfying the common law tests of surprise and affirmative harm, but that there was no such intent with regard to prior statements not falling within Rule 801(d)(1)(A). Graham adds:

> * * * If the witness does not give affirmatively damaging testimony, i.e., testimony of positive aid to the adversary, the party simply does not need to attack his credibility. If the witness' testimony does not surprise the party, the litigant should not be permitted to impeach his testimony by placing before the jury the witness' prior statement because he could have refrained from eliciting the statement he seeks to impeach. The requirement of surprise would prevent the party from consciously introducing affirmatively damaging testimony under the only circumstances in which he would do so— when the potential effect on the jury of the prior inconsistent statement outweighs the affirmatively damaging effect of the elicited testimony. (Id. at 230–31.)

Graham responds to the rejection of his position in the *Webster* case as follows:

> Judge Posner misses a very simple point. The government is not put to the choice he presents. It may elicit the helpful testimony without eliciting the known harmful testimony as well. If the defendant chooses to elicit the harmful testimony, the government can impeach with the prior inconsistent statement. If the defendant does not elicit such testimony, the prior inconsistent statement will never be presented to the jury. The only reason the government has to elicit the harmful testimony in the first instance is its belief that the effect of impeachment will more than nullify the harmful effect. (Id. at 424 n.17)

Who is right, Professor Graham or Judge Posner? Irrespective of the wisdom or lack of wisdom of Graham's position, he himself recognizes that the federal courts have interpreted Rule 607 literally and have not grafted on a surprise and affirmative harm limitation. But see Ohio R. Evid. 607(A) (requiring surprise and affirmative damage when a party impeaches its own witness with a prior inconsistent statement).

2. *Balancing.* The court in the principal case recognizes the rule that the prosecution may not call a witness for the primary purpose of using an inconsistent statement to impeach that witness' credibility. However, despite frequent statements of agreement with this rule, invocation of the rule has seldom resulted in a reversal. See, e.g., United States v. Crouch, 731 F.2d 621 (9th Cir.1984) (harmless error); United States v. Hogan, 763 F.2d 697 (5th Cir.1985) (witness not called as a subterfuge); State v. Lavaris, 721 P.2d 515 (Wash.1986) (same). But see United States v. Logan, 121 F.3d 1172, 1175–76

(8th Cir.1997) ("Although some courts focus on determining the 'true' purpose of the government in introducing testimony, we think that the relevant question is simply whether the evidence is admissible under Fed. R. Ev. 403. * * * Our assessment of the prior statements as creating a danger of unfair prejudice and jury confusion is reinforced by the fact that the government elicited, through the state police officer's testimony, additional inculpatory statements that Ms. Carlen allegedly made to the officer. * * * The only possible relevance that testimony could have had was as substantive evidence, yet it was clearly hearsay for those purposes. See Fed. R. Ev. 801(c). It was therefore manifestly inadmissible.").

(3) IMPEACHMENT: BIAS

ALFORD v. UNITED STATES
Supreme Court of the United States, 1931.
282 U.S. 687.

MR. JUSTICE STONE delivered the opinion of the Court. Petitioner was convicted in the District Court for southern California of using the mails to defraud in violation of section 215 of the Criminal Code (18 U.S.C.A. § 338). * * *

In the course of the trial the government called as a witness a former employee of petitioner. On direct examination he gave damaging testimony with respect to various transactions of accused, including conversations with the witness when others were not present, and statements of accused to salesmen under his direction, whom the witness did not identify. Upon cross-examination questions seeking to elicit the witness's place of residence were excluded on the government's objection that they were immaterial and not proper cross-examination. Counsel for the defense insisted that the questions were proper cross-examination, and that the jury was entitled to know "who the witness is, where he lives and what his business is." Relevant excerpts of the record are printed in the margin.[77]

---

[77] Q. Where do you live, Mr. Bradley?

Mr. Armstrong: That is objected to as immaterial and not proper cross-examination.

The Court: I cannot see the materiality.

Mr. Friedman: Why, I think the jury has a perfect right to know who the witness is, where he lives and what his business is, and we have the right to elicit that on cross-examination. I may say that this is the first witness the Government had called that they have not elicited the address from.

The Court: I will sustain the objection.

Q. By Mr. Friedman: What is your business, Mr. Bradley? A. My profession is an accountant, public accountant.

Q. What is your occupation now? A. I am not doing anything at the present time on account of this case.

Q. On account of this case? A. Yes.

Q. Do you live in Los Angeles?

Later, the jury having been excused, counsel for the defense urged, as an "additional" ground for asking the excluded questions, that he had been informed that the witness was then in the custody of the federal authorities, and that such fact might be brought out on cross-examination "for the purpose of showing whatever bias or prejudice he may have." But the court adhered to its previous rulings, saying that if the witness had been convicted of a felony that fact might be proved, but not that he was detained in custody.

* * *

Cross-examination of a witness is a matter of right. * * * Its permissible purposes, among others, are that the witness may be identified with his community so that independent testimony may be sought and offered of his reputation for veracity in his own neighborhood * * *; that the jury may interpret his testimony in the light, reflected upon it by knowledge of his environment * * *; and that facts may be brought out tending to discredit the witness by showing that his testimony in chief was untrue or biased * * *.

Counsel often cannot know in advance what pertinent facts may be elicited on cross-examination. For that reason it is necessarily exploratory; and the rule that the examiner must indicate the purpose of his inquiry does not, in general, apply. * * It is the essence of a fair trial that reasonable latitude be given the cross-examiner even though he is unable to state to the court what facts a reasonable cross-examination might develop. Prejudice ensues from a denial of the opportunity to place the witness in his proper setting and put the weight of his testimony and

---

Mr. Armstrong: That is objected to as immaterial and invading the Court's ruling.

The Court: I have ruled on that question.

Mr. Friedman: I will temporarily pass on to something else. I would like leave to submit authorities on my right to develop that on cross-examination. I haven't them with me.

The Court: All right. * * *

The jury were thereupon excused by the court until 9:30 o'clock on the morning of July 24, 1929, whereupon the jury retired after which the following proceedings were had relative to the materiality of the testimony, as to the residence and place thereof of Cameron Bradley.

The Court: So ordered. In what particular do you think that evidence is material?

Mr. Friedman: I think it is material for this purpose, first, not only on the general grounds I urged in asking the question, but on the additional grounds that I have been informed and caused to believe that this witness himself is now in the custody of the Federal authorities.

Mr. Armstrong: You mean Mr. Bradley? You mean by the Federal authorities here?

Mr. Friedman: I don't know by what authorities, but that is my impression, that he is here in the custody of the Federal authorities. If that is so, I have a right to show that for the purpose of showing whatever bias or prejudice he may have.

The Court: No; I don't think so. If you can prove he has ever been convicted of a felony, that is a different thing.

Mr. Friedman: I realize that is the rule. I may impeach him if he has been convicted of a felony.

The Court: No. You may prove that fact as going to his credibility, but you can't merely show that he is detained or in charge of somebody. Everybody is presumed to be innocent until proven guilty. * * *

his credibility to a test, without which the jury cannot fairly appraise them. * * * To say that prejudice can be established only by showing that the cross-examination, if pursued, would necessarily have brought out facts tending to discredit the testimony in chief, is to deny a substantial right and withdraw one of the safeguards essential to a fair trial. * * * In this respect a summary denial of the right of cross-examination is distinguishable from the erroneous admission of harmless testimony. * * *

The present case, after the witness for the prosecution had testified to uncorroborated conversations of the defendant of a damaging character, was a proper one for searching cross-examination. The question, "Where do you live?" was not only an appropriate preliminary to the cross-examination of the witness, but on its face, without any such declaration of purpose as was made by counsel here, was an essential step in identifying the witness with his environment, to which cross-examination may always be directed. * * *

But counsel for the defense went further, and in the ensuing colloquy with the court urged, as an additional reason why the question should be allowed, not a substitute reason, as the court below assumed, that he was informed that the witness was then in court in custody of the federal authorities, and that that fact could be brought out on cross-examination to show whatever bias or prejudice the witness might have. The purpose obviously was not, as the trial court seemed to think, to discredit the witness by showing that he was charged with crime (but) to show by such facts as proper cross-examination might develop, that his testimony was biased because given under promise or expectation of immunity, or under the coercive effect of his detention by officers of the United States, which was conducting the present prosecution. * * * Nor is it material, as the Court of Appeals said, whether the witness was in custody because of his participation in the transactions for which petitioner was indicted. Even if the witness were charged with some other offense by the prosecuting authorities, petitioner was entitled to show by cross-examination that his testimony was affected by fear or favor growing out of his detention. * * *

The extent of cross-examination with respect to an appropriate subject of inquiry is within the sound discretion of the trial court. It may exercise a reasonable judgment in determining when the subject is exhausted. * * * But no obligation is imposed on the court, such as that suggested below, to protect a witness from being discredited on cross-examination, short of an attempted invasion of his constitutional protection from self incrimination, properly invoked. There is a duty to protect him from questions which go beyond the bonds of proper cross-examination merely to harass, annoy, or humiliate him. * * * But no such case is presented here. The trial court cut off in limine all inquiry on a subject with respect to which the defense was entitled to a reasonable

cross-examination. This was an abuse of discretion and prejudicial error.
* * *

Reversed.

NOTES AND QUESTIONS

1. *Federal rule.* There is no federal rule on bias impeachment, although other rules refer to it. See Rule 411 (evidence of liability insurance inadmissible except if offered for another purpose such as "bias or prejudice"); Rule 801(d)(1)(B) (prior consistent statements admissible if offered to rebut an express or implied charge of recent fabrication, improper influence, or motive); Fed.R.Evid. 608(a) advisory committee's note ("corruption"). Should there be a federal rule? Other jurisdictions have such a rule. See Unif.R.Evid. 616 (rev. 1999); Haw.R.Evid. 609.1; Ohio R.Evid. 616(A); Utah R.Evid. 608(c); Mil.R.Evid. 608(c).

In United States v. Abel, 469 U.S. 45, 52 (1984), the Supreme Court held that the prosecution had properly been permitted to show that the defendant and a defense witness were both members of a secret prison organization whose members would lie, cheat, steal, and kill to protect each other. A full description of the organization was held to be justified as showing the source and strength of the witness' bias. The Court also stated that "proof of bias is almost always relevant because the jury, as finder of fact and weigher of credibility, has historically been entitled to assess all evidence which might bear on the accuracy and truth of a witness' testimony."

2. *Types of bias.* Other terms for bias are interest, partiality, and corruption. Facts that will suggest bias or interest on the part of a witness are so various as to defy cataloging. For illustrative listings see 3A Wigmore, Evidence §§ 948–969 (Chadbourn rev. 1970). See also *Abel*, note 1, supra, 469 U.S. at 52 ("Bias may be induced by a witness' like, dislike, or fear of a party, or by the witness' self-interest."); Brinson v. Walker, 547 F.3d 387, 393 (2d Cir.2008) ("It is hard to conceive of a more 'prototypical form of bias' than racial bias."); United States v. Figueroa, 548 F.3d 222, 228 (2d Cir.2008) ("Wright, who testified against Figueroa, bore two tattoos depicting swastikas. Inasmuch as the tattoos suggested that Wright harbored animus against racial or ethnic minority groups and their members, they were relevant to and probative of Wright's credibility, bias, and motive to lie when testifying against Figueroa."); United States v. Keys, 899 F.2d 983, 987 (10th Cir.1990) ("Keys' statement that he controlled sixty soldiers in the prison system who would do him favors, including breaking the law, is relevant to show that Kinnison's and Ward's testimony might have been influenced by their fear of Keys and his gang."); Longus v. United States, 52 A.3d 836, 849, 851 (D.C.2012) (right to confrontation violated because accused's precluded from asking Detective Brown whether he was under investigation for coaching a witness to provide untruthful information; "The fact that the detective was under investigation * * * provided a motive for the detective to

want to curry favor with the government and resist admitting that the witness had changed her story in that investigation.").

3. *Extrinsic evidence.* As held in the *Abel* case, note 1, supra, the courts have admitted extrinsic evidence (e.g., other witnesses) of bias as "non-collateral." 469 U.S. at 52 ("The 'common law of evidence' allowed the showing of bias by extrinsic evidence."). Does Rule 403 now replace the common law? See United States v. Vasquez, 635 F.3d 889, 897 (7th Cir.2011) ("Extrinsic evidence of a witness' bias, however, is admissible to impeach that witness and is never a collateral issue.").

4. *Foundation requirement.* Must a foundation for such evidence be laid by asking the witness about his bias on cross-examination? Apparently a majority of the courts say yes. See 1 McCormick, Evidence § 39 (7th ed. 2013). Is such an inquiry necessary under the Federal Rules? See United States v. Betts, 16 F.3d 748, 764 (7th Cir.1994) ("[T]he weight of authority supports the proposition that when a party seeks to prove bias through extrinsic evidence of a witness' prior statement, he must first give the witness the opportunity to explain or deny that statement, even though Rule 613(b) is not strictly applicable."). Rule 613 governs prior inconsistent statements.

5. *Right of confrontation.* The necessity of allowing reasonable scope for exercise of the right of cross-examination is constantly emphasized in the decisions. See Douglas v. Alabama, 380 U.S. 415, 418 (1965) ("Our cases construing the confrontation clause hold that a primary interest secured by it is the right of cross-examination.").

In Davis v. Alaska, 415 U.S. 308, 320 (1974), a defendant was prohibited from cross-examining a prosecution witness concerning that witness' status as a juvenile probationer. This curtailment of cross-examination was based on a state statute designed to protect the confidentiality of juvenile adjudications. The Supreme Court reversed: "The State's policy interest in protecting the confidentiality of a juvenile offender's record cannot require yielding of so vital a constitutional right as the effective cross-examination for bias of an adverse witness."

The Supreme Court, however, has recognized some limitations on the right of cross-examination: "It does not follow, of course, that the Confrontation Clause of the Sixth Amendment prevents a trial judge from imposing any limits on defense counsel's inquiry into the potential bias of a prosecution witness. On the contrary, trial judges retain wide latitude insofar as the Confrontation Clause is concerned to impose reasonable limits on such cross-examination based on concerns about, among other things, harassment, prejudice, confusion of the issues, the witness' safety, or interrogation that is repetitive or only marginally relevant." Delaware v. Van Arsdall, 475 U.S. 673, 679 (1986).

6. *Other causes for deprivation of right to cross-examine.* Loss of the opportunity to cross-examine can stem from causes other than judicial action. Occasionally a witness will die or become physically incapacitated during the

interval between direct and cross-examination. See Best v. Tavenner, 218 P.2d 471 (Or.1950); State v. Bigham, 131 S.E. 603 (S.C.1926); Note, 11 Okla.L.Rev. 452 (1958). More commonly, a claim of privilege by the witness during cross-examination precludes inquiry into otherwise appropriate matters. Although the matter has been said to be in the discretion of the trial judge, see United States v. Stubbert, 655 F.2d 453 (1st Cir.1981), the direct testimony of the witness may be stricken at least where the claim of privilege is shown to be unfounded. See Klein v. Harris, 667 F.2d 274 (2d Cir.1981). What if the privilege claim is valid? See United States v. Cardillo, 316 F.2d 606 (2d Cir.1963). Under what circumstances should the direct examination be stricken? See 1 McCormick, Evidence § 19 (7th ed. 2013).

7. *Harassment.* In accord with the principal case, it is commonly said that cross-examination cannot be used merely to humiliate, annoy, or disgrace the witness. See Rule 611(a). Would it be proper to inquire of a witness whether he had had an illicit relationship with one of the parties? See Annot., 25 A.L.R.3d 537. To go further and ask whether the witness was married at the time? See Ryan v. McEvoy, 315 N.E.2d 38 (Ill.App.Ct.1974).

8. *Broken witnesses?* In the popular lay view, effective cross-examination is equated with a broken witness crying *mea culpa* from the stand, or at the very least with the exposure by the cross-examiner of some powerful motive for prevarication on the part of the witness. Compare the following comments of one noted cross-examiner:

> No cause reaches the stage of litigation unless there are two sides to it. If the witnesses on one side deny or qualify the statements made by those on the other, which side is telling the truth? Not necessarily which side is offering perjured testimony,—there is far less intentional perjury in the courts than the inexperienced would believe. But which side is honestly mistaken,—for, on the other hand, evidence itself is far less trustworthy than the public usually realizes. The opinions of which side are warped by prejudice or blinded by ignorance? Which side has had the power or opportunity of correct observation? How shall we tell, how make it apparent to a jury of disinterested men who are to decide between the litigants? Obviously, by the means of cross-examination.

Wellman, The Art of Cross–Examination 27 (1st Collier ed. 1962). What potentially fruitful lines of cross-examination, other than inquiry into possible bias and interest, do Mr. Wellman's observations suggest? See generally Lezak, Some Psychological Limitations on Witness Reliability, 20 Wayne L.Rev. 117 (1973).

EDE v. ATRIUM SOUTH OB–GYN, INC.
Supreme Court of Ohio, 1994.
642 N.E.2d 365.

PFEIFER, JUSTICE.

This is a medical malpractice/wrongful death action brought by the plaintiff-appellant, Charles Ede, as administrator of the estate of his wife, Sheri Ede, who died on August 28, 1989. The defendants-appellees are George R. Dakoske, M.D., and the corporation of which he is the president, Atrium South OB–GYN, Inc. Dr. Dakoske performed surgery on Sheri Ede on August 24, 1989. Sheri had been scheduled to undergo an abdominal hysterectomy, but during that procedure Dakoske discovered a cancerous tumor on Sheri's right ovary which required further surgery. Sheri died four days later. Appellant alleges that Dakoske's negligent post-operative care caused Sheri's death. [Dr. Schneider testified on behalf of Dr. Dakoske.]

* * *

* * * The trial court in this case pointed to Evid.R. 403 in determining that the issue of the commonality of interests between Drs. Dakoske and Schneider could not be demonstrated through evidence of a common insurance carrier. The trial court ruled that the danger of prejudice outweighed the probative value of such testimony. We find that determination to be unreasonable, and therefore reversible error, for two reasons.

First, the trial court did not appreciate the probative value of establishing that Dakoske and Schneider were both insured by PIE [Physicians' Mutual Insurance Company.]. The trial court focused its inquiry on only one thing—whether a doctor's premiums could be raised by PIE if the doctor refused to testify on behalf of another PIE-insured doctor. Thus, the trial court sought to determine whether PIE coerced Schneider's testimony, but did not seem to consider Schneider's personal bias resulting from his insurance relationship. Satisfied by Dakoske's attorney's assurance that Schneider was not being coerced by PIE, the trial court failed to consider other possible biases created by Schneider's relationship with PIE. The trial court was not responsive to appellant's argument that as a fractional part-owner of PIE, Schneider's own premiums might fluctuate due to the result of the case. Such testimony would have been probative of bias.

Second, the trial court erred by grossly overestimating to what extent testimony that Dakoske was insured would prejudice the jury. The second sentence of Evid.R. 411 exists for a reason—it recognizes that testimony regarding insurance is not always prejudicial. However, too often courts have a Pavlovian response to insurance testimony—immediately assuming prejudice. It is naive to believe that today's jurors, bombarded for years with information about health care insurance, do not already assume in a malpractice case that the defendant doctor is covered by insurance. The legal charade protecting juries from information they already know keeps hidden from them relevant information that could assist them in making their determinations. Our Rules of Evidence are designed with truth and fairness in mind; they do not require that courts should be blind to reality.

* * *

Given the sophistication of our juries, the first sentence of Evid.R. 411 ("[e]vidence that a person was or was not insured against liability is not admissible upon the issue [of] whether he acted negligently or otherwise wrongfully") does not merit the enhanced importance it has been given. Instead of juries knowing the truth about the existence and extent of coverage, they are forced to make assumptions which may have more prejudicial effect than the truth.

Thus, the second sentence of Evid.R. 411, which allows courts to operate in a world free from truth-stifling legal fictions, ought to be embraced. In such instances as the case at hand, truth should win out over a naively inspired fear of prejudice.

Therefore, we hold that in a medical malpractice action, evidence of a commonality of insurance interests between a defendant and an expert witness is sufficiently probative of the expert's bias as to clearly outweigh any potential prejudice evidence of insurance might cause. Thus, in the present case, the trial court acted unreasonably in excluding evidence regarding the commonality of insurance interests of Drs. Dakoske and Schneider. * * *

Judgment reversed and cause remanded.

NOTES AND QUESTIONS

1. *Other cases on insurance.* See Bernal v. Lindholm, 727 N.E.2d 145, 172 (Ohio Ct.App.1999) ("We find that *Ede* is distinguishable from the case at hand because, in that case, the expert was insured by the same company as the doctor for whom he was testifying. Additionally, in *Ede*, the doctors participated in a mutual insurance company. Hence, because the expert and the defendant doctor for whom he was testifying shared in a common pool of liability loss, the expert stood to suffer an economic loss should the defendant doctor lose at trial. In this case, however, there is no evidence that Dr. Kunin shared a commonality of interest with any appellee with respect to insurance or otherwise."). See also Vasquez v. Rocco, 836 A.2d 1158, 1163–64 (Conn.2003) ("The majority of courts that have addressed this issue apply a 'substantial connection' test to determine whether evidence of an expert witness' relationship to the defendant's insurer is more probative of potential bias than it is prejudicial.").

2. *Expert compensation.* It may be assumed that the majority of experts appearing as witnesses in litigation today will receive compensation from the party calling them in addition to the statutory witness fee. Ford & Holmes, Exposure of Doctors' Venal Testimony, 32 Ins.C.J. 221 (1965). How

may cross-examining counsel be expected to phrase a question inquiring as to compensation?

Should it be permissible to bring out, if such is the fact, that the expert regularly testifies in litigation? That his testimony is always offered by plaintiffs rather than defendants, or vice versa? Compare Traders & Gen. Ins. Co. v. Robinson, 222 S.W.2d 266 (Tex.Civ.App.1949), with Schoolfield v. Witkowski, 203 N.E.2d 460 (Ill.Ct.App.1964). See also Collins v. Wayne Corp., 621 F.2d 777, 783 (5th Cir.1980) ("Counsel then brought out that the plaintiffs were paying Severy $95 an hour for his testimony, and that Severy had been testifying in accident cases for 20 years. Based on earlier deposition testimony that he worked around 12 hours a day, six days a week, counsel asked whether Severy earned $343,480 per year for testifying. * * * [C]ross-examination of an expert about fees earned in prior cases is not improper. The parties have not cited and our research has not uncovered any federal cases on this point. Cases from the state courts are split.").

3. *Religious belief.* Rule 610 provides that evidence of a witness' religious beliefs or opinions is not admissible either to attack or support the witness' credibility. However, the federal drafters stated: "While the rule forecloses inquiry into the religious beliefs or opinions of a witness for the purpose of showing that his character for truthfulness is affected by their nature, an inquiry for the purpose of showing interest or bias because of them is not within the prohibition. Thus disclosure of affiliation with a church which is a party to the litigation would be allowable under the rule." Fed.R.Evid. 610 advisory committee's note.

(4) IMPEACHMENT: MENTAL OR SENSORY CAPACITY

UNITED STATES v. HEINLEIN

United States Court of Appeals, District of Columbia Circuit, 1973.
490 F.2d 725.

[The opinion in United States v. Heinlein appears in Section A(5), supra].

NOTES AND QUESTIONS

1. *Heinlein case.* Note particularly in the principal case that despite the court's finding that the expert testimony concerning Harding's mental condition was insufficient to render him incompetent, the defense was allowed to present that testimony to the jury as potentially affecting credibility.

2. *Federal rule.* Like bias, there is no explicit provision in the Federal Rules for this type of impeachment. But see Ohio R.Evid. 616(B) ("A defect of capacity, ability, or opportunity to observe, remember, or relate may be shown to impeach the witness either by examination of the witness or by extrinsic evidence.").

3. *Mental condition.* See United States v. Sasso, 59 F.3d 341, 347–48 (2d Cir.1995) ("Evidence of a witness's psychological history may be admissible when it goes to her credibility. *See* Fed.R.Evid. 611(b). In assessing the probative value of such evidence, the court should consider such factors as the nature of the psychological problem, see, e.g., *Chnapkova v. Koh* (paranoid and delusional condition likely to be probative), the temporal recency or remoteness of the history, *see, e.g., id.* at 81–82 (paranoid delusions five years earlier not too remote); *United States v. Bari* (more than 10 years too remote); *United States v. Glover,* (12 years too remote), and whether the witness suffered from the problem at the time of the events to which she is to testify, so that it may have affected her 'ability to perceive or to recall events or to testify accurately'."); United States v. Butt, 955 F.2d 77, 82 (1st Cir.1992) ("For over forty years, federal courts have permitted the impeachment of government witnesses based on their mental condition at the time of the events testified to. *See United States v. Hiss,* 88 F.Supp. 559, 559–60 (S.D.N.Y.1950). * * * 'The readily apparent principle is that the jury should, within reason, be informed of all matters affecting a witness's credibility * * *.' *United States v. Partin,* 493 F.2d 750, 762 (5th Cir.1974). * * * Despite this precedent, we are aware of no court to have found relevant an informally diagnosed depression or personality defect. Rather, federal courts appear to have found mental instability relevant to credibility only where, during the time-frame of the events testified to, the witness exhibited a pronounced disposition to lie or hallucinate, or suffered from a severe illness, such as schizophrenia, that dramatically impaired her ability to perceive and tell the truth.").

See also United States v. Bari, 750 F.2d 1169, 1178–79 (2d Cir.1984) (finding no abuse of discretion when trial judge would not permit cross-examination on witness' prior hospitalization for schizophrenia); United States v. Dupree, 833 F.Supp.2d 255, 265 (E.D.N.Y.2011) ("First, the court finds that the witness's three psychiatrist visits from 1993 to 1994 for depression are so remote in time to the events at issue in the trial—approximately thirteen years before—that any probative value of allowing cross-examination regarding the psychiatric visits is outweighed by confusion to the jury and the embarrassment to the witness of having to reveal, at best marginally relevant, private medical information. * * * Second, the court will permit the defendants to cross-examine the witness regarding her use of anti-anxiety medication in 2009 for approximately six months. The period of time during which the witness used this medication occurred within the time period at issue in this case, from January 2007 to July 2010 * * * and is therefore probative of the witness's ability to perceive and recall the events about which she is expected to testify."); United States v. Falcon, 245 F.Supp.2d 1239, 1245 (S.D.Fla.2003) ("Only in rare cases, where there is temporally relevant and reliable documentation that a witness' capacity for perception and recollection is severely hampered, will a court permit an expert to testify to the witness' mental incapacity.").

4. *Psychiatric examinations.* Psychiatric opinion testimony to impeach, as well as to determine competency, has sometimes been admitted. Weihofen, Testimonial Competence and Credibility, 34 Geo.Wash.L.Rev. 53, 68 (1965) ("Because modern practice admits as competent to testify persons proved or conceded to be mentally ill to some degree, a liberal admission policy for evidence on the effect of mental conditions upon credibility is needed."). Helpful treatments of the question include: Juviler, Psychiatric Opinion as to Credibility, 48 Cal.L.Rev. 648 (1960); Slovenko, Witnesses, Psychiatry and the Credibility of Testimony, 19 Fla.L.Rev. 1 (1966). A significant countervailing consideration is the invasion of the privacy of the witness. See Nobrega v. Commonwealth, 628 S.E.2d 922, 926 (Va.2006) (rejecting a "compelling need" test that has been adopted in other jurisdictions, "a trial court has no authority to order a complaining witness in a rape case to undergo a psychiatric or psychological evaluation").

5. *Memory issues.* See United States v. Love, 329 F.3d 981, 985 (8th Cir.2003) ("Here the nature of the psychological problem in question is memory loss—a condition that implicates Thomas's ability 'to comprehend, know and correctly relate the truth.' "); United States v. Ciocca, 106 F.3d 1079, 1083 (1st Cir.1997) ("Ciocca was able to place before the jury ample evidence regarding Caporino's ability to remember the events that transpired prior to and after his accident.").

6. *Drug/alcohol use.* See Grimes v. Mazda North American Operations, 355 F.3d 566, 573 (6th Cir.2004) ("As to Gutierrez, the driver, the court ruled that the evidence of her drug and alcohol use on the night of the accident went to the credibility of her testimony describing the accident."); State v. Pond, 193 P.3d 368, 385 (Haw.2008) ("The circuit court committed reversible error in limiting the cross-examination of Ms. Russell as to her marijuana use. Pond was deprived of showing that Ms. Russell's perception of the events was altered through her alleged use of marijuana.").

7. *Time of trial.* See United States v. Spano, 421 F.3d 599, 606 (7th Cir.2005) ("Were there any indication that Taylor had been high when he was testifying, that would certainly have been appropriate to point out to the jury * * *."); State v. Reyes, 408 P.2d 400, 402 (Ariz.1965) ("Generally a witness may be cross-examined as to whether he is under the influence of drugs at the time of testifying.").

(5) IMPEACHMENT: UNTRUTHFUL CHARACTER, FEDERAL RULE 608(a)

STATE V. BAKER
Supreme Court of Wisconsin, 1962.
114 N.W.2d 426.

BROWN, JUSTICE. The complaint was signed by a police officer on information and belief. At the trial the only evidence of defendant's guilt was the uncorroborated testimony of James A., a fifteen year old boy, that defendant took James into a shed behind defendant's filling station and there they cooperated in the indecent liberties with which defendant was charged. Defendant denied James' accusations in every particular, and had a number of witnesses whose testimony tended to throw doubt on James' narrative.

Successful prosecution of the case, and likewise successful defense, depends completely on the jury's belief or disbelief in James' veracity. After the State had rested and the attorney for the defendant had called a number of witnesses whose evidence to some extent impeached James' story of his presence in the shed at the time in question, defendant's attorney called Rev. Clarence J. Schouten and then there occurred the following:

"DIRECT EXAMINATION BY MR. TIERNEY:

"I am the pastor of St. Joseph's Church which is one block north of the Baker filling station. I have been the pastor there since June, 1955.

"Q. Do you know Jimmy A.?

"A. I do.

"Q. And how long have you known him?

"A. I would say from September of '55.

"Q. Did he go to your school?

"A. He did.

"Q. Do you know what Jimmy A.'s reputation in the community there is as for truth and veracity?

"MR. MIECH: I am going to object; that's highly immaterial and irrelevant and its calling for a conclusion so far as the State's witness is concerned.

"THE COURT: Sustained."

* * *

On this appeal the State concedes that the court was in error in sustaining the objection, so no extensive research by us on the question is required for the purposes of this appeal. * * *

In our own state we find Duffy v. Radke (1909), 138 Wis. 38, 40, 119 N.W. 811, wherein we said:

"The contention that the court erred in the admission of evidence to impeach the defendant cannot be sustained. The record shows that a foundation for the reception of such evidence was properly laid by showing that the witnesses based their conclusions upon their knowledge of defendant's general reputation among those with whom he resided and the form of inquiry was properly restricted to the inquiry whether, in view of defendant's general reputation for truth and veracity the witness would believe him under oath."

When the court permitted the State to shut out evidence bearing upon James' reputation for truthfulness under the circumstances of the trial it was an error going to the heart of defendant's guilt or innocence.

* * *

Order reversed and cause remanded for a new trial.

NOTES AND QUESTIONS

1. *Character trait.* Where character evidence is offered for the purpose of impeaching credibility, most courts require that the evidence relate to the traits of truthfulness and veracity. A few jurisdictions, however, permit a witness to be impeached with regard to his morality generally. See 1 McCormick, Evidence § 43 (7th ed. 2013). Why would an offeror of character proof ever prefer the latter formulation to the former? See State v. Scott, 58 S.W.2d 275 (Mo.1933).

2. *Federal rule.* As with character evidence introduced for substantive purposes under Rules 404 and 405, the practice with regard to character proof for impeachment purposes has been liberalized by the adoption of the Federal Rules. Rule 608(a) allows impeaching evidence as to truthfulness to be given in terms of the witness' personal opinion. Testimony as to reputation for truthfulness remains admissible. A foundation must be laid to show the character witness' familiarity either with the witness and the relevant community in the case of reputation proof or with the witness himself or herself in the case of opinion evidence. See United States v. Turning Bear, 357 F.3d 730, 734 (8th Cir.2004) ("Such a foundation is laid by demonstrating that the opinion witness knows the relevant witness well enough to have formed an opinion. * * * Because Ms. Odens had had daily contact with N.T.B. over the four-to-six-month period that he lived in her home, she knew him well enough to have formed an opinion about his character for untruthfulness that was more than a 'bare assertion' or 'conclusory observation.' "); People v. Fernandez, 950 N.E.2d 126, 131 (N.Y.2011) (family and family friends can constitute a relevant community for purposes of introducing testimony pertaining to an opposing witness' bad reputation for truth and veracity).

3. *Impeaching the accused.* See United States v. McMurray, 20 F.3d 831, 834 (8th Cir.1994) ("McMurray next argues that the district court erred in allowing the government's rebuttal witness, Marjorie Carper, to express a negative opinion as to McMurray's truthfulness after he had testified in his own behalf at trial. We disagree. The credibility of a defendant who testifies may be attacked in the same manner as that of any other witness. * * * The

prosecutor asked Mrs. Carper whether she would believe McMurray's testimony under oath, based upon her opinion as to his truthfulness. This questioning is consistent with Rule 608(a).").

(6) IMPEACHMENT: CONVICTION OF CRIME, FEDERAL RULE 609

Pre–Rules law. In an article written prior to the adoption of the Federal Rules, Professor Slough, while noting wide agreement on allowing convictions to be introduced to affect credibility, found no agreement on the type of conviction receivable. He summarized the variations as follows:

> One formula adheres to common law terminology and requires the conviction to have been for an "infamous crime." Another formula limits scope of examination to conviction for "felonies" or "crimen falsi."[78] A third formula admits evidence of conviction for "felony" or "crime involving moral turpitude."[79] Finally, there are jurisdictions that allow evidence of conviction to enter without limitation, meaning that conviction of any crime will satisfy.[80] There is an increasing tendency to bar reference to traffic court convictions, and a declaration of delinquency in juvenile court will not ordinarily be classified with conviction for purposes of impeachment.

Slough, Impeachment of Witnesses: Common Law Principles and Modern Trends, 34 Ind.L.J. 1, 22 (1958).

If an accused is charged with driving while intoxicated, should the prosecutor be permitted to impeach the accused with a prior conviction for the same offense? See State v. Murdock, 174 N.E.2d 543 (Ohio 1961) (upholding use of any prior felony or misdemeanor for impeachment). What does a DUI conviction tell us about the witness' character for truthfulness?

Federal Rule 609. "In drafting Rule 609(a), Congress was torn between two conflicting interests. On the one hand, there was the interest in letting the jury have information regarding a prior conviction to the extent that it might bear on a defendant's credibility as a witness. On the other hand, there was the desire to avoid deterring the defendant,

---

[78] Commonwealth v. Kostan, 349 Pa. 560, 37 A.2d 606 (1944). "Crimen falsi" is a general designation of a class of offenses including those which involve deceit or falsification or affect the public administration of justice. Forgery, counterfeiting, and perjury are common examples.

[79] A * * * decision in Maine defines moral turpitude as being akin to baseness, vileness, or depravity. * * * State v. Jenness, 143 Me. 380, 62 A.2d 867 (1948).

[80] Way v. State, 224 Ind. 280, 66 N.E.2d 608 (1946) (convictions for speeding and disorderly conduct allowed despite slight probative values; discretion of lower court stressed); Fritch v. State, 199 Ind. 89, 155 N.E. 257 (1927) (cross-examination not confined to convictions for felony or infamous crimes); * * *

because of the obvious prejudice that might be caused by the jury's learning of his prior conviction, from testifying in his own defense, which might preclude the jury from having the benefit of his version of events." United States v. Ortiz, 553 F.2d 782, 785 (2d Cir.1977) (Mansfield, J., dissenting). [The congressional compromise that was finally reached recognized two types of convictions:] (1) those punishable by death or imprisonment for more than one year, and (2) those involving dishonesty or false statement ("crimen falsi").

UNITED STATES V. ALEXANDER
United States Court of Appeals, Ninth Circuit, 1995.
48 F.3d 1477.

DAVID R. THOMPSON, CIRCUIT JUDGE: These are the consolidated appeals of defendants Gary Edward Alexander, Jonathan Harrington, Anthony F. Hicks and Willie James Harris. The defendants appeal their convictions for conspiracy to commit robbery, [armed bank robbery, and use of a firearm during commission of a crime of violence].

* * *

Before trial, defendant Hicks filed a motion *in limine* to exclude evidence of his prior felony convictions for residential robbery and possession of rock cocaine for sale. The district court denied the motion, ruling that, if Hicks elected to testify, the evidence would be admissible for impeachment purposes, under Federal Rule of Evidence 609(a)(1), because its probative value outweighed its prejudicial effect. At trial, Hicks chose to take the stand and present an alibi defense. He testified that he was in the vicinity of the arrests on the day of the robbery because he was scheduled to meet a friend there. He also said he ran away when he heard sirens and saw police cars because he was afraid of being arrested on two outstanding warrants for traffic violations. Purportedly for the same reason, he also gave the arresting officer a false name. At the conclusion of his direct examination, Hicks again moved to exclude the evidence of his prior convictions. The district court adhered to its original ruling and denied the motion. On cross examination, the prosecution elicited testimony from Hicks regarding the nature and dates of both prior convictions.

Hicks contends the district court erred in allowing the jury to hear evidence of his prior convictions. With regard to his prior robbery conviction, he argues United States v. Brackeen, 969 F.2d 827, 830 (9th Cir.1992) (en banc) (per curiam), stands for the proposition that a prior robbery conviction cannot be used to attack a defendant's credibility. We disagree. Federal Rule of Evidence 609(a) provides, in pertinent part, that evidence of prior convictions is admissible for purposes of attacking the credibility of a witness if the crime "(1) was [a felony], and the court determines the probative value of admitting this evidence outweighs its prejudicial effect to the defendant, or (2) involved dishonesty or false statement* * *." *Brackeen* held only that, in this circuit, bank robbery is not per se a crime of dishonesty, and therefore prior robbery convictions are not admissible for impeachment purposes under Rule 609(a)(2). *Brackeen,* 969 F.2d at 829. We did not foreclose in *Brackeen* the admission of a prior robbery conviction under the balancing test of Rule 609(a)(1). Here, the government explicitly stated it intended to introduce both of Hicks's prior convictions under Rule 609(a)(1), and the district court specifically ruled on that basis by applying the appropriate balancing test. If the district court did not abuse its discretion * * *, the evidence of both of his prior convictions was properly admitted. *United States v. Browne,* 829 F.2d 760, 762 (9th Cir.1987) (noting that a district court's decision to admit evidence of prior convictions is reviewed for an abuse of discretion).

In *United States v. Cook,* 608 F.2d 1175, 1185 n.8 (9th Cir.1979) (en banc), we outlined five factors that should be considered in balancing the probative value of a prior conviction against its prejudicial impact for purposes of Rule 609(a)(1): (1) the impeachment value of the prior crime; (2) the point in time of conviction and the defendant's subsequent history; (3) the similarity between the past crime and the charged crime; (4) the importance of the defendant's testimony; and (5) the centrality of the defendant's credibility. The government bears the burden of showing, based on these factors, that the proffered evidence's probative value substantially [sic][81] outweighs its prejudicial effect. * * * Hicks does not dispute that the first factor favors admission of both his prior convictions. We have previously stated that "prior convictions for robbery are probative of veracity." *United States v. Givens,* 767 F.2d 574, 580 (9th Cir.1985). The same is true of prior convictions for drug offenses. Hicks stipulates that both his prior crimes were sufficiently recent to satisfy the second *Cook* factor. He was convicted of residential robbery, and was sentenced to a four-year prison term, in 1987. Shortly after his parole in 1988, he committed the drug offense, for which he received another four-year prison sentence. Less than a year later, he was arrested for the present crime. "By its terms, Rule 609 allows for admissibility of such * * * prior conviction[s] even where the defendant has been released for up to ten years." *Browne,* 829 F.2d at 763. *See* Fed.R.Evid. 609(b).

Hicks concedes that, as to his prior drug offense, the third factor is satisfied because the drug offense is sufficiently different from the present bank robbery. With regard to the prior residential robbery, the district court held that offense was similar to the charged bank robbery and, therefore, the third factor weighed in favor of excluding it. However,

---

[81] [The court incorrectly inserted the word "substantially" is stating the rule. See Note 3, infra. Ed.]

we have held that even "a prior 'bank robbery conviction [is] not inadmissable per se, merely because the offense involved was identical to that for which [the defendant] was on trial.' " *Browne,* 829 F.2d at 763 * * *. What matters is the balance of all five factors. Hicks contends that, contrary to the district court's determination, the related fourth and fifth factors weigh against admission of his prior convictions. He contends his trial testimony was not particularly important and his credibility was not central to the case, because other evidence corroborated his alibi defense.[82] We disagree. When a defendant takes the stand and denies having committed the charged offense, he places his credibility directly at issue. * * *

In *United States v. Bagley,* 772 F.2d 482, 488 (9th Cir.1985), we held that admission of the defendant's prior robbery convictions was an abuse of the district court's discretion. But in that case we emphasized "the record [was] devoid of any evidence that [the defendant] intended to misrepresent his character or to testify falsely as to his prior criminal record." *Id.* Here, Hicks testified he ran from the police because he was afraid of being arrested on outstanding warrants for traffic violations. This testimony could reasonably have misled the jury into believing that, with the exception of some minor traffic infractions, Hicks had no previous trouble with the police. As we said in *Cook:*

> [I]t is not surprising that the [district] court was unwilling to let a man with a substantial criminal history misrepresent himself to the jury, with the government forced to sit silently by, looking at a criminal record which, if made known, would give the jury a more comprehensive view of the trustworthiness of the defendant as a witness.

Cook, 608 F.2d at 1187.

We conclude that the district court properly balanced all five *Cook* factors and did not abuse its discretion * * *.

NOTES AND QUESTIONS

1. *Impeachment value of prior offense.* Remember that the most probative offenses (e.g., perjury) fall within Rule 609(a)(2) (crimes of dishonesty or false statement) and not this Rule. What is left? Burglary? Robbery? Drug offenses? See United States v. Brito, 427 F.3d 53, 64 (1st Cir.2005) ("Prior drug-trafficking crimes are generally viewed as having some bearing on veracity."); United States v. Ortiz, 553 F.2d 782, 784 (2d Cir.1977) ("a narcotics trafficker lives a life of secrecy and dissembling in the course of that activity, being prepared to say whatever is required by the demands of the moment, whether the truth or a lie").

---

[82] At trial, Hicks's attorney told the district court that Hicks's testimony was "central."

2. *Similarity.* In the principal case, which way does the similarity of the past crime (residential robbery) and the charged crime cut? In favor of probative value or in showing unfair prejudice? See United States v. Brito, 427 F.3d 53, 63 (1st Cir.2005) ("The offenses underlying the appellant's prior convictions are not similar to the offenses charged in this case. That is relevant because convictions for dissimilar crimes are customarily thought to be less prejudicial than convictions for similar crimes (which may run a risk of implying a propensity to commit the crime).").

3. *Different types of balancing tests.* How does the balancing in Rule 609(a)(1)(B) regarding the accused's prior convictions differ from the Rule 609(a)(1)(A) balancing that applies to all other witnesses? Which of the *Cook* factors would be relevant in the latter context? See United States v. Tse, 375 F.3d 148, 164 (1st Cir.2004) ("[T]he prior convictions of a government witness are unlikely to inflame the jury or invite a propensity inference: The probability that prior convictions of an ordinary government witness will be unduly prejudicial is low in most criminal cases.").

4. *Record findings.* How much of a record of its balancing process under Rule 609(a)(1) must a trial court make? Some courts have strongly recommended explicit findings if the evidence of convictions is admitted. See United States v. Mahone, 537 F.2d 922 (7th Cir.1976). Despite desires such as those expressed in the *Mahone* case, the appellate courts have generally not imposed a requirement of explicit findings on trial judges in connection with Rule 609(a) rulings. The matter is left in the discretion of the trial court judge, with or without explicit findings. See, e.g., United States v. Givens, 767 F.2d 574 (9th Cir.1985); United States v. Love, 746 F.2d 477 (9th Cir.1984). Such discretion will be held to have been abused if it is clear that the trial judge did not even consider the prejudice to the accused. See United States v. Mehrmanesh, 689 F.2d 822 (9th Cir.1982).

5. *State adoptions.* Many jurisdictions have adopted impeachment rules based on the balancing approach of Federal Rule 609, although there are variations. Other jurisdictions have blanket rules, which also vary significantly. Compare Mont.R.Evid. 609 ("For the purpose of attacking the credibility of a witness, evidence that the witness has been convicted of a crime is not admissible."), with N.C.R.Evid. 609(a) (all felonies and many misdemeanors, including simple assault and even some speeding convictions, shall be admitted).

6. *Ten-year rule.* In accord with the specific language of Rule 609(b), the courts have imposed a requirement of explicit findings in connection with rulings on the admissibility of convictions that are more than ten years old. See United States v. Portillo, 699 F.2d 461 (9th Cir.1982). Rule 609(b)'s relatively strict balancing test applies to all convictions more than ten years old—both "felony" convictions under Rule 609(a)(1) and otherwise automatically admissible "crimen falsi" convictions under Rule 609(a)(2).

The context of the witness' testimony may be a significant factor in weighing the probative value of the prior conviction against the unfair prejudice to the defendant. This is particularly true in cases involving convictions which are more than ten years old. The testimony of the defendant on direct examination may open the door for a finding that the probative value of the conviction substantially outweighs its prejudicial effect. See United States v. Ebner, 782 F.2d 1120 (2d Cir.1986) (defendant opened door to introduction of prior convictions by testifying that his conduct was attributable to advice from his lawyers).

7. *"Other acts" evidence compared.* In United States v. Valencia, 61 F.3d 616, 618–19 (8th Cir.1995), a prosecution for conspiracy, intent to distribute cocaine, and money laundering, the district court ruled that a prior conviction of the accused for unlawful possession for sale and purchase for sale of a controlled substance was inadmissible under Rule 404(b) ("other acts") evidence but was admissible under Rule 609. The accused appealed. The Eighth Circuit commented:

> The appellant contends that Rule 609(a)'s internalized balancing test is stricter in terms of admissibility in that a prior conviction is not admissible against the accused for impeachment purposes unless the probative value of the evidence outweighs its prejudicial effect. Appellant's argument is that after finding that the prejudice of the prior conviction *substantially* outweighed the probative value under 404(b), the district court abused its discretion in admitting the same evidence under Rule 609, where it would be excluded if the prejudice *merely* outweighed its probative effect. We disagree.

> * * * In a criminal setting, evidence offered under Rule 404(b) is substantive evidence against the accused, i.e., it is part of the government's case offered to prove his guilt beyond a reasonable doubt. Rule 609 evidence on the other hand has to do with the accused's ability to tell the truth when testifying on his or her own behalf. While both rules speak of "probative value" and "prejudice," it is critical to note that evidence offered under the respective rules is probative as to different matters. The probative character of evidence under Rule 609 has to do with credibility of a witness, while 404(b) "probativeness" essentially goes to the question of whether or not the accused committed the crime charged. Any similarity or overlap in the standards of admissibility under the respective rules is irrelevant because the rules apply to completely distinct situations.

ALTOBELLO v. BORDEN CONFECTIONARY PRODUCTS, INC.

United States Court of Appeals, Seventh Circuit, 1989.
872 F.2d 215.

POSNER, CIRCUIT JUDGE.

Guy Altobello brought this suit against his former employer, Borden, charging that Borden had fired him because of his age, in violation of the

Age Discrimination in Employment Act, 29 U.S.C. §§ 621 *et seq*. The jury brought in a verdict for the defendant at the end of a five-day trial. The evidence at trial had been in sharp conflict, with Borden presenting evidence that it had fired Altobello because he was a malingerer, and Altobello responding with evidence that his alleged malingering was merely the pretext for a discharge motivated by his age. The only issue on appeal that merits discussion is Altobello's claim that the district court erred in allowing Borden to impeach his credibility as a witness by asking him on the stand: "Mr. Altobello, in 1978 [ten years before the trial] you were convicted of the crime of tampering with electric meters of Commonwealth Edison, weren't you?"—to which Altobello had replied, "Yes."

* * * Rule 609(a)(2)—the provision applicable to this case—allows the witness to be impeached by proof that he was convicted of a crime that "involved dishonesty or false statement, regardless of the punishment," i.e., regardless of whether it was a felony or a misdemeanor. Altobello's conviction of meter tampering was a misdemeanor conviction, and therefore admissible if at all only under Rule 609(a)(2).

At trial Altobello argued that the conviction should be excluded under Fed.R.Evid. 403, which directs the exclusion of evidence the prejudicial effects of which substantially outweigh its probative value. Yet we held in *Campbell v. Greer,* 831 F.2d 700, 705–07 (7th Cir.1987), decided before the trial of this case, that Rule 403 is inapplicable to Rule 609(a)(2). On appeal, Altobello has abandoned Rule 403, and argues instead that Borden was obliged to show that the specific acts of meter tampering for which he was convicted involved dishonesty in the sense of a deceptive act—that, in an older jargon, the crime of which he was convicted was *crimen falsi.* * * *

Altobello's argument begins with the proposition that unless Borden is required to show that the specific acts for which Altobello was convicted involved dishonesty in the sense of deception, subsection (a)(2) of Rule 609 would swallow up (a)(1), making *any* misdemeanor conviction—any conviction, period—usable for impeachment regardless of how prejudice and probative value balanced out; for every crime is in a sense a dishonest act and 609(a)(2) contains no balancing test. But although acquisitive crimes are indeed dishonest, not all crimes are acquisitive, and those that are not are not "dishonest" unless honest and law-abiding are treated as synonyms. A man who kills his wife's lover *in flagrante delicto* is violent and lawless, but not necessarily dishonest as that word is normally understood, and there may be less reason to expect him to lie on the stand in a suit unrelated to his crime than to expect a lesser criminal, but one who has a history of seeking to enrich himself at others' expense, to lie on the stand.

The suggestion in short is that greed or *pleonexia* (wanting more than your fair share) is more highly correlated with willingness or propensity to lie under oath than wrath or passion is. Well, maybe; but a more plausible distinction—and the one that most courts have accepted * * * is between crimes that do not involve an element of deception and crimes that do. * * * It seems plausible (no stronger statement is possible) that a person who has used deceit to commit a crime is more likely than either another type of criminal or a law-abiding person to perceive the witness stand as an attractive site for further deceit—especially when as in this case he is a party to the suit in which he is testifying.

[In the case of some crimes, such as perjury, deceit is an element of the crime; conviction of the crime therefore imports the use of deceit.] In the case of other crimes, deceit is not an element, but the manner in which the witness committed the offense may have involved deceit, and if that is shown the conviction is admissible under Rule 609(a)(2). * * * The trial judge must not allow himself to be sidetracked into the details of the earlier conviction, but where as in this case the deceitful nature of the crime is admitted or is plain on the face of the indictment of other official record, the fact that the same type of offense can be committed in a manner not involving deceit does not make the conviction inadmissible.

[Altobello was convicted of a crime in the second category—the category of crimes that may or may not involve deceit, depending on the circumstances. In Altobello's case it was misdemeanor theft, which can be committed by obtaining property through deception, but alternatively by obtaining it through threat or force, or by receiving stolen property. See Ill.Rev.Stat. ch. 38, ¶ 16–1.

Which was it here? All the record discloses on this score is "tampering with electric meters of Commonwealth Edison." Apparently what happened is that Altobello helped several McDonald's franchisees in the Chicago area to alter the electric meters in their restaurants, in order to reduce their electric bills; but this was only told to us at argument and the record is limited to the bare question asked him at trial, to an unilluminating sidebar discussion of admissibility, and to the indictment, which is no more informative. [There was nevertheless an adequate foundation for the admission of the conviction.] An electric meter is not like a vending machine or a pay telephone, which you can jimmy to get out the coins. Tampering with an electric meter means altering the meter so that it records less use than the user is actually making of it. Meter tampering is *necessarily* a crime of deception; the goal is *always* to deceive the meter reader. It is therefore [securely within the scope of Rule 609(a)(2).]

The other errors claimed by Altobello are signally devoid of merit and require no discussion. The judgment is

Affirmed.

NOTES AND QUESTIONS

1. *Crimen falsi.* The Advisory Committee (2006) defined the term "crimen falsi":

> Rule 609(a)(2) mandates the admission of evidence of a conviction only when the conviction required the proof of (or in the case of a guilty plea, the admission of) an act of dishonesty or false statement. Evidence of all other convictions is inadmissible under this subsection, irrespective of whether the witness exhibited dishonesty or made a false statement in the process of the commission of the crime of conviction. Thus, evidence that a witness was convicted for a crime of violence, such as murder, is not admissible under Rule 609(a)(2), even if the witness acted deceitfully in the course of committing the crime.

> The amendment is meant to give effect to the legislative intent to limit the convictions that are to be automatically admitted under subdivision (a)(2). The Conference Committee provided that by "dishonesty and false statement" it meant "crimes such as perjury, subornation of perjury, false statement, criminal fraud, embezzlement, or false pretense, or any other offense in the nature of *crimen falsi*, the commission of which involves some element of deceit, untruthfulness, or falsification bearing on the [witness's] propensity to testify truthfully." Historically, offenses classified as *crimina falsi* have included only those crimes in which the ultimate criminal act was itself an act of deceit. * * *

2. *Petty theft.* In United States v. Mejia–Alaracon, 995 F.2d 982, 989–90 (10th Cir.1993), the court wrote that "crimes like burglary, robbery, and theft are not automatically admissible under Rule 609(a)(2)." Why doesn't "theft" fall within the Rule? See United States v. Washington, 702 F.3d 886, 893–94 (6th Cir.2012) ("We recognize that a crime that is ordinarily one of dishonesty, such as shoplifting, may in some circuits nonetheless be deemed such a crime on the particular facts of the case. However, in any event, that is not the situation here because Lipford appears to have stolen services through stealth, as opposed to misrepresentation or fraud.") (citation omitted). Some state courts disagree. See State v. Harrington, 800 N.W.2d 46, 50 (Iowa 2011) (theft and burglary are crimes of dishonesty)

3. *Going beyond the record.* The 2006 amendment added a phrase permitting the court to admit a prior conviction if it can "readily determine" (or the witness admits) that the crime involved a dishonest act or false statement. The Advisory Committee provided the following guidance on the new language:

> Evidence of crimes in the nature of *crimina falsi* must be admitted under Rule 609(a)(2), regardless of how such crimes are specifically

charged. For example, evidence that a witness was convicted of making a false claim to a federal agent is admissible under this subdivision regardless of whether the crime was charged under a section that expressly references deceit (e.g., 18 U.S.C. § 1001, Material Misrepresentation to the Federal Government) or a section that does not (e.g., 18 U.S.C. § 1503, Obstruction of Justice).

The amendment requires that the proponent have ready proof that the conviction required the factfinder to find, or the defendant to admit, an act of dishonesty or false statement. Ordinarily, the statutory elements of the crime will indicate whether it is one of dishonesty or false statement. Where the deceitful nature of the crime is not apparent from the statute and the face of the judgment—as, for example, where the conviction simply records a finding of guilt for a statutory offense that does not reference deceit expressly—a proponent may offer information such as an indictment, a statement of admitted facts, or jury instructions to show that the factfinder had to find, or the defendant had to admit, an act of dishonesty or false statement in order for the witness to have been convicted. * * * But the amendment does not contemplate a "mini-trial" in which the court plumbs the record of the previous proceeding to determine whether the crime was in the nature of *crimen falsi.*

See also United States v. Jefferson, 623 F.3d 227, 234 (5th Cir.2010) ("We turn to the indictment in the earlier case and conclude that Jefferson's convictions for obstruction of justice involve dishonesty or false statement."; "Jefferson knowingly and corruptly attempted to persuade another to lie to the authorities"). Is *Altobello* still good law?

4. *Pardons.* What effect does a pardon have on the use of a conviction for impeachment purposes? Does it matter why the pardon was given? See Rule 609(c).

5. *Juvenile adjudications.* See Rule 609(d), but see also *Davis v. Alaska,* note 5, following *Alford* v. *United States,* supra. See also People v. Harris, 901 N.E.2d 367, 372 (Ill.2008) (permitting impeachment with prior juvenile delinquency adjudications after defendant "opened the door" by testifying "I don't commit crimes"). Does this violate Rule 609(d)?

6. *Appeals.* Rule 609(e) is in accord with the generally held rule that the usability of a prior conviction to impeach is unaffected by the fact that the conviction is being appealed at the time the question is asked. See Suggs v. State, 250 A.2d 670 (Md.Ct.Spec.App.1969). But if the conviction has already been reversed a different result obtains. See State v. Hill, 520 P.2d 618 (Wash.1974). As to use of convictions on which judgment or sentence has not been imposed, see Annot., 28 A.L.R.4th 647.

7. *Method of proof.* One common technique of impeachment by showing prior conviction of crime is to inquire of the witness concerning the

fact of conviction on cross-examination and, if the conviction is denied, thereafter to establish the conviction by a certified record of the judgment or other extrinsic evidence. See, e.g., Mead v. State, 86 So.2d 773 (Fla.1956).

8.   *Foundation requirement.* Most jurisdictions hold that no foundation for producing documentary or other evidence of conviction need be laid, and that the evidence may be introduced without first having elicited a denial of the conviction from the witness. 1 McCormick, Evidence § 42 (7th ed. 2013). Should it be permissible, conversely, for a cross-examiner to inquire whether a witness has previously been convicted of crime without being prepared to introduce documentary or other evidence of such convictions in the event of a denial? See Ciravolo v. United States, 384 F.2d 54 (1st Cir.1967).

9.   *Details of crime.* In the event the witness concedes the fact of conviction in the first instance, it is generally held that additional questions concerning the nature and circumstances of the conviction are limited to those matters which are shown by the record of conviction. See Young v. James Green Management, Inc., 327 F.3d 616, 625–26 (7th Cir.2003) ("As a general rule, we have held that 'all that is needed to serve the purpose of challenging the witness's veracity is the elicitation of the crime charged, the date, and the disposition' and that 'it is error to elicit any further information for impeachment purposes.' "). See discussion in 1 McCormick, Evidence § 42 (7th ed. 2013).

10.   *Appellate review.* In Luce v. United States, 469 U.S. 38 (1984), the Supreme Court ruled that an accused had to testify in order to preserve the issue of admissibility for appeal. In Ohler v. United States, 529 U.S. 753 (2000), the Court held that bringing out the conviction on direct examination ("taking out the sting") waived the issue for appellate purposes. Both cases are found in Chapter 1, Section B, supra.

(7) IMPEACHMENT: UNTRUTHFUL CONDUCT, FEDERAL RULE 608(b)

STATE V. MORGAN

Supreme Court of North Carolina, 1986.
340 S.E.2d 84.

Before Owens, J., at the 15 October 1984 Criminal Session of Superior Court, Rutherford County, defendant was convicted of first-degree murder. Defendant appeals his sentence of life imprisonment as a matter of right * * *. * * *

MEYER, JUSTICE.

Defendant brings forth three assignments of error. First, defendant contends that the trial court committed reversible error in allowing the prosecutor, over objection, to cross-examine the defendant concerning a specific instance of prior assaultive conduct that was not probative of truthfulness or veracity. * * * For the reasons stated below, we find no reversible error.

* * *

Defendant's theory of the case was that he had shot Harrell in self-defense; that he reasonably felt it necessary to shoot Harrell in order to protect himself from Mr. Harrell, a 6–3, 280–pound manic depressive who was coming at him through the doorway of his home and business threatening to kill him. Defendant admitted on cross-examination, however, that at the time he shot Harrell, Harrell did not have a weapon in his hand.

During recross-examination of the defendant at trial, the following exchange took place:

> Q. Mr. Morgan, do you recall that on April 26th, 1984, less than three months before this incident, that you assaulted Mike Hall with a deadly weapon, a shotgun, by pointing it at Mr. Hall and stating that you would cut him in two with the shotgun there at this same place of business, did you not do that did you not do that [sic] with Mike Hall?

> MR. MITCHELL: Objection.

> THE COURT: Objection overruled.

> A. Mike Hall followed me from the station and come into my store [sic], yes sir, I remember that.

> Q. And then when Roger Poteat, the CHief [sic] of Police of Alexander Mills, came to serve the Warrant, did you not point the shotgun at Roger Poteat?

> A. No sir, I did not. I showed Roger the gun and it wouldn't [sic] even loaded.

The trial judge thus allowed the prosecutor to question defendant on cross-examination about a prior act of assaultive conduct not charged in the indictment upon which he was being tried. * * * Before analyzing the propriety of the trial judge's ruling here, we must be clear about what the transcript reveals.

This colloquy took place on recross-examination of the defendant by the prosecutor. The defendant had just testified on his own behalf and had admitted shooting Mr. Harrell but claimed he had done so in self-defense. Defendant testified that he would not have shot Mr. Harrell if he had not been afraid of him. During direct and redirect examination, defendant had testified as to Mr. Harrell's often violent behavior and his drinking during the days preceding his death. Apparently without having requested a ruling on admissibility prior to trial, the prosecutor on recross-examination then inquired of defendant whether he had engaged in a specific act of misconduct, which involved the same type of conduct (use of a shotgun at defendant's place of business) as that resulting in the charges for which defendant was being tried, but directed toward unrelated third parties at a time three months prior to the Harrell incident. Defendant admitted pointing the shotgun at Mike Hall but denied pointing the shotgun at Police Chief Poteat. The prosecutor did not then seek to further prove this conduct by extrinsic evidence; thus the record does not reveal the specific circumstances surrounding the 26 April 1984 incident. In the record before us, there is no indication why defendant pointed a gun at Mr. Hall, whether Chief Poteat ever served the warrant or even what or for whom the warrant was issued, or whether defendant was ever charged and convicted of pointing a gun at either man. For purposes of this discussion, we shall assume that defendant was not convicted of either alleged previous assault. Thus, this exchange informed the jury that defendant, at his place of business, may have pointed a shotgun at two men other than Mr. Harrell within three months of the 4 July tragedy when similar conduct resulted in Mr. Harrell's death and defendant's arrest therefor.

* * * Defendant argues that the prosecutor's questions were improper under N.C.G.S. § 8C–1, Rule 608(b) (evidence of specific instances of conduct for the purpose of proving credibility of witness or lack thereof). The State contends that the evidence was properly admitted pursuant to Rule 404(b) (evidence of specific instances of a party's conduct for the purpose of proving motive, opportunity, etc.) as well as Rule 608(b).

Although both rules concern the use of specific instances of a person's conduct, the two rules have very different purposes and are intended to govern entirely different uses of extrinsic conduct evidence.[83] * * * Our task on appellate review is complicated by the fact that there is nothing in the record indicating under which rule the prosecutor was proceeding or under which rule the trial judge overruled the objection. We must therefore consider the admissibility of the evidence under both Rule 404(b) and Rule 608(b).

Defendant correctly argues that the evidence of his alleged prior act of misconduct was inadmissible pursuant to Rule 608(b) (evidence of specific instances of conduct for the purpose of proving credibility of a witness or lack thereof). * * *

Rule 608(b) represents a drastic departure from the former traditional North Carolina practice which allowed a defendant to be cross-examined for impeachment purposes regarding any prior act of misconduct not resulting in conviction so long as the prosecutor had a

---

[83] "Extrinsic conduct evidence" refers to evidence of a specific prior or subsequent act, not charged in the indictment, which may be criminal but, as applied in Rule 608(b), does not result in a conviction. Criminal convictions are included in Rule 404(b).

good-faith basis for the questions. *E.g., State v. Dixon,* 77 N.C.App. 27, 334 S.E.2d 433 (1985).

Rule 608(b) addresses the admissibility of specific instances of conduct (as opposed to opinion or reputation evidence) only in the very narrow instance where (1) the *purpose* of producing the evidence is to impeach or enhance credibility by proving that the witness' conduct indicates his character for truthfulness or untruthfulness; and (2) the conduct in question *is in fact probative* of truthfulness or untruthfulness and is not too remote in time; and (3) the conduct in question did not *result in a conviction;* and (4) the inquiry into the conduct *takes place during cross-examination.* If the proffered evidence meets these four enumerated prerequisites, before admitting the evidence the trial judge must determine, in his discretion, pursuant to Rule 403, that the probative value of the evidence is not outweighed by the risk of unfair prejudice, confusion of issues or misleading the jury, and that the questioning will not harass or unduly embarrass the witness. Even if the trial judge allows the inquiry on cross-examination, extrinsic evidence of the conduct is not admissible. N.C.G.S. § 8C–1, Rule 608(b) and Commentary.

Because the only purpose for which this evidence is sought to be admitted is to impeach or to bolster the credibility of a witness, the only character trait relevant to the issue of credibility is veracity or the lack of it. The focus, then, is upon whether the conduct sought to be inquired into is of the type which is indicative of the actor's character for truthfulness or untruthfulness. Among the types of conduct most widely accepted as falling into this category are "use of false identity, making false statements on affidavits, applications or government forms (including tax returns), giving false testimony, attempting to corrupt or cheat others, and attempting to deceive or defraud others." 3 D. Louisell & C. Mueller, Federal Evidence § 305 (1979) (footnotes omitted). On the other hand, evidence routinely disapproved as irrelevant to the question of a witness' general veracity (credibility) includes specific instances of conduct relating to "sexual relationships or proclivities, the bearing of illigitimate [sic] children, the use of drugs or alcohol, * * * or *violence against other persons.*" *Id.* (footnotes omitted) (emphasis added). *See also* 3 J. Weinstein & M. Berger, Weinstein's Evidence ¶ 608[05] (1985) ("crimes primarily of force or intimidation * * * or crimes based on malum prohibitum are not included.") For example, in *United States v. Alberti,* 470 F.2d 878 (2d Cir.1972), cross-examination of a witness regarding a prior assault was properly disallowed because "the conduct involved does not relate to truthfulness or untruthfulness." *Id.* at 882. *See also United States v. Hill,* 550 F.Supp. 983 (E.D.Pa.1982), *aff'd,* 716 F.2d 893 (3d Cir.1983) ("acts of assault, force, or intimidation do not directly indicate an impairment of a witness' character for veracity." *Id.* at 990); *United States v. Kelley,* 545

F.2d 619 (8th Cir.1976) (evidence tending to show defendant had directed threats and violence toward these victims in the past properly excluded under Rules 607, 608, 609; court intimates that had defendant asserted self-defense at trial, the evidence might have been admissible under Rule 404(b)).

We conclude that the prosecutor's cross-examination of defendant in this case concerning an alleged specific instance of misconduct, i.e., two assaults by pointing a gun at two people during the same incident, was improper under Rule 608(b) because extrinsic instances of assaultive behavior, standing alone, are not in any way probative of the witness' character for truthfulness or untruthfulness.

[The court went on to hold that the evidence of the prior assaults was also inadmissible under Rule 404(b), but that the admission of the evidence in violation of both Rules 608(b) and 404(b) was harmless error under the facts of the case. A dissent by Exum, J., on the question of harmless error is omitted.]

NOTES AND QUESTIONS

1. *Other jurisdictions.* Although impeachment by prior misconduct is permitted by Rule 608 and state rules based on it, a number of American jurisdictions prohibit such impeachment. See 1 McCormick, Evidence § 41 (7th ed. 2013). What considerations might be suggested to support this minority view?

2. *Other examples.* United States v. Shinderman, 515 F.3d 5, 17 (1st Cir.2008) ("[A] witness's willingness to lie to the government in an application for a [medical] license is highly probative of his character for truthfulness."); United States v. Dawson, 434 F.3d 956, 959 (7th Cir.2006) ("[T]he decision whether to allow a witness to be cross-examined about a judicial determination finding him not to be credible is confided to the discretion of the trial judge; it is not barred by Rule 608(b), which, to repeat, is a rule about presenting extrinsic evidence, not about asking questions."); United States v. Whitmore, 359 F.3d 609, 619–22 (D.C.Cir.2004) (holding district court erred in refusing to allow the defendant to cross-examine an officer about a judge's conclusion that "I think [the officer] lied"); United States v. Thiongo, 344 F.3d 55, 60 (1st Cir.2003) ("Defendant's willingness to serve as a legal witness to a sham marriage designed to avoid immigration laws is fairly probative of Defendant's truthfulness."); Young v. James Green Management, Inc., 327 F.3d 616, 627 (7th Cir.2003) ("Stealing is probative of untruthfulness; therefore, the district court acted within the bounds of its discretion in allowing counsel to inquire on cross-examination with respect to this incident.").

3. *Rule 403 balancing.* Should the balancing test of Rule 403 be applied to evidence of misconduct offered under Rule 608(b)? See United States v. Thiongo, 344 F.3d 55, 59 (1st Cir.2003) ("The admissibility of such

evidence is determined by weighing several factors including whether the instances of prior conduct bear some similarity to the conduct at issue, whether they were recent or remote in time, and whether the evidence is cumulative of other evidence.").

4. _Extrinsic evidence._ As noted in the principal case, extrinsic evidence of misconduct not the subject of a conviction is not admissible. Obviously, if trials are ever to reach an end, it is not possible to permit contradictory evidence concerning every conceivable fact on which a witness may testify falsely or inaccurately. Thus the doctrine of "collateral issue," which precludes such contradictory proof unless the fact's importance looms large enough to justify the time required for contradiction. See State v. Long, 140 S.W.3d 27, 30–31 (Mo.2004) ("The bar on extrinsic evidence of prior, specific acts of misconduct furthers the general policy focusing the fact-finder [on] the most probative facts and conserving judicial resources by avoiding mini-trials on collateral issues. In some cases, however, the rule excluding extrinsic evidence of prior false allegations fails to serve this purpose by shielding the fact-finder not from collateral issues, but from a central issue in the case. An issue is not collateral if it is a 'crucial issue directly in controversy.' ").

5. _Good faith._ The Fourth Circuit found a due process violation where a prosecutor's questions concerning prior bad acts, offered to impeach the defendant, lacked a sufficient evidentiary foundation. Watkins v. Foster, 570 F.2d 501 (4th Cir.1978).

(8) IMPEACHMENT: SPECIFIC CONTRADICTION

UNITED STATES V. OPAGER

United States Court of Appeals, Fifth Circuit, 1979.
589 F.2d 799.

JOHN R. BROWN, CHIEF JUDGE:

On February 23, 1977, appellant Patricia Lynn Opager made the regrettable mistake of selling a pound of 90.4% [p]ure cocaine to three buyers, two of whom happened to be law enforcement officers, and the third a government informant and acquaintance of Opager. As a result of this incident, Opager was convicted by a jury of knowingly and intentionally possessing cocaine with the intent to distribute and knowingly and intentionally distributing cocaine * * *.

* * *

At her trial, Opager attempted to establish an entrapment defense. Opager took the stand, testifying that she had never sold cocaine before and that she was pressured into this sale by the informant, Phillip Posner, and the two police officers. In turn, Posner testified to show Opager's "predisposition" to sell cocaine. He stated that he had observed her engage in cocaine transactions in the past. On cross-examination,

Posner explained that he had worked at a beauty salon (the Clipper) with defendant in 1974 and again in 1976 and that during both times he had seen her use and sell cocaine. To impeach Posner's testimony, Opager presented five witnesses to attack Posner's character. By questioning witnesses and by attempting to offer into evidence business records from the beauty salon,[84] she also sought to prove that she and Posner had not worked together in 1974. The District Court ruled that the records were inadmissible under F.R.Evid. 608(b) as extrinsic evidence of a specific instance of conduct introduced to discredit the witness's testimony. * * *

Although the District Court refused to admit the records, the Court did indicate that it would accept into evidence two cancelled checks from the beauty salon to show when Opager started work there. Record at 375. The Record does not specify which checks these were. They apparently were not offered into evidence.

APPLICABILITY OF F.R.EVID. 608(b)

The District Court erred in applying F.R.Evid. 608(b) to determine the admissibility of the business records. The application of Rule 608(b) to exclude extrinsic evidence of a witness's conduct is limited to instances where the evidence is introduced to show a witness's general character for truthfulness. * * *

In this case, we are convinced that the records were not offered for such a purpose. The documents show and would permit the jury to find that, contrary to Posner's testimony, Posner and Opager did not work together in 1974 and that therefore Posner did not witness any of the drug transactions he described as occurring at that time. Thus, the records do more than indicate Posner's capacity to lie, about which five witnesses had testified. Instead, as Opager's counsel strenuously argued at trial The records were introduced to disprove a specific fact material to Opager's defense. * * * A.

1. We consider Rule 608(b) to be inapplicable in determining the admissibility of relevant evidence introduced to contradict a witness's testimony as to a material issue. So long as otherwise competent, such evidence is admissible. McCormick, Evidence § 47 (2d ed. 1972); 3A Wigmore, Evidence §§ 1000–1005 (Chadbourn rev. 1970). This was long the rule in this Circuit prior to the enactment of the Federal Rules of Evidence. * * *

In making this determination, we find helpful the Ninth Circuit's opinion in United States v. Batts, 558 F.2d at 513. In that case, the defendant on cross-examination testified that he had no knowledge of cocaine or its uses. To rebut this testimony, the trial court allowed the

---

[84] The documentary evidence consisted of cancelled checks, appointment books, various tax forms, and other business records of the beauty salon.

government to introduce evidence showing that the defendant had in fact ⌉ 2.
recently sold a large amount of cocaine to an undercover agent. * * *

* * *

That the payroll records are relevant evidence is unmistakable. * * *
Posner's testimony that he saw Opager deal in cocaine in 1974 was a
factor in establishing Opager's criminal "predisposition," itself a matter
clearly of consequence to her case. Hence, the payroll records, "as
indicative that a fact in issue did or did not exist," were clearly relevant.
United States v. Allison, 5 Cir., 1973, 474 F.2d 286, 289 * * *.

Reversed.

NOTES

1.   *No federal rule.* Because there is no Federal Rule on specific
contradiction, it was often confused with other methods of impeachment,
especially Rule 608(b), which prohibits the use of extrinsic evidence. Rule
608(b) was amended—substituting the phrase "character for untruthfulness"
for the term "credibility"—to eliminate this confusion. See Fed.R.Evid. 608
advisory committee's note (2003) ("The amendment restores the Rule to its
original intent, which was to impose an absolute bar on extrinsic evidence
only if the sole purpose of offering the evidence was to prove the witness'
character for veracity."). Specific contradiction involves present conduct (e.g.,
lying at trial), while Rule 608(b) concerns prior conduct (e.g., lying on an
earlier occasion). Specific contradiction would also apply if the witness was
simply mistaken at trial.

2.   *Other examples.* In United States v. Crockett, 435 F.3d 1305, 1312
(10th Cir.2006), the defendant was charged with defrauding the government
of taxes and of assisting others to do the same. He testified on direct
examination that he would never advise anyone to cheat on his or her taxes.
On cross-examination, he conceded that he had earned income assisting
individuals in preparing trusts but had not filed federal income tax returns.
According to the court, "when a defendant makes a false statement during
direct testimony, the prosecution is allowed to prove, either through cross-
examination or by rebuttal witnesses, that the defendant lied as to that fact.
* * * This is so even if the evidence elicited by the prosecution ordinarily
might be collateral or otherwise inadmissible. * * * This principle of cross-
examination is known as the doctrine of 'specific contradiction.'"

In United States v. Lopez, 979 F.2d 1024, 1034 (5th Cir.1992), which
involved the sale of 432 pounds of marihuana, Lopez asserted on direct
examination that he never had seen and could not recognize marihuana. The
government contradicted this testimony by introducing a 1974 conviction for
possession of marihuana. Objections were raised pursuant to Rules 608(b)
and 609. On appeal, however, the court stated: "Extrinsic evidence, which
includes prior convictions, is admissible under the general standards of Rules
402 and 403 to contradict specific testimony, as long as the evidence is

relevant and its probative value is not substantially outweighed by the danger of unfair prejudice."

In State v. Eddy, 895 A.2d 162, 165 (Vt.2006), an alibi witness (Labelle) testified that neither the defendant nor his confederate committed a burglary because they were both with her at the time. The prosecution called the confederate who admitted pleading guilty to the crime. The court held: "Ritchie's guilty plea was introduced not to show that Labelle was generally untrustworthy, but rather to contradict Labelle's assertion that neither Ritchie nor defendant could have committed the crime. Rule 609 simply does not address the use of a prior conviction for the purpose of impeachment by contradiction."

3. *Extrinsic evidence.* The Advisory Committee Note, note 1, supra, also addressed the admissibility of extrinsic evidence to prove specific contradiction:

> By limiting the application of the Rule [608(b)] to proof of a witness' character for truthfulness, the amendment leaves the admissibility of extrinsic evidence offered for other grounds of impeachment (such as contradiction, prior inconsistent statement, bias and mental capacity) to Rules 402 and 403. *See, e.g., United States v. Winchenbach*, 197 F.3d 548 (1st Cir.1999) (admissibility of a prior inconsistent statement offered for impeachment is governed by Rules 402 and 403, not Rule 608(b); *United States v. Tarantino*, 846 F.2d 1384 (D.C.Cir.1988) (admissibility of extrinsic evidence offered to contradict a witness is governed by Rules 402 and 403); *United States v. Lindemann*, 85 F.3d 1232 (7th Cir.1996) (admissibility of extrinsic evidence of bias is governed by Rules 402 and 403). Rules 402 and 403 displace the common-law rules prohibiting impeachment on "collateral" matters. * * *

4. *Sources.* Gilligan & Imwinkelried, Bringing the "Opening the Door" Theory to a Close: The Tendency to Overlook the Specific Contradiction Doctrine in Evidence Law, 41 Santa Clara L.Rev. 807 (2001); McMunigal & Sharpe, Reforming Extrinsic Impeachment, 33 Conn.L.Rev. 363 (2001).

(9) IMPEACHMENT: PRIOR INCONSISTENT STATEMENTS, FEDERAL RULE 613

UNITED STATES V. CATALAN–ROMAN

United States Court of Appeals, First Circuit, 2009.
585 F.3d 453.

LIPEZ, CIRCUIT JUDGE.

Appellants Lorenzo Catalán-Roman ("Catalán") and Hernaldo Medina–Villegas ("Medina") were convicted after a jury trial of several counts relating to a conspiracy to rob armored vehicles and the shooting death of an armored vehicle guard, Gilberto Rodríguez–Cabrera

("Rodríguez"), which occurred during a robbery committed in furtherance of the conspiracy.

* * *

[O]n March 27, 2002, [armored truck] guards Torres and Rodríguez were assigned to deliver $100,000 to the Saulo D. Rodríguez credit union in Gurabo. Torres, the driver, remained in the truck while Rodríguez, the messenger, exited with the money and walked towards the credit union. As Rodríguez approached the entrance, an assailant appeared and pointed a black, 9mm Glock pistol at his face and chest. A second assailant then appeared carrying a Beretta semi-automatic firearm. At trial, Torres identified the first assailant as Medina and the second as Catalán. Rodríguez raised his hands above his head in an act of surrender. As Catalán attempted to remove Rodríguez's firearm from its holster, Medina fired two shots at Rodríguez. Torres then opened the door of the armored truck and began firing at Catalán, who was hit and fell to the ground. Torres was shot in the left hand by a fourth indicted co-conspirator, Quester Sterling–Suarez ("Sterling"). Torres fell back into the truck and closed its doors.

* * *

3. THE TRIAL COURT'S RULING ON INCONSISTENCY

The court ruled that the statement made by Torres at the hospital following the March 27 murder of Rodríguez, recorded in a [Form] 302 by [FBI] agents Marerro and Cruz, was not inconsistent with Torres's trial testimony. The court concluded that in light of Torres's injured condition at the time of the [hospital] interview, the fact that he had taken pain medication, the short duration of the interview, and the fact that "we don't know what type of questions the agents asked," it would not have been "natural" for Torres to include the aggravating details. See United States v. Meserve, 271 F.3d 314, 320–21 (1st Cir.2001) ("Prior statements * * * that omit details included in a witness's trial testimony are inconsistent if it would have been 'natural' for the witness to include the details in the earlier statement."). The substance of defendants' proffer specifically stated, however, that Agent Cruz would testify that in her estimation Torres was an appropriate subject for an interview. Defense counsel proffered that Agent Cruz would testify as follows:

> She would say that she recognized that he was in pain, that he had been shot, I think it was in the left hand, that she, in accordance with procedure and policy, took notes during the interview, that she recorded all of the important things that he said about the event, that the notes were effectively transcribed into a written report which * * * she reviewed, initialed, as did Mr. Marrero, for accuracy.* * * She said that while he was in pain, in her opinion he was a subject

for an interview. She did not feel that he was incapacitated or incapable of being interviewed and providing information. That during the interview itself, as he described the events that took place on March 27th, at no time during that interview did he indicate Mr. Rodríguez [the victim] has his arms raised in a submissive mode prior to being shot. He did not at any time indicate that, prior to Mr. Rodríguez being shot, in the position with his arms raised, did he hear him say, please, no, please, no, please, no, and he did not indicate in any way that prior to that, in the mode with his hands raised, that the assailant, who he later identified in court as Mr. Hernaldo Medina Villegas, approached him from the front and shot him twice in the chest.

Unlike *Meserve*, on which the district court relied for its ruling that the omitted details were not inconsistent with Torres's trial testimony, the details omitted in Torres's earlier statement were not "peripheral" but went directly to the important element of premeditation as well as the possible imposition of the death penalty. Cf. *Meserve*, 271 F.3d at 321 (where "nuances [were] peripheral," district court did not abuse its discretion in excluding impeachment by omission through extrinsic evidence). As described in the discussion of the sufficiency of the evidence supporting Medina's conviction on the murder charge, see infra Part III(A), the indictment charged that the defendants had acted "with premeditation" in killing Rodríguez. With respect to premeditation, "it is the fact of deliberation, of second thought [,] that is important." United States v. Frappier, 807 F.2d 257, 261 (1st Cir.1986) * * *. The victim crying out for his life before he was shot by the defendant was some of the government's most persuasive evidence that Catalán had acted with premeditation in shooting Rodríguez.

* * *

4. THE TRIAL COURT'S COLLATERAL FACT RULINGS

Under the common law of evidence and the law of this circuit, impeachment by extrinsic evidence is normally restricted to impeachment on matters that are not collateral. United States v. Cruz–Rodriguez, 541 F.3d 19, 30 (1st Cir.2008) (" 'It is well established that a party may not present extrinsic evidence to impeach a witness by contradiction on a collateral matter.' ") (quoting United States v. Beauchamp, 986 F.2d 1, 3 (1st Cir.1993)).[85] A matter is considered collateral if " 'the matter itself is

---

[85] But see 1 McCormick on Evidence § 49 (6th ed. 2006) ("Given Rule 402 [which provides that "all relevant evidence is admissible"], there is a powerful argument that the collateral fact rule was impliedly repealed by enactment of the Federal Rules. Under this reading of the Federal Rules, there is no rigid prohibition on introducing extrinsic evidence to impeach a witness on a collateral matter; rather, under Rule 403, the judge would make a practical judgment as to whether the importance of the witness's testimony and the impeachment warrants the expenditure of the additional trial time. However, the collateral fact rule was so

not relevant in the litigation to establish a fact of consequence, i.e., not *A* · relevant for a purpose other than mere contradiction of the in-court testimony of the witness.'")Beauchamp, 986 F.2d at 4 (quoting 1 McCormick on Evidence § 45 (4th ed. 1992)).

The rule restricting impeachment to non-collateral matters is analogous to Rule 403's relevancy balancing test, which calls for relevant evidence to be excluded when its "probative value is substantially outweighed by * * * considerations of undue delay, [or] waste of time. . . ." Fed.R.Evid. 403; see also Beauchamp, 986 F.2d at 4. Although any *1* · demonstrated inconsistency in a witness's statement may impeach a witness's credibility, other concerns (such as wasting time and misleading the jury) become more important when the inconsistency at issue involves *a* · a statement relating to a matter that " 'is not relevant in the litigation to establish a fact of consequence.' " Beauchamp, 986 F.2d at 4 (quoting 1 McCormick on Evidence § 45, 169 (4th ed. 1992)). [On the other hand] *2* · when a statement that would be the subject of impeachment "is logically relevant to the merits of the case as well as the witness's credibility, it is worth the additional court time entailed in hearing extrinsic evidence." 1 McCormick on Evidence § 49 (6th ed. 2006).

Over defendants' protestations to the contrary, the trial court *F* · repeatedly ruled that evidence of Torres's prior inconsistent statements about the robberies was not admissible because it was "collateral." For example, in response to defendants' request to impeach Torres's claim that Rodríguez had pleaded for his life before being shot, the court said, "it's collateral source, collateral impeachment by extrinsic evidence because whether he said, no, no, or—yes, yes * * * that all doesn't go directly to the issues of guilt or innocence of the two defendants."

It is true that this circuit has said that ["[i]n light of the collateral issue rule, in order to be admissible, . . . testimony must not only *3* · contradict a statement . . . but also be material to [the defendant's] guilt or innocence." United States v. Mulinelli–Navas, 111 F.3d 983, 988 (1st Cir.1997) * * *. However, it appears that the district court may have interpreted that statement—or one like it—to mean that in order to be material here, the extrinsic evidence at issue must relate to whether the defendant did or did not shoot Rodríguez, or whether he stole the money, and not how the shooting or robbery were carried out.

This is too narrow a view. As has been noted, some of the details Catalán sought to impeach—such as the defendants' and victim's behavior during the shooting—plainly helped the government establish the premeditation that was charged as an aspect of the murder in count

ingrained at common law that many federal opinions continue to mention 'collateral' evidence."). This circuit continues to apply the collateral fact rule. See, e.g., Cruz–Rodriguez, 541 F.3d at 30; United States v. Marino, 277 F.3d 11, 24 (1st Cir.2002).

eight. Furthermore, several of the details were certainly relevant to the jury's consideration of the death penalty if the defendants were convicted. * * * Torres was the only eyewitness to the March 27 murder of his partner * * *. He had testified that the crimes were committed in a certain way, and the defendants sought to impeach him by introducing evidence through his prior inconsistent statements that the crimes were not committed that way. His accounts of the robberies and murder were unquestionably material to the government's case against Catalán, including its request for the death penalty, even if the impeachment of Torres on details of those accounts may not have exculpated Catalán from involvement in the crime.

* * *

For the reasons set forth above, we vacate the conviction and sentence of appellant Catalán on count nine and further direct that the special assessment on that count be removed. We further vacate Medina's sentence on count eight and remand for resentencing. All other convictions and sentences are affirmed.

NOTES AND QUESTIONS

1. *Theory of admissibility.* See 1 McCormick, Evidence § 34 (7th ed.2013) ("The attack by prior inconsistent statement is not based on the theory that the present testimony is false and the former statement true. Rather, the theory is that talking one way on the stand and another way previously is blowing hot and cold, raising a doubt as to the truthfulness of both statements.").

2. *Inconsistency requirement.* By definition, a prior inconsistent statement must be inconsistent with the testimony of the witness at the trial. Is a direct contradiction required? See United States v. Gravely, 840 F.2d 1156, 1163 (4th Cir.1988) ("The Federal Rules of Evidence, however, reject the view that the prior testimony must flatly contradict trial testimony. * * * It is enough if the 'proffered testimony, taken as a whole, either by what it says or by what it omits to say' affords some indication that the fact was different from the testimony of the witness whom it sought to contradict.").

3. *Lack of knowledge.* See United States v. Shoupe, 548 F.2d 636, 638–39 (6th Cir.1977) ("Adkins credibility as a witness was also challenged by the defense. He was confronted with prior grand jury testimony in which he had stated unequivocally that he had no recollection of finding a ski mask included in the contents of the duffle bag and that his agreement with Willison called for him to receive a fee for the use of his apartment which differed from the sum which he mentioned at trial.").

4. *Lack of memory.* See United States v. Knox, 124 F.3d 1360, 1364 (10th Cir.1997) ("A well-settled body of case law holds that where a declarant's memory loss is contrived it will be taken as inconsistent * * *."); United States v. Strother, 49 F.3d 869, 874 (2d Cir.1995) ("Under certain

circumstances, a witness's prior silence regarding critical facts may constitute a prior inconsistent statement where failure to mention those matters * * * conflicts with that which is later recalled. Where the belatedly recollected facts merely augment that which was originally described, the prior silence is often simply too ambiguous to have any probative force. * * * It would have been natural for Wollschleager to include Strother's request in her earlier statement.").

5. *Opinion rule.* It will frequently occur that a prior and allegedly inconsistent statement made by a witness will be phrased in terms which, if made on the stand, would violate the rule against opinions where it still prevails. May such a statement be used for impeachment? See Miller v. Lint, 404 N.E.2d 752 (Ohio 1980); Grady, The Admissibility of a Prior Statement of Opinion for Purposes of Impeachment, 41 Cornell L.Q. 224 (1956). Would exclusion of an opinion be consistent with the rationale underlying Federal Rule 701?

6. *Extrinsic evidence.* The common law rule prohibiting contradicting a witness on collateral matters by extrinsic evidence applied to prior inconsistent statements. Thus, although wide latitude was generally given on cross-examination with regard to the subject matter of prior inconsistent statements, extrinsic evidence of such statements was inadmissible unless the statement concerned facts relevant to the issues in the case or facts which themselves would be provable by extrinsic evidence, such as those involving bias or facts about which the witness would not be mistaken if his story were true. The classic case is Attorney–General v. Hitchcock, 154 Eng.Rep. 38 (1847). As the principal case indicates, Federal Rule 403 may have replaced the collateral issue rule. See also the discussion of this topic when specific contradiction is employed in the notes following *Opager*, Subsection 8, supra.

UNITED STATES V. HUDSON

United States Court of Appeals, First Circuit, 1992.
970 F.2d 948.

YOUNG, DISTRICT JUDGE.

Richard B. Hudson, Sr. ("appellant") here appeals from his conviction on two separate counts, each charging him with conspiracy to possess with intent to distribute in excess of five hundred grams of cocaine. * * * The first count alleged that during late 1986 and continuing through 1987, appellant engaged in a cocaine conspiracy with Henry Cormier, Robert Johnson, and others. The second count alleged another cocaine conspiracy, this one commencing in late 1988 and continuing through 1989, involving appellant with his brother, James Hudson, and others. [Cromier, Johnson, and the accused's brother, James Hudson, all testified pursuant to plea agreements. They all implicated the accused in the charged incidents.] * * *

Throughout, defense counsel had ably sought to impugn the motives of the government witnesses for testifying in a manner which inculpated appellant and had painted each of the government witnesses in the darkest possible hue. Defense counsel now prepared to present appellant's affirmative case.

At this point, the Assistant United States Attorney asked to approach the side bar and asked the Court to require defense counsel to make a proffer and to hear the testimony of the two defense witnesses outside the presence of the jury as it was "from the government's view, rank hearsay." Defense counsel represented that the two witnesses, Paul Whitten and Gregory Benson, were inmates in the South Windham Correctional Center where Henry Cormier and James Hudson had been held. Defense counsel said that one of the two witnesses would testify that he heard Cormier tell James Hudson that appellant "had nothing to do with drugs" but that he was angry with appellant over a gambling debt. What follows next in this side bar conference is vital to an understanding of appellant's claim here. We set forth the relevant colloquy * * *:

THE COURT: How do you overcome the hearsay?

DEFENSE COUNSEL: I think it's a situation—

CO–DEFENSE COUNSEL: I think it's evidence of impeachment of bias and motive for a witness who has previously testified that he doesn't have any bias, that he is telling the truth.

THE COURT: How do you get over the hearsay?

CO–DEFENSE COUNSEL: Prior inconsistent statement.

* * *

Whitten testified [on voir dire examination] that Cormier had told James Hudson that he "didn't believe that Dick Hudson had anything to do with drugs" but that Cormier was upset with appellant because "Dick had beat him in a game of gin and it cost him $5,000." Gregory Benson then testified that he had overheard the same conversation and that Cormier had said to James Hudson, "I never really thought your brother sold drugs but me and Robbie * * * said he did because he beat us out of a lot of money playing cards, gambling." Benson further testified that James Hudson "said he wanted to make sure the bastard got what he deserved" because "Dick was supposed to take care of [my] family and he never did." [The court sustained the government's hearsay objection.]

I.

Appellant first contends that the district court erred in excluding the testimony of the defense witnesses, Paul Whitten and Gregory Benson, contending that this aspect of the appeal is controlled by our decision in *United States v. Barrett,* 539 F.2d 244, 253–56 (1st Cir.1976).

* * *

Next, the government contends that the foundation for admitting extrinsic evidence through Benson about James Hudson's prior statement was never properly laid pursuant to Fed.R.Evid. 613(b), since James Hudson was never "afforded an opportunity to explain or deny [his earlier statement]." The government urges us to reconsider our ruling in *Barrett* in which we explained that the foundation requirements of 613(b) do not require that the witness be confronted with the statement while on the witness stand, but rather, only that the witness be available to be recalled in order to explain the statement during the course of the trial. *Barrett,* 539 F.2d at 254–56. The government properly notes that the Fifth, Ninth, and Tenth Circuits have upheld the refusal to admit proof through extrinsic evidence of prior inconsistent statements unless the witness has first been afforded the opportunity to deny or explain those statements. [Citations omitted.] The Eighth Circuit has followed suit, at least in circumstances in which there are considerable logistical difficulties in arranging for the recall of inmate witnesses sought to be impeached through extrinsic evidence of prior inconsistent statements. *United States v. Lynch,* 800 F.2d 765, 770 (8th Cir.1986). We decline the invitation. Assuming without deciding that James Hudson's expression of bias against appellant constituted a prior inconsistent statement with respect to his trial testimony, we reaffirm our earlier analysis as set forth in *Barrett.* The approach there taken is wholly consistent with the requirements of Fed.R.Evid. 613(b), as explained by the notes of the Advisory Committee: "the traditional insistence that the attention of the witness be directed to the statement on cross examination is relaxed in favor of simply providing the witness an opportunity to explain and the opposite party an opportunity to examine the statement, with no specification of any particular time or sequence," and is supported by the great weight of authority. * * *

Here, as in *Barrett,* we have no basis for assuming that James Hudson, a federal prisoner, was not available for recall or that the government would have been prejudiced by admission of the statement without the opportunity for adequate rebuttal and examination. Even though the district court possesses a substantial measure of discretion under Fed.R.Evid. 613(b), it would resurrect the now-discredited procedure laid down in *Queen Caroline's Case,* 2 Brod. & Bing. 284, 313, 129 Eng.Rep. 976 (1820), if we excluded James Hudson's statement on the ground of an inadequate evidentiary foundation when the district court acted without any evaluation of the availability of the witness sought to be impeached or, alternatively, without any expressed consideration of whatever delay or inconvenience might have been caused by defense counsel's failure to confront James Hudson, on cross-examination, with his allegedly inconsistent statement.[86] * * *

[Appellant's conviction on Count I was affirmed on harmless error grounds. The conviction on Count II was vacated and remanded for further proceedings.]

SELYA, CIRCUIT JUDGE (concurring).

* * * I concur in the judgment. I write separately, however, to express my thoughts as to why *Barrett* bears overruling and as to how Fed.R.Evid. 613(b) was meant to operate.

This court decided *Barrett* soon after the Federal Rules of Evidence took effect. Since that time, most (though not all) of the circuits have rejected *Barrett*'s rationale, deciding instead that the adoption of Rule 613(b) did not abolish the traditional common law requirement of laying a suitable foundation prior to the introduction of impeachment evidence. [Citations omitted.] In my estimation, the majority rule is sounder than the view espoused in *Barrett*. It works to avoid unfair surprise, gives the target of the impeaching evidence a timely opportunity to explain or deny the alleged inconsistency, facilitates judges' efforts to conduct trials in an orderly manner, and conserves scarce judicial resources. At the same time, insistence upon a prior foundational requirement, subject, of course, to relaxation in the presider's discretion if "the interests of justice otherwise require," Fed.R.Evid. 613(b), does not impose an undue burden on the proponent of the evidence. * * *

NOTES AND QUESTIONS

1. *Another example.* See Rush v. Illinois Cent. R. Co., 399 F.3d 705, 716, 720 (6th Cir.2005) (Defendant sought to impeach Lockett's direct testimony that he never saw "anybody running to get on the back of the train" with his post-accident statement that "Johnathan was running alongside the train trying to get on."; "Although unnecessary under the current version of Rule 613, defense counsel took the additional step of

---

[86] We think it is important to note that, both in *Barrett* and in the present case, the trial court's fundamental error lay not in a mistaken interpretation of Rule 613(b) but in its failure to exercise its discretion. Even if a proponent is not always required to lay a prior foundation under Rule 613(b), a trial court is free to use its informed discretion to exclude extrinsic evidence of prior inconsistent statements on grounds of unwarranted prejudice, confusion, waste of time, or the like. *See, e.g., Nachtsheim v. Beech Aircraft Corp.,* 847 F.2d 1261, 1276–77 (7th Cir.1988) (suggesting that trial court has discretion under Fed.R.Evid. 403 to exclude evidence not excluded by Fed.R.Evid. 613 [b]); * * * Moreover, *Barrett* notwithstanding, Fed.R.Evid. 611(a) allows the trial judge to control the mode and order of interrogation and presentation of evidence, giving him or her the discretion to impose the common-law "prior foundation" requirement when such an approach seems fitting. *See Nachtsheim,* 847 F.2d at 1276–77 (suggesting that trial court has broad discretion under Rules 611 and 403 to exclude evidence not barred by Rule 613[b]); *United States v. Marks,* 816 F.2d 1207, 1210–11 (7th Cir.1987) (stating that Rule 613 was not intended to eliminate trial judge's discretion to manage the trial in a way designed to promote accuracy and fairness). Here, however, there is no sign that the trial judge sought to exercise these powers.

revealing the prior inconsistent statement to Lockett during cross-examination and afforded Lockett with the opportunity to explain the apparent inconsistency."). Is there a tactical reason to do so?

2. *Written statements.* When the prior inconsistent statement with which the witness is sought to be impeached is a statement in writing, should the cross-examiner be required to show the statement to the witness before interrogating him concerning it? Such a requirement is commonly thought to have been laid down in The Queen's Case, 129 Eng.Rep. 976 (C.P.1820), and was widely applied in this country, at least prior to the adoption of the Federal Rules of Evidence. For an explanation and evaluation of the rule, see Ladd, Impeachment of Witness, 52 Cornell L.Q. 239, 246–77 (1967). As the principal case indicates, Rule 613(a) abolished this requirement.

3. *Hearsay.* The principal case and these notes concern statements offered for purposes of impeachment. Note that certain prior inconsistent statements are admissible as nonhearsay under Rule 801(d)(1)(A). See discussion in Chapter 13, Section B(1), infra.

4. *Constitutional issues.* Evidence obtained by the state in violation of the constitutional rights of a criminal accused is inadmissible as substantive evidence of the accused's guilt. Should such evidence be admissible for purposes of impeachment if the defendant chooses to testify in his own defense? In Walder v. United States, 347 U.S. 62 (1954), it was held proper, where the defendant testified that he had never possessed narcotics, to impeach him by evidence that an illegal search had disclosed the defendant in possession of narcotics. The Court qualified its holding by stating that the defendant "must be free to deny all the elements of the case against him without thereby giving leave to the Government to introduce by way of rebuttal evidence illegally secured by it * * *." Id. at 65.

Subsequent to *Miranda v. Arizona,* it was widely supposed that, *Walder* notwithstanding, statements obtained from a criminal accused in the absence of *Miranda* warnings would be inadmissible for impeachment as well as for substantive purposes. See, e.g., United States v. Fox, 403 F.2d 97 (2d Cir.1968). However, in Harris v. New York, 401 U.S. 222 (1971), the Supreme Court revived the *Walder* doctrine and arguably expanded it beyond its original compass. In *Harris,* the police had obtained statements from the defendant concerning two alleged narcotics sales, concededly without giving antecedent *Miranda* warnings. The state made no attempt to introduce these statements as part of its case in chief, but when defendant took the stand, denied one sale and asserted the other was of baking powder rather than heroin, the prosecution was allowed to use the statements for impeachment. A majority of the Court found no "difference in principle" between *Walder's* allowance of impeachment on a collateral matter and the instant case where the contradiction was as to facts relevant to the charge being tried. If there is no such difference, of what continuing significance is the statement in *Walder* that the defendant "must be free to deny all elements of the case against him?" See an able analysis of this and related questions in a Comment, The

Impeachment Exception to the Constitutional Exclusionary Rules, 73 Colum.L.Rev. 1476 (1973). See also Kansas v. Ventris, 556 U.S. 586, 594 (2009) ("[T]he informant's testimony, concededly elicited in violation of the Sixth Amendment [right to counsel], was admissible to challenge Ventris's inconsistent testimony at trial.").

However, an involuntary (coercive) confession may not be used to impeach, Mincey v. Arizona, 437 U.S. 385 (1978), nor may silence following the giving of *Miranda* warnings, Doyle v. Ohio, 426 U.S. 610 (1976). The exclusionary rule may also come into play where the prosecution seeks to impeach the testimony of a defense witness by use of accused's tainted statements. See James v. Illinois, 493 U.S. 307 (1990).

(10) IMPEACHMENT: LEARNED TREATISE

FRESHWATER V. SCHEIDT
Supreme Court of Ohio, 1999.
714 N.E.2d 891.

DOUGLAS, J.

[Plaintiff underwent surgery to remove her gallbladder. She subsequently filed a malpractice action against Dr. Scheidt, who had performed the laparoscopic cholecystectomy.]

Shortly after surgery, Kathleen had noticeable swelling of her body and severe abdominal pain. Kathleen was eventually transported by ambulance to another hospital, where she underwent further surgery to repair a perforation to her small bowel. The perforation occurred as a result of the laparoscopic procedure performed by Scheidt. During this time, Kathleen became seriously ill and almost died. She was hospitalized for seventy-seven days, the majority of which was spent in the intensive-care unit. She also incurred extensive medical bills.

* * *

Also at trial, Dr. Karl A. Zucker, an expert witness for appellees, testified that Scheidt did not deviate from accepted standards of medical care in removing Kathleen's gallbladder. Upon cross-examination of Zucker, counsel for appellants attempted to question Zucker about statements contained in a book entitled "Surgical Laparoscopy," which had been edited and written in part by Zucker. The statements were in a chapter entitled "Open Laparoscopy," written in part by a colleague of Zucker's, Dr. Fitzgibbons. Additionally, appellants' counsel also sought to cross-examine Zucker with respect to other medical literature authored by Fitzgibbons. This additional literature had apparently been referred to by Zucker in some of Zucker's other publications. When questioned about the writings that Fitzgibbons had authored, Zucker avoided answering whether Fitzgibbons was an "authority" in the field and he further refused to acknowledge whether the medical literature authored by Fitzgibbons was "authoritative" in nature:

"Q. When you have written articles on laparoscopic surgery, have you frequently cited Dr. Fitzgibbons as an authority on the open laparoscopic technique?

"A. I'm not sure the word 'authority' is one I'd use; but he's a colleague, a personal friend, my kids play with his kids. So he's a respected colleague, and I often will quote him. I think he's very honorable and honest individual with very good experience.

"Q. And you value his opinion?

"A. Yes.

"Q. And when you put out your book, he's the one who wrote the chapter with another doctor or two on open laparoscopic?

"A. Yes. * * *

"Q. * * * Doctor, I have—did you quote Dr. Fitzgibbons because you believed he was an authority in the area of open laparoscopic surgery?

"A. As I said, I'm not sure I used the word 'authority.'

"Q. Well, that's my question, though. It's of some legal significance as to the questions I can ask you or cannot ask you, and I'd like to know if you consider him an authority in the area of open laparoscopic surgery. * * *

"Q. * * * Have you relied upon Dr. Fitzgibbons at all in your profession of informing other doctors as to the open Hasson technique?

"A. I've quoted Dr. Fitzgibbons; but I don't always, you know, agree with his writing or what he advocates.

"Q. Did you rely upon, did you think he was authoritative enough to write a chapter in your book?

"A. Again, I'm not sure about the word 'authoritative,' but I value his opinion and his expertise. I invited him to write a chapter in a textbook that I wrote on laparoscopic surgery.

"Q. Did you rely upon the materials presented in that chapter of your book for any part of your testimony today?

"A. I certainly, I used part of that in coming up to my opinions and every day practice as well as in this testimony.

"Q. Did you rely upon his part of the chapter that dealt with complications and risk factors of not using the open technique?

" * * *

"Q. Did you rely upon any studies or statistics that he had as to the open Hasson technique versus the closed technique in coming to your conclusions for trial today?

"A. Well, as I said, I agree with some of the things and I disagree with other parts of his writings * * *."

The trial court prevented counsel for appellants from cross-examining Zucker with respect to statements in Zucker's book. * * *

* * *

The central issue in this case concerns the extent to which statements from learned treatises and other publications may be used to impeach the testimony of expert witnesses. * * * In *Hallworth v. Republic Steel Corp.* (1950), 153 Ohio St. 349 * * * the court held that learned treatises, even though properly identified, authenticated, and recognized as standard authority, are not admissible in evidence to prove the truth of the matter asserted therein. Rather, "learned treatises are considered hearsay, may not be used as substantive evidence, and are specifically limited to impeachment purposes only." Ramage v. Cent. Ohio Emergency Serv. Inc. (1992), 64 Ohio St.3d 97 * * *.

Later, in *Stinson v. England* (1994), 69 Ohio St.3d 451, 633 N.E.2d 532, this court set forth the conditions under which learned treatises can be used to impeach the credibility of expert witnesses. Counsel may use a learned treatise to impeach a testifying expert by establishing that the expert is either unaware of the text or unfamiliar with its contents. * * * Additionally, the substance of a learned treatise can be used to impeach the credibility of an expert witness if the expert has relied upon the treatise in forming his or her opinion or the expert has acknowledged the authoritative nature of the treatise. * * *

* * *

In the case at bar, both the trial court and court of appeals ruled that *Stinson* prevented appellants' counsel from cross-examining Scheidt and Zucker about the medical literature in question. On cross-examination, both Scheidt and Zucker would not explicitly concede the "authoritative" nature of the literature. Nevertheless, although Scheidt and Zucker refused to explicitly acknowledge the authoritative nature of the medical literature, they implicitly conceded as much. * * * Scheidt testified that he "hardly [knew] how to define authority," but that his teachers in the area of laparoscopic surgery were "helpful and useful," and that he looked to his teachers for "helpful suggestions." He also stated that the courses pertaining to laparoscopic cholecystectomies "were certainly helpful to me." With respect to Zucker, he testified that Fitzgibbons was a "respected colleague," "I often will quote him," and that he was "a very honorable and honest individual with very good experience." Zucker further stated that he valued Fitzgibbons's "opinions and his expertise," and had "invited him to write a chapter in a textbook that I wrote on laparoscopic surgery." Zucker also testified that he had relied upon materials presented in the chapter in that he "used part of that [chapter] in coming up to my opinions in everyday practice as well as in this testimony."

In *Stinson*, we determined that it was error to allow the medical treatise to be used for impeachment purposes because a proper foundation had not been laid establishing the text as a reliable authority. However, *Stinson* was not intended to allow testifying experts to adroitly evade cross-examination simply by avoiding such words as "rely" or "authority" or any forms of those words. Indeed, if an expert witness relies upon published medical literature in forming his or her opinion, or the expert provides testimony sufficient to establish that the literature is reliable authority, or the literature is part of the expert's own publication, statements contained in the literature can be used for purposes of impeachment. The requisite reliance upon published medical literature or its authoritative nature can be established without an express acknowledgement by the testifying expert that he or she had relied upon the literature or that it is authoritative.

The testimony of Scheidt and Zucker established that the medical literature at issue was reliable authority. Moreover, testimony and other evidence in the record indicate that Scheidt and Zucker also relied upon the literature in forming their opinions. The literature was not offered by appellants' counsel as substantive evidence. Instead, the literature was intended to call into question the weight to be attached by the fact finder to the testimony of Scheidt and Zucker. In this regard, the restricted cross-examination of Scheidt and Zucker by the trial court harmed the fact-finding process and prevented the jury from adequately assessing the credibility of the witnesses. * * *

Judgment reversed and cause remanded.

NOTE AND QUESTIONS

At the time *Freshwater* was decided, Ohio had a rule limiting the use of learned treatises to impeachment, which reflected the common law approach. The Ohio rule was based on Michigan Rule 707. In 2006, Ohio adopted the approach found in the Federal Rules, which create a hearsay exception for learned treatises. Under Rule 803(18), statements contained in treatises called to an expert's attention during cross-examination or relied upon in direct examination may be admissible as substantive evidence. By creating an exception to the hearsay rule, the Federal Rules avoid the awkwardness and futility of an instruction which tells the jury to consider the substance of the statement in the treatise for purposes of impeachment only.

Following the lead of the Supreme Court in Reilly v. Pinkus, 338 U.S. 269 (1949), Rule 803(18) provides that the authoritativeness of the treatise may be established by the testimony of the witness, by expert testimony or by judicial notice. Why must statements in authoritative treatises be called to the attention of an expert? Why not simply admit them on their own merit?

(11)   REHABILITATION

THOMAS, CROSS–EXAMINATION AND REHABILITATION OF WITNESSES[87]

14 Defense Law Journal 247, 261 (1965).

* * *

Rehabilitating the Cross–Examined Witness

Many of us have experienced instances where a devastating or skillful cross-examination has apparently made a shambles or wreckage of the "star witness" or other witnesses. The question then arises for the advocate, who vouches for said witness, to determine whether Humpty Dumpty really had a "great fall," and if he did, whether he can be "put together again," on re-direct or re-examination. For some unknown reason, the subject of re-direct examination, or rehabilitation of witnesses, has received but scant attention from the writers, yet it is here that we have a good indication of a trial lawyer's general ability and certainly an excellent test as to whether he has well prepared the facts of his case.

Admittedly, the proper function and scope of re-direct examination is to rebut, explain or avoid the effect of new matter brought out on cross-examination. Occasionally, in the discretion of the court, it has been utilized to propound forgotten questions.

Leaving Well Enough Alone May Be Best

At the outset, trial counsel must decide whether to proceed on re-direct. He should be mindful of the adage, "Let well enough alone" if his witness has not been seriously damaged, for he can over-try his case, and so doing "open the door" for a real time bomb. If the cross-examination has fallen short of the mark in reaching any material part of the story on direct, most skilled lawyers will waive re-direct, and seek to take care of his witness in summation if counsel opposite try to turn the spotlight on these immaterial contradictions or fallacies. * * *

NOTES AND QUESTIONS

1. *Limitations.* Having once made the determination that rehabilitation of a witness is essential, what evidence is admissible for the

---

[87] Copyright by the publisher, The Allen Smith Company, Indianapolis 46202. Reprinted by permission. [Ed.]

purpose? Few helpful generalizations are possible in the area, but if the courts recognize one cardinal principle it is that the permissible rehabilitation of a witness is a function of the type of impeachment to which that witness has been subjected. Therefore, since it is impossible to answer the general question, "How may a witness be rehabilitated?," it is fruitful only to inquire how a witness who has been impeached in a specific manner may be rehabilitated.

2. *Bolstering.* The first derivative of the proposition that rehabilitation is a function of impeachment is the universal rule that the credibility of an unimpeached witness cannot be supported. See material on bolstering at beginning of this Section.

3. *Sources.* As to rehabilitation generally, see Ladd, Techniques and Theory of Character Testimony, 24 Iowa L.Rev. 498 (1939); Orfield, Impeachment and Support of Witnesses in Federal Criminal Cases, 11 Kan.L.Rev. 477 (1963); Note, 36 Minn.L.Rev. 724 (1952); Mauet, Fundamentals of Trial Techniques 172 (1980).

RODRIGUEZ V. STATE

Court of Criminal Appeals of Texas, 1957.
305 S.W.2d 350.

WOODLEY, JUDGE. The offense is aggravated assault; the punishment, 9 months in jail and a fine of $750.

Appellant, aged 66 years, came to the home of Ramon Gavia on a Sunday afternoon to see Gavia.

Gavia was not at home and appellant was invited by Gavia's daughter, Cathalina, to wait for her father.

Cathalina Gavia testified that she left the room for a few minutes and upon her return appellant and her seven year old foster daughter were on the couch and appellant was holding one hand on the child's mouth and was taking her pants off, and she ran and got the child and called some friends who notified the officers.

The child was found not to be competent to testify.

Appellant testified and denied any assault was made on the child. His version was that the little girl went to the bathroom and returned with her panties down, and he called her to him to assist her in pulling them up which he was doing when Cathalina Gavia came into the room, ordered him to leave and called the officers.

Appellant further testified that on the previous day he had seen Cathalina in a car on a country road and a man was "lying down on her legs"; that when he came to see Cathalina's father, he spoke to her about what he had seen and she denied it and got mad, and shortly thereafter charged him with assaulting the child.

Cathalina was then recalled and denied that she had been on any country road or with a man on Saturday, and further denied that appellant had spoken to her about any such incident at her home on Sunday.

* * *

After the testimony above mentioned had been given by appellant and by the State's witness Cathalina Gavia, the State was permitted over objection to prove that Cathalina's reputation in the community for truth and veracity was good.

We are cited to the rule that where there is no evidence to impeach the testimony of a witness except contradictory evidence, it is not permissible to bolster the testimony of the witness by proof of his good reputation for truth and veracity. Jones v. State, 52 Tex.Cr.R. 206, 106 S.W. 126; Zysman v. State, 42 Tex.Cr.R. 432, 60 S.W. 669.

This rule has no application here for where an attack is made upon the veracity of a witness, such as by evidence that the witness has conspired with another to falsely accuse the defendant, or where it is attempted to be shown that the witness is testifying under corrupt motives, or is fabricating testimony, it is proper to permit testimony that the witness has a good reputation for truth and veracity. * * *

No reversible error appearing, the judgment is affirmed.

NOTES AND QUESTIONS

1. *Explaining or denying bias.* In accord with the principal case, facts alleged to have given rise to bias or interest may generally be denied or explained. 1 McCormick, Evidence § 47 (7th ed. 2013); 4 Wigmore, Evidence § 1119 (Chadbourn rev. 1970).

2. *Truthful character.* Should charges of bias or interest invariably authorize rebuttal in the form of evidence of good reputation for truth and veracity? What if the bias is alleged to arise from a familial relationship with a party? Lassiter v. State, 47 So.2d 230 (Ala.Ct.App.1950). See United States v. Medical Therapy Sciences, Inc., 583 F.2d 36 (2d Cir.1978), for discussion of when evidence of bias is an attack on truthful character. See also Renda v. King, 347 F.3d 550, 554 (3d Cir.2003) ("The reason that evidence of bias does not open the door for evidence of good character for truthfulness is because evidence of bias only relates to a motive to lie in the particular case, not a general predisposition to lie.").

UNITED STATES V. PLANTE
First Circuit, 1973.
472 F.2d 829.

ALDRICH, SENIOR JUDGE.

[The defendants were convicted of bank robbery.]

* * *

Plante next complains of the cross-examination of his witness Kedian. Kedian admitted a conviction for mail fraud on direct examination. On cross-examination, over objection, the government was permitted to inquire as to the details of the offense.[88] Certain formalized rules apply to impeachment of a witness. * * * [W]hile a conviction may be shown, it is generally not permissible to rehabilitate a witness by having him deny his guilt. The conventional reasons given for this are that the question is collateral, * * * and the opponent of the witness should not have to be prepared to try the criminal case. * * * *Contra*: United States v. Boyer, 1945, 80 U.S. App.D.C. 202, 150 F.2d 595. The frequent statement that the conviction is "conclusive," * * * merely states the rule, not the reason.

Within the limits of not disputing the offense, occasionally the opponent of the witness, and occasionally the proponent, wish to go into the details in order to enhance, or diminish the effect of the conviction. There is a split of authority as to whether the proponent may do so. Dryden v. United States, 5 Cir., 1956, 237 F.2d 517 (proponent may give brief explanatory or mitigating statement); United States v. Crisafi, 2 Cir., 1962, 304 F.2d 803 (proponent may explain, in court's discretion); Lamoureux v. New York, N. H. & H. RR., 1897, 169 Mass. 338, 47 N.E. 1009 (proponent may not); Rogers v. Baltimore & Ohio RR. Co., 6 Cir., 1963, 325 F.2d 134, 137 (proponent may not). The *Lamoureux* court reasoned that the opponent of the witness would normally not be in a position to contradict the explanation. We find this persuasive, although we note that the same reasoning would not apply to prevent the opponent of a witness asking the witness for the details. However, such decisions as there are appear to be uniform that the opponent of the witness may not do this. * * * We believe that neither party should be able to develop the details. To permit the opponent to do so tends unduly to prejudice the witness, * * * and in all cases it leads to a collateral issue, with frequently one party or the other being at a disadvantage.

In the present case we find no prejudice. In the first place, the witness was only a witness, and not the defendant. Secondly, the details of the witness' particular offense * * * seem very low on the scale of what a jury would normally consider mail fraud to constitute, and hence no threat to the evaluation of the witness' testimony. * * *

---

[88] The witness was not very specific, but apparently he had purchased, through the mail, a book of checks bearing the printed name of a fictitious person.

NOTES AND QUESTIONS

1. *Trial court discretion.* While some decisions support the admissibility of evidence in extenuation of a witness' prior conviction, exercise of trial court discretion to exclude is rarely held reversible error. See United States v. Crisafi, 304 F.2d 803, 804 (2d Cir.1962) ("No case has been called to our attention, and we have discovered none, in which a federal court has ever reversed a conviction against a defendant witness because he was not permitted to explain his [prior] conviction.").

2. *Double-edged sword?* Are there dangers in such an explanation? See United States v. Swanson, 9 F.3d 1354, 1357 (8th Cir.1993) ("Although we acknowledge the general rule of impropriety of inquiry by the prosecutor into specific details surrounding prior convictions, [a] different situation is presented when an accused, on direct examination, attempts to explain away the effect of the conviction or to minimize his guilt. In such cases, the defendant may be cross-examined on any facts which are relevant to the direct examination.").

3. *Truthful character.* Under Federal Rule 608(a)(2), evidence of truthful character is admissible "after the character of the witness for truthfulness has been attacked by opinion or reputation evidence or otherwise." Thus, evidence of good reputation for truthfulness is generally held admissible to rehabilitate a witness impeached by the showing of a prior conviction. 1 McCormick, Evidence § 47 (7th ed. 2013). See also United States v. Thomas, 768 F.2d 611, 618 (5th Cir.1985) ("Vigorous cross-examination and/or the fact that a witness is contradicted by other evidence in the case does not constitute such an attack.").

BRADFORD V. STATE
Court of Appeals of Alabama, 1956.
90 So.2d 96.

BONE, JUDGE. This appellant's jury trial on an indictment charging murder in the first degree resulted in his conviction of manslaughter in the first degree and a sentence of imprisonment in the state penitentiary for a term of ten years.

* * *

There were four witnesses who testified that they were eyewitnesses to the incidents and circumstances surrounding the actual shooting made the basis of the charges embodied in the indictment against the appellant. One was the wife of the deceased, another a friend and employee of the deceased, and the third was a witness called by the State.

One David Earl Trammell, the fourth witness, was the only one of the four testifying on behalf of the appellant. There was direct conflict between the testimony of Trammell on direct examination and the testimony of the other three witnesses. The testimony of Trammell on direct examination, if believed by the jury, corroborated the testimony of the appellant with respect to the evidence surrounding and leading up to the shooting and made out a case of self-defense. During cross-examination Trammell was asked twice if he did not tell Mr. Troy Tate that he was not at the scene of the homicide, and in both instances the witness answered in the affirmative.

On redirect examination of Trammell the following transpired:

"Q. (By Mr. Beddow): When Mr. Tate came to your brother's home was he at home? A. Yes, sir.

"Q. What did he have on? A. A gun.

"Q. Did you know he was an officer of the law? A. Yes, sir.

"Q. Had you heard that Jack Tate was his nephew? A. Yes, sir.

"Q. Now, were you afraid when Troy came there?

"Mr. Deason: Wait a minute. We object to that.

"The Court: Yes, sustain the objection.

"Mr. Beddow: We except.

"Q. I will ask you this question: Why did you tell him that you were not there?

"Mr. Deason: Don't answer that. We object to that, if the court please.

"The Court: Sustain the objection.

"Mr. Beddow: We except. Judge, I will call your attention to the case of Williams v. The State of Alabama, if this boy told Tate he wasn't there and didn't see anything, I think we have got a right to show the circumstances, that he was afraid, Troy Tate was armed, he knew this boy was kin to him, he knew he was his uncle, and we offer to show he was afraid.

"Mr. Deason: We object to that, if the court please.

"The Court: I have already ruled.

"Mr. Beddow: We except.

"Mr. Deason: Wait a minute, Roderick.

"The Court: Don't consider any of it, gentlemen.

"Mr. Deason: All right.

"The Court: Don't consider that for any purpose whatsoever."

Appellant's attorneys contend that: "Where, upon cross examination of the witness, he admitted having made statements which are contradictory to his testimony, he may on re-direct examination show what his motive or reason was for having made the statements even though his testimony is of an uncommunicated mental state."

Dean Wigmore states the rule in the following words: "The impeached witness *may always* endeavor to explain away the effect of the supposed inconsistency by relating whatever circumstances would naturally remove it." (Emphasis supplied.) 3 Wigmore on Evidence 1044, p. 737 (3rd ed. 1940).

* * *

One hundred and three years ago Chief Justice Chilton said: "It is a well established rule of law, that where a witness has been cross examined respecting his former statements with a view of impairing his credit, the counsel who called him has the right to reexamine him, so as to afford him an opportunity of explaining such statements, and it is also said by the same authority that he may be asked what induced him to give to the person or persons to whom he made the communication the account which he has stated in the cross examination." Campbell v. State, 23 Ala. 44, 76.

The principle involved, testimonial rehabilitation, is not only the law of Alabama, but it is elementary hornbook law as well. A Student's Textbook of the Law of Evidence, Wigmore, Sec. 175 (1935 Ed.).

* * *

Seneca once said: "He who decides a case without hearing the other side, though he decide justly, cannot be considered just." He might have added that where one side only is heard it is highly unlikely that the case will be decided justly. In the instant case the reason for the rule is well illustrated. The denial of the right to rehabilitate the witness could well have been the reason for the adverse verdict.

Ever mindful of Canon 5 of the Professional Ethics of the American Bar Association, which reads in part, "The primary duty of a lawyer engaged in public prosecution is not to convict, but to see that justice is done", and taking into consideration both the elementary principle involved and the expense involved in appealing a case, we are frankly shocked that error was not confessed by the prosecuting officers in this cause.

For the error of the court below in sustaining the objection of the State to the appellant's attorney's questions on redirect examination, the judgment is reversed and the cause remanded.

Reversed and remanded.

HARWOOD, P.J., and PRICE, J., concur in the conclusion.

NOTE

Truthful character. Although the witness may deny or explain the inconsistency, evidence of truthful character is generally not admissible to rehabilitate the witness. See United States v. Drury, 396 F.3d 1303, 1316 (11th Cir.2005) ("[T]he prosecution's questioning the veracity of the accused's testimony and calling attention to inconsistencies therein does not constitute an attack on the accused's reputation for truthfulness permitting rehabilitative testimony."); Renda v. King, 347 F.3d 550, 554 (3d Cir.2003) ("[P]rior inconsistent statements do not open the door for evidence of good character for truthfulness because there can be a number of reasons for the error, such as defects in knowledge or memory, a bias or interest to lie in this particular instance, or a general character trait for untruthfulness.").

NOTE ON PRIOR CONSISTENT STATEMENTS

When the credibility of a witness has been attacked, may credibility be buttressed through the introduction of prior statements consistent with his or her trial testimony? The great weight of state authority severely limits the use of such statements. Usually admissibility is limited to statements offered to rebut an express or implied charge of recent fabrication or improper motive, or to statements made relatively near the time of an alleged inconsistent statement that the witness has denied making. Certainly, the relevancy of consistent statements not offered for such purposes is questionable. See 4 Wigmore, Evidence § 1126 (Chadbourn rev. 1972); 1 McCormick, Evidence § 47 (7th ed. 2013). A few states broadly admit consistent statements. For a discussion of the wide latitude in one such state, see 1 Brandis & Broun, North Carolina Evidence §§ 162–65 (7th ed. 2011).

Most of the current questions involving prior consistent statements arise as a result of Rule 801(d)(1)(B) and identical state rules which provide that a statement is not hearsay if the declarant testifies at the trial and the statement is consistent with the declarant's testimony and is offered to rebut an express or implied charge against the declarant of recent fabrication or improper influence or motive. In essence, Rule 801(d)(1)(B) makes these consistent statements substantive evidence, rather than evidence simply affecting the credibility of the witness. What is the significance of that distinction? What is the status of consistent statements not falling within Rule 801(d)(1)(B)? Such issues are best developed in connection with a discussion of Rule 801. See Chapter 13, infra.

CHAPTER 13[1]

FOUNDATIONS OF THE HEARSAY RULE AND CONFRONTATION

■ ■ ■

A. DEFINITION AND RATIONALE: STATEMENTS FOR THE TRUTH OF THE MATTER ASSERTED

———

Federal Rule 801(a)–(c)

———

MOORE v. UNITED STATES

Supreme Court of the United States, 1976.
429 U.S. 20.

PER CURIAM.

John David Moore, Jr., was convicted in a bench trial of possession of heroin with intent to distribute it, in violation of 21 U.S.C. § 841(a)(1). * * *

In early January 1975, police officers received a tip from an informant that Moore and others were in possession of heroin at "Moore's apartment." The police obtained a search warrant and entered the apartment, where they found Moore lying face down near a coffee table in the living room. Also present in the apartment was a woman who was sitting on a couch in the same room. Bags containing heroin were found both on top of and beneath the coffee table, and they were seized along with various narcotics paraphernalia.

At a consolidated hearing on Moore's motion to suppress evidence and on the merits, the prosecution adduced no admissible evidence showing that Moore was in possession of the heroin in the apartment in

---

[1]   In the cases and materials throughout the chapter, some footnotes have been omitted and others have been renumbered. [Ed.]

which he and the woman were found other than his proximity to the narcotics at the time the warrant was executed. Indeed, one police officer testified that he did not find "any indications of ownership of the apartment." In his closing argument on the merits, however, the prosecutor placed substantial emphasis on the out-of-court declaration of the unidentified informant:

> "[A] confidential informant came to Detective Uribe and said, 'I have information or I have—through personal observation, know[ledge] that John David Moore resides at a certain apartment here in El Paso, Texas, and he is in possession of a certain amount of heroin.'"

In adjudging Moore guilty, the trial court found that he had been in close proximity to the seized heroin, that he was the tenant of the apartment in question, and that he had, therefore, been in possession of the contraband. In making these findings, the court *expressly* relied on the hearsay declaration of the informant * * *.

There can be no doubt that the informant's out-of-court declaration that the apartment in question was "Moore's apartment," either as related in the search warrant affidavit or as reiterated in live testimony by the police officers, was hearsay and thus inadmissible in evidence on the issue of Moore's guilt. Introduction of this testimony deprived Moore of the opportunity to cross-examine the informant as to exactly what he meant by "Moore's apartment," and what factual basis, if any, there was for believing that Moore was a tenant or regular resident there. Moore was similarly deprived of the chance to show that the witness' recollection was erroneous or that he was not credible. The informant's declaration falls within no exception to the hearsay rule recognized in the Federal Rules of Evidence, and reliance on this hearsay statement in determining petitioner's guilt or innocence was error.

* * *

The petition for a writ of certiorari is granted, the judgment of the Court of Appeals is vacated, and the case is remanded to that court so it may determine whether the wrongful admission of the hearsay evidence was harmless error.

It is so ordered.

TRIBE, TRIANGULATING HEARSAY[2]

87 Harv.L.Rev. 957, 958–59 (1974).

The Testimonial Triangle

The basic hearsay problem is that of forging a reliable chain of inferences, from an act or utterance of a person not subject to contemporaneous in-court cross-examination about that act or utterance, to an event that the act or utterance is supposed to reflect. Typically, the first link in the required chain of inferences is the link from the act or utterance to the belief it is thought to express or indicate. It is helpful to think of this link as involving a "trip" into the head of the person responsible for the act or utterance (the declarant) to see what he or she was really thinking when the act occurred. The second link is the one from the declarant's assumed belief to a conclusion about some external event that is supposed to have triggered the belief, or that is linked to the belief in some other way. This link involves a trip out of the head of the declarant, in order to match the declarant's assumed belief with the external reality sought to be demonstrated.

The trier must obviously employ such a chain of inferences whenever a witness testifies in court. But the process has long been regarded as particularly suspect when the act or utterance is not one made in court, under oath, by a person whose demeanor at the time is witnessed by the trier, and under circumstances permitting immediate cross-examination by counsel in order to probe possible inaccuracies in the inferential chain. These inaccuracies are usually attributed to the four testimonial infirmities of ambiguity, insincerity, faulty perception, and erroneous memory. In the absence of special reasons, the perceived untrustworthiness of such an out-of-court act or utterance has led the Anglo–Saxon legal system to exclude it as hearsay despite its potentially probative value.

There exists a rather simple way of schematizing all of this in terms of an elementary geometric construct that serves to structure its several related elements. The construct might be called the Testimonial Triangle. By making graphic the path of inferences, and by functionally grouping the problems encountered along the path, the triangle makes it easier both to identify when a hearsay problem exists and to structure consideration of the appropriateness of exceptions to the rule that bars hearsay inferences.

The diagram is as follows:

---

[2] Copyright © 1974 by the Harvard Law Review Association. Reprinted by permission of the Association and the author. [Ed.]

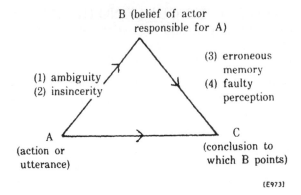

[E973]

If we use the diagram to trace the inferential path the trier must follow, we begin at the lower left vertex of the triangle (A), which represents the declarant's (X's) act or assertion. The path first takes us to the upper vertex (B), representing X's belief in what his or her act or assertion suggests, and then takes us to the lower right vertex (C), representing the external reality suggested by X's belief. When "A" is used to prove "C" along the path through "B," a traditional hearsay problem exists and the use of the act or assertion as evidence is disallowed upon proper objection in the absence of some special reason to permit it.

It is of course a simple matter to locate the four testimonial infirmities on the triangle to show where and how they might impede the process of inference. To go from "A" to "B," the declarant's belief, one must remove the obstacles of (1) ambiguity and (2) insincerity. To go from "B" to "C," the external fact, one must further remove the obstacles of (3) erroneous memory and (4) faulty perception.

NOTES AND QUESTIONS

1. *Oral and written statements.* As *Moore* demonstrates, hearsay may be either oral (testimony of police officers) or written (affidavit). Indeed, it may be presented in additional form, such as a tape recording or the audio component of a videotape.

2. *Hearsay for probable cause.* In *Moore,* the out-of-court declarations of the unidentified informant were admitted on both the issue of probable cause to search and the issue of Moore's guilt of heroin possession. While inadmissible on the issue of guilt, no objection was raised to its use to establish probable cause, a limited purpose for which it is generally admissible. See, e.g., United States v. Wilkes, 451 F.2d 938 (2d Cir.1971) (probable cause for arrest), and United States v. Cruz, 478 F.2d 408 (5th Cir.1973) (grand jury indictment).

3. *Different diagrams.* Other evidence scholars have offered modifications to Professor Tribe's method of diagraming hearsay. See

Friedman, Route Analysis of Credibility and Hearsay, 96 Yale L.J. 667 (1987); Graham, "Stickperson Hearsay": A Simplified Approach to Understanding the Rule Against Hearsay, 1982 U.Ill.L.Rev. 887; Lempert et al., A Modern Approach to Evidence 533 (4d ed. 2011); 6 Graham, Handbook of Federal Evidence § 801.1, at 12–17 (7th ed. 2012).

4.   *Edification, not agreement.* By helping to identify the hearsay dangers present in a particular out-of-court statement, Professor Tribe's diagram is useful in analyzing whether the statement is hearsay, and if hearsay, whether it should nevertheless be admitted under an exception to the rule. However, use of the diagram does not insure agreement on the appropriate definition of hearsay.

Tribe, for instance, interprets the Federal Rule definition to exclude a statement from hearsay when it is "seemingly nonassertive," thereby apparently, at least, reducing the sincerity concern on the left leg of the triangle. Tribe, Triangulating Hearsay, at 972. He disagrees, however, with this result since only one of the four hearsay dangers is eliminated or substantially reduced. Id. Professor Graham agrees with Tribe's view of how hearsay should be defined but disagrees that the Federal Rule definition has the effect Tribe ascribes to it. Under his view, only when all four hearsay dangers are eliminated is a statement not hearsay under that definition. 6 Graham, Handbook of Federal Evidence § 801.1, at 15 & § 801.7 (7th ed. 2012). Professor Lempert and his coauthors, on the other hand, contend that a statement is properly classified as not hearsay even if it depends upon the belief of the declarant as long as its relevance does not require that belief accurately to reflect reality. In such a situation, the dangers located on the left leg of the triangle are unaffected, but those on the right leg are eliminated, which they contend properly renders it not hearsay. Lempert et al., A Modern Approach to Evidence 532–34 (7th ed. 2011).

SILVER V. NEW YORK CENT. R.R.

Supreme Judicial Court of Massachusetts, 1952.
105 N.E.2d 923.

WILKINS, JUSTICE.

On January 14, 1948, Frances Silver became a passenger, bound from Boston to Cincinnati, on a train operated by the defendant railroad. The following morning the Pullman car in which she had a berth was detached at Cleveland and stood for nearly four hours in the yard to await connection with the next train to Cincinnati. She was suffering from a circulatory ailment known as Raynaud's disease. The temperature in the car became too cold for her, and she experienced ill effects. Mrs. Silver * * * brought this action against the defendant railroad and the Pullman Company. * * * The judge found for the plaintiff against the railroad. * * * The exceptions of the railroad * * * are to the denial of certain of its requests for rulings and to the exclusion of evidence.

Certain basic facts are not in dispute. The plaintiff, who was 58 years of age, boarded the train at Boston, on January 14, 1948, at 4:50 p.m. She occupied a lower berth in the rear car, which was the only through car to Cincinnati. The train was scheduled to arrive in Cleveland at 6:20 a.m. the following day, but did not do so until 8:40 a.m., too late for the intended connection for Cincinnati. This necessitated a lay-over in Cleveland until the next train for Cincinnati, which left at 12:30 p.m. In Cleveland the weather bureau records show that the temperature at 5:35 a.m. was one degree below zero Fahrenheit and 26 degrees above zero at 9 p.m. The plaintiff reached Cincinnati without further event, but because of her tendency to develop Raynaud's syndrome and the exposure to cold in Cleveland the condition of her hands required that she be hospitalized. * * *

Findings as to the plaintiff's experience at Cleveland could have been based upon statements she had made before suit was brought. She woke up about 9 a.m. because she was cold. She rang for the porter but no one came. She was alone in the car, which was standing in the yard and not at a platform. The station was inaccessible. She went to the washroom and got dressed. She "had to bundle up with her coat and furs," and put on a pair of woolen gloves. She rang twice more. Still no one came. She thought that the temperature was below freezing. She was extremely cold. She went back into her berth. The car remained in the same condition until connected with the Cincinnati train after 12 [noon]. At that time the temperature outside was 10 to 15 degrees, and the car had been "without any heat whatsoever" for about three hours with that temperature outside. * * *

We * * * turn to questions of evidence that may arise again. * * * The porter in the plaintiff's car was rightly allowed to testify as to the temperature conditions in that car. Leopold v. Van Kirk, 29 Wis. 548, 553–554. He was giving at first hand his experience with the same conditions which confronted the plaintiff. * * * But he was not permitted to give evidence that eleven other passengers in that car made no complaint to him as to the temperature while at Cleveland. This is a somewhat different proposition, as it was sought to draw from the silence of those passengers a deduction that the car was not too cold, otherwise they would have spoken. In certain courts evidence of absence of complaints by customers has been excluded on the issue of defective quality of goods sold, and the hearsay rule has been relied upon or referred to. * * * In Menard v. Cashman, 94 N.H. 428, 433–434, 55 A.2d 156, which was an action of tort arising out of a fall on a defective stairway in a business block, it was held proper to exclude testimony of a tenant that none of her customers had ever complained of any defects, the court saying that the testimony had the characteristics of hearsay, and that if it was not hearsay, it was only evidence of inconclusive silence, which might be excluded in the discretion of the trial judge.

Evidence as to absence of complaints from customers other than the plaintiff has been admitted in four cases, all relating to breach of warranty in the sale of food, in this Commonwealth. In three of them the testimony was apparently received without objection. Gracey v. Waldorf System, Inc., 251 Mass. 76, 78, 146 N.E. 232; Monahan v. Economy Grocery Stores Corp., 282 Mass. 548, 550, 185 N.E. 34; Schuler v. Union News Co., 295 Mass. 350, 352, 4 N.E.2d 465. In Landfield v. Albiani Lunch Co., 268 Mass. 528, 168 N.E. 160, the plaintiff alleged that he had been made ill by eating beans purchased at the defendant's restaurant. Subject to his exception, evidence was admitted that on that day and on the day preceding no complaint as to the beans was made by any other customer. In upholding the ruling on evidence, it was said, 268 Mass. at page 530, 168 N.E. at page 160: "The fact that others than the plaintiff ate of the food complained of without ill effects is competent evidence that it was not unwholesome. * * * There is a reasonable inference based on common experience that one who ate and suffered as he believed in consequence would make complaint. There is a further reasonable inference, based on logic, that if no one complained no one suffered. Obviously, the latter conclusion is not convincing that the food was wholesome, unless one is satisfied that both plaintiff and others ate of it. Evidence of no complaint is too remote and should not be admitted unless, in addition to the fact that no complaints were made, there is evidence of circumstances indicating that others similarly situated ate and had opportunity for complaining."

It has often been said that where collateral issues may be opened, much must rest in the discretion of the trial judge. * * * In the case at bar, should the circumstances of the plaintiff and of the other passengers as to exposure to the cold be shown to be substantially the same, the negative evidence that none of the others spoke of it to the porter might properly be admitted. The evidence would not be equivocal, and would then be offered on the basis of a common condition which all in the car encountered. The porter's duties should be shown to include the receipt of that sort of complaints from those passengers. It should appear that he was present and available to be spoken to, and that it was not likely that complaints were made by those passengers to other employees of the railroad or the sleeping car company. This would not seem to be a situation where one might prefer to remain silent rather than to make any statement. Indeed, if the car was too cold, ordinary prudence might seem to require that one speak out. There would be no ambiguity of inference. There would be at least as strong a case for admissibility as in the food cases, and a far stronger one than those relating to the sale of allegedly defective goods in which little may be known of the terms of sale to the noncomplaining buyers. Unlike the unknown users of a stairway in a business block, the uniform result of silence in the cases of a large number of passengers, here apparently eleven, would not be inconclusive. See Falknor, Silence as Hearsay, 89 U. of Pa.L.Rev. 192.

Exceptions sustained.

NOTES AND QUESTIONS

1.   *"Assertion."* Under the Rule 801, words and conduct are not defined as hearsay unless they are intended as assertions. The Advisory Committee Note places the burden on the party contending that an intention to assert is present: "The rule is so worded as to place the burden upon the party claiming that the intention existed; ambiguous and doubtful cases will be resolved against him and in favor of admissibility." The need for proof will be most obvious for non-verbal conduct.

2.   *Fainting rather than asserting.* People v. Clark, 86 Cal.Rptr. 106 (Cal.Ct.App.1970), provides a vivid example of nonassertive conduct. There a woman's partially decomposed body was discovered in an orchard. Witnesses reported that several days earlier they had been approached by a man seeking help in having his car pulled from a ditch near the orchard. They described the man, *inter alia,* as wearing a coat with a fur-lined collar. Clark was arrested at his home on the night the body was discovered. The court described the arrest as follows:

> The officers advised defendant of his constitutional rights and searched the premises and defendant's automobile. Traces of blood were found on defendant's shoes, and blood tracings were found in the interior of his automobile. Then, Sergeant Tabler asked defendant if he had a jacket with a fur-lined collar. Defendant turned to his wife and queried, "I don't have one like that, do I dear?" His wife fainted.

Id. at 108. Defendant's hearsay objection to Sergeant Tabler's description of Mrs. Clark's conduct was rejected by the court.

> The reaction of defendant's wife to this question was relevant to prove that defendant owned a coat with a fur-lined collar and that he had worn it on the night of the murder; and because it was nonassertive conduct it was not objectionable hearsay * * *.

Id. at 112.

3.   *Other hearsay dangers.* Assuming that dangers of insincerity are reduced when nonverbal, nonassertive conduct is involved, what other hearsay dangers remain and may even be exacerbated?

4.   *Conduct and silence as assertions.* Conduct can clearly be intended as an assertion. See, e.g., United States v. Aspinall, 389 F.3d 332, 342 (2d Cir.2004) (concluding that giving items to a police agent in response to the agent's inquiry was an assertive act); Clabon v. State, 111 S.W.3d 805, 808

(Tex.Ct.App.2003) (treating stabbing motion to the chest as asserting witness' knowledge about murders). When, if ever, will silence be assertive?

5. *Nonassertive nonverbal conduct and implied assertions.* Some commentators who question broad exclusion of assertive verbal conduct from the Federal Rules under the concept of implied assertions, discussed in the remainder of this section, view the exclusion of nonassertive nonverbal conduct more favorably. See, e.g., Rice, Should Unintended Implications of Speech Be Considered Nonhearsay? The Assertive/Nonassertive Distinction under Rule 801(a) of the Federal Rules of Evidence, 65 Temp.L.Rev. 529 (1992); Wellborn, The Definition of Hearsay in the Federal Rules of Evidence, 61 Tex.L.Rev. 49, 63–64 (1982); 6 Graham, Handbook of Federal Evidence § 801.3 (7th ed. 2012). When nonassertive nonverbal conduct is involved, the hearsay dangers of memory and perception are theoretically reduced. This is because the "declarant" has an enhanced incentive to verify the accuracy of perception and memory when translating his thoughts into action that is likely to carry more substantial consequences than typical speech alone. Lempert et al., A Modern Approach to Evidence 546 (4th ed. 2011). Moreover, by definition, if the conduct is truly not intended as an assertion, the hearsay danger of insincerity is greatly reduced.

PLAYER V. THOMPSON
Supreme Court of South Carolina, 1972.
193 S.E.2d 531.

[Bobby Thompson furnished an automobile to his then-estranged wife Geraldine, who entrusted the car to Nancy Carder. Plaintiff, a passenger in the car driven by Carder, was injured when the car skidded on wet pavement. She sued Carder and the Thompsons, and was nonsuited.]

PER CURIAM:

* * *

Inasmuch as the case must be tried again, we will rule upon evidentiary questions raised by plaintiff's exceptions. The complaint alleged:

(1) That Nancy Carder was heedless and reckless in driving the motor vehicle which she *"knew, or should have known, had worn and defective tires,* upon a wet and slippery street;" (emphasis added)

(2) That Geraldine Thompson was negligent, careless, reckless, wilful and wanton in providing an automobile to a driver when she *"knew or should have known, that the tires on said motor vehicle were worn, slippery, and in a defective condition."* (emphasis added)

Section 46–611, as amended, of the Code of Laws of South Carolina, requires that tires on motor vehicles "shall be in a safe operating condition." Section 46–644.1 makes it an offense to operate a vehicle not having a current inspection sticker issued by the State Highway

Department. The stickers are issued by authorized inspection stations throughout the State. Stickers are not issued for cars with defective or slick tires.

Subsequent to the collision and prior to suit, Carder gave a statement (to a representative of plaintiff's counsel) which was sworn to and recorded, concerning Geraldine Thompson and the car she was driving. In essence, she stated that she (Carder) went with Geraldine Thompson, two or three weeks before the collision, to a motor vehicle inspection station. She said that the inspector refused Mrs. Thompson a sticker because "she needed two tires." She stated she heard the inspector "tell her [Mrs. Thompson] and she [Mrs. Thompson] told me."—"The man told her that * * * she needed two more to pass inspection."

As a part of plaintiff's case in chief, counsel attempted to introduce the statement, or in the alternative call the court reporter who took the statement, to testify as to Carder's statement or read the questions and answers to the jury. Counsel conceded that "no portion of the statement is relevant as to the Thompsons." He stated: "I therefore in my proffer of proof have eliminated all references to the Thompsons and the portions that I now read includes only those words that I would think would be appropriate as to Miss Carder."

The proffer was refused because Carder had no personal knowledge of the tires being slick; because the inspection station incident was too remote in point of time; and because it was "hearsay against Thompson" and "prejudicial to Thompson."

There was testimony by Charles Player tending to prove that the tires on the car were slick when examined after the collision. We do not agree that evidence concerning the tires being defective two or three weeks before the collision was too remote in point of time.

It often happens that a statement which is inadmissible for one purpose is admissible for other purposes. We have held and we think it is indispensable that when a statement is admissible against one defendant and not against others, that the trial judge must admit the statement against the defendant and instruct the jury to disregard it as to the other defendants. Eberhardt v. Forrester, 241 S.C. 399, 128 S.E.2d 687 (1962); 1 Wigmore on Evidence § 13 (3d ed. 1940). The trial judge was in error in excluding the admission because it was hearsay against the Thompsons and prejudicial to them.

The admission as it affects Carder should not have been excluded because Carder did not have personal knowledge that the tires were slick. The rule is that personal knowledge of the person making an admission is immaterial. 4 Wigmore on Evidence § 1053 (3d ed. 1940).

At the new trial, if the statement can be dissected so as to eliminate mention of the Thompsons, its admission in that form would be the best procedure; on the other hand, if it cannot be dissected, the judge should admit the statement and charge the jury that it must not be considered against the Thompsons.

After the trial judge declined to admit the statement in evidence, counsel for plaintiff called defendant Carder as a witness. He attempted to ask her about the inspection station incident in an effort to show that both she (Carder), and Mrs. Thompson had notice of the slick tires. Defense counsel's objection was sustained on the ground that it was hearsay.

In C. McCormick, Law of Evidence § 225 (1954) hearsay evidence is defined:

> "Hearsay evidence is testimony in court or written evidence, of a statement made out of court, such statement being offered as an assertion to show the truth of matters asserted therein, and thus resting for its value upon the credibility of the out-of-court asserter."

Our Court has recognized this sound and very basic proposition in Watson v. Wall, 239 S.C. 109, 121 S.E.2d 427 (1961). Also see 5 Wigmore on Evidence § 1361 (3d ed. 1940).

> "If, then, an utterance can be used as circumstantial evidence, i.e. without inferring from it as an assertion to the fact asserted, the Hearsay rule does not oppose any barrier, because it is not applicable." 6 Wigmore on Evidence § 1788 (3d ed. 1940).

It would not be improper in this case for the plaintiff to elicit testimony from Nancy Carder that a filling station attendant stated to both Mrs. Thompson and her that the automobile had bad tires. It would be receivable, not as a testimonial assertion by the attendant to prove the fact of slick tires, but as indicating that Nancy Carder and Mrs. Thompson obtained knowledge of the slick tires, the fact of slick tires being proved by other evidence.

Inasmuch as the testimony was not offered to prove the truth of the matter stated, but solely to prove notice, which is a state of mind, the hearsay rule does not apply. Whether one is negligent or heedless or reckless in providing a car with slick tires to another or in driving a car with slick tires, depends at least to some degree on one's knowledge of the condition of the tires. Carder's testimony should have been admitted as it affects both Geraldine Thompson's and Carder's notice of slick tires. * * *

Reversed and remanded.

NOTES AND QUESTIONS

1. *Change the hypothetical.* Consider in each of the following situations whether hearsay is involved.

(a) The inspector, being called as a witness, testifies:

(i) He examined the tires, and they were slick;

(ii) He told Ms. Carder and Ms. Thompson that the tires were slick.

(b) Ms. Carder's statement to the adjuster is offered. It states:

(i) The inspector told Ms. Thompson and her that the tires were slick;

(ii) Ms. Thompson told her that the inspector said the tires were slick.

(c) Ms. Carder, being called as a witness, testifies:

(i) The inspector told them that the tires were slick;

(ii) Ms. Thompson told her that the inspector said the tires were slick.

2. *Hearsay and nonhearsay together.* For other cases in which the extrajudicial statement is admissible for a nonhearsay purpose and also contains an "assertion," see Rinehimer v. Cemcolift, Inc., 292 F.3d 375, 383 (3d Cir.2002) (finding statement as to what company doctor told manager about condition not hearsay because it explained why plaintiff employee was not permitted to return to his job as a working foreman and wear a respirator); Emich Motors Corp. v. General Motors Corp., 181 F.2d 70 (7th Cir.1950), rev'd on other grounds, 340 U.S. 558 (1951) (complaining letters from customers offered to show that cancellation of dealer's franchise was not motivated by dealer's refusal to finance car sales through defendant's finance affiliate).

In what ways can the evidence in these cases be used improperly? Can misuse be prevented by an instruction to the jury?

3. *Statements made in the presence of a party.* In *Player,* the statements were admissible because they were made in the presence of a party to the litigation to provide notice. Occasionally in other circumstances, statements are admissible because they were made in the presence of a party, as when they are adopted by the failure of the party to protest. See infra Section B. There is, however, no general basis for the contention, remarkably entrenched in the folklore of the profession, that extrajudicial statements should be excluded if not made in the presence of the party against whom offered. See Adkins v. Brett, 193 P. 251, 252 (Cal.1920); People v. Carpenter, 190 N.E.2d 738, 741 (Ill.1963).

UNITED STATES V. GIBSON

United States Court of Appeals, Ninth Circuit, 1982.
690 F.2d 697.

REINHARDT, CIRCUIT JUDGE:

Wilford R. Gibson was found guilty of * * * mail fraud, wire fraud, and inducing people to travel in interstate commerce for purposes of fraud. * * *

Background and Proceedings

In 1973, defendant incorporated Gibson Marketing International, Inc. (GMI), named himself president and chairman of that entity, and retained its entire capital stock. From its Phoenix, Arizona headquarters, GMI began a business of selling franchises and franchise distributorship rights ("area distributorships") to fast food restaurants which it called either "Burgher Haus" or "Kelly's Basket."

GMI's selling procedure was as follows. The company placed advertisements in newspapers and certain circulars for single unit franchises. Prospective investors dialed the toll free number printed in the ads and received an invitation to come to the Phoenix headquarters for a "personal interview." At these "personal interviews," GMI salesmen, sometimes including Gibson, urged investors to purchase "area distributorships" rather than the less expensive, single unit franchises. GMI personnel also outlined the "Burgher Haus" and/or "Kelly's Basket" programs. They promised that GMI would provide certain business services including personnel training, local advertising, site location and approvals and discounted national material purchasing accounts. * * *

Unfortunately, GMI did not provide certain of the promised business services. For example, in the course of its "site approval" service, for which it charged some investors a $1,000 fee, GMI approved a piece of unimproved underwater swamp land submitted as a test by a wary New York investor. * * * In addition, the evidence showed that Gibson spent substantial amounts of GMI's money in various Las Vegas gambling spots, [and] there was evidence that Gibson instructed GMI personnel to convey false information to complaining investors.

The Hearsay Argument

Gibson contends that the district court erred in admitting the testimony of investors regarding statements made by GMI's employees/salesmen. * * *

The Federal Rules of Evidence define hearsay as: "[A] statement, other than one made by the declarant while testifying at the trial or hearing, offered in evidence to prove the truth of the matter asserted."

Fed.R.Evid. 801(c). The government argues that the disputed testimony was not "offered in evidence to prove the truth of the matter asserted."

In their testimony, the investors related their discussions with GMI personnel. One witness testified that Gibson's brother, a GMI employee, told her that there were over 80 "Burgher Haus" restaurants in operation. Another witness said a GMI employee told him that GMI would finance 80% of his building and equipment costs. Other witnesses related assurances from GMI salesmen and officials regarding, *inter alia,* GMI's financial assets, the allegedly low failure rate of the restaurants, and the projected financial return on a franchise investment.

The investors' testimony was offered to prove the *existence* of a scheme; the statements were not offered for their truthfulness. The purpose of the testimony was solely to establish the fact that the salesmen and employees had made the statements. That fact was relevant to support the government's allegation that a scheme existed.[3]

* * *

We hold that these statements were not hearsay * * *.

[Affirmed.]

NOTES AND QUESTIONS

1. *Threats.* With regard to the "verbal act" element of *Gibson,* consider also United States v. Jones, 663 F.2d 567, 568–69, 571 (5th Cir.1981), a prosecution for threatening the lives of a federal judge and prosecutor:

> On May 4, 1979, appellant Lloyd Jones stood before the United States District Court, Northern District of Georgia, for sentencing in connection with his conviction for murder committed at the Atlanta Federal Penitentiary. Judge William C. O'Kelley addressed Jones, who appeared with counsel, to determine whether Jones wished to be heard on matters bearing upon his sentence. Jones responded:
>
>> Yes, sir. I'd like to say that * * * I don't think you passed sentence on me, you know, like, I think, during the process of the trial that I was totally insane, you know, which I also think that you should have looked over into the matter when I told you that them people out there was threatening me and stuff, which you said you would but you never have. But now today you bring me down here to pass sentence on me. It's nothing really too much I could do about it. When you can't beat them you join them. *So, Judge O'Kelley, U.S. Attorney, Mr. Bostic, I*

---

[3] Ultimately of course, the truth or falsity of the statements was important to the outcome of the case. However, the fact that the statements were made was not used to prove the truth of the content of the statements. Instead, the government sought to show their falsity through independent evidence.

pass sentence on you, the sentence would be death, you and all your relatives. Now you can pass your sentence. It is death to you, you, and you, and all your relatives by gunshot wound. Now do as you please. I don't give a * * * if you throw the whole Empire State building at me, the whole State of Georgia. * * *

The statement at issue is paradigmatic nonhearsay; it was offered because it contains threats made against officers of the federal courts, i.e., it contains the operative words of this criminal action. It was not "offered in evidence to prove the truth of the matter asserted," [Fed.R.Evid. 801(c)(2)].

2. *"Performative" utterances.* During trial, a marshal overheard the defendant state, "it's going to be $10,000," to a co-participant in crime who had earlier entered a guilty plea and testified that the defendant was innocent. Judge Posner accepted the government's position that the statement was a "verbal act," providing the following explanation:

The [remaining issue] * * * is the admissibility of the marshal's testimony that Dodd had told Montana that the price of Dodd's favorable testimony was $10,000. The government argues that it was admissible as a "verbal act" * * *, thus echoing the linguist's distinction between performative and illocutionary utterances. The latter narrate, describe, or otherwise convey information, and so are judged by their truth value (information is useful only if true—indeed is information only if it is true); the former—illustrated by a promise, offer, or demand—commit the speaker to a course of action. Performative utterances are not within the scope of the hearsay rule, because they do not make any truth claims. Had the marshal overheard Dodd tell Montana, "your father has promised me $10,000," Dodd's overheard statement would have been hearsay, because its value as evidence would have depended on its being truthful, that is, on such a promise having actually been made. But what in fact was overheard was merely a demand—in effect, "give me $10,000"—and so the only issue of credibility was whether the marshal was reporting the demand correctly, and his testimony was not hearsay.

United States v. Montana, 199 F.3d 947, 950 (7th Cir.1999).

3. *False statements.* Some constructions of the hearsay definition might mean that a statement that is false cannot be hearsay. Although this position may be too strong, when false statements are admitted, it is typically because they are introduced for another purpose than proving the matter asserted, which supports nonhearsay treatment even if not per se determinative of the issue. A false statement that is being admitted as a "verbal act" because it is false (e.g., a fraudulent sales offer in a fraud case or the false statement made under oath in a perjury prosecution) is nonhearsay based on its falsity. However, if the statement depends for its significance upon an inference about the reasons for the declarant's insincerity, as when

false alibi testimony is given by the defendant's spouse, nonhearsay treatment is not as clear. Compare Anderson v. United States, 417 U.S. 211 (1974), and United States v. Hackett, 638 F.2d 1179 (9th Cir.1980), with Park, McCormick on Evidence and the Concept of Hearsay: A Critical Analysis Followed by Suggestions to Law Teachers, 65 Minn.L.Rev. 423, 426 (1981), and Graham, "Stickperson Hearsay": A Simplified Approach to Understanding the Rule Against Hearsay, 1982 U.Ill.L.Rev. 887, 898–99. In this latter situation, all hearsay dangers are not eliminated and the evaluation involved is similar to that of "implied assertions," discussed later in this Section.

Professor Park has usefully categorized hearsay definitions as either assertion oriented, which "focuses on whether an out-of-court assertion will be used to prove the truth of what it asserts" or declarant oriented, which "focuses on whether the use of the utterance will require reliance on the credibility of the out-of-court declarant." 65 Minn.L.Rev. at 424. Under which of these categories would false statements be more broadly excluded from the hearsay rule?

4. *Major categories of nonhearsay.* Statements that are not hearsay because they are not offered for the truth of the matter asserted may be grouped under several general categories: (1) Some statements are relevant because of their effect on the hearer or reader. Common examples are statements providing notice or motive, or those showing reasonableness or good faith or the reason for taking action. See, e.g., United States v. Workman, 622 F.3d 969, 974–75 (8th Cir.2010) (ruling that rumors attributed to party were not hearsay since they provided motive for retaliation). (2) Verbal acts are statements that have operative legal effect. Examples include words of contract, slander, threats to do bodily harm, and the granting of authority to act as an agent. See 2 McCormick, Evidence § 249 (7th ed. 2013). Closely related to verbal acts are verbal parts of acts. These are words that accompany and characterize otherwise ambiguous nonverbal conduct, taking on with the act operative legal significance. The most common example is the words that accompany the handing over of money and characterize it as a loan, a bribe, a gift, etc. See id.; 6 Graham, Handbook of Federal Evidence § 801.5, at 64 (7th ed. 2012); 5 Weinstein's Federal Evidence § 801.11[4] (2d ed. 2013); State v. Harris, 789 N.W.2d 303, 309 (S.D.2010) (recorded statements by participant in a drug sale during the transaction). (3) A prior consistent or inconsistent statement of a witness likewise is not hearsay when offered for its impact upon the witness' credibility by showing that the witness previously made such a statement. See, e.g., United States v. Hudson, 970 F.2d 948, 956–57 (1st Cir.1992) (inconsistent statement not hearsay when used to affect credibility). Critically, the theory of impeachment does not depend on the premise that the testimony is false and the prior statement true but rather that the fact of an inconsistency ("blowing hot and cold") raises doubts as to the credibility of both statements. See 1 McCormick, Evidence § 34 (7th ed. 2013).

5.   *Common misuse of nonhearsay argument.* One area of frequent misuse of the argument that a statement is not used for the truth occurs when arresting or investigating officers recite what they were told about the crime as a reason why they came to the scene of a crime or why they conducted a specific type of investigation. The argument has obvious validity if properly applied. For example, officers should not be put in the misleading position of appearing to have happened upon the scene and therefore should be entitled to provide some explanation for their presence and conduct. They should not, however, be allowed to relate historical aspects of the case. The need for this evidence is slight, and the likelihood of misuse great, see Rule 403, particularly since a statement that an officer acted "upon information received," or words to that effect, would suffice. See, e.g., United States v. Silva, 380 F.3d 1018, 1019–20 (7th Cir.2004) (rejecting government argument that statements incriminating the defendant could be admitted as nonhearsay to show why the police investigated the defendant). Another ploy that should be ineffective is to offer an indirect version of hearsay statements. If the purpose or effect of testimony is to prove the truth of facts indirectly stated, an objection to the hearsay nature of the underlying facts cannot be eliminated by eliciting the content in summary form as "information received" or the result of investigation. See, e.g., United States v. Baker, 432 F.3d 1189, 1209 (11th Cir.2005) (investigator's statement about what he learned upon arrival at the scene of a shooting was inadmissible hearsay).

LOETSCH v. NEW YORK CITY OMNIBUS CORP.

Court of Appeals of New York, 1943.
52 N.E.2d 448.

THACHER, JUDGE.

Appeal by defendant from the nonunanimous judgment of the Appellate Division affirming a judgment of the Supreme Court, New York County, in favor of plaintiff in a wrongful death action.

Upon the trial of this action counsel for defendants-appellants offered in evidence the will of the decedent dated December 2, 1940, for the purpose of proving the statement of the decedent with respect to her relations with her husband. The statement was as follows: "Whereas I have been a faithful, dutiful, and loving wife to my husband, Dean Yankovich, and whereas he reciprocated my tender affections for him with acts of cruelty and indifference, and whereas he has failed to support and maintain me in that station of life which would have been possible and proper for him, I hereby limit my bequest to him to one dollar."

On plaintiffs' objection the will was excluded from evidence, and the exception taken presents the only question for our consideration. The will, executed within four months prior to decedent's death, was relevant to an understanding of the relations which existed between the decedent and her husband. It is always proper to make proof of the relations of the decedent to the person for whose benefit the action is maintained, because such proof has a bearing upon the pecuniary loss suffered by the person entitled to the recovery, and this is true whether the beneficiary is the surviving husband or wife or one or more of the next of kin. * * *

The measure of loss is to be determined solely from the standpoint of the surviving spouse and is strictly limited to compensation for pecuniary loss. Decedent Estate Law, § 132, Consol.Laws, c. 13. Accordingly, the amount recoverable in any particular case must be very largely influenced by the nature of the relationship between the beneficiary and the deceased. When the deceased is one who was under no legal obligation to provide support for the beneficiary during life, his or her disposition voluntarily to do so is of essential importance to the jury in determining pecuniary loss. Evidence showing such a disposition or the lack of it should not be excluded.

Question remains as to the character of the proof offered, which was a declaration in writing of the decedent made within four months of her death. Such declarations are evidence of the decedent's state of mind and are probative of a disposition on the part of the declarant which has a very vital bearing upon the reasonable expectancy, or lack of it, of future assistance or support if life continues. This expectancy, disappointed by death, is the basis of recovery * * * and is the measure of pecuniary loss for which the jury must award fair and just compensation. No testimonial effect need be given to the declaration, but the fact that such a declaration was made by the decedent, whether true or false, is compelling evidence of her feelings toward, and relations to, her husband. As such it is not excluded under the hearsay rule but is admissible as a verbal act. * * *

The judgments should be reversed and a new trial granted, with costs to the appellant to abide the event.

NOTES AND QUESTIONS

1. *"Whether or not true, that wasn't nice to say."* What does the court mean when it says, "No testimonial effect need be given to the declaration"? See State v. Newell, 710 N.W.2d 6, 18 (Iowa 2006) (ruling that derogatory names were not hearsay because not used to prove that victim was what the defendant called her). Note that what is being proven is the declarant's feelings or state of mind rather than the truth of some external fact, which is a key to the validity of the nonhearsay argument.

2. *A transition category.* The category created in *Loetsch* of nonhearsay statements can be viewed as something of a transition between different forms of statements not offered for their truth. We earlier examined statements that are nonhearsay because they are not offered for their truth

in what might be considered the "strong sense"—e.g., verbal acts, statements that have impact on the hearer, and inconsistent statements offered to impeach. In the two following cases, we examine a "weaker sense" of the not-for-the-truth-of-the-matter-asserted argument, labeled "implied assertions." These statements, the argument goes, are nonhearsay because they are not admitted for the truth of what is specifically asserted, but instead to prove some other fact that may be inferred from the asserted fact.

WRIGHT V. DOE DEM. TATHAM

Exchequer Chamber, 1837.
7 Adolph. & E. 313, 112 Eng.Rep. 488.

[In an ejectment action, the plaintiff's lessor claimed as heir, and the defendant, an employee, claimed through the will of John Marsden. The case hinged upon the testamentary capacity of Marsden. In support of competency, the defendant offered several letters received by Marsden from persons who had died by the time of trial. The first letter was from a cousin, describing his voyage to America and conditions found there; the second from Rev. Marton, vicar, asking that Marsden have his attorney propose terms of agreement as to an undescribed matter in dispute between Marsden and the parish; the third was a letter of gratitude from Rev. Ellershaw upon resigning a curacy to which Marsden had appointed him. The letters were excluded. A verdict was returned for plaintiff's lessor. On appeal, the judgment was affirmed by the Exchequer Chamber on an equally divided vote. The House of Lords also affirmed. 5 Cl. & F. 670, 47 Rev.Rep. 136 (1838). The following extract by Baron Parke in the Exchequer Chamber is selected from the numerous opinions delivered in the two courts of review.]

PARKE, B. * * * It is argued that the letters would be admissible because they are evidence of the treatment of the testator as a competent person by individuals acquainted with his habits and personal character, not using the word treatment in a sense involving any conduct of the testator himself; that they are more than mere statements to a third person indicating an opinion of his competence by those persons; they are acts done towards the testator by them, which would not have been done if he had been incompetent, and from which, therefore a legitimate inference may, it is argued, be derived that he was so.

Each of the three letters, no doubt, indicates that in the opinion of the writer the testator was a rational person. He is spoken of in respectful terms in all. Mr. Ellershaw describes him as possessing hospitality and benevolent politeness; and Mr. Marton addresses him as competent to do business to the limited extent to which his letter calls upon him to act; and there is no question but that, if any one of these writers had been living, his evidence, founded on personal observation, that the testator possessed the qualities which justified the opinion expressed or implied in his letters, would be admissible on this issue. * * *

But the question is, whether the contents of these letters are evidence of the fact to be proved upon this issue,—that is, the actual existence of the qualities which the testator is, in those letters, by implication, stated to possess: and those letters may be considered in this respect to be on the same footing as if they had contained a direct and positive statement that he was competent. For this purpose they are mere hearsay evidence, statements of the writers, not on oath, of the truth of the matter in question with this addition, that they have acted upon the statements on the faith of their being true, by their sending the letters to the testator. That the so acting cannot give a sufficient sanction for the truth of the statement is perfectly plain; for it is clear that, if the same statements had been made by parol or in writing to a third person, that would have been insufficient; and this is conceded by the learned counsel for the plaintiff in error. Yet in both cases there has been an acting on the belief of the truth, by making the statement, or writing and sending a letter to a third person; and what difference can it possibly make that this is an acting of the same nature by writing and sending the letter to the testator? It is admitted, and most properly, that you have no right to use in evidence the fact of writing and sending a letter to a third person containing a statement of competence, on the ground that it affords an inference that such an act would not have been done unless the statement was true, or believed to be true, although such an inference no doubt would be raised in the conduct of the ordinary affairs of life, if the statement were made by a man of veracity. But it cannot be raised in a judicial inquiry; and, if such an argument were admissible, it would lead to the indiscriminate admission of hearsay evidence of all manner of facts.

Further, it is clear that an acting to a much greater extent and degree upon such statements to a third person would not make the statements admissible. For example, if a wager to a large amount had been made as to the matter in issue by two third persons, the payment of that wager, however large the sum, would not be admissible to prove the truth of the matter in issue. You would not have had any right to present it to the jury as raising an inference of the truth of the fact, on the ground that otherwise the bet would not have been paid. It is, after all, nothing but the mere statement of that fact, with strong evidence of the belief of it by the party making it. Could it make any difference that the wager was between the third person and one of the parties to the suit? Certainly not. The payment by other underwriters on the same policy to the plaintiff could not be given in evidence to prove that the subject insured had been lost. Yet there is an act done, a payment strongly attesting the truth of the statement, which it implies, that there had been a loss. To illustrate this point still further, let us suppose a third person had betted a wager with Mr. Marsden that he could not solve some mathematical problem, the solution of which required a high degree of capacity; would payment of that wager to Mr. Marsden's banker be admissible evidence that he possessed that capacity? The answer is certain; it would not. It would be evidence of the fact of competence given by a third party not upon oath.

Let us suppose the parties who wrote these letters to have stated the matter therein contained, that is, their knowledge of his personal qualities and capacity for business, on oath before a magistrate, or in some judicial proceeding to which the plaintiff and defendant were not parties. No one could contend that such statement would be admissible on this issue; and yet there would have been an act done on the faith of the statement being true, and a very solemn one, which would raise in the ordinary conduct of affairs a strong belief in the truth of the statement, if the writers were faith-worthy. The acting in this case is of much less importance, and certainly is not equal to the sanction of an extra-judicial oath.

Many other instances of a similar nature, by way of illustration, were suggested by the learned counsel for the defendant in error, which, on the most cursory consideration, any one would at once declare to be inadmissible in evidence. Others were supposed on the part of the plaintiff in error, which, at first sight, have the appearance of being mere facts, and therefore admissible, though on further consideration they are open to precisely the same objection. Of the first description are the supposed cases of a letter by a third person to any one demanding a debt, which may be said to be a treatment of him as a debtor, being offered as proof that the debt was really due; a note, congratulating him on his high state of bodily vigour, being proposed as evidence of his being in good health; both of which are manifestly at first sight objectionable. To the latter class belong the supposed conduct of the family or relations of a testator, taking the same precautions in his absence as if he were a lunatic; his election, in his absence, to some high and responsible office; the conduct of a physician who permitted a will to be executed by a sick testator; the conduct of a deceased captain on a question of seaworthiness, who, after examining every part of the vessel, embarked in it with his family; all these, when deliberately considered, are, with reference to the matter in issue in each case, mere instances of hearsay evidence, mere statements, not on oath, but implied in or vouched by the actual conduct of persons by whose acts the litigant parties are not to be bound.

The conclusion at which I have arrived is that proof of a particular fact, which is not of itself a matter in issue, but which is relevant only as implying a statement or opinion of a third person on the matter in issue, is inadmissible in all cases where such a statement or opinion not on oath would be of itself inadmissible; and, therefore, in this case the letters which are offered only to prove the competence of the testator, that is the truth of the implied statements therein contained, were properly rejected, as the mere statement or opinion of the writer would certainly have been inadmissible. * * *

NOTES AND QUESTIONS

1. *Dangers perhaps reduced, not eliminated.* Are the hearsay dangers realistically present in the *Tatham* situation? Are they unquestionably absent?

2. *Is Tatham good law?* How should the issues in *Tatham* be decided under the Federal Rules of Evidence? For an answer, see the next principal case, *United States v. Zenni*, and the notes following that case.

3. *Metaphors, indirect statements, and delicate analysis.* Assertive conduct under the Federal Rules is not hearsay if not offered in evidence to prove "the truth of the matter asserted." Clearly, however, more is covered by the hearsay definition than direct, literal assertions of the matter to be proved. For example, "it will stop raining in an hour," if offered to prove that it was raining at the time of the statement, is hearsay because the matter to be proved is a "necessary implication" of the statement made. Wellborn, The Definition of Hearsay in the Federal Rules of Evidence, 61 Tex.L.Rev. 49, 75 (1982). Similarly, metaphorical speech must be included: A statement that the "sky is on fire" would be hearsay to prove that the sun was setting. Id. at 78.

Moving beyond these easy and somewhat unusual examples, when is a statement that is assertive for one proposition not hearsay because it is offered to prove another proposition? One potential way of addressing this question is to use the declarant's intent, or some objective manifestation of it, to determine what the statement asserts. Commentators have attempted various formulations of an intent-based test. Professor Saltzburg argues that "a statement should be treated as hearsay whenever it is offered to prove the truth of an express or implied assertion, so long as the Trial Judge finds that the declarant intended to communicate that assertion when he made the statement." 4 Saltzburg, Martin & Capra, Federal Rules of Evidence Manual § 801.02[1][i], at 801–25 (10th ed. 2011). Professor Park suggests a somewhat similar, albeit differently focused, approach: "If helpfulness depends on the trier's belief that the declarant intended to assert a fact that supports the proponent's case, then the court should consider the statement hearsay * * *." Park, "I Didn't Tell Them Anything About You": Implied Assertions as Hearsay Under the Federal Rules of Evidence, 74 Minn.L.Rev. 783, 800 (1990). These analytic methods are consistent with a view that the Federal Rules' definition of hearsay at least partially overrules *Tatham*. See generally 2 McCormick, Evidence § 250 (7th ed. 2013) (examining likelihood of purposeful deception in implied assertion).

By contrast, Professor Graham attempts to reconcile the Federal Rules' definition of hearsay with the result in *Tatham* by interpreting differently and more broadly when a statement is offered to prove the truth of the matter asserted. He contends that, if the truth of the matter directly asserted must be assumed in order for the nonasserted inference to be drawn, then the statement is offered for the truth of the matter asserted and is therefore properly considered hearsay under Rule 801's definition. 6 Graham, Handbook of Federal Rules of Evidence § 801.7, at 160–64 (7th ed. 2012). See also Rice, Should Unintended Implications of Speech Be Considered Nonhearsay? The Assertive/Nonassertive Distinction under Rule 801(a) of the Federal Rules of Evidence, 65 Temp.L.Rev. 529, 538–39 (1992) (assertion/nonassertion distinction should apply only to conduct that the actor did not intend to communicate anything).

4.   *Sources on a lively debate.* The academic debate on the proper treatment of implied assertions has continued since the time of *Tatham.* In addition to the sources cited in the preceding note, see Callen, Hearsay and Informal Reasoning, 47 Vand.L.Rev. 43 (1994); Falknor, The "Hear–Say" Rule as a "See–Do" Rule: Evidence of Conduct, 33 Rocky Mt.L.Rev. 133 (1966); Finman, Implied Assertions as Hearsay: Some Criticisms of the Uniform Rules of Evidence, 14 Stan.L.Rev. 682 (1962); Kirgis, Meaning, Intention, and the Hearsay Rule, 43 Wm. & Mary L.Rev. 275 (2001); Maguire, The Hearsay System: Around and Through the Thicket, 14 Vand.L.Rev. 741 (1961).

UNITED STATES V. ZENNI
United States District Court, Eastern District of Kentucky, 1980.
492 F.Supp. 464.

BERTELSMAN, DISTRICT JUDGE.

This prosecution for illegal bookmaking activities presents a classic problem in the law of evidence, namely, whether implied assertions are hearsay. The problem was a controversial one at common law, the discussion of which has filled many pages in the treatises and learned journals. Although the answer to the problem is clear under the Federal Rules of Evidence, there has been little judicial treatment of the matter, and many members of the bar are unfamiliar with the marked departure from the common law the Federal Rules have effected on this issue.

Facts

The relevant facts are simply stated. While conducting a search of the premises of the defendant, Ruby Humphrey, pursuant to a lawful search warrant which authorized a search for evidence of bookmaking activity, government agents answered the telephone several times. The unknown callers stated directions for the placing of bets on various sporting events. The government proposes to introduce this evidence to show that the callers believed that the premises were used in betting operations. The existence of such belief tends to prove that they were so used. The defendants object on the ground of hearsay.

Common Law Background

At common law, the hearsay rule applied "only to evidence of out-of-court statements offered for the purpose of proving that the facts are as asserted in the statement."[4]

On the other hand, not all out-of-court expression is common law hearsay. For instance, an utterance offered to show the publication of a slander, or that a person was given notice of a fact, or orally entered into a contract, is not hearsay.

In the instant case, the utterances of the absent declarants are not offered for the truth of the words,[5] and the mere fact that the words were uttered has no relevance of itself.[6] Rather they are offered to show the declarants' belief in a fact sought to be proved. At common law this situation occupied a controversial no-man's land. It was argued on the one hand that the out-of-court utterance was not hearsay, because the evidence was not offered for any truth stated in it, but for the truth of some other proposition inferred from it. On the other hand, it was also argued that the reasons for excluding hearsay applied, in that the evidence was being offered to show declarant's belief in the implied proposition, and he was not available to be cross-examined. Thus, the latter argument was that there existed strong policy reasons for ruling that such utterances were hearsay.

* * *

The court in *Wright v. Tatham* [7 Adolph. & E. 313, 112 Eng.Rep. 488 (Exchequer Chamber 1837)] held that implied assertions[7] of this kind were hearsay. * * * This was the prevailing common law view, where the hearsay issue was recognized. But frequently, it was not recognized. * * *

The Federal Rules of Evidence

The common law rule that implied assertions were subject to hearsay treatment was criticized by respected commentators for several reasons. A leading work on the Federal Rules of Evidence, referring to the hotly

---

[4] McCormick on Evidence § 250 (2d Ed. 1972) [hereinafter McCormick].

[5] That is, the utterance, "Put $2 to win on Paul Revere in the third at Pimlico," is a direction and not an assertion of any kind, and therefore can be neither true nor false.

[6] Cf. United States v. McLennan, 563 F.2d 943 (9th Cir.1977), in a criminal case, the defense was advice of counsel. Statements made by counsel to the defendant were not hearsay, because it was relevant what the advice was. Of a similar nature would be a policeman's statement. "Go through the stop sign," if it were illegal to go through it unless directed by an officer. Other examples of expression admissible as non-hearsay, because they are verbal acts, relevant merely because they occurred, are "I agree" offered to show a contract was made; or "He took a bribe," offered to show a slander was published.

[7] The problem is the same whether the relevant assertion is implied from verbal expression, such as that of the betters in the instant case or the letter writers in Wright, or from conduct, as in the sea captain example. See F.R.Ev. 801(a); Falknor, The "Hear–Say" Rule as a "See–Do" Rule: Evidence of Conduct, 33 Rocky Mt.L.Rev. 133, 134 (1961) [hereinafter Falknor].

debated question whether an implied assertion stands on better ground with respect to the hearsay rule than an express assertion, states:

"By the time the federal rules were drafted, a number of eminent scholars and revisers had concluded that it does. Two principal arguments were usually expressed for removing implied assertions from the scope of the hearsay rule. First, when a person acts in a way consistent with a belief but without intending by his act to communicate that belief, one of the principal reasons for the hearsay rule—to exclude declarations whose veracity cannot be tested by cross-examination—does not apply, because the declarant's sincerity is not then involved. In the second place, the underlying belief is in some cases self-verifying:

'There is frequently a guarantee of the trustworthiness of the inference to be drawn * * * because the actor has based his actions on the correctness of his belief, i.e. his actions speak louder than words.' "[8]

In a frequently cited article the following analysis appears:

"But ought the hearsay rule be deemed applicable to evidence of conduct? As McCormick has observed, the problem 'has only once received any adequate discussion in any decided case,' i.e., in *Wright v. Tatham,* already referred to. And even in that case the court did not pursue its inquiry beyond the point of concluding that evidence of an 'implied' assertion must necessarily be excluded wherever evidence of an 'express' assertion would be inadmissible. But as has been pointed out more than once (although I find no *judicial* recognition of the difference), the 'implied' assertion is, from the hearsay standpoint, not nearly as vulnerable as an express assertion of the fact which the evidence is offered to establish.

"This is on the assumption that the conduct was 'nonassertive;' that the passers-by had their umbrellas up for the sake of keeping dry, not for the purpose of telling anyone it was raining; that the truck driver started up for the sake of resuming his journey, not for the purpose of telling anyone that the light had changed; that the vicar wrote the letter to the testator for the purpose of settling the dispute with the latter, rather than with any idea of expressing his opinion of the testator's sanity. And in the typical 'conduct as hearsay' case this assumption will be quite justifiable.

---

[8] Weinstein's Evidence ¶ 801(a)[01], at 801–55 [hereinafter Weinstein]. * * *

"On this assumption, it is clear that evidence of conduct must be taken as freed from at least one of the hearsay dangers, *i.e.,* mendacity. A man does not lie to himself. Put otherwise, if in doing what he does a man has no intention of asserting the existence or non-existence of a fact, it would appear that the trustworthiness of evidence of this conduct is the same whether he is an egregious liar or a paragon of veracity. Accordingly, the lack of opportunity for cross-examination in relation to his veracity or lack of it, would seem to be of no substantial importance. Accordingly, the usual judicial disposition to equate the 'implied' to the 'express' assertion is very questionable."[9]

The drafters of the Federal Rules agreed with the criticisms of the common law rule that implied assertions should be treated as hearsay and expressly abolished it.[10] They did this by providing that no oral or written expression was to be considered as hearsay, unless it was an "assertion" concerning the matter sought to be proved and that no nonverbal conduct should be considered as hearsay, unless it was intended to be an "assertion" concerning said matter.[11] The relevant provisions are:

Rule 801. "(a) Statement.—A *'statement'* is (1) an oral or written *assertion* or (2) nonverbal conduct of a person, if it is *intended by him as an assertion.* * * *

(c) Hearsay. 'Hearsay' is a *statement,* other than one made by the declarant while testifying at the trial or hearing, offered in evidence to prove the truth of the matter asserted." * * *

"Assertion" is not defined in the rules, but has the connotation of a forceful or positive declaration.[12]

The Advisory Committee note concerning this problem states:

"The definition of 'statement' assumes importance because the term is used in the definition of hearsay in subdivision (c). *The effect of the definition of 'statement' is to exclude from the*

---

[9] Falknor, supra at 136. The context makes clear that the author would apply the same analysis "where the conduct, although 'verbal,' is relevant, not as tending to prove the truth of what was said, but circumstantially, that is, as manifesting a belief in the existence of the fact the evidence is offered to prove." Id. at 134.

[10] See Weinstein, ¶ 801(a)[01] at 801–55—801–56 * * *.

[11] See the sea captain illustration discussed, supra. In an unpublished ruling this court recently held admissible as non-hearsay the fact that a U.S. mining inspector ate his lunch in an area in a coal mine now alleged to have been unsafe, and that other inspectors who observed operations prior to a disastrous explosion issued no citations, when it would have been their duty to do so, if there had been safety violations. These non-assertive acts would have been hearsay under the rule of Wright v. Tatham but are not hearsay under Rule 801 of the Federal Rules of Evidence, because the inspectors did not intend to make assertions under the circumstances. Boggs v. Blue Diamond Coal Company (E.D.Ky. No. 77–69, Pikeville Division).

[12] Random House Dictionary of the English Language (1969 Ed.).

operation of the hearsay rule all evidence of conduct, verbal or nonverbal, not intended as an assertion. The key to the definition is that nothing is an assertion unless intended to be one.

"It can scarcely be doubted that an assertion made in words is intended by the declarant to be an assertion. Hence verbal assertions readily fall into the category of 'statement.' Whether nonverbal conduct should be regarded as a statement for purposes of defining hearsay requires further consideration. Some nonverbal conduct, such as the act of pointing to identify a suspect in a lineup, is clearly the equivalent of words, assertive in nature, and to be regarded as a statement. Other nonverbal conduct, however, may be offered as evidence that the person acted as he did because of his belief in the existence of the condition sought to be proved, from which belief the existence of the condition may be inferred. This sequence is, arguably, in effect an assertion of the existence of the condition and hence properly includable within the hearsay concept. *See* Morgan, "Hearsay Dangers and the Application of the Hearsay Concept," 62 Harv.L.Rev. 177, 214, 217 (1948), and the elaboration in Finman, "Implied Assertions as Hearsay: Some Criticisms of the Uniform Rules of Evidence," 14 Stan.L.Rev. 682 (1962). Admittedly evidence of this character is untested with respect to the perception, memory, and narration (or their equivalents) of the actor, *but the Advisory Committee is of the view that these dangers are minimal in the absence of an intent to assert and do not justify the loss of the evidence on hearsay grounds.* No class of evidence is free of the possibility of fabrication, but the likelihood is less with nonverbal than with assertive verbal conduct. The situations giving rise to the nonverbal conduct are such as virtually to eliminate questions of sincerity. Motivation, the nature of the conduct, and the presence or absence of reliance will bear heavily upon the weight to be given the evidence. Falknor, "The 'Hear–Say' Rule as a 'See–Do' Rule: Evidence of Conduct," 33 Rocky Mt.L.Rev. 133 (1961). *Similar considerations govern nonassertive verbal conduct and verbal conduct which is assertive but offered as a basis for inferring something other than the matter asserted,* also excluded from the definition of hearsay by the language of subdivision (c)." (Emphasis added).

This court, therefore, holds that, "Subdivision (a)(2) of Rule 801 removes implied assertions from the definition of statement and consequently from the operation of the hearsay rule."[13]

---

[13] Weinstein, ¶ 801(a)[01] at 801–56; McCormick § 250 at 599.

Applying the principles discussed above to the case at bar, this court holds that the utterances of the betters telephoning in their bets were nonassertive verbal conduct, offered as relevant for an implied assertion to be inferred from them, namely that bets could be placed at the premises being telephoned. The language is not an assertion on its face, and it is obvious these persons did not intend to make an assertion about the fact sought to be proved or anything else.[14]

As an implied assertion, the proffered evidence is expressly excluded from the operation of the hearsay rule by Rule 801 of the Federal Rules of Evidence, and the objection thereto must be overruled. An order to that effect has previously been entered.

NOTES AND QUESTIONS

1.   *Some dissenting voices.* Although *Zenni* rather than *Tatham* clearly represents the majority position in American jurisdictions that implied assertions are nonhearsay, see Mueller, Post–Modern Hearsay Reform: The Importance of Complexity, 76 Minn.L.Rev. 367, 413 n.133 (1992), there are occasionally explicitly dissenting voices. See Stoddard v. State, 887 A.2d 564 (Md.2005) (holding that question by 18–month–old child to her mother whether the defendant was "going to get" her was hearsay).

2.   *Tatham's only recent demise in England.* In Regina v. Kearley, 2 App.Cas. 228, 2 W.L.R. 656, 2 All E.R. 345 (H.L.1992), the House of Lords, adhered to the *Tatham* decision and reached the opposite conclusion from *Zenni.* It held that a series of calls asking to purchase drugs received by the police at the defendant's flat were hearsay and therefore inadmissible to prove the implied assertion that he was selling drugs. See generally Symposium on Hearsay and Implied Assertions: How Would (or Should) the Supreme Court Decide the *Kearley* Case?, 16 Miss.C.L.Rev. 1 (1995). However, that result was changed by provisions of the Criminal Justice Act of 2003. See Regina v. Singh, [2006] EWCA Crim. 660 (ruling that the legislation creates "a new rule against hearsay which does not extend to implied assertions" and would admit what was said by the callers in *Kearley*).

3.   *Linguistically not assertive or an implied assertion?* How is the result in *Zenni* that the phone calls are not hearsay best explained? Is it a linguistic explanation that they are "directions" that are not hearsay because

---

[14] A somewhat different type of analysis would be required by words non-assertive in form, but which under the circumstances might be intended as an assertion. For example, an inspector at an airport security station might run a metal detector over a passenger and say "go on through." In the absence of the inspector, would testimony of this event be objectionable hearsay, if offered for the proposition that the passenger did not have a gun on him at that time? Although Rule 801(a) does not seem to require a preliminary determination by the trial court whether verbal conduct is intended as an assertion, it is submitted that such a determination would be required in the example given. If an assertion were intended the evidence would be excluded. If not, it would be admissible. This result is implicit in the policy of the drafters of the Federal Rules of Evidence that the touchstone for hearsay is the intention to make an assertion. See S. Saltzburg and K. Redden, Federal Rules of Evidence Manual 456 (2d ed. 1977).

they are not assertive under Rule 801(a)? See United States v. Bailey, 270 F.3d 83, 87 (1st Cir.2001) (holding telephone call which summoned recipient to rendezvous point but did not by content identify the recipient, was a direction and not hearsay). Or are these calls more properly examined as assertions but not hearsay under an implied assertion analysis under Rule 801(c)(2)? Is it significant that several calls were received? Is there anything about the fact in *Zenni* that makes it more like conduct than the typical hearsay statement that is pure conversational speech?

HEADLEY V. TILGHMAN
United States Court of Appeals, Second Circuit, 1995.
53 F.3d 472.

McLAUGHLIN, CIRCUIT JUDGE:

[Headley was charged with possession of narcotics with intent to distribute and conspiracy to distribute narcotics.]

[At issue were statements from an unidentified Jamaican caller, which the trial court admitted as those of a co-conspirator made during and in furtherance of the conspiracy. The appellate court concluded that it did not need to struggle with the difficult co-conspirator argument because it could affirm on the alternative ground that "the statements were perfectly admissible as non-hearsay" under United States v. Oguns, 921 F.2d 442, 448–49 (2d Cir.1990).]

In Oguns, a police officer answered a telephone call while searching the defendant's house pursuant to a valid warrant. The unidentified caller asked, "Have the apples arrived there?" Id. at 448. The district court allowed the officer to recount this question, and admitted additional evidence demonstrating that narcotics traffickers often use code words when discussing drugs on the telephone. Id. at 445, 449. We affirmed, reasoning that:

> [t]he government legitimately used the phone call as circumstantial evidence of Oguns' knowledge and intent regarding the importation and distribution charges. The fact that an out-of-court statement is used to provide circumstantial evidence of a conspiracy does not require that the statement be analyzed under the co-conspirator exception to the hearsay rule.

Id. at 449 * * *.

Here, as in Oguns, the questions asked by the unidentified Jamaican caller—"Are you up? Can I come by? Are you ready?"—were not admitted for their truth, but rather as circumstantial evidence that Headley used his beeper to receive requests for drugs. Evidence scholars are wont to characterize such statements as "mixed acts and assertions," see generally 4 Christopher B. Mueller & Laird C. Kirkpatrick, Federal

Evidence 101–12 (2d ed. 1994), and admissibility is won by emphasizing the performance aspect of the statement. Thus, the question implies the speaker's belief that he is talking to a drug dealer; and that belief is regarded as circumstantial evidence of the nature of the business. By intellectual corner-cutting, the cases treat this as an assumption by the speaker that he has reached a drug den, rather than a direct assertion by him that "you are a drug dealer," an assertion that would surely trigger the hearsay rule, with its risks of insincerity, distorted perception, imperfect memory, and ambiguity of utterance. An assumption has a fair claim to be treated as non-hearsay since the attendant risks are not as intensively implicated as when the idea is directly enunciated in a statement. See United States v. Long, 905 F.2d 1572, 1579–80 (D.C.Cir.1990).

Accordingly, the questions are non-hearsay, the exclusion of which is not mandated by any other evidentiary rule. In addition, although, as in Oguns, the caller's questions were seemingly innocuous, Manzi's expert opinion that the caller was seeking to purchase cocaine provided an alternative interpretation based upon his experience eavesdropping on numerous drug deals between Jamaican individuals. The jury was free to reject the government's interpretation in favor of the defense's construction that the caller was merely asking Headley to go out for the night. * * *

UNITED STATES V. SUMMERS

United States Court of Appeals, Tenth Circuit, 2005.
414 F.3d 1287.

PAUL KELLY, JR., CIRCUIT JUDGE.

[Defendants Summers and Thomas appealed their convictions for bank robbery and aiding and abetting * * * and conspiracy to commit bank robbery * * *.]

Background

* * * [After investigation,] [t]he officers conducted a felony stop, handcuffing and frisking the four occupants of the vehicle. * * * The occupants were identified as Mr. Summers, Mr. Thomas, Mohammed, and Frazier. A search of the vehicle revealed evidence linked to the bank robbery. Officers discovered $5,142.10 in cash in Mr. Thomas's pockets, including ten "bait bills" subsequently identified by the Bank of America. * * * Mr. Thomas also possessed a key to Apartment 2013. * * * Officers also discovered zippered bank bags containing significant quantities of cash or cash equivalents, clothing and latex gloves resembling those used in the robbery, a purple pillowcase containing cash and coins, and a large amount of cash in the cargo area. * * *

Although Messrs. Summers and Thomas were apparently silent during the stop and search, Mohammed cannot be described as reticent. When an officer asked Mohammed to identify suspicious items in his front pocket during a pat down, Mohammed replied: "What do you think? It's bank money." * * * Later, while being led to a police car, Mohammed inquired of an attending officer: "How did you guys find us so fast?" * * *

Discussion

Hearsay Issues

Mr. Thomas first complains that the admission of a hearsay statement by co-defendant Mohammed violated his Sixth Amendment confrontation right. As noted above, over defense objection the district court permitted the following colloquy between the prosecution and Officer Daniel Wolf of the Albuquerque Police Department describing events immediately following the stop of the red Ford Escape:

* * *

Q.   And as you walked him over to the patrol car, did he say anything?

A.   Yes, sir, he did.

Q.   And tell the ladies and gentlemen of the jury what he said.

A.   He stated, "How did you guys find us so fast?"

* * *

A.   *Whether Mohammed's Question, "How Did You Guys Find Us So Fast?," Was Hearsay*

[In ruling on the constitutional challenge under the Confrontation Clause], [w]e must first ascertain whether the question, "How did you guys find us so fast?," is properly considered hearsay. It hardly needs stating that the admission of hearsay is frowned upon and generally inadmissible at trial. Fed.R.Evid. 802. Under the Federal Rules of Evidence, hearsay "is a statement, other than one made by the declarant while testifying at the trial or hearing, offered in evidence to prove the truth of the matter asserted." Fed.R.Evid. 801(c). A statement "is (1) an oral or written assertion or (2) nonverbal conduct of a person, if it is intended by the person as an assertion." *Id.* 801(a). The term "assertion" is not defined in Rule 801. "Assert" is generally defined as "to state or declare positively and often forcefully or aggressively" or "to demonstrate the existence of." *Webster's Ninth New Collegiate Dictionary* 109 (1991). To further guide our inquiry, the advisory notes to Rule 801 indicate that "[t]he key to the definition [of a statement] is that nothing is an assertion unless intended to be one." The government limits its argument on appeal to the contention that Mohammed's declaration is not hearsay because the declarant did not intend to make an assertion by uttering the words. We disagree.

In *United States v. Jackson,* 88 F.3d 845 (10th Cir.1996), we addressed for the first time whether the admission into evidence of a question posited by a non-testifying witness constituted hearsay within the meaning of Rules 801(c) and 802. In that case, officers recovered the pager of a suspected carjacker during a foot pursuit. *Id.* at 846. While an officer filled out a report on the carjacking, the pager went off and displayed a telephone number. *Id.* The officer called the displayed number and heard a voice say, "Is this Kenny?" The question was admitted over objection through the testimony of the officer, and the defendant was convicted of carjacking and related firearm offenses. *Id.* As in this case, the government argued that there was no error in the admission of the declaration because, as a question lacking assertive quality, it did not constitute hearsay under Rule 801(a)(1) and (c). *Id.* at 847. In determining that the question, "Is this Kenny?," did not constitute hearsay, we emphasized that such a declaration could not "reasonably be construed to be an assertion, either express or implied." *Id.* at 848. We explained that in analyzing the question, we found "it hard to believe in this case that the declarant *intended* to assert that Mr. Jackson was in possession of the pager and that he was responding to her call." *Id.* (emphasis added). We did not, however, foreclose the possibility that a question might indeed be construed as an assertion, either express or implied.

Our decision in *Jackson* relied in part on the District of Columbia Circuit's decision in *United States v. Long,* 905 F.2d 1572 (D.C.Cir.1990). In *Long,* the defendant was charged with various firearms and narcotics charges after a police search of the apartment in which Keith Long was arrested revealed a plethora of evidence related to the charged criminal conduct. *Id.* at 1575. While officers were searching the apartment, a telephone rang and police answered it. *Id.* at 1579. The unidentified caller first asked to speak with "Keith" and then inquired whether Keith "still had any stuff." *Id.* When queried as to the meaning of this question, the caller responded by indicating a quantity of crack cocaine. *Id.* Over defense objection, the police officer was permitted to testify concerning the conversation at trial. *Id.* Long argued that the caller's questions contained implicit assertions of his involvement in narcotics distribution and that the government introduced the statements to prove the truth of those assertions. *Id.* Writing for the court, then Circuit Judge Clarence Thomas rejected Long's argument. Noting that "[i]t is difficult to imagine any question, or for that matter any act, that does not in some way convey an implicit message," the court focused squarely on the intent of the caller. *Id.* at 1580. The court found that Long had failed to provide any evidence to suggest that the unidentified caller actually intended to assert that he was involved in narcotics distribution. *Id.*

Taken together, *Jackson* and *Long* do not foreclose the possibility that a declaration in the form of a question may nevertheless constitute an assertion within the meaning of Rule 801(a) and (c). Rather, both cases properly focus the inquiry on the declarant's intent. Furthermore, it is the party challenging admission of the declaration that bears the burden of demonstrating the declarant's requisite intent. *Jackson,* 88 F.3d at 848; *Long,* 905 F.2d at 1580; Rule 801 advisory committee's note ("The rule is so worded as to place the burden upon the party claiming that the intention existed; ambiguous and doubtful cases will be resolved against him and in favor admissibility.").

Turning to the facts of the instant case, we hold that Mr. Thomas has met his burden of demonstrating that by positing the question, "How did you guys find us so fast?," Mohammed intended to make an assertion. Unlike the rather innocuous and ambiguous question in *Jackson,* Mohammed's question clearly contained an inculpatory assertion. It begs credulity to assume that in positing the question Mohammed was exclusively interested in modern methods of law enforcement, including surveillance, communication, and coordination. Rather, fairly construed the statement intimated both guilt and wonderment at the ability of the police to apprehend the perpetrators of the crime so quickly. This in turn is distinguished from the questions in *Long* that were designed to elicit information and a response, rather than assert the defendant's involvement in criminal activity. Thus, on the face of the record, we hold that Mohammed's intent to make an assertion was apparent and that his question directed to police officers on the scene constituted hearsay for purposes of Rule 802.

[The court concluded admission of the hearsay was improper but found the error harmless. It reversed Summers' conviction on other grounds.]

NOTES AND QUESTIONS

1. *Almost a categorical exclusion for questions.* Although some courts treat questions as if they were categorically excluded from hearsay because not assertions, as *Summers* demonstrates, a more nuanced treatment may be appropriate. See also Martin v. United States, 991 A.2d 791, 796–97 (D.C.2010) (ruling question by defendant to police officer at time of arrest was intended as an assertion rather than a genuine request for information). However, when the question is truly a question "designed to elicit information and a response," courts readily find that questions are not statements and therefore not hearsay. See United States v. Love, 706 F.3d 832 839–40 (7th Cir.2013) (ruling that question by one of Love's associates whether the informant "was with" the defendant was not intended as an

assertion and therefore not hearsay). In what way is the effective inquiry similar to that involved in determining whether an implied assertion should be considered hearsay?

2. *Context and reducing hearsay dangers.* How might the context of these questions add critically to their superiority to the typical declarative sentence? See Park, The Definition of Hearsay: To Each His Own, 16 Miss.C.L.Rev. 125, 136–37 (1995).

UNITED STATES V. MUSCATO

United States District Court, Eastern District of New York, 1982.
534 F.Supp. 969.

Memorandum and Order

WEINSTEIN, CHIEF JUDGE.

Defendant was found guilty of conspiracy to unlawfully manufacture firearms and of related crimes. [Only the] claim that hearsay was improperly admitted [warrants discussion.] For the reasons stated below, this claim is rejected.

I.   Facts

The story begins with Walter Gollender, a self-styled part-time talent promotor. Though a fastidious and intelligent man, Gollender had been forced to leave the teaching profession by a psychiatric disability. In need of protection from Newark's dangers, real and imagined, he purchased a small, single shot firearm of simple design, in appearance resembling a large pen.

Gollender revealed his purchase to an acquaintance named Stanley Szostek, Jr., a former Newark police officer, who assisted his father in operating a neighborhood liquor and food store. In turn, Szostek showed the pen gun to his friend and business partner, Joseph Kirchner, a truck driver who delivered soft drinks to the store. Together, this enterprising pair had contrived to provide their community with a variety of services. They had invested in a rock concert, conducted a desultory loan-sharking business, and sold patent remedies as illicit drugs. Upon observing the simple construction of Gollender's weapon and learning that he had paid $40.00 for it, they decided to enter the arms trade.

Szostek took the prototype to a friend on the Newark police force, the defendant, John Muscato. Despairing of ever making the down payment for a new home on a modest policeman's salary, Muscato was moonlighting as a machinist in his father's basement. Muscato agreed to make copies of the pen gun in commercial quantities.

One problem with this plan was that it left Gollender defenseless. Accordingly, Muscato temporarily lent Gollender a twenty-five calibre pistol to replace his pen gun. Awed by the complexity and dangers of this new acquisition, Gollender carefully marked the pistol with a gummed label to indicate the safety position and the firing position. * * * After the model pen gun had served its purpose, it was returned to him and he relinquished the pistol to Szostek.

As Muscato began producing pen guns, Szostek and Kirchner began casting about for markets for their product. * * * To this end they contacted a business acquaintance, Patrick Monteforte. * * * He began looking for potential buyers of pen guns on Staten Island. * * * It was Monteforte's fortune to land as a customer one of the world's major armaments purchasers, the United States Government. Though presenting himself as the representative of a large New York area crime syndicate, the buyer was in fact Special Agent Matthew Raffa of the United States Treasury Department, Bureau of Alcohol, Tobacco and Firearms. As quickly as the basement factory could produce the pen guns, the Treasury Department bought them. Eventually, the government placed an order for 1,000 at $20,000. * * *

Delivery of the final shipment was arranged to be in neutral territory, a diner in the shadow of the George Washington Bridge, in Fort Lee, New Jersey. Szostek and Kirchner were armed and present. They were accompanied by a new recruit to the conspiracy, another former Newark policeman named Charles McDonald, now a hopeless alcoholic. His role was described as "riding shotgun," i.e., providing extra security. Muscato hid in the background with a high-powered rifle to "watch the deal go down."

To the surprise of Kirchner, Szostek and McDonald, instead of enriching them by $20,000, Raffa and his colleagues arrested them. From McDonald the federal agents recovered a .25 calibre pistol, bearing the remnants of a gummed label at the safety catch.

Eventually, all of the conspirators were rounded up and Kirchner, Gollender, Kasper and Monteforte agreed to testify for the government. During his debriefing by government officials, Gollender chanced to describe the gun that he claimed he had received from Muscato and returned to Szostek, recalling that he had placed a gummed label at the safety catch. At this point, the government agents retrieved from a safe the pistol found on McDonald. Gollender promptly identified it as the same pistol he had described.

Muscato did not cooperate with the United States Attorney. He was charged in a six count indictment [largely related to the unlawful manufacture and distribution of firearms.]

The evidence against Muscato at trial was overwhelming. He was directly implicated by Kirchner, Kasper and Gollender. Their testimony was corroborated by extensive circumstantial evidence, including damaged pen gun parts from the basement arsenal.

The defense consisted of a denial of criminal intent. The hypothesis suggested to the jury was that Muscato was a law-abiding policeman who had been making the various pen gun parts independently without knowing what they were or how they fit together. * * * [A]fter the jury had been exposed to pen guns in assembled and unassembled form over a period of days, they were probably predisposed to reject both Muscato's testimony that he was making parts without knowing their purpose and his attorney's argument that a reasonable policeman-machinist might believe he was helping manufacture pocket flashlights.

The defense position was, as noted, seriously undercut by the testimony of the other conspirators. Now, if these witnesses were not quite your run-of-the-mill mobsters, neither were they particularly solid citizens, and the defense attacked their credibility on cross-examination with considerable gusto.

Given Gollender's psychiatric history, he was by no means an ideal witness and the defense attorney had a field day with him on cross-examination. Particularly stressed was Gollender's difficulty in distinguishing reality from fancy and his suggestibility. The following exchanges are typical:

Mr. Richman: * * *

Q. You have many inordinate fears? * * *

A. I have had, yes. * * *

Q. * * * You have strong feelings of inadequacy and a terror that you will lose control of yourself?

A. Not ultimate control, but I have feelings like that, similar to those. Not total control, no. I have some good judgment I think sometimes.

Q. And it is true that * * * Dr. Howard Davidman, said that you have a great need to be noticed and appreciated which sometimes leads you to bizarre behavior? * * *

A. It has happened on occasion, yes.

Q. And on those occasions you don't know whether you behavior is bizarre or not, isn't that correct?

A. I would hope it would not be, but maybe perhaps it has been.

Q. You can't distinguish sometimes from reality to perhaps not so reality?

A. I can distinguish from reality but I can't always predict what effect my behavior would have on other people.

Q. Sometimes you become panicky and overdo some things, isn't that correct? * * *

A. Sometimes.

Given this attack on Gollender's credibility, one piece of real proof took on added weight. Linking Muscato to the conspiracy was the pistol he allegedly lent Gollender, which ultimately turned up in the hands of McDonald at the time of his arrest. Gollender identified the pistol in open court as follows:

Mr. [A.U.S.A.] Kirby: Did you have any conversation with Mr. Muscato at that time?

A. No, I did not. Except he gave me a .25 calibre gun while we were in the car. He came to an intersection in Irvington and he stopped and gave me the pistol. * * *

Q. Mr. Gollender, I show you what has been marked as Government's Exhibit 12.

Would you take a look at that object and tell the Court and jury whether you recognize it?

A. Yes, it's the gun.

Q. I'm sorry?

A. Yes, I recognize it as the .25 caliber pistol.

Q. How do you recognize it as such?

A. It has the same marking on it, same scuff mark and mainly the remnants of the gum label I marked it with, safe or unsafe. It still has a piece of paper indicating how it was safe or unsafe.

The fact that Gollender had provided an accurate description of the pistol prior to his being shown it or being told that it had been discovered on the person of Charles McDonald provided important confirmation of his testimony. The government [received] permission to elicit this fact from Special Agent Raffa. (It was clear that Muscato would deny from the witness stand Gollender's testimony about the source of the pistol.) The defense objected on the ground of hearsay. * * *

II. LAW * * *

B. *Hearsay* * * *

1) Was the extrajudicial declaration hearsay under the Federal Rules?

For purposes of analysis one way of treating the case with respect to the gun might be to consider only the following testimony: One member of the conspiracy testified that he had received a gun from the defendant, an alleged coconspirator, that this gun had a unique characteristic, observable upon examination, and that he had returned the gun to a third conspirator. The arresting officer testified that he had obtained a gun with the same unique characteristic from an alleged fourth conspirator. The jury could examine the gun, which had been admitted as an exhibit, to help it determine if the two witnesses were describing the same object. This part of the case presents no hearsay problem. Both witnesses testified with respect to characteristics and events they themselves observed.

The evidence was significant in two respects. First, the prosecution's ability to produce a gun matching Gollender's description lent circumstantial support to Gollender's story of having received such a gun from the defendant in furtherance of the conspiracy. Second, the fact that this gun was found on the person of another conspirator while engaged in acts furthering the conspiracy linked Muscato to the conspiracy.

What made the production of the gun useful as corroboration of Gollender's story is the improbability of his describing a gun with such a unique characteristic if he had not seen it. The physical evidence of the gun provided some assurance (unless the jury believed that this real evidence was fabricated by the prosecution) that the tale was not cut out of whole cloth. It did not by itself insure that Gollender saw the gun under the circumstances he related. If he first described the gun after having identified it while it was in the agent's possession, much of the effect of this line of proof would have been eroded. If, on the other hand, he described the gun before being shown it by a law enforcement official, production of the gun would have a substantial corroborative effect.

If we then add to the case the extrajudicial declaration of Gollender to the agent we have 1) testimony revealing the existence of a memory in the mind of a witness (a description of a gun with unique characteristics and its source), 2) a physical object matching that memory, and 3) an extrajudicial declaration made under circumstances indicating that the reported memory was acquired in a manner consistent with the witness' testimony.

It is the third leg which involved a hearsay danger since it depended on the truth of an extrajudicial declaration to the agent by Gollender. Gollender said outside of court, in essence, "the gun given to me by Muscato had a unique characteristic; this is that gun." On its face, thus parsed, his statement to the agent would appear to fall squarely within the definition of hearsay provided in rule 801(c) of the Federal Rules of Evidence:

"Hearsay" is a statement, other than one made by the declarant while testifying at the trial * * * offered in evidence to prove the truth of the matter asserted.

The fact that the extrajudicial declarant, like his auditor, was a witness subject to cross examination does not eliminate the hearsay problem. While many writers proposed treating extrajudicial declarations by witnesses as non-hearsay or as falling within a broad hearsay exception [citing authorities], the Federal Rules reject this approach except in special cases. *See* F.R.Evid. 801(d)(1); 803(5). * * *

Despite the fact that it could be analyzed as hearsay under the Federal Rules of Evidence, this extrajudicial declaration posed minimal hearsay dangers; it was highly probative while being essentially corroborative in function. Admitting it may be justified under a number of different theories: that it was circumstantial rather than testimonial evidence and, therefore, was not hearsay; that it was offered on the issue of credibility rather than for its truth as evidence-in-chief; and that it was admissible under Rule 803(24).

2) The extrajudicial declaration as circumstantial evidence

One way of characterizing the extrajudicial declaration in this case is as "circumstantial non-assertive use" of the utterance "to show state of mind." Statements used in this way, according to Professor McCormick, need not be denominated hearsay. This, he wrote, is especially true of "declarations evincing knowledge, notice, consciousness or awareness of some fact, which fact is established by other evidence in the case." McCormick, Evidence, § 249, p. 592 (2nd Cleary Ed. 1972). According to this analysis, the extrajudicial declaration was offered not to prove the truth of the proposition asserted—the description of the gun—but to prove that the declarant had knowledge of the truth of that proposition. Because McCormick's discussion of the "trace" on the mind theory has had great influence, it is set forth in its entirety:

> When the existence of knowledge is sought to be used as the basis for a further inference, caution is required lest the hearsay rule be infringed upon. Thus, in a Wisconsin case [*Bridges v. State,* 247 Wis. 350, 19 N.W.2d 529 (1945)] * * * evidence was received in a trial for mistreatment of a little girl, that the girl in reporting the incident gave a description of the house and its surroundings and of the room and its furnishings, where the mistreatment occurred. Other evidence showed that this description fitted exactly the house and room where the defendant lived. Morgan suggested that this evidence depended for its value upon "the observation, memory and veracity" of the girl and thus shared the hazards of hearsay. [Morgan, Evidence 1941–1945, 59 Harv.L.Rev. 481, 544 (1946). * * * It seems,

however, that the testimony had value without regard to her veracity. Other witnesses had described the physical characteristics of the house. Her testimony was not relied on for that, but to show her knowledge as a "trace," as it were, on her mind of her visit at the time of the crime. Significantly the undisputed proof excluded the possibility of other means by which she could have acquired the knowledge, and thus the hearsay dangers were eliminated.

The evidence before us is much like the extrajudicial declaration at issue in *Bridges v. State,* 247 Wis. 350, 19 N.W.2d 529, 534 (1945), the case McCormick cited as the paradigm. A seven year old child described to a police officer several exterior and interior details of the house in which she was allegedly assaulted. Subsequently, it was discovered that this description closely fit defendant's home. The court, relying on 6 Wigmore §§ 1788, 1790, 1791 (3rd Ed. 1940), reasoned that the statement to the police officer was circumstantial evidence of the child's state of mind which, in turn, was evidence of what caused that state of mind.

Additional support for such treatment of extrajudicial declarations (or behavior) evincing knowledge may be sought in *Kinder v. Commonwealth,* 306 S.W.2d 265 (Kentucky Court of Appeals, 1957), in which a defendant was convicted of larceny on the basis of his young son's knowledge of the location of the cache of stolen goods. Another such case is *State v. Galvan,* 297 N.W.2d 344 (Iowa Supreme Court, 1980), a murder case in which the court approved admission of a description by defendant's ex-wife of their two year old daughter's apparent unreflective re-enactment of the killing while the youngster was at play. While the *Galvan* court based its ruling on a "res gestae exception," *id.* at 347, and rejected the *Bridges* rationale, the fact pattern places the case in the *Bridges–Kinder* line. * * *

III. Conclusion

[The court concluded Gollender's out-of-court statement was properly admitted against the hearsay object and its probative value could be accurately evaluated by the jury. Accordingly, it denied the motion for a new trial.]

NOTES AND QUESTIONS

1. *Narrowing, not eliminating interpretative disagreement.* As the preceding cases make clear, enactment of the Federal Rules of Evidence has not eliminated major disagreements as to when a statement is not hearsay. See also United States v. Reynolds, 715 F.2d 99, 103 (3d Cir.1983) (finding a codefendant's statement that "I didn't tell them anything about you" hearsay under the theory that implied assertions are hearsay under the Federal Rules). While federal courts frequently analyze implied assertions as did

Zenni and treat them broadly as nonhearsay, others have either ignored the issue or, like *Reynolds*, have refused to recognize that the Federal Rules changed the result in *Tatham*. Callen, Hearsay and Informal Reasoning, 47 Vand.L.Rev. 43, 47 (1994). They have generally avoided decisions based on a literalistic distinction of how the utterance was phrased. Park, "I Didn't Tell Them Anything About You": Implied Assertions as Hearsay Under the Federal Rules of Evidence, 74 Minn.L.Rev. 783, 827–28 (1990).

2. *Brain teasers.* Consider whether hearsay is involved in each of the following cases: United States v. Sells, 496 F.2d 912 (7th Cir.1974) (name seen on driver's license to show identity of possessor); United States v. Snow, 517 F.2d 441 (9th Cir.1975) (defendant's name on tape affixed to gun case found on premises frequented by defendant as proof that he knowingly possessed firearm contained in case). Although typically considered not hearsay, the results are not always consistent. Compare Bernadyn v. State, 887 A.2d 602, 606–12 (Md.2005) (medical bill found at crime scene addressed to defendant considered hearsay as implied assertion), with United States v. Mejias, 552 F.2d 435, 446 (2d Cir.1977) (hotel receipt seized from defendant not hearsay when used to show defendant stayed at hotel but rather circumstantial evidence to connect him to that place).

3. *Some things can't be cross-examined.* A hearsay objection is sometimes made to "statements" by machines or animals, such as speed detecting devices or bloodhounds. In City of Webster Groves v. Quick, 323 S.W.2d 386, 390 (Mo.Ct.App.1959), the court rejected such a challenge to a speed detecting device:

> Evidence is called hearsay when its probative force depends, in whole or in part, on the competency and credibility of some person other than the witness by whom it is sought to be produced. * * * The hearsay rule cannot be applied to what the witness, on the stand and subject to cross-examination, observed, either through his own senses or through the use of scientific instruments.

See also United States v. Hamilton, 413 F.3d 1138, 1142–43 (10th Cir.2005) (ruling that header attached to photograph not hearsay when automatically created by computer without human input); State v. Kandutsch, 799 N.W.2d 865, 877–79 (Wis.2011) (ruling that computer generated logs, such as results of electronic monitoring device attached to defendant, are not hearsay because automatically generated by computer process). See generally 2 McCormick, Evidence § 249 (7th ed. 2013); 4 Mueller & Kirkpatrick, Federal Evidence § 8:13 (3d ed. 2007).

B. OTHER STATEMENTS THAT ARE NOT HEARSAY

(1) PRIOR STATEMENTS OF THE WITNESS

Federal Rule 801(d)(1)

COMMONWEALTH V. DAYE

Supreme Judicial Court of Massachusetts, 1984.
469 N.E.2d 483.

ABRAMS, JUSTICE.

We granted further appellate review to consider the Commonwealth's request that we adopt Proposed Mass.R.Evid. 801(d)(1)(A),[15] permitting the introduction of limited categories of prior inconsistent statements for their probative worth.

* * *

The evidence implicating the defendant consisted principally of one in-court identification of him as the gunman by an eyewitness who admitted on cross-examination that earlier he had identified a codefendant, Michael Prochilo as the gunman during a lineup conducted several days after the shooting. The victim and five other witnesses present at the scene of the shooting were unwilling or unable to identify the defendant in court. There was evidence that three of those witnesses, including the victim, also identified Prochilo as the gunman prior to trial. Statements elicited from some of the witnesses at trial suggest that their testimony may have been colored by fear of reprisals if they made an identification at trial.

The evidentiary issues we are asked to decide are affiliated with the Commonwealth's attempts to demonstrate that witnesses who did not identify the defendant at trial had done so from pretrial photographic arrays and before the grand jury.

[After concluding that the trial court committed reversible error by admitting testimony by a police officer concerning pretrial identifications of the defendant by two witnesses who denied at trial making such identifications, the court considered admission of identifications testimony given by one of those witnesses, Ciambelli, before the grand jury.]

---

[15] Proposed Mass.R.Evid. 801(d)(1)(A) reads as follows: "(d) Statements which are not hearsay. A statement is not hearsay if—(1) Prior statement by witness. The declarant testifies at the trial or hearing and is subject to cross-examination concerning the statement, and the statement is (A) inconsistent with his testimony and was given under oath subject to the penalty of perjury at a trial, hearing, or other proceeding, or in a deposition." Grand jury testimony falls within the "other proceeding" category.

2.   *Grand jury testimony.* After Ciambelli denied making a pretrial photographic identification of the defendant as the gunman, and stated that "I didn't know what he [the shooter] looks like," the prosecutor questioned him about his grand jury testimony. Over the defendant's objection, Ciambelli was permitted to read from the grand jury transcript that he had stated to the grand jury that he had identified Dennis Daye as the gunman. After reading the defendant's name from the transcript, Ciambelli volunteered that "I don't know Dennis Daye and I never seen him. That's just a name that was going around." Ciambelli stated he did not see Dennis Daye in the court room.

At side bar, the prosecutor specifically stated he did not intend to use the grand jury testimony for purposes of impeachment, but argued instead its probative admissibility as past recollection recorded. Admission of the testimony on that basis over the defendant's objection without a limiting instruction was error. We have previously expressed "serious doubt" whether grand jury testimony is admissible under the "past recollection recorded" exception to the hearsay rule. *Commonwealth v. Bookman,* 386 Mass. 657, 664–665, 436 N.E.2d 1228 (1982). We need not decide that question, however, because it is plain that the requirements of that exception are not met in this case. When a witness has no current recollection of a particular event, the witness may incorporate in his testimony "a writing expressive of his past knowledge," *Bendett v. Bendett,* 315 Mass. 59, 64, 52 N.E.2d 2 (1943), provided the witness, "having firsthand knowledge of the facts recorded in the memorandum, [is] able to testify that the memorandum written or observed by him was true at the time it was made." *Commonwealth v. Bookman, supra* 386 Mass. at 663, 436 N.E.2d 1228. See P.J. Liacos, Massachusetts Evidence 92–94 (5th ed. 1981). Ciambelli, however, denied at trial both first hand knowledge of the defendant's involvement in the crime and the truth of his statement to the grand jury implicating the defendant. Cf. *Commonwealth v. Greene,* 9 Mass.App. 688, 690, 404 N.E.2d 110 (1980).[16]

3.   *Probative use of prior inconsistent statements.* On the basis of the errors described above, we conclude that a new trial is required. We are unpersuaded by the Commonwealth's argument that any evidentiary errors relating to extrajudicial identifications of the defendant by Ciambelli and O'Connor should be treated as harmless because the identifications were cumulative of other evidence implicating the

---

[16] Ciambelli's grand jury testimony was likewise inadmissible as present recollection refreshed. A writing may be used to revive a witness's recollection of events observed by the witness, but, so utilized, the writing has no evidentiary value and should not be read to the jury. Commonwealth v. Parrotta, 316 Mass. 307, 312, 55 N.E.2d 456 (1944). Bendett v. Bendett, supra, 315 Mass. at 63, 52 N.E.2d 2. P.J. Liacos, Massachusetts Evidence, supra at 87. Moreover, it must be clear that when, assisted by the writing, the witness testifies in the presence of the jury, the witness is testifying from present memory rather than reciting the contents of the writing. Commonwealth v. Hoffer, 375 Mass. 369, 376, 377 N.E.2d 685 (1978).

defendant. In this case, only one witness identified the defendant in court as the gunman, and that identification was impeached by evidence of a prior identification by the same witness of another person as the gunman. The evidence, although sufficient to justify verdicts against the defendant, was not overwhelming. We are not persuaded that, in this context, it was harmless to permit the jury to consider at probative value evidence of independent identifications by other witnesses of the defendant as the gunman. * * *

The settled rule in this Commonwealth is the "orthodox" one that prior inconsistent statements, though admissible for the limited purpose of impeaching the credibility of a witness's testimony at trial, are inadmissible hearsay when offered to establish the truth of the matters asserted (citation omitted). By contrast, Fed.R.Evid. 801(d)(1)(A), incorporated verbatim in Proposed Mass.R.Evid. 801(d)(1)(A), permits probative use of inconsistent grand jury testimony, as well as other categories of inconsistent statements given under oath, in instances where "[t]he declarant testifies at the trial * * * and is subject to cross-examination concerning the statement." * * *

The orthodox view against probative admissibility of prior inconsistent statements is founded on the general rationale for the exclusion of hearsay, namely, that the reliability of a prior inconsistent statement "rests on the credit of the declarant, who was not (1) under oath, (2) subject to cross-examination, or (3) in the presence of the trier, when the statement was made." McCormick, Evidence § 251, at 601 (2d ed. 1972). This rationale for exclusion has come under attack from numerous prominent commentators, who think the dangers the hearsay rule was designed to protect against are dissipated to a large extent when, as in the case of prior inconsistent statements, the extrajudicial declarant is present at trial. See, e.g., 3A J. Wigmore, *supra* at 996; Morgan, Hearsay Dangers and the Application of the Hearsay Concept, 62 Harv.L.Rev. 177, 192 (1948); McCormick, The Turncoat Witness: Previous Statements as Substantive Evidence, 25 Tex.L.Rev. 573 (1947). Some proponents of the "modern view" advocate probative use of all prior inconsistent statements on the grounds that the oath is not a significant safeguard of reliability and that counsel's opportunity to cross-examine the declarant at trial, and the jury's opportunity to view the declarant's demeanor at trial, satisfy the other concerns. See Comment, Prior Inconsistent Statements: Conflict Between State and Federal Rules of Evidence, 34 Mercer L.Rev. 1495, 1498–1500 (1983). A less extreme "modern" position, reflected in the rule the Commonwealth advises us to adopt, accepts at probative value only those prior inconsistent statements given under oath in instances where a record of the statement is likely to be available.

The schism between adherents of the "orthodox" and "modern" doctrines is accounted for in large part by divergent viewpoints as to the validity of the premise that the presence of the extrajudicial declarant at trial constitutes adequate protection for the lack of contemporaneous cross-examination of the declarant at the time the subsequently disavowed statement was made.[17] Supporters of the modern view argue that, at least where the witness at trial does not disclaim memory of the circumstances under which the prior statement was made, the reliability of the statement can be tested notwithstanding the witness's recantation. "Cross-examination [at trial] can probe the witness' perception and memory and can develop all the reasons why the witness made a statement which he now insists was not true." 4 J. Weinstein & M. Berger, Evidence ¶ 801(d)(1)(A)[03] at 801–92. See McCormick, The Turncoat Witness: Previous Statements as Substantive Evidence, 25 Tex.L.Rev. 573, 577 (1947) (questioning at trial "will lay bare the sources of the change of face, in forgetfulness, carelessness, pity, terror or greed, and thus reveal which is the true story and which the false"). Partisans of the orthodox view retort that prior inconsistent statements, if admitted for probative purposes, are endowed with an "indestructible" quality superior to that of testimony at trial. "Nothing that happens to the witness inside the courtroom can deprive the fact finder of the right to believe the [extrajudicial statement]. Indeed, if the witness inside the courtroom were to be attacked with the usual devices of the cross-examiner and shown to be untrustworthy, that would merely make it all the more likely that the fact finder would decide to believe the [extrajudicial statement]." Blakey, Substantive Use of Prior Inconsistent Statements Under the Federal Rules of Evidence, 64 Ky.L.J. 3, 44–45 (1975–1976). A fact finder's disbelief of a witness's contradiction of a prior statement at trial, it is argued, "sheds no direct light on the accuracy of [the] pretrial statement," California v. Green, 399 U.S. 149, 193 * * * (1970) (Brennan, J., dissenting), and does not, therefore, adequately ensure the reliability of the extrajudicial statement's factual content.

The proponents of the modern view argue that doubts as to the effectiveness of cross-examination at trial should, as a matter of public policy, be resolved in favor of probative use of prior inconsistent statements because a contrary rule encourages witness intimidation and deprives the prosecution of evidence necessary to prove cases against criminal defendants in instances where key witnesses recant their testimony. To this policy argument is added the pragmatic argument that juries cannot, and perhaps should not, be expected to discriminate between impeachment and probative use of a prior inconsistent

---

[17] * * * Questions concerning the probative admissibility of prior inconsistent statements arise in instances where the witness denies, or asserts a lack of memory with regard to, the making of a statement or its veracity. See Ruhala v. Roby, 379 Mich. 102, 124, 150 N.W.2d 146 (1967) * * *

statement, and that formally conferring probative status to such statements does no more than legitimize current practice.

The orthodox view, on the other hand, is defended on the ground that a witness may recant former statements for reasons other than intimidation, see Blakey, *supra* at 46, and that probative use of prior inconsistent statements permits convictions based on ex parte statements to prosecutorial authorities that may be fabricated, distorted, or erroneous. See *State v. Spadafore,* 159 W.Va. 236, 220 S.E.2d 655 (1975). Further, the distinction between probative and impeachment use of prior inconsistent statements, it is argued, even if elusive to some jurors, is one of importance to the courts in adjudicating issues relating to sufficiency of the evidence. See *California v. Green, supra,* 399 U.S. at 194 n.6 * * * (Brennan, J., dissenting).

The history of Fed.R.Evid. 801(d)(1)(A) illuminates the controversy over the evidentiary status of prior inconsistent statements. In 1970, the United States Supreme Court, although not called on to decide, as between the orthodox and modern views, "which of these positions, purely as a matter of the law of evidence, is the sounder," *California v. Green, supra* at 155 * * *, held that, as a Federal constitutional matter, acceptance of prior inconsistent statements for their probative value does not violate the Sixth Amendment Confrontation Clause "as long as the declarant is testifying as a witness and subject to full and effective cross-examination." *Id.* at 158 * * *. See *Nelson v. O'Neil,* 402 U.S. 622 * * * (1971).

As drafted in the Proposed Federal Rules of Evidence promulgated by the Supreme Court in 1972, Fed.R.Evid. 801(d)(1)(A) would have sanctioned, as an evidentiary matter, the probative admissibility of prior inconsistent statements to the full extent constitutionally permissible. Rules of Evidence for United States Courts and Magistrates, 56 F.R.D. 183, 293 (1972). Although the United States Senate favored adoption of the Supreme Court rule, permitting probative use of prior inconsistent statements irrespective of the circumstances under which they were made, S.Rep. No. 1277, 93d Cong., 2d Sess. 13 (1974), reprinted in 1974 U.S.Code Cong. & Ad.News 7051, 7062–7063, the House Judiciary Committee advocated a stricter rule admitting only those statements made under oath and subject to cross-examination, H.R.Rep. No. 650, 93d Cong., 2d Sess. 13 (1974), reprinted in 1974 U.S.Code Cong. & Ad.News 7075, 7086–7087. Under the House version, inconsistent grand jury testimony would have remained within the hearsay category. As adopted, Fed.R.Evid. 801(d)(1)(A) constitutes a compromise between the two positions. The House requirement that the statement have been made under oath was retained, thereby eliminating the risk of manufactured third-party testimony by restricting probative admissibility to situations in which there is likely to be a written transcript or tape recording providing "overwhelming proof that the witness did in fact make the prior inconsistent statement," Blakey, *supra* at 10. The compromise version eliminated the requirement of contemporaneous cross-examination, however, thereby allowing the probative use of inconsistent grand jury testimony.

In the wake of the adoption of Fed.R.Evid. 801(d)(1)(A), other jurisdictions remain divided over the probative admissibility of prior inconsistent statements. * * * A majority of States permit the probative use of inconsistent grand jury testimony.

We take note of these developments and are persuaded that the reasoning favoring use of inconsistent grand jury statements as probative evidence is sound. * * * With regard to inconsistent grand jury statements, we are satisfied that the truth-seeking function of trials may be enhanced rather than diminished if consideration of their probative value is permitted. Where the presence of the declarant at trial creates an opportunity fully to explore the circumstances under which a grand jury statement was made and the veracity of its factual content, the absence of contemporaneous cross-examination does not in our opinion so impair the statement's reliability as to mandate that the fact finder be deprived of the right to accept the statement for its probative worth. "The jury is alerted by the inconsistency in the stories, and its attention is sharply focused on determining either that one of the stories reflects the truth or that the witness who has apparently lied once, is simply too lacking in credibility to warrant its believing either story." *California v. Green, supra* 399 U.S. at 160 * * *. We believe that a fact finder should be permitted to prefer a grand jury statement made closer in time to the events at issue over contradictory trial testimony that the passage of time and intervening influences may have affected. The prior statement will have been made in an atmosphere of formality impressing upon the declarant the need for accuracy, and will be memorialized in a manner eliminating subsidiary inquiries into whether the statement was actually made that would unacceptably attenuate the statement's probative worth.

Permitting probative use of an inconsistent grand jury statement also eliminates an unnecessary and unseemly legal fiction. "The rule limiting the use of prior statements by a witness subject to cross-examination to their effect on his credibility has been described by eminent scholars and judges as 'pious fraud,' 'artificial,' 'basically misguided,' 'mere verbal ritual,' and an anachronism 'that still impede[s] our pursuit of the truth.' * * * [T]o tell a jury it may consider the prior testimony as reflecting on the veracity of the later denial of relevant knowledge but not as the substantive evidence that alone would be pertinent is a demand for mental gymnastics of which jurors are happily incapable." *United States v. DeSisto,* 329 F.2d 929, 933 (2d Cir.1964).

* * *

Today, we do little more than harmonize the legal treatment of prior inconsistent statements with the practical effect of permitting the jury to consider such statements under the guise of impeachment. * * *

Although we today hold that inconsistent grand jury testimony may be admitted in limited circumstances for its probative worth, we will not permit convictions based exclusively on inconsistent extrajudicial testimony to stand. See *California v. Green, supra,* 399 U.S. at 170 and n.19. In this case the Commonwealth must produce identification evidence in addition to a prior inconsistent statement in order to meet its burden of proof. * * *

The judgments of the Superior Court are reversed, the verdicts set aside, and the case is remanded for a new trial. * * *

NOTES AND QUESTIONS

1. *The meaning of "other proceeding."* As *Daye* notes, grand jury proceedings satisfy the requirement of Rule 801(d)(1)(A) that the statement must be made "at a trial, hearing, or other proceeding." A number of courts have excluded statements given to investigative agents "under informal circumstances tantamount to a station house interrogation setting." United States v. Day, 789 F.2d 1217, 1222 (6th Cir.1986). See also United States v. Livingston, 661 F.2d 239 (D.C.Cir.1981); Santos v. Murdock, 243 F.3d 681, 684 (2d Cir.2001); United States v. Lloyd, 10 F.3d 1197, 1217 (6th Cir.1993). In United States v. Castro–Ayon, 537 F.2d 1055 (9th Cir.1976), the Ninth Circuit took a rather expansive view of what "other proceedings" would meet the requirements of the Rule. It held admissible statements taken under oath by a Border Patrol Agent in tape recorded interrogations during an "immigration proceeding." Compare State v. Smith, 651 P.2d 207 (Wash.1982) (holding admissible under the "other proceeding" requirement a notarized statement taken by a police detective where the court found the statement reliable under the particular circumstances of its making), with State v. Smith, 573 So.2d 306, 314–16 (Fla.1990) (rejecting Washington's approach).

2. *Inconsistency requirement flexibly applied.* Rule 801(d)(1)(A) requires that to be admissible, the statement must be "inconsistent with the declarant's testimony." Courts have generally interpreted the inconsistency requirement very flexibly. United States v. Dennis, 625 F.2d 782, 795 (8th Cir.1980), is reflective of the majority position: "The trial judge has considerable discretion in determining whether testimony is 'inconsistent' with prior statements; inconsistency is not limited to diametrically opposed answers but may be found in evasive answers, inability to recall, silence, or changes of position." A very well-settled body of case law treats a contrived memory loss as inconsistent, see, e.g., United States v. Knox, 124 F.3d 1360, 1364 (10th Cir.1997), but there is no requirement that the trial court

determine that the witness is lying about lack of memory, see United States v. Gajo, 290 F.3d 922, 930–32 (7th Cir.2002).

3. *Requiring little more than a human presence.* Rule 801(d)(1) generally requires that the declarant "testifies and is subject to cross-examination about a prior statement." The meaning of the term "subject to cross-examination" requires interpretation in the situation where a witness lacks memory of the prior statement and/or the underlying event or claims to have no memory. In United States v. Owens, 484 U.S. 554 (1988), the Supreme Court, in ruling admissible a prior statement of identification under Rule 801(d)(1)(C), provided a rather extreme interpretation of the term that largely eliminates the memory issue:

> Ordinarily a witness is regarded as "subject to cross-examination" when he is placed on the stand, under oath, and responds willingly to questions. Just as with [the Confrontation Clause], limitations on the scope of examination by the trial court or assertions of privilege by the witness may undermine the process to such a degree that meaningful cross-examination within the intent of the rule no longer exists. But that effect is not produced by the witness' assertion of memory loss—which * * * is often the very result sought to be produced by cross-examination, and can be effective in destroying the force of the prior statement. Rule 801(d)(1)(C) [like 801(d)(1)(A)], which specifies that the cross-examination need only "concer[n] the statement," does not on its face require more.

484 U.S. at 561–62. *Owens'* definition of "subject to cross-examination" allows extraordinarily few exceptions. United States v. Torrez–Ortega, 184 F.3d 1128, 1132–35 (10th Cir.1999), which found a witness who erroneously but persistently claimed the Fifth Amendment privilege did not satisfy the Rule, represents one of those unusual situations. See related discussion in Section C, infra.

4. *Sufficiency.* Admissibility of prior inconsistent statements as substantive evidence under the Rule does not necessarily mean that such statements alone are sufficient to sustain a conviction. See United States v. Bahe, 40 F.Supp.2d 1302, 1308–10 (D.N.M.1998) (describing the weight of authority that a prior inconsistent statement standing alone is insufficient to sustain a guilty verdict).

5. *Limits on statements admissible for impeachment only.* In spite of Rule 801(d)(1)(A), many prior inconsistent statements will remain admissible only for impeachment purposes because, to be substantively admissible, the prior inconsistent statements must have been made under oath, subject to penalty of perjury, and in certain types of proceedings. Where they are not substantively admissible, the basic principle remains that "[t]he prosecution may not call a witness it knows to be hostile for the *primary* purpose of eliciting otherwise inadmissible impeachment testimony, for such a scheme serves as a subterfuge to avoid the hearsay rule." United States v. Hogan, 763 F.2d 697, 702 (5th Cir.1985).

TOME V. UNITED STATES

Supreme Court of the United States, 1995.
513 U.S. 150.

JUSTICE KENNEDY delivered the opinion of the Court, except as to Part IIB.

Various federal Courts of Appeals are divided over the evidence question presented by this case. At issue is the interpretation of a provision in the Federal Rules of Evidence bearing upon the admissibility of statements, made by a declarant who testifies as a witness, that are consistent with the testimony and are offered to rebut a charge of a "recent fabrication or improper influence or motive." Fed. Rule Evid. 801(d)(1)(B). The question is whether out-of-court consistent statements made after the alleged fabrication, or after the alleged improper influence or motive arose, are admissible under the Rule.

I

Petitioner Tome was charged in a one-count indictment with the felony of sexual abuse of a child, his own daughter, aged four at the time of the alleged crime. * * *

Tome and the child's mother had been divorced in 1988. A tribal court awarded joint custody of the daughter, A.T., to both parents, but Tome had primary physical custody. In 1989 the mother was unsuccessful in petitioning the tribal court for primary custody of A.T., but was awarded custody for the summer of 1990. * * * On August 27, 1990, the mother contacted Colorado authorities with allegations that Tome had committed sexual abuse against A.T.

The prosecution's theory was that Tome committed sexual assaults upon the child while she was in his custody and that the crime was disclosed when the child was spending vacation time with her mother. The defense argued that the allegations were concocted so the child would not be returned to her father. At trial A.T., then six and one half years old, was the Government's first witness. For the most part, her direct testimony consisted of one- and two-word answers to a series of leading questions. Cross-examination took place over two trial days. The defense asked A.T. 348 questions. On the first day A.T. answered all the questions posed to her on general, background subjects.

The next day there was no testimony, and the prosecutor met with A.T. When cross-examination of A.T. resumed, she was questioned about those conversations but was reluctant to discuss them. Defense counsel then began questioning her about the allegations of abuse, and it appears she was reluctant at many points to answer. As the trial judge noted, however, some of the defense questions were imprecise or unclear. The judge expressed his concerns with the examination of A.T., observing there were lapses of as much as 40–55 seconds between some questions and the answers and that on the second day of examination the witness seemed to be losing concentration. The trial judge stated, "We have a very difficult situation here."

After A.T. testified, the Government produced six witnesses who testified about a total of seven statements made by A.T. describing the alleged sexual assaults: A.T.'s babysitter recited A.T.'s statement to her on August 22, 1990, that she did not want to return to her father because he "gets drunk and he thinks I'm his wife"; the babysitter related further details given by A.T. on August 27, 1990, while A.T.'s mother stood outside the room and listened after the mother had been unsuccessful in questioning A.T. herself; the mother recounted what she had heard A.T. tell the babysitter; a social worker recounted details A.T. told her on August 29, 1990 about the assaults; and three pediatricians, Drs. Kuper, Reich and Spiegel, related A.T.'s statements to them describing how and where she had been touched by Tome. All but A.T.'s statement to Dr. Spiegel implicated Tome. * * *

A.T.'s out-of-court statements, recounted by the six witnesses, were offered by the Government under Rule 801(d)(1)(B). The trial court admitted all of the statements over defense counsel's objection, accepting the Government's argument that they rebutted the implicit charge that A.T.'s testimony was motivated by a desire to live with her mother. * * * Following trial, Tome was convicted and sentenced to 12 years imprisonment.

On appeal, the Court of Appeals for the Tenth Circuit affirmed, adopting the Government's argument that all of A.T.'s out-of-court statements were admissible under Rule 801(d)(1)(B) even though they had been made after A.T.'s alleged motive to fabricate arose. The court reasoned that "the pre-motive requirement is a function of the relevancy rules, not the hearsay rules" and that as a "function of relevance, the pre-motive rule is clearly too broad * * * because it is simply not true that an individual with a motive to lie always will do so." 3 F.3d 342, 350 (C.A.10 1993). "Rather, the relevance of the prior consistent statement is more accurately determined by evaluating the strength of the motive to lie, the circumstances in which the statement is made, and the declarant's demonstrated propensity to lie." *Ibid.* * * * Applying this balancing test to A.T.'s first statement to her babysitter, the Court of Appeals determined that although A.T. might have had "some motive to lie, we do not believe that it is a particularly strong one." 3 F.3d, at 351. The court held that the district judge had not abused his discretion in admitting A.T.'s out-of-court statements. * * *

II

The prevailing common-law rule for more than a century before adoption of the Federal Rules of Evidence was that a prior consistent statement introduced to rebut a charge of recent fabrication or improper influence or motive was admissible if the statement had been made before the alleged fabrication, influence, or motive came into being, but it was inadmissible if made afterwards. As Justice Story explained: "[W]here the testimony is assailed as a fabrication of a recent date * * * in order to repel such imputation, proof of the *antecedent* declaration of the party may be admitted." *Ellicott v. Pearl*, 35 U.S. 412, 439 (1836) (emphasis supplied). See also *People v. Singer*, 300 N.Y. 120, 124–125, 89 N.E.2d 710, 712 (1949).

McCormick and Wigmore stated the rule in a more categorical manner: "[T]he applicable principle is that the prior consistent statement has no relevancy to refute the charge unless the consistent statement was made before the source of the bias, interest, influence or incapacity originated." E. Cleary, McCormick on Evidence § 49, p. 105 (2d ed. 1972) (hereafter McCormick). See also 4 J. Wigmore, Evidence § 1128, p. 268 (J. Chadbourn rev. 1972) (hereafter Wigmore) ("A consistent statement, at a *time prior* to the existence of a fact said to indicate bias * * * will effectively explain away the force of the impeaching evidence" (emphasis in original)). The question is whether Rule 801(d)(1)(B) embodies this temporal requirement. We hold that it does.

A

Rule 801 * * * defines prior consistent statements as nonhearsay only if they are offered to rebut a charge of "recent fabrication or improper influence or motive." Fed. Rule Evid. 801(d)(1)(B). Noting the "troublesome" logic of treating a witness prior consistent statements as hearsay at all (because the declarant is present in court and subject to cross-examination), the Advisory Committee decided to treat those consistent statements, once the preconditions of the Rule were satisfied, as nonhearsay and admissible as substantive evidence, not just to rebut an attack on the witness's credibility. See Advisory Committee Notes on Fed. Rule Evid. 801(d)(1), 28 U.S.C.App., p. 773. * * *

The Rules do not accord this weighty, nonhearsay status to all prior consistent statements. To the contrary, admissibility under the Rules is confined to those statements offered to rebut a charge of "recent fabrication or improper influence or motive," the same phrase used by the Advisory Committee in its description of the "traditiona[l]" common law of evidence, which was the background against which the Rules were drafted. See Advisory Committee Notes, *supra*, at 773. Prior consistent statements may not be admitted to counter all forms of impeachment or to bolster the witness merely because she has been discredited. In the present context, the question is whether A.T.'s out-of-court statements rebutted the alleged link between her desire to be with her mother and her testimony, not whether they suggested that A.T.'s in-court testimony was true. The Rule speaks of a party rebutting an alleged motive, not bolstering the veracity of the story told.

This limitation is instructive, not only to establish the preconditions of admissibility but also to reinforce the significance of the requirement that the consistent statements must have been made before the alleged influence, or motive to fabricate arose. That is to say, the forms of impeachment within the Rule's coverage are the ones in which the temporal requirement makes the most sense. Impeachment by charging that the testimony is a recent fabrication or results from an improper influence or motive is, as a general matter, capable of direct and forceful refutation through introduction of out-of-court consistent statements that predate the alleged fabrication, influence or motive. A consistent statement that predates the motive is a square rebuttal of the charge that the testimony was contrived as a consequence of that motive. By contrast, prior consistent statements carry little rebuttal force when most other types of impeachment are involved. McCormick § 49, p. 105 ("When the attack takes the form of impeachment of character, by showing misconduct, convictions or bad reputation, it is generally agreed that there is no color for sustaining by consistent statements. The defense does not meet the assault" (footnote omitted)); see also 4 Wigmore § 1131, p. 293 ("The broad rule obtains in a few courts that consistent statements may be admitted after impeachment of any sort—in particular after any impeachment by cross-examination. But there is no reason for such a loose rule" (footnote omitted)).

There may arise instances when out-of-court statements that postdate the alleged fabrication have some probative force in rebutting a charge of fabrication or improper influence or motive, but those statements refute the charged fabrication in a less direct and forceful way. Evidence that a witness made consistent statements after the alleged motive to fabricate arose may suggest in some degree that the in-court testimony is truthful, and thus suggest in some degree that that testimony did not result from some improper influence; but if the drafters of Rule 801(d)(1)(B) intended to countenance rebuttal along that indirect inferential chain, the purpose of confining the types of impeachment that open the door to rebuttal by introducing consistent statements becomes unclear. If consistent statements are admissible without reference to the time frame we find imbedded in the Rule, there appears no sound reason not to admit consistent statements to rebut other forms of impeachment as well. Whatever objections can be leveled against limiting the Rule to this designated form of impeachment and confining the rebuttal to those statements made before the fabrication or improper influence or motive arose, it is clear to us that the drafters of Rule 801(d)(1)(B) were relying upon the common-law temporal requirement.

The underlying theory of the Government's position is that an out-of-court consistent statement, whenever it was made, tends to bolster the testimony of a witness and so tends also to rebut an express or implied charge that the testimony has been the product of an improper influence. Congress could have adopted that rule with ease, providing, for instance, that "a witness' prior consistent statements are admissible whenever relevant to assess the witness's truthfulness or accuracy." The theory would be that, in a broad sense, any prior statement by a witness concerning the disputed issues at trial would have some relevance in assessing the accuracy or truthfulness of the witness's in-court testimony on the same subject. The narrow Rule enacted by Congress, however, cannot be understood to incorporate the Government's theory.

* * *

The language of the Rule, in its concentration on rebutting charges of recent fabrication, improper influence and motive to the exclusion of other forms of impeachment, as well as in its use of wording which follows the language of the common-law cases, suggests that it was intended to carry over the common-law pre-motive rule. * * *

B

Our conclusion that Rule 801(d)(1)(B) embodies the common-law premotive requirement is confirmed by an examination of the Advisory Committee Notes to the Federal Rules of Evidence. We have relied on those well-considered Notes as a useful guide in ascertaining the meaning of the Rules. * * *

* * *

Throughout their discussion of the Rules, the Advisory Committee Notes rely on Wigmore and McCormick as authority for the common-law approach. In light of the categorical manner in which those authors state the premotive requirement, * * * it is difficult to imagine that the drafters, who noted the new substantive use of prior consistent statements, would have remained silent if they intended to modify the premotive requirement. As we observed with respect to another provision of the Rules, "[w]ith this state of unanimity confronting the drafters of the Federal Rules of Evidence, we think it unlikely that they intended to scuttle entirely [the common-law requirement]." *United States v. Abel*, 469 U.S. 45, 50 (1984). Here, we do not think the drafters of the Rule intended to scuttle the whole premotive requirement and rationale without so much as a whisper of explanation.

Observing that Edward Cleary was the Reporter of the Advisory Committee that drafted the Rules, the Court has relied upon his writings as persuasive authority on the meaning of the Rules. See *Daubert v. Merrell Dow Pharmaceuticals, Inc.,* 509 U. S. 579 (1993); *Abel, supra,* at 51–52. Cleary also was responsible for the 1972 revision of McCormick's treatise, which included an examination of the changes introduced by the proposed federal rules to the common-law practice of impeachment and rehabilitation. The discussion, which occurs only three paragraphs after the treatise's categorical description of the common-law premotive rule, also lacks any indication that the proposed rules were abandoning that temporal limitation. See McCormick § 50, p. 107.

*   *   *

That Rule 801(d)(1)(B) permits prior consistent statements to be used for substantive purposes after the statements are admitted to rebut the existence of an improper influence or motive makes it all the more important to observe the preconditions for admitting the evidence in the first place. The position taken by the Rules reflects a compromise between the views expressed by the "bulk of the case law * * * against allowing prior statements of witnesses to be used generally as substantive evidence" and the views of the majority of "writers * * * [who] ha[d] taken the opposite position." [See Advisory Committee Notes on Rule 801(d)(1), 28 U.S.C.App., p. 773]. That compromise was one that the Committee candidly admitted was a "judgment * * * more of experience than of logic." *Ibid.*

C

The Government's final argument in favor of affirmance is that the common-law premotive rule advocated by petitioner is inconsistent with the Federal Rules' liberal approach to relevancy and with strong academic criticism, beginning in the 1940's, directed at the exclusion of out-of-court statements made by a declarant who is present in court and subject to cross-examination. This argument misconceives the design of the Rules' hearsay provisions.

* * * To be sure, certain commentators in the years preceding the adoption of the Rules had been critical of the common-law approach to hearsay, particularly its categorical exclusion of out-of-court statements offered for substantive purposes. See, e.g., Weinstein, The Probative Force of Hearsay, 46 Iowa L.Rev. 331, 344–345 (1961) (gathering sources). * * * As an alternative, they suggested moving away from the categorical exclusion of hearsay and toward a case-by-case balancing of the probative value of particular statements against their likely prejudicial effect. See Weinstein, *supra,* at 338; Ladd, The Relationship of the Principles of Exclusionary Rules of Evidence to the Problem of Proof, 18 Minn.L.Rev. 506 (1934). The Advisory Committee, however, was explicit in rejecting this balancing approach to hearsay: "The Advisory Committee has rejected this approach to hearsay as involving too great a measure of

judicial discretion, minimizing the predictability of rulings, [and] enhancing the difficulties of preparation for trial." Advisory Committee's Introduction, *supra*, at 771 (emphasis added). * * *

The statement-by-statement balancing approach advocated by the Government and adopted by the Tenth Circuit creates the precise dangers the Advisory Committee noted and sought to avoid: It involves considerable judicial discretion; it reduces predictability; and it enhances the difficulties of trial preparation because parties will have difficulty knowing in advance whether or not particular out-of-court statements will be admitted. See Advisory Committee's Introduction, *supra*, at 771.

D

The case before us illustrates some of the important considerations supporting the Rule as we interpret it, especially in criminal cases. If the Rule were to permit the introduction of prior statements as substantive evidence to rebut every implicit charge that a witness' in-court testimony results from recent fabrication or improper influence or motive, the whole emphasis of the trial could shift to the out-of-court statements, not the in-court ones. The present case illustrates the point. In response to a rather weak charge that A.T.'s testimony was a fabrication created so the child could remain with her mother, the Government was permitted to present a parade of sympathetic and credible witnesses who did no more than recount A.T.'s detailed out-of-court statements to them. Although those statements might have been probative on the question whether the alleged conduct had occurred, they shed but minimal light on whether A.T. had the charged motive to fabricate. At closing argument before the jury, the Government placed great reliance on the prior statements for substantive purposes but did not once seek to use them to rebut the impact of the alleged motive.

* * *

[Reversed and remanded.]

[JUSTICE SCALIA'S opinion, in which he disagrees with the "authoritative" weight given to the Advisory Committee Notes in Part IIB, is omitted.]

JUSTICE BREYER, with whom THE CHIEF JUSTICE, JUSTICE O'CONNOR and JUSTICE THOMAS join, dissenting.

The basic issue in this case concerns, not hearsay, but relevance. As the majority points out, the common law permitted a lawyer to rehabilitate a witness (after a charge of improper motive) by pointing to the fact that the witness had said the same thing earlier—but only if the witness made the earlier statement before the motive to lie arose. The reason for the time limitation was that, otherwise, the prior consistent statement had no relevance to rebut the charge that the in-court testimony was the product of the motive to lie. * * *

The majority believes that a hearsay-related rule, Federal Rule of Evidence 801(d)(1)(B), codifies this absolute timing requirement. I do not. Rule 801(d)(1)(B) has nothing to do with relevance. Rather, that Rule carves out a subset of prior consistent statements that were formerly admissible only to rehabilitate a witness (a nonhearsay use that relies upon the fact that the statement was made). It then says that members of that subset are "not hearsay." This means that, if such a statement is admissible for a particular rehabilitative purpose (to rebut a charge of recent fabrication, improper influence or motive), its proponent now may use it substantively, for a hearsay purpose (i.e., as evidence of its truth), as well.

The majority is correct in saying that there are different kinds of categories of prior consistent statements that can rehabilitate a witness in different ways, including statements (a) placing a claimed inconsistent statement in context; (b) showing that an inconsistent statement was not made; (c) indicating that the witness' memory is not as faulty as a cross-examiner has claimed; and (d) showing that the witness did not recently fabricate his testimony as a result of an improper influence or motive. See *United States v. Rubin,* 609 F.2d 51, 68 (C.A.2 1979) (Friendly, J., concurring). But, I do not see where, in the existence of several categories, the majority can find the premise, which it seems to think is important, that the reason the drafters singled out one category (category (d)) was that category's special probative force in respect to rehabilitating a witness. Nor, in any event, do I understand how that premise can help the majority reach its conclusion about the common-law timing rule.

* * *

Assuming Rule 801(d)(1)(B) does not codify the absolute timing requirement, I must still answer the question whether, as a relevance matter, the common-law statement of the premotive rule stands as an absolute bar to a trial court's admission of a postmotive prior consistent statement for the purpose of rebutting a charge of recent fabrication or improper influence or motive. * * *

[O]ne can find examples where the timing rule's claim of "no relevancy" is simply untrue. A post-motive statement is relevant to rebut, for example, a charge of recent fabrication based on improper motive, say, when the speaker made the prior statement while affected by a far more powerful motive to tell the truth. A speaker might be moved to lie to help an acquaintance. But, suppose the circumstances also make clear to the speaker that only the truth will save his child's life. Or, suppose the postmotive statement was made spontaneously, or when the speaker's motive to lie was much weaker than it was at trial. In these and similar situations, special circumstances may indicate that the prior statement was made for some reason other than the alleged improper motivation; it may have been made not because of, but despite, the improper motivation. Hence, postmotive statements can, in appropriate circumstances, directly refute the charge of fabrication based on improper motive, not because they bolster in a general way the witness' trial testimony, * * * but because the circumstances indicate that the statements are not causally connected to the alleged motive to lie.

* * *

Accordingly, I would hold that the Federal Rules authorize a district court to allow (where probative in respect to rehabilitation) the use of postmotive prior consistent statements to rebut a charge of recent fabrication, improper influence or motive (subject of course to, for example, Rule 403). * * *

NOTES AND QUESTIONS

1. *Substantial room for interpretation.* In an omitted portion of the opinion, Justice Kennedy acknowledges that determining precisely when a particular corrupting influence arose will sometimes be difficult. To what extent does *Tome* leave the lower courts free to shape admissibility through that factual determination? Compare United States v. Montague, 958 F.2d 1094, 1096–98 (D.C.Cir.1992) (warning that if consistent statements must predate the corrupting motive, statements made by accomplices during police interrogation will generally be inadmissible to support their testimony when testifying for the prosecution), with United States v. Prieto, 232 F.3d 816, 819–22 (11th Cir.2000) (rejecting bright-line rule that any statement after arrest is inadmissible because a motive to fabricate necessarily and automatically attaches, reasoning that determination regarding motive to fabricate is to be made on the basis of the circumstances of the individual case by the trial court, and concluding voluntary statement made after arrest and before any discussion of possible cooperation with the government was untainted by improper motive).

2. *Consistent statements still admissible to rehabilitate.* As Justice Breyer states in his dissent, prior consistent statements can rehabilitate a witness whose credibility has been attacked in several different ways. On this point, Breyer cites Judge Friendly's concurring opinion in United States v. Rubin, 609 F.2d 51, 68–70 (2d Cir.1979). Judge Friendly argued in *Rubin* that the specific timing requirement of Rule 801(d)(1)(B) was applicable exclusively to those prior consistent statements offered for their truth after an attack charging recent fabrication or improper motive or influence. When used only to rehabilitate after other types of attacks on credibility, such as when a consistent statement taken nearer the event is used to rehabilitate an attack based on poor memory, the statement is admissible under Rule 801(c)(2) for the limited purpose of affecting credibility rather than for the truth of the statement, and Friendly contended the timing restrictions of

Rule 801(d)(1)(B) were inapplicable. In such circumstances, no improper influence or motive is alleged, and the prior statement need not precede it. Judge Friendly's position is generally accepted in the federal courts. See United States v. Simonelli, 237 F.3d 19, 27–28 (1st Cir.2001) (consistent statements offered only for credibility are not governed by restrictions in Rule 801 but must have rebuttal force beyond mere fact that consistent statement was made). The most clearly accepted use of a prior consistent statement to rehabilitate is to clarify or rebut the impeaching effect of a prior inconsistent statement that was used to impeach the witness. See United States v. Santiago, 199 F.Supp.2d 101, 106–07 (S.D.N.Y.2002) (allowing government to admit statement to correct misleading impeaching claim regarding its contents).

3.   *Common law's perspective of the limited significance of typical prior consistent statement.* In determining whether a prior consistent statement is admissible when offered to rehabilitate, one should be cognizant of the common law position that mere repetition is valueless: "The witness is not helped by it; for, even if it is an improbable or untrustworthy story, it is not made more probable or more trustworthy by any number of repetitions of it." 4 Wigmore, Evidence § 1124, at 255 (Chadbourn rev. 1972). A simple example may be helpful in understanding this perspective. Learning that a witness gave the same version of her story moments before taking the witness stand would not be admissible regarding credibility; it would be excluded under Rule 403. In other situations, however, the particular circumstances under which the statement was made and its timing can make it sufficiently valuable in restoring credibility to satisfy the relevancy concerns of Rules 401 and 403.

4.   *Proposed expansion of receiving consistent statements for their truth.* The Evidence Rules Advisory Committee in 2013 proposed an amendment that would broaden this exemption beyond statements offered to rebut an express charge of fabrication or improper influence or motive. It would also include consistent statements offered "to rehabilitate the declarant's credibility as a witness when attached on another ground." The Committee's note explains that "[t]he amendment does not change the traditional and well-accepted limits on bringing prior consistent statements before the factfinder for credibility purposes." However, it would mean "that prior consistent statements are exempt from the hearsay rule [and admitted for their truth] whenever they are admissible to rehabilitate the witness." Although not overruling *Tome*, the impact of this amendment both to encourage introduction of consistent statements, which would be admissible not only to rehabilitate but for substantive purposes, and to erode the careful limitations of *Tome* remain to be determined.

UNITED STATES V. LEWIS

United States Court of Appeals, Second Circuit, 1977.
565 F.2d 1248.

FEINBERG, CIRCUIT JUDGE:

After a jury trial in the United States District Court for the Eastern District of New York before Thomas C. Platt, J., appellant Frank Tillman Lewis was convicted of armed bank robbery and conspiracy to commit that crime * * *.

The Photographic Identification

In his thorough brief and argument, appellant's counsel maintains that the district judge committed a number of errors of law. The most substantial arguments on appeal stem from Norma Sharpe's pre-trial identification of appellant from a display of photographs. At trial, Mrs. Sharpe was unable to identify appellant in the courtroom and mistakenly picked out a Deputy United States Marshal instead. When Mrs. Sharpe was then shown the photographic display, she testified that she had previously identified one of the bank robbers from the group of pictures, and she then picked out the photograph she had earlier selected. This picture, which was of appellant, was then admitted into evidence. After Mrs. Sharpe's testimony, FBI Agent Leo Farrell testified as to the way in which he had prepared the photographic spread. He also confirmed that Mrs. Sharpe had selected appellant's picture shortly after the bank robbery. * * *

Appellant next argues that the identification testimony should have been excluded as hearsay, and is not permitted by the new Federal Rules of Evidence. Appellant directs our attention to Rule 801(d), which contains various definitions, and provides in relevant part that:

(d) Statements which are not hearsay. A statement is not hearsay if—

(1) Prior statement by witness. The declarant testifies at the trial or hearing and is subject to cross-examination concerning the statement, and the statement is (A) inconsistent with his testimony, and was given under oath subject to the penalty of perjury at a trial, hearing, or other proceeding, or in a deposition, or (B) consistent with his testimony and is offered to rebut an express or implied charge against him of recent fabrication or improper influence or motive, or (C) *one of identification of a person made after perceiving him* * * * (Emphasis supplied).

Appellant argues that Agent Farrell's testimony should have been excluded because "identification of a person made after perceiving him" contemplates only corporeal, not photographic, identification; and because it was improper to allow Farrell to testify in the absence of an in-court identification by Mrs. Sharpe. Appellant also claims that Mrs. Sharpe's testimony about her prior identification after she erroneously identified someone else in court amounted to testimony about a prior inconsistent statement not made under oath, rendering it improper under subsection (A), which overrides subsection (C).

Subsection (C) of Rule 801(d)(1), the focal point of appellant's arguments, appeared in its present form in the Rules as promulgated by the Supreme Court in November 1972. However, the Senate deleted the subsection before the Rules were approved by Congress in December 1974. Not long thereafter, the subsection was resurrected in an amendment to Rule 801, effective October 31, 1975. The Senate Report on the 1975 amendment attributed the initial opposition to the subsection to concern over convicting a defendant solely on "unsworn, out-of-court testimony." The Report noted, however, that the Rule required the identifier to be available for cross-examination at the trial, and in support of the view that such evidence should be admissible, cited, among other recent decisions, the Supreme Court's discussion in *Gilbert v. California,* 388 U.S. 263, 272 n.3 * * * (1967), the opinion of Judge Friendly in *United States v. Miller,* 381 F.2d 529, 538 (2d Cir.1967), and the en banc decision of the Court of Appeals for the District of Columbia, *Clemons v. United States,* 408 F.2d 1230 (1968). The controversy over, and the rationale of, subsection (C) are both admirably summarized in 4 Weinstein's Evidence, 801–3ff., ¶ 801(d)(1)(C)[01]. We agree with the observation there made that

> Congress has recognized, as do most trial judges, that identification in the courtroom is a formality that offers little in the way of reliability and much in the way of suggestibility. The experienced trial judge gives much greater credence to the out-of-court identification.

Id. at 801–103. This court recently pointed out that "[t]he purpose of the rule was to permit the introduction of identifications made by a witness when memory was fresher and there had been less opportunity for influence to be exerted upon him." *United States v. Marchand,* 564 F.2d 983, 996 (2d Cir.1977).

With these considerations in mind, we turn to appellant's specific contentions. The legislative history makes clear that Congress intended "nonsuggestive * * * photographic," as well as lineup, identifications to be covered by subsection (C). Senate Report, at 2. This conclusion is confirmed by our recent holding in *United States v. Marchand, supra,* 564 F.2d at 996. We can see no sound principle for construing "identification of a person" to exclude identification by a photograph. True, there are dangers peculiar to photographic identification and these, like the dangers of a lineup or even those of an on-the-spot identification, must be taken into account in assessing reliability. But they do not justify a limiting construction of subsection (C).

Appellant's second argument on this point is that the failure of Mrs. Sharpe to identify appellant in court made inadmissible Agent Farrell's evidence that she had identified appellant a month or two earlier. Appellant may be confusing this situation with that posed by the failure or refusal of the identifying witness to recall in court the earlier identification, which is discussed in Judge Weinstein's treatise from which appellant's brief extensively quotes. In that situation, testimony like Agent Farrell's might well raise questions concerning the adequacy of cross-examination and the right to confront the original identifying witness. In this case, however, Mrs. Sharpe did recall her prior identification and so testified. Even before the new Rule, we approved of admitting evidence of prior identification, albeit corporeal, by the declarant's "own testimony and also by that of others corroborating his version of the details," see *United States v. Miller,* supra, 381 F.2d at 538, cited by the Senate Report in support of subsection (C). Cf. *United States v. Jenkins,* 496 F.2d 57, 68–70 (2d Cir.1974) (declarant could not recall prior photographic nonidentification of Jenkins and identification of another; evidence of same through third party excluded). If appellant is suggesting that under the new Rule testimony like Agent Farrell's may only be used to bolster an accurate in-court identification, we disagree. It seems clear both from the text and the legislative history of the amended Rule that testimony concerning extra-judicial identifications is admissible regardless of whether there has been an accurate in-court identification. The Senate Report recognizes the possibility that there may be a "di* * * between the witness's in-court and out-of-court testimony," and the House Report praises the amended Rule as a means of ensuring that "delays in the criminal justice system do not lead to cases falling through because the witness can no longer recall the identity of the person he saw commit the crime." The occurrence of the very contingency foreseen by the Congress will obviously not serve, of itself, to bar the Farrell testimony.

Appellant's final point seems to be that subsection (C) does not apply at all when the identifier has made an erroneous in-court identification because the prior identification is inconsistent with it and was not given under oath, as required by subsection (A). The Government responds that since appellant's appearance had changed significantly by the time of trial, there was no inconsistency. More significantly, even though Rule 801(d)(1) embraces subsection (C), the latter is not limited by the earlier subsections. Subsection (C) represents a legislative decision to admit statements of identification provided the declarant "testifies at * * * trial * * * and is subject to cross-examination concerning the statement." These conditions were met here, and we do not think that subsection (C) is rendered inoperative by Mrs. Sharpe's misidentification in court.

* * *

Judgment affirmed.

NOTES AND QUESTIONS

1. *Antecedents.* Prior to the enactment of the Federal Rules of Evidence, a number of courts had held pretrial identification evidence admissible as an "exception" to the hearsay rule. The most influential of these decisions was People v. Gould, 354 P.2d 865 (Cal.1960). There the Supreme Court of California recognized the superiority of pretrial identification testimony to the suggestive and unpersuasive in-court identification typically occurring at trial. This reliability would support an exception to the hearsay rule. *Gould* also concluded that "the principal danger of admitting hearsay is not present since the witness is available at the trial for cross-examination," which is the justification of the Federal Rules for treating prior identifications as falling outside the hearsay rule. Id. at 867.

2. *Improper and unconstitutional police identification methods.* In addition to the hearsay concern, the reliability of eyewitness identifications is the subject of great concern, particularly when the identification may be the product of improper police methods. The suggestiveness of pretrial identification procedures are at least partially addressed by a series of United States Supreme Court cases. See Manson v. Brathwaite, 432 U.S. 98 (1977); Simmons v. United States, 390 U.S. 377 (1968); Neil v. Biggers, 409 U.S. 188 (1972); United States v. Wade, 388 U.S. 218 (1967); Gilbert v. California, 388 U.S. 263 (1967); Stovall v. Denno, 388 U.S. 293 (1967). They guarantee a criminal defendant the right to counsel at pretrial identification procedures conducted after the initiation of formal adversarial proceedings, *Wade*, and exclude identification evidence where it is the result of suggestive police procedures that give rise to a "very substantial likelihood of irreparable misidentification." *Simmons,* 390 U.S. at 384. Despite these protections, commentators and courts, spurred by DNA exonerations of defendants wrongfully convicted by erroneous identifications, raise questions about the reliability of eyewitness identifications. See Chapter 12, Section E, supra (Hines v. United States and accompanying eyewitness identification note).

3. *"Subject to cross-examination" requirement.* Rule 801(d)(1)(C), which governs admission of prior statements of identification, like Rule 801(d)(1)(A) for prior inconsistent statements, requires that the declarant be subject to cross-examination. Here too issues of the adequacy of cross-examination arise if the witness claims at trial to have no memory. In United States v. Owens, 484 U.S. 554 (1988), the Supreme Court held that the victim of an assault, which resulted in severe memory impairment, was "subject to cross-examination" within the meaning of the Rule. While the victim remembered at trial previously identifying the defendant, he could not recall seeing his

attacker or the circumstances of the identification. The Court reasoned broadly that "[o]rdinarily a witness is regarded as 'subject to cross-examination' when he is placed on the stand, under oath, and responds willingly to questions. * * * [Absent limitations on cross-examination or assertion of privilege,] Rule 801(d)(1)(C) * * * does not * * * require more." 484 U.S. at 562.

4. *Composite drawing.* How should a composite drawing of the suspect prepared at the direction of the victim be treated? Compare State v. Motta, 659 P.2d 745 (Haw.1983) (drawing admissible under Rule for prior identifications), with United States v. Moskowitz, 581 F.2d 14 (2d Cir.1978) (drawing treated as nonhearsay; statements by victim identifying it admissible under instant Rule). How should statements describing the perpetrator be treated? See Morris v. United States, 398 A.2d 333 (D.C.1978) (treating victim's prior description of perpetrator as falling under the common law exception for identifications).

5. *Covering identification procedures, not prior statements that the witness knows the perpetrator.* A few courts have erroneously ignored the purpose and language of the Rule as to testimony about an identification of the defendant through an out-of-court identification procedure and instead allowed testimony that a certain person, known to the witness, committed a crime. See Bugh v. Mitchell, 329 F.3d 496, 505 n.2 (6th Cir.2003) (noting Ohio's brief use of the Rule in this fashion); United States v. Lopez, 271 F.3d 472, 484 (3d Cir.2001). The Rule should not be employed in this fashion. See United States v. Kaquatosh, 242 F.Supp.2d 562, 565–67 (E.D.Wis.2003). It is also not a proper way to introduce details of the crime. See Randolph v. United States, 882 A.2d 210, 220 (D.C.2005).

(2) ADMISSION OF THE PARTY OPPONENT

Federal Rule 801(d)(2)

EDMUND M. MORGAN, BASIC PROBLEMS OF EVIDENCE
(1962)[18]

The admissibility of an admission made by the party himself rests not upon any notion that the circumstances in which it was made furnish the trier means of evaluating it fairly, but upon the adversary theory of litigation. A party can hardly object that he had no opportunity to cross-examine himself or that he is unworthy of credence save when speaking under sanction of an oath. His adversary may use against him anything which he has said or done. Originally he had no chance to make an explanation, but since about the middle of the 1800's, he has been competent as a witness and can furnish the trier with all pertinent

---

[18] Copyright 1963 by The American Law Institute. Reprinted with the permission of the American Law Institute–American Bar Association Committee on Continuing Professional Education. [Ed.]

information within his knowledge. Consequently the orthodox decisions refuse to apply to evidence of personal admissions restrictions usually applicable to testimonial evidence.

OLSON V. HODGES

Supreme Court of Iowa, 1945.
19 N.W.2d 676.

[Personal injury action by passenger against driver of automobile. Defendant contends that his driving was not "reckless" within the meaning of the state's guest statute and appeals from a judgment entered on a verdict in favor of plaintiff.]

BLISS, JUSTICE. * * * As a part of plaintiff's cross-examination, defendant introduced a statement signed by plaintiff on March 14, 1944— nine days after the accident. In part it is as follows:

> "It is my understanding Hodges was going to Denison. My buddy, Clarence Salisbury, asked me to go along. He told me he would make it worth my while if I would go along to help lift a small piano out of the car. They made arrangements for the trip between themselves but in my presence.

> "At any rate we started for Denison. Just before the accident occurred the car started to skid, the back end started to slide around, and before Hodges could get the car under control it had skidded into a bridge bannister.

> "It was about five P.M. It was snowing a little. I had not noticed the pavement being slick. Hodges was a good, careful driver. He had not been driving fast or carelessly. He was only going twenty-seven or twenty-eight miles per hour when the accident happened. It happened right in front of some farm buildings and a drive into this place. There had been some dirt pulled out on the pavement, which caused the car to start skidding.

> "We were all sober, we had only a couple of beers. Neither of us were intoxicated in any way. * * *

> "Have you read this statement? Yes. Is it true? Yes."

Plaintiff's explanation of the statements in this writing which are contrary to his testimony was that a stranger, whom he supposed was an adjuster, interviewed him at the hospital, but he didn't remember what he told him, and he didn't read the statement which the man wrote, and it was not read to him, and he was in great pain and had been taking considerable opiates during that first month. * * *

II. Appellant assigned error because the court in instructing upon the signed statement of appellee, heretofore referred to, told the jury that it could be considered only as bearing upon the credibility of the plaintiff as a witness and not as proving any substantive fact. The instruction was duly excepted to. This statement was admitted generally without any restriction as to its consideration, over plaintiff's objection that it was incompetent. The instruction unduly and improperly limited the consideration of the statement by the jury. It was proper for the jury to consider it not only in its bearing upon plaintiff's credibility as a witness, because inconsistent with his testimony but since it was a deliberate statement over his own signature, it was admissible not merely as discrediting the testimony of plaintiff, if the statement was believed by the jury, but as substantive evidence against him, and as bearing upon the worthiness of his whole claim. Castner v. Chicago, B. & Q.R. Co., 126 Iowa 581, 585, 586, 102 N.W. 499. The plaintiff was not only a witness but a party-opponent of appellant, and even though he had not taken the stand as a witness, the statement was admissible against him and his case, as based upon his pleadings and the testimony relied upon him, as a discrediting inconsistency on his part. 2 Wigmore on Evidence, 2d Ed., §§ 1048, 1053. The giving of the instruction was reversible error.

NOTES AND QUESTIONS

1. *"Admissions"—a misnomer?* As traditionally used with regard to hearsay, "admissions" are the words or acts of a party or a party's representative that are offered as evidence by the opposing party. One could imagine that to constitute an "admission" a statement had to fully or at least substantially admit of liability or guilt. However, the only requirements are that the statement be inconsistent with the party's position at trial and that it be offered by the opponent, and there is no additional requirement concerning the degree of inconsistency between the prior statement and the party's present position. For this reason, the restyled Federal Rule 801(d)(2) no longer calls them "admissions" but uses the term "an opposing party's statement." See United States v. Reed, 227 F.3d 763, 770 (7th Cir.2000) (stating that admission need not be "incriminating, inculpatory, against interest, nor otherwise inherently damaging to the declarant's case" but merely be statements made by one party and offered as evidence by the opponent).

2. *Offered by the opponent.* An admission must be made by one party and offered by the opposing party. See United States v. McDaniel, 398 F.3d 540, 545 & n.2 (6th Cir.2005) (refusing to receive defendant's own statement as admission because not offered by party-opponent, observing that to receive such a statement would create an "end run" around the adversarial system).

3. *Admission "against interest"?* While most admissions are against the interest of the party making them at the time they were made (as opposed to the time of trial), there is no requirement for admissions that the statement must have been against interest when made. See 2 McCormick, Evidence § 254 (7th ed. 2013). Sometimes admissions are called "admissions

against interest," which is an inaccurate label. Statements against interest are examined in Chapter 14, Section J, and the differences between that exception and the admission exclusion should then be noted. Cf. Globe Savings Bank, F.S.B. v. United States, 61 Fed.Cl. 91, 94–95 (Fed.Cl.2004) (finding that deposition by party-opponent is admission and therefore unavailability is not required).

4. *Foundation requirement.* The final sentence of Rule 613(b) makes inapplicable to admissions the general requirement for inconsistent statements that a foundation must be laid before statements are admitted.

5. *Sharp practices in obtaining statements.* In some states, statutes deal with a side aspect of *Olson*, the taking of statements from persons in injured condition. See, e.g., Minn.Stat.Ann. § 602.01 (statement obtained from injured person within 30 days after injury presumably fraudulent).

6. *Examining another issue.* Refer to *Player v. Thompson*, Section A, supra, for its treatment of the out-of-court statement of Ms. Carder as an admission against her alone.

UNITED STATES V. MCKEON

United States Court of Appeals, Second Circuit, 1984.
738 F.2d 26.

WINTER, CIRCUIT JUDGE:

Following a trial before Judge Platt and a jury, appellant Bernard McKeon was convicted in the Eastern District of New York on one count of conspiracy to export firearms in violation of 18 U.S.C. § 371. McKeon was acquitted of eight substantive counts concerning the illegal exportation of firearms. The trial was McKeon's third on these charges, the first two having ended in mistrials. At issue on appeal is Judge Platt's admission into evidence at the third trial of portions of the opening statement made by McKeon's lawyer at the second trial and the resulting disqualification of that lawyer.

We affirm.

Background

On October 31, 1979, Irish police in Dublin found firearms in crates sent from New York supposedly containing electric paper drills. The alleged shipper of the crates, "Standard Tools," was a fictitious New York corporation which gave as its address a building in Queens, New York, owned by Bernard McKeon.

Officials of the United States Customs Service investigated the origin of the seized shipment and unearthed several shipping and warehousing documents relating to the shipment signed by one "John Moran." On at least one of these documents, which bore the Standard Tools letterhead, they discovered fingerprints of McKeon and his wife, Olive McKeon. * * *

McKeon's first trial on federal firearms charges took place in December, 1982 and ended in a mistrial when the jury was unable to reach a verdict. Prior to McKeon's second trial, a government handwriting and photocopy expert concluded that warehousing and shipping documents supposedly prepared by representatives of Standard Tools, were photocopies produced on the xerox machine located in the bank in which Olive McKeon worked. The defense was apprised both of the expert's identity and his conclusions. In his opening statement at the second trial, Michael Kennedy, McKeon's lawyer told the jury that the evidence would show that McKeon had innocently helped build packing crates for his tenant, John Moran, and that Moran alone was responsible for the Standard Tools' shipment of weapons. Kennedy then declared:

> With reference to the place where Olive McKeon works, expert testimony is going to be brought in to show that the Xerox machine * * * where Mrs. McKeon worked is not—I repeat—is not the same kind of Xerox machine that prepared any of the Standard Tools Xeroxed documents.

> The evidence will also indicate that Mrs. McKeon had absolutely nothing to do with this case other than doing what many wives do, which is, picking up mail and opening it. That is the extent, the sum and substance of her involvement.

The second trial ended in a mistrial before the conclusion of the prosecution's case-in-chief when the defense moved for access to classified documents regarding alleged foreign wiretaps. As a consequence, the expert testimony promised by Kennedy in his opening statement was never offered.

Kennedy's opening statement at the third trial depicted Olive McKeon's role in the events differently than had his opening statement at the second trial. At the third trial, Kennedy told the jury that Bernard McKeon gave his wife the warehouse receipt and some Standard Tools stationery so that she might make two photocopies on the stationery using the bank's xerox machine. This was done, Kennedy said, as a favor to John Moran. He thus continued to picture Bernard McKeon as the innocent dupe of John Moran.

The next day, outside the presence of the jury, the prosecution moved to introduce as evidence the above-quoted portion of Kennedy's opening statement from the second trial. Arguing that the statement was the admission of a party-opponent under Fed.R.Evid. 801(d)(2), the prosecution suggested that it should be imputed to McKeon for any of the following reasons: (i) it was a statement in which McKeon had "manifested his adoption or belief in its truth," *id.* 801(d)(2)(B); (ii) it was "a statement by a person authorized by [McKeon] to make a statement concerning the subject," *id.* 801(d)(2)(C); and (iii) it was "a statement made by [McKeon's] agent * * * concerning a matter within the scope of his agency," *id.* 801(d)(2)(D). The government argued that the inconsistencies in Kennedy's statements were relevant to prove McKeon's consciousness of guilt under Fed.R.Evid. 404(b). Judge Platt ruled that Kennedy's opening statement at the second trial was admissible as an admission under Rule 801(d)(2).

* * *

As part of its case-in-chief, the government introduced the above-quoted portions of Kennedy's opening statement from the second trial. It also put on its expert witness in photocopying, James Kelly, who testified that between the second and third trials he met a former student, Jim Horan, and told him that he, Kelly, had been hired by the prosecution to testify at the third McKeon trial. Horan had been hired as the expert witness for the defense; until his meeting with Kelly, the defense had believed that the prosecution's expert witness would be one Peter Tytell, another former Kelly student. In summation, the prosecution argued that so long as the defense believed that Horan and Tytell would offer conflicting testimony about the xerox machine on which the copies were produced, it was prepared to contend that Olive McKeon did not xerox the warehouse receipt. Once it discovered that the teacher, Kelly, would dispute his pupil, Horan, at the third trial, the defense elected to present a different version of the facts—*viz.* that the receipt had been xeroxed by Olive McKeon at her workplace but for innocent reasons. The prosecution's summation dwelt at length on the change in stories as manifested by the opening statements, arguing that it established McKeon's consciousness of guilt.

This appeal followed McKeon's conviction on a single count of conspiracy.

Discussion

1. *The Admissibility of the Opening Statement*

The parties agree that the evidentiary use against a criminal defendant of his counsel's argument to a jury in an earlier trial is without direct precedent. Although guidance is found in the rules and underlying policies of the law of evidence, the issue raises a number of difficulties since it touches upon numerous sensitive areas including: communications between criminal defendants and their attorneys, the privilege against self-incrimination, fear of impeachment by a prior conviction, the work product, legal theories and trial tactics of the attorney, the freedom of the attorney to engage in uninhibited and robust advocacy, the right to counsel of one's choice, and the usual issues of relevance, confusion and unfair prejudice as well.

We begin with the general proposition that "[s]tatements made by an attorney concerning a matter within his employment may be admissible against the party retaining the attorney," *United States v. Margiotta,* 662 F.2d 131, 142 (2d Cir.1981), a proposition which extends to arguments to a jury. The binding effect on a party of a clear and unambiguous admission of fact made by his or her attorney in an opening statement was acknowledged by the Supreme Court in *Oscanyan v. Arms Co.,* 103 U.S. 261, 263 * * * (1880) and has been frequently recognized in subsequent lower court decisions involving civil cases. *See, e.g., Rhoades, Inc. v. United Air Lines,* 340 F.2d 481, 484 (3d Cir.1965); *Collins v. Texas Company,* 267 F.2d 257, 258 (5th Cir.1959). An admission by a defense attorney in his opening statement in a criminal trial has also been held to eliminate the need for further proof on a given element of an offense. *Dick v. United States,* 40 F.2d 609, 611 (8th Cir.1930) (attorney's opening statement that defendant previously had been convicted of an offense involving sale of liquor sufficient evidence as to that fact).

The general admissibility of an attorney's statements, as well as the binding effect of an opening statement within the four corners of a single trial, are thus well established. The specific issue before us, however, is somewhat different. It involves not the binding effect of an attorney's statements within a trial, but rather the evidentiary use against a criminal defendant of an attorney's seemingly inconsistent statement at an earlier trial to prove that fundamental portions of the defendant's present case are fabricated. Authority on this specific issue is scant, although in at least one civil action it has been suggested that while a previous opening statement is not binding on a litigant, the statement can, under certain circumstances be considered by the trier of fact.[19] *Beyer Co. v. Fleischmann Co.,* 15 F.2d 465, 466 (6th Cir.1926).

We believe that prior opening statements are not *per se* inadmissible in criminal cases. To hold otherwise would not only invite abuse and sharp practice but would also weaken confidence in the justice system itself by denying the function of trials as truth-seeking proceedings. That function cannot be affirmed if parties are free, wholly without explanation, to make fundamental changes in the version of facts within their personal knowledge between trials and to conceal these changes from the final trier of fact.

Support for this conclusion may be found in the analogous issue of the admissibility of superseded pleadings in civil litigation. The law is

---

[19] A distinction is generally recognized between an attorney's judicial admissions, which, like any stipulation, can bind a party within a given lawsuit, and an attorney's less formal evidentiary admissions, which are statements made as a party's agent and which the trier of fact may evaluate as it sees fit. Note, Judicial Admissions, 64 Colum.L.Rev. 1121, 1121 (1964). We are of course concerned only with evidentiary admissions since no one claims that the opening statement from the second trial estopped McKeon from claiming that his wife had photocopied the receipts at his request.

quite clear that such pleadings constitute the admissions of a party-opponent and are admissible in the case in which they were originally filed as well as in any subsequent litigation involving that party. *Contractor Utility Sales Co. v. Certain–Teed Products Corp.*, 638 F.2d 1061, 1084 (7th Cir.1981); *Raulie v. United States*, 400 F.2d 487, 526 (10th Cir.1968); D. McCormick, *Handbook of the Law of Evidence* 633–36 (2d ed. 1972). A party thus cannot advance one version of the facts in its pleadings, conclude that its interests would be better served by a different version, and amend its pleadings to incorporate that version, safe in the belief that the trier of fact will never learn of the change in stories. As was explained in *Kunglig Jarnvagsstyrelsen v. Dexter & Carpenter, Inc.*, 32 F.2d 195, 198 (2d Cir. * * * (1929) by Judge Swan,

> Error is now assigned to the receipt in evidence of the original complaint, which was offered by the defendant both as evidence of agency, and as a formal ratification of the contract. One ground of objection to its admission was lack of proof of authority of the [party's] attorney to bind his client by the averments of the pleading. Such an objection is clearly not sustainable. A pleading prepared by an attorney is an admission by one presumptively authorized to speak for his principal.
>
> * * *
>
> A further objection was based upon the fact that the complaint had been superseded by an amended pleading. This objection is likewise unavailing. When a pleading is amended or withdrawn, the superseded portion ceases to be a conclusive judicial admission; but it still remains as a statement once seriously made by an authorized agent, and as such it is competent evidence of the facts stated, though controvertible, like any other extra-judicial admission made by a party or his agent. * * * If the agent made the admission without adequate information, that goes to its weight, not to its admissibility. There was no error in receiving the original complaint in evidence.

Although we by no means equate the admissibility of inconsistent pleadings with the admissibility of inconsistent opening statements, we believe the analogy is correct insofar as consideration of whether a *per se* rule against the admission of the latter exists.

We conclude, therefore, that there is no absolute rule preventing use of an earlier opening statement by counsel as an admission against a criminal defendant in a subsequent trial. We are not willing, however, to subject such statements to the more expansive practices sometimes permitted under the rule allowing use of admissions by a party-opponent. The rule itself has caused a substantial expenditure of ink by legal commentators seeking a coherent doctrinal theory explaining the use of admissions, D. McCormick, *supra* at 628–31, and has resulted in "a lengthy academic dispute in which most courts have evinced little interest." 4 J. Weinstein & M. Berger, *Evidence* 801–135 (rev.perm.ed. 1981).

Although we share that lack of interest, we note that the admissions rule is itself something of an anomaly since it is in some respects an exception to the general proposition that probative value and reliability are the touchstone of the law of evidence where non-privileged matters are concerned. Admissions may thus be used even though the statement was plainly self-serving when made, was not based upon the personal knowledge of the speaker and is in a form which would otherwise be inadmissible. D. McCormick, *supra* at 631–33; J. Weinstein & M. Berger, *supra* at 801–136. Why probative value and reliability carry so little weight in the case of the admissions rule is not clear, particularly since the use of admissions may be the trial equivalent of a deadly weapon. In all probability, these aspects of the rule are derived vestigially from an older, rough and ready view of the adversary process which leaves each party to bear the consequences of its own acts, no matter how unreliable these acts may be as proof. Whatever its derivation, however, we conclude that the evidentiary use of prior jury argument must be circumscribed in order to avoid trenching upon other important policies.

* * *

Before permitting such use, the district court must be satisfied that the prior argument involves an assertion of fact inconsistent with similar assertions in a subsequent trial. Speculations of counsel, advocacy as to the credibility of witnesses, arguments as to weaknesses in the prosecution's case or invitations to a jury to draw certain inferences should not be admitted. The inconsistency, moreover, should be clear and of a quality which obviates any need for the trier of fact to explore other events at the prior trial. The court must further determine that the statements of counsel were such as to be the equivalent of testimonial statements by the defendant. The formal relationship of the lawyer as agent and the client as principal by itself will rarely suffice to show this since, while clients authorize their attorneys to act on their behalf, considerable delegation is normally involved and such delegation tends to drain the evidentiary value from such statements. Some participatory role of the client must be evident, either directly or inferentially as when the argument is a direct assertion of fact which in all probability had to have been confirmed by the defendant.

Finally, the district court should, in a Fed.R.Evid. 104(a) hearing outside the presence of the jury, determine by a preponderance of the evidence that the inference the prosecution seeks to draw from the inconsistency is a fair one and that an innocent explanation for the inconsistency does not exist. Where the evidence is in equipoise or the preponderance favors an innocent explanation, the prior opening statement should be excluded. We impose this requirement so as to allow leeway for advocacy and to lessen the burden of choice between the defendant's not explaining the inconsistency to the jury or sacrificing other valuable rights.

* * *

Applying these principles to the present case, we conclude that the prior opening statement was properly admitted against McKeon under Fed.R.Evid. 801(d)(2)(B) and (C). The expert testimony about the xerox machine promised by Kennedy in the opening statement at the second trial was in support of a factual claim that Olive McKeon had not copied the documents. Kennedy's opening argument at the third trial, stating that Olive McKeon had indeed copied the documents at the request of her husband, was facially and irreconcilably at odds with the earlier assertion.

* * *

Affirmed.

NOTES AND QUESTIONS

1.   *Special concern for counsel in criminal cases.* The Second Circuit has wavered regarding its admonition in *McKeon* that in criminal cases care should be exercised lest the admissions by counsel concept that is expansively applied in the civil context impair the criminal defendant's constitutional rights under the Fifth and Sixth Amendments. Compare United States v. Valencia, 826 F.2d 169 (2d Cir.1987) (statements by defense counsel during informal conversations with a prosecutor not admissible as statements of an agent), with United States v. Arrington, 867 F.2d 122, 127–28 (2d Cir.1989) (no special procedures need be followed or analysis performed as prerequisite to evidentiary use of out-of-court statements by defense counsel).

2.   *Equal treatment.* The principle in *McKeon* may also be applied to statements by the prosecutor from a former trial. See, e.g., United States v. Ganadonegro, 854 F.Supp.2d 1088, 1115–28 (D.N.M.2012) (permitting use of prosecutor's closing statement as admission).

3.   *"Judicial" versus "evidentiary" admission.* A basic distinction exists between the "solemn judicial admission," which places the matter outside the area of controversy in the case, and the "evidentiary admission," which is admissible but not necessarily conclusive. In the "judicial admission" category fall admissions contained in the effective pleadings in the case, Foxmeyer Corp. v. General Elec. Capital Corp., 286 B.R. 546, 567–68 (Bankr.D.Del.2002), through a failure to deny under Fed.R.Civ.P. 8(d), admissions by stipulation, and admissions made pursuant to requests under Fed.R.Civ.P. 36. Superseded pleadings in the same case and pleadings in

other cases may be admitted but are given only the effect of evidentiary admissions. Annot., 52 A.L.R.2d 516. Similarly, a superseded bill of particulars in a criminal case may be received as an evidentiary admission of the government. United States v. GAF Corp., 928 F.2d 1253, 1258–62 (2d Cir.1991).

4. *Is party legally or practically "bound" by an admission?* Some courts treat a party's own statement at trial as conclusive on the issue, rather than as a simple evidentiary admission. See Bell v. Harmon, 284 S.W.2d 812 (Ky.1955) (party's statement in testimony concerning facts directly observed by him and establishing unequivocally that opponent was not negligent constitutes binding "judicial admission"). Cf. Fox v. Taylor Diving & Salvage Co., 694 F.2d 1349, 1355–56 (5th Cir.1983) (finding testimony of expert that was inconsistent with recovery under one theory held binding against plaintiff as adoptive admission because of high potential for jury prejudice likely from what the court viewed as a manipulative trial strategy). McCormick finds treating statements of a party as simple evidentiary admissions "preferable in policy and most in accord with the tradition of jury trial." 2 McCormick, Evidence § 258 (7th ed. 2013).

5. *Movement from evidentiary to judicial admission.* Answers to interrogatories have received the same treatment as a party's own testimony. Freed v. Erie Lackawanna Ry., 445 F.2d 619 (6th Cir.1971); Smith v. Trans World Airlines, Inc., 358 S.W.2d 91 (Mo.Ct.App.1962). In Ridley v. Young, 253 P.2d 433 (Colo.1953), the court permitted the defendant to contradict his response to an interrogatory admitting that he was driving the automobile that caused plaintiff's injuries even though it was a matter within the defendant's knowledge about which he could not be mistaken. Accordingly, a formal request to admit may be appropriate once an admission is obtained by deposition or interrogatory. See Fed.R.Civ.P. 36(b).

6. *Witness statements not admissions.* The fact that testimony given by a party's witnesses at a former trial was in conflict with testimony given by other witnesses now presented by the party is not admissible, much less binding upon the party. However, if the witnesses are the same, inconsistent testimony may be used for impeachment. Annot., 74 A.L.R.2d 521.

7. *Guilty plea as evidentiary admission.* A guilty plea in a criminal case may be received as a non-binding evidentiary admission where relevant in a civil case involving the party. See, e.g., State Farm Mut. Automobile Ins. Co. v. Worthington, 405 F.2d 683 (8th Cir.1968); Smith v. Southern Nat'l Life Ins. Co., 134 So.2d 337 (La.Ct.App.1961). Guilty pleas involving non-parties may be admissible under Rule 804(b)(3) as a statement against penal interest, discussed in Chapter 14, Section J.

8. *Exclusion under Rule 410.* A plea of nolo contendere, a withdrawn guilty plea, and statements made to prosecuting attorneys in conjunction with plea negotiations are generally inadmissible for policy reasons. See Rule 410. See also Kercheval v. United States, 274 U.S. 220 (1927).

9. *Impact of liberal pleading rules.* A few courts have accepted policy-based arguments that alternative and amended pleadings should not be admitted since to do so may thwart the liberal intent of modern civil pleading practices. See 2 McCormick, Evidence § 257 (7th ed. 2013).

10. *Admissibility of some criminal judgments.* Even without a guilty plea, a judgment of guilty rendered by a judge or jury of a crime punishable by imprisonment in excess of one year may be introduced in civil cases under Rule 803(22) as an exception to the hearsay rule to prove any fact essential to sustain the judgment. The effect of the judgment is similar to an admission; it has evidentiary, not conclusive, effect.

11. *Treatment of guilty pleas in traffic cases.* In terms of the principle of an admission, a plea of guilty to a traffic offense is no different than a plea of guilty to any other offense; it is admissible as evidence of the commission of the act in question in a companion civil case arising from the same event. However, the argument that people plead guilty to traffic charges for reasons of convenience and with little regard to guilt or the collateral consequences has led some commentators to argue for exclusion. See 6 Graham, Handbook of Federal Evidence § 801.17, at 339–40 (7th ed. 2012) (arguing that Rule 803(22), which excludes offenses punishable by less than a year, supports excluding pleas of guilty to minor traffic offenses). However, courts tend to admit such pleas as admissions. See 2 McCormick, Evidence § 257 (7th ed. 2013).

12. *Civil judgment not admission.* The admissibility of a prior civil judgment and its effect is largely a matter of the substantive law of res judicata and collateral estoppel.

MAHLANDT V. WILD CANID SURVIVAL & RESEARCH CENTER, INC.

United States Court of Appeals, Eighth Circuit, 1978.
588 F.2d 626.

VAN SICKLE, DISTRICT JUDGE.

This is a civil action for damages arising out of an alleged attack by a wolf on a child. The sole issues on appeal are as to the correctness of three rulings which excluded conclusionary statements against interest. Two of them were made by a defendant, who was also an employee of the corporate defendant; and the third was in the form of a statement appearing in the records of a board meeting of the corporate defendant.

On March 23, 1973, Daniel Mahlandt, then 3 years, 10 months, and 8 days old, was sent by his mother to a neighbor's home on an adjoining street to get his older brother, Donald. Daniel's mother watched him cross the street, and then turned into the house to get her car keys. Daniel's path took him along a walkway adjacent to the Poos' residence. Next to the walkway was a five foot chain link fence to which Sophie had been chained with a six foot chain. In other words, Sophie was free to move in a half circle having a six foot radius on the side of the fence opposite from Daniel.

Sophie was a bitch wolf, 11 months and 28 days old, who had been born at the St. Louis Zoo, and kept there until she reached 6 months of age, at which time she was given to the Wild Canid Survival and Research Center, Inc. It was the policy of the Zoo to remove wolves from the Children's Zoo after they reached the age of 5 or 6 months. Sophie was supposed to be kept at the Tyson Research Center, but Kenneth Poos, as Director of Education for the Wild Canid Survival and Research Center, Inc., had been keeping her at his home because he was taking Sophie to schools and institutions where he showed films and gave programs with respect to the nature of wolves. Sophie was known as a very gentle wolf who had proved herself to be good natured and stable during her contacts with thousands of children, while she was in the St. Louis Children's Zoo.

Sophie was chained because the evening before she had jumped the fence and attacked a beagle who was running along the fence and yapping at her.

A neighbor who was ill in bed in the second floor of his home heard a child's screams and went to his window, where he saw a boy lying on his back within the enclosure, with a wolf straddling him. The wolf's face was near Daniel's face, but the distance was so great that he could not see what the wolf was doing, and did not see any biting. Within about 15 seconds the neighbor saw Clarke Poos, about seventeen, run around the house, get the wolf off of the boy, and disappear with the child in his arms to the back of the house. Clarke took the boy in and laid him on the kitchen floor.

Clarke had been returning from his friend's home immediately west when he heard a child's cries and ran around to the enclosure. He found Daniel lying within the enclosure, about three feet from the fence, and Sophie standing back from the boy the length of her chain, and wailing. An expert in the behavior of wolves stated that when a wolf licks a child's face that it is a sign of care and not a sign of attack; that a wolf's wail is a sign of compassion, and an effort to get attention, not a sign of attack. No witness saw or knew how Daniel was injured. Clarke and his sister ran over to get Daniel's mother. She says that Clarke told her, "a wolf got Danny and he is dying." Clarke denies that statement. The defendant, Mr. Poos, arrived home while Daniel and his mother were in the kitchen. After Daniel was taken in an ambulance, Mr. Poos talked to everyone present, including a neighbor who came in. Within an hour after he arrived home, Mr. Poos went to Washington University to inform Owen Sexton, President of Wild Canid Survival and Research Center, Inc., of the incident. Mr. Sexton was not in his office so Mr. Poos left the following note on his door:

> Owen, would call me at home, 727–5080? Sophie bit a child that came in our back yard. All has been taken care of. I need to convey what happened to you. (Exhibit 11)

Denial of admission of this note is one of the issues on appeal.

Later that day, Mr. Poos found Mr. Sexton at the Tyson Research Center and told him what had happened. Denial of plaintiff's offer to prove that Mr. Poos told Mr. Sexton that, "Sophie had bit a child that day," is the second issue on appeal.

A meeting of the Directors of the Wild Canid Survival and Research Center, Inc., was held on April 4, 1973. Mr. Poos was not present at that meeting. The minutes of that meeting reflect that there was a "great deal of discussion * * * about the legal aspects of the incident of Sophie biting the child." Plaintiff offered an abstract of the minutes containing that reference. Denial of the offer of that abstract is the third issue on appeal.

Daniel had lacerations of the face, left thigh, left calf, and right thigh, and abrasions, and bruises of the abdomen and chest. Mr. Mahlandt was permitted to state that Daniel had indicated that he had gone under the fence. Mr. Mahlandt and Mr. Poos, about a month after the incident, examined the fence to determine what caused Daniel's lacerations. Mr. Mahlandt felt that they did not look like animal bites. The parallel scars on Daniel's thigh appeared to match the configuration of the barbs or tines on the fence. The expert as to the behavior of wolves opined that the lacerations were not wolf bites or wounds caused by wolf claws. Wolves have powerful jaws and a wolf bite will result in massive crushing or severing of a limb. He stated that if Sophie had bitten Daniel there would have been clear apposition of teeth and massive crushing of Daniel's hands and arms which were not injured. Also, if Sophie had pulled Daniel under the fence, tooth marks on the foot or leg would have been present, although Sophie possessed enough strength to pull the boy under the fence.

The jury brought in a verdict for the defense.

The trial judge's rationale for excluding the note, the statement, and the corporate minutes, was the same in each case. He reasoned that Mr. Poos did not have any personal knowledge of the facts, and accordingly, the first two admissions were based on hearsay; and the third admission contained in the minutes of the board meeting was subject to the same objection of hearsay, and unreliability because of lack of personal knowledge.

The Federal Rules of Evidence became effective in July 1975 (180 days after passage of the Act). Thus, at this time, there is very little case law to rely upon for resolution of the problems of interpretation.

The relevant rule here is: [801(d)(2)] * * * (A) his own statement, in either his individual or representative capacity or

I.

    (B) a statement of which he has manifested his adoption or belief in its truth, or

    (C) a statement by a person authorized by him to make a statement concerning the subject, or

    (D) a statement by his agent or servant concerning a matter within the scope of his agency or employment, made during the existence of the relationship * * *.

A.
So the statement in the note pinned on the door is not hearsay, and is admissible against Mr. Poos! It was his own statement, and as such was clearly different from the reported statement of another. Example, "I was told that * * *." See Cedeck v. Hamiltonian Fed. Sav. & L. Ass'n, 551 F.2d 1136 (8th Cir.1977). It was also a statement of which he had manifested his adoption or belief in its truth. And the same observations may be made of the statement made later in the day to Mr. Sexton that, "Sophie had bit a child * * *."

3.
Are these statements admissible against Wild Canid Survival and Research Center, Inc.? They were made by Mr. Poos when he was an agent or servant of the Wild Canid Survival and Research Center, Inc., and they concerned a matter within the scope of his agency, or employment, i.e., his custody of Sophie, and were made during the existence of that relationship.

Defendant argues that Rule 801(d)(2) does not provide for the admission of "in house" statements; that is, it allows only admissions made to third parties.

The notes of the Advisory Committee on the Proposed Rules * * * discuss the problem of "in house" admissions with reference to Rule 801(d)(2)(C) situations. This is not a (C) situation because Mr. Poos was not authorized or directed to make a statement on the matter by anyone. But the rationale developed in that comment does apply to this (D) situation. Mr. Poos had actual physical custody of Sophie. His conclusions, his opinions, were obviously accepted as a basis for action by his principal. See minutes of corporate meeting. As the Advisory Committee points out in its note on (C) situations.

    * * * communication to an outsider has not generally been thought to be an essential characteristic of an admission. Thus a party's books or records are usable against him, without regard

to any intent to disclose to third persons. V Wigmore on Evidence § 1557.

Weinstein's discussion of Rule 801(d)(2)(D) (Weinstein's Evidence § 801(d)(2)(D)(01), p. 801–137), states that:

> Rule 801(d)(2)(D) adopts the approach * * * which, as a general proposition, makes statement made by agents within the scope of their employment admissible * * *. Once agency, and the making of the statement while the relationship continues, are established, the statement is exempt from the hearsay rule so long as it relates to a matter within the scope of the agency.

After reciting a lengthy quotation which justifies the rule as necessary, and suggests that such admissions are trustworthy and reliable, Weinstein states categorically that although an express requirement of personal knowledge on the part of the declarant of the facts underlying his statement is not written into the rule, it should be. He feels that is mandated by Rules 805 and 403.

Rule 805 recites, in effect, that a statement containing hearsay within hearsay is admissible if each part of the statement falls within an exception to the hearsay rule. Rule 805, however, deals only with hearsay exceptions. A statement based on the personal knowledge of the declarant of facts underlying his statement is not the repetition of the statement of another, thus not hearsay. It is merely opinion testimony. Rule 805 cannot mandate the implied condition desired by Judge Weinstein.

Rule 403 provides for the exclusion of relevant evidence if its probative value is substantially outweighed by the danger of unfair prejudice, confusion of the issues, or misleading the jury, or by consideration of undue delay, waste of time, or needless presentation of cumulative evidence. Nor does Rule 403 mandate the implied condition desired by Judge Weinstein.

Thus, while both Rule 805 and Rule 403 provide additional bases for excluding otherwise acceptable evidence, neither rule mandates the introduction into Rule 801(d)(2)(D) of an implied requirement that the declarant have personal knowledge of the facts underlying his statement. So we conclude that the two statements made by Mr. Poos were admissible against Wild Canid Survival and Research Center, Inc.

As to the entry in the records of a corporate meeting, the directors as primary officers of the corporation had the authority to include their conclusions in the record of the meeting. So the evidence would fall within 801(d)(2)(C) as to Wild Canid Survival and Research Center, Inc., and be admissible. The "in house" aspect of this admission has already been discussed, Rule 801(d)(2)(D), supra.

But there was no servant, or agency, relationship which justified admitting the evidence of the board minutes as against Mr. Poos.

None of the conditions of 801(d)(2) cover the claim that minutes of a corporate board meeting can be used against a non-attending, non-participating employee of that corporation. The evidence was not admissible as against Mr. Poos.

There is left only the question of whether the trial court's rulings which excluded all three items of evidence are justified under Rule 403. He clearly found that the evidence was not reliable, pointing out that none of the statements were based on the personal knowledge of the declarant.

Again, that problem was faced by the Advisory Committee on Proposed Rules. In its discussion of 801(d)(2) exceptions to the hearsay rule, the Committee said:

> The freedom which admissions have enjoyed from technical demands of searching for an assurance of trustworthiness in some against-interest circumstances, and from the restrictive influences of the opinion rule and the rule requiring first hand knowledge, when taken with the apparently prevalent satisfaction with the results, calls for generous treatment of this avenue to admissibility. * * *

So here, remembering that relevant evidence is usually prejudicial to the cause of the side against which it is presented, and that the prejudice which concerns us is unreasonable prejudice; and applying the spirit of Rule 801(d)(2), we hold that Rule 403 does not warrant the exclusion of the evidence of Mr. Poos' statements as against himself or Wild Canid Survival and Research Center, Inc.

But the limited admissibility of the corporate minutes, coupled with the repetitive nature of the evidence and the low probative value of the minute record, all justify supporting the judgment of the trial court under Rule 403.

The judgment of the District Court is reversed and the matter remanded to the District Court for a new trial consistent with this opinion.

NOTES AND QUESTIONS

1. *No firsthand knowledge requirement.* As *Mahlandt* asserts, admissions under the Federal Rules are received despite lack of firsthand knowledge. This result represents the majority position under the common law. Annot., 54 A.L.R.2d 1069. But see Bein, Parties' Admissions, Agents' Admissions: Hearsay Wolves in Sheep's Clothing, 12 Hofstra L.Rev. 393 (1984) (proposing firsthand knowledge requirement for employee

admissions). Regarding *Mahlandt*, see generally Swift, The Story of *Mahlandt v. Wild Canid Survival & Research Center, Inc.*, in Evidence Stories 239 (Lempert ed., 2006).

2.   *Freedom from lay opinion rule.* The rule against opinions is another familiar landmark that disappears in connection with admissions. An admission couched in the form of an opinion is not objectionable. Cox v. Esso Shipping Co., 247 F.2d 629 (5th Cir.1957); 2 McCormick, Evidence § 256 (7th ed. 2013) (opinion rule is designed to "promote the concreteness of answers on the stand" and "is grotesquely misapplied to out-of-court statements such as admissions where the declarant's statements are made without thought of the form of courtroom testimony").

3.   *Changes in rules on statements by agents.* Conventional doctrine has determined the admissibility of agents' statements to third persons by referring to the scope of authority of the agent. Bristol Wholesale Grocery Co. v. Municipal Lighting Plant Comm'n of Taunton, 200 N.E.2d 260 (Mass.1964). That view is continued in Rule 801(d)(2)(C), but the range of admissions of agents expanded dramatically in 801(d)(2)(D).

> Rule 801(d)(2)(C), unlike 801(d)(2)(D), requires that a statement be "by a person authorized by him to make a statement concerning the subject." Rule 801(d)(2)(D), however, says nothing about an agent having authority to make a statement on a particular subject. After the fact of the agency is established, Rule 801(d)(2)(D) requires only that the statement "concern a matter within the scope of [the] agency or employment." * * * Rule 801(d)(2)(D) takes the broader view that an agent or servant who speaks on any matter within the scope of his agency or employment during the existence of that relationship, is unlikely to make statements damaging to his principal or employer unless those statements are true.

Nekolny v. Painter, 653 F.2d 1164, 1171 (7th Cir.1981). The scope of the agency relates to the authority "to speak" under Rule 801(d)(2)(C) and the scope of the individual's duties "to act" under Rule 801(d)(2)(D). As to the latter, see, e.g., Skay v. St. Louis Parking Co., 130 S.W.3d 22, 27 (Mo.Ct.App.2004) (finding statement of employee not an admission because that employee had no responsibilities for operating sprinkler system, which was the subject of the statement).

4.   *Alternate theory of respondeat superior.* Logically, when liability of the principal is predicated on respondeat superior, any evidence that would establish the liability of the agent should be acceptable, including any admissions by the agent. Madron v. Thomson, 419 P.2d 611 (Or.1966). However, some courts, apparently believing that this view would undermine their rule that unauthorized statements are not admissible against the principal, have insisted that the agent's liability be established by evidence also admissible against the principal. Annot., 27 A.L.R.2d 966.

5. *Privity not recognized.* Under common law analysis, some courts treated declarations by persons in "privity," such as persons jointly liable or interested with others, as another form of vicarious admission. See Belfield v. Coop, 134 N.E.2d 249 (Ill.1956). The Federal Rules contain no provision specifically governing privity-based admissions, which has been interpreted to omit from admissions statements made by those in privity or jointly interested with a party. See Calhoun v. Baylor, 646 F.2d 1158, 1162–63 (6th Cir.1981); Huff v. White Motor Corp., 609 F.2d 286, 290–91 (7th Cir.1979); In re Ty.B., 878 A.2d 1255, 1261–63 (D.C.2005) (ruling that privity concept inapplicable so that admission by mother improperly received against father under "privity of obligation"); 2 McCormick, Evidence § 260 (7th ed. 2013). However, many of the most powerful statements that would previously have been admitted under the privity concept will still be received as admissions by an agent (801(d)(2)(D)) or statements against interest (804(b)(3)) or admitted under the catchall exception (807).

6. *Agents for some, but not for all.* As *Mahlandt* indicates, not all statements made by corporate officers are admissible against other individuals in the corporation. For example, in United States v. Young, 736 F.2d 565, 567–68 (10th Cir.1983), rev'd on other grounds, 470 U.S. 1 (1985), the court noted that a statement of one corporate employee is not admissible against another simply because the latter is higher in the corporate chain of authority. Courts have looked instead for evidence of regular supervisory control. Lippay v. Christos, 996 F.2d 1490, 1498–99 (3d Cir.1993).

7. *Indirect importance of firsthand knowledge.* While firsthand knowledge is not required even for vicarious admissions, that fact does not relieve the party seeking to introduce the statement from demonstrating that the statements were made "concerning a matter within the scope of the agency or employment," which may have the effect of eliminating some putative admission where an employee has no personal knowledge. In this regard, consider Litton Systems, Inc. v. American Tel. & Tel. Co., 700 F.2d 785, 816–17 (2d Cir.1983):

> A Litton attorney, Norman Roberts, made notes of his interviews with various Litton employees during the course of [an internal] investigation. * * * AT & T's claim that Roberts' notes—which summarized what various Litton employees recounted to him about wrongdoing on the part of other Litton employees—were admissible because the multiple levels of hearsay were all made in the course and scope of employment, is not persuasive. * * * The fact that Roberts summarized what some Litton employees said about other employees in the course of his investigation does not bring the events he summarized within the "scope of his agency or employment" under 801(d)(2)(D). See J. Weinstein, 4 Evidence 801– 164 (1981) ("Gossip does not become reliable merely because it is heard in an office rather than a home.") The hearsay which he summarized may well have been inadmissible even if testified to by the employees interviewed.

The principle in *Litton* is recognized as limited and does not generally reimpose a firsthand knowledge requirement for vicarious admissions. See Brookover v. Mary Hitchcock Mem'l Hosp., 893 F.2d 411, 415–18 (1st Cir.1990).

8.   *Law enforcement personnel as agents.* Most courts do not treat the statements of law enforcement officials in criminal cases as admissions under Rule 801(d)(2)(D) as they would be if the statements had been made by employees of a corporate party. In United States v. Kampiles, 609 F.2d 1233, 1246 (7th Cir.1979), the court observed:

> Prior to adoption of the Federal Rules of Evidence, admissions by government employees in criminal cases were viewed as outside the admissions exception to the hearsay rule. * * * Because the agents of the G overnment are supposedly disinterested in the outcome of a trial and are traditionally unable to bind the sovereign * * *, their statements seem less the product of the adversary process and hence less appropriately described as admissions of a party. Nothing in the Federal Rules of Evidence suggests an intention to alter the traditional rule. * * *

However, in United States v. Morgan, 581 F.2d 933 (D.C.Cir.1978), the court held that a statement of a government agent was admissible against the government as an adoptive admission under Rule 801(d)(2)(B). There the statement of the agent was approved by an Assistant United States Attorney and presented as part of an affidavit to a magistrate to justify issuance of a warrant. Moreover, the court questioned whether special treatment of government admission survived generally under the Federal Rules: "As in the case of Rule 801(d)(2)(B), there is no indication in the history of the Rules that the draftsmen meant to except the government from operation of Rule 801(d)(2)(D) in criminal cases." 581 F.2d at 938 n.15. See also United States v. Lopez–Ortiz, 648 F.Supp.2d 241, 246–50 (D.P.R.2009) (treating affidavit of investigative agent as an adoptive admission when submitted by the government to support search warrant and in opposition to motion to suppress). Perhaps the two positions can be reconciled by basing admissibility on whether the statement was made by an attorney (admissible) rather than an investigative agent (inadmissible). See United States v. Yildiz, 355 F.3d 80, 81–82 (2d Cir.2004) (setting out majority view of the federal courts that excludes statements by informants and admits formally submitted statements by government attorneys); 2 McCormick, Evidence § 259 (7th ed. 2013); 5 Weinstein's Federal Evidence § 801.33[3] (2d ed. 2013) (noting admission particularly of statements by government attorneys).

9.   *Expert reports as admissions of agents?* Occasionally experts are considered agents so that the expert's analysis constitutes an admission of the party. See Collins v. Wayne Corp., 621 F.2d 777 (5th Cir.1980) (deposition of expert hired to investigate accident and to report conclusions constituted admission of party under Rule 801(d)(2)(C) that could be identified with party

in presentation to jury); Lear Automotive Dearborn, Inc. v. Johnson Controls, Inc., 789 F.Supp.2d 777, 785 (E.D.Mich.2011) (party adopted survey data when it provided that data to expert for use at trial). Cf. Rollins v. Board of Governors for Higher Educ., 761 F.Supp. 939, 942 (D.R.I.1991) (report of board of inquiry regarding accident treated as admission of principal). But statements by independent contractors or outside consultants typically do not qualify as admissions of the principal. See, e.g. United States v. Bonds, 608 F.3d 495, 505–06 (9th Cir.2010) (finding that Barry Bonds' trainer was an independent contractor rather than Bonds' employee and that the nature of the relationship did not render him an agent under 801(d)(1)(D)).

WILSON V. CITY OF PINE BLUFF

Court of Appeals of Arkansas, 1982.
641 S.W.2d 33.

COOPER, JUDGE.

The appellant was convicted of criminal trespass * * * and was fined $75.00, plus costs. From that decision, comes this appeal.

The Facts

On June 13, 1981, two Pine Bluff police officers, in response to radio instructions, went to a residence at 5704 Cheatham Street in Pine Bluff. Upon their arrival, they observed an injured woman being placed in an ambulance for transport to a hospital. The officers entered the residence to investigate the situation.

Inside the residence, the officers found the appellant and an unidentified woman. The officers testified that the woman claimed to live in the residence, and that she wanted the appellant to leave. They stated that the appellant did not respond to the woman's statement concerning her occupancy of the residence, even though he heard it. They further testified that the appellant stated that he was not going to leave the residence.

The officers testified that they explained to the appellant that if the woman wanted him to leave, then he would have to do so, or be arrested for criminal trespass. The officers verified that the woman did want the appellant to leave, and they requested that he do so on several occasions. The appellant refused to leave, and he was arrested for criminal trespass. The testimony shows that the appellant never claimed any possessory or ownership right to the premises.

The Admissibility of the Evidence

[C]riminal trespass is committed when an individual purposely enters or remains unlawfully on the premises of another person. The appellant argues that the only evidence which proved that the premises belonged to another person was the hearsay testimony of the officers concerning the woman's statements, and that this testimony was inadmissible hearsay. The appellant made a timely objection to the testimony, and the trial court ruled that the statements made by the woman, as testified to by the officers, were admissible as an adoptive admission of a party-opponent.

The Uniform Rules of Evidence, Rule 801(d)(2)(ii), Ark.Stat.Ann. § 28–1001 (Repl.1979), provides that a statement is not hearsay if the statement is offered against a party and is a statement of which that party has manifested his adoption or belief in its truth. Prior to the adoption of this rule, Arkansas law recognized a "tacit admission" as an exception to the hearsay rule. Under that exception, proof of damaging statements against an accused, made in his presence, were admissible in evidence, on the theory that the jury might find that the silence of the accused in the face of the accusation was a tacit admission. * * * Before hearsay evidence of an implied admission could fit within this exception, it must have been shown that the accused heard the statement, that he understood it, and that he failed to deny it.

The sole question in determining whether statements made by another person are admissible against a party as an admission by silence or acquiescence is whether a reasonable person, under the circumstances, would naturally have been expected to deny them, if the statements were untrue.[20] Some of the factors which should be considered in determining whether a party has impliedly admitted the statements are:

(1) The statement must have been heard by the party against whom it is offered;

(2) it must have been understood by him;

(3) the subject matter must have been within his personal knowledge;

(4) he must have been physically and psychologically able to speak;

(5) the speaker or his relationship to the party or event must be such as to reasonably expect a denial; and

(6) the statement itself must be such that, if untrue, under the circumstances, it would have been denied.

Other factors besides these may need to be considered, depending on the facts of a particular case. *See,* 4 J. Wigmore, Evidence §§ 1071–1073

---

[20] Silence by an accused or a claim of his Fifth Amendment right to remain silent made in response to a police accusation during custodial interrogation is inadmissible. Doyle v. Ohio, 426 U.S. 610 * * * (1976). Even silence by an accused in response to incriminating statements made by a third person, while he was in police custody and before he was advised of his Fifth Amendment right to remain silent, is inadmissible. Kagebein v. State, 254 Ark. 904, 496 S.W.2d 435 (1973).

(Chadbourn rev. 1972); C. McCormick, The Law of Evidence § 270 (2d ed. 1972).

The Uniform Rules of Evidence, Rule 801(d)(2)(ii), as adopted by the State of Arkansas, is identical to the Federal Rules of Evidence, Rule 801(d)(2)(B). The manner in which the federal courts have applied their rule is helpful.

The federal cases indicate that before a statement can fall under the adoptive admission rule, the trial court must find that sufficient foundational facts have been introduced so that the jury can reasonably infer that the accused heard and understood the statement and that the statement was such that, under the circumstances, if the accused were innocent he would normally respond. *United States v. Fortes*, 619 F.2d 108 (1st Cir.1980); *United States v. Moore*, 522 F.2d 1068 (9th Cir.1975). Once a foundation has been established, the question is left to the jury to determine whether the accused acquiesced in the statement.[21] *United States v. Moore, supra.*

The procedure used by the federal courts in applying rule 801 is appropriate to use in applying our rule, since it is entirely consistent with the approach followed in applying the "tacit admission" exception to the hearsay rule under prior Arkansas law. *Moore v. State, supra.*

In the case at bar, the testimony indicates that the appellant was present, and in fact was within two feet of the officers and the woman, when the statements were made. Further, he made no comment or objection to the woman's claim of right to occupy the residence. On these facts, adequate foundational facts were presented to the trial court so as to render the statements admissible. The trier of fact could reasonably infer that the appellant heard and understood the woman's statements, and that, had her statements been untrue, he would have responded with either a denial or an explanation.

Preliminary questions regarding the admissibility of evidence are decided by the trial court, and the appellate court will affirm such a decision unless it constitutes an abuse of discretion. Uniform Rules of Evidence, Rule 104(a, b), Ark.Stat.Ann. § 28–1001 (Repl.1979); *Derring v. State,* 273 Ark. 347, 619 S.W.2d 644 (1981). We hold that the trial court did not abuse his discretion by ruling that the officer's testimony was admissible.

* * *

The judgment appealed from is affirmed.

---

[21] Even though a statement may be admissible under the adoptive admission rule, the trial court may still exclude such a statement if he finds that the probative value of the statement is substantially outweighed by the danger of unfair prejudice, confusion of the issues, or misleading the jury. Uniform Rules of Evidence, Rule 403, Ark.Stat.Ann. § 28–1001 (Repl.1979).

Affirmed.

NOTES AND QUESTIONS

1. *Ambiguity of custodial silence.* When the declarant is aware of the presence of the police, separate from the constitutional concerns, silence may be considered too ambiguous to constitute an admission. United States v. Williams, 577 F.2d 188, 193–94 (2d Cir.1978), provides a useful discussion of the issues:

> In United States v. Flecha, [539 F.2d 874, 876–77 (2d Cir.1976)], this court addressed a situation in which one of several co-defendants under arrest apparently turned to another and said in Spanish, "Why so much excitement? If we are caught, we are caught." We there concluded that in light of the custodial circumstances it was not likely that the appellant would have responded to such a vaguely phrased comment and that, therefore, Rule 801(d)(2)(B) was inapplicable. Here, however, Williams and Simmons met in the street. If appellant had truly been an innocent bystander, it is more probable than not that he would have vigorously asserted his non-involvement in the conspiracy when told that, unlike those already arrested, he was in the clear because his larcenous participation had not been betrayed to the authorities. Since this natural reply was not forthcoming, we hold that the conversation constituted an adoptive admission within the circumscribed purview of Rule 801(d)(2)(B). * * *

2. *Application of Rules 104(a) or 104(b) to preliminary issues.* Whether the preliminary factual issues involved in adoptive admissions are questions of preliminary fact for the trial judge under Rule 104(a) or matters of conditional relevance under Rule 104(b) is subject to some disagreement. Among the various views on how these issues should be allocated between the judge and jury, *Wilson* clearly gives the principal role to the jury. See 5 Weinstein's Federal Evidence § 801.31[3][d] (2d ed. 2013) (treating issues of whether individual heard, understood, and acquiesced as matters of conditional relevance). Nevertheless, it allows for judicial control by authorizing the exclusion of evidence by balancing probativity versus prejudice under Rule 403. Other courts give the trial court a more substantial and direct role in deciding whether hearsay policy has been satisfied by placing these issues under the judge's determination through Rule 104(a). See, e.g., State v. Canady, 998 A.2d 1135, 1147 (Conn.2010); State v. Carlson, 808 P.2d 1002, 1007–09 (Or.1991). For an intermediate view, see 6 Graham, Handbook of Federal Evidence § 801.21, at 360–65 (7th ed. 2012) (whether the statement was made in the person's hearing, whether he or she understood it, and whether the person had an opportunity to reply are matters of conditional relevance decided under Rule 104(b), while the question of whether the ordinary pattern of human behavior would have

called for a response if the person believed the statement to be untrue is a preliminary question of fact decided by the court under Rule 104(a)).

3. *Not responding to accusatory letters.* Closely akin to the failure to respond to an oral accusation is the failure to respond to an accusatory letter or one that otherwise demands a response. Southern Stone Co., Inc. v. Singer, 665 F.2d 698 (5th Cir.1982), provides an example. There the court held inadmissible the failure of one of the defendants to respond to a letter by Southern Stone's counsel. The letter set out various allegations concerning the defendant's activities on behalf of a then defunct company and ended with the statement, "If any of the above is incorrect, please advise me." Id. at 702 n.4. Failure to respond to a letter constitutes an admission under Rule 801(d)(2)(B) only if "it was reasonable under the circumstances for the sender to expect the recipient to respond and correct the erroneous assertions." Id. at 703. The recipient testified that he did not respond because he was no longer involved with or concerned about the company, which he considered nonexistent. See also United States v. Ordonez, 737 F.2d 793, 800–01 (9th Cir.1983) (mere possession of a document does not constitute an adoptive admission).

4. *Forms of adoption.* Other actions manifesting adoption or belief, such as republication of material written by another, may qualify as an admission under this provision. See Wagstaff v. Protective Apparel Corp. of Am., Inc., 760 F.2d 1074, 1078 (10th Cir.1985) (newspaper articles received as adoptive admission in fraud case under theory that, "[b]y reprinting the newspaper articles and distributing them to persons with whom defendants were doing business, defendants unequivocally manifested their adoption of the inflated statements made in the newspaper articles"); Agriculture Ins. Co. v. Ace Hardware Corp., 214 F.Supp.2d 413, 416 (S.D.N.Y.2002) (drawing inferences from information provided by others constitutes adoption whereas merely repeating information may not); Gordon v. State, 40 A.3d 1093, 1101–02 (Md.Ct.Spec.App.2010) (defendant adopted the age shown on license by presenting it to a police officer in response to request for identification); Ten Broeck Dupont, Inc. v. Brooks, 283 S.W.3d 705, 724 (Ky.2009) (ruling that hospital adopted patient's complaints by acting on them).

5. *Constitutional considerations as to silence.* In *Wilson,* at the time the defendant made the adoptive admission, he was in the presence of the police but not in "custody." The Fifth Amendment right of the criminal defendant to remain silent after arrest under Miranda v. Arizona, 384 U.S. 436 (1966), means that constitutional principles must be considered before adoptive admissions are received. In Doyle v. Ohio, 426 U.S. 610 (1976), the Supreme Court held that once the defendant is warned of his *Miranda* rights "silence is insolubly ambiguous," and given the implicit assurance in the warnings that silence will carry no penalty, "it would be fundamentally unfair and a deprivation of due process to allow the arrested person's silence to be used to impeach." Id. at 617–18.

Silence after arrest while in police custody may not be used in the prosecution's case-in-chief in the absence of *Miranda* warnings and waiver. However, the Supreme Court has held that when the defendant's silence occurs before he or she is taken into custody and given *Miranda* rights, use of that silence to impeach offends neither the Fifth Amendment nor due process. Jenkins v. Anderson, 447 U.S. 231 (1980). Moreover, in Fletcher v. Weir, 455 U.S. 603, 607 (1982), the Court held that, where the defendant had been arrested but had not been advised of his rights, the absence of the "affirmative assurances" contained in *Miranda* warnings meant due process would not be offended by impeaching a defendant with his silence.

6.   *Flight.* Flight from custody or disappearance from one's usual haunts is frequently received as evidence of consciousness of guilt. See, e.g., United States v. Russell, 662 F.3d 831, 850–51 (7th Cir.2011) (admitting defendant's departure for Mexico shortly after learning of new incriminating evidence that increased the likelihood of conviction). In civil cases, flight from the scene of an accident has been admitted as proof of belief of fault as well. Harrington v. Sharff, 305 F.2d 333 (2d Cir.1962). The inference of a consciousness of guilt can be drawn from other conduct as well, such as the use of aliases, United States v. Clark, 184 F.3d 858, 869 (D.C.Cir.1999), or changing appearance, United States v. Felix–Gutierrez, 940 F.2d 1200, 1207–08 (9th Cir.1991) (cosmetic surgery). See generally 2 McCormick, Evidence § 263 (7th ed. 2013).

In discussing flight as evidence of guilt, the courts and writers have been prone to quote the Old Testament adage, "the wicked flee when no one pursues." Proverbs 28:1 (New Rev. Standard). See, e.g., Alberty v. United States, 162 U.S. 499, 509 (1896); 2 Wigmore, Evidence § 276, at 122 (Chadbourn rev. 1979). But with regard to silence as an admission, compare Matthew 27:11–14 (Christ stood silent before his accusers).

7.   *Spoliation.* "Admissions" by conduct also may occur in the form of "spoliation." This rubric includes fabrication of evidence, subornation of perjury, destruction of evidence, bribery, intimidation or other influences on a witness to testify favorably or to avoid testifying. The theory is that, by resorting to these means, the party demonstrates a belief that the case is weak or that he or she is at fault or guilty. Sanctions, including adverse jury instructions are imposed, particularly for intentional destruction potentially damaging evidence. *See* Goodman v. Praxair Servs., Inc., 632 F.Supp.2d 494, 522–23 (D.Md.2009). See generally 2 McCormick, Evidence § 265 (7th ed. 2013).

8.   *Missing witnesses and evidence.* Whether counsel should be permitted to argue to the jury that the failure of a party to produce witnesses or evidence within the party's control gives rise to an unfavorable inference and whether the court should instruct the jury on such an inference are hotly contested issues in many jurisdictions. Despite the frequency of the use these sanctions in some courts, many appellate decisions counsel caution because of

the almost inherent ambiguities involved. See generally 2 McCormick, Evidence § 264 (7th ed. 2013).

UNITED STATES V. CORNETT

United States Court of Appeals, Fifth Circuit, 1999.
195 F.3d 776.

DENNIS, CIRCUIT JUDGE:

This direct criminal appeal arises from the conviction following jury trial of Appellants Wendell Alboyd Cornett ("Cornett") and Mary Martillea Galloway ("Galloway") for conspiracy to distribute and possess with intent to distribute cocaine and cocaine base * * *. For the reasons assigned, we affirm the convictions and sentences of Appellant Cornett and reverse the conviction and sentence of Appellant Galloway and remand Galloway's case to the district court for further proceedings consistent with this opinion.

I.   Facts and Procedural History

This case presents a complicated set of facts that involve allegations of drug possession and distribution, money-laundering, tax evasion, police corruption and exploitation. The grand jury indicted ten co-conspirators as being part of an elaborate drug conspiracy. Appellants Cornett and Galloway were tried together and convicted of performing various roles in the drug conspiracy. * * *

Cornett owned and operated multiple businesses in the Houston area. Specifically, Cornett owned an automotive detailing shop called the House of Colors and a bowling alley pro shop. Galloway was one of Cornett's girlfriends. The government, believing that Cornett was running an elaborate drug smuggling operation behind the fronts of his legitimate businesses, began a three-year undercover investigation of Cornett and other suspects. In doing so, the government used undercover agents, cooperating witnesses, electronic monitoring and wire taps to gather evidence of Cornett's drug smuggling operation. * * *

Cornett used his wife and several girlfriends to assist his drug enterprise. Specifically, his girlfriend Kim Boutte ("Boutte") arranged drug transactions with customers and counted the cash receipts. Gradually Cornett used Boutte less and less, however, as his trust and interest in her waned. The government contends that Cornett then recruited Galloway to oversee the counting and storing of the drug money.

The facts surrounding Galloway's involvement in the drug conspiracy are disputed. The government's witnesses testified as to circumstantial evidence ambiguously suggesting differing degrees of Galloway's involvement with Cornett and his activities. Testimony from [several witnesses] suggested that Galloway was responsible for counting the money involved in the drug transactions. Specifically, one witness testified that, when he went to the hair salon where Galloway and Cornett worked for a rendezvous with Cornett, Galloway let him in the front door and escorted him to an upstairs room. He said he entered the room without Galloway and found Cornett counting, in his estimation, over $400,000. An audiotaped statement of a co-conspirator reported that Cornett had made a statement to her in which he mentioned Galloway in connection with "$500,000." Another witness testified that Cornett had told him that Galloway had a money counting machine and had accurately counted sums in excess of $21,000 for him. In an attempt to connect Galloway to the drug money, the government introduced evidence that Galloway received several expensive presents from Cornett, including a fur coat, a custom designed diamond ring and a Mercedes Benz; co-signed an automobile credit application as a reference for Cornett; and on two occasions wrote checks on her own account (for which Cornett supplied the cash) to pay Cornett's creditors. Galloway denied her involvement in the conspiracy, claiming that she had never seen more than $1,000 in cash in her life and that she never owned a money counting machine. It is undisputed, however, that she knew how to operate such a machine from her experience as a bank employee. She testified to her belief that any money or presents she had received from Cornett came from the operations of his legitimate businesses. Galloway's experience in bookkeeping and familiarity with Cornett's legitimate businesses tends to show that she knew Cornett's legal income from them was not sufficient to support their lifestyles.

As Cornett continued to engage in the drug conspiracy, the government arranged for cooperation with several of the participants. * * * Through its network of cooperating witnesses and undercover agents, the government compiled evidence of the drug conspiracy—recording over 100 audio tapes of conversation between the participants. The government argued at the end of the trial that one of these tapes, Exhibit 1.165, directly implicated Galloway in the conspiracy. Exhibit 1.165 involves a discussion between Boutte and a cooperating witness at the bowling alley pro shop. On the tape they discussed several topics—mostly limited to bowling scores and the appearance of persons on the scene. Part of the tape consisted of Boutte's laments over Cornett's exclusion of her from some of the drug activities and Cornett's relationship with Galloway. While mostly unintelligible, the government contends that this tape directly implicates Galloway because Boutte suggests her belief that Cornett had entrusted Galloway with storing and counting $500,000 of Cornett's drug money. Galloway's counsel objected to the admission of this tape, but the district court allowed the tape to be admitted as statements of co-conspirators in furtherance of the conspiracy under Federal Rules of Evidence 801(d)(2)(E).

*** Galloway was convicted on the sole count of conspiracy and sentenced to sixty months imprisonment. ***

2. *Co–Conspirator Statements*

***

I. Hearsay is not admissible under the Federal Rules of Evidence unless it fits an exception. Fed.R.Evid. 802. However, Rule 801 provides that certain statements which would otherwise constitute excludable hearsay under the general rule of Rule 801(c) are not hearsay by definition. One such definitional non-hearsay is found in Rule

A. 801(d)(2)(E) which provides:

> A statement is not hearsay if *** the statement is offered against a party and is *** a statement by a coconspirator of a party during the course and in furtherance of the conspiracy.

1. Under Rule 801(d)(2)(E), the proponent of admittance must prove by a preponderance of the evidence (1) the existence of the conspiracy (2) the statement was made by a co-conspirator of the party, (3) the statement was made during the course of the conspiracy, and (4) the statement was made in furtherance of the conspiracy. *See United States v. Broussard,* 80 F.3d 1025, 1038 (5th Cir.1996) (citing *Bourjaily v. United States,* 483 U.S. 171, 175 *** (1987)); *United States v. Means,* 695 F.2d 811, 818 (5th Cir.1983). There is no dispute as to the existence of the conspiracy, that the statements made in Exhibit 1.165 were made by a co-conspirator or that they were made during the course of the conspiracy—the only issue properly before the court is whether the statement was "in furtherance" of | *2.* the conspiracy.

2 3. The legal standards that define the "in furtherance" requirement are well-established. A statement must be "in furtherance" of the conspiracy in order to fit within the non-hearsay definition of Rule 801(d)(2)(E). However, this Circuit has consistently held that the "in furtherance" requirement is not to be construed too strictly lest the purpose of the exception be defeated. *See United States v. Lechuga,* 888 F.2d 1472, 1480 (5th Cir.1989); *United States v. Ascarrunz,* 838 F.2d 759, 763 (5th Cir.1988). This rule is not without its limits, however; a statement is not in furtherance of the conspiracy unless it advances the ultimate objects of the conspiracy. *See United States v. Snyder,* 930 F.2d 1090, 1095 (5th Cir.1991). "Mere idle chatter", even if prejudicial and made among co-conspirators, is not admissible under Rule 801(d)(2)(E). *See Means,* 695

b. F.2d at 818. Thus, while the in furtherance requirement is not a strict one, it is a necessary one, and the proponent of admissibility must satisfy it by a preponderance of the evidence. *See Broussard,* 80 F.3d at 1038; *see also United States v. Doerr,* 886 F.2d 944, 951 (7th Cir.1989).

Exhibit 1.165 involves a discussion between Boutte and a confidential informant that took place at the bowling alley pro shop. The tape is over 50 minutes long and the conversation recorded covers many topics. A significant portion of the tape involves discussions between the two co-conspirators on such diverse issues as the bowling prowess of certain friends and relatives, the appearance of some of the patrons at the bowling alley, the merits of certain designer outfits and the respective talents of certain exotic dancers. Amid these conversations, however, occurred the following dialogue which, although mostly unintelligible, was offered to connect Galloway to the conspiracy:

Boutte: Somebody taking me away from him.

Informant: Thought you was supposed to be his ace.

* * *

Boutte: ya'll can't be mad cause what's her name never stole for me * * *

Informant: If you going to bring * * * half a million dollars. Right ain't going to steal from you and he done counted it * * *

Boutte: Now she * * * because she take x amount of dollars with her * * * always comparing me to her likeness * * * he thought she was an angel.

* * *

Informant: She don't know what she's buying into * * * when I called up there yesterday I thought that was you.

Boutte: He told me he feel like I was just, he feels like I'm using him. What the hell am I using him * * *

Informant: It ain't all peach and cream * * *

Boutte: That's what I told him * * * me and Kevin ain't got no business sitting around talking about his business * * *

* * *

Boutte: [apparently quoting Cornett]—I don't trust nobody but my wife * * * well I mean there is other ladies I trust but I ain't got to tell you that cause we gonna get into it * * * Mary.

Informant: Mary.

The government contends that this interchange was intended to further the conspiracy in that it was meant to convey to a purchaser of the drugs that he should contact a new person (Galloway) for future drug deals because Boutte had lost favor with Cornett and Galloway had taken her place. The prosecution argued that this message is evidenced by the references to Galloway in connection with the drug money. In finding that the tape was admissible under Rule 801(d)(2)(E) the district court stated:

> The tape says that, essentially, Boutte feels like she's being compared to the woman who Cornett bought a Mercedes for. I hear the word "Mercedes" in there and then they say "who" and they say "Mary." And this was all in connection with the half-million dollars.

It is well-settled that a statement made among conspirators for the purpose of describing proper sources, avenues or conduits to promote the conspiracy is "in furtherance" for purposes of Rule 801(d)(2)(E). *See United States v. Lechuga,* 888 F.2d at 1480 (holding that during a conversation arranging a drug transaction, a reference to a "Wisconsin Source" as the source of the drugs in question was in furtherance of the conspiracy). However, in the cases in which a statement was found to be "in furtherance", either the statement itself or the conversation as a whole was intended to advance, facilitate or promote the ultimate conspiratorial objective. By way of contrast, conversations that represent "mere idle chatter" or which are mere narratives of past conduct are not in furtherance of the conspiracy because the statement and the conversation were not intended to further the conspiracy, regardless of whether an individual co-conspirator was implicated in the conversation. *See Means,* 695 F.2d at 818; *see also United States v. Phillips,* 664 F.2d 971, 1027 (5th Cir.1981) (abrogation on other grounds recognized by *United States v. Huntress,* 956 F.2d 1309 (5th Cir.1992)). The distinction between conversations in furtherance of the conspiracy and prejudicial statements made in conversations not in furtherance of the conspiracy has been recognized in other circuits as well. *See, e.g., United States v. Lieberman,* 637 F.2d 95, 102 (2d Cir.1980) ("The conversation * * * smacks of nothing more than casual conversation about past events. It is difficult to envision how it would have furthered the conspiracy"); *United States v. Santos,* 20 F.3d 280, 286 (7th Cir.1994) ("These statements are best described as narrative discussions of past events, which do not satisfy the 'in furtherance' requirement of Rule 801(d)(2)(E)"); *United States v. Roberts,* 14 F.3d 502, 514–515 (10th Cir.1993) ("mere narratives between co-conspirators or narrative declarations of past events are not in furtherance"); *United States v. Urbanik,* 801 F.2d 692, 698 (4th Cir.1986) ("We think that this statement can fairly be treated only as the sort of idle conversation which though it touches upon, does not 'further' a conspiracy").

In this respect, the present case is factually similar to the one addressed by the Fourth Circuit in *Urbanik.* In *Urbanik,* two co-conspirators conducted a conversation in furtherance of the conspiracy. Once they finished the business of the conspiracy, the two co-conspirators moved to a different part of the house and began lifting weights. During this weight lifting session one of the co-conspirators implicated a third co-conspirator. The Fourth Circuit held that this statement was inadmissible hearsay in that the statement was not in furtherance of the conspiracy. It was evident that the conversation was between two co-conspirators and that it was made during the course of the conspiracy in that they had just finished conducting the business of the conspiracy. However, it was also clear that the co-conspirators had ceased the operations of the conspiracy and had begun engaging in "mere idle chatter" as they pursued an unrelated activity. In the words of the Fourth Circuit:

> The statement identifying Urbanik as Pelino's "connection" for marijuana was merely a casual aside to the discussion of Urbanik the weight-lifter. In no sense but a most speculative one could it be thought to have been made to further the purposes of the conspiracy. Haselhuhn himself testified that this identification of Pelino's marijuana supplier could have had no effect on the conspiratorial relationship between him and Pelino. We think that this statement can fairly be treated only as the sort of idle conversation which though it touches upon, does not "further," a conspiracy, and which accordingly should not be admitted under Rule 801(d)(2)(E). *See United States v. Means,* 695 F.2d 811, 818 (5th Cir.1983)*; United States v. Lieberman,* 637 F.2d 95, 102 (2d Cir.1980)*; United States v. Eubanks,* 591 F.2d 513, 520 (9th Cir.1979). The requirement that the statements have been in furtherance of the conspiracy is designed both to assure their reliability and to be consistent with the presumption that the coconspirator would have authorized them* * *. The requirement is not satisfied by a conversation * * * which amounted to no more than idle chatter.

Urbanik, 801 F.2d at 698 * * *.

In the present case, the context of the admitted statements is that Boutte and the Informant were discussing a variety of subjects, which did not concern the conspiracy. The subject of whether Galloway enjoyed the confidence of Cornett arose out of a conversation about relationships and trust in relationships—the conversation turning to the specific trouble in Boutte's relationship with Cornett. The reference to the half-million dollars and then to Mary cannot reasonably be construed to convey to the Informant the message that future business in the conspiracy was to be conducted through Galloway instead of Boutte. Rather, the reference to Galloway and $500,000 was "a mere casual aside" in the conversation about Boutte the spurned lover and Galloway the other woman. That an allusion to the half-million dollars and Galloway was made in the statement is irrelevant for purposes of Rule 801(d)(2)(E) because the possible connection was not made in furtherance of the conspiracy and the statement was not part of a conversation that itself was in furtherance of the conspiracy.] While this may be the kind of conversation that touches upon the conspiracy, it cannot fairly be said that it furthered the conspiracy and thus its admissibility was not authorized by Rule 801(d)(2)(E).

[The court found the error was not harmless and reversed Galloway's conviction, stating *inter alia*: "The government's evidence against Galloway was 'thin' as the trial judge observed, because no item of evidence directly linked Galloway to the conspiracy. Further, the government relied heavily on the ambiguous audiotape Exhibit 1.165 to give meaning to all of its evidence concerning Galloway."]

NOTES AND QUESTIONS

1. *Kinship of "in furtherance" statements to verbal act.* [*Cornett* deals extensively with the meaning and application of the requirement of Rule 801(d)(2)(E) that co-conspirator statements must have been made "in furtherance" of the conspiracy.] United States v. Hassell, 547 F.2d 1048, 1052 (8th Cir.1977), suggests that when statements are made in furtherance of the conspiracy they are not hearsay at all but are rather verbal acts. Indeed, in United States v. Balthazard, 360 F.3d 309, 318 (1st Cir.2004), the court held that statements from one conspirator to another regarding the care and feeding of marijuana plants were not admissions but rather are nonhearsay verbal acts, or if in written form, real evidence of the crime. Is this an appropriate way to view the effect of the "in furtherance" requirement or does the in-furtherance requirement extend farther to include statements less directly involved in the conspiracy but facilitating its purpose?

2. *Narratives of past events and "idle chatter."* Under the "in furtherance" requirement, the narratives of past events are not generally admissible but may be admitted in appropriate circumstances. The test is whether they further the conspiracy, and in some types of conspiracies and under some circumstances, they will. See, e.g., United States v. Haldeman, 559 F.2d 31 (D.C.Cir.1976) (en banc) (concluding narratives of past events were in furtherance of the Watergate cover-up because they were necessary for planning strategy). Moreover, as *Cornett* notes, courts typically apply the "in furtherance" requirement generously. See United States v. Cruz Rea, 626 F.3d 929, 937–38 (7th Cir.2010) (applying a standard that statement may qualify as "in furtherance" if susceptible to alternative interpretations and that it need not have been made exclusively, or even primarily, to further conspiracy as long as some reasonable basis for concluding it furthered the conspiracy). Thus, to be excluded, the narratives of past events must be viewed roughly as "idle chatter." See, e.g., United States v. Warman, 578 F.3d 310 (6th Cir.2009) (finding context important and ruling that statements were inadmissible because they were bragging in the context of a casual conversation).

3. *Statements themselves usable but not sufficient to establish admissibility.* In Bourjaily v. United States, 483 U.S. 171 (1987), the Supreme Court held that under Rule 104(a) the trial judge is entitled to consider the purported hearsay statement in determining under Rule 801(d)(2)(E) the existence of a conspiracy and the participation in that conspiracy of the declarant and the defendant. The Court left undecided whether the statement standing alone was sufficient to establish these issues. A 1997 amendment to the Rule codified the admissibility holding in *Bourjaily* and extended it to establishing the declarant's authority as a "speaking" agent under subdivision (C) and the agency or employment relationship and its scope under subdivision (D). The amendment also resolved the undecided sufficiency issue, stating that the statement "does not by itself establish" these facts. See Back v. Nestle USA, Inc., 694 F.3d 571, 577–78 (6th Cir.2012) (ruling that statement was not admissible because no evidence was presented beyond the statement to establish that an unidentified declarant's statements concern a matter within the scope of employment under subdivision (D)); United States v. Liera, 585 F.3d 1237, 1246 (9th Cir.2009) (excluding statement when it was the only evidence establishing that the declarant was involved in the conspiracy under subdivision (E)).

4. *Burden of proof of conspiracy for admissibility. Bourjaily* holds that Rule 104(a) should be used in determining the existence of a conspiracy and its membership and that these facts are to be established by a preponderance of the evidence. As noted in Chapter 1, Section A, proof under Rule 104(a) is by a "preponderance of proof." How does this square with the requirement of proof beyond a reasonable doubt in criminal cases where co-conspirator statements are typically admitted?

5. *Adoption as alternative when co-conspirators are present.* The co-conspiracy provision (Rule 801(d)(2)(E)) is unnecessary when clearly incriminating statements are made in the presence of the other conspirators since those statements may be admitted as adoptive admissions (Rule 801(d)(2)(B)). See, e.g., State v. Alston, 47 A.3d 234, 246–47 (R.I.2012) (ruling that co-conspirator's statement made in the presence of another conspirator to which no objection is made is admissible as an adoptive admission of the latter).

6. *Co-conspirator statements to non-conspirators admissible.* To be admissible co-conspirator statements need not be made to members of the conspiracy, but they must be made during and in furtherance of the conspiracy, as would be the situation when statements are made in efforts to recruit new participants in the conspiracy. See, e.g., United States v. Dinwiddie, 618 F.3d 821, 836 (8th Cir.2010) (ruling that statements explaining to non-conspirator about need for gun used to aid conspiracy admissible); United States v. Haynes, 582 F.3d 686, 705 (7th Cir.2009) (finding that recruiting statement in furtherance of a conspiracy and during the course of the conspiracy admissible although made to government informer not a member of the conspiracy).

BLECHA V. PEOPLE

Supreme Court of Colorado, 1998.
962 P.2d 931.

JUSTICE BENDER delivered the Opinion of the Court.

We granted certiorari to review the court of appeals' decision in *People v. Blecha,* 940 P.2d 1070 (Colo.App.1996), to determine whether the hearsay statement of a previously acquitted co-defendant, Roger Younger (Younger), was properly admitted at the trial of the defendant-appellant, Clifton Blecha (Blecha). A jury convicted Blecha of first degree murder and conspiracy to commit first degree murder of a fellow inmate at the Limon Correctional Facility. The court of appeals held that the admission of Younger's statements was erroneous since the statements [did not qualify] as co-conspirator hearsay * * * [but found the error harmless and affirmed].

I.   Facts

At the trial, an inmate eyewitness to the murder, Joseph Bates (Bates), testified to two hearsay statements made by a previously acquitted co-defendant, Younger. These statements form the basis of Blecha's appeal * * *.

On July 13, 1992 at approximately 9:15 p.m., staff members of the Limon Correctional Facility (LCF) found inmate Daniel Shettler (the victim) dead in his cell, lying under the covers of his upper bunk bed. The staff members discovered the body as the result of a "lockdown" of the facility that occurred at 7:00 p.m. An investigation revealed that the victim was strangled by a ligature surrounding his neck, and that the time of death was approximately between 6:00 p.m. and 9:30 p.m. on July 13, 1992. * * *

The victim lived in a three-tiered pod that housed approximately fifty inmates, including Blecha, Younger, and Green. On the day of the murder, all fifty inmates were permitted to move freely throughout the pod between a lockdown that occurred at 4:00 p.m. and the lockdown that occurred at 7:00 p.m. In the days following the murder, investigators questioned all fifty inmates. During these interviews, the investigators learned of a rumor among the prisoners that the victim was killed because he was an informant in a murder that occurred six months earlier at a different prison, the Fremont Correctional Facility (FCF). Three inmates * * * told investigators that Blecha, Younger, and Green killed the victim. Another inmate, Michael Ford (Ford), implicated three other inmates. * * *

In August of 1992, Bates told the chief investigating officer that shortly after the murder, Younger threatened his life and told him to keep his mouth shut. The officer's opinion was that Bates feared for his life from the day of the murder until he was subsequently transferred from LCF to another facility.

In October of 1992, Blecha, Younger, and Green were charged with murder and conspiracy to commit murder. Blecha moved to exclude Younger's hearsay statements from trial, contending that the admission of these statements was prohibited by [Colorado hearsay rules] and by the confrontation clauses of the United States and Colorado Constitutions.

After a hearing, the district court ruled that Younger's statements were admissible as the nonhearsay statements of a co-conspirator under CRE 801(d)(2)(E).[22] The district court then addressed Blecha's assertion that admission of these statements violated the confrontation clauses of the United States and Colorado Constitutions under the two-part test articulated in *Ohio v. Roberts,* 448 U.S. 56, 65 * * * (1980). First, the district court found that Younger was not available to testify at trial because, at the time of the pre-trial hearing, Younger was protected by the Fifth Amendment privilege against self-incrimination due to the pending murder and conspiracy charges against him. Second, the district court determined that Younger's statements possessed sufficient independent indicia of reliability to overcome the presumption of unreliability that attaches to hearsay statements. Thus, the district court held that the admission of Younger's statements was appropriate under the Colorado and federal constitutions. * * * After this hearing, the district court severed the trials of each of the three co-defendants. In August of 1993, Younger was acquitted of all charges. Blecha's case proceeded to trial in November of 1993.

At Blecha's trial, the prosecution submitted the results of the investigation, set forth above, into evidence. The prosecution's theory was that the victim was killed pursuant to the order of the vice-president of the Aryan Brotherhood, a prison gang. Mike Schneider * * *, the vice-president of the gang and an inmate at FCF, believed that the victim was an informant in the unrelated prison murder that occurred at FCF. The defense's theory was that Blecha was in the gymnasium when the murder occurred, that the investigation overlooked inmate Ford's information that pointed to other suspects, and that the prosecution's case was based solely on the testimony of "liars, thieves and murderers."

Bates, who lived a few cells away from the victim, testified that on the evening of the murder he saw Younger, Green, and Blecha enter the victim's cell and shut the door. Bates testified that he walked by the victim's cell and saw Younger holding the victim in a headlock, Blecha standing in front of the victim with his hands up in the air, and Green standing behind Blecha holding a cord. Bates went to inmate Heath

---

[22] [Like Federal Rule 801(d)(2)(E), the Colorado Rule limits co-conspirator statements to those made during and in furtherance of the conspiracy. Ed.]

Pinion's * * * cell and told him "they were doing Danny." Bates returned to the victim's cell and saw Green, Blecha, and Younger putting the victim on the top bunk bed. Bates then informed three additional inmates * * * as to what he saw, and unsuccessfully attempted to rouse the victim by kicking the door to the victim's cell.

Bates further testified that the day after the murder Younger motioned to Bates by raising his index finger to his lips, indicating to Bates to be quiet. Three or four days after this incident, Younger told Bates that "[h]e knew I seen it, and he didn't want me to say anything."

[The court recounted testimony by several other witness that incriminated defendant Blecha as well as some testimony offered by the defense pointing to another group of inmates.]

II. Co–Conspirator Hearsay

Hearsay statements are out-of-court declarations offered into evidence for the truth of the matter asserted. *See* CRE 801(c). Hearsay statements are presumptively unreliable since the declarant is not present to explain the statement in context. Moreover, since the declarant is not subjected to cross-examination, the truthfulness of the statement is questionable. *See* Paul Marcus, *Prosecution and Defense of Criminal Conspiracy Cases* § 5.04[1], at 5–16 (1996). Due to this presumptive unreliability, hearsay statements are generally not admissible as evidence at trial. *See Bourjaily v. United States,* 483 U.S. 171, 179 * * * (1987). However, the out-of-court declarations of criminal conspirators "made during the course of and in furtherance of the conspiracy" are deemed non-hearsay under CRE 801(d)(2)(E) and may be admissible against all of the participants in the conspiracy.

The scope of the co-conspirator exception is narrow, *see Krulewitch v. United States,* 336 U.S. 440, 444 * * * (1949), and the requirement that the co-conspirator's statement be made during the course of and in furtherance of the conspiracy is a "prerequisite to admissibility" that must be "scrupulously observed." *Id.* The proponent must demonstrate the existence of both of these factors to overcome the presumption of unreliability that is the basis of the prohibition against the admission of hearsay. *See Williams v. People,* 724 P.2d 1279, 1285 (Colo.1986).

CRE 801(d)(2)(E)'s provision for the admission of co-conspirator statements is based on a theory of agency. Each conspirator is considered the agent of the other conspirators when acting or speaking to promote the conspiracy. *See* 5 Jack B. Weinstein & Margaret A. Berger, *Weinstein's Evidence* § 801.30, at 801–59 (Joseph M. McLaughlin, ed., 2d ed. 1998)*; United States v. Perez,* 989 F.2d 1574, 1577 (10th Cir.1993). However, just as an agent's responsibilities end upon the termination of the agency relationship, "all such responsibility is at an end when the conspiracy ends." *Fiswick v. United States,* 329 U.S. 211, 217 * * * (1946)*;

see also People v. Armstrong, 704 P.2d 877, 879 (Colo.App.1985). "There can be no furtherance of a conspiracy that has ended." *Lutwak v. United States,* 344 U.S. 604, 617–18 * * * (1953).

Thus, it is well-settled under Colorado and federal law that co-conspirator statements made after the conspirators attain the object of the conspiracy are not admissible under this exception unless the proponent demonstrates "an express original agreement among the conspirators to continue to act in concert in order to cover up, for their own self-protection, traces of the crime after its commission." *Grunewald v. United States,* 353 U.S. 391, 404 * * * (1957); *see also Villafranca v. People,* 194 Colo. 472, 474, 573 P.2d 540, 542 (1978). The proponent can satisfy this requirement by showing that the objectives of the original conspiracy include such an agreement or that there exists a separate conspiracy to conceal. *See Kolkman v. People,* 89 Colo. 8, 18, 300 P. 575, 579 (1931).

It is also well-settled that "secrecy plus overt acts of concealment" do not establish an express agreement to act in concert in order to conceal the crime. *Grunewald,* 353 U.S. at 403 * * *. Acts of concealment occur in every conspiracy case, *see id.* at 404 * * *, and admission of hearsay statements on this basis would impermissibly expand the narrow scope of the co-conspirator exception and further dilute the general prohibition against hearsay statements. *See Krulewitch,* 336 U.S. at 444 * * * (holding that statements aimed at preventing detection and punishment were not admissible under the co-conspirator exception). As the United States Supreme Court articulated in *Grunewald v. United States:*

> [A] subsidiary conspiracy to conceal may not be implied from circumstantial evidence showing merely that the conspiracy was kept a secret and that the conspirators took care to cover up their crime in order to escape detection and punishment* * *. Acts of covering up, even though done in the context of a mutually understood need for secrecy, cannot themselves constitute proof that concealment of the crime after its commission was part of the initial agreement among the conspirators* * *. [E]very conspiracy will inevitably be followed by actions taken to cover the conspirators' traces. Sanctioning the Government's theory would for all practical purposes wipe out the statute of limitations in conspiracy cases, as well as extend indefinitely the time within which hearsay declarations will bind co-conspirators.

Grunewald, 353 U.S. at 401–02 * * *. We adopted this view in *Villafranca v. People,* when we stated:

> Not every conspiracy continues beyond the time of the occurrence of the crime that is the object of the conspiracy. There

must be some specific evidence of a plan or agreement of concealment to demonstrate the pendency of the conspiracy at the time that the statements were made.

Villafranca, 194 Colo. at 474, 573 P.2d at 542.

Applying these principles to the facts of this case, the prosecution sought the admission of two hearsay statements made by Younger after the commission of the murder. Such statements are admissible only if the prosecution demonstrates the existence of an express agreement among the conspirators to continue to act in concert in order to conceal the crime.

The record shows that the conspirators disposed of the murder weapon and placed the victim's body in a manner that would give the appearance that the victim was asleep. "[A]cts of covering up, even though done in the context of a mutually understood need for secrecy, cannot themselves constitute proof that concealment of the crime after its commission was part of the initial agreement among the conspirators." *Grunewald,* 353 U.S. at 402 * * * (holding that conspirators' efforts to conceal irregularities in documents and attempts to silence witnesses were insufficient evidence of an explicit agreement to conceal the crime). The record also shows that in the days following the murder, Younger made two statements to Bates that could be construed as an attempt to silence Bates. While these statements may demonstrate Younger's purpose to conceal the murder conspiracy, they are not evidence that the murder conspiracy included the further agreement to conceal. *See Lutwak,* 344 U.S. at 616 * * * (explaining that statements "in the nature of an afterthought by the conspirator for the purpose of covering up" do not constitute evidence of an agreement to conceal). Other conspirators did not similarly attempt to silence witnesses. Review of the record discloses no evidence that concealment was an explicit objective of the murder conspiracy and no evidence of a separate conspiracy with the explicit objective of concealing the murder. Hence, we hold that Younger's statements were not admissible under the co-conspirator exception because they were not made during the course of and in furtherance of the conspiracy to murder as required by CRE 801(d)(2)(E), and we affirm the court of appeals' ruling that the district court's admission of these statements was error.

[Blecha argued that Younger's statements acknowledging that Bates witnessed the murder indirectly admitted Younger's guilt thereby bolstering Bates' credibility and contributing to Blecha's conviction. The Colorado Supreme Court nevertheless found admission of the statements harmless error because of the strength of the independent evidence linking Younger to the crime, other corroboration of Bates' account, and the relative lack of importance of Younger's statement to the prosecution's case.]

NOTES AND QUESTIONS

1.   *Frequently admitted.* In both *Cornett* and *Blecha*, the courts found error (albeit harmless error in *Blecha*) in the admission of the co-conspirator statements. Those results should not be read to suggest a general reticence of courts to receive such hearsay, which the Supreme Court observed "apparently is the most frequently used exception to the hearsay rule." United States v. Inadi, 475 U.S. 387, 398 (1986).

2.   *Determining when primary conspiracy ends.* Under Federal Rule 801(d)(2)(E), a co-conspirator's statements must have been made during the conspiracy and later concealment activities are not automatically included. Nevertheless, difficult issues arise concerning concealment because of the nature of some conspiracies, and in ordinary conspiracies dividing the primary conspiracy from concealment is often not obvious. Certainly some acts of concealment are treated as part of the "main" conspiracy in some cases. The Court in Grunewald v. United States, 353 U.S. 391, 405 (1957), gave the following examples: "Kidnapers in hiding, waiting for ransom, commit acts of concealment in furtherance of the objectives of the conspiracy itself, just as repainting a stolen car would be in furtherance of a conspiracy to steal; in both cases the successful accomplishment of the crime necessitates concealment." In a typical conspiracy, "in the course of" would more likely include dividing up the spoils of the crime (see United States v. Hickey, 596 F.2d 1082, 1089–90 (1st Cir.1979)) or a participant collecting payment for his part in the criminal enterprise (see United States v. Schwanke, 598 F.2d 575, 581–82 (10th Cir.1979)) than the subsequent arson of the getaway car (see United States v. Floyd, 555 F.2d 45, 48 (2d Cir.1977)).

Withdrawal from a conspiracy under the substantive criminal law test also has the effect of eliminating admissibility of statements by co-conspirators against the withdrawing party. United States v. Pratt, 239 F.3d 640, 644 (4th Cir.2001).

3.   *Concealment phase under state rules.* While federal evidentiary law will not permit admission of statements made during a broadly defined concealment phase, some states take a different view. See, e.g., State v. Helmick, 495 S.E.2d 262, 269 (W.Va.1997) ("we are persuaded by those jurisdictions that hold that '[a] conspiracy to commit a crime does not necessarily end with the commission of the crime' "). Moreover, the Federal Rule limitation is not constitutionally required. Dutton v. Evans, 400 U.S. 74 (1970) (affirming the constitutionality of admission of co-conspirator statement from state (Georgia) that automatically included concealment phase).

4.   *Conspiracy need not be charged.* A formal conspiracy charge is not required in order to admit the statement of a co-conspirator. 2 McCormick, Evidence § 259 (7th ed. 2013).

5.   *Admission despite acquittal.* The acquittal of a co-conspirator does not usually require exclusion of his or her statement because the standard of

proof for admissibility is less demanding than proof beyond a reasonable doubt required for conviction. See United States v. Peralta, 941 F.2d 1003, 1006–07 (9th Cir.1991); United States v. Gil, 604 F.2d 546, 549 (7th Cir.1979).

6.   *Extending an established conspiracy.* Some courts continue to state, despite the rather obvious flaw, that only slight evidence is required to connect a co-conspirator once a conspiracy is established. See, e.g., United States v. Andrews, 585 F.2d 961 (10th Cir.1978). But see United States v. Malatesta, 590 F.2d 1379 (5th Cir.1979) (banishing the rule).

C. CONFRONTATION

CALIFORNIA V. GREEN
Supreme Court of the United States, 1970.
399 U.S. 149.

MR. JUSTICE WHITE delivered the opinion of the Court.

Section 1235 of the California Evidence Code, effective as of January 1, 1967, provides that "[e]vidence of a statement made by a witness is not made inadmissible by the hearsay rule if the statement is inconsistent with his testimony at the hearing and is offered in compliance with Section 770."[23] In *People v. Johnson,* 68 Cal.2d 646, 441 P.2d 111 (1968), the California Supreme Court held that prior statements of a witness that were not subject to cross-examination when originally made, could not be introduced under this section to prove the charges against a defendant without violating the defendant's right of confrontation guaranteed by the Sixth Amendment and made applicable to the States by the Fourteenth Amendment.

* * *

The origin and development of the hearsay rules and of the Confrontation Clause have been traced by others and need not be recounted in detail here. It is sufficient to note that the particular vice that gave impetus to the confrontation claim was the practice of trying defendants on "evidence" which consisted solely of *ex parte* affidavits or depositions secured by the examining magistrates, thus denying the defendant the opportunity to challenge his accuser in a face-to-face encounter in front of the trier of fact. Prosecuting attorneys "would frequently allege matters which the prisoner denied and called upon them to prove. The proof was usually given by reading depositions, confessions of accomplices, letters, and the like; and this occasioned frequent

---

[23] * * * Section 770 merely requires that the witness be given an opportunity to explain or deny the prior statement at some point in the trial. * * *

demands by the prisoner to have his 'accusers,' *i.e.* the witnesses against him, brought before him face to face * * *."[24]

But objections occasioned by this practice appear primarily to have been aimed at the failure to call the witness to confront personally the defendant at his trial. So far as appears, in claiming confrontation rights no objection was made against receiving a witness' out-of-court depositions or statements, so long as the witness was present at trial to repeat his story and to explain or repudiate any conflicting prior stories before the trier of fact.

* * *

This conclusion is supported by comparing the purposes of confrontation with the alleged dangers in admitting an out-of-court statement. Confrontation: (1) insures that the witness will give his statements under oath—thus impressing him with the seriousness of the matter and guarding against the lie by the possibility of a penalty for perjury; (2) forces the witness to submit to cross-examination, the "greatest legal engine ever invented for the discovery of truth"[25]; (3) permits the jury that is to decide the defendant's fate to observe the demeanor of the witness in making his statement, thus aiding the jury in assessing his credibility.

It is, of course, true that the out-of-court statement may have been made under circumstances subject to none of these protections. But if the declarant is present and testifying at trial, the out-of-court statement for all practical purposes regains most of the lost protections. If the witness admits the prior statement is his, or if there is other evidence to show the statement is his, the danger of faulty reproduction is negligible and the jury can be confident that it has before it two conflicting statements by the same witness. Thus, as far as the oath is concerned, the witness must now affirm, deny, or qualify the truth of the prior statement under the penalty of perjury; indeed, the very fact that the prior statement was not given under a similar circumstance may become the witness' explanation for its inaccuracy—an explanation a jury may be expected to understand and take into account in deciding which, if either, of the statements represents the truth.

---

[24] 1 J. Stephen, A History of the Criminal Law of England 326 (1883). See also 9 [W.] Holdsworth, [A History of English Law] 225–228 [(3d ed. 1944)].

A famous example is provided by the trial of Sir Walter Raleigh for treason in 1603. A crucial element of the evidence against him consisted of the statements of one Cobham, implicating Raleigh in a plot to seize the throne. Raleigh had since received a written retraction from Cobham, and believed that Cobham would now testify in his favor. After a lengthy dispute over Raleigh's right to have Cobham called as a witness, Cobham was not called, and Raleigh was convicted. See 1 Stephen, supra, at 333–336; 9 Holdsworth, supra, at 216–217, 226–228. At least one author traces the Confrontation Clause to the common-law reaction against these abuses of the Raleigh trial. See F. Heller, The Sixth Amendment 104 (1951).

[25] 5 [J.] Wigmore [, Evidence] § 1367.

Second, the inability to cross-examine the witness at the time he made his prior statement cannot easily be shown to be of crucial significance as long as the defendant is assured of full and effective cross-examination at the time of trial. The most successful cross-examination at the time the prior statement was made could hardly hope to accomplish more than has already been accomplished by the fact that the witness is now telling a different, inconsistent story, and—in this case—one that is favorable to the defendant. * * *

The defendant's task in cross-examination is, of course, no longer identical to the task that he would have faced if the witness had not changed his story and hence had to be examined as a "hostile" witness giving evidence for the prosecution. This difference, however, far from lessening, may actually enhance the defendant's ability to attack the prior statement. For the witness, favorable to the defendant, should be more than willing to give the usual suggested explanations for the inaccuracy of his prior statement, such as faulty perception or undue haste in recounting the event. Under such circumstances, the defendant is not likely to be hampered in effectively attacking the prior statement, solely because his attack comes later in time.

Similar reasons lead us to discount as a constitutional matter the fact that the jury at trial is foreclosed from viewing the declarant's demeanor when he first made his out-of-court statement. The witness who now relates a different story about the events in question must necessarily assume a position as to the truth value of his prior statement, thus giving the jury a chance to observe and evaluate his demeanor as he either disavows or qualifies his earlier statement. * * *

It may be true that a jury would be in a better position to evaluate the truth of the prior statement if it could somehow be whisked magically back in time to witness a gruelling cross-examination of the declarant as he first gives his statement. But the question as we see it must be not whether one can somehow imagine the jury in "a better position," but whether subsequent cross-examination at the defendant's trial will still afford the trier of fact a satisfactory basis for evaluating the truth of the prior statement. On that issue, neither evidence[26] nor reason convinces us that contemporaneous cross-examination before the ultimate trier of fact

---

[26] The California Supreme Court in its earlier decision on this issue stated that "[t]his practical truth [the importance of immediate cross-examination] is daily verified by trial lawyers, not one of whom would willingly postpone to both a later date and a different forum his right to cross-examine a witness against his client." People v. Johnson, 68 Cal.2d 646, 655, 441 P.2d 111, 118 (1968). The citations that follow this sentence are to books on trial practice that shed little empirical light on the actual comparative effectiveness of subsequent, as opposed to timely, cross-examination. As the text suggests, where the witness has changed his story at trial to favor the defendant he should, if anything, be more rather than less vulnerable to defense counsel's explanations for the inaccuracy of his former statement.

is so much more effective than subsequent examination that it must be made the touchstone of the Confrontation Clause.

Finally, we note that none of our decisions interpreting the Confrontation Clause requires excluding the out-of-court statements of a witness who is available and testifying at trial. The concern of most of our cases has been focused on precisely the opposite situation—situations where statements have been admitted in the absence of the declarant and without any chance to cross-examine him at trial.

* * *

We find nothing, then, in either the history or the purposes of the Confrontation Clause, or in the prior decisions of this Court, that compels the conclusion reached by the California Supreme Court concerning the validity of California's § 1235. Contrary to the judgment of that court, the Confrontation Clause does not require excluding from evidence the prior statements of a witness who concedes making the statements, and who may be asked to defend or otherwise explain the inconsistency between his prior and his present version of the events in question, thus opening himself to full cross-examination at trial as to both stories.

[The Court remanded the case to the California courts to consider the narrow question of whether Porter's statement to Officer Wade, which had not been the subject of prior cross-examination, was inadmissible because of the witness' apparent memory lapse and the resulting limitation on cross-examination at trial.]

[In an omitted portion of the case, the Court approves admission of statements made by Porter at the preliminary hearing where he had been cross-examined by Green's counsel.]

NOTES AND QUESTIONS

1. *On remand.* In *Green*, the Supreme Court remanded to the state court the determination of whether Melvin Porter's claim that he could not remember the critical events covered by his prior statement to a police officer so affected Green's right of cross-examination as to deny effectively his confrontation rights. On remand, in People v. Green, 479 P.2d 998 (Cal.1971), the California court ruled that Porter's testimony amounted to an implied denial that defendant had furnished him with the marijuana and thus was inconsistent with his prior statements within the meaning of California Evidence Code. The court also held that the purposes of the Confrontation Clause had been satisfied, relying particularly upon the fact that Green's counsel had the opportunity to test the witness' memory concerning the prior statement but declined to take advantage of that opportunity.

2. *Availability for cross-examination, but not much more, required.* The Court in *Green* reserved judgment on whether the Confrontation Clause is violated if a witness who made a prior inconsistent statement is unable at

trial to recall the underlying event to which the statement refers. Similar issues arise when a witness has a memory of the underlying event but either has no memory of the prior statement or denies making it. See generally Graham, The Confrontation Clause, the Hearsay Rule, and the Forgetful Witness, 56 Tex.L.Rev. 151 (1978).

In United States v. Owens, 484 U.S. 554 (1988), the Court swept these various issues aside. It adopted the position of Justice Harlan in his concurring opinion in *Green* that "a witness's inability to 'recall either the underlying events that are the subject of an extra-judicial statement or previous testimony or recollect the circumstances under which the statement was given, does not have Sixth Amendment consequences.' " Id. at 558 (quoting *Green,* 399 U.S. at 188). See also United States v. Milton, 8 F.3d 39, 47 (D.C.Cir.1993) (prior statement receivable despite failure to remember both the events underlying statement and prior statement itself). *Owens* means that almost no matter what the witness' testimonial limitations, the physical availability and willing response to questions satisfies the Confrontation Clause. Compare United States ex rel. Hamilton v. Ellingsworth, 692 F.Supp. 356, 359 (D.Del.1988) (ruling that despite amnesia witness was "available"), with United States v. Spotted War Bonnet, 933 F.2d 1471, 1474 (8th Cir.1991) (stating that although a child's substantial forgetfulness regarding events or prior statement does not render opportunity for cross-examination constitutionally inadequate, simply putting child on stand who is so young that she could not be cross-examined at all would deny confrontation right). See similar discussion in Section(B)(1), supra.

3. *Calling witness or making available?* In order for *Green*'s rationale to apply, is it necessary that the prosecution call the declarant to testify on direct examination and the defendant then be given an opportunity for cross-examination, or is it sufficient if the prosecution simply produces the declarant and permits the defendant to conduct an examination? Compare People v. Bastien, 541 N.E.2d 670 (Ill.1989) (witness must be called as witness by state), with State v. Schaal, 806 S.W.2d 659 (Mo.1991) (en banc) (making witness available for examination is constitutionally sufficient).

4. *Part of the "new" system.* In *Crawford v. Washington,* infra, the Supreme Court established a new Confrontation Clause analysis that differs dramatically from its earlier analysis, particularly the general system described in *Ohio v. Roberts,* which is the next principal case. However, the theory of *California v. Green,* applicable when the declarant testifies at the current trial and is available for cross-examination about prior statements, remains valid under *Crawford.*

OHIO V. ROBERTS

Supreme Court of the United States, 1980.
448 U.S. 56.

MR. JUSTICE BLACKMUN delivered the opinion of the Court.

This case presents issues concerning the constitutional propriety of the introduction in evidence of the preliminary hearing testimony of a witness not produced at the defendant's subsequent state criminal trial.

I

Local police arrested respondent, Herschel Roberts, on January 7, 1975, in Lake County, Ohio. Roberts was charged with forgery of a check in the name of Bernard Isaacs, and with possession of stolen credit cards belonging to Isaacs and his wife Amy.

A preliminary hearing was held in Municipal Court on January 10. The prosecution called several witnesses, including Mr. Isaacs. Respondent's appointed counsel had seen the Isaacs' daughter, Anita, in the courthouse hallway, and called her as the defense's only witness. Anita Isaacs testified that she knew respondent, and that she had permitted him to use her apartment for several days while she was away. Defense counsel questioned Anita at some length and attempted to elicit from her an admission that she had given respondent checks and the credit cards without informing him that she did not have permission to use them. Anita, however, denied this. Respondent's attorney did not ask to have the witness declared hostile and did not request permission to place her on cross-examination. The prosecutor did not question Anita. * * *

Between November 1975 and March 1976, five subpoenas for four different trial dates were issued to Anita at her parents' Ohio residence. The last three carried a written instruction that Anita should "call before appearing." She was not at the residence when these were executed. She did not telephone and she did not appear at trial.

In March 1976, the case went to trial before a jury in the Court of Common Pleas. Respondent took the stand and testified that Anita Isaacs had given him her parents' checkbook and credit cards with the understanding that he could use them. Relying on Ohio Rev.Code Ann. § 2945.49 (1975), which permits the use of preliminary examination testimony of a witness who "cannot for any reason be produced at the trial," the State, on rebuttal, offered the transcript of Anita's testimony.

Asserting a violation of the Confrontation Clause and indeed, the unconstitutionality thereunder of § 2945.49, the defense objected to the use of the transcript. The trial court conducted a *voir dire* hearing as to its admissibility. Amy Isaacs, the sole witness at *voir dire*, was questioned by both the prosecutor and defense counsel concerning her daughter's whereabouts. Anita, according to her mother, left home for Tucson, Ariz., soon after the preliminary hearing. About a year before the trial, a San Francisco social worker was in communication with the Isaacs about a welfare application Anita had filed there. Through the social worker, the Isaacs reached their daughter once by telephone. Since then, however, Anita had called her parents only one other time and had not been in touch with her two sisters. When Anita called, some seven or eight months before trial, she told her parents that she "was traveling" outside Ohio, but did not reveal the place from which she called. Mrs. Isaacs stated that she knew of no way to reach Anita in case of an emergency. App. 9. Nor did she "know of anybody who knows where she is." *Id.* at 11. The trial court admitted the transcript into evidence. Respondent was convicted on all counts.

The Court of Appeals of Ohio reversed. * * * The Supreme Court of Ohio * * * affirmed * * *. It first held that * * * Anita was * * * unavailable. *Barber v. Page* was distinguished as a case in which "the government knew where the absent witness was," whereas Anita's "whereabouts were entirely unknown." 55 Ohio St.2d, at 194, 378 N.E.2d, at 495, "[T]he trial judge could reasonably have concluded from Mrs. Isaacs' *voir dire* testimony that due diligence could not have procured the attendance of Anita Isaacs"; he "could reasonably infer that Anita had left San Francisco"; and he "could properly hold that the witness was unavailable to testify in person." *Id.,* at 195, 378 N.E.2d, at 495–496.

The court, nonetheless, held that the transcript was inadmissible. Reasoning that normally there is little incentive to cross-examine a witness at a preliminary hearing, where the "ultimate issue" is only probable cause, *id.,* at 196, 378 N.E.2d, at 496 * * * the court held that the mere opportunity to cross-examine at a preliminary hearing did not afford constitutional confrontation for purposes of trial. * * * Since Anita had not been cross-examined at the preliminary hearing and was absent at trial, the introduction of the transcript of her testimony was held to have violated respondent's confrontation right. * * *

II

A

The Court here is called upon to consider once again the relationship between the Confrontation Clause and the hearsay rule with its many exceptions. The basic rule against hearsay, of course, is riddled with exceptions developed over three centuries. These exceptions vary among jurisdictions as to number, nature, and detail. But every set of exceptions seems to fit an apt description offered more than 40 years ago: "an old-fashioned crazy quilt made of patches cut from a group of paintings by cubists, futurists and surrealists." Morgan & Maguire, Looking Backward and Forward at Evidence, 50 Harv.L.Rev. 909, 921 (1937).

The Sixth Amendment's Confrontation Clause, made applicable to the States through the Fourteenth Amendment, *Pointer v. Texas,* 380 U.S. 400, 403–405 (1965) * * *, provides: "In all criminal prosecutions, the accused shall enjoy the right * * * to be confronted with the witnesses against him." If one were to read this language literally, it would require, on objection, the exclusion of any statement made by a declarant not present at trial. See *Mattox v. United States,* 156 U.S. 237, 243 (1895) ("[T]here could be nothing more directly contrary to the letter of the provision in question than the admission of dying declarations"). But, if thus applied, the Clause would abrogate virtually every hearsay exception, a result long rejected as unintended and too extreme.

The historical evidence leaves little doubt, however, that the Clause was intended to exclude some hearsay. See *California v. Green,* 399 U.S., at 156–157, and nn.9 and 10; see also McCormick § 252, p. 606. Moreover, underlying policies support the same conclusion. The Court has emphasized that the Confrontation Clause reflects a preference for face-to-face confrontation at trial, and that "a primary interest secured by [the provision] is the right of cross-examination." *Douglas v. Alabama,* 380 U.S. 415, 418 (1965).[27] In short, the Clause envisions

> "a personal examination and cross-examination of the witness, in which the accused has an opportunity, not only of testing the recollection and sifting the conscience of the witness, but of compelling him to stand face to face with the jury in order that they may look at him, and judge by his demeanor upon the stand and the manner in which he gives his testimony whether he is worthy of belief." *Mattox v. United States,* 156 U.S., at 242–243.

These means of testing accuracy are so important that the absence of proper confrontation at trial "calls into question the ultimate 'integrity of the fact-finding process.' " *Chambers v. Mississippi,* 410 U.S. 284, 295 (1973), quoting *Berger v. California,* 393 U.S. 314, 315 (1969). * * *

B

The Confrontation Clause operates in two separate ways to restrict the range of admissible hearsay. First, in conformance with the Framers' preference for face-to-face accusation, the Sixth Amendment establishes a rule of necessity. In the usual case (including cases where prior cross-examination has occurred), the prosecution must either produce, or demonstrate the unavailability of, the declarant whose statement it wishes to use against the defendant. See *Mancusi v. Stubbs,* 408 U.S. 204 (1972); *Barber v. Page,* 390 U.S. 719 (1968). * * *

---

[27] See also * * * California v. Green, 399 U.S., at 158 (cross-examination is the " 'greatest legal engine ever invented for the discovery of truth,' " quoting 5 J. Wigmore, Evidence § 1367 (3d ed. 1940)). Of course, these purposes are interrelated, since one critical goal of cross-examination is to draw out discrediting demeanor to be viewed by the factfinder. See Government of Virgin Islands v. Aquino, 378 F.2d 540, 548 (C.A.3 1967).

The second aspect operates once a witness is shown to be unavailable. Reflecting its underlying purpose to augment accuracy in the factfinding process by ensuring the defendant an effective means to test adverse evidence, the Clause countenances only hearsay marked with such trustworthiness that "there is no material departure from the reason of the general rule." *Snyder v. Massachusetts*, 291 U.S., at 107. The principle recently was formulated in *Mancusi v. Stubbs*:

> "The focus of the Court's concern has been to insure that there 'are indicia of reliability which have been widely viewed as determinative of whether a statement may be placed before the jury though there is no confrontation of the declarant,' *Dutton v. Evans, supra,* at 89 and to 'afford the trier of fact a satisfactory basis for evaluating the truth of the prior statement,' *California v. Green, supra,* 399 U.S., at 161. It is clear from these statements, and from numerous prior decisions of this Court, that even though the witness be unavailable his prior testimony must bear some of these 'indicia of reliability.' " 408 U.S., at 213.

The Court has applied this "indicia of reliability" requirement principally by concluding that certain hearsay exceptions rest upon such solid foundations that admission of virtually any evidence within them comports with the "substance of the constitutional protection." *Mattox v. United States,* 156 U.S., at 244. This reflects the truism that "hearsay rules and the Confrontation Clause are generally designed to protect similar values," *California v. Green,* 399 U.S., at 155, and "stem from the same roots," *Dutton v. Evans,* 400 U.S. 74, 86 (1970). It also responds to the need for certainty in the workaday world of conducting criminal trials.

In sum, when a hearsay declarant is not present for cross-examination at trial, the Confrontation Clause normally requires a showing that he is unavailable. Even then, his statement is admissible only if it bears adequate "indicia of reliability." Reliability can be inferred without more in a case where the evidence falls within a firmly rooted hearsay exception. In other cases, the evidence must be excluded, at least absent a showing of particularized guarantees of trustworthiness.

III

We turn first to [the adequacy of Anita's cross-examination]. Resolution of this issue requires a careful comparison of this case to *California v. Green, supra.*[28]

---

[28] [This element of the Green decision was omitted from the earlier treatment of the case. Ed.]

A

In *Green,* at the preliminary hearing, a youth named Porter identified Green as a drug supplier. When called to the stand at Green's trial, however, Porter professed a lapse of memory. Frustrated in its attempt to adduce live testimony, the prosecution offered Porter's prior statements. The trial judge ruled the evidence admissible, and substantial portions of the preliminary hearing transcript were read to the jury. This Court found no error. * * * It reasoned:

> "Porter's statement at the preliminary hearing had already been given under circumstances closely approximating those that surround the typical trial. Porter was under oath; respondent was represented by counsel—the same counsel in fact who later represented him at the trial; respondent had every opportunity to cross-examine Porter as to his statement; and the proceedings were conducted before a judicial tribunal, equipped to provide a judicial record of the hearings." 399 U.S., at 165.

These factors, the Court concluded, provided all that the Sixth Amendment demands: "substantial compliance with the purposes behind the confrontation requirement." *Id.,* at 166.

This passage and others in the *Green* opinion suggest that the *opportunity* to cross-examine at the preliminary hearing—even absent actual cross-examination—satisfies the Confrontation Clause. Yet the record showed, and the Court recognized, that defense counsel in fact had cross-examined Porter at the earlier proceeding. *Id.,* at 151. * * *

We need not decide whether the Supreme Court of Ohio correctly dismissed statements in *Green* suggesting that the mere opportunity to cross-examine rendered the prior testimony admissible. * * * Nor need we decide whether *de minimis* questioning is sufficient, for defense counsel in this case tested Anita's testimony with the equivalent of significant cross-examination.

B

Counsel's questioning clearly partook of cross-examination as a matter of *form.* His presentation was replete with leading questions, the principal tool and hallmark of cross-examination. In addition, counsel's questioning comported with the principal *purpose* of cross-examination: to challenge "whether the declarant was sincerely telling what he believed to be the truth, whether the declarant accurately perceived and remembered the matter he related, and whether the declarant's intended meaning is adequately conveyed by the language he employed." Davenport, The Confrontation Clause and the Co–Conspirator Exception in Criminal Prosecutions: A Functional Analysis, 85 Harv.L.Rev. 1378 (1972). Anita's unwillingness to shift the blame away from respondent became discernible early in her testimony. Yet counsel continued to explore the underlying events in detail. He attempted, for example, to establish that Anita and respondent were sharing an apartment, an assertion that was critical to respondent's defense at trial and that might have suggested ulterior personal reasons for unfairly casting blame on respondent. At another point, he directly challenged Anita's veracity by seeking to have her admit that she had given the credit cards to respondent to obtain a television. When Anita denied this, defense counsel elicited the fact that the only television she owned was a "Twenty Dollar * * * old model." App. 21. Cf. *Davis v. Alaska,* 415 U.S. 308, 316–317 (1974). * * *

In sum, we perceive no reason to resolve the reliability issue differently here than the Court did in *Green.* "Since there was an adequate opportunity to cross-examine [the witness], and counsel * * * availed himself of that opportunity * * *." 408 U.S., at 216.

IV

[Respondent also contends that the State] failed to lay a proper predicate for admission of the preliminary hearing transcript by its failure to demonstrate that Anita Isaacs was not available to testify in person at the trial. * * *

A

The basic litmus of Sixth Amendment unavailability is established: "[A] witness is not 'unavailable' for purposes of the * * * exception to the confrontation requirement unless the prosecutorial authorities have made a *good-faith effort* to obtain his presence at trial." *Barber v. Page,* 390 U.S., at 724–725 (emphasis added). * * *

Although it might be said that the Court's prior cases provide no further refinement of this statement of the rule, certain general propositions safely emerge. The law does not require the doing of a futile act. Thus, if no possibility of procuring the witness exists (as, for example, the witness' intervening death), "good faith" demands nothing of the prosecution. But if there is a possibility, albeit remote, that affirmative measures might produce the declarant, the obligation of good faith *may* demand their effectuation. "The lengths to which the prosecution must go to produce a witness * * * is a question of reasonableness." *California v. Green,* 399 U.S., at 189, n.22 (concurring opinion, citing *Barber v. Page, supra*). The ultimate question is whether the witness is unavailable despite good-faith efforts undertaken prior to trial to locate and present that witness. As with other evidentiary proponents, the prosecution bears the burden of establishing this predicate.

B

On the facts presented we hold that the trial court and the Supreme Court of Ohio correctly concluded that Anita's unavailability, in the constitutional sense, was established.

At the *voir dire* hearing, called for by the defense, it was shown that some four months prior to the trial the prosecutor was in touch with Amy Isaacs and discussed with her Anita's whereabouts. It may appropriately be inferred that Mrs. Isaacs told the prosecutor essentially the same facts to which she testified at *voir dire*: that the Isaacs had last heard from Anita during the preceding summer; that she was not then in San Francisco, but was traveling outside Ohio; and that the Isaacs and their other children knew of no way to reach Anita even in an emergency. This last fact takes on added significance when it is recalled that Anita's parents earlier had undertaken affirmative efforts to reach their daughter when the social worker's inquiry came in from San Francisco. This is not a case of parents abandoning all interest in an absent daughter.

The evidence of record demonstrates that the prosecutor issued a subpoena to Anita at her parents' home, not only once, but on five separate occasions over a period of several months. In addition, at the *voir dire* argument, the prosecutor stated to the court that respondent "witnessed that I have attempted to locate, I have subpoenaed, there has been a *voir dire* of the witness' parents, and they have not been able to locate her for over a year." App. 12.

Given these facts, the prosecution did not breach its duty of good-faith effort. To be sure, the prosecutor might have tried to locate by telephone the San Francisco social worker with whom Mrs. Isaacs had spoken many months before and might have undertaken other steps in an effort to find Anita. One, in hindsight, may always think of other things. Nevertheless, the great improbability that such efforts would have resulted in locating the witness, and would have led to her production at trial, neutralizes any intimation that a concept of reasonableness required their execution. We accept as a general rule, of course, the proposition that "the possibility of a refusal is not the equivalent of asking and receiving a rebuff." *Barber v. Page,* 390 U.S., at 724, quoting from the dissenting opinion in that case in the Court of Appeals (381 F.2d 479, 481 (C.A.10 1966)). But the service and ineffectiveness of the five subpoenas and the conversation with Anita's mother were far more than mere reluctance to face the possibility of a refusal. It was investigation at the last-known real address, and it was conversation with a parent who was concerned about her daughter's whereabouts.

Barber and *Mancusi v. Stubbs, supra,* are the cases in which this Court has explored the issue of constitutional unavailability. Although each is factually distinguishable from this case, *Mancusi* provides significant support for a conclusion of good-faith effort here,[29] and *Barber* has no contrary significance. Insofar as this record discloses no basis for concluding that Anita was abroad, the case is factually weaker than *Mancusi*; but it is stronger than *Mancusi* in the sense that the Ohio prosecutor, unlike the prosecutor in *Mancusi*, had no clear indication, if any at all, of Anita's whereabouts. In *Barber,* the * * * prosecution knew where the witness [who was incarcerated in a federal penitentiary in a neighboring state] was, procedures existed whereby the witness could be brought to the trial, and the witness was not in a position to frustrate efforts to secure his production. Here, Anita's whereabouts were not known, and there was no assurance that she would be found in a place from which she could be forced to return to Ohio.

We conclude that the prosecution carried its burden of demonstrating that Anita was constitutionally unavailable for purposes of respondent's trial.

The judgment of the Supreme Court of Ohio is reversed * * *.

MR. JUSTICE BRENNAN, with whom MR. JUSTICE MARSHALL and MR. JUSTICE STEVENS join, dissenting.

* * *

In the present case, I am simply unable to conclude that the prosecution met its burden of establishing Anita Isaacs' unavailability. From all that appears in the record—and there has been no suggestion that the record is incomplete in this respect—the State's *total* effort to secure Anita's attendance at respondent's trial consisted of the delivery of five subpoenas in her name to her parents' residence, and three of those were issued after the authorities had learned that she was no longer living there. At least four months before the trial began, the prosecution was aware that Anita had moved away; yet during that entire interval it did nothing whatsoever to try to make contact with her. It is difficult to believe that the State would have been so derelict in attempting to secure the witness' presence at trial had it not had her favorable preliminary hearing testimony upon which to rely in the event of her "unavailability." The perfunctory steps which the State took in this case can hardly qualify as a "good-faith effort." In point of fact, it was no effort at all. * * *

---

[29] In *Mancusi*, the declarant "who had been born in Sweden but had become a naturalized American citizen, had returned to Sweden and taken up permanent residence there." 408 U.S., at 209. While in this country, he had testified against Stubbs at his Tennessee trial for murder and kidnaping. Stubbs was convicted, but obtained habeas corpus relief 10 years later, and was retried by Tennessee. Before the second trial, the prosecution sent a subpoena to be served in Texas, the declarant's last place of residence in this country. It could not be served. The Court rejected Stubbs' assertion that the prosecution had not undertaken good-faith efforts in failing to do more. "Tennessee * * * was powerless to compel his attendance * * * either through its own process or through established procedures." Id., at 212.

NOTES AND QUESTIONS

1. *Constitutional unavailability. Roberts* treatment of prior cross-examined hearsay when the declarant is unavailable, like present cross-examination of the declarant about prior statements under *California v. Green*, remains solid precedent. The *Roberts* case discusses caselaw establishing two elements of unavailability analysis under the confrontation clause. As explicated by *Barber v. Page*, the Constitution requires that, before a witness outside the jurisdiction (or inside the jurisdiction but not readily findable) is determined to be unavailable, reasonable efforts must be made to secure the witness' presence. However, as *Mancusi v. Stubbs* holds, not all possible efforts are required. Indeed, the facts of *Roberts* suggest that a limited effort may be sufficient. Nevertheless, the constitutional requirement has teeth beyond mere inability to subpoena the witness. See, e.g., State v. Nobles, 584 S.E.2d 765, 770 (N.C.2003) (failure of prosecution to at least attempt to contact out-of-state witness and request presence violated requirement).

2. *The Roberts system. Roberts* is best known for the general system for handling hearsay under the Confrontation Clause. That system lasted almost a quarter of a century until it was replaced by *Crawford v. Washington*, the next principal case, and overruled as to its approach to confrontation by Whorton v. Bockting, 549 U.S. 406 (2007). To understand the historical context that *Crawford* dramatically altered, the general dimensions of its system are set out.

Roberts' general statement for Confrontation Clause treatment of hearsay is:

> In sum, when a hearsay declarant is not present for cross-examination at trial, the Confrontation Clause normally requires a showing that he is unavailable. Even then, his statement is admissible only if it bears adequate "indicia of reliability." Reliability can be inferred without more in a case where the evidence falls within a firmly rooted hearsay exception. In other cases, the evidence must be excluded, at least absent a showing of particularized guarantees of trustworthiness.

This produced two areas of analysis for statements—(1) reliability and (2) unavailability.

3. *Reliability—"Firmly rooted" hearsay.* Under *Roberts*, the "indicia of reliability" necessary for a hearsay statement to meet the Confrontation Clause was automatically established if the statement fell within a "firmly rooted" hearsay exception. A hearsay exception was held to be firmly rooted based on the exception's longevity and widespread acceptance. Bourjaily v. United States, 483 U.S. 171, 183 (1987). See also Idaho v. Wright, 497 U.S. 805, 817 (1990) ("Admission under a firmly rooted hearsay exception satisfies the constitutional requirement of reliability because of the weight accorded

longstanding judicial and legislative experience in assessing the trustworthiness of certain types of out-of-court statements.").

4.   *Unavailability—Generally need not be shown.* In United States v. Inadi, 475 U.S. 387 (1986) (co-conspirator statements), and White v. Illinois, 502 U.S. 346 (1992) (excited utterances and statements for medical treatment), the Court ruled that unavailability need not be shown under *Roberts* because the statements fell within these hearsay exceptions. It reasoned that the circumstances of the making of those out-of-court statements and/or the motivation of the declarant gave them "independent evidentiary significance," *Inadi,* 475 U.S. at 394, that could not likely be replicated if the declarant was asked to make the same statement in court. After *White, Roberts'* "unavailability" requirement was transformed and was not required for any of the specific hearsay exceptions contained in Federal Rule 803. Under the theory of Rule 803 exceptions as to which availability of the declarant is considered irrelevant, the out-of-court statement is in some way equal or superior to in-court testimony, which under the *Inadi/White* theory eliminated any constitutional requirement that unavailability be shown.

5.   *Confrontation challenge under Roberts typically resolved by hearsay admissibility.* After the clarifying cases, Confrontation Clause analysis under *Roberts* and admission under the hearsay rules largely merged into a single inquiry for most hearsay statements. The sole issue was whether the statement was admissible under an established hearsay exception. Statements admitted under newly created exceptions or through the residual or catchall exception still had to be independently and individually examined. However, for most hearsay, if the statement was admissible under an established evidentiary rule, the Confrontation Clause provided no additional barrier.

This was the state of the law when *Crawford v. Washington,* which follows, was decided.

CRAWFORD V. WASHINGTON
Supreme Court of the United States, 2004.
541 U.S. 36.

JUSTICE SCALIA delivered the opinion of the Court.

Petitioner Michael Crawford stabbed a man who allegedly tried to rape his wife, Sylvia. At his trial, the State played for the jury Sylvia's tape-recorded statement to the police describing the stabbing, even though he had no opportunity for cross-examination. The Washington Supreme Court upheld petitioner's conviction after determining that Sylvia's statement was reliable. The question presented is whether this procedure complied with the Sixth Amendment's guarantee that, "[i]n all criminal prosecutions, the accused shall enjoy the right * * * to be confronted with the witnesses against him."

I

On August 5, 1999, Kenneth Lee was stabbed at his apartment. Police arrested petitioner later that night. After giving petitioner and his wife *Miranda* warnings, detectives interrogated each of them twice. Petitioner eventually confessed that he and Sylvia had gone in search of Lee because he was upset over an earlier incident in which Lee had tried to rape her. The two had found Lee at his apartment, and a fight ensued in which Lee was stabbed in the torso and petitioner's hand was cut.

Petitioner gave the following account of the fight:

"Q. Okay. Did you ever see anything in [Lee's] hands?

"A. I think so, but I'm not positive.

"Q. Okay, when you think so, what do you mean by that?

"A. I coulda swore I seen him goin' for somethin' before, right before everything happened. He was like reachin', fiddlin' around down here and stuff * * * and I just * * * I don't know, I think, this is just a possibility, but I think, I think that he pulled somethin' out and I grabbed for it and that's how I got cut * * * but I'm not positive. I, I, my mind goes blank when things like this happen. I mean, I just, I remember things wrong, I remember things that just doesn't, don't make sense to me later." (punctuation added).

Sylvia generally corroborated petitioner's story about the events leading up to the fight, but her account of the fight itself was arguably different—particularly with respect to whether Lee had drawn a weapon before petitioner assaulted him:

"Q. Did Kenny do anything to fight back from this assault?

"A. pausing) I know he reached into his pocket * * * or somethin' * * * I don't know what.

"Q. After he was stabbed?

"A. He saw Michael coming up. He lifted his hand * * * his chest open, he might [have] went to go strike his hand out or something and then (inaudible).

"Q. Okay, you, you gotta speak up.

"A. Okay, he lifted his hand over his head maybe to strike Michael's hand down or something and then he put his hands in his * * * put his right hand in his right pocket * * * took a step back * * * Michael proceeded to stab him * * * then his hands were like * * * how do you explain this * * * open arms * * * with his hands open and he fell down * * * and we ran (describing subject holding hands open, palms toward assailant).

"Q. Okay, when he's standing there with his open hands, you're talking about Kenny, correct?

"A. Yeah, after, after the fact, yes.

"Q. Did you see anything in his hands at that point?

"A. (pausing) um um (no)." *Id.*, at 137 (punctuation added).

The State charged petitioner with assault and attempted murder. At trial, he claimed self-defense. Sylvia did not testify because of the state marital privilege, which generally bars a spouse from testifying without the other spouse's consent. See Wash. Rev.Code § 5.60.060(1) (1994). In Washington, this privilege does not extend to a spouse's out-of-court statements admissible under a hearsay exception, see *State v. Burden,* 120 Wash.2d 371, 377, 841 P.2d 758, 761 (1992), so the State sought to introduce Sylvia's tape-recorded statements to the police as evidence that the stabbing was not in self-defense. Noting that Sylvia had admitted she led petitioner to Lee's apartment and thus had facilitated the assault, the State invoked the hearsay exception for statements against penal interest, Wash. Rule Evid. 804(b)(3) (2003).

Petitioner countered that, state law notwithstanding, admitting the evidence would violate his federal constitutional right to be "confronted with the witnesses against him." Amdt. 6. According to our description of that right in *Ohio v. Roberts,* 448 U.S. 56 (1980), it does not bar admission of an unavailable witness's statement against a criminal defendant if the statement bears "adequate 'indicia of reliability.'" *Id.*, at 66. To meet that test, evidence must either fall within a "firmly rooted hearsay exception" or bear "particularized guarantees of trustworthiness." *Ibid.* The trial court here admitted the statement on the latter ground, offering several reasons why it was trustworthy: Sylvia was not shifting blame but rather corroborating her husband's story that he acted in self-defense or "justified reprisal"; she had direct knowledge as an eyewitness; she was describing recent events; and she was being questioned by a "neutral" law enforcement officer. The prosecution played the tape for the jury and relied on it in closing, arguing that it was "damning evidence" that "completely refutes [petitioner's] claim of self-defense." The jury convicted petitioner of assault.

The Washington Court of Appeals reversed. It applied a nine-factor test to determine whether Sylvia's statement bore particularized guarantees of trustworthiness, and noted several reasons why it did not: The statement contradicted one she had previously given; it was made in response to specific questions; and at one point she admitted she had shut her eyes during the stabbing. The court considered and rejected the State's argument that Sylvia's statement was reliable because it coincided with petitioner's to such a degree that the two "interlocked." The court determined that, although the two statements agreed about the events leading up to the stabbing, they differed on the issue crucial to petitioner's self-defense claim: "[Petitioner's] version asserts that Lee may have had something in his hand when he stabbed him; but Sylvia's version has Lee grabbing for something only after he has been stabbed."

The Washington Supreme Court reinstated the conviction, unanimously concluding that, although Sylvia's statement did not fall under a firmly rooted hearsay exception, it bore guarantees of trustworthiness: " '[W]hen a codefendant's confession is virtually identical [to, *i.e.,* interlocks with,] that of a defendant, it may be deemed reliable.' " * * *. The court explained:

> "Although the Court of Appeals concluded that the statements were contradictory, upon closer inspection they appear to overlap * * *.
>
> "[B]oth of the Crawfords' statements indicate that Lee was possibly grabbing for a weapon, but they are equally unsure when this event may have taken place. They are also equally unsure how Michael received the cut on his hand, leading the court to question when, if ever, Lee possessed a weapon. In this respect they overlap.
>
> "[N]either Michael nor Sylvia clearly stated that Lee had a weapon in hand from which Michael was simply defending himself. And it is this omission by both that interlocks the statements and makes Sylvia's statement reliable." 147 Wash.2d, at 438–439, 54 P.3d, at 664 (internal quotation marks omitted).[30]

We granted certiorari to determine whether the State's use of Sylvia's statement violated the Confrontation Clause. 539 U.S. 914 (2003).

II

The Sixth Amendment's Confrontation Clause provides that, "[i]n all criminal prosecutions, the accused shall enjoy the right * * * to be confronted with the witnesses against him." We have held that this bedrock procedural guarantee applies to both federal and state prosecutions. *Pointer v. Texas,* 380 U.S. 400, 406 (1965). As noted above, *Roberts* says that an unavailable witness's out-of-court statement may be admitted so long as it has adequate indicia of reliability—*i.e.,* falls within

---

[30] The court rejected the State's argument that guarantees of trustworthiness were unnecessary since petitioner waived his confrontation rights by invoking the marital privilege. It reasoned that "forcing the defendant to choose between the marital privilege and confronting his spouse presents an untenable Hobson's choice." * * * The State has not challenged this holding here. The State also has not challenged the Court of Appeals' conclusion (not reached by the State Supreme Court) that the confrontation violation, if it occurred, was not harmless. We express no opinion on these matters.

a "firmly rooted hearsay exception" or bears "particularized guarantees of trustworthiness." 448 U.S., at 66. Petitioner argues that this test strays from the original meaning of the Confrontation Clause and urges us to reconsider it.

A

The Constitution's text does not alone resolve this case. One could plausibly read "witnesses against" a defendant to mean those who actually testify at trial, cf. *Woodsides v. State,* 3 Miss. 655, 664–665 (1837), those whose statements are offered at trial, see 3 J. Wigmore, Evidence § 1397, p. 104 (2d ed.1923) (hereinafter Wigmore), or something in-between, see *infra,* at 52–53. We must therefore turn to the historical background of the Clause to understand its meaning.

The right to confront one's accusers is a concept that dates back to Roman times. * * *. The founding generation's immediate source of the concept, however, was the common law. English common law has long differed from continental civil law in regard to the manner in which witnesses give testimony in criminal trials. The common-law tradition is one of live testimony in court subject to adversarial testing, while the civil law condones examination in private by judicial officers. See 3 W. Blackstone, Commentaries on the Laws of England 373–374 (1768).

Nonetheless, England at times adopted elements of the civil-law practice. Justices of the peace or other officials examined suspects and witnesses before trial. These examinations were sometimes read in court in lieu of live testimony, a practice that "occasioned frequent demands by the prisoner to have his 'accusers,' *i.e.* the witnesses against him, brought before him face to face." 1 J. Stephen, History of the Criminal Law of England 326 (1883). In some cases, these demands were refused. See 9 W. Holdsworth, History of English Law 216–217, 228 (3d ed.1944)*; e.g., Raleigh's Case,* 2 How. St. Tr. 1, 15–16, 24 (1603) * * *.

Pretrial examinations became routine under two statutes passed during the reign of Queen Mary in the 16th century, 1 & 2 Phil. & M., c. 13 (1554), and 2 & 3 *id.,* c. 10 (1555). These Marian bail and committal statutes required justices of the peace to examine suspects and witnesses in felony cases and to certify the results to the court. It is doubtful that the original purpose of the examinations was to produce evidence admissible at trial. See J. Langbein, Prosecuting Crime in the Renaissance 21–34 (1974). Whatever the original purpose, however, they came to be used as evidence in some cases, see 2 M. Hale, Pleas of the Crown 284 (1736), resulting in an adoption of continental procedure. See 4 Holdsworth, *supra,* at 528–530.

The most notorious instances of civil-law examination occurred in the great political trials of the 16th and 17th centuries. One such was the 1603 trial of Sir Walter Raleigh for treason. Lord Cobham, Raleigh's alleged accomplice, had implicated him in an examination before the Privy Council and in a letter. At Raleigh's trial, these were read to the jury. Raleigh argued that Cobham had lied to save himself: "Cobham is absolutely in the King's mercy; to excuse me cannot avail him; by accusing me he may hope for favour." 1 D. Jardine, Criminal Trials 435 (1832). Suspecting that Cobham would recant, Raleigh demanded that the judges call him to appear, arguing that "[t]he Proof of the Common Law is by witness and jury: let Cobham be here, let him speak it. Call my accuser before my face * * *." 2 How. St. Tr., at 15–16. The judges refused, *id.*, at 24, and, despite Raleigh's protestations that he was being tried "by the Spanish Inquisition," *id.*, at 15, the jury convicted, and Raleigh was sentenced to death.

One of Raleigh's trial judges later lamented that " 'the justice of England has never been so degraded and injured as by the condemnation of Sir Walter Raleigh.' " 1 Jardine, *supra,* at 520. Through a series of statutory and judicial reforms, English law developed a right of confrontation that limited these abuses. For example, treason statutes required witnesses to confront the accused "face to face" at his arraignment. *E.g.,* 13 Car. 2, c. 1, § 5 (1661); see 1 Hale, *supra,* at 306. Courts, meanwhile, developed relatively strict rules of unavailability, admitting examinations only if the witness was demonstrably unable to testify in person. See *Lord Morley's Case,* 6 How. St. Tr. 769, 770–771 (H.L.1666); 2 Hale, *supra,* at 284; 1 Stephen, *supra,* at 358. Several authorities also stated that a suspect's confession could be admitted only against himself, and not against others he implicated. See 2 W. Hawkins, Pleas of the Crown c. 46, § 3, pp. 603–604 (T. Leach 6th ed. 1787) * * *.

B

Controversial examination practices were also used in the Colonies. Early in the 18th century, for example, the Virginia Council protested against the Governor for having "privately issued several commissions to examine witnesses against particular men *ex parte,*" complaining that "the person accused is not admitted to be confronted with, or defend himself against his defamers." A Memorial Concerning the Maladministrations of His Excellency Francis Nicholson, reprinted in 9 English Historical Documents 253, 257 (D. Douglas ed.1955). A decade before the Revolution, England gave jurisdiction over Stamp Act offenses to the admiralty courts, which followed civil-law rather than common-law procedures and thus routinely took testimony by deposition or private judicial examination. See 5 Geo. 3, c. 12, § 57 (1765); Pollitt, The Right of Confrontation: Its History and Modern Dress, 8 J. Pub.L. 381, 396–397 (1959). Colonial representatives protested that the Act subverted their rights "by extending the jurisdiction of the courts of admiralty beyond its ancient limits." Resolutions of the Stamp Act Congress § 8th (Oct. 19, 1765), reprinted in Sources of Our Liberties 270, 271 (R. Perry & J.

Cooper eds.1959). John Adams, defending a merchant in a high-profile admiralty case, argued: "Examinations of witnesses upon Interrogatories, are only by the Civil Law. Interrogatories are unknown at common Law, and Englishmen and common Lawyers have an aversion to them if not an Abhorrence of them." Draft of Argument in *Sewall v. Hancock* (1768–1769), in 2 Legal Papers of John Adams 194, 207 (K. Wroth & H. Zobel eds.1965).

Many declarations of rights adopted around the time of the Revolution guaranteed a right of confrontation [1776—Virginia, Pennsylvania, Delaware, Maryland, North Carolina; 1777 Vermont; 1780—Massachusetts; 1783—New Hampshire]. The proposed Federal Constitution, however, did not. At the Massachusetts ratifying convention, Abraham Holmes objected to this omission precisely on the ground that it would lead to civil-law practices: "The mode of trial is altogether indetermined; * * * whether [the defendant] is to be allowed to confront the witnesses, and have the advantage of cross-examination, we are not yet told * * *. [W]e shall find Congress possessed of powers enabling them to institute judicatories little less inauspicious than a certain tribunal in Spain, * * * the *Inquisition*." 2 Debates on the Federal Constitution 110–111 (J. Elliot 2d ed. 1863). Similarly, a prominent Antifederalist writing under the pseudonym Federal Farmer criticized the use of "written evidence" while objecting to the omission of a vicinage right: "Nothing can be more essential than the cross examining [of] witnesses, and generally before the triers of the facts in question * * *. [W]ritten evidence * * * [is] almost useless; it must be frequently taken ex parte, and but very seldom leads to the proper discovery of truth." R. Lee, Letter IV by the Federal Farmer (Oct. 15, 1787), reprinted in 1 Schwartz, *supra,* at 469, 473. The First Congress responded by including the Confrontation Clause in the proposal that became the Sixth Amendment.

Early state decisions shed light upon the original understanding of the common-law right. *State v. Webb,* 2 N.C. 103 (1794) *(per curiam),* decided a mere three years after the adoption of the Sixth Amendment, held that depositions could be read against an accused only if they were taken in his presence. Rejecting a broader reading of the English authorities, the court held: "[I]t is a rule of the common law, founded on natural justice, that no man shall be prejudiced by evidence which he had not the liberty to cross examine." *Id.,* at 104.

Similarly, in *State v. Campbell,* 1 Rich. 124, 1844 WL 2558 (S.C.1844), South Carolina's highest law court excluded a deposition taken by a coroner in the absence of the accused. * * * Many other decisions are to the same effect. Some early cases went so far as to hold that prior testimony was inadmissible in criminal cases *even if* the accused had a previous opportunity to cross-examine. See *Finn v. Commonwealth,* 26 Va. 701, 708 (1827) * * *. Most courts rejected that view, but only after reaffirming that admissibility depended on a prior opportunity for cross-examination. See *United States v. Macomb*, 26 F.Cas. 1132, 1133 (No. 15,702) (CC Ill. 1851); *State v. Houser,* 26 Mo. 431, 435–436 (1858) * * *.

III

This history supports two inferences about the meaning of the Sixth Amendment.

A

First, the principal evil at which the Confrontation Clause was directed was the civil-law mode of criminal procedure, and particularly its use of *ex parte* examinations as evidence against the accused. It was these practices that the Crown deployed in notorious treason cases like Raleigh's; that the Marian statutes invited; that English law's assertion of a right to confrontation was meant to prohibit; and that the founding-era rhetoric decried. The Sixth Amendment must be interpreted with this focus in mind.

Accordingly, we once again reject the view that the Confrontation Clause applies of its own force only to in-court testimony, and that its application to out-of-court statements introduced at trial depends upon "the law of Evidence for the time being." 3 Wigmore § 1397, at 101; accord, *Dutton v. Evans,* 400 U.S. 74, 94 (1970) (Harlan, J., concurring in result). Leaving the regulation of out-of-court statements to the law of evidence would render the Confrontation Clause powerless to prevent even the most flagrant inquisitorial practices. Raleigh was, after all, perfectly free to confront those who read Cobham's confession in court.

This focus also suggests that not all hearsay implicates the Sixth Amendment's core concerns. An off-hand, overheard remark might be unreliable evidence and thus a good candidate for exclusion under hearsay rules, but it bears little resemblance to the civil-law abuses the Confrontation Clause targeted. On the other hand, *ex parte* examinations might sometimes be admissible under modern hearsay rules, but the Framers certainly would not have condoned them.

The text of the Confrontation Clause reflects this focus. It applies to "witnesses" against the accused—in other words, those who "bear testimony." 1 N. Webster, An American Dictionary of the English Language (1828). "Testimony," in turn, is typically "[a] solemn declaration or affirmation made for the purpose of establishing or proving some fact." *Ibid.* An accuser who makes a formal statement to government officers bears testimony in a sense that a person who makes a casual remark to an acquaintance does not. The constitutional text, like the history underlying the common-law right of confrontation, thus reflects an especially acute concern with a specific type of out-of-court statement.

Various formulations of this core class of "testimonial" statements exist: "*ex parte* in-court testimony or its functional equivalent—that is, material such as affidavits, custodial examinations, prior testimony that the defendant was unable to cross-examine, or similar pretrial statements that declarants would reasonably expect to be used prosecutorially," Brief for Petitioner 23; "extrajudicial statements * * * contained in formalized testimonial materials, such as affidavits, depositions, prior testimony, or confessions," *White v. Illinois,* 502 U.S. 346, 365 (1992) (THOMAS, J., joined by SCALIA, J., concurring in part and concurring in judgment); "statements that were made under circumstances which would lead an objective witness reasonably to believe that the statement would be available for use at a later trial," Brief for National Association of Criminal Defense Lawyers et al. as *Amici Curiae* 3. These formulations all share a common nucleus and then define the Clause's coverage at various levels of abstraction around it. Regardless of the precise articulation, some statements qualify under any definition—for example, *ex parte* testimony at a preliminary hearing.

[Statements taken by police officers in the course of interrogations are also testimonial under even a narrow standard] Police interrogations bear a striking resemblance to examinations by justices of the peace in England. The statements are not *sworn testimon*y, but the absence of oath was not dispositive. Cobham's examination was unsworn, see 1 Jardine, Criminal Trials, at 430, yet Raleigh's trial has long been thought a paradigmatic confrontation violation, see, *e.g., Campbell,* 1 Rich., at 130. Under the Marian statutes, witnesses were typically put on oath, but suspects were not. See 2 Hale, Pleas of the Crown, at 52. Yet Hawkins and others went out of their way to caution that such unsworn confessions were not admissible against anyone but the confessor. See *supra,* at 45.

That interrogators are police officers rather than magistrates does not change the picture either. Justices of the peace conducting examinations under the Marian statutes were not magistrates as we understand that office today, but had an essentially investigative and prosecutorial function. See 1 Stephen, Criminal Law of England, at 221; Langbein, Prosecuting Crime in the Renaissance, at 34–45. England did not have a professional police force until the 19th century, see 1 Stephen, *supra,* at 194–200, so it is not surprising that other government officers performed the investigative functions now associated primarily with the police. The involvement of government officers in the production of testimonial evidence presents the same risk, whether the officers are police or justices of the peace.

rule

In sum, even if the Sixth Amendment is not solely concerned with testimonial hearsay, that is its primary object, and interrogations by law enforcement officers fall squarely within that class.[31]

5. ☆

B   B. - 2ⁿᵈ in first to he vice

The historical record also supports a second proposition: that the Framers would not have allowed admission of testimonial statements of a witness who did not appear at trial unless he was unavailable to testify, and the defendant had had a prior opportunity for cross-examination. The text of the Sixth Amendment does not suggest any open-ended exceptions from the confrontation requirement to be developed by the courts. Rather, the "right * * * to be confronted with the witnesses against him," Amdt. 6, is most naturally read as a reference to the right of confrontation at common law, admitting only those exceptions established at the time of the founding. See *Mattox v. United States,* 156 U.S. 237, 243 (1895); cf. *Houser,* 26 Mo., at 433–435. As the English authorities above reveal, the common law in 1791 conditioned admissibility of an absent witness's examination on unavailability and a prior opportunity to cross-examine. The Sixth Amendment therefore incorporates those limitations. The numerous early state decisions applying the same test confirm that these principles were received as part of the common law in this country.

1. ☆

a.

b. - exception permissible CL

We do not read the historical sources to say that a prior opportunity to cross-examine was merely a sufficient, rather than a necessary, condition for admissibility of testimonial statements. They suggest that this requirement was dispositive, and not merely one of several ways to establish reliability. This is not to deny, as THE CHIEF JUSTICE notes, that "[t]here were always exceptions to the general rule of exclusion" of hearsay evidence. * * * Several had become well established by 1791. See 3 Wigmore § 1397, at 101; Brief for United States as *Amicus Curiae* 13, n.5. But there is scant evidence that exceptions were invoked to admit *testimonial* statements against the accused in a *criminal* case.[32] Most of the hearsay exceptions covered statements that by their nature were not

2.

a.

---

[31] We use the term "interrogation" in its colloquial, rather than any technical legal, sense. Cf. Rhode Island v. Innis, 446 U.S. 291, 300–01 (1980). Just as various definitions of "testimonial" exist, one can imagine various definitions of "interrogation," and we need not select among them in this case. Sylvia's recorded statement, knowingly given in response to structured police questioning, qualifies under any conceivable definition.

[32] The one deviation we have found involves dying declarations. The existence of that exception as a general rule of criminal hearsay law cannot be disputed. See, e.g., Mattox v. United States, 156 U.S. 237, 243–44 (1895); King v. Reason, 16 How. St. Tr. 1, 24–38 (K.B.1722); 1 D. Jardine, Criminal Trials 435 (1832); Cooley, Constitutional Limitations, at *318; 1 G. Gilbert, Evidence 211 (C. Lofft ed. 1791); see also F. Heller, The Sixth Amendment 105 (1951) (asserting that this was the only recognized criminal hearsay exception at common law). Although many dying declarations may not be testimonial, there is authority for admitting even those that clearly are. See Woodcock, supra, at 501–504, 168 Eng. Rep., at 353–354; Reason, supra, at 24–38; Peake, Evidence, at 64; cf. Radbourne, supra, at 460–462, 168 Eng. Rep., at 332–333. We need not decide in this case whether the Sixth Amendment incorporates an exception for testimonial dying declarations. If this exception must be accepted on historical grounds, it is sui generis.

testimonial—for example, business records or statements in furtherance of a conspiracy. We do not infer from these that the Framers thought exceptions would apply even to prior testimony. Cf. *Lilly v. Virginia,* 527 U.S. 116, 134 (1999) (plurality opinion) ("[A]ccomplices' confessions that inculpate a criminal defendant are not within a firmly rooted exception to the hearsay rule").[33]

IV

Our case law has been largely consistent with these two principles. Our leading early decision, for example, involved a deceased witness's prior trial testimony. *Mattox v. United States,* 156 U.S. 237 (1895). In allowing the statement to be admitted, we relied on the fact that the defendant had had, at the first trial, an adequate opportunity to confront the witness: "The substance of the constitutional protection is preserved to the prisoner in the advantage he has once had of seeing the witness face to face, and of subjecting him to the ordeal of a cross-examination. This, the law says, he shall under no circumstances be deprived of * * *." *Id.,* at 244.

Our later cases conform to *Mattox's* holding that prior trial or preliminary hearing testimony is admissible only if the defendant had an adequate opportunity to cross-examine. See *Mancusi v. Stubbs,* 408 U.S. 204, 213–16 (1972); *California v. Green,* 399 U.S. 149, 165–68 (1970); *Pointer v. Texas,* 380 U.S., at 406–08; cf. *Kirby v. United States,* 174 U.S. 47, 55–61 (1899). Even where the defendant had such an opportunity, we excluded the testimony where the government had not established unavailability of the witness. See *Barber v. Page,* 390 U.S. 719, 722–25 (1968) * * *.

Even our recent cases, in their outcomes, hew closely to the traditional line. *Ohio v. Roberts,* 448 U.S., at 67–70, admitted testimony from a preliminary hearing at which the defendant had examined the witness. *Lilly v. Virginia, supra,* excluded testimonial statements that the defendant had had no opportunity to test by cross-examination. And *Bourjaily v. United States,* 483 U.S. 171, 181–84 (1987), admitted statements made unwittingly to an FBI informant after applying a more general test that did *not* make prior cross-examination an indispensable requirement.[34] * * *

---

[33] We cannot agree with THE CHIEF JUSTICE that the fact "[t]hat a statement might be testimonial does nothing to undermine the wisdom of one of these [hearsay] exceptions." Post, at 74. Involvement of government officers in the production of testimony with an eye toward trial presents unique potential for prosecutorial abuse—a fact borne out time and again throughout a history with which the Framers were keenly familiar. This consideration does not evaporate when testimony happens to fall within some broad, modern hearsay exception, even if that exception might be justifiable in other circumstances.

[34] One case arguably in tension with the rule requiring a prior opportunity for cross-examination when the proffered statement is testimonial is White v. Illinois, 502 U.S. 346 (1992), which involved, inter alia, statements of a child victim to an investigating police officer admitted

Our cases have thus remained faithful to the Framers' understanding: Testimonial statements of witnesses absent from trial have been admitted only where the declarant is unavailable, and only where the defendant has had a prior opportunity to cross-examine.[35]

V

Although the results of our decisions have generally been faithful to the original meaning of the Confrontation Clause, the same cannot be said of our rationales. *Roberts* conditions the admissibility of all hearsay evidence on whether it falls under a "firmly rooted hearsay exception" or bears "particularized guarantees of trustworthiness." 448 U.S., at 66. This test departs from the historical principles identified above in two respects. First, it is too broad: It applies the same mode of analysis whether or not the hearsay consists of *ex parte* testimony. This often results in close constitutional scrutiny in cases that are far removed from the core concerns of the Clause. At the same time, however, the test is too narrow: It admits statements that *do* consist of *ex parte* testimony upon a mere finding of reliability. This malleable standard often fails to protect against paradigmatic confrontation violations.

Members of this Court and academics have suggested that we revise our doctrine to reflect more accurately the original understanding of the Clause. See, *e.g., Lilly,* 527 U.S., at 140–43 (BREYER, J., concurring); *White,* 502 U.S., at 366 (THOMAS, J., joined by SCALIA, J., concurring in part and concurring in judgment); A. Amar, The Constitution and Criminal Procedure 125–131 (1997); Friedman, Confrontation: The Search for Basic Principles, 86 Geo. L.J. 1011 (1998). They offer two proposals: First, that we apply the Confrontation Clause only to testimonial statements, leaving the remainder to regulation by hearsay law—thus eliminating the overbreadth referred to above. Second, that we

---

as spontaneous declarations. Id., at 349–351. It is questionable whether testimonial statements would ever have been admissible on that ground in 1791; to the extent the hearsay exception for spontaneous declarations existed at all, it required that the statements be made "immediat[ely] upon the hurt received, and before [the declarant] had time to devise or contrive any thing for her own advantage." Thompson v. Trevanion, Skin. 402, 90 Eng. Rep. 179 (K.B.1694). In any case, the only question presented in White was whether the Confrontation Clause imposed an unavailability requirement on the types of hearsay at issue. See 502 U.S., at 348–49. The holding did not address the question whether certain of the statements, because they were testimonial, had to be excluded even if the witness was unavailable. We "[took] as a given * * * that the testimony properly falls within the relevant hearsay exceptions." Id., at 351, n.4.

[35] THE CHIEF JUSTICE complains that our prior decisions have "never drawn a distinction" like the one we now draw * * *. That the * * * cases did not extrapolate a more general class of evidence to which that criterion applied does not prevent us from doing so now. * * * If nothing else, the test we announce is an empirically accurate explanation of the results our cases have reached.

Finally, we reiterate that, when the declarant appears for cross-examination at trial, the Confrontation Clause places no constraints at all on the use of his prior testimonial statements. See California v. Green, 399 U.S. 149, 162 (1970). * * * The Clause does not bar admission of a statement so long as the declarant is present at trial to defend or explain it. (The Clause also does not bar the use of testimonial statements for purposes other than establishing the truth of the matter asserted. See Tennessee v. Street, 471 U.S. 409, 414 (1985).)

impose an absolute bar to statements that are testimonial, absent a prior opportunity to cross-examine—thus eliminating the excessive narrowness referred to above.

In *White,* we considered the first proposal and rejected it. 502 U.S., at 352–53. Although our analysis in this case casts doubt on that holding, we need not definitively resolve whether it survives our decision today, because Sylvia Crawford's statement is testimonial under any definition. This case does, however, squarely implicate the second proposal.

A

Where testimonial statements are involved, we do not think the Framers meant to leave the Sixth Amendment's protection to the vagaries of the rules of evidence, much less to amorphous notions of "reliability." Certainly none of the authorities discussed above acknowledges any general reliability exception to the common-law rule. Admitting statements deemed reliable by a judge is fundamentally at odds with the right of confrontation. To be sure, the Clause's ultimate goal is to ensure reliability of evidence, but it is a procedural rather than a substantive guarantee. It commands, not that evidence be reliable, but that reliability be assessed in a particular manner: by testing in the crucible of cross-examination. The Clause thus reflects a judgment, not only about the desirability of reliable evidence (a point on which there could be little dissent), but about how reliability can best be determined. Cf. 3 Blackstone, Commentaries, at 373 ("This open examination of witnesses * * * is much more conducive to the clearing up of truth"); M. Hale, History and Analysis of the Common Law of England 258 (1713) (adversarial testing "beats and bolts out the Truth much better").

The *Roberts* test allows a jury to hear evidence, untested by the adversary process, based on a mere judicial determination of reliability. It thus replaces the constitutionally prescribed method of assessing reliability with a wholly foreign one. In this respect, it is very different from exceptions to the Confrontation Clause that make no claim to be a surrogate means of assessing reliability. For example, the rule of forfeiture by wrongdoing (which we accept) extinguishes confrontation claims on essentially equitable grounds; it does not purport to be an alternative means of determining reliability. See *Reynolds v. United States,* 98 U.S. 145, 158–59 (1879).

The Raleigh trial itself involved the very sorts of reliability determinations that *Roberts* authorizes. In the face of Raleigh's repeated demands for confrontation, the prosecution responded with many of the arguments a court applying *Roberts* might invoke today: that Cobham's statements were self-inculpatory, 2 How. St. Tr., at 19, that they were not made in the heat of passion, *id.,* at 14, and that they were not "extracted from [him] upon any hopes or promise of Pardon," *id.,* at 29. It is not plausible that the Framers' only objection to the trial was that Raleigh's judges did not properly weigh these factors before sentencing him to death. Rather, the problem was that the judges refused to allow Raleigh to confront Cobham in court, where he could cross-examine him and try to expose his accusation as a lie.

Dispensing with confrontation because testimony is obviously reliable is akin to dispensing with jury trial because a defendant is obviously guilty. This is not what the Sixth Amendment prescribes.

B

The legacy of *Roberts* in other courts vindicates the Framers' wisdom in rejecting a general reliability exception. The framework is so unpredictable that it fails to provide meaningful protection from even core confrontation violations.

Reliability is an amorphous, if not entirely subjective, concept. There are countless factors bearing on whether a statement is reliable; the nine-factor balancing test applied by the Court of Appeals below is representative. * * *

The unpardonable vice of the *Roberts* test, however, is not its unpredictability, but its demonstrated capacity to admit core testimonial statements that the Confrontation Clause plainly meant to exclude. Despite the plurality's speculation in *Lilly*, 527 U.S., at 137, that it was "highly unlikely" that accomplice confessions implicating the accused could survive *Roberts*, courts continue routinely to admit them. See *Photogrammetric Data Servs., supra,* at 245–246; *Farrell, supra,* at 406–408; *Stevens, supra,* at 314–318 * * *. One recent study found that, after *Lilly*, appellate courts admitted accomplice statements to the authorities in 25 out of 70 cases—more than one-third of the time. Kirst, Appellate Court Answers to the Confrontation Questions in *Lilly v. Virginia*, 53 Syracuse L.Rev. 87, 105 (2003). Courts have invoked *Roberts* to admit other sorts of plainly testimonial statements despite the absence of any opportunity to cross-examine. See *United States v. Aguilar*, 295 F.3d 1018, 1021–1023 (C.A.9 2002) (plea allocution showing existence of a conspiracy) * * *.

To add insult to injury, some of the courts that admit untested testimonial statements find reliability in the very factors that *make* the statements testimonial. As noted earlier, one court relied on the fact that the witness's statement was made to police while in custody on pending charges—the theory being that this made the statement more clearly against penal interest and thus more reliable. *Nowlin, supra,* at 335–338, 579 S.E.2d, at 371–372. Other courts routinely rely on the fact that a prior statement is given under oath in judicial proceedings. *E.g., Gallego, supra,* at 168 (plea allocution); *Papajohn, supra,* at 1120 (grand jury testimony). That inculpating statements are given in a testimonial setting is not an antidote to the confrontation problem, but rather the trigger that makes the Clause's demands most urgent. It is not enough to point out that most of the usual safeguards of the adversary process attend the statement, when the single safeguard missing is the one the Confrontation Clause demands.

C

We readily concede that we could resolve this case by simply reweighing the "reliability factors" under *Roberts* and finding that Sylvia Crawford's statement falls short. But we view this as one of those rare cases in which the result below is so improbable that it reveals a fundamental failure on our part to interpret the Constitution in a way that secures its intended constraint on judicial discretion. Moreover, to reverse the Washington Supreme Court's decision after conducting our own reliability analysis would perpetuate, not avoid, what the Sixth Amendment condemns. The Constitution prescribes a procedure for determining the reliability of testimony in criminal trials, and we, no less than the state courts, lack authority to replace it with one of our own devising.

We have no doubt that the courts below were acting in utmost good faith when they found reliability. The Framers, however, would not have been content to indulge this assumption. They knew that judges, like other government officers, could not always be trusted to safeguard the rights of the people; the likes of the dread Lord Jeffreys were not yet too distant a memory. They were loath to leave too much discretion in judicial hands. Cf. U.S. Const., Amdt. 6 (criminal jury trial); Amdt. 7 (civil jury trial); *Ring v. Arizona*, 536 U.S. 584, 611–12 (2002) (SCALIA, J., concurring). By replacing categorical constitutional guarantees with open-ended balancing tests, we do violence to their design. Vague standards are manipulable, and, while that might be a small concern in run-of-the-mill assault prosecutions like this one, the Framers had an eye toward politically charged cases like Raleigh's—great state trials where the impartiality of even those at the highest levels of the judiciary might not be so clear. It is difficult to imagine *Roberts'* providing any meaningful protection in those circumstances. * * *

Where nontestimonial hearsay is at issue, it is wholly consistent with the Framers' design to afford the States flexibility in their development of hearsay law—as does *Roberts,* and as would an approach that exempted such statements from Confrontation Clause scrutiny altogether. Where testimonial evidence is at issue, however, the Sixth Amendment demands what the common law required: unavailability and a prior opportunity for cross-examination. We leave for another day any effort to spell out a comprehensive definition of "testimonial."[36] Whatever else the term covers, it applies at a minimum to prior testimony at a preliminary hearing, before a grand jury, or at a former trial; and to police interrogations. These are the modern practices with closest kinship to the abuses at which the Confrontation Clause was directed.

In this case, the State admitted Sylvia's testimonial statement against petitioner, despite the fact that he had no opportunity to cross-examine her. That alone is sufficient to make out a violation of the Sixth Amendment. *Roberts* notwithstanding, we decline to mine the record in search of indicia of reliability. Where testimonial statements are at issue, the only indicium of reliability sufficient to satisfy constitutional demands is the one the Constitution actually prescribes: confrontation.

The judgment of the Washington Supreme Court is reversed, and the case is remanded for further proceedings not inconsistent with this opinion.

CHIEF JUSTICE REHNQUIST, with whom JUSTICE O'CONNOR joins, concurring in the judgment.

I dissent from the Court's decision to overrule *Ohio v. Roberts,* 448 U.S. 56 (1980). I believe that the Court's adoption of a new interpretation of the Confrontation Clause is not backed by sufficiently persuasive reasoning to overrule long-established precedent. Its decision casts a mantle of uncertainty over future criminal trials in both federal and state courts, and is by no means necessary to decide the present case.

The Court's distinction between testimonial and nontestimonial statements, contrary to its claim, is no better rooted in history than our current doctrine. Under the common law, although the courts were far from consistent, out-of-court statements made by someone other than the accused and not taken under oath, unlike *ex parte* depositions or affidavits, were generally not considered substantive evidence upon which a conviction could be based.[37] See, *e.g., King v. Brasier,* 1 Leach 199, 200,

---

[36] We acknowledge THE CHIEF JUSTICE's objection * * * that our refusal to articulate a comprehensive definition in this case will cause interim uncertainty. But it can hardly be any worse than the status quo. * * * The difference is that the Roberts test is inherently, and therefore permanently, unpredictable.

[37] Modern scholars have concluded that at the time of the founding the law had yet to fully develop the exclusionary component of the hearsay rule and its attendant exceptions, and thus hearsay was still often heard by the jury. See Gallanis, The Rise of Modern Evidence Law, 84 Iowa L.Rev. 499, 534–535 (1999); Mosteller, Remaking Confrontation Clause and Hearsay Doctrine Under the Challenge of Child Sexual Abuse Prosecutions, 1993 U. Ill. L.Rev. 691, 738–746. In many cases, hearsay alone was generally not considered sufficient to support a conviction; rather, it was used to corroborate sworn witness testimony. See 5 J. Wigmore, Evidence, § 1364, pp. 17, 19–20, 19, n.33 (J. Chadbourn rev.1974) * * *; see also J. Langbein, Origins of Adversary Criminal Trial 238–239 (2003). Even when unsworn hearsay was proffered as substantive evidence, however, because of the predominance of the oath in society, juries were largely skeptical of it. See Landsman, Rise of the Contentious Spirit: Adversary Procedure in Eighteenth Century England, 75 Cornell L.Rev. 497, 506 (1990) (describing late 17th-century sentiments); Langbein, Criminal Trial before the Lawyers, 45 U. Chi. L.Rev. 263, 291–293

168 Eng. Rep. 202 (K.B.1779) * * *. Testimonial statements such as accusatory statements to police officers likely would have been disapproved of in the 18th century, not necessarily because they resembled *ex parte* affidavits or depositions as the Court reasons, but more likely than not because they were not made under oath. See *King v. Woodcock,* 1 Leach 500, 503, 168 Eng. Rep. 352, 353 (1789) * * *. Without an oath, one usually did not get to the second step of whether confrontation was required. * * *

[Doctrinal change is] * * * not in the least necessary to reverse the judgment of the Supreme Court of Washington in this case. The result the Court reaches follows inexorably from *Roberts* and its progeny without any need for overruling that line of cases. * * * A citation to *Idaho v. Wright,* [497 U.S. 805 (1990)], would suffice. * * *

DAVIS V. WASHINGTON & HAMMON V. INDIANA
Supreme Court of the United States, 2006.
547 U.S. 813.

JUSTICE SCALIA delivered the opinion of the Court.

These cases require us to determine when statements made to law enforcement personnel during a 911 call or at a crime scene are "testimonial" and thus subject to the requirements of the Sixth Amendment's Confrontation Clause.

I

A

The relevant statements in *Davis v. Washington,* No. 05–5224, were made to a 911 emergency operator on February 1, 2001. When the operator answered the initial call, the connection terminated before anyone spoke. She reversed the call, and Michelle McCottry answered. In the ensuing conversation, the operator ascertained that McCottry was involved in a domestic disturbance with her former boyfriend Adrian Davis, the petitioner in this case:

"911 Operator: Hello.

"Complainant: Hello.

"911 Operator: What's going on?

"Complainant: He's here jumpin' on me again.

"911 Operator: Okay. Listen to me carefully. Are you in a house or an apartment?

"Complainant: I'm in a house.

(1978). In the 18th century, unsworn hearsay was simply held to be of much lesser value than were sworn affidavits or depositions.

"911 Operator: Are there any weapons?

"Complainant: No. He's usin' his fists.

"911 Operator: Okay. Has he been drinking?

"Complainant: No.

"911 Operator: Okay, sweetie. I've got help started. Stay on the line with me, okay?

"Complainant: I'm on the line.

"911 Operator: Listen to me carefully. Do you know his last name?

"Complainant: It's Davis.

"911 Operator: Davis? Okay, what's his first name?

"Complainant: Adran[.]

"911 Operator: What is it?

"Complainant: Adrian.

"911 Operator: Adrian?

"Complainant: Yeah.

"911 Operator: Okay. What's his middle initial?

"Complainant: Martell. He's runnin' now." * * *

As the conversation continued, the operator learned that Davis had "just r[un] out the door" after hitting McCottry, and that he was leaving in a car with someone else. *Id.,* at 9–10. McCottry started talking, but the operator cut her off, saying, "Stop talking and answer my questions." *Id.,* at 10. She then gathered more information about Davis (including his birthday), and learned that Davis had told McCottry that his purpose in coming to the house was "to get his stuff," since McCottry was moving. *Id.,* at 11–12. McCottry described the context of the assault, *id.,* at 12, after which the operator told her that the police were on their way. "They're gonna check the area for him first," the operator said, "and then they're gonna come talk to you." *Id.,* at 12–13.

The police arrived within four minutes of the 911 call and observed McCottry's shaken state, the "fresh injuries on her forearm and her face," and her "frantic efforts to gather her belongings and her children so that they could leave the residence." * * *

The State charged Davis with felony violation of a domestic no-contact order. "The State's only witnesses were the two police officers who responded to the 911 call. Both officers testified that McCottry exhibited injuries that appeared to be recent, but neither officer could testify as to the cause of the injuries." *Ibid.* McCottry presumably could have testified as to whether Davis was her assailant, but she did not appear. Over

Davis's objection, based on the Confrontation Clause of the Sixth Amendment, the trial court admitted the recording of her exchange with the 911 operator, and the jury convicted him. * * * The Supreme Court of Washington * * * affirmed, concluding that the portion of the 911 conversation in which McCottry identified Davis was not testimonial, and that if other portions of the conversation were testimonial, admitting them was harmless beyond a reasonable doubt. * * *

B

In *Hammon v. Indiana*, No. 05–5705, police responded late on the night of February 26, 2003, to a "reported domestic disturbance" at the home of Hershel and Amy Hammon. 829 N.E.2d 444, 446 (Ind.2005). They found Amy alone on the front porch, appearing " 'somewhat frightened,' " but she told them that " 'nothing was the matter,' " *id.*, at 446, 447. She gave them permission to enter the house, where an officer saw "a gas heating unit in the corner of the living room" that had "flames coming out of the * * * partial glass front. There were pieces of glass on the ground in front of it and there was flame emitting from the front of the heating unit." * * *

Hershel, meanwhile, was in the kitchen. He told the police "that he and his wife had 'been in an argument' but 'everything was fine now' and the argument 'never became physical.' " 829 N.E.2d, at 447. By this point Amy had come back inside. One of the officers remained with Hershel; the other went to the living room to talk with Amy, and "again asked [her] what had occurred." Ibid. * * * Hershel made several attempts to participate in Amy's conversation with the police, see *id.*, at 32, but was rebuffed. The officer later testified that Hershel "became angry when I insisted that [he] stay separated from Mrs. Hammon so that we can investigate what had happened." *Id.*, at 34. After hearing Amy's account, the officer "had her fill out and sign a battery affidavit." Id., at 18. Amy handwrote the following: "Broke our Furnace & shoved me down on the floor into the broken glass. Hit me in the chest and threw me down. Broke our lamps & phone. Tore up my van where I couldn't leave the house. Attacked my daughter." *Id.*, at 2.

The State charged Hershel with domestic battery and with violating his probation. Amy was subpoenaed, but she did not appear at his subsequent bench trial. The State called the officer who had questioned Amy, and asked him to recount what Amy told him and to authenticate the affidavit. Hershel's counsel repeatedly objected to the admission of this evidence. * * *. At one point, after hearing the prosecutor defend the affidavit because it was made "under oath," defense counsel said, "That doesn't give us the opportunity to cross examine [the] person who allegedly drafted it. Makes me mad." *Id.*, at 19. Nonetheless, the trial court admitted the affidavit as a "present sense impression," *id.*, at 20, and Amy's statements as "excited utterances" that "are expressly permitted in these kinds of cases even if the declarant is not available to .testify." *Id.,* at 40. The officer thus testified that Amy⌉ ⎸ .

> "informed me that she and Hershel had been in an argument. That he became irrate [sic] over the fact of their daughter going to a boyfriend's house. The argument became * * * physical after being verbal and she informed me that Mr. Hammon, during the verbal part of the argument was breaking things in the living room and I believe she stated he broke the phone, broke the lamp, broke the front of the heater. When it became physical he threw her down into the glass of the heater. * * *

> "She informed me Mr. Hammon had pushed her onto the ground, had shoved her head into the broken glass of the heater and that he had punched her in the chest twice I believe." *Id.,* at 17–18.

The trial judge found Hershel guilty on both charges, *id.,* at 40, and the * * * Indiana Supreme Court * * * affirmed, concluding that Amy's ⌉ 2 . statement was admissible for state-law purposes as an excited utterance;⌋ 829 N.E.2d, at 449; that "a 'testimonial' statement is one given or taken in significant part for purposes of preserving it for potential future use in legal proceedings," where "the motivations of the questioner and 3 . declarant are the central concerns," *id.,* at 456, 457; and that Amy's oral statement was not "testimonial" under these standards⌋ *id.,* at 458. It also⌉ concluded that, although the affidavit was testimonial and thus wrongly⎸ admitted, it was harmless beyond a reasonable doubt * * *. 4 .

II

The Confrontation Clause of the Sixth Amendment provides: "In all criminal prosecutions, the accused shall enjoy the right * * * to be confronted with the witnesses against him." In *Crawford v. Washington,* 541 U.S. 36, 53–54 (2004), we held that this provision bars "admission of testimonial statements of a witness who did not appear at trial unless he was unavailable to testify, and the defendant had had a prior opportunity for cross-examination." A critical portion of this holding, and the portion central to resolution of the two cases now before us, is the phrase "testimonial statements." Only statements of this sort cause the declarant ⎸ . to be a "witness" within the meaning of the Confrontation Clause. See *id.,* at 51. It is the testimonial character of the statement that separates it from other hearsay that, while subject to traditional limitations upon hearsay evidence, is not subject to the Confrontation Clause.

Our opinion in *Crawford* set forth "[v]arious formulations" of the core class of " 'testimonial' " statements, *ibid.,* but found it unnecessary to endorse any of them, because "some statements qualify under any definition," *id.,* at 52. Among those, we said, were "[s]tatements taken by police officers in the course of interrogations," *ibid.;* see also *id.,* at 53.

The questioning that generated the deponent's statement in *Crawford*—which was made and recorded while she was in police custody, after having been given *Miranda* warnings as a possible suspect herself—"qualifies under any conceivable definition" of an " 'interrogation,' " 541 U.S., at 53, n.4. We therefore did not define that term, except to say that "[w]e use [it] * * * in its colloquial, rather than any technical legal, sense," and that "one can imagine various definitions * * *, and we need not select among them in this case." *Ibid.* The character of the statements in the present cases is not as clear, and these cases require us to determine more precisely which police interrogations produce testimony.

Without attempting to produce an exhaustive classification of all conceivable statements—or even all conceivable statements in response to police interrogation—as either testimonial or nontestimonial, it suffices to decide the present cases to hold as follows: Statements are nontestimonial when made in the course of police interrogation under circumstances objectively indicating that the primary purpose of the interrogation is to enable police assistance to meet an ongoing emergency. They are testimonial when the circumstances objectively indicate that there is no such ongoing emergency, and that the primary purpose of the interrogation is to establish or prove past events potentially relevant to later criminal prosecution.[38]

III

A

In *Crawford,* it sufficed for resolution of the case before us to determine that "even if the Sixth Amendment is not solely concerned with testimonial hearsay, that is its primary object, and interrogations by law enforcement officers fall squarely within that class." *Id.,* at 53. Moreover, as we have just described, the facts of that case spared us the need to define what we meant by "interrogations." The *Davis* case today does not permit us this luxury of indecision. The inquiries of a police operator in the course of a 911 call[39] are an interrogation in one sense, but not in a

---

[38] Our holding refers to interrogations because, as explained below, the statements in the cases presently before us are the products of interrogations—which in some circumstances tend to generate testimonial responses. This is not to imply, however, that statements made in the absence of any interrogation are necessarily nontestimonial. The Framers were no more willing to exempt from cross-examination volunteered testimony or answers to open-ended questions than they were to exempt answers to detailed interrogation. (Part of the evidence against Sir Walter Raleigh was a letter from Lord Cobham that was plainly not the result of sustained questioning. Raleigh's Case, 2 How. St. Tr. 1, 27 (1603).) And of course even when interrogation exists, it is in the final analysis the declarant's statements, not the interrogator's questions, that the Confrontation Clause requires us to evaluate.

[39] If 911 operators are not themselves law enforcement officers, they may at least be agents of law enforcement when they conduct interrogations of 911 callers. For purposes of this opinion (and without deciding the point), we consider their acts to be acts of the police. As in Crawford v. Washington, 541 U.S. 36 (2004), therefore, our holding today makes it unnecessary to consider whether and when statements made to someone other than law enforcement personnel are "testimonial."

sense that "qualifies under any conceivable definition." We must decide, therefore, whether the Confrontation Clause applies only to testimonial hearsay; and, if so, whether the recording of a 911 call qualifies.

The answer to the first question was suggested in *Crawford,* even if not explicitly held:

> "The text of the Confrontation Clause reflects this focus [on testimonial hearsay]. It applies to 'witnesses' against the accused—in other words, those who 'bear testimony.' 1 N. Webster, An American Dictionary of the English Language (1828). 'Testimony,' in turn, is typically 'a solemn declaration or affirmation made for the purpose of establishing or proving some fact.' *Ibid.* An accuser who makes a formal statement to government officers bears testimony in a sense that a person who makes a casual remark to an acquaintance does not." 541 U.S., at 51.

A limitation so clearly reflected in the text of the constitutional provision must fairly be said to mark out not merely its "core," but its perimeter.

We are not aware of any early American case invoking the Confrontation Clause or the common-law right to confrontation that did not clearly involve testimony as thus defined. Well into the 20th century, our own Confrontation Clause jurisprudence was carefully applied only in the testimonial context. * * *

Even our later cases, conforming to the reasoning of *Ohio v. Roberts,* 448 U.S. 56 (1980),[40] never in practice dispensed with the Confrontation Clause requirements of unavailability and prior cross-examination in cases that involved testimonial hearsay, see *Crawford,* 541 U.S., at 57–59 * * *. Where our cases did dispense with those requirements—even under the *Roberts* approach—the statements at issue were clearly nontestimonial. See, *e.g., Bourjaily v. United States,* 483 U.S. 171, 181–184 (1987) (statements made unwittingly to a Government informant); *Dutton v. Evans,* 400 U.S. 74, 87–89 (1970) (plurality opinion) (statements from one prisoner to another).

Most of the American cases applying the Confrontation Clause or its state constitutional or common-law counterparts involved testimonial statements of the most formal sort—sworn testimony in prior judicial proceedings or formal depositions under oath—which invites the argument that the scope of the Clause is limited to that very formal category. But the English cases that were the progenitors of the Confrontation Clause did not limit the exclusionary rule to prior court

---

[40] "Roberts condition[ed] the admissibility of all hearsay evidence on whether it falls under a 'firmly rooted hearsay exception' or bears 'particularized guarantees of trustworthiness.' " *Crawford,* 541 U.S., at 60 (quoting *Roberts,* 448 U.S., at 66). We overruled *Roberts* in *Crawford* by restoring the unavailability and cross-examination requirements.

testimony and formal depositions, see *Crawford, supra,* at 52, and n.3. In any event, we do not think it conceivable that the protections of the Confrontation Clause can readily be evaded by having a note-taking policeman *recite* the unsworn hearsay testimony of the declarant, instead of having the declarant sign a deposition. Indeed, if there is one point for which no case—English or early American, state or federal—can be cited, that is it.

The question before us in *Davis,* then, is whether, objectively considered, the interrogation that took place in the course of the 911 call produced testimonial statements. When we said in *Crawford, supra,* at 53, that "interrogations by law enforcement officers fall squarely within [the] class" of testimonial hearsay, we had immediately in mind (for that was the case before us) interrogations solely directed at establishing the facts of a past crime, in order to identify (or provide evidence to convict) the perpetrator. The product of such interrogation, whether reduced to a writing signed by the declarant or embedded in the memory (and perhaps notes) of the interrogating officer, is testimonial. It is, in the terms of the 1828 American dictionary quoted in *Crawford,* " '[a] solemn declaration or affirmation made for the purpose of establishing or proving some fact.' " 541 U.S., at 51. (The solemnity of even an oral declaration of relevant past fact to an investigating officer is well enough established by the severe consequences that can attend a deliberate falsehood. * * *) A 911 call, on the other hand, and at least the initial interrogation conducted in connection with a 911 call, is ordinarily not designed primarily to "establis[h] or prov[e]" some past fact, but to describe current circumstances requiring police assistance.

The difference between the interrogation in *Davis* and the one in *Crawford* is apparent on the face of things. In *Davis,* McCottry was speaking about events *as they were actually happening,* rather than "describ [ing] past events," *Lilly v. Virginia,* 527 U.S. 116, 137 (1999) (plurality opinion). Sylvia Crawford's interrogation, on the other hand, took place hours after the events she described had occurred. Moreover, any reasonable listener would recognize that McCottry (unlike Sylvia Crawford) was facing an ongoing emergency. Although one *might* call 911 to provide a narrative report of a crime absent any imminent danger, McCottry's call was plainly a call for help against bona fide physical threat. Third, the nature of what was asked and answered in *Davis,* again viewed objectively, was such that the elicited statements were necessary to be able to *resolve* the present emergency, rather than simply to learn (as in *Crawford*) what had happened in the past. That is true even of the operator's effort to establish the identity of the assailant, so that the dispatched officers might know whether they would be encountering a violent felon. See, *e.g., Hiibel v. Sixth Judicial Dist. Court of Nev., Humboldt Cty.,* 542 U.S. 177, 186 (2004). And finally, the difference in the level of formality between the two interviews is striking. Crawford was responding calmly, at the station house, to a series of questions, with the officer-interrogator taping and making notes of her answers; McCottry's frantic answers were provided over the phone, in an environment that was not tranquil, or even (as far as any reasonable 911 operator could make out) safe.

We conclude from all this that the circumstances of McCottry's interrogation objectively indicate its primary purpose was to enable police assistance to meet an ongoing emergency. She simply was not acting as a *witness;* she was not *testifying.* What she said was not "a weaker substitute for live testimony" at trial, *United States v. Inadi,* 475 U.S. 387, 394 (1986), like Lord Cobham's statements in *Raleigh's Case,* 2 How. St. Tr. 1 (1603), or Jane Dingler's *ex parte* statements against her husband in *King v. Dingler,* 2 Leach 561, 168 Eng. Rep. 383 (1791), or Sylvia Crawford's statement in *Crawford.* In each of those cases, the *ex parte* actors and the evidentiary products of the *ex parte* communication aligned perfectly with their courtroom analogues. McCottry's emergency statement does not. No "witness" goes into court to proclaim an emergency and seek help.

Davis seeks to cast McCottry in the unlikely role of a witness by pointing to English cases. None of them involves statements made during an ongoing emergency. In *King v. Brasier,* 1 Leach 199, 168 Eng. Rep. 202 (1779), for example, a young rape victim, "immediately on her coming home, told all the circumstances of the injury" to her mother. *Id.,* at 200, 168 Eng. Rep., at 202. The case would be helpful to Davis if the relevant statement had been the girl's screams for aid as she was being chased by her assailant. But by the time the victim got home, her story was an account of past events.

This is not to say that a conversation which begins as an interrogation to determine the need for emergency assistance cannot, as the Indiana Supreme Court put it, "evolve into testimonial statements," 829 N.E.2d, at 457, once that purpose has been achieved. In this case, for example, after the operator gained the information needed to address the exigency of the moment, the emergency appears to have ended (when Davis drove away from the premises). The operator then told McCottry to be quiet, and proceeded to pose a battery of questions. It could readily be maintained that, from that point on, McCottry's statements were testimonial, not unlike the "structured police questioning" that occurred in *Crawford,* 541 U.S., at 53, n.4. This presents no great problem. Just as, for Fifth Amendment purposes, "police officers can and will distinguish almost instinctively between questions necessary to secure their own safety or the safety of the public and questions designed solely to elicit testimonial evidence from a suspect," *New York v. Quarles,* 467 U.S. 649, 658–659 (1984), trial courts will recognize the point at which, for Sixth

Amendment purposes, statements in response to interrogations become testimonial. Through *in limine* procedure, they should redact or exclude the portions of any statement that have become testimonial, as they do, for example, with unduly prejudicial portions of otherwise admissible evidence. Davis's jury did not hear the *complete* 911 call, although it may well have heard some testimonial portions. We were asked to classify only McCottry's early statements identifying Davis as her assailant, and we agree with the Washington Supreme Court that they were not testimonial. That court also concluded that, even if later parts of the call were testimonial, their admission was harmless beyond a reasonable doubt. Davis does not challenge that holding, and we therefore assume it to be correct.

B

Determining the testimonial or nontestimonial character of the statements that were the product of the interrogation in *Hammon* is a much easier task, since they were not much different from the statements we found to be testimonial in *Crawford*. It is entirely clear from the circumstances that the interrogation was part of an investigation into possibly criminal past conduct—as, indeed, the testifying officer expressly acknowledged * * *. There was no emergency in progress; the interrogating officer testified that he had heard no arguments or crashing and saw no one throw or break anything. When the officers first arrived, Amy told them that things were fine, and there was no immediate threat to her person. When the officer questioned Amy for the second time, and elicited the challenged statements, he was not seeking to determine (as in *Davis*) "what is happening," but rather "what happened." Objectively viewed, the primary, if not indeed the sole, purpose of the interrogation was to investigate a possible crime—which is, of course, precisely what the officer *should* have done.

It is true that the *Crawford* interrogation was more formal. It followed a *Miranda* warning, was tape-recorded, and took place at the station house, see 541 U.S., at 53, n.4. While these features certainly strengthened the statements' testimonial aspect—made it more objectively apparent, that is, that the purpose of the exercise was to nail down the truth about past criminal events—none was essential to the point. It was formal enough that Amy's interrogation was conducted in a separate room, away from her husband (who tried to intervene), with the officer receiving her replies for use in his "investigat[ion]." * * * What we called the "striking resemblance" of the *Crawford* statement to civil-law *ex parte* examinations, 541 U.S., at 52, is shared by Amy's statement here. Both declarants were actively separated from the defendant—officers forcibly prevented Hershel from participating in the interrogation. Both statements deliberately recounted, in response to police questioning, how potentially criminal past events began and progressed. And both took place some time after the events described were over. Such statements under official interrogation are an obvious substitute for live testimony, because they do precisely *what a witness does* on direct examination; they are inherently testimonial.[41]

Both Indiana and the United States as *amicus curiae* argue that this case should be resolved much like *Davis.* For the reasons we find the comparison to *Crawford* compelling, we find the comparison to *Davis* unpersuasive. The statements in *Davis* were taken when McCottry was alone, not only unprotected by police (as Amy Hammon was protected), but apparently in immediate danger from Davis. She was seeking aid, not telling a story about the past. McCottry's present-tense statements showed immediacy; Amy's narrative of past events was delivered at some remove in time from the danger she described. And after Amy answered the officer's questions, he had her execute an affidavit, in order, he testified, "[t]o establish events that have occurred previously." * * *

Although we necessarily reject the Indiana Supreme Court's implication that virtually any "initial inquiries" at the crime scene will not be testimonial, see 829 N.E.2d, at 453, 457, we do not hold the opposite—that *no* questions at the scene will yield nontestimonial answers. We have already observed of domestic disputes that "[o]fficers called to investigate * * * need to know whom they are dealing with in order to assess the situation, the threat to their own safety, and possible danger to the potential victim." *Hiibel,* 542 U.S., at 186. Such exigencies may *often* mean that "initial inquiries" produce nontestimonial statements. But in cases like this one, where Amy's statements were neither a cry for help nor the provision of information enabling officers immediately to end a threatening situation, the fact that they were given at an alleged crime scene and were "initial inquiries" is immaterial. Cf. *Crawford, supra,* at 52, n.3.[42]

---

[41] The dissent criticizes our test for being "neither workable nor a targeted attempt to reach the abuses forbidden by the [Confrontation] Clause," * * * (opinion of THOMAS, J.). * * * The dissent, in attempting to formulate an exhaustive classification of its own, has not provided anything that deserves the description "workable"—unless one thinks that the distinction between "formal" and "informal" statements * * * qualifies. * * *

As for the charge that our holding is not a "targeted attempt to reach the abuses forbidden by the [Confrontation] Clause," which the dissent describes as the depositions taken by Marian magistrates, characterized by a high degree of formality * * *: We do not dispute that formality is indeed essential to testimonial utterance. But we no longer have examining Marian magistrates; and we do have, as our 18th-century forebears did not, examining police officers, * * * who perform investigative and testimonial functions once performed by examining Marian magistrates * * * Restricting the Confrontation Clause to the precise forms against which it was originally directed is a recipe for its extinction. Cf. Kyllo v. United States, 533 U.S. 27 (2001).

[42] Police investigations themselves are, of course, in no way impugned by our characterization of their fruits as testimonial. Investigations of past crimes prevent future harms and lead to necessary arrests. While prosecutors may hope that inculpatory "nontestimonial" evidence is gathered, this is essentially beyond police control. Their saying that an emergency exists cannot make it be so. The Confrontation Clause in no way governs police conduct, because it is the trial use of, not the investigatory collection of, ex parte testimonial statements which

IV

Respondents in both cases, joined by a number of their *amici,* contend that the nature of the offenses charged in these two cases— domestic violence—requires greater flexibility in the use of testimonial evidence. This particular type of crime is notoriously susceptible to intimidation or coercion of the victim to ensure that she does not testify at trial. When this occurs, the Confrontation Clause gives the criminal a windfall. We may not, however, vitiate constitutional guarantees when they have the effect of allowing the guilty to go free. Cf. *Kyllo v. United States,* 533 U.S. 27 (2001) (suppressing evidence from an illegal search). But when defendants seek to undermine the judicial process by procuring or coercing silence from witnesses and victims, the Sixth Amendment does not require courts to acquiesce. While defendants have no duty to assist the State in proving their guilt, they *do* have the duty to refrain from acting in ways that destroy the integrity of the criminal-trial system. We reiterate what we said in *Crawford:* that "the rule of forfeiture by wrongdoing * * * extinguishes confrontation claims on essentially equitable grounds." 541 U.S., at 62 (citing *Reynolds,* 98 U.S., at 158–159). That is, one who obtains the absence of a witness by wrongdoing forfeits the constitutional right to confrontation.

We take no position on the standards necessary to demonstrate such forfeiture, but federal courts using Federal Rule of Evidence 804(b)(6), which codifies the forfeiture doctrine, have generally held the Government to the preponderance-of-the-evidence standard, see, *e.g., United States v. Scott,* 284 F.3d 758, 762 (C.A.7 2002). State courts tend to follow the same practice, see, *e.g., Commonwealth v. Edwards,* 444 Mass. 526, 542, 830 N.E.2d 158, 172 (2005). Moreover, if a hearing on forfeiture is required, *Edwards,* for instance, observed that "hearsay evidence, including the unavailable witness's out-of-court statements, may be considered." *Id.,* at 545, 830 N.E.2d, at 174. The *Roberts* approach to the Confrontation Clause undoubtedly made recourse to this doctrine less necessary, because prosecutors could show the "reliability" of *ex parte* statements more easily than they could show the defendant's procurement of the witness's absence. *Crawford,* in overruling *Roberts,* did not destroy the ability of courts to protect the integrity of their proceedings.

We have determined that, absent a finding of forfeiture by wrongdoing, the Sixth Amendment operates to exclude Amy Hammon's affidavit. The Indiana courts may (if they are asked) determine on remand whether such a claim of forfeiture is properly raised and, if so, whether it is meritorious.

---

offends that provision. But neither can police conduct govern the Confrontation Clause; testimonial statements are what they are.

[JUSTICE THOMAS' concurring and dissent opinion is omitted.]

NOTES AND QUESTIONS

1. *The "Crawford" rule.* If the statement is "testimonial" and confrontation is not provided, *Crawford* interposes a huge "STOP SIGN" barring its admission in the absence of one of a few limited exceptions.

Crawford makes the key determination whether the statement is "testimonial." It described some testimonial statements: "Whatever else the term covers, [testimonial] applies at a minimum to prior testimony at a preliminary hearing, before a grand jury, or at a former trial; and to police interrogations." In the course of the opinion, the Court also included "plea allocution[s] showing existence of a conspiracy," which presumably includes all statements during guilty pleas, known as plea allocutions. In *Davis*, the Court added to the testimonial category statements made during police interrogation "when the circumstances objectively indicate that there is no * * * ongoing emergency, and that the primary purpose of the interrogation is to establish or prove past events potentially relevant to later criminal prosecution."

Although not technically an exception to the right of confrontation under *Crawford*, if the statement is determined not to be "testimonial," then the strong command to exclude absent confrontation is not triggered. Thus, the dimensions of the definition of testimonial and the determination of whether the statement falls within the definition are of paramount importance.

2. *Paradigm shift from focus on hearsay exceptions.* Under *Roberts*, the critical determination in most cases in satisfying the Confrontation Clause was the determination that a statement fit within a "firmly rooted" hearsay exception. *Crawford's* critical determination of the testimonial character of the statement is, by contrast, based on a very different model, which does not rest on hearsay exceptions and their guarantees of trustworthiness. The testimonial determination may sometimes overlap with hearsay theory as when the *Crawford* Court stated that "[m]ost of the hearsay exceptions covered statements that by their nature were not testimonial—for example, business records or statements in furtherance of a conspiracy." The statements in these hearsay categories are, however, not excluded from the testimonial category because they are within hearsay exceptions, but rather because statements within these categories are generally made for other purposes beside creating testimony. The Court indicated that White v. Illinois, 502 U.S. 346 (1992), where a firmly rooted excited utterance to a police officer was admitted, may have been wrongly decided. Indeed, in *Hammon*, the Court treated the state court's determination that the statement was an excited utterance as irrelevant to its conclusion that it was testimonial and violated the Constitution.

3. *The exceptions:* (A) *Present confrontation*. *Crawford* reaffirmed that the principles of *California v. Green* and *United States v. Owens* were valid in meeting the Confrontation Clause even as to testimonial statements.

Accordingly, whether the hearsay statement is testimonial or nontestimonial, the Confrontation Clause is satisfied if the person who made the out-of-court statement is present in court, testifies, and is subject to cross-examination.

4. *The exceptions: (B) Prior confrontation and unavailability. Crawford* also reaffirmed that if the witness has previously been subject to confrontation and is currently unavailable, then the prior testimonial statements may be received. Thus, the method of satisfying the Confrontation Clause illustrated by *Roberts*, where the preliminary hearing testimony of the defendant's unavailable former friend was received, remains sound.

5. *The exceptions: (C) Forfeiture by wrongdoing. Crawford* recognized an exception to the right of confrontation for "forfeiture by wrongdoing." That doctrine, which had been recognized in a nineteenth century decision, was largely undeveloped as a confrontation principle. In *Davis*, the Court invited attention to this task, suggesting that a preponderance-of-the-evidence standard applied and that the hearsay statements of the unavailable witness could be considered in making the determination. Neither case, however, answered the question of whether an intent to silence the witness was required for this Confrontation Clause exception to apply. For example, some decisions concluded that murdering the victim, albeit without intent to silence that person as a witness, constituted "forfeiture by wrongdoing" under the Confrontation Clause. See United States v. Garcia–Meza, 403 F.3d 364, 370 (6th Cir.2005); State v. Meeks, 88 P.3d 789, 794–95 (Kan.2004).

In answering the intent question, the Court, as in *Davis*, examined statements offered in a domestic violence case, this one ending in homicide. In *Giles v. California*, 554 U.S. 353 (2008), a sharply divided Court ruled that the forfeiture by wrongdoing exception was limited to those instances in which "the defendant engaged in conduct designed to prevent the witness from testifying." Id. at 359–60. However, the Court recognized that the intent to silence or dissuade a victim from testifying or cooperating with authorities might be found in the "domestic violence context" in prior acts of violence and threats. As long as the defendant intended to prevent the witness from testifying forfeiture applies even if he also has other motivations to harm the witness. See, e.g., United States v. Jackson, 706 F.3d 264, 267–69 (4th Cir.2013).

6. *The exceptions: (D) Statements not offered for the "truth of the matter asserted." In Crawford*, the Court stated that even if testimonial, statements were not barred if not offered for their truth. It cited the example of Tennessee v. Street, 471 U.S. 409 (1985), where a clearly testimonial confession by the codefendant was ruled admissible to refute a claim by the defendant. The defendant testified at trial that he had confessed only because the sheriff had told him to do so and had instructed him to "say the same thing" as the codefendant. The prosecution introduced the codefendant's statement, which contained quite different information, to refute the defendant's claim, and the trial court had given a limiting instruction that the jury was only to use it for that purpose. The Court in *Street* found the

Confrontation Clause was not violated, and *Crawford* explicitly approved this result.

7. *The exceptions: (E) Dying declarations (very likely).* In *Crawford*, the Court noted that at the time the Constitution was adopted, historical practice was to admit dying declarations as an exception to the principle of confrontation, which might mean it would be an exception to the Confrontation Clause. But it stated, "[i]f this exception must be accepted on historical grounds, it is *sui generis*."

Whether dying declarations are an exception to *Crawford*'s testimonial principle has still not been explicitly decided by the Supreme Court, but the likelihood appears high that it constitutes such an exception. While *Giles* did not decide the issue, the Court there used the existence of this common law exception so strongly to defeat the argument that killing a witness was sufficient for admission under the exception for forfeiture by wrongdoing that it would be difficult to imagine the Court now deciding that the dying declaration exception was not clearly recognized as its own exception to confrontation. Indeed, the lower courts have uniformly found dying declarations to be an exception. *See, e.g.*, State v. Beauchamp, 796 N.W.2d 780, 792–95 (Wis.2011) (concluding, along with every state to consider the issue, that dying declarations do not violate the Confrontation Clause under *Crawford*). Justice Scalia's opinion in *Giles* sets out the dimensions of the common law hearsay exception at the time of the framing, presumably imposing such limits on any modern-day exception.

8. *The exceptions: (F) Admissions by the defendant.* Although not mentioned by the Supreme Court, there can be no doubt that the defendant's own admissions, even if testimonial, are not barred by the Confrontation Clause. The explanation is the same as given by Morgan for receiving admissions when objected to on hearsay grounds: A party may not complain about not being able to cross-examine herself. See Section B(2), supra.

9. *Additional examples of testimonial and nontestimonial statements.* "An off-hand, overheard remark" may be a good candidate for exclusion under the hearsay rule, according to the Court, but bears little resemblance to the abuses that were the target of the Confrontation Clause. "An accuser who makes a formal statement to government officers bears testimony in a sense that a person who makes a causal remark to an acquaintance does not."

10. *Developing a general definition.* The Court in *Crawford* declined to give a definition of testimonial, but it has given some general guidance in *Crawford and Davis*. In *Crawford*, the Court provided three possible definitions:

> *ex parte* in-court testimony or its functional equivalent—that is, (1) material such as affidavits, custodial examinations, prior testimony that the defendant was unable to cross-examine, or similar pretrial statements that the declarant would reasonably expect to be used prosecutorially (Petitioner's Brief);

(2) extrajudicial statements * * * contained in formalized testimonial materials, such as affidavits, depositions, prior testimony, or confessions (Justice Thomas' concurring opinion in White v. Illinois, 502 U.S. 346, 365 (1992)); and

(3) statements that were made under circumstances which would lead an objective witness reasonably to believe that the statement would be available for use at a later trial (Defense Lawyers Amicus Brief).

In *Davis*, the Court's majority rejected the strict formality of the second definition, although it is still followed by Justice Thomas. *Davis* did not use the language of either of the other two possible definitions and again declined to give "an exhaustive classification" of all statements or even all police interrogations. It did, however, give guidance in the area of police interrogations, whether at the stationhouse or in the field:

> Statements are nontestimonial when made in the course of police interrogation under circumstances objectively indicating that the primary purpose of the interrogation is to enable police assistance to meet an ongoing emergency. They are testimonial when the circumstances objectively indicate that there is no such ongoing emergency, and that the primary purpose of the interrogation is to establish or prove past events potentially relevant to later criminal prosecution.

11. *Police "interrogation" and "structured questioning."* In *Crawford*, the Court used the terms "interrogation" and "structured questioning" to characterize the questioning of Sylvia Crawford but did not define or indicate the significance of either term in determining whether a response is testimonial. In *Davis*, the Court used the term interrogation, but stated while such questioning "in some circumstances tend to generate testimonial responses," it is not a requirement: "The Framers were no more willing to exempt from cross-examination volunteered testimony or answers to open-ended questions than they were to exempt answers to detailed interrogations."

12. *Significance of law enforcement involvement.* The Court in *Crawford* noted that government involvement in the creation of evidence is a particularly salient feature: "The involvement of government officers in the production of testimony with an eye toward trial presents *unique potential* for prosecutorial abuse—a fact borne out time and again throughout a history with which the Framers were keenly aware." (emphasis added). However, it did not state that government involvement in the creation of the evidence was required. In *Davis*, it treated 911 operators as agents of law enforcement, and thereby avoided deciding "whether and when" statements made to non-law enforcement personnel would be testimonial. The Court has avoided resolving this question in all subsequent cases as well, considering all statements as having been made to members of law enforcement. Would it matter if the videotaped statement of a victim of domestic violence was made by a privately funded group rather than by a police officer responding to the

victim's home an hour after the apparent assault or whether a child's statement regarding sexual abuse is made to a government doctor, or to a private doctor who works as part of a sexual abuse investigative team, or to the child's pediatrician during a routine exam?

13. *Declarant's knowledge of government involvement.* Must the statement be made with knowledge that the declarant is talking to a police or government officer? Apparently such knowledge may be an important factor at least in some contexts. In both *Crawford* and *Davis*, the Court noted that the co-conspirator statement in Bourjaily v. United States, 483 U.S. 171 (1987), which it considered correctly admitted, involved a statement "made unwittingly" to a government informant. Is the lack of knowledge of the speaker that the conversation is with a government agent dispositive in making the statement nontestimonial when the "primary purpose of the interrogation is to establish or prove past events potentially relevant to later criminal prosecution," which under *Davis* would ordinarily make it testimonial? Is this lack of knowledge that the apparent co-conspirator is in fact a government agent the reason for excluding co-conspirator statements from the testimonial category, or is it rather that the statement is made for the purpose of aiding the conspiracy ("in furtherance of") rather than for a testimonial purpose?

14. *Likely class of nontestimonial statements.* [Privately made statements without an intention for use at trial are unlikely to be considered testimonial, even if highly incriminating to another.]See, e.g., State v. Rivera, 844 A.2d 191, 202 (Conn.2004) (concluding "statement in confidence and on [the declarant's] own initiative to a close family member, almost eighteen months before the defendant was arrested and more than four years before his own arrest" not testimonial).

15. *Elimination of manipulation by police failure to formally record.* The *Crawford* opinion had left open the possibility that the formality of the statement might be given dispositive weight in determining its testimonial status, which could lead to manipulation by investigative officers in their decision to record a statement or to recite it from memory or informal notes. In *Davis*, the Supreme Court eliminated some of that concern: ["[W]e do not think it conceivable that the protections of the Confrontation Clause can readily be evaded by having a note-taking policeman *recite* the unsworn hearsay testimony of the declarant instead of having the declarant sign a deposition.]* * * The product of [police interrogation to prove or establish past crime], whether reduced to a writing signed by the declarant or embedded in the memory (and perhaps notes) of the interrogating officer is testimonial." *Davis*, 547 U.S. at 826.

16. *Ongoing emergency revisited and clarity eroded.* The nature of the ongoing emergency concept was expanded outside of the domestic violence context in Michigan v. Bryant, 131 S.Ct. 1143 (2011), which also eroded some of the clarity of the testimonial doctrine. In *Bryant*, the police spoke with a severely injured individual found in a gas station parking lot about the

circumstances of the shooting that caused his injury, which had occurred sometime earlier and at a different location. The Court ruled that statements made by the victim regarding the identification and description of the shooter and the location of the shooting were not testimonial statements because they had a "primary purpose * * * to enable police assistance to meet an ongoing emergency." Id. at 1167.

The *Bryant* opinion explained that the limited range of time involved in *Davis* was a function of the fact that the crime was an act of domestic violence targeted against a particular victim by an unarmed perpetrator. In *Bryant*, it reasoned that the perpetrator's use of a gun, his continued possession of that weapon, and his unknown motivation made more expansive inquiries pertinent to the ongoing emergency. The Court considered questions designed to identify and find the attacker legitimately related to concern for public safety regarding an armed attacker whose location and motivation were unknown and therefore did not consider those inquiries to have the primary purpose of developing evidence for trial but rather concerned the ongoing emergency.

Among the other factors the Court found pertinent in the testimonial determination were the serious medical condition of the victim and the informality of the police interrogation. The exact impact of *Bryant* is not clear, but it will permit a broader reading of the time period of an ongoing emergency in armed perpetrator situations, and its multi-factor analysis will effectively give broader discretion to trial judges in evaluating the primary purpose of the law enforcement inquiry and the declarant's motivation. Predictably, a larger group of statements will be ruled nontestimonial after *Bryant* generally, and particularly in armed, unidentified perpetrator cases.

More generally, *Bryant* appeared to open the determination of whether the statement is testimonial to a broad range of considerations. This prospect prompted Justice Scalia to write a blistering dissent, protesting that the opinion requires judges to conduct an open-ended balancing test that is amorphous, subjective, and looks to reliability and is no better than the *Roberts* balancing test that *Crawford* rejected. *See* Bryant, 131 S.Ct. at 1175–76 (Scalia, J., dissenting).

17. *Forensic certificates and reports. Crawford's* application to forensic certificates and expert reports has been examined in three cases that sharply divided the Court. While the first two brought many such documents within the testimonial concept, the third excluded some and left the issue muddled and confused. In *Melendez–Diaz v. Massachusetts*, 557 U.S. 305 (2009), the Supreme Court ruled that sworn certificates of analysis reporting the results of forensic analysis performed by a state laboratory at police request on seized material were testimonial and their admission without the testimony of the analysts violated the Confrontation Clause. The opinion, which was written by Justice Scalia for five members of the Court, concluded that these forensic certificates were in the core class of testimonial statements because they were functionally identical to live, in-court testimony. They stated that

the substance found was cocaine, which is the precise testimony the analysts would be expected to provide if called at trial.

In his dissenting opinion for four members of the Court, Justice Kennedy supported the argument of Massachusetts that the report should be admitted because it was a business or government record. The Court rejected this argument, which it characterized as misunderstanding the relationship between the business-and-official-records hearsay exceptions and the Confrontation Clause. It stated:

> Business and public records are generally admissible absent confrontation not because they qualify under an exception to the hearsay rules, but because—having been created for the administration of an entity's affairs and not for the purpose of establishing or proving some fact at trial—they are not testimonial. Whether or not they qualify as business or official records, the analysts' statements here—prepared specifically for use at petitioner's trial—were testimonial against petitioner, and the analysts were subject to confrontation under the Sixth Amendment.

Id. at 324. On the other hand, it described "medical reports created for treatment purposes [as not] * * * testimonial under our decision today." *Id.* at 312 n.2.

The Court also rejected statutes that require the defendant to subpoena and call forensic analysts. It characterized them as converting the duty under the Confrontation Clause into the defendant's privilege under the Compulsory Process Clause and declared them invalid as a possible alternative to the prosecution producing the analysts. The Court did, however, endorse the mechanism adopted in some states to lessen the burden of confrontation through notice-and-demand statutes. These require the prosecution to provide notice to the defendant of its intent to use an analyst's report as evidence after which the defendant is given a period of time to demand confrontation or lose the right to challenge admission of the evidence. In their "simplest form," the Court indicated these statutes are constitutional.

In *Melendez–Diaz,* the Court was not presented with the situation where the analyst who appears in court and is subject to cross-examination did not perform the underlying analysis. However, that was the situation in *Bullcoming v. New Mexico,* 131 S.Ct. 2705 (2011), which involved an unsworn lab report. There, the Court rejected surrogate examiner testimony as adequate. It ruled categorically that when the prosecution introduces the results of an examination "to prove a fact at a criminal trial" the Confrontation Clause is not satisfied by making available an uninvolved expert for cross-examination as a surrogate for the preparer of the report. Where the testifying expert did not sign the report or certificate and did not personally perform or observe performance of the test reported, cross-examination of the surrogate expert does not provide the confrontation required by the Constitution.

Bullcoming was a five-to-four decision, with Justice Sotomayor providing the decisive fifth vote. In her concurring opinion, she noted that this was not a case where the testifying expert relied upon a report produced by a non-testifying expert, not for its truth, but to form the basis of the testifying expert's opinion. Indeed, the testifying expert in *Bullcoming* had no independent opinion regarding the fact at issue—the defendant's blood alcohol level—but merely acted as a conduit for the admission of the non-testifying expert's results. The next term, the Court in *Williams v. Illinois*, 132 S.Ct. 2221 (2012), reached the unresolved issue of whether the Confrontation Clause was violated when the testifying expert relied on the forensic report of a non-testifying expert to provide the basis for the expert's opinion.

In *Williams*, four members of the Court concluded that *Crawford*'s exception for a statement not used "for the truth of the matter asserted" rendered nontestimonial the testifying expert's use of a report by a non-testifying expert where the report was neither admitted into evidence nor shown to the factfinder. Justice Alito, writing the plurality opinion, reasoned that while reliance on these documents might result in weaknesses in the proof or the irrelevance of inadequately supported propositions, those possible defects would be either matters of state law or due process, not the Confrontation Clause. He also concluded that, since the DNA report at issue was prepared without the primary purpose of accusing a targeted individual but rather to catch a dangerous unidentified rapist who was still at large, it was not testimonial.

Five Justices, four in dissent and one concurring in the result, concluded that the use of the report to support the testifying expert's opinion did not qualify as a "legitimate" or "plausible" nonhearsay purpose and that the use of the statement to provide the basis of the opinion was effectively to use it for the truth within the meaning of the Confrontation Clause. However, one of those five, Justice Thomas, found the report nontestimonial because, although the report was signed, it contained no certification. In his view, it lacked the requisite formality and solemnity to be considered testimonial. Accordingly, Justice Thomas concurred in the judgment reached by Justice Alito's plurality opinion, albeit on quite distinct grounds, that the use of the report did not violate the Confrontation Clause because it was insufficiently formal. Thus, *Williams* leaves the testimonial treatment of forensic reports badly confused in particular. See United States v. Pablo, 696 F.3d 1280, 1291–92 (10th Cir.2012) (affirming the trial court's admission of the expert evidence on the basis of this disjointed five-person majority). Moreover, *Williams* together with *Bryant* more broadly reveals a fundamentally divided Court on basic definitional issues.

18. *Statements not for the truth of the matter asserted revisited.* Given the divisions in *Williams*, how courts should treat other statements that under evidentiary law may arguably be used for a purpose other than their truth remains uncertain. As noted earlier, the Court in *Crawford* stated that the Confrontation Clause does not bar the use of testimonial statements for

purposes other than establishing the truth of the matter asserted, citing for that proposition Tennessee v. Street, 471 U.S. 409, 414 (1985), which all the justices endorsed in *Williams* as a proper use of the concept.

In principle, the exception for statements that are not offered for the truth is sound because such statements are supposed to make no claims that the declarant's out-of-court statement was truthful, which cross-examination could test. However, varying evidentiary definitions of this concept should not determine the Confrontation Clause exception. The specific argument in *Williams* regarding expert use of inadmissible hearsay statements presents one clear problem area but is not unique in challenging the absence of any significant truth claim for statements within this general nonhearsay category. *See, e.g.,* Jones v. Basinger, 635 F.3d 1030, 1040–51 (7th Cir.2011) (ruling that non-testifying informant's statements admitted to explain the "course of the investigation" were effectively used for the truth and violated defendant's confrontation rights); Jones v. Cain, 601 F.Supp.2d 769, 787–806 (E.D.La.2009) (ruling that statements admitted as prior consistent statements were subject to a Confrontation Clause challenge where the declarant did not testify, a conclusion that was buttressed by the lack of a limiting instruction and the prosecutor's use of the statements for their truth in closing argument).

19. *Problematic effect on some prosecutions: Domestic violence.* In general, *Crawford* has had a deleterious effect on domestic violence prosecutions. See generally Lininger, Prosecuting Batterers after *Crawford*, 91 Va.L.Rev. 747 (2005). As the facts of *Davis* and *Hammon* illustrate, emergency operators and police are frequently involved with frantic victims shortly after the incident, but some of these victims fail to appear at the time of trial or are unwilling witnesses against their partners or spouses. Prior to *Crawford*, many jurisdictions built prosecutions around 911 tapes, other excited utterances made to emergency workers and police, and special exceptions that relied on *Roberts*' individual indicia of reliability. After *Crawford*, some or all of that evidence was placed in doubt. *Davis* opens the door to many 911 calls, but closes it to many statements on the scene of a past assault made to the police. As *Davis* notes, domestic violence advocates sought greater flexibility for admission of hearsay under the testimonial definition, but the Court declined, offering instead the forfeiture by wrongdoing exception to the Confrontation Clause when silence is procured or coerced from victims and witnesses.

20. *Problematic effect on some prosecutions: Child sexual abuse cases.* For children's cases, many of the most serious being child sexual abuse prosecutions, clarity of *Crawford*'s application may exist for those statements clearly solicited for the purpose of admission at trial. See State v. Snowden, 867 A.2d 314 (Md.2005) (finding testimonial a statement obtained by social worker for express purpose of developing testimony under special hearsay exception). However, the coverage of the term testimonial is up in the air for many types of statements by children. The early revelations to parents and doctors may be good candidates for being considered nontestimonial, but after

Davis not some statements to the police. The decisive factors in rendering the statement testimonial are not clear. Whose intent regarding the purpose of the statement matters, the aware police or the perhaps unaware child? Will government involvement be required, and if so, to what degree? Did the expansion of Federal Rule 803(4) to cover statements made, not for treatment purposes, but exclusively for diagnosis mean that all such statements are testimonial since that expansion was intended to admit statements made to doctors whose only function is to give trial testimony?

21. *Alternatives of face-to-face confrontation at trial for children: Apparently unaffected by Crawford.* Child abuse cases raise other special Confrontation Clause issues. One of those concerns is the mode of presenting testimony: Where a child-witness would suffer psychological trauma from testifying in the presence of the criminal defendant, does the Constitution permit use of techniques that will eliminate the face-to-face confrontation? In Maryland v. Craig, 497 U.S. 836 (1990), the Court, over Justice Scalia's dissent, concluded that the Confrontation Clause permitted a child-witness to testify outside the physical presence of the defendant upon a case-specific showing that the child would suffer trauma interfering with the ability to testify that is not *de minimis*. See generally Marsil et al., Child Witness Policy: Law Interfacing with Social Science, 65 Law & Contemp.Probs., Winter 2002, at 209. This aspect of Confrontation Clause doctrine is apparently unaffected by *Crawford*, although its general approach was indirectly criticized in another recent Sixth Amendment case. See United States v. Gonzalez–Lopez, 548 U.S. 140, 146 (2006) ("abstract[ing] from the right to its purposes, and then eliminat[ing] the right"). See also Chapter 12, Section A(3), supra.

22. *General sources.* Friedman & McCormack, Dial–In Testimony, 150 U. Pa.L.Rev. 1171 (2002); Friedman, Confrontation: The Search for Basic Principles, 86 Geo.L.J. 1011 (1998); Friedman, The Story of *Crawford*, in Evidence Stories 335 (Lempert ed., 2006); Jonakait, "Witnesses" in the Confrontation Clause: *Crawford v. Washington,* Noah Webster, and Compulsory Process, 79 Temp.L.Rev. 155 (2006); Lininger, The Sound of Silence: Holding Batters Accountable for Silencing Victims, 87 Tex.L.Rev. 857 (2009); Lininger, Reconceptualizing Confrontation after *Davis,* 85 Tex.L.Rev. 271 (2006); Lininger, Prosecuting Batterers after *Crawford,* 91 Va.L.Rev. 747 (2005); Mosteller, *Crawford v. Washington*: Encouraging and Ensuring the Confrontation of Witnesses, 39 U.Rich.L.Rev. 511 (2005); Mosteller, Remaking Confrontation Clause and Hearsay Doctrine under the Challenge of Child Sexual Abuse Prosecutions, 1993 U.Ill.L.Rev. 691; Scallen, Coping with *Crawford*: Confrontation of Children and other Challenging Witnesses, 35 Wm. Mitchell L.Rev. 1558 (2009); Seaman, Triangulating Testimonial Hearsay: The Constitutional Boundaries of Expert Opinion Testimony, 96 Geo. L.J. 827 (2008); Sklansky, *Hearsay's Last Hurrah*, 2009 SUP. CT. REV. 1; Tuerkheimer, *Crawford* Triangle: Domestic Violence and the Right of Confrontation, 85 N.C.L.Rev. 1 (2006).

CHAPTER 14[1]

EXCEPTIONS TO THE HEARSAY RULE

■ ■ ■

A. PRESENT SENSE IMPRESSIONS AND EXCITED UTTERANCES

Federal Rules 803(1) & (2)

UNITED STATES V. CAIN

United States Court of Appeals, Fifth Circuit, 1979.
587 F.2d 678.

JAMES C. HILL, CIRCUIT JUDGE:

This appeal is from a conviction of interstate transportation of a stolen vehicle under the Dyer Act, 18 U.S.C. § 2312. The appellant seeks reversal of his conviction [, *inter alia*, on the ground that his] conviction was prejudiced by the trial judge's improperly receiving into evidence inadmissible hearsay. We find * * * that * * * his third argument is well-taken. Appellant's conviction is, therefore, reversed.

The appellant and a companion escaped from federal prison in Texarkana, Texas, during the early hours of August 21, 1977. On the following morning a pickup truck was reported missing from a residence approximately one mile from the prison.

At about the same time, a state trooper responding to a motorist's call on a citizens band radio concerning an abandoned truck found the pickup, with a khaki shirt and a tee shirt in it, on a bridge in Louisiana. A second unidentified "CB'er," responding to the state trooper's request for information, reported having seen two white, shirtless males walking from the place where the truck had been abandoned and attempting to hitch a ride toward the east. A call to police headquarters revealed that the truck had not been reported stolen, and the trooper then concluded that the truck had probably given out of gas. He sought, by way of a call

---

[1] In the cases and materials throughout the chapter, some footnotes have been omitted and others have been renumbered. [Ed.]

on his CB, to determine the present whereabouts of the two shirtless men so that he could help them remove the truck from the bridge, where it was blocking a lane of traffic. Other unidentified "CB'ers" informed him that two shirtless, white males were seen walking five to six miles east of the truck's location. Realizing that if these two men were from the truck, they had passed several service stations, the trooper used his police radio to request that anyone seeing them stop them for questioning. A deputy sheriff who was in the area where the two men had been reported to be walking was, at that moment, watching two shirtless, white males walk toward him. As it turned out, these two men were the appellant and his fellow escaped prisoner.

At the deputy sheriff's request, the appellant and his companion entered the deputy's car and were taken to the service station where the state trooper waited with the truck, which had been towed there. When the men refused to answer questions concerning their identity, their clothing, and their connection to the abandoned truck, they were transported to the parish jail, where it was learned that the pickup truck had been stolen in Texarkana and that the two men had escaped from the Texarkana prison.

* * *

Appellant's * * * third argument regarding the improper admission of hearsay into evidence requires that his conviction be reversed. The state trooper was allowed to testify, over objection, concerning the CB radio transmission he received regarding two white, shirtless males leaving the abandoned truck. There is no doubt and the government concedes that the statement constituted hearsay testimony, since it was offered for the truth of the matter therein. No limiting instruction regarding consideration of the statement for any purpose other than its truth was given. *See United States v. Gomez*, 529 F.2d 412, 416 (5th Cir.1976). The government contends that the statement was admissible under Rule 803(1) of the Federal Rules of Evidence and that no confrontation rights of the appellant were infringed. The trial judge agreed with the prosecutor's assertion that the "CB'er's" statement was admissible under the "present sense impression" exception to the hearsay rule. That exception reads as follows:

> (1) Present sense impression. A statement describing or explaining an event or condition made while the declarant was perceiving the event or condition or immediately thereafter.

Id. The appellant correctly points out, however, that his position five miles away within a few minutes of the statement contradicts the possibility that he could have been seen leaving the pickup truck at about that same time. Indeed, for the "CB'er" to have seen the appellant leave the truck immediately prior to his statement, one must make the unlikely assumption that Cain and his companion were transported at high speed immediately upon leaving the truck and resumed walking five miles later just prior to being observed by the deputy sheriff. The distances and time lapses involved make it impossible to determine whether the declaration by the "CB'er" was made immediately following the observation or not, but the chances that it was are slim. The exception to the hearsay rule found in Rule 803(1) is, therefore, inapplicable. The District of Columbia Circuit recently reached a similar conclusion in a case involving a hearsay statement that was calculated to have been made fifteen to forty-five minutes after the subject observation.

> This time span hardly qualifies as 'immediately' after the accident as that term is used in Rule 803(1), particularly in view of the commentary on that Rule contained in the Advisory Committee Notes. This states that the 'most significant practical difference [between 803(1) and 803(2)] will lie in the time lapse allowable between event and statement,' and that 803(1) 'recognizes that in many, if not most, instances, *precise contemporaneity* is impossible, and hence a *slight lapse* is allowable.' 56 F.R.D. 187, 304 (1973) (emphasis added). The thrust of this commentary is that in a circumstance such as that before us, an out-of-court statement made at least fifteen minutes after the event it describes is not admissible unless the declarant was still in a state of excitement resulting from the event.

Hilyer v. Howat Concrete Co., Inc., 578 F.2d 422, 426 n.7 (D.C.Cir.1978). *Accord, United States v. Kehoe,* 562 F.2d 65, 70 (1st Cir.1977); *United States v. Medico,* 557 F.2d 309 (2d Cir.1977). Since the declarant in this case had no reason to be in a state of excitement when he observed the two men or when he spoke and apparently was not in such a state, the "excited utterance" exception provided by Rule 803(2) is also inapplicable.

[The court also held that the evidence is inadmissible under the residual exception of Rule 803(24), now Rule 807.]

We conclude that the statement was inadmissible under the Federal Rules of Evidence and that, viewing the evidence as a whole, there is a significant possibility that the testimony had a substantial impact on the verdict of the jury. *See United States v. Gomez,* 529 F.2d 412, 416–17 (5th Cir.1976). The statement was the only evidence directly linking Cain to the pickup truck. It remains to be seen whether a new jury will consider the remaining evidence, circumstantial in nature, sufficient to connect Cain to the stolen truck and establish his guilt. Having reversed on the basis of the improper admission of hearsay testimony, we consider it unnecessary to decide whether or not Cain's confrontation rights were infringed.

Reversed.

NOTES AND QUESTIONS

1. *Time limitation.* The difference in time spans allowable where a statement is offered under the present sense impression as compared with the excited utterance exception is shown in Hilyer v. Howat Concrete Co., 578 F.2d 422 (D.C.Cir.1978), cited in *Cain*. Mr. Hilyer, a construction worker, was killed when he was struck by a concrete mixer truck. A fellow worker stated, somewhere between 15 and 45 minutes after the occurrence, that decedent had "backed into" the truck, a statement that supported defendant's contention that the decedent was contributorily negligent. The court expressed doubt that the statement could qualify under Rule 803(1), given the time span, but held the statement admissible as an excited utterance under Rule 803(2). Courts have not, however, required precise contemporaneity. See, e.g., Miller v. Crown Amusements, Inc., 821 F.Supp. 703, 706–07 (S.D.Ga.1993) (call made "in all likelihood, less than 10 minutes after the incident" received as present sense impression). A statement that involves the operation of memory is not admissible. See United States v. Hamilton, 948 F.Supp. 635, 639 (W.D.Ky.1996) (because it requires memory of what was previously seen, a photographic identification does not satisfy the exception). See generally McFarland, Present Sense Impressions Cannot Live in the Past, 28 Fla.St.L.Rev. 907 (2001).

2. *Subject matter.* The exception for present sense impressions ("statement describing or explaining an event or condition") is also more limited than the excited utterance exception ("statement relating to" an event or condition) in terms of the subject matter of the statement. As with the temporal element, the distinction between the two exceptions is based upon the theory that spontaneity has a more limited reach with regard to the statement's subject matter because the statement is not produced by an exciting event. 2 McCormick, Evidence § 271 (7th ed. 2013).

3. *Expanding opportunities for immediate statement through "e-hearsay."* Although the original formulation of the present sense impression assumed an oral communication, the expansion of modern forms of communication have multiplied the opportunities for immediate communication and preservation of hearsay assertions under this exception through computers and smartphones by e-mailing, tweeting, and texting. Commentators have noted that these technological developments that allow and social trends that encourage constant connection and communication are likely to increase the potential use of the present sense impressions in litigation. See Bellin, Facebook, Twitter, and the Uncertain Future of Present Sense Impressions, 160 U.Pa.L.Rev. 331, 332–35 (2012); Richter, Don't Just Do Something: E–Hearsay, the Present Sense Impression, and the Case for Caution in the Rulemaking Process, 61 Am.U.L.Rev. 1657, 1668–69 (2012).

4. *Corroboration.* Some commentators have argued that an additional requirement of the present sense exception is corroboration through the testimony of the declarant or another witness who perceived the events. See Bellin, Facebook, Twitter, and the Uncertain Future of Present Sense

Impressions, 160 U. Pa.L.Rev. 331, 370–72 (2012); Waltz, The Present Sense Impression Exception to the Rule Against Hearsay: Origins and Attributes, 66 Iowa L.Rev. 869 (1981). See also United States v. Blakey, 607 F.2d 779, 785 (7th Cir.1979) (noting the argument that corroboration is required). Despite these arguments, courts have not embraced a corroboration requirement for this exception. See United States v. Ruiz, 249 F.3d 643, 647 (7th Cir.2001); 2 McCormick, Evidence § 271 (7th ed. 2013).

MILLER V. KEATING

United States Court of Appeals, Third Circuit, 1985.
754 F.2d 507.

STERN, DISTRICT JUDGE:

The district court admitted into evidence a statement, made by an unidentified declarant at the scene of an automobile accident, amounting to an accusation that the accident was the fault of plaintiff Carol Miller. The district judge admitted the statement as *"res gestae,"* without making reference to any of the hearsay exceptions in Fed.R.Evid. 803, or any findings of fact on the issue of admissibility. Fed.R.Evid. 104(a). We conclude that the district judge erred.

I.

On January 18, 1982, Carol Miller was driving her white Ford LTD east on U.S. Route 22, a limited access highway, near Easton, Pennsylvania. She carried a passenger named Annette Vay. It is undisputed that Miller and Vay were traveling behind a UPS truck and that both vehicles switched into the lefthand lane to avoid a stalled vehicle in the righthand lane near the 25th Street exit ramp. It is also undisputed that, soon thereafter, the Miller car was struck from behind by defendant Texaco's tractor-trailer driven by co-defendant Lawrence Keating. The force of the collision propelled the Miller car first into the side of a car stopped in the righthand lane and then into the rear of the UPS truck. Mrs. Miller sustained serious injuries in the collision. The driver of the car stopped in the righthand lane was Kenneth Parris. His wife, Elfriede Parris, was a passenger.

One dispute at trial was over the amount of time that elapsed between the moment when Mrs. Miller pulled into the lefthand lane and the moment when her car was struck from the rear. Another conflict focused on whether the Miller car was stopped behind the UPS truck or was still moving when it was hit by the Texaco tractor-trailer.

Both Mrs. Miller and her passenger, Annette Vay, testified at trial that Miller had completely stopped her car before being rammed by the Texaco truck. According to Vay, the Miller car was stopped in the lefthand lane for "a few seconds" before the accident. Later, she testified that the time period could have been longer than "a second or two."

Lawrence Keating testified, however, that he was driving his Texaco tractor-trailer in the lefthand lane, slowing down in order to stop, and there was no vehicle between him and the UPS truck. He testified that he never saw the Miller car pull in front of him, and the first time he saw it was when it was in his lane. He said he saw only a "white blur" half or three-quarters of the way into his lane. He claimed that by the time he saw the Miller car in his lane, he was too close to it to avoid the collision.

There were other inconsistencies at trial of less relevance to the issue here, but several deserve mention because they illustrate the profusion of accounts before the jury. Mrs. Vay, who testified at length at the trial, had previously told police officer Young that she could not tell him what had happened, "[t]hat she did not know." The Parrises, who were stopped in the right lane, both testified that the Texaco truck had come to a full stop in the left lane behind the Parris car (and two car lengths behind the UPS truck, according to Mr. Parris), before the Miller car pulled in front of it. However, both Keating and the UPS driver, Neil Rasmussen, Jr., who was watching out of his side view mirror, depicted the Texaco truck as moving continuously toward the rear of the UPS truck. The UPS driver said, "it looked like I had better give Mr. Texaco all of the room he can have, you know, for stopping." And Keating said he was making "a gradual rolling stop."

There is also a dispute as to when the Parris car arrived alongside the Miller car. Vay and Miller both testified that the Parris car pulled up next to the Miller car during the few seconds it was stopped before being rammed by the Texaco truck. But the Parrises testified that they were stopped in the right lane for "several minutes" or "two minutes" before the accident.

It is the testimony of the Parrises about an incident occurring after the accident that gives rise to this appeal. After being hit in the left side, Mr. Parris pulled his car over. He testified that he left his car, comforted one of the victims in the Miller car, then walked to the rear of the Miller car where his wife was writing down the license plate number of the Miller car. At that point, a man approached and said, "the bastard tried to cut in." In somewhat inconsistent testimony, Mrs. Parris stated that she and her husband "were running towards the car, and I heard this person that was driving—running towards us—* * * [a]nd said the s.o.b. or some words like that, tried to cut in." Mr. Parris could not identify the declarant beyond saying that he was a white male. Mrs. Parris could do no better. There is no indication in the record why she thought the declarant was a driver or which vehicle he drove. Mr. Parris testified that he did not know what vehicle the declarant was driving.

Over objections, the trial judge allowed the Parrises to relate their versions of the declaration to the jury. He admitted the statements as "*res gestae.*" Parenthetically, we note that this terminology is inappropriate. As the trial judge implicitly recognized in his opinion denying post-trial relief, there is no such exception to the prohibition against hearsay. If admissible, the declaration must qualify under one of the genuine exceptions to the hearsay rule. The old catchall, *"res gestae,"* is no longer part of the law of evidence.[2]

As the trial judge also recognized, the excited utterance exception of Fed.R.Evid. 803(2) provides the most likely basis for admitting the statement. The question before us, therefore, is whether that statement by the unknown declarant should have been admitted under Fed.R.Evid. 803(2), which defines "excited utterance" as "[a] statement relating to a startling event or condition made while the declarant was under the stress of excitement caused by the event or condition."

II.

A.

[The court determined that admission of the statement was not harmless error because in] the thicket of conflicting accounts of the accident, the jurors may well have relied heavily on this apparent assignment of blame, made by an unknown person who was not under a duty to speak truthfully and who can never be confronted about his statement.

B.

The next question is whether the excited utterance exception may ever authorize the admission of a statement by an anonymous declarant. Fed.R.Evid. 806 provides that whenever a hearsay statement is admitted, the declarant's credibility may be attacked through cross-examination and the introduction of evidence of inconsistent statements. The rule confers no absolute right to cross-examination, because hearsay statements may often be admitted despite the unavailability of the declarant. For example, Fed.R.Evid. 804 defines various situations where hearsay testimony comes in even though the declarant is unavailable. Among these are dying declarations, former testimony, and declarations against interest. The unifying trait of all the Rule 803 exceptions is a circumstantial guarantee of trustworthiness sufficient to justify nonproduction of the declarant, whether available or not.[3] Although Rule

---

2   As Wigmore notes, "res gestae" means literally "the thing done" and properly applies only to words that accompany and aid in giving legal significance to the act. Such words are treated as "verbal acts." Before adoption of the Federal Rules of Evidence, courts applied "res gestae" with much confusion to hearsay statements of various sorts. 6 J. Wigmore, Evidence § 1745 (J. Chadbourn rev. 1976).

3   "The present rule proceeds upon the theory that under appropriate circumstances a hearsay statement may possess circumstantial guarantees of trustworthiness sufficient to justify nonproduction of the declarant at trial even though he may be available. The theory finds vast support in the many exceptions to the hearsay rule developed by the common law in which unavailability of the declarant is not a factor." Fed.R.Evid. 803 advisory committee note.

806 cannot be read to confer a right to any particular form of attack on the credibility of a hearsay declarant, it does confer a generalized right that is significantly diminished when the hearsay declarant is not only unavailable, but is also unidentified, and the party against whom the hearsay declarant's statement is introduced is thus deprived not only of the right to cross-examine, but of any meaningful prospect of finding evidence of inconsistency or bias.

We do not conclude, however, that statements by unidentified declarants are ipso facto inadmissible under Fed.R.Evid. 803(2). Such statements are admissible if they otherwise meet the criteria of 803(2). But unlike unavailability, which is immaterial to admission under Rule 803, the unidentifiability of the declarant is germane to the admissibility determination. A party seeking to introduce such a statement carries a burden heavier than where the declarant is identified to demonstrate the statement's circumstantial trustworthiness.

At minimum, when the declarant of an excited utterance is unidentified, it becomes more difficult to satisfy the established case law requirements for admission of a statement under Fed.R.Evid. 803(2). Wigmore defines these requirements as: (1) a startling occasion, (2) a statement relating to the circumstances of the startling occasion, (3) a declarant who appears to have had opportunity to observe personally the events, and (4) a statement made before there has been time to reflect and fabricate. 6 J. Wigmore, *Evidence* §§ 1750–51 (J. Chadbourn rev. 1976). *See* Fed.R.Evid. 803 advisory committee note; S. Saltzburg & K. Redden, *Federal Rules of Evidence Manual* 574–75 (3d ed. 1982); J. Weinstein, *Evidence* ¶ 803(2)[01] (1984). There is no doubt that the present case presents a startling occasion and little doubt that the declarant's statement relates to the circumstances of the occurrence. Partly because the declarant is unidentified, however, problems arise with the last two requirements: personal knowledge and spontaneity.

The first of these expresses the familiar principle that a witness may not testify about a subject without personal knowledge. Fed.R.Evid. 602. This rule applies with equal force to hearsay statements. *Kornicki v. Calmar Steamship Corporation,* 460 F.2d 1134, 1138 (3d Cir.1972). To be admissible, the declarant of an excited utterance must personally observe the startling event. *McLaughlin v. Vinzant,* 522 F.2d 448, 451 (1st Cir.1975). The burden of establishing perception rests with the proponent of the evidence. *David v. Pueblo Supermarkets of St. Thomas, Inc.,* 740 F.2d 230, 235 (3d Cir.1984). As in all questions of admissibility, the resolution of any dispute of fact necessary to the question is confided to the trial judge to be decided by a preponderance of the evidence. And while the trial judge is not confined to legally admissible evidence in making the determination, Fed.R.Evid. 104(a), still he must make the findings necessary to support admissibility.

Direct proof of perception, or proof that forecloses all speculation is not required. On the other hand, circumstantial evidence of the declarant's personal perception must not be so scanty as to forfeit the "guarantees of trustworthiness" which form the hallmark of all exceptions to the hearsay rule. Fed.R.Evid. 803 advisory committee note. When there is no evidence of personal perception, apart from the declaration itself, courts have hesitated to allow the excited utterance to stand alone as evidence of the declarant's opportunity to observe. *Garrett v. Howden,* 73 N.M. 307, 387 P.2d 874, 876–78 (1963); *Beck v. Dye,* 200 Wash. 1, 92 P.2d 1113, 1117 (1939). In some cases, however, the substance of the statement itself does contain words revealing perception. A statement such as, "I saw that blue truck run down the lady on the corner," might stand alone to show perception if the trial judge finds, from the particular circumstances, that he is satisfied by a preponderance that the declarant spoke from personal perception. * * *

In the present case, however, the record is empty of any circumstances from which the trial court could have inferred, by a preponderance, that the declarant saw Miller "cut in." The disputed declaration itself does not proclaim it. Indeed, the district judge acknowledged as much in his opinion denying plaintiffs' motion for a new trial. Nevertheless, he drew an inference of perception, reasoning that "the declarant would have made the declaration only if he was in a position to observe the collision." Yet the statements reported by the Parrises—"the bastard tried to cut in" and "the s.o.b., or some words like that, tried to cut in"—alone, do not show more likely than not that the declarant saw the event. The declarant might have been drawing a conclusion on the basis of what he saw as he approached the scene of the accident. He might have been hypothesizing or repeating what someone else had said. It is even possible that the declarant was talking about some other driver who had just cut in front of him. It is far from unlikely that the declarant was a participant in the accident, for the Parrises could never identify or exclude anyone as the speaker. And the tenor of the declaration, i.e., "the bastard tried to cut in," suggests at least the possibility that the declarant was a participant with a natural degree of bias. The self-serving exclamation by a participant in an auto accident "it was the other guy's fault," is hardly likely to qualify as trustworthy.

The circumstances external to the statement itself not only fail to demonstrate that the declarant was in a position to have seen what happened, they also fail to show that the declarant was excited when he spoke. No one so testified, and the trial judge made no finding of excitement. Thus, this last prong of the test for admissibility is also unsatisfied. The assumption underlying the hearsay exception of Rule 803(2) is that a person under the sway of excitement temporarily loses the capacity of reflection and thus produces statements free of fabrication.

See, e.g., Kornicki, 460 F.2d at 1138; *see also* 6 J. Wigmore *Evidence* § 1747 (Chadbourn rev. 1976). Since lack of capacity to fabricate is the justification for excited utterances, courts have recognized that the length of time separating the event from the statement may be considerably longer than for statements qualifying under the present sense impression exception of Rule 803(1), which is based on the lack of time to fabricate. *See* J. Weinstein, *Evidence* ¶ 803(2)[01] (1984). In *McCurdy v. Greyhound Corporation,* 346 F.2d 224, 226 (3d Cir.1965), for example, this Court approved admission of a statement made ten or fifteen minutes after an accident, recognizing that there can be no arbitrary time limits on the operation of Rule 803(2). Thus, even if several minutes elapsed between the exciting event and the utterance, it is not necessarily an abuse of discretion to admit the statement so long as the trial court explicitly finds it was not the product of conscious reflection. There is no such finding in this case.

We have considered appellants' other contentions and find them to be without merit. The judgment of the district court will be reversed and the case remanded for a new trial.

NOTES AND QUESTIONS

1. *Spontaneity.* Numerous criteria have been suggested as bearing upon the spontaneity of the utterance: lapse of time, place, content of the utterance, physical or mental condition of the declarant, whether made in response to an inquiry, and presence or absence of a motive to fabricate. See, e.g., Haywood v. State, 24 So. 3d 17, 30 (Fla.2009) (considering physical and emotional condition following devastating injuries to establish the declarant was still under the effect of startling event despite passage of time); State v. Delos Santos, 238 P.3d 162, 168–75 (Haw.2010) (admitting initial statement made by victim of violent domestic assault within a few minutes of event despite being in response to police officer's question but excluding subsequent extended narrative to the same officer because it summarized events and suggested reflective thought). Spontaneity is a preliminary question of fact for the trial judge, and the number of factors to be considered necessarily vests the judge with considerable discretion. 2 McCormick, Evidence § 272 (7th ed. 2013).

2. *Time requirement, children.* Where children are involved, a number of courts have liberally interpreted the allowable period of time between the exciting event and the child's description of it. See State v. Smith, 337 S.E.2d 833, 841–43 (N.C.1985). The theory is that the psychological characteristics of young children tend, as a general matter, to extend the period that is free of the dangers of conscious fabrication. *Smith,* 337 S.E.2d at 842; State v. Padilla, 329 N.W.2d 263, 266 (Wis.Ct.App.1982). In Morgan v. Foretich, 846 F.2d 941, 947 (4th Cir.1988), the court developed a new theory for further expansion of the time limitation for statements involving children. It looked, not to the time lapse since the abuse, but to the time lapse from the child's

first opportunity to report it. See Frye v. State, 313 S.W.3d 10, 14 (Ark.2009) (admitting statement made within 24 hours of a rape and likely the first real opportunity to report the event). Occasionally, courts generally question this broad expansion of exception to children, see Reed v. Thalacker, 198 F.3d 1058, 1062 (8th Cir.1999), or as applied to older children, see United States v. Marrowbone, 211 F.3d 452, 455 (8th Cir.2000), but the general pattern is expansive, see United States v. Hefferon, 314 F.3d 211, 222–23 (5th Cir.2002).

Approximately half of the states have enacted specific hearsay exceptions covering the statements of child-victims) Mosteller, Remaking Confrontation Clause and Hearsay Doctrine under the Challenge of Child Sexual Abuse Prosecutions, 1993 Ill.L.Rev. 691, 697. In State v. Myatt, 697 P.2d 836 (Kan.1985), the Supreme Court of Kansas noted that without a separate exception for statements by children, some courts had stretched the limits of existing hearsay exceptions, particularly the time limitation of the excited utterance exception, and had thereby undercut the certainty and integrity of the excited utterance exception. Id. at 842.

3.   *Independent evidence.* In *Miller,* the occurrence of a startling event was established independently of the statements by other witnesses. If this evidence had not been introduced, could the occurrence of a startling event be proved by the utterance of the witness alone? (Similarly, under Rule 803(1), does there need to be any proof beyond the statement that the described event in fact occurred?) Prior to the adoption of the Federal Rules of Evidence, there was considerable theoretical debate on this issue. See Slough, Res Gestae, 2 Kan.L.Rev. 41, 253–56 (1954) (noting the dangers to the hearsay rule in abolition of all corroboration requirements but recognizing that a substantial number of cases, particularly those involving workmen's compensation, admit excited utterances when the only evidence of the happening of the event is the utterance). Under Rule 104(a), contested evidence itself may be considered by the court in ruling upon admissibility. Bourjaily v. United States, 483 U.S. 171 (1987). Accordingly, the theoretical question of admissibility of the statement to prove the event has been resolved. Is the statement standing alone sufficient proof? "Under generally prevailing practice, the statement itself is taken as sufficient proof of the exciting event." 2 McCormick, Evidence § 272 (7th ed. 2013). See also United States v. Brown, 254 F.3d 454, 459–60 (3d Cir.2001).

A similar question is presented as to whether the words of the statement such as "I saw" are by themselves sufficient to prove the declarant's observation of the event. As *Miller* suggests, it will often be found adequate. Cf. State v. Phillips, 461 S.E.2d 75, 84 (W.Va.1995) (sufficiently descriptive statement may prove knowledge under identical requirements of Rule 803(1)).

4.   *Subject matter requirement.* The utterance must relate to the startling event. This terminology covers more than merely a description or explanation of the event, and courts have construed it quite liberally. 2

McCormick, Evidence § 272 (7th ed. 2013). See United States v. Moore, 791 F.2d 566, 572 (7th Cir.1986) (statements reflecting past events admissible under the exception if the subject matter likely evoked by the event). See also Murphy Auto Parts Co. v. Ball, 249 F.2d 508 (D.C.Cir.1957) (admitting a statement of agency by a driver following a collision, the court suggesting that whether the statement goes beyond a description of the exciting occurrence is merely another factor to be weighed in determining the existence of spontaneity).

5. *Unidentified declarant.* Excited utterances are not generally excluded because the declarant was a bystander rather than a participant. The declarant only has to be affected by the event, not involved in it. In most cases, the identity of the bystander is known, and he or she is often a witness at trial. As demonstrated in *Miller,* when the witness' identity is unknown, the cases show more reluctance to admit the declaration. See also State v. Harris, 531 S.E.2d 340, 345–46 (W.Va.2000) (court should ordinarily conclude statement does not satisfy requirements of rule in criminal case). But cf. Miller v. Crown Amusements, Inc., 821 F.Supp. 703 (S.D.Ga.1993) (statement by unidentified caller to 911 regarding accident admissible under similar requirements of Rule 803(1) where circumstantial evidence and content of call provided basis to satisfy requirements).

6. *Competency requirement.* Some courts find that for children excitement, which theoretically eliminates the concern about fabrication, also eliminates competency concerns related to truthfulness. See Morgan v. Foretich, 846 F.2d 941, 946–47 (4th Cir.1988) (nature of the utterance obviates the usual sources of untrustworthiness); State v. Bingham, 776 P.2d 424, 431 (Idaho 1989) (same). However, this logic should not apply to other sources of incompetency related to youthfulness.

7. *Other hearsay dangers ignored.* Excited utterances are received against a hearsay objection on the basis that the excitement temporarily reduces the capacity for reflection and thereby eliminates the danger of conscious fabrication. Long ago Hutchins and Slesinger pointed out the tendency of emotional stress, on the other hand, to increase another of the hearsay dangers by impairing the accuracy of perception. Some Observations on the Law of Evidence—Spontaneous Exclamations, 28 Colum.L.Rev. 432 (1928). Why should an exception be recognized where one hearsay danger is increased by the operation of the same factor that reduces another danger? In terms of Professor Tribe's hearsay triangle, is it more important to strengthen the left leg or may a hearsay exception rest on the presence of one strong leg, no matter which one it is?

8. *Sources.* Miller, A Shock to the System: Analyzing the Conflict Among Courts Over Whether and When Excited Utterances May Follow Subsequent Startling Events in Rape and Sexual Assault Cases, 12 Wm. & Mary J.Women & L. 49 (2005); Orenstein, "My God!": A Feminist Critique of the Excited Utterance Exception to the Hearsay Rule, 85 Cal.L.Rev. 159 (1997).

B. EXISTING MENTAL, EMOTIONAL, OR PHYSICAL CONDITION

Federal Rule 803(3)

WILKINSON V. SERVICE

Supreme Court of Illinois, 1911.
94 N.E. 50.

MR. JUSTICE CARTER delivered the opinion of the court:

Plaintiff in error, Carrie E. Wilkinson, filed her bill in the superior court of Cook county to set aside the will of her father, Charles D. Hews, on the ground that he was not of sound mind and memory when it was executed. A trial before a jury resulted in a verdict that the writing was the last will and testament of the testator, made while he was of sound mind and memory. A decree to that effect was thereafter entered and the bill dismissed for want of equity. From that decree this writ of error is sued out.

Charles D. Hews was a physician and resided and practiced in Chicago for many years. The plaintiff in error was his daughter and only child. At the time of the trial she had been married for some years and resided in St. Paul. By his will, dated March 23, 1909, Hews gave his small amount of household furniture and surgical and medical material to Dr. James W. Kelly, an intimate personal friend, and the remainder of his property, substantially all real estate, estimated by different witnesses to be worth from $8,000 to $12,000, to his sister, Mary J. Service, one of the defendants in error. The plaintiff in error received nothing under the will.
* * *

It is further insisted that portions of the evidence of this witness [the lawyer who drew the will] as to conversations with testator were inadmissible on the ground that they were hearsay, especially the statement of the testator that plaintiff in error's husband had written a letter in which he had directed the doctor not to communicate with the daughter in any way, the letter further stating that the testator had never treated his daughter right, and that when she wanted his assistance he was spending his money on whisky and fast women. The letter was also introduced in evidence. The rule is well established in this State that the declarations of the testator are competent, in a contest involving the validity of his will, to show the state of his mind but not to prove the facts stated. * * * Whatever is material to prove the state of a person's mind or what is passing in it, and what were his intentions, may be shown by his declarations and statements. The truth or falsity of such statements is of no consequence. They are to be used only as showing the condition of his mind. Declarations, prior to the execution of the will, that certain of the testator's children were wanting in natural affection are properly considered as showing his state of mind. * * * The testimony as to the doctor's feeling towards his daughter, and the causes for it, was properly admitted to show the condition of his mind at the time the will was executed. This evidence, taken in connection with the fact that he had several years before drawn two other wills, one giving his daughter $50 and the other $5, and also in connection with other declarations that he had given his divorced wife (the plaintiff in error's mother) quite an amount of property which she could give to plaintiff in error, was properly admitted as tending to show his reasons for disposing of his property as he did, under the will here in question.

* * *

Decree affirmed.

NOTES AND QUESTIONS

1. *Significance of indirect statement?* For the purpose of classification as hearsay, would it make any practical difference whether the testator's statement was, "My daughter does not love me," or "I believe that my daughter does not love me"? From the point of view of being classed as hearsay, is there any difference between the testimony of the lawyer about what the testator told him about the letter and the letter itself?

2. *Emotional condition v. its cause(s).* The principle that the mental or emotional condition of a person may be proved by his or her contemporaneous declarations is firmly established. Further illustration may be found in the alienation of affections cases. Declarations of the alienated spouse are inadmissible hearsay for the purpose of proving the actions of the defendant that are claimed to have resulted in alienation, but they are admissible to prove the state of mind of the alienated spouse before the separation, the effect produced on the alienated spouse, and the reason why the alienated spouse left. Adkins v. Brett, 193 P. 251 (Cal.1920); Glatstein v. Grund, 51 N.W.2d 162 (Iowa 1952).

3. *Alternative forms of expression.* Hinton, States of Mind and the Hearsay Rule, 1 U.Chi.L.Rev. 394 (1934), lists many states of mind and emotion and suggests various possible means of proving their existence: testimony of the person, proof of events conducive to the state, nonverbal conduct (kicking the cat), an assertive statement not offered to prove the truth of the matter asserted ("I am Napoleon" in a competency case), or an assertive statement of an existing state. Consider whether each of the above types of evidence is hearsay, and, if hearsay, whether it comes within the instant exception. See also Hutchins & Slesinger, Some Observations on the Law of Evidence: State of Mind in Issue, 29 Colum.L.Rev. 147 (1929).

4. *Complexity through inferences.* In most cases, rather than being directly relevant, a party is seeking to draw an inference from the existence of the state of mind. The inferences to be drawn increase in complexity in the

following cases. See generally Weissenberger, Hearsay Puzzles: An Essay on Federal Evidence Rule 803(3), 64 Temp.L.Rev. 145 (1991).

MUTUAL LIFE INS. CO. V. HILLMON

Supreme Court of the United States, 1892.
145 U.S. 285.

[Liability under policies insuring the life of Hillmon depended upon whether he was in fact dead. Plaintiff claimed that Hillmon was shot accidentally at Crooked Creek, about 175 miles west of Wichita, on March 18. The insurance companies contended that the person killed at Crooked Creek was one Walters, that Hillmon was still alive, and that he and others were engaged in a fraudulent conspiracy. Evidence as to the identity of the body was conflicting. The trial court excluded evidence offered by the insurance companies, consisting of letters written by Walters to his sister and to his fiancée stating that he planned to leave Wichita early in March for Colorado with Hillmon. Defendant insurance companies appeal from judgments rendered on verdicts against them.]

MR. JUSTICE GRAY.

* * *

Much conflicting evidence had been introduced as to the identity of the body. The plaintiff had also introduced evidence that Hillmon and one Brown left Wichita in Kansas on or about March 5, 1879, and travelled together through Southern Kansas in search of a site for a cattle ranch, and that on the night of March 18, while they were in camp at Crooked Creek, Hillmon was accidentally killed, and that his body was taken thence and buried. The defendants had introduced evidence, without objection, that Walters left his home and his betrothed in Iowa in March, 1878, and was afterwards in Kansas until March, 1879; that during that time he corresponded regularly with his family and his betrothed; that the last letters received from him were one received by his betrothed on March 3 and postmarked at Wichita March 2, and one received by his sister about March 4 or 5, and dated at Wichita a day or two before; and that he had not been heard from since.

The evidence that Walters was at Wichita on or before March 5, and had not been heard from since, together with the evidence to identify as his the body found at Crooked Creek on March 18, tended to show that he went from Wichita to Crooked Creek between those dates. Evidence that just before March 5 he had the intention of leaving Wichita with Hillmon would tend to corroborate the evidence already admitted, and to show that he went from Wichita to Crooked Creek with Hillmon. Letters from him to his family and his betrothed were the natural, if not the only attainable, evidence of his intention.

* * * A man's state of mind or feeling can only be manifested to others by countenance, attitude or gesture, or by sounds or words, spoken or written. The nature of the fact to be proved is the same, and evidence of its proper tokens is equally competent to prove it, whether expressed by aspect or conduct, by voice or pen. When the intention to be proved is important only as qualifying an act, its connection with that act must be shown, in order to warrant the admission of declarations of the intention. But whenever the intention is of itself a distinct and material fact in a chain of circumstances, it may be proved by contemporaneous oral or written declarations of the party.

The existence of a particular intention in a certain person at a certain time being a material fact to be proved, evidence that he expressed that intention at that time is as direct evidence of the fact, as his own testimony that he then had that intention would be. After his death there can hardly be any other way of proving it; and while he is still alive, his own memory of his state of mind at a former time is no more likely to be clear and true than a bystander's recollection of what he then said, and is less trustworthy than letters written by him at the very time and under circumstances precluding a suspicion of misrepresentation.

The letters in question were competent, not as narratives of facts communicated to the writer by others, nor yet as proof that he actually went away from Wichita, but as evidence that, shortly before the time when other evidence tended to show that he went away, he had the intention of going, and of going with Hillmon, which made it more probable both that he did go and that he went with Hillmon, than if there had been no proof of such intention. In view of the mass of conflicting testimony introduced upon the question whether it was the body of Walters that was found in Hillmon's camp, this evidence might properly influence the jury in determining that question. * * *

Upon principle and authority, therefore, we are of opinion that the two letters were competent evidence of the intention of Walters at the time of writing them, which was a material fact bearing upon the question in controversy; and that for the exclusion of these letters, as well as for the undue restriction of the defendants' challenges, the verdicts must be set aside, and a new trial had. * * *

Judgment reversed, and case remanded to the Circuit Court, with directions to set aside the verdict and to order a new trial.

NOTES AND QUESTIONS

1.   *Threats.* The authorities cited by the Court to support its decision have been omitted for brevity. Strangely enough, none of these authorities involves the admissibility of evidence of threats by an accused to prove that the acts threaten were taken, which involves a similar use of state of mind

and whose admissibility has never been doubted. 1A Wigmore, Evidence § 105 (Tillers rev. 1983); 6 Wigmore, Evidence § 1732 (Chadbourn rev. 1976). Similarly, to support a claim of self-defense in a homicide case, evidence is admissible that the victim made threats against the accused, although the accused had no knowledge of them. 1A Wigmore, Evidence § 110 (Tillers rev. 1983). It should be noted that a quite distinct theory—impact on the hearer that renders the statement nonhearsay because not offered for the truth of the matter asserted under Rule 801(c)(2)—supports the admission of threats actually communicated by the victim to the accused.

2. *Relevancy v. hearsay.* Once the soundness of establishing mental state by contemporaneous declarations is conceded, the next step in a *Hillmon* situation is relatively simple. As a matter of relevancy, the conclusion is difficult to escape that a person who intends to do an act is more likely to do so than one who has no such intent. 2 McCormick, Evidence § 275 (7th ed. 2013). While objections are often noted concerning the strength of such evidence given the possibility of intervening circumstances or changed intentions, these are more appropriately considered as issues involving relevancy rather than hearsay. See Lempert et al., A Modern Approach to Evidence 618 (4th ed. 2011). The hazard of giving the inference too great an effect is a real one. See United States v. Moore, 571 F.2d 76 (2d Cir.1978) (evidence of a statement by one of the defendants that kidnap victim would be taken out of the state held insufficient to prove interstate transportation).

3. *Dangers in backward-looking hearsay.* If a person's mental state in the form of a statement of intention to do an act in the future is admissible to prove the subsequent doing of an act, why should not the declarant's state of mind in the form of memory be admissible as evidence of the happening of the event? Are statements that a person intends to take action more reliable than statements that he or she has done so? Which is subject to greater hearsay dangers?

In general, while the *Hillmon* doctrine has permitted the use of state of mind to prove the declarant's future conduct, the proposition that a declaration of state of mind may be used to prove the happening of a prior act has been rejected, particularly the prior act of another person. One reason for this result is practical. In Shepard v. United States, 290 U.S. 96 (1933), the Supreme Court ruled inadmissible the statement of Mrs. Shepard that "Dr. Shepard has poisoned me" offered by the government under the state of mind exception. It noted, "[d]eclarations of intention, casting light upon the future, have been sharply distinguished from declarations of memory, pointing backwards to the past. There would be an end, or nearly that, to the rule against hearsay if the distinction were ignored." Id. at 105–06. The theoretical distinction is that when statements relate to an intention of the declarant to do a future act, the hearsay dangers of faulty memory and misperception are eliminated. In terms of Professor Tribe's hearsay triangle, the dangers located on the right leg are eliminated. Lempert et al., A Modern Approach to Evidence 618 (4th ed. 2011). Rule 803(3) writes this limitation into the text of the Rule through the provision "not including a statement of memory or belief to prove the fact remembered or believed."

4. *A piece of history.* A rich literature on the *Hillmon* case has developed. See Hutchins & Slesinger, Some Observations on the Law of Evidence—State of Mind to Prove an Act, 38 Yale L.J. 283 (1929); Maguire, The *Hillmon* Case—Thirty-three Years After, 38 Harv.L.Rev. 709 (1925); Payne, The *Hillmon* Case—An Old Problem Revisited, 41 Va.L.Rev. 1011 (1955); McFarland, Dead Men Tell Tales: Thirty Times Three Years of the Judicial Process After *Hillmon,* 30 Vill.L.Rev. 1 (1985); Wesson, The *Hillmon* Case, The Supreme Court, and The McGuffin, in Evidence Stories 277 (Lempert ed., 2006).

UNITED STATES V. DAY

United States Court of Appeals, District of Columbia Circuit, 1978.
591 F.2d 861.

["Beanny" Day and Eric Sheffey were indicted for the murder of Gregory Williams, who was killed by a shotgun blast fired from a person inside a parked car. Prior to trial, the district judge excluded proposed testimony by Mason, a government witness, that Williams, a few minutes before he was killed, gave Mason a slip of paper on which he had written "Beanny, Eric 635–3135" and told Mason "if he [Williams] wasn't back home by three the next day to call the police and tell them what he had told me and give them the number." The ruling also excluded testimony by Mason that at the same time Williams told him that Williams and "Beanny" had a fight over [stolen] guns and coats and that "Beanny" and "his boy" were trying to "get out on him." The government appealed.[4]]

MACKINNON, CIRCUIT JUDGE

* * *

We turn first to the Government's contention in their brief and at oral argument that the following testimony should be admitted: * * * the contemporaneous statement that if he (Williams) was not home by 3:00 o'clock the next day, Mason should call the police, tell them what he had said, and give them the number.

The Government, in arguing this point, does not seek to have admitted the content of "what he (Williams) had said," concerning the statements made prior to giving Mason the slip of paper about the fight and the dispute between him and Day, the robbery, and the location of the guns.

---

[4]   [A federal statute, 18 U.S.C.A. § 3731, allowed the prosecution to appeal before trial certain rulings excluding or suppressing evidence to avoid the bar that the Double Jeopardy Clause imposes on appeals by the government after acquittal. Ed.]

In arguing that the statement which immediately accompanied the delivery of the slip of paper is not hearsay, the Government states: "All that is sought to be proven in connection with the statement now under consideration, is that it was *in fact* made." Govt.Br. at 31 (emphasis in original). But in actuality, the Government seeks to have something more inferred from the content of the statement. The jury is being asked to infer from Williams' words that Day bore ill will toward Williams and had reason to cause him harm. Because this inference attaches to Williams' statement, the Government is seeking to use the statement for more than the mere fact that it was made.

The Government also contends that this statement is admissible as an utterance contemporaneous with a non-verbal act which relates to and elucidates that event, i.e., the giving of the piece of paper. Govt.Br. at 31 n.41. Professor Wigmore has described the limitations which attended the use of utterances forming the verbal part of an act. The first limitation is:

> [T]he conduct that is to be made definite must be independently material and provable under the issues, either as a fact directly in issue or as incidentally or evidentially relevant to the issue. The use of the words is wholly subsidiary and appurtenant to the use of the conduct. The former without the latter have no place in the case, and could only serve as a hearsay assertion in direct violation of the rule * * *.

VI Wigmore on Evidence, § 1773, at 268 (Chadbourn rev. 1976). In this case, the conduct to be made definite is that Williams gave Mason a slip of paper. Had Williams said "take this slip," that utterance would have been "wholly subsidiary and appurtenant" to the conduct. Here, Williams said more, and the inference from those words is not wholly incidental to the conduct. We conclude that the statement accompanying the delivery of the paper is inadmissible hearsay.

Our analysis does not end here, as Rule 803(3) provides an exception for evidence of state of mind. That rule provides: * * *

> (3) Then existing mental, emotional, or physical condition. A statement of the declarant's then existing *state of mind,* emotion, sensation, or physical condition (such as intent, plan, motive, design, *mental feeling,* pain, and bodily health), but not including a statement of memory or belief to prove the fact remembered or believed unless it relates to the execution, revocation, identification, or terms of declarant's will. [Emphasis added.]

We briefly summarized the purpose of the exception in United States v. Brown, 160 U.S.App.D.C. 190, 490 F.2d 758 (1973):

> [T]he state of mind exception to the hearsay rule allows the admission of extrajudicial statements to show the state of mind

of the declarant at that time *if that is the issue in the case.* * * *
It also allows such statements to show a future intent of the
declarant to perform an act if the occurrence of that act is at
issue.

160 U.S.App.D.C. at 194, 490 F.2d at 762 (emphasis added). We noted
that such statements invariably contain some extraneous factual
elements which necessitate limiting instructions to ensure that the
statements are considered solely on the issue of the declarant's mental
state and not for the truth of the matters contained therein. 160
U.S.App.D.C. at 195, 490 F.2d at 763. We also noted that whether such
evidence is admissible is subject to the rule of extrinsic policy, which is
now embodied in Rule 403:

> [*S*]*ome* evidence, while bearing some *logical* relevance to the
> case, may in the discretion of the judge nevertheless be excluded
> where its probative value is substantially outweighed by the
> danger of *unfair* prejudice, confusion or delay.

Id. (emphasis in original except "unfair").[5] While Williams' statements to
Mason are some indication of his state of mind, i.e., to fear of the future,
there is a danger that the jury would misuse such evidence. We described
the nature of the balancing process at length in *Brown,* supra, and we
need not restate that discussion here.

We think that the inference to be drawn from Williams' statement to
Mason which accompanied his handing over of the slip of paper, involving
as it did somewhat of a prophecy of what might happen to him, has too
great a potential for *unfair* prejudice, and we do not think that a limiting
instruction can correct that deficiency. As was the case in *Brown,* the
prejudicial dangers in the statement in question are substantial. Had
Williams referred to prior harmful acts or threats by Day, such
statements would be even more unfairly prejudicial, but even here "a
palpable danger exists" that the jury will infer from the statement, "if
anything happens to me, call the police and give them the names on this
slip [i.e., Day and Sheffey]," that Day and Sheffey were capable of
murder, or that they had done things in the past to justify Williams'
apprehension. Such inferences insofar as they reflect on defendants'

---

[5] We elaborated upon these dangers later in the opinion:

Quite a number of courts have confronted facts similar to those here involving hearsay
statements made by the victim of a homicide which inferentially implicate the defendant.
Such statements by the victims often include previous threats made by the defendant
towards the victim, narrations of past incidents of violence on the part of the defendant or
general verbalizations of fear of the defendant. While such statements are admittedly of
some value in presenting to the jury a complete picture of all the facts and circumstances
surrounding the homicide, it is generally agreed that their admissibility must be determined
by a careful balancing of their probative value against their prejudicial effect. Courts have
recognized that such statements are fraught with inherent dangers and require the
imposition of rigid limitations.

160 U.S.App.D.C. at 197–98, 490 F.2d at 765–66.

intentions or past conduct would be improperly drawn. See 160 U.S.App.D.C. at 210, 490 F.2d at 778. In fact, on the present record, Williams' state of mind, from which such inferences would be drawn, is immaterial. Of course, the situation will be different if the defendant seeks to adduce evidence tending to show self-defense or accident. Under the present circumstances of this case, we find the proffered evidence in this regard to be inadmissible at the outset of the Government's case in chief, and we would doubt the efficacy of a limiting instruction.

[The court held that the slip of paper itself with the names and telephone number on it was admissible because it was not offered for its truth under Rule 801(c)(2). It likewise concluded that Mason could testify that sometime in the hour before the shooting Williams gave him the slip of paper. The act of handing over the paper, while potentially communicative, was not assertive of a crime and was therefore admissible.]

* * * The ruling of the district court excluding the testimony of Kerry Mason is affirmed in part and reversed in part, as set forth in this opinion.

Judgment accordingly.

SPOTTSWOOD W. ROBINSON, III, CIRCUIT JUDGE, dissenting in part:

* * *

I am in complete accord with the court's application of Judge MacKinnon's perceptive opinion in *Brown* to the bulk of the statements made by Williams to Mason. I cannot, however, reconcile *Brown* with admission of (a) the slip bearing appellees' names and a telephone number, (b) testimony by Mason that when Williams turned the slip over he made a statement or (c), evidence that Mason called the police after the shooting and gave them the information on the slip—when it is combined with the first two.

* * *

NOTES AND QUESTIONS

1. *Why relevant?* An obvious condition of the admission of statements showing directly or circumstantially the declarant's state of mind is that such state of mind be relevant to the issues in the litigation. The declarant's fear is rarely directly relevant. In certain fact patterns, it may be indirectly useful in showing the declarant's likely conduct, which *Hillmon* shows is generally a permissible use of the exception. United States v. Green, 680 F.2d 520, 523 (7th Cir.1982), provides an example. There the victim's statements showing fear of the defendant were relevant to help prove she did not accompany him voluntarily, which was relevant to proving a kidnapping charge. See also United States v. Adcock, 558 F.2d 397 (8th Cir.1977) (victim's fear crucial in

extortion cases). *Day* states that the admissibility decision would be "different if the defendant seeks to adduce evidence tending to show self-defense or accident." In those two situations, the declarant's fear of the defendant would be relevant to show that it was unlikely, given his fear, that he attacked the defendant and the defendant responded in self-defense or that he was, for example, inspecting the defendant's gun collection and accidentally shot himself with defendant's gun.

In *Day*, other than to show indirectly that the victim had reasons to fear the defendants and thereby to communicate indirectly the historical facts that gave rise to his fear, fear had no relevance. As discussed in the notes following the *Hillmon* case, Rule 803(3) prohibits use of statements admissible under Rule 803(3) to prove past facts. Therefore, statements of fear relevant only to prove those past facts are inadmissible. Furthermore, if the jury is not inferring the defendant's likely future conduct from those past facts as proved through the declarant's fear, fear should be inadmissible as speculative, unless clairvoyance is accepted. It is important to note that under other hearsay exceptions, such as Rules 803(2) (excited utterances) or 804(b)(2) (dying declarations) that rely on other theories of trustworthiness, statements may prove events and the actions of others in the past.

2.   *Fear and domestic violence.* Statements of fear of a domestic partner are often found in domestic violence cases and are generally excluded to prove the perpetrator's identity. See State v. Canaday, 911 P.2d 104, 111–12 (Haw.Ct.App.1996). See also Commonwealth v. Laich, 777 A.2d 1057, 1060–61 (Pa.2001) (victim's prior statements regarding "state of the relationship" not admissible to show defendant's intent). However, the victim's state of mind statements regarding fear might be admitted where probably known to the defendant and potentially provided motive. See State v. Calleia, 20 A.3d 402,410–16 (N.J.2011). In part in response to exclusion of a statement of this sort by Nicole Brown Simpson, California created a hearsay exception for statements of past threats made by presently unavailable declarants that are recorded in writing or electronically or made to medical personnel or police officers. See Cal.Evid. Code § 1370. Without the benefit of a special rule, the North Carolina Supreme Court has repeatedly admitted statements of fear and related statements by those who later became victims under Rule 803(3) to establish the actions and intent of the defendant in domestic assaults, frequently homicides. See, e.g., State v. Alston, 461 S.E.2d 687 (N.C.1995). That analysis has been sharply criticized as a matter of both relevancy and hearsay theory. See 2 McCormick, Evidence § 276 (7th ed. 2013).

3.   *Events rather than emotions.* In *Day,* the declarant's state of mind could be inferred from his statements of fact, and the issue was whether the likely misuse of those statements in spite of a limiting instruction required their exclusion under Rule 403. A similar problem also frequently encountered is that even when the declarant has made direct statements of his or her state of mind or emotion, those statements are accompanied by descriptions of the event that gave rise to those feelings. See Adkins v. Brett, 193 P. 251 (Cal.1920) (in alienation of affection case, wife's admissible

statements of feelings contained inadmissible statements concerning automobile rides, dinners, and gifts involving defendant). With the exception of statements related to the declarant's last will, where admission is based on practical rather than theoretical grounds, Federal Rule 803(3) excludes statements concerning the cause of the state of mind.

United States v. Cohen, 631 F.2d 1223 (5th Cir.1980), provides a typical example of the operation of this restriction. Cohen defended on the ground of duress in that his alleged coconspirator, Galkin, had forced him to cooperate in the illegal scheme. The court upheld the exclusion of testimony under Rule 803(3) of Cohen's hearsay statements regarding Galkin's threats.

> [T]he state-of-mind exception does not permit the witness to relate any of the declarant's statements as to why he held the particular state of mind, or what he might have believed that would have induced the state of mind. If the reservation in the text of the rule is to have any effect, it must be understood to narrowly limit those admissible statements to declarations of condition—"I'm scared"— and not belief—"I'm scared because Galkin threatened me." Cohen's witnesses were permitted to relate any direct statements he had made concerning his state of mind but were prevented only from testifying to his statements of belief—that he believed that Galkin was threatening him.

Id. at 1225. *See also* United States v. Samaniego, 345 F.3d 1280, 1282–83 (11th Cir.2003) (finding an apology would be admissible to show the emotion of remorse, but inadmissible to prove why the declarant was remorseful).

STATE V. TERROVONA

Supreme Court of Washington, En Banc, 1986.
716 P.2d 295.

ANDERSEN, JUSTICE.

Facts of Case

At issue in this case is the admissibility of much of the State's evidence against the defendant, James R. Terrovona, who is appealing his conviction for the first degree murder of his stepfather, Gene Patton.

At about 8:15 p.m. on February 26, 1984, the decedent, Gene Patton, received a telephone call at his home. He told his girl friend that the phone call was from the defendant. He said that the defendant had apparently run out of gas on 116th in Marysville and wanted his (the decedent's) assistance. The decedent also said that he (the decedent) must be crazy, but left for the avowed purpose of helping the defendant.

At about 8:30 p.m., a passerby found a body lying alongside a car on 116th Street. Shortly after 9:00 p.m. Snohomish County deputies identified the deceased. He had been severely beaten and shot. The subsequent autopsy revealed that the cause of death was gun shots to the head and abdomen. * * *

ISSUE ONE. Did the trial court err in admitting hearsay evidence of the statements the decedent made as he left home to meet his death? * * *

CONCLUSION. Under ER 803(a)(3), the decedent's statements to his girl friend were admissible in evidence because they evinced his then state of mind.

A statement made out of court that is offered in court to prove the truth of the matter stated is inadmissible hearsay evidence unless it falls within one of the exceptions to the hearsay rule. One exception to the hearsay rule allows evidence of a declarant's state of mind * * * is ER 803(a)(3) * * *. This rule is in accord with previous Washington law providing that statements of a declarant's then existing state of mind are admissible in evidence if there is need for their use and if there is substantial probability of their trustworthiness.

Fed.R.Evid. 803(3) is the same as ER 803(a)(3). Under both rules, hearsay evidence is admissible if it bears on the declarant's state of mind and if that state of mind is an issue in the case.[6] Under the federal rule, the state of mind exception has also been held to authorize admission of evidence of a party's intentions as circumstantial evidence that he acted according to those intentions. This extension of the state of mind exception is known as the "*Hillmon* doctrine."

Long before the present evidentiary rules were adopted, the United States Supreme Court examined the state of mind rule in *Mutual Life Ins. Co. v. Hillmon,* 145 U.S. 285 * * * (1892). The issue in *Hillmon* was the identity of a body found at a campsite. The plaintiffs in that case contended that the body was that of a Mr. Hillmon. The defendants contended the body was that of a Mr. Walters and sought to introduce letters Walters had written stating that he intended to go to the area of the campsite with Hillmon. The Supreme Court found the letters admissible for two purposes:

> The letters in question were competent, * * * as evidence that, * * * [Walters] had the intention of going, and of going with Hillmon, which made it more probable both that he did go and that he went with Hillmon, than if there had been no proof of such intention.

Hillmon, at 295–96 * * *.

Although *Hillmon* was a civil case, the Court cited with approval a number of criminal cases in support of its decision.

---

[6] United States v. Pheaster, 544 F.2d 353, 376 (9th Cir.1976); State v. Parr, 93 Wash.2d 95, 98–99, 606 P.2d 263 (1980).

One such case was *Hunter v. State,* 40 N.J.L. 495 (1878). In that case, Hunter was indicted for the murder of Armstrong. At issue was the admissibility of Armstrong's letters and statements, conveyed to his wife and son on the date of his death, to the effect that he was going on a business trip with Hunter. The Court quoted as follows from *Hunter,* at 538:

> In the ordinary course of things, it was the usual information that a man about leaving home would communicate, for the convenience of his family, * * * At the time it was given, such declarations could * * * mean harm to no one; * * * If it is legitimate to show by a man's own declarations that he left his home to be gone a week, or for a certain destination, which seems incontestable, why may it not be proved in the same way that a designated person was to bear him company? * * * If it was in the ordinary train of events for this man to leave word or to state where he was going, it seems to me it was equally so for him to say with whom he was going.

Hillmon, at 299 * * *. A similar fact pattern, and much the same analysis, is found in *State v. Vestal,* 278 N.C. 561, 180 S.E.2d 755 (1971).

Under *Hillmon,* therefore, a declarant's statement of future intent is admissible to prove: (1) that the declarant went to the place indicated by his or her statement of intention, and (2) that the declarant went there with the other named party.

Most courts have expanded the "*Hillmon* doctrine" to admit hearsay statements of intent that implicate a third party's conduct. This expansion is commonly used in murder trials, where courts admit a decedent's hearsay statements that implicate the defendant in the murder.[7] Courts use such evidence despite conflicting guidance in the comments to Fed.R.Evid. 803(3). That rule itself makes no reference to *Hillmon,* but the comments contain this statement by the Advisory Committee: " 'The rule of *Mutual Life Ins. Co. v. Hillmon* * * *, allowing evidence of intention as tending to prove the doing of the act intended, is, of course, left undisturbed.' "[8] Following this observation is one from the House Judiciary Committee: " 'the Committee intends that the Rule be construed to limit the doctrine of [*Hillmon*], so as to render statements of intent by a declarant admissible only to prove *his* future conduct, not the future conduct of another person.' "[9]* * *

The defendant argues that under *State v. Parr,* 93 Wash.2d 95, 606 P.2d 263 (1980), the decedent's statements as to the defendant's phone call to him are inadmissible to show that the defendant met the decedent

---

[7] Note, 35 Vand.L.Rev. at 686 * * *.

[8] Id. 681.

[9] Id. at 681–82.

on 116th Street. At issue in *Parr* was the admissibility of a decedent's statements that she feared Parr and that he once threatened her. This evidence was introduced to rebut a claim that the defendant accidentally shot the victim in self-defense. We observed there that the inference to be drawn from such testimony was that the defendant wanted to and did kill the victim and was unduly prejudicial. *Parr* held that ER 803(a)(3) "permits statements reporting the declarant's state of mind, but does not permit statements reporting the conduct of another which might have induced that state of mind."[10]

Parr is distinguishable from the case before us. Here, the decedent's statements concerning his intention to take a certain action shortly before he was killed necessarily implicated the defendant's future conduct. The decedent said that because the defendant had called him, he (the decedent) was going to meet the defendant on 116th Street. Unlike *Parr,* the State is not relying on past incidents to prove the defendant's subsequent conduct.

The Ninth Circuit recognized that state of mind evidence used to prove subsequent conduct of the declarant and a third party is not foolproof, but concluded that any unreliability goes to the weight of the evidence rather than to its admissibility.

> Even where no actions by other parties are necessary in order for the intended act to be performed, a myriad of contingencies could intervene to frustrate the fulfillment of the intention. The fact that the cooperation of another party is necessary if the intended act is to be performed adds another important contingency, but the difference is one of degree rather than kind. The possible unreliability of the inference to be drawn from the present intention is a matter going to the weight of the evidence which might be argued to the trier of fact, but it should not be a ground for completely excluding the admittedly relevant evidence.

United States v. Pheaster, 544 F.2d 353, 376 n.14 (9th Cir.1976). We agree.

One New York court has found a greater degree of reliability in using *Hillmon* evidence to prove the conduct of a third person.

> Everyday experience confirms that people frequently express an intent to see another under circumstances that make it extremely likely that such a meeting will occur. Indeed, it is not uncommon for such expressions of intent to be more trustworthy evidence that the meeting took place than many statements of intent with regard to the performance of acts not involving any inference with regard to another person.

---

[10] Parr, at 104 n.1, 606 P.2d 263.

People v. Malizia, 92 A.D.2d 154, 460 N.Y.S.2d 23, 27 (1983), *aff'd,* 62 N.Y.2d 755, 476 N.Y.S.2d 825, 465 N.E.2d 364 * * * (1984).

The decedent's statements, made before leaving his house, about the phone call from the defendant and his intention to go help him, constituted the State's strongest evidence of the defendant's guilt. Neither this defendant's nor the decedent's states of mind were at issue in the trial. Under the *"Hillmon* doctrine", however, the decedent's intentions were admissible to infer that he acted according to those intentions, and that he acted with the person he mentioned. The conduct of the decedent and the defendant after the phone call was definitely at issue in the trial. The decedent's statements under the circumstances here created a trustworthy inference that the defendant met him on 116th Street where he was killed within a half hour of receiving the phone call and leaving his home. Those statements were properly admitted into evidence, the weight of such evidence being for the jury. * * *

Affirmed.

NOTES AND QUESTIONS

1. *Future actions of another.* The problem of admissibility was greatly simplified in *Hillmon* because the parties agreed that Hillmon went to Crooked Creek. The question was whether Walters went there. Some courts have reached the result in *Terrovona* by allowing the evidence of intention to show such things as opportunity, with a limiting instruction not to use the evidence as proof of any act by the nondeclarant. Can and will a jury make the distinction? See People v. Alcalde, 148 P.2d 627 (Cal.1944) (declarations by the murder victim that she was going out with the accused on the night of the killing admitted with a limiting instruction that the statement showed only decedent's intention). Is the limitation imposed in *Alcalde* that the statement shows only the intent of the declarant meaningful or valid? The Second Circuit permits the statement of intention of the declarant to establish the nature of the transaction contemplated where the third party's participation is proven by independent evidence. United States v. Cicale, 691 F.2d 95, 103–04 (2d Cir.1982). A minority of courts have excluded state of mind evidence when offered to show another person's conduct directly or indirectly through the intent of the declarant. See Clark v. United States, 412 A.2d 21, 29–30 (D.C.1980) (such statements excluded because inconsistent with theory of state of mind exceptions and because only reliable as to declarant's own intention).

2. *Will cases and other expansions of the doctrine.* Despite the limitation announced in Shepard v. United States, 290 U.S. 96 (1933), that the state of mind exception could not be used to show past acts, numerous decisions admitted subsequent declarations of testators to show an "influenced" state of mind and to show genuineness or due execution of a will. Rule 803(3) explicitly continues this practice of admitting statements of

memory or belief to prove past acts in cases relating to wills. However, the statement must still be a statement of then existing state of mind that can contain or be used to prove a fact remembered or believed, and it cannot be a later statement regarding intent at the earlier time when the will was made. *See* Estate of Grant v. Clemson Univ. Found., 725 S.E.2d 516, 521 (S.C.Ct.App.2012).

UNITED STATES V. VELTMANN
United States Court of Appeals, Eleventh Circuit, 1993.
6 F.3d 1483.

FAY, CIRCUIT JUDGE:

Defendants Chris Veltmann and Carl Veltmann were convicted of * * * [murder] and mail and wire fraud based on insurance claims arising from Elizabeth Veltmann's death and fire damage to the family home * * *. Defendants appeal their convictions based, [*inter alia*] on the trial court's * * * exclusion of state-of-mind evidence * * *. We REVERSE * * *.

Facts

Elizabeth Veltmann ("Elizabeth") died the evening of January 7, 1990 during a fire in the home she shared with her husband, Carl Veltmann ("Carl"). The couple had just returned from a week-long honeymoon cruise with Elizabeth's son, Christopher Veltmann ("Chris"), and his new bride.

The fire was caused by arson; the crux of the case is the identity of the arsonist(s). The government theorized that Carl and Chris set fire to the house with the knowledge that Elizabeth was inside and with intent to recover proceeds under various insurance policies. Defendants argued that Elizabeth, beset with fiscal worries and physical maladies, committed suicide after setting fire to the home. To evaluate the sufficiency of the evidence and harmlessness of evidentiary rulings, we must review in some detail the relevant facts pertaining to the fire, Elizabeth's state of mind, and the circumstantial case against the defendants.

I. The Fire

On January 7, 1990, at 9:41 p.m., a neighbor called 911 after hearing an alarm and seeing smoke and flames coming from a second floor window of the Veltmann's three story residence. Firefighters broke into the house through the locked front door and found Elizabeth unconscious in the third floor master bedroom. She could not be revived. No one else was found in the home. * * *

There was no forced entry into the house other than that made by firefighters. Although numerous people had access to keys, there were apparently no suspects other than Carl and Chris who had both access to the house and knowledge of the home protection systems.

II. *Elizabeth Veltmann's State-of-Mind*

The defense's case rested on proof that Elizabeth was suicidal. Elizabeth's autopsy revealed that her blood-alcohol level at death was .149, with a .33 level of Dalmane, a prescription sedative, in her system. Carbon monoxide test samples yielded a 73 to 75 percent result evidencing the cause of death as acute carbon monoxide intoxication from the inhalation of smoke and gases. The physician testified he did not consider suicide because it was not suggested by the police. Although Elizabeth was discovered two feet away from the sliding glass door, there is no forensic evidence that she was attempting to escape because her feet were not analyzed for soot deposits. She was found lying face down on the floor, clutching a tissue or handkerchief, nearby bills, bank statements, and family photos strewn across the floor. Approximately a year and a half after her death, Carl found an undated suicide note written by Elizabeth. The authenticity of the note was not challenged.

Contradictions permeate evidence of Elizabeth's physical and psychological condition. Elizabeth and Carl were married for twenty-five years, were business partners, and were described by a number of witnesses as a loving and devoted couple. Elizabeth was happy about Chris' recent marriage and excited about the honeymoon cruise. But numerous indicators point to Elizabeth's deep distress over her medical and financial problems.

Elizabeth suffered from a variety of physical maladies. She was treated for years with a variety of pain killers, and eventually became a prescription drug addict. In 1987, Elizabeth suffered respiratory arrest as a result of a self-induced drug overdose. Psychiatrists suspected a suicide attempt, but Elizabeth steadfastly refused to admit she was depressed and checked out of the hospital against medical advice. An addictionologist concluded that Elizabeth eventually became desperate for drugs as evidenced by stockpiling her supply, forging a prescription, obtaining drugs in her father's name, and trying to manipulate a nurse and another friend into providing her with drugs illegally. The expert postulated that she took most or all of the drugs in her system near the time of death. * * * The government's expert believed that given her level of drug intoxication, Elizabeth was not ambulatory during the time in which the fire must have been set.

In addition to being chemically dependent, Elizabeth was deeply troubled about what seemed to be impending financial ruin. She needed money for drugs and was trying to keep her dependency a secret. The Veltmann's corporation filed for bankruptcy in December, 1989. Their home, built in 1985 with Elizabeth as general contractor, was on the market. In the months preceding her death, Elizabeth tried to borrow money from a number of people.

The most telling indicator of Elizabeth's monetary dilemma and mental state was not admitted into evidence. In a videotaped deposition, Carl Engstrom testified that Elizabeth extracted $500,000 from him over the past twenty-five to thirty years. She was apparently blackmailing him based on their brief affair that took place when she was married to her first husband. Engstrom believed that Elizabeth would eventually pay him back because she frequently promised to do so. A few months before she died, Elizabeth talked to Engstrom about the possibility of her death, and instructed him to see Chris about being paid when she was gone. She mentioned suicide several times. In early December, 1989, Engstrom sent money which Elizabeth never picked up. She called him again for money on December 31 or January 1st, from Miami, where she was waiting to board the cruise ship. She called him collect from the Cayman Islands on January 6th, again demanding money. He refused. * * *

An addictionologist testified that suicidal ideation typically develops over two or three years, and that Elizabeth's earlier suicide threats to Engstrom were evidence of suicidal thinking. In the expert's view, Engstrom's cutting off of funds that Elizabeth could use for drugs was the "major precipitating event" in her suicide.

The financial picture was not entirely gloomy. The Veltmanns were willing to accept an incoming offer of $1,200,000 for the house and an adjacent lot. Carl testified that this money would be used to pay off mortgages with the balance infused into their failing corporation. But Elizabeth told friends that she did not want to live any longer, and that no one would have her house after she was gone; she believed Carl would remarry after her death, but "another Mrs. Veltmann" would not have what she had. Elizabeth said she would destroy everything.

III. The Evidence Against Carl and Chris Veltmann

* * * The government argued that the arson and murder were motivated by greed, and that defendants had the opportunity and knowledge to commit the crime. * * * David Meehan, Chris' cellmate, testified to admissions allegedly made by Chris while in custody. * * * Terry Price, Carl's cellmate, testified that Carl told him the fire was set with lighter fluid, but that he left for Montana the day before the fire and was hunting when the fire started. * * * Price testified that Carl said he dated the suicide note "January 7, 1990" because the insurance companies would not pay off otherwise; presumably Carl believed that the note should be dated, and that the date of death was most likely to promote payment by the insurers. * * * [Other incriminating evidence was also offered by the government.] Carl denied having anything to do with the arson to his residence and with the death of his wife. * * *

Discussion

The Evidentiary Rulings

A.   State of Mind Evidence

Defendants appeal the trial court's exclusion of Carl Engstrom's videotaped deposition. Defendants offered the deposition as relevant hearsay, admissible pursuant to Fed.R.Evid. 803(3), reflecting Elizabeth's state-of-mind. The government objected, claiming that decedent did not threaten suicide in the last phone call with Engstrom, and that threats of suicide in months preceding her death were inadmissible hearsay and irrelevant. The district court agreed with the government, also finding the information cumulative and collateral, and excluded the deposition testimony. We believe the trial court erred. The deposition was admissible under the state of mind exception, and while conceivably cumulative, its import was such that exclusion violated defendants' right to put on a defense. This abuse of discretion requires reversal.

Rule 803(3) of the Federal Rules of Evidence allows the admission of " * * *[a] statement of the declarant's then existing state of mind, emotion, sensation or physical condition (such as intent, plan, motive, design, mental feeling, pain and bodily health) * * *." The declarant's statement of mind must be relevant to some issue in the case before such testimony can be admitted under Rule 803(3). * * *.

A homicide victim's state of mind is unquestionably relevant to the defense theory that she committed suicide. The government maintains that Elizabeth's earlier suicide threats and references to dying were too remote to make Engstrom's testimony relevant. The time lag between Elizabeth's references to dying and her death warrants further examination.

In *In re Fill,* 68 B.R. 923 (Bankr.S.D.N.Y.1987), * * * the transferee was permitted to offer state of mind hearsay evidence of the debtor's declarations that he intended to repay the loans even though such statements were made six years before actual repayment. The court discussed a continuity of time concept relevant to the state of mind inquiry, quoting a leading commentator as follows:

> Although it is required that the statement describe a state of mind or feeling existing at the time of the statement, the evidentiary effect of the statement is broadened by the notion of the continuity of time in states of mind * * *. Since, however, the duration of state of mind or emotion varies with the particular attitudes or feelings at issue and with the cause, it is reasonable to require as a condition of invoking the continuity notion that the statement mirror a state of mind which, *in light of all the circumstances* including proxity [sic] in time, has some

probability of being the same condition existing at the material
time * * *.

Id. at 928, *citing McCormick,* Evidence, § 294, at 844–45 (Cleary, 3d ed.
1984) (emphasis added). * * *

The temporal relationship between Elizabeth's statements and her
death is far less attenuated than the six year time lag analyzed in *Fill.*
Where one threatens suicide, talks about what should be done in event of
her death, and dies within months under suspicious circumstances
including the presence of a suicide note and other witnesses corroborating
her depression and suicidal ideation, we do not believe uncertainty over
the exact date of the suicide threats should preclude admission of those
statements to show state of mind.

* * * We find that exclusion of this evidence impaired defendants'
right to fully present their defense, requiring reversal and remand for
new trial. * * *

NOTES AND QUESTIONS

1.   *Limitations recognized.* Although expanding the reach of the
exception, two basic limitations described earlier are honored by *Veltmann.*
First, the statement describes a then existing state of mind. Second, the
statement is used to prove the conduct of the declarant in the future rather
than past conduct or conduct of others.

2.   *Sincerity as a requirement?* May a trial court exclude a statement of
the declarant's then existing state of mind as not falling within Rule 803(3)
because it doubts the sincerity of the statement? The court in United States
v. DiMaria, 727 F.2d 265, 272 (2d Cir.1984), held that it was improper to
exclude the defendant's exculpatory statement of his reason for being in
possession of stolen cigarettes immediately upon his arrest by officers who
had the location of the cigarettes under surveillance. Speaking specifically as
to Rule 803(3), it stated:

> [T]he scheme of the Rules is to determine that issue [a particular
> guarantee of credibility] by categories; if a declaration comes within
> a category defined as an exception, the declaration is admissible
> without any preliminary finding of probable credibility by the judge,
> save for the "catch-all" exceptions * * * and the business records
> exceptions of Rule 803(6) ("unless the source of the information or
> the method or circumstance of preparation indicate lack of
> trustworthiness").

United States v. Ponticelli, 622 F.2d 985, 991–92 (9th Cir.1980), appears
to take a different position:

> In making the foundational inquiry on admissibility under * * *
> [803(1), 803(2), and 803(3)], the court must evaluate three factors:
> contemporaneousness, chance for reflection, and relevance. The

state of mind declaration has probative value, because the declarant presumably knows what his thoughts and emotions are at the time of his declarations. * * * The state of mind declaration also has probative value, because the declarant presumably has no chance for reflection and therefore for misrepresentation. * * * The greater the circumstances for misrepresentation, the less reliable is the declaration. * * *

In weighing these factors, the trial court did not abuse its discretion in concluding that Ponticelli had a chance for reflection and misrepresentation in making the proffered statements. Ponticelli's declarations came after his arrest; thus, he was aware that he was under investigation and that anything he said could be used against him. * * * Finally, Ponticelli made the statement while consulting an attorney. This fact implies that Ponticelli was considering the legal significance of his declarations at the time he made them.

One difference between the cases is the timing. However, even statements of intent made during a criminal conspiracy may not be admitted if they are construed as backward looking to characterize past acts rather than viewed as statements of current state of mind. See United States v. Cianci, 378 F.3d 71, 106–07 (1st Cir.2004). See also State v. Cosby, 262 P.3d 285, 292 (Kan.2011) (resting exclusion of the defendant's exculpatory statement on the ground that while phrased differently it in fact described his state of mind two days earlier).

Courts can exclude evidence under the concepts of relevance and prejudice contained in Rules 401–403. Rule 403 may provide an alternate way for courts to accomplish the result prohibited in *DiMaria* when it questions the trustworthiness of a self-serving statement. See United States v. Peak, 856 F.2d 825, 834 (7th Cir.1988); 2 McCormick, Evidence § 270 (7th ed. 2013) (suggesting use of Rule 403 to exclude as a preferable, although still somewhat controversial, approach).

3. *Physical condition.* In addition to mental and emotional conditions, Rule 803(3) covers statements of sensation and physical condition such as pain and bodily health. These statements, unlike those covered by Rule 803(4), need not be made to a physician or for the purpose of medical treatment or diagnosis. On the other hand, since contemporaneity is the guarantee of trustworthiness, statements concerning past sensations or conditions are inadmissible. Does contemporaneity provide sufficient protections against contrived statements? Should the exception be limited to admit only statements of sudden pain rather than reports of a chronic condition? Is there a realistic alternative to receiving such statements in spite of the dangers of conscious contrivance to establish the presence and effects of chronic pain? Issues of whether statements are self-serving and contrived arise not only in situations where intent is at issue but also in those where the declarant's statements establish existing physical condition. The

general answer provided by *DiMaria* regarding statements of mental conditions applies to physical conditions as well.

4. *Limited trustworthiness.* Exceptions to the hearsay rules are generally seen as based on some very rough mix of trustworthiness and necessity. See, e.g., *Dallas County v. Commercial Union Assur. Co.*, Section L, infra. For statements under Rule 803(3), how impressive is the guarantee of trustworthiness?

C. STATEMENTS FOR PURPOSE OF MEDICAL DIAGNOSIS OR TREATMENT

Federal Rule 803(4)

UNITED STATES V. IRON SHELL

United States Court of Appeals, Eighth Circuit, 1980.
633 F.2d 77.

STEPHENSON, CIRCUIT JUDGE.

Defendant, John Louis Iron Shell, appeals from a jury conviction of assault with intent to commit rape in violation of the Major Crimes Act, 18 U.S.C. § 1153 (1970).

* * *

The indictment in this case arose out of the defendant's acts on July 24, 1979, in the community of Antelope, which is within the Rosebud Indian Reservation and near Mission, South Dakota. The defense conceded at trial that Iron Shell had assaulted Lucy, a nine-year-old Indian girl. The key questions at trial concerned the nature of the assault and the defendant's intent.

* * *

Dr. Mark Hopkins, a physician with the Indian Health Service, examined Lucy at about 8:20 p.m. on the night of the assault. During his examination the doctor elicited a series of statements from Lucy concerning the cause of her injuries. Dr. Hopkins was only aware that Lucy was allegedly a rape victim and was not told of the details surrounding the assault. During the examination, in response to questions posed by the doctor, Lucy told Dr. Hopkins she had been drug into the bushes, that her clothes, jeans and underwear, were removed and that the man had tried to force something into her vagina which hurt. She said she tried to scream but was unable because the man put his hand over her mouth and neck.[11] The doctor, over objection, repeated Lucy's statement at trial.

Dr. Hopkins' examination also revealed that there was a small amount of sand and grass in the perineal area but not in the vagina. He also found superficial abrasions on both sides of Lucy's neck and testified that they were consistent with someone grabbing her but qualified his statement by adding that he could not absolutely determine that they were so caused. Dr. Hopkins also testified that there was no physical evidence of penetration, the hymen was intact and no sperm was located.

Lucy was able to add little and could only partially confirm the above record at trial. Lucy, a nine-year-old, was able to answer a number of preliminary questions demonstrating her ability to understand and respond to counsel but was unable to detail what happened after she was assaulted by the defendant. She did testify that she remembered something happening near the bushes and that a man had pushed her down. Lucy also said at trial that the man told her if she "didn't shut up he would choke me." In response to a series of leading questions she confirmed that the man had put his hand over her neck, hit her on the side of the face, held her down, taken her clothes off and that Mae Small Bear had scared the man, making him leave.[12] On cross-examination

-----

[11] Out of the presence of the jury, the doctor testified that he first asked Lucy "what happened" and she didn't answer. He asked whether she was in any pain and she pointed to her vaginal area. He asked if she hurt anywhere else and she didn't answer. Dr. Hopkins again asked "what happened" and Lucy said she had been drug into the bushes. The doctor then asked if the man "had taken her clothes off." She said yes, and then related the facts set out above. Dr. Hopkins testified that he was not "badgering" the patient, nor "dragging information out," but was asking "simple questions."

[12] The following is a representative sample of the prosecutor's direct examination of Lucy:

Q. What did the man do when he pushed you down, Lucy?

A. (Long hesitation)

Q. What did he do?

A. (Long hesitation)

Q. Did he hurt you any place?

A. (Long hesitation)

Q. Do you remember that?

A. (Long hesitation)

Q. Where did he put his hand, did he put his hand on your neck?

A. Yes

Q. Did you get hit on the side of the face?

A. Yes.

Q. When he pushed you down, did he hold you down?

A. Yes.

Q. Did you start crying?

A. Yes.

THE COURT: As much as you can, phrase your questions in a way to avoid any unnecessary leading.

Q. What else happened when he had you down, Lucy; did he say anything to you, do you remember?

defense counsel did not explore any of the substantive issues, nor did he examine Lucy concerning the statement she made to Dr. Hopkins, although he had the opportunity.

Dr. Hopkins' Testimony

* * *

Defendant challenges the admission of statements made by Lucy to Dr. Hopkins during his examination. The prosecution offered this testimony admittedly as hearsay but within the exception expressed in Rule 803(4). The rule states: * * *

> (4) * * * Statements made for purposes of medical diagnosis or treatment and describing medical history, or past or present symptoms, pain, or sensations, or the inception or general character of the cause or external source thereof insofar as reasonably pertinent to diagnosis or treatment.

Fed.R.Evid. 803(4). The defendant argues that the questions asked by Dr. Hopkins and the information received in response to those questions were not "reasonably pertinent" to diagnosis or treatment. The defense stresses Dr. Hopkins' question in which he asked Lucy whether the man had taken her clothes off and suggests that this was asked by one in the role of an investigator, seeking to solve the crime, rather than a doctor treating or diagnosing a patient. The defendant also asserts that the doctor's examination would have been the same whether or not this extra information had been received. The defense argues that this point supports his claim that the questions were not pertinent to treatment or diagnosis because they had no affect on the doctor's examination. Lastly, the defendant urges that the doctor was employed for the specific purpose of qualifying as an expert witness and as such his testimony should be more suspect.

It is clear that Rule 803(4) significantly liberalized prior practice concerning admissibility of statements made for purposes of medical diagnosis or treatment. *See* Notes of Advisory Committee on Proposed Rules, Rule 803 * * *. Rule 803(4) admits three types of statements: (1) medical history, (2) past or present sensations, and (3) inception or general cause of the disease or injury. All three types are admissible where they are "reasonably pertinent to diagnosis or treatment." The rule changed prior law in two main points. First, the rule adopted an

---

A. (Long hesitation)

Q. What did he say to you, can you tell me? Tell me what he said?

A. (Long hesitation)

Q. Could you do that for me?

A. Yes.

Q. Okay, tell me what he said?

A. If I didn't shut up he would choke me.

expansive approach by allowing statements concerning past symptoms and those which related to the cause of the injury. Second, the rule abolished the distinction between the doctor who is consulted for the purpose of treatment and an examination for the purpose of diagnosis only; the latter usually refers to a doctor who is consulted only in order to testify as a witness.[13] *See* Weinstein & Berger, *supra,* at 803–125.

Lucy's statements fall primarily within the third category listed by 803(4).[14] The key question is whether these statements were reasonably pertinent to diagnosis or treatment. The rationale behind the rule has often been stated. It focuses upon the patient and relies upon the patient's strong motive to tell the truth because diagnosis or treatment will depend in part upon what the patient says. It is thought that the declarant's motive guarantees trustworthiness sufficiently to allow an exception to the hearsay rule. *See Meaney v. United States,* 112 F.2d 538 (2d Cir.1940). Judge Weinstein, in his treatise, suggests another policy ground. He writes that "a fact reliable enough to serve as the basis for a diagnosis is also reliable enough to escape hearsay proscription." Weinstein & Berger, *supra,* at 803–129. This principle recognizes that life and death decisions are made by physicians in reliance on such facts and as such should have sufficient trustworthiness to be admissible in a court of law. This rationale closely parallels that underlying rule 703 and suggests a similar test should apply, namely—is this fact of a type reasonably relied upon by experts in a particular field in forming opinions. *See* Fed.R.Evid. 703 (Basis of Opinion Testimony by Experts). Thus, two independent rationales support the rule and are helpful in its application. A two-part test flows naturally from this dual rationale: first, is the declarant's motive consistent with the purpose of the rule; and second, is it reasonable for the physician to rely on the information in diagnosis or treatment.

We find no facts in the record to indicate that Lucy's motive in making these statements was other than as a patient seeking treatment. Dr. Hopkins testified that the purpose of his examination was two-fold. He was to treat Lucy and to preserve any evidence that was available.

---

[13] This is the first Eighth Circuit opinion to consider the effect of 803(4) on its pre–1975 case law. This circuit had followed the majority rule which prevented admission of testimony concerning the cause of the injury as not connected with treatment and excluded statements made to a physician who examined the patient solely for the purpose of testifying. * * * Some courts had also held that a physician could repeat a patient's statement regarding medical history or past symptoms for the limited purpose of explaining the basis of an opinion and not in order to prove the truth of the out-of-court declarations. This distinction was likewise rejected by the federal rules. Notes of Advisory Committee on Proposed Rules * * *.

[14] Dr. Hopkins testified that Lucy said she was experiencing pain in her vaginal area. This expression of a present symptom falls within the second category of 803(4) and would also be excepted from the hearsay rule under rule 803(3) covering a then existing physical condition. Fed.R.Evid. 803(3). The remainder of Lucy's statement concerns the general character and nature of the cause of the injury. Because of the result we reach in this case, it is not necessary to discuss this distinction at length.

There is nothing in the content of the statements to suggest that Lucy was responding to the doctor's questions for any reason other than promoting treatment. It is important to note that the statements concern what happened rather than who assaulted her. The former in most cases is pertinent to diagnosis and treatment while the latter would seldom, if ever, be sufficiently related.[15] *See United States v. Nick,* 604 F.2d 1199, 1201–02 (9th Cir.1979). All of Lucy's statements were within the scope of the rule because they were related to her physical condition and were consistent with a motive to promote treatment. The age of the patient also mitigates against a finding that Lucy's statements were not within the traditional rationale of the rule. The trial court placed special emphasis on this factor and we likewise find that it is important to our holding.

During an extensive examination outside the presence of the jury, Dr. Hopkins explained in detail the relevancy of his questions to the task of diagnosis and treatment. He testified that a discussion of the cause of the injury was important to provide guidelines for his examination by pinpointing areas of the body to be examined more closely and by narrowing his examination by eliminating other areas. It is not dispositive that Dr. Hopkins' examination would have been identical to the one he performed if Lucy had been unable to utter a word. The doctor testified that his examination would have been more lengthy had he been unable to elicit a description of the general cause, although he stated the exam would have been basically the same. The fact that in this case the discussion of the cause of the injury did not lead to a fundamentally different exam does not mean that the discussion was not pertinent to diagnosis. It is enough that the information eliminated potential physical problems from the doctor's examination in order to meet the test of 803(4). Discovering what is not injured is equally as pertinent to treatment and diagnosis as finding what is injured. Dr. Hopkins also testified, in response to specific questions from the court, that most doctors would have sought such a history and that he relied upon Lucy's statements in deciding upon a course of treatment.[16]

---

[15] The advisory committee notes on 803(4) provide that statements as to fault would not ordinarily qualify. The notes use this example: "a patient's statement that he was struck by an automobile would qualify but not his statement that the car was driven through a red light." Advisory Committee Notes, supra, at 585. Another example concludes that a statement by a patient that he was shot would be admissible but a statement that he was shot by a white man would not. United States v. Narciso, 446 F.Supp. 252, 289 (E.D.Mich.1977). And the fact that a patient strained himself while operating a machine may be significant to treatment but the fact that the patient said the machine was defective may not. See Stewart v. Baltimore & O.R. Co., 137 F.2d 527, 530 (2d Cir.1943).

[16] Judge Weinstein approached the problem as follows:

Much depends on the doctor's analysis. The doctor may or may not need to know that his patient was struck by a train and what caused him to fall under the train since dizziness before the accident may bear on diagnosis. A doctor consulted after the patient was involved in an automobile accident may need to know that the accident was precipitated when the

Weinstein & Berger, *supra,* at 803–130 (footnotes omitted). It is not necessary to find, and we do not hold in this case, that the fact that the doctor took the information is prima facie evidence that it was pertinent. Rather, we conclude that a close examination of the facts and circumstances in each case is required.

In light of this analysis we hold that it was not an abuse of discretion to admit the doctor's testimony. * * * Affirmed.

NOTES AND QUESTIONS

1.   *Three changes.* As *Iron Shell* notes, Rule 803(4) changed prior law in three ways: first, it admits statements concerning past symptoms; second, it permits admission of statements of causation of the condition or injury; and third, it abolishes the distinction between statements to a doctor consulted for the purpose of treatment and one who is consulted for the purpose of diagnosis only. These developments are considered in turn in the notes below.

2.   *Past symptoms.* On the admission of past symptoms, the Federal Rule followed the progressive trend of cases such as Peterson v. Richfield Plaza, Inc., 89 N.W.2d 712 (Minn.1958). As *Peterson* stated:

> [I]f the statements of the patient are deemed trustworthy for the reason that proper treatment rests on the truth of such statements, it is difficult to distinguish between the reliability of statements made in the doctor's presence as to subjective symptoms existing at that time and statements made which relate to similar symptoms, pertaining to the injury or ailment which the doctor seeks to diagnose, that the patient has experienced before coming to the doctor's office.

Id. at 721. See also 2 McCormick, Evidence § 277 (7th ed. 2013) (past symptoms received based on assurance of reliability arising from patient's belief that effective treatment requires accuracy as to past, as well as current, symptoms). This ability to receive evidence of past events under Rule 803(4) is one of the major differences between this exception and Rule 803(3) as applied to statements of physical and mental condition.

3.   *Causation.* Admitting statements of causation under the Rule constituted a more substantial change in existing law. The tradition had been to exclude the patient's statement regarding the cause of his or her condition on the theory that it was not relevant to diagnosis and treatment and thus not within the guarantee of trustworthiness. See, e.g., Clark v. People, 86 P.2d 257 (Colo.1939) (error to admit statement of deceased to physician that abortion had been performed by defendant). See also 6 Wigmore, Evidence § 1722 (Chadbourn rev. 1976). However, some cases reflected a trend to

---

patient fainted while driving. Since doctors may be assumed not to want to waste their time with unnecessary history, the fact that a doctor took the information is prima facie evidence that it was pertinent. Courtroom practice has tended to let in medical records and statements to nurses and doctors fairly freely, leaving it to the jury to decide probative force.

recognize that the manner in which an injury was sustained, short of excursions into fault and responsibility, could be relevant to diagnosis and treatment. See, e.g., Shell Oil Co. v. Industrial Comm'n, 119 N.E.2d 224 (Ill.1954) (proper to admit statement of claimant that he slipped and hurt his back while pulling pipe). Rule 803(4) includes statements of general causation under the theory that the guarantee of trustworthiness extends to such statements when reasonably pertinent to diagnosis or treatment. See State v. Cookson, 837 A.2d 101, 109 (Me.2003) (admitting statement by depressed patient to nurse practitioner that defendant had been following and stalking her as describing external source of depression and pertinent to treatment); State v. Momplaisir, 815 A.2d 65, 72 (R.I.2003) (admitting statement that injured patient had been struck by a club as medically pertinent).

4. *Fault.* However, as *Iron Shell* notes, while statements as to cause are admitted under this theory, statements as to fault or identity of the perpetrator are generally not. This is because statements in the second category would generally fail to satisfy either of the rationales for the exception. First, such statements are not likely to be motivated by the patient's selfish interest in facilitating proper treatment. Second, they are seldom, if ever, sufficiently related to proper diagnosis and treatment to be reasonably relied upon by the doctor. See also Cook v. Hoppin, 783 F.2d 684, 690 (7th Cir.1986) (putting prime emphasis on whether statements of fault are reasonably pertinent to diagnosis or treatment and observing that "much will depend on the treating physician's own analysis"). See also Doali–Miller v. Supervalu, Inc., 855 F.Supp.2d 510, 514–15 (D.Md.2012) (finding the location of the injury at a particular store was not pertinent to diagnosis or treatment and tended to impermissibly attribute fault).

5. *Identifying statements.* A substantial number of cases have recognized an exception to the general rule excluding statements that identify the perpetrator in cases involving sexual abuse of children where, the theory is, knowledge of identity may be relevant to issues of the child's placement, see United States v. Renville, 779 F.2d 430, 436–39 (8th Cir.1985); Goldade v. State, 674 P.2d 721, 726 (Wyo.1983), or treatment of continuing psychological problems, see United States v. Chaco, 801 F.Supp.2d 1200, 1213 (D.N.M.2011) (both placement and psychological treatment); Hawkins v. State, 72 S.W.3d 493, 498 (Ark.2002); State v. Robinson, 735 P.2d 801, 810 (Ariz.1987). But see Cassidy v. State, 536 A.2d 666, 682–83 (Md.Ct.Spec.App.1988) (finding child's placement outside scope of exception).

6. *Diagnosis-only statements.* The third change made by the Rule, which is probably the most dramatic, is to admit statements made to physicians consulted only for the purpose of diagnosis, which generally means a doctor who is consulted solely to testify at trial. Under traditional analysis, judicial attitudes changed radically when the physician to whom the statement was made was not the treating physician but one who makes an examination for the purpose of testifying. In the latter situation, it was

recognized that the declarant/"patient" might be motivated to embellish or fabricate symptoms and therefore trustworthiness was lacking. Although such statements were not admitted for their truth, statements made to a testifying physician were admissible as the basis for an opinion, a distinction in use that required a considerable intellectual feat by jurors. It was perceived futility of admitting testimony for the limited purpose of providing the basis of the doctor's diagnosis along with trust in medical experts to screen out unreliable statements that caused the drafters of the Federal Rule to admit statements made for diagnosis only as a hearsay exception. See Advisory Committee Note.

Are these sufficient justifications for admission of hearsay? Note that, when made for diagnosis only, the declarant's "selfish treatment interest" does not necessarily support the reliability of the statement since inaccurate declarations will not result in erroneous treatment because none is contemplated. Does acceptance of this rationale mean that statements received under Rule 703 to support the basis of the expert's opinion are also substantively admissible? Should the 2000 amendment to Rule 703 that restricts receipt of otherwise inadmissible evidence have any effect on this exception? Does the skill of the person who hears the statement provide a basis for admission of hearsay in any other situations? See generally Perrin, Expert Witnesses under Rules 703 and 803(4) of the Federal Rules of Evidence: Separating the Wheat from the Chaff, 72 Ind.L.J. 939 (1997).

Some jurisdictions differ from the Federal Rule and have limited the exception to situations where treatment is contemplated. See, e.g., State v. Hinnant, 523 S.E.2d 663, 669 (N.C.2000) (requiring satisfaction of common law treatment motivation); Pa.R.Evid. 803(4) ("medical diagnosis in contemplation of treatment"). See generally Mosteller, The Maturation and Disintegration of the Hearsay Exception for Statements for Medical Examination in Child Sexual Abuses Cases, 65 Law & Contemp.Probs., Winter 2002, at 47.

7. *Admissibility of statements to non-physicians.* The exception admits statements when made for the purpose of medical diagnosis even when not made to a physician. Such statements may be made directly by the patient to persons who are not doctors. See State v. Smith, 337 S.E.2d 833, 839–40 (N.C.1985) (statements of child sex victims to grandmother describing past assault and physical trauma admissible under this exception since children cannot independently seek medical treatment but must rely on their caretakers). Similarly, the motivation of the patient to speak truthfully to a treating physician is readily extended to include statements of parents or close family members relating the symptoms of a child. See United States v. Yazzie, 59 F.3d 807, 813 (9th Cir.1995) (in most circumstances, statements by parent of injured child to doctor will qualify); First Premier Bank v. Kolcraft Enters., Inc., 686 N.W.2d 430, 449 (S.D.2004) (admitting statement by parents as to cause of injury to child). As noted above, if the statement is one of current physical condition, it may be admitted regardless of to whom made under Rule 803(3).

8. *Meaning of "medical."* The exception admits statements made for the purpose of "medical" diagnosis or treatment. What range of professionals should be considered to provide "medical" services? In addition to medical doctors and nurses, courts have often included in this group psychologists and social workers. See Mosteller, Child Sexual Abuse and Statements for the Purpose of Medical Diagnosis or Treatment, 67 N.C.L.Rev. 257, 282–83 (1989). However, a minority has been unwilling to move beyond statements to physicians. See, e.g., State v. Zimmerman, 829 P.2d 861, 864 (Idaho 1992) (statements to psychologists inadmissible); State v. Huntington, 575 N.W.2d 268, 278 (Wis.1998) (statements to social workers and counselors inadmissible). See generally Capowski, An Interdisciplinary Analysis for Statements to Mental Health Professionals under the Diagnosis or Treatment Hearsay Exception, 33 Ga.L.Rev. 353 (1999).

9. *Statements to psychiatrists.* When the declarant is consulting a psychiatrist, almost all statements may be relevant to diagnosis or treatment. In this situation, the commentators note the discretion of the judge to exclude statements or to limit their admissibility for the purpose of supporting the diagnosis. See 5 Weinstein's Federal Evidence § 803.06[7] (2d ed. 2013); 2 McCormick, Evidence § 277 (7th ed. 2013).

10. *Interplay with Confrontation Clause and Crawford v. Washington.* Before *Crawford*, some courts restricted the exception under Ohio v. Roberts, 448 U.S. 56 (1980), on questions such as whether a treatment motivation had to be exhibited by the child. See United States v. Turning Bear, 357 F.3d 730, 738–39 (8th Cir.2004) (requiring understanding of treatment purpose in examination before statements of child admitted as firmly rooted hearsay exception). In extreme cases, statements made solely for diagnosis without a treatment purpose, which the Advisory Committee described as being made "only for the purpose of enabling him to testify," potentially could be viewed as testimonial and excluded by *Crawford*. See Mosteller, *Crawford v. Washington*: Encouraging and Ensuring the Confrontation of Witnesses, 39 U.Rich.L.Rev. 511, 600–11(2005).

11. *Importance in child sexual abuse cases.* As the above notes suggest, the expansions of this hearsay exception by the Federal Rules have seen frequent use and legal challenge in child sexual abuse cases. See generally Mosteller, Child Sexual Abuse and Statements for the Purpose of Medical Diagnosis or Treatment, 67 N.C.L.Rev. 257 (1989); Mosteller, The Maturation and Disintegration of the Hearsay Exception for Statements for Medical Examination in Child Sexual Abuses Cases, 65 Law & Contemp.Probs., Winter 2002, at 47; Symposium: Hearsay Testimony in Trials Involving Child Witnesses, 5 Psychol.Pub. Pol'y & L. 251 (1999); Symposium: What Have We Learned About Children as Victims and Witnesses in Criminal Trials?, 65 Law & Contemp.Probs., Winter 2002, at 1.

D. RECORDED RECOLLECTION

Federal Rule 803(5)

UNITED STATES V. BOOZ

United States Court of Appeals, Third Circuit, 1971.
451 F.2d 719.

SEITZ, CHIEF JUDGE. At around 8:30 a.m. on April 18, 1967, two armed men robbed the Dublin, Pennsylvania branch of the Bucks County Bank & Trust Company of $8,950.75. The appellant is alleged by the government to be one of the robbers; no other suspect has been charged. Included in the stolen money were twenty-five so-called bait bills, i.e., those whose serial numbers had been recorded. On June 12, 1967, the appellant deposited a large sum of money in the Girard Trust Bank which included eighteen of the bait bills. On June 14, 1967, FBI Agents executed a search warrant at appellant's home but apparently obtained no additional evidence. Approximately fourteen months later, in August, 1968, appellant was indicted by a grand jury for violating the Federal Bank Robbery Act, 18 U.S.C.A. § 2113 (1970). In January, 1971, approximately two years and five months after indictment, appellant was brought to trial, convicted by a jury and sentenced to fifteen years imprisonment. This appeal followed. The government's evidence showed that appellant had substantial opportunity to become acquainted with the pre-opening procedures of the bank's personnel, including the opening of the bank vault; that appellant's financial distress at about the time of the crime might have induced him to take this drastic step; that unusual activity in the area between appellant's home and the bank tended to place the perpetrators in that general area and hence, near appellant's home; and that appellant was seen in this area a few days after the robbery, perhaps to retrieve a hat, earlier found left at the scene. It was introduced in evidence and subsequently identified at trial as having been worn by one of the robbers.

* * *

Several witnesses testified about the movements of a tan car in the area of the bank and appellant's home in the early morning hours of the day of the robbery. Mrs. Kaprolet, who lived in the area, testified on behalf of the government to seeing the car around 8:00 a.m. However, FBI Agent Bass was called by the government to testify that Mrs. Kaprolet told him, on April 21, 1967, she had seen the tan car near her home twice, once at around 8:00 a.m. and a second time about 45 minutes later. Mrs. Kaprolet's testimony was important because a field search of this area turned up the hat allegedly worn by one of the robbers. We think it was error to permit the FBI agent to relate this hearsay statement of Mrs. Kaprolet. * * *

A farmer, Mr. Kulp, who also lived in this area, related that on April 21, 1967, he observed a white pickup truck stop where Mrs. Kaprolet said she had seen the tan car. A man got out of the truck, looked around and then left. Mr. Kulp recorded the license plate number, and FBI Agent Bass testified from his investigatory notes that Mr. Kulp gave him the number S0633. The evidence showed appellant owned two pickup trucks with plate numbers S6003R and S6002R.

* * *

Alleged Hearsay Nature of the License Number Evidence

A Mr. Kulp, who was a farmer living in the general vicinity of the crime, testified for the government that, on April 21, 1967, he observed a man in a white pickup truck stop and look around in the area where the farmer had seen police activity several days before. The hat allegedly worn by one of the robbers had been found there. This testimony was critical to the prosecution's case. If it could be established that the appellant was the man who searched the area on April 21, it would be if unexplained, a very strong circumstantial indication of appellant's involvement in the crime. The following colloquy occurred in the direct examination of Mr. Kulp:

"Q. Now, were you subsequently interviewed by an agent from the FBI?

"A. The FBI, yes.

"Q. Did you give him a license number that you had seen?

"A. Yes.

"Q. You did, all right. Now this was a little less than four years ago. Do you today remember that license plate number as you gave it to the FBI?

"A. No, I wouldn't remember that license number.

"Q. Did we discuss this matter within the past hour?

"A. What's that?

"Q. Did we discuss this matter of your testifying within the past hour up in my office?

"A. Yes.

"Q. Did I read you a report from the FBI regarding their interviewing you?

"A. That's right.

"Q. And did I read you that license number that was in that report?

"A. Yes, you did. I don't remember that number.

"Q. All right. The license number that I read to you from that report, did that jibe with your recollection of what you reported to the FBI?

"DEFENSE COUNSEL: I object, sir.

"A. That's right.

"THE COURT: Overruled.

"DEFENSE COUNSEL: He has already testified that he doesn't remember.

"THE COURT: Overruled. That is not the question.

"PROSECUTOR: Your Honor, I ask leave of the Court to tender to the witness the FBI report.

"THE COURT: No. You can call the FBI Agent if you wish."

After Mr. Kulp's cross-examination, FBI Agent Bass was called by the prosecution. Bass testified that Mr. Kulp had given him a license number. Using the written FBI report to refresh his recollection, Bass testified the license number was S0633. Subsequent testimony revealed that defendant's two trucks bore plate numbers S6003R and S6002R.

The objection to this part of the prosecution's case raised here by appellant is that FBI Agent Bass impermissibly testified as to hearsay, i.e., Mr. Kulp's oral statement to Agent Bass. The only question for us is whether one or more of the many exceptions to the hearsay rule applies.

Witnesses may use any aid to refresh their recollections. Reading Kulp's answer to the prosecution's question whether the report "jibed" with his recollection, it might be concluded that the witness' memory of the plate number was thereby revived. If so, Kulp should then have gone on to relate his revived memory of the number. In such circumstances, there was no need to admit the FBI report into evidence or to bring the Agent to the stand. The rule in cases of refreshed recollection is that the writing may not be admitted into evidence or its contents even seen by the jury. 3 Wigmore, Evidence § 763, (Chad.Rev.1970) and cases cited at 142 n.1.

It is not entirely clear on this record whether Kulp's memory had, in fact, been refreshed. If not, resort must be had by the prosecution to the hearsay exception for past recollection recorded. If Mr. Kulp's memory is not revived by the FBI Report, he may nevertheless testify from its contents if certain conditions are met. A prerequisite of such testimony is ascertaining the identity and accuracy of the record used. 3 Wigmore,

Evidence § 747, supra. If Kulp had testified that he read the report over after the FBI Agent made it and was, at that time, satisfied that it was correct, sufficient proof of the report's accuracy would have been made out. Since Kulp did not so testify, the more difficult question is whether there is any other basis for admitting the license plate number.

Some courts and textwriters have taken the view that where as here, a record is the joint product of two individuals, one who makes an oral statement and one who embodies it in a writing, if both parties are available to testify at trial as to the accuracy with which each performed his role, the recollection may be admitted. See, e.g., Swart v. United States, 394 F.2d 5 (9th Cir.1968); 3 Wigmore, Evidence § 751, supra; Morgan, *The Relation Between Hearsay and Preserved Memory*, 40 Harv.L.Rev. 712, 720 (1927). We think such an exception to the hearsay rule is sound and adopt it here. If Agent Bass can verify the accuracy of his transcription and if Kulp can testify he related an accurate recollection of the number to Agent Bass, we believe that, even though Kulp may not have read the report, sufficient indicia of its accuracy exist to let the evidence go to the jury. If the appropriate evidentiary basis is established at the retrial we think that the appellant would be entitled to an instruction on this point to the effect that in view of the elapsed time since Kulp reported to the FBI, the jurors should cautiously consider the degree of reliability the offered recollection deserves and that no more weight should be accorded it than such degree dictates.

* * *

[The defendant's conviction was reversed on other grounds and the case remanded to the trial court for examination of an unrelated issue.]

NOTES AND QUESTIONS

1. *Continuity of interpretation.* Rule 803(5) continues to receive two-party statements like the one discussed in *Booz.* See United States v. Hernandez, 333 F.3d 1168, 1178–79 (10th Cir.2003) (admitting two-party statement despite noting that most logical reading of Rule's language "made or adopted by the witness" would exclude such statements); 2 McCormick, Evidence § 283 (7th ed. 2013).

2. *Refreshing recollection.* The related but distinct doctrine of refreshing recollection is examined in Chapter 12, Section B(4), supra.

UNITED STATES V. FELIX–JEREZ
United States Court of Appeal, Ninth Circuit, 1982.
667 F.2d 1297.

SKELTON, SENIOR JUDGE:

In this case the facts are not in dispute and are generally as follows. Miguel Felix–Jerez (defendant) had been convicted in another proceeding of having entered the United States illegally and was sentenced to ninety days in prison and three years probation for that offense. He was serving his sentence as an inmate of the Federal Prison Camp at Stafford [sic], Arizona, when the events giving rise to the instant case occurred. The record shows that the defendant was arrested and indicted for escaping from the prison camp in violation of 18 U.S.C. § 751, and was convicted by a jury * * *. Because of the error of the court in admitting a hearsay statement into evidence over the timely objection of defendant, we reverse.

The prison camp at Stafford [sic] is a minimum security prison with no fences or enclosures and no armed guards. The prisoners are free to walk about the premises of the prison. While it was against the rules of the prison for the prisoners to leave the prison grounds without permission, the testimony of prison guards at the trial revealed that it was common knowledge at the prison that prisoners frequently went to a restaurant and bar about one-half mile from the camp to buy cigarettes, food and alcoholic beverages without obtaining permission to do so.

On November 5, 1980, during a 10:00 P.M. head count at the camp it was discovered that the defendant was not present, although he had not obtained permission to leave the prison grounds. He was discovered the next day walking along a road about 10 miles from the camp by an off-duty prison guard. The guard notified the local sheriff who arrested the defendant and returned him to the prison. At the time of his arrest, the defendant had two bottles of wine in his possession, one of which was unopened and the other was partly filled. He made no statement at the time he was picked up.

The next day, November 7th, the defendant was interrogated by Deputy United States Marshal Larry Hardeman at the prison. Because the defendant did not speak English and Hardeman did not speak Spanish, a camp guard named Daniel Tolavera served as an interpreter. The defendant was advised in Spanish of his *Miranda* rights and he waived them by signing a written form printed in Spanish.

The interrogation was conducted by Hardeman's asking questions in English which were translated into Spanish by Tolavera. The defendant answered the questions in Spanish and Tolavera translated the answers into English. Hardeman made notes of the questions and translated answers. Sometime later, after the interview had been concluded, Hardeman typed a statement containing the questions and translated answers as shown by his notes. As far as the record shows, the defendant was not present when the statement was typed by Hardeman, it was not read to him in Spanish, he did not sign it, and obviously did not know of its existence until the day of the trial.

At the trial, Tolavera was called as a witness. He testified that he acted as an interpreter at the interview between Hardeman and defendant in the manner described above because he spoke both Spanish and English, but that he had no independent recollection of the questions and answers and could not testify what they were. He said that his translations were accurate and that he had no difficulty in understanding the defendant's Spanish. He made no notes of the questions and answers.

The prosecutor then called Hardeman as a witness. He testified that he conducted the interrogation of the defendant as a United States Marshal with the assistance of camp guard Tolavera as an interpreter in the manner aforesaid. He said he did not know Spanish and did not know what the answers were that the defendant gave to Tolavera in Spanish, nor whether Tolavera correctly translated them into English. He testified further that he made notes of the questions and translated answers and later typed them himself in the form of a statement. He then compared the statement with his original notes and said that the statement was a true and accurate record and transcript of his original notes of the conversation with defendant. The prosecutor then offered the statement as evidence without asking Hardeman if he had an independent recollection of the questions he asked the defendant and of the answers the defendant gave, nor whether he could testify from his recollection what the questions and answers were. The defense counsel objected to the introduction of the statement on the ground that it was hearsay. The court overruled the objection and admitted the statement into evidence without giving any reason for his ruling. The statement was then read to the jury.

The questions and answers in the statement Hardeman had typed and which was read to the jury showed that the defendant had planned from the beginning of his incarceration at the Stafford [sic] prison camp to escape, and that he did escape on November 5, 1980, and that after drinking two six-packs of beer he bought at the nearby bar, he decided to remain away, and that he had no intention of returning to the camp.

After a careful review of the entire record and consideration of the briefs, argument of counsel and applicable authorities, we conclude that the Hardeman statement that was read to the jury was hearsay and inadmissible as evidence under Rule 802 of the Federal Rules of Evidence, unless it met the requirements of one of the 24 exceptions to the hearsay rule which are set forth in Rule 803(1)–(24).

[The court first concluded that the written statement did not constitute an adoptive admission of the defendant because he never saw, read, nor signed it. The court felt the involvement of a guard as a translator made treating the statement as an admission even more problematic.]

* * * We have carefully examined each of these exceptions in connection with the facts in this case and have concluded that none of them are applicable so as to make the Hardeman statement admissible as a non-hearsay document, except *arguendo* sub-paragraph (5) which provides:

> (5) Recorded recollection. A memorandum or record concerning a matter about which a witness once had knowledge but now has insufficient recollection to enable him to testify fully and accurately, shown to have been made or adopted by the witness when the matter was fresh in his memory and to reflect that knowledge correctly. If admitted, the memorandum or record may be read into evidence but may not itself be received as an exhibit unless offered by an adverse party.

The notes of the Advisory Committee found at the end of Rule 803 contain the following statement, in pertinent part, regarding this exception:

> The principal controversy attending the exception has centered, not upon the propriety of the exception itself, but upon the question whether a preliminary requirement of impaired memory on the part of the witness should be imposed. The authorities are divided. * * * Nevertheless, the absence of the requirement, it is believed, would encourage the use of statements carefully prepared for purposes of litigation under the supervision of attorneys, investigators, or claim adjusters. Hence the example includes a requirement that the witness not have "sufficient recollection to enable him to testify fully and accurately." * * * Title 28 U.S.C.A. Rule 803 at p. 586.

This circuit follows the rule set forth above that before a prior hearsay statement of a witness who is testifying can be admitted into evidence under this exception, it must first be shown that the witness does not now have sufficient recollection as to the matters contained in the statement to enable him to testify fully and accurately regarding them. See *United States v. Edwards,* 539 F.2d 689 (9 Cir.1976), where we held:

> Appellant also claims the trial court erred in admitting evidence of Newman's signed statement describing the events leading to the crime. At trial Newman denied any present recollection of the facts in question and the written statement was offered and admitted under the recorded recollection exception to the hearsay rule. F.R.Evid. 803(5).

Documents admitted pursuant to this rule must meet three requisites: (1) The document must pertain to matters about which the witness once had knowledge; (2) The witness must now have an insufficient recollection as to such matters; (3) The document must be shown to have been made by the witness and reflect his knowledge when the matters were fresh in his memory. 539 F.2d at 691–692.

It is clear that the second requirement set forth above in *Edwards* was not complied with in this case. Witness Hardeman did not testify that he now had an insufficient recollection as to the matters contained in the statement so as to be able to testify regarding them. In fact, he was not even asked if he now had an insufficient recollection as to such matters. The proper predicate was not laid for the introduction of the statement. Hardeman was on the witness stand and, as far as the record shows, he could have testified about the facts contained in the statement. Under these circumstances there was no need to introduce the statement, and it was error to do so.

Long before Rule 803(5) was adopted the Supreme Court set forth the substance of the rule in the case of *Vicksburg & Meridian R.R. Co. v. O'Brien,* 119 U.S. 99 * * * (1886). In that case, a physician was testifying as to the injuries to the plaintiff's wife in a railroad accident. The plaintiff offered a prior statement of the physician which he had made at the time of the accident regarding the wife's injuries. The court allowed the statement to be read to the jury over the hearsay objection of the defendant. There was no prior showing that the physician had no recollection of the facts so as to be able to testify regarding the facts in the statement. The Supreme Court held that it was error to read the hearsay statement to the jury under these circumstances, saying:

> We are of the opinion that this ruling cannot be sustained, upon any principle recognized in the law of evidence. The authorities are uniform in holding that a witness is at liberty to examine a memorandum prepared by him under the circumstances in which this one was, for the purpose of refreshing or assisting his recollection as to the facts stated in it. * * *

> There are, however, other cases, to the effect that where the witness states, under oath, that the memorandum was made by him presently after the transaction to which it relates, for the purpose of perpetuating his recollection of the facts, and that he knows it was correct when prepared, although after reading it he cannot recall the circumstances so as to state them alone from memory, the paper may be received as the best evidence of which the case admits.

The present case does not require us to enter upon an examination of the numerous authorities upon this general subject; for, it does not appear here but that at the time the witness testified he had, without even looking at his written statement, a clear, distinct recollection of every essential fact stated in it. If he had such present recollection, there was no necessity whatever for reading that paper to the jury. Applying, then, to the case the most liberal rule announced in any of the authorities, the ruling by which the plaintiffs were allowed to read the physician's written statement to the jury as evidence, in itself, of the facts therein recited, was erroneous. 119 U.S. at 102 * * *.

The decision in the *Judon* case, *supra,* contains a good discussion of Rule 803(5) and the reasoning therein is particularly applicable to our case. There a witness was present when a savings and loan branch was robbed. He wrote down on a piece of paper a description of the robber's car and its license number. The witness testified at the trial and his memorandum aforesaid was introduced into evidence over a hearsay objection and a further objection that a proper predicate had not been laid for its admission. The court held this was error, saying:

> The admissibility of this document is governed by Fed.R.Evid. 803(5), which prescribes the conditions under which recorded recollection qualifies as an exception to the hearsay rule * * *. It is clear from the second sentence of this rule that the admission of this memorandum as an exhibit was error. The drafters precluded the receipt of recorded recollection as an exhibit of the proponent of the memorandum in order to prevent the trier of fact from being overly impressed by the writing. 11 J. Moore, Federal Practice § 803(5)[5] (1976).

> *This memorandum may have qualified as a hearsay exception; however, the record reveals no proper predicate had been laid to show its admissibility as such. In particular, there was no showing that the witness had insufficient recollection to enable him to testify fully and accurately at trial.* The Advisory Committee deemed this requirement desirable, since its absence "would encourage the use of statements carefully prepared for purposes of litigation under the supervision of attorneys, investigators, or claim adjusters." See 11 J. Moore, Federal Practice § 803(5)[4] (1976). Additionally, we note that there was no specific testimony that the recording reflected the witness' knowledge correctly when the matter was fresh in his memory.

> This failure to adhere to the requirements of the Federal Rules of Evidence compounds the error in admitting the documents in evidence. (Emphasis supplied). 567 F.2d at 1294.

As stated in the notes of the Advisory Committee, and as repeated and approved by the court in the *Judon* case, the absence of a showing that the witness had insufficient recollection to enable him to testify fully and accurately at the trial, "would encourage the use of statements carefully prepared for purposes of litigation under the supervision of attorneys, investigators, or claim adjusters." That is exactly what happened in the instant case. Marshal Hardeman was an investigator. He prepared the statement for the express purpose of using it to prosecute the defendant. This is a classic example of the vice the Advisory Committee sought to prohibit by requiring proof of insufficient recollection by a witness before his hearsay statement can be admitted into evidence.

We conclude that the admission of Hardeman's statement into evidence without the proper predicate having been laid did not meet the requirements of Rule 803(5).

* * *

[The court concluded that the error was not harmless, and it reversed and remanded.]

NOTES AND QUESTIONS

1.   *Requirement of some failure of memory.* Wigmore notes two rationales for receiving recorded recollections. The first is that receipt of the memorandum is necessary because "there is not available a present actual recollection in the specific witness." The second is that "in the usual case a faithful record of past recollection, if it exists, is more trustworthy and desirable than a present recollection of greater or less vividness." 3 Wigmore, Evidence § 738, at 90 (Chadbourn rev. 1970). The second rationale, which was favored by Wigmore, id. at 91, would support admission of recorded recollections even when the witness claims no memory loss. Prior to the adoption of the Federal Rules, several states followed this second rationale, but apparently now only Colorado omits a requirement of some failure of present recollection. See Colo.R.Evid. 803(5).

2.   *Impaired not exhausted.* As explained in *Felix–Jerez,* Rule 803(5) requires some demonstration of impaired memory but does not require that it be totally exhausted. For a criticism of the federal approach, see Blakely, Past Recollection Recorded: Restrictions on Use as Exhibit and Proposals for Change, 17 Hous.L.Rev. 411 (1980).

3.   *Proving document's accuracy.* As a conceptual matter, witnesses may specifically remember that a statement they made about an event was accurate without remembering the event itself, but as a matter of everyday experience, one might assume witnesses who have forgotten the event, which is likely more memorable, would likewise have forgotten precisely what they said about it as well. One might suspect that sometimes the claims of a

specific memory about the accuracy of the statement are overstated. McCormick notes that such an attestation is not inevitably required.

> [I]f present memory is inadequate, the requirement may be met by testimony that the declarant knows [the document] is correct because of a habit or practice to record such matters accurately or to check them for accuracy. At the extreme, some courts find sufficient testimony that the individual recognizes his or her signature and believes the statement correct because the witness would not have signed it if he or she had not believed it true at the time.

2 McCormick, Evidence § 283 (7th ed. 2013). Some courts have been particularly liberal in finding an acknowledgment of accuracy with a reluctant witness. See United States v. Porter, 986 F.2d 1014, 1016–17 (6th Cir.1993); Isler v. United States, 824 A.2d 957, 960–61 (D.C.2003); State v. Gorman, 854 A.2d 1164, 1173 (Me.2004); State v. Marcy, 680 A.2d 76, 79 (Vt.1996).

4.   *Timeliness requirement.* The Rule requires that the memorandum must have been made or adopted when the matter was fresh in the witness' memory but provides no specific guidelines as to the degree of contemporaneity required. The courts have interpreted this requirement extremely generously. See, e.g., United States v. Smith, 197 F.3d 225, 231 (6th Cir.1999) (holding that trial court did not abuse its discretion in admitting statement made after fifteen months delay).

5.   *Prohibition on admitting document.* Rule 803(5) specifies that if admitted, the memorandum or record may be read into evidence but that the document itself can be received only if it is offered by the adverse party. Why does the Rule impose this restriction on admission of the document? Is it wise? See *Blakely*, note 2, supra.

6.   *Translators.* How to treat translated statements under the hearsay rules, raised in the *Felix–Jerez* case, presents an interesting question. Most courts consider the translator, even when not selected by the declarant, to be his or her agent, which allows the translation to be received as a vicarious admission where the declarant is a party. See, e.g., State v. Felton, 412 S.E.2d 344, 353–55 (N.C.1992). Other courts treat the translation as not hearsay at all, considering the interpreter as merely a "language conduit." See, e.g., United States v. Cordero, 18 F.3d 1248, 1253 (5th Cir.1994). A third, albeit rarely used, approach admits the translation under the hearsay exception for present sense impressions. United States v. Kramer, 741 F.Supp. 893, 896 (S.D.Fla.1990).

E. RECORDS OF REGULARLY CONDUCTED ACTIVITY

Federal Rules 803(6) & (7)

TRACY, THE INTRODUCTION OF DOCUMENTARY EVIDENCE

24 Iowa L.Rev. 436, 454 (1939).[17]

Business Records

To understand thoroughly the problems attendant upon the authentication of business records there must be borne in mind the development of the law as to the admissibility of such entries as an exception to the hearsay rule.

Under the rule which formerly excluded the testimony of interested parties, it was impossible for a tradesman doing business alone to prove even a simple case for goods sold and delivered. To remedy this situation, the courts developed the so-called "shop-book" rule, by which the tradesman's books of account were admissible in evidence to prove the facts stated therein, provided that the tradesman kept no clerk. At the same time this rule was being developed, the courts were confronted with other cases where the accounts of third parties and of tradesmen who did keep clerks were involved. In the first of these cases the tradesman was not ineligible as a witness, because he was not interested, and in the second class of cases the account could be proved by the clerks of the plaintiff, who also were not ineligible. In both classes of cases, however, the testimony of the person who knew about the transaction, whether proprietor or clerk, was often unobtainable because of death. In those cases the courts were able to work out a real exception to the hearsay rule, based on the necessity element arising from death. There thus grew up, side by side, two bodies of law, one for parties' books, where no clerks were employed, and the other as to the use of books of account in other cases. When the statutes were passed abolishing the disqualification of interest and making parties eligible to testify, the reasons for the shop-book rule vanished and the use of all book entries came to be governed by the same set of rules, except in a very few jurisdictions where legislation recognizing the shop-book rule has never been repealed.

NOTES AND QUESTIONS

1. *Historical perspective.* The excerpt from Tracy provides a bit of historical perspective on the modern "business records" exception found in Rule 803(6). See generally 2 McCormick, Evidence §§ 285 & 286 (7th ed. 2013).

---

[17] Copyright © by the State University of Iowa. Reprinted by permission. [Ed.]

2.   *Earlier requirements—unavailability and original records.* In a simpler day for business records, the exception required that before the records were received unavailability of the maker had to be demonstrated. As an occasional case showed, see Robertson v. Carson, 181 Ill.App. 251 (1913), the requirement helped eliminate inaccuracy, but particularly as the businesses increased in size and complexity, the requirement became unrealistic and less likely to provide benefits in terms of increased accuracy.

Similarly, the earlier requirement that the record contain "original entries" obviously raises problems of interpretation and realistic application. Should the books of a law firm, prepared from the time sheets submitted by various attorneys, be admissible in an action to recover a fee? What if the various attorneys prepare their time sheets weekly from notations on their desk calendars? Its relaxation was warranted by the nature of modern bookkeeping procedures and could not have survived the advent of computer records.

OLESEN V. HENNINGSEN
Supreme Court of Iowa, 1956.
77 N.W.2d 40.

PETERSON, JUSTICE. There is only one question in this case: was it reversible error for the trial court to admit in evidence a long distance telephone ticket on which was shown the time of the placing of a call?

[Plaintiff brought suit to recover damages for personal injuries sustained when the car he was driving struck the rear of a wagon load of corn which had been temporarily parked on a public highway by the defendant Simonson. The wagon was owned by the defendant Henningsen. At the time of the collision, no lighted red tail lamp was being exhibited on the rear of the wagon, and a principal issue of fact in the case was whether the collision had occurred at a time of day at which exhibition of such a light was required by Iowa statute. The jury found in favor of the defendants, and plaintiff appealed.]

The evidence in the case centered around the question as to whether or not it was earlier or later than 30 minutes after sunset when the collision occurred. There was a slight conflict as to the time of sunset. Each side had secured a report from the weather bureau and one report placed sunset at 4:45 and the other report placed it at 4:54.

The issue urged by appellant is that the trial court erred in admitting a certain telephone ticket, on which was stamped the time of a call. It appeared on the ticket that a long distance telephone call was placed from the Olesen farm residence near Graettinger to Emmetsburg to call the sheriff about the accident. It was not in dispute that the call was placed when plaintiff was brought home after the accident. The evidence was offered by defendants and the ticket showed that the call had been placed at 5:45 p.m. It was the claim of defendants that this was some evidence as to the accident having occurred prior to one half hour after sunset. Defendants also urge that it constituted an impeachment of the testimony of plaintiff's father and mother as to Richard being brought home at 6:05 p.m. The question of impeachment was settled by the verdict of the jury.

The testimony in connection with the call from the Olesen home to the sheriff at Emmetsburg is in substance that Mrs. Harry Fink was the operator at Graettinger, and that she kept the books and had charge of all records of the telephone office of Graettinge—Telephone Company. She testified that she held that position on November 17, 1950, the date involved in this case. When a long distance call came in for Emmetsburg she testified that the Graettinger operator made a report of the call and the long distance operator at Emmetsburg also made a record of the call, together with the time of the call and the length of the conversation. The Emmetsburg ticket as to the call was sent to Bell Telephone Company at Des Moines for record and was then sent back to Mrs. Fink, who checked it with her ticket, and then made it a part of the records of the office. This is the ticket offered in evidence. The Graettinger ticket was delivered to the customer with the charges for the month. Mrs. Fink does not testify that she handled the call. The chief operator at Emmetsburg supported the testimony of Mrs. Fink. She testified that it would be impossible to tell what operator at the Emmetsburg office handled the call, but as chief operator she had charge of the long distance records. Although she had not made the ticket, she identified it, and verified the time. In one part of the testimony they testified that the ticket was a part of their permanent records, but they also stated that the records were not necessarily permanent. However, the trial of the case was nearly three and one half years after the date of the telephone call, and the Graettinger operator and bookkeeper still had the ticket, so this in itself would be evidence of reasonable permanency of the records.

* * *

IV. Evidence as to long distance telephone tickets, railway-ticket records or hospital records is not the same as evidence concerning a book account. It does not need the same type of technical proof as the statute requires for proving an account, as set out in § 622.28. The <u>elements necessary for admission of a telephone ticket in a case such as this, are</u> identification by one or more telephone employees who either make or have supervision and charge of the records, and who know the ticket to be a genuine part of the records of the company, and who can testify it was made at or about the time shown thereon. The evidence submitted in this case meets this test. The trial court did not commit reversible error in admitting the telephone ticket. The question of admission of telephone tickets under the circumstances as herein offered has not heretofore been directly before this court. Some comparable matters have been considered, such as railroad-ticket records and hospital records. * * * There must be elements of precaution involved, because the admission creates an exception to the hearsay rule.

* * *

American Law Institute Model Code of Evidence, Rule 514 on page 270 provides as follows:

> "A writing offered as a memorandum or record of an act, event or condition is admissible as tending to prove the occurrence of the act or event or the existence of the condition if the judge finds that it was made in the regular course of a business and that it was the regular course of that business for one with personal knowledge of such an act, event or condition to make such a memorandum or record *or to transmit information thereof to be included in such a memorandum or record,* and for the memorandum or record to be made at or about the time of the act, event or condition or within a reasonable time thereafter." (Emphasis supplied.)

A comparable subject of hospital records was considered at length in Gearhart v. Des Moines R. Co., supra [21 N.W.2d 571]. In this case the court states:

> "The witness did not make any part of the records but testified as to the manner in which they were made and that they were made by the nurses and doctors in charge of the patient." One nurse testified as to part of the entries, but other entries were made by other nurses and doctors who did not testify. The court further states:

> "It is apparent that hospital records cannot be governed by the same rules or principles as applied to books of account nor admitted under our statute relating to such entries."

In this case the court based a substantial part of its argument upon provisions and quotations from Wigmore on Evidence.

Wigmore announces some tests, as quoted in the Gearhart case, supra, which apply in this case. In Wigmore on Evidence, 3d Ed., Volume V, § 1422, p. 204 it states as follows:

> "Further, in generalizing, the author states there is 'ample authority in judicial utterances for naming the following different classes of reasons underlying the exceptions:

> " 'a. Where the circumstances are such that a sincere and accurate statement would naturally be uttered, and no plan of falsification be formed.

" 'b. Where, even though a desire to falsify might present itself, other considerations, such as the danger of easy detection or the fear of punishment, would probably counteract its force.

" 'c. Where the statement was made under such conditions of publicity that an error, if it had occurred, would probably have been detected and corrected.' "

Exception "a" pertains to this case. The two operators were wholly disinterested witnesses. The circumstances were such that sincere and accurate statements were uttered. The evidence is such that it is clear no falsification plan was formed.

The greatest objection to evidence of this type is lack of opportunity for cross-examination, but the court quotes from Wigmore stating that "common sense and experience have from time to time pointed them out as practically adequate substitutes for the ordinary test" of cross-examination.

* * *

Several Federal Circuit Courts have approved the admission of long distance telephone tickets. The question has usually arisen in criminal cases, but the theory involved in cases of this type was analyzed and stated in the case of Valli v. United States, 1 Cir., 94 F.2d 687, 693, as follows:

> "While formerly at common law such evidence may not have been admissible under the hearsay rule, the law, however, is not static and the impossible is not required in these days of complicated business to meet the rules of evidence adopted when earlier and simpler methods of doing business were customary. With a business like that of the New England Telephone & Telegraph Company requiring many employees, who make records of hundreds of calls daily, if litigants were compelled to summon each employee engaged in making every record requiring proof, it would render the rules of evidence as originally recognized at common law an obstruction to justice instead of a means of promoting it. Funk v. United States, 290 U.S. 371, 381 * * *. We think it was within the sound discretion of the trial court to admit such evidence offered by the witness Buddington, especially since much of the evidence offered by him was corroborated by other testimony in the case."

In this case there is other testimony corroborating the information on the telephone ticket.

V. The argument and citations of attorneys for appellant are largely directed to specific identification of documents of evidence and to evidence necessary for proof of book accounts. Their argument is also directed along the line of the distinction between admission of evidence in states that have adopted what is known as Uniform Business Records as Evidence Act and the states which have not adopted same. Iowa has not adopted such an act. However, in view of the general statements of law, and decisions in Iowa heretofore cited, it is not necessary that evidence such as the long distance telephone ticket involved herein, be based on legislative enactment.

* * *

The judgment rendered, in accordance with the decision of the jury, is affirmed.

Affirmed.

<h2 style="text-align:center">NOTES AND QUESTIONS</h2>

1.   *Earlier formulations.* The Uniform Business Record as Evidence Act, referred to by the court in the *Olesen* case, provided in pertinent part as follows:

> § 1. Definition.—The term "business" shall include every kind of business, profession, occupation, calling or operation of institutions, whether carried on for profit or not.

> § 2. Business Records.—A record of an act, condition or event, shall, in so far as relevant, be competent evidence if the custodian or other qualified witness testifies to its identity and the mode of its preparation, and if it was made in the regular course of business, at or near the time of the act, condition or event, and if, in the opinion of the court, the sources of the information, method and time of preparation were such as to justify its admission.

The Uniform Act was adopted in more than half the states. Its substance was incorporated in Uniform Rule of Evidence 63(13) (1953). The essential features of the Act are incorporated in Federal Rule 803(6). See generally Kwestel, The Business Records Exception to the Hearsay Rule—New is Not Necessarily Better, 64 Mo.L.Rev. 595 (1999).

2.   *Scope of "business records."* Cases recognize an enormous scope in what is a record made in the regular course of activities covered by the exception. See United States v. Kaiser, 609 F.3d 556, 574 (2d Cir.2010) (business planner with contemporaneous handwritten notes regarding phone conversations); United States v. Kingston, 971 F.2d 481, 486 (10th Cir.1992) (loan counselor's notes of conversation with customer); United States v. McPartlin, 595 F.2d 1321 (7th Cir.1979) (combination appointment calendar and business diary); Stone v. Morris, 546 F.2d 730 (7th Cir.1976) (report of incident involving prisoner by prison counselor to staff psychiatrist); United Department of Pub. Safety & Correctional Servs. v. Cole, 672 A.2d 1115, 1123–24 (Md.1996) (videotape of removal of prisoner from his cell). This trend is clearly demonstrated in the admission of records of personal business

activities. For instance, in Keogh v. C.I.R., 713 F.2d 496, 499–500 (9th Cir.1983), the court held that a black-jack dealer's personal diary recording his tips at a Las Vegas casino was a business record. The court acknowledged that the diary was not a business record of the casino but found it was kept in the course of the dealer's own business activity or occupation. Moreover, records are covered even if such business activity is illegal. See United States v. Lizotte, 856 F.2d 341, 344 (1st Cir.1988) (calendar with notations of daily illegal drug sales); United States v. Hedman, 630 F.2d 1184, 1197–98 (7th Cir.1980) (diary recording illegal payoffs). However, personal records that are kept for non-business reasons do not qualify under the exception. Compare Clark v. City of Los Angeles, 650 F.2d 1033, 1037 (9th Cir.1981) (216–page diary recording encounters with police and city officials not business record since not used in witness' business of selling new and used merchandise), with Sabatino v. Curtiss Nat'l Bank of Miami Springs, 415 F.2d 632 (5th Cir.1969) (personal check record).

3.   *Liberal definition of foundation witness.* Under Rule 803(6), the foundation for admission of the business record may be shown by the testimony of the custodian of the record, or it may be established by another qualified witness. Courts have construed rather broadly the types of individuals who may lay a sufficient foundation. See United States v. Jenkins, 345 F.3d 928, 935–36 (6th Cir.2003) (concluding that postal inspector was qualified to lay foundation for express mailing labels because directly familiar with record keeping system at specific post office even though not employed there); *Keogh*, note 2, supra, 713 F.2d at 500 (wife of blackjack dealer laid adequate foundation to show regularity of entries recording tips in husband's diary); United States v. Veytia–Bravo, 603 F.2d 1187 (5th Cir.1979) (Bureau of Alcohol, Tobacco, and Firearms agent laid adequate foundation for regularity of records kept by defunct firearms dealer where records kept pursuant to federal statute).

4.   *Foundation by witnesses from another business.* Individuals who, for example, receive records will often not be able to establish the necessary foundation for records from the shipper's business because they do not have knowledge of their method of preparation and cannot verify their accuracy. See NLRB v. First Termite Control Co., 646 F.2d 424 (9th Cir.1981). There is some debate among the cases as to whether the receiving business' reliance on the preparer's records is sufficient foundation, but the better view is that, while reliance is an important part of establishing trustworthiness, it is not alone sufficient. See State v. Fitzwater, 227 P.2d 520, 551–52 (Haw.2010) (concluding that establishing trustworthiness is required); State v. Radley, 804 A.2d 1127, 1132 (Me.2002); 2 McCormick, Evidence § 292 (7th ed. 2013). Place of employment is not decisive if the witness has the requisite knowledge to establish the required foundational facts. See Phoenix Assocs. III v. Stone, 60 F.3d 95, 101–02 (2d Cir.1995) (partnership's accountant had sufficient knowledge).

5.   *Certification alternative.* Rule 803(6) allows the foundational facts required for admission under the Rule to be provided, not by a witness, but

by a certification authorized by law (e.g., Rules 902(11) or 902(12)). Because these provisions were only enacted in 2000, the case law interpreting them is not extensive. However, the cases generally accept as sufficient certifications tracking the specific terms of the Rule. See, e.g., DirecTV, Inc. v. Murray, 307 F.Supp.2d 764, 772 (D.S.C.2004) (relying on the precise terms of the certification to find e-mails admissible as created timely and kept in the regular course of business). They also enforce the notice requirement. See Latman v. Burdette, 366 F.3d 774, 787 (9th Cir.2004) (excluding records, *inter alia*, because requirement of written notice or opportunity to challenge was not met). Whether the courts will look behind a facially sufficient tracking of the Rule's requirements is unclear, but it is occasionally suggested. See Rambus, Inc. v. Infineon Techs. AG, 348 F.Supp.2d 698 (E.D.Va.2004). They exhibit some willingness, when challenged, to examine whether the certifying party is a "custodian or other qualified witness." See *Latman*, 366 F.3d at 786–87; *Rambus*, 348 F.Supp.2d at 702–03. See also Chapter 11, Section A, supra.

The admissibility of certificates of authenticity under Rules 902(4) & 902(11) may appear to be somewhat uncertain when offered in criminal cases against the criminal defendant because of the Supreme Court's recent confrontation cases, but it is likely not seriously challenged. See Melendez–Diaz v. Massachusetts, 557 U.S. 305, 336 (2009) (Kennedy, J., dissenting) ("Under one possible reading of the Court's opinion, recordkeepers will be required to testify."). Before *Melendez–Diaz* was decided, the consensus in the circuits was that such limited-purpose certificates do not render an otherwise nontestimonial document testimonial. See United States v. Adefehinti, 510 F.3d 319, 327–28 (D.C.Cir.2008) (certificates authenticating bank records may be admitted without confrontation); United States v. Ellis, 460 F.3d 920, 927 (7th Cir.2006) (not testimonial). Justice Kennedy's statement of uncertainty has not appeared to change that consensus, with courts noting the distinction between affidavits created to provide evidence against a defendant, which are testimonial, and affidavits created to authenticate an admissible record, which are not. See United States v. Yeley–Davis, 632 F.3d 673, 680 (10th Cir.2010) (citing Justice Scalia's majority opinion in *Melendez–Diaz*, 557 U.S. at 322–23). See also United States v. Johnson, 688 F.3d 494, 504–05 (8th Cir.2012) (finding such certificates nontestimonial); United States v. Anekwu, 695 F.3d 967, 975 (9th Cir.2012) (same).

UNITED STATES V. DE GEORGIA

United States Court of Appeals, Ninth Circuit, 1969.
420 F.2d 889.

HAMLEY, CIRCUIT JUDGE. Richard Allen De Georgia appeals from a judgment of conviction, entered on a jury verdict, for violating 18 U.S.C.A. § 2312 (Dyer Act). The offense involved a 1968 Mustang automobile allegedly stolen from the Hertz Corporation, in New York City, and thereafter driven to Tucson, Arizona. The car was recovered from De Georgia on September 9, 1968.

* * *

Defendant confessed in writing that he stole the automobile from the vicinity of John F. Kennedy Airport, New York, on or about July 2, 1968. However a confession does not constitute adequate proof of an element of an offense unless, as to that element, the confession is corroborated by other admissible evidence. While the Government did produce other evidence designed to corroborate the confession with regard to the element in question, defendant contends that this other evidence was inadmissible hearsay and his trial objection thereto should have been sustained.

The evidence offered by the Government in corroboration of defendant's confession that the Mustang was a stolen vehicle consisted of the testimony of Tony Gratta, the Hertz security manager for the company's New York zone. Gratta produced documentary evidence establishing that the Mustang was owned by Hertz, that it was rented to Edward P. Sweeney from John F. Kennedy Airport on June 28, 1968, and that Sweeney returned it to a Hertz station at the airport on June 30, 1968.

Gratta testified, in effect, that the vehicle was not rented or leased by Hertz after that date and therefore was a stolen vehicle when it was taken from the Hertz lot at the airport sometime after June 30, 1968. Gratta based his testimony that the Mustang had not been rented or leased by Hertz after June 30, 1968, upon information he obtained from the Hertz master computer control in Gratta's New York office.

According to Gratta, Hertz does not keep a running written business record of its rental and lease transactions but maintains this information in a computer system. Information concerning all automobile rental and lease agreements is fed into computer consoles located at each Hertz terminal and may be retrieved at the master computer control in Gratta's New York office. He explained that, under this system, one can check the master control to determine when and where a particular vehicle was last rented and when it was returned.

On July 26, 1968, Gratta received information from the Hertz office in Lincoln, Nebraska, that led him to believe that the Mustang might have been stolen. He thereupon checked the master computer control in his office and ascertained that the automobile in question had been returned to the Hertz office at the New York airport on June 30, 1968, and that there was no subsequent rental or lease activity recorded. Gratta testified that this indicated that the vehicle had been stolen.

[Counsel for defendant objected to the admission of this evidence upon the ground that it was hearsay.] As amplified in his motions for judgment of acquittal and in his briefs on appeal, counsel believes that the evidence was hearsay because it amounted to an assertion by those who placed rental and lease information into the Hertz computer system (and who were not called as witnesses) that no such transaction involving the Mustang occurred after June 30, 1968.[18]

This view finds support in the writings of Professor Wigmore. He has expressed the view that the absence of an entry concerning a particular transaction in a regularly-maintained business record of such transactions, is equivalent to an assertion by the person maintaining the record that no such transaction occurred. 5 Wigmore, Evidence (3d Ed.) §§ 1531, 1556, pages 392, 410.

But, assuming that the evidence was hearsay, this does not conclude the matter. There are many exceptions to the hearsay rule, one of which is the business records exception which, in the federal courts, is legislatively declared in the Business Records Act, 28 U.S.C.A. § 1732. See Phillips v. United States, 356 F.2d 297, 307 (9th Cir.1965). Professor Wigmore believes that negative testimony of the kind described above, based upon what regularly-maintained business records do not show, is admissible hearsay as a corollary to the exception that records made in the regular course of business are admissible. Wigmore, ibid.

A contrary view was stated in Shreve v. United States, 77 F.2d 2, 7 (9th Cir.1935), as one of several alternative reasons for reversing a district court judgment. * * *

All of the other United States Courts of Appeals which have passed upon the matter have held such evidence admissible. This is also the rule by statute in at least five states. This rule of admissibility was proposed in the Uniform Rules of Evidence, Rule 63(14), as drafted by the National Conference of Commissioners on Uniform State Laws, and approved by it at its annual conference in 1953. The Uniform Rules were also approved by the American Bar Association in 1953.

The rule that such evidence is admissible has also been proposed by the Committee on Rules of Practice and Procedure of the Judicial Conference of the United States. * * *

Regularly-maintained business records are admissible in evidence as an exception to the hearsay rule because the circumstance that they are

---

[18] Counsel did not make any point of the fact that the records examined by Gratta in reaching this conclusion were maintained in a computer system rather than in a running written business record of rental and lease transactions. In any event, paragraph (a) of 28 U.S.C.A. § 1732 * * * involves the admissibility of "any writing or record, whether in the form of an entry in a book or otherwise, made as a memorandum or record of any act, transaction * * *." (Emphasis supplied.)

regularly-maintained records upon which the company relies in conducting its business assures accuracy not likely to be enhanced by introducing into evidence the original documents upon which the records are based.

In our view, this same circumstance offers a like assurance that if a business record designed to note every transaction of a particular kind contains no notation of such a transaction between specified dates, no such transaction occurred between those dates. Moreover, in our opinion, that assurance is not likely to be enhanced by the only other means of proving such a negative; that is by bringing into court all of the documents involving similar transactions during the period in question to prove that there was no record of the transactions alleged not to have occurred, and calling as witnesses all company personnel who had the duty of entering into transactions of that kind during the critical period and inquiring whether the witnesses remembered any additional transactions for which no record had been produced.

As applied to the case now before us, this alternative method of proving the negative would have been singularly burdensome and unrewarding. An enormous volume of rental and lease contracts would have had to be brought into court. In addition, the Government would have been required to call as witnesses every Hertz employee who might have consummated a lease or rental of the Mustang during the period between June 30, 1968, the date the car was returned after its last recorded rental, and at least July 26, 1968, the date that Gratta first received information that the car was stolen. These employees would have had to be asked to state from memory whether, out of all of the lease and rental transactions which they had entered into during that time, there was any rental of this particular Mustang. Recourse to the Hertz computer avoided these difficulties.

We are in accord with the rule permitting admission of such hearsay evidence * * * which rule is supported by the weight of modern authority. With the knowledge and approval of all of the members of the court in active service, we therefore disapprove the holding in *Shreve* that such evidence is inadmissible.

It follows that Gratta's testimony to the effect that the Mustang was a stolen vehicle when it was transported across state lines after July 2, 1968, was properly received in evidence and provides adequate corroboration of defendant's confession to the same effect.

In his reply brief defendant argues, for the first time, that reception of Gratta's testimony violated the best evidence rule which required that the business records be introduced into evidence.

No such objection having been made in the trial court, we decline to consider the contention here.

Affirmed.

ELY, CIRCUIT JUDGE (concurring). [Omitted.]

NOTES AND QUESTIONS

1. *Hearsay exception for no record.* The Federal Rules define a separate hearsay exception, Rule 803(7), for admitting the absence of a "business records" to prove the "nonoccurrence or nonexistence of the matter." The facts of *De Georgia* show its use.

2. *Tangible record must exist.* While the absence of an entry in written records may be received, some tangible "record" must exist and oral statements are not admissible under the exception. See State v. Watkins, 224 P.3d 485, 493 (Idaho 2009). The restyled Federal Rule 803(6) refers to a "record," which is defined in Rule 101(b)(4) as "a memorandum, report, or data compliation."

POTAMKIN CADILLAC CORP. V. B.R.I. COVERAGE CORP.

United States Court of Appeals, Second Circuit, 1994.
38 F.3d 627.

KEARSE, CIRCUIT JUDGE:

Defendants B.R.I. Coverage Corp. *et al.* (collectively "BRI"), licensed commercial insurance brokers, appeal from so much of a judgment of the United States District Court for the Southern District of New York, Thomas P. Griesa, *Chief Judge,* as dismissed BRI's counterclaims against plaintiffs Potamkin Cadillac Corp. *et al.* (collectively "Potamkin") for $776,368 in insurance premiums allegedly advanced by BRI to insurers on behalf of Potamkin. The district court adopted the recommendation of a special master that BRI's counterclaims be denied because BRI failed to prove that it had advanced those premiums. On appeal, BRI contends principally that the district court erred in excluding a document on which it relied to prove its claims and that, in any event, Potamkin had admitted that BRI advanced the premiums in question. * * *

We reject BRI's contentions and affirm the judgment of the district court. * * *

I.   Background

Potamkin, a group of corporate entities engaged in the sale, lease, and servicing of automobiles, retained BRI as its insurance broker in 1980. In 1987, the relationship soured, and Potamkin commenced the present action * * * . Potamkin alleged that defendants had defrauded it through a scheme that included charging for insurance coverage that was not provided; charging "service fees" supposedly in lieu of commissions, while concealing percentage commissions in the premium charges it billed to Potamkin; and overstating premiums and converting payments made by Potamkin. BRI denied Potamkin's allegations and counterclaimed to recover amounts allegedly owed by Potamkin, including amounts for premiums allegedly advanced by BRI to insurance companies, for which Potamkin had never reimbursed BRI ("unreimbursed premium advances").

In November 1991, after four years of protracted and acrimonious discovery, the action came to trial. * * * The trial was terminated when the parties entered into a stipulation * * * leaving for adjudication only (a) an accounting with respect to Potamkin's claims for return of premiums, unapplied payments, overbillings, and overpayments, and (b) BRI's counterclaims for, *inter alia,* unreimbursed premium advances. [Both Potamkin and BRI submitted to the court evidence and summaries in support of their claims and agreed to appointment of a special master.]

A.   *The Proceedings Before the Special Master*

* * * In support of its counterclaims, BRI relied primarily on an accounting history prepared by the computer department of B.R.I. Coverage Corp. (the "company"), allegedly detailing all unreimbursed advanced premiums (the "Potamkin History" or the "History"). The affidavit of Edward DeLuca, the company's controller and the head of its accounting department, described the History's contents and compilation. DeLuca stated that the History "represent[ed] all business transacted between [the company] and the Potamkin organization over the course of the entirety of the[ir] relationship," and had been prepared "several years ago" by the company's computer department "by extracting information concerning the transactions from [the company's] computer history tapes." (Affidavit of Edward DeLuca, dated December 3, 1991 ("DeLuca Affidavit"), ¶¶ 7, 2.) DeLuca stated that this process required the computer department to program its computer system "to scan the history tapes, extract the pertinent information concerning the transactions between the parties," and create a printout. (*Id.* ¶ 2.) His affidavit was silent as to why the History had been prepared, what documents were the sources for the computer tapes from which the History had been prepared, and why, despite Potamkin's requests covering such documents, the tapes themselves had not been produced during the four years of discovery.

The DeLuca Affidavit stated that though DeLuca had found no "material financial improprieties" in the History (*id.* ¶ 9), a "test sample review" comparing parts of the History to the company's open ledger records had revealed a number of "keypunch errors, misapplication of cash or billings among policies, and policies mislabeled as unassigned. * * *

Potamkin, in support of its own claims and in support of its defenses to BRI's counterclaims, relied primarily on some of the evidence proffered by BRI. For example, Potamkin argued that portions of the History constituted admissions by BRI of Potamkin's payment of certain premiums.

Both sides also produced expert opinion evidence. BRI submitted affidavits of an independent accountant opining that the History was largely correct. Potamkin submitted reports of two academics opining that the History was self-serving and that BRI had not established the document's reliability.

After reviewing the presentations, the special master made tentative findings and circulated a draft report to the parties. Seeing that the special master intended to recommend denial of all of BRI's counterclaims for unreimbursed premium advances, BRI, with the master's permission, moved for reconsideration of the draft, arguing for the first time (a) that the History was presumptively reliable as a business record admissible under Fed.R.Evid. 803(6), and (b) that Potamkin had admitted in its complaint that BRI had made the pertinent premium advances on Potamkin's behalf.

B.   The Recommendations of the Special Master

In June 1993, the special master submitted to the district court his final report recommending the granting of certain of Potamkin's claims and the denial of all of BRI's counterclaims. (Recommendation of the Special Master ("Recommendation").) As to the counterclaims for unreimbursed premium advances, the master rejected BRI's contention that Potamkin had admitted those claims (Recommendation at 46–47), and concluded that the evidence produced by BRI was "insufficient to prove that it advanced moneys on behalf of Potamkin" (*id.* at 45). * * *

The master rejected BRI's contention that the History was admissible, and should be deemed reliable, as a business record. He found that "[f]ar from being a contemporaneous business record, the Potamkin History was prepared at the request of counsel." (*Id.* at 47.) He noted that in a November 1989 deposition, BRI had taken the position that the History was privileged as attorney work product. (*Id.*) He found that none of the affidavits submitted by BRI established that the History was a business record. Although the DeLuca Affidavit described the History as having been prepared from BRI's historical computer tapes, the master found that there was "no evidence presented of what information was the source of these computer tapes and indeed, the tapes themselves have apparently never been produced, despite their request by Potamkin." (*Id.* at 48.)

In sum, though the special master found that, where pertinent, the History could be relied on by Potamkin as admissions of BRI to support claims asserted by Potamkin (*id.* at 16), and though he gave some weight to the History in considering BRI's defenses against claims by Potamkin (*id.* at 45), he concluded that "the Potamkin History, by itself, is not sufficient to support BRI's claims against Potamkin * * * particularly * * * in the absence of any explanation for the failure to submit checks" (*id.* at 45–46). BRI had failed to meet its "burden of presenting competent evidence that it paid the money it seeks reimbursement for." (*Id.*) * * *

II. Discussion

On appeal, BRI principally pursues the contentions that its Potamkin History should have been admitted as a business record and that Potamkin admitted that BRI had paid the premiums for which BRI here seeks reimbursement. We find no merit in its contentions.

A.   The BRI History

The party proffering evidence has the burden of showing that the prerequisites for its admissibility are met. The district court's findings as to whether those prerequisites have been met may not be overturned unless they are clearly erroneous. *See, e.g., Gentile v. County of Suffolk,* 926 F.2d 142, 151 (2d Cir.1991); *United States v. Maldonado–Rivera,* 922 F.2d 934, 957 (2d Cir.1990). "The findings of a [special] master, to the extent that the court adopts them, shall be considered as the findings of the court," Fed.R.Civ.P. 52(a), and cannot be set aside unless they are clearly erroneous, *Mentor Insurance Co. v. Brannkasse,* 996 F.2d 506, 513 (2d Cir.1993). "Where there are two permissible views of the evidence, the factfinder's choice between them cannot be clearly erroneous." *Anderson v. Bessemer City,* 470 U.S. 564, 574 * * * (1985).

Rule 803(6) of the Federal Rules of Evidence excepts from the operation of the hearsay rule, *see* Fed.R.Evid. 802, any

> memorandum, report, record or data compilation, in any form, of acts [or] events * * * *made at or near the time by,* or from knowledge transmitted by, a person with knowledge, *if kept in the course of a regularly conducted business activity,* and if it was the regular practice of the business activity to make the memorandum, report, record or data compilation, * * * unless the source of information or the method or circumstances of preparation indicate lack of trustworthiness.

Fed.R.Evid. 803(6) (emphasis added). A business record may include data stored electronically on computers and later printed out for presentation in court, so long as the "original computer data compilation was prepared pursuant to a business duty in accordance with regular business practice." *United States v. Hernandez,* 913 F.2d 1506, 1512–13 (10th Cir.1990); see also Notes of Advisory Committee on 1972 Proposed Rules of Evidence. Data prepared or compiled for use in litigation are not admissible as business records. *See, e.g., Palmer v. Hoffman,* 318 U.S. 109, 114 * * * (1943). Thus, a document that constitutes attorney work product, *i.e.,* material prepared by or at the instance of an attorney during or in anticipation of litigation and reflecting the attorney's thought processes, *see, e.g., Hickman v. Taylor,* 329 U.S. 495, 510–11 * * * (1947), is not a business record within the meaning of Rule 803(6).

In all cases, "the principal precondition to admission of documents as business records pursuant to Fed.R.Evid. 803(6) is that the records have sufficient indicia of trustworthiness to be considered reliable." *Saks International, Inc. v. M/V "Export Champion",* 817 F.2d 1011, 1013 (2d Cir.1987). The determination of whether, in all the circumstances, the records are sufficiently reliable to warrant their admission in evidence is left to the sound discretion of the trial court. *See, e.g., id.; United States v. Lavin,* 480 F.2d 657, 662 (2d Cir.1973).

We see no error in the findings of the special master, which were adopted by the district court, that BRI did not show that its Potamkin History met the prerequisites for admissibility as a business record within the meaning of Rule 803. In concluding that BRI had not met its burden of showing that the History was prepared from original computer data compiled in accordance with regular business practice, the court was entitled to take into account BRI's refusal, despite discovery requests, to produce the computer tapes from which DeLuca asserted the History had been compiled. Further, the DeLuca Affidavit disclosed that the testing of the History showed that it contained inaccuracies resulting from, *e.g.,* keypunch errors, misapplication of cash or billings among policies, mislabeling of policies, and miscodings. Whether or not these errors were corrected, the fact that they were made suggests that the History required significant selection and interpretation of data, not simply a downloading of information previously computerized in the regular course of business. The view that the document was not prepared in the ordinary course of business was further supported by BRI's prior statements, recorded in a deposition transcript, that the History in fact constituted its attorney's work product.

* * *

Finally, we note that BRI contends that the special master could not reject the History as proof of BRI's payments on Potamkin's behalf because he relied on that document in granting certain claims of Potamkin. This argument is unsound. Assertions by a party in documents it has prepared and offers into evidence are admissible against it as admissions, *see* Fed.R.Evid. 801(d)(2)(A), and hence are evidence on the basis of which the court may make findings of fact. *See, e.g., United States v. Bedford Associates,* 713 F.2d 895, 905 (2d Cir.1983) (statements in answers to interrogatories or in proposed findings of fact are admissions admissible against the party that made them); *Bertha Building Corp. v. National Theatres Corp.,* 248 F.2d 833, 836 (1957). Such statements are nonhearsay admissions, however, only when offered against, not by, the party that made them. * * *

Conclusion

We have considered all of BRI's contentions on appeal and have found them to be without merit. The judgment of the district court is affirmed.

NOTES AND QUESTIONS

1. *Computer records viewed as modern standard.* Courts have treat computer records routinely under the basic requirements of business (or government) records. See United States v. Salgado, 250 F.3d 438, 453 (6th Cir.2001) (ruling that "government is not required to present expert testimony as to the mechanical accuracy of the computer where it presented evidence that the computer was sufficiently accurate that the company relied upon it in conducting its business"); United States v. Catabran, 836 F.2d 453, 458 (9th Cir.1988) (question regarding accuracy of printouts based on allegations of incorrect data entry or operation of computer program treated like similar claims for other types of business records); United States v. Vela, 673 F.2d 86, 90 (5th Cir.1982) (records received despite no specific showing that computers generating them were in proper working order—"computer evidence is not intrinsically unreliable"); People v. Martinez, 990 P.2d 563, 581–82 (Cal.2000) (admission of computer records under the hearsay rule for government records has no prerequisite of testimony regarding acceptability, accuracy, maintenance, and reliability of hardware or software). This result seems obvious today given the standard use of computers to make and store records.

2. *Printing stored data is not creating a report.* As *Potamkin* demonstrates, when information stored in computers is displayed, generally the act of display is not considered the creation of a record, but where significant selection and interpretation of data is involved, courts consider it a new record. Similarly, the printing of a report for litigation does not make it a "litigation records" with questionable motivation if the data was compiled in the regular course of the business and not with an eye on litigation. See U–Haul Intern., Inc. v. Lumbermans Mut. Cas. Co., 576 F.3d 1040, 1044 (9th Cir.2009).

3. *Timeliness requirement and printouts.* The creation of a printout to be used in evidence raises a set of issues under Rule 803(6) that barred admissibility in *Potamkin* but typically do not pose great obstacles to admission. These questions include: Does such a printout satisfy the Rule's requirement that it be "made at or near the time" of the act or event? Is such a printout prepared in the regular course of business? Is it a suspect "litigation record"? For routine records, the timeliness issue usually disappears when focus is placed on the time of data entry rather than its retrieval. See United States v. Russo, 480 F.2d 1228, 1240 (6th Cir.1973). The last two questions are in fact inter-related. Unlike the situation in *Potamkin*,

if the printout is simply ordering existing data rather than creating new information or, although done in this instance for evidence purposes, is the type of record that is part of the ordinary business routine, it should not be treated as suspect. See United States v. Sanders, 749 F.2d 195, 198 (5th Cir.1984) (contrasting programs that "only orders it [the data] out" rather than "sorting, compiling or summarizing information"); 4 Mueller & Kirkpatrick, Federal Evidence § 8.79 (3d ed. 2007) (test should be whether producing the printout is part of the business routine that gives basis for assuring reliability).

UNITED STATES V. BLECHMAN

United States Court of Appeals, Tenth Circuit, 2011.
657 F.3d 1052.

EBEL CIRCUIT JUDGE.

In January 2009, Defendant–Appellant Robert Andrew Blechman and a codefendant, Itsik ("Issac") Yass, were tried together in the District of Kansas on charges of mail fraud, aggravated identity theft, and conspiracy to commit mail fraud and aggravated identity theft. Evidence introduced at trial showed that Yass operated a business that he used to temporarily halt home foreclosures by "attaching" foreclosure properties to fraudulent bankruptcy cases in order to take advantage of the Bankruptcy Code's automatic stay provision. Several different pieces of evidence connected Blechman to Yass's scheme, including e-mails sent from "rablechman@aol.com" to Yass, Public Access to Court Electronic Records ("PACER") records suggesting that Blechman accessed fraudulent bankruptcies using both Yass's PACER account and his own PACER account, postal money orders that Blechman filled out and mailed to bankruptcy courts to pay filing fees on behalf of fictitious debtors, and Yass's trial testimony explaining Blechman's role in the scheme. After a two-week trial, the jury found Blechman and Yass guilty of all of the counts charged against them. * * *

Blechman now appeals, challenging the district court's admission of an America Online ("AOL") record that connected him to the e-mail address "rablechman@aol.com" and three PACER records revealing that he accessed fraudulent bankruptcy cases in Tennessee that were similar to the Kansas bankruptcies identified in the indictment. Blechman argues that these records contained double hearsay and that the district court erroneously admitted them under the business records exception to the hearsay rule. See Fed.R.Evid. 803(6). * * *

*** Layered Hearsay and the Business Records Exception*

The Federal Rules of Evidence define "hearsay" as "a statement, other than one made by the declarant while testifying at the trial or hearing, offered in evidence to prove the truth of the matter asserted."

Fed.R.Evid. 801(c). Hearsay is generally inadmissible unless it falls within a specific exception to the hearsay rule. *See* Fed.R.Evid. 802.

In this case, it is undisputed that the AOL record and PACER records were offered to prove the truth of the matters asserted in these documents—namely, that Blechman was the registered owner of the "rablechman@aol.com" e-mail address and that Blechman was associated with PACER account "RB 1071," which someone used to access fraudulent bankruptcy cases in Tennessee. Accordingly, the records constitute hearsay.

Nevertheless, the district court admitted the records under the business records exception to the hearsay rule, which provides that certain records of regularly conducted business activity are admissible for their truth even though they contain hearsay. Fed.R.Evid. 803(6). To satisfy the business records exception, a record

> must (1) have been prepared in the normal course of business; (2) have been made at or near the time of the events recorded; (3) be based on the personal knowledge of the entrant or of a person who had a business duty to transmit the information to the entrant; and (4) indicate the sources, methods and circumstances by which the record was made were trustworthy.

United States v. Ary, 518 F.3d 775, 786 (10th Cir.2008). Blechman argues that Exhibit 1–BBB [the AOL Records] and Exhibits 22, 23, and 24 [the PACER records] do not meet these requirements because the records feature "double" or "layered" hearsay in the form of unverified user-input information.

"Double hearsay in the context of a business record exists when the record is prepared by an employee with information supplied by another person." *United States v. Gwathney,* 465 F.3d 1133, 1141 (10th Cir.2006) (internal quotation marks omitted). If the person who provides the information is an outsider to the business who is not under a business duty to provide accurate information, then the reliability rationale that underlies the business records exception ordinarily does not apply. *See Ary,* 518 F.3d at 787 ("The essential component of the business records exception is that each actor in the chain of information is under a business duty or compulsion to provide accurate information. If any person in the process is not acting in the regular course of business, then an essential link in the trustworthiness chain fails."); *see also United States v. Snyder,* 787 F.2d 1429, 1433–34 (10th Cir.1986) ("The business records exception is based on a presumption of accuracy, accorded because the information is part of a regularly conducted activity, kept by those trained in the habits of precision, and customarily checked for correctness, and because of the accuracy demanded in the conduct of the nation's business. The reason underlying the business records exception

fails, however, if any of the participants is outside the pattern of
regularity of activity." (citation and internal quotation marks omitted)).
Accordingly, the general rule is that "[a]ny information provided by * * *
an outsider to the business preparing the record[ ] must itself fall within
a hearsay exception to be admissible." *Gwathney,* 465 F.3d at 1141; *see
also* Fed.R.Evid. 805 ("Hearsay included within hearsay is not excluded
under the hearsay rule if each part of the combined statements conforms
with an exception to the hearsay rule provided in these rules.").

This Court, however, has recognized one exception to the general
rule: information provided by an outsider that is included in a business
record may come in under the business records exception "[i]f the
business entity has adequate verification or other assurance of accuracy
of the information provided by the outside person." *United States v.
McIntyre,* 997 F.2d 687, 700 (10th Cir.1993); *see also United States v.
Cestnik,* 36 F.3d 904, 908 (10th Cir.1994). In the context of identity
information provided by an outsider, we have identified "two ways to
demonstrate this 'guarantee[ ] of trustworthiness': (1) proof that the
business has a policy of verifying [the accuracy of information provided by
someone outside the business]; or (2) proof that the business possesses 'a
sufficient self-interest in the accuracy of the [record]' to justify an
inference of trustworthiness." *Cestnik,* 36 F.3d at 908 (some alterations in
original) (quoting *McIntyre,* 997 F.2d at 700).

Applying these principles, we conclude that the district court erred in
admitting Exhibit 1–BBB and Exhibits 22, 23, and 24 under Rule 803(6).
It is undisputed that the crucial information in the AOL and PACER
records—specifically, the information concerning the identity of the user
of the "rablechman" AOL account and the user of PACER account "RB
1071"—was provided by a third party over the Internet, not by an
employee of AOL or PACER. Thus, the Government was required to
demonstrate the trustworthiness of the information in one of the two
ways mentioned above. *See United States v. Samaniego,* 187 F.3d 1222,
1224 (10th Cir.1999) ("The obligation of establishing the applicability of a
hearsay exception for these records falls upon the government as the
proponent of the evidence.").

But the record makes clear that neither AOL nor PACER made a
meaningful attempt to verify the identity of the person who submitted the
information. Beginning with AOL, Patricia Johnson, the AOL
investigator, admitted that AOL did not verify who input the "subscriber
information" contained on the third page of Exhibit 1–BBB and that it
could have been "anybody in the world who could access a computer."
(ROA, vol. V at 329.) Moreover, Exhibit 1–BBB states in no uncertain
terms that AOL made no effort to verify the identity of the individual who
registered the "rablechman" account: "Registration information is
recorded but not verified. Fictitious names and addresses are common."

(*Id.* vol. XI at 13 * * *). With respect to PACER, Ted Willmann, the PACER manager, acknowledged that PACER did no more than ensure that whoever created account "RB 1071" entered a valid mailing address and did not provide identifying information matching that of an existing user. PACER took no steps, however, to verify the authenticity of the identifying information. Furthermore, nothing in the record suggests— and the Government does not argue—that either AOL or PACER "had a sufficiently compelling self-interest in ensuring the accuracy of information filled out by [their] customers to justify an inference of reliability." *Cestnik,* 36 F.3d at 908. If anything, the record reveals that AOL and PACER were uninterested in the accuracy of the user-input information. For these reasons, the district court improperly admitted Exhibit 1–BBB and Exhibits 22, 23, 24 under the business records exception to the hearsay rule.

[Although finding error, the court affirmed defendant Bleckman's conviction because the error was found to be harmless.]

ECHO ACCEPTANCE CORP. V. HOUSEHOLD RETAIL SERVICES, INC.

United States Court of Appeals, Tenth Circuit, 2001.
267 F.3d 1068.

PAUL KELLEY, JR., CIRCUIT JUDGE.

Defendant Household Retail Services, Inc. ("HRSI" or "Household"), appeals from a jury verdict in favor of Plaintiffs Echo Acceptance Corporation and Echosphere Corporation (collectively, "Echo") on Echo's breach of contract claim. * * *

*** *Exclusion of Defense Exhibits 21, 23, and 25*

* * * HRSI claims that the district court erred in sustaining Echo's hearsay objections to the admission of three 1994 letters from HRSI. Inter alia, HRSI * * * claims that the letters were admissible as business records. Evidentiary rulings are reviewed for abuse of discretion. * * * We see no abuse of discretion here.

*** *Rule 803(6): Business Records Exception*

The district court * * * rejected HRSI's proffer of the letters under the business records exception to the hearsay rule. *See* Fed.R.Evid. 803(6). The court determined that the letters constituted legal "posturing," drafted by lawyers in anticipation of litigation, and that Rule 803(6) was therefore inapplicable. * * * Rule 803(6) "requires that the custodian or other qualified witness testify that (1) the records were made contemporaneously with the events and 'kept in the course of a regularly conducted business activity,' and (2) 'it was the regular practice of that business activity to make the [record].'" *United States v. Samaniego,* 187

F.3d 1222, 1224 (10th Cir.1999) (quoting Fed.R.Evid. 803(6)) (footnote omitted). Business records are inadmissible, however, where "the source of information or the method or *circumstances of preparation* indicate lack of trustworthiness." Fed.R.Evid. 803(6) (emphasis added); *see also id.* advisory committee notes (1972) (describing rationale underlying exception as "[t]he element of unusual reliability * * * said variously to be supplied by systematic checking, by regularity and continuity which produce habits of precision, by actual experience of business in relying upon them, or by a duty to make an accurate record as part of a continuing job or occupation") (citation omitted). Thus, the motivation of a record's author is relevant to admissibility. *Id.*

Not every item of business correspondence constitutes a business record. *See, e.g., Breeden v. ABF Freight System, Inc.,* 115 F.3d 749, 754 (10th Cir.1997) (sustaining exclusion of letter from chiropractor proffered as "medical business record"); *Timberlake Const. Co. v. U.S. Fidelity & Guar. Co.,* 71 F.3d 335, 342 (10th Cir.1995) (holding that court erred in admitting letters "written in anticipation of litigation" as business records). "It is well-established that one who prepares a document in anticipation of litigation is not acting in the regular course of business." *Timberlake,* 71 F.3d at 342 (citing *Palmer v. Hoffman,* 318 U.S. 109, 114 (1943); Fed.R.Evid. 803(6) advisory committee's note); *see also Certain Underwriters at Lloyd's, London v. Sinkovich,* 232 F.3d 200, 204 n.2 (4th Cir.2000) (noting that documents "prepared in view of litigation[ ] are not admissible as business records under Rule 803(6) and illustrate * * * that such documents prepared specifically for use in litigation are 'dripping with motivations to misrepresent' ") * * * *Noble v. Ala. Dep't of Envtl. Mgmt.,* 872 F.2d 361, 366 (11th Cir.1989) (holding that court erred in admitting letter as business record where "testimony was not adequate to establish that the letter was compiled as a matter of regular practice, as opposed to one prepared in anticipation of litigation"). Upon a thorough review of the exhibits and the testimony surrounding their proffer, we have found nothing to satisfy the foundational requirement that they were "kept in the course of a regularly conducted business activity." Fed.R.Evid. 803(6). Like the letters we found inadmissible in *Timberlake,* the exhibits at issue in this case "have all the earmarks of being motivated and generated to further [HRSI's] interest, with litigation * * * not far around the corner." 71 F.3d at 342. We see no abuse of discretion in the court's refusal to admit defense exhibits 21, 23, and 25 as business records under Rule 803(6).

NOTES AND QUESTIONS

1. *Hearsay within hearsay. Blechman* discusses the admission of multiple layers of hearsay, which in some situations is dealt with by multiple hearsay exceptions under Rule 805, see Section M, infra, and in others by the

single exception of business records. As *Blechman* notes, if each of the multiple layers of hearsay involve people within the business with a "business duty," then they are all admissible under Rule 803(6). However, if someone outside the business makes one of the statements (e.g., a bystander), then Rule 805 is involved and the statement cannot be received for its truth without another exception (e.g., excited utterance). See United States v. Sparkman, 235 F.R.D. 454, 460 (E.D.Mo.2006) (recognizing the distinction between two levels of hearsay when the source and the recorder are not the same person and the source is not acting in regular course of business, and a single level of hearsay under business records when, although different people, both the source and the recorder are acting within the regular course of business). Assuming an exception exists for the outsider's statement, note that the person within the business must have some business interest in hearing and recording the statement accurately. See Commonwealth v. Harris, 41 A.2d 688 (Pa.1945) (examining whether description of attacker should be admitted when contained in hospital record).

2.   *Verification.* As to requiring that persons furnishing information, as well as those recording it, be in the routine of the "business," consider United States v. Vigneau, 187 F.3d 70, 75–77 (1st Cir.1999) (ruling inadmissible defendant's name as sender on Western Union "To Send Money" forms since he was not part of business and company's practice was not to verify identity); United States v. Lieberman, 637 F.2d 95, 100–01 (2d Cir.1980) (admitting a hotel registration card under Rule 803(6) where the hotel employee verified the identification information supplied by the guest).

3.   *Ad hoc showing of lack of trustworthiness.* Rule 803(6) provides that a statement that meets the formal requirements of the Rule may be excluded if "neither the source of information nor the method or circumstances of preparation indicate a lack of trustworthiness." Courts have generally required the proponent of the evidence to initially bear the burden of establishing that the statement meets the Rule's general requirements and then shift the burden of demonstrating lack of trustworthiness to the party opposing admission. See, e.g., Shelton v. Consumer Prods. Safety Comm'n, 277 F.3d 998, 1010 (8th Cir.2002). In 2013, the Advisory Committee to the Federal Evidence Rules proposed an amendment to Rule 803(6)(E) that makes this burden shift to the opponent explicit, which the Committee notes is currently the view of most, but not all, courts.

4.   *Trustworthiness undercut by preparation for litigation.* In some cases, such as *Olesen v. Henningsen*, supra, the business that prepared the record has no interest in the litigation, but in others, such as *Echo Acceptance Corp.*, the entity preparing the record has a recognizable interest in the litigation. Lack of trustworthiness may be shown in a number of circumstances, and one given particular attention is that the record was prepared for litigation purposes. The seminal federal case is Palmer v. Hoffman, 318 U.S. 109 (1943), which excluded an accident report prepared by railroad employees with obvious motivation regarding fault in the accident. See Peat, Inc. v. Vanguard Research Inc., 378 F.3d 1154, 1159–61 (11th

Cir.2004) (excluding document prepared in response to discovery request by party to identify trade secrets allegedly misappropriated because prepared not in the regular course of business but for litigation); Paddack v. Dave Christensen, Inc., 745 F.2d 1254, 1258–59 (9th Cir.1984) (audit reports ordered by trustees of trust account only upon suspicion of deficiency were prepared for litigation and lacked trustworthiness); United States v. Williams, 661 F.2d 528, 531 (5th Cir.1981) (memorandum estimating value of company's trailer stolen three years earlier made by head of maintenance department lacked trustworthiness because it was not prepared in course of regularly conducted business but rather for trial); Pan–Islamic Trade Corp. v. Exxon Corp., 632 F.2d 539, 560 (5th Cir.1980) (memorandum drafted for purpose of preventing cancellation of contract prepared for litigation and lacked trustworthiness).

5.   *Admissible "litigation records."* The fact that a record may have value in the event of litigation does not, however, automatically exclude it from the exception as untrustworthy. In Lewis v. Baker, 526 F.2d 470 (2d Cir.1975), the court admitted as a business record an accident report prepared by railroad employees shortly after plaintiff's injury. In spite of the fact that the report was offered on behalf of the defendant railroad, the court found no lack of trustworthiness. The individual employees who prepared the report were neither personally involved in the accident nor potential targets of the suit, and such reports were regularly prepared both in response to federal regulations and because of their utility to the employer in preventing future accidents. See also S.E.C. v. Jasper, 678 F.3d 1116, 1123–24 (9th Cir.2012) (ruling that corporation's yearly filing with SEC restating its financial statements was admissible as business record despite its potential to be used in litigation because the filing is a legal requirement and the prospect of litigation involving such a statement is always possible).

6.   *Hospitals as businesses.* Hospital records may contain a variety of entries, as in United States v. Bohle, 445 F.2d 54, 61 (7th Cir.1971):

> It contains material in the nature of a case history consisting largely of statements made by Bohle and third parties, principally his mother, and recorded by members of the hospital staffs. It also contains records concerning the treatment given Bohle and concerning observations made of him which require no special skill and as to which there is little likelihood of disagreement among trained observers [sic]. Finally, Exhibit A contains diagnoses, and similar judgment opinions, of Bohle's condition prepared by those who attended him while he was hospitalized.

The court in *Bohle* reached the conclusion that different treatment is required depending upon the nature of the entry. Rule 803(6) specifically includes opinions or diagnoses within its scope and draws no distinction based on their objective or judgmental character. Does this mean that all opinions are admissible under the Rule or does the court retain discretion to exclude those that are questionable under the trustworthiness rubric? Some commentators argue that courts can require the testimony of the expert before admitting the record in situations where the opinion is especially contestable. See 5 Weinstein's Federal Evidence § 803.08[6][b] (2d ed. 2013); 2 McCormick, Evidence § 293 (7th ed. 2013).

7. *Diagnoses and opinions.* In general, expert opinions in business records should not be admissible if the person rendering the opinion is unqualified or the topic is not a proper one for expert testimony. 2 McCormick, Evidence § 287 (7th ed. 2013). It makes little sense that an opinion that could not be received under Rule 702 if the expert testified, for example, were admissible from the same individual through a business record. See related discussion of expert opinions that are part of evaluative reports in Section F, infra, following *Bridgeway.*

Whether the party who offers the record or the opponent who would challenge it bears the burden of proving issues regarding expertise is not entirely clear, and perhaps which party has the burden should not receive uniform treatment. Courts have reached different conclusions. Compare United States v. Licavoli, 604 F.2d 613, 622–23 (9th Cir.1979) (no inflexible rule that qualifications be affirmatively established, but trial judge has discretion to exclude opinion where qualifications are seriously challenged), with Forward Communications Corp. v. United States, 608 F.2d 485, 510–11 (Ct.Cl.1979) (opinions that are not part of factual reports of contemporaneous events but are prepared for the purpose of stating or supporting expert opinions are inadmissible unless preparer testifies and establishes qualifications). Which approach is more consistent with the general structure of Rule 803(6)? Perhaps a sensible pattern can be seen in pre-Rules cases involving diagnostic entries contained in hospital records. They have frequently been admitted, at least where the entrants are shown to be members of the hospital staff, with the competency of the doctor presumed from the position held. See Allen v. St. Louis Pub. Serv. Co., 285 S.W.2d 663 (Mo.1956). A similar presumption appears to attach to technicians whose laboratory findings are incorporated in such record. See Webber v. McCormick, 164 A.2d 813 (N.J.Super.1960). But, a presumption of competency may not be appropriate for records of privately practicing physicians. See Falcone v. New Jersey Bell Tel. Co., 236 A.2d 394 (N.J.Super.1967).

F. PUBLIC RECORDS AND REPORTS

Federal Rules 803(8), (9) & (10)

CHESAPEAKE & DELAWARE CANAL CO. v. UNITED STATES
Supreme Court of the United States, 1919.
250 U.S. 123.

[Action by the Government to recover dividends claimed to be due and unpaid on shares of stock held by it in defendant corporation.]

MR. JUSTICE CLARKE delivered the opinion of the court: * * *

The government produced a witness who testified that he, in conspiracy with another employee of the Canal Company, embezzled the amount of these dividends, and that, to conceal their crime, they placed in the files of the Canal Company, from which they were produced in evidence, forged drafts purporting to have been drawn by Assistant Treasurers of the United States upon the treasurer of the Canal Company for payment of these dividends, and also what purported to be receipts therefor. This witness testified that until 1886, when he left the employ of the Canal Company, no notice of the declaration of the three dividends in controversy had been sent to the government, as had been the practice when earlier dividends were declared; that until that time no payment of them had been made, and that the names signed to the drafts and receipts were fictitious.

The government also produced the notices by the Canal Company of the declaration of each of the fourteen earlier dividends and the record of the payment of them.

To supplement this evidence the books were produced in evidence, the admission of which is assigned as error.

Employees of the Department of the Treasury, who produced the books, testified: that they were records of the Department, compiled by authority of law under the direction of the Secretary of the Treasury, and were the volumes in daily use by officials and employees in the discharge of their duties; that part of them were printed from the original records of miscellaneous revenues, in which such dividends would be classed, while others were printed compilations from books not of original entry, and the testimony was that the volumes produced were intended to, and the witnesses believed did, show all of the miscellaneous receipts and disbursements of the government from 1848 to 1914. They showed the receipt by the government of fourteen dividends paid by the Canal Company prior to those in controversy, and the witnesses testified that a careful search made by them failed to discover any record in the books of the receipt of any of the three dividends sued for. There was an elaborate description of the method employed by the Department of the Treasury in keeping its accounts, and of the necessarily contemporaneous character of the original entries, which it is not necessary to rehearse. The copies produced were printed by the Public Printer.

The objection is that these are not books of original entry, and that they are not certified as copies of public records are required to be by Rev.Stat. 882, Comp.Stat.1916, § 1494, 3 Fed.Stat.Anno.2d ed. p. 197.

It is enough to say of this last contention that although the books admitted were printed from written public records, they were so printed by authority of law, and were produced from the custody of the

Department of the Treasury, where they were used as original records in the transaction of the daily business of the Department, and therefore they did not require certification.

They were public records, kept pursuant to constitutional and statutory requirement. Constitution of the United States, Article 1, § 9, cl. 7; Act of Congress, approved September 2, 1789, * * * Thus, their character as public records required by law to be kept, the official character of their contents, entered under the sanction of public duty, the obvious necessity for regular contemporaneous entries in them, and the reduction to a minimum of motive on the part of public officials and employees to either make false entries or to omit proper ones, all unite to make these books admissible as unusually trustworthy sources of evidence. * * * Obviously such books are not subject to the rules of restricted admissibility applicable to private account books. The considerations which we have found rendered the books admissible in evidence as tending to prove the truth of the statements of entries contained in them also make them admissible as evidence tending to show that because the receipt of the dividends was not entered in them, they were not received, and therefore were not paid. The evidence may not be as persuasive in the latter case as in the former, but that it was proper evidence to be submitted to the jury for the determination of its value we cannot doubt. Such books so kept presumptively contained a record of all payments made, and the absence of any entry of payment, where it naturally would have been found if it had been made, was evidence of nonpayment, proper for the consideration of the jury. * * *

The judgment of the Circuit Court of Appeals is affirmed.

NOTES

1. *Records of agency activities not restricted in criminal prosecutions.* Rule 803(8)(A)(i), unlike subparts (ii) and (iii), has no restrictions on admission in criminal cases, even against the criminal defendant. See United States v. Clarke, 628 F.Supp.2d 15, 19–20 (D.D.C.2009) (ruling that certificate was admissible in criminal case against the defendant as a record of INS with respect to the issue of the issuance of a certificate of naturalization rather than the factual finding that an individual was qualified for citizenship).

2. *Public official requirement.* Rules 803(8) creates a exceptions for records and reports made by public officers or agencies pursuant to a statutory authorization or mandate. The Rule does not directly authorize admission of statements made by private individuals to public officials, although this may be accomplished in some circumstances through Rule 805. It also does not provide a blanket exception for statements by private individuals to public officials even when those statements are made pursuant

to statutory duty, although a limited exception is created under Rule 803(9) for records of vital statistics.

UNITED STATES V. QUEZADA

United States Court of Appeals, Fifth Circuit, 1985.
754 F.2d 1190.

JOHN R. BROWN, CIRCUIT JUDGE:

In this appeal from a conviction under 8 U.S.C. § 1326 for illegal reentry after deportation, appellant challenges the admission of certain evidence at his bench trial. We review the proceedings below, find that properly admitted evidence sufficiently supports the conviction, and affirm.

Background

Appellant Oscar Ramos Quezada, an illegal alien, was deported from this country on April 25, 1982, pursuant to a warrant of deportation (Form I–205) issued by the United States Immigration and Naturalization Service (INS). Seven months later, on November 17, 1983, a Border Patrol officer arrested Quezada at the El Paso County Jail, where he was incarcerated on a public intoxication charge. Quezada was subsequently indicted by a federal grand jury for illegally reentering the country after having been previously arrested and deported, in violation of 8 U.S.C. § 1326. After a bench trial, he was convicted and sentenced to a prison term of two years, all but six months of which were suspended in lieu of supervised probation.

At trial, the principal part of the government's case was devoted to proving that Quezada had been "deported and arrested" as required for conviction under the statute. In order to establish these statutory requisites, the government called as a witness Border Patrol Agent David Meshirer. Agent Meshirer first testified that he had been designated the custodian of appellant's immigration file. The government then used the witness to introduce its exhibits.

Two exhibits are of particular importance in this appeal. The first is INS Form I–205, the warrant of deportation which authorized the deportation of appellant. The second, INS Form I–294, is a letter to appellant in his native language, warning him of the penalties for illegal reentry after deportation. Both exhibits were admitted into evidence over appellant's objections.

The testimony of Agent Meshirer also figures prominently in this appeal. His testimony described the use and function of the INS forms put in evidence. First, he explained that on the back of Form I–205 are spaces to be filled out by the deporting officer, as well as a space for the thumbprint of the deportee. Agent Meshirer also observed that the back of Form I–205 reflected that appellant had been deported on April 25, 1982, and that this deportation had been witnessed by an immigration officer whose signature appeared on the exhibit. Finally, he pointed out a thumbprint on the back of the exhibit, which subsequent testimony established to be that of appellant.

Agent Meshirer next testified as to the normal procedure followed in executing warrants of deportation. He stated that when a person has been ordered deported, an immigration officer will pick up the deportee, fill in the blanks on the back of the warrant, and sign the warrant as having witnessed the departure. He also testified that in the course of a normal deportation, the deportee's right thumbprint is taken. As to Form I–294, the letter informing the deportee of the penalties for illegal reentry, Agent Meshirer observed that it is given to the deportee along with a copy of the warrant of deportation. Thus, according to this testimony, the deported individual is fully apprised of the fact of his deportation, and that he is subject to criminal penalties for illegal reentry.

* * *

Discussion

Appellant urges that the evidence below was insufficient to prove the "arrest" necessary for prosecution under 8 U.S.C. § 1326, as that term has been interpreted by this court. In *United States v. Wong Kim Bo*, 466 F.2d 1298 (5th Cir.1972) *rehearing denied,* 472 F.2d 720 (5th Cir.1972), we discussed that term as it fits into the scheme of the statute in question. First, we observed that there are five elements which the government must prove in order to obtain a conviction for illegal reentry after deportation: [i] that defendant was an alien; [ii] that he was "arrested" and [iii] "deported" as those terms are contemplated by the statute; [iv] that he was subsequently found within this country and [v] that he did not have consent from the Attorney General to reapply for admission. *Id.* at 1303.[19]

We next turned to an analysis of the "arrest" requirement. After examining the legislative and Congressional purpose underlying the Act, we concluded that an "arrest" under the statute is accomplished by service on the alien of the warrant of deportation, thus providing the requisite notice to trigger criminal sanctions for illegal reentry thereafter. *Id.* at 1304–05. This notice is critical, we observed, for it insures that criminal sanctions are not imposed for reentry where the alien does not know that he has previously been officially deported. *Id.* at 1304.

---

[19] Of these five elements, appellant challenges only the second, whether or not he was properly "arrested."

The argument presented on appeal is that the government failed to prove that appellant was actually served with a warrant of deportation issued by INS. This argument implicates important questions respecting the use of public documents in criminal proceedings * * *.

Documentary Evidence

Initially, our attention is drawn to the question of the admissibility of INS Form I–205, the warrant of deportation. This document is crucial to the government's case, as it contains virtually all of the information proving appellant's prior arrest and deportation. Thus is implicated F.R.Evid. 803(8)(B), the public records exception to the hearsay rule, which provides as follows: * * *

> (8) Public records and reports. Records, reports, statements, or data compilations, in any form, of public offices or agencies setting forth * * * (B) matters observed pursuant to duty imposed by law as to which matters there was a duty to report, excluding, however, in criminal cases matters observed by police officers and other law enforcement personnel.

Two principal reasons underlie this exception to the general rule excluding hearsay: the presumed trustworthiness of public documents prepared in the discharge of official functions, and the necessity of using such documents, due to the likelihood that a public official would have no independent memory of a particular action or entry where his duties require the constant repetition of routine tasks. *See generally,* 4 D. Louisell and C. Mueller, Federal Evidence, Public Records § 454.

Despite this policy favoring the admissibility of public records, Congress was also obviously concerned about the use of such documents in criminal cases. In an apparent attempt to avoid a collision between the hearsay rule and the confrontation clause of the Sixth Amendment, Congress excluded from the public records exception "in criminal cases matters observed by police officers and other law enforcement personnel. * * * " Rule 803(8)(B). In so doing, however, Congress did not make clear whether the Rule was designed to exclude all reports made by a government employee which are offered against a criminal defendant, or whether only certain types of reports were intended to be excluded.

While some courts have inflexibly applied the Rule 803(8)(B) proscription to all law enforcement records in criminal cases, *see, e.g., United States v. Oates,* 560 F.2d 45, 83–84 (2d Cir.1977), we are not persuaded that such a narrow application of the rule is warranted here. The law enforcement exception in Rule 803(8)(B) is based in part on the presumed unreliability of observations made by law enforcement officials at the scene of a crime, or in the course of investigating a crime:

[o]stensibly, the reason for this exclusion is that observations by police officers at the scene of the crime or the apprehension of the defendant were not as reliable as observations by public officials in other cases because of the adversarial nature of the confrontation between the police and the defendant in criminal cases.

Senate Report No. 1277, 93d Cong.2d Sess., *reprinted in* [1974] U.S.Code Cong. & Ad.News 7051, 7064. Thus, a number of courts have drawn a distinction for purposes of Rule 803(8)(B) between law enforcement reports prepared in a routine, non-adversarial setting, and those resulting from the arguably more subjective endeavor of investigating a crime and evaluating the results of that investigation. *See, e.g., United States v. Orozco,* 590 F.2d 789, 793–94 (9th Cir.1979) (admitting computer records of license plates on cars crossing the border due to non-adversarial setting in which information was gathered); *United States v. Union Nacional de Trabajadores,* 576 F.2d 388, 390–91 (1st Cir.1978) (admitting Marshal's return of service); *United States v. Grady,* 544 F.2d 598 (2d Cir.1976) (admitting reports on firearms serial numbers for Northern Ireland law enforcement agency on basis that they were records of a routine function).

Under this analysis, a warrant of deportation was deemed properly admissible in a § 1326 action in *United States v. Hernandez–Rojas,* 617 F.2d 533 (9th Cir.1980). The Ninth Circuit there concluded that the notations on the warrant indicating the defendant's deportation were the result of a ministerial, objective observation, and thus had none of the subjective features of reports made in a more adversarial setting, such as an investigation of a crime scene. *Id.* at 535.

We find the reasoning of these cases persuasive. This circuit has recognized that Rule 803(8) is designed to permit the admission into evidence of public records prepared for purposes independent of specific litigation. *United States v. Stone,* 604 F.2d 922 (5th Cir.1979) (Rule 803(8)(A)). In the case of documents recording routine, objective observations, made as part of the everyday function of the preparing official or agency, the factors likely to cloud the perception of an official engaged in the more traditional law enforcement functions of observation and investigation of crime are simply not present. Due to the lack of any motivation on the part of the recording official to do other than mechanically register an unambiguous factual matter (here, appellant's departure from the country), such records are, like other public documents, inherently reliable. *See Smith v. Ithaca,* 612 F.2d 215, 222 (5th Cir.1980) (records trustworthy where recording official has no reason to be other than objective).

We further believe that the warrant of deportation in this case establishes the service required by *Wong Kim Bo.* Appellant's thumbprint on the warrant indicates that the warrant was presented to him prior to departure. Additionally, testimony of Border Patrol Agent Meshirer conclusively established the authenticity and reliability of this record of deportation. *See* F.R.Evid. 901(b)(7). He testified that the warrants of deportation are kept in the normal course of business of the INS. Trial Transcript at 11. He further testified that the warrants of deportation are kept as a matter of course with the individual file maintained for each alien being processed. *Id.* at 9–10. This testimony clearly indicated the extent to which such records are relied on by the INS in its day-to-day operations.

Moreover, in a case like the one at bar, the absolute necessity of proving the government's case through the use of public records is unquestionable. In the years 1977–1981, the INS processed for departure from the country, on average, more than 1,000,000 aliens annually. In 1981, more than 260,000 aliens were processed in the State of Texas alone, with over 6,000 of those having been officially deported. Given these numbers, it is unlikely that testimony by an INS officer as to the deportation of a particular individual could be based on anything other than recorded observations, with such testimony being merely cumulative to the more reliable written record of deportation.

We thus conclude that the warrant of deportation, containing appellant's thumbprint and indicating the date and location of his deportation, sufficiently established the arrest requirement contemplated by the statute. Given the overwhelming number of immigration cases processed each year, the INS must be permitted to rely on such records to establish certain elements of a violation of § 1326.

* * *

Affirmed.

NOTES AND QUESTIONS

1. *Admissibility of "ministerial" records.* As *Quezada* notes, a number of other courts have disagreed with United States v. Oates, 560 F.2d 45, 83–84 (2d Cir.1977), as to its extremely broad reading of the exclusion of public reports when offered against a criminal defendant under Rule 803(8)(A)(ii), formerly 803(8)(B). The clear majority view is that the Rule does not bar use of "ministerial" as opposed to "investigative" reports. See, e.g., United States v. Dowdell, 595 F.3d 50, 70–72 (1st Cir.2010) (finding routine booking records admissible under the exception when offered by the government against the defendant). Is this a sensible result? See Alexander, The Hearsay Exception for Public Records in Federal Criminal Trials, 47 Albany L.Rev. 699, 716–17 (1983) (finding "the majority view" preferable and consistent with legislative

intent). In getting a sense of the distinction between ministerial and adversarial records, compare United States v. Brown, 315 F.3d 929, 931 (8th Cir.2003) (admitting information from Secret Service database on location of counterfeit bills with same serial numbers because records were both objective and not adversarial in that they were not collected in anticipation of defendant's trial) with United States v. Orellana–Blanco, 294 F.3d 1143, 1150 (9th Cir.2002) (ruling that interview with INS agent about nature of marriage was adversarial in nature, rather than ministerial or objective observation, and therefore not admissible under Rule 803(8)(B) against the defendant).

2.   *Limitations on police records as business records.* Substantial pre-Federal Rules authority supported the admissibility of police reports under the hearsay exception for business records. *Oates* reasoned that, since a public report is not admissible against a criminal defendant under Rule 803(8) by virtue of Congress' explicit prohibition, the same document may not properly be received under Rule 803(6). The reasoning of *Oates* that Rule 803(6) should not provide a "back door" method of admitting statements by the police against criminal defendants has been generally followed. See, e.g., United States v. Cain, 615 F.2d 380, 382 (5th Cir.1980). However, if the declarant testifies, courts frequently find the prohibition, which is seen as protecting confrontation rights, inapplicable. See United States v. Sokolow, 91 F.3d 396, 404–05 (3d Cir.1996); United States v. Hayes, 861 F.2d 1225, 1230 (10th Cir.1988). Also, some courts hold that Rule 803(6) can be used when the record is not being offered by the prosecution against the defendant in a criminal case. See, e.g., United States v. Carneglia, 356 F.R.D. 384, 391 (E.D.N.Y.2009) (admitting statement offered by the defendant against the prosecution); Johnson v. O'Farrell, 787 N.W.2d 307 (S.D.2010) (admitting police report as business record in civil case).

3.   *Police records and other exceptions. Oates* also argued that a public report may likewise not be admitted under any other hearsay exception. 560 F.2d at 78. Some courts have disagreed and admitted statements under several other exceptions, principally based on the declarant's presence on the stand. See United States v. Arias–Santana, 964 F.2d 1262, 1264–65 (1st Cir.1992) (police report, which is generally inadmissible against criminal defendant, may be admitted as a prior consistent statement under Rule 801(d)(1)(B)); United States v. Sawyer, 607 F.2d 1190, 1193 (7th Cir.1979) (prohibition inapplicable to Rule 803(5) when police officer testifies). But others follow *Oates* in this regard. See United States v. Pena–Gutierrez, 222 F.3d 1080, 1086–87 (9th Cir.2000) (ruling that law enforcement reports are not admissible under Rule 803(5) because they are admissible only under Rule 803(8)). Statutory construction arguments have also been used to permit alternative admission. See United States v. Metzger, 778 F.2d 1195, 1201–02 (6th Cir.1985) (prohibition not included in Rule 803(10), an exception equally specific to Rule 803(8), and therefore *Oates* argument is not applicable).

4.   *Laboratory reports in criminal cases.* United States v. Baker, 855 F.2d 1353, 1359–60 (8th Cir.1988), presents a more general challenge to

Oates in holding a police department lab report, made on a routine basis, admissible against the criminal defendant. See also United States v. Rosa, 11 F.3d 315, 331–33 (2d Cir.1993) (restriction meant to focus on police officers, accusers, and adversaries and not to public servants who have no law enforcement duties). A number of state courts have ruled in favor of admitting routine laboratory or similar reports against the defendant following analysis similar to that in *Quezada*. See, e.g., Ealy v. State, 685 N.E.2d 1047, 1054–55 (Ind.1997) (autopsy report admissible because not prepared for advocacy purposes); State v. Dilliner, 569 S.E.2d 211, 215–17 (W.Va.2002) (finding intoxilyzer accuracy report admissible as governmental record in criminal case). Again, however, other states disagree. See State v. Sandoval–Tena, 71 P.3d 1055, 1058–59 (Idaho 2003) (holding police crime lab report inadmissible as either governmental or business record).

5. *Admission by the defense of government reports against the prosecution and the unfortunate wording of Rule 803(8)(a)(ii)[formerly 803(8)(B)].* While Rule 803(8)(a)(iii) allows admission of evaluative reports if offered by the defense against the government, Rule 803(8)(a)(ii), if read literally, would exclude law enforcement reports even when offered by the criminal defendant. In United States v. Smith, 521 F.2d 957 (D.C.Cir.1975), the court concluded that the Rule should not be read to prohibit admission of reports offered by the defendant since such a reading was inconsistent with the obvious legislative intent. Accord United States v. Versaint, 849 F.2d 827, 831 (3d Cir.1988). But see United States v. Sharpe, 193 F.3d 852, 868 (5th Cir.1999) (treating exception as excluding records under Rule 803(8)(B) when offered against the government in accord with its literal wording). *Sharpe's* "plain meaning" analysis is criticized in 2 McCormick, Evidence § 296 (7th ed. 2013).

BRIDGEWAY CORP. V. CITIBANK

United States Court of Appeals, Second Circuit, 2000.
201 F.3d 134.

CALABRESI, CIRCUIT JUDGE:

Bridgeway Corp. ("Bridgeway"), a Liberian corporation seeking to enforce a final judgment rendered by the Supreme Court of Liberia, appeals from the district court's decision denying Bridgeway's motion for summary judgment and granting, *sua sponte,* summary judgment in favor of the nonmoving party, Citibank. The district court held * * * that the evidence in the record established, as a matter of law, that the Liberian judicial system was not "a system that * * * provide[s] impartial tribunals or procedures compatible with the requirements of due process." *Bridgeway Corp. v. Citibank,* 45 F.Supp.2d 276, 288 (S.D.N.Y.1999). We affirm.

I.   Background

Overview of Liberian History

This appeal derives from an action by Bridgeway to enforce a money judgment against Citibank entered by the Supreme Court of Liberia on July 28, 1995. Because the merits of this case turn on the events surrounding the Liberian civil war during the first half of the 1990s, it is helpful to provide a brief overview of those circumstances before proceeding to discuss the case. * * *

From 1980 to 1989, Samuel Kanyon Doe headed a Liberian government marked by corruption and human rights abuses, as well as by rampant inflation. In 1989, a group of dissidents seized power and, in 1990, executed Doe. Doe's death marked the beginning of a violent seven-year civil war. By 1991, Liberia was in effect ruled by two governments: one controlled Monrovia, the capital, while the other controlled the remainder of the country. Following several short-lived cease fires, a formal peace accord was signed in August 1995. After another outbreak of violence in 1996, elections were held in July 1997. In August 1997, Charles Taylor was inaugurated and the 1986 Constitution was reinstated.

Throughout the period of civil war, Liberia's judicial system was in a state of disarray and the provisions of the Constitution concerning the judiciary were no longer followed. Instead, under an agreement worked out among the warring parties in 1992, the Supreme Court was reorganized, with various factions each unilaterally appointing a specified number of justices. The U.S. State Department Country Reports for Liberia during this period paint a bleak picture of the Liberian judiciary. The 1994 Report observed that "corruption and incompetent handling of cases remained a recurrent problem." The 1996 Report stated that, "the judicial system, already hampered by inefficiency and corruption, collapsed for six months following the outbreak of fighting in April."

In 1997, before elections were held, the leaders of the various factions acknowledged that the integrity of the Supreme Court had been compromised by factional loyalties since 1992 and agreed that the Court would have to be reconstituted so that it might gain the legitimacy that would enable it to resolve successfully disputes that might arise concerning the elections. The members of the Court were therefore dismissed and new members were appointed based on the recommendations of the Liberian National Bar Association.

This Case

* * * For many years Citibank maintained a branch in Monrovia, but it closed that branch in January 1992 and completely withdrew from Liberia by 1995. As required by Liberian law, Citibank, before

withdrawing, formulated a plan of liquidation, which was approved by the National Bank of Liberia. According to this plan, funds were to be remitted by Citibank to Meridian Bank Liberia Ltd., in order to meet Citibank's obligations to depositors. Citibank alerted its customers to its plans so that they could withdraw their funds. On April 21, 1995, the National Bank of Liberia indicated by letter that Citibank had satisfactorily completed the liquidation plan and was no longer licensed to do business in Liberia.

Bridgeway had an account at Citibank's Liberian branch with a balance of $189,376.66. In November 1992, Bridgeway brought suit in Liberia against Citibank, seeking a declaration that Citibank was obligated to pay Bridgeway its balance in U.S. (rather than Liberian) dollars. In August 1993, the trial court ruled in favor of Citibank. The court found that, under Liberian law, a person may not refuse to accept Liberian dollars for the discharge of an obligation unless there is an express agreement to the contrary and that Liberian law gives the Liberian dollar a par value equal to the value of the U.S. dollar. The trial court also found that under Bridgeway's contract with Citibank, the latter had the right to decide the currency in which a withdrawal would be paid. Bridgeway appealed to the Liberian Supreme Court, which reversed the lower court's decision and entered judgment for Bridgeway.

Bridgeway filed suit in New York state court to enforce the Liberian Supreme Court judgment, and Citibank removed the case to the federal district court. When it became apparent that Citibank was going to defend itself by challenging the legitimacy of the Liberian judicial system, Bridgeway moved for summary judgment—arguing that Citibank was estopped from questioning the fairness of the Liberian judiciary. But the district court denied that motion and, *sua sponte,* granted summary judgment for Citibank. Specifically, the court found that, as a matter of law, Liberia's courts did not constitute "a system of jurisprudence likely to secure an impartial administration of justice" and that, as a result, the Liberian judgment was unenforceable in the United States. *See Bridgeway,* 45 F.Supp.2d at 287. Bridgeway now appeals.

II. Discussion

[The court found no error in the trial court's action to grant summary judgment *sua sponte* against the moving party and found no merit in Bridgeway's argument that by voluntarily participating in litigation in the Liberian courts Citibank was estopped from challenging the impartiality of those courts.]

Fairness of Liberian Courts

* * *

Burden

The parties strenuously dispute who bears the ultimate burden of proof with respect to the fairness of the Liberian judicial system. Although there are cases in which the question of the burden might be significant, it does not ultimately matter here. Accordingly, we express no opinion on it. Even if Citibank were to bear both the burden of production and that of persuasion, it has come forward with sufficiently powerful and uncontradicted documentary evidence describing the chaos within the Liberian judicial system during the period of interest to this case to have met those burdens and to be entitled to judgment as a matter of law. Thus, the U.S. State Department Country Reports presented by Citibank indicate that the Liberian judicial system was in a state of disarray, as do, more subtly, the affidavits by Citibank's Liberian counsel, H. Varney G. Sherman.

The only evidence Bridgeway has introduced in support of its position are three statements by Liberian attorneys. * * * The first statement concerns the design of the Liberian judicial system, but says nothing about its practice during the period in question. The second, in addition to suffering from the same defect as the first, does not even discuss the Liberian judicial system directly. And the third is purely conclusory. *See Kulak v. City of New York,* 88 F.3d 63, 71 (2d Cir.1996) ("[C]onclusory statements, conjecture, or speculation by the party resisting the motion will not defeat summary judgment.").

Evidence

Summary judgment cannot be granted on the basis of inadmissible evidence. *See* Fed.R.Civ.P. 56(e). And Bridgeway raises many objections to the evidence relied upon by the district court in determining that Liberia's courts were, as a matter of law, unlikely to render impartial justice. Although the parties argue over a variety of different pieces of evidence, in the absence of any proof supporting Bridgeway's position, we need only consider whether Citibank adduced admissible evidence in sufficient amount to make the district court's decision regarding the performance of the Liberian judiciary during the civil war be supportable as well as uncontroverted. In fact, all of the district court's conclusions concerning this issue can be derived from just two sources: the affidavits of H. Varney G. Sherman ("Sherman affidavits") and the U.S. State Department Country Reports for Liberia for the years 1994–1997 ("Country Reports" or "Reports"). * * *

The district court also relied quite heavily on the Country Reports. Bridgeway argues that these Reports constitute excludable hearsay.

Citibank replies that the Reports are admissible under Federal Rule of Evidence 803(8)(C), which allows the admission of "factual findings resulting from an investigation made pursuant to authority granted by law, unless the sources of information or other circumstances indicate lack of trustworthiness." *See* Fed.R.Evid. 803(8)(C).

Rule 803(8) "is based upon the assumption that public officers will perform their duties, that they lack motive to falsify, and that public inspection to which many such records are subject will disclose inaccuracies." 31 Michael H. Graham, Federal Practice and Procedure § 6759, at 663–64 (Interim ed. 1992). " 'Factual finding' includes not only what happened, but how it happened, why it happened, and who caused it to happen." *Id.* at 689. The rule therefore renders presumptively admissible "not merely * * * factual determinations in the narrow sense, but also * * * conclusions or opinions that are based upon a factual investigation." *Gentile v. County of Suffolk,* 926 F.2d 142, 148 (2d Cir.1991).

In order to fit within the purview of the Rule, the evidence must (1) contain factual findings, and (2) be based upon an investigation made pursuant to legal authority. Once a party has shown that a set of factual findings satisfies the minimum requirements of Rule 803(8)(C), the admissibility of such factual findings is presumed. The burden to show "a lack of trustworthiness" then shifts to the party opposing admission. *See Ariza v. City of New York,* 139 F.3d 132, 134 (2d Cir.1998).

In this case, there is little doubt that the Country Reports constitute "factual findings." Moreover, the Reports are certainly gathered pursuant to legal authority: federal law requires that the State Department submit the Reports annually to Congress * * * . They are therefore presumptively admissible.

Bridgeway attempts to rebut this presumption by arguing that the Reports are untrustworthy, and it points to language in the State Department's description of their preparation. The State Department says that "[w]e have given particular attention to attaining a high standard of consistency despite the multiplicity of sources and the obvious problems related to varying degrees of access to information, structural differences in political and social systems, and trends in world opinion regarding human rights practices in specific countries." Although this constitutes a frank recognition of the shortcomings intrinsic in any historical investigation, it does not amount (as Bridgeway argues) to an admission of the lack of trustworthiness required to reject the admissibility of these documents.

When evaluating the trustworthiness of a factual report, we look to (a) the timeliness of the investigation, (b) the special skills or experience of the official, (c) whether a hearing was held and the level at which it was conducted, and (d) possible motivation problems. *See* Fed.R.Evid. 803(8)(C) advisory committee's note. With the exception of (c), which is not determinative by itself, *cf. id.* ([T]he rule * * * assumes admissibility in the first instance but with ample provision for escape if *sufficient negative factors* are present. (emphasis added)), nothing about the Reports calls into question their reliability with respect to these factors. The Reports are submitted annually, and are therefore investigated in a timely manner. They are prepared by area specialists at the State Department. And nothing in the record or in Bridgeway's briefs indicates any motive for misrepresenting the facts concerning Liberia's civil war or its effect on the judicial system there. *See Bank Melli Iran v. Pahlavi,* 58 F.3d 1406, 1411 (9th Cir.1995) (relying on Country Reports in granting summary judgment on the issue of the fairness of Iranian courts).

In addition to its reliance on the Sherman affidavits and the Country Reports, the district court took judicial notice of historical facts drawn from a variety of sources. *See Bridgeway,* 45 F.Supp.2d at 278 n.2. Bridgeway objects to this. Even if we agreed with Bridgeway's objection, we would affirm the district court's decision because the facts of which the district court took judicial notice were merely background history and of no moment to the ultimate determination of the fairness of Liberia's courts during the period of the civil war. The information in the district court's opinion concerning the functioning of the Liberian courts during the war is drawn (or could easily be drawn) entirely from the Sherman affidavits and the Country Reports, both of which were clearly admissible. * * *

Having found all of Bridgeway's contentions to be without merit, we AFFIRM the judgment of the district court.

NOTES AND QUESTIONS

1. *Scope of "investigative reports."* In *Bridgeway,* the court describes the scope of "investigative reports" under Rule 803(8)(a)(iii) [formerly 803(8)(C)] to properly include not only "factual determinations in a narrow sense" but also "conclusions or opinions that are based upon a factual investigation." While it cites an earlier Second Circuit case for this proposition, the authority for this broad view of the scope of such reports is the United States Supreme Court decision in Beech Aircraft Corp. v. Rainey, 488 U.S. 153 (1988). In that decision, the Court resolved the split between the circuits, rejecting the narrow view that "factual findings" under Rule 803(8)(C) "did not encompass 'opinions' or 'conclusions' " and adopting the broader view that "factually based conclusions or opinions" are within its scope. 488 U.S. at 162. *Beech Aircraft* held such opinions and conclusions admissible as long as they: (1) are based on a factual investigation and (2) satisfy the Rule's trustworthiness requirement. Id. at 170.

2. *Reliance on unreliable data.* In addition to the four factors listed in *Bridgeway* to determine whether the report lacks trustworthiness, reliance upon unreliable data is sometimes treated almost as a fifth factor. However, reliance on hearsay does not necessarily result in exclusion. For example, in Kehm v. Procter & Gamble Mfg. Co., 724 F.2d 613, 618 (8th Cir.1983), Proctor & Gamble challenged the admission of epidemiological studies conducted by the Center for Disease Control on the toxic shock syndrome. It based its challenge to the evidence, *inter alia*, on the preparer's lack of firsthand knowledge of the data used. In rejecting the company's argument, the court stated, "We agree with the district court that once a report is conclusively shown to represent findings of a public agency made pursuant to an investigation authorized by law, the central inquiry becomes whether the report is trustworthy." The court placed the burden on the party opposing admission to demonstrate untrustworthiness beyond the mere fact that the report relied in part on hearsay. See also Robbins v. Whelan, 653 F.2d 47 (1st Cir.1981) (Department of Transportation report on automobile stopping distances admissible despite reliance on data provided by automobile manufacturers of which the agency had no firsthand knowledge because other factors helped insure trustworthiness).

On the other hand, when the report relies upon unverified evidence or when it depends on the data of parties whose motivation may be questionable and merely repeats that data without independent evaluation, the weakness of the underlying data may render the report inadmissible. See, e.g., United States v. Jackson–Randolph, 282 F.3d 369, 381 (6th Cir.2002) (agreeing with exclusion of examiner's report that relied on testimony of witness with motive to lie because unreliable); Barlow v. Connecticut, 319 F.Supp.2d 250, 258 (D.Conn.2004) (excluding report because based largely on unreliable hearsay). Whether this provision allows the court to exclude the evidence because it simply doubts the result is questionable. See Blake v. Pellegrino, 329 F.3d 43, 48 (1st Cir.2003).

3. *Guidance from rules on expert witnesses.* Where opinions or conclusions are reached, the principles of Rules 702 and 703 are helpful in determining admissibility. The lack of expertise of those preparing the report may be critical. See Jenkins v. Whittaker Corp., 785 F.2d 720, 725–27 & n.18 (9th Cir.1986) (Investigative reports were properly excluded where they included opinions rendered by investigators without expertise: "it would be anomalous if [the investigator's] opinions were allowed into evidence as part of a report that is not subject to cross-examination when [he] lacked the expertise to testify to those same opinions at trial where he *could* be cross-examined."). See also Matthews v. Ashland Chem., Inc., 770 F.2d 1303, 1309–10 (5th Cir.1985) (report properly rejected where record revealed no special skill or experience of fire investigator who prepared report). Also, the data upon which the investigator relies must be of a satisfactory character. See Faries v. Atlas Truck Body Mfg. Co., 797 F.2d 619 (8th Cir.1986) (where state trooper performed incomplete personal investigation and relied upon potentially interested eyewitnesses, report lacked trustworthiness, and under

Rule 703, trooper's testimony was inadmissible because not based on information reasonably relied upon).

4. *Final report requirement.* Reports that are tentative, are merely accumulations of information rather than the conclusion of a government agency, or do not reflect a comprehensive investigation may also be rejected. See Smith v. Isuzu Motors Ltd., 137 F.3d 859, 862–63 (5th Cir.1998) (opinions of individual staff members not accepted by agency do not qualify as factual findings of agency); Alexander v. FBI, 691 F.Supp.2d 182, 195 (D.D.C.2010) (finding interim report from committee of House of Representatives insufficiently trustworthy); *but cf.* English v. District of Columbia, 651 F.3d 1, 7–8 (D.C.Cir.2011) (final report of public official conducting an investigation authorized by law is admissible under the exception even if the agency does not adopt the finding).

5. *Other admissibility concerns.* In Chandler v. Roudebush, 425 U.S. 840, 863 n.39 (1976), the Supreme Court ruled that administrative findings of racial discrimination are admissible under the Rule in a subsequent federal trial de novo. Does this mean that the findings are per se admissible in non-jury trials under Title VII? Are there additional concerns that might warrant exclusion when the report is offered in a related civil rights action tried before a jury? The circuits are in some conflict on these issues. See Barfield v. Orange County, 911 F.2d 644, 649–50 (11th Cir.1990) (discussing positions of courts, which most often afford the trial judge some discretion in determining whether to admit the findings).

G. UNAVAILABILITY

Federal Rule 804(a)

UNITED STATES V. MACCLOSKEY

United States Court of Appeals, Fourth Circuit, 1982.
682 F.2d 468.

MURNAGHAN, CIRCUIT JUDGE:

* * *

Count Two of the indictment charged MacCloskey and others (the same alleged coconspirators as in Count One) with conspiracy to obstruct the administration of justice by killing Steve Lansley, a potential government witness (by blowing him up with dynamite), in violation of 18 U.S.C. §§ 371, 1503 and 844(d). * * *

MacCloskey appeals his conviction raising a number of contentions * * * [, including his contention] that the district court's failure to admit prior testimony of a key defense witness, Patsey Elaine Edwards, [at a voir dire hearing] was prejudicial error. * * *

Admission of Edwards' Prior Testimony

* * * [W]e are of the opinion that a new trial is required because MacCloskey was improperly denied the complete testimony of his major defense witness, Patsey Elaine Edwards.

Edwards was originally indicted with MacCloskey and others for conspiring to murder Lansley and Skaggs. At the beginning of the trial, which commenced on January 19, 1981, the defense made known its intention of calling Edwards as a defense witness. Before trial, MacCloskey's attorneys were advised by the federal prosecutor that the indictment against Edwards would be dropped prior to the commencement of MacCloskey's trial. On January 21, 1981, the U.S. Attorney, David Smith, telephoned Edwards' attorney, Michael Greeson. In essence, Smith told Greeson that he would be well-advised to remind his client that, if she testified at MacCloskey's trial, she could be reindicted if she incriminated herself during that testimony. The attorneys defending MacCloskey were apprised of the conversation (presumably by Greeson) the same evening.

The next morning defense counsel brought the conversation containing Smith's warning to the attention of the trial court. Later that afternoon, Edwards agreed to testify out of the jury's presence in a *voir dire* hearing. She was warned of her *Miranda* rights by the trial judge before she testified. She nevertheless testified and was cross-examined by the U.S. Attorney. Reduced to its basics, her testimony was that she knew nothing about any scheme to kill either Skaggs or Lansley and that MacCloskey never discussed the matter with her. In short, the testimony contradicted [the testimony of the government's informant, Pete Honeycutt,] of Edwards' involvement and was completely exculpatory of both her and MacCloskey. After the *voir dire* hearing, the indictment against Edwards was dismissed.

On January 26, the day the defense began its case, MacCloskey's counsel advised the trial court that they had been advised that Edwards might not testify on advice from an attorney identified as Gary Vannoy.

On January 27, defense counsel told the trial judge that they had been advised by Edwards and her attorney that Edwards would invoke her Fifth Amendment privilege. They requested a *voir dire* if she so invoked her rights. In addition, defense counsel requested that, if she refused to testify, her prior *voir dire* testimony be admitted pursuant to Fed.R. of Evid. 804.

The trial judge stated that if she invoked the Fifth Amendment he would not pursue the matter because he felt that he had no right to determine whether a person was properly pleading the Fifth Amendment. In addition, he refused to admit Edwards' prior testimony because it was his belief that a person's testimony was not "unavailable," as required by

Rule 804, merely because the person has invoked the Fifth Amendment. Thereafter, Edwards was called to the stand by the defense and she answered many questions in the jury's presence but refused to answer some questions, invoking the Fifth Amendment. She had testified in great detail to virtually identical questions at the *voir dire* held earlier that week and at that time she answered all the questions which she subsequently refused to answer at trial.

Before cross-examination by the prosecutor, *voir dire* was held. Edwards said that she truthfully testified at the *voir dire* earlier in the week. She testified that she nevertheless now was invoking the Fifth Amendment because she was afraid that her indictment would not be dismissed.[20] She stated she was not concerned about incriminating herself but was not testifying because her attorney told her that the U.S. Attorney's office suggested that she had "better remember the privilege of the Fifth Amendment." At that point, defense counsel moved for a mistrial on the ground that MacCloskey had been denied the use of his witness as a result of the prosecutor's call. In addition, defense counsel renewed their motion that the prior *voir dire* testimony be admitted pursuant to Rule 804. Both motions were denied. After the evidence closed, Edwards' former attorney, Michael Greeson, testified, out of the presence of the jury, concerning the details of the phone call he received from Mr. Smith.

The defense sought to get Edwards' prior testimony (which was exculpatory to both her and MacCloskey) into evidence under Fed.Rule of Evid. 804, [which requires that the declarant must be unavailable] * * *. No dispute existed that the *voir dire* testimony could be admitted under the Rule if Edwards was found unavailable. Rule 804(a) defines unavailability as including situations in which the declarant:

> (1) is exempted by ruling of the court on the ground of privilege from testifying concerning the subject matter of his statement; or

> (2) persists in refusing to testify concerning the subject matter of his statement despite an order of the court to do so. * * *

The district court refused to admit the prior testimony of Edwards on the erroneous ground that Edwards' invocation of her right against self-incrimination did not render her unavailable. The law is clear that a witness is unavailable under Rule 804(a)(1) when he invokes the Fifth Amendment privilege and the claim is sustained by the trial court. *See, e.g., United States v. Zurosky,* 614 F.2d 779, 792 (1st Cir.1979); *United States v. Toney,* 599 F.2d 787, 789–90 (6th Cir.1979).

The Rule requires, however, that the court first rule the declarant exempt from testifying on the ground of privilege. We think the

---

[20]   * * * Her indictment had been dismissed * * * [but], her fear of reindictment lingered.

requirement was met when the district judge informed counsel that, if Edwards pleaded the Fifth Amendment, the judge "would not pursue it;" i.e. would allow Edwards to stand mute, because he thought he did not have the authority to determine whether she was properly invoking the Fifth Amendment. That view was also erroneous. *See, e.g., Roberts v. United States,* 445 U.S. 552, 560 n.7 * * * (1980) ("It is the duty of a court to determine the legitimacy of a witness' reliance upon the Fifth Amendment."); *United States v. Klauber,* 611 F.2d 512, 514 (4th Cir.1979) ("The right to invoke the Fifth Amendment as to any question put is not absolute. The trial judge in appropriate cases may determine that a foundation for invocation of the Fifth Amendment does not exist."); McCormick, *Handbook of the Law of Evidence* § 139 at 293 ("[T]he court itself has the obligation to determine whether the refusal to answer is in fact justifiable under the privilege.").

Arguing that a witness can be unavailable under Rule 804 only if he *properly* invokes the Fifth Amendment, the government contends that Edwards waived her Fifth Amendment privilege by virtue of her testimony during the *voir dire* and at trial. *See Rogers v. United States,* 340 U.S. 367 * * * (1951). We think the government is, as a general proposition, correct in asserting that a witness must properly invoke his Fifth Amendment right for him to be unavailable under Rule 804(a)(1).[21]

Nevertheless, we still think reversible error occurred. Assuming Edwards waived her Fifth Amendment privilege during either her *voir dire* testimony, her trial testimony or both,[22] the trial judge should have compelled her to testify. If she still refused to testify after being ordered to do so and threatened with contempt if she did not, she would be unavailable under Rule 804(a)(2) and her *voir dire* testimony then should have been admitted under Rule 804(b)(1). Of course, if she testified because of the court order, her complete testimony would have been before the jury.

Edwards was the primary defense witness. The testimony she gave in the first *voir dire* was detailed and contradicted, or offered innocent explanations to, Honeycutt's damaging testimony. In short, her *detailed* testimony was vital to MacCloskey's defense. Since the evidence against MacCloskey was not overwhelming and consisted largely of Honeycutt's

---

[21] * * * The commentators suggest that the privilege must be properly invoked for a witness to be unavailable under Rule 804(a)(1). See, e.g., 4 D. Louisell & C. Mueller, Federal Evidence § 486 at 1027–29. * * * Note, however, that the case does not fall within Rule 804(a)(2) because, instead of ordering Edwards to testify, the district judge made clear that he would not so order her. * * * [I]f as the judge should have done, he "had ordered Edwards to testify, and she then refused, she would have been unavailable under Rule 804(a)(2). * * *.

[22] The fact that she testified at the voir dire hearing does not, by itself, mean that she waived her Fifth Amendment privilege. The privilege is waived only if the prior testimony revealed incriminating facts. See, e.g., McCarthy v. Arndstein, 262 U.S. 355, 359 * * * (1923). * * *

testimony concerning Edwards' statements and actions, we are unable to say that the error was harmless. * * *

Reversed and Remanded.

NOTES AND QUESTIONS

1. *Necessity.* When the declarant is unavailable, as is required under the exceptions found in Rule 804(b), the choice is between receiving no evidence and admission of the hearsay evidence, rather than between ideally presented evidence and imperfectly presented evidence. Unavailability of the witness obviously adds nothing to the trustworthiness of his or her extrajudicial statement. With regard to former testimony, the unavailability requirement, which originally was perhaps only satisfied by the witness' death, now may be met by other types of unavailability, such as claims of privilege, inability to locate, and insanity. 5 Wigmore, Evidence §§ 1402–1410 (Chadbourn rev. 1974).

2. *Judicial ruling on privilege.* Rule 804(a)(1) defines a witness to be unavailable where the witness "is exempted by ruling of the court" on the grounds of an asserted privilege. Does this language mean that the witness must formally invoke a privilege and the court rule favorably? An affirmative answer is clearly indicated by the Advisory Committee Note: "A ruling by the judge is required, which clearly implies an actual claim of privilege must be made." See United States v. Pelton, 578 F.2d 701, 709–10 (8th Cir.1978) (unavailability not established by proffer that witness' counsel would advise witness to assert Fifth Amendment). In some instances, however, the validity of the claim is so certain that the court may dispense with formal invocation. See, e.g., United States v. Lieberman, 637 F.2d 95, 103 (2d Cir.1980) (declarant, a defendant in the case, could not even be called by government to the stand and was therefore unavailable); United States v. Chan, 184 F.Supp.2d 337, 341 (S.D.N.Y.2002) (accepting representation by lawyers for coconspirators).

3. *Refusal to testify as alternative to privilege and verification of memory loss claim.* When the judge rules against the existence of a privilege and the witness persists in his or her refusal to testify, unavailability is established whether or not the appellate court determines the privilege claim was properly made. In *MacCloskey,* the appellate court notes that, where a claim of privilege is denied by the trial court, the court should order the witness to testify before finding the witness unavailable because of refusal to testify under Rule 804(a)(2). While the trial judge's misunderstanding of the law removed this issue from *MacCloskey,* an order to testify is generally considered a prerequisite when the claim of privilege is properly denied and the witness persists in her refusal to testify based on that erroneous claim. See State v. Cox, 779 N.W.2d 844, 852 (Minn.2010) (ruling that unavailability not established where witness showed reluctance to testify during closed evidentiary hearing but was never called as a witness by the prosecution and refusal not established); State v. Finney, 591 S.E.2d 863,

866–67 (N.C.2004) (ruling that reluctant witness not unavailable where she never definitively refused to testify and sufficient effort was not made by the court to determine persistence in resistance to testimony). Similarly, under Rule 804(a)(3), when a witness claims loss of memory, testimony by the witness and judicial verification is required. See Turner v. Commonwealth, 726 S.E.2d 325, 330 (Va.2012) (ruling that trial court may not rely on the witness' bare assertion to memory loss but is obligated to conduct an inquiry, observing the demeanor of the witness, to determine whether the loss of memory is feigned in an attempt to evade the obligation to testify).

4. *Immunity.* The claim of privilege under the Fifth Amendment, which renders the declarant unavailable, is eliminated when the government grants immunity. Under special circumstances, a criminal defendant may be able to compel the granting of immunity and thereby make the witness available. See United States v. Bahadar, 954 F.2d 821, 825–26 (2d Cir.1992).

CAMPBELL V. COLEMAN CO.

United States Court of Appeals, Eighth Circuit, 1986.
786 F.2d 892.

DIANA E. MURPHY, DISTRICT JUDGE.

Minor plaintiffs July A. Campbell and James E. Campbell, by and through their next friend, Janet M. Campbell, brought this action for strict liability against defendant The Coleman Company, Inc. (Coleman), alleging that they were severely burned because of a defective gasoline lantern. A jury trial was held and a verdict returned in favor of Coleman. * * *

[Plaintiff claimed that the two Campbell children were injured when a lantern manufactured by Coleman exploded as a result of its defective manufacture, a claim they supported by expert testimony.]

Coleman has a different theory of the case. It contends that the lantern ignited after Johnnie Lee Hayes had filled it with gasoline, that he threw the burning lantern out of the house, and that it accidentally hit the children. At the start of its case, Coleman informed the trial judge that it had subpoenaed Hayes but failed to locate him. It therefore proposed to call three witnesses to testify to out-of-court statements made by Hayes. Over plaintiffs' objection, the trial court permitted these witnesses to testify under the "statements against interest" exception to the hearsay rule, Fed.R.Evid. 804(b)(3).

The first of these witnesses, Jerry Lee Davis, was a neighbor who drove the children to the hospital. He testified that at the hospital he asked Hayes what had happened. He reported that Hayes "said something about he lit the lantern after he just filled it up and they lit it and they had it outside and it blowed up, that's all I know." Transcript, Vol. III, p. 7. Davis added: "[H]e [Hayes] lit it and he set it down there and then it blowed up and then he threw it to the yard or whatever." Transcript, Vol. III, p. 8.

The second witness was Lilly Salts, a sister of Mildred Warren. Salts testified that she drove to the Warren home and asked Hayes what happened and he told her that the lantern had "blew up." Salts was not sure whether Hayes said at that time whether the lantern was in the house or whether it was on the front porch when it exploded. Salts also stated that Hayes told her that "he was putting unleaded gas in this Coleman lantern so they would have a light and it blowed up * * * [h]e said he pitched it out the door * * * [h]e said the little girl was in the line of fire." Transcript, Vol. III, p. 18.

The third witness was Morgan Pruett, who testified to a conversation with Hayes which apparently took place about one week after the incident. "He told me that he filled up the lantern, and was filling it up, and I understand him to say he overfilled it or something and he lit it, it caught on fire, and he picked it up and threw it out in the yard." Transcript, Vol. III, p. 46. Pruett said that Hayes did not tell him where the kids were when he threw the lantern, and he [Pruett] thought the kids were burned when the lantern blew up as it hit the ground. Plaintiffs moved to strike Pruett's testimony about the conversation on the ground that the statements attributable to Hayes were not against his interest within the meaning of the rule. The court denied the motion.

* * *

The record indicates that both sides attempted to subpoena Hayes without success. At the time of trial, neither side knew where he was. Coleman had taken his deposition, but it was not introduced at trial. In his deposition, Hayes testified that he was in the yard when he saw the children were on fire and the lantern was shooting flames from its upright position on the front porch. He said he then picked up the lantern and threw it into the yard. He denied ever making any contradictory statements as to how the plaintiffs were burned.

II. Discussion

Plaintiffs contend that the trial court erred in admitting the out-of-court statements of Hayes as exceptions to the hearsay rule under Fed.R.Evid. 804(b)(3). They claim that the requirements of the rule were not met as Hayes was not "unavailable" and several of his statements were not against his interest.

* * *

Before a statement against interest may be admitted, the proponent of the evidence must demonstrate that the declarant is "unavailable." *United States v. Pelton,* 578 F.2d 701 (8th Cir.1978). Rule 804(a)(5) provides that a declarant is "unavailable" if "absent from the hearing and the proponent of his statement has been unable to procure his attendance (or in the case of a hearsay exception under subdivision (b)(2), (3) or (4), his attendance or testimony) by process or other reasonable means." This subsection is concerned with the absence of testimony, rather than the physical absence of the declarant. *See generally* H.R. 1597, 93d Cong., 2d Sess. 12 (1974), U.S.Code Cong. & Admin.News 1974, p. 7051; Cotchett and Elkund, *Federal Courtroom Evidence,* 163 (1984). Hayes was absent from the trial, but his testimony was available. Coleman had taken his deposition on July 5, 1984, eight months before trial. Since Hayes was not unavailable within the meaning of Rule 804(a)(5) and (b), his hearsay statements could not be admitted under the "statement against interest" exception in Rule 804(b)(3).

Coleman argues that plaintiffs failed to make a timely objection and conceded Hayes' unavailability. The record indicates, however, that plaintiffs objected to the admission of the hearsay statements with enough specificity. Plaintiffs did not dispute that Hayes himself was unavailable at trial, but they informed the court several times that the deposition of Hayes was available. To be sure, the objection could have been phrased in a more clear manner. The repeated references to the deposition were sufficient, however, to focus the trial court's attention on the nature of the unavailability requirement in Rule 804.

Coleman next argues that even if the trial court erred in admitting the hearsay statements, it was harmless error. We cannot agree. At the close of plaintiffs' case-in-chief, no evidence had been introduced from which Coleman could have argued that plaintiffs' injuries were caused by the negligent actions of a non-party. Introduction of the inadmissible hearsay created a substantive defense for Coleman, allowing it to present to the jury another explanation for plaintiffs' injuries. Admission of the testimony enabled the jury to consider improper evidence in deciding causation, one of the central issues. Plaintiffs were thereby prejudiced. Nor can we find that the error is harmless because testimony about Hayes' prior statements would have been admissible to impeach him. Before the statements could have been admitted under this alternative theory, Coleman would have first been compelled to produce Hayes or read his sworn deposition testimony. If the deposition had been read, the jury would have heard Hayes flatly denying that he caused plaintiffs' injuries. The deposition would have corroborated plaintiffs' theory of the case. The jury also would have been instructed that the prior inconsistent statements were not received to prove the truth of the assertions, but only for impeachment purposes. *See United States v. Rogers,* 549 F.2d 490, 497 (8th Cir.1976). Thus, the circumstances under which the testimony about Hayes' statements could have properly come in would have been very different than those under which it was actually presented. The fact that some of the testimony might ultimately have been admissible for impeachment purposes does not mitigate the prejudice to the plaintiffs. The admission of the hearsay statements under Fed.R.Evid. 804(b)(3) was therefore reversible error. * * *

[Reversed and remanded.]

NOTES AND QUESTIONS

1. *Limited deposition requirement.* The requirement that a party use a deposition of an unavailable witness applies only if unavailability arises under Rule 804(a)(5) and applies to hearsay admitted under Rules 804(b)(2), (3), and (4), but not under 804(b)(1) or (6). Why the requirement is not imposed for prior testimony under Rule 804(b)(1) is easily understood since there is no argument for the superiority of one type of prior testimony (a deposition) over another. Requiring a deposition when forfeiture by wrongdoing is involved would make little sense practically or theoretically.

Should the deposition requirement be applied to bar admission of hearsay by a presently unavailable declarant who was available for a deposition while the litigation was pending but was not deposed? Although rarely raised in the cases, it is possible that a deposition must be attempted if the declarant is outside the subpoena power of the court but at a location where the declarant could be deposed, and if not done, other hearsay will be excluded. See 1337523 Ontario, Inc. v. Golden State Bancorp, Inc., 163 F.Supp.2d 1111, 1120 (N.D.Cal.2001) (holding failure to attempt to take deposition of witness who could not be compelled to attend because living in another state barred receipt of statement against interest because testimony was not unavailable); 4 Saltzburg, Martin & Capra, Federal Rules of Evidence Manual § 804.02[3], at 804–10–11 (10th ed. 2011) (arguing for such a requirement). Other courts have appeared cold to the requirement. See United States v. McHan, 101 F.3d 1027, 1037 (4th Cir.1996) (hearsay admitted under Rule 804(b)(5) not excluded under Confrontation Clause despite government's failure to depose unavailable witness it knew was approaching death); United States v. Yonkers Contracting Co., Inc., 701 F.Supp. 431, 433–34 (S.D.N.Y.1988) (no requirement of taking deposition before death of terminally ill declarant).

2. *Degree of "permanency" of infirmity required.* Subsection (a)(4) defines as unavailable persons who are unable to testify because of illness or infirmity. Issues arise under these provisions concerning the degree of permanency required of the disabling condition. When the disability is apparently temporary, the trial court may be required to grant a continuance. See United States v. Faison, 679 F.2d 292 (3d Cir.1982) (trial court abused discretion in failing to grant continuance since witness, who was hospitalized with heart attack, was important witness against defendant). In United States v. Amaya, 533 F.2d 188, 191 (5th Cir.1976), the court set out a general standard that "[t]he duration of the illness need only be in probability long enough so that, with proper regard to the importance of the testimony, the trial cannot be postponed." Several commentators have suggested that,

because of the Confrontation Clause, the standard must be applied in a much more exacting fashion in criminal cases where hearsay from an unavailable witness is offered against the defendant. 2 McCormick, Evidence § 253 (7th ed. 2013); 5 Weinstein's Federal Evidence § 804.03[5][b] (2d ed. 2013).

3. *Testimony as to lack of memory.* Lack of memory must be established by the declarant's testimony. See State v. Thoma, 834 P.2d 1020, 1025 (Or.1992). The Rule is silent on the nature of proof required for other types of unavailability. See In re Complaint of Bankers Trust Co., 752 F.2d 874, 888 (3d Cir.1984) (counsel's representations of physical infirmity held insufficient in absence of affidavit from witness). When unavailability is predicated on the lack of memory, loss of memory about some details covered by the statement is not sufficient. State v. Miller, 408 S.E.2d 846, 849–50 (N.C.1991).

4. *Discretion in judging adequacy of effort.* The trial court has substantial discretion in determining that the party seeking to admit an absent witness' statement has been unable to secure this testimony by process or other reasonable means under Rule 804(a)(5). See Bailey v. Southern Pac. Transp. Co., 613 F.2d 1385 (5th Cir.1980) (trial court has discretion to accept counsel's assertion that witness was not subject to process and opponent has burden of demonstrating an abuse of that discretion). That discretion is not unbounded, however. See Perricone v. Kansas City S. Ry., 630 F.2d 317, 320–21 (5th Cir.1980) (trial court erred in finding absent witness unavailable where opponent was able after trial easily to locate witness through telephone listing).

5. *Non-impact of Crawford.* While Crawford v. Washington, 541 U.S. 36 (2004), profoundly changed much of confrontation law, see Chapter 13, Section C, supra, the requirements respecting when a witness is unavailable appear unchanged.

6. *Implicit impact of Confrontation Clause.* The effort that must be exerted to find or secure the presence of the declarant may differ between criminal and civil cases. The Advisory Committee Note refers to Barber v. Page, 390 U.S. 719 (1968), a Confrontation Clause case, for the standard for reasonableness of efforts to secure declarants. That standard, either as a matter of rule interpretation or as required by the Confrontation Clause, applies when statements are offered against the criminal defendant. See United States v. Kehm, 799 F.2d 354, 360 (7th Cir.1986). In civil cases and in criminal cases when the statement is offered against the prosecution, there is some authority that the "inability to procure the declarant's attendance by reasonable means is equivalent to inability to serve a subpoena." 5 Weinstein's Federal Evidence § 804.03[6][a] (2d ed. 2013). But see Kirk v. Raymark Indus., Inc., 61 F.3d 147, 165–65 (3d Cir.1995) (ruling expert witness in civil case not unavailable despite being beyond subpoena power where party failed to offer normal witness fee and request attendance).

7. *Effect of "unclean hands."* Rule 804 states that, where the proponent of the witness' statement procured or wrongfully caused the absence, a

witness is not unavailable. Where the party procures unavailability, the Rule disables the party from admitting hearsay under Rule 804 even though the actions were not "wrongful." See United States v. Bollin, 264 F.3d 391, 414 (4th Cir.2001) (defendant could not assert his Fifth Amendment privilege and then claim unavailability). However, refusal of the government to grant immunity, which would eliminate unavailability under the Fifth Amendment, is not treated as causing the unavailability. See United States v. Dolah, 245 F.3d 98, 102–03 (2d Cir.2001).

Where the conduct is wrongful, it will frequently not only bar admission of hearsay by the party who is responsible for rendering the declarant unavailable, but also affirmatively permit admission of statements by that declarant against him or her under Rule 804(b)(6). See Section K, infra.

8. *Unavailability under other rules.* In addition to Rule 804(b)(1), depositions are admissible under the terms of the Federal Rules of Civil and Criminal Procedure. Under Rule 802, if admissible under such rules or under federal statute, the prior testimony is separately admissible. See Advisory Committee Note to Rule 802. These separate rules and statutes frequently impose conditions different than the evidence rules for admission of what would otherwise constitute hearsay. For example, "unavailability" under Federal Rule of Civil Procedure 32(a)(3)(B) permits admission of a deposition where the witness is 100 miles from the place of trial or is out of the United States, unless the party offering the deposition secured that absence. Thus, the unavailability requirement for former testimony generally under Rule 804 is more demanding than the unavailability requirement for former testimony of a witness in the form of a deposition under Civil Procedure Rule 32. Is the difference justified?

H. FORMER TESTIMONY

Federal Rule 804(b)(1)

UNITED STATES V. DUENAS
United States Court of Appeals, Ninth Circuit, 2012.
691 F.3d 1070.

OPINION

WARDLAW, CIRCUIT JUDGE:

These consolidated appeals arise from the chaotic two-day execution of a search warrant by the Guam Police Department's ("GPD") SWAT team, in coordination with federal DEA and ATF agents. * * *

Ray and Lou [Duenas] were arrested and separately gave statements to police officers. The district court denied their motions to suppress evidence of the drugs and stolen goods seized in the raid and their statements. A jury convicted each of the Duenases on multiple counts.

Both appeal their convictions, contending that the suppression motions should have been granted, that former testimony of by-then-deceased Officer Frankie Smith should not have been admitted at trial * * *

* * * Officer Smith's Former Testimony

* * * [W]e are compelled to conclude that the district court should not have admitted Officer Smith's suppression hearing testimony following his unfortunate demise. The district court admitted the testimony as "former testimony" under Federal Rule of Evidence 804(b)(1), reasoning that Ray "had a meaningful opportunity to cross-examine Officer Smith" about the "context and details" of Officer Smith's testimony at the suppression hearing, but made "a tactical decision" not to do so. We disagree, because the district court failed to compare Ray's "fundamental objectives" at each hearing to find a similar motive under Rule 804(b)(1).

"Former testimony" is not hearsay if a declarant is unavailable. "Former testimony" is testimony that:

> (A) was given as a witness at a trial, hearing, or lawful deposition, whether given during the current proceeding or a different one; and
>
> (B) is now offered against a party who had—or, in a civil case, whose predecessor in interest had—an opportunity and similar motive to develop it by direct, cross-, or redirect examination.

Fed.R.Evid. 804(b)(1). Smith was "unavailable" because he was deceased, and his former testimony was given during the pre-trial suppression hearing. *See* Fed.R.Evid. 804(a)(4). Thus, the critical question is whether Ray had the "opportunity and similar motive" to develop Officer Smith's testimony by direct, cross-, or redirect examination at the suppression hearing as he would have had at trial. *See United States v. Salerno,* 505 U.S. 317, 321 (1992) (holding that former testimony may not be introduced under Rule 804(b)(1) without a showing of "similar motive"). Because Ray's motive at the suppression hearing was solely to demonstrate that his statements were involuntary and obtained in violation of *Miranda*, and thus inadmissible, his motive for cross-examining Officer Smith at trial, to challenge the substance of the statements as opposed to the circumstances in which they were given, was substantially dissimilar.

In *Salerno*, the only Supreme Court decision to address the "similar motive" requirement, the Court clarified that "similar motive" is a necessary element of Rule 804(b)(1). However, it did not explain how courts should determine whether a party's motives are "similar." Justice Blackmun, concurring, provided some guidance by noting that "similar motive" does not mean "identical motive," and that the "similar motive" analysis is "inherently a *factual* inquiry" based on "the similarity of the underlying issues and on the context of the * * * questioning." *Id.* at 326 (emphasis in original).

We have twice addressed whether, under Rule 804(b)(1), suppression hearing testimony is admissible at a later proceeding. *See United States v. Geiger,* 263 F.3d 1034 (9th Cir.2001); *United States v. Poland,* 659 F.2d 884 (9th Cir.1981) (per curiam). The government argues that these cases dictate the outcome of our "similar motive" analysis. We find *Poland* and *Geiger* to be factually inapposite, however, and conclude that neither decision controls our "inherently * * * factual inquiry." *Salerno,* 505 U.S. at 326 (emphasis omitted).

In *Poland,* an eye-witness identified the defendant in a line-up. 659 F.2d at 896. A suppression hearing, at which the defense cross-examined the witness, was held to determine whether the line-up was impermissibly suggestive. Denying the motion to suppress, the district court concluded that the lineup was "fair and not unjust." *Id.* at 895. The witness died before trial, and the district court granted the prosecution's motion to admit a transcript of the suppression hearing testimony at trial. On appeal, the defendant argued that he would have been motivated at trial to test the witness's reliability by cross-examining him about his eyesight, whether he was intoxicated, and the distance from which he observed the defendant, inquiries that he was not motivated to make at the suppression hearing. We rejected this argument and concluded that the "similar motive" requirement was satisfied, noting that pretrial identifications are admissible if they are reliable, even if the identification procedure is unduly suggestive. Thus the defendant's motive in cross-examining the witness at both the suppression hearing and trial was the same: to cast doubt on the witness's reliability with questions about his eyesight, intoxication, and the like.

In *Geiger,* the question was not whether suppression hearing testimony was admissible at trial, but rather whether an officer's testimony at a state suppression hearing was admissible at a subsequent federal suppression hearing. 263 F.3d at 1038. The defendant in *Geiger* admitted in a taped confession taken by Officer Churchill that he had placed a bomb in the victim's truck. Before Geiger was indicted in federal court, the state of Alaska charged him with first degree murder. Geiger successfully sought suppression of the recorded confession in state court, because the arresting officers, including Officer Churchill, had failed to comply with Alaska's custodial interrogation requirements. Officer Churchill, who testified at the state suppression hearing, died before the federal suppression hearing. The magistrate judge admitted his testimony at the federal hearing under Rule 804(b)(1). Geiger contended that the court erred in admitting the former testimony, because the state hearing focused on Alaska's custodial interrogation requirements, while the federal suppression hearing concerned the sufficiency of his *Miranda* warning, the voluntariness of his statement, and his request for counsel. We rejected Geiger's argument, reasoning that the similarity of his state and federal motions to suppress belied his claim of dissimilar motives: "Both motions to suppress presented virtually the same issues: whether Geiger's taped confession was coerced and involuntary; whether Geiger had been properly *Mirandized;* whether the arrest was pretextual; and whether Geiger had been unlawfully detained." *Id.* Geiger also introduced the exact same detailed affidavit in both hearings. Moreover, Churchill's testimony at the state hearing addressed issues pertinent to the federal hearing, such as his role in the interrogation, whether Geiger asked for an attorney or refused to speak, whether he coerced Geiger into confessing, and whether he threatened Geiger's family. Because the legal and factual issues in both hearings were "substantially similar," we concluded that Geiger had a "similar motive" at both hearings.

We have also addressed the "similar motive" prong in other contexts. In *United States v. McFall,* 558 F.3d 951 (9th Cir.2009), we examined whether exculpatory grand jury testimony is admissible at trial against the prosecution, an issue on which the courts of appeals are split. The First and Second Circuits examine whether the government "t[ook] the same side on the same issue" and whether it had the same degree of interest to prevail at each proceeding. *Id.* at 962 (citing *United States v. DiNapoli,* 8 F.3d 909 (2d Cir.1993) (en banc); *United States v. Omar,* 104 F.3d 519, 522–24 (1st Cir.1997)). In *McFall,* we rejected this "fine-grained" method and followed the D.C. and Sixth Circuits in comparing motives at a "high level of generality." *Id.* * * * We noted that the government need not have the same "intensity" of motivation at each proceeding, because the plain language of Rule 804(b)(1) requires similar, but not identical, motivation. *Id.* at 963.

McFall was charged with conspiracy to commit extortion. McFall's co-conspirator, Sawyer, at that point uncharged, appeared before a grand jury and offered a first-person account of key events that contradicted the testimony of the government's primary witness and corroborated McFall's version of the events. Sawyer died before trial, and McFall sought to introduce a transcript of the exculpatory grand jury testimony under Rule 804(b)(1). The district court did not admit the transcript, concluding that the government's motive at trial was "completely different" than its motive before the grand jury because Sawyer was not a suspect at the time of his testimony and because the grand jury was a fact-finding investigation, not an adversarial proceeding. *Id.* at 962. We held that the district court "erred in concluding that the government's respective motives were 'completely different,' and the exclusion of Sawyer's grand jury testimony as hear-say amounted to an abuse of discretion." *Id.* at 963. Although we noted that the government's incentive to develop incriminating testimony before the grand jury was "likely not as intense as it would have been at trial," we nevertheless held that the government's "fundamental objective" was the same at each proceeding. *Id.* That "fundamental objective" was "to draw out testimony that would support its theory that McFall conspired with Sawyer to commit extortion—the same motive it possessed at trial." *Id.*

Finally, we recently had occasion to address the issue of "similar motive" in the context of an SEC investigation of a CFO involved in a stock option back-dating scandal. *See Sec. & Exch. Comm'n v. Jasper,* 678 F.3d 1116 (9th Cir.2012). The SEC alleged that Jasper engaged in an illegal scheme to back-date stock options granted to employees and directors. The company's former treasurer, Ruehle, made exculpatory statements in sworn testimony taken in connection with the SEC's fact-gathering investigation. Because Ruehle was unavailable at the time of trial, Jasper attempted to introduce his testimony under Rule 804(b)(1). The district court found the testimony inadmissible, concluding that the SEC had a different motive at the accusatory stage of the proceedings than it did during the investigatory stage. We affirmed, because the district court did not abuse its discretion based on the inherently different motives involved in an early investigation, at which "open-ended questions are typically asked without expectation the witness will be needed at trial," and a cross-examination of an adverse witness. *Id.* at 1128–29.

As the foregoing cases demonstrate, we have not developed a bright-line test for determining similarity of motive. Nor should we. As Justice Blackmun instructed, the "similar motive" analysis is "inherently a factual inquiry" based on "the similarity of the underlying issues and on the context of the * * * questioning." *Salerno,* 505 U.S. at 326 (emphasis omitted). Here we are faced with a unique set of facts that does not fit squarely within the ambit of any of our aforementioned precedent.

The transcript of Ray's suppression hearing demonstrates that his counsel did not have a similar motive in questioning Officer Smith at the suppression hearing as at trial. Ray's "fundamental objective," *McFall,* 558 F.3d at 963, in questioning Officer Smith at the suppression hearing was to elicit testimony to prove that his statements to Smith were involuntary and obtained in violation of *Miranda.* This was Ray's sole purpose in examining Smith, a point Ray's counsel made emphatically when the prosecution veered into the substance of the statement and sought details about Ray's meetings with his drug source. Ray's counsel objected to this inquiry as "having no relevance or bearing on" the only question at issue—whether Ray voluntarily spoke with Smith. After the district court overruled Ray's objection, Ray's counsel offered to enter the written statement into evidence for purposes of the suppression hearing, rather than to permit the prosecutor to go into detail about the substance of the statement. The prosecutor acquiesced to the defense's limitation on its inquiry and simply asked Officer Smith to identify Ray's statement before introducing it into evidence.

During the cross-examination of Officer Smith at the suppression hearing, Ray's counsel inquired only about the circumstances under which Ray was arrested and made the statement. Counsel asked about the duration of Smith's interview with Ray, whether Ray was under the influence of any drugs or medication at the time of the statement, whether he had consumed alcohol the night before giving the statement, whether Smith offered leniency if Ray cooperated in finding an alleged associate, and whether Smith threatened Ray. The record of the suppression hearing plainly shows that Ray's motive at that proceeding was to question Officer Smith about circumstances bearing on the voluntariness of the statement, and not to delve into the contents of the statement.

Ray's written motion to suppress confirms that his motive was confined to demonstrating involuntariness and a *Miranda* violation. *See Geiger,* 263 F.3d at 1038 (comparing defendant's state and federal motions to dismiss to determine similarity of motive). The motion argues only that Ray was improperly *Mirandized* and that his statement was involuntary. The motion makes no reference to the substance of Ray's statement.

Ray's fundamental objective at the suppression hearing was not the same as his motive would have been had Smith testified at trial. The issue at trial was whether the evidence proved Ray's guilt beyond a reasonable doubt, not the circumstances of his confession. By the time of trial, neither voluntariness nor the alleged *Miranda* violation was even at issue. Rather, Ray's objective at trial would have been to vigorously challenge Officer Smith on the details of the oral and written statements, to cast doubt on his credibility and on the reliability and completeness of his version of Ray's statement. For instance, Ray's written statement says that "[f]irearms found on property were traded with meth." The statement does not indicate which particular firearms were acquired via methamphetamine trafficking. Similarly, although the statement makes clear that Ray traded methamphetamine for stolen items, it never refers to a specific quantity of drugs.

Ray's counsel also would have had a motive to question Officer Smith about the substance of Ray's oral statements to Smith. In Smith's suppression hearing testimony, Smith "summarize[d]" Ray's oral statements. He testified that Ray admitted to trading methamphetamine for jewelry, tools, and recreational vehicles, and named his source of methamphetamine. Smith also testified to a purported admission that Ray knew the items he was receiving were stolen. Had Smith testified at trial, Ray's counsel certainly would have been motivated to develop more than a "summary" of Ray's oral statement. Counsel would have had a strong motive to cast doubt on Officer Smith's summary, by determining the specific questions that Smith asked Ray, testing the accuracy of Smith's recollection, and seeking to learn Ray's full responses to those questions. Smith's account of Ray's oral statement makes no reference to the quantity of methamphetamine being sold or exchanged, nor to the value of the stolen items received in exchange; a thorough cross-examination of Smith regarding his interview with Ray might have drawn out such facts. Ray's counsel also would have been motivated on cross-examination to reveal inconsistencies between Ray's written statement and Smith's version of Ray's oral statement. These motives stand in stark contrast to Ray's motive at the suppression hearing, which was limited to developing testimony concerning voluntariness and whether Ray was properly *Mirandized.*

We therefore conclude that the district court's "similar motive" determination must be reversed. The district court failed to properly compare Ray's "fundamental objective" at the suppression hearing to his motive at trial, and instead focused on Ray's *opportunity* to cross-examine Officer Smith. The district court noted that the government had a motive to explore the details of Ray's statements and, from that, apparently inferred that Ray also had a motive to delve into the substance of the statements. But the government's only purpose in questioning Officer Smith about the details of the statement was to demonstrate voluntariness, under the theory that "[t]he detail that a person goes into is an indicia of how open, how comfortable they feel with the person that they're talking to." Thus, only the amount of detail—and not the accuracy of those details—was relevant to the suppression motion, and even after the district court permitted the government to explore the details of the statement, Ray continued to lack any motive to probe Officer Smith about the accuracy of the statement or about Smith's recollection.

The extent of the district court's comparison of Ray's motives is contained in its conclusory statement that "[a] purely tactical decision not to develop particular testimony despite the same issue and level of interest at each proceeding does not constitute a lack of opportunity or a dissimilar motive for purposes of Rule 804(b)(1)." This is of course circular, in that it predicates its conclusion that Ray's counsel's decision was tactical on the unfounded assumption that the same issue and level of interest existed at each proceeding. Because it failed to directly compare Ray's "fundamental objectives" at trial and at the suppression hearing, the district court abused its discretion by admitting Smith's testimony. * * * *See McFall,* 558 F.3d at 963 (district court's decision to admit or exclude evidence under Rule 804(b)(1) is reviewed for abuse of discretion).

* * * [B]ecause Ray did not have a "similar motive" to cross-examine Officer Frankie Smith at the suppression hearing as at the trial, the district court erred in admitting Officer Smith's suppression-hearing testimony into evidence. Ray's conviction must therefore be reversed.

NOTES AND QUESTIONS

1.   *Satisfying hearsay protections?* Are depositions and former testimony actually hearsay under conventional definitions? Wigmore was the leading proponent of the view that prior testimony should not be classified as hearsay. 5 Wigmore, Evidence § 1370 (Chadbourn rev. 1974). United States v. Inadi, 475 U.S. 387, 394 (1986), took a very different perspective, figuratively treating former testimony as a particularly inferior form of hearsay from the perspective of the Confrontation Clause. It required a showing of unavailability for this type of hearsay while eliminating the requirement for coconspirator statements: "former testimony often is only a weaker substitute for live testimony." What is a sensible justification for limiting admissibility of former testimony since it has been previously subjected to cross-examination when considered purely as a matter of hearsay policy? See 2 McCormick, Evidence § 301 (7th ed. 2013) (antipathy to trial by presentation of prepared statement, perhaps?).

2.   *Similarity of motive, not identity of issues.* While some rigid formulations of the exception for prior testimony have required identity of issues in the two proceedings, even before the Federal Rules the trend was to require substantial rather than technical identity. Rule 804(b)(1) imposes no direct requirement concerning identity or similarity of issues. Rather, the Rule requires that the party against whom the testimony is offered have a similar motive to develop the testimony. "Since identity of issues is significant only in that it bears on motive and interest in developing fully the testimony of the witness, expressing the matter in the latter terms is preferable." Advisory Committee Note to Rule 804(b)(1). See also 2 McCormick, Evidence § 304 (7th ed. 2013). See, e.g., United States v. Licavoli, 725 F.2d 1040, 1048 (6th Cir.1984) (almost identical issues in state criminal prosecutions that formed predicate acts for federal RICO prosecution provided similar motive for cross-examination); United States v. Poland, 659 F.2d 884, 896 (9th Cir.1981) (testimony offered at hearing on defendant's motion to suppress identification evidence admissible at trial since motive of cross-examination at hearing was to challenge the reliability of the identification); Commonwealth v. Sena, 809 N.E.2d 505, 515–16 (Mass.2004) (finding that additional evidence regarding new witness at subsequent trial did not substantially affect motive to challenge witness at the first trial as to what he saw).

3.   *Emphasis on opportunity.* Whether the opportunity and motive for cross-examination at a preliminary hearing in a criminal case or at a discovery deposition in a civil case is sufficient to permit admission of the testimony has been frequently litigated. As a general matter, courts have

ruled that testimony from such prior proceedings is admissible in spite of some rather obvious differences in tactical and strategic interests at those proceedings as contrasted with the interests at trial. See, e.g., United States v. Avants, 367 F.3d 433, 444 (5th Cir.2004) (finding preliminary hearing in 1966 state case admissible in 2003 civil rights prosecution); DeLuryea v. Winthrop Labs., 697 F.2d 222, 226–27 (8th Cir.1983) (deposition); People v. Zapien, 846 P.2d 704, 728–30 (Cal.1993) (preliminary hearing); United States v. Carneglia, 256 F.R.D. 366, 375–76 (E.D.N.Y.2009) (preliminary hearing).

4. *Major limits on cross-examination.* Restrictions on the scope or extent of cross-examination at the prior proceeding may render the testimony inadmissible. See United States v. Jackson, 335 F.3d 170, 177–78 (2d Cir.2003) (holding statements by defendant during plea colloquy inadmissible because the Rule directs that examination be conducted by the court rather than the prosecutor and prosecution questioning is limited and typically perfunctory); United States v. Smith, 231 F.3d 800, 817 (11th Cir.2000) (finding opportunity to cross-examine inadequate where witness asserted Fifth Amendment privilege during government's cross-examination); In re Complaint of Paducah Towing Co., 692 F.2d 412, 418–19 (6th Cir.1982) (opportunity to cross-examine held inadequate where conducted by nonlawyer in administrative proceeding and where both redirect examination and opportunity to impeach witness were improperly limited); Butler v. Comm'r of Internal Revenue, 103 T.C.M. (CCH) 1359, at *45 (T.C.2012) (ruling that IRS interview did not qualify because it was not a hearing and the opposing party did not have an opportunity to examine the declarant under oath); Williams v. State, 7 A.3d 1038, 1054 (Md.2010) (ruling opportunity inadequate where defendant had not been informed that the witness was "legally blind" before conducting earlier cross-examination); Commonwealth v. Arrignton, 917 N.E.2d 734, 739–40 (Mass.2009) (ruling witness' medications and medical condition prohibited vigorous cross-examination); Commonwealth v. Ramtahal, 33 A.3d 602, 610 (Pa.2011) (finding opportunity inadequate when defendant took Fifth Amendment privilege during cross-examination). At the same time, the courts have held that the opportunity for cross-examination need not be unbounded. See United States v. King, 713 F.2d 627, 630 (11th Cir.1983) (limitations imposed by court on cross-examination at prior trial were reasonable and permitted "adequate" or "meaningful," if not unlimited, cross-examination).

5. *Unimportance (but not irrelevancy) of actual motivation.* Courts generally pay little attention to arguments that the party's actual motivation differed at the prior proceeding. A frequent response to such arguments is that "tactical decisions" or "selection of a trial strategy" are not considered sufficient to eliminate the motive for cross-examination. United States v. Pizarro, 717 F.2d 336, 349 (7th Cir.1983); United States v. Zurosky, 614 F.2d 779, 793 (1st Cir.1979). However, as reflected in cases like United States v. Feldman, 761 F.2d 380 (7th Cir.1985 (deposition in a civil deposition taken in federal agency action ruled inadmissible in criminal prosecution from the same transaction), the greater the facial dissimilarity between the issues, the

more likely the court is to examine the adequacy of the party's actual motivation. See Hannah v. City of Overland, Missouri, 795 F.2d 1385, 1390–91 (8th Cir.1986) (prosecutor in homicide case lacked significant motive to challenge testimony of witnesses at civil deposition that posed little threat to government's case).

    6. *Application to grand jury testimony.* In United States v. Salerno, 505 U.S. 317 (1992), the Supreme Court rejected the argument that grand jury testimony of a declarant who asserts a Fifth Amendment privilege at trial should be automatically admissible against the government under the principle of "adversarial fairness," regardless of whether the prosecutor could be shown to have had a "similar motive" when examining the witness before the grand jury. The Court believed it was not free to alter the literal terms of the Rule's requirements. Id. at 322. On remand, the Second Circuit rejected any automatic position about the similarity of the prosecutor's motivation before the grand jury and at a subsequent trial, considering that inquiry to be fact specific in each case. United States v. DiNapoli, 8 F.3d 909, 914 (2d Cir.1993) (en banc). On the particular facts of *DiNapoli*, the court found the motive to be dissimilar and excluded the hearsay. Id. at 915. However, in some cases, exculpatory grand jury testimony has been found admissible against the government. See United States v. McFall, 558 F.3d 951, 963 (9th Cir.2009); United States v. Foster, 128 F.3d 949, 955–56 (6th Cir.1997).

DYKES V. RAYMARK INDUSTRIES, INC.
United States Court of Appeals, Sixth Circuit, 1986.
801 F.2d 810.

ENGEL, CIRCUIT JUDGE.

National Gypsum Company appeals a judgment entered against it after a jury awarded plaintiffs $300,000.00 in compensatory damages and $200,000.00 in punitive damages for injuries suffered by Mr. Eulis Dykes from exposure to asbestos-containing products while on the job.

* * *

Eulis Dykes worked as a plasterer at Gilbert Plastering Company in Knoxville, Tennessee, from 1947 through the mid–1960's. He used the spray gun method of applying plaster which involved using an applicator attached to a hose immersed in liquid plaster. The acoustical plaster he used in some of his work contained asbestos. The district court expressly found that on several occasions Mr. Dykes was exposed to Gold Bond Sprayolite, an acoustical plaster manufactured by National Gypsum. * * * [Around 1965, he] became a utility mechanic at Union Carbide. His work at Union Carbide included some plastering as well as the replacement of asbestos pipe insulation and asbestos boiler linings. The trial court found that Mr. Dykes' last possible exposure to asbestos was in 1967, and this finding is not challenged on appeal. He left Union Carbide in 1982 after he was diagnosed as suffering from mesothelioma, a form of chest cancer associated with the inhalation of asbestos. Mr. Dykes died from complications of his disease in November 1983, shortly after the present suit was filed in the district court. * * *

Sufficiency of Evidence of Punitive Damages.

Punitive damages are available under Tennessee law for conduct "involving fraud, malice, gross negligence or oppression * * * or where a wrongful act is done with a bad motive or so recklessly as to imply a disregard for social obligations. * * * *"Island Container Corp. v. March,* 529 S.W.2d at 45. Mrs. Dykes attempted to meet this standard by establishing that National Gypsum was aware of the dangers of asbestos exposure during and after her husband's exposure but did nothing to protect or inform employees of those dangers. She also attempted to establish that National Gypsum suppressed studies and reports documenting the risks associated with asbestos exposure. The parties do not dispute the trial court's finding that the last possible year in which Mr. Dykes was exposed to asbestos is 1967.

National Gypsum challenges * * * the admission by the trial court of * * * the deposition of Dr. Kenneth Wallace Smith, the medical director of the Johns–Manville Corporation from 1953 to 1966 * * *.

Dr. Kenneth Wallace Smith joined Canadian Johns–Manville in 1942 as a medical officer, became medical director there in 1946 or 1947, corporate director in 1951, and in 1953 he became the medical director for Johns–Manville Corporation. He held that post until 1966. Dr. Smith was deposed on January 13, 1976, in relation to the case *DeRocco v. Forty–Eight Insulation, Inc.,* Nos. 7880, 7281 (Pa.Ct.Common Pleas, Allegheny County 1974). The entire deposition was read into the record before the jury in the present case.

National Gypsum objects to the admission of Dr. Smith's testimony on the ground that it is hearsay, and is inadmissible former testimony under Rule 804(b)(1) * * *

There is no dispute that Dr. Smith's deposition was not previously offered by or against National Gypsum. Absent these circumstances, former testimony of an unavailable declarant is admissible only if National Gypsum can be said to be a "predecessor in interest" to Johns–Manville, against whom the deposition was originally offered.

The Sixth Circuit addressed this same issue with respect to *this same deposition* in *Clay v. Johns–Manville Sales Corp.,* 722 F.2d 1289 (1983). There, the issue was whether Dr. Smith's deposition was admissible against Raybestos–Manhattan, which likewise was not a party in *DeRocco.*

In *Clay,* our court speaking through Judge Edwards adopted the Third Circuit's construction of Rule 804(b)(1) and the following language:

While we do not endorse an extravagant interpretation of who or what constitutes a "predecessor in interest," we prefer one that is realistically generous over one that is formalistically grudging. We believe that what has been described as "the practical and expedient view" expresses the congressional intention: "if it appears that in the former suit a party having a like motive to cross-examine about the same matters as the present party would have, was accorded an adequate opportunity for such examination, the testimony may be received against the present party." Under these circumstances, the previous party having like motive to develop the testimony about the same material facts is, in the final analysis, a predecessor in interest to the present party.

722 F.2d at 1295 (citing *Lloyd v. American Export Lines, Inc.*, 580 F.2d 1179, 1185 (3d Cir.1978)).

In a more recent decision, *Murphy v. Owens–Illinois, Inc.*, 779 F.2d 340 (6th Cir.1985), our court, speaking through Judge Kennedy, upheld the exclusion of the same deposition of Dr. Smith involved in *Clay* and involved here when it was offered to show the state of the art against a manufacturer which withdrew from the asbestos product market in 1953. We there held that although the company was a predecessor in interest under Rule 804(b)(1) and *Clay,* the admissibility of Dr. Smith's deposition must still be subject to the balancing test of Rule 403, Fed.R.Evid. * * *, to determine whether its relevance was out-weighed by its prejudicial effect. Since in *Murphy* we agreed with the district judge that the particular circumstances were different from those in *Clay,* we upheld his exclusion there of Dr. Smith's deposition. Judge Kennedy for the court in *Murphy* recognized as *stare decisis* the continuing viability of *Clay.* She characterized its holding as having "collapsed the two criteria, i.e., whether the defendant was a predecessor in interest, and whether he had an opportunity and similar motive to develop the testimony by cross-examination into one test." 779 F.2d at 343. We view the net effect of *Clay* and *Murphy* as holding that in our circuit the fact of being a predecessor in interest is not limited to a legal relationship, but is also to be determined by the second aspect of the test under the rule: whether the defendant had an opportunity and similar motive to develop the testimony by cross-examination. In the instant case, the record shows that the trial judge was familiar with *Clay* and that he had examined the deposition before he concluded that the Smith deposition ought to be admitted. He further held that any differences in the interests of the defendants here and the defendants in *DeRocco* was a matter of degree but did not affect his decision that they were sufficiently similar to justify the use of the Smith deposition.

We might normally be concerned with the ruling of the trial judge here. We do not view our decision in *Clay* as establishing the admissibility of Dr. Smith's deposition for all purposes in all asbestos cases. *Clay* did not rule the deposition admissible as a matter of law. It only held that it was the type of deposition which was subject to the application of Rule 804(b)(1), and thus should have been admissible under the particular facts in *Clay*. While we agree with *Clay* that a realistic application of the rule is to be preferred over one which is formalistically grudging, we believe also that the preferred approach in determining admissibility is for the attorneys to present to the court and for the court to consider the circumstances under which the original deposition was taken so that a full understanding of the motives in the first case can be obtained. Some of the motives of the defendants can be understood from the very limited cross-examination which appears in the Smith deposition, but very little otherwise is shown in our record or is shown either in *Clay* or in *Murphy*.

What is more important, however, is the question of potential prejudice that can accrue to a defendant against whom a deposition is introduced which the defendant never had an opportunity to adequately refute. Under such circumstances, we think it is incumbent upon counsel for the defendant when objecting to the admissibility of such proof to explain as clearly as possible to the judge precisely why the motive and opportunity of the defendants in the first case was not adequate to develop the cross-examination which the instant defendant would have presented to the witness. Thus, we would have been much more impressed with the defense's objections had they articulated before the trial court in the first instance, and later before us, precisely what lines of questioning they would have pursued. While National Gypsum here points to certain areas of difference between its situation and that of Johns–Manville, much of its argument before us was not presented to the district court, nor are we told precisely what lines of questioning National Gypsum would have pursued had it had the opportunity. We do not doubt that the trial judge here understood that he was not bound as a matter of law to admit the document in every case and we do not doubt he would have carefully considered any such factors, if they existed and had been pointed out to him at the time. We believe that it was the responsibility of National Gypsum to make this showing in the district court if it wished later to seek a retrial in which the evidence was to be excluded.

We further comment that we are aware of the great risk which might normally attend the use of a deposition of an expert who is no longer available for cross-examination. Expert witnesses all too often may be obtained on any subject and may speak with great authority and express opinions very wide in scope. When they are not adequately cross-examined, even though an opportunity is present, experts are often prone to create too heavy an aura of authoritativeness. Further, it should rarely be necessary to use the purely opinion testimony of an expert who testified in an entirely different case; and the dangers are correspondingly great that, where there exists a wide variety of opinion, an alert attorney may simply search out expert testimony which he conceives to be favorable to his cause and which he knows to have been made by a witness who is no longer, through death or otherwise, available to testify. Obviously, Rule [804] is not designed to deprive the opposite party of the historic right of cross-examination; rather, it is intended to permit parties to employ proof and testimony which is essentially reliable, cannot be effectively obtained in any other manner, and whose relevancy and probity is such that its introduction outweighs the possible prejudicial value which may result from denying cross-examination.

Here, the testimony of Dr. Smith is not so much the testimony of any expert who is giving opinions, as it is the testimony of a very knowledgeable person who was aware of the historical development of the specialized subject matter under examination. We believe that the very limited cross-examination of which the counsel in the original *DeRocco* case availed itself reflects its correct conclusion that most of Dr. Smith's testimony did relate to historical facts and was of a type which was not subject to refutation. Indeed, nothing in the argument before us or before the district court challenges the accuracy of the historical statements made by Dr. Smith, and for this additional reason we believe it was not an abuse of discretion for the trial judge here to have admitted the deposition. As observed by Judge Kennedy, "Smith, as former Medical Director of the leading manufacturer of asbestos-containing products, was in a unique position to discuss the scope of knowledge available to the industry during his 20–year tenure at Johns–Manville." *Murphy,* 779 F.2d at 343.

* * * [Remanded on damages issue.]

NOTES AND QUESTIONS

1.   *Progression of party identity requirement.* "Identity of parties" has been, on occasion, given as a requirement for admission of prior testimony. However, the modern trend, as reflected in Rule 804(b)(1), is to eliminate such a requirement in a number of situations. See 2 McCormick, Evidence § 303 (7th ed. 2013). First, there is no requirement of mutuality. Only identity of the party against whom the testimony is offered is required. See Bailey v. S. Pac. Transp. Co., 613 F.2d 1385, 1390 (5th Cir.1980) (testimony by plaintiff in another civil action against the railroad concerning malfunctioning signal light admissible in second suit against same defendant). Also, where the party against whom the prior testimony is offered is in privity with a party in the prior proceeding, the testimony is admissible.

Creamer v. General Teamsters Local Union 326, 560 F.Supp. 495, 499 (D.Del.1983) (owner of company is predecessor in interest to company).

An arguably distinct rationale covers cases where the government is placed in a position akin to the predecessor in interest when its public duty is to protect private interests. See In re Master Key Antitrust Litig., 72 F.R.D. 108, 109 (D.Conn.1976) (unique relationship between government's antitrust suits and private actions that follow); Lloyd v. Am. Export Lines, Inc., 580 F.2d 1179, 1185–86 (3d Cir.1978) (testimony at Coast Guard inquiry admissible because of community of interest between victim of assault and Coast Guard, which has overlapping duty to protect both private interest of alleged victim and public interest in unimpeded merchant marine service). The line of cases culminating in *Dykes* relies heavily upon the *Lloyd* case. Was the extension proper?

2. *Party identity issues in civil cases.* *Dykes* teaches that the predecessor-in-interest language should not be applied too strictly, but it concerned a rather unique situation. Does *Dykes* mean that testimony offered against similarly situated but entirely separate parties is freely admissible? Consider the following: Suppose two bus passengers are injured in a collision and file separate actions against the bus company. Should the testimony of a witness called by the defense in the suit of the first passenger be admissible against the second passenger, the witness having become unavailable? *Dykes* suggests that protection against unfairness is provided by giving the new party the opportunity to explain why cross-examination was not adequate. See also Horne v. Owens–Corning Fiberglas Corp., 4 F.3d 276, 283 (4th Cir.1993) (employee opposing admission must point up distinctions not evident in earlier litigation involving different employees that would preclude similar motive); O'Banion v. Owens–Corning Fiberglas Corp., 968 F.2d 1011, 1015 (10th Cir.1992) (finding no harm in admitting prior testimony where opponent offered no basis to find prior examination inadequate). Does this opportunity provide sufficient protection against unfairness to the opponent of the evidence given that the alternative is the total loss of the evidence (witness is by definition unavailable), which may lead to unfairness to the other party?

3. *Criminal cases.* When evidence is offered against the defendant in a criminal case, the "predecessor in interest" concept has no place. Under Rule 804(b)(1), the defendant must have been a party in the prior proceeding. "Another party, no matter how closely allied in interest or motive, will not do." 5 Weinstein's Federal Evidence § 804.04[6] (2d ed. 2013). Whether the predecessor-in-interest concept applies when the statement is offered against the government is subject to debate. Compare United States v. McDonald, 837 F.2d 1287, 1291 (5th Cir.1988) (open question), with United States v. Peterson, 100 F.3d 7, 12–13 (2d Cir.1996) (assuming admissibility only if federal prosecutor controlled state prosecution or had opportunity to develop testimony). See also 2 McCormick, Evidence § 303 (7th ed. 2013) (exclusion probably not intended by Congress and may violate due process under some circumstances).

I. DYING DECLARATIONS

Federal Rule 804(b)(2)

SHEPARD V. UNITED STATES

Supreme Court of the United States, 1933.
290 U.S. 96.

MR. JUSTICE CARDOZO delivered the opinion of the Court.

The petitioner, Charles A. Shepard, a major in the medical corps of the United States Army, has been convicted of the murder of his wife, Zenana Shepard, at Fort Riley, Kan., a United States military reservation. The jury having qualified their verdict by adding thereto the words "without capital punishment" (18 U.S.C. § 567 [18 USCA § 567]), the defendant was sentenced to imprisonment for life.

* * *

The crime is charged to have been committed by poisoning the victim with bichloride of mercury. The defendant was in love with another woman, and wished to make her his wife. There is circumstantial evidence to sustain a finding by the jury that to win himself his freedom he turned to poison and murder. Even so, guilt was contested, and conflicting inferences are possible. The defendant asks us to hold that by the acceptance of incompetent evidence the scales were weighted to his prejudice and in the end to his undoing.

The evidence complained of was offered by the government in rebuttal when the trial was nearly over. On May 22, 1929, there was a conversation in the absence of the defendant between Mrs. Shepard, then ill in bed, and Clara Brown, her nurse. The patient asked the nurse to go to the closet in the defendant's room and bring a bottle of whisky that would be found upon a shelf. When the bottle was produced, she said that this was the liquor she had taken just before collapsing. She asked whether enough was left to make a test for the presence of poison, insisting that the smell and taste were strange. And then she added the words, "Dr. Shepard has poisoned me."

The conversation was proved twice. After the first proof of it, the government asked to strike it out, being doubtful of its competence, and this request was granted. A little later, however, the offer was renewed; the nurse having then testified to statements by Mrs. Shepard as to the prospect of recovery. "She said she was not going to get well; she was going to die." With the aid of this new evidence, the conversation already summarized was proved a second time. There was a timely challenge of the ruling.

She said, "Dr. Shepard has poisoned me." The admission of this declaration, if erroneous, was more than unsubstantial error. As to that the parties are agreed. The voice of the dead wife was heard in accusation of her husband, and the accusation was accepted as evidence of guilt. If the evidence was incompetent, the verdict may not stand.

1. Upon the hearing in this court the government finds its main prop in the position that what was said by Mrs. Shepard was admissible as a dying declaration. This is manifestly the theory upon which it was offered and received. The prop, however, is a broken reed. To make out a dying declaration, the declarant must have spoken without hope of recovery and in the shadow of impending death. The record furnishes no proof of that indispensable condition. So, indeed, it was ruled by all the judges of the court below, though the majority held the view that the testimony was competent for quite another purpose, which will be considered later on.

We have said that the declarant was not shown to have spoken without hope of recovery and in the shadow of impending death. Her illness began on May 20. She was found in a state of collapse, delirious, in pain, the pupils of her eyes dilated, and the retina suffused with blood. The conversation with the nurse occurred two days later. At that time her mind had cleared up, and her speech was rational and orderly. There was as yet no thought by any of her physicians that she was dangerously ill, still less that her case was hopeless. To all seeming she had greatly improved, and was moving forward to recovery. There had been no diagnosis of poison as the cause of her distress. Not till about a week afterwards was there a relapse, accompanied by an infection of the mouth, renewed congestion of the eyes, and later hemorrhages of the bowels. Death followed on June 15.

Nothing in the condition of the patient on May 22 gives fair support to the conclusion that hope had then been lost. She may have thought she was going to die and have said so to her nurse, but this was consistent with hope, which could not have been put aside without more to quench it. Indeed, a fortnight later, she said to one of her physicians, though her condition was then grave, "You will get me well, won't you?" Fear or even belief that illness will end in death will not avail of itself to make a dying declaration. There must be "a settled hopeless expectation" (Willes, J. in Reg. v. Peel; 2 F. & F. 21, 22) that death is near at hand, and what is said must have been spoken in the hush of its impending presence. Mattox v. United States, 146 U.S. 140, 151 * * * ; 3 Wigmore on Evidence, §§ 1440, 1441, 1442, collating the decisions. Despair of recovery may indeed be gathered from the circumstances if the facts support the inference. Carver v. United States, supra; Wigmore, Evidence, § 1442. There is no unyielding ritual of words to be spoken by the dying. Despair may even be gathered, though the period of survival outruns the bounds of expectation. Wigmore, § 1441. What is decisive is the state of mind. Even so, the state of mind must be exhibited in the evidence, and not left to conjecture. The patient must have spoken with the consciousness of a swift and certain doom.

What was said by this patient was not spoken in that mood. There was no warning to her in the circumstances that her words would be repeated and accepted as those of a dying wife, charging murder to her husband, and charging it deliberately and solemnly as a fact within her knowledge. To the focus of that responsibility her mind was never brought. She spoke as one ill, giving voice to the beliefs and perhaps the conjectures of the moment. The liquor was to be tested, to see whether her beliefs were sound. She did not speak as one dying, announcing to the survivors a definitive conviction, a legacy of knowledge on which the world might act when she had gone.

The petitioner insists that the form of the declaration exhibits other defects that call for its exclusion, apart from the objection that death was not imminent and that hope was still alive. Homicide may not be imputed to a defendant on the basis of mere suspicions, though they are the suspicions of the dying. To let the declaration in, the inference must be permissible that there was knowledge or the opportunity for knowledge as to the acts that are declared. Wigmore, § 1445(2). The argument is pressed upon us that knowledge and opportunity are excluded when the declaration in question is read in the setting of the circumstances (citations omitted). The form is not decisive, though it be that of a conclusion, a statement of the result with the antecedent steps omitted. Wigmore, § 1447. "He murdered me," does not cease to be competent as a dying declaration because in the statement of the act there is also an appraisal of the crime. State v. Mace, 118 N.C.1244, 24 S.E. 798; State v. Kuhn, supra. One does not hold the dying to the observance of all the niceties of speech to which conformity is exacted from a witness on the stand. What is decisive is something deeper and more fundamental than any difference of form. The declaration is kept out if the setting of the occasion satisfies the judge, or in reason ought to satisfy him, that the speaker is giving expression to suspicion or conjecture, and not to known facts. The difficulty is not so much in respect of the governing principle as in its application to varying and equivocal conditions. In this case, the ruling that there was a failure to make out the imminence of death and the abandonment of hope relieves us of the duty of determining whether it is a legitimate inference that there was the opportunity for knowledge. We leave that question open.

[The Court determined that the statements to the nurse were not admissible under other hearsay exceptions.]

Reversed.

NOTES AND QUESTIONS

1. *Relaxing standard. Shepard*, which was decided long before the development of the Federal Rules, is generally consistent with the requirements of Rule 804(b)(2). However, the Rule's provision, "believing that the declarant's death to be imminent," is somewhat less emphatic than the "swift and certain doom" of *Shepard*. Cases decided over the past two decades have slightly relaxed the previous extremely demanding standard, see, e.g., Burks v. State, 876 S.W.2d 877, 901 (Tex.Crim.App.1994), perhaps in recognition of the increasing effectiveness of modern medicine. See Johnson v. State, 579 P.2d 20, 25 (Alaska 1978); 2 McCormick, Evidence § 310 (7th ed. 2013).

2. *Methods of proof of declarant's belief that death imminent.* As *Shepard* states, the declarant's belief that death is imminent need not necessarily be proved by his or her direct statements of that belief. It may also be established circumstantially by evidence such as the apparently fatal nature of the wounds or statements made to the declarant by others. See State v. Stanford, 695 S.E.2d 579, 583 (Ga.2010) (extremely serious wounds, question by declarant to 911 operator whether she was going to die, and statement of operator to "stay alive"); People v. Clay, 926 N.Y.S.2d 598, 610 (App.Div.2011) (detective told victim who was having trouble breathing as a result of multiple gunshot wounds that he did not think the victim would live); 2 McCormick, Evidence § 310 (7th ed. 2013). However, the burden is on the party offering the statement to show declarant's recognition of the dire nature of the situation, see United States v. Lawrence, 349 F.3d 109, 117 (3d Cir.2003) (ruling statement inadmissible under exception where no statements by medical staff or police indicated declarant was going to die and all medical statements were upbeat), and dire medical evaluations that are neither obvious nor communicated are insufficient, see Bell v. United States, 801 A.2d 117, 126–27 (D.C.2002) (excluding statements by patient whom medical staff understood had little chance of recovery where not shown that he understood more than that his condition was serious and perhaps fatal or that visible nature of the injuries conveyed that he assuredly would die); Hayward v. State, 24 So. 3d 17, 31 (Fla.2009) (ruling statement inadmissible even though declarant knew "something was radically wrong" when he also knew the ambulance had arrived and he was receiving medical attention).

3. *Requirement of belief that death is "near at hand."* See, e.g. Trascher v. Territo, 89 So. 3d 357, 365 (La.2012) (ruling that deposition taken from declarant who was not expected to live more than six months was not admissible under the exception because death was not "imminent"); Roby v. State, 808 N.W.2d 20, 28 (Minn.2011) (concluding affidavit made by declarant while dying of colon cancer was not made with belief in impending death).

4. *Application to atheists?* Lack of religious belief in a hereafter on the part of the declarant would seem to require exclusion of his or her declaration if the guarantee of trustworthiness is theological. The Advisory Committee

Note suggests that "powerful psychological pressures" provide an alternative guarantee of trustworthiness. Is this guarantee sufficient? Does necessity for the statement provide the additional justification that renders this exception rational? Some common law authority permits lack of religious belief to be used to impeach the credibility of the declaration. Does Rule 610, which prohibits admission of evidence of religious beliefs to impeach credibility, have an impact on such impeachment?

5. *Concern about trustworthiness.* Courts and commentators have remained concerned about the reliability of dying declarations, recognizing that (1) powerful human motivations such as revenge or favoritism do not necessarily cease to have sway as death approaches, (2) the condition of the declarant may distort the reliability of the statement, and (3) the statement may be the product of prompting by interested questioners. See Quick, Some Reflections on Dying Declarations, 6 How.L.J. 109, 111–12 (1960); 5 Weinstein's Federal Evidence § 804.05[1] (2d ed. 2013).

6. *Applicability outside homicide cases.* Standard doctrine in this country for many years limited dying declarations to those of the victim in homicide prosecutions. Thus, dying declarations of the victim in a prosecution for rape were held inadmissible where death resulted from a fever following the birth of a child so conceived, Hansel v. Commonwealth, 84 S.W.2d 68 (Ky.1935), and where another victim died from ingesting the same poisonous liquor, People v. Cox, 172 N.E. 64 (Ill.1930). Dying declarations were also held generally inadmissible in civil cases. Carver v. Howard, 280 S.W.2d 708 (Ky.1955). Federal Rule 804(b)(2) permits admission of dying declarations in civil cases generally and in homicide prosecutions. As proposed, the Rule would have admitted such statements in all criminal cases, but concerns about reliability of statements under this exception, see note 5, supra, prompted the House of Representatives to limit its application in criminal cases to homicide prosecutions where the need for the statement was considered greatest. Under the wording of the Rule, must the declarant be the homicide victim for the statement to be admissible, or can the declarant survive in a multiple victim case where one victim is killed?

7. *Belief, rather than death, required.* While death will frequently render the declarant unavailable when statements are admitted under this exception, the Rule does not require that death actually ensue—only that the declarant believe that it is imminent.

8. *Exculpatory statements.* In the nature of things, the declarations ordinarily are damaging to the accused. However, if the statement is helpful to the accused, it may be received if it otherwise meets the requirements of the exception. State v. Proctor, 269 S.W.2d 624 (Mo.1954); Commonwealth v. Plubell, 80 A.2d 825 (Pa.1951).

9. *Subject matter limitation.* Under common law development, the subject matter of the declaration was usually limited to the circumstances surrounding the killing, but the interpretation of the scope of that limitation provided opportunity for "prolific quibbling." 5 Wigmore, Evidence § 1434, at

284 (Chadbourn rev. 1974). Perhaps typical under the common law was the exclusion of a reference to previous threats by the accused. State v. Chaplin, 286 A.2d 325 (Me.1972). While still limiting the subject matter of the statement to reduce the dangers of fabrication, the modern trend under the Federal Rule is more liberal and admits statements concerning the "cause or circumstances" of the declarant's apparently impending death. See 5 Mueller & Kirkpatrick, Federal Evidence § 8:124 (3d ed. 2007) (arguing that prior threats admissible under Rule 804(b)(2)).

10. *Death by suicide.* Should a suicide note ever properly qualify for admission as a dying declaration? See State v. Satterfield, 457 S.E.2d 440, 447–50 (W.Va.1995) (admitting suicide note). But see United States v. Angleton, 269 F.Supp.2d 878, 882–87 (S.D.Tex.2003) (ruling that suicide notes were inadmissible because unrelated to cause or circumstances of death and because of doubt that the declarant believed death would be swift and certain when the statements were made since it was unknown precisely when the notes were written).

J. STATEMENTS AGAINST INTEREST

Federal Rule 804(b)(3)

HASKELL V. SIEGMUND
Appellate Court of Illinois, Third District, 1960.
170 N.E.2d 393.

[Haskell recovered a judgment for $35,000 against Siegmund for injuries sustained from the latter's driving of an automobile owned by Peterson. He then sought by appropriate ancillary proceedings to collect the judgment from Peterson's liability insurance company. Liability under the policy depended upon whether Siegmund was driving with Peterson's permission. Following the accident, Klophel, an investigator for the insurance company obtained statements from Peterson to the effect that he had given Siegmund permission to use the automobile. The insurance company appeals from a judgment entered on a verdict against it.]

REYNOLDS, JUSTICE. * * * Peterson died before trial of the garnishment action. Siegmund, who was 19 years old at the time of the accident, left Peterson's employ shortly after August 6, 1955. He was thereafter convicted of the crime of forgery and was incarcerated. Neither Peterson nor Siegmund testified at either trial. * * *

* * * Peterson's written statements to Klophel that he loaned the 1942 Chevrolet to Siegmund were admissible as declarations against his pecuniary interest, a well established exception to the hearsay rule. * * * The tests for admissibility of declarations against pecuniary interest are

set forth in German Insurance Co. v. Bartlett, 1900, 188 Ill. 165, 173, 58 N.E. 1075, 1077:

> " * * * (1) The declarant must be dead; (2) the declaration must have been against the pecuniary interest of the declarant at the time it was made; (3) the declaration must be of a fact in relation to a matter concerning which the declarant was immediately and personally cognizable; and (4) the court should be satisfied that the declarant had no probable motive to falsify the fact declared."

I.

Peterson's statements to Klophel meet these tests: (1) Peterson was dead at the time of the trial below. (2) It is presumed that one who is driving another's vehicle is the owner's agent. Parrino v. Landon, 1956, 8 Ill.2d 468, 470, 134 N.E.2d 311, 313; Howard v. Amerson, 1st Dist.1925, 236 Ill.App. 587, 593–594. Hence, when Peterson stated that he owned the car being driven by Siegmund on the night of the accident, Peterson was exposing himself, *prima facie,* to liability for Siegmund's negligence. (3) Peterson had personal knowledge of the circumstances under which he gave the car to Siegmund. (4) No proof was adduced as to any reason why Peterson should falsify for a part-time employee, who did not even return to work after the accident. * * *

Judgment affirmed.

NOTES AND QUESTIONS

1. *Admissions and against interest statements compared.* The distinction between statements against interest and admissions of a party should clearly be noted. Statements against interest require that the declarant be unavailable, he or she must have personal knowledge of the matters asserted, and the statement must be against the declarant's interest when made. These are not requirements of admissions. On the other hand, admissions must have been made by a party and must be offered by the opposing party, while the statement against interest exception applies to any declarant and may be offered by either party. 2 McCormick, Evidence § 316 (7th ed. 2013).

2. *How against interest?* What should satisfy the against-interest test? There are at least three possibilities: (1) that the facts stated be against interest; (2) that the statement itself create an obligation; or (3) that the declarant be creating evidence which may be used to his or her detriment. Furthermore, how should we evaluate the mental attitude of the declarant— by actually attempting to ascertain it or by using a reasonable person standard as contained in Rule 804(b)(3)? Consider Commonwealth Life Ins. Co. v. Clarke, 123 S.W.2d 811 (Ky.1938) (an action on a life insurance policy defended on the ground of suicide, holding it error to exclude a declaration of the insured that he had shot himself since the policy was still effectively his

property under a reservation of right to change the beneficiary). The cases are generally far from clear when closely scrutinized as to theory.

3.   *What interests?* As to the nature of the interest involved, Rule 804(b)(3) is broadly drawn, and while excluding statements incurring social disapproval, the Rule "occupies the entire area developed by the common law except for some of the more fanciful English decisions in tenancy cases." 2 McCormick, Evidence § 317 (7th ed. 2013). Substantial issues will still remain, however, as to whether the statement in question is sufficiently contrary to such interest that "a reasonable person in the declarant's position would not have made the statement unless believing it to be true." See, e.g., Donovan v. Crisostomo, 689 F.2d 869, 876–77 (9th Cir.1982) (statements of alien workers that they did not work overtime not admissible under Rule 804(b)(3) since workers might feel it was in their interest to claim they were properly paid to avoid wrath of employer that might result in their deportation); State v. Lynch, 854 A.2d 1022, 1036–39 (R.I.2004) (concluding that statement by 14–year–old male of consensual sex was not against his interest, despite financial implications given that his partner became pregnant, considering the greater likelihood that statement was made to avoid more substantial criminal liability).

KNAPP V. ST. LOUIS TRUST CO.

Supreme Court of Missouri, 1906.
98 S.W. 70.

GANTT, J. This is an action to contest the validity of the will of Mrs. Margaret Gaffey. The grounds of contest were and are that the testatrix at the time of executing the alleged will was not of sound and disposing mind and memory and was under undue influence. * * *

As the case must be reversed it is proper that we should note another assignment of error, to-wit: That the circuit court improperly held that the entries in the account book of Dr. McWilliams were only admissible for the purpose of showing that at certain dates the doctor made certain charges for visits to Mrs. Gaffey. It is insisted by the learned counsel for the plaintiff that these entries were admissible as evidence of the other fact stated therein, to-wit, the nature of the disease for which he treated Mrs. Gaffey. Dr. McWilliams, who made the entry, was shown to be dead. The first entry is a fair sample of the others and was in this form:

"1890. Mrs. Marg. Gaffey, 5886 Cabanne Place:

June 24, Hyperaemia of Brain, 1 visit and med.............................$2.00

June 24, By cash paid...$2.00"

In Higham v. Ridgway, 10 East 109, the proposition now urged by the appellant received great consideration by the court of King's Bench in 1808. In that case the question was as to the date of the birth of a child. There was offered in evidence an entry from the book of a man mid-wife, in which he had entered a charge, stating the services, and acknowledged the receipt of the payment. It was objected to and discussed at great length by counsel pro and con, and it was held by the court, all the judges concurring, that the entry was admissible as evidence of the birth and the time, as well as of the receipt of the payment. Lord Ellenborough, C.J., said: "I think the evidence here was properly admitted upon the broad principle on which receivers' books have been admitted; namely, that the entry was made in the prejudice of the party making it. * * * It is idle to say that the word *paid* only shall be admitted in evidence without the context, which explains to what it refers."

LE BLANC, J., states: "But here the entries were made by a person who, so far from having any interest to make them, had an interest the other way; and such entries against the interest of the party making them are clearly evidence of the fact stated, on the authority of Warren v. Greenville, and of all those cases where the books of receivers have been admitted." * * * In 16 Cyclopedia of Law and Procedure, p. 1218, it is said: "Declarations against interest are not only received as evidence of the fact directly asserted, but of incidental facts fairly embraced within the scope of the declaration." In view of this practically unanimous statement of the rule, we think that the entries were admissible not only for the purpose of showing that at certain dates Dr. McWilliams rendered medical services to Mrs. Gaffey, and was paid therefor, but also for the purpose of showing that he treated her for hyperaemia of the brain and for softening of the brain and paralysis, and the circuit court erred in holding otherwise.

For the errors noted, the judgment of the circuit court is reversed and the cause is remanded for a new trial in accordance with the views herein expressed.

WILLIAMSON V. UNITED STATES

Supreme Court of the United States, 1994.
512 U.S. 594.

[JUSTICE O'CONNOR, for six justices, delivered the opinion of the Court as to Parts I, II–A, and II–B. JUSTICES SCALIA, GINSBURG (for four justices), and KENNEDY (for three justices) filed concurring opinions.]

JUSTICE O'CONNOR * * *.

In this case we clarify the scope of the hearsay exception for statements against penal interest. Fed. Rule Evid. 804(b)(3).

I

A deputy sheriff stopped the rental car driven by Reginald Harris for weaving on the highway. Harris consented to a search of the car, which revealed 19 kilograms of cocaine in two suitcases in the trunk. Harris was promptly arrested.

Shortly after Harris' arrest, Special Agent Donald Walton of the Drug Enforcement Administration (DEA) interviewed him by telephone. During that conversation, Harris said that he got the cocaine from an unidentified Cuban in Fort Lauderdale; that the cocaine belonged to petitioner Williamson; and that it was to be delivered that night to a particular dumpster. Williamson was also connected to Harris by physical evidence [in the car] * * *.

Several hours later, Agent Walton spoke to Harris in person. During that interview, Harris said he had rented the car a few days earlier and had driven it to Fort Lauderdale to meet Williamson. According to Harris, he had gotten the cocaine from a Cuban who was Williamson's acquaintance, and the Cuban had put the cocaine in the car with a note telling Harris how to deliver the drugs. Harris repeated that he had been instructed to leave the drugs in a certain dumpster, to return to his car, and to leave without waiting for anyone to pick up the drugs.

Agent Walton then took steps to arrange a controlled delivery of the cocaine. But as Walton was preparing to leave the interview room, Harris "got out of [his] chair * * * and * * * took a half step toward [Walton] * * * and * * * said, * * * 'I can't let you do that,' threw his hands up and said 'that's not true, I can't let you go up there for no reason.' 'Harris told Walton he had lied about the Cuban, the note, and the dumpster. The real story, Harris said, was that he was transporting the cocaine to Atlanta for Williamson, and that Williamson was traveling in front of him in another rental car. Harris added that after his car was stopped, Williamson turned around and drove past the location of the stop, where he could see Harris' car with its trunk open. Because Williamson had apparently seen the police searching the car, Harris explained that it would be impossible to make a controlled delivery.

Harris told Walton that he had lied about the source of the drugs because he was afraid of Williamson. Though Harris freely implicated himself, he did not want his story to be recorded, and he refused to sign a written version of the statement. Walton testified that he had promised to report any cooperation by Harris to the Assistant United States Attorney. Walton said Harris was not promised any reward or other benefit for cooperating.

Williamson was eventually convicted of possessing cocaine with intent to distribute, conspiring to possess cocaine with intent to distribute, and traveling interstate to promote the distribution of cocaine * * *. When called to testify at Williamson's trial, Harris refused, even though the prosecution gave him use immunity and the court ordered him to testify and eventually held him in contempt. The District Court then ruled that, under Rule 804(b)(3), Agent Walton could relate what Harris had said to him: "The ruling of the Court is that the statements * * * are admissible under [Rule 804(b)(3)], which deals with statements against interest." * * * Williamson appealed his conviction [and the Court of Appeals affirmed].

II

A

The hearsay rule, Fed. Rule Evid. 802, is premised on the theory that out-of-court statements are subject to particular hazards. The declarant might be lying; he might have misperceived the events which he relates; he might have faulty memory; his words might be misunderstood or taken out of context by the listener. And the ways in which these dangers are minimized for in-court statements—the oath, the witness' awareness of the gravity of the proceedings, the jury's ability to observe the witness' demeanor, and, most importantly, the right of the opponent to cross-examine—are generally absent for things said out of court.

Nonetheless, the Federal Rules of Evidence also recognize that some kinds of out-of-court statements are less subject to these hearsay dangers, and therefore except them from the general rule that hearsay is inadmissible. One such category covers statements that are against the declarant's interest: "statement[s] which * * * at the time of [their] making * * * so far tended to subject the declarant to * * * criminal liability * * * that a reasonable person in the declarant's position would not have made the statement[s] unless believing [them] to be true." Fed. Rule Evid. 804(b)(3).

To decide whether Harris' confession is made admissible by Rule 804(b)(3), we must first determine what the Rule means by "statement," which Federal Rule of Evidence 801(a)(1) defines as "an oral or written assertion." One possible meaning, "a report or narrative," Webster's Third New International Dictionary 2229, defn. 2(a) (1961), connotes an extended declaration. Under this reading, Harris' entire confession—even if it contains both self-inculpatory and non-self-inculpatory parts—would be admissible so long as in the aggregate the confession sufficiently inculpates him. Another meaning of "statement," "a single declaration or remark," *ibid.*, defn. 2(b), would make Rule 804(b)(3) cover only those declarations or remarks within the confession that are individually self-inculpatory. See also *id.*, at 131 (defining "assertion" as a "declaration"); *id.*, at 586 (defining "declaration" as a "statement").

Although the text of the Rule does not directly resolve the matter, the principle behind the Rule, so far as it is discernible from the text, points clearly to the narrower reading. Rule 804(b)(3) is founded on the commonsense notion that reasonable people, even reasonable people who are not especially honest, tend not to make self-inculpatory statements unless they believe them to be true. This notion simply does not extend to the broader definition of "statement." The fact that a person is making a broadly self-inculpatory confession does not make more credible the confession's non-self-inculpatory parts. One of the most effective ways to lie is to mix falsehood with truth, especially truth that seems particularly persuasive because of its self-inculpatory nature.

In this respect, it is telling that the non-self-inculpatory things Harris said in his first statement actually proved to be false, as Harris himself admitted during the second interrogation. And when part of the confession is actually self-exculpatory, the generalization on which Rule 804(b)(3) is founded becomes even less applicable. Self-exculpatory statements are exactly the ones which people are most likely to make even when they are false; and mere proximity to other, self-inculpatory, statements does not increase the plausibility of the self-exculpatory statements.

We therefore cannot agree with JUSTICE KENNEDY's suggestion that the Rule can be read as expressing a policy that collateral statements— even ones that are not in any way against the declarant's interest—are admissible. Nothing in the text of Rule 804(b)(3) or the general theory of the hearsay Rules suggests that admissibility should turn on whether a statement is collateral to a self-inculpatory statement. The fact that a statement is self-inculpatory does make it more reliable; but the fact that a statement is collateral to a self-inculpatory statement says nothing at all about the collateral statement's reliability. We see no reason why collateral statements, even ones that are neutral as to interest, should be treated any differently from other hearsay statements that are generally excluded.

Congress certainly could, subject to the constraints of the Confrontation Clause, make statements admissible based on their proximity to self-inculpatory statements. But we will not lightly assume that the ambiguous language means anything so inconsistent with the Rule's underlying theory. See *Cooter & Gell v. Hartmarx Corp.*, 496 U.S. 384, 394–395, 408–409 (1990). In our view, the most faithful reading of Rule 804(b)(3) is that it does not allow admission of non-self-inculpatory statements, even if they are made within a broader narrative that is generally self-inculpatory. The district court may not just assume for purposes of Rule 804(b)(3) that a statement is self-inculpatory because it is part of a fuller confession, and this is especially true when the statement implicates someone else. "[T]he arrest statements of a codefendant have traditionally been viewed with special suspicion. Due to his strong motivation to implicate the defendant and to exonerate himself, a codefendant's statements about what the defendant said or did are less credible than ordinary hearsay evidence." *Lee v. Illinois*, 476 U.S. 530, 541 (1986) (internal quotation marks omitted) * * *.

JUSTICE KENNEDY suggests that the Advisory Committee Notes to Rule 804(b)(3) should be read as endorsing the position we reject—that an entire narrative, including non-self-inculpatory parts (but excluding the clearly self-serving parts), may be admissible if it is in the aggregate self-inculpatory. The Notes read, in relevant part:

> "[T]he third-party confession * * * may include statements implicating [the accused], and under the general theory of declarations against interest they would be admissible as related statements * * *. [*Douglas v. Alabama*, 380 U.S. 415 (1965), and *Bruton v. United States*, 391 U.S. 123 (1968)] * * * by no means require that all statements implicating another person be excluded from the category of declarations against interest. Whether a statement is in fact against interest must be determined from the circumstances of each case. Thus a statement admitting guilt and implicating another person, made while in custody, may well be motivated by a desire to curry favor with the authorities and hence fail to qualify as against interest * * *. On the other hand, the same words spoken under different circumstances, e.g., to an acquaintance, would have no difficulty in qualifying * * *. The balancing of self-serving against dissenting [sic] aspects of a declaration is discussed in McCormick § 256." 28 U.S.C. App., p. 790.

This language, however, is not particularly clear, and some of it—especially the Advisory Committee's endorsement of the position taken by Dean McCormick's treatise—points the other way:

> "A certain latitude as to contextual statements, neutral as to interest, giving meaning to the declaration against interest seems defensible, but bringing in self-serving statements contextually seems questionable * * *. [A]dmit[ting] the disserving parts of the declaration, and exclud[ing] the self-serving parts * * * seems the most realistic method of adjusting admissibility to trustworthiness, where the serving and disserving parts can be severed." See C. McCormick, Law of Evidence § 256, pp. 551–553 (1954) (footnotes omitted).

Without deciding exactly how much weight to give the Notes in this particular situation * * *, we conclude that the policy expressed in the statutory text points clearly enough in one direction that it outweighs whatever force the Notes may have. * * *

B

We also do not share JUSTICE KENNEDY's fears that our reading of the Rule "eviscerate[s] the against penal interest exception," or makes it lack "meaningful effect." There are many circumstances in which Rule 804(b)(3) does allow the admission of statements that inculpate a criminal defendant. Even the confessions of arrested accomplices may be admissible if they are truly self-inculpatory, rather than merely attempts to shift blame or curry favor.

For instance, a declarant's squarely self-inculpatory confession—"yes, I killed X"—will likely be admissible under Rule 804(b)(3) against accomplices of his who are being tried under a co-conspirator liability theory. See *Pinkerton v. United States*, 328 U.S. 640, 647 (1946). Likewise, by showing that the declarant knew something, a self-inculpatory statement can in some situations help the jury infer that his confederates knew it as well. And when seen with other evidence, an accomplice's self-inculpatory statement can inculpate the defendant directly: "I was robbing the bank on Friday morning," coupled with someone's testimony that the declarant and the defendant drove off together Friday morning, is evidence that the defendant also participated in the robbery.

Moreover, whether a statement is self-inculpatory or not can only be determined by viewing it in context. Even statements that are on their face neutral may actually be against the declarant's interest. "I hid the gun in Joe's apartment" may not be a confession of a crime; but if it is likely to help the police find the murder weapon, then it is certainly self-inculpatory. "Sam and I went to Joe's house" might be against the declarant's interest if a reasonable person in the declarant's shoes would realize that being linked to Joe and Sam would implicate the declarant in Joe and Sam's conspiracy. And other statements that give the police significant details about the crime may also, depending on the situation, be against the declarant's interest. The question under Rule 804(b)(3) is always whether the statement was sufficiently against the declarant's penal interest "that a reasonable person in the declarant's position would not have made the statement unless believing it to be true," and this question can only be answered in light of all the surrounding circumstances.

C

In this case, however, we cannot conclude that all that Harris said was properly admitted. Some of Harris' confession would clearly have been admissible under Rule 804(b)(3); for instance, when he said he knew there was cocaine in the suitcase, he essentially forfeited his only possible defense to a charge of cocaine possession, lack of knowledge. But other parts of his confession, especially the parts that implicated Williamson, did little to subject Harris himself to criminal liability. A reasonable person in Harris' position might even think that implicating someone else would decrease his practical exposure to criminal liability, at least so far as sentencing goes. Small fish in a big conspiracy often get shorter sentences than people who are running the whole show, see, e.g., United

States Sentencing Commission, Guidelines Manual § 3B1.2 (Nov. 1993), especially if the small fish are willing to help the authorities catch the big ones, see, e.g., *id.*, at § 5K1.1.

Nothing in the record shows that the District Court or the Court of Appeals inquired whether each of the statements in Harris' confession was truly self-inculpatory. * * * [W]e therefore remand to the Court of Appeals to conduct this inquiry in the first instance.

* * *

JUSTICE SCALIA, concurring.

* * * [A] declarant's statement is not magically transformed from a statement against penal interest into one that is inadmissible merely because the declarant names another person or implicates a possible co-defendant. For example, if a lieutenant in an organized crime operation described the inner workings of an extortion and protection racket, naming some of the other actors and thereby inculpating himself on racketeering and/or conspiracy charges, I have no doubt that some of those remarks could be admitted as statements against penal interest. Of course, naming another person, if done, for example, in a context where the declarant is minimizing culpability or criminal exposure, can bear on whether the statement meets the Rule 804(b)(3) standard. The relevant inquiry, however—and one that is not furthered by clouding the waters with manufactured categories such as "collateral neutral" and "collateral self-serving"—must always be whether the particular remark at issue (and not the extended narrative) meets the standard set forth in the Rule.

JUSTICE GINSBURG, * * * concurring in part and concurring in the judgment.

* * * I agree with the Court that Federal Rule of Evidence 804(b)(3) excepts from the general rule that hearsay statements are inadmissible only "those declarations or remarks within [a narrative] that are individually self-inculpatory." As the Court explains, the exception for statements against penal interest "does not allow admission of non-self-inculpatory statements, even if they are made within a broader narrative that is generally self-inculpatory"; the exception applies only to statements that are "sufficiently against the declarant's penal interest 'that a reasonable person in the declarant's position would not have made the statement unless believing it to be true * * * ' "

Further, the Court recognizes the untrustworthiness of statements implicating another person. A person arrested in incriminating circumstances has a strong incentive to shift blame or downplay his own role in comparison with that of others, in hopes of receiving a shorter sentence and leniency in exchange for cooperation. * * *

Unlike JUSTICE O'CONNOR, however, I conclude that Reginald Harris' statements, as recounted by DEA Special Agent Donald E. Walton, do not fit, even in part, within the exception described in Rule 804(b)(3), for Harris' arguably inculpatory statements are too closely intertwined with his self-serving declarations to be ranked as trustworthy. Harris was caught red-handed with 19 kilos of cocaine-enough to subject even a first-time offender to a minimum of 12 1/2 years' imprisonment. * * * He could have denied knowing the drugs were in the car's trunk, but that strategy would have brought little prospect of thwarting a criminal prosecution. He therefore admitted involvement, but did so in a way that minimized his own role and shifted blame to petitioner Fredel Williamson (and a Cuban man named Shawn).

* * *

To the extent some of these statements tended to incriminate Harris, they provided only marginal or cumulative evidence of his guilt. They project an image of a person acting not against his penal interest, but striving mightily to shift principal responsibility to someone else. See *United States v. Sarmiento–Perez*, 633 F.2d 1092, 1102 (C.A.5 1981) ("[The declarant] might well have been motivated to misrepresent the role of others in the criminal enterprise, and might well have viewed the statement[s] as a whole—including the ostensibly disserving portions—to be in his interest rather than against it.").

For these reasons, I would hold that none of Harris' hearsay statements were admissible under Rule 804(b)(3). * * *

JUSTICE KENNEDY, * * * concurring in the judgment.

I

* * * There has been a long-running debate among commentators over the admissibility of collateral statements. Dean Wigmore took the strongest position in favor of admissibility, arguing that "the statement may be accepted, not merely as to the specific fact against interest, but also as to every fact contained in the same statement." 5 J. Wigmore, Evidence § 1465, p. 271 (3d ed. 1940) (emphasis deleted); see also 5 J. Wigmore, Evidence § 1465, p. 339 (J. Chadbourn rev. 1974); *Higham v. Ridgway*, 10 East. 109, 103 Eng.Rep. 717 (K.B. 1808). According to Wigmore, because "the statement is made under circumstances fairly indicating the declarant's sincerity and accuracy," the entire statement should be admitted. 5 J. Wigmore § 1465, p. 271 (3d ed. 1940). Dean McCormick's approach regarding collateral statements was more guarded. He argued for the admissibility of collateral statements of a neutral character; and for the exclusion of collateral statements of a self-serving character. For example, in the statement "John and I robbed the bank," the words "John and" are neutral (save for the possibility of conspiracy charges). On the other hand, the statement "John, not I, shot

the bank teller" is to some extent self-serving and therefore might be inadmissible. See C. McCormick, Law of Evidence § 256, pp. 552–553 (1954) (hereinafter McCormick). Professor Jefferson took the narrowest approach, arguing that the reliability of a statement against interest stems only from the disserving fact stated and so should be confined "to the proof of the fact which is against interest." Jefferson, Declarations Against Interest: An Exception to the Hearsay Rule, 58 Harv.L.Rev. 1, 62–63 (1944). Under the Jefferson approach, neither collateral neutral nor collateral self-serving statements would be admissible.

Enacted by Congress in 1975, Rule 804(b)(3) establishes a hearsay exception for statements against penal, proprietary, pecuniary, and legal interest (and does not distinguish among those interests). The text of the Rule does not tell us whether collateral statements are admissible, however. * * *. The Court resolves the issue, as I understand its opinion, by adopting the extreme position that no collateral statements are admissible under Rule 804(b)(3). * * * The Court reaches that conclusion by relying on the "principle behind the Rule" that reasonable people do not make statements against their interest unless they are telling the truth, and reasons that this policy "expressed in the statutory text" "simply does not extend" to collateral statements. * * *

With respect, I must disagree with this analysis. All agree that the justification for admission of hearsay statements against interest was, as it still is, that reasonable people do not make those statements unless believing them to be true, but that has not resolved the long-running debate over the admissibility of collateral statements, as to which there is no clear consensus in the authorities. * * * The Rule's silence no more incorporates Jefferson's position respecting collateral statements than it does McCormick's or Wigmore's.

II

Because the text of Rule 804(b)(3) expresses no position regarding the admissibility of collateral statements, we must determine whether there are other authoritative guides on the question. In my view, three sources demonstrate that Rule 804(b)(3) allows the admission of some collateral statements * * *.

First, the Advisory Committee Note establishes that some collateral statements are admissible. In fact, it refers in specific terms to the issue we here confront: "[o]rdinarily the third-party confession is thought of in terms of exculpating the accused, but this is by no means always or necessarily the case: it may include statements implicating him, and under the general theory of declarations against interest they would be admissible as related statements." * * *

Second, even if the Advisory Committee Note were silent about collateral statements, I would not adopt a rule excluding all statements collateral or related to the specific words against penal interest. Absent contrary indications, we can presume that Congress intended the principles and terms used in the Federal Rules of Evidence to be applied as they were at common law. * * * Application of that interpretive principle indicates that collateral statements should be admissible. "From the very beginning of this exception, it has been held that a declaration against interest is admissible, not only to prove the disserving fact stated, but also to prove other facts contained in collateral statements connected with the disserving statement." Jefferson, 58 Harv.L.Rev., at 57 * * *.

There is yet a third reason weighing against the Court's interpretation, one specific to statements against penal interest that inculpate the accused. There is no dispute that the text of Rule 804(b)(3) contemplates the admission of those particular statements. Absent a textual direction to the contrary, therefore, we should assume that Congress intended the penal interest exception for inculpatory statements to have some meaningful effect. * * * That counsels against adopting a rule excluding collateral statements. As commentators have recognized, "the exclusion of collateral statements would cause the exclusion of almost all inculpatory statements." Comment, 66 Calif.L.Rev. at 1207 * * *

I note finally that the Court's decision applies to statements against penal interest that exculpate the accused as well as to those that inculpate the accused. Thus, if the declarant said, "I robbed the store alone," only the portion of the statement in which the declarant said "I robbed the store" could be introduced by a criminal defendant on trial for the robbery. See Note, Declarations Against Penal Interest: Standards of Admissibility Under an Emerging Majority Rule, 56 B.U.L.Rev. 148, 165, n.95 (1976). That seems extraordinary. The Court gives no justification for such a rule and no explanation that Congress intended the exception for exculpatory statements to have this limited effect. See *id.*, at 166 ("A strict application of a rule excluding all collateral statements can lead to the arbitrary rejection of valuable evidence").

III

Though I would conclude that Rule 804(b)(3) allows admission of statements collateral to the precise words against interest, that conclusion of course does not answer the remaining question whether all collateral statements related to the statement against interest are admissible; and if not, what limiting principles should apply. The Advisory Committee Note suggests that not all collateral statements are admissible. The Note refers, for example, to McCormick's treatise, not to Wigmore's, for guidance as to the "balancing of self-serving against dis[serving] aspects of a declaration." * * * McCormick stated that "[a] certain latitude as to contextual [i.e., collateral] statements, neutral as to interest, giving meaning to the declaration against interest seems defensible, but bringing in self-serving statements contextually seems questionable." McCormick § 256, p. 552. McCormick further stated that, within a declaration containing self-serving and disserving facts, he would "admit the disserving parts of the declaration, and exclude the self-serving parts" at least "where the serving and disserving parts can be severed." *Id.* § 256, p. 553. It thus appears that the Advisory Committee Note, by its reference to (and apparent incorporation of) McCormick, contemplates exclusion of a collateral self-serving statement, but admission of a collateral neutral statement. * * *

NOTES AND QUESTIONS

1.   *Collateral statements in civil cases. Knapp* and *Higham v. Ridgway,* cited in *Knapp* and by Justice Kennedy in *Williamson,* reflect a longstanding practice of receiving collateral statements in civil cases. Collateral statements were not an issue in criminal cases until relatively recently because statements against penal interest were until then excluded from the exception. While the Supreme Court in *Williamson* recognized special concern with the trustworthiness of collateral statements that incriminate another, its analysis should also exclude collateral statements in civil contexts as well. See Silverstein v. Chase, 260 F.3d 142, 146–48 (2d Cir.2001) (applying *Williamson* analysis in civil case and finding collateral statements inadmissible).

2.   *Separating different parts.* Does *Williamson* mean that the self-serving and disserving parts of the statement must always be severed? Is it ever impossible to do? Given that she joined the part of Justice O'Connor's opinion that requires severing the two types of statements, why does Justice Ginsburg then argue that the inculpatory statements must be excluded because they "are too closely intertwined with his self-serving declarations"?

3.   *Impact of identity of hearer on reasonable belief.* The requirement of Rule 804(b)(3) is written in terms of the reasonable person in the position of the declarant, requiring that such a person believe the statement to be against interest. One factor logically important in determining whether the declarant believed the statement was against interest is the identity of the person to whom the statement was made. However, the fact that the statement was made to a friend, who might be expected (or hoped) to keep the damaging information secret, is typically not considered to eliminate the disserving quality of the statement. See, e.g., United States v. Lang, 589 F.2d 92, 97 (2d Cir.1978) (statement admitting crime against interest when made to undercover agent whom the defendant thought was a confederate). Although the fact the statement was made to a friend or relative may make it less against interest, see Santiago v. O'Brien, 628 F.3d 30, 35 (1st Cir.2010), the private status of the individual helps eliminate the argument that it was made to curry favor with authorities, see United States v. Pelletier, 666 F.3d 1, 8 (1st Cir.2011), and the trusted nature of the individual helps provide

corroboration. See United States v. US Infrastructure, Inc., 576 F.3d 1195, 1209 (11th Cir.2009).

4. *Corroboration requirement.* Under Rule 804(b)(3)(B), in addition to being against interest, a statement exposing the declarant to criminal liability is not to be admitted unless "corroborating circumstances clearly indicate its trustworthiness." Initially the corroboration requirement applied only to statements that exculpated the defendant. The legislative history of the original rule shows that Congress recognized the potential unfairness of excluding statements that exculpated the defendant but feared fabricated confessions, and it added this requirement to guard against manufactured evidence. In 2010, the Rule was amended to require corroboration for all declarations against penal interest, applying the requirement to statements inculpating the defendant as well. The Advisory Committee note to the amendment rejects the position taken by some courts that the corroboration requirement applies not only to the declarant but also to the person who claims to have heard the statement, finding the "ear witness" credibility to be a matter for jury determination. A few jurisdictions continue to make an issue of corroborating the "ear witness". See, e.g., Zanders v. United States, 999 A.2d 149, 159 (D.C.2010); State v. Stridiron, 777 N.W.2d 892, 902 (N.D.2010).

5. *Limited corroboration.* While some courts have applied an inappropriately strict level of corroboration, corroboration appropriately goes beyond a minimal level, but it should not be made unrealistically severe. 5 Weinstein's Federal Evidence § 804.06[5][b][iii] (2d ed. 2013) (suggesting showing of motive and opportunity should be sufficient).

6. *Impact of Williamson.* After *Williamson*, it seems safe to say that fewer statements against interest, both inculpatory and exculpatory, will be admitted. However, is Justice Kennedy correct that from the statement "I robbed the store alone," only "I robbed the store" could now be introduced by a criminal defendant on trial for that robbery? Does the addition of the word "alone" add to the incriminating nature of the statement? Is it "collateral"? On the other hand, arguments can be made that statements inculpating others should be admissible. See United States v. Manfre, 368 F.3d 832, 841–43 (8th Cir.2004) (admitting statements made to fiancee when declarant not under threat of prosecution and to friend in setting where no incentive to shift blame); United States v. Barone, 114 F.3d 1284, 1294–99 (1st Cir.1997) (arguing that statements implicating others are self-incriminating in showing insider's knowledge). Moreover, Justices O'Connor and Scalia argued that statements incriminating others might be against the declarant's interest by implicating him in a larger conspiracy. When might that larger conspiracy argument, which is often available, be rejected? See United States v. Mendoza, 85 F.3d 1347, 1351–52 (8th Cir.1996) (statements inculpating higher up that only confirm facts of crime already known held to be currying favor and ruled inadmissible). Is the typical ("reasonable person") criminal likely to anticipate being charged with conspiracy?

7.   *Impact of Crawford.* Even if the statements of co-participants implicating others in criminal activity satisfy the requirements of this hearsay exception, to be admitted against the defendant in a criminal case, they must not violate the Confrontation Clause. After Crawford v. Washington, 541 U.S. 36 (2004), such statements made to the police while in custody will generally be found testimonial and excluded unless meeting one of the limited *Crawford* exceptions. This change in Confrontation Clause analysis has had a profound effect on this particular type of hearsay, and Supreme Court dissatisfaction with the failure of the earlier doctrine under Ohio v. Roberts, 448 U.S. 56 (1980), to exclude such statements appears to have been a major motivating factor in jettisoning that doctrine. See *Crawford*, 541 U.S. at 63–64 ("The unpardonable vice of the *Roberts* test, however, is not its unpredictability, but its demonstrated capacity to admit core testimonial statements that the Confrontation Clause plainly meant to exclude * * * [—] accomplice statements implicating the accused.").

However, statements of this type made in confidence to private individuals are not testimonial and therefore are not excluded by *Crawford*. See, e.g., United States v. Manfre, 368 F.3d 832, 838 n.1 (8th Cir.2004) (finding *Crawford* inapplicable to statements made to friends). As noted earlier, the fact the statement is made to a private individual and not to a police officer also helps to establish that it was not made to curry favor. See, e.g., United States v. Pelletier, 666 F.3d 1, 8 (1st Cir.2011); United States v. US Infrastructure, Inc., 576 F.3d 1195, 1209 (11th Cir.2009). Such private statements are frequently admitted. See, e.g., United States v. Persico, 645 F.3d 85, 98–103 (2d Cir.2011) (statement to wife); State v. Usee, 800 N.W.2d 192, 198–99 (Minn.2011) (statement to fellow prisoner).

8.   *Impact on state law.* Although *Williamson* is not binding on the states, a number have adopted its analysis for their hearsay exception for statements against interest. See McCormick, Evidence § 319 (7th ed. 2013). Prior to *Crawford*, the result was likely influenced by the Supreme Court's decision in Lilly v. Virginia, 527 U.S. 116 (1999), where the Supreme Court ruled that admission of statements violated the Confrontation Clause but satisfied Virginia's exception for statements against interest when it placed sole blame on an accomplice. Id. at 146–48 (Rehnquist, C.J., concurring). After *Crawford*, one may expect less interest in state courts following *Williamson* since its hearsay-based analysis was abandoned by *Crawford* and is no longer controlling on the states.

K. FORFEITURE BY WRONGDOING

Federal Rule 804(b)(6)

UNITED STATES V. GRAY

United States Court of Appeals, Fourth Circuit, 2005.
405 F.3d 227.

SHEDD, CIRCUIT JUDGE:

A grand jury indicted Josephine Gray on five counts of mail fraud and three counts of wire fraud relating to her receipt of insurance proceeds following the deaths of her second husband [Robert Gray] and a former paramour [Andre Savoy]. Gray was convicted on all counts * * * Gray now challenges her conviction, arguing * * * [*inter alia* that] the district court improperly permitted the Government to reopen its case to prove the alleged mailings; and the district court improperly admitted "other crimes" and hearsay evidence against Gray. We find no reversible error * * * and affirm Gray's conviction. * * *

* * *

In late August 1990, Robert Gray brought criminal charges against Gray, alleging that Gray had assaulted him at his workplace by swinging at him with a club and lunging at him with a knife. Robert Gray also brought charges against [Clarence Goode, Gray's cousin and boyfriend] alleging that Goode had threatened him with a 9–millimeter handgun. Robert Gray appeared in court on October 5, 1990, but the case against Gray and Goode was continued. Later that same day, Robert Gray was driving home when he noticed his wife's car behind him. She was flashing her lights and signaling her husband to pull over. When Robert Gray did not pull over, Gray drove her car alongside her husband's car. As Robert Gray turned to look toward his wife, Goode sat up (from a reclined position) in the front passenger seat and pointed a gun at him. Robert Gray reported this incident to police, and a warrant was issued for the arrests of Gray and Goode. One week before the November 16, 1990 trial date, Robert Gray was discovered dead in his new apartment, shot once in the chest and once in the neck with a .45 caliber handgun.

* * * Gray challenges her conviction [on fraud] on several grounds [including admission of] hearsay testimony from Robert Gray * * * [concerning his] fear for his safety. * * * The district court * * * admitted into evidence several out-of-court statements made by Robert Gray during the three months preceding his murder:

Robert Gray's criminal complaint alleging that Goode had tossed a 9–millimeter handgun on the table at his house to provoke an argument;

Robert Gray's criminal complaint alleging that Gray had tried to stab him with a knife and attack him with a club;

Statements made by Robert Gray to Darnell Gray and a police detective, claiming that Gray and Goode had assaulted him in October 1990; and

Statements made by Robert Gray to Rodney Gray claiming that Goode had pulled a gun on him outside a restaurant in September or October 1990.

Although out-of-court statements ordinarily may not be admitted to prove the truth of the matters asserted, the doctrine of forfeiture by wrongdoing allows such statements to be admitted where the defendant's own misconduct rendered the declarant unavailable as a witness at trial. The Supreme Court applied this doctrine in *Reynolds v. United States,* 98 U.S. 145 (1878), stating that "[t]he Constitution gives the accused the right to a trial at which he should be confronted with the witnesses against him; but if a witness is absent by [the accused's] own wrongful procurement, he cannot complain if competent evidence is admitted to supply the place of that which he has kept away." *Id.* at 158. By 1996, every circuit to address the issue had recognized this doctrine. * * *.

Fed.R.Evid. 804(b)(6), which took effect in 1997, codifies the common-law doctrine of forfeiture by wrongdoing as an exception to the general rule barring admission of hearsay evidence. Fed.R.Evid. 804(b)(6) advisory committee note. Under Rule 804(b)(6), "[a] statement offered against a party that has engaged or acquiesced in wrong-doing that was intended to, and did procure the unavailability of the declarant as a witness" is admissible at trial. In order to apply the forfeiture-by-wrongdoing exception, the district court must find, by the preponderance of the evidence, *see United States v. Scott,* 284 F.3d 758, 762 (7th Cir.2002), that (1) the defendant engaged or acquiesced in wrongdoing (2) that was intended to render the declarant unavailable as a witness and (3) that did, in fact, render the declarant unavailable as a witness. The district court need not hold an independent evidentiary hearing if the requisite findings may be made based upon evidence presented in the course of the trial. *United States v. Johnson,* 219 F.3d 349, 356 (4th Cir.2000).

Gray contends that Rule 804(b)(6) should not apply in this case because she did not intend to procure Robert Gray's unavailability as a witness at *this* trial. "Because the Federal Rules of Evidence are a legislative enactment, we turn to the traditional tools of statutory construction in order to construe their provisions. We begin with the language itself." *Beech Aircraft Corp. v. Rainey,* 488 U.S. 153, 163 (1988). The text of Rule 804(b)(6) requires only that the defendant intend to render the declarant unavailable "as a witness." The text does not require that the declarant would otherwise be a witness at any *particular* trial, nor does it limit the subject matter of admissible statements to events distinct from the events at issue in the trial in which the statements are offered. Thus, we conclude that Rule 804(b)(6) applies *whenever* the defendant's wrongdoing was intended to, and did, render the declarant unavailable as a witness against the defendant, without regard to the nature of the charges at the trial in which the declarant's statements are offered. *Accord United States v. Dhinsa,* 243 F.3d 635, 652–53 (2d Cir.2001); *United States v. Emery,* 186 F.3d 921, 926 (8th Cir.1999); 4 C. Mueller & L. Kirkpatrick, *Federal Evidence* § 507.1, at 268 (2d ed. Supp.2004) ("It seems that there is no limit on the subject matter of statements that can be admitted under this exception, which means that statements in which the declarant implicates a defendant in a plot to kill the declarant himself can fit the exception.").

Our interpretation of Rule 804(b)(6) advances the clear purpose of the forfeiture-by-wrongdoing exception. The advisory committee noted its specific goal to implement a "prophylactic rule to deal with abhorrent behavior which strikes at the heart of the system of justice itself." Fed.R.Evid. 804(b)(6) advisory committee note (internal quotations omitted); *see also United States v. Thompson,* 286 F.3d 950, 962 (7th Cir.2002) (stating that "the primary reasoning behind this rule" is "to deter criminals from intimidating or 'taking care of' potential witnesses against them"). More generally, federal courts have recognized that the forfeiture-by-wrongdoing exception is necessary to prevent wrongdoers from profiting by their misconduct. *See Reynolds,* 98 U.S. at 158–59 (holding that a criminal defendant waives his right to confront a witness whose absence his own misconduct procured and stating that this rule "has its foundation in the maxim that no one shall be permitted to take advantage of his own wrong"); *Emery,* 186 F.3d at 926 (stating that the Rule "establishes the general proposition that a defendant may not benefit from his or her wrongful prevention of future testimony from a witness or potential witness"); *United States v. White,* 116 F.3d 903, 911 (D.C.Cir.1997) (stating that "where the defendant has silenced a witness through the use of threats, violence or murder, admission of the victim's prior statements at least partially offsets the perpetrator's rewards for his misconduct"); *United States v. Houlihan,* 92 F.3d 1271, 1279 (1st Cir.1996) (applying the forfeiture-by-wrongdoing exception and noting that "courts will not suffer a party to profit by his own wrongdoing").

Federal courts have sought to effect the purpose of the forfeiture-by-wrongdoing exception by construing broadly the elements required for its application. *See, e.g., Dhinsa,* 243 F.3d at 652 (noting that the Rule may apply where the declarant was only a potential witness, *i.e.,* "there was no ongoing proceeding in which the declarant was scheduled to testify"); *United States v. Cherry,* 217 F.3d 811, 820 (10th Cir.2000) (holding that the declarant's statements may be admitted against a person who participated in a conspiracy to silence the declarant even if that person did not himself engage in witness intimidation or other wrongdoing); *Steele v. Taylor,* 684 F.2d 1193, 1201 (6th Cir.1982) (stating that "any significant interference" with the declarant's appearance as a witness, including the exercise of "persuasion and control" or an instruction to invoke the Fifth Amendment privilege, amounts to wrongdoing that forfeits the defendant's right to confront the declarant). Although the Rule requires that the wrongdoing was *intended* to render the declarant unavailable as a witness, we have held that a defendant need only intend "in part" to procure the declarant's unavailability. *Johnson,* 219 F.3d at 356; *accord Dhinsa,* 243 F.3d at 654; *Houlihan,* 92 F.3d at 1279.

Like these applications of the forfeiture-by-wrongdoing exception, our interpretation of Rule 804(b)(6) ensures that a defendant will not be permitted to avoid the evidentiary impact of statements made by his victim, whether or not he suspected that the victim would be a witness at the trial in which the evidence is offered against him. A defendant who wrongfully and intentionally renders a declarant unavailable as a witness in any proceeding forfeits the right to exclude, on hearsay grounds, the declarant's statements at that proceeding and any subsequent proceeding. *See United States v. Aguiar,* 975 F.2d 45, 47 (2d Cir.1992) (affirming the district court's admission of hearsay testimony to prove witness tampering as well as an underlying drug conspiracy, and stating that "[a] defendant who procures a witness's absence waives the right of confrontation for all purposes with regard to that witness").[23]

Having rejected Gray's interpretation of Rule 804(b)(6), we need only determine whether the district court properly applied the Rule in admitting Robert Gray's out-of-court statements. Those statements were admissible only if the district court properly found, by a preponderance of the evidence, that (1) Gray engaged in some wrongdoing (2) that was intended to procure Robert Gray's unavailability as a witness and (3) that did, in fact, procure his unavailability as a witness. The district court in this case found that Robert Gray "was killed prior to the court date on November 15 and 16, and after the defendant was well aware of his status as a witness, justifies the inference that * * * the killing was motivated * * * to prevent [Robert Gray] from being available * * * at court proceedings." J.A. 205. These findings are supported by the evidence and are sufficient to warrant application of the Rule 804(b)(6). Accordingly, the district court did not abuse its discretion in admitting testimony concerning out-of-court statements made by Robert Gray.

---

[23] We emphasize that the intent requirement in Rule 804(b)(6) continues to limit application of the forfeiture-by-wrongdoing exception to those cases in which the defendant intended, at least in part, to render the declarant unavailable as a witness against him. *See Johnson,* 219 F.3d at 356. Absent such intent, Rule 804(b)(6) has no application.

NOTES AND QUESTIONS

1. *Wrongful intent.* Rule 804(b)(6) requires an intent to procure the absence of the witness. It also requires "wrongdoing" to procure that result, but as the Committee Note states, wrongdoing need not necessarily involve criminal conduct. See United States v. Scott, 284 F.3d 758, 763–64 (7th Cir.2002) (concluding that "wrongdoing," which the Advisory Committee states need not be a criminal act, also need not include murder, physical assault, or bribery, but would be satisfied by coercion, undue influence, or pressure to silence testimony).

2. *Murder to eliminate witness(es).* *Gray* rules that the hearsay statements may be admitted not only as to the crimes as to which the witness would have testified, but also to criminal conduct, such as murder, through which the witness' absence was procured. The exception does not, however, apply to the murder of all potential witnesses. By its terms, the Rule should be inapplicable to a murder committed during a robbery for the purpose of overcoming the victim's physical resistance. The Committee Note states that it "applies to actions taken after the event to prevent a witness from testifying." In many cases, the wrongful conduct will occur long after the original crime (the event) when the witness' identity becomes known to the defendant. Would the exception apply to a murder committed during a robbery if the perpetrator killed the victim in order to eliminate any witnesses? What is the result if the purpose is to both overcome resistance and to eliminate a potential witness?

3. *No trustworthiness requirement.* Rule 804(b)(6) operates under the rationale of forfeiture rather than the typical mix of trustworthiness and necessity involved in most hearsay exceptions. As a consequence, it requires no explicit showing of trustworthiness. See United States v. Scott, 284 F.3d 758, 765 (7th Cir.2002) (ruling that, to the extent the unreliability challenge depends on lack of cross-examination, admission under wrongdoing renders that objection unavailing); People v. Hanson, 939 N.E.2d 238, 252–53 (Ill.2010) (admitting statements as long as relevant and otherwise admissible without reflecting additional indicia of reliability). A somewhat related examination is required under Rule 403, which considers probativity, a factor that rests in part on trustworthiness. However, the review under Rule 403 is a forgiving one, requiring admission of evidence unless its probativity is substantially outweighed by its prejudicial impact.

4. *Procedures for finding intent.* In line with preliminary factfinding generally under the hearsay rules, this Rule requires the trial court to find the required intent, for example, by a preponderance of the evidence. The circuits differ on whether this finding must be made before admission and outside the presence of the jury or whether the evidence may be admitted conditionally upon subsequent proof of the requisite facts. While United States v. Dhinsa, 243 F.3d 635, 653–54 (2d Cir.2001), holds that the trial court must hold a hearing outside the presence of the jury prior to admitting

hearsay under this exception, the Eighth Circuit rejects this requirement. See United States v. Emery, 186 F.3d 921, 926 (8th Cir.1999).

5. *Procurement "through others."* Action "through others" producing unavailability may be directly arranged by the defendant. Direct proof of procurement is often difficult to obtain. Thus, it is important that actions may be "counted against" the defendant if (1) the actions were taken by coconspirators, (2) the wrongful procurement was within the scope and in furtherance of the conspiracy, and (3) it was reasonably foreseeable as a natural consequence of the conspiracy. Several courts have held that such indirect involvement of the defendant in the declarant's unavailability of the type that satisfies conspiratorial liability for such unavailability (frequently through murder) is sufficient. See, e.g., United States v. Thompson, 286 F.3d 950, 963 (7th Cir.2002).

6. *Relationship to Confrontation Clause.* In Giles v. California, 554 U.S. 353 (2008), the Supreme Court ruled that a key requirement of Rule 804(b)(6) that the party intended to render the declarant unavailable as a witness applied also under the Confrontation Clause. This decision ran contrary to that of a number of courts, which had ruled that wrongful actions that procured absence, such as killing the declarant, automatically operated as a forfeiture of confrontation rights. See, e.g., United States v. Garcia–Meza, 403 F.3d 364, 370–71 (6th Cir.2005); State v. Meeks, 88 P.3d 789 (Kan.2004). In general, the requirements of the evidence rule and confrontation track very closely.

7. *Antecedents and state adoptions.* Prior to the adoption of Rule 804(b)(6) in 1997, some courts had admitted hearsay when a party wrongfully caused the declarant's unavailability under the theory of waiver or forfeiture of hearsay and Confrontation Clause objections. See, e.g., United States v. Smith, 792 F.2d 441, 442 (4th Cir.1986); Steele v. Taylor, 684 F.2d 1193, 1202 (6th Cir.1982). A number of states have adopted a form of this hearsay exception by rule or court decision. See 2 McCormick, Evidence § 253 (7th ed. 2013).

L. CATCHALL OR RESIDUAL EXCEPTION

Federal Rules 807 (Formerly 803(24) & 804(b)(5))

DALLAS COUNTY V. COMMERCIAL UNION ASSUR. CO.

United States Court of Appeals, Fifth Circuit, 1961.
286 F.2d 388.

WISDOM, CIRCUIT JUDGE. This appeal presents a single question—the admissibility in evidence of a newspaper to show that the Dallas County Courthouse in Selma, Alabama, was damaged by fire in 1901. We hold that the newspaper was admissible, and affirm the judgment below.

On a bright, sunny morning, July 7, 1957, the clock tower of the Dallas County Courthouse at Selma, Alabama, commenced to lean, made loud cracking and popping noises, then fell and telescoped into the courtroom. Fortunately, the collapse of the tower took place on a Sunday morning; no one was injured, but damage to the courthouse exceeded $100,000. An examination of the tower debris showed the presence of charcoal and charred timbers. The State Toxicologist, called in by Dallas County, reported the char was evidence that lightning struck the courthouse. Later, several residents of Selma reported that a bolt of lightning struck the courthouse July 2, 1957. On this information, Dallas County concluded that a lightning bolt had hit the building causing the collapse of the clock tower five days later. Dallas County carried insurance for loss to its courthouse caused by fire or lightning. The insurers' engineers and investigators found that the courthouse collapsed of its own weight. They reported that the courthouse had not been struck by lightning; that lightning could not have caused the collapse of the tower; that the collapse of the tower was caused by structural weaknesses attributable to a faulty design, poor construction, gradual deterioration of the structure, and overloading brought about by remodeling and the recent installation of an air-conditioning system, part of which was constructed over the courtroom trusses. In their opinion, the char was the result of a fire in the courthouse tower and roof that must have occurred many, many years before July 2, 1957. The insurers denied liability.

The County sued its insurers in the Circuit Court of Dallas County. As many of the suits as could be removed, seven, were removed to the United States District Court for the Southern District of Alabama, and were consolidated for trial. The case went to the jury on one issue: did lightning cause the collapse of the clock tower?

The record contains ample evidence to support a jury verdict either way. The County produced witnesses who testified they saw lightning strike the clock tower; the insurers produced witnesses who testified an examination of the debris showed that lightning did not strike the clock tower. Some witnesses said the char was fresh and smelled smoky; other witnesses said it was obviously old and had no fresh smoky smell at all. Both sides presented a great mass of engineering testimony bearing on the design, construction, overload or lack of overload. All of this was for the jury to evaluate. The jury chose to believe the insurers' witnesses and brought in a verdict for the defendants.

During the trial the defendants introduced a copy of the Morning Times of Selma for June 9, 1901. This issue carried an unsigned article describing a fire that occurred at two in the morning of June 9, 1901, while the courthouse was still under construction. The article stated, in part: "The unfinished dome of the County's new courthouse was in flames at the top, and * * * soon fell in. The fire was soon under control and the main building was saved. * * * "The insurers do not contend that the collapse of the tower resulted from unsound charred timbers used in the repair of the building after the fire; they offered the newspaper account to show there had been a fire long before 1957 that would account for charred timber in the clock tower.

As a predicate for introducing the newspaper in evidence, the defendants called to the stand the editor of the Selma Times–Journal who testified that his publishing company maintains archives of the published issues of the Times–Journal and of the Morning Times, its predecessor, and that the archives contain the issue of the Morning Times of Selma for June 9, 1901, offered in evidence. The plaintiff objected that the newspaper article was hearsay; that it was not a business record nor an ancient document, nor was it admissible under any recognized exception to the hearsay doctrine. The trial judge admitted the newspaper as part of the records of the Selma Times–Journal. The sole error Dallas County specifies on appeal is the admission of the newspaper in evidence.

In the Anglo–American adversary system of law, courts usually will not admit evidence unless its accuracy and trustworthiness may be tested by cross-examination. Here, therefore, the plaintiff argues that the newspaper should not be admitted: "You cannot cross-examine a newspaper."[24] Of course, a newspaper article *is* hearsay, and in almost all circumstances is inadmissible. However, the law governing hearsay is somewhat less than pellucid.[25] And, as with most rules, the hearsay rule is not absolute; it is replete with exceptions. Witnesses die, documents are lost, deeds are destroyed, memories fade. All too often, primary evidence is not available and courts and lawyers must rely on secondary evidence.

---

[24] This argument, a familiar one, rests on a misunderstanding of the origin and the nature of the hearsay rule. The rule is not an ancient principle of English law recognized at Runnymede. And, gone is its odor of sanctity.

Wigmore is often quoted for the statement that "cross-examination is beyond any doubt the greatest legal engine ever invented for the discovery of the truth". 5 Wigmore § 1367 (3d ed.). In over 1200 pages devoted to the hearsay rule, however, he makes it very clear that: "[T]he rule aims to insist on testing all statements by cross-examination, if they can be. * * * No one could defend a rule which pronounced that all statements thus untested are worthless; for all historical truth is based on uncross-examined assertion; and every day's experience of life gives denial to such an exaggeration. What the Hearsay Rule implies—and with profound verity—is that all testimonial assertions ought to be tested by cross-examination, as the best attainable measure; and it should not be burdened with the pedantic implication that they must be rejected as worthless if the test is unavailable." 1 Wigmore § 8c. In this connection see Falknor, The Hearsay Rule and Its Exceptions, 2 U.C.L.A.L.Rev. 43 (1954). * * *

[25] "The fact is, then, that the law governing hearsay today is a conglomeration of inconsistencies, developed as a result of conflicting theories. Refinements and qualifications within the exceptions only add to its irrationality. The courts by multiplying exceptions reveal their conviction that relevant hearsay evidence normally has real probative value, and is capable of valuation by a jury as well as by other triers of fact. * * * "ALI Model Code of Evidence, p. 223 (1942).

* * *

We turn now to a case * * * in which the court used an approach we consider appropriate for the solution of the problem before us. G. & C. Merriam Co. v. Syndicate Pub. Co., 2nd Cir., 1913, 207 F. 515, 518, concerned a controversy between dictionary publishers over the use of the title "Webster's Dictionary" when the defendant's dictionary allegedly was not based upon Webster's dictionary at all. The bone of contention was whether a statement in the preface to the dictionary was admissible as evidence of the facts it recited. Ogilvie, the compiler of the dictionary, stated in his preface that he used Webster's Dictionary as the basis for his own publication. The dictionary, with its preface, was published in 1850, sixty-three years before the trial of the case. Ogilvie's published statement was challenged as hearsay. Judge Learned Hand, then a district judge, unable, as we are here, to find a case in point, for authority relied solely on Wigmore on Evidence (then a recent publication), particularly on Wigmore's analysis that "the requisites of an exception to the hearsay rule are necessity and circumstantial guaranty of trustworthiness." Wigmore on Evidence, §§ 1421, 1422, 1690 (1st ed. 1913). Applying these criteria, Judge Hand held that the statement was admissible as an exception to the hearsay rule:

> "Ogilvie's preface is of course an unsworn statement and as such only hearsay testimony, which may be admitted only as an exception to the general rule. The question is whether there is such an exception. I have been unable to find any express authority in point and must decide the question upon principle. In the first place, I think it fair to insist that to reject such a statement is to refuse evidence about the truth of which no reasonable person should have any doubt whatever, because it fulfills both the requisites of an exception to the hearsay rule, necessity and circumstantial guaranty of trustworthiness. Wigmore, §§ 1421, 1422, 1690 * * *. Besides Ogilvie, everyone else is dead who ever knew anything about the matter and could intelligently tell us what the fact is. * * * As to the trustworthiness of the testimony, it has the guaranty of the occasion, at which there was no motive for fabrication." 207 F. 515, 518.

The Court of Appeals adopted the district court's opinion in its entirety.

The first of the two requisites is necessity. As to necessity, Wigmore points out this requisite means that unless the hearsay statement is admitted, the facts it brings out may otherwise be lost, either because the person whose assertion is offered may be dead or unavailable, or because the assertion is of such a nature that one could not expect to obtain evidence of the same value from the same person or from other sources. *1 1.* Wigmore, § 1421 (3d ed.).

The fire referred to in the newspaper account occurred fifty-eight *a.* years before the trial of this case. Any witness who saw that fire with sufficient understanding to observe it and describe it accurately, would have been older than a young child at the time of the fire. We may reasonably assume that at the time of the trial he was either dead or his faculties were dimmed by the passage of fifty-eight years. It would have been burdensome, but not impossible, for the defendant to have discovered the name of the author of the article (although it had no by-line) and, perhaps, to have found an eye-witness to the fire. But it is improbable—so it seems to us—that any witness could have been found whose recollection would have been accurate at the time of the trial of this case. And it seems impossible that the testimony of any witness would have been as accurate and as reliable as the statement of facts in the contemporary newspaper article.

The rationale behind the "ancient documents" exception is applicable here: after a long lapse of time, ordinary evidence regarding signatures or handwriting is virtually unavailable, and it is therefore permissible to resort to circumstantial evidence. Thus, in Trustees of German Township, Montgomery County v. Farmers & Citizens Savings Bank Co., Ohio Com.Pl.1953, 113 N.E.2d 409, 412, affirmed Ohio App., 115 N.E.2d 690, the court admitted as ancient documents newspapers eighty years old containing notices of advertisements for bids relating to the town hall: "Such exhibits, by reason of age, alone, and unquestioned authenticity, qualify as ancient documents." The ancient documents rule applies to documents a generation or more in age. Here, the Selma Times–Journal article is almost two generations old. The principle of necessity, not requiring absolute impossibility or total inaccessibility of first-hand knowledge, is satisfied by the practicalities of the situation before us.

The second requisite for admission of hearsay evidence is *B.* trustworthiness. According to Wigmore, there are three sets of circumstances when hearsay is trustworthy enough to serve as a practicable substitute for the ordinary test of cross-examination: "Where *(1)* the circumstances are such that a sincere and accurate statement would naturally be uttered, and no plan of falsification be formed; where, even though a desire to falsify might present itself, other considerations, such *(2)* as the danger of easy detection or the fear of punishment, would probably counteract its force; where the statement was made under such conditions *(3)* of publicity that an error, if it had occurred, would probably have been detected and corrected." 5 Wigmore, Evidence § 1422 (3d ed.). These circumstances fit the instant case.

There is no procedural canon against the exercise of common sense in deciding the admissibility of hearsay evidence. In 1901 Selma, Alabama, was a small town. Taking a common sense view of this case, it is inconceivable to us that a newspaper reporter in a small town would report there was a fire in the dome of the new courthouse—if there had been no fire. He is without motive to falsify, and a false report would have subjected the newspaper and him to embarrassment in the community. The usual dangers inherent in hearsay evidence, such as lack of memory, faulty narration, intent to influence the court proceedings, and plain lack of truthfulness are not present here. To our minds, the article published in the Selma Morning–Times on the day of the fire is more reliable, more trustworthy, more competent evidence than the testimony of a witness called to the stand fifty-eight years later.

We hold, that in matters of local interest, when the fact in question is of such a public nature it would be generally known throughout the community, and when the questioned fact occurred so long ago that the testimony of an eye-witness would probably be less trustworthy than a contemporary newspaper account, a federal court, under Rule 43(a), may relax the exclusionary rules to the extent of admitting the newspaper article in evidence. We do not characterize this newspaper as a "business record", nor as an "ancient document", nor as any other readily identifiable and happily tagged species of hearsay exception. It is admissible because it is necessary and trustworthy, relevant and material, and its admission is within the trial judge's exercise of discretion in holding the hearing within reasonable bounds.

Judgment is affirmed.

BOHLER–UDDEHOLM AMERICA, INC. v. ELLWOOD GROUP, INC.

United States Court of Appeals, Third Circuit, 2001.
247 F.3d 79.

BECKER, CHIEF JUDGE.

This is an appeal by defendant Ellwood Group, Inc., (Ellwood) from a final judgment entered against it by the District Court for the Western District of Pennsylvania in favor of plaintiff Uddeholm Tooling AB (Uddeholm). This complicated commercial case emerges from the disintegration of a joint venture entered into by Ellwood, a Pennsylvania corporation in the business of forging steel ingots into various components of heavy machinery, and Uddeholm, a Swedish company that produces specialty tool steels. Uddeholm brought numerous claims against Ellwood, including breach of contract, breach of fiduciary duty, misappropriation of trade secrets, and civil conspiracy. Resolution of this appeal requires us to address a number of questions of Pennsylvania contract, business tort, and damages law, along with two questions on the application of the Federal Rules of Evidence.

[The portions of the opinion treating issues other than the admission of a hearsay statement have been omitted.]

Evidentiary Challenges

* * * We review the District Court's evidentiary rulings for abuse of discretion. *See Walden v. Georgia–Pacific Corp.*, 126 F.3d 506, 517 (3d Cir.1997).

The Jonsson affidavit

The District Court admitted into evidence portions of an affidavit of Bo Jonsson, a former President of Uddeholm, under Federal Rule of Evidence 807, the catchall exception to the hearsay rule. Jonsson attested to the affidavit in 1994 and died in 1996, before the trial. Uddeholm used the affidavit to counter assertions by Ellwood about what transpired at certain directors meetings that Jonsson attended in a representative capacity for Uddeholm. Rule 807 provides that

> [a] statement not specifically covered by Rule 803 or 804 but having equivalent circumstantial guarantees of trustworthiness, is not excluded by the hearsay rule, if the court determines that (A) the statement is offered as evidence of a material fact; (B) the statement is more probative on the point for which it is offered than any other evidence which the proponent can procure through reasonable efforts; and (C) the general purposes of these rules and the interests of justice will best be served by admission of the statement into evidence. However, a statement may not be admitted under this exception unless the proponent of it makes known to the adverse party sufficiently in advance of the trial or hearing to provide the adverse party with a fair opportunity to prepare to meet it, the proponent's intention to offer the statement and the particulars of it, including the name and address of the declarant.

Ellwood argues that the District Court's admission of the Jonsson affidavit under Rule 807 was error, because Rule 807 is meant to be used only in the rare case, which, it argues, this is not. *See United States v. Bailey,* 581 F.2d 341, 347 (3d Cir.1978) (stating that the residual hearsay exception is "to be used only rarely, and in exceptional circumstances," and is meant to "apply only when certain exceptional guarantees of trustworthiness exist and when high degrees of probativeness and necessity are present"). Specifically, Ellwood takes issue with the District Court's findings that the Jonsson affidavit was exceptionally trustworthy and that it was more probative than any other evidence that Uddeholm could present.

While Ellwood is correct that Rule 807 should only be used in rare situations, the District Court made careful and extensive findings in support of its conclusion that this was such a situation. * * *. First, the District Court ascertained that the requirements of Rule 807 were met. The court specifically found that

- the affidavit was offered as evidence on a material fact, namely the parties' course of dealings, which bears upon the interpretation of the Agreement;

- the affidavit was more probative on the point for which it is offered than any other evidence which the proponent could procure through reasonable efforts: it was highly probative because Jonsson was the only representative of Uddeholm on the EUS board of directors at the time in question, and, as such, this evidence was the only evidence that Uddeholm could present to counter the Ellwood's allegation that Uddeholm understood the Agreement to permit sales to third parties and reimbursement for those sales;

- the general purpose of the rules, fairness and the administration of justice, would be served by admitting the affidavit, because it would assist the jury in determining the truth;

- there was sufficient notice to Ellwood that it would be used, as Uddeholm proffered the affidavit months prior to trial, and there was argument and briefs filed on the issue.

The District Court found that the following factors also militated in favor of admitting the Jonsson affidavit:

- Ellwood had ways to rebut the affidavit: its witnesses were present at the meetings discussed therein, and these witnesses could present their testimony, while Uddeholm's only witness to these meetings (Jonsson) was dead;

- the affidavit was trustworthy because: (1) the declarant was known and named, (2) the statement was made under oath and penalty of perjury, (3) the declarant "was aware of the pending litigation at the time he made the declaration and thus knew that his assertions were subject to cross examination," (4) the statements were based on personal observation, (5) the declarant was not employed by the plaintiff at the time of the statements, and thus had no financial interest in the litigation's outcome, (6) the affidavit was corroborated, partially, by minutes of directors meetings (some statements Jonsson said were made match others' notations), and (7) his position and background qualified him to make the assertions.

The District Court then acknowledged that Rule 807 should only be used sparingly, but opined that this affidavit presented "a rather unique combination of circumstances where a material fact can be proved only through one method, or, in this case, rebutted by only one method." The court was also swayed by the fact that it was Ellwood that first argued that Uddeholm knew of Ellwood's interpretation of the Agreement because Jonsson must have gained this knowledge at the directors meetings; the only way Uddeholm could rebut this claim was via Jonsson's affidavit, given that he was not available to testify.

These findings are sufficient for us to hold that the District Court did not abuse its discretion when it admitted the Jonsson affidavit under Rule 807. In *Copperweld Steel Co. v. Demag–Mannesmann–Bohler,* 578 F.2d 953 (3d Cir.1978), this Court upheld a district court's admission of a similar item—a memorandum prepared by a lawyer of an executive who was later killed—on a weaker showing by the district court under the predecessor rule to Rule 807 (Rule 804(b)(5)). *See id.* at 964. We therefore hold that the admission of the Jonsson affidavit was not error.

NOTES AND QUESTIONS

1.   *Trustworthiness factors.* Trustworthiness under the catchall exception involves the circumstances under which the declarant made the statements and his or her incentives to speak truthfully. The factors that may establish such trustworthiness are so varied that providing useful categorization is difficult, but some factors repeatedly found to be important are:

> whether the declarant had a motivation to speak truthfully or otherwise; the spontaneity of the statement, including whether it was elicited by leading questions, and generally the time lapse between event and statement; whether the statement was under oath; whether the declarant was subject to cross-examination at the time the statement was made; the relationship between the declarant and the person to whom the statement was made; whether the declarant has recanted or reaffirmed the statement; whether the statement was recorded and particularly whether it was videotaped; and whether the declarant's firsthand knowledge is clearly demonstrated.

2 McCormick, Evidence § 324 (7th ed. 2013). See also 4 Saltzburg, Martin & Capra, Federal Rules of Evidence Manual § 807.02[4] (10th ed. 2011) (providing lengthy list of factors supporting trustworthiness). Whether the reliability of the report of the hearsay statement is an appropriate factor is subject to dispute between the circuits. Compare Huff v. White Motor Corp., 609 F.2d 286, 293 (7th Cir.1979) (inappropriate), and 2 McCormick, supra, § 324 (inappropriate), with United States v. Bailey, 581 F.2d 341, 349 (3d Cir.1978) (proper), and 7 Graham, Handbook of Federal Evidence § 807.1, at 802 (7th ed. 2012) (considering certainty that statement was made, including evaluation of in-court witness).

2.   *Meaning of "not specifically covered"; Is a "near miss" bad or good for admissibility?* When a statement fails to meet the requirements of a

hearsay exception, should that not mean it is excluded? On the other hand, when a statement is offered under the residual exception, one of its characteristics is that the statement is "not specifically covered by Rule 803 or 804." Should there be a difference in treatment depending on whether the statement appears to fall within a category governed by a specific rule but fails to qualify versus a statement that is unlike any of the specific exceptions? Is it a favorable factor for admission of a statement that fails to qualify that it just barely missed admission under one of the specific rules, or is the fact that it is a "near miss" a factor disqualifying the statement?

In a concurring opinion in United States v. Dent, 984 F.2d 1453, 1465 (7th Cir.1993), which concerned the admissibility of grand jury testimony, Judge Easterbrook argued that the language of the catchall "reads more naturally if we understand the introductory clause to mean that evidence of a kind specifically addressed ("covered") by one of the four other subsections must satisfy the conditions laid down for its admission, and that other kinds of evidence not covered (because the drafters could not be exhaustive) are admissible if the evidence is approximately as reliable as evidence that would be admissible under the specific subsections." That is not, however, the dominant position. See, e.g., United States v. Laster, 258 F.3d 525, 530 (6th Cir.2001) (rejecting exclusionary argument that had been suggested in an earlier opinion in the circuit); People v. Katt, 662 N.W.2d 12, 18–23 (Mich.2003) (rejecting "near miss" exclusion after extensive discussion).

The term "near miss" is sometimes applied to the above argument or a slight extension of it. It is occasionally used by courts to deny admissibility under the catchall exception, but the predominant use is to provide support for admissibility. Courts have frequently found statements admissible where the statement narrowly misses qualifying under one of the specific exceptions, and the court determines by analogy, that the statement has substantial guarantees of trustworthiness, almost satisfying the "equivalent circumstantial guarantees of trustworthiness" requirement of the catchall. See United States v. Valdez–Soto, 31 F.3d 1467, 1471 (9th Cir.1994); State v. Anderson, 695 N.W.2d 731, 749 (Wis.2005); 7 Graham, Handbook of Federal Evidence § 807.1, at 833 & n.30 (7th ed. 2012). A few courts have followed Judge Easterbrook's analysis and held that, where a specific exception is available and the evidence "misses" admission under its requirements, the residual exception should be rejected. See Acme Printing Ink Co. v. Menard, Inc., 812 F.Supp. 1498, 1527 (E.D.Wis.1992).

Is there at least a little possible common ground between these approaches when legislative intent of the drafters gives concrete indication that failure to satisfy a specific exception demonstrates a lack of trustworthiness? Compare United States v. Bailey, 581 F.2d 341, 349 n.12 (3d Cir.1978) (rejection by Congress of exception for statements of recent perception gives guidance as to whether similar statement has equivalent trustworthiness to other Rule 804(b) exceptions), with Robinson v. Shapiro, 646 F.2d 734, 742 n.6 (2d Cir.1981) (rejection of recent perception exception meant only that Congress was unwilling to admit all such statements, not a legislative intent to exclude any statements if offered under appropriate circumstances through the residual exception).

3. *Corroboration?* Can corroborating evidence external to the statement establishing the accuracy of the statement establish its trustworthiness under the catchall rule? Idaho v. Wright, 497 U.S. 805 (1990), appeared to answer the question "no." While *Wright* decided an issue under the Confrontation Clause, see Chapter 13, Section C, supra, its conclusion that "particularized guarantees of trustworthiness" "include only those [circumstances] that surround the making of the statement and that render the declarant particularly worthy of belief" rested on "the rationale for permitting exceptions to the general rule against hearsay." *Id.* at 819. In *Wright*, the Supreme Court appeared to endorse not only a Confrontation Clause theory, but also a hearsay rationale, that excludes corroboration as a source of trustworthiness. Whether *Wright*'s analysis should carry any weight, however, is uncertain since it was part of the *Ohio v. Roberts* mode of analysis that was thoroughly rejected by *Crawford*.

4. *Impact of declarant's unavailability.* The catchall exception under Rule 807 covers both situations where the declarant is available (formerly 803(24)) and where he or she is unavailable (formerly 804(b)(5)). One clear difference between these situations is that an unavailable declarant cannot testify, which might in general suggest a greater likelihood to receive the hearsay because it is more "necessary." Courts have treated the significance of the declarant's availability in very different ways. Some have ruled that, with available declarants, the requirement that the statement be "more probative on the point for which it is offered than any other evidence that the proponent can procure through reasonable efforts" is difficult to meet because the available declarant could give live testimony as an alternative to the hearsay statement. See United States v. Mathis, 559 F.2d 294, 298–99 (5th Cir.1977); State v. Smith, 337 S.E.2d 833, 846 (N.C.1985). This concern should not apply where the statement, as is often the case with the exceptions under Rule 803, is clearly superior in terms of its trustworthiness to the testimony of the declarant at the time of trial. The *Dallas County* case, presented at the beginning of this Section, provides an example. Other courts have taken a different tack and have concluded that, where the declarant is available and does testify, the required showing of trustworthiness is more easily met. See, e.g., United States v. Leslie, 542 F.2d 285, 290 (5th Cir.1976); United States v. Iaconetti, 406 F.Supp. 554, 559 (E.D.N.Y.), aff'd, 540 F.2d 574 (2d Cir.1976).

5. *Analyzing "necessity."* On the question of whether the hearsay statement satisfies the requirement of Rule 807(B)—that the statement must be more probative on the point than other available evidence—courts have used different methods of analysis. For example, in United States v. Simmons, 773 F.2d 1455, 1459 (4th Cir.1985), the court found the hearsay more probative than other available evidence by balancing the trustworthiness of the hearsay against the cost of alternative proof. It held that the government was not required to assemble witnesses from across the

country to establish the state in which the weapons had been manufactured, given the likely accuracy of standard government "trace forms" completed by the manufacturer. In United States v. Welsh, 774 F.2d 670 (4th Cir.1985), the court held that the requirement is not met simply because an unavailable declarant is a more credible witness than the witness who would otherwise testify for the government. And in United States v. Vretta, 790 F.2d 651, 658–59 (7th Cir.1986), the court held that the statement may be more probative than other available evidence, even if some other nonhearsay evidence is available on the issue when the hearsay statements complete the picture of a pattern of conduct otherwise not established.

6.   *Application to grand jury testimony.* Prior to the Supreme Court's decision in Crawford v. Washington, 541 U.S. 36 (2004), a number of courts had admitted grand jury testimony under the cathcall exception. See, e.g., United States v. Earles, 113 F.3d 796 (8th Cir.1997). Although *Crawford* does not change the hearsay analysis, it makes the hearsay analysis irrelevant because grand jury testimony is undeniably testimonial and therefore excluded by the Confrontation Clause.

7.   *Children's cases.* Another general area where courts have rather liberally used the catchall exception involves the statements of children who are the victims of sexual offenses. Relying upon research that shows children are unlikely to fabricate claims of sexual abuse and corroborating circumstances, such as knowledge about anatomy and sexual functioning typically foreign to one of tender years, many courts have found the statements trustworthy. See, e.g., United States v. Dunford, 148 F.3d 385, 392–94 (4th Cir.1998); United States v. NB, 59 F.3d 771, 775–78 (8th Cir.1995); State v. McCafferty, 356 N.W.2d 159, 164 (S.D.1984). Whether the witness' availability should weigh heavily against admission is subject to some disagreement. Compare United States v. Cree, 778 F.2d 474, 478–79 (8th Cir.1985) (young child need not be unavailable and prosecution not required to call child as witness before testimony concerning sexual assault admissible under catchall exception), with State v. Fearing, 337 S.E.2d 551 (N.C.1985) (child must be unavailable before testimony meets requirement that it be more probative than other available evidence). *Crawford* will have an impact in cases of this type, although statements by children are generally not as clearly testimonial.

About half the states have followed a different course and created a new exception for statements of youthful victims of sexual abuse where the statement is shown to bear indicia of trustworthiness. See, e.g., State v. Myatt, 697 P.2d 836 (Kan.1985). These statutes create for child abuse cases an exception that, like the catchall exception, allows the court to find trustworthiness from any available factor. See generally Mosteller, Remaking Confrontation Clause and Hearsay Doctrine Under the Challenge of Child Sexual Abuse Prosecutions, 1993 Ill.L.Rev. 691, 698–99.

8.   *Admission not so rare.* As the two preceding notes suggest, the drafters' admonition that the residual hearsay exceptions should "be used

very rarely, and only in exceptional circumstances" has not been followed. Evidence is rather frequently admitted under the catchall exception in federal litigation, and it has been used more heavily in criminal than in civil cases. Raeder, The Effect of the Catchalls on Criminal Defendants: Little Red Riding Hood Meets the Hearsay Wolf and Is Devoured, 25 Loy.L.A.L.Rev. 925, 933–34 (1992).

9. *Notice requirement.* Rule 807 requires that the proponent of the evidence provide notice to the adverse party of the particulars of the statement and the identity of the declarant to allow a fair opportunity to meet the statement. Generally, courts have interpreted this notice requirement flexibly. See, e.g., Furtado v. Bishop, 604 F.2d 80, 92 (1st Cir.1979). However, courts have occasionally demanded strict compliance with the notice requirement. See United States v. Ruffin, 575 F.2d 346, 358 (2d Cir.1978). See generally Grant, The Pre–Trial Notice Requirement of Federal Rule of Evidence 803(24), 36 Drake L.Rev. 91 (1986–87).

M. NOTES ON OTHER SELECTED EXCEPTIONS AND MISCELLANEOUS PROVISIONS

NOTES AND QUESTIONS ON FEDERAL RULES 803(16), (18) & (22)

A number of other hearsay exceptions are defined under Rules 803 and 804 besides those discussed above. These include:

1. *Ancient Documents* (Rule 803(16)). This exception permits the admission of documents that have been in existence twenty years or more. Traditionally, the ancient document doctrine established only authenticity and did not constitute a hearsay exception. See, e.g., Town of Ninety Six v. Southern Ry. Co., 267 F.2d 579 (4th Cir.1959), Chapter 11, Section A, supra. The rationale for the hearsay exception is somewhat related to the authentication theory. As to both, it is unlikely that witnesses will be available or will reliably recall the events recorded. Trustworthiness is supplied by the requirements that the statement must be in writing and that it must have been created years earlier, presumably long before the beginning of litigation. See generally 2 McCormick, Evidence § 323 (7th ed. 2013).

2. *Learned Treatises* (Rule 803(18)). This exception adopts the position long advocated by many of the major commentators that learned treatises should be admissible substantively and should not be limited to use for impeachment purposes. 6 Wigmore on Evidence §§ 1690–92 (Chadbourn rev. 1976).

The Rule requires that the treatise be established as a "reliable authority." This can be done by the expert's reliance on the treatise during direct examination or, when used in the cross-examination of the expert, by that witness' admission, the testimony of another expert, or judicial notice. In order to reduce the possibility of over-valuing or misunderstanding the treatise, the Rule permits the treatise only to be read to the jury and not to be received as an exhibit. See generally 2 McCormick, Evidence § 321 (7th ed. 2013). In addition to "published treatises, periodicals, or pamphlets," the learned treatise exception may also encompass videotapes prepared by authoritative sources. Constantino v. Herzog, 203 F.3d 164, 170–73 (2d Cir.2000). Note that while the Federal Rules permit learned treatises to be used, not only to impeach an expert's testimony, but also to be admitted for their truth as an exception to the hearsay rule, some states continue to limit their use to affect credibility, either for impeachment, see Michigan Evidence Rule 707, or to support the opinion of the expert, see Aldridge v. Edmunds, 750 A.2d 292, 296–98 (Pa.2000). See also Chapter 12, Section E(10) (discussion in connection with *Freshwater v. Scheidt*).

3.   *Judgment of Felony Conviction* (Rule 803(22)). The Rule permits the admission of a conviction for a crime punishable by imprisonment of more than a year to prove any fact essential to the judgment. Limiting the Rule to crimes carrying a potential punishment of felony grade is intended to exclude from the Rule's operation minor offenses where the motivation to defend is "often minimal or nonexistent." Advisory Committee Note to Rule 803(22). The Rule only authorizes the conviction to be admitted as an item of evidence and does not accord it binding effect. Furthermore, in order to avoid conflict with the Confrontation Clause, Rule 803(22) prohibits use of the conviction of a third party to establish a fact against a criminal defendant.

NOTES AND QUESTIONS ON RULES 805 & 806

Rules 805 and 806 map out an important procedural framework for certain aspects of the application of the hearsay rules.

1.   *Rule 805—Double hearsay.* Rule 805 makes explicit the unassailable position that, where a statement that is itself hearsay contains another hearsay statement, the entire statement may be admitted if both parts of it are admissible because they either satisfy a hearsay exception or they are excluded from the hearsay rule, as are admissions of parties and inconsistent statements used to impeach. See, e.g., Wright v. Farmers Co–Op, 681 F.2d 549 (8th Cir.1982) (statement of employee admissible as admission of party's agent and document containing it admissible as business record of insurance adjuster who secured the statement). See also discussion in Section E, supra, following the *Blechman* case.

2.   *Rule 806—Practical difficulties of impeaching "virtual" witness.* Rule 806 permits the opponent of a hearsay statement to attack the credibility of its declarant to the same extent as would have been permitted if the declarant had testified at trial. The opponent also may call the declarant to the stand and examine him or her concerning the statement in the manner permitted during cross-examination. A difficulty with the Rule in practice arises when the government introduces the statements of codefendants as statements of coconspirators. Can one defendant impeach the testimony

offered by the non-testifying codefendant by offering his prior convictions? Compare United States v. Bovain, 708 F.2d 606 (11th Cir.1983) (giving affirmative answer), with United States v. Robinson, 783 F.2d 64 (7th Cir.1986) (sustaining trial court's exercise of discretion against permitting impeachment). Similarly, how is the prohibition in Rule 608(b) against use of extrinsic evidence affected when the hearsay declarant is unavailable and therefore cannot be asked about the "bad act" on cross-examination? See United States v. Saada, 212 F.3d 210, 221 (3d Cir.2000) (ruling that the prohibition is not modified by Rule 806 but finding a conflict between the circuits). See generally Condray, Evidence Rule 806 and the Problem of Impeaching the Nontestifying Declarant, 56 Ohio St.L.J. 495 (1995); Douglass, Virtual Cross–Examination: The Art of Impeaching Hearsay, 34 J.Mar.L. & Com. 149 (2003); Sonenshein, Impeaching the Hearsay Declarant, 74 Temp.L.Rev. 163 (2001).

3. *Rule 806—Implications of the impeachment rationale.* Rule 806 treats the declarant as a witness when a hearsay statement is admitted. If the statement is not admitted for its truth, such as to explain why the person hearing the statement took an action, impeachment of the declarant is not appropriate. See United States v. Arthur Andersen, LLP, 374 F.3d 281, 292 (5th Cir.2004). Conversely, use of prior testimonial statements for the limited purpose of impeaching the declarant under Rule 806 should constitute an exception to the Confrontation Clause under Crawford v. Washington, 541 U.S. 36, 59 n.9 (2004) (recognizing an exception to the confrontation right when statements are not admitted for their truth); Le v. State, 913 So.2d 913, 940–43 (Miss.2005) (applying this principle).

CHAPTER 15[1]

PRIVATE PRIVILEGES

■ ■ ■

A. INTRODUCTION

STATE V. 62.96247 ACRES OF LAND
Superior Court of Delaware, 1963.
193 A.2d 799.

LYNCH, JUDGE.

* * *

There are many exclusionary rules of evidence that are intended to withhold evidence which is regarded as unreliable or regarded as prejudicial or misleading, but rules of privileged communications have no such purpose. Such rules of privilege preclude the consideration of competent evidence which could aid in determining the outcome of a case, and privilege in no way can be justified as a means of promoting a fair settlement of disputes.

Privileges have been traced to the Roman law, where the basis for exclusion was the general moral duty not to violate the underlying fidelity upon which the protected relation was built.[2]

At early common law, the obligations of honor among gentlemen were advanced as the basis for maintaining silence[3], however, in 1776 the House of Lords made it clear that the communicant was the holder of the privilege and the policy was to protect his interests.[4] Some courts have

---

[1] Throughout this chapter some footnotes from the cases and materials have been omitted; others have been renumbered. [Ed.]

[2] Radin, The Privilege of Confidential Communication Between Lawyer and Client, 16 Calif.L.Rev. 487 (1928).

It was written long ago, Gospel of St. Matthew, Chap. 6, 24th verse:

> "No man can serve two masters; for either he will hate the one, and love the other; or else he will hold to the one, and despise the other. * * * "

[3] 8 Wigmore, Evidence, § 2286 (3d Ed. 1940).

[4] Duchess of Kingston's Case, 20 How.St.Tr. 586; Notable British Trial Series (Melville ed. 1927); see also City and County of San Francisco v. Superior Court, 37 Cal.2d 227, 231 P.2d 26, 25 A.L.R.2d 1418 (1951) (to preclude the humiliation of the patient that might follow disclosure of his ailments); Woernley v. Electromatic Typewriters, 271 N.Y. 228, 2 N.E.2d 638 (1936) (to prevent the physician from disclosing information which might result in humiliation, embarrassment, or disgrace to the patient); Annesley v. Earl of Anglesea, 17 How.St.Tr. 1139, 1225 (1743) (inability of client to carry on his own legal business).

justified a particular privilege in the interest of justice,[5] public health[6] or some similar goal.[7]

Thus, the duty of the confidant of nondisclosure of confidential communications is imposed to protect the reliance interest of the communicant, with an assent of the community. This reliance interest is protected because such protection will encourage certain communications. Encouraging these communications is desirable because the communications are necessary for the maintenance of certain relationships. It is socially desirable to foster the protected relationships because other beneficial results are achieved, such as the promotion of justice, public health and social stability. These goals are promoted in furtherance of a well-organized, peaceful society, which in turn is considered necessary for human survival.

NOTE AND QUESTIONS

The foregoing statement is a succinct summarization of the generally accepted concept underlying the recognition of relational privileges in the present day. It is a concept that has proved strongly attractive to American legislators (though somewhat less to American judges) and a greater or lesser number of privileges adorn the statute books of every state.

How effective is an evidentiary privilege likely to be in promoting the types of confidences that society deems desirable? It is doubtful whether anyone can, or at least should, feel confident in answering this question since a satisfactory answer is arguably discoverable only through the use of empirical research techniques that have only begun to be applied to the problem. In the face of this uncertainty might it be argued that at least some of the currently widely recognized privileges actually should be viewed as resting on some other alternative basis?

The Federal Rules of Evidence, as proposed by the Supreme Court, Prop. Fed.R.Evid., 56 F.R.D. 183 (1973), contained a set of rules on privilege that attempted to codify several well-entrenched common law privileges while rejecting others either that were fixtures of the common law or of the statutory schemes of most states. Specifically, the proposed rules codified the private privileges concerning communications between attorney and client,

---

[5] Anderson v. Bank of British Columbia, 2 Ch.D. 644 (1876); Greenough v. Gaskell, 1 Myl. & K. 98, 103 (1833) ("But it is out of regard to the interests of justice, which cannot be upholden, and to the administration of justice, which cannot go on without the aid of men skilled in jurisprudence * * *.")

[6] "To open the door to the disclosure of secrets revealed on the sickbed, or when consulting a physician, would destroy confidence between the physician and the patient, and, it is easy to see, might tend very much to prevent the advantages and benefits which flow from this confidential relationship." Edington v. Mutual Life Ins. Co., 67 N.Y. 185, 194 (1876) [sic].

[7] " * * * the reason of the rule for excluding the confidences between husband and wife * * * is found to rest in that public policy that seeks to preserve inviolate the peace, good order, and limitless confidence between the heads of the family circle so necessary to every well-ordered civilized society." Mercer v. State, 40 Fla. 216, 227, 24 So. 154, 157 (1898).

psychotherapist and patient, spousal testimony, and to clergy, as well as several privileges concerning governmental activities. Glaringly absent from the proposed rules were privileges for marital communications and for communications generally between physicians and patients. Congress ultimately rejected the codification and substituted current Rule 501, which leaves the development of privileges either to the federal common law, or, where state law supplies the rule of decision, to state law.

Among the many criticisms of the privilege rules proposed by the Supreme Court were those directed to the elimination of the privileges referred to above. As part of his criticism of the Supreme Court proposals, one prominent legal academic set forth a rationale for privileges significantly different from the traditional one:

BLACK, THE MARITAL AND PHYSICIAN PRIVILEGES—A REPRINT OF A LETTER TO A CONGRESSMAN[8]
1975 Duke Law Journal 45, 48, 49–50.

Let me first consider the near-elimination of the marital-confidentiality privilege (Rule 505). There remains a narrow privilege in proceedings where one spouse is a criminal defendant. Aside from this, the meaning of the Rule (made entirely clear in the Advisory Committee's comments) is that, however intimate, however private, however embarrassing may be a disclosure by one spouse to another, or some fact discovered, within the privacies of marriage, by one spouse about another, that disclosure or fact can be wrung from the spouse under penalty of being held in contempt of court, if it is thought barely relevant to the issues in anybody's lawsuit for breach of a contract to sell a carload of apples. It ought to be enough to say of such a rule that it could easily— even often—force any decent person—anybody any of us would want to associate with—either to lie or to go to jail. No rule can be good that has that consequence—that compels the decent and honorable to evade or to disobey it. It seems clear to me that this Rule trenches on the area of marital privacy so staunchly defended by the Supreme Court, and especially by the late Mr. Justice Harlan's concurrence in *Griswold v. Connecticut*, [381 U.S. 479 (1965)]; certainly it is arguable that it does so. Even if *Griswold* had never been decided, it would be an entirely viable contention that the "scheme of ordered liberty," sanctioned in much earlier cases, forbade this nearly complete destruction of the privacy of marriage, in the interest of the conduct of ordinary litigation.

* * *

Hardly less grave is the invasion of central human privacy involved in the root-and-branch abolition of the physician-patient privilege. The question here is not only whether people might be discouraged from making full communication to physicians, though it seems flatly

---

8 Copyright © 1975 Duke Law Journal. Reprinted by permission. [Ed.]

impossible that this would not sometimes happen—a consideration which would in itself be enough to make incomprehensible the absolute subordination of this privacy interest to any trivial interest arising in litigation. But evaluation of a rule like this entails not only a guess as to what conduct it will motivate, but also an estimate of its intrinsic decency. All of us would consider it indecent for a doctor, in the course, say, of a television interview, or even a textbook, to tell all he knows, naming names, about patients who have been treated by him. Why does this judgment of decency altogether vanish from sight, sink to absolute zero, as soon as somebody files any kind of a non-demurrable complaint in a federal court? Here, again, can a rule be a good one when the ethical doctor *must* violate it, or hedge, or evade?

NOTE AND QUESTIONS

Is Professor Black's articulation of a privacy rationale the only reasonable alternative to the utilitarian rationale set forth by Judge Lynch, above, that can be put forward as the basis for the law of evidentiary privileges? Consider the lively debate between the student editors of the Harvard Law Review, Comment, Developments in the Law—Privileged Communications, 98 Harv.L.Rev. 1450 (1985), and the authors of Wright & Graham, Federal Practice and Procedure § 5422 (2012).

For a thorough and thoughtful discussion of the various rationales for evidence privileges, see Imwinkelried, The New Wigmore: Evidentiary Privileges ch. 5 (2d ed. 2010). Professor Imwinkelried suggests a humanistic theory of privilege that emphasizes autonomy—the creation of privacy enclaves with particular types of consultants to enable the citizen to make more intelligent, independent life preference choices. Id. § 5.3.3.

Consider whether the comments of Professor Black apply to any or all of the privileges considered in this chapter. If such considerations are applicable to existing privileges, do they also suggest the creation of privileges not so commonly recognized such as communications between parents and children? How about communications between lovers or good friends?

Professor Black's argument assumes a compulsion to testify in a whole range of legal actions, including the most mundane. Should the same considerations apply in cases involving serious crime or devastating personal injury? Should the value of privilege, whether based on considerations of privacy, protection of a relationship or any other reason, be weighed against the particularized need in a particular litigation? What effect would such an uncertain privilege have on the considerations giving rise to the privilege?

B. HUSBAND–WIFE

TRAMMEL V. UNITED STATES

Supreme Court of the United States, 1980.
445 U.S. 40.

MR. CHIEF JUSTICE BURGER delivered the opinion of the Court.

We granted certiorari to consider whether an accused may invoke the privilege against adverse spousal testimony so as to exclude the voluntary testimony of his wife. 440 U.S. 934 (1979). This calls for a re-examination of Hawkins v. United States, 358 U.S. 74 (1958).

I

On March 10, 1976, petitioner Otis Trammel was indicted with two others, Edwin Lee Roberts and Joseph Freeman, for importing heroin into the United States from Thailand and the Philippine Islands and for conspiracy to import heroin in violation of 21 U.S.C.A. §§ 952(a), 962(a), and 963. The indictment also named six unindicted co-conspirators, including petitioner's wife Elizabeth Ann Trammel.

According to the indictment, petitioner and his wife flew from the Philippines to California in August 1975, carrying with them a quantity of heroin. Freeman and Roberts assisted them in its distribution. Elizabeth Trammel then travelled to Thailand where she purchased another supply of the drug. On November 3, 1975, with four ounces of heroin on her person, she boarded a plane for the United States. During a routine customs search in Hawaii, she was searched, the heroin was discovered, and she was arrested. After discussions with Drug Enforcement Administration agents, she agreed to cooperate with the Government.

Prior to trial on this indictment, petitioner moved to sever his case from that of Roberts and Freeman. He advised the court that the Government intended to call his wife as an adverse witness and asserted his claim to a privilege to prevent her from testifying against him. At a hearing on the motion, Mrs. Trammel was called as a Government witness under a grant of use immunity. She testified that she and petitioner were married in May 1975 and that they remained married.[9] She explained that her cooperation with the Government was based on assurances that she would be given lenient treatment.[10] She then described, in considerable detail, her role and that of her husband in the heroin distribution conspiracy.

---

[9] In response to the question whether divorce was contemplated, Mrs. Trammel testified that her husband had said that "I would go my way and he would go his." (App., at 27).

[10] The Government represents to the Court that Elizabeth Trammel has not been prosecuted for her role in the conspiracy.

After hearing this testimony, the District Court ruled that Mrs. Trammel could testify in support of the Government's case to any act she observed during the marriage and to any communication "made in the presence of a third person"; however, confidential communications between petitioner and his wife were held to be privileged and inadmissible. The motion to sever was denied.

At trial, Elizabeth Trammel testified within the limits of the court's pretrial ruling; her testimony, as the Government concedes, constituted virtually its entire case against petitioner. He was found guilty on both the substantive and conspiracy charges and sentenced to an indeterminate term of years pursuant to the Federal Youth Corrections Act, 18 U.S.C.A. § 5010(b).

In the Court of Appeals petitioner's only claim of error was that the admission of the adverse testimony of his wife, over his objection, contravened this Court's teaching in Hawkins v. United States, 358 U.S. 74 (1958), and therefore constituted reversible error. The Court of Appeals rejected this contention. It concluded that *Hawkins* did not prohibit "the voluntary testimony of a spouse who appears as an unindicted co-conspirator under grant of immunity from the Government in return for her testimony." 583 F.2d 1166, 1168 (C.A.10 1978).

II

The privilege claimed by petitioner has ancient roots. Writing in 1628, Lord Coke observed that "it hath been resolved by the Justices that a wife cannot be produced either against or for her husband." 1 Coke, A Commentarie upon Littleton 6b (1628). See, generally, 8 J. Wigmore, Evidence § 2227, (McNaughton rev. 1961). This spousal disqualification sprang from two canons of medieval jurisprudence: first, the rule that an accused was not permitted to testify in his own behalf because of his interest in the proceeding; second, the concept that husband and wife were one, and that since the woman had no recognized separate legal existence, the husband was that one. From those two now long-abandoned doctrines, it followed that what was inadmissible from the lips of the defendant-husband was also inadmissible from his wife.

Despite its medieval origins, this rule of spousal disqualification remained intact in most common-law jurisdictions well into the 19th century. See 8 Wigmore, § 2333. It was applied by this Court in Stein v. Bowman, 10 L.Ed. 129, 13 Pet. 209, 220–223 (1839), in Graves v. United States, 150 U.S. 118 (1893), and again in Jin Fuey Moy v. United States, 254 U.S. 189, 195 (1920), where it was deemed so well established a proposition as to "hardly requir[e] mention." Indeed, it was not until 1933, in Funk v. United States, 290 U.S. 371, that this Court abolished the testimonial disqualification in the federal courts, so as to permit the spouse of a defendant to testify in the defendant's behalf. *Funk,* however,

left undisturbed the rule that either spouse could prevent the other from]
giving adverse testimony. Id., at 373. The rule thus evolved into one of
privilege rather than one of absolute disqualification. See J. Maguire,
Evidence, Common Sense and Common Law, at 78–92 (1947).

The modern justification for this privilege against adverse spousal]
testimony is its perceived role in fostering the harmony and sanctity of
the marriage relationship. Notwithstanding this benign purpose, the rule
was sharply criticized. Professor Wigmore termed it "the merest
anachronism in legal theory and an indefensible obstruction to truth in
practice." 8 Wigmore, § 2228, at 221. The Committee on the Improvement
of the Law of Evidence of the American Bar Association called for its
abolition. 63 American Bar Association Reports, at 594–595 (1938). In its
place, Wigmore and others suggested a privilege protecting only private
marital communications, modeled on the privilege between priest and
penitent, attorney and client, and physician and patient. See 8 Wigmore,
§ 2332 et seq.[11]

These criticisms influenced the American Law Institute, which, in its
1942 Model Code of Evidence advocated a privilege for marital
confidences, but expressly rejected a rule vesting in the defendant the
right to exclude all adverse testimony of his spouse. See American Law
Institute, Model Code of Evidence, Rule 215 (1942). In 1953 the Uniform
Rules of Evidence, drafted by the National Conference of Commissioners
on Uniform State Laws, followed a similar course; it limited the privilege
to confidential communications and "abolishe[d] the rule, still existing in
some states, and largely a sentimental relic, of not requiring one spouse
to testify against the other in a criminal action." See Rule 23(2) and
comments. Several state legislatures enacted similarly patterned
provisions into law.

In Hawkins v. United States, 358 U.S. 74 (1958), this Court
considered the continued vitality of the privilege against adverse spousal
testimony in the federal courts. There the District Court had permitted
petitioner's wife, over his objection, to testify against him. With one
questioning concurring opinion, the Court held the wife's testimony
inadmissible; it took note of the critical comments that the common-law
rule had engendered, id., at 76, and n.4, but chose not to abandon it. Also
rejected was the Government's suggestion that the Court modify the
privilege by vesting it in the witness spouse, with freedom to testify or not
independent of the defendant's control. The Court viewed this proposed
modification as antithetical to the widespread belief, evidenced in the

---

[11] This Court recognized just such a confidential marital communications privilege in
Wolfle v. United States, 291 U.S. 7 (1934), and in Blau v. United States, 340 U.S. 332 (1951). In
neither case, however, did the Court adopt the Wigmore view that the communications privilege
be substituted *in place of* the privilege against adverse spousal testimony. The privilege as to
confidential marital communications is not at issue in the instant case; accordingly, our holding
today does not disturb *Wolfle* and *Blau*.

rules then in effect in a majority of the States and in England, "that the law should not force or encourage testimony which might alienate husband and wife, or further inflame existing domestic differences." Id., at 79.

Hawkins, then, left the federal privilege for adverse spousal testimony where it found it, continuing "a rule which bars the testimony *a.* of one spouse against the other unless both consent." Id., at 78. Accord, Wyatt v. United States, 362 U.S. 525, 528 (1960).[12] However, in so doing, the Court made clear that its decision was not meant to "foreclose *b.* whatever changes in the rule may eventually be dictated by 'reason and experience.'" 358 U.S., at 79.

III

A

B . The Federal Rules of Evidence acknowledge the authority of the federal courts to continue the evolutionary development of testimonial privileges in federal criminal trials "governed by the principles of the common law as they may be interpreted * * * in the light of reason and experience." Fed.Rule Evid. 501. Cf. Wolfle v. United States, supra, 291 U.S., at 12 (1934). The general mandate of Rule 501 was substituted by the Congress for a set of privilege rules drafted by the Judicial Conference Advisory Committee on Rules of Evidence and approved by the Judicial Conference of the United States and by this Court. That proposal defined nine specific privileges, including a husband-wife privilege which would have codified the *Hawkins* rule and eliminated the privilege for confidential marital communications. See Fed.Rule of Evid., Proposed Rule 505. In rejecting the proposed rules and enacting Rule 501, Congress manifested an affirmative intention not to freeze the law of privilege. Its purpose rather was to "provide the courts with the flexibility to develop rules of privilege on a case-by-case basis," 120 Cong.Rec. 40891 (1974) (statement of Rep. Hungate), and to leave the door open to change. See also S.Rep. No. 93–1277, 93d Cong., 2d Sess., 11 (1974); H.R.Rep. No. 93–650, 93d Cong., 1st Sess., 8 (1973),[13] U.S.Code Cong. & Admin.News 1974, p. 7051.

---

[12] The decision in *Wyatt* recognized an exception to *Hawkins* for cases in which one spouse commits a crime against the other. 362 U.S., at 526. This exception, placed on the ground of necessity, was a longstanding one at common law. See *Lord Audley's Case,* 123 Eng.Rep. 1140 (1931); 8 Wigmore § 2239. It has been expanded since then to include crimes against the spouse's property, see Herman v. United States, 220 F.2d 219, 226 (C.A.4 1955), and in recent years crimes against children of either spouse, United States v. Allery, 526 F.2d 1362 (C.A.8 1975). Similar exceptions have been found to the confidential marital communications privilege. See 8 Wigmore, § 2338.

[13] Petitioner's reliance on 28 U.S.C.A. § 2076 for the proposition that this Court is without power to reconsider *Hawkins* is ill founded. That provision limits this Court's *statutory* rulemaking authority by providing that rules "creating, abolishing, or modifying a privilege shall have no force or effect unless * * * approved by act of Congress." It was enacted principally to insure that state rules of privilege would apply in diversity jurisdiction cases unless Congress

Although Rule 501 confirms the authority of the federal courts to reconsider the continued validity of the *Hawkins* rule, the long history of the privilege suggests that it ought not to be casually cast aside. That the privilege is one affecting marriage, home, and family relationships—already subject to much erosion in our day—also counsels caution. At the same time we cannot escape the reality that the law on occasion adheres to doctrinal concepts long after the reasons which gave them birth have disappeared and after experience suggests the need for change. This was recognized in *Funk* where the Court "decline[d] to enforce * * * ancient rule[s] of the common law under conditions as they now exist." 290 U.S., at 382. For, as Mr. Justice Black admonished in another setting, "[w]hen precedent and precedent alone is all the argument that can be made to support a court-fashioned rule, it is time for the rule's creator to destroy it." Francis v. Southern Pacific Co., 333 U.S. 445, 471 (1948) (Black, J., dissenting).

B   *C.*

[Since 1958, when *Hawkins* was decided, support for the privilege against adverse spousal testimony has been eroded further] Thirty-one jurisdictions, including Alaska and Hawaii, then allowed an accused a privilege to prevent adverse spousal testimony. 358 U.S., at 81, n.3, (Stewart, J., concurring). The number has now declined to 24.[14] In 1974, the National Conference on Uniform States Laws revised its Uniform Rules of Evidence, but again rejected the *Hawkins* rule in favor of a limited privilege for confidential communications. See Uniform Rules of Evidence, Rule 504. That proposed rule has been enacted in Arkansas, North Dakota, and Oklahoma—each of which in 1958 permitted an accused to exclude adverse spousal testimony.[15] The trend in state law

---

authorized otherwise. In Rule 501 Congress makes clear that § 2076 was not intended to prevent the federal courts from developing testimonial privilege law in federal criminal cases on a case-by-case basis "in light of reason and experience"; indeed Congress encouraged such development.

[14] Eight states provide that one spouse is incompetent to testify against the other in a criminal proceeding * * *. Sixteen states provide a privilege against adverse spousal testimony and vest the privilege in both spouses or in the defendant-spouse alone * * *. Nine states entitle the witness-spouse alone to assert a privilege against adverse spousal testimony * * *. The remaining 17 states have abolished the privilege in criminal cases * * *.

In 1901, Congress enacted a rule of evidence for the District of Columbia that made husband and wife "competent but not compellable to testify for or against each other," except as to confidential communications. This provision, which vests the privilege against adverse spousal testimony in the witness spouse, remains in effect.* * *

[15] In 1965, California took the privilege from the defendant-spouse and vested it in the witness-spouse, accepting a study commission recommendation that the "latter [was] more likely than the former to determine whether or not to claim the privilege on the basis of the probable effect on the marital relationship." See Cal.Evid.Code §§ 970–973 and 1 California Law Revision Commission, Recommendation and Study relating to The Marital "For or Against" Testimonial Privilege at F–5 (1956). * * *

Support for the common-law rule has also diminished in England. In 1972 a study group there proposed giving the privilege to the witness-spouse, on the ground that "if [the wife] is willing to give evidence * * * the law would be showing excessive concern for the preservation of toward divesting the accused of the privilege to bar adverse spousal testimony has special relevance because the law of marriage and domestic relations are concerns traditionally reserved to the states. See Sosna v. Iowa, 419 U.S. 393, 404 (1975). Scholarly criticism of the *Hawkins* rule has also continued unabated.

C

Testimonial exclusionary rules and privileges contravene the fundamental principle that "the public * * * has a right to every man's evidence." United States v. Bryan, 339 U.S. 323, 331 (1950). As such, they must be strictly construed and accepted "only to the very limited extent that permitting a refusal to testify or excluding relevant evidence has a public good transcending the normally predominant principle of utilizing all rational means for ascertaining truth." Elkins v. United States, 364 U.S. 206, 234 (1960) (Frankfurter, J., dissenting). Accord, United States v. Nixon, 418 U.S. 683, 709–710 (1974). Here we must decide whether the privilege against adverse spousal testimony promotes sufficiently important interests to outweigh the need for probative evidence in the administration of criminal justice.

It is essential to remember that the *Hawkins* privilege is not needed to protect information privately disclosed between husband and wife in the confidence of the marital relationship—once described by this Court as "the best solace of human existence." Stein v. Bowman, 13 Pet., at 223. Those confidences are privileged under the independent rule protecting confidential marital communications. Blau v. United States, 340 U.S. 332 (1951). The *Hawkins* privilege is invoked, not to exclude private marital communications, but rather to exclude evidence of criminal acts and of communications made in the presence of third persons.

No other testimonial privilege sweeps so broadly. The privileges between priest and penitent, attorney and client, and physician and patient limit protection to private communications. These privileges are rooted in the imperative need for confidence and trust. The priest-penitent privilege recognizes the human need to disclose to a spiritual counselor, in total and absolute confidence, what are believed to be flawed acts or thoughts and to receive priestly consolation and guidance in return. The lawyer-client privilege rests on the need for the advocate and counselor to know all that relates to the client's reasons for seeking representation if the professional mission is to be carried out. Similarly, the physician must know all that a patient can articulate in order to identify and to treat disease; barriers to full disclosure would impair diagnosis and treatment.

---

marital harmony if it were to say she must not do so." Criminal Law Revision Committee, Eleventh Report Evidence (General), at 93.

The *Hawkins* rule stands in marked contrast to these three privileges. Its protection is not limited to confidential communications; rather it permits an accused to exclude all adverse spousal testimony. As Jeremy Bentham observed more than a century and a half ago, such a privilege goes far beyond making "every man's house his castle," and permits a person to convert his house into "a den of thieves." 5 Rationale of Judicial Evidence 340 (1827). It "secures, to every man, one safe and unquestionable and ever ready accomplice for every imaginable crime." Id., at 338.

The ancient foundations for so sweeping a privilege have long since disappeared. Nowhere in the common-law world—indeed in any modern society—is a woman regarded as chattel or demeaned by denial of a separate legal identity and the dignity associated with recognition as a whole human being. Chip by chip, over the years those archaic notions have been cast aside so that "[n]o longer is the female destined solely for the home and the rearing of the family, and only the male for the marketplace and the world of ideas." Stanton v. Stanton, 421 U.S. 7, 14, 15 (1975).

The contemporary justification for affording an accused such a privilege is also unpersuasive. When one spouse is willing to testify against the other in a criminal proceeding—whatever the motivation— their relationship is almost certainly in disrepair; there is probably little in the way of marital harmony for the privilege to preserve. In these circumstances, a rule of evidence that permits an accused to prevent adverse spousal testimony seems far more likely to frustrate justice than to foster family peace.[16] Indeed, there is reason to believe that vesting the privilege in the accused could actually undermine the marital relationship. For example, in a case such as this the Government is unlikely to offer a wife immunity and lenient treatment if it knows that her husband can prevent her from giving adverse testimony. If the Government is dissuaded from making such an offer, the privilege can have the untoward effect of permitting one spouse to escape justice at the expense of the other. It hardly seems conducive to the preservation of the marital relation to place a wife in jeopardy solely by virtue of her husband's control over her testimony.

IV

Our consideration of the foundations for the privilege and its history satisfy us that "reason and experience" no longer justify so sweeping a rule as that found acceptable by the Court in *Hawkins*. Accordingly, we

---

[16] It is argued that abolishing the privilege will permit the Government to come between husband and wife, pitting one against the other. That, too, misses the mark. Neither *Hawkins,* nor any other privilege, prevents the Government from enlisting one spouse to give information concerning the other or to aid in the other's apprehension. It is only the spouse's testimony in the courtroom that is prohibited.

conclude that the existing rule should be modified so that the witness spouse alone has a privilege to refuse to testify adversely; the witness may be neither compelled to testify nor foreclosed from testifying. This modification—vesting the privilege in the witness spouse—furthers the important public interest in marital harmony without unduly burdening legitimate law enforcement needs.

Here, petitioner's spouse chose to testify against him. That she did so after a grant of immunity and assurances of lenient treatment does not render her testimony involuntary. Cf. Bordenkircher v. Hayes, 434 U.S. 357 (1978). Accordingly, the District Court and the Court of Appeals were correct in rejecting petitioner's claim of privilege, and the judgment of the Court of Appeals is affirmed.

Affirmed.

MR. JUSTICE STEWART, concurring in the judgment.

Although agreeing with much of what the Court has to say, I cannot join an opinion that implies that "reason and experience" have worked a vast change since the *Hawkins* case was decided in 1958. In that case the Court upheld the privilege of a defendant in a criminal case to prevent adverse spousal testimony, in an all-but-unanimous opinion, by Mr. Justice Black. Today the Court, in another all-but-unanimous opinion, obliterates that privilege because of the purported change in perception that "reason and experience" have wrought.

The fact of the matter is that the Court in this case simply accepts the very same arguments that the Court rejected when the Government first made them in the *Hawkins* case in 1958. I thought those arguments were valid then, and I think so now.

The Court is correct when it says that "[t]he ancient foundations for so sweeping a privilege have long since disappeared." * * * But those foundations had disappeared well before 1958; their disappearance certainly did not occur in the few years that have elapsed between the *Hawkins* decision and this one. To paraphrase what Mr. Justice Jackson once said in another context, there is reason to believe that today's opinion of the Court will be of greater interest to students of human psychology than to students of law.

NOTES AND QUESTIONS

1. *"Marrying the witness into silence."* See also the English case of Hoskyn v. Metropolitan Police Comm'r, 2 W.L.R. 695 (H.L.(E.) 1978), where the House of Lords found a victim who had married the accused two days before trial was not compellable to testify. As illustrated by a case such as *Hoskyn*, the *Trammel* decision does not of itself render impossible the time-honored practice of "marrying the witness into silence." Should this practice

be prevented and, if so, by what rule? Proposed Federal Rule 505, which would have codified the spousal testimony privilege, excepted matters occurring prior to marriage. See also United States v. Clark, 712 F.2d 299 (7th Cir.1983). Uniform Rule 504, dealing with the same privilege, contains no such limitation, and the holding of the *Clark* case has been rejected, at least in dicta, by the Seventh Circuit. See United States v. Byrd, 750 F.2d 585, 590 (7th Cir.1984); United States v. Lofton, 957 F.2d 476, 477 (7th Cir.1992). See also A.B. v. United States, 24 F.Supp.2d 488 (D.Md.1998) (noting that *Clark* has been relegated to the status of an isolated artifact by later Seventh Circuit cases). Should the rule be different if the marriage is a sham? See Osborne v. State, 623 P.2d 784 (Alaska 1981); Annot., 13 A.L.R.4th 1305.

2.   *Requirement of a valid marriage.* Given the rationale for excluding adverse spousal testimony, should a valid marriage constitute a *sine qua non* of the privilege? Most courts have held that it should. See, e.g., United States v. Snyder, 707 F.2d 139 (5th Cir.1983); United States v. Lustig, 555 F.2d 737 (9th Cir.1977). By whom and by what standard should the existence of marriage be ascertained? See Chapter 1, supra.

3.   *Exceptions.* Various exceptions exist to the spousal privilege. Some, but not all, courts recognize an exception where the spouses were joint participants in the crime. Compare United States v. Van Drunen, 501 F.2d 1393 (7th Cir.1974) (joint participants exception to privilege), with United States v. Ramos–Oseguera, 120 F.3d 1028 (9th Cir.1997) (no joint participants exception). Most jurisdictions provide that the privilege does not exist where one spouse is charged with a crime against the person or property of the other or against a child of either. See, e.g., United States v. Allery, 526 F.2d 1362 (8th Cir.1975).

4.   *Scholarly debate.* Some commentators advocate abolition of the adverse spousal testimony privilege in its entirety. See Medine, The Adverse Testimony Privilege: Time to Dispose of a Sentimental Relic, 67 Or.L.Rev. 519 (1988). Others take an opposite tack, believing that the Court went too far in *Trammel* in precluding the defendant/spouse from claiming the privilege. See Mullane, *Trammel v. United States*: Bad History, Bad Policy, and Bad Law, 47 Me.L.Rev. 105 (1995). Still others see the existence or nonexistence of the privilege as an important cultural statement of how our society views marriage and call for a continued study of the issue. See Regan, Spousal Privilege and the Meanings of Marriage, 81 Va.L.Rev. 2045 (1995). See also Ortiz, Making Marriage, 81 Va.L.Rev. 2157 (1995), and Williams, The Adverse Testimony Privilege, Inalienable Entitlements, and the "Internal Stance:" A Response to Professor Regan, 81 Va.L.Rev. 2167 (1995).

5.   *The other privilege.* As indicated in *Trammel*, the spousal or testimonial privilege involved in that case is a very different rule from the rule that provides a privilege for confidential communications made during the marriage. The next case discusses that other privilege.

UNITED STATES v. ESTES

United States Court of Appeals, Second Circuit, 1986.
793 F.2d 465.

VAN GRAAFEILAND, CIRCUIT JUDGE:

Kenneth Estes appeals from a judgment of the United States District Court for the District of Vermont convicting him, after a jury trial before Judge Franklin S. Billings, Jr., of violating 18 U.S.C. § 1623 by testifying falsely before a grand jury concerning his involvement in a theft. For reasons hereafter assigned, we reverse the conviction and remand for a new trial.

Appellant's principal contention on appeal is that testimony of his former wife, Lydia, concerning confidential communications between them was introduced erroneously before both the grand jury and the trial jury. * * *

On February 23, 1982, the Purolator Armored Car Service, for whom appellant worked as a driver-guard, was the victim of a $55,000 theft. Appellant's estranged wife, Lydia, testified willingly before the grand jury and at trial that appellant returned home on the day of the theft carrying a motorcycle bag full of money. In response to Lydia's inquiry, appellant told her that he had taken the money from Purolator. Lydia also testified that she helped appellant count the money and hide a portion of it behind a stair panel. At a subsequent time, she "laundered" some of the money by exchanging small bills for larger ones.

Appellant contends that all of Lydia's testimony should have been excluded on the ground that it involved the disclosure of confidential communications between them. The district court rejected this contention, citing cases from other circuits which hold that "confidential marital communications concerning ongoing criminal activity are not protected by the privilege" and opining that this is likely to be the rule followed by the Second Circuit. * * * The district court's very statement of the rule shows, however, that it does not apply to the most damning testimony given by Lydia, viz., that appellant brought home a bag of money and told her that he had taken it from the Purolator truck.

[At that time, the theft of the money had been completed and Lydia's involvement could be only as an accessory after the fact] *United States v. Barlow,* 470 F.2d 1245, 1249, 1252–53 (D.C.Cir.1972). Lydia could not become such an accessory until she knew that the theft had taken place. *Id.* at 1252; 18 U.S.C. 3. The communication to her of that knowledge was a necessary precursor to her involvement and therefore could not have been made as part of an ongoing joint criminal activity. Under the normal evidentiary rule applicable to confidential marital communications, this portion of Lydia's testimony should not have been admitted. *See Blau v. United States,* 340 U.S. 332 * * * (1951). To the extent that *United States* *v. Neal,* 743 F.2d 1441 (10th Cir.1984) * * * (1985), the case upon which the Government places main reliance, holds to the contrary, we decline to follow it.

* * *

Normally, the confidential communication privilege extends only to utterances and not to acts. *Pereira v. United States,* 347 U.S. 1, 6 * * * (1954); * * * Testimony concerning a spouse's conduct can be precluded upon the spouse's challenge only in the rare instances where the conduct was intended to convey a confidential message from the actor to the observer. *United States v. Mitchell,* 137 F.2d 1006, 1009 (2d Cir.), *aff'd on reh'g,* 138 F.2d 831 (1943); * * * *United States v. Lewis,* 433 F.2d 1146, 1150–51 (D.C. Cir.1970) (per curiam). The counting, hiding and laundering of the money conveyed no confidential message from appellant to Lydia. Acts do not become privileged communications simply because they are performed in the presence of the actor's spouse. *United States v. Lustig,* 555 F.2d 737, 748 n.13 (9th Cir.1977). "Nor does it appear that the essential qualities of communication and confidentiality flow automatically from the fact that the act seen by the other spouse is one that connotes criminal conduct." *United States v. Lewis, supra,* 433 F.2d at 1151. Lydia's testimony concerning the handling and disposition of the money, much of which was done by Lydia herself, was properly heard by both the grand and petit juries.

Assuming for the argument that one or more of appellant's acts which followed the original disclosure of his theft might be construed as additional confidential communications of wrongdoing, we agree with so much of the opinion in *United States v. Neal, supra,* 743 F.2d at 1446–47, as would support the district court's holding that Lydia's testimony concerning those acts was admissible as evidence of joint criminal activity. There are a number of cases, including *In re Grand Jury Subpoena United States,* 755 F.2d 1022 (2d Cir.1985) * * *, which refuse to apply the "partnership in crime" exception to the marital testimonial privilege. However, because an accused cannot invoke marital testimonial privilege to prevent his or her spouse from testifying, *Trammel v. United States,* 445 U.S. 40 * * * (1980), those cases have little precedential significance where the spouse chooses to testify voluntarily. Although an accused does have the right to object to spousal testimony which violates confidential communications privilege, a number of circuits, in addition to the Tenth Circuit which decided *United States v. Neal, supra,* refuse to recognize that right where the testimony is not given under compulsion and the communications in question were made in furtherance of unlawful joint criminal activity. *See, e.g., United States v. Sims,* 755 F.2d 1239, 1240–43 (6th Cir.1985) * * *. Indeed, our own decision in *In re Grand Jury Subpoena United States, supra,* suggests that a joint participation exception makes sense in the context of the marital confidential communications privilege. 755 F.2d at 1027.

There is sound reasoning behind these holdings. As we stated in *In re Grand Jury Subpoena United States, supra,* 755 F.2d 1022, public policy may militate against subjecting a marriage to the possible disruptive influence of compelled adverse spousal testimony. However, testimonial privileges "must be strictly construed and accepted 'only to the very limited extent that permitting a refusal to testify or excluding relevant evidence has a public good transcending the normally predominant principle of utilizing all rational means for ascertaining truth.' " *Trammel v. United States, supra,* 445 U.S. at 50 * * * (quoting *Elkins v. United States,* 364 U.S. 206, 234 * * * (1960) (Frankfurter, J., dissenting)). The above-cited courts which recognize the "partnership in crime" exception to the confidential communication privilege believe that greater public good will result from permitting the spouse of an accused to testify willingly concerning their joint criminal activities than would come from permitting the accused to erect a roadblock against the search for truth. We agree.

For all the reasons above stated, we hold that Lydia's testimony concerning appellant's initial disclosure of his theft should not have been admitted but that it was not error to admit the balance of Lydia's testimony dealing with the handling and disposition of the stolen money.

* * *

The judgment of conviction is reversed and the matter is remanded to the district court with instructions to grant appellant a new trial.

NOTES AND QUESTIONS

1. *Difference from spousal testimony privilege.* In what respects does the privilege applied in the principal case differ from that recognized in *Trammel v. United States*? Would a *Trammel*-type privilege have been of any value to the defendant in the principal case?

2. *Acts as communications.* As to whether acts performed by one spouse come within the scope of a "communications" privilege, compare the holding of the principal case with Shepherd v. State, 277 N.E.2d 165 (Ind.1971) (communication privilege applicable to husband's observation of defendant's driving a car). Many courts support the more expansive view reflected in cases such as *Shepherd.* 1 McCormick, Evidence § 79 (7th ed. 2013). Cases are collected in Annot., 23 A.L.R.6th 1. Even in jurisdictions limiting the privilege to communications rather than acts, certain acts without words may be viewed as communications. See, e.g., United States v. Bahe, 128 F.3d 1440 (10th Cir.1997).

3. *Confidentiality.* In what instances will communications between spouses possess the confidentiality universally required for application of the

communications privilege? It is often stated that inter-spousal communications are "assumed" to be confidential, Wolfle v. United States, 291 U.S. 7 (1934), but it is clear from the decisions that a variety of factual patterns, if present, will destroy the presumption. Thus threats to harm or kill the spouse if he or she "talks" are frequently held incompatible with "reliance on the confidence which exists between husband and wife." See, e.g., People v. Dudley, 248 N.E.2d 860 (N.Y.1969). Similarly, the question whether privacy from eavesdropping was reasonably to be expected at the locus of the conversation may be determinative. North v. Superior Court, 502 P.2d 1305 (Cal.1972). The known presence of third persons generally precludes confidentiality, and this has been held true even where the third person is the minor child of the spouses. See, e.g., People v. Sanders, 457 N.E.2d 1241 (Ill.1983) (communication in presence of children, the eldest 13, not privileged). For additional cases, see Annot., 39 A.L.R.4th 480. See also Story, Twenty–First Century Pillow–Talk: Applicability of the Marital Communications Privilege to Electronic Mail, 58 S.C.L.Rev. 275 (2006).

4. *Revelations to third persons.* It will sometimes occur that a spouse, whose testimony would come within either the adverse spousal testimony privilege or the privilege for marital communications, has revealed matters to some other person. If otherwise admissible and unprivileged, would testimony from such a third person violate the adverse spousal testimony privilege? Wigmore believed that it should. See 8 Wigmore, Evidence § 2232, at 225–26 (McNaughton rev. 1961). See also Imwinkelried, The New Wigmore: Evidentiary Privileges § 6.6.5 (2d ed. 2010), where the author examines both sides of the issue, but ultimately reaches the same conclusion as Wigmore. But see United States v. Archer, 733 F.2d 354 (5th Cir.1984) (third party could testify to spouse's statement); State v. Burden, 841 P.2d 758 (Wash.1992) (same).

5. *Requirement of a valid marriage.* Like the privilege dealing with adverse spousal testimony, the marital communications privilege also requires a valid marriage. See 1 McCormick, Evidence § 81 (7th ed. 2013). But see Glover, Evidentiary Privileges for Cohabiting Parents: Protecting Children Inside and Outside of Marriage, 70 La.L.Rev. 751 (2010)(arguing for expanding the privilege to include unmarried cohabiting parents).

6. *Marital disharmony.* Should marital disharmony that has not yet resulted in a divorce decree serve to remove the privileged character of communications between the spouses? Compare United States v. Roberson, 859 F.2d 1376 (9th Cir.1988), with People v. Vermeulen, 438 N.W.2d 36 (Mich.1989). What problems arise under a rule that the privilege is terminated by marital discord short of divorce? See Blazek v. Superior Court, 869 P.2d 509 (Ariz.Ct.App.1994).

7. *Crime or fraud exception.* Should the marital communications privilege be qualified by a crime or fraud exception? Remember that some, but not all, courts engraft such an exception onto the adverse testimony privilege. See Note 3 following *Trammel v. United States.* Are there

differences between the rules that would call for the existence of such an exception in one privilege but not the other. See discussion in 2 Saltzburg, Martin & Capra, Federal Rules of Evidence Manual § 501.02[8], at 501–84—501–85 (10th ed. 2011). Many courts, including all federal circuits to address the question, have held that such an exception should apply to the marital communications privilege, although the test for determining when the exception applies has varied from circuit to circuit. See, e.g., United States v. Darif, 446 F.3d 701, 706–07 (7th Cir. 2006) (communications between husband and wife not privileged where both implicated in marriage fraud scheme); United States v. Hill, 967 F.2d 902 (3d Cir.1992) (commission of a crime in which both spouses are participants); United States v. Evans, 966 F.2d 398 (8th Cir.1992) (exception limited to communications regarding "patently illegal activity"). Does the creation of a crime or fraud exception effectively abolish the communications privilege? See United States v. Neal, 743 F.2d 1441, 1448 (10th Cir.1984) (Logan, J., concurring).

Uniform Rules of Evidence

RULE 504. SPOUSAL PRIVILEGE.

(a) Confidential communication. A communication is confidential if it is made privately by an individual to the individual's spouse and is not intended for disclosure to any other person.

(b) Marital communications. An individual has a privilege to refuse to testify and to prevent the individual's spouse or former spouse from testifying as to any confidential communication made by the individual to the spouse during their marriage. The privilege may be waived only by the individual holding the privilege or by the holder's guardian or conservator, or the individual's personal representative if the individual is deceased.

(c) Spousal testimony in criminal proceeding. The spouse of an accused in a criminal proceeding has a privilege to refuse to testify against the accused spouse.

(d) Exceptions. There is no privilege under this rule:

> (1) in any civil proceeding in which the spouses are adverse parties;

> (2) in any criminal proceeding in which an unrefuted showing is made that the spouses acted jointly in the commission of the crime charged;

> (3) in any proceeding in which one spouse is charged with a crime or tort against the person or property of the other, a minor child of either, an individual residing in the household of either, or a third person if the crime or tort is committed in the course of committing a crime or tort

against the other spouse, a minor child of either spouse, or an individual residing in the household of either spouse; or

(4) in any other proceeding, in the discretion of the court, if the interests of a minor child of either spouse may be adversely affected by invocation of the privilege.

C. ATTORNEY–CLIENT AND "WORK PRODUCT"

DENVER TRAMWAY CO. V. OWENS

Supreme Court of Colorado, 1894.
36 P. 848.

[Action by passenger for personal injuries allegedly sustained in alighting from a cable car.]

MR. JUSTICE ELLIOTT delivered the opinion of the court.

* * *

Mr. C.V. Mead, an attorney at law of several years in Denver, was called as a witness for defendant. He testified that shortly after the accident, plaintiff came to his office and that he had a talk with her "about the facts of this case." He was then asked to state what that conversation was.

Plaintiff's counsel being permitted to first cross-examine, the witness testified that the conversation between himself and plaintiff was in his "professional capacity;" that she was consulting him "as an attorney in relation to her case."

On further examination in chief he stated that he had never before seen plaintiff on professional business; that she had never been a client of his before that time; that the relation of attorney and client never existed between them prior to that time; that she did not pay nor agree to pay any retainer fee; that there was no talk about fees or compensation, and no contract or agreement with her at all.

The witness was then asked if he made any charge against plaintiff for the consultation. This was objected to as immaterial, and the objection was sustained.

Counsel for defendant then stated to Mr. Mead the substance of plaintiff's testimony as to the manner in which she had been injured, and thereupon asked if plaintiff's statement to him as to the occurrence resulting in her injury was materially or substantially different from what she had thus testified. The court sustained plaintiff's objection to the testimony thus sought to be elicited. These rulings are assigned for error.

At common law *professional communications* between an attorney and his client relating to the business affairs of the latter were privileged. Lord Brougham states the reason of the rule as follows:

"The foundation of this rule is not difficult to discover. It is not (as has sometimes been said) on account of any particular importance which the law attributes to the business of legal professors, or any particular disposition to afford them protection, though certainly it may not be very easy to discover, why a like privilege has been refused to others, and especially to medical advisers.

"But it is out of regard to the interests of justice which cannot be upholden and to the administration of justice, which cannot go on without the aid of men skilled in jurisprudence, in the practice of the courts, and in those matters affecting rights and obligations which form the subject of all judicial proceedings. If the privilege did not exist at all, every one would be thrown upon his own legal resources. Deprived of all professional assistance, a man would not venture to consult any skillful person, or would only dare to tell his counselor half his case. If the privilege were confined to communications connected with suits begun, or intended, or expected, or apprehended, no one could safely adopt such precautions as might eventually render any proceedings successful, or all proceedings superfluous." Greenough v. Gaskell, 1 My. & K. (7 Eng.Ch.) 103.

According to one author the rule had its origin in the fact that at common law parties were not competent witnesses in their own behalf, and could not be compelled to disclose facts known only to themselves. Weeks on Attorneys, § 142. The general rule now being that parties are competent witnesses, and that they may be compelled to testify in civil cases, it is urged that the rule in regard to professional communications should be relaxed. *Cessante ratione, cessat lex.* There would be some force in this argument if the rule rested alone upon the common law; but we have a statute passed long after parties were made competent witnesses in this state, which reads as follows:

"An attorney shall not, without the consent of his client, be examined as to any communication made by the client to him, or his advice given thereon in the course of professional employment." Gen.Statutes, § 3649.

When a party invokes the protection of the statute, it should not be unduly extended or restricted, but should be fairly construed and applied according to the plain import of its terms so as to effectuate its intent and purpose. The statute is intended for the benefit of the client, not the attorney.

In determining whether or not an attorney should be required or permitted to testify to a conversation between himself and another person without the consent of the latter, the test is: Had such person at the time of the conversation employed the attorney in his professional capacity in respect to the subject-matter of the conversation? If yes, the testimony would not be admissible; otherwise, it would be. It becomes necessary, therefore, to determine whether plaintiff had employed Mr. Mead in his professional capacity as attorney at the time of the conversation inquired about.

To constitute professional employment, it is not essential that the client should have employed the attorney professionally on any previous occasion. Such a limitation of the rule would bear hard upon a person involved in legal controversy for the first time, and also upon an attorney with his first cause. It is not necessary that any retainer should have been paid, promised, or charged for; nor are such matters of any importance except as they may tend to show whether the attorney was or was not professionally employed; neither is it material that there was a suit pending at the time of the consultation, nor that the attorney consulted did not afterwards undertake the case about which the consultation was had.

If a person, in respect to his business affairs or troubles of any kind, consults with an attorney in his professional capacity with the view to obtaining professional advice or assistance, and the attorney voluntarily permits or acquiesces in such consultation, then the professional employment must be regarded as established; and the communication made by the client or advice given by the attorney under such circumstances is privileged.

An attorney is employed—that is, he is engaged in his professional capacity as a lawyer or counselor—when he is listening to his client's preliminary statement of his case, or when he is giving advice thereon, just as truly as when he is drawing his client's pleadings, or advocating his client's cause in open court. It is the consultation between attorney and client which is privileged, and which must ever remain so, even though the attorney, after hearing the preliminary statement, should decline to be retained further in the cause, or the client, after hearing the attorney's advice, should decline to further employ him. The general rule undoubtedly is that a breach of professional relations between attorney and client, whatever may be the cause, does not of itself remove the seal of silence from the lips of the attorney in respect to matters received by him in confidence from his client. Foster v. Hall, 12 Pick. 89; Hunter v. Van Bomhorst, 1 Md. 504; Cross v. Riggins, 50 Mo. 335. * * *

Affirmed.

NOTE

See generally Fried, The Lawyer as Friend: The Moral Foundations of the Attorney–Client Relation, 85 Yale L.J. 1060 (1976); Hazard, An Historical Perspective on the Attorney–Client Privilege, 66 Cal.L.Rev. 1061 (1978).

5 BENTHAM, RATIONALE OF JUDICIAL EVIDENCE 302
(J.S. Mill, Ed.1827).

When, in consulting with a law adviser, attorney or advocate, a man has confessed his delinquency, or disclosed some fact which, if stated in court, might tend to operate in proof of it, such law adviser is not to be suffered to be examined as to any such point. The law adviser is neither to be compelled, nor so much as suffered, to betray the trust thus reposed in him. Not suffered? Why not? Oh, because to betray a trust is treachery; and an act of treachery is an immoral act.

An immoral sort of act, is that sort of act, the tendency of which is, in some way or other, to lessen the quantity of happiness in society. In what way does the supposed cause in question tend to the production of any such effect? The conviction and punishment of the defendant, he being guilty, is by the supposition an act the tendency of which, upon the whole, is beneficial to society. Such is the proposition which for this purpose must be assumed. Some offences (it will be admitted by every body) are of that sort and quality, that the acts by which they are punished do possess this beneficial tendency. Let the offence in question be of the number: it is of such only as are of that number that I speak. The good, then, that results from the conviction and punishment, in the case in question, is out of dispute: where, then is the additional evil of it when produced by the cause in question? Nowhere. The evil consists in the punishment: but the punishment a man undergoes is not greater when the evidence on which the conviction and punishment are grounded happens to come out of the mouth of a law adviser of his, than if it had happened to come out of his own mouth, or that of a third person.

But if such confidence, when reposed, is permitted to be violated, and if this be known, (which, if such be the law, it will be), the consequence will be, that no such confidence will be reposed. Not reposed?—Well: and if it be not, wherein will consist the mischief? The man by the supposition is guilty; if not, by the supposition there is nothing to betray: let the law adviser say every thing he has heard, every thing he can have heard from his client, the client cannot have any thing to fear from it. That it will often happen that in the case supposed no such confidence will be reposed, is natural enough: the first thing the advocate or attorney will say to his client, will be,—Remember that, whatever you say to me, I shall be obliged to tell, if asked about it. What, then, will be the consequence? That a guilty person will not in general be able to derive quite so much assistance from his law adviser, in the way of concerting a false defence, as he may do at present.

Except the prevention of such pernicious confidence, of what other possible effect can the rule for the requisition of such evidence be productive? Either of none at all, or of the conviction of delinquents, in some instances in which, but for the lights thus obtained, they would not have been convicted. But in this effect, what imaginable circumstance is there that can render it in any degree pernicious and undesirable? None whatever. The conviction of delinquents is the very end of penal justice.

NOTES AND QUESTIONS

1.   *Attacks on the privilege.* Frontal attacks on the attorney-client privilege are not limited to the nineteenth century. See the different, but equally scathing, attack on both the attorney-client and the work product privileges in Fischel, Lawyers and Confidentiality, 65 U.Chi.L.Rev. 1 (1998). What rebuttal is there to Bentham's attack? Wigmore was somewhat more sympathetic to the privilege, arguing in essence that Bentham's points were well taken only with regard to a certain proportion of cases. He argues that the privilege may serve a more valid societal function in a civil case where right and wrong are not so clear. 8 Wigmore, Evidence § 2291 (McNaughton rev. 1961). But he concludes his lukewarm defense with the observation that the benefits of the privilege are "all indirect and speculative; its obstruction is plain and concrete."

2.   *Other rationales.* Are there other, better arguments for the privilege than those suggested by the *Denver Tramway* case? Is there a need for a free flow of information between lawyer and client even when the client is in fact guilty of a crime or misconduct? Do considerations of privacy or personal autonomy, as suggested in by Professor Black and the following notes in Section A of this chapter, come into play with regard to this privilege? What impact might the elimination of the privilege have on how clients view their lawyers? On how they view the judicial system? See also Freedman, Lawyers' Ethics in an Adversary System (1975); Fuller, The Adversary System, in Talks on American Law 30, 32–38 (1961).

SWIDLER & BERLIN V. UNITED STATES
Supreme Court of the United States, 1998.
524 U.S. 399.

CHIEF JUSTICE REHNQUIST delivered the opinion of the Court.

Petitioner, James Hamilton, an attorney, made notes of an initial interview with a client shortly before the client's death. The Government, represented by the Office of Independent Counsel, now seeks his notes for use in a criminal investigation. We hold that the notes are protected by the attorney-client privilege.

This dispute arises out of an investigation conducted by the Office of the Independent Counsel into whether various individuals made false statements, obstructed justice, or committed other crimes during investigations of the 1993 dismissal of employees from the White House Travel Office. Vincent W. Foster, Jr., was Deputy White House Counsel when the firings occurred. In July 1993, Foster met with petitioner Hamilton, an attorney at petitioner Swidler & Berlin, to seek legal representation concerning possible congressional or other investigations of the firings. During a 2–hour meeting, Hamilton took three pages of handwritten notes. One of the first entries in the notes is the word "Privileged." Nine days later, Foster committed suicide.

In December 1995, a federal grand jury, at the request of the Independent Counsel, issued subpoenas to petitioners Hamilton and Swidler & Berlin for, inter alia, Hamilton's handwritten notes of his meeting with Foster. Petitioners filed a motion to quash, arguing that the notes were protected by the attorney-client privilege and by the work-product privilege. The District Court, after examining the notes in camera, concluded they were protected from disclosure by both doctrines and denied enforcement of the subpoenas.

The Court of Appeals for the District of Columbia Circuit reversed. In re Sealed Case, 124 F.3d 230 (1997). While recognizing that most courts assume the privilege survives death, the Court of Appeals noted that holdings actually manifesting the posthumous force of the privilege are rare. Instead, most judicial references to the privilege's posthumous application occur in the context of a well-recognized exception allowing disclosure for disputes among the client's heirs. Id., at 231–232. It further noted that most commentators support some measure of posthumous curtailment of the privilege. Id., at 232. The Court of Appeals thought that the risk of posthumous revelation, when confined to the criminal context, would have little to no chilling effect on client communication, but that the costs of protecting communications after death were high. It therefore concluded that the privilege was not absolute in such circumstances, and that instead, a balancing test should apply. Id., at 233–234. It thus held that there is a posthumous exception to the privilege for communications whose relative importance to particular criminal litigation is substantial. Id., at 235. While acknowledging that uncertain privileges are disfavored, Jaffee v. Redmond, 518 U.S. 1, 17–18 (1996), the Court of Appeals determined that the uncertainty introduced by its balancing test was insignificant in light of existing exceptions to the privilege. 124 F.3d, at 235. The Court of Appeals also held that the notes were not protected by the work-product privilege.

The dissenting judge would have affirmed the District Court's judgment that the attorney-client privilege protected the notes. Id., at 237. He concluded that the common-law rule was that the privilege survived death. He found no persuasive reason to depart from this accepted rule, particularly given the importance of the privilege to full and frank client communication. Id., at 237.

Petitioners sought review in this Court on both the attorney-client privilege and the work-product privilege.[17] We granted certiorari, 523 U.S. 1045 (1998), and we now reverse.

Issue

The attorney-client privilege is one of the oldest recognized privileges for confidential communications. Upjohn Co. v. United States, 449 U.S. 383, 389 (1981); Hunt v. Blackburn, 128 U.S. 464, 470 (1888). The privilege is intended to encourage "full and frank communication between attorneys and their clients and thereby promote broader public interests in the observance of law and the administration of justice." Upjohn, supra, at 389. The issue presented here is the scope of that privilege; more particularly, the extent to which the privilege survives the death of the client. Our interpretation of the privilege's scope is guided by "the principles of the common law * * * as interpreted by the courts * * * in the light of reason and experience." Fed.Rule Evid. 501; Funk v. United States, 290 U.S. 371 (1933).

I.

A.

The Independent Counsel argues that the attorney-client privilege should not prevent disclosure of confidential communications where the client has died and the information is relevant to a criminal proceeding. There is some authority for this position. One state appellate court, Cohen v. Jenkintown Cab Co., 238 Pa.Super. 456, 357 A.2d 689 (1976), and the Court of Appeals below have held the privilege may be subject to posthumous exceptions in certain circumstances. In Cohen, a civil case, the court recognized that the privilege generally survives death, but concluded that it could make an exception where the interest of justice was compelling and the interest of the client in preserving the confidence was insignificant. Id., at 462–464, 357 A.2d, at 692–693.

Ind. Couns. Arg.

But other than these two decisions, cases addressing the existence of the privilege after death—most involving the testamentary exception—uniformly presume the privilege survives, even if they do not so hold. See, e.g., Mayberry v. Indiana, 670 N.E.2d 1262 (Ind.1996); Morris v. Cain, 39 La. Ann. 712, 1 So. 797 (1887); People v. Modzelewski, 611 N.Y.S.2d 22, 203 A.D.2d 594 (1994). Several State Supreme Court decisions expressly hold that the attorney-client privilege extends beyond the death of the client, even in the criminal context. See In re John Doe Grand Jury Investigation, 408 Mass. 480, 481–483, 562 N.E.2d 69, 70 (1990); State v. Doster, 276 S.C. 647, 650–651, 284 S.E.2d 218, 219 (1981); State v. Macumber, 112 Ariz. 569, 571, 544 P.2d 1084, 1086 (1976). In John Doe Grand Jury Investigation, for example, the Massachusetts Supreme

1.

---

[17] Because we sustain the claim of attorney-client privilege, we do not reach the claim of work-product privilege.

Judicial Court concluded that survival of the privilege was "the clear implication" of its early pronouncements that communications subject to the privilege could not be disclosed at any time. 408 Mass., at 483, 562 N.E.2d, at 70. The court further noted that survival of the privilege was "necessarily implied" by cases allowing waiver of the privilege in testamentary disputes. Ibid.

Such testamentary exception cases consistently presume the privilege survives. See, e.g., United States v. Osborn, 561 F.2d 1334, 1340 (C.A.9 1977); DeLoach v. Myers, 215 Ga. 255, 259–260, 109 S.E.2d 777, 780–781 (1959); Doyle v. Reeves, 112 Conn. 521, 152 A. 882 (1931); Russell v. Jackson, 9 Hare 387, 68 Eng. Rep. 558 (V.C.1851). They view testamentary disclosure of communications as an exception to the privilege: "[T]he general rule with respect to confidential communications * * * is that such communications are privileged during the testator's lifetime and, also, after the testator's death unless sought to be disclosed in litigation between the testator's heirs." Osborn, 561 F.2d, at 1340. The rationale for such disclosure is that it furthers the client's intent. Id., at 1340, n.11.[18]

Indeed, in Glover v. Patten, 165 U.S. 394, 406–408 (1897), this Court, in recognizing the testamentary exception, expressly assumed that the privilege continues after the individual's death. The Court explained that testamentary disclosure was permissible because the privilege, which normally protects the client's interests, could be impliedly waived in order to fulfill the client's testamentary intent. Id., at 407–408 (quoting Blackburn v. Crawford, 3 Wall. 175, 18 L.Ed. 186 (1865), and Russell v. Jackson, supra).

The great body of this case law supports, either by holding or considered dicta, the position that the privilege does survive in a case such as the present one. Given the language of Rule 501, at the very least the burden is on the Independent Counsel to show that "reason and experience" require a departure from this rule.

The Independent Counsel contends that the testamentary exception supports the posthumous termination of the privilege because in practice

---

[18] About half the States have codified the testamentary exception by providing that a personal representative of the deceased can waive the privilege when heirs or devisees claim through the deceased client (as opposed to parties claiming against the estate, for whom the privilege is not waived). See, e.g., Ala.Rule Evid. 502 (1996); Ark.Code Ann. § 16–41–101, Rule 502 (Supp.1997); Neb.Rev.Stat. § 27–503, Rule 503 (1995). These statutes do not address expressly the continuation of the privilege outside the context of testamentary disputes, although many allow the attorney to assert the privilege on behalf of the client apparently without temporal limit. See, e.g., Ark.Code Ann. § 16–41–101, Rule 502(c) (Supp.1997). They thus do not refute or affirm the general presumption in the case law that the privilege survives. California's statute is exceptional in that it apparently allows the attorney to assert the privilege only so long as a holder of the privilege (the estate's personal representative) exists, suggesting the privilege terminates when the estate is wound up. See Cal.Code Evid.Ann. §§ 954, 957 (West 1995). But no other State has followed California's lead in this regard.

most cases have refused to apply the privilege posthumously. He further argues that the exception reflects a policy judgment that the interest in settling estates outweighs any posthumous interest in confidentiality. He then reasons by analogy that in criminal proceedings, the interest in determining whether a crime has been committed should trump client confidentiality, particularly since the financial interests of the estate are not at stake.

But the Independent Counsel's interpretation simply does not square with the case law's implicit acceptance of the privilege's survival and with the treatment of testamentary disclosure as an "exception" or an implied "waiver." And the premise of his analogy is incorrect, since cases consistently recognize that the rationale for the testamentary exception is that it furthers the client's intent, see, e.g., Glover, supra. There is no reason to suppose as a general matter that grand jury testimony about confidential communications furthers the client's intent.

Commentators on the law also recognize that the general rule is that the attorney-client privilege continues after death. See, e.g., 8 Wigmore, Evidence § 2323 (McNaughton rev. 1961); Frankel, The Attorney–Client Privilege After the Death of the Client, 6 Geo.J.Legal Ethics 45, 78–79 (1992); 1 J. Strong, McCormick on Evidence § 94, p. 348 (4th ed. 1992). Undoubtedly, as the Independent Counsel emphasizes, various commentators have criticized this rule, urging that the privilege should be abrogated after the client's death where extreme injustice would result, as long as disclosure would not seriously undermine the privilege by deterring client communication. See, e.g., C. Mueller & L. Kirkpatrick, 2 Federal Evidence § 199, pp. 380–381 (2d ed. 1994); Restatement (Third) of the Law Governing Lawyers § 127, Comment d (Proposed Final Draft No. 1, Mar. 29, 1996). But even these critics clearly recognize that established law supports the continuation of the privilege and that a contrary rule would be a modification of the common law. See, e.g., Mueller & Kirkpatrick, supra, at 379; Restatement of the Law Governing Lawyers, supra, § 127, Comment c; 24 C. Wright & K. Graham, Federal Practice and Procedure § 5498, p. 483 (1986).

[Despite the scholarly criticism, we think there are weighty reasons that counsel in favor of posthumous application.] Knowing that communications will remain confidential even after death encourages the client to communicate fully and frankly with counsel. While the fear of disclosure, and the consequent withholding of information from counsel, may be reduced if disclosure is limited to posthumous disclosure in a criminal context, it seems unreasonable to assume that it vanishes altogether. Clients may be concerned about reputation, civil liability, or possible harm to friends or family. Posthumous disclosure of such communications may be as feared as disclosure during the client's lifetime.

The Independent Counsel suggests, however, that his proposed exception would have little to no effect on the client's willingness to confide in his attorney. He reasons that only clients intending to perjure themselves will be chilled by a rule of disclosure after death, as opposed to truthful clients or those asserting their Fifth Amendment privilege. This is because for the latter group, communications disclosed by the attorney after the client's death purportedly will reveal only information that the client himself would have revealed if alive.

The Independent Counsel assumes, incorrectly we believe, that the privilege is analogous to the Fifth Amendment's protection against self-incrimination. But as suggested above, the privilege serves much broader purposes. Clients consult attorneys for a wide variety of reasons, only one of which involves possible criminal liability. Many attorneys act as counselors on personal and family matters, where, in the course of obtaining the desired advice, confidences about family members or financial problems must be revealed in order to assure sound legal advice. The same is true of owners of small businesses who may regularly consult their attorneys about a variety of problems arising in the course of the business. These confidences may not come close to any sort of admission of criminal wrongdoing, but nonetheless be matters which the client would not wish divulged.

The contention that the attorney is being required to disclose only what the client could have been required to disclose is at odds with the basis for the privilege even during the client's lifetime. In related cases, we have said that the loss of evidence admittedly caused by the privilege is justified in part by the fact that without the privilege, the client may not have made such communications in the first place. See Jaffee, 518 U.S., at 12; Fisher v. United States, 425 U.S. 391, 403 (1976). This is true of disclosure before and after the client's death. Without assurance of the privilege's posthumous application, the client may very well not have made disclosures to his attorney at all, so the loss of evidence is more apparent than real. In the case at hand, it seems quite plausible that Foster, perhaps already contemplating suicide, may not have sought legal advice from Hamilton if he had not been assured the conversation was privileged.

The Independent Counsel additionally suggests that his proposed exception would have minimal impact if confined to criminal cases, or, as the Court of Appeals suggests, if it is limited to information of substantial importance to a particular criminal case.[19] However, there is no case authority for the proposition that the privilege applies differently in

---

[19] Petitioners, while opposing wholesale abrogation of the privilege in criminal cases, concede that exceptional circumstances implicating a criminal defendant's constitutional rights might warrant breaching the privilege. We do not, however, need to reach this issue, since such exceptional circumstances clearly are not presented here.

criminal and civil cases, and only one commentator ventures such a suggestion, see Mueller & Kirkpatrick, supra, at 380–381. In any event, a client may not know at the time he discloses information to his attorney whether it will later be relevant to a civil or a criminal matter, let alone whether it will be of substantial importance. Balancing ex post the importance of the information against client interests, even limited to criminal cases, introduces substantial uncertainty into the privilege's application. For just that reason, we have rejected use of a balancing test in defining the contours of the privilege. See Upjohn, 449 U.S., at 393; Jaffee, supra, at 17–18.

In a similar vein, the Independent Counsel argues that existing exceptions to the privilege, such as the crime-fraud exception and the testamentary exception, make the impact of one more exception marginal. However, these exceptions do not demonstrate that the impact of a posthumous exception would be insignificant, and there is little empirical evidence on this point.[20] The established exceptions are consistent with the purposes of the privilege, see Glover, 165 U.S., at 407–408; United States v. Zolin, 491 U.S. 554, 562–563 (1989), while a posthumous exception in criminal cases appears at odds with the goals of encouraging full and frank communication and of protecting the client's interests. A "no harm in one more exception" rationale could contribute to the general erosion of the privilege, without reference to common-law principles or "reason and experience."

Finally, the Independent Counsel, relying on cases such as United States v. Nixon, 418 U.S. 683, 710 (1974), and Branzburg v. Hayes, 408 U.S. 665 (1972), urges that privileges be strictly construed because they are inconsistent with the paramount judicial goal of truth seeking. But both Nixon and Branzburg dealt with the creation of privileges not recognized by the common law, whereas here we deal with one of the oldest recognized privileges in the law. And we are asked, not simply to

---

[20] Empirical evidence on the privilege is limited. Three studies do not reach firm conclusions on whether limiting the privilege would discourage full and frank communication. Alexander, The Corporate Attorney Client Privilege: A Study of the Participants, 63 St. John's L.Rev. 191 (1989); Zacharias, Rethinking Confidentiality, 74 Iowa L.Rev. 352 (1989); Comment, Functional Overlap Between the Lawyer and Other Professionals: Its Implications for the Privileged Communications Doctrine, 71 Yale L.J. 1226 (1962). These articles note that clients are often uninformed or mistaken about the privilege, but suggest that a substantial number of clients and attorneys think the privilege encourages candor. Two of the articles conclude that a substantial number of clients and attorneys think the privilege enhances open communication, Alexander, supra, at 244–246, 261, and that the absence of a privilege would be detrimental to such communication, Comment, 71 Yale L.J., supra, at 1236. The third article suggests instead that while the privilege is perceived as important to open communication, limited exceptions to the privilege might not discourage such communication, Zacharias, supra, at 382, 386. Similarly, relatively few court decisions discuss the impact of the privilege's application after death. This may reflect the general assumption that the privilege survives—if attorneys were required as a matter of practice to testify or provide notes in criminal proceedings, cases discussing that practice would surely exist.

"construe" the privilege, but to narrow it, contrary to the weight of the existing body of case law.

It has been generally, if not universally, accepted, for well over a century, that the attorney-client privilege survives the death of the client in a case such as this. While the arguments against the survival of the privilege are by no means frivolous, they are based in large part on speculation—thoughtful speculation, but speculation nonetheless—as to whether posthumous termination of the privilege would diminish a client's willingness to confide in an attorney. In an area where empirical information would be useful, it is scant and inconclusive.

Rule 501's direction to look to "the principles of the common law as they may be interpreted by the courts of the United States in the light of reason and experience" does not mandate that a rule, once established, should endure for all time. Funk v. United States, 290 U.S. 371, 381 (1933). But here the Independent Counsel has simply not made a sufficient showing to overturn the common-law rule embodied in the prevailing caselaw. Interpreted in the light of reason and experience, that body of law requires that the attorney-client privilege prevent disclosure of the notes at issue in this case.

The judgment of the Court of Appeals is

Reversed.

JUSTICE O'CONNOR, with whom JUSTICE SCALIA and JUSTICE THOMAS join, dissenting.

Although the attorney-client privilege ordinarily will survive the death of the client, I do not agree with the Court that it inevitably precludes disclosure of a deceased client's communications in criminal proceedings. In my view, a criminal defendant's right to exculpatory evidence or a compelling law enforcement need for information may, where the testimony is not available from other sources, override a client's posthumous interest in confidentiality.

We have long recognized that "[t]he fundamental basis upon which all rules of evidence must rest—if they are to rest upon reason—is their adaptation to the successful development of the truth." Funk v. United States, 290 U.S. 371, 381 (1933). In light of the heavy burden that they place on the search for truth, see United States v. Nixon, 418 U.S. 683, 708–710 (1974), "[e]videntiary privileges in litigation are not favored, and even those rooted in the Constitution must give way in proper circumstances," Herbert v. Lando, 441 U.S. 153 (1979). Consequently, we construe the scope of privileges narrowly. See Jaffee v. Redmond, 518 U.S. 1, 19 (1996) (SCALIA, J., dissenting); see also University of Pennsylvania v. EEOC, 493 U.S. 182, 189 (1990). We are reluctant to recognize a privilege or read an existing one expansively unless to do so will serve a "public good transcending the normally predominant principle of utilizing all rational means for ascertaining truth." Trammel v. United States, 445 U.S. 40, 50 (1980) (internal quotation marks omitted).

The attorney-client privilege promotes trust in the representational relationship, thereby facilitating the provision of legal services and ultimately the administration of justice. See Upjohn Co. v. United States, 449 U.S. 383, 389 (1981). The systemic benefits of the privilege are commonly understood to outweigh the harm caused by excluding critical evidence. A privilege should operate, however, only where "necessary to achieve its purpose," see Fisher v. United States, 425 U.S. 391, 403 (1976), and an invocation of the attorney-client privilege should not go unexamined "when it is shown that the interests of the administration of justice can only be frustrated by [its] exercise," Cohen v. Jenkintown Cab Co., 238 Pa.Super. 456, 464, 357 A.2d 689, 693–694 (1976).

I agree that a deceased client may retain a personal, reputational, and economic interest in confidentiality * * *. But, after death, the potential that disclosure will harm the client's interests has been greatly diminished, and the risk that the client will be held criminally liable has abated altogether. Thus, some commentators suggest that terminating the privilege upon the client's death "could not to any substantial degree lessen the encouragement for free disclosure which is [its] purpose." 1 J. Strong, McCormick on Evidence § 94, p. 350 (4th ed. 1992); see also Restatement (Third) of the Law Governing Lawyers § 127, Comment d (Proposed Final Draft No. 1, Mar. 29, 1996). This diminished risk is coupled with a heightened urgency for discovery of a deceased client's communications in the criminal context. The privilege does not "protect disclosure of the underlying facts by those who communicated with the attorney," Upjohn, supra, at 395, and were the client living, prosecutors could grant immunity and compel the relevant testimony. After a client's death, however, if the privilege precludes an attorney from testifying in the client's stead, a complete "loss of crucial information" will often result, see 24 C. Wright & K. Graham, Federal Practice and Procedure § 5498, p. 484 (1986).

As the Court of Appeals observed, the costs of recognizing an absolute posthumous privilege can be inordinately high. See In re Sealed Case, 124 F.3d 230, 233–234 (C.A.D.C.1997). Extreme injustice may occur, for example, where a criminal defendant seeks disclosure of a deceased client's confession to the offense. See State v. Macumber, 112 Ariz. 569, 571, 544 P.2d 1084, 1086 (1976); cf. In the Matter of John Doe Grand Jury Investigation, 408 Mass. 480, 486, 562 N.E.2d 69, 72 (1990) (Nolan, J., dissenting). In my view, the paramount value that our criminal justice system places on protecting an innocent defendant should outweigh a deceased client's interest in preserving confidences. See, e.g.,

Schlup v. Delo, 513 U.S. 298, 324–325 (1995); In re Winship, 397 U.S. 358, 371 (1970) (Harlan, J., concurring). Indeed, even petitioners acknowledge that an exception may be appropriate where the constitutional rights of a criminal defendant are at stake. An exception may likewise be warranted in the face of a compelling law enforcement need for the information. "[O]ur historic commitment to the rule of law * * * is nowhere more profoundly manifest than in our view that the twofold aim of criminal justice is that guilt shall not escape or innocence suffer." Nixon, supra, at 709 (internal quotation marks omitted); see also Herrera v. Collins, 506 U.S. 390, 398 (1993). Given that the complete exclusion of relevant evidence from a criminal trial or investigation may distort the record, mislead the factfinder, and undermine the central truth-seeking function of the courts, I do not believe that the attorney-client privilege should act as an absolute bar to the disclosure of a deceased client's communications. When the privilege is asserted in the criminal context, and a showing is made that the communications at issue contain necessary factual information not otherwise available, courts should be permitted to assess whether interests in fairness and accuracy outweigh the justifications for the privilege.

A number of exceptions to the privilege already qualify its protections, and an attorney "who tells his client that the expected communications are absolutely and forever privileged is oversimplifying a bit." 124 F.3d, at 235. In the situation where the posthumous privilege most frequently arises—a dispute between heirs over the decedent's will—the privilege is widely recognized to give way to the interest in settling the estate. See Glover v. Patten, 165 U.S. 394, 406–408 (1897). This testamentary exception, moreover, may be invoked in some cases where the decedent would not have chosen to waive the privilege. For example, "a decedent might want to provide for an illegitimate child but at the same time much prefer that the relationship go undisclosed." 124 F.3d, at 234. Among the Court's rationales for a broad construction of the posthumous privilege is its assertion that "[m]any attorneys act as counselors on personal and family matters, where, in the course of obtaining the desired advice, confidences about family members or financial problems must be revealed * * * which the client would not wish divulged." * * * That reasoning, however, would apply in the testamentary context with equal force. Nor are other existing exceptions to the privilege—for example, the crime-fraud exception or the exceptions for claims relating to attorney competence or compensation—necessarily consistent with "encouraging full and frank communication" or "protecting the client's interests." * * * Rather, those exceptions reflect the understanding that, in certain circumstances, the privilege " 'ceases to operate' " as a safeguard on "the proper functioning of our adversary system." See United States v. Zolin, 491 U.S. 554, 562–563 (1989).

Finally, the common law authority for the proposition that the privilege remains absolute after the client's death is not a monolithic body of precedent. Indeed, the Court acknowledges that most cases merely "presume the privilege survives," * * * and it relies on the case law's "implicit acceptance" of a continuous privilege * * *. Opinions squarely addressing the posthumous force of the privilege "are relatively rare." See 124 F.3d, at 232. And even in those decisions expressly holding that the privilege continues after the death of the client, courts do not typically engage in detailed reasoning, but rather conclude that the cases construing the testamentary exception imply survival of the privilege. See, e.g., Glover, supra, at 406–408; see also Wright & Graham, supra, § 5498, at 484 ("Those who favor an eternal duration for the privilege seldom do much by way of justifying this in terms of policy").

Moreover, as the Court concedes * * *, there is some authority for the proposition that a deceased client's communications may be revealed, even in circumstances outside of the testamentary context. California's Evidence Code, for example, provides that the attorney-client privilege continues only until the deceased client's estate is finally distributed, noting that "there is little reason to preserve secrecy at the expense of excluding relevant evidence after the estate is wound up and the representative is discharged." Cal. Evid. Code Ann. § 954, and comment, p. 232, § 952 (West 1995). And a state appellate court has admitted an attorney's testimony concerning a deceased client's communications after "balanc[ing] the necessity for revealing the substance of the [attorney-client conversation] against the unlikelihood of any cognizable injury to the rights, interests, estate or memory of [the client]." See Cohen, supra, at 464, 357 A.2d, at 693. The American Law Institute, moreover, has recently recommended withholding the privilege when the communication "bears on a litigated issue of pivotal significance" and has suggested that courts "balance the interest in confidentiality against any exceptional need for the communication." Restatement (Third) of the Law Governing Lawyers § 127, at 431, Comment d; see also 2 C. Mueller & L. Kirkpatrick, Federal Evidence, § 199, p. 380 (2d ed. 1994) ("[I]f a deceased client has confessed to criminal acts that are later charged to another, surely the latter's need for evidence sometimes outweighs the interest in preserving the confidences").

Where the exoneration of an innocent criminal defendant or a compelling law enforcement interest is at stake, the harm of precluding critical evidence that is unavailable by any other means outweighs the potential disincentive to forthright communication. In my view, the cost of silence warrants a narrow exception to the rule that the attorney-client privilege survives the death of the client. Moreover, although I disagree with the Court of Appeals' notion that the context of an initial client interview affects the applicability of the work product doctrine, I do not believe that the doctrine applies where the material concerns a client who is no longer a potential party to adversarial litigation.

Accordingly, I would affirm the judgment of the Court of Appeals. Although the District Court examined the documents in camera, it has not had an opportunity to balance these competing considerations and decide whether the privilege should be trumped in the particular circumstances of this case. Thus, I agree with the Court of Appeals' decision to remand for a determination whether any portion of the notes must be disclosed.

With respect, I dissent.

NOTES AND QUESTIONS

1. *More on rationale.* Does the Court's opinion in the *Swidler & Berlin* case shed any further light on the reasons behind the attorney-client privilege? Is the Court's posthumous recognition of the privilege based on the utilitarian notion that the continuation of the privilege after death fosters better communications between lawyer and client or considerations of privacy or some of both? See generally Broun, The Story of *Swidler & Berlin v. United States*, in Evidence Stories 127 (Lempert ed., 2006).

2. *Constitutional limitations?* The majority brushes off the dissent's concern that a continuation of the privilege after death may deprive a criminal defendant of a full defense to a crime by suggesting that there may be constitutional limits on the privilege in some circumstances. In what circumstances could you foresee a constitutional challenge to the exercise of the privilege? See Chambers v. Mississippi, 410 U.S. 284 (1973); Davis v. Alaska, 415 U.S. 308 (1974). Might not those same considerations apply in the case of the exercise of the privilege before the death of the client?

3. *Using evidence obtained as a result of a breach of an evidentiary privilege.* The courts have generally held that evidence derived from a breach of an evidentiary privilege such as the attorney-client privilege is admissible. See, e.g. Nickel v. Hannigan, 97 F.3d 403, 408–09 (10th Cir.1996) (even if attorney's testimony should have been suppressed because of the attorney-client privilege, evidence derived from that testimony should not have been suppressed). See Mosteller, Admissibility of Fruits of Breached Evidentiary Privileges: The Importance of Adversarial Fairness, Party Culpability, and Fear of Immunity, 81 Wash.U.L.Q. 961 (2003).

UPJOHN CO. V. UNITED STATES

Supreme Court of the United States, 1981.
449 U.S. 383.

JUSTICE REHNQUIST delivered the opinion of the Court.

We granted certiorari in this case to address important questions concerning the scope of the attorney-client privilege in the corporate context and the applicability of the work-product doctrine in proceedings to enforce tax summonses. With respect to the privilege question the parties and various *amici* have described our task as one of choosing between two "tests" which have gained adherents in the courts of appeals. We are acutely aware, however, that we sit to decide concrete cases and not abstract propositions of law. We decline to lay down a broad rule or series of rules to govern all conceivable future questions in this area, even were we able to do so. We can and do, however, conclude that the attorney-client privilege protects the communications involved in this case from compelled disclosure and that the work-product doctrine does apply in tax summons enforcement proceedings.

I

Petitioner Upjohn manufactures and sells pharmaceuticals here and abroad. In January 1976 independent accountants conducting an audit of one of petitioner's foreign subsidiaries discovered that the subsidiary made payments to or for the benefit of foreign government officials in order to secure government business. The accountants so informed Mr. Gerard Thomas, petitioner's Vice–President, Secretary, and General Counsel. Thomas is a member of the Michigan and New York bars, and has been petitioner's General Counsel for 20 years. He consulted with outside counsel and R.T. Parfet, Jr., petitioner's Chairman of the Board. It was decided that the company would conduct an internal investigation of what were termed "questionable payments." As part of this investigation the attorneys prepared a letter containing a questionnaire which was sent to "all foreign general and area managers" over the Chairman's signature. The letter began by noting recent disclosures that several American companies made "possibly illegal" payments to foreign government officials and emphasized that the management needed full information concerning any such payments made by Upjohn. The letter indicated that the Chairman had asked Thomas, identified as "the company's General Counsel," "to conduct an investigation for the purpose of determining the nature and magnitude of any payments made by the Upjohn Company or any of its subsidiaries to any employee or official of a foreign government." The questionnaire sought detailed information concerning such payments. Managers were instructed to treat the investigation as "highly confidential" and not to discuss it with anyone other than Upjohn employees who might be helpful in providing the requested information. Responses were to be sent directly to Thomas. Thomas and outside counsel also interviewed the recipients of the questionnaire and some 33 other Upjohn officers or employees as part of the investigation.

On March 26, 1976, the company voluntarily submitted a preliminary report to the Securities and Exchange Commission on Form 8–K disclosing certain questionable payments. A copy of the report was simultaneously submitted to the Internal Revenue Service, which immediately began an investigation to determine the tax consequences of the payments. Special agents conducting the investigation were given lists by Upjohn of all those interviewed and all who had responded to the questionnaire. On November 23, 1976, the Service issued a summons pursuant to 26 U.S.C.A. § 7602 demanding production of:

> "All files relative to the investigation conducted under the supervision of Gerard Thomas to identify payments to employees of foreign governments and any political contributions made by the Upjohn Company or any of its affiliates since January 1, 1971 and to determine whether any funds of the Upjohn Company had been improperly accounted for on the corporate books during the same period.

> "The records should include but not be limited to written questionnaires sent to managers of the Upjohn Company's foreign affiliates, and memoranda or notes of the interviews conducted in the United States and abroad with officers and employees of the Upjohn Company and its subsidiaries." App. 17a–18a.

The company declined to produce the documents specified in the second paragraph on the grounds that they were protected from disclosure by the attorney-client privilege and constituted the work product of attorneys prepared in anticipation of litigation. On August 31, 1977, the United States filed a petition seeking enforcement of the summons under 26 U.S.C.A. §§ 7402(b) and 7604(a) in the United States District Court for the Western District of Michigan. That court adopted the recommendation of a magistrate who concluded that the summons should be enforced. Petitioner appealed to the Court of Appeals for the Sixth Circuit which rejected the magistrate's finding of a waiver of the attorney-client privilege, 600 F.2d 1223, 1227, n.12, but agreed that the privilege did not apply "to the extent the communications were made by officers and agents not responsible for directing Upjohn's actions in response to legal advice * * * for the simple reason that the communications were not the 'client's.'" Id., at 1225. The court reasoned that accepting petitioner's claim for a broader application of the privilege would encourage upper-echelon management to ignore unpleasant facts and create too broad a "zone of silence." Noting that petitioner's counsel had interviewed officials such as the Chairman and President, the Court of Appeals remanded to the District Court so that a determination of who was within the "control group" could be made. In a concluding footnote the court stated that the work-product doctrine "is not applicable to administrative summonses issued under 26 U.S.C.A. § 7602." Id., at 1228, n.13.

II

Federal Rule of Evidence 501 provides that "the privilege of a witness * * * shall be governed by the principles of the common law as they may be interpreted by the courts of the United States in light of reason and experience." The attorney-client privilege is the oldest of the privileges for confidential communications known to the common law. 8 Wigmore, Evidence § 2290 (McNaughton rev. 1961). Its purpose is to encourage full and frank communication between attorneys and their clients and thereby promote broader public interests in the observance of law and administration of justice. The privilege recognizes that sound legal advice or advocacy serves public ends and that such advice or advocacy depends upon the lawyer being fully informed by the client. As we stated last Term in Trammel v. United States, 445 U.S. 40, 51 (1980), "The attorney-client privilege rests on the need for the advocate and counselor to know all that relates to the client's reasons for seeking representation if the professional mission is to be carried out." And in Fisher v. United States, 425 U.S. 391, 403 (1976), we recognized the purpose of the privilege to be "to encourage clients to make full disclosures to their attorneys." This rationale for the privilege has long been recognized by the Court, see Hunt v. Blackburn, 128 U.S. 464, 470 (1888) (privilege "is founded upon the necessity, in the interest and administration of justice, of the aid of persons having knowledge of the law and skilled in its practice, which assistance can only be safely and readily availed of when free from the consequences or the apprehension of disclosure"). Admittedly complications in the application of the privilege arise when the client is a corporation, which in theory is an artificial creature of the law, and not an individual; but this Court has assumed that the privilege applies when the client is a corporation, United States v. Louisville & Nashville R. Co., 235 U.S. 318, 336 (1915), and the Government does not contest the general proposition.

The Court of Appeals, however, considered the application of the privilege in the corporate context to present a "different problem," since the client was an inanimate entity and "only the senior management, guiding and integrating the several operations, * * * can be said to possess an identity analogous to the corporation as a whole." 600 F.2d, at 1226. The first case to articulate the so-called "control group test" adopted by the court below, City of Philadelphia v. Westinghouse Electric Corp., 210 F.Supp. 483, 485 (E.D.Pa.1962), reflected a similar conceptual approach:

> "Keeping in mind that the question is, Is it the corporation which is seeking the lawyer's advice when the asserted privileged communication is made?, the most satisfactory solution, I think, is that if the employee making the communication, of whatever rank he may be, is in a position to control or even to take a

substantial part in a decision about any action which the
corporation may take upon the advice of the attorney, * * * then,
in effect, *he is (or personifies) the corporation* when he makes his
disclosure to the lawyer and the privilege would apply."
(Emphasis supplied.)

Such a view, we think, overlooks the fact that the privilege exists to
protect not only the giving of professional advice to those who can act on
it but also the giving of information to the lawyer to enable him to give
sound and informed advice. See *Trammel,* 445 U.S., at 51; *Fisher,* 425
U.S., at 403. The first step in the resolution of any legal problem is
ascertaining the factual background and sifting through the facts with an
eye to the legally relevant. See ABA Code of Professional Responsibility,
Ethical Consideration 4–1:

> "A lawyer should be fully informed of all the facts of the matter
> he is handling in order for his client to obtain the full advantage
> of our legal system. It is for the lawyer in the exercise of his
> independent professional judgment to separate the relevant and
> important from the irrelevant and unimportant. The observance
> of the ethical obligation of a lawyer to hold inviolate the
> confidences and secrets of his client not only facilitates the full
> development of facts essential to proper representation of the
> client but also encourages laymen to seek early legal assistance."

See also Hickman v. Taylor, 329 U.S. 495, 511 (1947).

[In the case of the individual client the provider of information and
the person who acts on the lawyer's advice are one and the same.] In the
corporate context, however, it will frequently be employees beyond the
control group as defined by the court below—"officers and agents * * *
responsible for directing [the company's] actions in response to legal
advice"—who will possess the information needed by the corporation's
lawyers. Middle-level—and indeed lower-level—employees can, by actions
within the scope of their employment, embroil the corporation in serious
legal difficulties, and it is only natural that these employees would have
the relevant information needed by corporate counsel if he is adequately
to advise the client with respect to such actual or potential difficulties.
This fact was noted in Diversified Industries, Inc. v. Meredith, 572 F.2d
596 (C.A.8 1977) (en banc):

> "In a corporation, it may be necessary to glean information
> relevant to a legal problem from middle management or non-
> management personnel as well as from top executives. The
> attorney dealing with a complex legal problem 'is thus faced with
> a "Hobson's choice." If he interviews employees not having "the
> very highest authority" their communications to him will not be
> privileged. If, on the other hand, he interviews *only* those

employees with the "very highest authority," he may find it extremely difficult, if not impossible, to determine what happened.' " Id., at 608–609 (quoting Weinschel, Corporate Employee Interviews and the Attorney–Client Privilege, 12 B.C.Ind. & Comm.L.Rev. 873, 876 (1970)).

The control group test adopted by the court below thus frustrates the very purpose of the privilege by discouraging the communication of relevant information by employees of the client to attorneys seeking to render legal advice to the client corporation. The attorney's advice will also frequently be more significant to noncontrol group members than to those who officially sanction the advice, and the control group test makes it more difficult to convey full and frank legal advice to the employees who will put into effect the client corporation's policy. See, e.g., Duplan Corp. v. Deering Milliken, Inc., 397 F.Supp. 1146, 1164 (SC 1974) ("After the lawyer forms his or her opinion, it is of no immediate benefit to the Chairman of the Board or the President. It must be given to the corporate personnel who will apply it.").

The narrow scope given the attorney-client privilege by the court below not only makes it difficult for corporate attorneys to formulate sound advice when their client is faced with a specific legal problem but also threatens to limit the valuable efforts of corporate counsel to ensure their client's compliance with the law. In light of the vast and complicated array of regulatory legislation confronting the modern corporation, corporations, unlike most individuals, "constantly go to lawyers to find out how to obey the law," Burnham, The Attorney–Client Privilege in the Corporate Arena, 24 Bus.Law. 901, 913 (1969), particularly since compliance with the law in this area is hardly an instinctive matter, see, e.g., United States v. United States Gypsum Co., 438 U.S. 422, 440–441 (1978) ("the behavior proscribed by the [Sherman] Act is often difficult to distinguish from the gray zone of socially acceptable and economically justifiable business conduct").[21] The test adopted by the court below is difficult to apply in practice, though no abstractly formulated and unvarying "test" will necessarily enable courts to decide questions such as this with mathematical precision. But if the purpose of the attorney-client privilege is to be served, the attorney and client must be able to predict with some degree of certainty whether particular discussions will be protected. An uncertain privilege, or one which purports to be certain but results in widely varying applications by the courts, is little better than

---

[21] The Government argues that the risk of civil or criminal liability suffices to ensure that corporations will seek legal advice in the absence of the protection of the privilege. This response ignores the fact that the depth and quality of any investigations to ensure compliance with the law would suffer, even were they undertaken. The response also proves too much, since it applies to all communications covered by the privilege; an individual trying to comply with the law or faced with a legal problem also has strong incentive to disclose information to his lawyer, yet the common law has recognized the value of the privilege in further facilitating communications.

no privilege at all. The very terms of the test adopted by the court below suggest the unpredictability of its application. The test restricts the availability of the privilege to those officers who play a "substantial role" in deciding and directing a corporation's legal response. Disparate decisions in cases applying this test illustrate its unpredictability. Compare, e.g., Hogan v. Zletz, 43 F.R.D. 308, 315–316 (N.D.Okla.1967), aff'd in part sub nom. Natta v. Hogan, 392 F.2d 686 (C.A.10 1968) (control group includes managers and assistant managers of patent division and research and development department) with Congoleum Industries, Inc. v. GAF Corp., 49 F.R.D. 82, 83–85 (E.D.Pa.1969), aff'd 478 F.2d 1398 (C.A.3 1973) (control group includes only division and corporate vice-presidents, and not two directors of research and vice-president for production and research).

The communications at issue were made by Upjohn employees[22] to counsel for Upjohn acting as such, at the direction of corporate superiors in order to secure legal advice from counsel. As the magistrate found, "Mr. Thomas consulted with the Chairman of the Board and outside counsel and thereafter conducted a factual investigation to determine the nature and extent of the questionable payments *and to be in a position to give legal advice to the company with respect to the payments.*" (Emphasis supplied.) Pet. App. 13a. Information, not available from upper-echelon management, was needed to supply a basis for legal advice concerning compliance with securities and tax laws, foreign laws, currency regulations, duties to shareholders, and potential litigation in each of these areas. The communications concerned matters within the scope of the employees' corporate duties and the employees themselves were sufficiently aware that they were being questioned in order that the corporation could obtain legal advice. The questionnaire identified Thomas as "the company's General Counsel" and referred in its opening sentence to the possible illegality of payments such as the ones on which information was sought. App. 48a. A statement of policy accompanying the questionnaire clearly indicated the legal implications of the investigation. The policy statement was issued "in order that there be no uncertainty in the future as to the policy with respect to the practices which are the subject of this investigation." It began "Upjohn will comply with all laws and regulations," and stated that commissions or payments "will not be used as a subterfuge for bribes or illegal payments" and that all payments must be "proper and legal." Any future agreements with foreign distributors or agents were to be approved "by a company attorney" and any questionsconcerning the policy were to be referred "to

---

[22] Seven of the 86 employees interviewed by counsel had terminated their employment with Upjohn at the time of the interview. App. 33a–38a. Petitioner argues that the privilege should nonetheless apply to communications by these former employees concerning activities during their period of employment. Neither the District Court nor the Court of Appeals had occasion to address this issue, and we decline to decide it without the benefit of treatment below.

the company's General Counsel." App. 165a–166a. This statement was issued to Upjohn employees worldwide, so that even those interviewees not receiving a questionnaire were aware of the legal implications of the interviews. Pursuant to explicit instructions from the Chairman of the Board, the communications were considered "highly confidential" when made, App. 39a, 43a, and have been kept confidential by the company.[23] Consistent with the underlying purposes of the attorney-client privilege, these communications must be protected against compelled disclosure.

The Court of Appeals declined to extend the attorney-client privilege beyond the limits of the control group test for fear that doing so would entail severe burdens on discovery and create a broad "zone of silence" over corporate affairs. Application of the attorney-client privilege to communications such as those involved here, however, puts the adversary in no worse position than if the communications had never taken place. The privilege only protects disclosure of communications; it does not protect disclosure of the underlying facts by those who communicated with the attorney:

> "The protection of the privilege extends only to *communications* and not to facts. A fact is one thing and a communication concerning that fact is an entirely different thing. The client cannot be compelled to answer the question, 'What did you say or write to the attorney?' but may not refuse to disclose any relevant fact within his knowledge merely because he incorporated a statement of such fact into his communication to his attorney." City of Philadelphia v. Westinghouse Electric Corp., 205 F.Supp. 830, 831 (E.D.Pa.1962).

See also *Diversified Industries,* 572 F.2d, at 611; State v. Circuit Court, 34 Wis.2d 559, 580, 150 N.W.2d 387, 399 (1967) ("the courts have noted that a party cannot conceal a fact merely by revealing it to his lawyer"). Here the Government was free to question the employees who communicated with Thomas and outside counsel. Upjohn has provided the IRS with a list of such employees, and the IRS has already interviewed some 25 of them. While it would probably be more convenient for the Government to secure the results of petitioner's internal investigation by simply subpoenaing the questionnaires and notes taken by petitioner's attorneys, such considerations of convenience do not overcome the policies served by the attorney-client privilege. As Justice Jackson noted in his concurring opinion in Hickman v. Taylor, 329 U.S., at 516: "Discovery was hardly intended to enable a learned profession to perform its functions * * * on wits borrowed from the adversary."

---

[23] See magistrate's opinion * * *: "The responses to the questionnaires and the notes of the interviews have been treated as confidential material and have not been disclosed to anyone except Mr. Thomas and outside counsel."

Needless to say, we decide only the case before us, and do not undertake to draft a set of rules which should govern challenges to investigatory subpoenas. Any such approach would violate the spirit of F.R.E. 501. See S.Rep. No. 93–1277, 93d Cong., 2d Sess., 13 ("the recognition of a privilege based on a confidential relationship * * * should be determined on a case-by-case basis"); *Trammel,* 445 U.S. at 47; United States v. Gillock, 445 U.S. 360, 367 (1980). While such a "case-by-case" basis may to some slight extent undermine desirable certainty in the boundaries of the attorney-client privilege, it obeys the spirit of the Rules. At the same time we conclude that the narrow "control group test" sanctioned by the Court of Appeals in this case cannot, consistent with "the principles of the common law as * * * interpreted * * * in light of reason and experience," F.R.E. 501, govern the development of the law in this area.

III

Our decision that the communications by Upjohn employees to counsel are covered by the attorney-client privilege disposes of the case so far as the responses to the questionnaires and any notes reflecting responses to interview questions are concerned. The summons reaches further, however, and Thomas has testified that his notes and memoranda of interviews go beyond recording responses to his questions. App. 27a–28a, 91a–93a. To the extent that the material subject to the summons is not protected by the attorney-client privilege as disclosing communications between an employee and counsel, we must reach the ruling by the Court of Appeals that the work-product doctrine does not apply to summonses issued under 26 U.S.C.A. § 7602.

The Government concedes, wisely, that the Court of Appeals erred and that the work-product doctrine does apply to IRS summonses. Gov.Br., at 16, 48. This doctrine was announced by the Court over 30 years ago in Hickman v. Taylor, 329 U.S. 495 (1947). In that case the Court rejected "an attempt, without purported necessity or justification, to secure written statements, private memoranda, and personal recollections prepared or formed by an adverse party's counsel in the course of his legal duties." Id., at 510. The Court noted that "it is essential that a lawyer work with a certain degree of privacy" and reasoned that if discovery of the material sought were permitted

> "much of what is now put down in writing would remain unwritten. An attorney's thoughts, heretofore inviolate, would not be his own. Inefficiency, unfairness and sharp practices would inevitably develop in the giving of legal advice and in the preparation of cases for trial. The effect on the legal profession would be demoralizing. And the interests of the clients and the cause of justice would be poorly served." Id., at 511.

The "strong public policy" underlying the work-product doctrine was reaffirmed recently in United States v. Nobles, 422 U.S. 225, 236–240 (1975), and has been substantially incorporated in Federal Rule of Civil Procedure 26(b)(3).[24]

As we stated last Term, the obligation imposed by a tax summons remains "subject to the traditional privileges and limitations." United States v. Euge, 444 U.S. 707, 714 (1980). Nothing in the language of the IRS summons provisions or their legislative history suggests an intent on the part of Congress to preclude application of the work-product doctrine. Rule 26(b)(3) codifies the work-product doctrine, and the Federal Rules of Civil Procedure are made applicable to summons enforcement proceedings by Rule 81(a)(3). See Donaldson v. United States, 400 U.S. 517, 528 (1971). While conceding the applicability of the work-product doctrine, the Government asserts that it has made a sufficient showing of necessity to overcome its protections. The magistrate apparently so found. Pet. App. 30a. The Government relies on the following language in *Hickman*:

> "We do not mean to say that all written materials obtained or prepared by an adversary's counsel with an eye toward litigation are necessarily free from discovery in all cases. Where relevant and nonprivileged facts remain hidden in an attorney's file and where production of those facts is essential to the preparation of one's case, discovery may properly be had. * * * And production might be justified where the witnesses are no longer available or may be reached only with difficulty." 329 U.S., at 511.

The Government stresses that interviewees are scattered across the globe and that Upjohn has forbidden its employees to answer questions it considers irrelevant. The above-quoted language from *Hickman,* however, did not apply to "oral statements made by witnesses * * * whether presently in the form of [the attorney's] mental impressions or memoranda." Id., at 512. As to such material the Court did "not believe that any showing of necessity can be made under the circumstances of this case so as to justify production. * * * If there should be a rare situation justifying production of these matters, petitioner's case is not of

---

[24] This provides, in pertinent part:

"[A] party may obtain discovery of documents and tangible things otherwise discoverable under subdivision (b)(1) of this rule and prepared in anticipation of litigation or for trial by or for another party or by or for that other party's representative (including his attorney, consultant, surety, indemnitor, insurer, or agent) only upon a showing that the party seeking discovery has substantial need of the materials in the preparation of his case and that he is unable without undue hardship to obtain the substantial equivalent of the materials by other means. In ordering discovery of such materials when the required showing has been made, the court shall protect against disclosure of the mental impressions, conclusions, opinions, or legal theories of an attorney or other representative of a party concerning the litigation."

that type." Id., at 512–513. See also *Nobles,* supra, at 252–253 (White, J., concurring). Forcing an attorney to disclose notes and memoranda of witnesses' oral statements is particularly disfavored because it tends to reveal the attorney's mental processes, 329 U.S., at 513 ("what he saw fit to write down regarding witnesses' remarks"); id., at 516–517 ("the statement would be his [the attorney's] language, permeated with his inferences") (Jackson, J., concurring).[25]

Rule 26 accords special protection to work product revealing the attorney's mental processes. The Rule permits disclosure of documents and tangible things constituting attorney work product upon a showing of substantial need and inability to obtain the equivalent without undue hardship. This was the standard applied by the magistrate, Pet. App. 26a–27a. Rule 26 goes on, however, to state that "[i]n ordering discovery of such materials when the required showing has been made, the court shall protect against disclosure of the mental impressions, conclusions, opinions or legal theories of an attorney or other representative of a party concerning the litigation." Although this language does not specifically refer to memoranda based on oral statements of witnesses, the *Hickman* court stressed the danger that compelled disclosure of such memoranda would reveal the attorney's mental processes. It is clear that this is the sort of material the draftsmen of the Rule had in mind as deserving special protection. See Notes of Advisory Committee on 1970 Amendment to Rules, reprinted in 48 F.R.D. 487, 502 ("The subdivision * * * goes on to protect against disclosure the mental impressions, conclusions, opinions, or legal theories * * * of an attorney or other representative of a party. The *Hickman* opinion drew special attention to the need for protecting an attorney against discovery of memoranda prepared from recollection of oral interviews. The courts have steadfastly safeguarded against disclosure of lawyers' mental impressions and legal theories * * * ").

Based on the foregoing, some courts have concluded that *no* showing of necessity can overcome protection of work product which is based on oral statements from witnesses. See, e.g., In re Grand Jury Proceedings, 473 F.2d 840, 848 (C.A.8 1973) (personal recollections, notes and memoranda pertaining to conversation with witnesses); In re Grand Jury Investigation, 412 F.Supp. 943, 949 (E.D.Pa.1976) (notes of conversation with witness "are so much a product of the lawyer's thinking and so little probative of the witness's actual words that they are absolutely protected from disclosure"). Those courts declining to adopt an absolute rule have nonetheless recognized that such material is entitled to special protection. See, e.g., In re Grand Jury Investigation, 599 F.2d, at 1231 ("special

---

[25] Thomas described his notes of the interviews as containing "what I consider to be the important questions, the substance of the responses to them, my beliefs as to the importance of these, my beliefs as to how they related to the inquiry, my thoughts as to how they related to other questions. In some instances they might even suggest other questions that I would have to ask or things that I needed to find elsewhere." Pet. App. 13a.

considerations * * * must shape any ruling on the discoverability of interview memoranda * * * such documents will be discoverable only in a 'rare situation' "); cf. In re Grand Jury Subpoena, 599 F.2d, at 511–512.

We do not decide the issue at this time. It is clear that the magistrate applied the wrong standard when he concluded that the Government had made a sufficient showing of necessity to overcome the protections of the work-product doctrine. The magistrate applied the "substantial need" and "without undue hardship" standard articulated in the first part of Rule 26(b)(3). The notes and memoranda sought by the Government here, however, are work product based on oral statements. If they reveal communications, they are, in this case, protected by the attorney-client privilege. To the extent they do not reveal communications, they reveal the attorneys' mental processes in evaluating the communications. As Rule 26 and *Hickman* make clear, such work product cannot be disclosed simply on a showing of substantial need and inability to obtain the equivalent without undue hardship.

While we are not prepared at this juncture to say that such material is always protected by the work-product rule, we think a far stronger showing of necessity and unavailability by other means than was made by the Government or applied by the magistrate in this case would be necessary to compel disclosure. Since the Court of Appeals thought that the work-product protection was never applicable in an enforcement proceeding such as this, and since the magistrate whose recommendations the District Court adopted applied too lenient a standard of protection, we think the best procedure with respect to this aspect of the case would be to reverse the judgment of the Court of Appeals for the Sixth Circuit and remand the case to it for such further proceedings in connection with the work-product claim as are consistent with this opinion.

Accordingly, the judgment of the Court of Appeals is reversed, and the case remanded for further proceedings.

CHIEF JUSTICE BURGER, concurring in part and concurring in the judgment.

I join in Parts I and III of the opinion of the Court and in the judgment. As to Part II, I agree fully with the Court's rejection of the so-called "control group" test, its reasons for doing so, and its ultimate holding that the communications at issue are privileged. As the Court states, however, "if the purpose of the attorney-client privilege is to be served, the attorney and the client must be able to predict with some degree of certainty whether particular discussions will be protected." * * * For this very reason, I believe that we should articulate a standard that will govern similar cases and afford guidance to corporations, counsel advising them, and federal courts.

The Court properly relies on a variety of factors in concluding that the communications now before us are privileged. * * * Because of the great importance of the issue, in my view the Court should make clear now that, as a general rule, a communication is privileged at least when, as here, an employee or former employee speaks at the direction of the management with an attorney regarding conduct or proposed conduct within the scope of employment. The attorney must be one authorized by the management to inquire into the subject and must be seeking information to assist counsel in performing any of the following functions: (a) evaluating whether the employee's conduct has bound or would bind the corporation; (b) assessing the legal consequences, if any, of that conduct; or (c) formulating appropriate legal responses to actions that have been or may be taken by others with regard to that conduct. See, e.g., Diversified Industries, Inc. v. Meredith, 572 F.2d 596, 609 (C.A.8 1977) (en banc); Harper & Row Publishers, Inc. v. Decker, 423 F.2d 487, 491–492 (C.A.7 1970), aff'd by an equally divided Court, 400 U.S. 348 (1971); Duplan Corp. v. Deering Milliken, Inc., 397 F.Supp. 1146, 1163–1165 (SC 1974). Other communications between employees and corporate counsel may indeed be privileged—as the petitioners and several *amici* have suggested in their proposed formulations—but the need for certainty does not compel us now to prescribe all the details of the privilege in this case.

Nevertheless, to say we should not reach all facets of the privilege does not mean that we should neglect our duty to provide guidance in a case that squarely presents the question in a traditional adversary context. Indeed, because Federal Rule of Evidence 501 provides that the law of privileges "shall be governed by the principles of the common law as they may be interpreted by the courts of the United States in light of reason and experience," this Court has a special duty to clarify aspects of the law of privileges properly before us. Simply asserting that this failure "may to some slight extent undermine desirable certainty," * * * neither minimizes the consequences of continuing uncertainty and confusion nor harmonizes the inherent dissonance of acknowledging that uncertainty while declining to clarify it within the frame of issues presented.

NOTES AND QUESTIONS

1. *Sources.* See generally Rothstein, *Upjohn v. United States:* The Story of One Man's Journey to Extend Lawyer–Client Confidentiality and the Social Forces That Affected It, in Evidence Stories 151 (Lempert ed., 2006).

2. *State decisions.* Note that the Supreme Court's decision in *Upjohn* is predicated on common law and not upon federal constitutional grounds. Accordingly the decision does not compel state abandonment of the control group test, which was widely followed prior to *Upjohn*. Although many states have adopted the *Upjohn* approach, see Southern Bell Telephone &

Telegraph Co. v. Deason, 632 So.2d 1377 (Fla.1994), some states have continued to adhere to their earlier standard. Consolidation Coal Co. v. Bucyrus–Erie Co., 432 N.E.2d 250 (Ill.1982). Compare Uniform Rules of Evidence 502, infra.

What problems arise from recognition of different forms of the privilege by state and federal courts? See McCormick, Evidence § 76 (7th ed. 2013). One state court, attempting to minimize such problems by affording "rough comparability with federal common law," Samaritan Foundation v. Goodfarb, 862 P.2d 870 (Ariz.1993), found its solution quickly nullified by legislative action. See Ariz.Rev.Stat. § 12–2234.

3.   *Empirical study.* An interesting (and rare) empirical study of the actual operation of the privilege in the corporate context is Alexander, The Corporate Attorney–Client Privilege: A Study of the Participants, 63 St. John's L.Rev. 191 (1989) (proposing that the privilege for non-control group employees be only a qualified one).

4.   *Other problems in the corporate context.* Among the many problems raised by application of the attorney-client privilege in the corporate context some of the most troublesome concern the question of who should be viewed as representing the corporation in a variety of situations. Should the privilege be available to management in a derivative stockholders action? See Garner v. Wolfinbarger, 430 F.2d 1093 (5th Cir.1970) (privilege held by management but may become unavailable upon stockholder showing of "good cause"). See also Saltzburg, Corporate Attorney–Client Privilege in Shareholder Litigation and Similar Cases: *Garner* Revisited, 12 Hofstra.L.Rev. 817 (1984); Friedman, Is the *Garner* Qualification of the Corporate Attorney–Client Privilege Viable after *Jaffee v. Redmond*, 55 Bus. Law. 243 (1999). *Garner* has been extended to a variety of situations other than derivative suits. See, e.g., Solis v. Food Employers Labor Relations Ass'n, 644 F.3d 221 (4th Cir.2011) (adopts the fiduciary exception for documents subpoenaed in response to ERISA investigations); In re Occidental Petroleum Corp., 217 F.3d 293 (5th Cir.2000) (employees who were participants in stock ownership plan suing for breaches of fiduciary duty relating to the plan); Fausek v. White, 965 F.2d 126 (6th Cir.1992) (minority shareholders suing for own benefit rather than corporation's). Who should hold the privilege as between management and a trustee in bankruptcy? Commodity Futures Trading Comm'n v. Weintraub, 471 U.S. 343 (1985). Problems of this sort will obviously be compounded if the communicating employee asserts that he was also personally the client of the attorney.

5.   *Work product privilege.* The *Upjohn* case involved the work product privilege as well as the attorney-client privilege. See 1 McCormick, Evidence § 96 (7th ed. 2013), for a comparison of these related, overlapping and often confused doctrines.

Uniform Rules of Evidence

RULE 502. LAWYER–CLIENT PRIVILEGE.

(a) Definitions. In this rule:

(1) "Client" means a person for whom a lawyer renders professional legal services or who consults a lawyer with a view to obtaining professional legal services from the lawyer.

(2) A communication is "confidential" if it is not intended to be disclosed to third persons other than those to whom disclosure is made in furtherance of the rendition of professional legal services to the client or those reasonably necessary for the transmission of the communication.

(3) "Lawyer" means a person authorized, or reasonably believed by the client to be authorized, to engage in the practice of law in any State or country.

(4) "Representative of the client" means a person having authority to obtain professional legal services, or to act on legal advice rendered, on behalf of the client or a person who, for the purpose of effectuating legal representation for the client, makes or receives a confidential communication while acting in the scope of employment for the client.

(5) "Representative of the lawyer" means a person employed, or reasonably believed by the client to be employed, by the lawyer to assist the lawyer in rendering professional legal services.

(b) General rule of privilege. A client has a privilege to refuse to disclose and to prevent any other person from disclosing a confidential communication made for the purpose of facilitating the rendition of professional legal services to the client:

(1) between the client or a representative of the client and the client's lawyer or a representative of the lawyer;

(2) between the lawyer and a representative of the lawyer;

(3) by the client or a representative of the client or the client's lawyer or a representative of the lawyer to a lawyer or a representative of a lawyer representing another party in a pending action and concerning a matter of common interest therein;

(4) between representatives of the client or between the client and a representative of the client; or

(5) among lawyers and their representatives representing the same client.

(c) Who may claim privilege. The privilege under this rule may be claimed by the client, the client's guardian or conservator, the personal representative of a deceased client, or the successor, trustee, or similar representative of a corporation, association, or other organization, whether or not in existence. A person who was the lawyer or the lawyer's representative at the time of the communication is presumed to have authority to claim the privilege, but only on behalf of the client.

(d) Exceptions. There is no privilege under this rule:

(1) if the services of the lawyer were sought or obtained to enable or aid anyone to commit or plan to commit what the client knew or reasonably should have known was a crime or fraud;

(2) as to a communication relevant to an issue between parties who claim through the same deceased client, regardless of whether the claims are by testate or intestate succession or by transaction inter vivos;

(3) as to a communication relevant to an issue of breach of duty by a lawyer to the client or by a client to the lawyer;

(4) as to a communication necessary for a lawyer to defend in a legal proceeding an accusation that the lawyer assisted the client in criminal or fraudulent conduct;

(5) as to a communication relevant to an issue concerning an attested document to which the lawyer is an attesting witness;

(6) as to a communication relevant to a matter of common interest between or among two or more clients if the communication was made by any of them to a lawyer retained or consulted in common, when offered in an action between or among any of the clients; or

(7) as to a communication between a public officer or agency and its lawyers unless the communication concerns a pending investigation, claim, or action and the court determines that disclosure will seriously impair the ability of the public officer or agency to act upon the claim or conduct a pending investigation, litigation, or proceeding in the public interest.

NOTES AND QUESTIONS

1. *Comparison with Upjohn.* Prior to 1986, Revised Uniform Rule of Evidence 502 embodied the "control group" test rejected in *Upjohn Co. v. United States.* The rule was amended in 1987 to track the *Upjohn* holding. Uniform Rule of Evidence 502 (amended 1986), Comment. To what extent does it do so? Are all aspects of the rule suggested by the *Upjohn* decision?

2. *Subject matter.* What should be the result if the subject matter of the corporate employee's communication to the corporate attorney has no connection with the employee's corporate duties? A subject matter limitation where the privilege is claimed for communications by corporate employees has frequently been advocated. See, e.g., D.I. Chadbourne, Inc. v. Superior Court, 388 P.2d 700 (Cal.1964). Would such a limitation invite unduly restricted applications of the privilege? In Leer v. Chicago, M., St. P. & Pac. Ry., 308 N.W.2d 305 (Minn.1981), the court first argued, conventionally, that "communications about events which are within the employee's knowledge simply because he witnessed an accident" should not be privileged. The court then applied this rule to deny privilege to statements of the members of a railway switching crew concerning a switching accident, stating that "the witnessing of an accident was not within the scope of the employees' duties."

3. *Representatives of the client.* Cases considering who is a "representative" of the client under rules similar to Uniform Rule 502 are collected in Annot., 66 A.L.R.4th 1227. Should the expansive definition of "representative of the client" now contained in Uniform Rule 502 apply, as the text of the rule would justify, to individuals as well as to corporate clients? Should it matter whether the communication concerns the principal's business or private affairs? In State v. Jancsek, 730 P.2d 14 (Or.1986) (en banc), the privilege was held inapplicable to a letter written by the defendant to a former employer which contained incriminating statements and empowered the addressee to secure legal representation. The court held that while the terms of the statute (similar to Uniform Rule 502) would support availability of the privilege to a non-business entity, the legislative history did not.

Compare Sexton, A Post *Upjohn* Consideration of the Corporate Attorney–Client Privilege, 57 N.Y.U.L.Rev. 443 (1982) (suggesting that *Upjohn* may foreshadow the development of an "enterprise" privilege, extending to the non-managerial employees of labor unions, government agencies, partnerships, and other entities).

STATE V. PRATT

Court of Appeals of Maryland, 1979.
398 A.2d 421.

DIGGES, JUDGE.

The question presented by this criminal cause is one of first impression in this State, and yet, it involves "the oldest of the privileges for confidential communications"—that which exists between an attorney and his client. 8 J. Wigmore, *Evidence in Trials at Common Law* § 2290, at 542 (McNaughton rev. 1961). Stated succinctly, we are asked to decide whether this privilege was violated when, over objection, a psychiatrist, who was retained by defense counsel to examine his client in preparing an insanity defense, was permitted to testify at the instance of the prosecution. Because we conclude that this fundamental privilege was invaded, we will direct a new trial.

The factual background here is uncomplicated and may be briefly related. On the morning of October 23, 1976, respondent Margaret Melton Pratt, after a sleepless night during which she contemplated the taking of her own life, shot and killed her still-slumbering husband, William S. Pratt, in their Montgomery County apartment. After the shooting, the wife packed an overnight bag and drove to a friend's farm near Front Royal, Virginia, to visit the gravesite of her dog; she stayed several hours and then proceeded to a nearby motel to spend the night. The next morning Mrs. Pratt returned to her home and, after a short stay there, began driving aimlessly around the Bethesda–Rockville area. Realizing she would eventually be apprehended, the respondent went to the Montgomery County police and informed them of her husband's death. The officers, after verifying Mrs. Pratt's story concerning what had taken place, arrested her for murder.

* * *

Throughout the trial, Mrs. Pratt did not dispute that she had killed her husband but, instead, strenuously urged that she was insane at the time she fired the fatal shots. In support of her insanity plea, respondent presented two psychiatrists, Dr. Gerald Polin and Dr. Leon Yochelson, who testified that at the time of the act Mrs. Pratt was, in their opinion, suffering from a mental illness of such severity that she lacked substantial capacity to conform her conduct to the requirements of the law. *See* Md.Code (1957, 1972 Repl. Vol.), Art. 59, § 25(a). In rebuttal, the State produced three psychiatrists, all of whom agreed that the respondent was suffering from some degree of mental disorder when the shooting took place. Nonetheless, two of these medical experts testified that, under Maryland law, Mrs. Pratt was legally responsible for her act. Of these two, one, Dr. Brian Crowley, had examined the accused at the request of her attorney after being retained by him to aid in preparing support for Mrs. Pratt's insanity plea. It is the evidence given by Dr. Crowley, who testified during the trial at the request of the State and over the objection of the defense, that precipitated the controversy now before us. On appeal to the Court of Special Appeals, that court concluded that the permitting of Dr. Crowley's testimony violated the attorney-client privilege and ordered a new trial. *Pratt v. State,* 39 Md.App. 442, 387 A.2d 779 (1978). We agree.

In this State the attorney-client privilege, deeply rooted in common law and now memorialized in section 9–108 of the Maryland Code's (1974) Courts Article, is a rule of evidence that forever bars disclosure, without the consent of the client, of all communications that pass in confidence between the client and his attorney during the course of professional employment or as an incident of professional intercourse between them. *See Harrison v. State,* 276 Md. 122, 135, 345 A.2d 830, 838 (1975); 3 B. Jones, *The Law of Evidence* § 21:8–:10, at 762–71 (6th ed. S. Gard 1972); 8 J. Wigmore, *supra,* § 2292, at 554. The privilege is based upon the public policy that " 'an individual in a free society should be encouraged to consult with his attorney whose function is to counsel and advise him and he should be free from apprehension of compelled disclosures by his legal advisor.' " *Harrison v. State, supra,* 276 Md. at 135, 345 A.2d at 838 (quoting *Morris v. State,* 4 Md.App. 252, 254, 242 A.2d 559, 560 (1968)); *accord,* 8 J. Wigmore, *supra,* § 2291, at 545. While never given an explicit constitutional underpinning, the privilege is, nevertheless, closely tied to the federal, as well as this State's, constitutional guarantees of effective assistance of counsel and could, if limited too severely, make these basic guarantees virtually meaningless. *Harrison v. State, supra,* 276 Md. at 133–34, 345 A.2d at 837; *United States v. Alvarez,* 519 F.2d 1036, 1045–47 (3d Cir.1975); *see* U.S.Const., amend. VI; Md.Decl. of Rts., Art. 21.

Initially we observe that, given the complexities of modern existence, few if any lawyers could, as a practical matter, represent the interest of their clients without a variety of nonlegal assistance. Recognizing this limitation, it is now almost universally accepted in this country that the scope of the attorney-client privilege, at least in criminal causes, embraces those agents whose services are required by the attorney in order that he may properly prepare his client's case. Consequently, in line with the views of the vast majority of the courts in our sister jurisdictions, we have no hesitancy in concluding that in criminal causes communications made by a defendant to an expert in order to equip that expert with the necessary information to provide the defendant's attorney with the tools to aid him in giving his client proper legal advice are within the scope of the attorney-client privilege. *E.g., United States v. Alvarez, supra,* 519 F.2d at 1046 (psychiatrist); *United States v. Kovel,* 296 F.2d 918, 922 (2d Cir.1961) (accountant); *People v. Lines,* 13 Cal.3d 500, 119 Cal.Rptr. 225, 232–35, 531 P.2d 793, 800–03 (1975) (psychiatrist); *accord,* 3 B. Jones, *supra,* § 21:15, at 786–87. *But cf. State v. Mingo,* 143 N.J.Super. 411, 363 A.2d 369, 370–71 (1976) (per curiam) (because defendant's handwriting exemplars not privileged communications, State's solicitation at trial of opinion of defense-hired graphologist as to identity of handwriting on note sent to assault victim not barred by attorney-client privilege). This is uniquely so in cases concerning the question of a criminal defendant's sanity, because the need of an attorney to consult with a qualified medical expert is paramount. Such a medical expert not only provides testimony that usually is necessary at trial to support an insanity defense, but also "attunes the lay attorney to unfamiliar but central medical concepts and enables him, as an initial matter, to assess the soundness and advisability of offering the defense * * * and perhaps most importantly, * * * permits a lawyer inexpert in the science of psychiatry to probe intelligently the foundations of adverse testimony." *United States v. Taylor,* 437 F.2d 371, 377 n.9 (4th Cir.1971).

The State here does not dispute the inclusion of psychiatric communications within the scope of the attorney-client privilege; instead, it contends that when Mrs. Pratt interposed a defense of insanity, she waived the privilege with respect to all statements she may have made to any medical expert, whether in her employ or in that of the State.[26] While there is little doubt that a client may waive this right to confidentiality, which may be done either expressly or impliedly, *see, e.g., Harrison v. State, supra,* 276 Md. at 136–38, 345 A.2d at 839; 8 J. Wigmore, *supra,* § 2327, at 634–39; *but see* 2 H. Underhill, *Criminal Evidence* § 333, at 841 (5th ed. P. Herrick 1956) (doubtful if any waiver of the privilege should be implied in criminal cause), we have been made aware of only one decision in which a court, the New York Court of Appeals, has held that raising the defense of insanity, without more, is a relinquishment of the attorney-client privilege as to communications between the client and his alienist. In its opinion the court justified its conclusion that a defendant's insanity plea waived the attorney-client privilege on the following basis:

> A defendant who seeks to introduce psychiatric testimony in support of his insanity plea may be required to disclose prior to trial the underlying basis of his alleged affliction to a prosecution psychiatrist. Hence, where, as here, a defendant reveals to the prosecution the very facts which would be secreted by the exercise of the privilege, reason does not compel the exclusion of expert testimony based on such facts, or cross-examination concerning the grounds for opinions based thereon. It follows that no harm accrues to the defense from seeking pretrial psychiatric advice where an insanity plea is actually entered, for in such circumstances, the underlying factual basis will be revealed to the prosecution psychiatrist. (*People v. Edney,* 39 N.Y.2d 620, 385 N.Y.S.2d 23, 26, 350 N.E.2d 400, 403 (1976). * * *)

While there appears to be some logic, at least in a technical sense, to New York's highest court's reasoning, nonetheless we find that the chilling effect such a result would have upon a client's willingness to confide in his attorney or any defense-employed consultants requires that we align ourselves with the overwhelming body of authority and reject that court's conclusion. *See United States v. Alvarez, supra,* 519 F.2d at 1046; *United States ex rel. Edney v. Smith,* 425 F.Supp. 1038, 1039, 1053

---

[26] In effect, the State asks us, by judicial decision, to create a waiver of the attorney-client privilege as the General Assembly has done by providing that, in the case of the psychiatrist/psychologist-patient privilege, if the patient "introduces his mental condition as an element of his claim or defense * * *," the privilege is waived. *See* Md.Code (1974, 1978 Cum.Supp.), § 9–109(d)(3)(i) of the Courts Article.

(E.D.N.Y.1976) (dicta); *People v. Lines, supra,* 531 P.2d at 800–03, 119 Cal.Rptr. at 232–35; *Pouncy v. State,* 353 So.2d 640, 641–42 (Fla.Dist.Ct.App.1977); *People v. Hilliker,* 29 Mich.App. 543, 185 N.W.2d 831, 833 (1971); *State v. Kociolek,* 23 N.J. 400, 129 A.2d 417, 423–26 (1957).

Moreover, a further drawback to the New York rule is the prejudice inherent in disclosing to the trier of fact that the source of this adverse testimony is an expert originally employed by the defendant. This factor will almost certainly carry added weight with the jury, which usually is the prosecution's principal purpose for producing the defense-employed psychiatrist as a witness. *See United States ex rel. Edney v. Smith, supra,* 425 F.Supp. at 1053; Note, *Protecting the Confidentiality of Pretrial Psychiatric Disclosures: A Survey of Standards,* 51 N.Y.U.L.Rev. 409, 411 (1976). The potential for prejudice inherent in such evidence, as demonstrated by the State's closing argument to the jury in this case,[27] graphically illustrates that the attorney-client privilege protecting such potential testimony from disclosure should remain intact. Though the State points out that this Court previously has recognized the existence of a discretion in the trial court to permit the introduction of evidence concerning the employment posture of an expert because such evidence is frequently a useful factor in evaluating the credibility of the expert witness's testimony, *City of Baltimore v. Zell,* 279 Md. 23, 28, 367 A.2d 14, 17 (1977), that decision arose in a civil context and does not provide a persuasive basis for employing a waiver of the attorney-client privilege in criminal causes.[28]

* * *

* * * Breaching the attorney-client privilege in this situation also would have the effect of inhibiting the free exercise of a defense attorney's

---

[27] Concerning the testimony of Dr. Crowley, the State's Attorney argued to the jury:

Mr. Heeney [, the defendant's attorney,] said he was glad he didn't use Dr. Crowley. If Dr. Crowley had given a different opinion, Dr. Crowley would have been in here so fast it would have made your head spin and not in my case but in Mr. Heeney's case. *They hired Dr. Crowley.* Dr. Crowley was the first defense psychiatrist to see Mrs. Pratt. He said she did not lack substantial capacity * * *. *What do they do after that? They kept looking and finally they found him. How many people didn't show up here?* I don't know the answer to that. Were there any others we don't know about? I don't know. We know they found two. [(Emphasis added.)]

[28] In reaching the result we do in this case, we confine our holding to criminal causes and specifically reserve for another time the question of the scope of the attorney-client privilege when an attorney hires an expert to aid in the preparation of civil matters. Though an opponent called as his witness at trial an expert appraiser hired by his adversary in *City of Baltimore v. Zell,* 279 Md. 23, 367 A.2d 14 (1977), he did so without objection and thus, in *Zell,* the question of the impact upon the attorney-client privilege of allowing that testimony was not determined by this Court. For differing views among our sister states on this subject compare *People v. Donovan,* 57 Cal.2d 346, 369 P.2d 1, 5–7, 19 Cal.Rptr. 473, 477–79 (1962) (appraiser's opinion not covered by attorney-client privilege) with *State v. 62.96247 Acres of Land in New Castle County,* 193 A.2d 799, 810, 7 Storey 40 (Del.Super.Ct.1963) (attorney-client privilege bars party from compelling testimony of appraiser hired by opponent) and *Lindsay v. Lipson,* 367 Mich. 1, 116 N.W.2d 60, 62–63 (1962) (to allow physician hired by plaintiff in tort action to testify for defendant, over opponent's objection, violates attorney-client privilege).

informed judgment by confronting him with the likelihood that, in taking a step obviously crucial to his client's defense, he is creating a potential government witness who theretofore did not exist. *Id.* The possible impact upon the federal and State constitutional rights of the defendant of a rule permitting such testimony further persuades us that we should be reluctant to hold there is a waiver, under the circumstances here, of the attorney-client privilege.

Accordingly, we affirm the judgment of the Court of Special Appeals, which comports with the ruling we make here.

NOTES AND QUESTIONS

1. *Insanity defense.* Courts are split on the issue of whether defendant presenting an insanity defense waives the attorney-client privilege as to nontestifying defense retained psychiatrists. In addition to *Pratt*, compare State v. Pawlyk, 800 P.2d 338 (Wash.1990) (assertion of an insanity defense waives privilege), with United States v. Alvarez, 519 F.2d 1036 (3d Cir.1975) (privilege applies despite assertion of insanity defense). See generally Note, Witness for the Prosecution: Prosecutorial Discovery of Information Generated by Non-testifying Defense Psychiatric Experts, 62 Fordham L.Rev. 653 (1993).

2. *Waivers based on claims or defenses. Pratt* is extensively discussed and criticized in Saltzburg, Privileges and Professionals: Lawyers and Psychiatrists, 66 Va.L.Rev. 597 (1980). Professor Saltzburg advocates the view that raising the defense of insanity should, in effect, waive the attorney-client privilege insofar as it might cover psychiatric testimony from experts initially retained by the defense. Should the commencement of an action by the beneficiary of a double indemnity life insurance contract, contested on grounds of suicide, waive the attorney-client privilege as to statements by the deceased to his attorney? Martin v. John Hancock Mut. Life Ins. Co., 466 N.Y.S.2d 596 (Gen.Term.1983), held in the affirmative. On what ground, if any, can this result be justified?

Certain defenses, too, may if asserted waive the privilege. Not surprisingly, asserting a defense of advice of counsel waives the privilege. See United States v. Workman, 138 F.3d 1261 (8th Cir.1998).

3. *Work product privilege.* To what extent should the work product privilege bar access to expert testimony which will be used at trial? See Federal Rule of Civil Procedure 26(b)(4). See generally Imwinkelried, The Applicability of the Attorney–Client Privilege to Non–Testifying Experts: Reestablishing the Boundaries Between the Attorney–Client Privilege and the Work Product Protection, 68 Wash.U.L.Q. 19 (1990), where the author asserts that the attorney-client privilege applies to communications between the client and the psychiatrist but that only the work product privilege applies to the expert's other information. See also State v. Pawlyk, note 1, supra (work-product privilege also inapplicable); Friedenthal, Discovery and

Use of Adverse Party's Expert Information, 14 Stan.L.Rev. 455 (1962); Graham, Discovery of Experts under Rule 26(b)(4) of the Federal Rules of Civil Procedure, 1976 U.Ill.L.F. 895.

HENKE V. IOWA HOME MUT. CAS. CO.

Supreme Court of Iowa, 1958.
87 N.W.2d 920.

LARSON, JUSTICE. The principal issue involved in this appeal is whether correspondence, reports and communications are confidential and privileged between an insurer and the attorney employed by it to defend an insured in litigation resulting from an automobile accident insofar as it pertains to that litigation.

Plaintiff brought an action at law asking damages against the defendant, an automobile liability insurance company, referred to herein as the insurer, for bad faith and negligence in failing to settle two cases against plaintiff within the limits of the policy and in which judgment was rendered against him in an amount greatly in excess of the limits of the policy. After the issues were resolved, plaintiff filed an application asking for an order directing the defendant company to produce for plaintiff's inspection, copying, or photostating "all letters, correspondence, reports, communications and copies of the same," concerning the two previously tried cases in Floyd County, Iowa. Defendant's resistance was on the sole ground that each and every item which plaintiff asked an order to produce "is privileged" under the laws of the State of Iowa, and is therefore not available to plaintiff for his use in the trial of this cause.

In its ruling the court found that the insurer employed a Mason City law firm in accordance with its obligation under an insurance contract with plaintiff's decedent, to defend in any action for damages resulting from such an accident; that said firm did defend the administrator in the trial of the two cases, and further that said firm "did defend and represent both parties, that is E.W. Henke, Administrator, and Iowa Home Mutual Casualty Company in the two cases against * * * E.W. Henke, Administrator."

The trial court then said: "The Court finds that this being true, the letters and documents which the plaintiff in this cause wishes to inspect, copy or photostat, are not privileged," and it entered an order for the defendant to deposit within fifteen days with the clerk, for inspection, copying or photostating by plaintiff, *all letters, correspondence, reports, communications* and *copies* of same, concerning the causes of action heretofore mentioned, sent by the defendant company to the Mason City attorneys who tried the cases, and received by the company from said attorneys, as it concerned the two causes of action already tried. * * *

I. Defendant denies there is any attorney-client relationship between a lawyer, hired by an insurer and who defends the insured under the terms of the insurance policy, and the insured. The contention is without merit. * * *

II. We have consistently held that when two or more parties consult an attorney for their mutual benefit, the testimony as to the communications between the parties or the attorney as to that transaction is not privileged in a later action between such parties or their representatives. In our latest reference to this matter in England v. England, 243 Iowa 274, 282, 51 N.W.2d 437, 442, we said:

> "Notwithstanding section 622.10, Code 1950 (now 1954), I.C.A., prohibiting testimony as to confidential communications, (the attorney's) testimony would have been admissible since, as (he) testifies, he acted as adviser to both plaintiff and defendant who went together to his office, if indeed he was more than primarily a scrivener of the deeds."

The rule is quite clear that to constitute a privileged communication to an attorney there must be some element of confidence imposed in the attorney himself, and for him to accept that relationship it must be apparent that the transaction or his action in relation thereto is for the mutual benefit of the parties, knowingly and willingly seeking his professional services.

It is true that in most, if not in all, of our previously-decided cases, both parties went together to the attorney for advice and guidance. Defendant vigorously contends that even if insurer and insured were both clients of one attorney in regard to the actions, the confidential nature of their respective communications with the attorney must be respected and be held privileged unless (1) they are made in the presence of the other or (2) are made with the intent that they be communicated. Such exceptions to the confidential nature of attorney-client communications, if adopted, might be justified as waivers. * * *

While there is respectable authority holding that communications between joint clients and their attorney are not privileged on the basis of waiver, Allen v. Ross, 199 Wis. 162, 225 N.W. 831, 64 A.L.R. 180; State v. Rogers, 226 Wis. 39, 51, 275 N.W. 910, and other cases cited in annotation, 22 A.L.R.2d 662–664, we are convinced there is a more compelling reason the general rule prohibiting disclosures of information received in confidence by one of two or more joint clients in regard to a transaction for their mutual benefit, is not privileged. It is simply that if it appears the secret or imparted communication is such that the attorney is under a duty to divulge it for the protection of the others he has undertaken to represent in the involved transaction, then the communication is not privileged. It would be shocking indeed to require an attorney who had assumed such a duty to act for the mutual benefit of both or several parties to be permitted or compelled to withhold vital information affecting the rights of others because it involves the informant. * * * The rule is based on much firmer ground than waiver, that of duty, loyalty and fairness, as well as on substantial public policy.

In the fast-moving economic world of today it seems desirable and proper to permit and encourage the consultation of an attorney by several parties on matters or transactions in which they have joint and mutual interests, although in almost every such case there is a potential conflict of interest and, if and when it develops, that lawyer cannot and should not try to render further service or advice therein.

In the case of Kilgo v. Continental Casualty Co., 140 Ark. 336, 215 S.W. 689, we find a situation somewhat in reverse of the case at bar. There the insured communicated the information to the attorney representing both the insured and insurer, in a personal damage action, that his former statements given the insurance company were false. That communication was held not privileged and the attorney's testimony concerning same admissible in an action between the parties and their representatives or assigns. * * *

Such being the case before us, we conclude the trial court was correct in holding that the papers requested were not as between the parties confidential, and that the claim of privilege was invalid.

Affirmed.

NOTES AND QUESTIONS

1. *Communications between insured and insurance company.* Should communications between an insured and representatives of his or her insurance company be privileged as against third persons? Compare Asbury v. Beerbower, 589 S.W.2d 216 (Ky.1979) (privileged), with Varuzza v. Bulk Materials, Inc., 169 F.R.D. 254 (N.D.N.Y.1996) (no privilege). Should it matter with whom the insured communicates—an attorney, claims representative, outside adjuster? Cases dealing with the existence of the privilege in a variety of situations involving the insured and insurer are collected in Annot., 55 A.L.R.4th 336. If not within the attorney-client privilege, should work product protection apply? See Menton v. Lattimore, 667 S.W.2d 335 (Tex.App.1984).

2. *Presence of third persons.* The presence of a third person who is not an agent of either the client or the attorney is usually taken as an indication of lack of confidentiality, precluding the application of the privilege. Mitchell v. Towne, 87 P.2d 908 (Cal.Ct.App.1939); People v. Buchanan, 39 N.E. 846 (N.Y.1895). However, the cases have been generous in including within the privilege agents employed in effecting the communication. Thus State v. Loponio, 88 A. 1045 (N.J.1913), applied the privilege to communications by

an illiterate accused to a fellow prisoner who acted as his amanuensis in writing a letter for the purpose of retaining a lawyer. What about the presence of the client's family members during the conference with the attorney? Compare United States v. Bigos, 459 F.2d 639 (1st Cir.1972) (presence of father did not vitiate privilege), with Cafritz v. Koslow, 167 F.2d 749 (D.C.Cir.1948) (sister's presence destroyed privilege).

3. *Joint defense or common interest.* Meetings between clients and their lawyers planning a joint defense or the exchange of statements between attorneys representing different parties with a common interest have generally been held not to constitute a waiver of attorney-client privilege applicable to the statements in the first instance. See, e.g., United States v. McPartlin, 595 F.2d 1321 (7th Cir.1979); Continental Oil Co. v. United States, 330 F.2d 347 (9th Cir.1964); Hanover Ins. Co. v. Rapo & Jepsen Ins. Services, Inc., 870 N.E.2d 1105 (Mass. 2007) (joint defense exception applied despite lack of clients' express consent to such an agreement). But see United States v. Evans, 113 F.3d 1457 (7th Cir.1997) (common interest did not arise until after meeting with attorney); Vance v. State, 230 S.W.2d 987 (Tenn.1950) (meeting not for purpose of planning a joint defense). If there is a common interest, will communications between clients concerning their legal representation outside the presence of the attorney for either be privileged? The court in United States v. Gotti, 771 F.Supp. 535 (E.D.N.Y.1991), suggested that there would be no privilege.

4. *Inadvertent disclosure and Federal Rule 502.* Conventional doctrine dictates that disclosure of privileged matter to third persons, and particularly opponents in litigation, constitutes waiver. See Unif.R.Evid. 510 (1999). However, the realities of modern discovery practice, in which thousands of documents may be required to be produced, obviously raise unprecedented possibilities of inadvertent disclosure. Should waiver automatically result from even inadvertent disclosure, or should additional conditions be attached? Courts are divided on the issue. See generally Marcus, The Perils of Privilege: Waiver and the Litigator, 84 Mich.L.Rev. 1605 (1986); Kiker, Waiving the Privilege in a Storm of Data: An Argument for Uniformity and Rationality in Dealing with the Inadvertent Production of Privileged Materials in the Age of Electronically Stored Information, 12 Rich.J.L. & Tech. 15 (2006). The Federal Rules of Evidence were amended in 2008 to add Rule 502, providing that inadvertent disclosures do not operate as waivers, provided the privilege holder took reasonable steps to prevent disclosure and to rectify the error. The rule applies in federal courts to disclosures made in either federal or state proceedings. Rule 502 also provides that a federal court order, including those incorporating party agreements, finding that there is no waiver is binding in other federal or state proceedings, even with regard to third parties. See also Grimm, Bergstrom & Kraeuter, Federal Rule of Evidence 502: Has It Lived Up To Its Potential?, 17 Rich. J.L. & Tech. 8 (2011); Murphy, Federal Rule of Evidence 502: The "Get Out of Jail Free" Provision—Or Is It?, 41 N.M. L.Rev. 193 (2011). Several courts have used a five-part test to determine the reasonableness of the producing parties

actions. The * * * test requires the court to balance the following factors to determine whether inadvertent production of attorney-client privileged materials waives the privilege: (1) the reasonableness of the precautions taken to prevent inadvertent disclosure; (2) the number of inadvertent disclosures; (3) the extent of the disclosures; (4) any delay in measures taken to rectify the disclosure; and (5) overriding interests in justice." Victor Stanley, Inc. v. Creative Pipe, Inc., 250 F.R.D. 251, 259 (D.Md. 2008). *See also* Felman Production, Inc. v. Industrial Risk Insurers, 2010 WL 2944777 at *3 (S.D.W.Va.2010).

5. *Partial disclosure.* Waiver will generally not result from disclosure of the underlying facts, but only if the communication itself is disclosed. Commonwealth v. Goldman, 480 N.E.2d 1023 (Mass.1985). Should disclosure of a portion of the communication result in waiver of the privilege with respect to the remainder? Should the answer depend upon whether the partial disclosure is made judicially or extrajudicially? See von Bulow v. von Bulow, 828 F.2d 94 (2d Cir.1987); Marcus, note 4, supra. Fed.R.Evid. 502, note 4, supra, provides that a waiver extends to undisclosed communication or information "concerning the same subject matter only if that undisclosed communication or information ought in fairness to be considered with the disclosed communication or information."

UNITED STATES V. KENDRICK

United States Court of Appeals, Fourth Circuit, 1964.
331 F.2d 110.

PER CURIAM.

This is an appeal from the District Court's decision denying, after hearing, the petitioner's motion under 28 U.S.C.A. § 2255 to vacate an illegal sentence on the grounds that the petitioner was incompetent to stand trial. * * *

The Government's case consisted of the testimony of counsel appointed by the Court to represent the petitioner at his trial in 1960 and of the F.B.I. Agent who arrested him. Both of these witnesses testified to the extent of their contacts with the petitioner and stated over objection from petitioner's present counsel that in their opinion he was sane and competent to stand trial. * * *

We do not agree with the petitioner that the testimony of his trial counsel should have been excluded at the post-conviction hearing on the basis of the attorney-client privilege.

We need not now consider whether the assertion that he was incapable of effective communication and cooperation with trial counsel is a waiver of the attorney-client privilege on the ground that the petitioner has flung open the curtain of secrecy which otherwise would conceal his actual communications. Nor need we enter the controversy as to whether such an assertion is always so necessarily an implicit attack upon the competence of trial counsel as to amount to a waiver of the privilege to the extent necessary to enable trial counsel to defend himself and his reputation. See Gunther v. United States, 97 U.S.App.D.C. 254, 230 F.2d 222 (1956); cf. United States v. Wiggins, 184 F.Supp. 673 (D.C.1960); United States v. Bostic, 206 F.Supp. 855 (D.C.1962). We do not here consider the question of waiver on either ground, for the attorney's testimony was well within an established exception to the privilege.

Communications made in confidence by a client to his attorney are protected by the attorney-client privilege. It is the substance of the communications which is protected, however, not the fact that there have been communications. Excluded from the privilege, also, are physical characteristics of the client, such as his complexion, his demeanor, his bearing, his sobriety and his dress. Such things are observable by anyone who talked with the client, and there is nothing, in the usual case, to suggest that the client intends his attorney's observations of such matters to be confidential.[29] In short, the privilege protects only the client's confidences, not things which, at the time, are not intended to be held in the breast of the lawyer, even though the attorney-client relation provided the occasion for the lawyer's observation of them. See generally VIII Wigmore, Evidence (McNaughton Revision) § 2306.

Here the attorney testified to just such nonconfidential matters. Petitioner, the attorney testified, was responsive, readily supplied the attorney with his version of the facts and the names of other people involved, was logical in his conversation and his reasoning, and appeared to know and understand everything that went on before and during the trial. No mention was made of the substance of any communication by client to attorney; the witness testified only about his client's cooperativeness and awareness.

All of the matters to which the attorney testified are objectively observable particularizations of the client's demeanor and attitude. Made at a time when neither client nor lawyer manifested any reason to suppose they were confidential, they were not within the privilege. Certainly, the client was then making no secret of his capacity, or want of capacity to communicate with his attorney and to cooperate in his defense.

It is suggested that, in these circumstances, adequate cross-examination of attorney-witness might require the petitioner to inquire into the substance of his communications. That is speculative, however. Effective cross-examination need not go so far. And, if difficulty inheres in

---

[29] Particular circumstances may alter the rule. If the client reveals to the attorney a physical defect, usually concealed by clothing, which may be relevant to the attorney's representation of him, it well may be a confidential and protected communication.

the situation, it is no more than if the question were the client's sobriety or inebriety at the time of an otherwise unrelated consultation. If the attorney who testifies his client's hair was blonde when she consulted him had confused her with another client, inquiry as to the substance of the communication might be the only effective means of revealing his confusion, but his testimony is not drawn within the privilege on that account.

We have not heretofore considered this particular question when it was contested, but we have tacitly assumed that the trial attorney may be examined as to such matters, indeed, that the postconviction court should seek such light as the trial attorney can throw upon the question. United States v. Pledger, 301 F.2d 906 (4 Cir.1962); United States v. Taylor, 303 F.2d 165 (4 Cir.1962); United States v. McNicholas, 298 F.2d 914 (4 Cir.1962). Our tacit assumption does not foreclose reconsideration, but after thorough reconsideration in this contested case, we adhere to it.

However persuasive the highly relevant testimony of the attorney, which we now hold properly received, it does not militate against our conclusion that a further hearing should be held to inquire into the petitioner's medical history, diagnosis, treatment and response after his reception in Atlanta. * * *

The judgment is vacated and the case remanded for further proceedings in accordance with this opinion.

Vacated and remanded.

SOBELOFF, CHIEF JUDGE, and J. SPENCER BELL, CIRCUIT JUDGE (concurring specially).

In full accord with the majority in vacating the judgment and remanding the case, we nevertheless cannot agree that the attorney's testimony was admissible in the proceeding under review, or that it should be admitted in the proceedings to follow.

We agree that an attorney may testify as to "facts observable by anyone," but we refuse to accept the characterization of the lawyer's testimony here as merely reporting "facts observable by anyone." If nothing were involved beyond observations open to anyone, it is doubtful that the attorney would have been called to the stand. His testimony was desired for a purpose more far-reaching. Any expression as to the client's mental competency necessarily embraced more than facts observable by anyone; it comprehended conclusions drawn in the course of an association that is uniquely regarded in the law.

The lawyer's observations were inextricably intertwined with communications which passed between him and his client. It cannot be said that the testimony was confined to nonconfidential matters. This being so, the well-established privilege which protects the client against disclosure was violated. * * *

Consider the practical difficulty that arises when an attorney is permitted to testify on such an issue as the section 2255 hearing presented. The attorney testifies baldly that his client was "cooperative" and mentally competent. No meaningful cross-examination is possible without inquiring what his client said to him and what he said to his client. The client finds himself on the horns of a dilemma: Either he must forego raising the issue of his incapacity or he must surrender the protection of the privilege the law accords him—a choice he should not have to make. The lawyer's conclusory opinion thus stands without possibility of effective challenge.

The new hearing which the court awards the appellant will, therefore, do him little or no good.

NOTES AND QUESTIONS

1. *Litigation between attorney and client.* The privilege has generally been viewed as inapplicable in an action by an attorney to recover a fee, or by a client to recover damages for the attorney's malpractice. See 1 McCormick, Evidence § 91(7th ed. 2013). See also Uniform Rule of Evidence 502(d)(3), supra. Should institution of such a malpractice action simultaneously waive the privilege in litigation between the client and third parties concerning the same subject matter? See Industrial Clearinghouse v. Browning Mfg., 953 F.2d 1004 (5th Cir.1992). See also Willy v. Administrative Review Board, 423 F.3d 483, 494–501 (5th Cir.2005) (privilege did not protect communications in retaliatory discharge claim brought by in-house counsel).

2. *Client's location.* Should the privilege apply to preclude an attorney's testimony that he informed the client as to the time and date of a required court appearance? See State v. Breazeale, 713 P.2d 973 (Kan.Ct.App.1986) (holding testimony not privileged). What of an attorney's testimony concerning the whereabouts of the client? Fellerman v. Bradley, 493 A.2d 1239 (N.J.1985) (denying privilege on facts but stating that a client's address may be privileged in some circumstances).

IN RE GRAND JURY INVESTIGATION NO. 83–2–35 (DURANT)

United States Court of Appeals, Sixth Circuit, 1983.
723 F.2d 447.

KRUPANSKY, CIRCUIT JUDGE.

Attorney Richard Durant (Durant) appeals a finding of contempt for failure to disclose to the grand jury upon order of court the identity of his client. On March 1, 1983, Special Agent Edwards (Edwards), of the Federal Bureau of Investigation (FBI), visited Durant's office and explained that the FBI was investigating the theft of numerous checks made payable to International Business Machines, Inc. (IBM). He advised that a number of the stolen checks had been traced and deposited into various banking accounts under names of non-existent organizations, at least one of which included the initials "IBM". Edwards produced a photostatic copy of a check drawn upon one of these fictitious accounts which check was made payable to Durant's law firm. Upon FBI inquiry, Durant conceded that this check for $15,000 had been received and endorsed by his firm for services rendered to a client in two cases, one of which was "finished" and the other of which was "open". Durant refused to disclose the identity of his client to whose credit the proceeds had been applied, asserting the attorney-client privilege.

Durant was subpoenaed to appear before the grand jury the following day, March 2, 1983, where he again refused to identify his client, asserting the attorney-client privilege. The government immediately moved the United States District Court for the Eastern District of Michigan for an Order requiring Durant to provide the requested information. At a hearing that same afternoon, Durant informed the court that disclosure of his client's identity could incriminate that client in criminal activity so as to justify invoking the attorney-client privilege. Citing to the court: *In re Grand Jury Appearance (Michaelson),* 511 F.2d 882 (9th Cir.1975); *Baird v. Koerner,* 279 F.2d 623 (9th Cir.1960). Durant additionally stated that "I do not know any of the facts about this theft or anything else", and suggested that the requested information should be obtained through other methods.[30] The court adjudged that the privilege did not attach and ordered Durant to identify his client. Upon refusal to comply with this Order, Durant was held in contempt. Further proceedings (e.g. bond) were stayed until March 16, 1983, and subsequently stayed until March 22, 1983.

In an obvious attempt to ascertain the identity of Durant's client in an alternate manner, the United States issued a second subpoena to Durant on March 9, 1983, ordering him to appear before the grand jury on March 16, 1983, and produce * * * [certain] documents * * * Durant moved to quash this subpoena duces tecum, again asserting the attorney-client privilege. At the March 22, 1983 hearing on this motion, Durant re-asserted that production of the subpoenaed documents could implicate his client in criminal activity. He additionally observed that the FBI had admitted before Durant and the district court judge in-chambers that an

---

[30] Durant stated:

> I should add that if the facts as the agents have discussed them with me are correct and there is a substantial number of checks flowing around the city, all those checks come back to the drawee bank with bank endorsements on the back. It should be, it seems to me, equally possible, without violating the attorney-client privilege, for the agents to find out who presented, who cashed and to trace the money through normal commercial channels, to say nothing of the fact that who opens the mail at IBM now obviously becomes of significant importance.

arrest would be effected by the FBI immediately following disclosure.[31]
* * *

The Court was informed that disclosure of the requested information
would not only implicate Durant's client in criminal activity, but it would
implicate that client in the very criminal activity for which legal advice
had been sought.

> COURT: Do you contend and do you submit that the disclosure
> of the information which is sought by this subpoena, quote,
> would implicate your client in the very criminal activity for
> which legal advice was sought?
>
> MR. DURANT: Yes, Your Honor, I do.
>
> COURT: Other than—in what way do you contend that it would?
>
> MR. DURANT: Sir, I'm in a catch–22 position again. I can't tell
> you. If I tell you, I have explained things that my client obviously
> doesn't wish to be disclosed.
>
> COURT: All right.

Durant failed to move the court for an *ex parte in camera* submission of
evidence or testimony to establish that his client had indeed sought legal
advice relating to past criminal activity involving theft of IBM checks.
Nor did the district court, *sua sponte,* suggest an *ex parte in camera*
submission of evidence to probe Durant's blanket statements.

The United States then introduced the check into evidence in support
of the proposition that it was improbable that Durant's client had
engaged Durant's services to defend against impending charges of theft. A
notation on the lower left hand corner of the check stated "corporate legal
services". The United States observed "That doesn't say anything about
crimes committed or to be committed or legal services in connection with
criminal matters. It is 'corporate legal services'; no suggestion of any
criminal investigation." It was additionally noted by the government that
the FBI had not initiated the investigation nor had it been informed of
the theft of the IBM checks until March 1st, approximately two weeks
after the check had been received by Durant. Durant offered the following
rebuttal:

> I don't know when IBM knew it (i.e. knew that checks had been
> stolen), but Mr. Edwards, when he appeared at my office, told

---

[31] Durant stated:

> I would remind the Court that when, through the courtesy of the Court, we had a
> session in-chambers with the members of the FBI present, as well as the U.S. Attorney
> and myself, the FBI members specifically said—I can't remember which one—
> specifically said that as soon as we get the name of that client, we are going to arrest
> the client * * *.

me that it did involve checks from IBM, and I said that on March 2nd, when I appeared here.

I think the mere fact that the check says for "corporate legal services" when it has been admitted by the U.S. Attorney that such a corporation doesn't even exist, it is a fictional entity, doesn't deny what I am representing to the Court.

The district court, opining that the issues joined in the first and second subpoenas served upon Durant were "essentially the same", withheld a decision of Durant's motion to quash the second subpoena duces tecum pending appellate resolution of the court's contempt Order of March 2, 1983.

Confronting the applicability of the attorney-client privilege as urged by Durant, it is initially observed that the privilege is recognized in the federal forum. See: *Fisher v. United States,* 425 U.S. 391 * * * (1976); Rule 501, Federal Rules of Evidence. * * *

The federal forum is unanimously in accord with the general rule that the identity of a client is, with limited exceptions, not within the protective ambit of the attorney-client privilege. *See: In re Grand Jury Proceedings (Pavlick),* 680 F.2d 1026, 1027 (5th Cir.1982) (en banc) * * *.[32]

The Circuits have embraced various "exceptions" to the general rule that the identity of a client is not within the protective ambit of the attorney-client privilege. All such exceptions appear to be firmly grounded in the Ninth Circuit's seminal decision in *Baird v. Koerner,* 279 F.2d 623 (9th Cir.1960). In *Baird* the IRS received a letter from an attorney stating that an enclosed check in the amount of $12,706 was being tendered for additional amounts due from undisclosed taxpayers. When the IRS summoned the attorney to ascertain the identity of the delinquent taxpayers the attorney refused identification asserting the attorney-client privilege. The Ninth Circuit, applying California law, adjudged that the "exception" to the general rule as pronounced in *Ex parte McDonough,* 170 Cal. 230, 149 P. 566 (1915) controlled:

The name of the client will be considered privileged matter where the circumstances of the case are such that the name of

---

[32] This general rule applies equally to fee arrangements:

In the absence of special circumstances, the amount of money paid or owed to an attorney by his client is generally not within the attorney-client privilege. *In re Michaelson,* 511 F.2d 882, 888 (9th Cir.1975); *see In re Grand Jury Proceedings,* 517 F.2d 666, 670–71 (5th Cir.1975). The receipt of fees from a client is not usually within the privilege because the payment of a fee is not normally a matter of confidence or a communication. *United States v. Hodgson,* 492 F.2d 1175 (10th Cir.1974). This Court has held that ministerial or clerical services of an attorney in transferring funds to or from a client is not a matter of confidence protected by the attorney-client privilege. *United States v. Bartone,* 400 F.2d 459 (6 Cir.1968).

United States v. Haddad, 527 F.2d 537, 538–39 (6th Cir.1975).

the client is material only for the purpose of showing an acknowledgement of guilt on the part of such client of the very offenses on account of which the attorney was employed.

Baird, supra, 279 F.2d at 633. The identity of the *Baird* taxpayer was adjudged within this exception to the general rule. The Ninth Circuit has continued to acknowledge this exception.

> A significant exception to this principle of non-confidentiality holds that such information may be privileged when the person invoking the privilege is able to show that a strong possibility exists that disclosure of the information would implicate the client in the very matter for which legal advice was sought in the first case.

In re Grand Jury Subpoenas Duces Tecum (Marger/Merenbach), 695 F.2d 363, 365 (9th Cir.1982). * * * This exception, which can perhaps be most succinctly characterized as the "legal advice" exception, has also been recognized by other circuits. *See: In re Walsh,* 623 F.2d 489, 495 (7th Cir.1980); *In re Grand Jury Investigation (Tinari),* 631 F.2d 17, 19 (3d Cir.1980). Since the legal advice exception is firmly grounded in the policy of protecting confidential communications, this Court adopts and applies its principles herein. *See: In re Grand Jury Subpoenas Duces Tecum (Marger/Merenbach), supra.*

> It should be observed, however, that the legal advice exception may be defeated through a *prima facie* showing that the legal representation was secured in furtherance of present or intended continuing illegality, as where the legal representation itself is part of a larger conspiracy. *See: In re Grand Jury Subpoenas Duces Tecum (Marger/Merenbach), supra,* 695 F.2d at 365 n.1. * * *

Another exception to the general rule that the identity of a client is not privileged arises where disclosure of the identity would be tantamount to disclosing an otherwise protected confidential communication. In *Baird, supra,* the Ninth Circuit observed:

> If the identification of the client conveys information which ordinarily would be conceded to be part of the usual privileged communication between attorney and client, then the privilege should extend to such identification in the absence of other factors.

Id., 279 F.2d at 632. Citing *Baird,* the Fourth Circuit promulgated the following exception:

> To the general rule is an exception, firmly bedded as the rule itself. The privilege may be recognized where so much of the actual communication has already been disclosed that

identification of the client amounts to disclosure of a confidential communication.

NLRB v. Harvey, 349 F.2d 900, 905 (4th Cir.1965). *Accord: United States v. Tratner,* 511 F.2d 248, 252 (7th Cir.1975); * * * The Seventh Circuit has added to the *Harvey* exception the following emphasized caveat:

> The privilege may be recognized where so much of the actual communication has already been disclosed [*not necessarily by the attorney, but by independent sources as well*] that identification of the client [*or of fees paid*] amounts to disclosure of a confidential communication.

United States v. Jeffers, 532 F.2d 1101, 1115 (7th Cir.1976) (emphasis added). The Third Circuit, applying this exception, has emphasized that it is the link between the client and the *communication,* rather than the link between the client and the possibility of potential criminal *prosecution,* which serves to bring the client's identity within the protective ambit of the attorney-client privilege. *See: In re Grand Jury Empanelled February 14, 1978 (Markowitz),* 603 F.2d 469, 473 n.4 (3d Cir.1979). Like the "legal advice" exception, this exception is also firmly rooted in principles of confidentiality.

Another exception, articulated in the Fifth Circuit's *en banc* decision of *In re Grand Jury Proceedings (Pavlick),* 680 F.2d 1026 (5th Cir.1982) (*en banc*), is recognized when disclosure of the identity of the client would provide the "last link" of evidence:

> We have long recognized the general rule that matters involving the payment of fees and the identity of clients are not generally privileged. *In re Grand Jury Proceedings, (United States v. Jones),* 517 F.2d 666 (5th Cir.1975); see cases collected *id.* at 670 n.2. There we also recognized, however, a limited and narrow exception to the general rule, one that obtains when the disclosure of the client's identity by his attorney would have supplied the last link in an existing chain of incriminating evidence likely to lead to the client's indictment.

Id. at 1027. Upon careful consideration this Court concludes that, although language exists in *Baird* to support validity of *Pavlick's* "last link" exception,[33] the exception is simply not grounded upon the preservation of confidential *communications* and hence not justifiable to support the attorney-client privilege. Although the last link exception

---

[33] Although *Baird* observed in passing that disclosure of the identity of the clients "may well be the link that could form the chain of testimony necessary to convict [the taxpayers] of a federal crime", 279 F.2d at 633, the Court repeatedly emphasized that the retention of the attorney and remission of a check to the IRS was tantamount to a *communication* or admission from the clients to the attorney that "they had not paid a sufficient amount in income taxes some one or more years in the past". *Id.*

may promote concepts of fundamental fairness against self-incrimination, these concepts are not proper considerations to invoke the attorney-client privilege. Rather, the focus of the inquiry is whether disclosure of the identity would adversely implicate the confidentiality of communications. Accordingly, this Court rejects the last link exception as articulated in *Pavlick.*

Turning to the facts at bar, it is observed that Durant asserted three justifications for invocation of the attorney-client privilege. First, at the March 2 hearing, he stated that disclosure might possibly implicate the client in criminal activity. As this justification has no roots in concepts of confidentiality or communication, it cannot be advanced to support an abdication of the general rule that identity of a client is not privileged. Second, at the March 22 hearing, Durant informed the Court that the FBI had informed him that an arrest would be effected upon disclosure of the identity of Durant's client. This is simply an assertion that disclosure would provide the last link of evidence to support an indictment as articulated in *Pavlick*—a precedent which is herein rejected.

Third, at the March 22 hearing, Durant submitted that disclosure was justified under the "legal advice" exception embraced by the Ninth Circuit. Seeking to invoke this exception, it was incumbent upon Durant to "show that a *strong possibility* exist[ed] that disclosure of the information would implicate the client in the very matter for which legal advice [had been] sought in the first case". *In re Grand Jury Subpoenas Duces Tecum (Marger/Merenbach), supra,* 695 F.2d at 365 (emphasis added). A well recognized means for an attorney to *demonstrate* the existence of an exception to the general rule, while simultaneously preserving confidentiality of the identity of his client, is to move the court for an *in camera ex parte* hearing. *See: In re Grand Jury Witness (Salas),* [695 FP.2d 3594, 362 (5th Cir. 1982)]; (proper procedure to establish existence of "legal advice" exception was to make an *in camera* showing); *In re Grand Jury Empanelled February 14, 1978 (Markowitz), supra,* 603 F.2d at 474 (referring to procedure to be employed by an attorney who asserts Fifth Amendment privilege); *In re Grand Jury Subpoena (Slaughter),* [694 F.2d 1258, 1260 n.2 (11th Cir. 1982)] (United States requested in its subpoena that any averred privileged matters be deleted and the original copy retained intact for possible *in camera* inspection by the district court); *In re Walsh, supra,* 623 F.2d at 494 n.5; *United States v. Tratner, supra,* 511 F.2d at 252.

Since the burden of establishing the existence of the privilege rests with the party asserting the privilege, it is incumbent upon the attorney to move for an *in camera ex parte* hearing if one is desired. In the action *sub judice,* Durant failed to so move. Rather, he rested on his blanket assertion that his client had initially sought legal advice relating to matters involving the theft of IBM checks. Such unsupported assertions of privilege are strongly disfavored. *See: United States v. Cromer,* 483 F.2d 99, 102 (9th Cir.1973); *United States v. Davis,* 636 F.2d 1028, 1044 n.20 (5th Cir.1981); *In re Grand Jury Witness (Salas), supra,* 695 F.2d at 362. Further, it is pertinent to observe that at the first hearing on March 2 Durant had expressly disavowed knowledge of the existence of stolen IBM checks. This statement significantly diminishes the credibility of Durant's subsequent March 22 representation that his client had indeed engaged Durant's services for past activity relating to stolen IBM checks. Accordingly, Durant clearly failed to satisfy his burden of demonstrating a "strong possibility" that disclosure of the identity of his client would implicate that client in the very matter for which legal advice had been initially sought.

Last, it is observed that Durant did not represent to the district court that disclosure of the identity of his client would amount to a disclosure of a confidential communication. *See: NLRB v. Harvey, supra; United States v. Jeffers, supra.* Not having advanced this exception to the general rule, it follows axiomatically that Durant failed to satisfy the burden of establishing its existence. Nor does the record suggest the viability of this exception so as to justify a remand.

In sum, Durant has failed to establish the existence of any exception to the general rule that disclosure of the identity of a client is not within the protective ambit of the attorney-client privilege. Therefore the Contempt Order of the district court issued against Durant is hereby AFFIRMED.

NOTES AND QUESTIONS

1. *Client identity.* As suggested by the principal case, the leading decision in Baird v. Koerner, 279 F.2d 623 (9th Cir.1960), has given rise to a miscellany of exceptions to the general rule that client identity is not protected by the privilege. For criticisms of these derivatives of *Baird,* see Comment, Developments in the Law—Privileged Communications, 98 Harv.L.Rev. 1450, 1522–24 (1985) (suggesting that protection vel non of client identity should depend essentially upon the client's intent in seeking legal services). See also In re Grand Jury Subpoenas, 803 F.2d 493 (9th Cir.1986) (characterizing *Baird* facts as "unique" and holding privilege inapplicable to protect identity of anonymous payer of fees for criminal defense because no legitimate attorney-client relationship was shown to exist between fee-payer and attorney; alternate holding); United States v. Goldberger & Dubin, 935 F.2d 501 (2d Cir.1991) (holding neither federal nor state attorney-client privilege exempted attorneys from federal statutory obligation to report cash fee payments in excess of $10,000); Goode, Identity, Fees, and the Attorney–Client Privilege, 59 Geo.Wash.L.Rev. 307 (1991); Annot., 84 A.L.R.Fed. 852.

2. *Confidentiality distinguished/* The attorney-client privilege must be distinguished from the rule governing a lawyer's professional conduct that requires that information received in the course of a lawyer's representation of a client be kept confidential. What differences might you suspect there are between a rule that governs whether a court can compel the disclosure of communications between lawyer and her client and a rule governing a lawyer's professional obligation to keep such communications secret? See Model Rules of Professional Conduct, Rule 1.6. A useful contrast of the differences between the privilege rule and confidentiality imposed by the rules of professional conduct is contained in Zacharias, Privilege and Confidentiality in California, 28 U.C.Davis L.Rev. 367 (1995).

Both rules may be implicated by the problem suggested in the principal case, which arises when physical evidence, or the key to its discovery, is delivered by the client to the attorney. Is the attorney under legal or ethical obligation to deliver the evidence to the authorities and, if so, what use may the latter make of it at trial? Is it possible to separate the "communication" of a murder weapon, effected by its delivery to the attorney, from the evidentiary entity itself? For helpful treatments of these and related questions, suggesting somewhat contrasting responses, see Lefstein, Incriminating Physical Evidence, The Defense Attorney's Dilemma, and the Need for Rules, 64 N.C.L.Rev. 897 (1986); Saltzburg, Communications Falling Within the Attorney–Client Privilege, 66 Iowa L.Rev. 811 (1981). Discussions focusing primarily upon the ethical problems arising from possession of the client's guilty secrets are found in Noonan, The Purposes of Advocacy and the Limits of Confidentiality, 64 Mich.L.Rev. 1485 (1966); Callan & David, Professional Responsibility and the Duty of Confidentiality: Disclosure of Client Misconduct in an Adversary System, 29 Rutgers L.Rev. 332 (1976). A further complicating factor has appeared in the form of required reporting statutes. See Mosteller, Child Abuse Reporting Laws and Attorney–Client Confidences: The Reality and the Specter of Lawyer as Informant, 42 Duke L.J. 203 (1992). See also discussion in Chapter 2, note 2 after *Napue v. Illinois*, supra.

IN RE SEALED CASE

United States Court of Appeals, District of Columbia Circuit, 1997.
107 F.3d 46.

RANDOLPH, CIRCUIT JUDGE:

This appeal arises out of ongoing grand jury proceedings. The grand jury is investigating violations of federal election laws. The record is sealed. The appellant is a corporation, which we shall call the "Company." The Company refused to produce two subpoenaed documents, for which it was held in contempt. One of the documents is a memorandum from a Company vice president to the president, with a copy to the Company's general counsel. The memorandum reflects a conversation between the vice president and the Company's general counsel about campaign finance laws. The Company withheld it on the basis of the attorney-client privilege. The other document is a memorandum written by the general counsel, apparently at the request of outside counsel. The Company withheld it on the basis of the attorney-client privilege and work product immunity.

The district court examined both documents *in camera* (*see United States v. Zolin,* 491 U.S. 554 * * * 1989)), and, without deciding whether they were covered by the privilege or the work product doctrine, ordered the Company to turn them over. The court found that the crime-fraud exception applied because of these circumstances. In late June 1994, the Company's political action committee contributed the maximum amount permitted by law to a former candidate for federal office who was seeking to retire his campaign debt. The vice president wrote his memorandum and had his discussion with the general counsel in early August 1994. Later in the same month, the vice president called two individuals who did business with the Company and asked them to contribute to the former candidate. The individuals and their wives made the contributions. After several weeks had passed, the vice president authorized checks to be drawn from his department's budget to reimburse these individuals not only for the amount of their contributions, but also to make up for the additional taxes they would incur from reporting the reimbursement as income. The vice president's solicitation may have been permissible but, according to the government, this use of corporate funds was illegal.

The other subpoenaed document—the general counsel's memorandum to the file—was written more than a year later. It mentions dates in November 1995, and according to the Company's appellate counsel, recites actions the Company took to correct the vice president's use of corporate funds to reimburse the donors.

In addition to appealing from the order to produce the documents and the contempt citation, the Company appeals the district court's order compelling the vice president to testify in the grand jury about a late August 1994 meeting between him, the Company's president, and its general counsel. The participants at the meeting discussed certain facts and the general counsel gave legal advice about federal election laws. In the grand jury, the vice president—who had been granted immunity—invoked the attorney-client privilege on behalf of the Company. Again, the district court ruled that the crime-fraud exception applied and ordered him to testify about the late August 1994 meeting. The vice president then signed an affidavit stating that he would honor the court's directive. The court stayed its order pending the outcome of the Company's appeal.

I

We will take up first the vice president's early August 1994 memorandum and his meeting in late August 1994 with the president and general counsel. Both the memorandum and the meeting, as the Company sees it, are covered by the attorney-client privilege. Since the district court has yet to pass on this question, we will assume the Company is correct. The "privilege of a witness," Fed.R.Evid. 501 tells us, is "governed by the principles of the common law as they may be interpreted by the courts of the United States in the light of reason and experience." Those principles recognize the importance of maintaining the confidentiality of attorney-client communications in order to promote the rendering of legal services. In modern society, legal advice and assistance is often essential. To provide effective representation, attorneys need "full and frank" disclosures from their clients. *Upjohn Co. v. United States,* 449 U.S. 383, 389 * * * (1981). Clients, it has been thought, might not be forthright if their lawyers could be turned into witnesses against them or if they could be forced to disclose their conversations with their lawyers.

The relationship between client and counsel may, however, be abused. And so the attorney-client privilege is subject to what is known as the crime-fraud exception. Two conditions must be met. First, the client must have made or received the otherwise privileged communication with the intent to further an unlawful or fraudulent act.[34] *In re Sealed Case,* 754 F.2d 395, 399 (D.C.Cir.1985) (*Sealed Case II*); *United States v. White,* 887 F.2d 267, 271 (D.C.Cir.1989). Second, the client must have carried out the crime or fraud. In other words, the exception does not apply even though, at one time, the client had bad intentions. Otherwise "it would penalize a client for doing what the privilege is designed to encourage— consulting a lawyer for the purpose of achieving law compliance." *See* Restatement of the Law Governing Lawyers § 142 cmt. c, at 461 (Proposed Final Draft No. 1, 1996).[35]

The privilege is the client's, and it is the client's fraudulent or criminal intent that matters. A third party's bad intent cannot remove

---

[34] In nearly all cases, a client's innocence will bar application of the crime-fraud exception. We say "nearly all" because there may be rare cases—this is not one of them—in which the attorney's fraudulent or criminal intent defeats a claim of privilege even if the client is innocent. *See, e.g., Moody v. IRS,* 654 F.2d 795, 800–01 (D.C.Cir.1981); *In re Impounded Case (Law Firm),* 879 F.2d 1211, 1213–14 (3d Cir.1989).

[35] To this the Restatement drafters added: "By the same token, lawyers might be discouraged from giving full and candid advice to clients about legally questionable courses of action." *Id.* This seems to us rather doubtful. Why would a lawyer put his client—and himself— at such risk? Fully advising the client may prevent possibly unlawful action. On the other hand, if the lawyer gives less than "full and candid" advice, the client may rely on it, wind up violating the law and thus lose the privilege anyway. A lawyer representing such a client would have reason to be concerned about his own personal civil and criminal liability. Rather than discouraging full advice, that prospect plus the danger to the client provides a strong incentive for the lawyer to advise the client clearly and firmly.

the protection of the privilege.[36] For example, a stenographer hired to record a meeting between an attorney and a client might intend to use his notes to commit some kind of crime—say extortion—but the contents of the meeting would not therefore cease to be privileged. Otherwise, existence of the attorney-client privilege would be unpredictable and the interest of "full and frank communication" between client and counsel would be undermined. *See Upjohn Co.,* 449 U.S. at 389 * * *.[37]

As the party seeking to overcome the privilege, the government had the burden of showing that the crime-fraud exception applied to the memorandum and the meeting. What was the nature of that burden? Here we encounter some confusion. This court and others have described the required showing in terms of establishing a "prima facie" case. *See, e.g., Sealed Case II,* 754 F.2d at 399. The formulation can be traced to the Supreme Court's opinion in *Clark v. United States,* 289 U.S. 1, 14 * * * (1933). The problem is, as the Supreme Court mentioned in *Zolin,* 491 U.S. at 563 n.7 * * *, that "prima facie" evokes the concept, familiar in civil litigation, of shifting the burden from one party to another. Yet it is altogether clear where the burden in these cases lies—on the party invoking the crime-fraud exception. In terms of the level of proof, is a "prima facie showing" a preponderance of the evidence, clear and convincing evidence, or something else?

Our opinion in *Sealed Case II* contains this answer: "The government satisfies its burden of proof if it offers evidence that if believed by the trier of fact would establish the elements of an ongoing or imminent crime or fraud." 754 F.2d at 399. We appended a footnote to this statement explaining that although the Second Circuit had "framed the test in terms of probable cause to believe that a crime or fraud had been committed and that the communications were in furtherance thereof" (*see In re John Doe Corp.,* 675 F.2d 482, 491 & n.7 (2d Cir.1982)), there was "little practical difference" between that standard and the one just quoted from *Sealed Case II.* 754 F.2d at 399 n.3. We confess some difficulty in understanding why the differences between the two formulations were considered slight, but there is no reason to dwell on the matter. It is apparent here that the government failed to make the sort of probable cause showing the Second Circuit would demand, or the showing *Sealed Case II* contemplated.[38]

---

[36] Of course, in many cases, a third party's access to a communication may destroy the confidentiality required for the attorney-client privilege, *see, e.g., In re Sealed Case,* 877 F.2d 976, 980 (D.C.Cir.1989) (*Sealed Case III*), but that is a separate problem.

[37] At least one district court seems to have said that anyone's use of a communication to further a crime or fraud defeats the attorney-client privilege, regardless of the innocence of the attorney and the client. *See Duttle v. Bandler & Kass,* 127 F.R.D. 46, 53, 55–56 (S.D.N.Y.1989). We think this is incorrect.

[38] *Zolin* left the standard of proof question for another day. The Supreme Court decided only that the crime-fraud exception need not be established entirely with independent evidence; that courts may review allegedly privileged materials *in camera* in order to determine whether the crime-fraud exception applies, 491 U.S. at 565–70 * * *; and that before "engaging in *in*

The critical consideration is that the government's presentation had to be aimed at the intent and action of the client. It was not enough for the government to show that the vice president committed a crime after he wrote his memorandum and attended the late August meeting with Company counsel. The holder of the privilege is the client and, in this case, the client was the Company, not the vice president. Unless the government made some showing that the Company intended to further and did commit a crime, the government could not invoke the crime-fraud exception to the privilege.

As to the late August meeting, the government's evidence reveals that the participants discussed campaign finance laws. That is not enough. One cannot reasonably infer from the meeting that the Company was consulting its general counsel with the intention of committing a crime, or even that the vice president was then doing so. Companies operating in today's complex legal and regulatory environments routinely seek legal advice about how to handle all sorts of matters, ranging from their political activities to their employment practices to transactions that may have antitrust consequences. There is nothing necessarily suspicious about the officers of this corporation getting such advice. True enough, within weeks of the meeting about campaign finance law, the vice president violated that law. But the government had to demonstrate that the Company sought the legal advice with the intent to further its illegal conduct. Showing temporal proximity between the communication and a crime is not enough. *Sealed Case II,* 754 F.2d at 402; *In re Grand Jury Subpoenas Duces Tecum,* 798 F.2d 32, 34 (2d Cir.1986).

Moreover, from the material before the district court, there was no way of knowing or even guessing whether the vice president was on a frolic of his own, against the advice of Company counsel, when he reimbursed the donors with corporate funds. The government suggested at oral argument that even if he was, the Company still could be held criminally liable. There are circumstances under which corporations are responsible for the crimes of their agents. * * * But neither in this court nor in the district court did the government offer anything in terms of evidence or law to support the idea that the Company bore criminal responsibility for the acts of this officer. * * * The government therefore did not sustain its burden. In so holding, we express no view on the Company's ultimate criminal liability. The law of corporate criminality is not well developed in this circuit. Given the government's complete failure to address the subject, this is not the case to develop it.

---

camera review * * *, the judge should require a showing of a factual basis adequate to support a good faith belief by a reasonable person that *in camera* review of the materials may reveal evidence to establish the claim that the crime-fraud exception applies," *id.* at 572 * * * (internal quotation marks and citation omitted).

Many of the same points can be made about the vice president's memorandum. Like the district court, we have examined this document, which the Company submitted *in camera* and *ex parte*. From the memorandum and the other information the government presented, all that can be discerned is that the Company's vice president and its general counsel discussed federal election laws in early August 1994, perhaps at the suggestion of the Company's president. The memorandum reflected that discussion. Again, given the need for corporations and their officers to seek legal advice about activities like political contributions, there is nothing suspect about this discussion. And the fact that the vice president broke the law weeks later does not, without more, demonstrate the validity of the government's assumption that the Company intended or probably intended to further that crime.

II

This brings us to the second of the two documents the Company withheld. We have examined the document. It is a memorandum by the Company's general counsel, written to the file and relating to matters that occurred one year after the vice president's illegal action. As Company counsel seemed to agree at oral argument, the document is covered by work product immunity rather than the attorney-client privilege. The protection for attorney work product is broader than the attorney-client privilege, but less absolute. Work product immunity covers not only confidential communications between the attorney and client. It also attaches to other materials prepared by attorneys (and their agents) in anticipation of litigation. *Cf.* Fed.R.Civ.P. 26(b)(3). Like the attorney-client privilege, work product immunity promotes the rendering of effective legal services. *See Hickman v. Taylor,* 329 U.S. 495, 510–11 * * * (1947). And as with the privilege, the interests in favor of work product immunity are overcome when the client uses the attorney to further a crime or fraud. *See In re Sealed Case,* 676 F.2d 793, 811, 812 (D.C.Cir.1982) (*Sealed Case I*); 1 Scott N. Stone & Robert K. Taylor, Testimonial Privileges § 2.11, at 2–67 & n.284 (2d ed. 1993) (collecting cases).

With respect to work product immunity, the crime-fraud exception calls for a somewhat different inquiry than with the attorney-client privilege. The focus is not on the client's intent regarding a particular communication, but on the client's intent in consulting the lawyer or in using the materials the lawyer prepared. The question is: Did the client consult the lawyer or use the material for the purpose of committing a crime or fraud?[39]

---

[39] So long as the client had the requisite intent, the proposed Restatement removes work product immunity—but not the attorney-client privilege—even if the client never carries out the crime or fraud. *Compare* § 132 with § 142 of the Restatement of the Law Governing Lawyers,

In light of these principles, the government's argument for invoking the crime-fraud exception goes nowhere. As is apparent from the nature of the inquiry, the crime-fraud exception for work product immunity cannot apply if the attorney prepared the material after his client's wrongdoing ended. *See, e.g., Zolin,* 491 U.S. at 562–63 * * *; *Sealed Case II,* 754 F.2d at 402; *In re Grand Jury Subpoena 92–1(SJ),* 31 F.3d 826, 831 (9th Cir.1994); *In re Federal Grand Jury Proceedings 89–10(MIA),* 938 F.2d 1578, 1581 (11th Cir.1991). Here, the general counsel wrote the memorandum long after the vice president committed the offenses. The government points out that work product might still be in furtherance of a crime or fraud even if the client's original offense was complete. The client could be using the attorney to cover up or conceal his first crime. The trouble is that the government has made no such allegation here and, even if it did, we have spotted nothing in the record that would support it. And if the government cannot show that the Company or any of its officers tried to or intended to cover up the vice president's illegality, it surely cannot show that the Company used its general counsel for that purpose.

* * *

The district court decided this case by assuming that the meeting and the memoranda fell under either the attorney-client privilege or the work product doctrine and then finding that the crime-fraud exception applied. Since we disagree with the district court's conclusions regarding the crime-fraud exception, we reverse and remand the case.

NOTES AND QUESTIONS

1. *Procedure for determining existence of crime-fraud exception.* As noted in the principal case, the procedure for determining whether a communication comes within the crime-fraud exception to the attorney-client privilege was established for the federal courts in United States v. Zolin, 491 U.S. 554 (1989). Chapter 1, supra. The judge may inspect documents *in camera* when there is a "factual basis adequate to support a good faith belief by a reasonable person" that such an inspection "may reveal evidence to establish the claim that the crime-fraud exception applies." Id. at 572. See 1 McCormick, Evidence § 95 (7th ed. 2013). For state treatments of the issue see, e.g., First Union Nat'l Bank of Florida v. Whitener, 715 So.2d 979 (Fla.Dist.Ct.App.1998); State ex rel. Nix v. Cleveland, 700 N.E.2d 12 (Ohio 1998). See also Bricker, Revisiting the Crime Fraud Exception to the Attorney Client Privilege: A Proposal to Remedy the Disparity in Protections for Civil and Criminal Privilege Holders, 82 Temple L. Rev. 149 (2009) (discussion of procedure in civil and criminal cases for determining the

---

supra. Why the crime-fraud exception differs in these two contexts is not explained in the draft's commentary or in the reporter's notes.

existence of the crime-fraud exception and proposing legislation to provide more safeguards in summary judgment cases).

2. *Work product privilege.* The court in the principal case considers the crime-fraud exception to be applicable to both the attorney-client and the work product privileges. However, it notes that there has been a difference in application of the exception between the two privileges where the client never in fact commits the crime or fraud. The court did not explain the difference. Can you? For a case holding that the crime-fraud exception does not apply to a state created work product privilege, see Menton v. Lattimore, 667 S.W.2d 335 (Tex.App.1984).

3. *Intentional torts.* Should the crime-fraud exception also apply to communications in furtherance of intentional torts other than fraud? Some courts have so held. See, e.g., Recycling Solutions, Inc. v. District of Columbia, 175 F.R.D. 407 (D.D.C.1997); Horizon of Hope Ministry v. Clark County, Ohio, 115 F.R.D. 1 (S.D.Ohio 1986). *Contra* Motley v. Marathon Oil Co., 71 F.3d 1547 (10th Cir.1995).

4. *The Bentham criticisms.* To what extent are the criticisms leveled by Jeremy Bentham, above, at the attorney-client privilege adequately addressed by recognition of a crime or fraud exception? To what extent are Bentham's criticisms not met by such an exception? Should the exception have been applied to permit the attorney's testimony in *Denver Tramway v. Owens*?

D. ADDITIONAL PRIVILEGES

IN THE MATTER OF MYRON FARBER
Supreme Court of New Jersey, 1978.
394 A.2d 330.

MOUNTAIN, J.

In these consolidated appeals The New York Times Company and Myron Farber, a reporter employed by the newspaper, challenged judgments entered against them in two related matters—one a proceeding in aid of a litigant (civil contempt), the other for criminal contempt of court. The proceedings were instituted in an ongoing murder trial now in its seventh month, as a result of the appellants' failure to comply with two *subpoenas duces tecum,* directing them to produce certain documents and materials compiled by one or both of these appellants in the course of Farber's investigative reporting of certain allegedly criminal activities. Farber's investigations and reporting are said to have contributed largely to the indictment and prosecution of Dr. Mario E. Jascalevich for murder. * * *

I

The First Amendment

Appellants claim a privilege to refrain from revealing information sought by the *subpoenas duces tecum* essentially for the reason that were they to divulge this material, confidential sources of such information would be made public. Were this to occur, they argue, newsgathering and the dissemination of news would be seriously impaired, because much information would never be forthcoming to the news media unless the persons who were the sources of such information could be entirely certain that their identities would remain secret. The final result, appellants claim, would be a substantial lessening in the supply of available news on a variety of important and sensitive issues, all to the detriment of the public interest. They contend further that this privilege to remain silent with respect to confidential information and the sources of such information emanates from the "free speech" and "free press" clauses of the First Amendment.[40]

In our view the Supreme Court of the United States has clearly rejected this claim and has squarely held that no such First Amendment right exists. In Branzburg v. Hayes, 408 U.S. 665 * * * (1972), three news media representatives argued that, for the same reason here advanced, they should not be required to appear and testify before grand juries, and that this privilege to refrain from divulging information, asserted to have been received from confidential sources, derived from the First Amendment. Justice White, noting that there was no common law privilege, stated the issue and gave the Court's answer in the first paragraph of his opinion:

> The issue in these cases is whether requiring newsmen to appear and testify before state or federal grand juries abridges the freedom of speech and press guaranteed by the First Amendment. We hold that it does not. [Branzburg v. Hayes, supra, 408 U.S. at 667 * * * (1972).]

In that case one reporter, from Frankfort, Kentucky, had witnessed individuals making hashish from marijuana and had made a rather comprehensive survey of the drug scene in Frankfort. He had written an article in the Louisville Courier–Journal describing this illegal activity. Another, a newsman-photographer employed by a New Bedford, Massachusetts television station, had met with members of the Black Panther movement at the time that certain riots and disorders occurred in New Bedford. The material he assembled formed the basis for a

---

[40] The First Amendment of the United States Constitution reads as follows:

Congress shall make no law respecting an establishment of religion, or prohibiting the free exercise thereof; or abridging the freedom of speech, or of the press; or the right of the people peaceably to assemble, and to petition the Government for a redress of grievances.

television program that followed. The third investigative reporter had met with members of the Black Panthers in northern California and had written an article about the nature and activities of the movement. In each instance there had been a commitment on the part of the media representative that he would not divulge the source of his article or story.

By a vote of 5 to 4 the Supreme Court held that newspaper reporters or other media representatives have no privilege deriving from the First Amendment to refrain from divulging confidential information and the sources of such information when properly subpoenaed to appear before a grand jury. The three media representatives were directed to appear and testify. The holding was later underscored and applied directly to this case by Justice White in a brief opinion filed in this cause upon the occasion of his denial of a stay sought by these appellants. He said,

> There is no present authority in this Court either that newsmen are constitutionally privileged to withhold duly subpoenaed documents material to the prosecution or defense of a criminal case or that a defendant seeking the subpoena must show extraordinary circumstances before enforcement against newsmen will be had. [New York Times and Farber v. Jascalevich, 439 U.S. 1317, [1322] * * * (1978)]

We pause to point out that despite the holding in *Branzburg,* those who gather and disseminate news are by no means without First Amendment protections. Some of these are referred to by Justice White in the *Branzburg* opinion. See 408 U.S. at 681–2 * * *. They include, among others, the right to publish what the press chooses to publish, to refrain from publishing what it chooses to withhold, to seek out news in any legal manner and to refrain from revealing its sources except upon legitimate demand. Demand is not legitimate when the desired information is patently irrelevant to the needs of the inquirer or his needs are not manifestly compelling. Nor will the First Amendment sanction harassment of the press. These do not exhaust the list of such First Amendment protective rights.

The point to be made, however, is that among the many First Amendment protections that may be invoked by the press, there is not to be found the privilege of refusing to reveal relevant confidential information and its sources to a grand jury which is engaged in the fundamental governmental function of "[f]air and effective law enforcement aimed at providing security for the person and property of the individual * * * " [408 U.S. at 690 * * *]. The reason this is so is that a majority of the members of the United States Supreme Court have so determined.

Faced with this conclusion, appellants appear to argue that Justice Powell's concurring opinion in *Branzburg* somehow fails to support this result. The argument is without merit. We do not read Justice Powell's opinion as in any way disagreeing with what is said by Justice White. But even if it did, it would not matter for present purposes. The important and conclusive point is that five members of the Court have all reached the conclusion that the First Amendment affords no privilege to a newsman to refuse to appear before a grand jury and testify as to relevant information he possesses, even though in so doing he may divulge confidential sources. The particular path that any Justice may have followed becomes unimportant when once it is seen that a majority have reached the same destination.

Thus we do no weighing or balancing of societal interests in reaching our determination that the First Amendment does not afford appellants the privilege they claim. The weighing and balancing has been done by a higher court. Our conclusion that appellants cannot derive the protection they seek from the First Amendment rests upon the fact that the ruling in *Branzburg* is binding upon us and we interpret it as applicable to, and clearly including, the particular issue framed here. It follows that the obligation to appear at a criminal trial on behalf of a defendant who is enforcing his Sixth Amendment rights is at least as compelling as the duty to appear before a grand jury.

II

The Shield Law[41]

In Branzburg v. Hayes, supra, the Court dealt with a newsman's claim of privilege based solely upon the First Amendment. As we have seen, this claim of privilege failed. In *Branzburg* no shield law was involved. Here we have a shield law, said to be as strongly worded as any in the country.

---

[41] The term "shield law" is commonly and widely applied to statutes granting newsmen and other media representatives the privilege of declining to reveal confidential sources of information. The New Jersey shield law reads as follows:

> Subject to Rule 37, a person engaged on, engaged in, connected with, or employed by news media for the purpose of gathering, procuring, transmitting, compiling, editing or disseminating news for the general public or on whose behalf news is so gathered, procured, transmitted, compiled, edited or disseminated has a privilege to refuse to disclose, in any legal or quasi-legal proceeding or before any investigative body, including, but not limited to, any court, grand jury, petit jury, administrative agency, the Legislature or legislative committee, or elsewhere:
>
> a. The source, author, means, agency or person from or through whom any information was procured, obtained, supplied, furnished, gathered, transmitted, compiled, edited, disseminated, or delivered; and
>
> b. Any news or information obtained in the course of pursuing his professional activities whether or not it is disseminated.
>
> The provisions of this rule insofar as it relates to radio or television stations shall not apply unless the radio or television station maintains and keeps open for inspection, for a period of at least 1 year from the date of an actual broadcast or telecast, an exact recording, transcription, kinescopic film or certified written transcript of the actual broadcast or telecast.
>
> Unless a different meaning clearly appears from the context of this act, as used in this act:
>
> a. "News media" means newspapers, magazines, press associations, news agencies, wire services, radio, television or other similar printed, photographic, mechanical or electronic means of disseminating news to the general public.
>
> b. "News" means any written, oral or pictorial information gathered, procured, transmitted, compiled, edited or disseminated by, or on behalf of any person engaged in, engaged on, connected with or employed by a news media [sic] and so procured or obtained while such required relationship is in effect.
>
> c. "Newspaper" means a paper that is printed and distributed ordinarily not less frequently than once a week and that contains news, articles of opinion, editorials, features, advertising, or other matter regarded as of current interest, has a paid circulation and has been entered at a United States post office as second class matter.
>
> d. "Magazine" means a publication containing news which is published and distributed periodically, has a paid circulation and has been entered at a United States post office as second class matter.
>
> e. "News agency" means a commercial organization that collects and supplies news to subscribing newspapers, magazines, periodicals and news broadcasters.
>
> f. "Press association" means an association of newspapers or magazines formed to gather and distribute news to its members.
>
> g. "Wire service" means a news agency that sends out syndicated news copy by wire to subscribing newspapers, magazines, periodicals or news broadcasters.
>
> h. "In the course of pursuing his professional activities" means any situation, including a social gathering, in which a reporter obtains information for the purpose of disseminating it to the public, but does not include any situation in which a reporter intentionally conceals from the source the fact that he is a reporter, and does not include any situation in which a reporter is an eyewitness to, or participant in any act involving physical violence or property damage. [N.J.S.A. 2A:84A–21 and 21a].

We read the legislative intent in adopting this statute in its present form as seeking to protect the confidential sources of the press as well as information so obtained by reporters and other news media representatives to the greatest extent permitted by the Constitution of the United States and that of the State of New Jersey. It is abundantly clear that appellants come fully within the literal language of the enactment. Extended discussion is quite unnecessary. Viewed solely as a matter of statutory construction, appellants are clearly entitled to the protections afforded by the act unless statutory exceptions including waiver are shown to apply. In view of the fundamental basis of our decision today, the question of waiver of privilege under the Shield Law need not be addressed by us.

III

The Sixth Amendment[42] and its New Jersey Counterpart[43]

Viewed on its face, considered solely as a reflection of legislative intent to bestow upon the press as broad a shield as possible to protect against forced revelation of confidential source materials, this legislation is entirely constitutional. Indeed, no one appears to have attacked its facial constitutionality.

It is however, argued, and argued very strenuously, that if enforced under the facts of this case, the Shield Law violates the Sixth Amendment of the Federal Constitution as well as Article 1, ¶ 10 of the New Jersey Constitution. These provisions are set forth above. Essentially the argument is this: The Federal and State Constitutions each provide that in all criminal prosecutions the accused shall have the right "to have compulsory process for obtaining witnesses in his favor." Dr. Jascalevich seeks to obtain evidence to use in preparing and presenting his defense in the ongoing criminal trial in which he has been accused of multiple murders. He claims to come within the favor of these constitutional provisions—which he surely does. Finally, when faced with the Shield Law, he invokes the rather elementary but entirely sound proposition that where Constitution and statute collide, the latter must yield. Subject to what is said below, we find this argument unassailable.

---

[42] The Sixth Amendment of the United States Constitution reads as follows:

> In all criminal prosecutions, the accused shall enjoy the right to a speedy and public trial, by an impartial jury of the State and district wherein the crime shall have been committed, which district shall have been previously ascertained by law, and to be informed of the nature and cause of the accusation; to be confronted with the witnesses against him; to have compulsory process for obtaining witnesses in his favor, and to have the Assistance of Counsel for his defence.

[43] Article 1, ¶ 10 of the Constitution of the State of New Jersey reads as follows:

> In all criminal prosecutions the accused shall have the right to a speedy and public trial by an impartial jury; to be informed of the nature and cause of the accusation; to be confronted with the witnesses against him; to have compulsory process for obtaining witnesses in his favor; and to have the assistance of counsel in his defense.

The compulsory process clause of the Sixth Amendment has never been elaborately explicated by the Supreme Court. Not until 1967, when it decided Washington v. Texas, 388 U.S. 14 * * * had the clause been directly construed. Westen, *Confrontation and Compulsory Process: A Unified Theory of Evidence for Criminal Cases,* 91 Harv.L.Rev. 567, 586 (1978). In *Washington* the petitioner sought the reversal of his conviction for murder. A Texas statute at the time provided that persons charged or convicted as co-participants in the same crime could not testify for one another. One Fuller, who had already been convicted of the murder, was prevented from testifying by virtue of the statute. The record indicated that had he testified his testimony would have been favorable to petitioner. The Court reversed the conviction on the ground that petitioner's Sixth Amendment right to compulsory process had been denied. At the same time it determined that the compulsory process clause in the Sixth Amendment was binding on state courts by virtue of the due process clause of the Fourteenth Amendment. It will be seen that *Washington* is like the present case in a significant respect. The Texas statute and the Sixth Amendment could not both stand. The latter of course prevailed. So must it be here.

Quite recently, in United States v. Nixon, 418 U.S. 683 * * * (1974), the Court dealt with another compulsory process issue. There the Special Prosecutor, Leon Jaworski, subpoenaed various tape recordings and documents in the possession of President Nixon. The latter claimed an executive privilege and refused to deliver the tapes. The Supreme Court conceded that indeed there was an executive privilege and that although "[n]owhere in the Constitution * * * is there any explicit reference to a privilege of confidentiality, yet to the extent this interest relates to the effective discharge of a President's powers, it is constitutionally based." 418 U.S. at 711 * * *. Despite this conclusion that at least to some extent a president's executive privilege derives from the Constitution, the Court nonetheless concluded that the demands of our criminal justice system required that the privilege must yield.

> We have elected to employ an adversary system of criminal justice in which the parties contest all issues before a court of law. The need to develop all relevant facts in the adversary system is both fundamental and comprehensive. The ends of criminal justice would be defeated if judgments were to be founded on a partial or speculative presentation of the facts. The very integrity of the judicial system and public confidence in the system depend on full disclosure of all the facts, within the framework of the rules of evidence. To ensure that justice is done, it is imperative to the function of courts that compulsory process be available for the production of evidence needed either

by the prosecution or by the defense. [United States v. Nixon, supra, 418 U.S. at 709 * * *.]

It is important to note that the Supreme Court in this case compelled the production of privileged material—the privilege acknowledged to rest in part upon the Constitution—even though there was no Sixth Amendment compulsion to do so. The Sixth Amendment affords rights to an accused but not to a prosecutor. The compulsion to require the production of the privileged material derived from the necessities of our system of administering criminal justice.

Article 1, ¶ 10 of the Constitution of the State of New Jersey contains, as we have seen, exactly the same language with respect to compulsory process as that found in the Sixth Amendment. There exists no authoritative explication of this constitutional provision. Indeed it has rarely been mentioned in our reported decisions. We interpret it as affording a defendant in a criminal prosecution the right to compel the attendance of witnesses and the production of documents and other material for which he may have, or may believe he has, a legitimate need in preparing or undertaking his defense. It also means that witnesses properly summoned will be required to testify and that material demanded by a properly phrased *subpoena duces tecum* will be forthcoming and available for appropriate examination and use.

Testimonial privileges, whether they derive from common law or from statute, which allow witnesses to withhold evidence seem to conflict with this provision. This conflict may arise in a variety of factual contexts with respect to different privileges.[44] We confine our consideration here to the single privilege before us—that set forth in the Shield Law. We hold that Article 1, ¶ 10 of our Constitution prevails over this statute, but in recognition of the strongly expressed legislative viewpoint favoring confidentiality we prescribe the imposition of the safeguards set forth in Point IV below.

IV

Procedural Mechanism

Appellants insist that they are entitled to a full hearing on the issues of relevance, materiality and overbreadth of the subpoena. We agree. The trial court recognized its obligation to conduct such a hearing, but the appellants have aborted that hearing by refusing to submit the material subpoenaed for an *in camera* inspection by the court to assist it in determining the motion to quash. That inspection is no more than a procedural tool, a device to be used to ascertain the relevancy and materiality of that material. Such an *in camera* inspection is not in itself

---

[44] Compare the informer's privilege where disclosure of identity may sometimes be required. State v. Milligan, 71 N.J. 373, 365 A.2d 914 (1976); State v. Oliver, 50 N.J. 39, 231 A.2d 805 (1967); Roviaro v. United States, 353 U.S. 53 * * * (1957).

an invasion of the statutory privilege. Rather it is a preliminary step to determine whether, and if so to what extent, the statutory privilege must yield to the defendant's constitutional rights.

Appellants' position is that there must be a full showing and definitive judicial determination of relevance, materiality, absence of less intrusive access, and need, prior to any *in camera* inspection. The obvious objection to such a rule, however, is that it would, in many cases, effectively stultify the judicial criminal process. It might well do so here. The defendant properly recognizes Myron Farber as a unique repository of pertinent information. But he does not know the extent of this information nor is it possible for him to specify all of it with particularity, nor to tailor his subpoena to precise materials of which he is ignorant. Well aware of this, Judge Arnold refused to give ultimate rulings with respect to relevance and other preliminary matters until he had examined the material. We think he had no other course. It is not rational to ask a judge to ponder the relevance of the unknown.

* * *

The judgment of conviction of criminal contempt and that in aid of litigants' rights are affirmed. Stays heretofore entered are vacated effective as of 4:00 p.m., Tuesday, September 26, 1978.

[The concurring opinion of HUGHES, C.J., and the dissenting opinions of PASHMAN, J., and HANDLER, J., are omitted. The dissents contended that the procedure followed was inadequate.]

NOTES AND QUESTIONS

1. *The New Jersey aftermath.* Following the decision in the principal case the New Jersey legislature amended the state shield law in an attempt to afford the broadest protection possible to newspersons consistent with the Sixth Amendment. See N.J.S.A. 2A:84A–21.1 et seq. The amended statute codified the tripartite showing required by *Farber* for penetration of the qualified privilege, but it also mandated that such a showing must be made *before* even an *in camera* inspection is ordered. Despite the observation in the principal case that such a requirement would "effectively stultify the judicial criminal process," the court subsequently acceded to the legislative will. State v. Boiardo, 414 A.2d 14 (N.J.1980). The resulting balance between First and Sixth Amendment concerns is criticized in Comment, Sixth Amendment Limitations on the Newsperson's Privilege: A Breach in the Shield, 13 Rutgers L.J. 361 (1982).

2. *Other state statutes.* State statutes conferring the privileges are common. See Monk, Evidentiary Privilege for Journalists' Sources: Theory and Statutory Protection, 51 Mo.L.Rev. 1 (1986). Where extant, they have typically received broad interpretation. Henderson v. People, 879 P.2d 383

(Colo.1994) (en banc) (privilege extended to pilot's knowledge of flight plan of news helicopter from which police officer observed marijuana plants).

The Commissioners on Uniform State Laws decided to abandon consideration of a uniform news gatherer's privilege, being unable to agree on either the content of or need for such an act. Uniform Laws Commissioners at Work, 61 A.B.A.J. 1399 (1975).

3. *Federal cases.* Despite the Supreme Court's rejection of a constitutionally based privilege in Branzburg v. Hayes, 408 U.S. 665 (1972), many federal courts, noting that this rejection did not command an absolute majority of the Court, have undertaken to recognize a qualified privilege penetrable upon bases much the same as those set out in *Farber.* See, e.g., United States v. Cuthbertson, 651 F.2d 189 (3d Cir.1981); Shoen v. Shoen, 5 F.3d 1289 (9th Cir.1993). In the federal courts, the requirements of relevance and need have been seen as heightened in civil cases. See Baker v. F & F Inv., 470 F.2d 778 (2d Cir.1972); Silkwood v. Kerr–McGee Corp., 563 F.2d 433 (10th Cir.1977). Compare Maressa v. New Jersey Monthly, 445 A.2d 376 (N.J.1982) (holding New Jersey privilege "absolute in the context of a libel action").

A few federal circuits have refused to recognize even a qualified privilege in connection with grand jury proceedings. See In re Grand Jury Proceedings, 810 F.2d 580 (6th Cir.1987); In re Grand Jury Proceedings, 5 F.3d 397 (9th Cir.1993). See generally Note, Journalist's Privilege: When Deprivation is a Benefit, 108 Yale L.J. 1449 (1999).

4. *The newsperson's privilege and the headlines.* Not surprisingly, claims of privilege by news people often involve situations of intense public interest—with reporters willing to suffer time in jail for contempt rather than divulge information concerning hot news stories. See, e.g., In re Grand Jury Subpoena, Judith Miller, 438 F.3d 1141 (D.C.Cir.2005) (court rejected argument on both constitutional and common law grounds that identity of sources for stories concerning disclosure of Valerie Plame as a CIA operative was confidential; grand jury subpoena had to obeyed). For a further discussion of this incident, see Nestler, Comment, The Underprivileged Profession: The Case for Supreme Court Recognition of the Journalist's Privilege, 154 U.Pa.L.Rev. 201 (2005). See generally Larsen, Note, The Demise of the First Amendment–Based Reporter's Privilege: Why This Current Trend Should Not Surprise the Media, 37 Conn.L.Rev. 1235 (2005).

5. *What about bloggers?* Who is a newsperson or journalist entitled to the protection of any privilege? For two different solutions to the question of who can claim protection, compare Alexander, Looking Out for the Watchdogs: A Legislative Proposal Limiting the Newsgathering Privilege to Journalists in the Greatest Need of Protection for Sources and Information, 20 Yale L. & Pol'y Rev. 97, 130 (2002) (claimant must have a substantial connection with an established news organization and the end product must be found to include information of public interest or concern) with Berger, Shielding the UnMedia: Using the Process of Journalism to Protect the

Journalist's Privilege in an Infinite Universe of Publication, 39 Hous.L.Rev. 1371, 1411 (2003) (any individual engaged in "journalism" should be protected by journalists' shield laws; "An individual is 'engaged in journalism' when he or she is involved in a process that is intended to generate and disseminate truthful information to the public on a regular basis.").

6.   *Sixth Amendment questions.* For discussions of the problem of reconciling testimonial privilege with the requirements of the Sixth Amendment, see Hill, Testimonial Privilege and Fair Trial, 80 Colum.L.Rev. 1173 (1980); Westen, Reflections on Alfred Hill's "Testimonial Privilege and Fair Trial," 14 U.Mich.J.L.Ref. 371 (1981); 1 McCormick, Evidence § 76.2 (7th ed. 2013).

JAFFEE V. REDMOND

Supreme Court of the United States, 1996.
518 U.S. 1.

JUSTICE STEVENS delivered the opinion of the Court.

After a traumatic incident in which she shot and killed a man, a police officer received extensive counseling from a licensed clinical social worker. The question we address is whether statements the officer made to her therapist during the counseling sessions are protected from compelled disclosure in a federal civil action brought by the family of the deceased. Stated otherwise, the question is whether it is appropriate for federal courts to recognize a "psychotherapist privilege" under Rule 501 of the Federal Rules of Evidence.

I

Petitioner is the administrator of the estate of Ricky Allen. Respondents are Mary Lu Redmond, a former police officer, and the Village of Hoffman Estates, Illinois, her employer during the time that she served on the police force. Petitioner commenced this action against respondents after Redmond shot and killed Allen while on patrol duty.

On June 27, 1991, Redmond was the first officer to respond to a "fight in progress" call at an apartment complex. As she arrived at the scene, two of Allen's sisters ran toward her squad car, waving their arms and shouting that there had been a stabbing in one of the apartments. Redmond testified at trial that she relayed this information to her dispatcher and requested an ambulance. She then exited her car and walked toward the apartment building. Before Redmond reached the building, several men ran out, one waving a pipe. When the men ignored her order to get on the ground, Redmond drew her service revolver. Two other men then burst out of the building, one, Ricky Allen, chasing the other. According to Redmond, Allen was brandishing a butcher knife and disregarded her repeated commands to drop the weapon. Redmond shot Allen when she believed he was about to stab the man he was chasing.

Allen died at the scene. Redmond testified that before other officers arrived to provide support, "people came pouring out of the buildings," App. 134, and a threatening confrontation between her and the crowd ensued.

Petitioner filed suit in Federal District Court alleging that Redmond had violated Allen's constitutional rights by using excessive force during the encounter at the apartment complex. The complaint sought damages under Rev. Stat. § 1979, 42 U.S.C. § 1983, and the Illinois wrongful-death statute, Ill. Comp. Stat., ch. 740, § 180/1 *et seq.* (1994). At trial, petitioner presented testimony from members of Allen's family that conflicted with Redmond's version of the incident in several important respects. They testified, for example, that Redmond drew her gun before exiting her squad car and that Allen was unarmed when he emerged from the apartment building.

During pretrial discovery petitioner learned that after the shooting Redmond had participated in about 50 counseling sessions with Karen Beyer, a clinical social worker licensed by the State of Illinois and employed at that time by the Village of Hoffman Estates. Petitioner sought access to Beyer's notes concerning the sessions for use in cross-examining Redmond. Respondents vigorously resisted the discovery. They asserted that the contents of the conversations between Beyer and Redmond were protected against involuntary disclosure by a psychotherapist-patient privilege. The district judge rejected this argument. Neither Beyer nor Redmond, however, complied with his order to disclose the contents of Beyer's notes. At depositions and on the witness stand both either refused to answer certain questions or professed an inability to recall details of their conversations.

In his instructions at the end of the trial, the judge advised the jury that the refusal to turn over Beyer's notes had no "legal justification" and that the jury could therefore presume that the contents of the notes would have been unfavorable to respondents. The jury awarded petitioner $45,000 on the federal claim and $500,000 on her state-law claim.

The Court of Appeals for the Seventh Circuit reversed and remanded for a new trial. Addressing the issue for the first time, the court concluded that "reason and experience," the touchstones for acceptance of a privilege under Rule 501 of the Federal Rules of Evidence, compelled recognition of a psychotherapist-patient privilege. * * * "Reason tells us that psychotherapists and patients share a unique relationship, in which the ability to communicate freely without the fear of public disclosure is the key to successful treatment." * * * As to experience, the court observed that all 50 States have adopted some form of the psychotherapist-patient privilege. * * * The court attached particular significance to the fact that Illinois law expressly extends such a privilege to social workers like

Karen Beyer. * * * The court also noted that, with one exception, the federal decisions rejecting the privilege were more than five years old and that the "need and demand for counseling services has skyrocketed during the past several years."

The Court of Appeals qualified its recognition of the privilege by stating that it would not apply if, "in the interests of justice, the evidentiary need for the disclosure of the contents of a patient's counseling sessions outweighs that patient's privacy interests." * * * Balancing those conflicting interests, the court observed, on the one hand, that the evidentiary need for the contents of the confidential conversations was diminished in this case because there were numerous eyewitnesses to the shooting, and, on the other hand, that Officer Redmond's privacy interests were substantial. * * * Based on this assessment, the court concluded that the trial court had erred by refusing to afford protection to the confidential communications between Redmond and Beyer.

The United States Courts of Appeals do not uniformly agree that the federal courts should recognize a psychotherapist privilege under Rule 501. Compare *In re Doe,* 964 F.2d 1325 (C.A.2 1992) (recognizing privilege); * * * Because of the conflict among the Courts of Appeals and the importance of the question, we granted certiorari. 516 U.S. 930 (1995). We affirm.

II

Rule 501 of the Federal Rules of Evidence authorizes federal courts to define new privileges by interpreting "common law principles * * * in the light of reason and experience." The authors of the Rule borrowed this phrase from our opinion in *Wolfle v. United States,* 291 U.S. 7, 12 (1934), which in turn referred to the oft-repeated observation that "the common law is not immutable but flexible, and by its own principles adapts itself to varying conditions." *Funk v. United States,* 290 U.S. 371, 383 (1933). See also *Hawkins v. United States,* 358 U.S. 74, 79 (1958) (changes in privileges may be "dictated by 'reason and experience' "). The Senate Report accompanying the 1975 adoption of the Rules indicates that Rule 501 "should be understood as reflecting the view that the recognition of a privilege based on a confidential relationship * * * should be determined on a case-by-case basis." S.Rep. No. 93–1277, p. 13 (1974) U.S.Code Cong. & Admin.News 1974, pp. 7051, 7059. The Rule thus did not freeze the law governing the privileges of witnesses in federal trials at a particular point in our history, but rather directed federal courts to "continue the evolutionary development of testimonial privileges." *Trammel v. United States,* 445 U.S. 40, 47 (1980); see also *University of Pennsylvania v. EEOC,* 493 U.S. 182, 189 (1990).

The common-law principles underlying the recognition of testimonial privileges can be stated simply. " 'For more than three centuries it has now been recognized as a fundamental maxim that the public * * * has a right to every man's evidence. When we come to examine the various claims of exemption, we start with the primary assumption that there is a general duty to give what testimony one is capable of giving, and that any exemptions which may exist are distinctly exceptional, being so many derogations from a positive general rule.' " *United States v. Bryan,* 339 U.S. 323, 331 (1950) (quoting 8 J. Wigmore, Evidence § 2192, p. 64 (3d ed. 1940)). See also *United States v. Nixon,* 418 U.S. 683, 709 (1974). Exceptions from the general rule disfavoring testimonial privileges may be justified, however, by a " 'public good transcending the normally predominant principle of utilizing all rational means for ascertaining truth.' " *Trammel,* 445 U.S., at 50(quoting *Elkins v. United States,* 364 U.S. 206, 234(1960) (Frankfurter, J., dissenting)).

Guided by these principles, the question we address today is whether a privilege protecting confidential communications between a psychotherapist and her patient "promotes sufficiently important interests to outweigh the need for probative evidence * * *." 445 U.S., at 51. Both "reason and experience" persuade us that it does.

III

Like the spousal and attorney-client privileges, the psychotherapist-patient privilege is "rooted in the imperative need for confidence and trust." * * *. Treatment by a physician for physical ailments can often proceed successfully on the basis of a physical examination, objective information supplied by the patient, and the results of diagnostic tests. Effective psychotherapy, by contrast, depends upon an atmosphere of confidence and trust in which the patient is willing to make a frank and complete disclosure of facts, emotions, memories, and fears. Because of the sensitive nature of the problems for which individuals consult psychotherapists, disclosure of confidential communications made during counseling sessions may cause embarrassment or disgrace. For this reason, the mere possibility of disclosure may impede development of the confidential relationship necessary for successful treatment. As the Judicial Conference Advisory Committee observed in 1972 when it recommended that Congress recognize a psychotherapist privilege as part of the Proposed Federal Rules of Evidence, a psychiatrist's ability to help her patients

> " 'is completely dependent upon [the patients'] willingness and ability to talk freely. This makes it difficult if not impossible for [a psychiatrist] to function without being able to assure * * * patients of confidentiality and, indeed, privileged communication. Where there may be exceptions to this general

rule * * *, there is wide agreement that confidentiality is a *sine qua non* for successful psychiatric treatment.' " Advisory Committee's Notes to Proposed Rules, 56 F.R.D. 183, 242 (1972) (quoting Group for Advancement of Psychiatry, Report No. 45, Confidentiality and Privileged Communication in the Practice of Psychiatry 92 (June 1960)).

By protecting confidential communications between a psychotherapist and her patient from involuntary disclosure, the proposed privilege thus serves important private interests.

Our cases make clear that an asserted privilege must also "serv[e] public ends." *Upjohn Co. v. United States,* 449 U.S. 383, 389 (1981). Thus, the purpose of the attorney-client privilege is to "encourage full and frank communication between attorneys and their clients and thereby promote broader public interests in the observance of law and administration of justice." *Ibid.* And the spousal privilege, as modified in *Trammel,* is justified because it "furthers the important public interest in marital harmony," 445 U.S., at 53. See also *United States v. Nixon,* 418 U.S., at 705; *Wolfle v. United States,* 291 U.S., at 14. The psychotherapist privilege serves the public interest by facilitating the provision of appropriate treatment for individuals suffering the effects of a mental or emotional problem. The mental health of our citizenry, no less than its physical health, is a public good of transcendent importance.[45]

In contrast to the significant public and private interests supporting recognition of the privilege, the likely evidentiary benefit that would result from the denial of the privilege is modest. If the privilege were rejected, confidential conversations between psychotherapists and their patients would surely be chilled, particularly when it is obvious that the circumstances that give rise to the need for treatment will probably result in litigation. Without a privilege, much of the desirable evidence to which litigants such as petitioner seek access—for example, admissions against interest by a party—is unlikely to come into being. This unspoken "evidence" will therefore serve no greater truth-seeking function than if it had been spoken and privileged.

That it is appropriate for the federal courts to recognize a psychotherapist privilege under Rule 501 is confirmed by the fact that all 50 States and the District of Columbia have enacted into law some form of psychotherapist privilege. We have previously observed that the policy decisions of the States bear on the question whether federal courts should

[45] This case amply demonstrates the importance of allowing individuals to receive confidential counseling. Police officers engaged in the dangerous and difficult tasks associated with protecting the safety of our communities not only confront the risk of physical harm but also face stressful circumstances that may give rise to anxiety, depression, fear, or anger. The entire community may suffer if police officers are not able to receive effective counseling and treatment after traumatic incidents, either because trained officers leave the profession prematurely or because those in need of treatment remain on the job.

recognize a new privilege or amend the coverage of an existing one. See *Trammel,* 445 U.S., at 48–50; *United States v. Gillock,* 445 U.S. 360, 368, n.8 (1980). Because state legislatures are fully aware of the need to protect the integrity of the factfinding functions of their courts, the existence of a consensus among the States indicates that "reason and experience" support recognition of the privilege. In addition, given the importance of the patient's understanding that her communications with her therapist will not be publicly disclosed, any State's promise of confidentiality would have little value if the patient were aware that the privilege would not be honored in a federal court. Denial of the federal privilege therefore would frustrate the purposes of the state legislation that was enacted to foster these confidential communications.

It is of no consequence that recognition of the privilege in the vast majority of States is the product of legislative action rather than judicial decision. Although common-law rulings may once have been the primary source of new developments in federal privilege law, that is no longer the case. In *Funk v. United States,* 290 U.S. 371 (1933), we recognized that it is appropriate to treat a consistent body of policy determinations by state legislatures as reflecting both "reason" and "experience." *Id.,* at 376–381. That rule is properly respectful of the States and at the same time reflects the fact that once a state legislature has enacted a privilege there is no longer an opportunity for common-law creation of the protection. The history of the psychotherapist privilege illustrates the latter point. In 1972 the members of the Judicial Conference Advisory Committee noted that the common law "had indicated a disposition to recognize a psychotherapist-patient privilege when legislatures began moving into the field." Proposed Rules, 56 F.R.D., at 242 (citation omitted). The present unanimous acceptance of the privilege shows that the state lawmakers moved quickly. That the privilege may have developed faster legislatively than it would have in the courts demonstrates only that the States rapidly recognized the wisdom of the rule as the field of psychotherapy developed.[46]

---

[46] Petitioner acknowledges that all 50 state legislatures favor a psychotherapist privilege. She nevertheless discounts the relevance of the state privilege statutes by pointing to divergence among the States concerning the types of therapy relationships protected and the exceptions recognized. A small number of state statutes, for example, grant the privilege only to psychiatrists and psychologists, while most apply the protection more broadly. Compare Haw. Rules Evid. 504, 504.1 and N.D. Rule Evid. 503 (privilege extends to physicians and psychotherapists), with Ariz.Rev.Stat. Ann. § 32–3283 (1992) (privilege covers "behavioral health professional[s]"); Tex. Rule Civ. Evid. 510(a)(1) (privilege extends to persons "licensed or certified by the State of Texas in the diagnosis, evaluation or treatment of any mental or emotional disorder" or "involved in the treatment or examination of drug abusers"); Utah Rule Evid. 506 (privilege protects confidential communications made to marriage and family therapists, professional counselors, and psychiatric mental health nurse specialists). The range of exceptions recognized by the States is similarly varied. Compare Ark.Code Ann. § 17–46–107 (1987) (narrow exceptions); Haw. Rules Evid. 504, 504.1 (same), with Cal. Evid.Code Ann. §§ 1016–1027 (West 1995) (broad exceptions); R.I. Gen. Laws § 5–37.3–4 (1995) (same). These variations in the scope

The uniform judgment of the States is reinforced by the fact that a psychotherapist privilege was among the nine specific privileges recommended by the Advisory Committee in its proposed privilege rules. In *United States v. Gillock,* 445 U.S., at 367–368, our holding that Rule 501 did not include a state legislative privilege relied, in part, on the fact that no such privilege was included in the Advisory Committee's draft. The reasoning in *Gillock* thus supports the opposite conclusion in this case. In rejecting the proposed draft that had specifically identified each privilege rule and substituting the present more open-ended Rule 501, the Senate Judiciary Committee explicitly stated that its action "should not be understood as disapproving any recognition of a psychiatrist-patient * * * privileg[e] contained in the [proposed] rules." S.Rep. No. 93–1277, at 13, U.S.Code Cong. & Admin.News 1974, pp. 7051, 7059.

Because we agree with the judgment of the state legislatures and the Advisory Committee that a psychotherapist-patient privilege will serve a "public good transcending the normally predominant principle of utilizing all rational means for ascertaining truth," *Trammel,* 445 U.S., at 50, we hold that confidential communications between a licensed psychotherapist and her patients in the course of diagnosis or treatment are protected from compelled disclosure under Rule 501 of the Federal Rules of Evidence.

IV

All agree that a psychotherapist privilege covers confidential communications made to licensed psychiatrists and psychologists. We have no hesitation in concluding in this case that the federal privilege should also extend to confidential communications made to licensed social workers in the course of psychotherapy. The reasons for recognizing a privilege for treatment by psychiatrists and psychologists apply with equal force to treatment by a clinical social worker such as Karen Beyer.[47] Today, social workers provide a significant amount of mental health treatment. See, *e.g.,* U.S. Dept. of Health and Human Services, Center for Mental Health Services, Mental Health, United States, 1994, pp. 85–87, 107–114; Brief for National Association of Social Workers et al. as *Amici Curiae* 5–7 (citing authorities). Their clients often include the poor and those of modest means who could not afford the assistance of a psychiatrist or psychologist, *id.,* at 6–7 (citing authorities), but whose

---

of the protection are too limited to undermine the force of the States' unanimous judgment that some form of psychotherapist privilege is appropriate.

[47] If petitioner had filed her complaint in an Illinois state court, respondents' claim of privilege would surely have been upheld, at least with respect to the state wrongful-death action. An Illinois statute provides that conversations between a therapist and her patients are privileged from compelled disclosure in any civil or criminal proceeding. Ill. Comp. Stat., ch. 740, § 110/10 (1994). The term "therapist" is broadly defined to encompass a number of licensed professionals including social workers. Ch. 740, § 110/2. Karen Beyer, having satisfied the strict standards for licensure, qualifies as a clinical social worker in Illinois. 51 F.3d 1346, 1358, n.19 (C.A.7 1995) * * *.

counseling sessions serve the same public goals.[48] Perhaps in recognition of these circumstances, the vast majority of States explicitly extend a testimonial privilege to licensed social workers. * * * We therefore agree with the Court of Appeals that "[d]rawing a distinction between the counseling provided by costly psychotherapists and the counseling provided by more readily accessible social workers serves no discernible public purpose." 51 F.3d, at 1358, n.19.

We part company with the Court of Appeals on a separate point. We reject the balancing component of the privilege implemented by that court and a small number of States. Making the promise of confidentiality contingent upon a trial judge's later evaluation of the relative importance of the patient's interest in privacy and the evidentiary need for disclosure would eviscerate the effectiveness of the privilege. As we explained in *Upjohn,* if the purpose of the privilege is to be served, the participants in the confidential conversation "must be able to predict with some degree of certainty whether particular discussions will be protected. An uncertain privilege, or one which purports to be certain but results in widely varying applications by the courts, is little better than no privilege at all." 449 U.S., at 393.

These considerations are all that is necessary for decision of this case. A rule that authorizes the recognition of new privileges on a case-by-case basis makes it appropriate to define the details of new privileges in a like manner. Because this is the first case in which we have recognized a psychotherapist privilege, it is neither necessary nor feasible to delineate its full contours in a way that would "govern all conceivable future questions in this area." *Id.,* at 386.[49]

V

The conversations between Officer Redmond and Karen Beyer and the notes taken during their counseling sessions are protected from compelled disclosure under Rule 501 of the Federal Rules of Evidence. The judgment of the Court of Appeals is affirmed.

---

[48] The Judicial Conference Advisory Committee's proposed psychotherapist privilege defined psychotherapists as psychologists and medical doctors who provide mental health services. Proposed Rules, 56 F.R.D., at 240. This limitation in the 1972 recommendation does not counsel against recognition of a privilege for social workers practicing psychotherapy. In the quarter century since the Committee adopted its recommendations, much has changed in the domains of social work and psychotherapy. See generally Brief for National Association of Social Workers et al. as *Amici Curiae* 5–13 (and authorities cited). While only 12 States regulated social workers in 1972, all 50 do today. See American Association of State Social Work Boards, Social Work Laws and Board Regulations: A State Comparison Study 29, 31 (1996). Over the same period, the relative portion of therapeutic services provided by social workers has increased substantially. See U.S. Dept. of Health and Human Services, Center for Mental Health Services, Mental Health, United States, 1994, pp. 85–87, 107–114.

[49] Although it would be premature to speculate about most future developments in the federal psychotherapist privilege, we do not doubt that there are situations in which the privilege must give way, for example, if a serious threat of harm to the patient or to others can be averted only by means of a disclosure by the therapist.

JUSTICE SCALIA, with whom the CHIEF JUSTICE joins as to Part III, dissenting.

The Court has discussed at some length the benefit that will be purchased by creation of the evidentiary privilege in this case: the encouragement of psychoanalytic counseling. It has not mentioned the purchase price: occasional injustice. That is the cost of every rule which excludes reliable and probative evidence—or at least every one categorical enough to achieve its announced policy objective. In the case of some of these rules, such as the one excluding confessions that have not been properly "Mirandized," see *Miranda v. Arizona,* 384 U.S. 436 (1966), the victim of the injustice is always the impersonal State or the faceless "public at large." For the rule proposed here, the victim is more likely to be some individual who is prevented from proving a valid claim—or (worse still) prevented from establishing a valid defense. The latter is particularly unpalatable for those who love justice, because it causes the courts of law not merely to let stand a wrong, but to become themselves the instruments of wrong.

In the past, this Court has well understood that the particular value the courts are distinctively charged with preserving—justice—is severely harmed by contravention of "the fundamental principle that ' "the public * * * has a right to every man's evidence." ' " *Trammel v. United States,* 445 U.S. 40, 50 (1980) (citation omitted). Testimonial privileges, it has said, "*are not lightly created nor expansively construed,* for they are in derogation of the search for truth." *United States v. Nixon,* 418 U.S. 683 (1974) (emphasis added). Adherence to that principle has caused us, in the Rule 501 cases we have considered to date, to reject new privileges, see *University of Pennsylvania v. EEOC,* 493 U.S. 182 (1990) (privilege against disclosure of academic peer review materials); *United States v. Gillock,* 445 U.S. 360 (1980) (privilege against disclosure of "legislative acts" by member of state legislature), and even to construe narrowly the scope of existing privileges, see, *e.g., United States v. Zolin,* 491 U.S. 554, 568–570 (1989) (permitting *in camera* review of documents alleged to come within crime-fraud exception to attorney-client privilege); *Trammel, supra* (holding that voluntary testimony by spouse is not covered by husband-wife privilege). The Court today ignores this traditional judicial preference for the truth, and ends up creating a privilege that is new, vast, and ill defined. I respectfully dissent.

* * *

III

Turning from the general question that was not involved in this case to the specific one that is: The Court's conclusion that a social-worker psychotherapeutic privilege deserves recognition is even less persuasive. In approaching this question, the fact that five of the state legislatures that have seen fit to enact "some form" of psychotherapist privilege have elected not to extend *any form* of privilege to social workers, * * * ought to give one pause. So should the fact that the Judicial Conference Advisory Committee was similarly discriminating in its conferral of the proposed Rule 504 privilege * * *. The Court, however, has "no hesitation in concluding * * * that the federal privilege should also extend" to social workers, * * * and goes on to prove that by polishing off the reasoned analysis with a topic sentence and two sentences of discussion, as follows (omitting citations and nongermane footnote):

> "The reasons for recognizing a privilege for treatment by psychiatrists and psychologists apply with equal force to treatment by a clinical social worker such as Karen Beyer. Today, social workers provide a significant amount of mental health treatment. Their clients often include the poor and those of modest means who could not afford the assistance of a psychiatrist or psychologist, but whose counseling sessions serve the same public goals." * * *

So much for the rule that privileges are to be narrowly construed.

Of course this brief analysis—like the earlier, more extensive, discussion of the general psychotherapist privilege—contains no explanation of why the psychotherapy provided by social workers is a public good of such transcendent importance as to be purchased at the price of occasional injustice. Moreover, it considers only the respects in which social workers providing therapeutic services are *similar* to licensed psychiatrists and psychologists; not a word about the respects in which they are different. A licensed psychiatrist or psychologist is an expert in psychotherapy—and that may suffice (though I think it not so clear that this Court should make the judgment) to justify the use of extraordinary means to encourage counseling with him, as opposed to counseling with one's rabbi, minister, family, or friends. One must presume that a social worker does *not* bring this greatly heightened degree of skill to bear, which is alone a reason for not encouraging that consultation as generously. Does a social worker bring to bear at least a significantly heightened degree of skill—more than a minister or rabbi, for example? I have no idea, and neither does the Court. The social worker in the present case, Karen Beyer, was a "licensed clinical social worker" in Illinois, * * * a job title whose training requirements consist of a "master's degree in social work from an approved program," and "3,000 hours of satisfactory, supervised clinical professional experience." Ill. Comp. Stat., ch. 225, § 20/9 (1994). It is not clear that the degree in social work requires *any* training in psychotherapy. The "clinical professional experience" apparently will impart some such training, but only of the vaguest sort, judging from the Illinois Code's definition of "[c]linical social work practice," viz., "the providing of mental health services for the evaluation, treatment, and prevention of mental and emotional disorders in individuals, families and groups based on knowledge and theory of psychosocial development, behavior, psychopathology, unconscious motivation, interpersonal relationships, and environmental stress." Ch. 225, § 20/3(5). But the rule the Court announces today—like the Illinois evidentiary privilege which that rule purports to respect, ch. 225, § 20/16—IS not limited to "licensed clinical social workers," but includes all "licensed social worker[s]." "Licensed social worker[s]" may also provide "mental health services" as described in § 20/3(5), so long as it is done under supervision of a licensed clinical social worker. And the training requirement for a "licensed social worker" consists of either (a) "a degree from a graduate program of social work" approved by the State, or (b) "a degree in social work from an undergraduate program" approved by the State, plus "3 years of supervised professional experience." Ch. 225, § 20/9A. With due respect, it does not seem to me that any of this training is comparable in its rigor (or indeed in the precision of its subject) to the training of the other experts (lawyers) to whom this Court has accorded a privilege, or even of the experts (psychiatrists and psychologists) to whom the Advisory Committee and this Court proposed extension of a privilege in 1972. Of course these are only *Illinois'* requirements for "social workers." Those of other States, for all we know, may be even less demanding. Indeed, I am not even sure there is a nationally accepted definition of "social worker," as there is of psychiatrist and psychologist. It seems to me quite irresponsible to extend the so-called "psychotherapist privilege" to all licensed social workers, nationwide, without exploring these issues.

Another critical distinction between psychiatrists and psychologists, on the one hand, and social workers, on the other, is that the former professionals, in their consultations with patients, *do nothing but psychotherapy.* Social workers, on the other hand, interview people for a multitude of reasons.

* * *

Thus, in applying the "social worker" variant of the "psychotherapist" privilege, it will be necessary to determine whether the information provided to the social worker was provided to him *in his capacity as a psychotherapist,* or in his capacity as an administrator of social welfare, a community organizer, etc. Worse still, if the privilege is to have its desired effect (and is not to mislead the client), it will presumably be necessary for the social caseworker to advise, as the conversation with his welfare client proceeds, which portions are privileged and which are not.

Having concluded its three sentences of reasoned analysis, the Court then invokes, as it did when considering the psychotherapist privilege, the "experience" of the States—once again an experience I consider irrelevant (if not counter-indicative) because it consists entirely of legislation rather than common-law decision. It says that "the vast majority of States explicitly extend a testimonial privilege to licensed social workers." * * * There are two elements of this impressive statistic, however, that the Court does not reveal.

First—and utterly conclusive of the irrelevance of this supposed consensus to the question before us—the majority of the States that accord a privilege to social workers do *not* do so as a subpart of a "psychotherapist" privilege. The privilege applies to *all* confidences imparted to social workers, and not just those provided in the course of psychotherapy. In Oklahoma, for example, the social-worker-privilege statute prohibits a licensed social worker from disclosing, or being compelled to disclose, *"any information* acquired from persons consulting the licensed social worker in his or her professional capacity" (with certain exceptions to be discussed *infra,* at 1939). Okla. Stat., Tit. 59, § 1261.6 (1991) (emphasis added). The social worker's "professional capacity" [in Oklahoma] is expansive. * * *

Thus, in Oklahoma, as in most other States having a social-worker privilege, it is not a subpart or even a derivative of the psychotherapist privilege, but rather a piece of special legislation similar to that achieved by many other groups, from accountants, see, *e.g.,* Miss. Code Ann. § 73–33–16(2) (1995) (certified public accountant "shall not be required by any court of this state to disclose, and shall not voluntarily disclose," client information), to private detectives, see, *e.g.,* Mich. Comp. Laws § 338.840(2) (1979) ("Any communications * * * furnished by a professional man or client to a [licensed private detective], or any information secured in connection with an assignment for a client, shall be deemed privileged with the same authority and dignity as are other privileged communications recognized by the courts of this state").[50] These social-worker statutes give no support, therefore, to the theory (importance of psychotherapy) upon which the Court rests its disposition.

Second, the Court does not reveal the enormous degree of disagreement among the States as to the scope of the privilege. It concedes that the laws of four States are subject to such gaping exceptions that they are " 'little better than no privilege at all,' " * * * so that they should more appropriately be categorized with the five States whose laws contradict the action taken today. * * * In adopting *any* sort of a social-worker privilege, then, the Court can at most claim that it is following the legislative "experience" of 40 States, and contradicting the "experience" of 10.

---

[50] These ever-multiplying evidentiary-privilege statutes, which the Court today emulates, recall us to the original meaning of the word "privilege." It is a composite derived from the Latin words "privus" and "lex": private law.

But turning to those States that do have an appreciable privilege of some sort, the diversity is vast * * *.

* * *

Thus, although the Court is technically correct that "the vast majority of States explicitly extend a testimonial privilege to licensed social workers," * * * that uniformity exists only at the most superficial level. No State has adopted the privilege without restriction; the nature of the restrictions varies enormously from jurisdiction to jurisdiction; and 10 States, I reiterate, effectively reject the privilege entirely. It is fair to say that there is scant national consensus even as to the propriety of a social-worker psychotherapist privilege, and none whatever as to its appropriate scope. In other words, the state laws to which the Court appeals for support demonstrate most convincingly that adoption of a social-worker psychotherapist privilege is a job for Congress.

* * *

The question before us today is not whether there should be an evidentiary privilege for social workers providing therapeutic services. Perhaps there should. But the question before us is whether (1) the need for that privilege is so clear, and (2) the desirable contours of that privilege are so evident, that it is appropriate for this Court to craft it in common-law fashion, under Rule 501. Even if we were writing on a clean slate, I think the answer to that question would be clear. But given our extensive precedent to the effect that new privileges "in derogation of the search for truth" "are not lightly created," *United States v. Nixon,* 418 U.S., at 710, the answer the Court gives today is inexplicable.

In its consideration of this case, the Court was the beneficiary of no fewer than 14 *amicus* briefs supporting respondents, most of which came from such organizations as the American Psychiatric Association, the American Psychoanalytic Association, the American Association of State Social Work Boards, the Employee Assistance Professionals Association, Inc., the American Counseling Association, and the National Association of Social Workers. Not a single amicus brief was filed in support of petitioner. That is no surprise. There is no self-interested organization out there devoted to pursuit of the truth in the federal courts. The expectation is, however, that this Court will have that interest prominently—indeed, primarily—in mind. Today we have failed that expectation, and that responsibility. It is no small matter to say that, in some cases, our federal courts will be the tools of injustice rather than unearth the truth where it is available to be found. The common law has identified a few instances where that is tolerable. Perhaps Congress may conclude that it is also tolerable for the purpose of encouraging psychotherapy by social workers. But that conclusion assuredly does not burst upon the mind with such clarity that a judgment in favor of suppressing the truth ought to be pronounced by this honorable Court. I respectfully dissent.

NOTES AND QUESTIONS

1. *Further development of the privilege.* As is apparent from the principal case, unlike the comparable privilege existing in most states, the federal psychotherapist privilege is a judicial creation. The dimensions of the federal privilege are now being developed through the judicial process. See, e.g., United States v. Auster, 517 F.3d 312 (5th Cir.2008) (communications not privileged where patient knew that psycho-therapist would communicate his threats to the victims); Speaker v. County of San Bernardino, 82 F.Supp. 2d 1105 (C.D.Cal.2000) (mandatory counseling sessions within privilege; privilege exists so long as patient believes counselor was a psychotherapist); Barrett v. Vojtas, 182 F.R.D. 177 (W.D.Pa.1998) (privilege did not apply where examination ordered by public officials). See generally Amann & Imwinkelried, The Supreme Court's Decision to Recognize a Psychotherapist Privilege in *Jaffee v. Redmond*, 116 S.Ct. 1923 (1996): The Meaning of "Experience" and the Role of "Reason" Under Federal Rule of Evidence 501, 65 U.Cin.L.Rev. 1019 (1997); Courville, Note, Rationales for the Confidentiality of Psychotherapist—Patient Communications: Testimonial Privilege and the Constitution, 35 Hous.L.Rev. 187 (1998).

2. *Persons covered.* The dissent in the principal case is particularly concerned about the expansion of the privilege to cover social workers. Even under the majority view of the privilege, should there be a limit as to which counselors are covered by the privilege? If so, on what should that limit be based? Licensing? Education? See United States v. Schwensow, 942 F.Supp. 402 (E.D.Wis.1996) (privilege did not apply where communications made to persons who were not physicians, psychotherapists, counselors or social workers); Poulin, The Psychotherapist–Patient Privilege After *Jaffee v. Redmond*: Where Do We Go From Here?, 76 Wash.U.L.Q. 1341 (1998).

3. *General physician-patient privilege in the states.* Approximately forty states recognize a general physician-patient privilege in addition to a psychotherapist privilege. The privileges vary substantially among the states. Most provide that the privilege is absolute, with specific exceptions. See Cal. Evid. Code §§ 990–1007. Others provide for a qualified privilege, such as North Carolina Gen. Stat. § 8–53 (disclosure may be required by a judge if "necessary to a proper administration of justice"). Remember that, in the principal case, the Court rejected a qualified psychotherapist's privilege and instead opted for an absolute privilege. What are the advantages and disadvantages of a qualified privilege? See generally 1 McCormick, Evidence ch. 11 (7th ed. 2013).

4. *General physician-patient privilege in the federal courts.* As did the proposed Federal Rules of Evidence governing privilege, the federal courts have uniformly rejected a general physician-patient privilege. See, e.g., United States v. Bercier, 848 F.2d 917 (8th Cir.1988). What is the rationale

for rejecting a general physician-patient privilege, while accepting a psychotherapist-patient privilege? See the criticism of such a choice in 25 Wright & Graham, Federal Practice and Procedure § 5522 (1989) and the proposal for a general physician-patient privilege in the federal courts, modeled after the privilege created in *Jaffee* in Broun, The Medical Privilege in the Federal Courts—Should It Matter Whether Your Ego or Your Elbow Hurts?, 38 Loy.L.A.L.Rev. 657 (2004).

Uniform Rules of Evidence

RULE 503. [PSYCHOTHERAPIST][51] [PHYSICIAN AND PSYCHOTHERAPIST] [PHYSICIAN AND MENTAL–HEALTH PROVIDER] [MENTAL–HEALTH PROVIDER]—PATIENT PRIVILEGE.

(a) Definitions. In this rule:

(1) A communication is "confidential" if it is not intended to be disclosed to third persons, except those present to further the interest of the patient in the consultation, examination, or interview, those reasonably necessary for the transmission of the communication, and persons who are participating in the diagnosis and treatment of the patient under the direction of a [psychotherapist] [physician or psychotherapist] [physician or mental-health provider] [mental-health provider], including members of the patient's family.

[(2) "Mental-health provider" means a person authorized, in any State or country, or reasonably believed by the patient to be authorized, to engage in the diagnosis or treatment of a mental or emotional condition, including addiction to alcohol or drugs.]

[(3) "Patient" means an individual who consults or is examined or interviewed by a [psychotherapist] [physician or psychotherapist] [physician or mental-health provider] [mental-health provider].]

[(4) "Physician" means a person authorized in any State or country, or reasonably believed by the patient to be authorized to practice medicine.]

[(5) "Psychotherapist" means a person authorized in any State or country, or reasonably believed by the patient to be authorized, to practice medicine, while engaged in the diagnosis or treatment of a mental or emotional condition, including addiction to alcohol or drugs, or a person licensed or certified under the laws of any State or country, or reasonably believed by

---

[51] [The language in brackets was provided by the drafters to give jurisdictions options when adopting this privilege. Ed.]

the patient to be licensed or certified, as a psychologist, while similarly engaged.]

(b) General rule of privilege. A patient has a privilege to refuse to disclose and to prevent any other person from disclosing confidential communications made for the purpose of diagnosis or treatment of the patient's [physical,] mental[,] or emotional condition, including addiction to alcohol or drugs, among the patient, the patient's [psychotherapist] [physician or psychotherapist] [physician or mental-health provider] [mental-health provider] and persons, including members of the patient's family, who are participating in the diagnosis or treatment under the direction of the [psychotherapist] [physician or psychotherapist] [physician or mental-health provider] [mental-health provider].

(c) Who may claim the privilege. The privilege under this rule may be claimed by the patient, the patient's guardian or conservator, or the personal representative of a deceased patient. The person who was the [psychotherapist] [physician or psychotherapist] [physician or mental-health provider] [mental-health provider] at the time of the communication is presumed to have authority to claim the privilege, but only on behalf of the patient.

(d) Exceptions. There is no privilege under this rule for a communication:

(1) relevant to an issue in proceedings to hospitalize the patient for mental illness, if the [psychotherapist] [physician or psychotherapist] [physician or mental-health provider] [mental-health provider], in the course of diagnosis or treatment, has determined that the patient is in need of hospitalization;

(2) made in the course of a court-ordered investigation or examination of the [physical,] mental[,] or emotional condition of the patient, whether a party or a witness, with respect to the particular purpose for which the examination is ordered, unless the court orders otherwise;

(3) relevant to an issue of the [physical,] mental[,] or emotional condition of the patient in any proceeding in which the patient relies upon the condition as an element of the patient's claim or defense or, after the patient's death, in any proceeding in which any party relies upon the condition as an element of the party's claim or defense;

(4) if the services of the [psychotherapist] [physician or psychotherapist] [physician or mental-health provider] [mental-health provider] were sought or obtained to enable or aid anyone to commit or plan to commit what the patient knew, or

reasonably should have known, was a crime or fraud or mental or physical injury to the patient or another individual;

(5) in which the patient has expressed an intent to engage in conduct likely to result in imminent death or serious bodily injury to the patient or another individual;

(6) relevant to an issue in a proceeding challenging the competency of the [psychotherapist] [physician or psychotherapist] [physician or mental-health provider] [mental-health provider];

(7) relevant to a breach of duty by the [psychotherapist] [physician or psychotherapist] [physician or mental-health provider] [mental-health provider]; or

(8) that is subject to a duty to disclose under [statutory law].

NOTE ON THE CLERGY–COMMUNICANT PRIVILEGE

Though some authorities have questioned the existence of a clergy-communicant privilege at common law, it would appear that such a privilege was recognized before the Reformation and only dropped from view after that era had substantially reduced the importance of confession in England. Yellin, The History and Current Status of the Clergy–Penitent Privilege, 23 Santa Clara L.Rev. 95 (1983). Whatever its recognition at common law, the privilege is now recognized by statute in all but three states. 8 Wigmore, Evidence § 2395 (McNaughten rev. 1961). The statutory forms vary widely, however, and it has been said that "there is no typical clergy privilege statute." Mitchell, Must Clergy Tell? Child Abuse Reporting Requirements Versus the Clergy Privilege and Free Exercise of Religion, 71 Minn.L.Rev. 723 (1987). Similarly the justifications advanced for the privilege have varied. See Reece, Confidential Communications to the Clergy, 24 Ohio St.L.J. 55 (1963).

Problems arising from attempts to invoke the privilege have frequently centered on who is a "clergyman," Annot., 101 A.L.R.5th 619, and what types of communications are covered, Annot., 93 A.L.R. 5th 327. See also Kuhlman, Communications to Clergyman—When Are They Privileged?, 2 Val.U.L.Rev. 265 (1968).

Many of the priest-penitent statutes incorporate the requirement that the communication, to be privileged, must be made "in the course of discipline enjoined by the church or denomination" of the clergyman. Should this language be construed to extend the privilege only to communicants of a church in which confession is required? Compare In re Swenson, 237 N.W. 589 (Minn.1931) (holding the quoted statutes not to be so restricted), with Sherman v. State, 279 S.W. 353 (Ark.1926). See also State v. Martin, 959 P.2d 152 (Wash.Ct.App.1998) (language interpreted as requiring only that clergy member be required by the member's religion to receive the confidential communication and to provide spiritual counseling).

What of the constitutionality of any priest-penitent privilege, even one available to members of all denominations and sects? See Durrant, Where There's Smoke, There's Fire (And Brimstone): Is It Time to Abandon the Clergy–Penitent Privilege?, 39 Loy.L.A.L.Rev. 1339 (2006) (arguing that the privilege violates the Establishment Clause); Smith, The Pastor on the Witness Stand: Toward a Religious Privilege in the Courts, 29 Cath.Law. 1 (1984); Stoyles, The Dilemma of the Constitutionality of the Priest–Penitent Privilege, 29 U.Pitt.L.Rev. 27 (1967).

NOTE ON MISCELLANEOUS STATUTORY PRIVILEGES

A state by state survey of various and sundry evidentiary privileges can be found in Imwinkelried, The New Wigmore: Evidentiary Privilege, App. D (2d ed. 2010).

Among the more common statutory privileges listed by Professor Imwinkelried is the accountant-client's privilege, existing in more than half the states.

Increased awareness of the problems facing victims of rape has found expression not only in rules such as Fed.R.Evid. 412, but in advocacy for, and occasional adoption of, a rape victim-counselor privilege. See Comment, Rape Victim—Crisis Counselor Communications: An Argument for an Absolute Privilege, 17 U.C. Davis L.Rev. 1213 (1984).

A parent-child privilege has been adopted by statute in at least three states, Idaho Code § 9–203(7); Minn.Stat.Ann. § 595.02(j); Mass.Gen.L. ch. 233, § 20; though appeals for the judicial creation of such a privilege have been almost universally rejected. See In re Grand Jury, 103 F.3d 1140 (3d Cir.1997) (listing cases rejecting the privilege). The literature, generally in support of some form of the privilege, is extensive. A representative selection includes Coburn, Child–Parent Communications: Spare the Privilege and Spoil the Child, 74 Dick.L.Rev. 599 (1970); Kraft, The Parent–Child Testimonial Privilege: Who's Minding the Kids?, 18 Fam.L.Q. 505 (1985) (advocating non-traditional privilege protecting child as opposed to parent testimony); Schlueter, The Parent–Child Privilege: A Response to Calls for Adoption, 19 St. Mary's L.J. 35 (1987); Stanton, Child–Parent Privilege for Confidential Communications, An Examination and Proposal, 16 Fam.L.Q. 1 (1982); Stern, Don't Tell Mom the Babysitter's Dead: Arguments for a Federal Parent–Child Privilege and a Proposal to Amend Article V, 99 Geo.L.J. 605 (2011).

Creation of still other privileges has been advocated, Nejelski & Lerman, A Researcher–Subject Testimonial Privilege, 1971 Wis.L.Rev. 1085; Delgado & Miller, God, Galileo, and Government: Toward Constitutional Protection for Scientific Inquiry, 53 Wash.L.Rev. 349 (1978). For a tentative suggestion that creation of a librarian-patron privilege might be sought, together with discussion of several incidents giving rise to the idea, see 1 American Libraries 749 (1970).

CHAPTER 16[1]

PRIVILEGES DESIGNED TO SAFEGUARD GOVERNMENTAL OPERATIONS

■ ■ ■

A. STATE SECRETS AND EXECUTIVE PRIVILEGE

UNITED STATES V. REYNOLDS

Supreme Court of the United States, 1953.
345 U.S. 1.

MR. CHIEF JUSTICE VINSON delivered the opinion of the Court.

These suits under the Tort Claims Act arise from the death of three civilians in the crash of a B–29 aircraft at Waycross, Georgia, on October 6, 1948. Because an important question of the Government's privilege to resist discovery is involved, we granted certiorari. 343 U.S. 918.

The aircraft had taken flight for the purpose of testing secret electronic equipment, with four civilian observers aboard. While aloft, fire broke out in one of the bomber's engines. Six of the nine crew members and three of the four civilian observers were killed in the crash.

The widows of the three deceased civilian observers brought consolidated suits against the United States. In the pretrial stages the plaintiffs moved, under Rule 34 of the Federal Rules of Civil Procedure, for production of the Air Force's official accident investigation report and the statements of the three surviving crew members, taken in connection with the official investigation. The Government moved to quash the motion, claiming that these matters were privileged against disclosure pursuant to Air Force regulations promulgated under R.S. § 161. The District Judge sustained plaintiffs' motion, holding that good cause for production had been shown. The claim of privilege under R.S. § 161 was rejected on the premise that the Tort Claims Act, in making the Government liable "in the same manner" as a private individual, had waived any privilege based upon executive control over governmental documents.

---

[1]   In the cases and materials throughout the chapter, some footnotes have been omitted and others have been renumbered. [Ed.]

Shortly after this decision, the District Court received a letter from the Secretary of the Air Force, stating that "it has been determined that it would not be in the public interest to furnish this report. * * * " The court allowed a rehearing on its earlier order, and at the rehearing the Secretary of the Air Force filed a formal "Claim of Privilege." This document repeated the prior claim based generally on R.S. § 161, and then stated that the Government further objected to production of the documents "for the reason that the aircraft in question, together with the personnel on board, were engaged in a highly secret mission of the Air Force." An affidavit of the Judge Advocate General, United States Air Force, was also filed with the court, which asserted that the demanded material could not be furnished "without seriously hampering national security, flying safety and the development of highly technical and secret military equipment." The same affidavit offered to produce the three surviving crew members, without cost, for examination by the plaintiffs. The witnesses would be allowed to refresh their memories from any statement made by them to the Air Force, and authorized to testify as to all matters except those of a "classified nature."

The District Court ordered the Government to produce the documents in order that the court might determine whether they contained privileged matter. The Government declined, so the court entered an order, under Rule 37(b)(2)(i), that the facts on the issue of negligence would be taken as established in plaintiffs' favor. After a hearing to determine damages, final judgment was entered for the plaintiffs. The Court of Appeals affirmed, both as to the showing of good cause for production of the documents, and as to the ultimate disposition of the case as a consequence of the Government's refusal to produce the documents.

We have had broad propositions pressed upon us for decision. On behalf of the Government it has been urged that the executive department heads have power to withhold any documents in their custody from judicial view if they deem it to be in the public interest.[2] Respondents have asserted that the executive's power to withhold documents was waived by the Tort Claims Act. Both positions have constitutional overtones which we find it unnecessary to pass upon, there being a narrower ground for decision. * * * .

The Tort Claims Act expressly makes the Federal Rules of Civil Procedure applicable to suits against the United States. The judgment in this case imposed liability upon the Government by operation of Rule 37, for refusal to produce documents under Rule 34. Since Rule 34 compels

---

[2]   While claim of executive power to suppress documents is based more immediately upon R.S. § 161 * * *, the roots go much deeper. It is said that R.S. § 161 is only a legislative recognition of an inherent executive power which is protected in the constitutional system of separation of power.

production only of matters "not privileged," the essential question is whether there was a valid claim of privilege under the Rule. We hold that there was, and that, therefore, the judgment below subjected the United States to liability on terms to which Congress did not consent by the Tort Claims Act.

We think it should be clear that the term "not privileged," as used in Rule 34, refers to "privileges" as that term is understood in the law of evidence. When the Secretary of the Air Force lodged his formal "Claim of Privilege," he attempted therein to invoke the privilege against revealing military secrets, a privilege which is well established in the law of evidence.[3] * * *

[T]he principles which control the application of the privilege emerge quite clearly from the available precedents. The privilege belongs to the Government and must be asserted by it; it can neither be claimed nor waived by a private party. It is not to be lightly invoked.[4] There must be a formal claim of privilege, lodged by the head of the department which has control over the matter, after actual personal consideration by that officer. The court itself must determine whether the circumstances are appropriate for the claim of privilege, and yet do so without forcing a disclosure of the very thing the privilege is designed to protect.[5] The latter requirement is the only one which presents real difficulty. As to it, we find it helpful to draw upon judicial experience in dealing with an analogous privilege, the privilege against self-incrimination.

The privilege against self-incrimination presented the courts with a similar sort of problem. Too much judicial inquiry into the claim of privilege would force disclosure of the thing the privilege was meant to protect, while a complete abandonment of judicial control would lead to intolerable abuses. Indeed, in the earlier stages of judicial experience with the problem, both extremes were advocated, some saying that the bare assertion by the witness must be taken as conclusive, and others saying that the witness should be required to reveal the matter behind his claim of privilege to the judge for verification.[6] Neither extreme

---

[3]   Totten v. United States, 92 U.S. 105, 107 (1875); Firth Sterling Steel Co. v. Bethlehem Steel Co., 199 F. 353 (D.C.E.D.Pa.1912) * * *.

[4]   Marshall, C.J., in the *Aaron Burr* trial, I Robertson's Reports 186: "That there may be matter, the production of which the court would not require, is certain. * * * What ought to be done, under such circumstances, presents a delicate question, the discussion of which, it is hoped, will never be rendered necessary in this country."

[5]   [Duncan v. Cammell, Laird & Co., [1942] A.C. 624,] at pp. 638–642; cf. the language of this Court in Hoffman v. United States, 341 U.S. 479, 486 (1951), speaking to the analogous hazard of probing too far in derogation of the claim of privilege against self-incrimination:

"However, if the witness, upon interposing his claim, were required to prove the hazard in the sense in which a claim is usually required to be established in court, *he would be compelled to surrender the very protection which the privilege is designed to guarantee.*" (Emphasis supplied.)

[6]   Compare the expressions of Rolfe, B. and Wilde, C.J., in Regina v. Garbett, 2 Car. & K. 474, 492 (1847); see 8 Wigmore on Evidence (3d ed.) § 2271.

prevailed, and a sound formula of compromise was developed. This formula received authoritative expression in this country as early as the *Burr* trial.[7] There are differences in phraseology, but in substance it is agreed that the court must be satisfied from all the evidence and circumstances, and "from the implications of the question, in the setting in which it is asked, that a responsive answer to the question or an explanation of why it cannot be answered might be dangerous because injurious disclosure could result." Hoffman v. United States, 341 U.S. 479, 486–487 (1951). If the court is so satisfied, the claim of the privilege will be accepted without requiring further disclosure.

Regardless of how it is articulated, some like formula of compromise must be applied here. Judicial control over the evidence in a case cannot be abdicated to the caprice of executive officers. Yet we will not go so far as to say that the court may automatically require a complete disclosure to the judge before the claim of privilege will be accepted in any case. It may be possible to satisfy the court, from all the circumstances of the case, that there is a reasonable danger that compulsion of the evidence will expose military matters which, in the interest of national security, should not be divulged. When this is the case, the occasion for the privilege is appropriate, and the court should not jeopardize the security which the privilege is meant to protect by insisting upon an examination of the evidence, even by the judge alone, in chambers.

In the instant case we cannot escape judicial notice that this is a time of vigorous preparation for national defense. Experience in the past war has made it common knowledge that air power is one of the most potent weapons in our scheme of defense, and that newly developing electronic devices have greatly enhanced the effective use of air power. It is equally apparent that these electronic devices must be kept secret if their full military advantage is to be exploited in the national interests. On the record before the trial court it appeared that this accident occurred to a military plane which had gone aloft to test secret electronic equipment. Certainly there was a reasonable danger that the accident investigation report would contain references to the secret electronic equipment which was the primary concern of the mission.

Of course, even with this information before him, the trial judge was in no position to decide that the report was privileged until there had been a formal claim of privilege. Thus it was entirely proper to rule

[7] I Robertson's Reports 244:

"When a question is propounded, it belongs to the court to consider and to decide, whether any direct answer to it can implicate the witness. If this be decided in the negative, then he may answer it without violating the privilege which is secured to him by law. If a direct answer to it *may* criminate himself, then he must be the sole judge what his answer would be. The court cannot participate with him in this judgment, because they cannot decide on the effect of his answer without knowing what it would be; and a disclosure of that fact to the judges would strip him of the privilege which the law allows, and which he claims."

initially that petitioner had shown probable cause for discovery of the documents. Thereafter, when the formal claim of privilege was filed by the Secretary of the Air Force, under circumstances indicating a reasonable possibility that military secrets were involved, there was certainly a sufficient showing of privilege to cut off further demand for the documents on the showing of necessity for its compulsion that had then been made.

In each case, the showing of necessity which is made will determine how far the court should probe in satisfying itself that the occasion for invoking the privilege is appropriate. Where there is a strong showing of necessity, the claim of privilege should not be lightly accepted, but even the most compelling necessity cannot overcome the claim of privilege if the court is ultimately satisfied that military secrets are at stake.[8] *A fortiori,* where necessity is dubious, a formal claim of privilege, made under the circumstances of this case, will have to prevail. Here, necessity was greatly minimized by an available alternative, which might have given respondents the evidence to make out their case without forcing a showdown on the claim of privilege. By their failure to pursue that alternative, respondents have posed the privilege question for decision with the formal claim of privilege set against a dubious showing of necessity.

There is nothing to suggest that the electronic equipment, in this case, had any causal connection with the accident. Therefore, it should be possible for respondents to adduce the essential facts as to causation without resort to material touching upon military secrets. Respondents were given a reasonable opportunity to do just that, when petitioner formally offered to make the surviving crew members available for examination. We think that offer should have been accepted.

Respondents have cited us to those cases in the criminal field, where it has been held that the Government can invoke its evidentiary privileges only at the price of letting the defendant go free.[9] The rationale of the criminal cases is that, since the Government which prosecutes an accused also has the duty to see that justice is done, it is unconscionable to allow it to undertake prosecution and then invoke its governmental privileges to deprive the accused of anything which might be material to his defense. Such rationale has no application in a civil forum where the Government is not the moving party, but is a defendant only on terms to which it has consented.

---

[8]   See Totten v. United States, 92 U.S. 105 (1875), where the very subject matter of the action, a contract to perform espionage, was a matter of state secret. The action was dismissed on the pleadings without ever reaching the question of evidence, since it was so obvious that the action should never prevail over the privilege.

[9]   United States v. Andolschek, 142 F.2d 503 (C.A.2d Cir.1944); United States v. Beekman, 155 F.2d 580 (C.A.2d Cir.1946).

The decision of the Court of Appeals is reversed and the case will be remanded to the District Court for further proceedings consistent with the views expressed in this opinion.

Reversed and remanded.

MR. JUSTICE BLACK, MR. JUSTICE FRANKFURTER, and MR. JUSTICE JACKSON dissent, substantially for the reasons set forth in the opinion of Judge Maris below. 192 F.2d 987.

NOTES AND QUESTIONS

1. *Uncertainty on conclusiveness of executive determination of privilege.* In *Reynolds,* the Supreme Court provides inconsistent indications as to whether the trial court must accept as virtually conclusive the executive determination of privilege or whether it has the right to determine independently the validity of the claim on the basis of an *in camera* inspection. In Ellsberg v. Mitchell, 709 F.2d 51 (D.C.Cir.1983), the court of appeals, while recognizing the dangers involved, stated the test for determining whether an *in camera* inspection should be conducted as follows:

> Whether (and in what spirit) the trial judge in a particular case should examine the materials sought to be withheld depends upon two critical considerations. First, the more compelling a litigant's showing of need for the information in question, the deeper "the court should probe in satisfying itself that the occasion for invoking the privilege is appropriate." Second, the more plausible and substantial the government's allegations of danger to national security, in the context of all circumstances surrounding the case, the more deferential should be the judge's inquiry into the foundations and scope of the claim.

709 F.2d at 58–59 (quoting *Reynolds*, 345 U.S. at 11).

The court then dealt with the requester's argument that a decision by the court based solely upon an *ex parte in camera* inspection was inadequate. It concluded that in ruling upon the validity of the claim, the court should not permit the requester's counsel to participate in the *in camera* proceedings since "our nation's security is too important to be entrusted to the good faith and circumspection of a litigant's lawyer (whose sense of obligation to his client is likely to strain his fidelity to his pledge of secrecy) or to the coercive power of a protective order." 709 F.2d at 61. However, the court concluded that the government should be required to provide as complete a public account of the materials as possible to assist adversary analysis of the claim:

> [T]he trial judge should insist (1) that the formal claim of privilege be made on the public record and (2) that the government either (a) publicly explain in detail the kinds of injury to national security it seeks to avoid and the reason those harms would result from the revelation of the requested information or (b) indicate why such an explanation would itself endanger national security. * * * [B]efore

> conducting an *in camera* examination of the requested materials, the trial judge should be sure that the government has justified its claim in as much detail as is feasible (and would be helpful) without undermining the privilege itself.

Id. at 63–64. See also Northrop Corp. v. McDonnell Douglas Corp., 751 F.2d 395, 401 (D.C.Cir.1984) (describing court's determination of whether to conduct *in camera* inspection as application of "sliding scale").

2. *Limited judicial role. Reynolds* has been "extensively mined" for its analysis of the role of the judge in military or diplomatic secrets cases. 1 McCormick, Evidence § 110 (7th ed. 2013). "Whatever material is considered by the court the standard applied is whether there exists a reasonable danger that disclosure will damage national security. If this danger is found, the privilege is absolute and is not affected by the extent of the litigants need for the confidential information." Id. § 110, at 53. All other governmental privileges are qualified. As will be seen throughout the rest of the Chapter, these cases necessitate a greater role for the judiciary, which must weigh the competing interests of government secrecy against a litigant's interest in obtaining the evidentiary information. *In camera* inspection of the disputed evidence is often the means of accomplishing this task, but it "is not a necessary or inevitable tool in every case. Others are available." EPA v. Mink, 410 U.S. 73, 93 (1973) (noting that the agency may sometimes satisfy its burden by means such as a detailed affidavit or oral testimony).

3. *Government invocation of privilege where non-party.* As *Reynolds* notes, the state secrets privilege may be invoked only by the government. There are often significant consequences when it does so. Where the government is not a party, the result in most instances is as if the witness possessing the evidence were dead—the evidence is simply unavailable. *Ellsberg,* note 1, supra, 709 F.2d at 64. In some circumstances, the impact may be far more drastic. In Fitzgerald v. Penthouse Int'l, Ltd., 776 F.2d 1236 (4th Cir.1985), the court held that, where trial of a libel action would require proof of the truth or falsity of classified materials, the government's invocation of the state secrets privilege required dismissal since litigation would compromise military secrets. See also Mohamed v. Jeppesen Dataplan, Inc., 614 F.3d 1070, 1087–89 (9th Cir.2010) (en banc) (dismissing action by foreign national against company allegedly aiding the extraordinary rendition program because no feasible way to litigate the case without unjustified risk of divulging state secrets); El–Masri v. United States, 479 F.3d 296, 306–11 (4th Cir.2007) (ruling that dismissal was required because litigation could not be fairly conducted without disclosure of material covered by the state secrets privilege).

4. *Government invocation of privilege where civil defendant.* Where the government is a civil defendant, the results remain essentially the same as if it were not a party: there is no direct penalty for invoking the privilege, and the evidence is treated simply as unavailable. "The rationale for this doctrine is that the United States, while waiving its sovereign immunity for many

purposes, has never consented to an *increase* in its exposure to liability when it is compelled, for reasons of national security, to refuse to release relevant evidence." *Ellsberg,* 709 F.2d at 64. In some circumstances, the government may be able to use the materials submitted *in camera* to establish a defense. See Molerio v. Federal Bureau of Investigation, 749 F.2d 815, 825 (D.C.Cir.1984) (summary judgment properly granted against plaintiff when privileged information provided *in camera* established a valid defense).

5. *Government invocation where civil plaintiff or criminal prosecutor.* When the government is the moving party as civil plaintiff or prosecutor in a criminal case, assertion of privilege may result in direct sanctions. In a civil case, dismissal of the government's complaint will frequently be required but will not always be an appropriate remedy. Compare United States v. Cotton Valley Operators Comm'n, 9 F.R.D. 719 (W.D.La.1949), aff'd by equally divided court, 339 U.S. 940 (1950) (dismissal appropriate remedy), with Republic of China v. Nat'l Union Fire Ins., 142 F.Supp. 551 (D.Md.1956) (dismissal inappropriate). In the criminal context, when the government denies the defendant information material to the defense or bearing directly on the merits of the charge, dismissal is appropriate. United States v. Reynolds, 345 U.S. 1, 12 (1953). While changing neither the state secrets privilege nor the consequences of the government withholding classified materials, the procedures followed when such information is withheld is now governed by the Classified Information Procedures Act. 18 U.S.C.App. § 1, et seq.

6. *Classified material in criminal defense.* Criminal defendants will on occasion, chiefly in espionage cases, possess classified information they contend must be revealed in the presentation of their defense. A defendant in such circumstances has the ability to place the government in the position of continuing the prosecution at the cost of the revelation of state secrets. This situation, which may arise either from the bogus claims of the unscrupulous or through wholly proper efforts of counsel to present a defense, is given the label "graymail." This problem was a principal reason for passage of the Classified Information Procedures Act (CIPA). CIPA has been part of several high profile cases. See United States v. Noriega, 117 F.3d 1206, 1215–17 (11th Cir.1997) (former Panamanian strongman arguing unsuccessfully that intelligence work performed for the United States should have been admitted at trial); United States v. Ho Lee, 90 F.Supp.2d 1324 (D.N.M.2000) (rejecting espionage defendant's argument that CIPA was unconstitutional as applied to him).

CIPA establishes procedures to litigate such claims in an effort to remedy one of the critical inadequacies of the then existing procedures, the lack of opportunity for the government to obtain an advance ruling concerning admissibility of the classified material. Prosecutors often cited this feature of the law as the reason they dismissed charges rather than risking disclosure of the information at trial. CIPA provides that a defendant must give advance notice to the prosecution if he or she intends to disclose classified information in connection with litigation of the criminal trial. The court then holds an *in camera* hearing to determine issues involving relevance and admissibility of the classified information. As a consequence of the hearing, the court may deny the defendant the right to disclose the information or, if it finds disclosure proper, order, at the government's request, that either a statement admitting relevant facts or a summary of the specific information be received as a substitute for the classified information. See United States v. Moussaoui, 382 F.3d 453, 471–82 (4th Cir.2004) (finding dismissal not appropriate sanction for government refusal to produce enemy combatant witness where substitutes for testimony were adequate). If the court denies the government's request to accept a substitute, upon objection by the Attorney General, the court orders the defendant not to disclose the information and either dismisses the charges or fashions other appropriate relief.

The prospect of a defendant's use of state secrets may justify resort to unusual procedural devices to protect the privileged information. In Loral Corp. v. McDonnell Douglas Corp., 558 F.2d 1130 (2d Cir.1977), the court upheld the trial court's action in striking a jury trial demand where the litigation involved large amounts of classified material. The case involved an action by a subcontractor producing classified equipment for the Air Force against the prime contractor for breach of contract. Both parties already had access to the classified material, and the court pointed out that the Department of Defense would grant security clearance to the judge and magistrate to whom the case was assigned but that such a course was not feasible with respect to jurors. See also Halpern v. United States, 258 F.2d 36 (2d Cir.1958). These unusual steps may be preferable to the option of dismissing the action.

7.   *Sources.* 2 Imwinkelried, The New Wigmore: Evidentiary Privileges, ch. 8 (2d ed. 2010); Askin, Secret Justice and the Adversary System, 18 Hastings Const.L.Q. 745 (1991); Gardner, The State Secret Privilege Invoked in Civil Litigation: A Proposal for Statutory Relief, 29 Wake Forest L.Rev. 567 (1994); Pilchen & Klubes, Using the Classified Information Procedures Act in Criminal Cases: A Primer for Defense Counsel, 31 Am.Crim.L.Rev. 191 (1994); Schmidt & Dratel, Turning the Tables: Using the Government's Secrecy and Security Arsenal for the Benefit of the Client in Terrorism Prosecutions, 48 N.Y.L.Sch.L.Rev. 69 (2003/2004); Stracher, Eyes Tied Shut: Litigating for Access under CIPA in the Government's "War on Terror," 48 N.Y.L.Sch.L.Rev.173 (2003/2004).

UNITED STATES V. NIXON

Supreme Court of the United States, 1974.
418 U.S. 683.

MR. CHIEF JUSTICE BURGER delivered the opinion of the Court.

* * *

On March 1, 1974, a grand jury of the United States District Court for the District of Columbia returned an indictment charging seven named individuals[10] with various offenses, including conspiracy to defraud United States and to obstruct justice. Although he was not designated as such in the indictment, the grand jury named the President, among others, as an unindicted coconspirator. On April 18, 1974, upon motion of the Special Prosecutor, * * * a subpoena *duces tecum* was issued pursuant to Rule 17(c) to the President by the United States District Court and made returnable on May 2, 1974. This subpoena required the production, in advance of the September 9 trial date, of certain tapes, memoranda, papers, transcripts or other writings relating to certain precisely identified meetings between the President and others. The Special Prosecutor was able to fix the time, place and persons present at these discussions because the White House daily logs and appointment records had been delivered to him. On April 30, the President publicly released edited transcripts of 43 conversations; portions of 20 conversations subject to subpoena in the present case were included. On May 1, 1974, the President's counsel, filed a "special appearance" and a motion to quash the subpoena, under Rule 17(c). This motion was accompanied by a formal claim of privilege. At a subsequent hearing, further motions to expunge the grand jury's action naming the President as an unindicted coconspirator and for protective orders against the disclosure of that information were filed or raised orally by counsel for the President.

On May 20, 1974, the District Court denied the motion to quash and the motions to expunge and for protective orders. 377 F.Supp. 1326 (1974). It further ordered "the President or any subordinate officer, official or employee with custody or control of the documents or objects subpoenaed," id., at 1331, to deliver to the District Court, on or before May 31, 1974, the originals of all subpoenaed items, as well as an index and analysis of those items, together with tape copies of those portions of the subpoenaed recordings for which transcripts had been released to the public by the President on April 30. The District Court rejected jurisdictional challenges based on a contention that the dispute was

---

[10] The seven defendants were John N. Mitchell, H.R. Haldeman, John D. Ehrlichman, Charles W. Colson, Robert C. Mardian, Kenneth W. Parkinson, and Gordon Strachan. Each had occupied either a position of responsibility on the White House staff or the Committee for the Re-election of the President. Colson entered a guilty plea on another charge and is no longer a defendant.

nonjusticiable because it was between the Special Prosecutor and the Chief Executive and hence "intra-executive" in character; it also rejected the contention that the judiciary was without authority to review an assertion of executive privilege by the President. The court's rejection of the first challenge was based on the authority and powers vested in the Special Prosecutor by the regulation promulgated by the Attorney General; the court concluded that a justiciable controversy was presented. The second challenge was held to be foreclosed by the decision in Nixon v. Sirica, 159 U.S.App.D.C. 58, 487 F.2d 700 (1973).

The District Court held that the judiciary, not the President, was the final arbiter of a claim of executive privilege. The court concluded that under the circumstances of this case the presumptive privilege was overcome by the Special Prosecutor's prima facie "demonstration of need sufficiently compelling to warrant judicial examination in chambers * * *." 377 F.Supp., at 1330. The court held, finally, that the Special Prosecutor had satisfied the requirements of Rule 17(c). The District Court stayed its order pending appellate review on condition that review was sought before 4 p.m., May 24. The court further provided that matters filed under seal remain under seal when transmitted as part of the record.

On May 24, 1974, the President filed a timely notice of appeal from the District Court order, and the certified record from the District Court was docketed in the United States Court of Appeals for the District of Columbia Circuit. On the same day, the President also filed a petition for writ of mandamus in the Court of Appeals seeking review of the District Court order.

Later on May 24, the Special Prosecutor also filed, in this Court, a petition for a writ of certiorari before judgment. On May 31, the petition was granted with an expedited briefing schedule, 417 U.S. 927 (1974). On June 6, the President filed, under seal, a cross-petition for writ of certiorari before judgment. This cross-petition was granted June 15, 1974, 417 U.S. 960 (1974), and the case was set for argument on July 8, 1974. * * *

[The Court overruled jurisdictional objections that were based on lack of a final and appealable judgment in the absence of an adjudication of contempt and on lack of a case or controversy since the dispute was within the Executive Branch. The Court also overruled the claim that Criminal Rule 17(c) had not been satisfied.]

IV

The Claim of Privilege

A

* * *

Notwithstanding the deference each branch must accord the others, the "judicial power of the United States" vested in the federal courts by Art. III, § 1 of the Constitution can no more be shared with the Executive Branch than the Chief Executive, for example, can share with the Judiciary the veto power, or the Congress share with the Judiciary the power to override a presidential veto. Any other conclusion would be contrary to the basic concept of separation of powers and the checks and balances that flow from the scheme of a tripartite government. The Federalist, No. 47, p. 313 (C.F. Mittel ed. 1938). We therefore reaffirm that it is the province and duty of this Court "to say what the law is" with respect to the claim of privilege presented in this case. Marbury v. Madison, supra, 1 Cranch, at 177.

B

In support of his claim of absolute privilege, the President's counsel urges two grounds one of which is common to all governments and one of which is peculiar to our system of separation of powers. The first ground is the valid need for protection of communications between high government officials and those who advise and assist them in the performance of their manifold duties; the importance of this confidentiality is too plain to require further discussion. Human experience teaches that those who expect public dissemination of their remarks may well temper candor with a concern for appearances and for their own interests to the detriment of the decision-making process.[11] Whatever the nature of the privilege of confidentiality of presidential communications in the exercise of Art. II powers the privilege can be said to derive from the supremacy of each branch within its own assigned area of constitutional duties. Certain powers and privileges flow from the nature of enumerated powers; the protection of the confidentiality of presidential communications has similar constitutional underpinnings.

The second ground asserted by the President's counsel in support of the claim of absolute privilege rests on the doctrine of separation of powers. Here it is argued that the independence of the Executive Branch

---

[11] There is nothing novel about governmental confidentiality. The meetings of the Constitutional Convention in 1787 were conducted in complete privacy. 1 Farrand, The Records of the Federal Convention of 1787, xi–xxv (1911). Moreover, all records of those meetings were sealed for more than 30 years after the Convention. See 3 U.S.Stat. At Large, p. 475, 15th Cong. 1st Sess., Res. 8 (1818). Most of the Framers acknowledged that without secrecy no constitution of the kind that was developed could have been written. Warren, The Making of the Constitution, 134–139 (1937).

within its own sphere, Humphrey's Executor v. United States, 295 U.S. 602, 629–630; Kilbourn v. Thompson, 103 U.S. 168, 190–191 (1880), insulates a president from a judicial subpoena in an ongoing criminal prosecution, and thereby protects confidential presidential communications.

However, neither the doctrine of separation of powers, nor the need for confidentiality of high level communications, without more, can sustain an absolute, unqualified presidential privilege of immunity from judicial process under all circumstances. The President's need for complete candor and objectivity from advisers calls for great deference from the courts. However, when the privilege depends solely on the broad, undifferentiated claim of public interest in the confidentiality of such conversations, a confrontation with other values arises. Absent a claim of need to protect military, diplomatic or sensitive national security secrets, we find it difficult to accept the argument that even the very important interest in confidentiality of presidential communications is significantly diminished by production of such material for *in camera* inspection with all the protection that a district court will be obliged to provide.

The impediment that an absolute, unqualified privilege would place in the way of the primary constitutional duty of the Judicial Branch to do justice in criminal prosecutions would plainly conflict with the function of the courts under Art. III. * * * To read the Art. II powers of the President as providing an absolute privilege as against a subpoena essential to enforcement of criminal statutes on no more than a generalized claim of the public interest in confidentiality of nonmilitary and nondiplomatic discussions would upset the constitutional balance of "a workable government" and gravely impair the role of the courts under Art. III.

C

Since we conclude that the legitimate needs of the judicial process may outweigh presidential privilege, it is necessary to resolve those competing interests in a manner that preserves the essential functions of each branch. The right and indeed the duty to resolve that question does not free the judiciary from according high respect to the representations made on behalf of the President. United States v. Burr, 25 Fed.Cas. pp. 187, 190, 191–192 (No. 14,694) (CCVa.1807).

The expectation of a President to the confidentiality of his conversations and correspondence, like the claim of confidentiality of judicial deliberations, for example, has all the values to which we accord deference for the privacy of all citizens and added to those values the necessity for protection of the public interest in candid, objective, and even blunt or harsh opinions in presidential decisionmaking. A President and those who assist him must be free to explore alternatives in the process of shaping policies and making decisions and to do so in a way many would be unwilling to express except privately. These are the considerations justifying a presumptive privilege for presidential communications. The privilege is fundamental to the operation of government and inextricably rooted in the separation of powers under the Constitution.[12] In Nixon v. Sirica, 159 U.S.App.D.C. 58, 487 F.2d 700 (1973), the Court of Appeals held that such presidential communications are "presumptively privileged," id., at 717, and this position is accepted by both parties in the present litigation. We agree with Mr. Chief Justice Marshall's observation, therefore, that "in no case of this kind would a court be required to proceed against the President as against an ordinary individual." United States v. Burr, 25 Fed.Cas., at 192.

But this presumptive privilege must be considered in light of our historic commitment to the rule of law. This is nowhere more profoundly manifest than in our view that "the twofold aim [of criminal justice] is that guilt shall not escape or innocence suffer." Berger v. United States, 295 U.S. 78, 88 (1935). We have elected to employ an adversary system of criminal justice in which the parties contest all issues before a court of law. The need to develop all relevant facts in the adversary system is both fundamental and comprehensive. The ends of criminal justice would be defeated if judgments were to be founded on a partial or speculative presentation of the facts. The very integrity of the judicial system and public confidence in the system depend on full disclosure of all the facts, within the framework of the rules of evidence. To ensure that justice is done, it is imperative to the function of courts that compulsory process be available for the production of evidence needed either by the prosecution or by the defense.

Only recently the Court restated the ancient proposition of law, albeit in the context of a grand jury inquiry rather than a trial,

> " 'that the public * * * has a right to every man's evidence' except for those persons protected by a constitutional, common law, or statutory privilege, United States v. Bryan, 339 U.S. [323], at 331 (1950) * * *." Branzburg v. [Hayes] United States, 408 U.S. 665, 688 (1972).

The privileges referred to by the Court are designed to protect weighty and legitimate competing interests. Thus, the Fifth Amendment to the Constitution provides that no man "shall be compelled in any criminal case to be a witness against himself." And, generally, an attorney or a priest may not be required to disclose what has been revealed in professional confidence. These and other interests are recognized in law by privileges against forced disclosure, established in the Constitution, by

---

[12] "Freedom of communication vital to fulfillment of the aims of wholesome relationships is obtained only by removing the specter of compelled disclosure * * * [G]overnment * * * needs open but protected channels for the kind of plain talk that is essential to the quality of its functioning." Carl Zeiss Stiftung v. V.E.B. Carl Zeiss, Jena, 40 F.R.D. 318, 325 (D.C.1966). * *

statute, or at common law. Whatever their origins, these exceptions to the demand for every man's evidence are not lightly created nor expansively construed, for they are in derogation of the search for truth.[13]

In this case the President challenges a subpoena served on him as a third party requiring the production of materials for use in a criminal prosecution on the claim that he has a privilege against disclosure of confidential communications. He does not place his claim of privilege on the ground they are military or diplomatic secrets. As to these areas of Art. II duties the courts have traditionally shown the utmost deference to presidential responsibilities. In C. & S. Air Lines v. Waterman Steamship Corp., 333 U.S. 103, 111 (1948), dealing with presidential authority involving foreign policy considerations, the Court said:

> "The President, both as Commander-in-Chief and as the Nation's organ for foreign affairs, has available intelligence services whose reports are not and ought not to be published to the world. It would be intolerable that courts, without the relevant information, should review and perhaps nullify actions of the Executive taken on information properly held secret." Id., at 111.

In United States v. Reynolds, 345 U.S. 1 (1952), dealing with a claimant's demand for evidence in a damage case against the Government the Court said:

> "It may be possible to satisfy the court, from all the circumstances of the case, that there is a reasonable danger that compulsion of the evidence will expose military matters which, in the interest of national security, should not be divulged. When this is the case, the occasion for the privilege is appropriate, and the court should not jeopardize the security which the privilege is meant to protect by insisting upon an examination of the evidence, even by the judge alone, in chambers."

No case of the Court, however, has extended this high degree of deference to a President's generalized interest in confidentiality. Nowhere in the Constitution, as we have noted earlier, is there any explicit reference to a privilege of confidentiality, yet to the extent this interest relates to the effective discharge of a President's powers, it is constitutionally based.

The right to the production of all evidence at a criminal trial similarly has constitutional dimensions. The Sixth Amendment explicitly confers upon every defendant in a criminal trial the right "to be

---

[13] Because of the key role of the testimony of witnesses in the judicial process, courts have historically been cautious about privileges. Justice Frankfurter, dissenting in Elkins v. United States, 364 U.S. 206, 234 (1960), said of this: "Limitations are properly placed upon the operation of this general principle only to the very limited extent that permitting a refusal to testify or excluding relevant evidence has a public good transcending the normally predominant principle of utilizing all rational means for ascertaining truth."

confronted with the witnesses against him" and "to have compulsory process for obtaining witnesses in his favor." Moreover, the Fifth Amendment also guarantees that no person shall be deprived of liberty without due process of law. It is the manifest duty of the courts to vindicate those guarantees and to accomplish that it is essential that all relevant and admissible evidence be produced.

In this case we must weigh the importance of the general privilege of confidentiality of presidential communications in performance of his responsibilities against the inroads of such a privilege on the fair administration of criminal justice.[14] The interest in preserving confidentiality is weighty indeed and entitled to great respect. However we cannot conclude that advisers will be moved to temper the candor of their remarks by the infrequent occasions of disclosure because of the possibility that such conversations will be called for in the context of a criminal prosecution.

On the other hand, the allowance of the privilege to withhold evidence that is demonstrably relevant in a criminal trial would cut deeply into the guarantee of due process of law and gravely impair the basic function of the courts. A President's acknowledged need for confidentiality in the communications of his office is general in nature, whereas the constitutional need for production of relevant evidence in a criminal proceeding is specific and central to the fair adjudication of a particular criminal case in the administration of justice. Without access to specific facts a criminal prosecution may be totally frustrated. The President's broad interest in confidentiality of communications will not be vitiated by disclosure of a limited number of conversations preliminarily shown to have some bearing on the pending criminal cases.

We conclude that when the ground for asserting privilege as to subpoenaed materials sought for use in a criminal trial is based only on the generalized interest in confidentiality, it cannot prevail over the fundamental demands of due process of law in the fair administration of criminal justice. The generalized assertion of privilege must yield to the demonstrated, specific need for evidence in a pending criminal trial.

D

We have earlier determined that the District Court did not err in authorizing the issuance of the subpoena. If a President concludes that compliance with a subpoena would be injurious to the public interest he may properly, as was done here, invoke a claim of privilege on the return

---

[14] We are not here concerned with the balance between the President's generalized interest in confidentiality and the need for relevant evidence in civil litigation, nor with that between the confidentiality interest and congressional demands for information, nor with the President's interest in preserving state secrets. We address only the conflict between the President's assertion of a generalized privilege of confidentiality against the constitutional need for relevant evidence in criminal trials.

of the subpoena. Upon receiving a claim of privilege from the Chief Executive, it became the further duty of the District Court to treat the subpoenaed material as presumptively privileged and to require the Special Prosecutor to demonstrate that the Presidential material was 'essential to the justice of the (pending criminal) case.' United States v. Burr, 25 Fed.Cas., at 192. Here the District Court treated the material as presumptively privileged, proceeded to find that the Special Prosecutor had made a sufficient showing to rebut the presumption, and ordered an in camera examination of the subpoenaed material. On the basis of our examination of the record we are unable to conclude that the District Court erred in ordering the inspection. Accordingly we affirm the order of the District Court that subpoenaed materials be transmitted to that court. We now turn to the important question of the District Court's responsibilities in conducting the *in camera* examination of presidential materials or communications delivered under the compulsion of the subpoena *duces tecum*.

E

Enforcement of the subpoena *duces tecum* was stayed pending this Court's resolution of the issues raised by the petitions for certiorari. Those issues now having been disposed of, the matter of implementation will rest with the District Court. "[T]he guard, furnished to [the President] to protect him from being harassed by vexatious and unnecessary subpoenas, is to be looked for in the conduct of the [district] court after the subpoenas have issued; not in any circumstance which is to precede their being issued." United States v. Burr, [25 F.Cas. pp. 30, 34 (No. 14,692d) (CC Va.1807)]. Statements that meet the test of admissibility and relevance must be isolated; all other material must be excised. At this stage the District Court is not limited to representations of the Special Prosecutor as to the evidence sought by the subpoena; the material will be available to the District Court. It is elementary that *in camera* inspection of evidence is always a procedure calling for scrupulous protection against any release or publication of material not found by the court, at that stage, probably admissible in evidence and relevant to the issues of the trial for which it is sought. That being true of an ordinary situation, it is obvious that the District Court has a very heavy responsibility to see to it that presidential conversations, which are either not relevant or not admissible, are accorded that high degree of respect due the President of the United States. Mr. Chief Justice Marshall sitting as a trial judge in the *Burr* case, supra, was extraordinarily careful to point out that:

> "[I]n no case of this kind would a court be required to proceed against the President as against an ordinary individual." United States v. Burr, 25 Fed.Cas. pp. 187, 192 (No. 14,694).

Marshall's statement cannot be read to mean in any sense that a President is above the law, but relates to the singularly unique role under Art. II of a President's communications and activities, related to the performance of duties under that Article. Moreover, a President's communications and activities encompass a vastly wider range of sensitive material than would be true of any "ordinary individual." It is therefore necessary in the public interest to afford presidential confidentiality the greatest protection consistent with the fair administration of justice. The need for confidentiality even as to idle conversations with associates in which casual reference might be made concerning political leaders within the country or foreign statesmen is too obvious to call for further treatment. We have no doubt that the District Judge will at all times accord to presidential records that high degree of deference suggested in United States v. Burr, supra and will discharge his responsibility to see to it that until released to the Special Prosecutor no *in camera* material is revealed to anyone. This burden applies with even greater force to excised material; once the decision is made to excise, the material is restored to its privileged status and should be returned under seal to its lawful custodian.

Since this matter came before the Court during the pendency of a criminal prosecution, and on representations that time is of the essence, the mandate shall issue forthwith.

Affirmed. * * *

NOTES AND QUESTIONS

1. *Sources on United States v. Nixon.* Berger, Executive Privilege: A Constitutional Myth (1974); Cox, Executive Privilege, 122 U.Pa.L.Rev. 1383 (1974); Freund, Foreword: On Presidential Privilege, in The Supreme Court, 1973 Term, 88 Harv.L.Rev. 13 (1974); Symposium, United States v. Nixon: Presidential Power and Executive Privilege Twenty–Five Years Later, 85 Minn.L.Rev. 1061 (1999); Symposium: United States v. Nixon, 22 UCLA L.Rev. 1 (1974).

2. *Executive privilege in recent presidencies.* During President Clinton's second term, a variety of privilege claims made their way from the White House into the legal system. See Clinton v. Jones, 520 U.S. 681 (1997); *In re* Lindsey, 148 F.3d 1100 (D.C.Cir.1998); *In re* Sealed Case, 121 F.3d 729 (D.C.Cir.1997); *In re* Grand Jury Subpoena Duces Tecum, 112 F.3d 910 (8th Cir.1997). See Kelley, The Constitutional Dilemma of Litigation Under the Independent Counsel System, 83 Minn.L.Rev. 1197, 1201–15 (1999) (briefly summarizing the Clinton privilege claims and their resolution). For direction, the courts often looked to *Nixon* and two United States v. Burr decisions (25 F.Cas. 30 (C.C.D.Va.1807) & 25 F.Cas. 187 (C.C.D.Va.1807)), cited in *Nixon*. See Yoo, The First Claim: The Burr Trial, *United States v. Nixon*, and Presidential Power, 83 Minn.L.Rev. 1435 (1999) (discussing *Burr* cases, their

historical context, and their use in *Nixon* and the Clinton cases). During the Bush presidency, see Cheney v. United States Dist. Court, 542 U.S. 367 (2004) (ruling that separation of powers argument could be raised without first invoking executive privilege).

3. *Analysis of claim of executive privilege. In re* Sealed Case, 121 F.3d 729 (D.C.Cir.1997), is the most comprehensive judicial treatment of executive privilege since *Nixon* and also extensively examines the deliberative process privilege, treated in the next principal case. *In re Sealed Case* deals with White House documents related to allegations that former Secretary of Agriculture Mike Espy improperly accepted a gift. The Office of the Independent Counsel (OIC) sought all relevant White House documents. The White House provided several documents but withheld others under claim of privilege.

> * * * [A]t the OIC's request, the White House produced a privilege log identifying the date, author, and recipient of each document withheld as well as a general statement of the nature of each document and the basis for the privilege on which the document was withheld. This privilege log indicated that 84 documents were withheld on grounds of the deliberative process privilege, with one document additionally withheld on grounds of attorney-client privilege. In a later draft of the privilege log, the White House lists the privilege basis of all 84 documents as being "executive/deliberative privilege."

> The OIC negotiated with the White House for access to the withheld documents for several months, finally filing a motion to compel production on June 7, 1995. The White House resisted the motion, arguing that the withheld documents came within both the privilege for presidential communications, recognized in *United States v. Nixon*, 418 U.S. 683 (1974) (*Nixon*), and the deliberative process privilege that protects the deliberations and decisionmaking process of executive officials generally. After a hearing on the motion to compel, the district court ordered the White House to produce the withheld documents for *in camera* review and the White House complied. Each document produced was accompanied by an *ex parte* cover sheet that explained the purpose of the document. The OIC also made an *ex parte* submission justifying the grand jury's need for the documents. On September 30, 1996, the court denied the motion to compel. The memorandum opinion accompanying the denial quoted from *Nixon* to the effect that the "generalized assertion of privilege [for presidential communications] must yield to the demonstrated, specific need for evidence in a pending criminal trial," 418 U.S. at 713, but then concluded that the White House had properly asserted the claimed privileges in this case. In reaching this conclusion, the court stated that it had carefully reviewed the documents, but did not discuss the

documents in any further detail and provided no analysis of the grand jury's asserted need for the documents.

121 F.3d at 735–36.

On appeal, the D.C. Circuit analyzed the issues as follows:

While the presidential communications privilege and the deliberative process privilege are closely affiliated, the two privileges are distinct and have different scopes. Both are executive privileges designed to protect executive branch decisionmaking, but one applies to decisionmaking of executive officials generally, the other specifically to decisionmaking of the President. The presidential privilege is rooted in constitutional separation of powers principles and the President's unique constitutional role; the deliberative process privilege is primarily a common law privilege. *See* [*Nixon v. Fitzgerald*, 457 U.S. 731, 753 & n.35 (1982)]. Consequently, congressional or judicial negation of the presidential communications privilege is subject to greater scrutiny than denial of the deliberative privilege. * * *

In addition, unlike the deliberative process privilege, the presidential communications privilege applies to documents in their entirety, and covers final and post-decisional materials as well as pre-deliberative ones. Even though the presidential privilege is based on the need to preserve the President's access to candid advice, none of the cases suggest that it encompasses only the deliberative or advice portions of documents. Indeed, *Nixon* argued that the presidential privilege must be qualified to ensure full access to facts in judicial proceedings, thereby assuming that factual material comes under the privilege. 418 U.S. at 709; *but see* LARKIN, [FEDERAL TESTIMONIAL PRIVILEGES] § 6.01 at 6–1 [(1996)] (asserting, without explanation, that the presidential privilege does not "protect purely factual material"). There is no indication either that the presidential privilege is restricted to pre-decisional materials. GSA cautioned that the privilege only applies to communications made in the process of arriving at presidential decisions, but by this we believe the Court meant that the privilege was limited to materials connected to presidential decisionmaking, as opposed to other executive branch decisionmaking, and not that only pre-decisional materials were covered. 433 U.S. at 449. Nor would exclusion of final or post-decisional materials make sense, given the *Nixon* cases' concern that the President be given sufficient room to operate effectively. These materials often will be revelatory of the President's deliberations— as, for example, when the President decides to pursue a particular course of action, but asks his advisers to submit follow-up reports so that he can monitor whether this course of action is likely to be successful. The release of final and post-decisional materials would also limit the President's ability to communicate his decisions privately, thereby interfering with his ability to exercise control over the executive branch.

Finally, while both the deliberative process privilege and the presidential privilege are qualified privileges, the *Nixon* cases suggest that the presidential communications privilege is more difficult to surmount. In regard to both, courts must balance the public interests at stake in determining whether the privilege should yield in a particular case, and must specifically consider the need of the party seeking privileged evidence. But this balancing is more ad hoc in the context of the deliberative process privilege, and includes consideration of additional factors such as whether the government is a party to the litigation. Moreover, the privilege disappears altogether when there is any reason to believe government misconduct occurred. On the other hand, a party seeking to overcome the presidential privilege seemingly must always provide a focused demonstration of need, even when there are allegations of misconduct by high-level officials. In holding that the Watergate Special Prosecutor had provided a sufficient showing of evidentiary need to obtain tapes of President Nixon's conversations, the Supreme Court made no mention of the fact that the tapes were sought for use in a trial of former presidential assistants charged with engaging in a criminal conspiracy while in office. *Accord Senate Committee*, 498 F.2d at 731 (noting that presidential privilege is not intended to shield governmental misconduct but arguing that showing of need turns on extent to which subpoenaed evidence is necessary for government institution to fulfill its responsibilities, not on type of conduct evidence may reveal); *contra* 26A WRIGHT & GRAHAM, [FEDERAL PRACTICE AND PROCEDURE] § 5673, at 53–54 (quoting *Senate Committee's* not-a-shield language and arguing that allegations of misconduct qualify the privilege, but not addressing *Senate Committee's* comment that need showing turns on function for which evidence is sought and not on conduct revealed by evidence).

These differences between the presidential communications privilege and the deliberative privilege demonstrate that the presidential privilege affords greater protection against disclosure. Consequently, should we conclude as to any document that the presidential privilege applies but that the OIC has demonstrated a sufficient showing of need, there is no reason to examine whether the documents also come under the deliberative process privilege. *A fortiori*, if release is required under the presidential privilege, it will certainly be required under the deliberative process privilege. Hence, we would need to address application of the deliberative process privilege as to any document only if we determine that the withheld document is not subject to the presidential privilege.

121 F.3d at 745–46. After a review of the precedents, the court stated:

> Based on our review of the Nixon cases and the purpose of the presidential communications privilege, we conclude that this privilege extends to cover communications which do not themselves directly engage the President, provided the communications are either authored or received in response to a solicitation by presidential advisers in the course of gathering information and preparing recommendations on official matters for presentation to the President. The privilege also extends to communications authored or solicited and received by those members of an immediate White House advisor's staff who have broad and significant responsibility for investigating and formulating the advice to be given to the President on a particular matter. We also hold that in order to overcome a claim of presidential privilege raised against a grand jury subpoena, it is necessary to specifically demonstrate why it is likely that evidence contained in presidential communications is important to the ongoing grand jury investigation and why this evidence is not available from another source.

Id. at 757.

Applying these principles to the case at hand, the court found "that all of the documents withheld by the White House here are subject to the presidential communications privilege," and as a result, it did not need to determine whether the documents would qualify for the "deliberative process privilege." Id. at 758. The court then balanced the presidential communications privilege against the OIC's "demonstration of need," id. at 759, and concluded that

> the OIC has demonstrated sufficient need in order to overcome the presidential communications privilege in regard to evidence of statements made by Espy or his counsel and contained in the withheld documents, and that the OIC should be given an opportunity to make out a sufficient showing of need in regard to other evidence more generally. On remand, the district court should identify and release specific items of evidence that might reasonably be relevant to the grand jury's investigation into the potential false statements charge. If the court deems any additional showing of need presented by the OIC to be sufficient, it should also identify any new items of information that merit release. We are submitting a sealed appendix to assist the district court with its review. * * *

This case forces us to engage in the difficult business of delineating the scope and operation of the presidential communications privilege. In holding that the privilege extends to communications authored by or solicited and received by presidential advisers and that a specified demonstration of need must be made even in regard to a grand jury subpoena, we are ever mindful of the dangers involved in cloaking governmental operations in secrecy and in placing obstacles in the path of the grand jury in its investigatory mission. There is a powerful counterweight to these concerns, however, namely the public and constitutional interest in preserving the efficacy and quality of presidential decisionmaking. We believe that the principles we have outlined in this opinion achieve a delicate and appropriate balance between openness and informed presidential deliberation.

Id. at 762. Accordingly, it reversed the District Court's decision.

4.   *Sources on executive privilege.* Chemerinsky, Constitutional Law: Principles and Policies § 4.3 (4th ed. 2011); 2 Imwinkelried, The New Wigmore: Evidentiary Privileges § 7.6 (2d ed. 2010); Rozell, Executive Privilege: The Dilemma of Secrecy and Democratic Accountability (1994); Miller, Congressional Inquests: Suffocating the Constitutional Prerogative of Executive Privilege, 81 Minn.L.Rev. 631 (1997); Symposium, *United States v. Nixon*: Presidential Power and Executive Privilege Twenty–Five Years Later, 83 Minn.L.Rev.1061 (1999); Symposium: Executive Privilege and the Clinton Presidency, 8 Wm. & Mary Bill of Rts.J. 535 (2000). For further discussion of Clinton and "executive privilege," see Miller, Presidential Sanctuaries after the Clinton Sex Scandals, 22 Harv.J.L. & Pub. Pol'y 647 (1999); Turley, Paradise Lost: The Clinton Administration and the Erosion of Executive Privilege, 60 Md.L.Rev. 205 (2001).

DEPARTMENT OF THE INTERIOR AND BUREAU OF INDIAN AFFAIRS V. KLAMATH WATER USERS PROTECTIVE ASS'N

Supreme Court of the United States, 2001.
532 U.S. 1.

JUSTICE SOUTER delivered the opinion of the Court.

Documents in issue here, passing between Indian Tribes and the Department of the Interior, addressed tribal interests subject to state and federal proceedings to determine water allocations. The question is whether the documents are exempt from the disclosure requirements of the Freedom of Information Act, as "intra-agency memorandums or letters" that would normally be privileged in civil discovery. 5 U.S.C. § 552(b)(5). We hold they are not.

I

Two separate proceedings give rise to this case, the first a planning effort within the Department of the Interior's Bureau of Reclamation, and the second a state water rights adjudication in the Oregon courts. Within the Department of the Interior, the Bureau of Reclamation (Reclamation) administers the Klamath Irrigation Project (Klamath Project or Project), which uses water from the Klamath River Basin to irrigate territory in Klamath County, Oregon, and two northern California counties. In 1995, the Department began work to develop a long-term operations plan for the Project, to be known as the Klamath Project Operation Plan (Plan), which would provide for allocation of water among competing uses and competing water users. The Department asked the Klamath as well as the Hoopa Valley, Karuk, and Yurok Tribes (Basin Tribes) to consult with Reclamation on the matter, and a memorandum of understanding between the Department and the Tribes recognized that "[t]he United States Government has a unique legal relationship with Native American tribal governments," and called for "[a]ssessment, in consultation with the Tribes, of the impacts of the [Plan] on Tribal trust resources." App. 59, 61.

During roughly the same period, the Department's Bureau of Indian Affairs (Bureau) filed claims on behalf of the Klamath Tribe alone in an Oregon state-court adjudication intended to allocate water rights. Since the Bureau is responsible for administering land and water held in trust for Indian tribes, 25 U.S.C. § 1a; 25 CFR subch. H., pts. 150–181 (2000), it consulted with the Klamath Tribe, and the two exchanged written memorandums on the appropriate scope of the claims ultimately submitted by the United States for the benefit of the Klamath Tribe. The Bureau does not, however, act as counsel for the Tribe, which has its own lawyers and has independently submitted claims on its own behalf.

Respondent, the Klamath Water Users Protective Association is a nonprofit association of water users in the Klamath River Basin, most of whom receive water from the Klamath Project, and whose interests are adverse to the tribal interests owing to scarcity of water. The Association filed a series of requests with the Bureau under the Freedom of Information Act (FOIA), 5 U.S.C. § 552, seeking access to communications between the Bureau and the Basin Tribes during the relevant time period. The Bureau turned over several documents but withheld others as exempt under the attorney work-product and deliberative process privileges. These privileges are said to be incorporated in FOIA Exemption 5, which exempts from disclosure "inter-agency or intra-agency memorandums or letters which would not be available by law to a party other than an agency in litigation with the agency." § 552(b)(5). The Association then sued the Bureau under FOIA to compel release of the documents.

By the time of the District Court ruling, seven documents remained in dispute, three of them addressing the Plan, three concerned with the Oregon adjudication, and the seventh relevant to both proceedings. * * * . Six of the documents were prepared by the Klamath Tribe or its representative and were submitted at the Government's behest to the Bureau or to the Department's Regional Solicitor; a Bureau official prepared the seventh document and gave it to lawyers for the Klamath and Yurok Tribes. * * * .

The District Court granted the Government's motion for summary judgment. It held that each document qualified as an inter-agency or intra-agency communication for purposes of Exemption 5, and that each was covered by the deliberative process privilege or the attorney work product privilege, as having played a role in the Bureau's deliberations about the Plan or the Oregon adjudication. * * * The Court of Appeals for the Ninth Circuit reversed. 189 F.3d 1034 (C.A.9 1999). It recognized that some Circuits had adopted a "functional" approach to Exemption 5, under which a document generated outside the Government might still qualify as an "intra-agency" communication. See *id.,* at 1037–1038. The court saw no reason to go into that, however, for it ruled out any application of Exemption 5 on the ground that "the Tribes with whom the Department has a consulting relationship have a direct interest in the subject matter of the consultations." *Id.,* at 1038. The court said that "[t]o hold otherwise would extend Exemption 5 to shield what amount to ex parte communications in contested proceedings between the Tribes and the Department." *Ibid.* * * * We granted certiorari in view of the decision's significant impact on the relationship between Indian tribes and the Government * * *, and now affirm.

II

Upon request, FOIA mandates disclosure of records held by a federal agency, see 5 U.S.C. § 552, unless the documents fall within enumerated exemptions, see § 552(b). "[T]hese limited exemptions do not obscure the basic policy that disclosure, not secrecy, is the dominant objective of the Act," *Department of Air Force v. Rose,* 425 U.S. 352, 361 (1976); "[c]onsistent with the Act's goal of broad disclosure, these exemptions have been consistently given a narrow compass," *U.S. Department of Justice v. Tax Analysts,* 492 U.S. 136, 151 (1989) * * * .

A

Exemption 5 protects from disclosure "inter-agency or intra-agency memorandums or letters which would not be available by law to a party other than an agency in litigation with the agency." 5 U.S.C. § 552(b)(5). To qualify, a document must thus satisfy two conditions: its source must be a Government agency, and it must fall within the ambit of a privilege against discovery under judicial standards that would govern litigation against the agency that holds it.

Our prior cases on Exemption 5 have addressed the second condition, incorporating civil discovery privileges. See, *e.g., United States v. Weber Aircraft Corp.,* 465 U.S. 792, 799–800 (1984); *NLRB v. Sears, Roebuck & Co.,* 421 U.S. 132, 148 (1975) ("Exemption 5 withholds from a member of the public documents which a private party could not discover in litigation with the agency."). So far as they might matter here, those privileges include the privilege for attorney work-product and what is sometimes called the "deliberative process" privilege. Work product protects "mental processes of the attorney," *United States v. Nobles,* 422 U.S. 225, 238 (1975), while deliberative process covers "documents reflecting advisory opinions, recommendations and deliberations comprising part of a process by which governmental decisions and policies are formulated," *Sears, Roebuck & Co.,* 421 U.S., at 150 (internal quotation marks omitted). The deliberative process privilege rests on the obvious realization that officials will not communicate candidly among themselves if each remark is a potential item of discovery and front page news, and its object is to enhance "the quality of agency decisions," *id.,* at 151, by protecting open and frank discussion among those who make them within the Government, see *EPA v. Mink,* 410 U.S. 73, 86–87 (1973); see also *Weber Aircraft Corp., supra,* at 802.

The point is not to protect Government secrecy pure and simple, however, and the first condition of Exemption 5 is no less important than the second; the communication must be "inter-agency or intra-agency." 5 U.S.C. § 552(b)(5). Statutory definitions underscore the apparent plainness of this text. With exceptions not relevant here, "agency" means "each authority of the Government of the United States," § 551(1), and "includes any executive department, military department, Government corporation, Government controlled corporation, or other establishment in the executive branch of the Government * * *, or any independent regulatory agency," § 552(f).

Although neither the terms of the exemption nor the statutory definitions say anything about communications with outsiders, some Courts of Appeals have held that in some circumstances a document prepared outside the Government may nevertheless qualify as an "intra-agency" memorandum under Exemption 5. See, *e.g., Hoover v. U.S. Dept. of Interior,* 611 F.2d 1132, 1137–1138 (C.A.5 1980); *Lead Industries Assn. v. OSHA,* 610 F.2d 70, 83 (C.A.2 1979); *Soucie v. David,* 448 F.2d 1067 (C.A.D.C.1971). In *United States Department of Justice v. Julian,* 486 U.S. 1 (1988), JUSTICE SCALIA, joined by JUSTICES O'CONNOR and WHITE, explained that "the most natural meaning of the phrase 'intra-agency memorandum' is a memorandum that is addressed both to and from employees of a single agency," *id.,* at 18, n.1 (dissenting opinion). But his opinion also acknowledged the more expansive reading by some Courts of Appeals:

> "It is textually possible and * * * in accord with the purpose of the provision, to regard as an intra-agency memorandum one that has been received by an agency, to assist it in the performance of its own functions, from a person acting in a governmentally conferred capacity other than on behalf of

another agency—*e.g.*, in a capacity as employee or consultant to the agency, or as employee or officer of another governmental unit (not an agency) that is authorized or required to provide advice to the agency." *Ibid.*

Typically, courts taking the latter view have held that the exemption extends to communications between Government agencies and outside consultants hired by them. See, *e.g., Hoover, supra,* at 1138 ("In determining value, the government may deem it necessary to seek the objective opinion of outside experts rather than rely solely on the opinions of government appraisers"); *Lead Industries Assn., supra,* at 83 (applying Exemption 5 to cover draft reports "prepared by outside consultants who had testified on behalf of the agency rather than agency staff") * * * . In such cases, the records submitted by outside consultants played essentially the same part in an agency's process of deliberation as documents prepared by agency personnel might have done. To be sure, the consultants in these cases were independent contractors and were not assumed to be subject to the degree of control that agency employment could have entailed; nor do we read the cases as necessarily assuming that an outside consultant must be devoid of a definite point of view when the agency contracts for its services. But the fact about the consultant that is constant in the typical cases is that the consultant does not represent an interest of its own, or the interest of any other client, when it advises the agency that hires it. Its only obligations are to truth and its sense of what good judgment calls for, and in those respects the consultant functions just as an employee would be expected to do.

B

The Department purports to rely on this consultant corollary to Exemption 5 in arguing for its application to the Tribe's communications to the Bureau in its capacity of fiduciary for the benefit of the Indian Tribes. The existence of a trust obligation is not, of course, in question, see *United States v. Cherokee Nation of Oklahoma,* 480 U.S. 700, 707 (1987); *United States v. Mitchell,* 463 U.S. 206, 225 (1983); *Seminole Nation v. United States,* 316 U.S. 286, 296–297 (1942). The fiduciary relationship has been described as "one of the primary cornerstones of Indian law," F. Cohen, Handbook of Federal Indian Law 221 (1982), and has been compared to one existing under a common law trust, with the United States as trustee, the Indian tribes or individuals as beneficiaries, and the property and natural resources managed by the United States as the trust corpus. See, *e.g., Mitchell, supra,* at 225. Nor is there any doubt about the plausibility of the Government's assertion that the candor of tribal communications with the Bureau would be eroded without the protections of the deliberative process privilege recognized under Exemption 5. The Department is surely right in saying that confidentiality in communications with tribes is conducive to a proper discharge of its trust obligation.

From the recognition of this interest in frank communication, which the deliberative process privilege might protect, the Department would have us infer a sufficient justification for applying Exemption 5 to communications with the Tribes, in the same fashion that Courts of Appeals have found sufficient reason to favor a consultant's advice that way. But the Department's argument skips a necessary step, for it ignores the first condition of Exemption 5, that the communication be "intra-agency or inter-agency." The Department seems to be saying that "intra-agency" is a purely conclusory term, just a label to be placed on any document the Government would find it valuable to keep confidential.

There is, however, no textual justification for draining the first condition of independent vitality, and once the intra-agency condition is applied,[15] it rules out any application of Exemption 5 to tribal communications on analogy to consultants' reports (assuming, which we do not decide, that these reports may qualify as intra-agency under Exemption 5). As mentioned already, consultants whose communications have typically been held exempt have not been communicating with the Government in their own interest or on behalf of any person or group whose interests might be affected by the Government action addressed by the consultant. In that regard, consultants may be enough like the agency's own personnel to justify calling their communications "intra-agency." The Tribes, on the contrary, necessarily communicate with the Bureau with their own, albeit entirely legitimate, interests in mind. While this fact alone distinguishes tribal communications from the consultants' examples recognized by several Courts of Appeals, the distinction is even sharper, in that the Tribes are self-advocates at the expense of others seeking benefits inadequate to satisfy everyone.[16]

As to those documents bearing on the Plan, the Tribes are obviously in competition with nontribal claimants, including those irrigators represented by the respondent. App. 66–71. The record shows that documents submitted by the Tribes included, among others, "a position paper that discusses water law legal theories" and "addresses issues related to water rights of the tribes," App. to Pet. for Cert. 42a–43a, a

---

[15] Because we conclude that the documents do not meet this threshold condition, we need not reach step two of the Exemption 5 analysis and enquire whether the communications would normally be discoverable in civil litigation. *See United States v. Weber Aircraft Corp.*, 465 U.S. 792, 799 (1984).

[16] Courts of Appeals have recognized at least two instances of intra-agency consultants that arguably extend beyond what we have characterized as the typical examples. [*E.g.*] *Public Citizen, Inc. v. Department of Justice,* 111 F.3d 168 (C.A.D.C.1997)[;] * * * *Ryan v. Department of Justice,* 617 F.2d 781 (C.A.D.C.1980) * * * . We need not decide whether either instance should be recognized as intra-agency * * * [because] the intra-agency condition excludes, at the least, communications to or from an interested party seeking a Government benefit at the expense of other applicants.

memorandum "contain[ing] views on policy the BIA could provide to other governmental agencies," "views concerning trust resources," *id.,* at 44a, and a letter "conveying the views of the Klamath Tribes concerning issues involved in the water rights adjudication," *id.,* at 47a. While these documents may not take the formally argumentative form of a brief, their function is quite apparently to support the tribal claims. The Tribes are thus urging a position necessarily adverse to the other claimants, the water being inadequate to satisfy the combined demand. As the Court of Appeals said, "[t]he Tribes' demands, if satisfied, would lead to reduced water allocations to members of the Association and have been protested by Association members who fear water shortages and economic injury in dry years." 189 F.3d, at 1035.

The Department insists that the Klamath Tribe's consultant-like character is clearer in the circumstances of the Oregon adjudication, since the Department merely represents the interests of the Tribe before a state court that will make any decision about the respective rights of the contenders. Brief for Petitioners 42–45; Reply Brief for Petitioners 4–6. But it is not that simple. Even if there were no rival interests at stake in the Oregon litigation, the Klamath Tribe would be pressing its own view of its own interest in its communications with the Bureau. Nor could that interest be ignored as being merged somehow in the fiduciary interest of the Government trustee; the Bureau in its fiduciary capacity would be obliged to adopt the stance it believed to be in the beneficiary's best interest, not necessarily the position espoused by the beneficiary itself. Cf. Restatement (Second) of Trusts § 176, Comment *a* (1957) ("[I]t is the duty of the trustee to exercise such care and skill to preserve the trust property as a man of ordinary prudence would exercise in dealing with his own property * * * ").

But, again, the dispositive point is that the apparent object of the Tribe's communications is a decision by an agency of the Government to support a claim by the Tribe that is necessarily adverse to the interests of competitors. Since there is not enough water to satisfy everyone, the Government's position on behalf of the Tribe is potentially adverse to other users, and it might ask for more or less on behalf of the Tribe depending on how it evaluated the tribal claim compared with the claims of its rivals. The ultimately adversarial character of tribal submissions to the Bureau therefore seems the only fair inference, as confirmed by the Department's acknowledgement that its "obligation to represent the Klamath Tribe necessarily coexists with the duty to protect other federal interests, including in particular its interests with respect to the Klamath Project." Reply Brief 8; cf. *Nevada v. United States,* 463 U.S. 110, 142 (1983) ("[W]here Congress has imposed upon the United States, in addition to its duty to represent Indian tribes, a duty to obtain water rights for reclamation projects, and has even authorized the inclusion of reservation lands within a project, the analogy of a faithless private fiduciary cannot be controlling for purposes of evaluating the authority of the United States to represent different interests"). The position of the Tribe as beneficiary is thus a far cry from the position of the paid consultant.

Quite apart from its attempt to draw a direct analogy between tribes and conventional consultants, the Department argues that compelled release of the documents would itself impair the Department's performance of a specific fiduciary obligation to protect the confidentiality of communications with tribes. Because, the Department argues, traditional fiduciary standards forbid a trustee to disclose information acquired as a trustee when it should know that disclosure would be against the beneficiary's interests, excluding the Tribes' submissions to the Department from Exemption 5 would handicap the Department in doing what the law requires. Brief for Petitioners 36–37. And in much the same vein, the Department presses the argument that "FOIA is intended to cast light on existing government practices; it should not be interpreted and applied so as to compel federal agencies to perform their assigned substantive functions in other than the normal manner." *Id.,* at 29.

All of this boils down to requesting that we read an "Indian trust" exemption into the statute, a reading that is out of the question for reasons already explored. There is simply no support for the exemption in the statutory text, which we have elsewhere insisted be read strictly in order to serve FOIA's mandate of broad disclosure,[17] which was obviously expected and intended to affect Government operations. In FOIA, after all, a new conception of Government conduct was enacted into law, " 'a general philosophy of full agency disclosure.' " *U.S. Department of Justice v. Tax Analysts,* 492 U.S., at 142 (quoting S.Rep. No. 813, 89th Cong., 1st Sess., at 3 (1965)). "Congress believed that this philosophy, put into practice, would help 'ensure an informed citizenry, vital to the functioning of a democratic society.' " *Ibid.* (quoting *NLRB v. Robbins Tire & Rubber Co.,* 437 U.S. 214, 242 (1978)). Congress had to realize that not every secret under the old law would be secret under the new.

The judgment of the Court of Appeals is affirmed.

It is so ordered.

---

[17] The Department does not attempt to argue that Congress specifically envisioned that Exemption 5 would cover communications pursuant to the Indian trust responsibility, or any other trust responsibility. Although as a general rule we are hesitant to construe statutes in light of legislative inaction, see *Bob Jones Univ. v. United States,* 461 U.S. 574, 600 (1983), we note that Congress has twice considered specific proposals to protect Indian trust information, see Indian Amendment to Freedom of Information Act: Hearings on S. 2652 before the Subcommittee on Indian Affairs of the Senate Committee on Interior and Insular Affairs, 94th Cong., 2d Sess. (1976); Indian Trust Information Protection Act of 1978, S. 2773, 95th Cong., 2d Sess. (1978). We do so because these proposals confirm the commonsense reading that we give Exemption 5 today, as well as to emphasize that nobody in the Federal Government should be surprised by this reading.

NOTES AND QUESTIONS

1. *General scope.* The "deliberative process" privilege covers opinion or evaluation that the agency sought to keep confidential prior to finalization of the policy decision. See, e.g., McKinley v. Bd. of Governors of Fed. Reserve Sys., 647 F.3d 331, 340 (D.C.Cir. 2011) (ruling that Board had sufficiently demonstrated that disclosure of the withheld material would discourage candid internal discussion and undermine policy development and also made a specific showing disclosure would harm the decision-making process); Hongsermeir v. Comm'r of Internal Revenue, 621 F.3d 890, 904 (9th Cir.2010) (ruling that the material must be both pre-decisional and deliberative). The privilege in general does not cover the mere reporting of objective facts. However, factual information that "reflects or reveals the deliberative process of the agency is protected." 1 McCormick, Evidence § 108 (7th ed. 2013).

2. *Maintaining the intra-agency or inter-agency requirement.* In *Klamath,* the Supreme Court feared that an opposite ruling would "drain[ ] the first condition"—that the evidence be intra- or inter-agency—"of independent vitality." Would this fear be realized given the Tribe's unique fiduciary relationship to the government?

3. *Relationship of privilege to FOIA exemption.* The decision in *Klamath* notes that the deliberative process privilege is "said to be incorporated in FOIA Exemption 5." In 1966 Congress enacted the so-called Freedom of Information Act (or Right to Know Act). No standing or special need is required to invoke the provisions of the Act. The Act provides that each agency shall make available to the public information subject to nine exemptions, including Exemption 5, which are listed in the next note.

The principal distinction between Exemption 5 and the deliberative process privilege has been explained as follows:

> FOIA does not address the question of admissibility of evidence, and therefore Exemption 5 should not be considered a congressional enactment of the deliberative process privilege, even though it may incorporate the rationale of the privilege. FOIA protects materials subject to "routine disclosure" by the government. Any material that is protected by a privilege, whether absolute or qualified, is clearly not subject to routine disclosure under FOIA. In other words, once the government makes a prima facie showing for invoking the privilege, analysis under FOIA Exemption 5 stops and does not proceed to the balancing of interests. This is an important distinction between the deliberative process privilege and FOIA. While a litigant's need for information may be sufficient to override the privilege, such need would not remove that information from the category of material that is normally privileged. Therefore, while FOIA may properly be viewed as defining the maximum limits of the privilege, the privilege itself should be interpreted as being somewhat less protective than Exemption 5.

Note, The Reasonable Government Official Test: A Proposal for the Treatment of Factual Information Under the Federal Deliberative Process Privilege, 49 Duke L.J. 561, 580–81 (1999).

4. *FOIA exemptions.* The Freedom of Information Act (FOIA) was originally enacted in 1966 as an amendment to the Administrative Procedure Act. The exemptions, now found in 5 U.S.C. § 552(b)(1), are as follows:

This section does not apply to matters that are—

(1)(A) specifically authorized under criteria established by an Executive order to be kept secret in the interest of national defense or foreign policy and (B) are in fact properly classified pursuant to such Executive order;

(2) related solely to the internal personnel rules and practices of an agency;

(3) specifically exempted from disclosure by statute (other than section 552b of this title), provided that such statute (A) requires that the matters be withheld from the public in such a manner as to leave no discretion on the issue, or (B) establishes particular criteria for withholding or refers to particular types of matters to be withheld;

(4) trade secrets and commercial or financial information obtained from a person and privileged or confidential;

(5) inter-agency or intra-agency memorandums or letters which would not be available by law to a party other than an agency in litigation with the agency;

(6) personnel and medical files and similar files the disclosure of which would constitute a clearly unwarranted invasion of personal privacy;

(7) records or information compiled for law enforcement purposes, but only to the extent that the production of such law enforcement records or information (A) could reasonably be expected to interfere with enforcement proceedings, (B) would deprive a person of a right to a fair trial or an impartial adjudication, (C) could reasonably be expected to constitute an unwarranted invasion of personal privacy, (D) could reasonably be expected to disclose the identity of a confidential source, including a State, local, or foreign agency or authority or any private institution which furnished information on a confidential basis, and, in the case of a record or information compiled by criminal law enforcement authority in the course of a criminal investigation or by an agency conducting a lawful national security intelligence investigation, information furnished by a confidential source, (E) would disclose techniques and procedures for law enforcement investigations or prosecutions, or would disclose guidelines for law enforcement investigations or prosecutions if such disclosure could reasonably be

expected to risk circumvention of the law, or (F) could reasonably be expected to endanger the life or physical safety of any individual;

(8) contained in or related to examination, operating, or condition reports prepared by, on behalf of, or for the use of an agency responsible for the regulation or supervision of financial institutions; or

(9) geological and geophysical information and data, including maps, concerning wells.

5. *Exemptions as maximum limits of privilege.* While designed to make information available to the public generally, and to the mass media in particular, the Act has clear relevance to matters of governmental privilege. It defines what may be termed the maximum limits of any privilege for governmental information, for if the information is available to the public generally, it would be anomalous to prohibit the use of that information in litigation on the ground of an evidentiary privilege. On the other hand, the fact that the information is not generally available, while giving some insight into a relevant legislative judgment that the information is sensitive and not generally disclosable, does not necessarily mean that access to such evidence for litigation purposes will be denied since the need of the litigant may be substantially greater. 1 McCormick, Evidence § 108 (7th ed. 2013). Consistent with this view, the Court in United States v. Weber Aircraft Corp., 465 U.S. 792, 802 n.20 (1984), made clear that particularized need in litigation may require discovery in connection with the litigation process but that possibility does not authorize disclosure under the Act.

6. *Machin privilege under Exemption 5.* In *Weber*, note 5, supra, 465 U.S. at 799–800, cited in *Klamath*, respondents "sought discovery of all Air Force investigative reports pertaining to [an airplane] accident." Id. at 796. The Air Force claimed exemption from disclosure under the so-called *Machin* privilege (from Machin v. Zuckert, 316 F.2d 336 (D.C.Cir.1963)), which protects confidential statements to air crash investigators, and from Exemption 5. The Ninth Circuit reversed a lower court ruling in favor of the Air Force, arguing that while "the requested documents were intra-agency memorandums within the meaning of Exemption 5 and that they were protected from civil discovery under the *Machin* privilege," they were not covered under FOIA since "the statutory phrase 'would not be available by law' did not encompass every civil discovery privilege but rather reached only those privileges explicitly recognized in the legislative history of the FOIA." *Weber*, 465 U.S. at 797–98. The Supreme Court in turn reversed the Ninth Circuit on the basis that

the legislative history of Exemption 5 does not contain the kind of compelling evidence of congressional intent that would be necessary to persuade us to look beyond the plain statutory language. Because of the difficulty inherent in compiling an exhaustive list of evidentiary privileges, it would be impractical to treat the legislative history of Exemption 5 as containing a comprehensive list of all privileges Congress intended to adopt. Rather, the history of Exemption 5 can be understood by means of "rough analogies." EPA v. Mink, 410 U.S. 73, 86. The legislative history of Exemption 5 indicates that Congress intended to incorporate governmental privileges analogous to the *Machin* privilege. That history recognizes a need for claims of privilege when confidentiality is necessary to ensure frank and open discussion and hence efficient governmental operations. * * * The *Machin* privilege was recognized for precisely this reason. Thus, the *Machin* privilege is sufficiently related to the concerns expressed in the legislative history that we cannot say that the legislative history demonstrates that the statute should not be construed to mean what it says with respect to the *Machin* privilege.

465 U.S. at 802–03.

How can this aspect of *Weber* be reconciled with the Court's assertion near the end of the *Klamath* opinion that "[a]ll of this boils down to requesting that we read an 'Indian trust' exemption into the statute"? Why does the Court in *Klamath* rule out such a reading?

7. *Meaning of "memorandum."* For a comprehensive presentation of the often inconsistent treatment of what has and has not counted as "memorandum" under Exemption 5, see Annot., 168 A.L.R.Fed. 143.

8. *Sources.* Weaver & Jones, The Deliberative Process Privilege, 54 Mo.L.Rev. 279 (1989); Wetlaufer, Justifying Secrecy: An Objection to the General Deliberative Privilege, 65 Ind.L.J. 845 (1990); Note, The Reasonable Government Official Test: A Proposal for the Treatment of Factual Information Under the Federal Deliberative Process Privilege, 49 Duke L.J. 561 (1999); Greenwald et al., Testimonial Privileges §§ 9:8 to 9:13 (2012 ed.); 2 Imwinkelried, The New Wigmore: Evidentiary Privileges § 7.7 (2d ed. 2010); 1 McCormick, Evidence § 108 (7th ed. 2013); 3 Weinstein's Federal Evidence §§ 509.23 & 509.24 (2d ed. 2013); 2 Mueller & Kirkpatrick, Federal Evidence §§ 5:56–5:57 (3d ed. 2007).

B. PROCEEDINGS OF PETIT AND GRAND JURIES

TANNER V. UNITED STATES
Supreme Court of the United States, 1987.
483 U.S. 107.

JUSTICE O'CONNOR delivered the opinion of the Court.

Petitioners William Conover and Anthony Tanner were convicted [after jury trial] of conspiring to defraud the United States in violation of 18 U.S.C. § 371, and of committing mail fraud in violation of 18 U.S.C. § 1341. * * *

The day before petitioners were scheduled to be sentenced, Tanner filed a motion, in which Conover subsequently joined, seeking continuance of the sentencing date, permission to interview jurors, an evidentiary hearing, and a new trial. According to an affidavit accompanying the motion, Tanner's attorney had received an unsolicited telephone call from one of the trial jurors, Vera Asbul. App. 246. Juror Asbul informed Tanner's attorney that several of the jurors consumed alcohol during the lunch breaks at various times throughout the trial, causing them to sleep through the afternoons. *Id.,* at 247. The District Court continued the sentencing date, ordered the parties to file memoranda, and heard argument on the motion to interview jurors. The District Court concluded that juror testimony on intoxication was inadmissible under Federal Rule of Evidence 606(b) to impeach the jury's verdict. The District Court invited petitioners to call any nonjuror witnesses, such as courtroom personnel, in support of the motion for new trial. Tanner's counsel took the stand and testified that he had observed one of the jurors "in a sort of giggly mood" at one point during the trial but did not bring this to anyone's attention at the time. *Id.,* at 170.

Earlier in the hearing the judge referred to a conversation between defense counsel and the judge during the trial on the possibility that jurors were sometimes falling asleep. During that extended exchange the judge twice advised counsel to immediately inform the court if they observed jurors being inattentive, and suggested measures the judge would take if he were so informed:

"MR. MILBRATH [defense counsel]: But, in any event, I've noticed over a period of several days that a couple of jurors in particular have been taking long naps during the trial.

"THE COURT: Is that right. Maybe I didn't notice because I was—

"MR. MILBRATH: I imagine the Prosecutors have noticed that a time or two.

"THE COURT: What's your solution?

"MR. MILBRATH: Well, I just think a respectful comment from the Court that if any of them are getting drowsy, they just ask for a break or something might be helpful.

"THE COURT: Well, here's what I have done in the past—and, you have to do it very diplomatically, of course: I once said, I remember, 'I think we'll just let everybody stand up and stretch, it's getting a little sleepy in here,' I said, but that doesn't sound good in the record.

"I'm going to—not going to take on that responsibility. If any of you think you see that happening, ask for a bench conference and come up and tell me about it and I'll figure out what to do about it, and I won't mention who suggested it.

"MR. MILBRATH: All right.

"THE COURT: But, I'm not going to sit here and watch. I'm— among other things, I'm not going to see—this is off the record.

"(Discussion had off the record.)

" * * * [T]his is a new thing to this jury, and I don't know how interesting it is to them or not; some of them look like they're pretty interested.

* * *

"And, as I say, if you don't think they are, come up and let me know and I'll figure how—either have a recess or—which is more than likely what I would do." Tr. 12–100–12–101.

As the judge observed during the hearing, despite the above admonitions counsel did not bring the matter to the court again. App. 147.

The judge also observed that in the past courtroom employees had alerted him to problems with the jury. "Nothing was brought to my attention in this case about anyone appearing to be intoxicated," the judge stated, adding, "I saw nothing that suggested they were." *Id.*, at 172.

Following the hearing the District Court filed an order stating that "[o]n the basis of the admissible evidence offered I specifically find that the motions for leave to interview jurors or for an evidentiary hearing at which jurors would be witnesses is not required or appropriate." The District Court also denied the motion for new trial. *Id.*, at 181–182.

While the appeal of this case was pending before the Eleventh Circuit, petitioners filed another new trial motion based on additional evidence of jury misconduct. In another affidavit, Tanner's attorney stated that he received an unsolicited visit at his residence from a second juror, Daniel Hardy. *Id.*, at 241. Despite the fact that the District Court had denied petitioners' motion for leave to interview jurors, two days after Hardy's visit Tanner's attorney arranged for Hardy to be interviewed by two private investigators. *Id.*, at 242. The interview was transcribed, sworn to by the juror, and attached to the new trial motion. In the interview Hardy stated that he "felt like * * * the jury was on one big party." *Id.*, at 209. Hardy indicated that seven of the jurors drank alcohol during the noon recess. Four jurors, including Hardy, consumed between them "a pitcher to three pitchers" of beer during various recesses. *Id.*, at 212. Of the three other jurors who were alleged to have consumed alcohol, Hardy stated that on several occasions he observed two jurors having one or two mixed drinks during the lunch recess, and one other juror, who was also the foreperson, having a liter of wine on each of three occasions. *Id.*, at 213–215. Juror Hardy also stated that he and three other jurors smoked marijuana quite regularly during the trial. *Id.*, at 216–223. Moreover, Hardy stated that during the trial he observed one juror ingest cocaine five times and another juror ingest cocaine two or three times. *Id.*, at 227. One juror sold a quarter pound of marijuana to another juror during the trial, and took marijuana, cocaine and drug paraphernalia into the courthouse. *Id.*, at 234–235. Hardy noted that some of the jurors were falling asleep during the trial, and that one of the jurors described himself to Hardy as "flying." *Id.*, at 229. Hardy stated that before he visited Tanner's attorney at his residence, no one had contacted him concerning the jury's conduct, and Hardy had not been offered anything in return for his statement. *Id.*, at 232. Hardy said that he came forward "to clear my conscience" and "[b]ecause I felt * * * that the people on the jury didn't have no business being on the jury. I felt * * * that Mr. Tanner should have a better opportunity to get somebody that would review the facts right." *Id.*, at 231–232.

The District Court, stating that the motions "contain supplemental allegations which differ quantitatively but not qualitatively from those in the April motions," *id.*, at 256, denied petitioners' motion for a new trial.

The Court of Appeals for the Eleventh Circuit affirmed. 772 F.2d 765 (1985). We granted certiorari * * * to consider whether the District Court was required to hold an evidentiary hearing, including juror testimony, on juror alcohol and drug use during the trial, and to consider whether petitioners' actions constituted a conspiracy to defraud the United States within the meaning of 18 U.S.C. § 371.

II

Petitioners argue that the District Court erred in not ordering an additional evidentiary hearing at which jurors would testify concerning drug and alcohol use during the trial. Petitioners assert that, contrary to the holdings of the District Court and the Court of Appeals, juror testimony on ingestion of drugs or alcohol during the trial is not barred by Federal Rule of Evidence 606(b). Moreover, petitioners argue that whether or not authorized by Rule 606(b), an evidentiary hearing including juror testimony on drug and alcohol use is compelled by their Sixth Amendment right to trial by a competent jury.

By the beginning of this century, if not earlier, the near-universal and firmly established common-law rule in the United States flatly prohibited the admission of juror testimony to impeach a jury verdict. See 8 J. Wigmore, Evidence § 2352, pp. 696–697 (McNaughton rev. ed. 1961) (common-law rule, originating from 1785 opinion of Lord Mansfield, "came to receive in the United States an adherence almost unquestioned").

Exceptions to the common-law rule were recognized only in situations in which an "extraneous influence," *Mattox v. United States,* 146 U.S. 140, 149 (1892), was alleged to have affected the jury. In *Mattox,* this Court held admissible the testimony of jurors describing how they heard and read prejudicial information not admitted into evidence. The Court allowed juror testimony on influence by outsiders in *Parker v. Gladden,* 385 U.S. 363, 365 (1966) (bailiff's comments on defendant), and *Remmer v. United States,* 347 U.S. 227, 228–230 (1954) (bribe offered to juror). See also *Smith v. Phillips,* 455 U.S. 209 (1982) (juror in criminal trial had submitted an application for employment at the District Attorney's office). In situations that did not fall into this exception for external influence, however, the Court adhered to the common-law rule against admitting juror testimony to impeach a verdict. *McDonald v. Pless,* 238 U.S. 264 (1915); *Hyde v. United States,* 225 U.S. 347, 384 (1912).

Lower courts used this external/internal distinction to identify those instances in which juror testimony impeaching a verdict would be admissible. The distinction was not based on whether the juror was literally inside or outside the jury room when the alleged irregularity took place; rather, the distinction was based on the nature of the allegation. Clearly a rigid distinction based only on whether the event took place inside or outside the jury room would have been quite unhelpful. For example, under a distinction based on location a juror could not testify concerning a newspaper read inside the jury room. Instead, of course, this has been considered an external influence about which juror testimony is admissible. See *United States v. Thomas,* 463 F.2d 1061 (C.A.7 1972). Similarly, under a rigid locational distinction jurors could be regularly required to testify after the verdict as to whether they heard and comprehended the judge's instructions, since the charge to the jury takes place outside the jury room. Courts wisely have treated allegations of a juror's inability to hear or comprehend at trial as an internal matter. See *Government of the Virgin Islands v. Nicholas,* 759 F.2d 1073 (C.A.3 1985); *Davis v. United States,* 47 F.2d 1071 (C.A.5 1931) (rejecting juror testimony impeaching verdict, including testimony that jurors had not heard a particular instruction of the court).

Most significant for the present case, however, is the fact that lower federal courts treated allegations of the physical or mental incompetence of a juror as "internal" rather than "external" matters. In *United States v. Dioguardi,* 492 F.2d 70 (C.A.2 1974), the defendant Dioguardi received a letter from one of the jurors soon after the trial in which the juror explained that she had "eyes and ears that * * * see things before [they] happen," but that her eyes "are only partly open" because "a curse was put upon them some years ago." *Id.,* at 75. Armed with this letter and the opinions of seven psychiatrists that the letter suggested that the juror was suffering from a psychological disorder, Dioguardi sought a new trial or in the alternative an evidentiary hearing on the juror's competence. The District Court denied the motion and the Court of Appeals affirmed. The Court of Appeals noted "[t]he strong policy against any post-verdict inquiry into a juror's state of mind," *id.*, at 79, and observed:

> "The quickness with which jury findings will be set aside when there is proof of tampering or *external* influence, * * * parallel the reluctance of courts to inquire into jury deliberations when a verdict is valid on its face. * * * Such exceptions support rather than undermine the rationale of the rule that possible *internal* abnormalities in a jury will not be inquired into except 'in the gravest and most important cases.' " *Id.*, at 79, n.12, citing *McDonald v. Pless, supra,* 238 U.S., at 269 (emphasis in original).

The court of appeals concluded that when faced with allegations that a juror was mentally incompetent, "courts have refused to set aside a verdict, or even to make further inquiry, unless there be proof of an adjudication of insanity or mental incompetence closely in advance * * * of jury service," or proof of "a closely contemporaneous and independent post-trial adjudication of incompetency." 492 F.2d, at 80. See also *Sullivan v. Fogg,* 613 F.2d 465, 467 (C.A.2 1980) (allegation of juror insanity is internal consideration); *United States v. Allen,* 588 F.2d 1100, 1106, n.12 (C.A.5 1979) (noting "specific reluctance to probe the minds of jurors once they have deliberated their verdict"); *United States v. Pellegrini,* 441 F.Supp. 1367 (E.D.Pa.1977), aff'd, 586 F.2d 836 (C.A.3 1978) (whether juror sufficiently understood English language was not a question of "extraneous influence"). This line of federal decisions was reviewed in *Government of the Virgin Islands v. Nicholas, supra,* in which the Court of Appeals concluded that a juror's allegation that a hearing impairment interfered with his understanding of the evidence at trial was not a matter of "external influence." *Id.*, at 1079.

Substantial policy considerations support the common-law rule against the admission of jury testimony to impeach a verdict. As early as 1915 this Court explained the necessity of shielding jury deliberations from public scrutiny:

> "[L]et it once be established that verdicts solemnly made and publicly returned into court can be attacked and set aside on the testimony of those who took part in their publication and all verdicts could be, and many would be, followed by an inquiry in the hope of discovering something which might invalidate the finding. Jurors would be harassed and beset by the defeated party in an effort to secure from them evidence of facts which might establish misconduct sufficient to set aside a verdict. If

evidence thus secured could be thus used, the result would be to make what was intended to be a private deliberation, the constant subject of public investigation—to the destruction of all frankness and freedom of discussion and conference." *McDonald v. Pless,* 238 U.S., at 267–268.

See also *Mattox v. United States,* 146 U.S. 140 (1892).

The Court's holdings requiring an evidentiary hearing where extrinsic influence or relationships have tainted the deliberations do not detract from, but rather harmonize with, the weighty government interest in insulating the jury's deliberative process. See *Smith v. Phillips,* 455 U.S. 209 (1982) (juror in criminal trial had submitted an application for employment at the District Attorney's office); *Remmer v. United States,* 347 U.S. 227 (1954) (juror reported attempted bribe during trial and was subjected to investigation). The Court's statement in *Remmer* that "[t]he integrity of jury proceedings must not be jeopardized by unauthorized invasions," *id.,* at 229, could also be applied to the inquiry petitioners seek to make into the internal processes of the jury.

There is little doubt that post-verdict investigation into juror misconduct would in some instances lead to the invalidation of verdicts reached after irresponsible or improper juror behavior. It is not at all clear, however, that the jury system could survive such efforts to perfect it. Allegations of juror misconduct, incompetency, or inattentiveness, raised for the first time days, weeks, or months after the verdict seriously disrupt the finality of the process. See, *e.g., Government of Virgin Islands v. Nicholas,* 759 F.2d, at 1081 (one year and eight months after verdict rendered, juror alleged that hearing difficulties affected his understanding of the evidence). Moreover, full and frank discussion in the jury room, jurors' willingness to return an unpopular verdict, and the community's trust in a system that relies on the decisions of laypeople would all be undermined by a barrage of post verdict scrutiny of juror conduct. * * *

Federal Rule of Evidence 606(b) is grounded in the common-law rule against admission of jury testimony to impeach a verdict and the exception for juror testimony relating to extraneous influences. See *Government of Virgin Islands v. Gereau,* 523 F.2d 140, 149, n.22 (C.A.3 1975); S.Rep. No. 93–1277, p. 13 (1974), U.S.Code Cong. & Admin.News 1974, p. 7051 (observing that Rule 606(b) "embodied long-accepted Federal law").

Rule 606(b) states:

"Upon an inquiry into the validity of a verdict or indictment, a juror may not testify as to any matter or statement occurring during the course of the jury's deliberations or to the effect of anything upon his or any other juror's mind or emotions as influencing him to assent to or dissent from the verdict or indictment or concerning his mental processes in connection therewith, except that a juror may testify on the question whether extraneous prejudicial information was improperly brought to the jury's attention or whether any outside influence was improperly brought to bear upon any juror. Nor may his affidavit or evidence of any statement by him concerning a matter about which he would be precluded from testifying be received for these purposes."

Petitioners have presented no argument that Rule 606(b) is inapplicable to the juror affidavits and the further inquiry they sought in this case, and, in fact, there appears to be virtually no support for such a proposition. See 3 D. Louisell & C. Mueller, Federal Evidence § 287, pp. 121–125 (1979) (under Rule 606(b), "proof to the following effects is excludable * * * that one or more jurors was inattentive during trial or deliberations, sleeping or thinking about other matters"); cf. Note, Impeachment of Verdicts by Jurors—Rule of Evidence 606(b), 4 Wm. Mitchell L.Rev. 417, 430–431 and n.88 (1978) (observing that under Rule 606(b), "juror testimony as to * * * juror intoxication probably will be inadmissible"; note author suggests that "[o]ne possibility is for the courts to determine that certain acts, such as a juror becoming intoxicated outside the jury room, simply are not within the rule," but cites no authority in support of the suggestion). Rather, petitioners argue that substance abuse constitutes an improper "outside influence" about which jurors may testify under Federal Rule of Evidence 606(b). In our view the language of the Rule cannot easily be stretched to cover this circumstance. However severe their effect and improper their use, drugs or alcohol voluntarily ingested by a juror seems no more an "outside influence" than a virus, poorly prepared food, or a lack of sleep.

In any case, whatever ambiguity might linger in the language of Rule 606(b) as applied to juror intoxication is resolved by the legislative history of the Rule. In 1972, following criticism of a proposed rule that would have allowed considerably broader use of juror testimony to impeach verdicts, the Advisory Committee drafted the present version of Rule 606(b). Compare 51 F.R.D. 315, 387 (1971) with 56 F.R.D. 183, 265 (1972); see 117 Cong.Rec. 33642, 33645 (1971) (letter from Sen. McClellan to Advisory Committee criticizing earlier proposal); *id.,* at 33655 (letter from Department of Justice to Advisory Committee criticizing earlier proposal and arguing that "[s]trong policy considerations continue to support the rule that jurors should not be permitted to testify about what occurred during the course of their deliberations"). This Court adopted the present version of Rule 606(b) and transmitted it to Congress.

The House Judiciary Committee described the effect of the version of Rule 606(b) transmitted by the Court as follows:

"As proposed by the Court, Rule 606(b) limited testimony by a juror in the course of an inquiry into the validity of a verdict or indictment. He could testify as to the influence of extraneous prejudicial information brought to the jury's attention (e.g. a radio newscast or a newspaper account) or an outside influence which improperly had been brought to bear upon a juror (e.g. a threat to the safety of a member of his family), but he could not testify as to other irregularities which occurred in the jury room. Under this formulation a quotient verdict could not be attacked through the testimony of juror, *nor could a juror testify to the drunken condition of a fellow juror which so disabled him that he could not participate in the jury's deliberations.*" H.R.Rep. No. 93–650, pp. 9–10 (1973), U.S.Code Cong. & Admin.News 1974, p. 7083 (emphasis supplied).

The House Judiciary Committee, persuaded that the better practice was to allow juror testimony on any "objective juror misconduct," amended the Rule so as to comport with the more expansive versions proposed by the Advisory Committee in earlier drafts[18] and the House passed this amended version.

The Senate Judiciary Committee did not voice any disagreement with the House's interpretation of the Rule proposed by the Court, or the version passed by the House. Indeed, the Senate Report described the House version as "considerably broader" than the version proposed by the Court, and noted that the House version "would permit the impeachment of verdicts by inquiry into, not the mental processes of the jurors, but what happened in terms of conduct in the jury room." S.Rep. No. 93–1277, p. 13 (1974), U.S.Code Cong. & Admin.News 1974, p. 7060. With this understanding of the differences between the two versions of Rule 606(b)—an understanding identical to that of the House—the Senate decided to reject the broader House version and adopt the narrower version approved by the Court. The Senate Report explained:

"[The House version's] extension of the ability to impeach a verdict is felt to be unwarranted and ill-advised.

"The rule passed by the House embodies a suggestion by the Advisory Committee of the Judicial Conference that is considerably broader than the final version adopted by the Supreme Court, which embodied long-accepted Federal law. Although forbidding the

---

[18] The House version, which adopted the earlier Advisory Committee proposal, read as follows:

"Upon an inquiry into the validity of a verdict or indictment, a juror may not testify concerning the effect of anything upon his or any other juror's mind or emotions as influencing him to assent to or dissent from the verdict or indictment or concerning his mental processes in connection therewith. Nor may his affidavit or evidence of any statement by him indicating an effect of this kind be received for these purposes." H.R. 5463, 93d Cong., 2d Sess. (1974).

impeachment of verdicts by inquiry into the jurors' mental processes, it deletes from the Supreme Court version the proscription against testimony 'as to any matter or statement occurring during the course of the jury's deliberations.' This deletion would have the effect of opening verdicts up to challenge on the basis of what happened during the jury's internal deliberations, for example, where a juror alleged that the jury refused to follow the trial judge's instructions or that some of the jurors did not take part in deliberations.

"Permitting an individual to attack a jury verdict based upon the jury's internal deliberations has long been recognized as unwise by the Supreme Court.

* * *

"As it stands then, the rule would permit the harassment of former jurors by losing parties as well as the possible exploitation of disgruntled or otherwise badly-motivated ex-jurors.

"Public policy requires a finality to litigation. And common fairness requires that absolute privacy be preserved for jurors to engage in the full and free debate necessary to the attainment of just verdicts. Jurors will not be able to function effectively if their deliberations are to be scrutinized in post-trial litigation. In the interest of protecting the jury system and the citizens who make it work, rule 606 should not permit any inquiry into the internal deliberations of the jurors." *Id.,* at 13–14, U.S.Code Cong. & Admin.News 1974, p. 7060.

The Conference Committee Report reaffirms Congress' understanding of the differences between the House and Senate versions of Rule 606(b): "[T]he House bill allows a juror to testify about objective matters occurring during the jury's deliberation, such as the misconduct of another juror or the reaching of a quotient verdict. The Senate bill does not permit juror testimony about any matter or statement occurring during the course of the jury's deliberations." H.R.Conf.Rep. No. 93–1597, p. 8 (1974), U.S.Code Cong. & Admin.News 1974, p. 7102. The Conference Committee adopted, and Congress enacted, the Senate version of Rule 606(b).

Thus, the legislative history demonstrates with uncommon clarity that Congress specifically understood, considered, and rejected a version of Rule 606(b) that would have allowed jurors to testify on juror conduct during deliberations, including juror intoxication. This legislative history provides strong support for the most reasonable reading of the language of Rule 606(b)—that juror intoxication is not an "outside influence" about which jurors may testify to impeach their verdict.

Finally, even if Rule 606(b) is interpreted to retain the common-law exception allowing post verdict inquiry of juror incompetence in cases of "substantial if not wholly conclusive evidence of incompetency," *Dioguardi,* 492 F.2d, at 80, the showing made by the petitioners falls far short of this standard. The affidavits and testimony presented in support of the first new trial motion suggested, at worst, that several of the jurors fell asleep at times during the afternoons. The District Court judge appropriately considered the fact that he had "an unobstructed view" of the jury, and did not see any juror sleeping. App. 147–149, 167–168; See *Government of Virgin Islands v. Nicholas,* 759 F.2d, at 1077 ("[I]t was appropriate for the trial judge to draw upon his personal knowledge and recollection in considering the factual allegations * * * that related to events that occurred in his presence"). The juror affidavit submitted in support of the second new trial motion was obtained in clear violation of the District Court's order and the court's local rule against juror interviews, MD Fla.Rule 2.04(c); on this basis alone the District Court would have been acting within its discretion in disregarding the affidavit. In any case, although the affidavit of juror Hardy describes more dramatic instances of misconduct, Hardy's allegations of *incompetence* are meager. Hardy stated that the alcohol consumption he engaged in with three other jurors did not leave any of them intoxicated. App. to Pet. for Cert. 47 ("I told [the prosecutor] that we would just go out and get us a pitcher of beer and drink it, but as far as us being drunk, no we wasn't"). The only allegations concerning the jurors' ability to properly consider the evidence were Hardy's observation that some jurors were "falling asleep all the time during the trial," and that Hardy's own reasoning ability was affected on one day of the trial. App. to Pet. for Cert. 46, 55. These allegations would not suffice to bring this case under the common-law exception allowing post verdict inquiry when an extremely strong showing of incompetency has been made.

Petitioners also argue that the refusal to hold an additional evidentiary hearing at which jurors would testify as to their conduct "violates the sixth amendment's guarantee to a fair trial before an impartial and *competent* jury." Brief for Petitioners 34 (emphasis in original).

This Court has recognized that a defendant has a right to "a tribunal both impartial and mentally competent to afford a hearing." *Jordan v. Massachusetts,* 225 U.S. 167, 176 (1912). In this case the District Court held an evidentiary hearing in response to petitioners' first new trial motion at which the judge invited petitioners to introduce any admissible evidence in support of their allegations. At issue in this case is whether the Constitution compelled the District Court to hold an additional evidentiary hearing including one particular kind of evidence inadmissible under the Federal Rules.

As described above, long-recognized and very substantial concerns support the protection of jury deliberations from intrusive inquiry.

Petitioners' Sixth Amendment interests in an unimpaired jury, on the other hand, are protected by several aspects of the trial process. The suitability of an individual for the responsibility of jury service, of course, is examined during *voir dire.* Moreover, during the trial the jury is observable by the court, by counsel, and by court personnel. See *United States v. Provenzano,* 620 F.2d 985, 996–997 (C.A.3 1980) (marshal discovered sequestered juror smoking marijuana during early morning hours). Moreover, jurors are observable by each other, and may report inappropriate juror behavior to the court *before* they render a verdict. See *Lee v. United States,* 454 A.2d 770 (D.C.App.1982) (on second day of deliberations, jurors sent judge a note suggesting that foreperson was incapacitated). Finally, after the trial a party may seek to impeach the verdict by nonjuror evidence of misconduct. See *United States v. Taliaferro,* 558 F.2d 724, 725–726 (C.A.4 1977) (court considered records of club where jurors dined, and testimony of marshal who accompanied jurors, to determine whether jurors were intoxicated during deliberations). Indeed, in this case the District Court held an evidentiary hearing giving petitioners ample opportunity to produce nonjuror evidence supporting their allegations.

In light of these other sources of protection of the petitioners' right to a competent jury, we conclude that the District Court did not err in deciding, based on the inadmissibility of juror testimony and the clear insufficiency of the nonjuror evidence offered by petitioners, that an additional post verdict evidentiary hearing was unnecessary. * * *

[Affirmed. Remanded on other issues.]

JUSTICE MARSHALL, with whom JUSTICE BRENNAN, JUSTICE BLACKMUN, and JUSTICE STEVENS join, concurring in part and dissenting in part.

Every criminal defendant has a constitutional right to be tried by competent jurors. This Court has long recognized that "[d]ue process implies a tribunal both impartial and mentally competent to afford a hearing," *Jordan v. Massachusetts,* 225 U.S. 167, 176 (1912), "a jury capable and willing to decide the case solely on the evidence before it." *Smith v. Phillips,* 455 U.S. 209, 217 (1982). If, as is charged, members of petitioners' jury were intoxicated as a result of their use of drugs and alcohol to the point of sleeping through material portions of the trial, the verdict in this case must be set aside. In directing district courts to ignore sworn allegations that jurors engaged in gross and debilitating misconduct, this Court denigrates the precious right to a competent jury. Accordingly, I dissent from that part of the Court's opinion.

I

At the outset, it should be noted that petitioners have not asked this Court to decide whether there is sufficient evidence to impeach the jury's verdict. The question before us is only whether an evidentiary hearing is required to explore allegations of juror misconduct and incompetency.

The allegations of juror misconduct in this case are profoundly disturbing. * * *

II

Despite the seriousness of the charges, the Court refuses to allow petitioners an opportunity to vindicate their fundamental right to a competent jury. The Court holds that petitioners are absolutely barred from exploring allegations of juror misconduct and incompetency through the only means available to them—examination of the jurors who have already voluntarily come forward. The basis for the Court's ruling is the mistaken belief that juror testimony concerning drug and alcohol abuse at trial is inadmissible under Federal Rule of Evidence 606(b) and is contrary to the policies the Rule was intended to advance. * * *

In this case, however, we are not faced with a conflict between the policy considerations underlying Rule 606(b) and petitioners' Sixth Amendment rights. Rule 606(b) is not applicable to juror testimony on matters *unrelated* to the jury's deliberations. * * *

It is undisputed that Rule 606(b) does not exclude juror testimony as to matters occurring before or after deliberations. See 3 D. Louisell & C. Mueller, Federal Evidence § 290, p. 151 (1979) * * * . But, more particularly, the Rule only "operates to prohibit testimony as to *certain conduct by the jurors which has no verifiable manifestations*," 3 J. Weinstein & M. Berger, Weinstein's Evidence ¶ 606[04], p. 606–28 (1985) (emphasis added); as to other matters, jurors remain competent to testify. See Fed.Rule Evid. 601. Because petitioners' claim of juror misconduct and incompetency involves objectively verifiable conduct occurring prior to deliberations, juror testimony in support of the claims is admissible under Rule 606(b).

The Court's analysis of legislative history confirms the inapplicability of Rule 606(b) to the type of misconduct alleged in this case. As the Court emphasizes, the debate over two proposed versions of the Rule—the more restrictive Senate version ultimately adopted and the permissive House version * * *, focused on the extent to which jurors would be permitted to testify as to what transpired *during the course of the deliberations themselves*. Similarly, the Conference Committee Report, quoted by the Court * * *, compares the two versions solely in terms of the admissibility of testimony as to matters occurring during, or relating to, the jury's deliberations: "[T]he House bill allows a juror to testify about objective matters occurring during the jury's deliberation, such as the misconduct of another juror or the reaching of a quotient verdict. The Senate bill does not permit juror testimony about any matter or statement occurring *during the course of the jury's deliberations*." H.R.Conf.Rep. No. 93–1597,

p. 8 (1974), U.S.Code Cong. & Admin.News 1974, p. 7102 (emphasis added). The obvious conclusion, and the one compelled by Rule 601, is that *both* versions of Rule 606(b) would have permitted jurors to testify as to matters not involving deliberations. The House Report's passing reference to juror intoxication during deliberations * * * is not to the contrary. Reflecting Congress' consistent focus on the deliberative process, it suggests only that the authors of the House Report believed that the Senate version of Rule 606(b) did not allow testimony as to juror intoxication during deliberations. * * *

Even if I agreed with the Court's expansive construction of Rule 606(b), I would nonetheless find the testimony of juror intoxication admissible under the Rule's "outside influence" exception.[19] As a common sense matter, drugs and alcohol *are* outside influences on jury members. Commentators have suggested that testimony as to drug and alcohol abuse, even during deliberations, falls within this exception. "[T]he present exception paves the way for proof by the affidavit or testimony of a juror that one or more jurors became intoxicated during deliberations. * * * Of course the use of hallucinogenic or narcotic drugs during deliberations should similarly be provable." 3 Louisell & Mueller, Federal Evidence, § 289, pp. 143–145 (footnote omitted). See 3 Weinstein & Berger, Weinstein's Evidence, *supra,* ¶ 606[04], pp. 606–29—606–32 ("Rule 606(b) would not render a witness incompetent to testify to juror irregularities such as intoxication * * * regardless of whether the jury misconduct occurred within or without the jury room"). The Court suggests that, if these are outside influences, "a virus, poorly prepared food, or a lack of sleep" would also qualify. [483 U.S.] at 122. Distinguishing between a virus, for example, and a narcotic drug is a matter of line-drawing. Courts are asked to make these sorts of distinctions in numerous contexts; I have no doubt they would be capable of differentiating between the intoxicants involved in this case and minor indispositions not affecting juror competency.

The Court assures us that petitioners' Sixth Amendment interests are adequately protected by other aspects of the trial process: *voir dire*; observation during trial by the court, counsel, and courtroom personnel; and observation by fellow jurors (so long as they report inappropriate juror behavior to the court before a verdict is rendered). * * * Reliance on these safeguards, to the exclusion of an evidentiary hearing, is misguided. *Voir dire* cannot disclose whether a juror will choose to abuse drugs and

---

[19] The sole support for the Court's cramped interpretation of this exception is the isolated reference to juror intoxication *at deliberations,* contained in the House Report, quoted *supra* * * * . The source for the reference is a letter to the House Subcommittee, to the effect that the version of the Rule adopted by the Senate would not allow inquiry into juror consumption of alcohol during deliberations. * * * In a subsequent letter, the writer dropped any reference to the question of intoxication, focusing exclusively on the issue of quotient verdicts. * * * Moreover, this reference is hardly dispositive. * * * None of the subsequent Committee Reports make any allusion to juror intoxication.

alcohol during the trial. Moreover, the type of misconduct alleged here is not readily verifiable through nonjuror testimony. The jurors were not supervised by courtroom personnel during the noon recess, when they consumed alcoholic beverages and used drugs. Hardy reported that he and his three companions purposely avoided observation. They smoked marijuana and used cocaine first in a municipal parking garage and later "[d]own past the Hyatt Regency" because it was "away from everybody." App. 218, 222. * * *

I dissent.

NOTES AND QUESTIONS

1. *Litigating effect of improper influence. Tanner* deals only with the issue of whether the testimony concerning "substance abuse" constitutes an "improper outside influence" available to impeach the jury's verdict. Even where an event is considered admissible as an outside influence, a juror may still not testify concerning the effect of that influence upon his or her mind under Rule 606(b) and long-standing case law. See, e.g., Mattox v. United States, 146 U.S. 140, 149 (1892). Accordingly, if evidence is admitted, the court must determine whether a new trial should be granted based upon objective circumstances. See, e.g., United States v. Vasquez, 597 F.2d 192, 194 (9th Cir.1979) (where file containing inadmissible evidence left in jury room, court examined prejudicial potential of information, period of time file left in room, and extent of exposure to jurors, but could not consider subjective effect on jurors). This means that direct testimony regarding the prejudicial impact of the outside influence will generally be unavailable, and as a result, the burden of proof regarding prejudice and presumptions of prejudice take on special importance in determining the outcome. The Supreme Court has on several occasions addressed improper outside influences: Remmer v. United States, 347 U.S. 227, 229 (1954) (any private communication about matter pending before jury is presumptively prejudicial, placing burden on government to show harmlessness), and Smith v. Phillips, 455 U.S. 209 (1982) (defendant has opportunity to prove actual bias of juror who applied for employment with district attorney's office during trial). Lower courts have struggled with precisely what these cases mean with respect to the burden of proof and presumptions. See United States v. Maree, 934 F.2d 196, 201 (9th Cir.1991) (where extraneous material about the case is submitted to jury, defendant receives a new trial if the court finds a "reasonable possibility" that the material could have affected the verdict, but where *ex parte* contacts do not pertain to the law or facts of the case, a new trial is to be granted only if the court finds "actual prejudice"); Stockton v. Virginia, 852 F.2d 740, 743–44 (4th Cir.1988) (*Remmer* creates presumption of prejudice where third party communicates with a juror about the case and neither *Tanner* nor *Phillips* eliminates that presumption).

2. *Racists comments.* If the internal deliberations of the jury, as reported by one of the jurors after the verdict of guilty, included extremely

racist remarks by jurors in a case involving a minority defendant, would the rationale of the *Tanner* Court hold? If not, what rationale might be used? See Developments in the Law: Race and the Criminal Process: VII. Racist Juror Misconduct During Deliberations, 101 Harv.L.Rev. 1595 (1988). For an argument that jury deliberations are too secretive and should be transcribed and made part of the record, see Ruprecht, Are Verdicts, Too, Like Sausages?: Lifting the Cloak of Jury Secrecy, 146 U.Pa.L.Rev. 217 (1997).

3. *False or incomplete answers on voir dire.* Where a juror fails to respond fully and truthfully to questions on voir dire, are the limitations of Rule 606 inapplicable? See Urseth v. City of Dayton, 680 F.Supp. 1084 (S.D.Ohio 1987). Is a new trial justified on a lesser showing of prejudice? See McCoy v. Goldston, 652 F.2d 654 (6th Cir.1981).

4. *Interviewing jurors.* In *Tanner,* the Supreme Court noted that the trial judge denied counsel's motion to interview jurors. If counsel is prohibited from interviewing jurors, how is misconduct to be discovered? With regard to the practical problem of discovering whether improprieties occurred that might serve as grounds for setting aside a verdict, compare United States v. Moten, 582 F.2d 654 (2d Cir.1978) (recognizing that notice must be given to the court and opposing counsel before jurors are contacted and that district court has the power to order that all post-trial investigation be conducted under judicial supervision), with Model Code of Professional Responsibility DR 7–108(D) (prohibiting the questioning of jurors only where done for the purpose of harassing or embarrassing juror or influencing future jury service). The Model Rules of Professional Conduct have no provision dealing with this issue. See generally 3 Mueller & Kirkpatrick, Federal Evidence § 6:23 (3d ed. 2007); 3 Weinstein's Federal Evidence § 606.06 (2d ed. 2013).

5. *Correcting mistake in verdict form.* In 2006, Rule 606(b) was amended to clarify that juror testimony could be received to prove that there was a mistake made in entering the verdict on the verdict form.

6. *Sources.* Alschuler, The Supreme Court and the Jury: Voir Dire, Peremptory Challenges, and the Review of Jury Verdicts, 56 U.Chi.L.Rev. 153 (1989); Cammack, The Jurisprudence of Jury Trials: The No Impeachment Rule and the Conditions for Legitimate Legal Decisionmaking, 64 U.Colo.L.Rev. 57 (1993); Crump, Jury Misconduct, Jury Interviews, and the Federal Rules of Evidence: Is the Broad Exclusionary Principle of Rule 606(b) Justified?, 66 N.C.L.Rev. 509 (1988); Diehm, Impeachment of Jury Verdicts: *Tanner v. United States* and Beyond, 65 St. John's L.Rev. 389 (1991); Mueller, Jurors' Impeachment of Verdicts and Indictments in Federal Courts Under Rule 606(b), 57 Neb.L.Rev. 920 (1978); ABA Standards for Criminal Justice, Trial by Jury, Standard 15–5.7 (3d ed. 1996).

DOUGLAS OIL CO. OF CALIFORNIA V. PETROL STOPS NORTHWEST

Supreme Court of the United States, 1979.
441 U.S. 211.

MR. JUSTICE POWELL delivered the opinion of the Court.

This case presents two intertwined questions concerning a civil litigant's right to obtain transcripts of federal criminal grand jury proceedings. First, what justification for disclosure must a private party show in order to overcome the presumption of grand jury secrecy applicable to such transcripts? Second, what court should assess the strength of this showing—the court where the civil action is pending, or the court that acts as custodian of the grand jury documents?

I

Respondent Petrol Stops Northwest is a gasoline retailer unaffiliated with any major oil company. In 1973, it operated 104 service stations located in Arizona, California, Oregon, Washington, and several other States. On December 13, 1973, respondent filed an antitrust action in the District of Arizona against 12 large oil companies, including petitioners Douglas Oil Company of California and Phillips Petroleum Company. In its complaint, respondent alleged that on January 1, 1973, there had been a sharp reduction in the amount of gasoline offered for sale to it, and that this reduction had resulted from a conspiracy among the oil companies to restrain trade in gasoline, in violation of §§ 1 and 2 of the Sherman Act. 26 Stat. 209, 15 U.S.C.A. §§ 1, 2. As a part of this conspiracy, respondent charged, petitioners and their codefendants had fixed the prices of gasoline at the retail and wholesale distribution levels in California, Oregon and Washington.

Respondents Gas–A–Tron of Arizona and Coinoco also independently sell gasoline through service stations they own or lease. Unlike respondent Petrol Stops Northwest, however, their operations are limited to the vicinity of Tucson, Ariz. On November 2, 1973, Gas–A–Tron and Coinoco filed an antitrust complaint in the District of Arizona naming as defendants nine large oil companies, including petitioner Phillips Petroleum Company. Like respondent Petrol Stops Northwest, Gas–A–Tron and Coinoco alleged that as of January 1, 1973, their supply of gasoline had been sharply reduced, and attributed this reduction to a conspiracy to restrain trade in violation of the Sherman Act. The specific charges of illegal behavior asserted by the two retailers substantially paralleled those made by Petrol Stops Northwest in its complaint, and included an allegation that the defendants had fixed the price of gasoline at the wholesale and retail levels.

Although the issues and defendants in the two actions were substantially the same, the cases were assigned to two different judges in the District of Arizona. In February 1974, respondents served upon petitioners a set of interrogatories which included a request that petitioners state whether either of their companies at any time between January 1, 1968, and December 14, 1974, had had any communication with any of their competitors concerning the wholesale price of gasoline to be sold to unaffiliated retailers. Petitioners also were asked to produce any documents they had concerning such communications. Petitioners responded that they were aware of no such communications, and therefore could produce no documents pertinent to the request.

In the meantime, the Antitrust Division of the Department of Justice had been investigating since 1972 the pricing behavior on the West Coast of several major oil companies including petitioners. See App. 26. As part of this investigation, employees of petitioners were called to testify before a grand jury empanelled in the Central District of California. The Government's investigation culminated on March 19, 1975, when the grand jury returned an indictment charging petitioners and four other oil companies with having conspired to fix the price of "rebrand gasoline" in California, Oregon, Washington, Nevada, and Arizona. The indictment alleged that the price-fixing conspiracy had begun in July 1970 and had continued at least until the end of 1971.

Although initially all six defendants charged in the criminal indictment pled not guilty, by December of 1975, each had pled *nolo contendere* and was fined $50,000. Before changing their pleas, petitioners, acting pursuant to Fed.Rule Crim.Proc. 16(a)(1)(A), asked the District Court for the Central District of California to give them copies of the transcripts of testimony given by their employees before the grand jury. Their request was granted, and it appears that petitioners continue to possess copies of these transcripts.

In October of 1976 respondents served upon petitioners requests under Fed.Rule Civ.Proc. 34 for production of the grand jury transcripts in petitioners' possession. Petitioners objected to the requests for production, arguing that the transcripts were not relevant to the private antitrust actions and that they were not likely to lead to any admissible evidence. Respondents did not pursue their discovery requests by making a motion in the Arizona trial court under Fed.Rule Civ.Proc. 37 to compel discovery. * * * Rather, they filed a petition in the District Court for the Central District of California asking that court, as guardian of the grand jury transcripts under Fed.Rule Crim.Proc. 6(e), to order them released to respondents. An attorney from the Antitrust Division of the Department of Justice appeared and indicated that the Government had no objection to respondents' receiving the transcripts already made available to petitioners under Fed.Rule Crim.Proc. 16(a)(1)(A). He suggested to the court, however, that the real parties in interest were petitioners, and therefore that they should be given an opportunity to be heard. The

California District Court accepted this suggestion, and petitioners participated in the proceedings as parties adverse to respondents.

After briefing and oral argument, the court ordered the Chief of the Antitrust Division's Los Angeles Office "to produce for [respondents'] inspection and copying all grand jury transcripts previously disclosed to Phillips Petroleum Company or Douglas Oil Company of California or their attorneys relating to the indictment in United States v. Phillips, et al., Criminal Docket No. 75–377." App. 48–49. The production order was subject, however, to several protective conditions. The transcripts were to "be disclosed only to counsel for [respondents] in connection with the two civil actions" pending in Arizona. Furthermore, under the court's order the transcripts of grand jury testimony "may be used * * * solely for the purpose of impeaching or refreshing the recollection of a witness, either in deposition or at trial" in the Arizona actions. Finally, the court forbade any further reproduction of the matter turned over to respondents, and ordered that the material be returned to the Antitrust Division "upon completion of the purposes authorized by this Order."

On appeal the Ninth Circuit affirmed the disclosure order. 571 F.2d 1127 (1978). The Court of Appeals noted that under United States v. Procter & Gamble Co., 356 U.S. 677 (1958), a party seeking access to grand jury transcripts must show a "particularized need." In evaluating the strength of the need shown in the present case, the Ninth Circuit considered two factors: the need for continued grand jury secrecy and respondents' need for the requested material. The court found the former need to be insubstantial, as the grand jury proceeding had concluded three years before and the transcripts already had been released to petitioners. As to respondents' claim, the court conceded that it knew little about the Arizona proceedings, but speculated that the transcripts would facilitate the prosecution of respondents' civil suits: Petitioners' answers to the 1974 interrogatories concerning price communications with competitors appeared to be at odds with their pleas of *nolo contendere* in the California criminal action.

II

Petitioners contend that the courts below erred in holding that, because the grand jury had dissolved and the requested material had been disclosed already to the defendants, respondents had to show only a "slight need" for disclosure. According to petitioners, this approach to disclosure under Fed.Rule Crim.Proc. 6(e) is contrary to prior decisions of this Court indicating that, "a civil litigant must demonstrate a compelling necessity for specified grand jury materials before disclosure is proper." Brief for Petitioners 16.

We consistently have recognized that the proper functioning of our grand jury system depends upon the secrecy of grand jury proceedings.

See, e.g., United States v. Procter & Gamble, 356 U.S. 677 (1958).[20] In particular, we have noted several distinct interests served by safeguarding the confidentiality of grand jury proceedings. First, if preindictment proceedings were made public, many prospective witnesses would be hesitant to come forward voluntarily, knowing that those against whom they testify would be aware of that testimony. Moreover, witnesses who appeared before the grand jury would be less likely to testify fully and frankly, as they would be open to retribution as well as to inducements. There also would be the risk that those about to be indicted would flee, or would try to influence individual grand jurors to vote against indictment. Finally, by preserving the secrecy of the proceedings, we assure that persons who are accused but found innocent by the grand jury will not be held up to public ridicule.[21]

For all of these reasons, courts have been reluctant to lift unnecessarily the veil of secrecy from the grand jury. At the same time, it has been recognized that in some situations justice may demand that discrete portions of transcripts be made available for use in subsequent proceedings. See, e.g., United States v. Socony–Vacuum, 310 U.S. 150, 233–234 (1940). Indeed, recognition of the occasional need for litigants to have access to grand jury transcripts led to the provision in Fed.Rule Crim.Proc. 6(e)(2)(C)(i) that disclosure of grand jury transcripts may be made "when so directed by a court preliminarily to or in connection with a judicial proceeding."

---

[20] Since the 17th century, grand jury proceedings have been closed to the public, and records of such proceedings have been kept from the public eye. See Calkins, Grand Jury Secrecy, 63 Mich.L.Rev. 455, 457 (1965). The rule of grand jury secrecy was imported into our federal common law and is an integral part of our criminal justice system. See Costello v. United States, 350 U.S. 359, 362 (1956); United States v. Johnson, 319 U.S. 503, 513 (1943). Rule 6(e) of the Federal Rules of Criminal Procedure codifies the requirement that grand jury activities generally be kept secret, by providing that,

"A grand juror, an interpreter, a stenographer, an operator of a recording device, a typist who transcribes recorded testimony, [or] an attorney for the Government * * * shall not disclose matters occurring before the grand jury, except as otherwise provided for in these rules. * * * A knowing violation of rule 6 may be punished as a contempt of court."

Although the purpose for grand jury secrecy originally was protection of the criminally accused against an overreaching Crown, see Calkins, Grand Jury Secrecy, supra, with time it came to be viewed as necessary for the proper functioning of the grand jury. * * *

[21] In United States v. Procter & Gamble, 356 U.S. 677, 681–682, n.6 (1958), we said that the reasons for grand jury secrecy had been summarized correctly in United States v. Rose, 215 F.2d 617, 628–629 (C.A.3 1954):

"(1) To prevent the escape of those whose indictment may be contemplated; (2) to insure the utmost freedom to the grand jury in its deliberations, and to prevent persons subject to indictment or their friends from importuning the grand jurors; (3) to prevent subornation of perjury or tampering with the witnesses who may testify before the grand jury and later appear at the trial of those indicted by it; (4) to encourage free and untrammeled disclosures by persons who have information with respect to the commission of crimes; (5) to protect innocent accused who is exonerated from disclosure of the fact that he has been under investigation, and from the expense of standing trial where there was no probability of guilt."

In United States v. Procter & Gamble, supra, the Court sought to accommodate the competing needs for secrecy and disclosure by ruling that a private party seeking to obtain grand jury transcripts must demonstrate that "without the transcript a defense would be greatly prejudiced or that without reference to it an injustice would be done." 356 U.S., at 682. Moreover, the Court required that the showing of need for the transcripts be made "with particularity" so that "the secrecy of the proceedings [may] be lifted discretely and limitedly." Id., at 683. Accord, Pittsburgh Plate Glass Co. v. United States, 360 U.S. 395, 400 (1959).

In Dennis v. United States, 384 U.S. 855 (1966), the Court considered a request for disclosure of grand jury records in quite different circumstances. It was there held to be an abuse of discretion for a district court in a criminal trial to refuse to disclose to the defendants the grand jury testimony of four witnesses who some years earlier had appeared before a grand jury investigating activities of the defendants. The grand jury had completed its investigation, and the witnesses whose testimony was sought already had testified in public concerning the same matters. The Court noted that "[n]one of the reasons traditionally advanced to justify nondisclosure of grand jury minutes" was significant in those circumstances, 384 U.S., at 872 n.18, whereas the defendants had shown it to be likely that the witnesses' testimony at trial was inconsistent with their prior grand jury testimony.

From *Procter & Gamble* and *Dennis* emerges the standard for determining when the traditional secrecy of the grand jury may be broken: Parties seeking grand jury transcripts under Rule 6(e) must show that the material they seek is needed to avoid a possible injustice in another judicial proceeding, that the need for disclosure is greater than the need for continued secrecy, and that their request is structured to cover only material so needed.[22] Such a showing must be made even when the grand jury whose transcripts are sought has concluded its operations, as it had in *Dennis.* For in considering the effects of disclosure on grand jury proceedings, the courts must consider not only the immediate effects upon a particular grand jury, but also the possible effect upon the functioning of future grand juries. Persons called upon to testify will consider the likelihood that their testimony may one day be disclosed to outside parties. Fear of future retribution or social stigma may act as powerful deterrents to those who would come forward and aid the grand jury in the performance of its duties. Concern as to the future consequences of frank and full testimony is heightened where the witness

---

[22] As noted in United States v. Procter & Gamble, 356 U.S. 677, 683 (1958), the typical showing of particularized need arises when a litigant seeks to use "the grand jury transcript at the trial to impeach a witness, to refresh his recollection, to test his credibility and the like." Such use is necessary to avoid misleading the trier of fact. Moreover, disclosure can be limited strictly to those portions of a particular witness' testimony that bear upon some aspect of his direct testimony at trial.

is an employee of a company under investigation. Thus, the interests in grand jury secrecy, although reduced, are not eliminated merely because the grand jury has ended its activities.[23]

It is clear from *Procter & Gamble* and *Dennis* that disclosure is appropriate only in those cases where the need for it outweighs the public interest in secrecy, and that the burden of demonstrating this balance rests upon the private party seeking disclosure. It is equally clear that as the considerations justifying secrecy become less relevant, a party asserting a need for grand jury transcripts will have a lesser burden in showing justification. Accord, Illinois v. Sarbaugh, 552 F.2d 768, 774 (C.A.7 1977); U.S. Industries Inc. v. United States District Court, 345 F.2d 18, 21 (C.A.9 1965); 1 C. Wright, Federal Practice & Procedure § 106, at 173 (1969). In sum, as so often is the situation in our jurisprudence, the court's duty in a case of this kind is to weigh carefully the competing interests in light of the relevant circumstances and the standards announced by this Court. And if disclosure is ordered, the court may include protective limitations on the use of the disclosed material, as did the District Court in this case. Moreover, we emphasize that a court called upon to determine whether grand jury transcripts should be released necessarily is infused with substantial discretion. See Pittsburgh Plate Glass Co. v. United States, 360 U.S. 395, 399 (1959).

Applying these principles to the present case, we conclude that neither the District Court nor the Court of Appeals erred in the standard by which it assessed the request for disclosure under Rule 6(e). The District Court made clear that the question before it was whether a particularized need for disclosure outweighed the interest in continued grand jury secrecy. See App. 53–55. Similarly, the Court of Appeals correctly understood that the standard enunciated in *Procter & Gamble* requires a court to examine the extent of the need for continuing grand jury secrecy, the need for disclosure, and the extent to which the request was limited to that material directly pertinent to the need for disclosure.[24]

---

[23] The transcripts sought by respondents already had been given to the target companies in the grand jury investigation. Thus, release to respondents will not enhance the possibility of retaliatory action by employers in this case. But the other factors supporting the presumption of secrecy remain and must be considered.

[24] As petitioners point out, the Court of Appeals did say that, because of the circumstances, "the party seeking disclosure should not be required to demonstrate a large compelling need," and that a "minimal showing of particularized need" would suffice. In a different context, these statements could be read as an unjustified lowering of the standard of proof required by *Procter & Gamble* and *Dennis*. We cannot say, however, that the Court of Appeals applied an incorrect standard in view of the circumstances of this case and the discussion thereof in the opinion below.

III

Petitioners contend, irrespective of the legal standard applied, that the District Court for the Central District of California was not the proper court to rule on respondents' motion for disclosure. Petitioners note that the Court of Appeals and the District Court both purported to base their decisions in part upon the need for use of the requested material in the civil antitrust proceedings pending in Arizona. This determination necessarily involved consideration of the nature and status of the Arizona proceedings, matters peculiarly within the competence of the Arizona District Court.

* * * The federal courts that have addressed the question generally have said that the request for disclosure of grand jury minutes under Rule 6(e) must be directed toward the court under whose auspices the grand jury was impanelled. * * * Indeed, those who seek grand jury transcripts have little choice other than to file a request with the court that supervised the grand jury, as it is the only court with control over the transcripts.[25] * * *

It does not follow, however, that in every case the court in which the grand jury sat should make the final decision whether a request for disclosure under Rule 6(e) should be granted. Where, as in this case, the request is made for use in a case pending in another district, the judges of the court having custody of the grand jury transcripts will have no first-hand knowledge of the litigation in which the transcripts allegedly are needed, and no practical means by which such knowledge can be obtained. In such a case, a judge in the district of the grand jury cannot weigh in an informed manner the need for disclosure against the need for maintaining grand jury secrecy. Thus, it may well be impossible for that court to apply the standard required by the decisions of this Court, reiterated above, for determining whether the veil of secrecy should be lifted. * * *

In the present case, the District Court for the Central District of California was called upon to make an evaluation entirely beyond its expertise. The District Judge readily conceded that he had no knowledge of the civil proceedings pending several hundred miles away in Arizona. App. 58. Nonetheless, he was asked to rule whether there was a "particularized need" for disclosure of portions of the grand jury

---

[25] As we have noted, by virtue of a prior order petitioners have possession of the transcripts sought by respondents. * * * We were informed at argument by counsel for the Government that under the terms of that order, the transcripts were to be returned upon completion of the criminal proceeding in the Central District of California and were to be used only for purposes of defending against the criminal charges in that case. * * * It appears, therefore, that if the District Court in Arizona had the authority to order disclosure by the petitioners, this power was derived from petitioners' unlawful retention of the transcripts. Indeed, as the Government suggests, it is questionable whether the Arizona District Court properly could have ordered production of the documents in direct violation of the California District Court order.

transcript and whether this need outweighed the need for continued grand jury secrecy. Generally we leave it to the considered discretion of the District Court to determine the proper response to requests for disclosure under Rule 6(e). See Pittsburgh Plate Glass Co. v. United States, 360 U.S. 395, 399 (1959). We have a duty, however, to guide the exercise of discretion by district courts, and when necessary to overturn discretionary decisions under Rule 6(e). See, e.g., Dennis v. United States, 384 U.S. 855 (1966).

We find that the District Court here abused its discretion in releasing directly to respondents the grand jury minutes they requested. Appreciating that it was largely ignorant of the Arizona civil suits, the court nonetheless made a judgment concerning the relative needs for secrecy and disclosure. The court based its decision largely upon the unsupported assertions of counsel during oral argument before it, supplemented only by the criminal indictment returned by the grand jury, the civil complaints, and petitioners' response to a single interrogatory that appeared to be inconsistent with petitioners' *nolo contendere* plea in the criminal case. Even the court's comparison of the criminal indictment and the civil complaints did not indicate unambiguously what, if any, portions of the grand jury transcripts would be pertinent to the subject of the Arizona actions, as only some of the same parties were named and only some of the same territory was covered.

The possibility of an unnecessary breach of grand jury secrecy in situations such as this is not insignificant. A court more familiar with the course of the antitrust litigation might have seen important differences between the allegations of the indictment and the contours of the conspiracy respondents sought to prove in their civil actions—differences indicating that disclosure would likely be of little value to respondents, save perhaps as a mechanism for general discovery. Alternatively, the courts where the civil proceedings were pending might have considered disclosure at that point in the litigation to be premature; if there were to be conflicts between petitioners' statements and their actions in the criminal proceedings, the court might have preferred to wait until they ripened at depositions or even during testimony at trial.

Under these circumstances, the better practice would have been for the District Court, after making a written evaluation of the need for continued grand jury secrecy and a determination that the limited evidence before it showed that disclosure might be appropriate, to have sent the requested materials to the courts where the civil cases were pending. The Arizona court, armed with their special knowledge of the status of the civil actions, then could have considered the requests for disclosure in light of the California court's evaluation of the need for continued grand jury secrecy. In this way, both the need for continued secrecy and the need for disclosure could have been evaluated by the courts in the best position to make the respective evaluations.

We do not suggest, of course, that such a procedure would be required in every case arising under Rule 6(e). Circumstances that dictate the need for cooperative action between the courts of different districts will vary, and procedures to deal with the many variations are best left to the rulemaking procedures established by Congress. Undoubtedly there will be cases in which the court to whom the Rule 6(e) request is directed will be able intelligently on the basis of limited knowledge to decide that disclosure plainly is inappropriate or that justice requires immediate disclosure to the requesting party, without reference of the matter to any other court. Our decision today therefore is restricted to situations, such as that presented by this case, in which the District Court having custody of the grand jury records is unlikely to have dependable knowledge of the status of, and the needs of the parties in, the civil suit in which the desired transcripts are to be used.

The judgment of the Court of Appeals is reversed, and the case remanded for further proceedings consistent with this opinion.

[JUSTICE REHNQUIST'S concurring opinion is omitted.]

MR. JUSTICE STEVENS, with whom THE CHIEF JUSTICE and MR. JUSTICE STEWART join, dissenting.

Although I join all but the last nine paragraphs of the Court's opinion, I cannot agree with the conclusion that the District Judge sitting in the Central District of California should not have granted access to the grand jury transcripts subject to the conditions stated in his order. More fundamentally, I do not share the Court's readiness to review the District Judge's exercise of his broad discretion in this matter in the absence of any allegation of egregious abuse on his part and in the face of the confirmation of his conclusion by the Court of Appeals. * * *

NOTES AND QUESTIONS

1. *Principles of grand jury secrecy.* The common law principle of grand jury secrecy, noted in *Douglas Oil,* has been codified in Rule 6(e) of the Federal Rules of Criminal Procedure as well as numerous state statutes and rules. For a comprehensive treatment of issues of grand jury secrecy, see 2 Beale et al., Grand Jury Law and Practice ch. 5 (2d ed. 2012).

2. *Procedures for determining disclosure.* Effective in 1983, Federal Rule of Criminal Procedure was amended by adding subsections (3)(D) & (E) to codify and amplify the procedural aspects of *Douglas Oil.* Under these provisions, a petition for disclosure must be filed in the district where the grand jury is convened. Except when the hearing is *ex parte,* which may in some circumstances occur when the government seeks disclosure, notice and a reasonable opportunity to be heard is to be provided to the government and

to the parties in the other judicial proceeding. Unless that court can reasonably obtain sufficient information concerning the other judicial proceeding to determine if disclosure is proper, it must transfer the petition to the district court where that case is pending. The transferring court is to forward, together with the material sought to be disclosed, a written assessment of the need for continued secrecy.

3.   *Witness disclosure.* Federal Rule of Criminal Procedure 6(e) does not prohibit a witness who testifies before the grand jury from revealing his or her own testimony. See, e.g., In re Grand Jury Investigation (Lance), 610 F.2d 202, 217 (5th Cir.1980). However, if the witness declines to provide the information, the party seeking the information generally has no right to compel disclosure. In re Swearingen Aviation Corp., 605 F.2d 125, 127 (4th Cir.1979). Moreover, principles restricting discovery in connection with criminal litigation may even prevent disclosure. In re Application of Eisenberg, 654 F.2d 1107, 1113 (5th Cir.1981). When the witness does not wish to disclose his or her testimony, is it appropriate to consider the witness as holder of the privilege?

4.   *Showing required for disclosure. Douglas Oil* requires a civil litigant to show "particularized need" before obtaining information from a grand jury investigation for use in connection with another judicial proceeding. Related issues arise when government attorneys, other than those handling the grand jury investigation, seek grand jury information for use in connection with enforcement activities by an administrative agency or in civil litigation where the government is a party. The Supreme Court has held generally that many of the same principles apply to disclosure to other government attorneys as apply in private civil litigation under *Douglas Oil.* In United States v. Baggot, 463 U.S. 476 (1983), the Court held that disclosure in connection with a civil tax audit was not "preliminar[y] to or in connection with a judicial proceeding" under Fed.R.Crim.P. 6(e)(3)(C)(i) and therefore was not authorized under the Rule. In United States v. Sells Eng'g, Inc., 463 U.S. 418 (1983), it held that attorneys in the civil division of the Justice Department were not entitled to automatic disclosure of grand jury information under Rule 6(e)(3)(A)(i), which permits disclosure to "attorneys for the government," but rather they must obtain the transcripts by court order upon a showing of particularized need under Rule 6(e)(3)(C)(i). However, in United States v. John Doe, Inc. I, 481 U.S. 102 (1987), the Court relaxed the strictness of its earlier rulings. First, it held that the same government attorney who conducted the grand jury investigation involving potential criminal antitrust violations could use the grand jury information in connection with a resulting civil antitrust action without demonstrating particularized need since continued use did not amount to disclosure under the Rule. Second, the Court recognized that the concerns underlying grand jury secrecy are "implicated to a much lesser extent when the disclosure merely involves Government attorneys," id. at 112, thereby rendering the required showing less onerous when disclosure is sought for a related government civil enforcement action than for private civil litigation.

5. *Meaning of particularized need.* For an extended treatment of the factors examined by courts in determining "particularized need" as required by *Douglas Oil* for disclosure, see 2 Beale et al., Grand Jury Law and Practice § 7:12 (2d ed. 2012).

C. INFORMERS

MCCRAY v. ILLINOIS

Supreme Court of the United States, 1967.
386 U.S. 300.

MR. JUSTICE STEWART delivered the opinion of the Court.

The petitioner was arrested in Chicago, Illinois, on the morning of January 16, 1964, for possession of narcotics. The Chicago police officers who made the arrest found a package containing heroin on his person and he was indicted for its unlawful possession. Prior to trial he filed a motion to suppress the heroin as evidence against him, claiming that the police had acquired it in an unlawful search and seizure in violation of the Fourth and Fourteenth Amendments. See Mapp v. Ohio, 367 U.S. 643. After a hearing, the court denied the motion, and the petitioner was subsequently convicted upon the evidence of the heroin the arresting officers had found in his possession. The judgment of conviction was affirmed by the Supreme Court of Illinois, and we granted certiorari to consider the petitioner's claim that the hearing on his motion to suppress was constitutionally defective.

[On the hearing of the motion to suppress, the two police officers who had arrested and searched petitioner testified that they had done so pursuant to a tip from an informer who had told them that petitioner had narcotics on his person and could be found in the area of 47th and Calumet Streets. Both officers further testified that the same informer who had supplied the information which led to petitioner's arrest had on numerous previous occasions supplied them with information concerning narcotics activities which had proved accurate and which had led to convictions. On cross-examination of the officers, petitioner's counsel attempted to elicit the informer's identity but was prevented from doing so when prosecution objections to this line of questioning were sustained.][26]

---

[26] "Q. What is the name of this informant that gave you this information?

"Mr. Engerman: Objection, Your Honor.

"The Court: State for the record the reasons for your objection.

"Mr. Engerman: Judge, based upon the testimony of the officer so far that they had used this informant for approximately a year, he has worked with this individual, in the interest of the public, I see no reason why the officer should be forced to disclose the name of the informant, to cause harm or jeopardy to an individual who has cooperated with the police. The City of Chicago has a tremendous problem with narcotics. If the police are not able to

There can be no doubt, upon the basis of the circumstances related by Officers Jackson and Arnold, that there was probable cause to sustain the arrest and incidental search in this case. Draper v. United States, 358 U.S. 307. Unlike the situation in Beck v. Ohio, 379 U.S. 89, each of the officers in this case described with specificity "what the informer actually said, and why the officer thought the information was credible." 379 U.S., at 97. The testimony of each of the officers informed the court of the "underlying circumstances from which the informant concluded that the narcotics were where he claimed they were, and some of the underlying circumstances from which the officer concluded that the informant * * * was 'credible' or his information 'reliable.' " Aguilar v. Texas, 378 U.S. 108, 114. See United States v. Ventresca, 380 U.S. 102. Upon the basis of those circumstances, along with the officers' personal observations of the petitioner, the court was fully justified in holding that at the time the officers made the arrest "the facts and circumstances within their knowledge and of which they had reasonably trustworthy information were sufficient to warrant a prudent man in believing that the petitioner had committed or was committing an offense. Brinegar v. United States, 338 U.S. 160, 175–176; Henry v. United States, 361 U.S. 98, 102." Beck v. Ohio, supra, 379 U.S. 91. It is the petitioner's claim, however, that even though the officers' sworn testimony fully supported a finding of probable cause for the arrest and search, the state court nonetheless violated the Constitution when it sustained objections to the petitioner's questions as to the identity of the informant. We cannot agree.

In permitting the officers to withhold the informant's identity, the court was following well-settled Illinois law. When the issue is not guilt or innocence, but, as here, the question of probable cause for an arrest or search, the Illinois Supreme Court has held that police officers need not invariably be required to disclose an informant's identity if the trial judge is convinced, by evidence submitted in open court and subject to cross-examination, that the officers did rely in good faith upon credible information supplied by a reliable informant. This Illinois evidentiary rule is consistent with the law of many other States. In California, the State Legislature in 1965 enacted a statute adopting just such a rule for cases like the one before us:

　　"[I]n any preliminary hearing, criminal trial, or other criminal proceeding, for violation of any provision of Division 10 (commencing

---

withhold the name of the informant they will not be able to get informants. They are not willing to risk their lives if their names become known.

　　"In the interest of the City and the law enforcement of this community, I feel the officer should not be forced to reveal the name of the informant. And I also cite People vs. Durr.

　　"The Court: I will sustain that.

　　"Mr. Adam: Q. Where does this informant live?

　　"Mr. Engerman: Objection, your Honor, same basis.

　　"The Court: Sustained."

with § 11000) of the Health and Safety Code, evidence of information communicated to a peace officer by a confidential informant, who is not a material witness to the guilt or innocence of the accused of the offense charged, shall be admissible on the issue of reasonable cause to make an arrest or search without requiring that the name or identity of the informant be disclosed if the judge or magistrate is satisfied, based upon evidence produced in open court, out of the presence of the jury, that such information was received from a reliable informant and in his discretion does not require such disclosure." California Evid.Code § 1042(c).

The reasoning of the Supreme Court of New Jersey in judicially adopting the same basic evidentiary rule was instructively expressed by Chief Justice Weintraub in State v. Burnett, 42 N.J. 377, 201 A.2d 39:

> "If a defendant may insist upon disclosure of the informant in order to test the truth of the officer's statement that there is an informant or as to what the informant related or as to the informant's reliability, we can be sure that every defendant will demand disclosure. He has nothing to lose and the price may be the suppression of damaging evidence if the State cannot afford to reveal its source, as is so often the case. And since there is no way to test the good faith of a defendant who presses the demand, we must assume the routine demand would have to be routinely granted. The result would be that the State could use the informant's information only as a lead and could search only if it could gather adequate evidence of probable cause apart from the informant's data. Perhaps that approach would sharpen investigatorial techniques, but we doubt that there would be enough talent and time to cope with crime upon that basis. Rather we accept the premise that the informer is a vital part of society's defensive arsenal. The basic rule protecting his identity rests upon that belief.

> * * *

> "We must remember also that we are not dealing with the trial of the criminal charge itself. There the need for a truthful verdict outweighs society's need for the informer privilege. Here, however, the accused seeks to avoid the truth. The very purpose of a motion to suppress is to escape the inculpatory thrust of evidence in hand, not because its probative force is diluted in the least by the mode of seizure, but rather as a sanction to compel enforcement officers to respect the constitutional security of all of us under the Fourth Amendment. State v. Smith, 37 N.J. 481, 486, 181 A.2d 761 (1962). If the motion to suppress is denied, defendant will still be judged upon the untarnished truth.

* * *

"The Fourth Amendment is served if a judicial mind passes upon the existence of probable cause. Where the issue is submitted upon an application for a warrant, the magistrate is trusted to evaluate the credibility of the affiant in an *ex parte* proceeding. As we have said, the magistrate is concerned, not with whether the informant lied, but with whether the affiant is truthful in his recitation of what he was told. If the magistrate doubts the credibility of the affiant, he may require that the informant be identified or even produced. It seems to us that the same approach is equally sufficient where the search was without a warrant, that is to say, that it should rest entirely with the judge who hears the motion to suppress to decide whether he needs such disclosure as to the informant in order to decide whether the officer is a believable witness." 42 N.J., at 385–388, 201 A.2d, at 43–45.

What Illinois and her sister States have done is no more than recognize a well-established testimonial privilege, long familiar to the law of evidence. Professor Wigmore, not known as an enthusiastic advocate of testimonial privileges generally,[27] has described that privilege in these words—

"A genuine privilege, on * * * fundamental principle * * *, must be recognized for the *identity of persons supplying the government with information concerning the commission of crimes.* Communications of this kind ought to receive encouragement. They are discouraged if the informer's identity is disclosed. Whether an informer is motivated by good citizenship, promise of leniency or prospect of pecuniary reward, he will usually condition his cooperation on an assurance of anonymity—to protect himself and his family from harm, to preclude adverse social reactions and to avoid the risk of defamation or malicious prosecution actions against him. The government also has an interest in nondisclosure of the identity of its informers. Law enforcement officers often depend upon professional informers to furnish them with a flow of information about criminal activities. Revelation of the dual role played by such persons ends their usefulness to the government and discourages others from entering into a like relationship.

"That the government has this privilege is well established and its soundness cannot be questioned" (footnotes omitted). 8 Wigmore, Evidence § 2374 (McNaughton rev. 1961).

In the federal courts the rules of evidence in criminal trials are governed "by the principles of the common law as they may be interpreted

---

27 See 8 Wigmore, Evidence § 2192 (McNaughton rev. 1961).

by the courts of the United States in the light of reason and experience."[28] This Court, therefore, has the ultimate task of defining the scope to be accorded to the various common law evidentiary privileges in the trial of federal criminal cases. See Hawkins v. United States, 358 U.S. 74. This is a task which is quite different, of course, from the responsibility of constitutional adjudication. In the exercise of this supervisory jurisdiction the Court had occasion 10 years ago, in Roviaro v. United States, 353 U.S. 53, to give thorough consideration to one aspect of the informer's privilege, the privilege itself having long been recognized in the federal judicial system.[29]

The *Roviaro* case involved the informer's privilege, not at a preliminary hearing to determine probable cause for an arrest or search, but at the trial itself where the issue was the fundamental one of innocence or guilt. The petitioner there had been brought to trial upon a two-count federal indictment charging sale and transportation of narcotics. According to the prosecution's evidence, the informer had been an active participant in the crime. He "had taken a material part in bringing about the possession of certain drugs by the accused, had been present with the accused at the occurrence of the alleged crime, and might be a material witness as to whether the accused knowingly transported the drugs as charged." 353 U.S., at 55. The trial court nonetheless denied a defense motion to compel the prosecution to disclose the informer's identity.

This Court held that where, in an actual trial of a federal criminal case,

> "the disclosure of an informer's identity * * * is relevant and helpful to the defense of an accused, or is essential to a fair determination of a cause, the privilege must give way. In these situations the trial court may require disclosure and, if the Government withholds the information, dismiss the action. * * *

> "We believe that no fixed rule with respect to disclosure is justifiable. The problem is one that calls for balancing the public interest in protecting the flow of information against the individual's right to prepare his defense. Whether a proper balance renders nondisclosure erroneous must depend on the particular circumstances of each case, taking into consideration the crime charged, the possible defenses, the possible significance of the informer's testimony, and other relevant factors." 353 U.S., at 60–61, 62 (footnotes omitted).

The Court's opinion then carefully reviewed the particular circumstances of Roviaro's trial, pointing out that the informer's "possible

---

[28] Rule 26, Fed.Rules Crim.Proc.

[29] See Scher v. United States, 305 U.S. 251; In re Quarles & Butler, 158 U.S. 532; Vogel v. Gruaz, 110 U.S. 311.

testimony was highly relevant * * *," that he "might have disclosed an entrapment * * *," "might have thrown doubt upon petitioner's identity or on the identity of the package * * *," "might have testified to petitioner's possible lack of knowledge of the contents of the package that he 'transported' * * *," and that the "informer was the sole participant, other than the accused, in the transaction charged." 353 U.S., at 63–64. The Court concluded "that, under these circumstances, the trial court committed prejudicial error in permitting the Government to withhold the identity of its undercover employee in the face of repeated demands by the accused for his disclosure." 353 U.S., at 65.

What *Roviaro* thus makes clear is that this Court was unwilling to impose any absolute rule requiring disclosure of an informer's identity even in formulating evidentiary rules for federal criminal trials. Much less has the Court ever approached the formulation of a federal evidentiary rule of compulsory disclosure where the issue is the preliminary one of probable cause, and guilt or innocence is not at stake. Indeed, we have repeatedly made clear that federal officers need *not* disclose an informer's identity in applying for an arrest or search warrant. As was said in United States v. Ventresca, 380 U.S. 102, 108, we have "recognized that 'an affidavit may be based on hearsay information and need not reflect the direct personal observations of the affiant,' so long as the magistrate is 'informed of some of the underlying circumstances' supporting the affiant's conclusions and his belief that any informant involved *'whose identity need not be disclosed * * ** was "credible" or his information "reliable." ' Aguilar v. Texas, supra, 378 U.S., at 114." (Emphasis added.) See also Jones v. United States, 362 U.S. 257, 271–272; Rugendorf v. United States, 376 U.S. 528, 533. And just this Term we have taken occasion to point out that a rule virtually prohibiting the use of informers would "severely hamper the Government" in enforcement of the narcotics laws. Lewis v. United States, 385 U.S. 206, 210.

In sum, the Court in the exercise of its power to formulate evidentiary rules for federal criminal cases has consistently declined to hold that an informer's identity need always be disclosed in a federal criminal trial, let alone in a preliminary hearing to determine probable cause for an arrest or search. Yet we are now asked to hold that the Constitution somehow compels Illinois to abolish the informer's privilege from its law of evidence, and to require disclosure of the informer's identity in every such preliminary hearing where it appears that the officers made the arrest or search in reliance upon facts supplied by an informer they had reason to trust. The argument is based upon the Due Process Clause of the Fourteenth Amendment, and upon the Sixth Amendment right of confrontation, applicable to the States through the Fourteenth Amendment. Pointer v. Texas, 380 U.S. 400. We find no support for the petitioner's position in either of those constitutional provisions.

The arresting officers in this case testified, in open court, fully and in precise detail as to what the informer told them and as to why they had reason to believe his information was trustworthy. Each officer was under oath. Each was subjected to searching cross-examination. The judge was obviously satisfied that each was telling the truth, and for that reason he exercised the discretion conferred upon him by the established law of Illinois to respect the informer's privilege.

Nothing in the Due Process Clause of the Fourteenth Amendment requires a state court judge in every such hearing to assume the arresting officers are committing perjury. "To take such a step would be quite beyond the pale of this Court's proper function in our federal system. It would be a wholly unjustifiable encroachment by this Court upon the constitutional power of States to promulgate their own rules of evidence * * * in their own state courts * * *." Spencer v. Texas, 385 U.S. 554, 568–569.

The petitioner does not explain precisely how he thinks his Sixth Amendment right to confrontation and cross-examination was violated by Illinois' recognition of the informer's privilege in this case. If the claim is that the State violated the Sixth Amendment by not producing the informer to testify against the petitioner, then we need no more than repeat the Court's answer to that claim a few weeks ago in Cooper v. California:

> "Petitioner also presents the contention here that he was unconstitutionally deprived of the right to confront a witness against him, because the State did not produce the informant to testify against him. This contention we consider absolutely devoid of merit." 386 U.S. 58, at 62.

On the other hand, the claim may be that the petitioner was deprived of his Sixth Amendment right to cross-examine the arresting officers themselves, because their refusal to reveal the informer's identity was upheld. But it would follow from this argument that no witness on cross-examination could ever constitutionally assert a testimonial privilege, including the privilege against compulsory self-incrimination guaranteed by the Constitution itself. We have never given the Sixth Amendment such a construction, and we decline to do so now.

Affirmed.

MR. JUSTICE DOUGLAS, with whom THE CHIEF JUSTICE, MR. JUSTICE BRENNAN and MR. JUSTICE FORTAS concur, dissenting.

* * *

In Roviaro v. United States, 353 U.S. 53, 61, we held that where a search *without a warrant* is made on the basis of communications of an informer and the Government claims the police had "probable cause," disclosure of the identity of the informant is normally required. In no other way can the defense show an absence of "probable cause." By reason of Mapp v. Ohio, supra, that rule is now applicable to the States.

In Beck v. Ohio, 379 U.S. 89, 96, we said:

> "An arrest without a warrant bypasses the safeguards provided by an objective predetermination of probable cause, and substitutes instead the far less reliable procedure of an after-the-event justification for the arrest or search, too likely to be subtly influenced by the familiar shortcomings of hindsight judgment."

For that reason we have weighted arrests with warrants more heavily than arrests without warrants. See United States v. Ventresca, 380 U.S. 102, 106. Only through the informer's testimony can anyone other than the arresting officers determine "the persuasiveness of the facts relied on * * * to show probable cause." Aguilar v. Texas, 378 U.S. 108, 113. Without that disclosure neither we nor the lower courts can ever know whether there was "probable cause" for the arrest. Under the present decision we leave the Fourth Amendment exclusively in the custody of the police. As stated by Mr. Justice Schaefer dissenting in People v. Durr, 28 Ill.2d 308, 318, 192 N.E.2d 379, 384, unless the identity of the informer is disclosed "the policeman himself conclusively determines the validity of his own arrest." That was the view of the Supreme Court of California in Priestly v. Superior Court, 50 Cal.2d 812, 818, 330 P.2d 39, 43:

> "Only by requiring disclosure and giving the defendant an opportunity to present contrary or impeaching evidence as to the truth of the officer's testimony and the reasonableness of his reliance on the informer can the court make a fair determination of the issue. Such a requirement does not unreasonably discourage the free flow of information to law enforcement officers or otherwise impede law enforcement. Actually its effect is to compel independent investigations to verify information given by an informer or to uncover other facts that establish reasonable cause to make an arrest or search."

There is no way to determine the reliability of Old Reliable, the informer, unless he is produced at the trial and cross-examined. Unless he is produced, the Fourth Amendment is entrusted to the tender mercies of the police. What we do today is to encourage arrests and searches without warrants. The whole momentum of criminal law administration should be in precisely the opposite direction, if the Fourth Amendment is to remain a vital force. Except in rare and emergency cases, it requires magistrates to make the findings of "probable cause." We should be mindful of its command that a judicial mind should be interposed between the police and the citizen. We should also be mindful that "disclosure, rather than suppression, of relevant materials ordinarily promotes the proper administration of criminal justice." Dennis v. United States, 384 U.S. 855, 870.

NOTES AND QUESTIONS

1. *Validity and wisdom of balancing test.* Despite the narrowly divided vote in *McCray*, its balancing test has remained the law, almost without challenge. For strong criticism of the opinion, see Grano, A Dilemma for Defense Counsel: *Spinelli–Harris* Search Warrants and the Possibility of Police Perjury, 1971 U.Ill.L.F. 405. See generally Quinn, *McCray v. Illinois*: Probable Cause and the Informer's Privilege, 45 Denv. L.J. 399 (1968); 2 Imwinkelried, The New Wigmore: Evidentiary Privileges § 7.3 (2d ed. 2010); 2 LaFave, Search and Seizure § 3.3(g) (5th ed. 2012); 1 McCormick, Evidence § 111 (7th ed. 2013).

2. *Alternative of in camera inspection.* Where an informer's identity is relevant to the existence of probable cause for an arrest or search without a warrant, the dissenting Justices suggest that the choice available is between allowing cross-examination of the informer and entrusting the Fourth Amendment to the "tender mercies of the police." A number of courts have concluded that an *in camera* examination by the court offers an intermediate alternative between disclosure and accepting blindly the word of the officer. See, e.g., United States v. Moore, 522 F.2d 1068, 1072 (9th Cir.1975) ("The *in camera* procedure provides an equally-acceptable accommodation of the competing interests of the Government and the accused * * * [where] the question is whether a law enforcement officer has lied."). Does this procedure adequately protect the defendant's interest since cross-examination will not be possible in the absence of defense counsel? Compare Quinn, note 1, supra, 45 Denv. L.J. at 420 (arguing that procedure is ineffective without cross-examination), with Grano, note 1, supra, 1971 U.Ill.L.F. at 447 (arguing that, since the issue at the suppression hearing is limited to whether the officer lied, *in camera* proceedings are sufficient).

3. *Procedures for in camera inspection.* State v. Casal, 699 P.2d 1234, 1238 (Wash.1985) (en banc), sets out procedures for the *in camera* proceedings: (1) the prosecutor may be present but defendant and counsel are strictly excluded; (2) defense counsel may submit written questions to be asked by the court; (3) a transcript shall be prepared for appellate review; and (4) precautions are to be taken to protect the informant. See also People v. Darden, 313 N.E.2d 49, 52 (N.Y.1974). Would it not be appropriate to permit the attendance of defense counsel under a protective order? See United States v. Anderson, 509 F.2d 724, 729–30 (9th Cir.1974) (approving counsel's presence); State v. Russell, 580 S.W.2d 793, 794

(Tenn.Crim.App.1978) (same). But see 2 LaFave, Search and Seizure § 3.3(g) (5th ed. 2012) (arguing that most informants will not believe that defense counsel will keep their identities confidential from the defendant). See also State v. Richardson, 529 A.2d 1236, 1241 (Conn.1987) (expressing concern that requiring informer to attend any hearing entails substantial risk of disclosure of identity).

4. *Showing required for in camera inspection.* An *in camera* inspection clearly need not be held in every case. What is the nature of the showing that the defendant must make in order to require such a hearing? Professor LaFave argues that the showing should not be onerous:

> [B]ecause the protection-of-informer-anonymity interest and protection-against-police-perjury interest do not collide head on as they do when he questions whether full disclosure of the informant's identity should be made, it should not take much to prompt the suppression hearing judge to order such a hearing. If the defendant "has fairly put in issue" the existence of the informant, whether the officer's report of the informer's prior reliability is truthful, or whether the officers recitation of what the informant told him is correct, then an in camera hearing should be held.

2 LaFave, Search and Seizure § 3.3(g) (5th ed. 2012). See also People v. Vauzanges, 634 N.E.2d 1085 (Ill.1994) (court may order *in camera* hearing if it doubts the credibility of the affiant with respect to the existence of the informant). But see People v. Luttenberger, 784 P.2d 633 (Cal.1990) (imposing rather onerous standard for *in camera* hearing).

5. *Privilege in civil cases.* The privilege is also available in civil cases. See, e.g., Hoffman v. Reali, 973 F.2d 980 (1st Cir.1992); Coughlin v. Lee, 946 F.2d 1152 (5th Cir.1991); Holman v. Cayce, 873 F.2d 944 (6th Cir.1989); Cullen v. Margiotta, 811 F.2d 698 (2d Cir.1987).

6. *Privilege for surveillance location.* Courts have developed an analogous privilege applicable to police surveillance locations. United States v. Green, 670 F.2d 1148 (D.C.Cir.1981); Valentin v. United States, 15 A.3d 270, 273–75 (D.C.2011); Church v. State, 971 A.2d 280, 290–93 (Md.2009); Commonwealth v. Lugo, 548 N.E.2d 1263 (Mass.1990); State v. Garcia, 618 A.2d 326 (N.J.1993). The government's strongest interest is in insuring the safety of private citizens who permit the police to use their property. United States v. Harley, 682 F.2d 1018, 1020 (D.C.Cir.1982). For limitations on this privilege, see United States v. Foster, 986 F.2d 541, 542–44 (D.C.Cir.1993). For a contrary view, see State v. Darden, 41 P.3d 1189, 1196–97 (Wash.2002) (ruling that no surveillance location privilege exists under state statutory or common law and that the court has no authority to create such a privilege).

INDEX

References are to Pages

Rape-victim-counselor, 1193
Rationale for, generally, 1089–90, 1176–
1183

PRIVILEGE
See also Governmental Privileges; Private
Privileges

PROCEDURAL DEFAULT
Barring collateral challenge to conviction,
103
Innocence exception to habeas procedural
default, 95–101

PROOF OF INNOCENCE
Innocence exception to habeas procedural
default, 95–101
Right of the defendant to present evidence to
prove innocence, 84–92

PROSECUTION
Obligation to disclose evidence favorable to
defendant, 72–84
Statements to as offers of plea, 390–91

PSYCHIATRIST–PATIENT PRIVILEGE
See Private Privileges

**PSYCHOTHERAPIST–PATIENT
PRIVILEGE**
See Private Privileges

PUBLIC RECORDS
Accused, offer of by, 1015
Administrative studies and investigations,
reports of, 1015–22
Criminal cases, reports of police
investigation, 1008
Hearsay exception for, generally, 1006–22
Immigration records, 1008–13
Rationale of hearsay exception for, 1006–08
Records of regularly conducted activity as
alternative ground for admission of,
1014
Statements of private individuals in, 1008

QUESTIONS
See also Examination of Witnesses
Leading, 576–83
Objections to form of, generally, 576

RAPE SHIELD STATUTES
Adoption of, 317–31

**REAL AND DEMONSTRATIVE
EVIDENCE**
Attorney-client privilege as applicable to, 72
Chain of custody requirement, 422–426
Computer simulations, 432–44
"Day in the Life" films, as, 455
Directed to various senses, 448
Distinguished, 419–423
Duplicates as, 427
Exhibiting injuries and disabilities as, 452–
54
Experimentation with by jury, 459–62
Motion pictures and video tapes as, 429–48

Photographs, 427–29
Reenactments, 429–32
Sound recordings as, 448
Views, 454–57
X-rays, 446

RECORDED RECOLLECTION
Generally, 971–982
Evidentiary status of, 980–81
Foreign language, problems raised by
recordation in, 982
Memory of witness, impairment required,
980–81
Multiple participants, 971–974
Prohibition on admitting document
containing, 982–83
Rationales for exception in favor of, 981–82
Time of recordation, 982

**RECORDS OF REGULARLY
CONDUCTED ACTIVITY**
Generally, 983–1006
Best evidence rule, application to summaries
used in, 523
Certification alternative, 988–89
Computer records as, 989–92
Foundation witness testimony for, 988
Historical development, 983–87
Hospital records as, 1005
Motive for preparation, 1004–05
Police records as, 1041
Source of information contained in, 998–04
Telephone records as, 983–87
Trustworthiness requirement, 1004–05
Types of activity qualifying, 987–88
Uniform Business Records as Evidence Act,
text of, 987

REFRESHING RECOLLECTION
See also Witnesses
Generally, 583–95
Hypnosis, used for, 587–95

REHABILITATION
Generally, 766–773
Bias and interest, after showing of, 767–68
Convictions of crime, explanations of for,
768–69
Determining when to attempt, 766–767
Prior consistent statements admissible for
as hearsay, 823–33
Prior consistent statements, by, 772–73
Prior inconsistent statement, showing
circumstances of for, 770–72

RELATIONAL PRIVILEGES
See Private Privileges

RELEVANCY
Admissions and stipulations as affecting,
247–60
Animal behavior, 284–86
Character, of, in civil cases, 286–90
Character, of, in criminal cases, 303–43
Defined, 223